PAGET'S LAW OF BANKING

FIRST EDITION	February	1904	Sir John Paget, KC
Reprinted	September	1904	
SECOND EDITION	September	1908	Sir John Paget, KC
THIRD EDITION	August	1922	Sir John Paget, KC
FOURTH EDITION	March	1930	Sir John Paget, KC
FIFTH EDITION	April	1947	Maurice Megrah
Amended Reprint	November	1948	
SIXTH EDITION	April	1961	Maurice Megrah
SEVENTH EDITION	July	1966	Maurice Megrah
EIGHTH EDITION	July	1972	Maurice Megrah & Frank Ryder
Reprinted	May	1976	
NINTH EDITION	November	1982	Maurice Megrah & Frank Ryder
Reprinted	November	1983	
TENTH EDITION	November	1989	Mark Hapgood

PAGET'S
LAW OF BANKING

TENTH EDITION

Mark Hapgood
of Gray's Inn, Barrister

With specialist contributions from
Neil Levy
Mark Phillips
David Beales

Butterworths
London & Edinburgh
1989

United Kingdom	Butterworth & Co (Publishers) Ltd, 88 Kingsway, LONDON WC2B 6AB and 4 Hill Street, EDINBURGH EH2 3JZ
Australia	Butterworths Pty Ltd, SYDNEY, MELBOURNE, BRISBANE, ADELAIDE, PERTH, CANBERRA and HOBART
Canada	Butterworths Canada Ltd, TORONTO and VANCOUVER
Ireland	Butterworth (Ireland) Ltd, DUBLIN
Malaysia	Malayan Law Journal Sdn Bhd, KUALA LUMPUR
New Zealand	Butterworths of New Zealand Ltd, WELLINGTON and AUCKLAND
Puerto Rico	Equity de Puerto Rico, Inc, HATO REY
Singapore	Malayan Law Journal Pte Ltd, SINGAPORE
USA	Butterworth Legal Publishers, AUSTIN, Texas; BOSTON, Massachusetts; CLEARWATER, Florida (D & S Publishers); ORFORD, New Hampshire (Equity Publishing); ST PAUL, Minnesota; and SEATTLE, Washington

A CIP Catalogue record for this book is available from the British Library.

ISBN 0 406 33353 X

Printed by Butler & Tanner Ltd, Frome and London

PREFACE

The death of Maurice Megrah on 23 March 1985 left a gap in the scholarship of banking law which cannot be filled. Nowhere has the gap been felt more acutely than in the preparation of the present edition of *Paget*. Maurice Megrah assumed the editorship of *Paget* following the death of Sir John Paget in 1938. He was the editor of the 5th edition published in 1947 and the four succeeding editions ending with the 9th edition published in 1982.

Maurice Megrah's contribution to legal literature in the field of banking law is quite extraordinary. In addition to his editorship of *Paget*, he was for many years the co-editor of *Byles on Bills of Exchange*; he was co-author of the leading work on letters of credit, Gutteridge & Megrah on the *Law of Bankers' Commercial Credits*; he contributed the banking titles to the 3rd and 4th editions of *Halsbury's Laws of England* and the *Encyclopaedia of Forms and Precedents*; and he wrote many other published works on the law of banking.

Maurice Megrah was assisted in the preparation of the 7th edition of *Paget* by Frank Ryder, who went on to become joint editor of the 8th and 9th editions. Maurice Megrah and Frank Ryder were a formidable and unrivalled team. The preparation of the present edition has suffered from the additional loss of the services of Frank Ryder following his decision to stand down after so many years of close involvement with this work.

The loss of the services of Maurice Megrah and Frank Ryder has led to an unsatisfactorily long gap between the last edition and the present one. This has, however, provided the opportunity to introduce a considerable amount of new material. There is a new group of opening chapters dealing with the statutory framework within which the law of banking now exists, including a chapter on the Banking Act 1987. The chapters dealing with the relation of banker and customer include new chapters covering interest on debts, and insolvency of the customer. There has been brought forward into this part of the book the chapter on the general duties of the paying banker, this being a subject which is more appropriately dealt with at this point than in the more limited context of cheques. There is a new Part III covering interference by third parties. This includes new chapters on Mareva injunctions and other freezing orders, and disclosure and discovery orders, both of which are today subjects of considerable practical importance. The group of chapters covering cheques and other orders for payment has been heavily revised to eliminate material which has ceased to be relevant. Sadly, much of this deleted material was written by Sir John Paget himself, but inevitably some of the issues which benefited from his lucid style and penetrating analysis have now ceased to be relevant with the passage of time.

The chapters dealing with security for advances have been largely re-written. There is a new chapter on the important subject of the taking of security. The treatment of lien and set-off has been considerably expanded. There is a new chapter concerning charges over book debts, and conditional debt obligations ('flawed assets'), and also on mortgages over interests in land. The chapter on guarantees has been revised and expanded to include a section of letters of comfort. The chapter on letters of credit has been substantially updated in the light of the 1983 Revision of the Uniform Customs and Practice for Documentary Credits, and a section has been added on performance bonds.

The law is stated as at 1 June 1989. The responsibility for any errors is, of course, mine alone.

1, Brick Court,
Temple.   M B H

October 1989

ACKNOWLEDGMENTS

The preparation of this edition is a task which I could not have completed without the assistance, advice and encouragement of a great many people.

I have had the invaluable benefit of assistance from **Neil Levy** of Lloyds Bank Plc Legal Department, **Mark Phillips** and **David Beales** of Slaughter and May, who contributed chapters in their respective areas of expertise, namely the Consumer Credit Act 1984, the law of insolvency and the law of mortgage.

The following have also made important contributions: **Richard Slade** wrote the section on the paying banker as constructive trustee; **Hodge Malek** assisted in the preparation of Chapter 19 (Mareva and Other Freezing Orders); **Peter Havey,** contributed Chapter 30 (Taking of Security), and also assisted with the revision of several of the chapters relating to cheques; **Richard McManus** revised and largely re-wrote Chapter 25 (Money Paid by Mistake); **Francis Neate** of Slaughter and May, assisted by **Patrick Clancy** and **Eryl Cottrell,** revised Chapter 33 (Pledges of Goods, Documents of Title and Negotiable Instruments); **Ruth Fox** of Slaughter and May, assisted by **Brian Henderson** and **Gilbert McClung,** revised Chapter 35 (Guarantees), and contributed a new section on letters of comfort.

There are two persons to whom I owe a special debt which goes far beyond their assistance and advice with the preparation of this edition. The first is **Richard Yorke QC,** who introduced me to the intricacies of banking law, encouraged me to take on the task of updating *Paget,* and has always found time to share with me his vast knowledge of this fascinating subject. The second is **Francis Neate** of Slaughter and May, now Chairman of the Banking Committee of the IBA's Section on Business Law, who for many years has with unfailing kindness given me the benefit of his great expertise and experience, in particular on the subjects of set-off and letters of credit.

To all the above I am deeply indebted; and there are many others, too numerous to name individually, who have helped to bring this edition to press.

Finally, I wish to acknowledge with gratitude the inexhaustible patience of my Publishers since they commissioned this edition some years ago, and the efficiency and speed with which they completed the various steps between submission of manuscripts and publication.

M B H

CONTENTS

PART IV
CHEQUES AND OTHER ORDERS FOR PAYMENT

PART V
SECURITY FOR ADVANCES

TABLE OF STATUTES

References in this Table of Statutes are to Halsbury's Statutes of England (Fourth Edition) showing the volume and page at which the annotated text of the Act will be found.

TABLE OF CASES

J

PAGE

L

PAGE

M

PAGE

U

PART 1

THE STATUTORY FRAMEWORK

SUMMARY OF CONTENTS

CHAPTER 1

THE BANKING ACT 1987

1 INTRODUCTION

(a) Commencement and background

The Banking Act 1987 ('the Act') received the Royal Assent on 15 May 1987. The Act was brought into force in stages[1] and was not fully in force until 29 April 1988. The Act repeals the whole of the Banking Act 1979 save for s 38 (Amendment of ss 74, 114(3)(a) and 185(2) of the Consumer Credit Act 1974); s 47 (Defence of contributory negligence available to bankers notwithstanding s 11(1) of the Torts (Interference with Goods) Act 1977); s 51 and Sch 6 (Consequential amendments and repeals); and s 52 (Short title, commencement and extent).

The Act follows generally the recommendations of a Committee on the System of Banking Supervision chaired by the Governor of the Bank of England.[2] It has introduced several important changes into the statutory regulation of deposit-taking. In particular:

(1) The former two-tier system comprising 'recognised banks' and 'licensed institutions' has been replaced by a single category of 'authorised institutions'.
(2) Authorised institutions have become subject to a requirement to make reports of large exposures.
(3) The powers of the Bank of England to obtain information, require production of documents, carry out investigations and make disclosure of information to third parties have been extended.

---

1 Section 91 (Powers for securing reciprocal facilities for banking and other financial services) came into force on the passing of the Act (s 110(2)). Part V (ss 82–87: Restriction on Disclosure of Information) and certain general provisions came into force on 1 July 1987 (Banking Act 1987 (Commencement No 1) Order 1987, SI 1987/1189). The remaining provisions, save for s 38 (Reports on large exposures) and the repeal of s 193 of the Financial Services Act 1986, came into force on 1 October 1987 (Banking Act 1987 (Commencement No 2) Order 1987, SI 1987/1664). Section 38 came into force on 1 April 1988 (Banking Act 1987 (Commencement No 3) Order 1988, SI 1988/502). The repeal of s 193 of the Financial Services Act 1986 came into force on 29 April 1988 (Banking Act 1987 (Commencement No 4) Order 1988, SI 1988/644).
2 Report of the Committee set up to Consider the System of Banking Supervision dated 5 June 1985, Cmnd 9550.

3

(b) Scope of the Act

The Act is principally concerned with regulating the acceptance of deposits in the course of a deposit-taking business (Part I, ss 1–49). Its other provisions concern the Deposit Protection Scheme (Part II, ss 50–66), banking names and descriptions (Part III, ss 67–73), overseas institutions with representative offices (Part IV, ss 74–81), restriction on disclosure of information (Part V, ss 82–87) and miscellaneous related matters (Part VI, ss 88–110). Although the Act affects important aspects of banking business, it does no more than provide a statutory framework. It does not, save in relation to deposit advertisements and banking names and descriptions, prescribe how a deposit-taking business is to be carried on, nor does it restrict banking activities unconnected with deposit-taking.

(c) Relation between the 1979 and 1987 Acts

Section 107 and Sch 5 to the 1987 Act contain provisions governing the transition from the 1979 Act. The most important is that any institution (within s 106(1) of the 1987 Act) which at 1 October 1987[3] was a recognised bank or a licensed institution under the 1979 Act is to be deemed to have been granted an authorisation under the 1987 Act (Sch 5 para 2(1)).

At the dates of repeal of the 1979 Act[4] there were in force various regulations made under that Act, in particular the Banking Act 1979 (Advertisement) Regulations 1985[5] and the Banking Act 1979 (Exempt Transactions) Regulations 1986.[6] These regulations have since been replaced by fresh regulations made under the 1987 Act, namely the Banking Act 1987 (Advertisements) Regulations 1988[7] and the Banking Act 1987 (Exempt Transactions) Regulations 1988.[8]

(d) Key definitions

Certain definitions are central to the 1987 Act:

 (i) *The Bank* means the Bank of England: ss 1(1), 106(1).
 (ii) *Institution*, except in the expression 'overseas institution', means (a) a body corporate wherever incorporated; (b) a partnership formed under the law of any part of the United Kingdom; (c) a partnership or other unincorporated association of two or more persons formed under the law of a member state of the EEC[9] other than the United Kingdom; or (d) a Scottish 1819 savings bank: s 106(1).
 (iii) *Director*, in relation to an institution, includes (a) any person who occupies the position of a director, by whatever name called; (b) in the case of an institution established in a country or territory outside the United Kingdom, any person including a member of the managing board, who occupies a position appearing to the Bank to be analogous

---

3 Ie the date of coming into force of the Banking Act 1987, s 3.
4 The repeal of the Banking Act 1979, s 20 came into force on 15 July 1987; the remaining repeals of that Act came into force on 1 October 1987.
5 SI 1985/220, amended by SI 1987/64.
6 SI 1986/1712.
7 SI 1988/645.
8 SI 1988/646, amended by SI 1989/465.
9 The meaning of 'member state' derives from the Interpretation Act 1978, s 5, Sch 1; European Communities Act 1972, s 1, Sch 1, Pt 2.

to that of a director of a company registered under the Companies Act 1985; (c) in the case of a partnership, a partner, but only in s 105(6) and (7) (meaning of 'chief executive'): s 105(2).

(iv) *Controller*, in relation to an institution, means (a) a managing director of the institution or of another institution of which it is a subsidiary or, in the case of an institution which is a partnership, a partner; (b) a chief executive of the institution or of another institution of which it is a subsidiary; (c) a person who, either alone or with any associate or associates (see s 105(9)) is entitled to exercise, or control the exercise of, 15% or more of the voting power at any general meeting of the institution or of another institution of which it is a subsidiary (*a shareholder controller*: s 105(4)); (d) a person in accordance with whose directions or instructions the directors of the institution or of another institution of which it is a subsidiary or persons who are controllers of the institution by virtue of paragraph (c) above (or any of them) are accustomed to act (*an indirect controller*: s 105(5)): s 105(3).

(v) *Minority/majority/principal shareholder controller* mean, respectively, a shareholder controller in whose case the percentage of the voting power at any general meeting of the institution or of another institution of which it is a subsidiary:
   (a) in the case of a minority shareholder controller, does not exceed 50;
   (b) in the case of a majority shareholder controller, exceeds 50 but not 75;
   (c) in the case of a principal shareholder controller, exceeds 75: s 105(4).

(vi) *Associate*, in relation to a person entitled to exercise or control the exercise of voting power in relation to, or holding shares in, a body corporate, means (a) the wife or husband or son or daughter of that person; (b) any company of which that person is a director; (c) any person who is an employee or partner of that person; (d) if that person is a company (i) any director of that company; (ii) any subsidiary of that company; and (iii) any director or employee of any such subsidiary; and (e) if that person has with any other person an agreement or arrangement with respect to the acquisition, holding or disposal of shares or other interests in that body corporate or under which they undertake to act together in exercising their voting power in relation to it, that other person: s 105(9).

(vii) *Manager*, in relation to an institution, means a person (other than a chief executive) who, under the immediate authority of a director or chief executive of the institution (a) exercises managerial functions; or (b) is responsible for maintaining accounts or other records of the institution: s 105(6).

(viii) *Subsidiary* and *holding company* have the same meaning as in s 736 of the Companies Act 1985: s 106(2).

2   REGULATION OF DEPOSIT-TAKING BUSINESS

(a) Bank of England's duty of supervision

(i) Powers and duties of the Bank

The Bank of England ('the Bank') has the powers conferred on it by the Act and the duty generally to supervise the institutions authorised by it in the exercise of those powers (s 1(1)). It is also the duty of the Bank to keep under review the operation of the Act and developments in the field of banking which appear to it to be relevant to the exercise of its powers and the discharge of its duties (s 1(2)). Neither the Bank nor any person who is a member of its Court of Directors or who is, or is acting as, an officer or servant of the Bank is liable in damages for anything done or omitted in the discharge or purported discharge of the Bank's functions under the Act unless it is shown that the act or omission was in bad faith (s 1(4)).

(ii) The Board of Banking Supervision

The Act required the Bank to establish as soon as practicable after 1 October 1987 (the date on which s 2 came into force) a committee to be known as the Board of Banking Supervision (s 2(1)). The Board was in fact established (on a non-statutory basis) in May 1986, and accordingly the Bank's duty under s 2(1) was de facto discharged as soon as it became operative.

The Board consists of three ex officio members (the Bank's Governor, Deputy Governor and executive director responsible for the supervision of authorised institutions) and six independent members (s 2(2)). It is the duty of the independent members to give such advice to the ex officio members as they think fit on the exercise by the Bank of its functions under the Act and on any matter relating to or arising out of the exercise of those functions (s 2(3)). Although the ex officio members are not bound to act on the advice of the independent members, they must in any case in which it is decided not to follow such advice give written notice to the Chancellor of the Exchequer and the independent members are entitled to place before the Chancellor the reasons for their advice (s 2(5)). The Board enjoys immunity from liability similar to that which exists in favour of the Bank (s 2(7)).

(b) Restriction on acceptance of deposits

The restriction is imposed by s 3(1) of the Act;

> '... no person shall in the United Kingdom accept a deposit in the course of carrying on (whether there or elsewhere) a business which for the purposes of this Act is a deposit-taking business unless that person is an institution for the time being authorised by the Bank. ...'

(i) Exempted persons

The restriction does not apply to the acceptance of a deposit by the Bank itself or by a *person* specified in Sch 2 to the Act. These include the National Savings Bank; a building society incorporated (or deemed to be incorporated) under the Building Societies Act 1986; a friendly society within the meaning of s 7(1)(a) of the Friendly Societies Act 1974 (exemption limited to acceptance of deposits in the course of carrying out transactions permitted by the rules of the society); and any institution which is for the time being authorised under ss 3 or 4 of the Insurance Companies Act 1982 to carry on an insurance business of a class specified in Sch 1 (Long Term Business) or Sch 2 (General Business) to that Act (Banking Act 1987, Sch 2, paras 2, 5, 6 and 8).

(ii) Exempted transactions

In addition to exemptions in favour of specified persons, the Act empowers the Treasury to prescribe *transactions* to which s 3 shall not apply (s 4(4)). Such prescription may be by reference to any factors appearing to the Treasury to be appropriate, in particular: (a) the amount of the deposit; (b) the total liability of the persons accepting the deposit to his depositors and any other creditors; (c) the circumstances in which or the purpose for which the deposit is made; (d) the identity of the person by whom the deposit is made or accepted, including his membership of a class whose membership is determined otherwise than by the Treasury; and (e) the number of, or the amount involved in, transactions of any particular description carried out by the person accepting the deposit or the frequency with which he carries out transactions of any particular description (s 4(5)). This provision substantially re-enacts ss 2(1) and (5) of the Banking Act 1979, save that the 1979 Act made no reference to factor '(e)'.

The power to exempt transactions enables the Treasury to place sensible limits on the scope of the statutory regulation of deposit-taking. The practical importance of such limits is apparent from the regulations presently in force, the Banking Act 1987 (Exempt Transactions) Regulations 1988,[10] which exempt deposit-taking in specified circumstances by such diverse institutions as charities, the Central Board of Finance of the Church of England, industrial and provident societies, specified public undertakings, solicitors and estate agents, and authorised and exempted persons under the Financial Services Act 1986.

(iii) Meaning of 'deposit'

The definition of 'deposit' in the Act has two limbs. The first is positive: a deposit is a sum of money paid on terms under which it will be *repaid*, with or without interest or a premium, and either on demand or at a time or in circumstances agreed by or on behalf of the person making the payment and the person receiving it (s 5(1)(a)). The second is negative: a deposit is a sum of money paid on terms which are *not referable to the provision of property or services or the giving of security* (s 5(1)(b)). By s 5(2), money is paid on terms which are so referable if and only if:

(a) it is paid by way of *advance or part payment* under a contract for the sale, hire or other provision of property or services, and is repayable only in the event that the property or services is not or are not in fact sold, hired or otherwise provided;

(b) it is paid by way of *security* for the performance of a contract or by way of *security* in respect of loss which may result from the non-performance of a contract; or

(c) without prejudice to paragraph (b) above, it is paid by way of *security*

10 SI 1988/646.

for the delivery up or return of any property, whether in a particular state of repair or otherwise.

The words in paragraph (b): 'security in respect of loss which may result from the non-performance of a contract', make express that which the Court of Appeal in *SCF Finance v Masri (No 2)*[11] held to be included in the words in s 1(6)(b) of the 1979 Act 'paid by way of security for payment for the provision of property or services'.

By s 5(3), unless otherwise provided in the Act, 'deposit' does not include:

(a) a sum paid by the Bank or any authorised institution;
(b) a sum paid by an exempted person;
(c) a sum paid by a person, not falling within (a) or (b) above, in the course of carrying on a business consisting wholly or mainly of lending money;
(d) a sum which is paid by one company to another at a time when:
    (i) one is a subsidiary of the other; or
    (ii) both are subsidiaries of another company; or
    (iii) the same individual is a majority shareholder controller or a principal shareholder controller of both of them;
(e) a sum which is paid by a person who, at the time when it is paid, is a close relative (ie spouse, or child, step-child, parent, step-parent, mother, sister, step-brother, step-sister or spouse of any of them: s 5(5)) of the person receiving it or who is, or is a close relative of, a director, controller or manager of that person.

(iv) Meaning of 'deposit-taking business'

The Act does not restrict the acceptance of deposits simpliciter, but rather the acceptance of deposits *in the course of carrying on a deposit-taking business*. A business is a deposit-taking business for the purposes of the Act if (a) in the course of the business money received by way of deposit is lent to others; or (b) any other activity of the business is financed, wholly or to any material extent, out of the capital of or the interest on money received by way of deposit (s 6(1), re-enacting s 1(2) of the 1979 Act). In the great majority of cases the first of these alternatives is likely to be satisfied, as it was in *SCF Finance v Masri (No 2)* (see above) in respect of deposits paid to futures brokers which were commingled with other monies in a general account and from time to time lent to others.[12] Insofar as the definition of 'deposit-taking business' narrows the ambit of the Act, this results more from s 6(2), which provides that a business is not a deposit-taking business for the purposes of the Act if (a) the person carrying it on does not *hold himself out* as accepting deposits on a day to day basis; *and* (b) any deposits which are received are accepted only on *particular occasions*, whether or not involving the issue of debentures or other securities. The Act has introduced a new provision that, in determining whether deposits are accepted only on particular occasions, regard must be had to the frequency of those occasions and to any characteristics distinguishing them from each other (s 6(4)). This weakens the statement in *SCF Finance v Masri (No 2)*, supra, that the mere fact that the occasions on which deposits are accepted may be numerous does not render

11 [1987] QB 1002 at 1020H, [1987] 1 All ER 175 at 188–189.
12 Ibid at 1021G, 189f.

them any less 'particular'.[13] The Act clearly contemplates that the mere frequency of occasions *may* render them less particular.

It was further held in *SCF Finance v Masri (No 2),* supra, without attempting any comprehensive definition of the phrase, that on the ordinary meaning of the words, a person 'holds himself out to accept deposits' only if, by way of an express or implied invitation, he holds himself out as being generally willing on any normal working day to accept such deposits from those persons to whom the invitation is addressed who may wish to place monies with him by way of deposit.[14]

The restriction in s 3(1) is on the acceptance of a deposit *in the United Kingdom* in the course of carrying on *whether there or elsewhere* a deposit-taking business. The italicised words did not appear in the equivalent section of the 1979 Act. Their inclusion in the 1987 Act makes definite the territorial limits of the restriction and its applicability to institutions which carry on a deposit-taking business overseas, but not in the United Kingdom.

(c) Authorisations

(i) Grant of authorisation

Any institution may make an application for authorisation to the Bank (s 8(1)), but the Bank may not grant an application unless satisfied that the criteria specified in Sch 3 to the Act are fulfilled with respect to the applicant (s 9(?)) Schedule 3 sets out six criteria:

1 Every person who is, or is to be, a director, controller or manager of the institution must be a fit and proper person to hold the particular position which he holds or is to hold.
2 At least two individuals must effectively direct the business of the institution.
3 In the case of an institution incorporated in the United Kingdom, the directors must include such number (if any) of directors without executive responsibility for the management of its business as the Bank considers appropriate having regard to the circumstances of the institution and the nature and scale of its operations.
4 The institution must conduct its business in a prudent manner.
5 The business of the institution must be carried on with integrity and the professional skills appropriate to the nature and scale of its activities.
6 The institution must at the time when authorisation is granted have net assets amounting to not less than £1 m (or an amount of equivalent value denominated wholly or partly otherwise than in sterling).

The requirement that an institution must conduct its business in a prudent manner is supplemented in Sch 3 by a list of circumstances in which an institution will *not* be regarded as so conducting its business. These include the failure to maintain (a) net assets sufficient to safeguard the interests of depositors and potential depositors, (b) adequate liquidity and (c) accounting and other business records and adequate systems of control of its business and records; and also the making of adequate provision for depreciation or diminution in the value of assets and for future liabilities and losses. On a

13 Ibid at 1023A, 190e.
14 Ibid at 1022E, 190b.

number of these matters the Bank is entitled to take into account factors appearing to it to be relevant.

(ii) Revocation of authorisation

The Bank has power to revoke an authorisation in a wide range of circumstances. First, there are circumstances where the interests of depositors or potential depositors are threatened. By s 11(1), the Bank may revoke an authorisation if it appears that:

(a) any of the criteria specified in Sch 3 is not or has not been fulfilled, or may not be fulfilled;
(b) the institution has failed to comply with any obligation imposed on it by the Act;
(c) a person has become a controller of the institution in contravention of s 21 or has become or remained a controller after being given a notice of objection under ss 22, 23 or 24 (see infra);
(d) the Bank has been provided with false, misleading or inaccurate information by or on behalf of the institution or, in connection with an application for authorisation, by or on behalf of a person who is or is to be a director, controller or manager of the institution;
(e) the interests of depositors or potential depositors are in any other way threatened.

The power of revocation is also exercisable in other circumstances relating to the non-acceptance of deposits, the revocation of an authorisation granted under the Financial Services Act 1986, the making of compositions or arrangements with creditors, the appointment of a receiver or manager, the taking of possession of property subject to a charge in favour of debenture-holders and the making of an administration order under the Insolvency Act 1986 (s 11(2) (4) (7) and (8)).

The Bank *must* revoke the authorisation of an institution wherever incorporated if it appears to the Bank that a winding-up order has been made against it in the United Kingdom or a resolution for its voluntary winding up in the United Kingdom has been passed (s 11(6)).

(iii) Restriction of authorisation

Where it appears to the Bank that there are grounds on which its power to revoke an authorisation is exercisable, but that the circumstances are not such as to justify revocation, the Bank may restrict the authorisation instead of revoking it (s 12(1)). An authorisation may be restricted by limiting its duration, and/or by imposing such conditions as the Bank thinks desirable for the protection of the institution's depositors or potential depositors (s 12(2)). By s 12(4), such conditions may in particular:

(a) require the institution to take certain steps or to refrain from adopting or pursuing a particular course of action or to restrict the scope of its business in a particular way;
(b) impose limitations on the acceptance of deposits, the granting of credit or the making of investments;
(c) prohibit the institution from soliciting deposits, either generally or from persons who are not already depositors;

(d) prohibit it from entering into any other transaction or class of trans-
    actions;
(e) require the removal of any director, controller or manager;
(f) specify requirements to be fulfilled otherwise than by action taken by the
    institution.

(iv) Statement of principles

The Bank was required as soon as practicable after 1 October 1987 (the date
of coming into force of s 16) to publish a statement of principles in accordance
with which it acts (a) in interpreting the criteria specified in Sch 3 and the
grounds of revocation specified in s 11, and (b) in exercising its power to grant,
revoke or restrict an authorisation (s 16(1)). The Statement of Principles was
not in fact issued until May 1988.[15]

If the Bank makes a material change in the published principles, it must
include a statement of the change in its Annual Report (s 16 (2)). Although
the Bank has power to publish an up-dated statement of principles (s 16 (3))
it is apparently under no obligation to do so.

(v) Institutions whose principal place of business is outside the UK

Institutions whose principal place of business is in a country or territory
outside the United Kingdom are treated differently in relation to authorisations in two respects. First, in the case of such an applicant for authorisation, the Bank may regard itself as satisfied that the criteria specified in
Sch 3, para 1 (directors, etc to be fit and proper persons), para 4 (business to
be conducted in prudent manner) and para 5 (integrity and skill) are fulfilled
if (a) the relevant supervisory authority in that country or territory (ie the
authority discharging in that place functions corresponding to those of the
Bank under the Act: s 106(1)) is satisfied with respect to the prudent management and skill and overall financial soundness of the applicant; and (b)
the Bank is satisfied as to the nature and scope of the supervision exercised
by that authority (s. 9(3)).

Secondly, if it appears to the Bank that the relevant supervisory authority
has withdrawn from the institution an authorisation corresponding to that
conferred by the Bank, the Bank may revoke the institution's authorisation,
and must do so if the relevant supervisory authority is that of a country or
territory which is a member state of the EEC.

(vi) Notification procedures

The Act provides in s 13 a notification procedure where the Bank proposes
to revoke or restrict an authorisation or to vary the restrictions imposed on
an authorisation otherwise than with the institution's agreement. The Bank
must then give a notice specifying the proposed restrictions or variation,
stating the grounds on which the Bank proposes to act, and giving particulars
of the institution's right to make representations (ss 13(2) and (3)). Where
the ground or a ground of a proposed restriction or variation is that it appears
to the Bank that a person who is or is to be a director, controller or manager
of the institution is not a fit and proper person to hold the particular position

---

15 Copies are obtainable from the Banking Supervision Department, Bank of England,
   Threadneedle Street, London EC2R 8AH.

which he holds or is to hold, the Bank must give that person a copy of the notice, together with a statement of his right to make representations (s 13(4)). Representations may be made within the period of 14 days beginning with the day on which notice was given by the Bank (s 13(5)). The Bank must give the institution and any person on whom the notice was served written notice of its decision within the period of 28 days beginning with the day on which the original notice was given, failing which the Bank will be treated as having at the end of that period given a notice that no further action is to be taken (s 13(10)). Except where the Bank's decision is to take no further action, the decision notice must state the reasons for the decision and give particulars, in the case of a decision to restrict or to vary otherwise than as stated in the original notice, of the right to make further representations, and in all cases, of the right of appeal (s 13(7)).

The Act also makes provision for the surrender of authorisation (s 15).

(vii) Directions

The Bank has power in specified circumstances to give an institution such directions as appear to the Bank to be desirable in the interests of the institution's depositors or potential depositors, whether for the purpose of safeguarding its assets or otherwise (s 19(2)). The Bank may give directions, among other times, when giving an institution notice that it proposes to revoke its authorisation or at any time thereafter (including after revocation), and when giving a notice of revocation to an institution in the case of a members' voluntary winding up (s 19(1)).

(viii) Appeals

By s 27(1), an institution which is aggrieved by a decision of the Bank:

(a) to refuse an application by the institution for authorisation;
(b) to revoke its authorisation otherwise than in a case in which revocation is mandatory under s 11;
(c) to restrict its authorisation, to restrict it in a particular manner or to vary any restrictions of its authorisation; or
(d) to give it a direction under s 19 or to vary a direction given to it under that section,

may appeal against that decision.

Where the ground or a ground for the decision to refuse, revoke, restrict or vary an authorisation is that a person who is, or is to be, a director, controller or manager of the institution is not a fit and proper person to hold the particular position which he holds or is to hold, or where the effect of a decision to restrict or vary an authorisation or to give or vary a direction is to require the removal of a person as director, controller or manager, the person to whom the ground relates or whose removal is required also has a right of appeal against the finding of such a ground or, as the case may be, the decision to require his removal (s 27(2)). On such an appeal the institution concerned is itself entitled to be heard (s 30(2)).

Appeal lies in the first instance to a banking appeal tribunal consisting of a chairman appointed by the Lord Chancellor and two other members appointed by the Chancellor of the Exchequer (s 28(2)). The chairman must be a barrister or solicitor of at least seven years' standing, and the other two members must be persons appearing to the Chancellor of the Exchequer to have respectively experience of accountancy and experience of banking (s 28(3)). Regulations have now been made governing the procedure on such appeals.[16] The tribunal may give such directions as it thinks fit for the payment of costs or expenses by any party to the appeal (s 30(1)).

Further appeal on any question of law lies to the High Court at the instance of an institution or other person who has appealed to a banking appeal tribunal, or at the instance of the Bank; and if the High Court is of opinion that the decision was erroneous, it is required to remit the matter to the tribunal for re-hearing and determination by it (s 31(1)). No appeal to the Court of Appeal may be brought except with leave of that court or of the court from whose decision the appeal is brought (s 31(3)).

(d) Objections to controllers

By s 21(1) and (2), no person may become a minority, majority or principal shareholder controller or an indirect controller of an institution *incorporated in the United Kingdom* (or a partner in an authorised institution which is a United Kingdom partnership) unless:

(a) he has served on the Bank a written notice stating that he intends to become such a controller of the institution; and
(b) either the Bank has, before the end of a period of three months beginning with the date of service of that notice, notified him that there is no objection to his becoming such a controller, or that period has elapsed without the bank having served on him under s 22 or 23 a written notice of objection.

The Bank may serve a notice of objection unless it is satisfied as to three matters: that the person is a fit and proper person to become a controller of the description in question of the institution; that the interests of depositors and potential depositors would not thereby be in any other manner threatened; and that the criteria in Sch 3 would continue to be fulfilled or, if not, that that person is likely to undertake adequate remedial action (s 22(1)). The Bank must first serve a preliminary written notice stating that it is considering service of a notice of objection, and this preliminary notice must specify the matters about which the Bank is not satisfied and its reasons, and must also give particulars of the right to make written representations to the Bank (s 22(2)). The notice of objection itself must similarly specify the Bank's reasons, and must also give particulars of the right of appeal (s 22(4)).

Where a person required to give a notice under s 21 becomes a controller of any description without having given notice, the Bank may serve him with a notice of objection at any time within three months after becoming aware of his having done so (s 22(6)).

The Bank has a similar power of objection if it appears that a person who is a shareholder controller of any description of an authorised institution incorporated in the United Kingdom is no longer a fit and proper person to be such a controller (s 24(1)).

Where a person becomes or continues to be a shareholder controller of any description after being served with a notice of objection to his becoming or continuing to be a controller of that description, then by s 26(2) the Bank may by notice in writing direct that any specified shares to which s 26

16 Banking Appeal Tribunal Regulations 1987, SI 1987/1299.

applies shall, until further notice, be subject to one or more of the following restrictions:

(a) any transfer of, or agreement to transfer, those shares or, in the case of unissued shares, any transfer of or agreement to transfer the right to be issued with them shall be void;
(b) no voting rights shall be exercisable in respect of the shares;
(c) no further shares shall be issued in right of them or in pursuance of any offer made to their holder;
(d) except in a liquidation, no payment shall be made of any sums due from the institution on the shares, whether in respect of capital or otherwise.

These restrictions in the nature of a freezing order are unmistakably modelled on s 454 of the Companies Act 1985. The shares which may be made subject to such an order are, by s 26(7): (a) all the shares in the institution of which the person is a controller of the relevant description which are held by him or any associate of his and were not so held immediately before he became such a controller; and (b) where the person in question became a controller of the relevant description as a result of the acquisition by him or any associate of shares in another company, to all the shares in that other company which are held by him or any associate and were not so held immediately before he became such a controller. In relation to both classes of shares, the effect of the concluding words 'and were not so held ...' is to exclude from any freezing order shares which were held by the person in question immediately before he became a shareholder of the relevant description. If, for example, the relevant description is 'principal shareholder controller', the jurisdiction to impose restrictions does not extend to any shareholding by virtue of which immediately before he became a principal shareholder controller, he was a majority shareholder controller. This is not unreasonable because either the Bank had no power to object to his becoming a majority shareholder controller, or if it did, ex hypothesi it failed to exercise that power.

The court may, on the application of the Bank, order the sale of any specified shares to which s 26 applies and, if they are subject to restrictions, that they shall cease to be subject to those restrictions (s 26(3)). There is no provision for such an application to be made by the shareholder himself.

A person on whom a notice of objection is served may appeal to a banking appeal tribunal (see supra), but not if he has failed to give a notice under s 21 or has unlawfully become or continued to be a controller (s 27(3)).

(e) Invitations to make deposits

The Treasury may after consultation with the Bank and the Building Societies Commission make regulations for regulating (1) the issue, form and content of deposit advertisements (s 32(1)) and (2) the making of unsolicited calls on persons in the United Kingdom or from the United Kingdom on persons elsewhere (s 34(1)). The regulations presently in force are the Banking Act 1987 (Advertisements) Regulations 1988.[17] If the Bank considers that any deposit advertisement issued or proposed to be issued by or on behalf of an authorised institution is misleading, then by s 33(1) and (2), the Bank may by notice in writing give the institution a direction containing any or all of the following prohibitions or requirements:

17 SI 1988/645.

(a) a prohibition on the issue of advertisements of a specified kind;
(b) a requirement that advertisements of a particular description shall be modified in a specified manner;
(c) a prohibition on the issue of any advertisements which are, wholly or substantially, repetitions of an advertisement which has been issued and which is identified in the direction;
(d) a requirement to take all practical steps to withdraw from display in any place any advertisements or any advertisements of a particular description specified in the direction.

The Act contains provisions as to the giving of a preliminary notice, and the right to make representations, similar to those in relation to notices of objection to new or increased control (see supra). There is, however, no right of appeal against the Bank's decision to give a s 33 direction.

(f) Information

(i) Duties of disclosure

The Act imposes duties of disclosure in addition to the duty to give notification of new or increased control. These duties are:

1 An authorised institution must give written notice to the Bank of the fact that any person has become or ceased to be a director, controller or manager (s 36(1)).
2 A person who becomes a significant shareholder (ie a person who, either alone or with any associate or associates, is entitled to exercise or control the exercise of 5% or more, but less than 15%, of the voting power at any general meeting of the institution or of another institution of which it is a subsidiary) in relation to an authorised institution incorporated in the United Kingdom must within seven days give written notice of that fact to the Bank (s 37(1)).
3 An authorised institution, other than one whose principal place of business is outside the United Kingdom, must make a report to the Bank if (a) it *has* entered into a transaction or transactions relating to any one person as a result of which it is exposed to the risk of incurring losses in excess of 10% of its available capital resources; or (b) it *proposes* to enter into a transaction or transactions relating to any one person which, either alone or together with a previous transaction or transactions in relation to that person, would result in its being exposed to the risk of incurring losses in excess of 25% of those resources (s 38(1)).
4 An authorised institution incorporated in the United Kingdom must forthwith give written notice to the Bank if the institution proposes to give special notice to its shareholders of an ordinary resolution removing an auditor before the expiration of his term, or notice replacing an auditor at the expiration of his term of office with a different auditor (s 46(1)).
5 An auditor of an authorised institution appointed under s 384 of the Companies Act 1985 (Annual appointment of auditors) must forthwith give written notice to the Bank if he resigns before the expiration of his term of office, or does not seek to be re-appointed, or decides to include in his report on the institution's accounts any qualification as to a matter mentioned in s 236 (Auditor's report) or s 237 (Auditor's duties and powers)

of the Companies Act 1985 (s 46(2)). The Act confers certain protection upon auditors in relation to communications with the Bank (s 47).

(ii) Powers to obtain information and documents

The Act also confers on the Bank wide powers to obtain information and require production of documents. As regards *information*, the Bank may by notice in writing require an institution to provide the Bank with (a) such information as it may reasonably require for the performance of its functions under the Act and (b) a report by an accountant or other person with relevant professional skill on, or on any aspect of, any matter about which the Bank has required or could require the institution to provide information under (a) above (s 39(1)). The Act confers certain protection upon persons making such a report (s 47).

As regards *documents* (which includes information recorded in any form: s 106(1)) the Bank may by notice in writing require an authorised institution to produce such document or documents of such description as may be specified in the notice, being such documents as the Bank may reasonably require for the performance of its functions under the Act (s 39(3)(a)).

As regard both *information and documents* the Bank may authorise an officer, servant or agent of the Bank, on producing evidence of his authority, to require an authorised institution to provide him forthwith with such information, or to produce to him forthwith such documents, as he may specify, being such information or documents as the Bank may reasonably require for the performance of its functions under the Act (s 39(3)(b)).

The power to order production of documents includes power, if documents are produced, to take copies and require an explanation of them, and, if documents are not produced, to require the person who was required to produce them to state, to the best of his knowledge and belief, where they are (s 39(5)).

The above powers are exercisable not only in relation to an authorised institution, but if it appears to the Bank to be desirable to do so in the interests of depositors or potential depositors, in relation to any body corporate which is or has at any relevant time been a holding company, subsidiary company or related company of that institution, or a body corporate falling within any of three other specified classes (s 39(6)). Similarly wide powers exist in relation to an authorised institution which is a partnership (s 39(7)).

The Bank's powers to obtain information and documents are also exercisable in relation to any person who is a significant shareholder of an authorised institution within s 37 (see supra) if the Bank considers that the exercise of those powers is desirable in the interests of depositors or potential depositors (s 39(10)). The Bank has similar powers to require a person who is or is to be a director, controller or manager of an authorised institution to provide the Bank with such information or documents as the Bank may reasonably require for determining whether he is a fit and proper person to hold the particular position which he holds or is to hold (s 39(9)).

(iii) Right to enter premises

The Bank is also given rights to enter premises to obtain information and documents. It has two such rights. The first is the right of any officer, servant or agent of the Bank, on producing if required evidence of his authority, to enter any premises occupied by any person on whom a s 39 notice *has been* served for the purpose of obtaining there the information or documents required by that notice or of taking copies etc (s 40(1)). The second right is to enter for these purposes any premises occupied by a person on whom a s 39 notice *could be* served, but the Bank may not authorise anyone so to act unless it has reasonable cause to believe that if such a notice were served, it would not be complied with or that any documents to which it would relate would be removed, tampered with or destroyed (s 40(2)).

(g) Investigations

The Bank has power, if it appears desirable to do so in the interests of depositors or potential depositors of an authorised institution, to appoint one or more competent persons to investigate and report to it on (a) the nature, conduct or state of the institution's business or any particular aspect of it, or (b) the ownership or control of the institution; and the Bank must give written notice of any such appointment to the institution concerned (s 41(1)). If he thinks it necessary for the purposes of his investigation, a person so appointed may also investigate the business of any body corporate which is or has at any relevant time been a holding company, subsidiary or related company of the institution under investigation, or a body corporate falling within any of three other specified classes (s 41(2)). Similarly wide powers exist in relation to an authorised institution which is a partnership (s 41(3)).

The Act confers upon a person so appointed a right to enter premises (s 41(7)) and imposes a duty on every person who is or was a director, controller, employee, agent, banker, solicitor or significant shareholder of a body under investigation (including holding companies, etc) a duty to produce documents, to attend before the person so appointed, and otherwise to give that person all reasonable assistance in connection with the investigation (s 41(5)).

The Bank is also given by s 42 wide powers to investigate suspected contraventions of s 3 (restriction on deposit-taking) and s 35 (fraudulent inducement to make a deposit).

(h) Consequences of unauthorised acceptance of deposits, etc

The Act contains the following provisions as to the consequences of the unauthorised acceptance of a deposit and other unlawful acts:

 (i) The fact that a deposit has been taken in contravention of s 3 does not affect any civil liability arising in respect of the deposit or the money deposited (s 3(3)).

 (ii) A contravention of a prohibition imposed by a direction under s 19 does not invalidate any transaction (s 19(7)).

 (iii) On the application of the Bank, the High Court may, if it appears that a person has accepted deposits in contravention of s 3, order him and any other person who appears to the court to have been knowingly concerned in the contravention to repay the depositor, or appoint a receiver to recover those deposits (s 48(1)).

 (iv) On the application of the Bank, the High Court may, if it appears that profits have accrued to a person as a result of deposits having been accepted in contravention of s 3, order him to pay into court, or appoint a receiver to recover from him, such sum as appears to the court to be just having regard to the profits appearing to the court to have accrued to him (s 49(1)).

In *SCF Finance v Masri (No 2)*,[18] the Court of Appeal held that s 1(8) of the 1979 Act (now s 3(3) of the 1987 Act) referred to the civil liability of the depositor as well as that of the depositee. The Court expressly left open any consideration of the position if the parties were to enter into a transaction in contravention of the restriction on deposit-taking and one or both parties were aware that illegality was involved.[19]

3   DEPOSIT PROTECTION SCHEME

The Act continues the existence of the Deposit Protection Board ('the Board') and the Deposit Protection Fund ('the Fund') established by s 21 of the 1979 Act. The object of the Scheme is to ensure that in the event of the insolvency of an authorised institution, there will be paid out of the Fund three-quarters of the amount of any protected deposit.

(a) The Fund

The Fund consists of (a) any money which formed part of it on 1 October 1987 (the date on which s 51 came into force); (b) initial, further and special contributions; (c) money borrowed by the Board under s 64; and (d) any other money required or directed by the Board to be credited to the Fund.

The Scheme operates on a system of contributions, which may be initial, further or special. All authorised institutions are liable to contribute to the Fund and are referred to in Part II of the Act as 'contributory institutions' (s 52(1)). Subject to a right of waiver (s 53(4)), the Board is required to levy an *initial* contribution where an institution becomes a contributory institution after 1 October 1987 (s 53(1)). The Act contains provisions as to the calculation of such contributions (s 53(2) and (3)), and fixes the minimum initial contribution at £10,000 (s 56(1)).

If at the end of any financial year of the Board the amount standing to the credit of the Fund is less than £3 m, the Board may, with the approval of the Treasury, levy *further* contributions so as to restore the amount to a minimum of £5 m and a maximum of £6 m (s 54(1)). The total amount of the initial contribution and any further contribution from a contributory institution must not exceed £300,000 (s 56(2)). If it appears that payments out of the Fund under s 58 are likely to exhaust it, the Board may, with the approval of the Treasury, levy *special* contributions to meet the Fund's commitments under that section (s 55(1)).

The Act fixes a limit calculated by reference to deposit base on the amount of further and special contributions which an institution can be required to pay (s 56(3)).

Subject to that maximum limit, on each occasion on which further or special contributions are levied, a contribution must be levied from each contributory institution, and the amount of the contribution of each institution is to be fixed by applying to the institution's deposit base the percentage

18 [1987] QB 1002 at 1026D, [1987] 1 All ER 175, 192j.
19 Ibid at 1026G, 192b.

determined by the Board for the purpose of the contribution levied on that occasion.

The Board has power to borrow up to a total outstanding at any time of £10 m if in the course of operating the Fund it appears desirable to do so (s 64(1)). The Board also has power to require contributory institutions to provide such information and to produce such documents, or documents of such a description, as it may reasonably require for the purpose of determining the contribution of the institution (s 65(1)).

(b) Protected deposits

References in the Act to a depositor's protected deposit are to the total liability of an insolvent institution, or an institution subject to an administration order, to him immediately before the time when it became insolvent, or the making of the administration order, limited to a maximum of £20,000 in respect of the principal amount of and accrued interest on sterling deposits made with the United Kingdom offices of the institution (s 60(1)).

No account is to be taken of any liability of the institution unless a proof of debt has been lodged with its liquidator, or (in the case of an institution formed outside the United Kingdom) a corresponding act has been done, or (in the case of an institution subject to an administration order) demand for repayment has been lodged with the administrator (s 60(3) and (4)). No account is to be taken of any liability in respect of a deposit if (among other circumstances) it is a secured deposit or a deposit with an original term to maturity of more than five years (s 60(6)). There also has to be deducted any liability of the depositor to the institution in respect of which a right of set-off existed immediately before insolvency, or could have existed if the deposit in question had been repayable on demand and the liability in question had fallen due (s 60(7)).

(c) Payments out of the Fund

If at any time an authorised institution becomes insolvent or subject to an administration order under s 8 of the Insolvency Act 1986 the Board must pay out of the Fund to each depositor who has a protected deposit with that institution an amount equal to three-quarters of his protected deposit. Payment must be made, in the case of an insolvent institution, as soon as practicable, and in the case of an institution subject to an administration order, as soon as practicable after the deposit is or becomes due and payable under the terms on which it was made or, if later, the approval of the administrator's proposals under s 24 of the Insolvency Act 1986 (s 58(1) and (2)).

The Act provides for the Board to make deductions from the payment that would otherwise have been made to a depositor if the Board is satisfied that a payment has been or will be made to him under a comparable scheme or under a guarantee given by a government or other authority (s 58(3)); and in the case of an institution subject to an administration order, to deduct any payment in respect of that deposit already made by the administrator (s 58(6)). The Act contains no comparable provisions in respect of dividends paid by the liquidator of an insolvent institution.

The Board has a discretion to decline to make any payment to a person whom it considers has any responsibility for, or may have profited directly or indirectly from, the circumstances giving rise to the institution's financial difficulties (s 58(5)).

Even before it has become liable to make a payment out of the Fund, in respect of a deposit with an insolvent institution the Board is entitled to receive any notice or other document required to be sent to a creditor of the institution whose debt has been proved, to attend and make representations at any meeting of creditors and to be a member of any committee established under specified sections of the Insolvency Act 1986 (s 58(8)). Similar provisions apply in relation to an institution which is subject to an administration order (s 58(10)).

'Insolvency' for the above purposes is defined in s 59 of the Act.

4   BANKING NAMES AND DESCRIPTIONS

(a) Restriction on use of banking names

Notwithstanding the abandonment of the former two-tier system comprising recognised banks and licensed institutions, the Act retains a two-tier system in relation to the restriction on the use of banking names. A banking name is any name which indicates or may reasonably be understood to indicate (whether in English or any other language) that a person is a bank or banker or is carrying on banking business (s 67(1)). Subject to certain exemptions, no person carrying on business in the United Kingdom may use any banking name *unless* he is an authorised institution which:

(a) is a company incorporated in the United Kingdom which has
   (i) an issued share capital in respect of which the amount paid up is not less than £5 m (or an amount of equivalent value denominated wholly or partly otherwise than in sterling); or
   (ii) undistributable reserves falling within s 264(3)(a), (b) or (d) of the Companies Act 1985 of not less than that sum (or such an equivalent amount); or
   (iii) such undistributable reserves of an amount which together with the amount paid up in respect of its issued share capital equals not less than that sum (or such an equivalent amount); or
(b) is a partnership formed under the law of any part of the United Kingdom in respect of which one or more designated fixed capital accounts (defined in s 67(4)) are maintained to which there has been credited not less than £5 m (or such an equivalent amount).

'Share capital' does not include redeemable share capital (s 67(3)). An institution whose share capital, etc is denominated wholly or partly otherwise than in sterling is not to be regarded as ceasing to satisfy any of the above conditions by reason only of a fluctuation in the rate of exchange of sterling unless and until it has ceased to satisfy any of them for a continuous period of three months (s 67(5)).

The exemptions fall into two categories. First, there are certain *institutions* to which the restriction does not apply at all. These include the Bank of England, the central bank of a member state of the EEC and various international economic and development banks (s 68(6)). Secondly, there are certain *uses* of names which s 67 does not prohibit. These include (1) the use by an authorised institution which is a company incorporated under the law of a country or territory *outside* the United Kingdom, or is formed under the law of a member state other than the United Kingdom, of a name under which it carries on business in that country, territory or state (or an approximate translation in English of that name) (s 68(3)); (2) the use by an authorised institution which is a wholly-owned subsidiary of an authorised institution to which s 67 or s 68(3) applies, or a company which has a wholly-owned subsidiary which is an authorised institution to which either of those provisions applies, of a name which includes the name of the authorised institution for the purpose of indicating the connection between the two companies (s 68(4)).

In summary, the basic position in relation to the restriction on the use of banking names by authorised institutions which are companies is that:

(1) An authorised institution which does not carry on any business in the United Kingdom is not subject to the restriction.
(2) An authorised institution which is a company incorporated in the United Kingdom with issued paid up share capital, etc of not less than £5 m may use any banking name, but such a company which does not satisfy this condition may not use any such name.
(3) An authorised institution which is a company incorporated outside the United Kingdom may only use a banking name under which it carries on business in the country or territory of its incorporation.

(b) Restriction on use of banking descriptions

The Act also imposes a restriction on the use of banking descriptions. Subject to certain exemptions, no person carrying on business in the United Kingdom may so describe himself or hold himself out as to indicate or reasonably be understood to indicate (whether in English or any other language) that he is a bank or banker or is carrying on a banking business unless he is an authorised institution (s 69(1)). An authorised institution to which the prohibition on the use of banking names applies may not use a banking description which is in such immediate conjunction with the name of the institution that the description might reasonably be thought to be part of it (s 69(2)).

There is again an exemption in favour of the Bank of England, the central bank of any member state and certain international economic and development banks (s 69(6)).

The restriction does not prohibit a person from using the expression 'bank' or 'banker' (or a similar expression) where it is necessary for him to do so in order to be able to assert that he is complying with, or entitled to the advantage of, any enactment, statutory instrument, international agreement, rule of law or commercial usage or practice which applies to a person by virtue of his being a bank or banker (s 69(4)). This is potentially an important provision in relation to banker's set-off and to enactments such as the Bills of Exchange Act 1882 and the Cheques Act 1957 which use the term 'banker'.

(c) Power to object to notified name

Where an institution applies for authorisation under the Act, it must give notice to the Bank of any name it is using or proposing to use for the purpose of or in connection with any business carried on by it and the Bank may give the institution notice in writing that it objects to that name (s 70(1)). Similar provisions apply where an authorised institution proposes to change any name it uses (s 70(2)). The Bank must not give notice of objection to a name unless it considers that the name is misleading to the public or otherwise undesirable (s 70(3)). The institution may not use a name to which the Bank has objected for the purposes of or in connection with any business carried on in the United Kingdom after the objection has taken effect (s 71(1)). An institution on which a notice of objection is served under ss 70(1) and (2) has three weeks within which to apply to the High Court to have it set aside and on such an application the court may set it aside or confirm it (s 71(3)). The Act makes no provision for further appeal to the Court of Appeal.

5   OVERSEAS INSTITUTIONS WITH REPRESENTATIVE OFFICES

A number of overseas institutions have established representative offices in the United Kingdom for purposes which do not include the acceptance of deposits. Such institutions fall outside the ambit of Part I of the Act, but are brought under the supervision of the Bank by Part IV.

(a) Meaning of 'representative office'

'Representative office' is defined to mean premises from which the deposit-taking (presumably non-UK deposit-taking) lending or other financial or banking activities of the overseas institution are promoted or assisted in any way; and 'establishment', in relation to such an office includes the making of any arrangement by virtue of which such activities are promoted or assisted from it (s 74(3)). 'Overseas institution' for these purposes means a person, *other than an authorised institution or an exempted person*, which is a body corporate incorporated, or a partnership formed, in a country or territory outside the United Kingdom, or which has its principal place of business in such a country or territory (s 74(1)). To avoid casting the net too wide, the Act goes on to provide that such a person must also satisfy one of the following conditions to be an overseas institution:

(a) the person's principal place of business must be outside the United Kingdom and the person must be authorised by the relevant supervisory authority in a country or territory outside the United Kingdom;

(b) the person must describe or hold himself out as being authorised by such an authority in a country or territory outside the United Kingdom;

(c) the person must use a name or in some other way so describe or hold himself out as to indicate or reasonably be understood to indicate (whether in English or any other language) that he is a bank or banker or is carrying on a banking business (whether in the United Kingdom or elsewhere) (s 74(2)).

(b) Notice of establishment

An overseas institution may not establish a representative office in the United Kingdom unless it has given not less than two months' notice to the Bank, and such notice must specify (a) any name the institution proposes to use in relation to activities conducted by it in the United Kingdom after the establishment of that office and (b) any name disclosable by virtue of s 4 of the Business Names Act 1985 (s 75(1)). Institutions which established a representative office before 1 October 1987 (the date on which Part IV came into force) and had not given notice of that fact to the Bank under s 40 of the Banking Act 1979 were required to give written notice to the Bank of the continued existence of that office by 1 December 1987 (s 75(2)).

(c) Restriction on use of names and power to object to notified names

The restriction on the use of banking names (see supra) does not prohibit the use by an overseas institution which has its principal place of business in a country or territory outside the United Kingdom and a representative office in the United Kingdom, of the name under which it carries on business in that country or territory if (a) the name is used in immediate conjunction with the description 'representative office' and (b) where the name appears in writing, that description is at least as prominent as the name (s 68(5)).

The Bank has power in certain circumstances to object to a name which appears to be misleading to the public or otherwise undesirable. These circumstances are:

(1) Where notice of a name is given to the Bank by an overseas institution before establishing a representative office, or before changing the name used by it in relation to activities conducted by a representative office (s 76(1) and (2));
(2) In the case of a representative office established before 1 October 1987, within the period of six months of the establishment of the office coming to the Bank's knowledge (s 76(3)).
(3) Where there has been a material change in circumstances since the giving of a notice referred to in (1) above, or further information has become available to the Bank since that time (s 76(4)).

Where the Bank gives notice of objection, s 694(4) of the Companies Act 1985 applies as it applies to a notice served under s 694(1) and (2) (s 78(1)). The effect of this is that a corporate overseas institution may deliver to the registrar of companies for registration a statement in the prescribed form specifying a name approved by the Secretary of State other than its corporate name under which it proposes to carry on business in Great Britain. However, no such statement may be delivered unless the Bank (presumably in addition to the Secretary of State) has signified that it does not object to the specified name (s 78(2)).

Appeal against objection lies to the High Court, which may set it aside or confirm it (s 77(3)).

(d) Power to obtain information and to require production of documents

The Bank has power by notice in writing to require any overseas institution which has established or has given notice of its intention to establish a representative office to provide the Bank with such information or documents as the Bank may require (s 79(1)). Although the Act does not confer on the Bank the same back-up powers as it has under ss 39 and 40 in relation to obtaining information and documents from authorised institutions, provision is made for the Treasury to order that those sections shall apply to overseas institutions (s 79(7)).

6   RESTRICTION ON DISCLOSURE OF INFORMATION

The Act imposes a restriction on disclosure of information. This restriction applies to (a) persons who *under* or *for the purposes of* the Act receive information relating to the business or other affairs of any person and (b) persons who obtain any such information directly or indirectly from a person who has so received it. Such persons may not disclose such information without the consent of the person to whom it relates and (if different) the person from whom it was received (s 82(1)).

The restriction does not apply to information which at the time of disclosure is or has already been made available to the public from other sources, nor to information in the form of a summary or collection of information so framed as not to enable information relating to any particular person to be ascertained from it (s 82(2)).

The Act then goes on to set out disclosures which are not precluded by the general restriction. These disclosures fall into five categories. First, the disclosure of information in any case in which disclosure is for the purpose of enabling or assisting the Bank to discharge its functions under the Act (s 83(1)). This is clearly wide enough to cover disclosure to the Bank as well as disclosure by the Bank. The Act makes specific provision for two such situations: disclosure by the Bank to the auditor of an authorised institution (s 83(2)), and disclosure by the Bank if it considers it necessary to seek advice from any qualified person on any matter of law, accountancy, valuation or other matter (s 83(3)).

The second category of permitted disclosures is disclosure by the Bank of information to specified persons if the Bank considers that disclosure would enable or assist them to discharge specified statutory functions. The specific persons and functions are set out in a Table contained in s 84(1) of the Act, to which there has now been added the Panel on Take-overs and Mergers, in relation to all its functions.[20] A person so specified may in turn disclose information so obtained by him if he does so with the consent of the Bank and for the purpose of enabling or assisting him to discharge any functions specified in relation to him (s 84(4)).

The third category is disclosure by the Bank to the Treasury if disclosure appears to the Bank to be desirable or expedient in the interests of depositors or in the public interest, and disclosure to the Secretary of State, but in more limited circumstances (s 84(5)).

The fourth category is disclosure for the purpose of enabling or assisting an authority in a country or territory outside the UK to exercise: (a) functions corresponding to those of (i) the Bank under the Act, (ii) the Secretary of State under the Insurance Companies Act 1982, Part XIII of the Insolvency Act 1986 or the Financial Services Act 1986, or (iii) the competent authority under Part IV of the Financial Services Act 1986; (b) functions in connection with rules of law corresponding to any of the provisions of the Company Securities (Insider Dealing) Act 1985 or Part VII of the Financial Services Act 1986; or (c) supervisory functions in respect of bodies carrying on business corresponding to that of building societies (s 84(6)).

Fifthly, there are miscellaneous permitted disclosures, including disclosure with a view to the institution of, or otherwise for the purposes of, any criminal

20 Banking Act 1987 (Disclosure of Information) (Specified Persons) Order 1987, SI 1987/1292.

proceedings, whether under the Act or otherwise, and disclosure in connection with any other proceedings arising out of the Act (s 85(1)).

The restriction on disclosure also applies by s 86 to information supplied to the Bank for the purpose of its functions under the Act by a relevant supervisory authority in a country or territory outside the UK (ie the authority discharging in that place functions corresponding to those of the Bank under the Act: s 106(1)). Section 86 goes on to provide that such information may not be disclosed except as provided in s 82 or for the purpose of enabling or assisting the Bank to discharge its functions under the Act, or with a view to the institution of, or otherwise for the purposes of, criminal proceedings under the Act or otherwise. The effect of this provision is to make the categories of permitted disclosures of information received from relevant overseas supervisory authorities more limited than the categories relating to other information.

The Act contains further provisions in respect of information disclosed to the Bank under s 449(1) of the Companies Act 1985 (which authorises disclosure to, among others, the Bank of information obtained by the Secretary of State under ss 447 and 448 of the 1985 Act). Such information may be disclosed by the Bank in any case in which information to which s 82 applies could be disclosed, save that disclosure to the persons specified in s 84(1) may only be made with the consent of the Secretary of State (s 87(2)).

Any information which has been lawfully disclosed to the Bank may be disclosed by it to the Board of Banking Supervision so far as necessary for enabling or assisting the Board to discharge its functions under the Act (s 87(4)).

7 MISCELLANEOUS PROVISIONS

(a) Winding up on the petition of the Bank

The court having jurisdiction under the Insolvency Act 1986 may wind up an authorised institution on a petition presented by the Bank if the institution is unable to pay its debts within ss 123 or 221 of that Act, or the court is of the opinion that it is just and equitable that the institution be wound up. An institution which defaults in an obligation to pay any sum due and payable in respect of a deposit is to be deemed to be unable to pay its debts (s 92(1)). For these purposes, 'deposit' has an extended meaning to include any sum that would otherwise be excluded by s 5(3)(a), (b) or (c) (sums paid by the Bank, an authorised institution, an exempted person or a person carrying on a money-lending business) (s 92(5)).

(b) Injunctions relating to contraventions

The Act confers on the High Court jurisdiction to grant an injunction on the application of the Bank or the DPP in three circumstances, namely:

(1) If it is satisfied that there is a reasonable likelihood that a person *will* contravene ss 3, 18, 35, 67, 69, 71 or 77 of the Act, or a direction under s 19, or regulations under ss 32, 34 or 80, it may grant an injunction restraining the contravention (s 93(1)(a)).
(2) If it is satisfied that any person *has been* guilty of any such contravention

and that the contravention will continue or be repeated, it may grant an injunction restraining the contravention (s 93(1)(b));
(3) If it appears to the court that a person *may have been* guilty of any such contravention, it may grant an injunction restraining him from disposing or otherwise dealing with any of his assets while the suspected contravention is investigated.

(c) Evidence in proceedings

In any proceedings, a certificate purporting to be signed by the Bank is admissible in evidence if it certifies any of the following: (a) that a particular person is or is not an authorised institution or was or was not such an institution at a particular time; (b) the date on which a particular institution became or ceased to be authorised; (c) whether or not a particular institution's authorisation is or was restricted; (d) the date on which a restricted authorisation expires; or (e) the date on which a particular institution became or ceased to be a recognised bank or licensed institution under the Banking Act 1979 (s 101(1)).

A certificate purporting to have been signed by the Bank is to be deemed to have been duly signed unless the contrary is shown.

(d) Notices

No notice required by the Act to be given to or served on the Bank is regarded as given or served until it is received, but subject to that, notice may be given or served by telex or similar means which produce a document containing the text of the communication (s 99(1) and (2)). A facsimile transmission appears to meet this requirement.

The Act makes provision in relation to the giving or serving on any person other than the Bank of any notice, direction or other document (s 100).

(e) Criminal liability

The Act creates some 28 criminal offices. It further provides that where any such offence committed by a body corporate is proved to have been committed with the consent or connivance of, or to be attributable to any neglect on the part of any director, manager or secretary or other similar officer of that body corporate or any person who was purporting to act in any such capacity, he, as well as the body corporate, is guilty of that offence and liable to be prosecuted accordingly (s 96(1)). Where the affairs of a body corporate are managed by its members, this applies in relation to the acts and defaults of a member in connection with his management functions as if he were a director (s 96(2)). For the above purposes the definitions of 'director' and 'manager' in s 105 do not apply (s 105(1)).

In any proceedings for an offence, it is a defence for the person charged to prove that he took all reasonable precautions and exercised due diligence to avoid the commission of the offence by himself or any other person under his control (s 96(4)).

No proceedings may be brought in England and Wales without the consent of the DPP (s 96(5)), and any proceedings for an offence alleged to have been committed by an unincorporated association must be brought in the name of that association (s 98(1)).

(f) Treasury's powers to make orders and regulations

The Treasury has powers under the Act to make orders and regulations and to give directions. These include the power:

(i) To amend Sch 2 (Exempted persons): s 4(3).

(ii) To prescribe transactions to which the restriction on deposit-taking will not apply: s 4(4).

(iii) To amend the meaning of 'deposit' and 'deposit-taking business': s 7(1).

(iv) To make provision corresponding to s 11(4) in relation to any authorisation or licence granted under such other enactments as may appear appropriate: s 11(5).

(v) To direct the Bank to serve a s 22 notice of objection: s 23(1).

(vi) To make regulations with respect to appeals under Part 1 of the Act: s 30(3).

(vii) To make regulations for regulating the issue, form and content of deposit advertisements: s 32(1).

(viii) To make regulations for regulating the making of unsolicited calls: s 34(1).

(ix) To amend the percentages specified in s 38(1) and to make provision with respect to the transactions and risks to be taken into account for the purposes of s 38 (Reports of large exposures): s 38(11).

(x) To make regulations applying to any accountants or class of accountants to whom s 47(1) applies specifying circumstances in which matters are to be communicated to the Bank as mentioned in that subsection: s 47(5).

(xi) To amend the sums mentioned in s 54(1) (Further contributions): s 54(2).

(xii) To amend the sums and the percentage specified in s 56(1), (2) and (3) (Maximum and minimum contributions): s 56(5).

(xiii) To amend the fraction specified in s 58(1), (2) and (6) (Compensation payments to depositors): s 58(7).

(xiv) To amend the sum specified in s 60(1) and (2) (Protected deposits): s 60(5).

(xv) To amend the sum specified in respect of unissued share capital, undistributable reserves and designated fixed capital accounts in s 67(2): s 67(6).

(xvi) To provide that the prohibitions in s 67 (Restriction on use of banking names) and s 68 (Restriction on use of banking descriptions) shall not apply to any person or class of persons or that it shall apply to a person previously exempted: ss 68(7), 69(7).

(xvii) To order that s 39 (Power to obtain information and require production of documents) and s 40 (Right of entry) shall apply in relation to overseas institutions: s 79(7).

(xviii) To impose on overseas institutions which have established or propose to establish representative offices in the United Kingdom such requirements as the Treasury considers appropriate in connection with those officers or the activities conducted from them: s 80(1).

(xix) To amend the Table of specified persons and functions in s 84(1) (disclosure for facilitating discharge of functions by other supervisory authorities): s 84(2).

The powers of the Treasury to make orders or regulations under the Act are exercisable by statutory instrument (s 102).

CHAPTER 2

THE COMPANIES ACT 1985

This Chapter considers the provisions of the Companies Act 1985 which are specific to authorised institutions and banking companies. 'Authorised institution' is defined in the Act to mean a company which is an institution authorised under the Banking Act 1987 (s 744); 'banking company' means a company which is an authorised institution (s 257(1)(a)).

1 DISCLOSURE OF INTERESTS IN SHARES

Part VI of the Companies Act 1985 (ss 198–220) makes provision for the disclosure of interests in shares in a public company. Where a person either (a) to his knowledge acquires an interest in shares comprised in a public company's relevant share capital, or ceases to be interested in shares so comprised, or (b) becomes aware that he has acquired an interest in shares so comprised or that he has ceased to be interested in shares so comprised in which he was previously interested, then in certain circumstances he comes under an obligation to make notification to the company of the interests which he has, or had, in the shares (s 198(1)). The obligation of disclosure arises where a person has a notifiable interest immediately after the relevant time,[1] but did not have such an interest immediately before that time (s 199(4)), and in the converse case (s 199(5)(a)), and where there is a change in the percentage level of a person's notifiable interest (s 199(5)(b)). A person has a notifiable interest at any time when he is interested in shares comprised in the relevant share capital[2] of the company concerned of an aggregate nominal value equal to or more than the percentage of the nominal value of that share capital which is for the time being the notifiable percentage (s 199(2)). The notifiable percentage is 5% or such other percentage as may from time to time be prescribed by statutory instrument (s 201(1)).

The words 'an interest in shares' include an interest of any kind whatsoever in the shares (s 208(1)). Where shares comprised in a public company's relevant share capital are pledged or charged to a bank as security, the bank clearly acquires 'an interest in shares' for the purposes of ss 198 to 202. However, there are certain acquisitions which fall outside the mischief at

1 'Relevant time' is defined in s 198(4).
2 'Relevant share capital' is defined in s 198(2).

29

which Part VI is directed, and accordingly the Act goes on to provide that certain interests are to be disregarded for the purposes of the above sections. These interests include *an exempt security interest* (s 209(1)(g)). An interest is an exempt security interest if (a) it is held by (inter alios) a person who is an authorised institution and (b) it is held by way of security only for the purpose of a transaction entered into in the ordinary course of its business as such a person (s 209(5)).

2   ACCOUNTS OF AUTHORISED INSTITUTIONS

(a) Disclosure of dealings with and for directors

A holding company's group accounts for a financial year and, in the case of a company other than a holding company, its individual accounts, are required to comply with the Companies Act 1985, Sch 6, Part 1 as regards the disclosure of transactions, arrangements and agreements there mentioned (loans, quasi-loans and other dealings in favour of directors and connected persons) (s 232(1),(2)). These requirements apply with such exceptions as are mentioned in Sch 6, Part 1, including, in particular, exceptions for and in respect of authorised institutions (s 232(5)).

By Sch 6, paras 1 and 2, group accounts and the accounts prepared by a company other than a holding company are required to contain particulars of any transactions, arrangements and agreements described in those paragraphs. However, paras 1 and 2 do not apply for the purposes of accounts prepared by a company which is, or is the holding company of, an authorised institution in relation to a transaction or arrangement of a kind described in s 330, or an agreement to enter into such a transaction or arrangement, to which that authorised institution is a party (Sch 6, para 4). The application of Sch 6, Part 1 to such accounts is thus effectively limited to transactions or arrangements outside s 330, being: (1) in relation to group accounts, any transaction or arrangement with a *company* or *its subsidiary* in which a person who was at any time during the financial year a director of the *company* or *its holding company*, had, directly or indirectly, a material interest (Sch 6, para 1(c)); and (2) in relation to accounts prepared by an authorised institution other than a holding company, any transaction or arrangement with the *company* in which a person who at any time during the financial year was a director of the *company* or its *holding company* had, directly or indirectly, a material interest (Sch 6, para 2(c)). An interest in such a transaction or arrangement is not material for these purposes if that is the opinion of the board (meaning the director of the company preparing the accounts, or a majority of those directors, but excluding in either case the director whose interest it is), but this is without prejudice to the question whether or not such an interest is material in a case where the board do not consider the matter (Sch 6, para 3). The particulars required to be disclosed by Sch 6, Part 1 are those of the principal terms of the transaction, arrangement or agreement (Sch 6, para 9).

The exception in favour of authorised institutions as regards disclosure of particulars in relation to s 330 transactions, arrangements and agreements is narrowed by s 234. This provides that the group accounts of a company which is, or is the holding company of, an authorised institution, and the individual accounts of any other company which is an authorised institution, are required to comply with Sch 6, Part III as regards transactions, arrangements and agreements made by the company preparing the accounts (if it is an authorised institution) and, in the case of a holding company, by any of its subsidiaries which is an authorised institution, for persons[3] who at any time during the financial year were *directors of the company* or *connected with a director of it.*[4]

Schedule 6, Part III applies to the following classes of transactions, arrangements and agreements (paras 15(a), 18):

(1) (a) loans, guarantees and securities relating to loans;
    (b) arrangements relating to loans, being arrangements of a kind described in s 330(6) (assignment to a company or assumption by it of any rights, obligations or liabilities under a transaction) or s 330(7) (arrangement whereby a person obtaining a benefit from a company enters into a transaction);
    (c) agreements to enter into any of the foregoing transactions and arrangements;
(2) (a) quasi-loans;[5]
    (b) guarantees and securities relating to quasi-loans;
    (c) arrangements of a kind described in either of s 330(6) or (7) relating to quasi-loans;
    (d) agreements to enter into any of the foregoing transactions and arrangements;
(3) (a) credit transactions;
    (b) guarantees and securities relating to credit transactions;
    (c) arrangements of a kind described in either of s 330(6) or (7) relating to credit transactions;
    (d) agreements to enter into any of the foregoing transactions and arrangements;

To comply with the Sch 6, Part III the accounts must contain a statement in relation to transactions, arrangements and agreements made as mentioned in s 234(1) of (a) the aggregate *amount* outstanding (defined in Sch 6, para 21) at the end of the financial year under transactions, arrangements and agreements to which Sch 6, Part III applies (see supra), and (b) the *number of persons* for whom the transactions, arrangements and agreements falling within each of sub-paragraphs (1), (2) and (3) above were made (Sch 6, para 19).

In summary, the accounts prepared by a company which is, or is the holding company of, an authorised institution are not required to contain particulars of the principal terms of any transaction, etc of a kind described in s 330, or an agreement to enter into such a transaction, but such accounts must contain in relation to loans, quasi-loans, credit transactions, etc, made by the company for directors or connected persons a statement of the aggre-

3 As to the meaning of 'for persons', see s 331(9); Sch 6, para 21(b).
4 As to the meaning of a person being 'connected' with a director, see s 346; Sch 6, paras 20 and 21(c).
5 'Quasi-loan' means a transaction under which one party ('the creditor') agrees to pay, or pays otherwise than in pursuance of an agreement, a sum for another ('the borrower') or agrees to reimburse, or reimburses otherwise than in pursuance of an agreement, expenditure incurred by a third party for another ('the borrower'), on terms that the borrower will reimburse the creditor, or in circumstances giving rise to a liability to reimburse: s 331(3); Sch 6 para 21(a).

gate outstanding amounts thereof and the number of persons for whom such transactions were made. As regards any transaction outside s 330 in which a director had a material interest, such accounts must comply with Sch 6, Part I, which requires disclosure of the terms of the transaction.

(b) Loans, etc to officers of an authorised institution

The Companies Act 1985, s 233(1) and (2) require a holding company's group accounts for a financial year and, in the case of a company other than a holding company, its individual accounts, to comply with Sch 6, Part II as regards loans, quasi-loans, credit transactions, etc made by the company or a subsidiary of it for persons who at any time during that financial year were officers of the company, but not directors. 'Officer' is defined in s 744 to include a director, manager or secretary. However, these requirements do not apply in relation to any transaction, arrangement or agreement made by an authorised institution for any of its officers or for any officer of its holding company unless the officer is a chief executive or manager within the meaning of the Banking Act 1987 (s 233(3), as substituted by the Banking Act 1987, s 90(1)).

(c) Authorised institutions as special category companies

For the purposes of the Companies Act 1985, 'special category companies' include banking companies, and a banking company means a company which is an authorised institution (s 257(1)(a)). The individual accounts of a special category company and the group accounts of a holding company which is, or has as its subsidiary, a special category company, may be prepared either under ss 221–256 and Sch 4 or under ss 257–262 and Sch 9 (s 257(3)).

Where accounts are prepared under Sch 9, para 27 of that Schedule applies to any banking company (if not subject to the Banking Companies (Accounts) Regulations 1970[6]) which satisfies the Secretary of State that it ought to have the benefit of that paragraph, in which event the company is not subject to the requirements of Sch 9, Part 1 (General provisions as to balance sheet and profit and loss account) save in certain respects set out in paras 27(2) and (3). Furthermore, the company's accounts are not to be deemed, by reason only of the fact that they do not comply with any requirements of Sch 9, Part 1 from which the company is exempt, not to give the true and fair view required by the Act (para 29(4)).

3   RESTRICTION OF LOANS, ETC TO DIRECTORS AND CONNECTED PERSONS

Section 330 of the Companies Act 1985 prohibits a company from making a loan to a director of the company or its holding company and from entering into any guarantee or providing any security in respect of such a loan

---

6 SI 1970/327. The Regulations apply to any banking company which is for the time being one of the London Clearing Banks or represented on the Committee of Scottish Bank General Managers.

(s 330(2)). It also prohibits a public company and a company falling within any of three other specified classes ('*a relevant company*') (a) from making a 'quasi-loan'[7] to a director of the company or its holding company, and (b) from making loans, etc to a person connected with a director (s 330(3)); and also from entering into a credit transaction, etc for such a director or a person so connected (s 330(4)). These prohibitions are subject to the exceptions contained in ss 332 to 338 (s 330(1)). The following exceptions relate specifically to authorised institutions.

(a) Exception in respect of loans, etc (other than housing loans)

There is excepted (a) a loan or quasi-loan made by a money-lending company to *any* person, and (b) a money-lending company entering into a guarantee in connection with any loan or quasi-loan (s 338(1)). 'Money-lending company' means a company whose ordinary business includes the making of loans or quasi-loans, or the giving of guarantees in connection with loans or quasi-loans. As regards *relevant companies*, authorised institutions enjoy a wider exception than other money-lending companies because they are not subject to the £50,000 limit imposed by s 338(4). Thus all authorised institutions which are money-lending companies enjoy an unlimited exception from the s 330 prohibitions as regards loans and quasi-loans to any person and guarantees given in connection with any loan or quasi-loan.

(b) Housing loans, etc

Although authorised institutions are exempted from the £50,000 limit imposed by s 338(4), they are subject to a limit in respect of one particular type of loan, namely a loan for the purpose of facilitating the purchase or improvement for use as a director's only or main residence of a dwelling-house, together with any land to be occupied and enjoyed with it (s 338(6)). However, here too authorised institutions enjoy a specific exemption. The £50,000 limit in s 338(6) is expressed by reference to 'the aggregate of the relevant amounts', which means, in essence, the aggregate of amounts lent under any other exceptions from the prohibitions in s 330. As regards an authorised institution, where it proposes to make a house loan, etc, any other transaction or arrangement which would otherwise fall within the transactions or arrangements by reference to which the relevant amounts are ascertained, is excluded unless it was also a housing loan (s 339(4)).

4 RECORD OF TRANSACTIONS NOT DISCLOSED IN COMPANY ACCOUNTS

Authorised institutions and their holding companies must maintain a register containing a copy of every transaction, arrangement or agreement of which particulars would, but for Sch 6 para 4 (see supra) be required by s 232 to be disclosed in the company's accounts or group accounts for the current financial year and for each of the preceding 10 years (s 343(1) and (2)). In the case

---

7 For the meaning of 'quasi-loan', see note 5, ante.

of a transaction which is not in writing, the register must contain a written memorandum setting out its terms (s 343(3)). The Act provides an exception in favour of certain transactions made or subsisting during a financial year if the aggregate values do not exceed £1,000 (s 344(1)).

CHAPTER 3

THE FINANCIAL SERVICES ACT 1986

The Financial Services Act 1986 ('the FSA') regulates the carrying on of investment business in the United Kingdom. 'Investment' for these purposes means any asset, right or interest falling within Sch 1, Part 1 of the Act (s 1(1)). 'Investment business' means the business of engaging in one or more activities falling within Sch 1, Part II, if not excluded by Sch 1, Part III (s 1(2)). The basic position is that it is unlawful to carry on an investment business in the UK without being either an authorised or an exempted person. Exempted persons include the Bank of England (s 35) and, in respect of specified transactions only, listed money market institutions (s 43). The Act has specific application to authorised institutions under the Banking Act 1987 in the following respects.

1 CLIENTS' MONEY

Section 55 of FSA, which came into force on 4 June 1988,[1] empowers the Secretary of State to make regulations with respect to money held by authorised persons in such circumstances as are specified in the regulations.

Regulations have been made by The Securities and Investments Board Ltd ('the SIB') as a designated agency under s 114 of the Act. The principal regulations are the Financial Services (Clients' Money) Regulations 1987 (as amended),[2] which came into operation on 29 April 1988.[3] The regulations provide that a firm which receives or holds client money must open one or more client bank accounts (reg 3.1(1)).

Each of the expressions 'a firm', 'client money' and 'client bank account' are defined, but the precise definitions are not relevant for present purposes. The regulations provide for the opening of a client bank account with an *approved bank*, which is defined to include, in the case of an account opened at a branch in the United Kingdom, an authorised institution under the Banking Act 1987 (reg 1.3).

1 The Financial Services Act 1986 (Commencement) (No 5) Order 1987, SI 1987/907.
2 The Financial Services (Clients' Money) Regulations were amended by the Financial Services (Miscellaneous Amendments) (No 5) Rules and Regulations 1988.
3 Ie the day on which s 3 came into force: Financial Services Act 1986 (Commencement) (No 8) Order 1988, SI 1988/740.

On opening a client bank account with an approved bank, a firm must give written notice to the bank concerned:

(a) that all money standing to the credit of that account is held by the firm as a trustee (or agent) and that the bank is not entitled to combine the account with any other account or to exercise any right of set-off or counterclaim against money in that account in respect of any sum owed to it on any other account of the firm;
(b) that interest payable in respect of sums credited to the account shall be credited to that account; and
(c) requiring the bank to acknowledge in writing that it accepts the terms of the notice (reg 3.1(4)).

Where the firm itself is an approved bank, a client bank account may be held with it as a segregated trust or agency account subject to the regulations, and, subject to observing normal banking practice and complying with the regulations, it is not liable to account for any profits made by its use as banker of the funds in the account (reg 3.1(5)).

The SIB has also made the Financial Services (Investment Business Clients' Money) (Chartered Accountants) Regulations 1988, which came into operation on 1 October 1988, and contain provisions similar to those contained in the Financial Services (Clients' Money) Regulations 1987.

The FSA provides a limitation on liability in respect of client accounts. By s 55(4), an institution with which an account is kept in pursuance of regulations made under s 55 does not incur any liability as constructive trustee where money is wrongfully paid from the account unless the institution permits the payment knowing that it is wrongful or having deliberately failed to make enquiries in circumstances in which a reasonable and honest person would have done so. This appears to remove as a ground of liability (if such a ground exists) knowledge within categories (iv) and (v) set out in *Baden, Delvaux v Société General pour Favoriser le Developpement du Commerce et de l'Industrie en France SA*,[4] viz (iv) knowledge of circumstances which would have indicated the facts to an honest and reasonable man, and (v) knowledge of circumstances which would have put an honest and reasonable man on inquiry.

2   COLLECTIVE INVESTMENT SCHEMES

The basic position under the FSA is that it is unlawful for an authorised institution to market in the United Kingdom a collective investment scheme unless the scheme is an authorised unit trust scheme or a recognised scheme under Chapter VIII of Part I (ss 75–95).

A collective investment scheme means, essentially, any arrangements (1) with respect to property, the purpose or effect of which is to enable persons taking part to participate in or receive profits or income arising therefrom (s 75(1)); (2) under which the participants do not have day to day control over the management of the property (s 75(2)); and (3) in which the contributions of participants, and the profits or income out of which payments are to be made to them, are pooled (s 75(3)).

4 [1983] BLCL 325 at 407.

The FSA goes on to provide that certain arrangements do not constitute a collective investment scheme. These include arrangements where the receipt of the participants' contributions:

(i) constitutes the acceptance of deposits in the course of a deposit-taking business for the purposes of the Banking Act 1987; and
(ii) does not constitute a transaction prescribed by regulations made by the Treasury for the purposes of s 4(4) of that Act (an exempt transaction) (s 75(6)(e)).

3 RECIPROCAL FACILITIES FOR BANKING BUSINESS

The Act contains provisions to ensure that countries outside the United Kingdom provide reciprocal facilities for banking business.

If it appears to the Treasury that by reason of (a) the law of any country outside the United Kingdom or (b) any action taken by or the practices of the government or any authority or body in that country, persons connected[5] with the United Kingdom are unable to carry on banking business in (or in relation to) that country on terms as favourable as those on which persons connected with that country are able to carry on business in the United Kingdom, the Treasury may serve a notice ('a s 183 notice') on any person connected with that country who is carrying on or intends to carry on any such business in the United Kingdom (s 183(1)). A s 183 notice may only be served if the Treasury considers that it is in the national interest to do so (s 183(2)).

Section 91 of the Banking Act 1987 declares that a s 183 notice may be served on any person connected with the country in question who is carrying on or appears to intend to carry on in the United Kingdom business of *any* of the descriptions specified in s 183(1), whether or not it is of the same description as that affected by the less favourable terms which are the occasion of the service of the notice. Section 183(1) specifies investment, insurance and banking business. Thus a s 183 notice may be served on a person carrying on banking business in the United Kingdom if the country with which he is connected does not provide reciprocal facilities to those in the United Kingdom in respect of investment or insurance business.

A s 183 notice relating to the carrying on of a deposit-taking business may be either a disqualification notice or a partial restriction notice (s 185(1)). A *disqualification* notice has the effect of cancelling any authorisation granted to the person concerned under the Banking Act 1987 and disqualifying him from becoming an authorised institution within the meaning of that Act (s 185(2)). A *partial restriction* notice may:

(a) prohibit the person concerned from dealing with or disposing of his assets in any manner specified in the direction;
(b) impose limitations on the acceptance by him of deposits;
(c) prohibit him from soliciting deposits either generally or from persons who are not already depositors;

5 As to the meaning for these purposes of a person being 'connected with' a country, see s 183(4).

(d) prohibit him from entering into any other transaction or class of trans-
    actions;
(e) require him to take certain steps, to pursue or refrain from pursuing a
    particular course of activities, or to restrict the scope of his business in a
    particular way (s 185(3)).

The Treasury has power to vary a partial restriction notice and to revoke
either a disqualification notice or a partial restriction notice; and it must
revoke a notice if it appears that the grounds specified in s 183(1) no longer
exist (s 186(1) and (2)). The revocation of a disqualification notice does not
have the effect of reviving the deposit-taking authorisation which it cancelled,
but a person who has been subject to a disqualification notice which was
revoked may again become authorised (s 186(4) and (5)).

The service of a s 183 notice has two further consequences under the Banking
Act 1987. First, the service of a disqualification notice is a ground on which
the Bank of England may exercise its power to give directions under s 19 of
that Act (s 19(1)(f)). Secondly, the Treasury has the power to direct the Bank
of England to serve a notice of objection under s 23(1) of that Act on a person
who has given notice of his intention to become a shareholder controller of
any description of an institution, or who has become such a controller without
giving the required notice, if it appears that in the event of his becoming (or
having become) such a controller, a s 183 notice could be served on the
institution by the Treasury (s 23(1)). More generally, the Bank of England
may revoke the deposit-taking authorisation of an institution if it appears
that the institution has ceased to be an authorised institution under the FSA
otherwise than at its request or with its consent (Banking Act 1987, s 11(4)).

4   INTER-RELATION BETWEEN AUTHORISATIONS

Some institutions carry on both a deposit-taking business and an investment
business. To meet this situation, the FSA was enacted with a provision (s 193)
that the restriction on deposit-taking in s 1(1) of the Banking Act 1979 was
not to apply to the acceptance of a deposit by an authorised or exempted
person (under the FSA) in the course of or for the purpose of engaging in
any activity within Sch 1, paras 12, 13, 14 or 16 on behalf of the depositor.

The Banking Act 1987, Sch 7, Part I has repealed both the Banking Act
1979 and s 193 of the FSA.[6] The interrelation between authorisations under
the Banking Act 1987 and the FSA is now governed by the Banking Act 1987
(Exempt Transactions) Regulations 1988,[7] which provide that the acceptance
of a deposit by a person who is an authorised or an exempted person under
the FSA is an exempt transaction (under the Banking Act 1987) if the deposit
is accepted in the course of or for the purpose of engaging in any dealing
activity with or on behalf of the person by whom or on whose behalf the
deposit is made or any service activity on behalf of that person.[8] The exemption applies to an FSA *authorised* person only if the activity is one in which
he may engage without contravening the rules (made by the appropriate
authority or a recognised organisation) of the kind described in s 48(2)(a)

6 See Ch 1, ante.
7 SI 1988/646, amended by SI 1989/465.
8 Ibid, reg 14(1).

and (b) of the FSA (rules as to type of business carried on or the persons in relation to whom business is carried on) or any prohibition of the kind described in s 65 of the FSA.[9] The exemption applies to an FSA *exempted* person only if the activity is one in respect of which he is exempt under the FSA.[10]

---

9 Ibid, reg 14(2). The FSA, s 65 empowers the Secretary of State to prohibit an authorised person from (1) entering into transactions of any specified kind or entering into them except in specified circumstances or to a specified extent; (2) soliciting business from persons of a specified kind or otherwise than from such persons or in a specified country or territory outside the United Kingdom; (3) carrying on business in a specified manner or otherwise than in a specified manner.

10 Ibid, reg 14(3).

CHAPTER 4

THE INSURANCE COMPANIES ACT 1982

It is necessary to consider certain limited provisions of the Insurance Companies Act 1982 because the classes of insurance business specified in Sch 1 are so wide as to catch certain types of transaction which are commonplace in modern commercial banking, in particular the issue of bank guarantees and the writing of cap agreements. It is presumably in recognition of this difficulty that the Act contains an exemption in favour of bankers.

The Act provides a system of authorisation broadly similar to that which exists under the Financial Services Act 1986 and the Banking Act 1987. By s 2(1), no person may carry on any insurance business in the United Kingdom unless authorised to do so under ss 3 or 4.[1] The Act contains a non-exhaustive definition of insurance business (s 95), and a specification of classes of long-term business (Sch 1), and classes and groups of general business (Sch 2). The classes of general business include classes 14 (Credit), 15 (Suretyship), 16 (Miscellaneous financial loss) and 17 (Legal expenses). The description of each class is supplemented by a definition of the nature of the insurance business falling within it.

Although some of the business within classes 14 to 17 appears to be largely unconnected with the business of banking, it must have been contemplated by the legislature that each class is at least capable of being carried on in the course of a banking business. This is apparent from s 2(4), which provides:

'(4) Subsection (1) above [restriction on carrying on insurance business] shall not apply to general business of class 14, 15, 16 or 17 if it is carried on solely in the course of carrying on, and for the purposes of, banking business.'

There are, then, three conditions to be satisfied by a person claiming the benefit of this exemption:

1 He must be carrying on general business of one or more of the specified classes.
2 He must be carrying on a banking business.
3 The general business must be carried on in the course of carrying on, and for the purposes of, a banking business.

1 For the effects of illegality, see *Phoenix General Insurance Co of Greece SA v Halvanon Insurance Co Ltd* [1988] QB 216, [1987] 2 All ER 152, CA.

1   CARRYING ON GENERAL BUSINESS OF CLASSES 14–17

For a complete definition of classes 14–17, reference must be made to Sch 2, Part 1 of the Act. It may, however, be helpful to set out here the two sub-classes (15(b) and 16(c)) which appear to have by far the closest connection with banking:

Class	Description	Nature of business
15	Suretyship	Effecting and carrying out –
		....
		(b) contracts of fidelity bonds, performance bonds, administration bonds, bail bonds or customs bonds or similar contracts of guarantee.
16	Miscellaneous financial loss	Effecting and carrying out contracts of insurance against any of the following risks, namely –
		....
		(c) risks neither falling within paragraph 16(a) [Business interruption] or (b) [Unforeseen expense] nor being of a kind such that the carrying on of the business of effecting and carrying out contracts of insurance against them constitutes the carrying on of insurance business of some other class.

Class 15(b) appears to include the issue of performance bonds, standby letters of credit and bank guarantees. Class 16(c) appears to include the writing of cap agreements, whether in respect of interest rates or exchange rates.

The types of business covered by class 15(b) are referred to again in s 95(a), which provides:

'95. For the purposes of this Act 'insurance business' includes –
(a) the effecting and carrying out, *by a person not carrying on a banking business*, of contracts for fidelity bonds, performance bonds, administration bonds, bail bonds or customs bonds or similar contracts of guarantee, being contracts effected by way of business (and not merely incidentally to some other business carried on by the person effecting them) in return for the payment of one or more premiums;'

The purpose of this provision is not entirely clear. Insofar as it defines insurance business, it restates with modifications the definition in Class 15(b). Insofar as the italicised words are intended to protect bankers, the provision overlaps with s 2(4), supra.

The expression 'carry on [a trade or business]' and related expressions have appeared in numerous statutes.[2] It has been said that there is no principle of law which decides what 'carrying on' trade is – it is a compound fact made up of a variety of things.[3] In the present context it is perhaps pertinent to note the observation of Lord Loreburn LC in *Kirkwood v Gadd*, that carrying on a business imports a series or repetition of acts,[4] the relevant acts in this context being the effecting and carrying out of specified contracts of insurance.

2 See *Stroud's Judicial Dictionary* (5th edn, 1986), vol 1, pp. 364–368.
3 *Erichsen v Last* (1881) 8 QBD 414 at 416 per Jessel MR.
4 [1910] AC 422 at 423.

2   CARRYING ON A BANKING BUSINESS

The Act does not define 'banking business'. At common law, there is no exhaustive definition of 'banking business', but there are established characteristics of such business. These characteristics, and the relevance of authorisation under the Banking Act 1987 to the determination of banking status at law, are considered in Ch 6, post.

3   IN THE COURSE OF CARRYING ON, AND FOR THE PURPOSES OF, BANKING BUSINESS

There is considerable overlap between the expressions 'in the course of carrying on banking business' and 'for the purposes of banking business'. Both seem to require that the carrying on of insurance business should be in some way incidental[5] or connected with[6] the carrying on of banking business, and not simply an independent business which happens to be carried on by a bank. The distinction between the expressions is perhaps best illustrated by *Havering London Borough v Stevenson*,[7] where it was held that the sale, by a person who carried on a car-hire business, of a car which had been used in the business was a sale in the course of trade or business, but not for its purpose.

Although each case must no doubt turn on its own particular facts, two general points can be made. First, once the court is satisfied that the relevant person carries on a banking business, it then appears to be necessary to establish the scope of that business. A banking business may, of course, comprise more than the essential characteristics of banking. As it was put in *Royal Bank of Canada v IRC*,[8] a statement of the essentials of a business is not, without more, exhaustive of all that is ordinary in that business. This observation was made with reference to the words 'ordinary banking transactions' in s 414(5) of the Income Tax Act 1952, but the reasoning is of general application. Indeed, it is difficult to see that general insurance business within classes 14 to 18 could ever be carried on solely in the course of carrying on, and for purposes of, the essentials of a banking business, ie the conduct of current accounts, and the payment and collection of cheques.

Secondly s 2(4) does not, it is submitted, impose a requirement that the insured should be a customer of the bank. The wording of the section does not on its ordinary construction impose any such requirement. Nor would the drawing of a distinction between customers and non-customers accord with the apparent purpose of the exemption, namely to place exempted persons, most of whom will be authorised institutions under the Banking Act 1987, wholly outside the authorisation procedure under the 1982 Act. It is noteworthy that the Banking Act 1987 contains a matching exemption in favour of any institution which is for the time being authorised under s 3 or

---

5 Nb the expression in s 95(a) 'contracts effected by way of business (and not merely *incidentally* to some other business carried on by the person effecting them) . . . .'

6 In *Re Pryce, ex p Rensburg* (1877) 4 Ch D 685, it was held that the words in the Bankruptcy Act 1883, s 44(2)(iii) 'Debts due to the bankrupt in the course of his trade' included only debts connected with the trade.

7 [1970] 3 All ER 609, [1970] 1 WLR 1375.

8 [1972] Ch 665 at 679, [1972] 1 All ER 225 at 235, per Megarry J.

4 of the Insurance Companies Act 1982 to carry on insurance business of a class specified in Sch 1 or 2 to that Act, the exception being limited to the acceptance of deposits in the course of carrying on the authorised insurance business.[9]

9 Banking Act 1987, s 4(1), Sch 2, para 8.

CHAPTER 5

THE CONSUMER CREDIT ACT 1974[1]

The Consumer Credit Act regulates lending to non-corporate persons of up to a prescribed sum (currently £15,000[2]) and the hiring of goods to such persons for payments not exceeding the same prescribed sum. The system is administered by the Director General of Fair Trading and the Act prescribes the role of the Director, the persons who may properly provide regulated credit and hire services and the manner in which they may offer and supply their services. There are also provisions of general application to the advertising of credit and to so-called 'extortionate credit bargains'. The Act was passed to give effect to recommendations made by the Crowther Committee on Consumer Credit[3] for the protection of the debtor or hirer and, in particular, to replace the then existing regulation contained in the Pawnbrokers Acts 1872 and 1960, Moneylenders Acts 1900 and 1927, and Hire Purchase Act 1965.

1 THE DIRECTOR GENERAL OF FAIR TRADING

The duties of the Director specified in Part I of the Act (ss 1–7) relate to licensing, adjudication, policing and review. As regards licensing, his duty is to administer the licensing system established by the Act (s 1(1)(a)). He must adjudicate upon the issue, renewal, variation, suspension and revocation of licences and other matters (s 1(1)(b)). The policing function is expressed in terms of a duty generally to superintend the working and enforcement of the Act and if necessary to initiate enforcement (s 1(1)(c),(d)). His duties of review are qualified to the extent that he is only required, so far as appears to him to be practicable, to keep under review social and commercial developments relating to the provision of credit or bailment and the working and enforcement of the Act (s 1(2)).

The functions of the Director may be supervised by the Secretary of State by means of orders and directions. By order the Secretary of State may expand the functions of the Director and regulate the way he carries them out (s 2(1)). Such orders are made by statutory instruments which are subject

1 The editor gratefully acknowledges that this chapter has been contributed by Mr Neil Levy, LLB, of Lincoln's Inn, Barrister.
2 SI 1983/1878.
3 Cmnd 4596, March 1971.

to annulment by either House of Parliament (s 182(1)), with the exception of orders expanding the functions of the Director, which must be by statutory instrument approved by both Houses of Parliament (s 2(6)). Directions may also be given as to the way in which the Director carries out his functions but may not affect determinations and decisions which he makes against which there lies an appeal to the Secretary of State (s 2(2), (7)). Subject to this, directions may be general or specific. General directions indicate considerations to which the Director should pay particular regard; specific directions may be given on any matter (s 2(2)). The Secretary of State is obliged to publish all directions (s 2(3)) and the Act amends s 125 of the Fair Trading Act 1973 so that directions are set out in the Director's annual report to the Secretary of State, which is also published (s 5).

The Act also amended the Tribunals and Inquiries Act 1971[4] so that in carrying out his functions under the Consumer Credit Act the Director and his authorised staff are treated as a tribunal under the supervision of the Council on Tribunals (s 3(c)). But the provisions of the 1971 Act requiring the Secretary of State to apply to court to remove a tribunal member do not apply, nor does the 1971 Act regulate the exercise by the Director of executive functions (s 3(b)).[5] This means that insofar as the Director exercises executive functions he does not have to give reasons for his decisions. However the Director's adjudicating functions seem to be judicial rather than executive, in which case he would be subject to the requirement to give reasons for his determinations in any event.[6]

It is provided that the Director shall disseminate such information as appears to him expedient to give to the UK public about the operation of the Act, credit facilities available to them and other matters within his functions (s 4).

With the approval of the Secretary of State and Treasury, the Director may charge fees for services he provides under the Act. The level of fees must be specified in general notices published by the Director, and may be reduced or nil for persons of a specified description (s 2(4), (5)). Applications to the Director are of no effect unless in the form prescribed by general notice published by the Director and accompanied by the specified fee (s 6(1), (2)). The Director may request such further information as the notice specifies, require any information given to be verified, and by notice in writing to the applicant require details of the application to be published (s 6(3), (4)). Knowingly or recklessly giving materially false or misleading information to the Director in connection with an application or request is an offence with maximum penalties of a fine of the prescribed sum[7] upon summary conviction or two years' imprisonment and an unlimited fine upon conviction on indictment (ss 7, 167 and Sch 1).

4 By the addition of para 5A in Sch 1, new para 6A in Sch 1.
5 Amending Tribunals and Inquiries Act 1971, ss 8(2), 19(4).
6 s 12(1) Tribunals and Inquiries Act 1971, s 12(1).
7 Currently £2,000: SI 1984/447, made under Magistrates' Courts Act 1980, s 143.

2 TERMINOLOGY

The types of credit agreements, hire agreements and linked transactions to which the Act applies are set out in Part II (ss 8–20).

(a) Regulated consumer credit agreement

The Act defines a consumer credit agreement as a personal credit agreement by which the creditor provides the debtor with credit not exceeding £15,000[8] (s 8(2)). A personal credit agreement is an agreement between an individual ('the debtor') and any other person ('the creditor') by which the creditor provides the debtor with credit (s 8(1)).

'Individual' includes a partnership or other unincorporated body of persons not consisting entirely of bodies corporate (s 189(1)). Thus although one might expect the Act to apply only to protect consumers in the sense of individuals dealing other than in the course of a business or profession, in practice it applies for the protection of all non-corporate borrowers[9]. Moreover, an agreement for the provision of credit to two or more persons jointly where one or more of them is an individual and one or more a body corporate, is a consumer credit agreement if it would have been had they all been individuals, and in this event the body or bodies corporate qualify as debtors under the agreement (s 185(5)).

The terms 'creditor' and 'debtor' are also given extended meanings so as to apply not only to the persons providing and receiving (respectively) the credit under a consumer credit agreement, but also to any person to whom their rights and duties under the agreement have passed by assignment or operation of law (s 189(1)). It has been suggested that policy considerations should determine whether an equitable assignee who does not give notice of assignment to the debtor should be treated as the creditor in any particular case by virtue of this provision, since the debtor will continue to deal with the assignor. If so, the assignee might be treated as the creditor for the purpose of provisions restricting the rights of the creditor for the protection of the debtor but not for the purpose of provisions imposing obligations upon the creditor to provide information to the debtor.[10] The better view is thought to be that everything depends upon the terms of the assignment and, in particular, which rights and duties have been assigned. If all the rights and duties of the original creditor have been assigned in equity it is difficult to see why even an equitable assignee should not be treated as the creditor for the purpose of all the provisions of the Act.

'Credit' includes a cash loan and any other form of financial accommodation (s 9(1)). Cash includes money in any form (s 189(1)). Although financial accommodation could cover transactions which do not constitute the provision of credit in its accepted sense (eg a gift), it is thought that, construed in context, these words must be limited to financial accommodation provided on terms that the accommodated party incurs an unconditional

---

8 SI 1983/1878; the monetary limit may be amended by the Secretary of State by order made by statutory instrument approved by both Houses of Parliament: (s 181).
9 It is understood that an amendment may be made to the Act so that it will no longer apply to business lending.
10 Guest *Encyclopedia of Consumer Credit Law* para 2–190.

monetary repayment obligation with the right to defer repayment.[11] Credit
would not therefore be provided where there is no repayment obligation (eg
gifts, advance payments for goods or services) nor if the obligation to repay
may never arise (eg payments by way of security). Nor is credit provided
under a hire or leasing agreement.[12] Credit provided otherwise than in sterling
is treated as provided in the sterling equivalent (s 9(2)). Credit does not
include items entering into the total charge for credit (s 9(4)).

A person who bails goods under a hire-purchase agreement is deemed to
provide credit to the purchaser of a fixed sum equal to the total price of the
goods less any deposit and the total charge for credit (s 9(3)). A hire-purchase
agreement is an agreement, other than a conditional sale agreement, under
which goods are bailed in return for periodical payments by the person to
whom they are bailed and under which the property in the goods will pass
to that person if the terms of the agreement are complied with and either an
option to purchase is exercised by that person or some other specified act is
done by any party to the agreement or some other specified event occurs
(s 189(1)). A conditional sale agreement is an agreement for the sale of goods
or land under which the purchase price is payable by instalments and the
property in the goods or land is to remain in the seller (despite the buyer
being in possession) until such conditions as to the payment of instalments
or otherwise as specified in the agreement are fulfilled (s 189(1)). Most sale
agreements on retention of title terms would fall within the latter definition
and consequently outside the definition of hire-purchase, but if there is a
contractual deferment of the price payable, credit (within s 9(1)) would usually
be provided under a conditional sale agreement in any event. 'Total price'
means the total sum payable by the debtor under a hire-purchase or conditional sale agreement, including any sum payable on the exercise of an
option to purchase, but excluding any sum payable as a penalty or as
compensation or damages for breach of the agreement (s 189(1)).

A consumer credit agreement is a regulated agreement if it is not within
the categories of exempt agreements (s 8(3)).

(b) Running-account credit

This is a facility under a personal credit agreement whereby the debtor is
able to receive from time to time from the creditor or a third party cash,
goods or services to an amount or value such that, taking into account credits
paid in, the credit limit (if any) is not at any time exceeded (s 10(1)(a)). Credit
provided by way of overdraft on a bank current account, or on a retailer
budget account or credit card account is running-account credit (Examples
15, 16, 18 and 23, Part II, Sch 2). The credit limit for any period is the
maximum debit balance which under the credit agreement is permitted on
the account for that period, disregarding any term permitting temporary
excesses (s 10(2)). If there is a credit limit, running-account credit is deemed
not to exceed £15,000[13] if the credit limit does not exceed £15,000 (s 10(3)(a)).
But even if the credit limit does exceed £15,000 or if there is no credit limit,

---

11 Guest ibid para 2–010; *R v Mitchell* [1955] 3 All ER 263, [1955] 1 WLR 1125; *R v Garlick*
(1958) 42 Cr App Rep 141; *Fisher v Raven* [1964] AC 210, [1963] 2 All ER 389.
12 *Moorgate Mercantile Leasing Ltd v Isobel Gell and Ugolini Dispensers (UK) Ltd* [1986] CLY
371, 40 Consumer Credit, No 3, p 16.
13 Ie for the purposes of s 8(2).

it is also deemed not to exceed £15,000 in three cases. Firstly, if the debtor is not able to draw at any one time an amount of credit which exceeds £15,000 (s 10(3)(b)(i)). Secondly, if the agreement provides that if the debit balance rises above a given amount (not exceeding £15,000), the rate of the total charge for credit increases or any other condition favouring the creditor or his associate[14] comes into operation (s 10(3)(b)(ii)). Thirdly, if when the agreement is made it is probable that the debit balance will not rise above £15,000 (s 10(3)(b)(iii) and Example 7, Part II Sch 2), but in this case if the agreement contains a term that in the opinion of the parties this provision does not apply to the agreement, it is taken not to apply unless the contrary is proved (s 171(1)).

(c) Fixed-sum credit

This is credit under a personal credit agreement which is not running-account credit (s 10(1)(b)). Credit provided by way of personal loan on a bank or other account, or in a credit sale is fixed-sum credit (Examples 9, 10, 17 and 23, Part II, Sch 2). As seen above, the Act also deems credit provided on hire-purchase to be fixed-sum credit (s 9(3)). But permitting the credit limit of an agreement for running-account credit to be temporarily exceeded is not treated as providing fixed-sum credit in respect of the excess (s 18(5)).

(d) Restricted and unrestricted-use credit

A restricted-use credit agreement is a regulated consumer credit agreement to finance (whether wholly or partly) a transaction between the debtor and the creditor or between the debtor and a person other than the creditor whose identity need not be known at the time the agreement is made (s 11(4)), or to refinance (whether wholly or partly) any existing indebtedness of the debtor (s 11(1)). If the transaction financed is between the debtor and creditor, the creditor is a 'supplier' for the purposes of the Act (s 189(1)); if it is with a person other than the creditor, that person is a 'supplier' (s 11(1)(b)).[15] Credit provided under a hire-purchase agreement, or by way of a loan for payments direct to suppliers of goods or services, or on a credit card account when the card is used to obtain goods from suppliers, restricted-use credit agreement (Examples 10, 12, 13, 14 and 16 Part II, Sch 2).

A consumer credit agreement which is not a restricted-use credit agreement is an unrestricted-use credit agreement (s 11(2)), as is an agreement under which the credit is in fact provided in such a way as to leave the debtor free to use it as he chooses (even if certain uses are prohibited) (s 11(3)). Credit provided by way of a personal loan (without restriction on the use to which the funds are to be put), or on a credit card account when the card is used to obtain cash from the creditor,[16] or by way of overdraft on a bank current

---

14 Associate is defined in wide terms in s 184 and generally covers (a) an individual's family, relatives and business partners, and (b) a company's controllers and companies under the same control. 'Controller' means a person on whose instructions the company or a company which is its controller is accustomed to act or a person who controls at least one third of the votes in a general meeting of the company or of the company which is its controller.

15 'Supplier' includes any person to whom the supplier's rights and duties under the agreement have passed by assignment or operation of law (s 189(1)).

16 Quaere if the card is used to obtain cash from a third party. Probably such credit is restricted-use credit, by analogy with refinancing.

account is also unrestricted-use credit (Examples 8, 12, 16, 17, 18 and 21, Part II, Sch 2).

(e) Debtor-creditor-supplier agreement

This is a regulated consumer credit agreement taking one of three forms.

Firstly, a restricted-use credit agreement to finance (wholly or partly) a transaction between the debtor and the creditor (s 12(a)).

Secondly, a restricted-use credit agreement to finance (wholly or partly) a transaction between the debtor and supplier and which is made by the creditor under pre-existing arrangements, or in contemplation of future arrangements, between the creditor and supplier (s 12(b), Example 16, Part II, Sch 2). A consumer credit agreement is treated as entered into under pre-existing arrangements between a creditor and supplier if entered into in accordance with or in furtherance of arrangements previously made between either the creditor and supplier or between one of them and an associate[17] of the other or between associates of each of them (s 187(1), (4)). Such arrangements clearly exist between a credit card issuer and suppliers who are parties to the issuer's scheme (Example 16, Part II, Sch 2). But it will often be difficult to assess what constitutes arrangements when dealings between the creditor and supplier are informal or one-off (see Example 8, Part II, Sch 2). On the face of it, any dealing between potential supplier and creditor (acting as such) which materially facilitates the proposed consumer credit agreement could constitute such an arrangement. If the creditor is an associate of the supplier the agreement is presumed entered into under pre-existing arrangements between them unless the contrary is proved (s 187(5)). A consumer credit agreement is treated as entered into in contemplation of future arrangements between a creditor and supplier if entered into in the expectation that arrangements for the supply of cash, goods or services to be financed (wholly or partly) by the agreement will be made between either the creditor and supplier or between one of them and an associate of the other or between associates of each of them (s 187(2)). For the purposes of both of these deeming provisions arrangements for the creditor to make payments to the supplier in specified circumstances are disregarded if the creditor holds himself out as willing to make payments of that kind to suppliers generally in such circumstances (s 187(3), Example 21, Part II, Sch 2). This prevents the issue of a cheque guarantee card to a customer from constituting a debtor-creditor-supplier agreement. Further, by an amendment made by the Banking Act 1987, arrangements for the electronic transfer of funds from a current account at a bank within the Bankers' Books Evidence Act 1879 are also disregarded (s 187(3A)). This prevents agreements for electronic funds transfer facilities such as EFTPOS or EFTPOL from constituting debtor-creditor-supplier agreements.

The third form of debtor-creditor-supplier agreement is an unrestricted-use credit agreement made by the creditor under pre-existing arrangements between himself and a person other than the debtor in the knowledge that the credit is to be used to finance (wholly or partly) a transaction between the debtor and that person (who is a supplier for the purposes of the Act) (s 12(c), Example 8, Part II, Sch 2).

17 See n 14, p 48, above.

(f) Debtor-creditor agreement

This is a regulated consumer credit agreement taking one of three forms.

Firstly, a restricted-use credit agreement to finance (wholly or partly) a transaction between the debtor and supplier which does not fall within the second category of debtor-creditor-supplier agreements (s 13(a)). For example, a loan for payments to be made direct to a supplier (in the absence of pre-existing arrangements between creditor and supplier).

Secondly, a restricted-use credit agreement to refinance (wholly or partly) any existing indebtedness of the debtor (s 13(b)).

Thirdly, an unrestricted-use credit agreement which is not made by the creditor under pre-existing arrangements between himself and a person (the 'supplier') other than the debtor in the knowledge that the credit is to be used to finance (wholly or partly) a transaction between the debtor and the supplier (s 13(c)). For example, a loan provided without restriction on the use to which the funds are to be put, a credit card account when the card is used to obtain cash from the creditor, or a bank current account overdraft (Examples 8, 16, 17, 18 and 21, Part II, Sch 2).

(g) Credit-token agreement

This is a regulated agreement for the provision of credit in connection with the use of a credit-token (s 14(2)).

A credit-token is anything given to an individual[18] by a person carrying on a consumer credit business[19] who undertakes that on production of it (whether or not some other action is also required) either he will supply cash, goods or services on credit, or if a third party supplies any of these he will pay the third party for them in return for payment to him by the individual (s 14(1)). Examples of the former type of credit-token are bank credit cards which can be used to obtain cash on credit from the bank (Example 16, Part II, Sch 2) or a retailer's credit card which can be used to obtain goods or services from the retailer; examples of the latter type are credit cards which can be used to make payments to third party suppliers within the scheme (Examples 3, 16 and 22, Part II, Sch 2) or trading checks of a specified value issued by a creditor and which suppliers within the scheme will accept as payment up to that value (Example 14, Part II, Sch 2). A bank automated teller machine (ATM) card which can be used to obtain cash from ATMs of other banks probably falls within the first type of credit-token if, in dispensing cash, the other banks act as agents for the bank which issued the card. If the other banks act as principals, it would be a credit-token of the second type. Cheque guarantee cards are not credit-tokens even if the relevant account is in debit, for the guarantor undertakes to pay the cheques rather than to supply cash or pay for goods etc supplied by third parties (Example 21, Part II, Sch 2). The same reasoning would seem to prevent cheques themselves being treated as credit-tokens.

'Some other action' can include completion of the credit agreement. So the fact that use of a card to obtain credit is conditional upon completion of a credit agreement does not prevent the card from being a credit-token and,

18 See p 46, above.
19 See p 57, below.

further, the undertaking given by the person offering the credit need not be a contractually binding undertaking.[20]

It is expressly provided that the use of an object to operate a machine is treated as production of that object to the person providing the machine (s 14(3)). So, for example, use of a bank credit-card to obtain a rail ticket from a ticket machine is treated as production of the card to the railway company. In cases such as this, where a credit-token is produced to a third party, the person who issued the credit-token is taken to provide credit to the individual whenever the third party supplies the cash, goods or services (s 14(4)).

(h) Regulated consumer hire agreement

A consumer hire agreement is an agreement made by a person with an individual[21] (the 'hirer') for the bailment of goods to the hirer, which is not a hire-purchase agreement, is capable of subsisting for more than three months and does not require the hirer to make payments exceeding £15,000[1] (s 15(1)).

Although 'bailment' potentially has a very wide meaning (eg a deposit of goods with a mandate to perform work on them), it seems that consumer hire agreements should be limited to agreements for the letting of goods on hire,[2] for example equipment leasing agreements (Example 24, Part II, Sch 2). Hire-purchase agreements are not covered since the Act treats them as consumer credit agreements for fixed sum credit (see s 9(3), above).

An agreement does not 'require' payments exceeding £15,000 if, for example, it permits the hirer to terminate the agreement before the £15,000 limit is exceeded (Example 24, Part II, Sch 2). But for this purpose a statutory right of termination (eg that contained in s 101, below) is irrelevant (Example 20, Part II, Sch 2): only requirements embodied in the terms of the agreement are taken into account. It has been held that VAT on rentals, if charged under the agreement to the hirer, should be taken into account in calculating the £15,000 limit.[3] By analogy maintenance charges should probably also be taken into account.

A consumer hire agreement is a regulated agreement if it is not within the categories of exempt agreements (s 15(2)).

(i) Exempt agreement

An exempt agreement is a consumer credit or hire agreement which is not a regulated agreement (ss 8(3), 15(2), 16(1)). There are four categories of exempt agreements.

The first category covers certain types of consumer credit agreements made with a creditor of a specified class. The relevant classes of creditor are (s 16(1))

---

20 *Elliot v Director General of Fair Trading* [1980] 1 WLR 977.
21 See p 46, above.
1 For the financial limit see SI 1983/1878.
2 See Palmer and Yates [1979] Camb LJ 180; *General Motors Acceptance Corpn (UK) Ltd v IRC* [1987] STC 122, CA (agreement under which motor cars not to be driven pending sale or return not let on hire for the purposes of the Finance Act 1976, Sch 5, para 29(2)(c)). And see Example 20, Part II, Sch 2.
3 *Apollo Leasing Ltd v Scott* 1984 SLT (Sh Ct) 90.

a local authority or a body specified in an order made by the Secretary of State[4] being an insurance company (within s 96(1) of the Insurance Companies Act 1982), friendly society (registered under the Friendly Societies Acts 1896–1971), an organisation of employers or workers, a charity (registered under or exempt under the Charities Act 1960), a land improvement company (within s 7 of the Improvement of Land Act 1899), a corporation specifically referred to in any public general Act or in an order made under ss 156(4), 444(1) or 447(2)(a) of the Housing Act 1985, a building society (within the Building Societies Act 1986), an authorised institution (within the Banking Act 1987) or a wholly-owned subsidiary (within the meaning of the Companies Act 1985) of such an authorised institution.

The types of agreement which may qualify for exemption within this first category are (s 16(2)): (a) debtor-creditor-supplier agreements financing (wholly or partly) the purchase of land or the provision of dwellings on land and secured by a land mortgage on that land (in the Act land includes any interest in land and land mortgage includes any security[5] charged on land (s 189(1))); (b) debtor-creditor agreements secured by any land mortgage; and (c) debtor-creditor-supplier agreements financing (wholly or partly) any transaction which is a linked transaction either in relation to an agreement within (a) and secured by a land mortgage on the land referred to in (a), or in relation to an agreement within (b) which finances (wholly or partly) the purchase of land or the provision of dwellings on land and which is secured by a land mortgage on that land. However, an order of the Secretary of State specifying a body as being within the relevant classes of creditor may be limited so as to provide that only certain of the qualifying types of agreements made by that body are exempt (s 16(4)).[6] Under this power the Secretary of State has exempted certain consumer credit agreements secured on land where the creditor is a bank, building society or other body specified in the Schedule to the Order.[7]

The second category of exempt agreements covers consumer credit agreements which the Secretary of State has by order provided should not be regulated where the number of payments to be made by the debtor or the rate of the total charge for credit does not exceed that specified in the order (s 16(5)(a), (b))[8] or where the agreement has a connection with a country outside the UK (s 16(5)(c)).[9]

The third category of exempt agreements covers consumer hire agreements which the Secretary of State has by order provided should not be regulated where the owner is a corporation authorised by statute to supply electricity, gas or water and the agreement is a meter or metering agreement or the owner is a public telecommunication operator specified in the order (s 16(6)).[10]

The final category of exempt agreements covers consumer credit agreements where the creditor is a housing authority within s 80(1) of the Housing

---

4 The Consumer Credit (Exempt Agreements) Order 1989 SI 1989/869 has been made.
5 See p 92.
6 For the policy adopted by the Secretary of State in limiting such orders see para 9 and Annex A of the Department of Trade circular 'Exemption of Certain Consumer Credit Agreements under section 16(1)'.
7 SI 1989/869 ibid, art 2.
8 SI 1989/869 ibid, arts 3 and 4.
9 SI 1989/869 ibid, art 5.
10 SI 1989/869 ibid, art 6.

Act 1985 (not being a charitable housing association or housing trust) and the agreement is secured by a land mortgage of a dwelling (s 16(6A), (6B)).

It should be noted that even exempt agreements are subject to the provisions of the Act (ss 137–140) relating to extortionate credit bargains (s 16(7)).

(j) Small agreement

This is a regulated consumer credit agreement which is unsecured or secured[11] only by a guarantee or indemnity (whether or not the guarantee or indemnity is itself secured) and which (not being a hire-purchase or conditional sale agreement[12]) is for credit not exceeding £50[13] (s 17(1)) or which is a regulated consumer hire agreement not requiring the hirer to make payments exceeding £50 (s 17(1)). Small agreements would, for example, include loan agreements for credit of up to £50 or an agreement by a bank to permit a specified overdraft on a current account to meet payment of a cheque of up to £50 (Example 17, Part II, Sch 2).

If a small agreement is for running-account credit and there is a credit limit, the credit is deemed not to exceed £50 if the credit limit does not exceed £50[13] (s 17(2), Example 16, Part II, Sch 2).

If two or more small agreements are made at about the same time between the same parties and it appears probable that they would have been made as a single agreement but for the desire to avoid the operation of the Act as it would have applied to a single agreement, the Act applies to the small agreements as if they were regulated agreements other than small agreements (s 17(3)). Further, for the purpose of determining whether an agreement is made between the same parties an associate[14] of a party may be substituted for that party (s 17(4)).

(k) Multiple agreement

This is an agreement the terms of which either place a part of it within one category of agreement mentioned in the Act and another part of it within a different category of agreement (whether mentioned in the Act or not) or place it or a part of it within two or more categories of agreement mentioned in the Act (s 18(1)).

An example of an agreement falling into two categories, one within and one outside those mentioned in the Act, is an agreement to provide a bank current account and overdraft facility, for only the overdraft element is a debtor-creditor agreement (cf Example 18, Part II, Sch 2). An example of an agreement placed within two or more categories mentioned in the Act is a credit card agreement, which is a credit-token agreement, a debtor-creditor-supplier agreement (insofar as the card can be used to purchase goods) and a debtor-creditor agreement (insofar as the card can be used to obtain cash from the creditor) (Example 16, Part II, Sch 2).

If a part of an agreement falls within the definition of multiple agreement, that part is treated by the Act as a separate agreement (s 18(2)) and any sum payable under such an agreement, if not apportioned by the parties, will be

11 See p 92, below.
12 See p 47, above.
13 For the financial limits see SI 1983/1878.
14 See n 14, p 48, above.

apportioned by the court for the purposes of any proceedings (s 18(4)). Furthermore, if an agreement is in parts, each part (since it is treated as a separate agreement) might be required to be documented separately and if part falls outside the financial limits or within the categories of exempt agreements the agreement might be only partly regulated by the Act. This will not apply if the whole (rather than a part) of an agreement falls within the definition of multiple agreement. But there is no indication as to how to determine when an agreement is to be treated as unitary or in parts. It has been suggested that if the agreement could not be split up without affecting the character of the transaction it will be treated as a unitary agreement.[15] It has also been suggested that regard should be had to whether the terms of the agreement treat the elements differently and whether they are distinct in terms of subject-matter, legal classification and their operation under the Act.[16] Since the section is expressed to apply to an agreement 'if its terms are such as to' put it within one of the definitions, it is thought that the correct approach is to look primarily at whether the terms of the agreement treat the elements differently.

On either basis it is thought that a current account overdraft would be only partly within the definition of multiple agreement, the overdraft facility being treated as a separate agreement. It is difficult to know whether a credit card agreement would be treated as being in parts. A number of major credit card companies have assumed their agreements are unitary, and therefore give no separate treatment to the debtor-creditor and debtor-creditor-supplier elements. This is thought to be the correct view on the basis that in practice a credit card agreement is presented as a package which is not severable.

Other terms also give rise to difficulty. For example, it is unclear whether a provision for payment protection insurance (against the risk that payments cannot be maintained as a result of illness, unemployment and the like) would be a separate part of a regulated agreement. If the premium is financed by the creditor, the arrangement would constitute a debtor-creditor-supplier agreement, for there will be 'pre-existing arrangements' between the creditor and insurer. It is thought that such insurance is properly treated as a separate part of an agreement, for it is often offered as an 'option' and the nature of the rest of the agreement is unlikely to be affected by its exclusion. If a loan is made partly to refinance an existing facility and partly to provide additional cash, the arrangement would constitute an agreement for restricted and unrestricted-use credit respectively. It is thought that the arrangement can be treated as a unitary agreement if the same conditions (eg interest rate and repayment terms) apply to the two elements of the agreement.

The Act further provides that if the terms of the agreement place it or a part of it within two or more categories of agreement mentioned in the Act, it is treated as an agreement in each of the categories in question (s 18(3)). This will apply even if the agreement is not in parts and consequently does not fall to be treated as embodying separate agreements. For example, a credit card agreement would be treated as a credit-token agreement embodying both a debtor-creditor agreement for unrestricted-use credit (insofar as the card can be used to obtain cash from the creditor) and a debtor-creditor-supplier

15 Goode, *Consumer Credit Legislation* para I/564.
16 *Guest* ibid, para 2–019.

agreement for restricted-use credit (insofar as the card can be used to purchase goods on credit from third parties).

It is specifically provided that a term of an agreement for running-account credit allowing the credit limit to be exceeded temporarily is not treated as a separate agreement or as providing fixed-sum credit in respect of the excess (s 18(5)). Nor does the Act apply to a multiple agreement so far as it relates to goods if under the agreement payments are to be made in respect of the goods in the form of rent (other than a rentcharge) issuing out of land (s 18(6)). Therefore an agreement for the letting of furnished premises will not be treated as including a separate consumer hire agreement insofar as rent is paid for hire of furniture.

(l) Linked transactions

A transaction (other than for the provision of security[17]) entered into by the debtor or hirer with any person ('the other party') is linked to an actual or prospective regulated agreement (the 'principal agreement') of which it does not form part in three situations. Firstly, if the transaction is entered into in compliance with a term of the principal agreement (s 19(1)(a)). Secondly, if the principal agreement is a debtor-creditor-supplier agreement which finances or is to finance the transaction (wholly or partly) (s 19(1)(b)). For example, a purchase of goods using a credit card is a transaction linked to the debtor-creditor-supplier agreement by which the credit card is provided to the purchaser. Thirdly, if the other party is within specified categories of persons and initiated the transaction by suggesting it to the debtor, hirer or his associate[18] who enters it either to induce the creditor or owner to enter the principal agreement or for another purpose related to the principal agreement or (if the principal agreement is for restricted-use credit) for a purpose related to a transaction financed or to be financed (wholly or partly) by the principal agreement (s 19(1)(c)). The specified categories of persons are the creditor, owner or his associate (s 19(2)(a)), a person who in negotiations for the transaction, is represented by a credit-broker[19] who is also a negotiator in antecedent negotiations[20] for the principal agreement (s 19(2)(b)), or a person who, at the time the transaction is initiated, knows that the principal agreement has been made or contemplates that it might be made (s 19(2)(c)). For example, life insurance taken out by the debtor would be a linked transaction with a loan agreement if required by the creditor as a condition of the creditor lending or if taken out at the creditor's suggestion to induce the creditor to make the loan (Example 11, Part II, Sch 2).

A linked transaction entered into before the making of the principal agreement has no effect until such time as the principal agreement is made (s 19(3)). However, the Secretary of State may make regulations[1] to exclude prescribed linked transactions from this provision (s 19(4)).

---

17 See p 92, below.
18 See n 14, p 48, above.
19 See p 106, below.
20 See p 67, below.
1 The Consumer Credit (Linked Transactions) (Exemptions) Regulations 1983, SI 1983/1560 have been made and exclude linked transactions consisting of contracts of insurance, other contracts insofar as they contain a guarantee of goods, and transactions comprising or effected under agreements for the operation of accounts for the deposit of money or current accounts ((reg 2(2)).

(m) Total charge for credit

The Act provides for the Secretary of State to make regulations for determining the total charge for credit, for these to prescribe items to be taken into account (including any amounts payable under any linked transaction: s 20(2)), their calculation, and the method of calculating the rate of total charge for credit (s 20)(1)).

Under this power the Secretary of State has made the Consumer Credit (Total Charge for Credit) Regulations 1980.[2] Part II (regs 3–5) deals with the total charge for credit. This is intended to represent the true cost to the debtor of the credit (s 20(1)) and is the total (determined as at the date of making the agreement) of the interest on the credit which may be provided under the agreement and other charges at any time payable under the transaction by or on behalf of the debtor or his associate,[3] whether to the creditor or to any other person, notwithstanding that the charge (or part of it) may be repayable or that the consideration for the charge may include matters outside the transaction (regs 3–4). So, for example, commitment, redemption, legal, valuation/survey and search fees could be included along with stamp duty and finance and installation charges and (subject as follows) maintenance charges and insurance premiums. Furthermore, 'transaction' is defined in wide terms to mean a consumer credit agreement, any linked transaction, any contract for the provision of security[4] relating to the agreement and any other contract which the creditor requires to be made by the debtor or his relative as a condition to making the agreement (reg 1(2)). However, certain charges are specifically excluded.[5] These include charges payable upon default by the debtor, charges for incidental services contracted for prior to the debtor applying for credit, certain charges under arrangements for the maintenance of land or goods, charges for money transmission services relating to use of a current account which vary according to the debtor's use of the services, and certain insurance premiums.

Part III (regs 6–11) deals with the rate of total charge for credit. This is the annual percentage rate of charge ('APR') determined (to one decimal place) in accordance with the appropriate formula. There are two specific formulae for agreements under which the charge is a constant period rate of charge for periods of equal length (reg 7) or fixed-sum credit is provided and repayable at the end of a specified period in a single lump sum representing repayment of both credit and the total charge for credit (reg 8). A third formula can be used for any agreement (reg 9). The rate applicable to certain agreements can be found in the Consumer Credit Tables published by HMSO (reg 10).

Part IV (regs 12–18) deals with the assumptions to be made when calculating the total charge for credit or the APR if the creditor cannot at the date the agreement is made ascertain the amount of the credit (reg 13), the period for which the credit is provided (reg 14), any amount ascertained by

---

2 SI 1980/51 as amended by SI 1985/1192 and SI 1989/596. It is understood that an EC Directive on the calculation of APR is in preparation.

3 See n 14, p 48, above.

4 See p 92, below.

5 See reg 5 for a full list.

reference to the level of any index or other factor (reg 15), the rate of any item in the total charge for credit which will change within one year in cases where the period of the credit is unknown (reg 16), the time of provision of credit (reg 17) or the time of payment of charges (reg 18).

3 LICENSING OF CREDIT AND HIRE BUSINESS

Licensing requirements, the forms of licence available and the basis upon which licences are issued are set out in Part III of the Act (ss 21–42).

(a) Licensing principles

A licence is required to carry on a consumer credit or consumer hire business (s 21(1)), unless the business is carried on by a local authority (s 21(2)) or by a body corporate empowered by public general Act to carry on business (s 21(3)).

Consumer credit business means any business so far as it comprises or relates to the provision of credit under regulated consumer credit agreements (s 189(1)). Consumer hire business means any business insofar as it comprises or relates to the bailment of goods under regulated consumer hire agreements (s 189(1)). So a business providing credit of, or bailing goods for payments of, more than £15,000 or providing credit or bailing goods to companies only or only under exempt agreements does not require a licence, for such agreements are not regulated.

'Business' includes profession or trade (s 189(1)). In other contexts the word has been interpreted either restrictively as a commercial activity carried on with a view to profit[6] or expansively as any occupation, other than a pleasure, which requires attention.[7] The Act seems to assume an expansive interpretation[10] as does the Director.[11] But a person is not treated as carrying on a particular business merely because occasionally he enters into transactions belonging to a business of that type (s 189(2)). Therefore, even assuming an expansive interpretation of the word 'business', whether that business is 'carried on' depends upon the frequency of transactions belonging to such business.

The Director may issue either a standard or a group licence (s 22). A standard licence is to a named person for a prescribed period (currently 15 years from the date specified in the licence)[12] and specifies the activities covered (s 22(1)(a)). So, for example, a standard licence issued to a parent company would not cover its subsidiaries. A standard licence can be issued

6 *Smith v Anderson* (1880) 15 ChD 247 at 258; *R v Crayden* [1978] 2 All ER 700, [1978] 1 WLR 604.
7 *Rolls v Miller* (1884) 27 ChD 71 at 88; *Town Investments Ltd v Department of the Environment* [1978] AC 359 at 383; *Blakemore v Bellamy* [1983] RTR 303.
10 Eg s 21(2).
11 See General Notices Nos 1004 and 1005 (issuance of group licences to the National Association of Citizens Advice Bureaux and to Age Concern to carry on the business of debt-adjusting and debt-counselling).
12 SI 1975/2124 as amended by SI 1986/1016.

to a partnership or unincorporated body (in which case it is issued in the name of the partnership or body) but otherwise cannot be issued to more than one person (s 22(3), (4)). A standard licence will be issued if the applicant satisfies the Director that he is fit to engage in the activities covered by the licence and any name to be licensed is not misleading or undesirable (s 25(1)). In determining the applicant's fitness, the Director may have regard to any circumstances he considers relevant, including evidence tending to show that the applicant, its employees, agents, associates[13] (including, for this purpose, business associates) or (in the case of companies) controllers, has committed an offence involving fraud, dishonesty or violence, has breached a provision in the Act, practised discrimination or engaged in deceitful, oppressive or unfair business practices (s 25(2)).

A group licence is for an indefinite period and specifies the persons and activities covered (s 22(1)(b)). The Director may only issue a group licence if he considers it better in the public interest than to require each individual to apply (s 22(5)). A group licence is issued to the applicant and the Director must publish a notice of its issue (s 22(8)). Group licences have, for example, been issued to solicitors, executors, trustees, liquidators, administrators and chartered accountants for specified business activities.

A licence is not assignable or transmissable (s 22(2)) and if issued to an individual will terminate if the individual dies, is adjudged bankrupt or becomes a mental patient[14] (s 37(1)). But in relation to standard licences regulations may specify other events of termination, provide for termination to be deferred for up to 12 months and authorise the licensee's business to be carried on by another person during that period of deferment (s 37(2), (3)). The Consumer Credit (Termination of Licences) Regulations 1976[15] made under this provision specify as additional events of termination the making of certain compositions, schemes or deeds of arrangement by the licensee, the bankruptcy of unincorporated licensees and the relinquishment of licences. The regulations also provide for a 12-month period of deferment of termination in all cases (except relinquishment of licences, when the period is one month) and specify the persons authorised to carry on the licensee's business during the period of deferment: generally the personal representative of a deceased licensee and in other cases the trustee or other representative appointed.

A licence may limit the activities it covers (s 23(2)). Accordingly the Director issues licences by reference to six categories of business: A. consumer credit business, B. consumer hire business, C. credit brokerage,[16] D. debt-adjusting and debt-counselling,[17] E. debt-collecting,[18] and F. credit reference agency.[19] A licence does not cover canvassing off trade premises debtor-creditor-supplier agreements or regulated consumer hire agreements unless it specifically so provides and a group licence cannot so provide (s 23(3)). Regulations may specify other activities requiring specific provision in licences

13 See n 14, p 48, above.
14 Ie within Part VIII of the Mental Health Act 1959, now Part VII of the Mental Health Act 1983.
15 SI 1976/1002 as amended by SI 1981/614.
16 See p 106, below.
17 See pp 106–107, below.
18 See p 107, below.
19 See p 107, below.

(s 23(4)). A licence authorises the licensee to carry on a business only under the name or names specified in it (s 24).

Although employees will be covered by their employer's licence, there is doubt as to the position of agents who are not employees. One view (apparently adopted by the Office of Fair Trading) is that if an agent acts for only one principal it is covered by that principal's licence. This may be doubted on the basis that the legal relationship of agent and principal is not affected by the circumstance that the agent has more than one principal: nor ought the scope of a licence be construed by reference to such circumstance. Accordingly it is suggested that the prudent course is for an agent to obtain a licence in every case.

Regulations may be made as to the conduct of a licensee's business, including records to be kept, information to be given to those dealing with him (s 26) and as to the seeking of business by a licensee who carries on a consumer credit or hire business (s 54).[20]

(b) Issue of licences

Unless the Director determines to issue a licence, before determining an application he must give the applicant written notice stating that he is minded to refuse the application or grant it on terms differing from the application made, stating his reasons, specifying any differing terms, and inviting the applicant to submit representations (s 27(1)). If the Director grants the application on terms differing from the application made, a licence must be issued on those terms whether or not the applicant appeals, unless the applicant notifies the Director that he does not want such a licence (s 27(2)).

If the Director proposes to issue a group licence but to exclude any named person, before making a determination he must give that person written notice stating his reasons for the proposed exclusion, and invite that person to submit representations (s 28).

(c) Renewal, variation, suspension and revocation of licences

A licensee must apply to the Director for renewal of a licence (s 29(1)). In the case of renewal of a standard licence, the application must be made on a prescribed form[21] and in the period beginning three months and ending one month before the licence expires. In the case of renewal of a group licence, the application must contain prescribed particulars.[1] The Director has power to renew a group licence of his own motion (s 29(2)). The procedure upon renewal is the same as upon issue of a licence (s 29(3)). After determination of the application, if an appeal lies the old licence continues in force even if it would otherwise have expired (s 29(4)). If renewal is refused, the Director must give directions authorising the carrying into effect of agreements made before the licence expired (s 29(5)).[2] The Director must publish a general notice of the renewal of a group licence (s 29(6)).

20 The Consumer Credit (Conduct of Business) (Credit References) Regulations 1977, SI 1977/330 and Consumer Credit (Conduct of Business) (Pawn Records) Regulations 1982, SI 1982/1565 have been made. But neither include regulations as to seeking business. See also p 67, below.
21 General Notice No 14, 3 April 1979 made under s 6.
1 General Notice No 16, 3 April 1979 made under s 6.
2 Consumer Credit Licensing (Representations) Order 1976 SI 1976/191, art 5.

On application by the licensee in prescribed form,[3] the Director may vary a standard licence (s 30(1)). An application to vary a group licence may be made by the person who applied for the licence (s 30(2)) and must contain prescribed particulars.[4] The Director may not vary a group licence by excluding a named person other than the applicant unless that person consents in writing to exclusion (s 30(2)). On application by a person excluded from a group licence, the Director may remove the exclusion (s 30(3)). Unless the Director determines to vary a licence in accordance with an application, before determining the application he must give the applicant written notice stating that he is minded to refuse the application, stating his reasons and inviting the applicant to submit representations (s 30(4)). The Director must publish a general notice of the variation of a group licence (s 30(5)).

If during the currency of a licence the Director considers that if the licence had expired he would have renewed it on different terms or not have renewed it, he must, in the case of a standard licence, give written notice to the licensee of his proposal compulsorily to vary, or to suspend or revoke the licence (as the case may be), stating his reasons and inviting the licensee to submit representations (s 31(1), (2), s 32(1), (2)). In the case of a group licence the Director must publish a general notice of the proposed compulsory variation, suspension or revocation, stating his reasons and inviting any licensee to submit representations (s 31(1), (3), s 32(1), (3)). If the group licence was issued on application, the Director must also inform the original applicant of the proposed compulsory variation, suspension or revocation, stating his reasons and inviting the applicant to submit representations (s 31(4), s 32(4)). If the proposal is compulsorily to vary a group licence by excluding a named person other than the original applicant, before making a determination the Director must give that person written notice stating his reasons for the proposed exclusion, and invite him to submit representations against his exclusion (s 31(5), s 28). If the Director suspends or revokes a licence he must give directions authorising the licensee to carry into effect agreements made before the suspension or revocation (s 32(5)).[5] The Director must publish a general notice of any compulsory variation or suspension or revocation of a group licence made under the above provisions (s 31(6), s 32(6)).[6] The compulsory variation or suspension or revocation does not take effect before the end of the appeal period (s 31(7), s 32(7)).[7]

A licensee under a suspended licence is treated as if the licence had not been issued (s 32(8)). If the suspension was not for a specified period the Director may end the suspension by written notice to the licensee or in the case of a group licence by publishing a general notice (s 32(8)). The Director may also end the suspension of a standard licence on an application in prescribed form[8] by the licensee; and in the case of a group licence issued on application, the Director may end suspension on application by either the licensee or the original applicant (s 33(1), s 33(4)(a)) containing prescribed

---

3 General Notice No 32, 1 May 1986 made under s 6.
4 General Notice No 17, 3 April 1979 made under s 6.
5 Consumer Credit Licensing (Representations) Order above, art 5.
6 Consumer Credit Licensing (Representations) Order above, art 6, specifies details to be included in notices of an adverse decision.
7 Note that authorisation under the Banking Act may be revoked if a consumer credit licence held by an authorised institution is revoked: s 11(4) Banking Act 1987.
8 General Notice No 7, 28 September 1977 made under s 6.

particulars.[9] Unless the Director determines to end the suspension in accordance with an application, before determining the application he must give the applicant written notice stating that he is minded to refuse the application, stating his reasons and inviting the applicant to submit representations (s 33(2)). The Director must publish a general notice that suspension of a group licence has been ended in this way (s 33(3)) and, in the case of a group licence issued on application, inform the original applicant (s 33(4)(b)).

(d) Miscellaneous

Where the Director invites a person to submit representations, he must require that person within 21 days to submit representations in writing and to notify the Director whether he wishes to make oral representations (in which case the Director must also arrange for these to be heard) (s 34(1)).[10] In making a determination, the Director must take into account any representations so submitted or made (s 34(2)) and give notice of his determination to the persons invited to submit them or, if the invitation was given by general notice, he must publish his determination in a general notice (s 34(3)).[11]

The Act directs the Director to maintain a register of (a) applications for the issue, variation, renewal or ending suspension of a licence; (b) licences in force, suspended or revoked (with details of variations); (c) decisions of the Director and appeals from them; and (d) any other matters he thinks fit and which he has specified in a general notice (s 35(1), (2)).[12] On payment of the prescribed fee anyone can inspect the register, take copies of any entry and obtain certified copies of any entry at the place and times prescribed by the Director by general notice (s 35(3), (5)).[13] If there is a change in any particulars entered in the register in relation to a standard licence (other than as a result of action by the Director), the licensee must within 21 working days notify the Director and the Director must amend the register (s 36(1)). There are further provisions for notification to the Director within 21 working days of certain other changes by specified bodies which hold standard licences: an incorporated or unincorporated body must notify changes in its officers; an incorporated body must also notify changes in its controllers[14] and their officers; a partnership must notify changes in its members (s 36(2)). If the Director receives such notice he may by notice require the licensee to provide details (s 36(6)). A controller of a body corporate which has a standard licence must within 14 working days notify the licensee of his becoming or ceasing to be a controller and (if the controller is a body corporate) of changes in the controller's officers (s 36(3), (4)). A standard licence held by a partnership

9 General Notice No 18, 3 April 1979 made under s 6.
10 The Consumer Credit Licensing (Representations) Order, above, provides for the Director to notify a person wishing to make oral representations of the date, time and place of the hearing (art 3) and for the conduct of the hearing (art 4).
11 Consumer Credit Licensing (Representations) Order, above art 6 specifies details to be included in notices of an adverse decision.
12 See General Notices No 5, 29 January 1976 and No 28, 3 November 1983 made under s 6.
13 See General Notices No 24, 14 May 1982 and No 25, 11 October 1982 made under s 6 and Leaflet No CCP9 ('The Consumer Credit Public Register') issued by the Office of Fair Trading.
14 See n 14, p 48, above.

ceases to have effect if the business of the partnership ceases to be carried on under any name(s) specified in the licence (s 36(5)).

A person who engages in activities requiring a licence when he is not a licensee under a licence covering those activities commits an offence (s 39(1)) as does a holder of a standard licence who carries on business under a name not specified in the licence (s 39(2)) and a person who fails to give the Director or a licensee notice of the changes as detailed above (s 39(3)). The maximum penalties are a fine of the prescribed sum[15] upon summary conviction and two years' imprisonment or an unlimited fine upon conviction on indictment (s 167(1) and Schedule 1).

Further, a regulated agreement (other than a non-commercial agreement)[16] made when the creditor or owner was unlicensed is enforceable against the debtor or hirer only if the Director so orders (s 40(1)). 'Unlicensed' means without a licence and only applies in relation to acts for which a licence is required (s 189(1)). The creditor or owner may apply to the Director for an order on the prescribed form[17] (s 40(2)). Unless the Director determines to make an order in accordance with an application, before determining the application he must give the applicant written notice stating that he is minded to refuse the application or grant it on different terms, stating his reasons and inviting the applicant to submit representations (s 40(3)). In making his determination the Director must consider how far debtors or hirers have been prejudiced, whether he would have granted a licence for the relevant period if an application had been made and the degree of culpability for failure to obtain a licence (s 40(4)). The Director may limit any order by reference to specified agreements, types of agreement or the time of their making (s 40(5)(a)); he may also make an order conditional on the applicant doing specified acts (s 40(5)(b)). Since a regulated agreement made by an unlicensed trader is potentially enforceable in this way, the fact that the trader has committed an offence in making the agreement cannot render the agreement automatically void for illegality (as was previously the case[18]), for it is expressly provided that no civil or criminal sanctions should be incurred except as provided by the Act (s 170(1)). But it should be noted that this does not prevent the grant of an injunction or prerogative order (s 170(3)) and it has also been held that it does not prevent aiders or abettors being liable under s 8 of the Accessories and Abettors Act 1861 and s 44 of the Magistrates' Courts Act 1980.[19] A regulated agreement made by a trader who is licensed but is otherwise committing a licensing offence (eg carrying on business under a name not specified in the licence or failing to notify changes in particulars entered on the register) may be enforceable without an order of the Director, for such a trader is not strictly unlicensed.[20]

Certain persons aggrieved by a determination of the Director may appeal to the Secretary of State in the prescribed period and manner (s 41(1)).[1] The persons are: the applicant in the case of a determination to refuse to issue,

15 Currently £2,000: SI 1984/447, made under Magistrates' Courts Act, 1980 s 143.
16 A non-commercial agreement is a consumer credit or consumer hire agreement not made by the creditor or owner in the course of a business carried on by him (s 189(1)).
17 General Notice No 22, 8 May 1980 made under s 6.
18 See Moneylenders Act 1927, s 1(3)(b).
19 *Brookes v Retail Credit Card Ltd* [1986] Crim LR 327 (where it was stated obiter that other inchoate offences (eg attempts) could also be committed).
20 See *Guest* para 2–025.
 1 The Consumer Credit Licensing (Appeals) Regulations 1976, SI 1976/837 have been made.

renew, vary or end suspension of a licence or to grant an order for enforcement of an agreement made by an unlicensed trader in accordance with the application; the licensee in the case of a determination to refuse to give directions in rejecting an application to renew a licence or in compulsorily varying, or suspending or revoking a licence; the original applicant or any licensee in the case of a determination for compulsory variation or to suspend or revoke a group licence; and the person excluded in the case of a determination to exclude him from a group licence (Table to s 41). Regulations may provide for the persons to hear and the conduct of such appeals (s 41(2))[1] and the Secretary of State may give directions for disposing of any such appeal, including for the payment of any party's costs (s 41(4)). The Act also amends the Tribunals and Inquiries Act 1971[2] so that in hearing such appeals the Secretary of State is treated as a tribunal from which an appeal lies on a point of law to the High Court (s 42(1)).

4 SEEKING BUSINESS

Provisions covering the advertising and canvassing of, and the giving of quotations in relation to, credit and hire agreements are set out in Part IV of the Act (ss 43–54).

(a) Advertising

The provisions in Part IV of the Act apply to any advertisement published for the purposes of a business carried on by the advertiser, indicating that he is willing to provide credit or to enter into an agreement for the bailment of goods by him (s 43(1)). The Act can therefore apply even to advertising of agreements which are not regulated agreements or consumer credit or consumer hire agreements. The ambit of Part IV is only limited by the specific exclusion from regulation of advertisements in certain circumstances. Firstly, if the advertiser does not carry on a consumer credit or consumer hire business,[3] a business in which he provides credit to individuals secured on land (or an interest in land), or a business relating to unregulated agreements the proper law of which is that of a country outside the United Kingdom but which would have been regulated agreements if their proper law had been the law of a part of the United Kingdom (s 43(2)). Secondly, advertisements which indicate that the credit must exceed £15,000[4] and that no security[5] is required or the security is to consist of property other than land, or which indicate that the credit is available only to a body corporate (s 43(3)). Thirdly, bailment advertisements indicating that the advertiser is not willing to enter into consumer hire agreements (s 43(4)). Finally, the Secretary of State may by order provide that Part IV shall not apply to other advertisements of a specified description (s 43(5)). Under this power the Secretary of State has made the Consumer Credit (Exempt Advertisements) Order 1985.[6] This provides that Part IV shall not apply to a further six types of advertisements

1 The Consumer Credit Licensing (Appeals) Regulations 1976, SI 1976/837 have been made.
2 By the addition of s 13(5A).
3 See p 57, above.
4 For the financial limit see SI 1983/1878.
5 See p 92, below.
6 SI 1985/621.

(art 2). The first four are advertisements relating to consumer credit and consumer hire agreements within the second and third categories of exempt agreements.[7] The remaining two are advertisements relating to consumer credit or consumer hire agreements which would have fallen within the first four types of advertisement had the credit provided or the payments required to be made not exceeded £15,000.

There is no comprehensive definition of 'advertisement', although it is stated to include every form of advertising, whether in a publication, by TV, radio, display of notices or goods, distribution of any material, exhibition of pictures, models or films. 'Advertiser' means any person indicated by the advertisement as willing to enter into transactions to which the advertisement relates (s 189(1)) and does not, therefore, necessarily mean the person who publishes the advertisement. There is no definition of 'published'. It could be interpreted expansively to mean 'made known to a third party', in which case even an advertisement addressed only to a single individual would be 'published'. A restrictive interpretation would be 'made known to the public', in which case an advertisement to a defined group (eg the employees of a company) might not be 'published'. An intermediate interpretation would be 'make generally known', which would require a degree of general distribution. It is suggested that in the context of advertising this latter interpretation is the most appropriate and it would be a question of fact as to whether there had been a sufficiently wide distribution for it to be held that an advertisement had been published. It has been held that Part IV of the Act does not apply to an advertisement in the form of a sticker bearing only a company name and logo since it did not indicate that the advertiser was willing to provide credit.[8]

The Secretary of State must make regulations as to the form and content of advertisements to which Part IV applies to ensure that they convey a fair and reasonably comprehensive indication of the nature of the credit or hire facilities offered by the advertiser and their true cost to persons using them (s 44(1)). Accordingly, the Secretary of State has made the Consumer Credit (Advertisements) Regulations 1980.[9] These regulations apply to every advertisement to which Part IV applies except advertisements which indicate clearly (whether expressly or by implication) that the advertiser is willing to provide credit or enter into bailment agreements only for the purposes of the business carried on by a person other than the advertiser or any person acting as a credit-broker[10] in relation to the agreements to which the advertisement relates and not otherwise (reg 2). Advertisements to which the regulations apply which indicate that the advertiser is willing to provide credit must comply with the requirements in the regulations for simple, intermediate or full credit advertisements (reg 5).[11]

It is an offence to publish an advertisement to which Part IV of the Act applies and which indicates that the advertiser is willing to provide credit under a restricted-use credit agreement relating to goods or services to be

---

7 See pp 51–52, above.
8 *Jenkins v Lombard North Central plc* [1984] 1 All ER 828, [1984] 1 WLR 307.
9 SI 1980/54, as amended by SI 1980/1360, SI 1983/110, SI 1983/1721, SI 1984/1055 and SI 1985/619. SI 1980/54 will be revoked and replaced by the Consumer Credit (Advertisements) Regulations 1989, SI 1989/1125 with effect from 1 February 1990.
10 See p 106, below.
11 Reference should be made to the regulations for full details.

supplied by any person if at the time of publication that person is not holding himself out as prepared to sell the goods or provide the services for cash (s 45). It is also an offence to publish an advertisement to which Part IV applies if it conveys information which is false or misleading in a material respect (s 46(1)). Information stating or implying an intention on the advertiser's part which he has not got is false (s 46(2)). The maximum penalties are a fine of the prescribed sum[12] upon summary conviction or two years imprisonment and an unlimited fine upon conviction on indictment (s 167 and Sch 1). If an advertiser commits either of these offences or an offence against the advertising regulations (or would have been taken to have committed such an offence if he had not been able to rely upon a statutory defence,[13] a like offence (with the same maximum penalties) is committed by the publisher, by anyone who, in the course of his business, devised the advertisement or the part relevant to the offence, and the person who procured publication of the advertisement (if not the advertiser) (s 47(1)). But it is a defence for the person charged under this provision to prove that he received and published the advertisement in the course of his business and did not know and had no reason to suspect that its publication would be an offence under Part IV (s 47(2)).

(b) Canvassing etc

It is an offence to canvass debtor-creditor agreements off trade premises (s 49(1)). An individual canvasses if he solicits the entry of an individual ('the consumer') into a regulated agreement by making oral representations to the consumer, or any other individual, during a visit by the canvasser to a place where the consumer or that individual is, being a visit for the purpose of making such representations to individuals there and which is not made in response to a prior request (s 48(1)). Canvassing is off trade premises if not at a place where a business is carried on[14] (whether temporarily or permanently) by the creditor or owner, a supplier,[15] the canvasser (or his employer or principal) or the consumer (s 48(2)). It is also an offence to solicit the entry of an individual into a debtor-creditor agreement during a visit in response to a prior request where the request was not in writing signed by the person making it and, had no request been made, the soliciting would have constituted canvassing off trade premises (s 49(2)). However, neither of these offences can be committed in soliciting for an agreement enabling the debtor to overdraw on a current account kept with the creditor where the Director has determined that such accounts are excluded and the debtor already keeps an account (whether or not a current account) with the creditor (s 49(3)). The Director can only make a determination under this provision if of the opinion that it is not against the interests of debtors (s 49(4)). The Director has determined[16] that such accounts are excluded if they satisfy two criteria. Firstly, that through the account the debtor can, by means of cheques or similar orders which are honoured, obtain or have the use of funds held by the creditor and received from the debtor, a third party on his behalf or made available by the creditor. Secondly, that the account records alterations

12 Currently £2,000: SI 1984/447, made under Magistrates' Courts Act 1980, s 143.
13 See p 115, below.
14 See p 57, above.
15 Ie within ss 11, 12 and 13.
16 Determination issued under s 49(3) dated 1 June 1977.

in the financial relationship between the creditor and the debtor. However, this exclusion is on condition that any attempt to solicit an agreement enabling the debtor to overdraw on such an account is carried out only by the creditor or his employees and the determination would not apply to soliciting in breach of this condition (s 49(5)).

A person commits an offence if, with a view to financial gain, he sends to a minor a document inviting him to borrow money, obtain goods on credit or hire, obtain services on credit, or apply for information or advice on borrowing money or otherwise obtaining credit or hiring goods (s 50(1)). Sending to a minor a document which makes it clear that the recipient must be 18 or over to apply would not seem to be an offence as no invitation has been addressed to him. It is also a defence for the person charged to prove that he did not know and had no reasonable cause to suspect that the recipient was a minor (s 50(2)), but he is taken to have had reasonable cause so to suspect if he sent the document to the minor at an establishment which he knew or suspected to be an educational establishment for minors (s 50(3)).

It is also an offence to deliver or send by post to a person a credit-token[17] if he has not asked for it (s 51(1)). Except where the credit-token agreement is a small debtor-creditor-supplier agreement, a person does not ask for a credit-token unless his request is contained in a document which he has signed (s 51(2)). The offence can be committed even if the credit-token relates to credit to be provided under an agreement not regulated by the Act. But no offence is committed if the credit-token is given either for use under a credit-token agreement already made or in renewal or replacement of a credit-token previously accepted for use under a credit-token agreement which continues in force, whether or not varied (s 51(3)). In proceedings brought by the creditor under a credit-token agreement the onus is on the creditor to prove that the credit-token was lawfully supplied to the debtor and was accepted by him (s 171(4)(a)).

The maximum penalties for these canvassing and related offences are a fine of the prescribed sum[18] upon summary conviction or one year's imprisonment and an unlimited fine upon conviction on indictment (s 167(1) and Schedule 1). However, the commission of such an offence does not render an agreement made as a consequence unenforceable (s 170(1)).

(c) Miscellaneous

The Act provides that the Secretary of State may make regulations as to the form and content of a document ('quotation') which the regulations require to be provided by a person carrying on a consumer credit or consumer hire business[19] or a business in the course of which he provides credit to individuals secured on land (or an interest in land) to give prospective customers information about the terms upon which he is prepared to do business (s 52(1)).[1]

It is also provided that regulations made by the Secretary of State may prescribe information required to be displayed in a prescribed manner at any premises to which the public may have access and from which a person is

17 See p 50, above.
18 Currently £2,000: SI 1984/447, made under Magistrates' Courts Act 1980, s 143.
19 See p 57, above.
 1 The Consumer Credit (Quotations) Regulations 1980, SI 1980/55 (as amended by SI 1983/110 and SI 1983/1721) have been made. SI 1980/55 will be revoked and replaced by the Consumer Credit (Quotations) Regulations 1989, SI 1989/1126 with effect from 1 February 1990.

carrying on a consumer credit or hire business or a business in the course of which he provides credit to individuals secured on land (s 53). However, no regulations have been made to date.

Regulations made (under s 26) as to the conduct of a licensee's business may include provisions regulating the seeking of business by a licensee who carries on a consumer credit or consumer hire business (s 54).[2] Again no such provisions have been included to date.

It is an offence to contravene these quotations and related regulations (s 167(2)). The maximum penalties are a fine of the prescribed sum[3] upon summary conviction or two years' imprisonment and an unlimited fine upon conviction on indictment (s 167(1) and Sch 1). However, the commission of such an offence does not render an agreement made as a consequence unenforceable (s 170(1)).

5 ENTRY INTO CREDIT OR HIRE AGREEMENTS

Provisions covering matters preliminary to and to be complied with in making credit and hire agreements and dealing with cancellation rights are set out in Part V of the Act (ss 55–74). It should be noted that certain agreements are excluded from these provisions (s 74) and these are dealt with at the end of this section of the text (pp 76–77, below).

(a) Preliminary matters

Regulations may require specified information to be disclosed in the prescribed manner to the debtor or hirer before a regulated agreement is made (s 55(1)). A regulated agreement is not properly executed unless such regulations are complied with before it is made (s 55(2)) and an improperly executed agreement is enforceable against the debtor or hirer only on an order of the court (s 65(1)) unless he consents to enforcement. However no regulations have been made to date.

The Act also provides that certain persons who act as a 'negotiator' with a debtor or hirer are deemed to conduct negotiations as agent for the creditor as well as in their own right (s 56(2)). A negotiator is a person who conducts antecedent negotiations with the debtor or hirer (s 56(1)). 'Antecedent negotiations' means any negotiations with the debtor or hirer conducted by any of three categories of persons: (a) the creditor or owner in relation to the making of a regulated agreement; or (b) a credit-broker[4] in relation to goods sold or proposed to be sold by the credit-broker to the creditor before forming the subject matter of a debtor-creditor-supplier agreement of the first type;[5] or (c) the supplier[6] in relation to a transaction financed (wholly or partly) or proposed to be so financed by a debtor-creditor-supplier agreement of the second or third type[5] (s 56(1), Examples 1, 2, 3 & 4, Part II, Sch 2). Antecedent negotiations are taken to begin when the negotiator and the debtor or hirer first enter into communication (including communication by advertisement),[7]

2 See p 57, above.
3 Currently £2,000: SI 1984/447, made under Magistrates' Courts Act 1980, s 143.
4 See p 106, below.
5 See p 49, above.
6 Ie within ss 11, 12 or 13.
7 See p 64, above.

and to include any representations made by the negotiator to the debtor or hirer and any other dealings between them (s 56(4)). So, for example, a misrepresentation by a supplier in antecedent negotiations with the debtor will be taken to be made on behalf of the creditor and could therefore entitle the debtor to rescind the credit agreement. Furthermore, an agreement is void if, and to the extent that, it purports either to provide that a person acting as, or on behalf of, a negotiator in relation to an actual or prospective regulated agreement is to be treated as the agent of the debtor or hirer, or to relieve a person from liability for acts or omissions of any person acting as, or on behalf of, a negotiator in relation to such an agreement (s 56(3)). Although this has the effect that the creditor cannot prevent the deemed agency arising, he may be able to exempt his liability for the defaults for which he is thereby rendered responsible to the extent that he is able to do so according to the Misrepresentation Act 1967 and Unfair Contract Terms Act 1977. It is unclear to what extent the deemed agency would render a creditor liable for torts or criminal offences committed by a negotiator. It has been suggested that the effect could be that any act of the negotiator would be deemed to have been authorised by the creditor.[8] But the better view is thought to be that the creditor will only be liable for those acts of the negotiator for which he would have been liable if he had actually appointed the negotiator as his agent.[9]

The question has arisen as to whether negotiations by a motor car dealer concerning the trade-in of an existing vehicle were conducted in relation to the hire-purchase of a new one so as to constitute antecedent negotiations with a credit-broker within the second category mentioned above. On the facts it was held that the hire-purchase and trade-in were both part of a single transaction and accordingly negotiations concerning the trade-in were conducted in relation to the sale of the new one.[10]

If a party withdraws from a prospective regulated agreement the provisions of Part V of the Act apply to the agreement, any linked transaction and anything done in anticipation of the making of the agreement in the same way as they apply if the agreement had been made but cancelled in accordance with the Act (s 57(1)) even if the agreement would not have been a cancellable agreement[11] had it been made (s 57(4)). The giving of written or oral notice indicating an intention to withdraw from a prospective regulated agreement operates as a withdrawal from it (s 57(2)) and a credit-broker[12] or supplier[13] who is a negotiator in antecedent negotiations and any person who, in the course of a business carried on by him,[14] acts on behalf of the debtor or hirer[15] in any negotiations for the agreement are each deemed to be the agent of the creditor or owner for the purpose of receiving such notice (s 57(3)).

---

8 *Guest* para 2–057.
9 See *Bowstead on Agency* (15th edn) pp 287ff.
10 *UDT v Whitfield* [1986] CLY 375; *cf Northgran Finance Ltd v Ashley* [1963] 1 QB 476, [1962] 3 All ER 973, CA.
11 As to which see s 69 (p 72, below).
12 See p 106, below.
13 Ie within ss 11, 12 or 13.
14 See p 57, above.
15 It seems surprising that a debtor can give notice to a person who has been his agent in negotiations. But a person deemed by the Act to receive a notice as agent of the creditor or owner under a regulated agreement is also deemed to be under a contractual duty to the creditor or owner to transmit the notice to him forthwith (s 175).

Before sending to the debtor or hirer for signature an unexecuted agreement to be secured on land (or an interest in land), the creditor or owner must (subject to the exceptions mentioned below) give the debtor or hirer a copy of it containing a notice in prescribed form indicating the right of the debtor or hirer to withdraw from the prospective agreement and how and when the right is exercisable, together with a copy of any other document referred to in it (s 58(1)).[16] 'Unexecuted agreement' means a document embodying the terms of a prospective regulated agreement, or such of them as it is intended to reduce to writing (s 189(1)). It is to be noted that security to be provided by the debtor or hirer must be set out or referred to in the agreement,[17] and consequently copies of such security documents will have to be provided (unless within the exceptions). These provisions can present a problem if a debtor has executed a land mortgage in favour of a creditor which secures existing and future advances, for a future regulated loan may be secured on land in which case advance copies may need to be given. To avoid this it is advisable for such a mortgage to state that it will not secure any regulated loan unless otherwise specified in the loan agreement.

The Act specifies two exceptional cases in which advance copies need not be given. These are where the prospective agreement is either for restricted-use credit to finance (wholly or partly) the purchase of the mortgaged land or for a bridging loan in connection with the purchase of the mortgaged or other land (s 58(2)). Further exceptions are contained in regulations.[18]

An agreement is void if, and to the extent that, it purports to bind a person to enter as debtor or hirer into a prospective regulated agreement (s 59(1)), but regulations may exclude specified agreements from this provision (s 59(2)).[19] A prospective regulated agreement could, however, be conditional upon some event occurring or the creditor or owner could bind himself to enter the agreement (with, for example, an option for the prospective debtor or hirer to take up the offer), for in both cases the debtor would not be bound before the regulated agreement took effect.

(b) Making the agreement

The Act sets out a number of requirements which must be satisfied for a regulated agreement to be properly executed. It is important that these requirements are satisfied, for an improperly executed regulated agreement is enforceable against the debtor or hirer on an order of the court only (s 65(1)), unless he consents to enforcement (s 173(3)). A retaking of goods or land to which a regulated agreement relates is an enforcement of the agreement (s 65(2)).[20]

16 Regulations made by the Secretary of State may prescribe the form and content of copy documents and exclude the duty to provide copies of specified documents (s 180). The Consumer Credit (Cancellation Notices and Copies of Documents) Regulations 1983, SI 1983/1557 (as amended by SI 1984/1108, SI 1985/666, SI 1988/2047, and SI 1989/591) have been made.
17 See pp 92ff.
18 See n 16, above.
19 The Consumer Credit (Agreements to Enter Prospective Agreements) (Exemptions) Regulations 1983, SI 1983/1552 have been made. They exclude certain consumer hire agreements and agreements for restricted-use fixed sum credit.
20 See also s 113(2), p 94 below (effect on security) and *Eastern Distributors Ltd v Goldring* [1957] 2 QB 600, [1957] 2 All ER 525; *North West Securities v Alexander Breckon Ltd* [1981] RTR 518 (rights of creditor/owner against third parties).

The Secretary of State may make regulations as to the form and content of documents embodying regulated agreements (s 60(1)).[1] A document embodies a provision if the provision is set out either in the document itself or in another document referred to in it (s 189(4)). If, on an application in prescribed form[2] to the Director by a person carrying on a consumer credit or hire business,[3] it appears to the Director impracticable for the applicant to comply with any requirement of the regulations in a particular case, he may, by notice in writing to the applicant direct that the requirement be waived or waived in relation to such agreements, and subject to such conditions, as he may specify (s 60(3)). The Director must only give such a notice if satisfied that to do so would not prejudice the interests of debtors or hirers (s 60(4)).

A regulated agreement is not properly executed unless it satisfies three documentary conditions (s 61(1)). Firstly, a document in the prescribed form itself containing all the prescribed terms and conforming with the agreements regulations must be signed in the prescribed manner by the debtor or hirer and by or on behalf of the creditor or owner (s 61(1)(a)). If the debtor or hirer is a partnership or unincorporated body, the agreement must be signed by or on behalf of the debtor or hirer (s 61(4)). Secondly, the document must embody all the terms of the agreement, other than implied terms (s 61(1)(b)). So in addition to containing the prescribed terms, the agreement must contain any other terms or a reference to any document(s) in which other terms are contained. Thirdly, when presented to the debtor or hirer for signature the document must be in such a state that all its terms are readily legible (s 61(1)(c)). It is often possible to incorporate all the terms of the agreement into the application form itself so that it will be executed once signed, returned to and accepted by the creditor or owner (credit card agreements are often executed on this basis). This probably cannot be done if the agreement is for fixed-sum credit as it is not usually possible to pre-print terms specifying the amount of credit, the repayment period or the amount of repayments: such terms will need to be filled in by the debtor (perhaps by reference to a repayment table) and consequently will not be readily legible when the agreement is presented for signature. It may be possible for the agreement simply to include a term to the effect that these details will be such amounts as are filled in by the debtor in the appropriate boxes and in accordance with the creditor's repayment tables (if applicable). However it is preferable to require the debtor to complete a separate application form from which it will be possible for the creditor to prepare a complete agreement document ready for signature.

If the agreement is to be secured on land (or an interest in land), four additional conditions apply (s 61(2)): (a) the debtor must be given the appropriate advance copy document(s) where required (ie under s 58(1)); (b) the unexecuted agreement[4] must be sent, for signature, to the debtor or hirer by post not less than seven days after the copy was given to him; (c) during the consideration period, the creditor or owner must refrain from approaching

---

1 The Consumer Credit (Agreements) Regulations 1983, SI 1983/1553 (as amended by SI 1984/1600, SI 1985/666 and SI 1988/2047) have been made.
2 General Notice No 27, 3 November 1983, made under s 6; and Form Nos CCD 30, 31/83.
3 See p 57, above.
4 See p 69, above.

the debtor or hirer except in response to a specific request made by the debtor or hirer after the beginning of the consideration period; (d) no notice of withdrawal by the debtor or hirer must be received by the creditor or owner before sending the unexecuted agreement. The consideration period for this purpose is the time between the giving of the copy prior to execution and the earlier of the expiry of seven days after the unexecuted agreement was sent or the return of the signed agreement (s 61(3)). Although there is no qualification to the prohibition on approaches to the debtor or hirer during the consideration period, it is thought that this must be restricted to approaches in connection with the proposed agreement and would not prohibit approaches on unrelated matters. It would, however, probably extend to prohibit approaches concerning the proposed agreement to an agent of the debtor or hirer (eg a solicitor) in his capacity as such.

An agreement document which contains a material error is unlikely to be considered properly executed since it will not embody all the terms of the agreement. Cases decided under the Moneylenders Acts suggest that errors which are not material will probably not render an agreement unenforceable.[5]

A copy[6] of an unexecuted agreement and of any other document referred to in it must be provided to the debtor or hirer in two cases (s 62). Firstly, if the unexecuted agreement is presented personally to him for his signature, but on the occasion when he signs it the document does not become an executed agreement, the copy document(s) must be 'there and then' delivered to the debtor or hirer (s 62(1)). An executed agreement is a document, signed by or on behalf of the parties, embodying the terms of a regulated agreement or such of them as have been reduced to writing (s 189(1)). It is unclear whether the obligation is to deliver the copy document(s) when presenting the unexecuted agreement or at the time of signing, but the former seems to read more naturally. Further, an unexecuted agreement handed to the debtor or hirer for him to take away to sign would seem to fall within this provision, in which case it could be impracticable to deliver the copy document(s) at the time when he signs. Secondly, the copy document(s) must be sent to the debtor or hirer if (and at the same time as) the unexecuted agreement is sent to him for his signature (s 62(2)). A regulated agreement is not properly executed unless these requirements are observed (s 62(3)).

A copy of an executed agreement and of any other document referred to in it must also be provided to the debtor or hirer in two cases (s 63). Firstly, if the unexecuted agreement is presented personally to him for his signature, and on the occasion when he signs it it becomes an executed agreement, the copy document(s) must be there and then delivered to the debtor or hirer (s 63(1)). Similar questions of interpretation arise as discussed above. Secondly, the copy document(s) must be delivered or sent by post to the debtor or hirer within seven days following the making of the agreement unless they were given in accordance with the first case or the unexecuted agreement was sent to the debtor or hirer for his signature and when he signed it it became an executed agreement (s 63(2)), but this does not apply in the case of a credit-token agreement if copies are given before or at the same

---

5 *Reading Trust Ltd v Spero* [1930] 1 KB 492 at 505; *Temperance Loan Fund Ltd v Rose* [1932] 2 KB 522 at 526; *Re a Debtor (No 18 of 1937)* [1938] Ch 645 at 651; *London and Harrogate Securities Ltd v Pitts* [1976] 3 All ER 809, [1976] 1 WLR 1063.
6 See n 16, p 69, above.

time as the credit-token is given to the debtor. Copies given in accordance with the second case must, in the case of cancellable agreements,[7] be sent by post (s 66(3)). A regulated agreement is not properly executed unless these requirements are satisfied (s 63(5)).

In the case of a cancellable agreement,[7] a notice in prescribed form indicating the right of the debtor or hirer to cancel the agreement, how and when that right is exercisable, and the name and address of a person to whom notice of cancellation may be given must be included in any copy given under the above provisions (ie ss 62 or 63). Such notice must also be sent by post to the debtor or hirer within seven days following the making of the agreement (s 64(1)) unless either a copy is given in accordance with the second case in s 63 or, in the case of a credit-token agreement, such notice is sent by post to the debtor or hirer either before the credit-token is given to him or with the credit-token (s 64(2)). Regulations may provide for the notice sent by post in accordance with this provision to be accompanied by a further copy of the executed agreement and of any document referred to in it (s 64(3)). To date no such regulations have been made. Regulations may also provide that notice need not be sent by post in accordance with this provision if on an application by a particular person the Director has determined that the requirement can be dispensed with in relation to agreements made by that person without prejudicing the interests of debtors or hirers (s 64(4)).[8] A cancellable agreement is not properly executed unless these requirements are satisfied (s 64(5)).

The Act specifically provides that the debtor should not be liable under a credit-token agreement for use made of the credit-token by any person unless the debtor had previously accepted the credit-token, or the use constituted an acceptance of it by him (s 66(1)). The debtor accepts a credit-token when it or a receipt for it is signed or when it is first used by the debtor or a person who, pursuant to the agreement, is authorised by him to use it (s 66(2)).

(c) Cancellation of certain agreements within cooling-off period

A cancellable agreement is a regulated agreement which may be cancelled by the debtor or hirer in accordance with the Act (s 189(1)). A regulated agreement may be cancelled by the debtor or hirer in accordance with Part V of the Act if the antecedent negotiations[9] included oral representations made when in the presence of the debtor or hirer by an individual acting as, or on behalf of, the negotiator (s 67(1)). There are, however, two excepted categories. Firstly, where the agreement is secured on land, or is a restricted-use credit agreement to finance (wholly or in part) the purchase of land (or an interest in land) or is an agreement for a bridging loan in connection with the purchase of land (or an interest in land) (s 67(1)(9)). Secondly, where the unexecuted agreement is signed by the debtor or hirer at premises at which any business[10] (whether permanent or temporary) is carried on by the creditor or owner, any party to a linked transaction (other than the debtor or hirer or an associate[11] of his), or the negotiator in any antecedent negotiations

---

7 See below.
8 The Consumer Credit (Notice of Cancellation Rights) (Exemptions) Regulations 1983, SI 1983/1558 have been made. They cover certain mail order consumer credit agreements.
9 See p 67, above.
10 See p 57, above.
11 See n 14, p 48, above.

(s 67(1)(b)), Example 4, Part II, Sch 2).[12] An agreement will not be cancellable within this provision if the only oral representations made to the debtor or hirer were made over the telephone, since such representations are not made in the presence of the debtor or hirer.

The debtor or hirer may serve notice of cancellation of a cancellable agreement between his signing the unexecuted agreement and (a) the end of the fifth day after he received the obligatory second copy (ie under s 63(2)) or notice (ie under s 64(1)); or (b) if by regulations (ie under s 64(4))[13] no further copy or notice is required, the end of the fourteenth day after he signed (s 68).

If within the appropriate period the debtor or hirer serves on the creditor or owner, an agent of either, or on a person specified in a statutory notice of cancellation rights, a cancellation notice indicating an intention to withdraw from a cancellable agreement, the notice operates to cancel the agreement and any linked transaction and to withdraw any offer by him or his associate[14] to enter into any linked transaction (s 69(1)). But if the agreement sought to be cancelled is a debtor-creditor-supplier agreement for restricted-use credit financing (wholly or partly) the doing of work or supply of goods to meet an emergency, or the supply of goods which have become incorporated by the act of the debtor or his associate into anything not comprised in the agreement or any linked transaction, a cancellation notice cancels only those provisions of the agreement and linked transactions relating to the provision of credit, requiring the debtor to pay any item in the total charge for credit, or subjecting the debtor to any obligation other than to pay for the work done or goods supplied (s 69(2)). Goods installed by, for example, a supplier at the request of the debtor or hirer might fall within this provision if the phrase 'by the act of the debtor' includes acts attributable to him. A credit-broker[15] or supplier[16] who is the negotiator in antecedent negotiations,[17] and any person who, in the course of a business carried on by him,[18] acts on behalf of the debtor or hirer[19] in any negotiations for the agreement are each deemed to be the agent of the creditor or owner for the purpose of receiving a cancellation notice (s 69(6)). A cancellation notice sent by post is deemed served on the addressee at the time of posting, whether or not he actually receives it (s 69(7)).

Unless otherwise provided by the Act, a cancelled agreement or transaction is treated as if it had never been entered into (s 69(4)), although regulations made by the Secretary of State may exclude specified linked transactions from the effects of cancellation[1] (s 69(5)).

On cancellation of a regulated agreement and any linked transaction, any sum paid by the debtor or hirer or his associate[14] under or in contemplation

12 See also the Consumer Protection (Cancellation of Contracts Concluded away from Business Premises) Regulations 1987, SI 1987/2117, which implement Council Directive 85/577/EEC and provide the consumer with rights to cancel certain credit and hire agreements which would not be cancellable under the Consumer Credit Act 1974.
13 See n 8, p 72, above.
14 See n 14, p 48, above.
15 See p 106, below.
16 Ie within ss 11, 12 or 13.
17 See p 67, above.
18 See p 57, above.
19 See n 15, p 68, above.
 1 See n 1, p 56, above.

of the agreement or transaction must be repaid (s 70(1)(a)) by the person to whom it was originally paid (s 70(3)). Any sum which but for the cancellation might become payable by the debtor or his associate under the agreement or transaction is not payable (s 70(1)(b)). If the agreement is a debtor-creditor-supplier agreement of the second type (ie within s 12(b)),[2] any sum paid on the debtor's behalf by the creditor to the supplier must also be repaid (s 70(1)(c)) by the person to whom it was originally paid, and the creditor and supplier are under a joint and several liability to repay sums paid by the debtor or his associate under the agreement or a linked transaction entered into in compliance with a term of the agreement (s 70(2)). The creditor is entitled to have the supplier made a party to any proceedings brought against the creditor where the supplier is liable with him in this way (s 70(3)) and, subject to any agreement between them, the creditor is also entitled to an indemnity from the supplier for loss suffered in satisfying any such liability, including costs reasonably incurred by him in defending proceedings by the debtor (s 70(4)). In all cases, the debtor or hirer has a statutory lien for repayable sums on any goods of which he or his associate has possession under the agreement or transaction (s 70(2)). However, these provisions do not apply to any sum which, if not paid by a debtor, would be payable under the repayment of credit provisions (ie s 71) mentioned below (s 70(5)). Nor do these provisions apply to a sum paid or payable by a debtor for the issue of a credit-token[3] unless the credit-token has been returned to the creditor or surrendered to a supplier[4] (s 70(5)). Further, only the excess over £3[5] of any fee or commission charged by a credit-broker[6] and entering into the total charge for credit is repayable (s 70(6)) and for this purpose any sum payable or paid by the debtor to the credit-broker and entering into the total charge for credit is treated as if it were such a fee or commission (s 70(6)). Finally, if an agreement or transaction is only partly cancellable (ie under s 69(2)), these provisions apply insofar as it is cancelled (s 70(8)).

To cover cases in which a debtor has received credit prior to cancellation, the Act provides that a regulated consumer credit agreement (other than a debtor-creditor-supplier agreement for restricted-use credit) continues in force, despite cancellation, so far as it relates to the repayment of credit and the payment of interest (s 71(1)). Since restricted-use credit debtor-creditor-supplier agreements are excluded, a creditor under such an agreement has no statutory right to recover the credit from the debtor, although he might be able to rely upon a right to restitution under the general law or to recover from the supplier either under his contract with him or under the Act (ie s 70(1)(c), supra). If, after cancellation, the debtor repays all or part of the credit before the expiry of one month from service of the cancellation notice or (if the credit is repayable by instalments) before the date on which the first instalment is due, no interest is payable on the amount repaid (s 71(2)). If the whole of a credit repayable by instalments is not repaid on or before the date on which the first instalment is due, the debtor is not liable to make any repayments unless he receives a written request in prescribed form[7] signed by

2 See p 49, above.
3 See p 50, above.
4 Ie within ss 11, 12 or 13.
5 For the financial limit see SI 1983/1571.
6 See p 106, below.
7 See SI 1983/1559.

or on behalf of the creditor, stating the amounts outstanding (recalculated by the creditor as nearly as possible in accordance with the agreement without extending the repayment period) but excluding any sum other than principal and interest (s 71(3)). Repayment of credit or payment of interest under a cancelled agreement is treated as duly made if made to any person on whom the cancellation notice could have been served (other than an agent of the debtor).

If a debtor or hirer or an associate[8] of either ('the possessor'), acquired possession of goods prior to cancellation of and by virtue of a restricted-use debtor-creditor-supplier agreement, a consumer hire agreement, or a linked transaction to which the possessor is a party, he is treated as having been under a duty from the time he acquired possession to retain possession and take reasonable care of the goods (s 72(1)–(4), (8)). On cancellation, the possessor is under a duty, subject to any lien, to restore the goods to the person from whom he acquired possession ('the other party') (s 72(4)), but he is not under a duty to deliver them except at his own premises pursuant to a written request signed by or on behalf of the other party and served on the possessor either before, or at the time when, the goods are collected from those premises (s 72(5)). If the possessor's address is specified in the executed agreement, for the purpose of this provision his premises are deemed to be at that address and no other (s 72(10)). If the possessor does not receive the appropriate written request for delivery of the goods within 21 days of cancellation his duty to take reasonable care of the goods ceases (s 71(8)). Furthermore, all of these statutory duties imposed upon the possessor cease if he delivers the goods (at his own premises or elsewhere), or sends them at his own expense, to any person (other than an agent of the debtor) on whom a cancellation notice could have been served (s 72(6)). But if he sends them, he is under a duty to take reasonable care to see that they are received by the other party and not damaged in transit (s 72(7)). Breach of any of these duties is actionable as a breach of statutory duty (s 72(11)). However, none of the duties apply to perishables, goods which by their nature are consumed by use and which were consumed before cancellation, goods supplied to meet an emergency or goods which before cancellation had become incorporated in any land or thing not comprised in the cancelled agreement or a linked transaction (s 72(9)).

Special provisions apply to goods which, in antecedent negotiations,[9] the negotiator agreed to take in part-exchange and which have been delivered to him before cancellation (s 73(1)). A negotiator is treated as having agreed to take goods in part-exchange, if, in pursuance of antecedent negotiations, he agreed to purchase or accept those goods as part of the consideration for the cancelled agreement (s 73(7)(a)). Unless such goods are returned to the debtor or hirer before the end of 10 days from the date of cancellation and in a condition substantially as good as when they were delivered to the negotiator, the debtor or hirer is entitled to recover from the negotiator a sum ('part-exchange allowance') equal to the amount agreed in the antecedent negotiations as a part-exchange allowance or, if no sum was agreed, such sum as it would have been reasonable to allow in respect of the part-exchanged goods if the agreement had not been cancelled (s 73(2), (7)(b)). If, in the 10

8 See n 14, p 48, above.
9 See p 67, above.

day period beginning on the date of cancellation, the debtor or hirer is in possession of goods to which the cancelled agreement relates, he has a lien on them for return of part-exchanged goods or payment of the part-exchange allowance (s 73(5)). In any action against the creditor for a sum recoverable in respect of a part-exchange allowance, the creditor is entitled to have the negotiator made a party (s 73(8)). If the debtor or hirer recovers from the negotiator or creditor (or both jointly) a sum equal to the part-exchange allowance, his title to the part-exchanged goods vests in the negotiator if it has not already done so (s 73(6)).

(d) Exclusion of certain agreements from Part V

The documentation and cancellation provisions in Part V of the Act (except those relating to antecedent negotiations in s 56) do not apply to three categories of agreement.

The first category covers non-commercial agreements[10] (s 74(1)(a)).

The second category covers debtor-creditor agreements enabling the debtor to overdraw on a current account (s 74(1)(b), Examples 17 and 18, Part II, Sch 2). Agreements within this category are only exempted if the Director makes a determination to that effect, which may be subject to conditions and may only be made if the Director is of the opinion that to exempt such agreements would not be against the interests of debtors (s 74(3)). But the Director is obliged to make a determination covering such agreements where the creditor is the Bank of England or a bank within the meaning of the Bankers' Books Evidence Act 1879 unless he considers it would be against the public interest to do so (s 74(3A)). The Director has in fact determined[11] that debtor-creditor agreements enabling the debtor to overdraw on a current account where the creditor is such a bank are exempt on condition that the creditor shall have informed the Office of Fair Trading in writing of his general intention to enter into such agreements.

The third category covers debtor-creditor agreements to finance (wholly or partly) the making of such payments arising on, or connected with, the death of a person as may be prescribed by regulations made by the Secretary of State (s 74(1)(c)). However, agreements within this category are again only exempted if the Director makes a determination, which may be subject to conditions and may only be made if the Director is of the opinion that to exempt such agreements would not be against the interests of debtors (s 74(3)). Furthermore, if any term of such an agreement is in fact expressed in writing, regulations as to the form and content of regulated agreements[12] apply to that term as if the agreement were a regulated agreement not falling within the above exemptions (s 74(4)). The payments prescribed[13] as being within the third category are payments made to discharge capital transfer tax, payments to a surety in connection with a guarantee required as a condition to a grant of Letters of Administration or fees payable to a court for a grant of probate or Letters of Administration. The Director has determined[14] that the exemption should apply to debtor-creditor agreements to finance such

10 See n 16, p 62, above.
11 Determination issued under s 74(1)(b) dated 3 November 1983.
12 See n 1, p 70, above.
13 Consumer Credit (Payments Arising on Death) Regulations 1983, SI 1983/1554.
14 Determination issued under s 74(1)(c) dated 3 November 1983.

payments if the creditor is the Bank of England or a bank within the Bankers' Books Evidence Act 1879. However, this is on condition that interest due under the agreement is calculated on a daily, weekly or monthly basis on the outstanding balance shown on the account (or some lesser amount), that interest is charged only to the date of repayment, and that the creditor has informed the Office of Fair Trading in writing of his general intention to enter into agreements of this type.

In addition, the documentation and cancellation provisions in Part V (except those relating to disclosure of information in s 55 and antecedent negotiations in s 56) do not apply to small debtor-creditor-supplier agreements for restricted-use credit (s 74(2)). For the purpose of this provision, the financial limit mentioned in the definition of small agreements is reduced from £50 to £35 if the agreement is also within the Consumer Protection (Cancellation of Contracts Concluded away from Business Premises) Regulations 1987 (s 74(2A)). This ensures that the cancellation requirements of the Act are in line with those of the Regulations which apply to agreements for credit of over £35. But again, if any term of an agreement within the third category mentioned above or of a small debtor-creditor-supplier agreement for restricted-use credit is expressed in writing, regulations as to the form and content of regulated agreements[15] apply to that term as if the agreement were a regulated agreement not falling within the above exemptions (s 74(4)).

6 MATTERS ARISING DURING THE CURRENCY OF CREDIT OR HIRE AGREEMENTS

Provisions concerning connected lender liability, the giving of information, variation of agreements and miscellaneous other matters arising during the currency of credit or hire agreements are contained in Part VI of the Act (ss 75–86).

(a) Connected lender liability

If the debtor under a debtor-creditor-supplier agreement of the second or third types (ie within s 12(b) or (c))[16] has, in relation to a transaction financed (wholly or partly) by the agreement, any claim against the supplier in respect of a misrepresentation or breach of contract, he has a like claim against the creditor, who, with the supplier, is jointly and severally liable to the debtor (s 75(1)). So, for example, a debtor who purchases goods by use of a credit card issued under a regulated agreement may have a claim against the creditor as well as the supplier for defects in the goods. Such liability is usually referred to as 'connected lender' liability. Although the form of statement of this remedy which regulations require to be contained in the agreement refers only to a right to sue the supplier and/or creditor for 'unsatisfactory goods or services',[17] connected lender liability can apply to claims in respect of any land or other things. But it does not apply to a claim under a non-commercial

15 See n 1, p 70, above.
16 See p 49, above.
17 Consumer Credit (Agreements) Regulations 1983, SI 1983/1553, Sch 2, Form 12.

agreement[18] or so far as the claim relates to any single item to which the supplier has attached a cash price of under £100 or over £30,000 (s 75(3)).[19]

Since there must be a claim for misrepresentation or breach of contract it would not seem that claims in tort give rise to connected lender liability. Furthermore, if the supplier has effectively limited, exempted, compromised, or released his liability to the debtor, the connected lender's liability will be limited, exempted, compromised or released to the same extent. The fact that the debtor has obtained a judgment against the supplier would not prevent him from obtaining a judgment against the creditor (unless the judgment against the supplier had been satisfied) but the debtor would not be entitled to costs of the second action unless he could show reasonable grounds for bringing it.[1]

It has been held that if the debtor has a claim to rescind the transaction with the supplier by virtue of connected lender liability he will also be able to rescind his agreement with the creditor.[2] However, the section does not mention any effect upon the associated credit agreement: on the contrary the claim which the debtor has against the creditor is said to be 'like' to his claim against the supplier which must be a claim 'in relation to a transaction financed by the agreement'. The better view is, therefore, that connected lender liability does not directly affect the associated credit agreement.[3] The creditor's connected lender liability is probably sufficiently closely related to the creditor's claim under the associated credit agreement for the debtor to claim a set-off. It is also to be noted that connected lender liability arises even if the debtor, in entering into the transaction, exceeded the credit limit or otherwise contravened the agreement (s 75(4)).

A creditor who suffers loss in satisfying connected lender liability is entitled to be indemnified by the supplier, subject to any agreement between them, for such loss including any costs he reasonably incurred in defending proceedings instituted by the debtor (s 75(2)) and to have the supplier made a party to such proceedings (s 75(5)). This indemnity is wide enough to cover loss arising from a judgment or settlement.

It is unclear whether connected lender liability would extend to a claim by the debtor in respect of a transaction conducted abroad and subject to a foreign law. Although the statutory wording seems wide enough to cover such a case, it is suggested that the application of the section ought to be limited unless clear and unambiguous, particularly because it imposes an artificial liability without fault upon the creditor which would not otherwise arise. This adverse effect is mitigated by the creditor's right to join the supplier into proceedings and to recover from him by virtue of the statutory indemnity, but these rights may not be capable of effective enforcement against a foreign supplier. In addition, the use of the terms 'misrepresentation or breach of contract' may also be read as suggesting that only claims under English or Scottish law were contemplated by Parliament as giving rise to connected lender liability.

---

18 See n 16, p 62, above.
19 For the financial limits see SI 1983/1878.
 1 Civil Liability (Contribution) Act 1978, ss 3, 4.
 2 *United Dominions Trust v Taylor* 1980 SLT 28.
 3 Davidson (1980) 96 LQR 343; Lowe (1981) 97 LQR 532; Dobson [1981] JBL 179; *Guest* para 2–076.

There is also doubt as to whether a person who has taken an assignment of the credit agreement from the creditor will incur connected lender liability. It has been suggested that he should not, on the basis that connected lender liability is only intended to arise when a credit agreement has been made under arrangements between the creditor and supplier and an assignee would not usually have been a party to such arrangements.[4]

(b) Notices and the provision of information

A creditor or owner is not entitled to enforce a term of a regulated agreement by demanding earlier payment of any sum, recovering possession of any goods or land, or treating any right conferred on the debtor or hirer by the agreement as terminated, restricted or deferred, except by or after delivering or sending by post to the debtor not less than seven days' written notice of his intention to do so (s 76(1)). A notice is ineffective unless in the form prescribed by the Secretary of State (s 76(3)).[5]

There are, however, certain limitations upon the application of this provision. Firstly, it applies only if the agreement specifies the period of its duration and that period has not ended (even if under its terms it can be terminated beforehand) (s 76(2)). So, for example, it will not apply to a loan which is only repayable on demand by the creditor or to enforcement of any term upon or after the expiry of the period of the agreement. Secondly, it does not prevent a creditor from treating the right to draw on any credit as restricted or deferred and taking such steps as may be necessary to make the restriction or deferment effective (s 76(4)). Thirdly, it does not apply to a right of enforcement arising by reason of any breach by the debtor or hirer of the regulated agreement (s 76(6)).[6] Finally, regulations made by the Secretary of State may provide that it should not apply to prescribed agreements (s 76(5)) and under this power the Secretary of State has exempted non-commercial agreements[7] where no security[8] is provided.[9]

A creditor under a regulated agreement for fixed-sum or running-account credit, and an owner under a regulated consumer hire agreement, within the period prescribed by regulations made by the Secretary of State[10] after receiving a request in writing to that effect from the debtor and payment of a fee of 50p,[11] must deliver or send by post to the debtor a copy of the executed agreement (if any) and of any other document referred to in it, together with a statement signed by or on behalf of the creditor showing, according to information to which it is practicable for him to refer, certain information (ss 77(1), 78(1), 79(1)). In the case of a fixed-sum credit agreement, the information is: (a) the total sum paid under the agreement by the debtor; (b) the total sum which has become payable under the agreement by the debtor but remains unpaid and the various amounts comprised in that

---

4 Guest para 2–076; but see p 46 above.
5 The Consumer Credit (Enforcement, Default and Termination Notices) Regulations 1983, SI 1983/1561 have been made.
6 But see the provisions covering default notices in s 87 (p 85, below).
7 See n 16, p 62, above.
8 Se p 92, below.
9 SI 1983/1561 (as amended by SI 1984/1109), reg 2(9).
10 12 working days: Consumer Credit (Prescribed Periods for Giving Information) Regulations 1983, SI 1983/1569, reg 2.
11 SI 1983/1571.

total with the date when each became due; and (c) the total sum which is to become payable under the agreement by the debtor, and the various amounts comprised in that total with the date (or mode of determining the date) when each becomes due (s 77(1)). In the case of running-account credit, the information is: (a) the state of the account; (b) the amount, if any, currently payable under the agreement by the debtor to the creditor; and (c) the amounts and dates of any payments which, if the debtor does not draw further on the account, will later become payable under the agreement by the debtor to the creditor (s 78(1)). In the case of a consumer hire agreement, the information is the total sum which has become payable under the agreement by the hirer but remains unpaid and the various amounts comprised in that total sum, with the dates when each became due (s 79(1)). However, there are certain tolerances and exceptions. In the case of both fixed-sum and running-account credit agreements if the creditor possesses insufficient information to enable him to ascertain any of the amounts or dates within (c) above, he is taken to have complied if his statement gives the basis on which, under the agreement, they fall to be ascertained (s 77(2), 79(2)). Furthermore, in all cases the duties do not apply in three circumstances. Firstly, if the agreement is one under which no sum is, will or may become payable by the debtor (ss 77(3)(a), 78(3)(a), 79(2)(a)). Secondly, if the request for information is made less than one month after a previous request relating to the same agreement was complied with (ss 77(3)(b), 78(3)(b), 79(2)(b)). Thirdly, if the agreement is a non-commercial agreement[12] (s 77(5)). But if the creditor or owner fails to comply with the duties in a case where they apply he is not entitled, while default continues, to enforce the agreement and if the default continues for one month he commits an offence (ss 77(4), 78(6), 79(3)) for which the maximum penalty is a fine of level 4 on the standard scale[13] upon summary conviction (s 167 and Sch 1).

When running-account credit is provided under a regulated agreement, the creditor must also give the debtor statements in the form prescribed by regulations made by the Secretary of State[14] and with the prescribed contents showing (according to information to which it is practicable for the creditor to refer): (a) the state of the account at regular intervals of not more than 12 months; and (b) if the agreement provides for payments to be made by the debtor or for interest (or any other sum) to be charged in specified periods, the state of the account at the end of each of those periods during which there is any movement in the account (s 78(4)). This statement must be given within the prescribed time[15] after the end of the period to which it relates (s 78(5)). However, no penalties are specified for default in providing this statement.

Finally, where a regulated agreement, other than a non-commercial agreement,[12] requires the debtor or hirer to keep goods to which the agreement relates in his possession or control, he must, within seven days after receiving a request in writing to that effect from the creditor or owner, tell the creditor or owner where the goods are (s 80(1)). If he fails to do so, and the default

---

12 See n 16, p 62, above.
13 Currently £1,000: SI 1984/447, made under Magistrates' Courts Act 1980, s 143.
14 The Consumer Credit (Running-Account Credit Information) Regulations 1983 SI 1983/1570 have been made.
15 The period can be 1, 6 or 12 months depending on the circumstances: SI 1983/1570, reg 3.

continues for 14 days, he commits an offence (s 80(2)) for which the maximum penalty is a fine of level 4 on the standard scale[16] upon summary conviction (s 167, Sch 1).

(c) Appropriation of payments

If the debtor or hirer is liable to make payments in respect of two or more regulated agreements to the same person, he is entitled, on making any payment which is not sufficient to discharge the total amount then due under all the agreements, to appropriate the sum so paid in or towards satisfaction of the sum due under any one or more of the agreements in such proportions as he thinks fit (s 81(1)). If he does not do so in cases where one or more of the agreements is a hire-purchase, conditional sale,[17] or consumer hire agreement or an agreement in relation to which any security[18] is provided, the payment must be appropriated towards satisfaction of sums due under each agreement in the proportions which they bear to one another (s 81(2)). This overrides the general common law rule that a creditor may appropriate payments if the debtor does not do so.

(d) Variation of agreements

The Act deals with two methods of variation: firstly, under a power contained in the agreement (ie unilateral variation by the creditor or owner) and secondly, by the making of a new ('modifying') agreement. But these provisions do not apply to non-commercial agreements[19] (s 82(7)).

If the creditor or owner varies a regulated agreement under a power contained in it, the variation does not take effect before notice of it is given to the debtor or hirer in the manner prescribed by regulations made by the Secretary of State (s 82(1)). The Consumer Credit (Notice of Variation of Agreements) Regulations 1977[20] have been made and provide that notice of variation of any regulated agreement must set out particulars of the variation and be served on the debtor or hirer not less than seven days before the variation takes effect (reg 2). An exception is made for cases where under the agreement the amount of interest payments is determined, before and after the variation takes effect, by reference to the amount of the balance outstanding at daily intervals and the variation is a variation of the rate of interest payable under the agreement (reg 3(1)). In such cases the particulars of variation are treated as properly served upon the debtor or hirer if published in at least three national daily newspapers (printed in no less than 3 mm type and in a space of no less than 10 sq cm) or, if this is not reasonably practicable, if it is published in the appropriate Gazette (ie if the creditor has a place of business in England or Wales, the *London Gazette*: reg 1(2)) and in either case, if reasonably practicable to do so, the notice must also be prominently displayed, so that it may easily be read, in a part (if any) open to the public of the premises of the creditor where the agreement to which the variation relates is maintained (reg 3(2)). There is also an exception for certain variations in the amount payable under a regulated consumer hire agreement

16 Currently £1,000: SI 1984/447 made under Magistrates' Courts Act 1980, s 143.
17 See p 47, above.
18 See p 92, below.
19 See n 16, p 62 above.
20 SI No 328, as amended by SI 1979/661 and SI 1979/667.

(reg 4). Although it is possible to include in any agreement a term providing that the creditor or owner may vary any of the terms from time to time, reliance upon such a power to effect a substantial variation might be considered an unfair or improper business practice (ie within s 25(2))[21] and such a term could not properly be relied upon to effect variations which, by their very nature, are consensual: for example, the making of a further advance under a fixed-sum credit agreement. Such variations would therefore fall to be treated as modifying agreements.

If a modifying agreement varies or supplements an earlier agreement, it is treated for the purposes of the Act as revoking the earlier agreement and containing provisions reproducing the combined effect of the two agreements so that obligations outstanding in relation to the earlier agreement are treated as outstanding in relation to the modifying agreement (s 82(2)). Examples of a modifying agreement made between the parties to an earlier agreement would be an agreement to increase the credit limit applicable under a credit card agreement or under an agreement for an overdraft facility (Examples 22 and 23, Part II, Sch 2), or an agreement to take substitute security. A variation which does not involve agreement (eg a waiver or forbearance by a creditor or owner) would probably not be covered. Moreover, since the modifying agreement must vary or supplement an earlier agreement, an agreement made between parties to an earlier agreement but intended to rescind and replace the earlier agreement (ie a novation) would not be covered (such an agreement would be treated as a new agreement for the purposes of the Act). But there is no restriction that the modifying agreement must be one between the parties to the original agreement. So an assignment by either of them to a third party would probably be treated as a modifying agreement since even if it does not strictly vary the earlier agreement it would seem to supplement it. It has also been suggested that any form of variation must be contractually binding for there to be a modifying agreement,[1] so that, for example, an arrangement to reduce the number of repayments would not be a modifying agreement if unsupported by consideration. But presumably an agreed variation could become binding even if unsupported by consideration: for example as a result of estoppel.

Since a modifying agreement is treated in effect as a new agreement, it must, if regulated, comply with all the provisions concerning the entry into credit or hire agreements.[2] Furthermore, since it reproduces the combined effect of the earlier agreement and variations, an earlier unregulated agreement could become a regulated agreement. For example if an earlier loan in excess of £15,000 has been reduced below that limit by repayment, the making of a further advance under that agreement which does not take the total amount of the loan over £15,000 produces a regulated agreement. If the further advance was itself less than £15,000 but took the total amount of the loan over £15,000 it is thought that the agreement would continue to be unregulated. But if the earlier agreement is regulated, the modifying agreement is also treated as regulated (even if it would not otherwise be) unless it is for running-account credit (s 82(3)). So a further advance which takes the

---

21 See p 58, above.
1 *Guest* para 2–083.
2 See p 67ff, above. The documentary requirements for modifying agreements are particularly complicated and for this reason modifying agreements are to be avoided where possible.

total amount of a loan for fixed-sum credit over £15,000 remains regulated. In the case of a regulated agreement for running-account credit, if by the modifying agreement the creditor allows the credit limit to be exceeded but intends the excess to be merely temporary, the documentation and cancellation provisions in Part V of the Act (except those relating to antecedent negotiations in s 56) do not apply to the modifying agreement (s 82(4)). So, for example, if a customer is permitted to exceed the agreed credit limit applicable under a credit card agreement, or if a bank honours a cheque which takes the customer's overdraft beyond the agreed facility, it will not be necessary to go through the formalities for execution of a modifying agreement if the creditor intends the excess to be temporary (Examples 22 and 23, Part II, Sch 2). In all cases, if the earlier agreement is cancellable[3] and the modifying agreement is made within the cooling-off period applicable (under s 68) to the earlier agreement, then the modifying agreement is treated as a cancellable agreement (even if it would not otherwise be) and notice of cancellation may be served (also under s 68) not later than the end of the cancellation period applicable to the earlier agreement (s 82(5)). Otherwise modifying agreements are not cancellable (s 82(6)).

A variation for which an agreement provides but which is not made by the creditor or owner (eg movements in an applicable rate of interest which are beyond the creditor's control) would seem to fall outside these provisions.

(e) Miscellaneous

The Act provides that a debtor under a regulated consumer credit agreement shall not be liable to the creditor for any loss arising from use of the credit facility by another person not acting (or treated as acting)[4] as the debtor's agent (s 83(1)). This provision is very wide. It could, for example, cover unauthorised withdrawals from a customer's current account which happens to be (or thereby becomes) overdrawn. But there are certain exceptions to this provision. Firstly, it does not apply to a non-commercial agreement[5] or to any loss in so far as it arises from misuse of an instrument to which s 4 of the Cheques Act 1957[6] applies (s 83(4)). Secondly, there are exceptions relating to misuse of credit-tokens.[7] The debtor under a credit-token agreement can incur liability of up to £50[8] (or the credit limit, if lower) for loss to the creditor arising from use of the credit-token by other persons during any time when it is not in the possession of the debtor, creditor or anyone authorised by the debtor to use it (s 84(1), (7)) and unlimited liability for loss to the creditor from use of the credit-token by a person who acquired possession of it with the debtor's consent (s 84(2)). But the exceptions for credit-token misuse only apply if the credit-token agreement contains in the manner prescribed by

---

3 See p 72, above.
4 It is unclear when a person will be 'treated as' the debtor's agent. Presumably an agent whose actual authority has been withdrawn should be treated as the debtor's agent if he has ostensible authority: eg by continued possession of a credit card issued to him for use on the debtor's account (in which case the debtor could incur unlimited liability for use of the card by such a person).
5 See n 16, p 62, above.
6 See chapter 23.
7 See p 50, above.
8 SI 1983/1571.

regulations made by the Secretary of State[9] details of the name, address and telephone number of a person to whom oral or written notice may be given by the debtor that the card is lost, stolen or for any other reason liable to misuse (s 84(4)) and such notice has not been given (s 84(3)). For this purpose notice is effective when received, but if given orally and the agreement so requires it is treated as ineffective unless confirmed in writing within seven days (s 84(5)). It should be noted that in proceedings brought by the creditor under a credit-token agreement, if the debtor alleges that any use of the credit-token was not authorised by him, the onus is on the creditor to prove either that the use was authorised or occurred before the creditor had been given the notice mentioned above (s 171(4)(b)). Further, if the debtor is liable under one of the credit-token misuse exceptions, any sum he paid for the issue of the credit-token (eg a subscription fee), to the extent (if any) that it has not been previously offset by use made of the credit-token, must be treated as paid towards satisfaction of his liability (s 84(6)). Finally, where two or more credit-tokens are given under one credit-token agreement, the above provisions apply to each credit-token separately (s 84(8)).

Whenever, in connection with a credit-token agreement which is not a small agreement, a credit-token (other than the first) is given by the creditor to the debtor, the creditor must also give the debtor a copy[10] of the executed agreement (if any) and any other document referred to in it (s 85(1), (2)). If the creditor fails to do so he is not entitled, while the default continues, to enforce the agreement and if the default continues for one month he commits an offence with a maximum penalty of a fine of level 4 on the standard scale[11] upon summary conviction (s 167 and Sch 4).

If a regulated agreement specifies the period of its duration and that period has not come to an end, the creditor or owner is not entitled, by reason of the death of the debtor or hirer, to do any act which requires service of a default notice (as specified in s 87(1), below) if at the death the agreement is fully secured, notwithstanding that the agreement provides that it may be terminated by any party before the end of its duration (s 86(1), (3)). Even if such an agreement is only partly secured or unsecured, the creditor or owner is only entitled, by reason of the death, to do any act which requires prior service of a default notice on an order of the county court (s 86(2)). An act is done by reason of the death if done under a power conferred by the agreement which is exercisable on the death of the debtor or hirer or exercisable at will but actually exercised after his death (s 86(6)). It is thought that an agreement will be treated as secured if security has been provided as defined in the Act (which provides an extended definition of security).[12] Presumably the security must be valued to determine whether the creditor is fully or partly secured. The county court may only make an order if the creditor or owner proves that he has been unable to satisfy himself that the present and future obligations of the debtor or hirer under the agreement are likely to be discharged (s 128). But these provisions do not affect the operation of any agreement providing for payment of sums already due under the

9 The Consumer Credit (Credit-Token Agreements) Regulations 1983, SI 1983/1555 have been made and provide that the relevant details must be prominent and easily legible.
10 See n 16, p 69, above.
11 Currently £1,000: SI 1984/447, made under Magistrates' Courts Act 1980, s 143.
12 See p 92, below.

agreement or becoming due under it on the death of the debtor or hirer if in either case those sums are payable out of the proceeds of a policy of life assurance on his life (s 86(5)). This would cover, for example, an endowment or repayment protection policy. Further, the creditor is not prevented from treating the right to draw on any credit as restricted or deferred, and taking such steps as may be necessary to make this effective (eg preventing further withdrawals) (s 86(4)) and if default occurs the creditor or owner will have the usual remedies (see below).

7 DEFAULT AND TERMINATION

Provisions covering default notices, restrictions upon remedies for default, early payment by the debtor and termination of agreements are contained in Part VII of the Act (ss 87–104).

(a) Default notices

Service of a default notice on the debtor or hirer is necessary before the creditor or owner can become entitled, by reason of any breach by the debtor or hirer of a regulated agreement, to terminate the agreement, demand early payment of any sum, recover possession of any goods or land, treat any right conferred on the debtor or hirer by the agreement as terminated, restricted or deferred, or to enforce any security[12a] (s 87(1)). It is specifically provided that the doing of an act by which a floating charge becomes fixed is not enforcement of a security (s 87(3)) and regulations made by the Secretary of State may exempt specified agreements from the requirement for service of default notices (s 87(4)).[13] Furthermore, the creditor is not prevented from treating the right to draw upon any credit as restricted or deferred and taking such steps as may be necessary to make this effective (eg preventing further withdrawals) (s 87(2)) nor from claiming arrears or damages for breach of the agreement.[14]

A default notice must be in the form prescribed by regulations made by the Secretary of State,[15] contain prescribed information about the consequences of failure to comply with it, and specify the nature of the alleged breach and, if the breach is capable of remedy,[16] what action is required to remedy it and the date by which this is to be done or, if the breach is not capable of remedy, the sum (if any) required to be paid as compensation for the breach and the date by which it is to be paid (s 88(1), (4)). Any date specified in the notice must be not less than seven days after the date it is served and the creditor or owner cannot take any action which requires prior service of a default notice (as specified in s 87(1)) before that date; if no date is specified in the notice, no such action can be taken before seven days have elapsed from the date of service (s 88(2)). A default notice must not treat as

12a See p 92 below.
13 The Consumer Credit (Enforcement, Default and Termination Notices) Regulations 1983, SI 1983/1561 have been made and exempt non-commercial agreements (as to which see n 16, p 62, above) in relation to which no security has been provided.
14 Quaere whether the creditor could also claim rescission for misrepresentation without serving a default notice.
15 See the Consumer Credit (Enforcement, Default and Termination Notices) Regulations 1983, n 13 above.
16 Cf the similar wording in s 146 Law of Property Act 1925 and cases thereon.

a breach a failure to comply with a provision of the agreement which becomes operative only on breach of some other provision, but if the breach of that other provision is not duly remedied, or compensation demanded (under s 88(1)) not paid, or (if no requirement is made under s 88(1)) the seven day period has elapsed, the creditor or owner may treat the failure as a breach (ie for the purposes of s 87(1)) (s 88(3)). If the notice imposes a requirement (under s 88(1)), it may include a provision that action will be taken (as mentioned in s 87(1)), at any time after the appropriate time restriction ceases, together with a statement that the provision will be ineffective if the breach is duly remedied or the compensation duly paid (s 88(5)).

If before the date specified for that purpose in the default notice the debtor or hirer remedies the breach or pays the compensation as required by the notice, the breach is treated as not having occurred (s 89(1)). But partial compliance is not sufficient for this purpose.[17]

(b) Further restrictions on remedies for default

There are special provisions restricting the right of a creditor under a regulated hire-purchase or conditional sale agreement[18] to retake the goods ('protected goods': s 90(7)) from the debtor. In these cases, at any time when the debtor is in breach of the agreement, if he has paid to the creditor one-third or more of the total price[18] of the goods but the property in them remains with the creditor, the creditor is not entitled to recover possession of the goods from the debtor except on an order of the county court (s 90(1)). In making the calculation, if the creditor under the agreement is required to carry out any installation and the total price includes an amount to be paid in respect of the installation ('installation charge'), the reference to one-third of the total price is construed as a reference to the aggregate of the installation charge and one-third of the remainder of the total price (s 90(2)). 'Installation' means the installing of any electric line or any gas or water pipe, the fixing of goods to the premises where they are to be used, the alteration of premises to enable goods to be used in them, and (if it is reasonably necessary that the goods should be constructed or erected on the premises where they are to be used) any work carried out for the purpose of constructing or erecting them on those premises (s 189(1)). If the debtor is in breach, has not paid the creditor one-third or more of the total price, but has done so on a previous occasion in relation to an earlier hire-purchase or conditional sale agreement between the same parties and relating to any of the goods comprised in the later agreement (whether or not other goods were also included) the requirement (in s 90(1) that one third or more of the total price of the goods should have been paid does not apply (s 90(3)). The same applies if the later agreement was a modifying agreement (s 90(4)). It should, however, be noted that all of these provisions only apply if the goods are in the possession of the debtor. Further, they cease to apply if the debtor terminates the agreement (s 90(5)), and do not apply if the debtor, although in possession, consents to repossession at the time when it is sought (s 173(3)). Such consent must be unqualified and informed.[19] If these provisions apply at the death of the debtor, they continue to apply (in relation to the possessor of the goods) until the grant

17 *Price v Romilly* [1960] 3 All ER 429, [1960] 1 WLR 1360.
18 See p 47, above.
19 *Chartered Trust plc v Pitcher* (1987) 131 Sol Jo 503.

of probate or administration (s 90(6)). If the goods are recovered by the creditor in breach of these provisions, the regulated agreement terminates (if it has not already been terminated), the debtor is released from all liability under the agreement and is entitled to recover from the creditor all sums he has paid under the agreement (s 91). These consequences cannot be remedied by returning the goods to the debtor.[1]

Furthermore, a creditor or owner is not entitled to enter any premises to take possession of any goods subject to a regulated hire-purchase, conditional sale or consumer hire agreement, except under an order of the county court (s 92(1)). Such an order is also necessary before a creditor under a regulated conditional sale agreement relating to land is entitled to recover possession of the land from the debtor when the latter is in breach of the agreement (s 92(2)). Any entry upon land in contravention of these provisions is actionable as a breach of statutory duty (s 92(3)). Again, however, they do not prevent entry with the consent of the debtor or hirer given at that time (s 173(3)).

Finally, if the total charge for credit includes an item in respect of interest, the debtor under any regulated consumer credit agreement cannot be required to pay interest on sums which, in breach of the agreement, are unpaid by him at a rate exceeding the rate of that interest (s 93(9). If no such item is included in the total charge for credit, the debtor cannot be required to pay interest on such sums at a rate exceeding what would be the rate of total charge for credit if any items which regulations (under s 20(2))[2] provide to be included in respect of linked transactions were disregarded (s 93). A term which offends against this provision is probably void only to the extent that the rate of interest exceeds that permitted. Furthermore, a term requiring immediate payment of principal and interest if the borrower defaults would not appear to be caught, since such sums are not unpaid in breach of the agreement (although such a term might be construed as a penalty).[3] If the applicable rate of total charge for credit is 0% (ie an interest free facility), no interest could apparently be charged upon default: although it may be possible to get around this consequence by specifying a commercial interest rate in the agreement but waiving the right to interest payments unless the debtor defaults.

(c) Early payment by debtor

The debtor under a regulated consumer credit agreement is entitled at any time, by notice in writing to the creditor and payment to the creditor of all amounts payable by the debtor to him under the agreement (less any rebate, as mentioned below) to discharge the debtor's indebtedness under the agreement (s 94(1)). The notice required may embody the exercise by the debtor of any option to purchase goods conferred on him by the agreement and deal with any other matter arising on, or in relation to, termination of the agreement (s 94(2)).

1 Cf *Capital Finance Co Ltd v Bray* [1964] 1 All ER 603, [1964] 1 WLR 323.
2 See p 56, above.
3 But see for example *The Angelic Star* [1988] 1 Lloyd's Rep 122 (acceleration of principal and accrued interest not penal). Note also that such clauses are subject to the rebate provisions mentioned below.

Regulations made by the Secretary of State may provide for a rebate of charges for credit to the debtor under a regulated consumer credit agreement where the debtor's indebtedness is discharged or becomes payable before the time fixed by the agreement, or any sum becomes payable by him before the time so fixed, whether as a result of the debtor having made early repayment (under s 94) or on refinancing (wholly or partly), breach of the agreement or for any other reason (s 95(1)). The regulations may also provide for calculation of the rebate by reference to any sums paid or payable by the debtor or his associate[4] under or in connection with the agreement (whether to the creditor or some other person), including sums under linked transactions and other items in the total charge for credit (s 95(2)). The Consumer Credit (Rebate on Early Settlement) Regulations 1983[5] have been made. They cover (inter alia) accelerated payment clauses. Nevertheless, judgment in respect of the accelerated sums may be given without deduction of the rebate on those sums (although the judgment is satisfied by payment of the judgment debt, less the rebate for early settlement).[6]

Where for any reason the debtor's indebtedness under a regulated consumer credit agreement is discharged before the time fixed by the agreement, he and any associate[4] of his is at the same time discharged from any liability under a linked transaction (s 96(1)). But this does not apply to a linked transaction which is a debt which has already become payable (s 96(1)) or a linked transaction which is an agreement providing the debtor or his associate with credit (s 96(2)), and regulations[7] made by the Secretary of State may exclude other prescribed linked transactions (s 96(3)).

Finally, the creditor under a regulated consumer credit agreement must, within the period prescribed (by regulations made by the Secretary of State)[8] after receiving a request in writing to that effect from the debtor, deliver or send by post to the debtor a statement in the form prescribed by the regulations indicating (according to information to which it is practicable for him to refer) the amount of the payment required to discharge the debtor's indebtedness under the agreement, together with particulars prescribed by the regulations showing how the amount is arrived at (s 97(1)). But this does not apply to a request made less than one month after a previous request relating to the same agreement was complied with (s 97(2)). If the creditor fails to comply with a request when obliged to do so he is not entitled, while the default continues, to enforce the agreement and if the default continues for one month he commits an offence for which he can incur a fine of level 3 on the standard scale[9] upon summary conviction (ss 97(3), 167 and Sch 1).

(d) Termination of agreements

A creditor or owner who wishes to terminate a regulated agreement (otherwise than by reason of any breach[10] by the debtor or hirer: s 98(6)) is not entitled

4 See n 14, p 48, above.
5 SI 1983/1562, as amended by SI 1989/596.
6 *Forward Trust v Wymark* (1989) Times, 25 July.
7 See n 1, p 55, above.
8 The Consumer Credit (Settlement Information) Regulations 1983, SI 1983/1564 have been made. The prescribed period is 12 working days: reg 4.
9 Currently £400: SI 1984/447, made under Magistrates' Courts Act 1980, s 143.
10 Equivalent provisions for cases of default are in s 87 (see p 85, above). The provisions for enforcement notices in s 76(1) (see p 79, above) may also apply.

to terminate the agreement except by or after delivering or sending by post to the debtor or hirer not less than seven days' notice of termination (s 98(1)). Such notice is ineffective unless in the form prescribed by regulations made by the Secretary of State.[11] But the requirement to serve notice only applies where a period for the duration of the agreement is specified in the agreement and that period has not ended when the creditor or owner terminates the agreement (s 98(2)). It does not prevent a creditor from treating the right to draw on any credit as restricted or deferred or from taking such steps as may be necessary to make the restriction or deferment effective (s 98(4)). In addition, the regulations may provide that the requirement does not apply to prescribed agreements (s 76(5)) and under this power the Secretary of State has exempted non-commercial agreements[12] where no security[13] is provided.[14]

At any time before the final payment by the debtor falls due under a regulated hire-purchase or conditional sale agreement,[15] the debtor is entitled to terminate the agreement by delivering or sending by post notice in writing to any person entitled or authorised to receive the sums payable under the agreement (s 99(1)). But termination does not affect any liability under the agreement which has accrued beforehand (s 99(2)). It has been held that the final payment under an agreement has 'fallen due' if the agreement provides for future instalments to become immediately payable upon default and a default occurs.[16] The right to terminate does not, however, apply to a conditional sale agreement relating to land after title to the land has passed to the debtor (s 99(3)). Not does it apply to a conditional sale agreement relating to goods the property in which has vested in the debtor and which he has transferred to another person, unless the transferee becomes the debtor under the agreement (s 99(4)). But if the debtor under a conditional sale agreement has the right to terminate and exercises the right after the property in the goods has vested in him, the property thereupon vests in the person in whom it was previously vested ('the previous owner'); if the previous owner has died or some other event has occurred by which the property (had it been vested in him immediately before the event) would have vested in somebody else, the property is treated as having devolved as if it had vested in the previous owner immediately before his death or the event (s 99(5)).

If a regulated hire-purchase or conditional sale agreement[15] is terminated under the above provisions, the debtor is liable to pay to the creditor the amount (if any) by which one-half of the total price exceeds the aggregate of the sums paid and the sums due in respect of the total price immediately before termination, unless the agreement provides for a smaller payment (s 100(1)). Usually, therefore, the creditor will not be entitled to any payment if the debtor has paid (or become liable to pay) over half of the sums payable (the so-called '50% rule'). If the agreement requires the creditor to carry out any installation and specifies as part of the total price an installation charge, the reference (in s 100(1)) to one-half of the total price must be construed as

---

11 The Consumer Credit (Enforcement, Default and Termination Notices) Regulations 1983, SI 1983/1561 (as amended by SI 1984/1109) have been made. For the prescribed form see reg 2(3) and Sch 3.
12 See n 16, p 62, above.
13 See p 92, below.
14 SI 1983/1561, reg 2(9).
15 See p 47, above.
16 *Wadham Stringer Finance Ltd v Meaney* [1980] 3 All ER 789, [1981] 1 WLR 39.

a reference to the aggregate of the installation charge and one-half of the remainder of the total price (s 100(2)). But if in any action the court is satisfied that the loss to the creditor as a result of the termination is less than this amount, the court may order payment of that lesser sum instead (s 100(3)). If the debtor has breached an obligation to take reasonable care of the goods or land, the amount to which the creditor is entitled must be increased by the sum required to compensate him for the breach (s 100(4)). Finally, if the debtor, on termination, wrongfully retains possession of the goods to which the agreement relates, in any action by the creditor to recover possession the court must order delivery up of the goods to the creditor without giving the debtor an option to pay their value, unless the court is satisfied that having regard to the circumstances it would not be just to make such an order (s 100(5)). But these provisions would not seem to prevent the creditor from claiming fully compensatory damages[17] if termination by the debtor constitutes a repudiatory breach.

The hirer under a regulated consumer hire agreement is entitled to terminate the agreement by delivering or sending by post a notice in writing to any person entitled or authorised to receive the sums payable under the agreement (s 101(1)), but termination does not affect any liability under the agreement which has occurred beforehand (s 101(2)). There is a general limitation that notice of termination cannot expire earlier than 18 months after the making of the agreement (which means the original agreement if it has been modified: s 101(9)). The statutory right is not, therefore, available if the agreement cannot last for 18 months. Subject to this, the following provisions determine the minimum period, unless the agreement provides for a shorter period (s 101(3)). If the agreement provides for the making of payments by the hirer to the owner at equal intervals, the minimum period of notice is the length of one such interval or three months (whichever is less) (s 101(4)). If the agreement provides for the making of such payments at differing intervals, the minimum period of notice is the length of the shortest interval or three months (whichever is less) (s 101(5)). In all other cases the minimum period is three months (s 101(6)). These provisions do not, however, apply in three cases. Firstly, if the agreement provides for the making by the hirer of payments which in total (without breach of the agreement) exceed £900)[1] in any year (s 101(7)(a)). Secondly, if the agreement is for the bailment[2] of goods to the hirer for the purposes of a business carried on by him[3] (or the hirer holds himself out as requiring the goods for those purposes) and the goods are selected by the hirer, and acquired by the owner, for the purposes of the agreement at the hirer's request from any person other than an associate[4] of the hirer (s 101(7)(b)). Thirdly, if the hirer requires (or holds himself out as requiring) the goods for the purpose of bailing them to other persons in the course of a business carried on by him (s 101(7)(c)). In addition, on an application to the Director by a person carrying on a consumer hire business,[2] if the Director considers it would be in the interests of hirers he

---

17 As to which see eg *Yeoman Credit Ltd v Waragowski* [1961] 3 All ER 145, [1961] 1 WLR 1124; *Lombard North Central plc v Butterworth* [1987] QB 527, [1987] 1 All ER 267.
1 For the financial limit see SI 1983/1571.
2 See p 51, above.
3 See p 57, above.
4 See n 14, p 48, above.

may direct in a notice to the applicant that the right to terminate should not apply to consumer hire agreements made by the applicant, subject to such conditions (if any) as the Director may specify (s 101(8)).

A credit-broker[5] or supplier[6] who was a negotiator in antecedent negotiations[7] and any person who, in the course of a business carried on by him,[8] acted on behalf of the debtor or hirer[9] in any negotiations for an agreement are each deemed to be the agent of the creditor or owner for the purpose of receiving any notice from the debtor or hirer rescinding any regulated agreement (s 102(1)). For this purpose rescission does not cover service of a cancellation notice (as to which see the equivalent provisions in s 69(5), supra) or notice of termination of a hire-purchase, conditional sale[10] or consumer hire agreement (whether under ss 99 or 101 or by the exercise of a right or power conferred by the agreement) (s 102(2)). If construed expansively, as is thought appropriate, rescission would cover not only rescission in the strict sense (eg for fraud, misrepresentation, or mistake) but also in the looser sense of acceptance by the innocent party of a repudiatory breach of an agreement.

If an individual (the 'customer') delivers or sends by post to any person (the 'trader') written notice of termination, the trader must, within the prescribed period[11] after receiving the notice, either comply with it or serve on the customer a counter-notice stating that he disputes its correctness or asserts that the customer is not indebted to him under the agreement (s 103(1)). 'Notice of termination' means a notice stating that the customer was the debtor or hirer and the trader the creditor or owner under a regulated agreement described in the notice, that the customer has discharged his indebtedness to the trader under the agreement and that the agreement has ceased to have any operation, and requiring the trader to give the customer notice in writing, signed by or on behalf of the trader, confirming that these statements are correct (s 103(1)). If the trader disputes the correctness of the notice he must give particulars of the way in which he alleges it is wrong (s 103(2)). If the trader fails to comply with the notice or serve a counter-notice and the default continues for one month, he commits an offence with a maximum penalty of a fine of level 3 on the standard scale[12] upon summary conviction (ss 103(5), 167 and Sch 1). However, these provisions do not apply to a non-commercial agreement,[13] nor do they apply to an agreement if the trader has previously complied with them on service of a notice with respect to that agreement (s 103(3), (4)).

5 See p 106, below.
6 Ie within ss 11, 12 or 13.
7 See p 67, above.
8 See p 57, above.
9 See n 15, p 68, above.
10 See p 47, above.
11 12 working days: Consumer Credit (Prescribed Periods for Giving Information) Regulations 1983, SI 1983/1569, reg 2.
12 Currently £400: SI 1984/447, made under Magistrates' Courts Act 1980, s 143.
13 See n 16, p 62, above.

8 SECURITY

Provisions concerning security generally, and, in particular, pledges, negotiable instruments and land mortgages are set out in Part VIII of the Act (ss 105–126).

(a) General

Any security provided by a person (other than the debtor or hirer: s 105(6)) in relation to a regulated agreement must be expressed in writing (s 105(1)) and regulations made by the Secretary of State may prescribe the form and content of such documents ('security instruments') (s 105(2)).[14] 'Security' means a mortgage, charge, pledge, bond, debenture, indemnity, guarantee, bill, note or other right provided by the debtor or hirer or at his request to secure the carrying out of his obligations under the agreement. It should be noted that 'security instrument' only covers security provided by a third party. Since the definition of security covers third party securities only if provided at the request of the debtor or hirer to secure the carrying out of his obligations, any security which is not provided at the debtor's request would not be a security instrument, nor would a charge in support of a guarantor's own obligations under the guarantee. The reason why the meaning of security instrument is limited in this way is because regulations made as to the form and content of regulated agreements[15] must include provision requiring documents embodying regulated agreements also to embody any security provided in relation to them by the debtor or hirer (s 105(9)).

A security instrument is not properly executed unless certain conditions are satisfied. Firstly, a document in the prescribed form, itself containing all the prescribed terms, and conforming with the regulations must be signed in the prescribed manner by or on behalf of the surety[16] (s 105(4)(a)). Secondly, the document must embody all the terms of the security, other than implied terms (s 105(4)(b)). A document embodies a provision if the provision is set out either in the document itself or in another document referred to in it (s 189(4)). Thirdly, when presented or sent to be signed by or on behalf of the surety the document must be in such a state that all its terms are readily legible (s 105(4)(c)) and at the same time a copy[1] of the document must also be presented or sent to the surety (s 105(4)(d)). In addition, if the security is provided after, or at the time when, the regulated agreement is made, a copy of the executed agreement and any other document referred to in it must be delivered or sent by post to the surety at the time the security is provided (s 105(5)(a)). If the security is provided before the regulated agreement is made, a copy of the executed agreement and any other document referred to in it must be delivered or sent by post to the surety within seven days after the regulated agreement is made (s 105(5)(b)).

If security is not expressed in writing when required to be, or if a security

---

14 The Consumer Credit (Guarantees and Indemnities) Regulations 1983, SI 1983/1556 have been made, but (as their name suggests) cover only guarantees and indemnities.

15 See n 1, p 70, above.

16 Surety means the person by whom any security is provided, or the person to whom his rights and duties in relation to the security have passed by assignment or operation of law s 189(1).

1 See n 16, p 69, above.

instrument is not properly executed, insofar as it has been provided in relation to a regulated agreement it is enforceable against the surety on an order of the court only (s 105(7)). If an application for such an order is dismissed the security is treated as ineffective (ie for the purposes of s 106, below), unless the court certifies it is dismissed on technical grounds only (s 105(8)).

Where under any provision of the Act a security provided in relation to a regulated agreement is to be treated as ineffective (within s 106) then (subject to s 177, below) the security, insofar as it is so provided, is treated as never having effect (s 106(a)) and the creditor or owner must return forthwith any property lodged with him solely for the purposes of the security so provided (s 106(b)), take any necessary action to remove or cancel an entry in any register, insofar as it relates to the security (s 106(c)), and repay to the surety any amount received by the creditor or owner from the surety on realisation of the security insofar as it is referable to the agreement (s 106(d)).

If security has been provided in relation to a regulated agreement for fixed-sum or running-account credit or in relation to a consumer hire agreement, the creditor or owner must, within the period prescribed by regulations made by the Secretary of State[2] after receiving a request in writing to that effect from the surety and payment of a fee of 50p,[3] deliver or send by post to the surety (if a different person from the debtor or hirer) a copy[4] of the executed agreement (if any) and any other document referred to in it, a copy of the security instrument (if any) and a statement signed by or on behalf of the creditor or owner showing (according to information to which it is practicable to refer) certain information (ss 107(1), 108(1), 109(1)). This is the same information as required to be given (under ss 77, 78, 79)[5] in response to a similar request from the debtor or hirer. The same tolerances and exceptions apply and the same penalties (ss 107(2)–(5), 108(2)–(5), 109(2)–(4)).

In addition, the creditor or owner under a regulated agreement must, within the period prescribed by regulations made by the Secretary of State[2] after receiving a request in writing to that effect from the debtor or hirer and payment of a fee of 50p,[6] deliver or send by post to the debtor or hirer a copy[4] of any security instrument[7] executed in relation to the agreement after the making of the agreement (s 110(1)). The same exceptions and penalties as mentioned above (in relation to ss 107–9) apply (s 110(2), (3)).

When a default notice (under ss 76(1) or 98(1)) is served on the debtor or hirer, a copy[4] must be served by the creditor or owner on any surety (if a different person from the debtor or hirer) (s 111(1)). If the creditor or owner fails to comply with this duty, the security is enforceable against the surety (in respect of the breach or other matter to which the notice relates) on an order of the county court only (s 111(2)).

Regulations made by the Secretary of State[8] may (subject to s 121, infra), provide for any matters relating to the sale or other realisation by the creditor or owner of property over which any right has been provided by way of

2 12 working days: Consumer Credit (Prescribed Periods for Giving Information) Regulations 1983, SI 1983/1569, reg 2.
3 SI 1983/1571.
4 See n 16, p 69, above.
5 See pp 71–80 above.
6 SI 1983/1571.
7 See p 92, above.
8 No regulations have been made to date.

security in relation to an actual or prospective agreement, other than a non-commercial agreement[9] (s 112).

There are also provisions (in s 113) intended to prevent evasion of the Act by use of security. If a security is provided in relation to an actual or prospective regulated agreement, the security cannot be enforced so as to benefit the creditor or owner, directly or indirectly, to an extent greater (whether as respects the amount of any payment or the time or manner of its being made) than would be the case if the security were not provided and any obligations of the debtor, hirer, or his associate,[10] under or in relation to the agreement were carried out to the extent (if any) to which they would be enforced under the Act (s 113(1)). So, for example, a creditor cannot avoid the 50% rule (as to which see s 100, above) by realising any security to recover more than the rule permits. If an indemnity or guarantee is given in a case where the debtor or hirer is a minor, or an indemnity is given in a case where he is otherwise not of full capacity, the reference (in s 113(1)) to the extent to which his obligations would be enforced must be read as a reference to the extent to which those obligations would be enforced if he were of full capacity (s 113(7)). This is intended to ensure that a guarantee or indemnity of the liabilities of, for example, a minor is not unenforceable by reason only of his minority.[11] Where a regulated agreement is enforceable on an order of the county court or the Director only, any security provided in relation to the agreement is enforceable (insofar as provided in relation to the agreement) where such an order has been made in relation to the agreement, but not otherwise (s 113(2)). In addition, a security is treated as ineffective (within s 106) in four cases (s 113(3)). Firstly, if a regulated agreement is cancelled (under s 69(1) or (2)), in which case the duty imposed on the debtor or hirer to repay the credit (under s 71) or return the goods (under s 72) is not enforceable before the creditor or owner has discharged any duty imposed on him (under s 106) as a result of the agreement being treated as ineffective (s 113(5)). Secondly, if a regulated agreement is terminated (under s 91). Thirdly, if an application for an enforcement order (under ss 40(2) (agreements made by unlicensed traders), 65(1) (improperly executed agreements), 124(1) (restrictions on taking cheques and negotiable instruments as security) or 149(2) (agreements made on introductions by unlicensed credit-brokers))[12] in relation to any agreement is dismissed, unless the court certifies that it is dismissed on technical grounds only. Finally, if a declaration is made by the court (under s 142(1) (refusal of enforcement order) as regards any regulated agreement. In the latter case, if the declaration relates to a part only of the agreement, the security is only ineffective insofar as it concerns that part (s 112(4)). These provisions (s 113(1)–(3)) also apply where a security is provided in relation to an actual or prospective linked transaction, and in that case references to the agreement must be read as references to the linked transaction and references to the creditor or owner to any person (other than the debtor, hirer or his associate)[10] who is a party or prospective party to the linked transaction (s 113(8)). If security is provided in relation to a prospective agreement or transaction, the security is enforceable in relation to the agree-

9   See n 16, p 62, above.
10   See n 14, p 48, above.
11   Cf Minors' Contracts Act 1987, s 2.
12   See p 106, below.

ment or transaction only after the time (if any) when the agreement is made and until that time the person providing the security is entitled, by notice in writing to the creditor or owner, to require that the security should thereupon be treated as ineffective (within s 106) (s 113(6)).

(b) Pledges

The Act contains specific provisions (ss 114–122) regulating pledges. These replace the system of regulation previously contained in the Pawnbrokers Acts 1872 to 1960. It should, however, be noted that these provisions do not apply to pledges of documents of title[13] or of bearer bonds, nor to non-commercial agreements[14] (s 114(3)).

A person who takes any article in pawn under a regulated agreement must, at the time he receives it, deliver or send by post to the person from whom he receives it a receipt in the form prescribed by regulations made by the Secretary of State[15] (a 'pawn-receipt') (s 114(1)). 'Pawn' means any article subject to a pledge and 'pledge' means the pawnee's rights over an article taken in pawn (s 189(1)). It has been held that a pledge must relate to personal chattels capable of delivery.[16] A person who takes any article in pawn from an individual whom he knows to be, or who appears to be and is, a minor, commits an offence for which the maximum penalties are a fine of the prescribed sum[17] upon summary conviction or one year's imprisonment and an unlimited fine upon conviction on indictment (ss 114(2), 167 and Sch 1). If the creditor under a regulated agreement to take any article in pawn fails to observe the requirements of the Act regarding the duty to supply copies and give notice of cancellation rights (in ss 62–64 and 114(1)) in relation to the agreement, he commits an offence for which the maximum penalties are a fine of level 4 on the standard scale[18] upon summary conviction (ss 115, 167 and Sch 1).

A pawn is redeemable at any time within six months after it was taken (s 116(1)). Subject to this, the period within which a pawn is redeemable is the same as the period fixed by the parties for the duration of the credit secured by the pledge, or such longer period as they may agree (s 116(2)). If the pawn is not redeemed within the period determined in accordance with these rules (the 'redemption period'), it nevertheless remains redeemable until realised by the pawnee (under s 120(1)(a), below) (s 116(3)). No special charge can be made for redemption of a pawn after the end of the redemption period, and charges for its safe keeping cannot be at a higher rate after the end of the redemption period than before (s 116(4)).

13 'Documents of title' is not defined; at common law they comprise only bills of lading and documents treated as documents of title by mercantile custom: see Benjamin *Sale of Goods* (3rd edn) §1433.
14 See n 16, p 62, above.
15 The Consumer Credit (Pawn-Receipts) Regulations 1983, SI 1983/1566 prescribe the form if the pawn-receipt is separate from the document embodying the regulated agreement and the Consumer Credit (Agreements) Regulations 1983, SI 1983/1553 (as amended by SI 1984/1600, SI 1985/666 and SI 1988/2047) prescribe the form if the pawn-receipt is not separate (see reg 4).
16 *Harrold v Plenty* [1901] 2 Ch 314 (chose in action not capable of being pledged); *Swanley Coal Co v Denton* [1906] 2 KB 873 (deposit of documents of title to land creates a charge, not a pledge).
17 Currently £2,000: SI 1984/447, made under Magistrates' Courts Act 1980, s 143.
18 Currently £1,000: SI 1984/447, ibid.

On surrender of the pawn-receipt and payment of the amount owing at any time when the pawn is redeemable, the pawnee must deliver the pawn to the bearer of the pawn-receipt (s 117(1)), unless the pawnee knows or has reasonable cause to suspect that the bearer of the pawn-receipt is neither the owner of the pawn nor authorised by the owner to redeem it (s 117(2)). The pawnee is not liable in tort or delict for delivering the pawn if he is obliged to do so (under s 117(1)) or for refusing to deliver the pawn if he is not obliged to do so under the Act (s 117(2)). A person (the 'claimant') who is not in possession of the pawn-receipt but claims to be the owner of the pawn or to be otherwise entitled to redeem it, may do so at any time when it is redeemable by tendering to the pawnee in place of the pawn-receipt either a statutory declaration made by the claimant in the form prescribed by regulations made by the Secretary of State[19] and with the prescribed contents or, if the pawn is security for fixed-sum credit not exceeding £25 or running-account credit on which the credit limit does not exceed £25[20] and the pawnee agrees, a statement in writing in the form prescribed by the regulations and with the prescribed contents, signed by the claimant (s 118(1)). On compliance by the claimant with either of these requirements, the redemption procedure provisions (in s 117) apply as if the declaration or statement were the pawn-receipt, and the pawn-receipt becomes inoperative for the purposes of those provisions (s 118(2)). If a person who has taken a pawn under a regulated agreement refuses without reasonable cause to allow the pawn to be redeemed, he commits an offence with maximum penalties of a fine of level 4 on the standard scale[21] upon summary conviction (ss 119(1), 167 and Sch 1) and on conviction, even if the offence does not amount to theft, s 28 Theft Act 1968 (orders for restitution) and any provision of the Theft Act 1968 relating to s 28 apply as if the pawnee had been convicted of stealing the pawn (s 119(2)). Essentially this gives the court the power to make an order for restitution of the pawn, of goods which directly or indirectly represent it or for payment of its value.

If at the end of the redemption period the pawn has not been redeemed, then (notwithstanding s 113, above) the property in the pawn passes to the pawnee if the redemption period is six months and the pawn is security for fixed-sum credit not exceeding £25 or running-account credit on which the credit limit does not exceed £25[20] (s 120(1)(a)). In any other case where the redemption period has ended but the pawn has not been redeemed, the pawn becomes realisable (pursuant to s 121, below) by the pawnee (s 120(1)(b)). But if the debtor or hirer is entitled to apply to court for a time order (under s 129, below), the property passes or the pawn becomes realisable (as the case may be) after the expiry of the five days following the end of the redemption period (s 120(2)). When a pawn has become realisable by him, the pawnee may sell it after giving to the pawnor (except in such cases as may be prescribed by regulations made by the Secretary of State)[1] not less than the

19 The Consumer Credit (Loss of Pawn-Receipt) Regulations 1983, SI 1983/1567 have been made.
20 For the financial limits see SI 1983/1571.
21 The Consumer Credit (Realisation of Pawn) Regulations 1982, SI 1983/1568 have been made and except cases in which the pawn is security for fixed-sum credit not exceeding £50 or running-account credit on which the credit limit does not exceed £50: reg 3.
 1 Currently £1,000: SI 1984/447 made under Magistrates' Courts Act 1980, s 143.

prescribed period of notice[2] of the intention to sell, indicating in the notice the asking price and any other prescribed particulars[3] (s 121(1)). In addition, within the prescribed period[4] after the sale takes place, the pawnee must give to the pawnor the prescribed information in writing as to the sale, its proceeds and expenses[5] (s 121(2)). If the net proceeds of sale are not less than the sum which, if the pawn had been redeemed on the date of the sale, would have been payable for its redemption, the debt secured by the pawn is discharged and any surplus must be paid by the pawnee to the pawnor (s 121(3)). Otherwise the debt is treated as equal to the amount by which the net proceeds of sale fall short of the sum which would have been payable for the redemption of the pawn on that date (s 121(4)). For this purpose 'net proceeds of sale' is the amount realised (the 'gross amount') less the expenses (if any) of the sale (s 121(5)). If the pawnor alleges that the gross amount is less than the true market value of the pawn on the date of the sale, the burden is on the pawnee to prove that he and any agents employed by him in the sale used reasonable care to ensure that the true market value was obtained and if he fails to prove this the gross amount is taken to be the true market value (s 121(6)). Similarly, if the pawnor alleges that the expenses of the sale were unreasonably high, the burden is on the pawnee to prove that they were reasonable and if he fails to prove this the net proceeds of sale is the gross amount less the reasonable expenses of the sale (s 121(7)).

(c) Negotiable instruments

A creditor or owner must not take a negotiable instrument, other than a bank note or cheque,[6] in discharge of any sum payable either by the debtor or hirer under a regulated agreement or by any person as surety[6a] in relation to the agreement (s 123(1)). In addition a creditor or owner must not negotiate a cheque taken in discharge of any sum so payable except to a banker (within the meaning of the Bills of Exchange Act 1882) (s 123(2)) nor must he take a negotiable instrument as security for the discharge of any sum so payable (s 123(3)). A person takes a negotiable instrument as security for the discharge of a sum if the sum is intended to be paid in some other way, and the negotiable instrument is to be presented for payment only if the sum is not paid in that way (s 123(4)). However, these provisions do not apply if the regulated agreement is a non-commercial agreement[7] (s 123(5)) and the Secretary of State may by order provide that they do not apply where the regulated agreement has a connection with a country outside the United Kingdom[8] (s 123(6)).

2 14 days minimum: ibid reg 2(1).
3 See ibid, reg 4 and Sch 1.
4 20 working days: ibid, reg 1(2).
5 See reg 5 and Sch 2.
6 'Cheque' is not defined. If construed in accordance with Bills of Exchange Act, s 73 it would not include a post-dated cheque, since such a cheque is not payable on demand: eg *Forster v Mackreth* (1867) LR 2 Exch 163 at 166, 167; *Re Palmer ex p Richdale* (1882) 19 ChD 409 at 417. But see Goode [1975] Camb LJ 79 at 114n.
6a See n 17 p 92, above.
7 See n 16, p 62, above.
8 The Consumer Credit (Negotiable Instruments) (Exemption) Order 1984, SI 1984/435 has been made and provides that the provisions do not apply to consumer hire agreements connected with a country outside the UK if the goods are hired in the course of the hirer's business.

If a contravention of these provisions occurs in relation to a sum payable by the debtor or hirer under a regulated agreement, the agreement under which the sum is payable is enforceable against the debtor or hirer on an order of the court only (s 124(1)). If the contravention occurs in relation to a sum payable by a surety, the security is enforceable on an order of the court only (s 124(2)) and if an application for enforcement of the security is dismissed the security is treated as ineffective (within s 106, supra), unless the court certifies that it is dismissed on technical grounds only (s 124(3)). Furthermore, a person who takes a negotiable instrument when this is not permitted (ie by s 123(1) or (3)), is not a holder in due course and is not entitled to enforce the instrument (s 125(1)) (although it seems that there is nothing to prevent him from subsequently negotiating it). If, on the other hand, he negotiates a cheque when this is not permitted (ie by s 123(2)), his doing so constitutes a defect in title within the meaning of the Bills of Exchange Act 1882 (s 125(2)) and consequently the person to whom he negotiates it will be presumed to be a holder in due course[9] unless it is shown that at the time the cheque was negotiated he had notice of the defect.

If the debtor or hirer under a regulated agreement or any person as surety in relation to the agreement (the 'protected person') becomes liable to a holder in due course of an instrument taken from the protected person when this is not permitted (ie by s 123(1) or (3)), or taken from the protected person and negotiated when this is not permitted (ie by s 123(2)), the creditor must indemnify the protected person in respect of that liability (s 125(3)). It is, however, expressly provided that nothing in the Act affects the rights of a holder in due course of any negotiable instrument (s 125(4)).

(d) Land mortgages

A land mortgage[10] securing a regulated agreement is enforceable (insofar as provided in relation to the agreement) on an order of the court only (s 126). This provision effectively prevents a creditor under a regulated agreement secured by a mortgage of land from exercising any right conferred by the mortgage to sell the land without a court order. The same would also apply in relation to any right conferred by a mortgage for the creditor to take possession of the land, if this constitutes enforcement of the mortgage. In the absence of contrary agreement, a legal mortgagee or chargee is entitled to take possession of the land at any time even if the mortgagor is not in default,[11] which would seem to indicate that his taking possession is not enforcement. But it is likely that the term 'enforcement' would be given a wide interpretation for the purposes of the Act[12] and accordingly it is advisable to obtain a court order in any event.

9 Bills of Exchange Act 1882, s 30(2).
10 See p 52, above.
11 Eg *Birch v Wright* (1786) 1 Term Rep 378 at 383; *Western Bank Ltd v Schindler* [1977] Ch 1, [1976] 2 All ER 393; Law of Property Act 1925, s 87(1).
12 Cf s 65(2), above (although this may only apply in relation to improperly executed agreements).

9 JUDICIAL CONTROL

Provisions relating to judicial enforcement of certain regulated agreements and securities, the making of time and property protection orders, powers of the courts over goods bailed or sold under regulated agreements, and extortionate credit bargains are contained in Part IX of the Act (ss 127–144).

(a) Enforcement of certain regulated agreements and securities

The Act directs a court only to dismiss certain applications for enforcement orders in certain circumstances (s 127(1)). The relevant applications are for enforcement orders in relation to improperly executed agreements (under s 65(1)) or improperly executed security instruments (under s 105(7)(a) or (b)), or in cases where the creditor or owner has failed to serve a notice on a surety (under s 111(2)), or taken a negotiable instrument when this is not permitted (under s 124(1) or (2)). These applications must only be dismissed (subject to s 127(3) and (4), below) if the court considers it just to do so, having regard to prejudice caused to any person by the contravention in question, the degree of culpability for it, and the powers conferred on the court to reduce or discharge any sum payable, impose conditions or suspend the operation of an order, and to vary agreements and securities (under ss 127(2), 135 and 136, below). If it appears to the court just to do so, it may in an enforcement order reduce or discharge any sum payable by the debtor or hirer, or by any surety, so as to compensate him for prejudice suffered as a result of the contravention in question (s 127(2)). But the court cannot make an enforcement order in relation to an improperly executed agreement (under s 65(1)) unless a document (whether or not in the form prescribed by and complying with regulations[13] made under s 60(1)) itself containing all the prescribed terms of the agreement[14] was signed by the debtor or hirer (whether or not in the prescribed manner) (s 127(3)) (and if an enforcement order is made in such a case the court may direct that the regulated agreement is to have effect as if it did not include a term omitted from the document signed by the debtor or hirer: s 127(5)). Nor can the court make an enforcement order in relation to an improperly executed agreement (under s 65(1)) which is a cancellable agreement if the duty to supply a copy of the unexecuted or executed agreement (under ss 62 or 63) was not complied with and the creditor or owner did not deliver or send by post to the debtor or hirer a copy of the executed agreement and any document referred to in it before the commencement of the proceedings in which the order is sought, or if the duty to give notice of cancellation rights (under s 64(1)) was not complied with (s 127(4)). Finally, the court can only make an order (under s 86(2)) entitling a creditor or owner to do an act requiring prior service of a default notice (as specified in s 87(1)) in relation to a partly secured or unsecured agreement after the death of the debtor or hirer if the creditor or owner proves that he has been unable to satisfy himself that the present and future obligations of the debtor under the agreement are likely to be discharged (s 128).

---

13 See n 1, p 70, above.
14 For the 'prescribed terms' see SI 1983/1553, Sch 6. These relate to the amount of credit/credit limit, interest rate and repayments.

(b) Time orders

A time order may provide for one or both of two things (s 129(2)): either payment by the debtor or hirer or any surety[15] of any sum owed under a regulated agreement or a security[15] by such instalments, payable at such times as the court considers reasonable having regard to the means of the debtor or hirer and any surety (s 129(2)(a)) or the remedying by the debtor or hirer of any breach of a regulated agreement (other than non-payment of money) within such period as the court may specify (s 129(2)(b)). Such an order may be made by the court if it considers it just to do so in three cases (s 129(1)). Firstly, on an application for an enforcement order. Secondly, on an application by the debtor or hirer after service on him by the creditor or owner of various notices: namely a default notice or any notice required to be served (under s 76(1)) before demanding early payment of any sum, recovering possession of any goods or treating any right conferred on the debtor or hirer by the agreement as terminated, restricted or deferred, or required to be served (under s 98(1)) before terminating a regulated agreement. Thirdly, in an action brought by a creditor or owner to enforce a regulated agreement or any security or to recover possession of any goods or land to which the agreement relates.

If an offer made by the debtor or hirer in accordance with rules of court to pay any sum by instalments is accepted by the creditor or owner, the court may make a time order (under s 129(2)(a)) giving effect to the offer without hearing evidence of means (s 130(1)). In the case of a hire-purchase or conditional sale agreement,[16] a time order (under s 129(2)(a)) may deal with sums which, although not payable by the debtor at the time the order is made, would subsequently become payable under it if the agreement continued in force (s 130(2)). But a time order (under s 129(2)(a)) cannot be made where the regulated agreement is secured by a pledge if, by virtue of regulations (made under ss 76(5), 87(4) or 98(5))[17] service of a notice is not necessary for enforcement of the pledge (s 130(3)). Finally, on the application of any person affected by a time order, the court may vary or revoke the order (s 130(6)).

(c) Property protection orders

On the application of the creditor or owner under a regulated agreement the court may make such orders as it thinks just to protect any property of the creditor or owner, or property subject to any security,[15] from damage or depreciation pending the determination of any proceedings under the Act, including orders restricting or prohibiting use of the property or giving directions as to its custody (s 131).

(d) Special powers over goods under consumer-hire, hire-purchase and conditional sale agreements

If the owner under a regulated consumer hire agreement recovers possession of the goods to which the agreement relates otherwise than by action, the hirer may apply to the court for an order that the whole or part of any sum

15 See p 92, above.
16 See p 47, above.
17 No relevant regulations have been made to date.

paid by the hirer to the owner in respect of the goods be repaid and that the obligation to pay the whole or part of any sum owed by the hirer to the owner in respect of the goods cease. If it appears to the court just to do so, having regard to the extent of the enjoyment of the goods by the hirer, it may grant such an application in full or in part (s 132(1)). So, for example, the court could order an owner who has retaken goods to repay to the hirer any deposit or rentals paid by the hirer. But the power to order 'sums owed' may only cover sums which are due and payable and not sums which have not become payable at the date when the order is made. These orders may also be included in any order the court makes in proceedings (eg under s 3 of the Torts (Interference with Goods) Act 1977) relating to a regulated consumer hire agreement for delivery to the owner of goods to which the agreement relates (s 132(2)).

If in relation to a regulated hire-purchase or conditional sale agreement it appears to the court just to do so, on an application for an enforcement or time order, or in an action brought by the creditor to recover possession of goods to which the agreement relates, the court may also make an order for the return to the creditor of the goods to which the agreement relates (a 'return order'), or an order for the transfer to the debtor of the creditor's title to certain goods to which the agreement relates (the 'transferred goods') and the return to the creditor of the remainder of the goods (a 'transfer order') (s 133(1)). If a transfer order is made, the transferred goods are such of the goods to which the agreement relates as the court thinks just; but a transfer order can only be made if the total price[1] paid (the 'paid-up sum') exceeds the part of the total price referable to the transferred goods by an amount equal to at least one-third of the unpaid balance of the total price (s 133(3)). In determining the paid-up sum, the court may treat any sum paid by the debtor, or owed by the creditor, in relation to the goods as part of the paid-up sum, deduct any sum owed by the debtor, or owed in relation to the goods (otherwise than as part of the total price) from the paid-up sum, and make corresponding reductions in amounts so owed (s 133(2)). The part of the total price referable to any goods is the part assigned to those goods by the agreement or, if no such assignment is made, the part determined by the court as reasonable (s 133(7)). But notwithstanding the making of a return or transfer order, the debtor may, at any time before the goods enter the creditor's possession, on payment of the balance of the total price and fulfilment of any other necessary conditions, claim the goods ordered to be returned to the creditor (s 133(4)). Further, if the total price of goods under a regulated hire-purchase or conditional sale agreement is paid pursuant to a time order or under this section and any other necessary conditions fulfilled, the creditor's title to the goods vests in the debtor (s 133(5)). If any goods are not returned to the creditor in contravention of a return or transfer order, on an application by the creditor the court may revoke so much of the order as relates to those goods and order the debtor to pay the creditor the unpaid portion of so much of the total price as is referable to them (s 133(7)).

Finally, if goods are comprised in a regulated hire-purchase, conditional sale or consumer hire agreement and the creditor or owner brings an action or makes an application to enforce a right to recover possession of the goods

1 See p 47, above.

from the debtor or hirer, then for the purposes of the proceedings the possession of the goods by the debtor or hirer is deemed to be adverse to the creditor or owner if the latter proves one of two things (s 134(1)). This is either that a demand for delivery of the goods was included in the default notice (under s 88(5), above) or that after the right to recover possession of the goods accrued but before the action was begun or made, he made a request in writing to the debtor or hirer to surrender the goods. For this purpose the debtor or hirer includes a person in possession of the goods at any time between the death of the debtor or hirer and the grant of probate or administration (s 134(2)). However, nothing in this provision affects a claim for damages for conversion (s 134(3)).

(e) Supplemental provisions as to orders

If it considers it just to do so, the court may in an order it makes in relation to a regulated agreement include two supplemental provisions (s 351(1)). These are either provisions making the operation of any term of the order conditional on the doing of specified acts by any party to the proceedings (s 135(1)(a)), or suspending the operation of any term of the order either until such time as the court subsequently directs or until the occurrence of a specified act or omission (s 135(1)(b)). The court cannot, however, suspend the operation of a term requiring the delivery up of goods by any person unless satisfied that the goods are in his possession or control (s 135(2)). Nor, in the case of a consumer hire agreement, can the court use its powers of suspension (under s 135(1)(b)) so as to extend the period for which, under the terms of the agreement, the hirer is entitled to possession of the goods to which the agreement relates (s 135(2)). On the application of any person affected by any such supplemental provision included in an order, the court may vary the provision (s 135(4)).

Finally, there is a general power for the court to include in any order it makes under the Act such provisions as it considers just for amending any agreement or security[2] in consequence of a term of the order (s 136).

(f) Extortionate credit bargains

If the court finds a credit bargain extortionate, it may re-open the credit agreement so as to do justice between the parties (s 137(1)). For this purpose (and for the purposes of ss 138–140) a credit agreement is any agreement between an individual (the 'debtor') and any other person (the 'creditor') by which the creditor provides the debtor with credit of any amount. In cases where no transaction other than the credit agreement is to be taken into account in computing the total charge for credit, 'credit bargain' means the credit agreement; in cases where one or more other transactions are to be so taken into account, 'credit bargain' means the credit agreement and the other transactions taken together (s 137(2)). These provisions replace those previously contained in s 1 of the Moneylenders Act 1900 and s 10 of the Moneylenders Act 1927 which prohibited harsh and unconscionable transactions by moneylenders. However, it seems that no assistance in the interpretation of the term extortionate credit bargain can be had from the

2 See p 92, above.

old provisions.[3] It should be noted that the definitions of credit agreement and credit bargain are not limited to regulated agreements or consumer credit agreements and a credit bargain extends to cover not only the credit agreement but also any other transaction affecting the total charge for credit. If the credit agreement is not a regulated agreement, expressions used in the provisions concerning extortionate credit bargains (ss 137–9) which would otherwise apply only to regulated agreements must be construed as nearly as may be as if the credit agreement were a regulated agreement (s 140).

A credit bargain is extortionate either if it requires the debtor or his associate[4] to make payments (whether unconditionally, or on certain contingencies) which are grossly exorbitant, or if it otherwise grossly contravenes ordinary principles of fair dealing (s 138(1)). A payment on a contingency might cover a default clause requiring the debtor to make a payment if he breaches the agreement. But it is thought unlikely that such a term would render the credit bargain extortionate unless it is in the nature of a penalty (and therefore unenforceable in any event). Unreasonably large sums which become payable on events other than breach are more likely to be affected. It has been held that this definition contemplates 'a substantial imbalance in bargaining power of which one party has taken advantage', but that the mere fact that a credit bargain is unwise or improvident for the debtor to have undertaken is not, of itself, enough to show that it is extortionate.[5] In determining whether a credit bargain is extortionate, regard must be had to such evidence as is adduced concerning interest rates prevailing at the time it was made, certain specified 'factors', and any other relevant considerations (s 138(2)).

Looking firstly at the question of interest rates, although the Act mentions only the rate prevailing at the time, subsequent movements in the rate could be taken into account as an 'other relevant consideration'. It has been held that in considering interest rates, like is to be compared with like, in the sense that the rate must be seen in the context of the transaction[5] and cannot be compared with rates applied by different institutions to different transactions.[6] Similarly, an unsecured loan may justify a higher interest rate than a secured loan[7] and the adequacy of any security is also relevant.[8]

The Act mentions three 'factors' to be taken into account. Firstly, factors in relation to the debtor, including his age, experience, business capacity, state of health, the degree to which (at the time of making the credit bargain) he was under financial pressure and the nature of that pressure (s 138(3)). Secondly, factors in relation to the creditor, including the degree of risk accepted by him (having regard to the value of any security provided), his relationship to the debtor, and whether or not a colourable cash price was quoted for any goods or services included in the credit bargain (s 138(4)). The risk factor was taken into account under the old law, and it was held that the risk had to be viewed as it would have been viewed by the lender at

3 *A Ketley Ltd v Scott* [1981] ICR 241; *Davies v Directloans Ltd* [1986] 1 WLR 823 at 831B–C.
4 See n 14, p 48, above.
5 *Wills v Wood* (1984) 128 Sol Jo 222, CA.
6 *A Ketley Ltd v Scott* ibid (in which a 48% interest rate was found acceptable).
7 Eg *Verner-Jeffreys v Pinto* [1929] 1 Ch 401, CA.
8 See n 6, above.

the time of the loan with the lender's experience of borrowers.[9] The reference to 'colourable cash price' is intended to provide for cases in which credit charges are disguised by an artificially high cash price. The third set of factors relate to any linked transaction, including the question how far it was reasonably required for the protection of the debtor or creditor, or was in the interest of the debtor (s 138(5)).

Under the saving for 'any other relevant considerations', the court has had regard to whether the creditor has had time to enquire as to the debtor's financial circumstances.[10] Although the exercise of undue influence on the debtor can be a relevant consideration, it will not be if exercised by a third party who is not acting in any sense as an agent for the creditor.[11]

If the court thinks it just, it may reopen a credit agreement on the ground that the credit bargain is extortionate in three circumstances[12] (s 139(1)). Firstly, on an application made for that purpose by the debtor or any surety[14] to the High Court or county court (s 139(1)(a)). But such an application can only be brought in the county court in the case of a regulated agreement or an agreement (other than a regulated agreement) under which the creditor provides the debtor with fixed-sum credit not exceeding the county court limit or running-account credit on which the credit limit does not exceed the county court limit (s 139(5)). For this purpose the county court limit is that for the time being specified by Order in Council under s 145 of the County Courts Act 1984[13] (s 139(5A)). Secondly, at the instance of the debtor or a surety in any proceedings to which the debtor and creditor are parties, being proceedings to enforce the credit agreement, any security[14] relating to it, or any linked transaction (s 139(1)(b)). Thirdly, at the instance of the debtor or a surety in other proceedings in any court where the amount paid or payable under the credit agreement is relevant (s 139(1)(c)). In reopening the agreement the court may, for the purpose of relieving the debtor or a surety from payment of any sum in excess of that fairly and reasonably due, make an order providing for any of the following (s 139(2)): namely, for accounts to be taken between any persons, the setting aside of the whole or any part of any obligation imposed on the debtor or a surety by the credit bargain or any related agreement, repayment by the creditor of the whole or part of any sum paid under the credit bargain or any related agreement by the debtor or a surety (whether paid to the creditor or any other person), return to the surety of any property provided for the purposes of security, or for the alteration of the terms of the credit agreement or any security instrument.[14] Any such order may be made notwithstanding that its effect is to place a burden on the creditor in respect of an advantage unfairly enjoyed by another person who is a party to a linked transaction (s 139(3)), but may not alter the effect of any judgment (s 139(4)). It is thought that these provisions probably empower the court to reopen an agreement even after the credit has been

9 *Carringtons Ltd v Smith* [1906] 1 KB 79 at 84.
10 *A Ketley Ltd v Scott*, ibid.
11 *Coldunell Ltd v Gallon* [1986] 2 WLR 466 at 481, 490.
12 Note that if in any of these circumstances the debtor or any surety alleges that the credit bargain is extortionate, the burden is on the creditor to prove the contrary (s 171(7)). It has been held that the burden is discharged if the creditor shows that the bargain was on its face a proper commercial bargain in which the creditor acted as an ordinary lender would be expected to act: *Caldinell v Gallon* ibid.
13 Currently £5,000: SI 1981/1123.
14 See p 92, above.

repaid or the agreement otherwise discharged.[15] Furthermore, they apply to agreements 'whenever made' (Sch 3, para 42) and could therefore even apply to agreements made before they came into force.[16]

Neither the trustee of a bankrupt's estate, nor an undischarged bankrupt is entitled to make an application to reopen a credit agreement (under s 139(1)(a)) by which credit has been provided to the bankrupt (s 343(6) Insolvency Act 1986). But there are broadly similar provisions in the Insolvency Act (s 343) empowering the court, on the application of the trustee of the bankrupt's estate, to reopen extortionate credit transactions which the bankrupt entered into in the three years before the commencement of the bankruptcy.

(g) Miscellaneous

The county court has jurisdiction to hear and determine any action by the creditor or owner to enforce a regulated agreement or any security[17] relating to it and any action to enforce any linked transaction against the debtor, hirer or his associate,[18] and any such action cannot be brought in any other court (s 141(1)). Since this provision only relates to actions brought by the creditor or owner, an action brought by the debtor or hirer should be brought in the court with jurisdiction under the normal rules. If an action or application which the Act requires to be brought in the county court is brought in the High Court, it is not treated as improperly brought but must be transferred to the county court (s 141(2)). Unless otherwise provided by rules of court,[19] all the parties to a regulated agreement and any surety must be made parties to any proceedings relating to the agreement (s 141(5)).

If under any provision of the Act a thing can be done by a creditor or owner on an enforcement order only, in two circumstances the court may if it thinks just make a declaration that the creditor or owner is not entitled to do that thing, and thereafter no application for an enforcement order can be entertained (s 142(1)). The two circumstances are where either the court dismisses an application for an enforcement order (other than on grounds which the court certifies as technical grounds only) or (if such an application has not been made or has been dismissed on grounds which the court certifies as technical grounds only), where an interested party applies to the court for a declaration. Finally, if a regulated agreement or linked transaction is cancelled (under s 69) or a regulated agreement is terminated (under s 91), the county court may make a declaration on the application of an interested party (s 142(2)).

10 ANCILLARY CREDIT BUSINESS

Provisions relating to licensing of, seeking and making agreements in the course of so-called ancillary credit businesses are contained in Part X of the Act (ss 145–160).

15 See eg *Davies v Directloans Ltd* [1986] 2 All ER 783, [1986] 1 WLR 823.
16 16 May 1977: SI 1977/325.
17 See p 92, above.
18 See n 14 p 48, above.
19 See CCR Ord 49, rr 4(3) and 4(4).

(a) Definitions

An ancillary credit business is any business[20] insofar as it comprises or relates to credit brokerage, debt-adjusting, debt-counselling, debt-collecting, or the operation of a credit reference agency (s 145(1)).

Credit brokerage is (subject to s 146(5), below) the effecting of introductions in four types of case (s 145(2)). Firstly, introductions of individuals desiring to obtain credit to persons carrying on consumer credit businesses,[20] businesses which comprise or relate to consumer credit agreements being exempt agreements (otherwise than by virtue of s 16(5)(a)) or to unregulated agreements the proper law of which is that of a country outside the United Kingdom but which would have been regulated agreements if their proper law had been the law of a part of the United Kingdom (s 145(2)(a)(i), 145(3)). In this limb of the definition the references to 'persons' carrying on 'businesses' seem to indicate that only introductions to more than one person carrying on such businesses will constitute credit brokerage. It is also arguable that introductions to persons carrying on consumer credit businesses (within the first part of this limb) will not constitute credit brokerage unless effected in relation to the making of regulated consumer credit agreements since a consumer credit business is any business so far as it comprises or relates to the provision of credit under regulated consumer credit agreements (s 189(1)). The second case covers introductions of individuals desiring to obtain credit to finance the acquisition or provision of a dwelling occupied or to be occupied by himself or his associate[21] to any person carrying on a business in the course of which he provides credit secured on land (or an interest in land) (s 145(2)(a)(ii)). There is no financial limit to this limb of the definition, which consequently will cover the activities of many estate agents, solicitors and the like (but see s 145(6), below). The third case covers introductions of individuals desiring to obtain goods on hire to persons carrying on consumer hire businesses or businesses which comprise or relate to unregulated agreements the proper law of which is that of a country outside the United Kingdom but which would have been regulated agreements if their proper law had been the law of a part of the United Kingdom (s 145(2)(b), (4)). Again, it seems that only introductions to more than one person will fall within this definition. The last case of credit-broking covers introductions to other credit-brokers of individuals desiring to obtain credit or goods on hire (s 145(2)(c)).[1] A person who carries on a credit brokerage business is a credit-broker (s 189(1)). It should be noted that only introductions of individuals[2] can fall within the definition of credit brokerage. It has been held that the provision by a retailer of display boxes containing a third party's credit application forms does not of itself constitute an introduction for this purpose.[3]

Debt-adjusting is (subject to s 146(6), below), in relation to debts due under consumer credit agreements or consumer hire agreements, either negotiating with the creditor or owner, on behalf of the debtor or hirer, terms for the discharge of a debt, or taking over the obligation of the debtor or hirer to

20 See p 57, above.
21 See n 14, p 48, above.
 1 See eg *Hicks v Walker and Frank Reynolds Ltd* [1984] Crim LR 495.
 2 See p 46, above.
 3 *Brookes v Retail Credit Card Ltd* [1986] Crim LR 327, DC.

discharge a debt in return for payments by the debtor or hirer, or any similar activity concerned with the liquidation of a debt (s 145(5)). So, for example, a motor vehicle dealer probably engages in debt-adjusting in agreeing to settle any outstanding sums due in relation to a motor car which he takes in part-exchange for the sale of a new vehicle. Debt-counselling is (subject to s 146(6)), the giving of advice to debtors or hirers about the liquidation of debts due under consumer credit or hire agreements (s 145(6)). Accountants, solicitors and bankers could, for example, fall within this category (but see s 146(6), below). Debt-collecting is (subject to s 146(6)), the taking of steps to procure payment of debts due under consumer credit or hire agreements (s 145(7)). This could, for example, cover factoring such debts. Finally, a credit reference agency is a person carrying on a business comprising the furnishing of persons with information relevant to the financial standing of individuals, being information collected by the agency for that purpose (s 145(8)). Banks and other financial institutions which obtain such information in the course of providing services to customers or an employer who maintains records regarding his employees' finances do not act as credit reference agencies in providing references from that information, since the information has not been collected for the purpose of providing references.

The Act goes on to list certain exceptional cases which are not to be treated as ancillary credit business. Firstly, a barrister acting in that capacity is not to be treated as doing so in the course of any ancillary credit business (s 146(1)). Nor is a solicitor engaging in contentious business (as defined in s 86(1) of the Solicitors Act 1957) (s 146(2)). Furthermore, introductions effected by an individual by canvassing off trade premises[4] either debtor-creditor-supplier agreements of the first type (ie within s 12(a)) or regulated consumer hire agreements are disregarded (for the purposes of s 145(2)) if the introductions are not effected by him in the capacity of an employee and he does not by any other method effect introductions (within s 145(2)) (s 146(5)). This could, for example, cover an agent who canvasses debtor-creditor-supplier agreements on behalf of a suppliers.[5] Finally, it is not debt-adjusting, debt-counselling or debt-collecting for a person to do anything in relation to a debt arising under an agreement in certain circumstances (s 146(6)). These are where he is the creditor or owner under the agreement otherwise than by assignment (unless the assignment was made in connection with the transfer to the assignee of any business other than a debt-collecting business) or where he is a supplier[5] in relation to the agreement, a credit-broker who has acquired the business of the person who was such a supplier, or, if the agreement was made in consequence of an introduction which (under s 146(5)) is to be disregarded, a person thereby prevented from being treated as a credit-broker.

(b) Licensing

The provisions of Part III of the Act[6] (except s 40) apply to an ancillary credit business as they apply to a consumer credit business (s 147(1)). A day has

4 See p 65, above; and Dobson (1980) 130 NLJ 528.
5 Ie within ss 11, 12 or 13.
6 See pp 57–63, above; the categories of licence required for ancillary credit businesses are set out at p 58. Group licences have been issued covering solicitors, Citizens' Advice Bureaux, and certain other specified persons for debt-adjusting and/or debt-counselling.

not yet been appointed for the commencement of this provision insofar as it applies the licensing provisions to credit brokerage businesses carried on by individuals wishing to enter certain debtor-creditor-supplier agreements not exceeding £30. In addition, regulations made by the Secretary of State in relation to the conduct of a licensee's business (under s 26)[7] may include provisions regulating the collection and dissemination of information by credit reference agencies (s 147(2)).

An agreement for the services of a person carrying on an ancillary credit business (the 'trader') made when the trader was unlicensed, is enforceable against the other party (the 'customer') only if the Director so orders (s 148(1)). This effectively prevents the unlicensed trader from suing to recover, without first obtaining an order, his fees and/or commission from the customer (who could, for example, be a creditor who has engaged his services). The trader or his successor in title may apply to the Director for an order on the prescribed form.[8] Furthermore, if during any period individuals were introduced to a person carrying on a consumer credit or hire business by an unlicensed credit-broker for the purpose of making regulated agreements with the person carrying on that business, that person or his successor in title may apply to the Director, on the prescribed form,[8] for an order that regulated agreements so made are to be treated as if the credit-broker had been licensed at the time of the introduction (s 149(2)). The procedure following either of these applications is the same as that which applies to the equivalent application for enforcement of regulated agreements made by unlicensed creditors/owners (ie s 40(3)–(5), above), (ss 148(3)–(5) and 149(3)–(5)).

A regulated agreement made by a debtor or hirer who, for the purpose of making that agreement, was introduced to the creditor or owner by an unlicensed credit-broker is enforceable against the debtor or hirer only if the Director has made an order (under s 148(2)) covering the time when the introduction was made and not excluding the agreement in question, or an order (under s 149(2)) that the credit-broker is to be treated as having been licensed at the time when the introduction was made (s 149(1).[9] Those who engage in consumer credit and hire business must therefore ensure that any credit-broker with whom they deal is licensed.

If the director refuses to make an order (under ss 148(2)–149(2)) in accordance with an application, the applicant may, if aggrieved by the determination, appeal to the Secretary of State (pursuant to s 41, as applied by s 147(1)) (s 150).

(c) Seeking business

The advertisement provisions of the Act (in ss 44–47, above) apply to an advertisement published for the purpose of a credit brokerage business carried on by any person, whether it advertises the services of that person or of persons to whom he effects introductions, as they apply to an advertisement to which Part IV of the Act applies (s 151(1)). In addition, certain of the

---

7 See n 20, p 59, above.
8 See General Notice No 22, 18 May 1980 made under s 6.
9 In the absence of such an order, any security provided in relation to a regulated agreement made after an introduction by an unlicensed credit-broker is also unenforceable: s 113(2), above.

advertisement provisions (namely ss 44, 46 and 47, above) apply to an advertisement published for the purpose of a business carried on by the advertiser indicating that he is willing to advise on debts, or engage in transactions concerned with the liquidation of debts, as they apply to an advertisement to which Part IV of the Act applies (s 151(2)). This latter provision is wide enough to cover such advertisements even if they relate purely to unregulated agreements, but in such circumstances the advertisement should indicate that the advertiser is not willing to act in relation to consumer credit or hire agreements, for advertisements containing such an indication are not caught (by s 151(2)) (s 151(4)). Furthermore, the Secretary of State may by order provide that an advertisement published for the purpose of any credit brokerage, debt-adjusting or debt-counselling business is exempt (from both s 151(1) and (2)) if it is of a description specified in the order (s 151(3)). For the purpose of this section, the meaning of credit brokerage is extended to include the effecting of introductions of individuals desiring to obtain credit to any person carrying on a business in the course of which he provides credit secured on land (s 151(5)). Consequently advertisements of mortgage brokers are covered.

The miscellaneous provisions in the Act relating to seeking business (ss 52–54, above) apply to credit brokerage, debt-adjusting or debt-counselling business as they apply to a consumer credit business (s 152(1)) and in their application to a credit brokerage business, they apply to the giving of quotations and information about the business of any person to whom the credit-broker effects introductions as well as about his own business (s 152(2)).

The offence of 'canvassing off trade premises' is also applied to ancillary credit business, in that it is an offence to canvass off trade premises the services of a person carrying on a business of credit brokerage, debt-adjusting or debt-counselling (s 154). The definition of canvassing off trade premises is identical to the equivalent offence in relation to regulated agreements (in s 48, above), except that it involves the canvasser soliciting entry of the consumer into an agreement for the provision of the services mentioned above rather than into regulated agreements and 'off trade premises' means not at a place where either the ancillary credit business is carried on (whether temporarily or permanently) or a business is carried on by the canvasser (or his employer or principal) or by the consumer (s 153(1) (2)). The same maximum penalties apply and the commission of the offence does not render the agreement unenforceable (as under s 48).

The excess over £3[10] of a fee or commission charged by a credit-broker for his services to certain individuals ceases to be payable or (as the case may be) is recoverable by the individual if the introduction does not result in his entering into a relevant agreement within six months following the introduction (disregarding any agreement cancelled under s 69) (s 155(1)). An individual falls within this provision if he sought an introduction for a purpose which would have been fulfilled by his entry into one of three types of relevant agreements (s 155(2)). Firstly, a regulated agreement; secondly, (in the case of an individual within s 145(2)(a)(ii), above) an agreement for credit secured on land (or an interest in land); thirdly, certain agreements made after introductions which can constitute credit-broking (namely agreements mentioned in ss 145(3)(b), (c) or (4)(b), above) (s 155(3)). It seems that entry into

10 For the financial limit see SI 1983/1571.

any such agreement after an introduction has the effect that this provision does not apply even if it is a different type of agreement from that in relation to which the introduction was made. In the case of an individual desiring to obtain credit under a consumer credit agreement, any sum payable or paid by him to a credit-broker otherwise than as a fee or commission for the credit-broker's services are treated, for the purpose of this section, as such a fee or commission if it enters, or would enter, into the total charge for credit (s 155(4)). So, for example, sums paid to a credit-broker under a linked transaction (eg insurance premiums) or by way of payment in respect of surveyor's or valuer's fees, could be recoverable by the debtor.

(d) Entry into agreements

Regulations made by the Secretary of State may make provision, in relation to agreements entered into in the course of a credit brokerage, debt-adjusting or debt-counselling business, corresponding (with such modifications as the Secretary of State thinks fit) to regulations made under certain of the provisions of the Act relating to entry into regulated agreements (namely ss 55, 60, 61, 62, 63, 65, 127, 179 and 180) (s 156). No regulations have been made to date.

(e) Credit reference agencies

The Act specifies certain obligations to disclose information relating to or held by credit reference agencies. It should be noted that these provisions are additional to any other similar obligations imposed by other statutes, such as the Data Protection Act 1984. In addition, further obligations as to disclosure in connection with credit reference agencies are contained in the Consumer Credit (Conduct of Business) (Credit References) Regulations 1971.[11]

A creditor, owner or negotiator[12] must, within the period prescribed by regulations made by the Secretary of State,[13] after receiving a request in writing to that effect from the debtor or hirer, deliver or send by post to him notice in writing of the name and address of any credit reference agency from which the creditor, owner or negotiator has, during antecedent negotiations,[12] applied for information about his financial standing (s 157(1)). However, this does not apply to a request received more than 28 days after the termination of the antecedent negotiations, whether on the making of the regulated agreement or otherwise (s 157(2)). If only one of the parties mentioned in this section applied to an agency, the better view is thought to be that the other parties mentioned in the section (assuming they did not apply to an agency) are not obliged to give notice, although this is not clear from the wording of the section. It should also be noted that the obligation is limited to cases in which information has been applied for from an agency in connection with the making of a regulated agreement, for antecedent negotiations can only be conducted in relation to a regulated agreement. If the creditor or owner fails to comply with the obligation to give notice under this section when required to do so, he commits an offence (s 157(3)) for which the maximum

11 SI 1977/330 made under ss 26 and 147(2).
12 See p 67, above.
13 The Consumer Credit (Credit Reference Agency) Regulations 1977, SI 1977/329 have been made and prescribe the period of seven working days.

penalty is a fine of level 4 on the standard scale[15] upon summary conviction (s 167 and Sch 1).

A credit reference agency must deliver or send by post to any individual (the 'consumer') a copy[16] of the file relating to him kept by the agency within the period prescribed by regulations made by the Secretary of State[17] after receiving a request in writing to that effect from the consumer, together with such particulars as the agency reasonably requires to enable them to identify the file, and a £1 fee[18] (s 158(1)). When giving a copy of the file, the agency must also give the consumer a statement of his rights (under s 159, below) in the form prescribed by the regulations[19] (s 158(2)). If the agency does not keep a file relating to the customer it must deliver or send by post to him written notice of that fact, but need not return any money paid (s 158(3)). For the purpose of these provisions, 'file' means, in relation to an individual, all the information about him kept by the agency, regardless of how the information is stored, and if information is not in plain English, a copy of it means a transcript reduced into plain English (s 158(5)). If an agency contravenes these provisions it commits an offence (s 158(4)) for which the maximum penalty is a fine of level 4 on the standard scale[1] upon summary conviction (s 167 and Sch 1).

A consumer given information (under s 158) who considers that an entry on his file is incorrect and that if it is not corrected he is likely to be prejudiced, may deliver or send by post to the agency notice in writing requiring it either to remove the entry from the file or amend it (s 159(1)). Within 28 days after receiving such a notice, the agency must inform the consumer by notice in writing that it has either removed the entry from the file, amended the entry (in which case it must include a copy[16] of the file insofar as it comprises the amended entry) or taken no action (s 159(2)). Within 28 days after receiving this notice from the agency, or (if no notice was given by the agency) within 28 days after the expiry of the time for the agency to return a notice, the consumer may (unless the agency has informed him that it has removed the entry from his file) serve a further notice on the agency requiring it to add to the file an accompanying notice of correction (not exceeding 200 words) drawn up by the consumer, and include a copy of it when furnishing information included in or based upon that entry (s 159(3)). Within a further 28 days of receiving such a correction notice the agency must (unless it intends to apply to the Director under s 159(5), below) inform the customer by notice in writing that it has received the correction notice and intends to comply with it (s 159(4)). If the consumer has not received such a counter notice (under s 159(4)) within the time required, or if for any reason it appears to the agency that it would be improper for it to publish the consumer's notice of correction, the consumer or the agency (as the case may be) may apply to the Director in the manner prescribed by regulations made by the Secretary

15 Currently £1,000: SI 1984/447, made under Magistrates' Courts Act 1980, s 143.
16 See n 16, p 69, above.
17 Seven working days: Consumer Credit (Credit Reference Agency) Regulations 1977, SI 1977/329, reg 3.
18 SI 1983/1571.
19 Consumer Credit (Credit Reference Agency) Regulations 1977, ibid, reg 3.
 1 Currently £1,000: SI 1984/447, ibid.

of State[2] and on payment of the specified fee[3] and the Director may make such order on the application as he thinks fit (s 159(5)). If a person to whom such an order is directed fails to comply with it within the period specified in the order he commits an offence (s 159(6)) with a maximum penalty of a fine of level 4 in the standard scale[4] upon summary conviction (s 167 and Sch 1).

If on an application[5] by a credit reference agency the Director is satisfied that compliance with the duty to disclose information (under s 158) in the case of consumers who carry on a business[6] would adversely affect the service provided by the agency to its customers, and that, having regard to the methods employed by the agency and other relevant factors, it is probable that consumers carrying on a business would not be prejudiced, then the Director can direct that the alternative procedure set out below should apply to the agency (s 160(1)). This procedure is designed to avoid a situation in which, for example, disclosure of the file of a business consumer would reveal sources of information which might not wish their identity to be revealed to business consumers. If an agency which is the subject of a direction by the director in this respect receives a request, particulars and a fee (in accordance with s 158(1)) from a consumer who carries on a business and the agency has a file relating to that consumer, it may, instead of complying with the normal procedure (in s 158), elect to deal with the matter as follows (s 160(2)). Instead of giving the consumer a copy of the file, the agency must, within the period prescribed by regulations made by the Secretary of State,[7] deliver or send by post to the consumer notice in writing that it is proceeding under the alternative procedure (in s 160) and containing such information included in or based on entries in the files as the Director may direct, together with a statement in the form prescribed by the regulations[8] of the consumer's rights (under s 166(4) and (5), below). If, within 28 days after receiving such information or such longer period as the Director may allow, the consumer delivers or sends by post notice in writing to the Director that he is dissatisfied with the information, satisfies the Director that he has taken such steps in relation to the agency as may be reasonable with a view to removing the cause of his dissatisfaction and pays the specified fee,[9] the Director may direct the agency to give him (the Director) a copy[10] of the file and he may disclose such information on the file as he thinks fit (s 160(4)). The provisions for correction of wrong information (in s 159) apply with any necessary modifications to information given to the consumer under this procedure as it applies to information given after normal disclosure (s 160(5)). Finally, if an agency which has made an election for the alternative procedure (under s 160(2)) fails to comply with its obligations (under s 160(3) or (4)) it commits an

2 See Consumer Credit (Credit Reference Agency) Regulations 1977, ibid reg 4; General Notices Nos 11 (applications by consumers) and 12 (applications by credit reference agencies), 12 June 1977 made under s 6.

3 There is currently no fee: General Notice No 15, 3 April 1979, para 22, made under s 2.

4 Currently £1,000: SI 1984/447, made under Magistrates' Courts Act 1980, s 143.

5 See General Notice No 3, 12 April 1976 made under s 6 (form of application); there is currently a £25 fee: General Notice No 15, 3 April 1979, para 2, made under s 2.

6 See p 57, above.

7 Seven working days: Consumer Credit (Credit Reference Agency) Regulations 1977, ibid, reg 3.

8 Consumer Credit (Credit Reference Agency) Regulations, ibid, reg 2 and Sch 2.

9 There is currently no fee: General Notice No 15, para 23, ibid.

10 See n 16, p 69, above.

offence (s 160(6)) with a maximum penalty of a fine of level 4 on the standard scale[11] upon summary conviction (s 167 and Sch 1).

11 ENFORCEMENT OF THE ACT

Miscellaneous provisions relating to the enforcement of the Act are contained in Part XI (ss 161–173).

Enforcement authorities

The Director and local weights and measures authorities ('enforcement authorities') are under a duty to enforce the Act and regulations made under it (s 161(1)). Before instituting proceedings for an offence under the Act (other than under ss 162(6), 165(1) or (2) or 174(5), below) a local weights and measures authority is under a duty to the Director to give him notice of the intended proceedings together with a summary of the facts on which the charges are to be founded, and to postpone taking proceedings for 28 days after giving the notice or until the Director has notified them of its receipt (s 161(2)). Local weights and measures authorities must also report to the Director on the exercise of their functions under the Act if he so requires (s 161(3)).

A duly authorised officer of an enforcement authority, at all reasonable hours and on production (if required) of his credentials, may take certain action (s 162(1)). Firstly, he may inspect any goods and enter any premises (other than premises used only as a dwelling) to ascertain whether a breach of the Act has been committed (s 162(1)(a)). Secondly, if he has reasonable cause to suspect that a breach of the Act has been committed, to ascertain whether it has been committed he may either require any person carrying on, or employed in connection with, a business[11a] to produce any books or documents relating to it or require any person with control of any information relating to a business recorded otherwise than in legible form to provide a document containing a legible reproduction of the whole or any part of the information and, in either case, take copies of, or of an entry in, the books or documents (s 162(1)(b)). Thirdly, if he has reasonable cause to believe that a breach of the Act has been committed, he may seize and detain any goods to ascertain (by testing or otherwise) whether such a breach has been committed (s 162(1)(c)). Fourthly, he may seize and detain any goods, books or documents which he has reason to believe may be required as evidence in proceedings for an offence under the Act (s 162(1)(d)). Finally, for the purpose of exercising these powers to seize and detain any goods, books or documents, he may require any person with authority to do so to break open any container and, if that person does not comply, he may break it open himself, but in either case only if and to the extent reasonably necessary to secure that the provisions of the Act and any regulations made under it are duly observed (s 162(1)(e)). If he does seize any goods, books or documents under these powers, the officer must inform the person from whom he seizes them (s 162(2)). Upon being satisfied of various matters (set out in s 162(3)), a justice of the peace may, on sworn affirmation in writing, issue a warrant (valid for one month) authorising an officer of an enforcement authority to

---

11 Currently £1,000: SI 1984/447, made under Magistrates' Courts Act 1980, s 143.
11a See p 57 above.

enter premises (by force if need be) (s 162(3)). An officer entering premises (by virtue of s 162) may take such other persons and equipment with him as he thinks necessary; and on leaving premises entered by virtue of a warrant (issued under s 162(3)) he must (if they are unoccupied or the occupier is temporarily absent) ensure they are left as effectively secured against trespassers as he found them (s 162(4)). Regulations made by the Secretary of State[12] may provide that in specified cases an officer of a local weights and measures authority is not to be taken to be duly authorised (within s 162) unless authorised by the Director (s 162(5)). A person who is not a duly authorised officer of an enforcement authority, but purports to act as such (under s 162) commits an offence (s 162(6)) with maximum penalties of a fine of the prescribed sum[13] upon summary conviction or two years' imprisonment and an unlimited fine upon conviction on indictment (s 167 and Sch 1). It is, however, specifically provided that nothing in these provisions compels a barrister or solicitor to produce a document containing a privileged communication made by or to him in that capacity or authorises the seizing of any such document in his possession (s 167(7)).

Where, in exercising his powers (under s 162), an officer of an enforcement authority seizes and detains goods and their owner suffers loss by reason of the seizure or by reason of the loss, damage or deterioration of the goods during detention, then, unless the owner is convicted of an offence in relation to the goods, the authority must compensate him for the loss so suffered (s 163(1)). Any dispute as to the right to or amount of such compensation must be determined by arbitration (s 163(2)).

An enforcement authority may make, or authorise any of their officers to make on their behalf, such purchases of goods and authorise any of their officers to procure the provision of such services or facilities or to enter into such agreements or other transactions as may appear to them expedient for determining whether any provisions made by or under the Act are being complied with (s 164(1)). Any act done by an officer so authorised is treated for the purposes of the Act as done by him as an individual on his own behalf (s 164(2)). Thus an officer can enter into a consumer credit or hire agreement to ensure that the Act is being complied with by the creditor or owner, and the officer qualifies as a debtor or hirer under such agreements. Any goods seized by an officer under the Act may be tested, and in the event of such a test he must inform the person from whom he seized them of the test results (s 164(3)). If any test leads to proceedings under the Act, the enforcement authority must (if the goods were purchased) inform the person they were purchased from of the test results and allow any person against whom the proceedings are taken to have the goods tested on his behalf if it is reasonably practicable to do so (s 164(4)).

Any person who wilfully obstructs an officer of an enforcement authority acting in pursuance of the Act, or wilfully fails to comply with any requirement properly made to him by an officer (under s 162), or who without reasonable cause fails to give such an officer (so acting) other assistance or information he may reasonably require in performing his functions under the

---

12 The Consumer Credit (Entry and Inspection) Regulations 1977, SI 1977/331 (as amended by SI 1984/1046) have been made and specify (inter alia) cases involving bankers' records and certain credit reference agency files.
13 Currently £2,000: SI 1984/447, made under Magistrates' Courts Act 1980, s 143.

Act, commits an offence (s 165(1)) with a maximum penalty of a fine of level 4 on the standard scale[14] upon summary conviction (s 167 and Sch 1). It is also an offence for a person to make a statement he knows to be false in giving information which such an officer reasonably requires to perform his functions under the Act (s 165(2)) with maximum penalties of a fine of the prescribed sum[15] upon summary conviction or two years imprisonment and an unlimited fine upon conviction on indictment (s 167 and Sch 1). However, these provisions do not require a person to answer any question or give any information if to do so might incriminate that person or that person's spouse (s 165(3)).

If a person is convicted of an offence or has a judgment given against him by a court in the United Kingdom and it appears to the court that the conviction or judgment ought to be brought to the Director's attention and that this may not happen unless the court so arranges, the court may make such arrangements notwithstanding that the proceedings have been finally disposed of (s 166). The judgment or conviction need not relate to matters arising under the Act: for example, any criminal conviction may be taken into account by the Director in considering a licensing application.

In any proceedings for an offence under the Act it is a statutory defence for the person charged to prove that his act or omission was due to a mistake, or to reliance on information supplied to him, or to an act or omission by another person, or to an accident or some other cause beyond his control and in addition that he took all reasonable precautions and exercised all due diligence to avoid such an act or omission by himself of any person under his control (s 168(1)).[16] But if in any case this defence involves the allegation that the act or omission was due to an act or omission by another person, the person charged is not entitled, without leave of the court, to rely on that defence unless, within a period ending seven clear days before the hearing, he has served on the prosecutor a written notice giving such information identifying or assisting in the identification of that other person as was then in his possession (s 168(2)).

If at any time a body corporate commits an offence under the Act with the consent or connivance of, or because of neglect by, any individual, the individual commits the like offence if at that time he is a director, manager, secretary or similar officer of the body corporate, or he is purporting to act as such an officer, or the body corporate is managed by its members of whom he is one (s 169).[17]

The Act also provides that a breach of any requirement made (otherwise than by any court) by or under the Act should incur no civil or criminal sanction, except to the extent (if any) which the Act expressly provides (s 170(1)). However, it has been held that this does not prevent accessories from incurring liability and it was suggested that the same would apply

14 Currently £1,000: SI 1984/447, made under Magistrates' Courts Act 1980, s 143.
15 Currently £2,000: SI 1984/447, ibid.
16 Cf the similar wording in Trade Descriptions Act 1968, s 24 and Fair Trading Act 1973, s 25 and the cases thereon.
17 For the meaning of 'manager' and 'officer' see eg *Registrar of Restrictive Trading Agreements v WH Smith & Son Ltd* [1969] 3 All ER 1065, [1969] 1 WLR 1460; *Tesco Supermarkets Ltd v Nattrass* [1971] 1 QB 133, [1970] 3 All ER 357; *Re a Company* [1980] Ch 138, [1980] 1 All ER 284 (revsd on other grounds).

to other inchoate offences (eg attempts and conspiracy).[18] Furthermore, in exercising his functions under the Act the Director may take into account any matter appearing to him to constitute a breach of a requirement made by or under the Act, whether or not any sanction for that breach is provided by or under the Act, and, if a sanction is so provided, whether or not proceedings have been brought in respect of that breach (s 170(2)). Nor does this provision prevent the grant of an injunction or the making of an order of certiorari, mandamus or prohibition (s 170(3)).

The Act deems certain statements by a creditor or owner as binding on him (namely those made under ss 77(1), 78(1), 79(1), 97(1), 107(1)(c), 108(1)(c) or 109(1)(c)) (s 172(1)). In addition, a trader is bound by a notice which he gives a customer as required in response to the customer's termination statement (under s 103(1)(b)) or a notice (under s 103(1)) asserting that the customer is not indebted to him (s 172(2)). But if in any proceedings it is sought to rely on any of these statements or notices and the statement is known to be incorrect, the court may direct such relief (if any) to be given to the creditor or owner from the operation of these deeming provisions as appears to the court to be just (s 172(3)). It is thought that the court should grant relief unless the person against whom relief is claimed has altered his position in reliance upon the original statement or notice.

Finally, a term contained in a regulated agreement or linked transaction or in any other agreement relating to an actual or prospective regulated agreement or linked transaction, is void if, and to the extent that, it is inconsistent with a provision for the protection of the debtor or hirer or his associate[19] or any surety[20] contained in the Act or in any regulation made under the Act (s 173(1)). For this purpose if a provision specifies the duty or liability of the debtor or hirer or his associate or any surety in certain circumstances, a term is inconsistent with that provision if it purports to impose, directly or indirectly, an additional duty or liability on him in those circumstances (s 173(2)). However, notwithstanding this section, a provision of the Act under which a thing may be done in relation to any person on an order of the court or the Director only is not to be taken to prevent its being done at any time with that person's consent given at that time, although the refusal of such consent cannot give rise to any liability (s 173(3)).

12 SUPPLEMENTAL

Supplemental provisions relating to the Act generally, to regulations and orders and interpretation are contained in Part XII of the Act (ss 174–193).

(a) General

No information obtained under or by virtue of the Act about any individual may be disclosed without his consent (s 174(1)) and no information similarly obtained about any business[21] may be disclosed, so long as the business continues to be carried on, except with the consent of the person for the time being carrying it on (s 174(2)). Any person who discloses information in

18 *Brookes v Retail Credit Card Ltd* [1986] Crim LR 327.
19 See n 14, p 48, above.
20 See p 92, above.
21 See p 57.

contravention of these provisions commits an offence (s 174(5)) with maximum penalties of a fine of the prescribed sum[22] upon summary conviction or two years' imprisonment and an unlimited fine upon conviction on indictment (s 167 and Sch 1). These provisions do not, however, apply to disclosure of information made for the purpose of various statutes (listed in s 174(3)(a)), or made in connection with the investigation of any criminal offence or for the purposes of any criminal proceedings (s 174(3)(b)), or any civil proceedings brought under or by virtue of the Act or Part III of the Fair Trading Act 1973 or under the Control of Misleading Advertisements Regulations 1988 (s 174(3)(c)). Nor do they apply to any disclosure of information by the Director to the Bank of England for the purpose of enabling or assisting the Bank to discharge its functions under the Banking Act 1987 or the Director to discharge his function under the Act (s 174(3A)). Finally, they are not to be taken as limiting the particulars which may be entered in the register kept by the Director (under s 35, above) or as applying to any information which has been made public as part of the register (s 174(4)).

There are provisions relating to the service of documents (contained in s 176).

The Act expressly provides that it is not to affect the rights of a proprietor of a registered charge (within the meaning of the Land Registration Act 1925), who became the proprietor under a transfer for valuable consideration without notice of any defect in the title arising by virtue of the Act (apart from this section) or who derives title from such a proprietor (s 177(1)) (although this does not apply to a proprietor carrying on a business of debt-collecting:[23] s 177(3)). This provision is designed to protect a transferee of a mortgage of registered land which is defective under the Act, by treating him, if he qualifies as a proprietor within the section, as unaffected by the defect. A land mortgage[1] probably gives rise to a defect in title if it is to be treated as ineffective (under s 106, above). It is unclear whether a land mortgage which is only potentially ineffective (eg because it has been improperly executed but no order for its enforcement has been sought) gives rise to a defect: but it probably does. It is also unclear how far the operation of the Act is excluded in cases to which this provision applies. It seems likely that it is not altogether excluded: for example, the transferee could still be obliged to serve any notices as required by the Act prior to enforcing the mortgage. It is also provided that the Act does not affect the operation of s 104 of the Law of Property Act 1925 (protection of purchaser where mortgagee exercises power of sale) (s 177(2)). Thus a purchaser of land sold under a power contained in a land mortgage need not be concerned to enquire whether the power is being properly invoked (unless he has actual notice of an irregularity). If (by virtue of s 177(1)) a land mortgage is enforced which otherwise would be treated as never having effect, the original creditor or owner must indemnify the debtor or hirer against any loss thereby suffered by him (s 177(4)).

(b) Regulations and orders

Regulations may be made by the Secretary of State as to the form and content of credit-cards, trading-checks, receipts, vouchers and other documents or

---

22 Currently £2,000: SI 1984/447 made under Magistrates' Courts Act 1980, s 143.
23 See p 107, above.
 1 See p 52, above.

things issued by creditors, owners or suppliers[2] under or in connection with regulated agreements or by other persons in connection with linked transactions (s 179(1)). If a person issues any document or thing in contravention of any such regulations, then as from the time of the contravention but without prejudice to anything done before it, the Act applies as if the regulated agreement had been improperly executed by reason of a contravention of regulations as to the form and content of agreements (ie made under s 60(1), above) (s 179(2)). However, no regulations (ie under s 179(1)) have been made to date.

Further provisions concerning regulations in this Part of the Act (ss 180–183) have been dealt with in the text.

(c) Interpretation

Where an actual or prospective regulated agreement has two or more debtors or hirers (not being a partnership or unincorporated body of persons) anything required by or under the act to be done to or in relation to the debtor must be done to or in relation to each of them (s 185(1)(a)), and anything done under the Act by or on behalf of one of them has effect as if done by or on behalf of all of them (s 185(1)(b)). However, there are certain exceptions to these provisions. Firstly, where running-account credit is provided to two or more debtors jointly, any of them may by written notice signed by him (a 'dispensing notice') authorise the creditor not to comply in his case with the requirement to give a periodical statement of account (in s 78(4)); and the dispensing notice has that effect until revoked by a further notice given by the debtor to the creditor (s 185(2)). A dispensing notice cannot take effect if previous dispensing notices are operative in the case of the other debtor(s), any dispensing notices cease to have effect if any of the debtors dies, and a dispensing notice operative in relation to an agreement is operative also in relation to any subsequent modifying agreement[3] (s 185(2)). Secondly, the requirement (in s 185(1)(a)) to do acts in relation to each debtor does not apply in relation to signing of agreements (under s 61(1)(a)) nor does it affect the conditions (in s 127(3)) for the making of enforcement orders (s 185(3)). If an agreement has two or more debtors or hirers (not being a partnership or unincorporated body of persons) the provisions of the Act (in s 86) concerning the death of the debtor or hirer apply to the death of any of them (s 185(4)).

Similarly, if an actual or prospective regulated agreement has two or more creditors or owners, anything required by or under the Act to be done to, in relation to, or by, the creditor or owner is effective if done to, in relation to, or by any one of them (s 186).

The remaining interpretation provisions (ss 187–189) have been dealt with in the text.

---

2 Ie within ss 11, 12 or 13.
3 See p 81, above.

PART II

THE RELATION OF BANKER AND CUSTOMER

SUMMARY OF CONTENTS

CHAPTER 6

BANKS, BANKERS AND THE BUSINESS OF BANKING

The following issues are considered in this Chapter:

1 What is the relevance of the definition at common law of 'bank', and related expressions?
2 What is the common law definition?
3 Are (1) banks at common law and (2) institutions which carry on a lawful deposit-taking business pursuant to the Banking Act 1987 ('lawful deposit-takers'[1]) now one and the same class, and if not, what is the relation between them?

1 RELEVANCE OF THE COMMON LAW DEFINITION OF 'BANK'

The definition is relevant for two main reasons:

(1) There exist several statutes which use one or more of the expressions 'bank', 'banker' and 'banking business' without positive or useful definition. The more important statutes within this category are identified below.
(2) There exist rights under the general law which are available to a person by virtue of his being a bank or banker. These rights are the banker's lien and the banker's right of set-off.

The importance of the common law definition has, however, declined somewhat since the introduction in 1979 of statutory regulation of the acceptance of deposits. The Banking Act 1979 introduced a two-tier structure comprising recognised banks and licensed deposit-takers, and the opportunity was taken to amend several earlier enactments to define 'bank' by reference to recognised banks and (in some instances) licensed deposit-takers, and specified institutions such as the National Savings Bank. The Banking Act 1987 replaced the two-tier structure with a single tier of authorised institutions. By s 108 and Sch 6, the enactments which had been amended by the 1979 Act were re-amended to make reference to authorised institutions under the 1987 Act. The principal pre-1979 statutes which have been re-amended in this way are as follows:

---

1 Ie, authorised institutions and exempted persons – see ch 1, ante.

(i) The Bankers' Books Evidence Act 1879, which provides:
     '9(1) In this Act the expressions 'bank' and 'banker' mean –
>   (a) an institution authorised under the Banking Act 1987 or a municipal bank within the meaning of that Act;
>   [(b) ...;   ][3]
>   (c) the National Savings Bank; and
>   (d) the Post Office, in the exercise of its powers to provide banking services.'

(ii) The Agricultural Credits Act 1928, which provides:
      '5(7) For the purposes of this Part of this Act [Part II, ss. 5–14] –

      ....

      'Bank' means the Bank of England, an institution authorised under the Banking Act 1987, ...,[4] or the Post Office in the exercise of its powers to provide banking services.'

(iii) The Solicitors Act 1974, which provides:
       '87(1) In this Act, except where the context otherwise requires, 'bank' means –
>   (a) the Bank of England, the Post Office, in the exercise of its powers to provide banking services, or an institution authorised under the Banking Act 1987
>   [(b) ...].'[5]

In addition to these pre-1979 statutes, there is an important group of post-1979 statutes which conspicuously avoid usage of the expression 'bank' and refer instead to authorised institutions under the Banking Act 1987. The most important statutes are the Companies Act 1985, the Insolvency Act 1986, the Building Societies Act 1986 and the Financial Services Act 1986. These statutes were, of course, originally enacted with references to recognised banks and licensed deposit-takers, but were amended to refer to authorised institutions by the Banking Act 1987, s 108(1) and Sch 6. The British Tele-communication Act 1981 does refer to 'bank', but it also provides a definition[6] similar to that in the Solicitors Act 1974.

This important post-1979 trend toward certainty of expression is unfortunately not without exception, and there exist several statutes enacted both before and after 1979 where the expression 'bank' or 'banker' or a similar expression is used without proper definition. It is in relation to these statutes that the common law definition remains of paramount importance. They include the following:

(i) The Bills of Exchange Act 1882, which provides:
     '2. In this Act, unless the context otherwise requires –

     ....

     "Banker" includes a body of persons whether incorporated or not who carry on the business of banking.'

---

3 Para (b) was repealed by the Trustee Savings Banks Act 1985, ss 4(3), 7(3), Sch 4.
4 Certain words were repealed by the Trustee Savings Banks Act 1985, ss 4(3), 7(3), Sch 4.
5 Paragraph (b) was repealed by the Banking Act 1987, s 108(1), Sch 6, para 5.
6 See s 67(4), which, as amended by the Trustee Savings Banks Act 1985, ss 4(3), 7(3), Sch 4 and the Banking Act 1987, s 108(1), Sch 6, para 10, provides: 'In this section ..."bank" means (a) the Bank of England; (b) an authorised institution under the Banking Act 1987; (c) the Post Office; or (d) the central bank of a member State other than the United Kingdom.'

(ii) The Cheques Act 1957, which by virtue of s 6(1) is to be construed as one with the Bills of Exchange Act 1882.

(iii) The Post Office Act 1969, discussed in ch 7, post.

(iv) The Insurance Companies Act 1982, which refers to 'banking business' without definition.[7]

(v) The Building Societies Act 1986, discussed in ch 7, post.

(vi) The Income and Corporation Taxes Act 1988, a consolidating enactment, which refers variously to 'a bank carrying on a bona fide banking business',[8] 'a person carrying on a banking business',[9] 'any transaction entered into by [bankers] in the ordinary course of their business as bankers',[10] 'deposit-taker'[11] and 'an institution authorised under the Banking Act 1987'.[12]

A hybrid form of wording, and one which presupposes that the expressions 'bank' and 'deposit-taker' are not synonymous, is found in the Supreme Court Act 1981, s 40 which, as amended by the Banking Act 1987, provides:

'40(1) ... this section applies to the following accounts, namely –
(a) any deposit account with a bank or other deposit-taking institution. ...
....
(6) In this section, "deposit-taking institution" means any person carrying on a business which is a deposit-taking business for the purposes of the Banking Act 1987.'

Where a statute uses the expression 'bank', the restriction imposed by s 69(1) of the Banking Act 1987 on the use of banking descriptions by persons who are not authorised institutions will rarely (if ever) apply, for s 69(4) provides:

'(4) Subsection (1) above does not prohibit a person from using the expression "bank" or "banker" (or a similar expression) where it is necessary for him to do so in order to be able to assert that he is complying with, or entitled to take advantage of, any enactment, any instrument made under any enactment, any international agreement, any rule of law or any commercial usage or practice which applies to a person by virtue of his being a bank or banker.'

The most obvious provisions which make it necessary for a person to assert that he is a 'bank' etc, in order to be entitled *to take advantage* of an enactment are the Bills of Exchange Act 1882, ss 60, 73–77, 79, 80, the Cheques Act 1957, ss 1–4 and the Income and Corporation Taxes Act 1988, ss 473, 765. The most obvious provision which makes it necessary for a person to assert that he is a banker in order to assert that he is *complying with* an enactment

---

7 See s 2(4), and ch 2, ante.
8 S 353(1).
9 Ss 473(1)(a), 808. See also s 794(2)(c)(i) ('a company which ... carries on a banking business').
10 S 765(2).
11 Ss 479, 480, 481, 483(5). 'Deposit-taker' is defined by s 481(2) to mean any of the following: '(a) the Bank of England; (b) any institution authorised under the Banking Act 1987 or municipal bank within the meaning of that Act; (c) the Post Office; (d) any company to which property and rights belonging to a trustee savings bank were transferred by s 3 of the Trustee Savings Banks Act 1985; (e) any bank formed under the Savings Bank (Scotland) Act 1819; and (f) any person or class of person who receives deposits in the course of his business or activities and which is for the time being prescribed by order made by the Treasury for the purposes of this paragraph.'
12 Ss 481(2)(b), 632(1)(c).

is the Insurance Companies Act 1982, s 2(4).[13] The rules of law which apply to a person by virtue of his being a bank or banker include the banker's lien and the banker's right of set-off.

2   COMMON LAW DEFINITION OF 'BANK' AND RELATED EXPRESSIONS

At common law, there is no exhaustive definition of 'bank', but in *United Dominions Trust Ltd v Kirkwood*[14] the Court of Appeal defined certain characteristics of the business of banking. Lord Denning MR held[15] that the *usual* characteristics are much as stated in the 6th edition of *Paget*, ie:

1 The conduct of current accounts
2 The payment of cheques drawn on bankers
3 The collection of cheques for customers.

Diplock LJ, having held it to be *essential* to the business of banking that a banker should accept money from his customers upon a running account into which sums of money are from time to time paid by the customer and from time to time withdrawn by him (ie the first of the above characteristics), went on to adopt the second and third characteristics:[16]

'I am inclined to agree with the Master of the Rolls and the author of the current edition of *Paget on Banking* (6th edn, 1961) p 8, that to constitute the business of banking to-day the banker must also undertake to pay cheques drawn upon himself (the banker) by his customers in favour of third parties up to the amount standing to their credit in their "current accounts" and to collect cheques for his customers and credit the proceeds to their current accounts.'

It was further held that a lacuna in the evidence relating to these characteristics is capable of being filled by evidence that the relevant person enjoys in banking and commercial circles the reputation of being a banker.[17] It is in this connection that the difference between *usual* and *essential* characteristics becomes material. In the view of Lord Denning MR:[18]

'... it must be remembered that a recital of *usual* characteristics is not equivalent to a definition. The *usual* characteristics are not the *sole* characteristics. There are other characteristics which go to make a banker. In particular stability, soundness

---

13 See ch 2, ante.
14 [1966] 2 QB 431, [1966] 1 All ER 968, CA. The principal authorities which led to the decision in *UDT v Kirkwood* are *Richardson v Bradshaw* (1752) 1 Atk 128; *Re District Savings Bank Ltd, ex p Coe* (1861) 3 De GF & J 335; *Davies v Kennedy* (1868) 3 IR Eq 31; affd on appeal sub nom *Copland v Davies* (1872) LR 5 HL 358 at 375; *Halifax Union v Wheelwright* (1875) LR 10 Exch 183; *Re Bottomgate Industrial Co-operative Society* (1891) 65 LT 712; *Re Shield's Estate* [1901] 1 IR 172; *Furber v Fieldings Ltd* (1907) 23 TLR 362; *Re Birkbeck Permanent Benefit Building Society* [1912] 2 Ch 183 CA; *Edgelow v MacElwee* [1918] 1 KB 205; *Bank of Chettinad Ltd of Colombo v IT Comrs of Colombo* [1948] AC 378, PC; *Commercial Banking Co Ltd v Hartigan* (1952) 86 ILT 109; *R v Industrial Disputes Tribunal, ex p East Anglian Trustee Savings Bank* [1954] 2 All ER 730, [1954] 1 WLR 1093; *Official Assignee of Property of Koh Hor Khoon v EK Liong Hin Ltd* [1960] AC 178, [1960] 1 All ER 440, PC. A review of most of these authorities can be found in *Paget* (8th edn, 1972) pp 8–12.
15 [1966] 2 QB 431 at 447, [1966] 1 All ER 968 at 975, CA.
16 [1966] 2 QB 431 at 465, [1966] 1 All ER 968 at 986–987, CA.
17 [1966] 2 QB 431 at 453–455 (per Lord Denning MR), 473–474 (per Diplock LJ), [1966] 1 All ER 968 at 979–980, 991–992, CA.
18 [1966] 2 QB 431 at 453–454, [1966] 1 All ER 968 at 979, CA.

usual

and probity ... Like many other beings, a banker is easier to recognise than to define. In case of doubt it is, I think, permissible to look at the reputation of the firm amongst ordinary intelligent commercial men.'

On this approach, the evidence of reputation which had been adduced by UDT was of itself sufficient to establish UDT's status as a banker. Diplock LJ took a different view. Having held that the three above-mentioned characteristics are essential, it followed that UDT's evidence had to be relevant to the existence of those characteristics if it was to be relevant at all.[19]

Whichever view is preferred, it is a point of some importance that, in the words of Megarry J in *Royal Bank of Canada v IRC*,[20] a statement of the essentials of a business is not, without more, exhaustive of all that is ordinary in that business. This point has already been made[1] in considering the Insurance Companies Act 1982, with its usage of the imprecise expression 'in the course of carrying on, and for the purpose of banking business'.

Where a statute refers to the carrying on of the business of banking, it is a matter of construction whether the description only applies if banking is the primary object of the business carried on. For example, s 6(d) of the Moneylenders Act 1900 (now repealed) excepted from the definition of moneylenders 'any person bona fide carrying on the business of moneylending'. It was held in *UDT v Kirkwood* that for a person to fall within this definition, banking need not be the primary object of the business carried on by him: he might carry on a composite business of which the accepting of deposits might be only a minor part.[2]

The words 'bona fide', which are perhaps implicit in every statutory reference to carrying on a banking business, were held in *UDT v Kirkwood* to involve two requirements. First, that the banking transactions must not be negligible in size when compared to the rest of the business; second, that the transactions relied upon as constituting the acceptance of deposits of money from customers must be genuinely of this legal nature and not a mere disguise for transactions of a different legal nature.[3] It was emphasised in *Re Roe's Legal Charge*[4] that the court is not concerned to compare the number of clearances of an alleged bank with the number of clearances of other recognised banks.

3 RELATION BETWEEN THE COMMON LAW AND THE BANKING ACT 1987

Given that the characteristics of a banking business at common law laid down in *UDT v Kirkwood* are not prerequisites to authorisation under the Banking Act 1987, it cannot be said that every authorised institution or other lawful deposit-taker is a bank at law. That the categories are not co-extensive

---

19 [1966] 2 QB 431 at 473–474 [1966] 1 All ER 968 at 991–992, CA, referring to 'reasons which differ from those which have commended themselves to the Master of the Rolls, for which, with great respect, I cannot find sufficient authority in the cases which he cites'.
20 [1972] Ch 665 at 679, [1972] 1 All ER 225 at 235.
 1 See ch 2, ante.
 2 [1966] 2 QB 431 at 466, [1966] 1 All ER 968 at 987, CA, per Diplock LJ. Cf *Halifax Union v Wheelwright* (1875) LR 10 Exch 183; *Re Shield's Estate* [1901] 1 IR 172 at 199; *Paget* (8th edn, 1972) pp 12–13.
 3 *UDT v Kirkwood*, supra, loc cit.
 4 [1982] 2 Lloyd's Rep 370 at 381, CA.

is implicitly recognised both in s 40(1) of the Supreme Court Act 1981 and in s 69(4) of the Banking Act 1987, and also in the non-amendment of references to banks in certain pre-1979 statutes. In practice, it is likely that the class of deposit-takers (ie authorised institutions and exempted persons) generally embraces, and is wider than, the class of banks at law. This is because almost every institution which operates current accounts, etc also accepts deposits, but there are probably some deposit-taking institutions which do not operate current accounts. This view derives support from the reference in the Supreme Court Act 1981, s 40(1) to 'bank or *other* deposit-taking institution'. There is, however, a high degree of overlap, and this is perhaps illustrated by the fact that whereas the Companies Act 1948 referred to 'banking company' without definition,[5] the Companies Act 1985 defines 'banking company' as a company which is an authorised institution under the Banking Act 1987.[6]

It was pointed out by the Privy Council in *Bank of Chettinad Ltd of Colombo v I T Comrs of Colombo*,[7] that the words 'bank' and 'banker' may bear different shades of meaning at different periods of history. The authorities cited in *UDT v Kirkwood* show that before the First World War, banking was defined principally by reference to the acceptance of deposits. Thus in 1901, in the Irish case of *Re Shield's Estate, Governor and Co of Bank of Ireland, Petitioners*,[8] Holmes LJ said: 'The real business of the banker is to obtain deposits of money which he may use for his profit by lending it out again.' If and when electronic fund transfers render the payment and collection of cheques a less prominent feature of banking practice, the *UDT v Kirkwood* criteria may need to be reformulated, and that may be an appropriate time to assimilate banks at law with deposit-takers under the 1987 Act. Indeed, on the approach taken by Lord Denning MR in *UDT v Kirkwood* to the relevance of reputation, there is no reason why every lawful deposit-taker should not now be recognised as a bank at law.

5 See, eg Companies Act 1948, Sch 8, para 23.
6 Companies Act 1985, ss 257(1)(a), 744.
7 [1948] AC 378
8 [1901] 1 IR 172 at 182.

CHAPTER 7

THE TSB, THE NATIONAL SAVINGS BANK, BUILDING SOCIETIES AND THE POST OFFICE

1 THE TSB

The long existence of trustee savings banks as a separate form of legal organisation came to an end with their privatisation under the Trustee Savings Banks Act 1985. An illuminating description of the legislative history of trustee savings banks from 1817 until their reorganisation under the 1985 Act can be found in the speech of Lord Templeman in *Ross v Lord Advocate*.[1]

The formal reorganisation was carried through on the vesting day appointed[2] by the Treasury pursuant to s 1(4), namely 21 July 1986. On that date there were transferred from each of the existing trustee savings banks certified under the Trustee Savings Banks Act 1969 and 1981 to a successor company all its property, rights, liabilities and obligations, 'whether or not capable of being transferred or assigned'.[3] The successor to the existing bank for England and Wales ('Trustee Savings Bank England and Wales') was required to be a company registered in England and Wales, and was in fact TSB England and Wales plc, a company formed under the Companies Act 1985.

The metamorphosis from the relationship of savings banks and member to the exclusively contractual relationship of banker and customer was achieved by s 3(4), which provides:

'(4) The liabilities referable to a depositor's deposit with a bank which are transferred ... to the bank's successor are liabilities to return his deposit and to pay interest on it (if it was payable) at the rate prevailing immediately before the vesting day, but, as from that day, the rights, liabilities and obligations referable to the deposit shall become instead, rights, liabilities, and obligations incident to the relationship of customer and banker (and variable accordingly).'

It was held in *Ross v Lord Advocate*[4] that at the date of the passing of the 1985 Act depositors had no proprietary interest in the surplus assets of the existing banks and that, accordingly, by s 3(3) such assets were transferred to the successor companies.

---

1 [1986] 3 All ER 79 at 84–93, [1986] 1 WLR 1077 at 1084–1085, HL.
2 Trustee Savings Banks Act 1985 (Appointed Day) (No 3) Order 1986, SI 1986/1222, art 2.
3 Trustee Savings Banks Act 1985, s 3(3)(6).
4 [1986] 3 All ER 79, [1986] 1 WLR 1077, HL.

TSB England and Wales plc is an authorised institution under the Banking Act 1987.

2   THE NATIONAL SAVINGS BANK

The National Savings Bank was established by s 94(1) of the Post Office Savings Bank Act 1969 and is now regulated by the National Savings Bank Act 1971 and regulations made by the Treasury thereunder. The Bank exists for the receipt and repayment of deposits and its business is carried on by the Director of Savings (s 1(1)(2)).

A deposit may be made either as an ordinary deposit or as an investment deposit (s 3(1)). An ordinary deposit must be of at least £1, and an investment deposit of at least £5, if made at any savings bank office other than the principal offices of the National Savings Bank.[5] Where an account is opened, a deposit book must be issued to the depositor, and where investment deposits are made, a separate account must be opened and a separate deposit book issued in respect of those deposits.[6]

Subject to specified exceptions, the maximum amount which may be received from any person by way of ordinary deposit is limited to £10,000.[7]

The rate of interest payable on ordinary deposits is specified by the Treasury, but the rate may not be reduced below $2\frac{1}{2}\%$ per annum (s 5(1), (5)). The depositor is entitled to repayment of an ordinary deposit (or part thereof) within ten days after demand, and in specified circumstances withdrawals of smaller sums (£100 and £250) may be made without previous notice if, as regards any particular office, payment can be made at that office without inconvenience.[8]

The maximum amount which may be received from any person by way of investment deposit is limited to £100,000.[9] Interest is payable on investment deposits at rates determined by the Treasury, and different rates may be determined in relation to different descriptions of investment deposits and different periods of notice of withdrawal.[10] Investment deposits may not be withdrawn unless one month's prior notice of withdrawal has been given.[11]

The National Savings Bank is an exempted person for the purposes of the Banking Act 1987.[12] By s 68(1) of that Act, the prohibition on the use of banking names imposed by s 67(1) does not prohibit the use of the name 'National Savings Bank'.

---

5 NSB Regulations 1972, SI 1972/764, regs 20, 28(5), as amended by SI 1978/1594; SI 1982/294.
6 Ibid, regs 16, 28.
7 Savings Bank (Ordinary Deposits) (Limits) Order 1969, SI 1969/939, as amended by SI 1969/1699; SI 1987/330.
8 NSB Regulations 1972, reg 22(1)(1A), as substituted and added to by SI 1982/1762.
9 NSB (Investment Deposits) (Limits) Order 1977, SI 1977/1210, as amended by SI 1986/1217.
10 NSB Act 1971, s 6(2), as amended by the Finance Act 1982, Sch 20, para 5(2).
11 NSB Regulations 1972, reg 29(1).
12 Banking Act 1987, s 4(1), Sch 2, para 2.

3 BUILDING SOCIETIES

The Building Societies Act 1986 now permits building societies to provide banking services (s 34(1), Sch 8, Part I). The Act also confers powers to provide banking services which powers must, in order to be exercisable, be adopted by the building society (s 34(5)).

By Sch 8, Part II, para 1,[13] the power to provide banking services does not of itself confer power (1) to accept deposits in circumstances which require authorisation under the Banking Act 1987 (or would require authorisation were the taker not a building society); or (2) to make advances or loans of any description. But this general restriction on the power to provide banking services does not prevent that power 'from conferring the power' to *arrange* the taking of deposits from individuals or to arrange the lending of money to individuals, or, where the lending is on security and the security comprises or includes land, to persons other than individuals (Sch 8, Part II, para 2(a); Part III, para 1(a)(b)). The word 'arrange' is defined to include (a) arranging the performance of any activity on behalf of the person in respect of whom the activity is performed as well as the person who performs the activity and (b) acting as agent on behalf of either such person.[14] It does not follow from the existence of this general restriction that a building society can never have the capacity to perform the restricted activities, for the restriction is subject to the qualification that it does not prohibit performance of any activity which is within the capacity of a building society by virtue of any power arising otherwise than under Sch 8 (Sch 8, Part II, para 1). Additional specific restrictions are imposed in relation to, inter alia, the provision of guarantees and the provision of foreign exchange services (Sch 8, Part III, para 1).

Schedule 8, Part IV contains supplementary 'particular provisions' relating to the provision of banking services including the following provision:

'3 (1) A building society shall, so far as regards the carrying on of an activity which comprises provision of a banking service for the purposes of this Schedule, be treated for all purposes as a bank and a banker and as carrying on the business of banking or a banking undertaking whether or not it would be so treated apart from this paragraph.
(2) This paragraph does not affect the determination of any question as to the status of a building society as a bank or banker for other purposes.'

The effect of para 3(1) seems to be that a building society is to be treated as a bank in the provision of banking services by virtue of powers arising under Sch 8. Banking services are not, however, defined and therefore the provision solves one problem at the cost of raising another. Para 3(2) appears to apply whenever banking services are provided otherwise than by virtue of a power arising under Sch 8. As to the common law definition of 'bank' and related expressions, see ch 6 ante.

A building society incorporated (or deemed to be incorporated) under the Building Societies Act 1986 is an exempted person for the purposes of the Banking Act 1987.[15] By s 69(3) of the 1987 Act, the restriction on the use of banking descriptions imposed by s 69(1) does not prohibit the use by a

13 Sch 8 was substituted by the Building Societies (Commercial Assets and Services) Order 1988, SI 1988/1141, art 5, Sch 5.
14 Sch 8, Pt IV, para 8.
15 Banking Act 1987, s 4(1), Sch 2, para 5.

building society authorised under the Building Societies Act 1986 of any description of itself as providing banking services unless the description is in such immediate conjunction with its name that it might reasonably be thought to be part of it.

4 THE POST OFFICE

The Post Office is empowered to provide banking services by s 7(1)(b) of the Post Office Act 1969 (as substituted by s 58(1) of the British Tele-communications Act 1981), which provides:

> 'The Post Office shall have power:
> (b) to provide banking services and such other services by means of which money may be remitted (whether by means of money orders, postal orders or other-wise) as it thinks fit.'

Section 40 of the 1969 Act (as amended by Sch 7 to the Banking Act 1979) declares:

> 'So far as regards the provision by it, in exercise of the power conferred on it by virtue of s 7(1)(b) of this Act, of a banking service, the Post Office shall be deemed for all purposes to be a banker and to be carrying on the business of banking and a banking undertaking. . . .'

'Banker' is defined, somewhat unhelpfully, to include a body of persons, whether incorporated or not, who carry on the business of banking (s 86(1)).

The Post Office provides a banking service through the National Girobank. Starting in 1968 as a simple current account service (with the facility of cheque drawing), National Girobank has since offered most of the other banking facilities, including deposit and budget accounts, personal loans, guarantee cards and the issue of foreign currency. By using postcheques its customers can also obtain cash at post offices in many overseas countries.

CHAPTER 8

THE CUSTOMER

What constitutes a customer

The law of banking proper is the law of the relationship between a banker and his customer. Basically the relationship is that of mandator (the customer) and mandatory (the bank), but it is nonetheless a relationship which embraces mutual duties and obligations and offers privileges to both parties. It is a relationship peculiar to banking, giving rise to a contract between the two parties. The relationship is enjoyed by no one but a bank with reference to a customer and thus it is necessary to know what in law is a customer. Nowhere is it defined, not even in the Bills of Exchange Act 1882, which to a large extent is based on the relationship, nor in the Cheques Act 1957 which in its entirety is dependent upon it.

'Customer' is probably impossible to define with exactness, but the chief criterion is that there exists an account with a bank through which transactions are passed. It was at one time thought that the account had to be of some duration before the status of customer could be achieved,[1] but this view no longer holds, largely because of the Privy Council decision in *Taxation Comrs v English, Scottish and Australian Bank Ltd*,[2] in which it was held that duration of the relationship was not of the essence.

This was a decision of the Judicial Committee of the Privy Council in 1920 on a colonial enactment corresponding verbatim with s 82 of the Bills of Exchange Act 1882, and was to the effect that a man was a 'customer' whose only connection with the bank at the material date was the payment in of a single cheque for collection, a typical case of a first transaction. The material portion of the judgment is as follows:[3]

'Their Lordships are of opinion that the word 'customer' signifies a relationship in which duration is not of the essence. A person whose money has been accepted by the bank on the footing that they undertake to honour cheques up to the amount standing to his credit is, in the view of their Lordships, a customer of the bank in the sense of the statute, irrespective of whether his connection is of short or long standing. The contrast is not between an habitué and a newcomer, but

---

1 See *Mathews v Brown & Co* (1894) 63 LJQB 494; *Lacave & Co v Crédit Lyonnais* [1897] 1 QB 148; *Great Western Rly Co v London and County Banking Co Ltd* [1901] AC 414, HL.
2 [1920] AC 683.
3 [1920] AC 683 at 687.

between a person for whom the bank performs a casual service, such as, for instance, cashing a cheque for a person introduced by one of their customers, and a person who has an account of his own at the bank.'

The same line was taken by Bailhache J in *Ladbroke & Co v Todd*,[4] where a person was told by a bank that he could not draw against a cheque until cleared. It was held that it was not necessary before he became a customer that 'he should have drawn any money or even that he should be in a position to draw money'.

In *Tate v Wilts and Dorset Bank*[5] Darling J said of a man asking the defendant bank to cash a cheque for him, the cheque being drawn in favour of a person under whose name he had traded, which the bank agreed to do only after ascertaining that the cheque would be paid:

'He was not a customer at the moment, but he was going to become a customer if that cheque was collected.'

The man had said that he might open an account with the cheque, which may have been reason for the judge's comment. A somewhat similar situation was present in *Woods v Martins Bank Ltd*,[6] where Salmon J held that the relationship of banker and customer existed between the parties from the time when the bank accepted instructions from the plaintiff to collect moneys from a building society, to pay part to a company he was going to finance and 'retain to my order the balance of the proceeds', although there was at that time no account. There was the likelihood that an account would be opened, as shortly after it was. There were early negotiations from which it could normally be inferred that Woods would open an account with the bank and that the bank was willing for him to do so, so that a contract was concluded between them.

The proper view would seem to be that expressed in the *Taxation Comrs* case as augmented in *Woods v Martins Bank Ltd* that this is not really a legal question but one to be solved by what an ordinary intelligent business man would understand by 'a bank's customer'. If a banker may rely on statutory protection in respect of the acceptance of a cheque for collection on the understanding that relations will proceed if references are found to be satisfactory, it would follow that when both parties contemplate such a relationship, the one party is entitled to be treated by the bank as if he were a customer, rendering the statutory protection available.

A course of dealing not distinctly related to banking business is not sufficient to create the relation of banker and customer. This is shown by *Great Western Rly Co v London and County Banking Co Ltd*, where a man had for some years been in the habit of getting crossed cheques exchanged for cash at a bank where he had no account, and which charged him nothing for the service. It was held by the House of Lords, reversing the Court of Appeal, that he was not a customer. Such expedients as making him draw a counter cheque or entering the transaction under 'sundry customers' will not make him a customer.[7]

It appears that a person who is a customer of a bank in a general sense

---

4 (1914) 19 Com Cas 256.
5 (1899) 1 Legal Decisions Affecting Bankers 286.
6 [1959] 1 QB 55 at 63, [1958] 3 All ER 166 at 173, approved in *Warren Metals Ltd v Colonial Catering Co Ltd* [1975] 1 NZLR 273.
7 [1901] AC 414 at 425, HL; cf *Mathews v Brown & Co* (1894) 63 LJQB 494.

may not be a customer in relation to particular transactions. This proposition is implicit in a view tentatively expressed by Lawrence LJ on a point on which no argument was addressed in *Lloyds Bank Ltd v E B Savory & Co.*[8] The case involved the collection of stolen cheques through the branch clearing system, ie the cheques were paid in at a branch other than that at which the persons paying in maintained their accounts. Referring to *Lacave & Co v Crédit Lyonnais*,[9] *Great Western Rly Co v London and County Banking Co Ltd*[10] and *Taxation Comrs v English, Scottish and Australian Bank*[11] Lawrence LJ said:

> 'In the present case neither Perkins nor Mrs Smith had any account at the respondent bank's office which collected the stolen cheques for them; they were not known at those offices and those offices did not charge them for the accommodation thus afforded; in no real sense were they customers of the collecting offices. So far as the substance of the matter is concerned, Perkins and Mrs Smith might just as well have been customers of some other bank than Lloyds'.[12]

Neither Scrutton LJ nor Greer LJ dealt with the question, and nor was it dealt with on appeal to the House of Lords.[13]

A bank is not a philanthropic institution. Banks perform gratuitously for their customers many useful functions for which those customers would elsewhere have specifically to pay. But it is the business relation, the facilities for depositing moneys, the convenience of the cheque book on the one hand and the beneficial use of the money deposited on the other hand, which is at the root of the conception of a customer. This was recognised in *Great Western Rly Co v London and County Banking Co Ltd*,[14] though Lord Brampton was inclined to hold any pecuniary interest immaterial. It is immaterial that the account to which cheques are credited is overdrawn; that, per se, does not render the account-holder any less a customer.[15] A continued practice of getting bills discounted by a bank would probably be enough and similarly the keeping of a deposit account,[16] and where an English bank, acting as agent for a foreign bank, habitually collected cheques drawn on other English banks and paid into the foreign bank by that bank's customers, the English bank so collecting a crossed cheque was held by the Court of Appeal to be collecting for a customer within the predecessor to s 4 of the Cheques Act 1957 (s 82 of the Bills of Exchange Act 1882).[17] In that case, Atkin LJ said:[18]

> '. . . it seems to me that if a non-clearing bank regularly employs a clearing bank to clear its cheques, the non-clearing bank is the 'customer' of the clearing bank'.

and Bankes LJ said:[19]

> 'In this case this class of business of collecting cheques was done between bank

8 [1932] 2 KB 122, CA.
9 [1897] 1 QB 148.
10 [1901] AC 414.
11 [1920] AC 683.
12 [1932] 2 KB 122 at 141.
13 [1933] AC 201.
14 [1901] AC 414.
15 *Clarke v London and County Banking Co* [1897] 1 QB 552.
16 Per Lord Davey, *Great Western Rly Co v London and County Banking Co Ltd* [1901] AC 414 at 421.
17 *Importers Co Ltd v Westminster Bank Ltd* [1927] 2 KB 297.
18 Ibid, at 310.
19 Ibid at 305.

and bank, and it seems to me impossible to contend, as a matter of law, that the bank for which the respondents were doing business were not, in reference to that business, their customer.'

The deposit of a sum of money by a foreign bank with an English bank, with instructions that it be transferred to another foreign bank, does not, without more, make the person at whose request the transfer is made a customer of the English bank.[20]

The banker–customer relationship does not arise where an account is opened on false documents and without authority.[1]

20 *Aschkenasy v Midland Bank Ltd* (1934) 50 TLR 209; cf also *Kahler v Midland Bank Ltd* [1948] 1 All ER 811, CA; affd [1950] AC 24, [1949] 2 All ER 621, HL.
 1 See *Robinson v Midland Bank Ltd* (1925) 41 TLR 402, CA; *Stoney Stanton Supplies (Coventry) Ltd v Midland Bank Ltd* [1966] 2 Lloyd's Rep 373, CA.

CHAPTER 9

SPECIAL CUSTOMERS

1 COMPANIES

In its dealings with a company,[1] a bank is generally concerned with one or more of three matters: (a) the company's capacity to maintain an account, borrow and create security; (b) the authority of persons purporting to act on behalf of the company to exercise its powers for the purpose of a particular transaction; (c) the form of the company's cheques.

(a) Capacity

(i) Ultra vires

In the context of companies, an ultra vires transaction is one which it is beyond the capacity of a company to enter into. An ultra vires transaction is to be distinguished from an unauthorised transaction, ie a transaction which, although within the capacity of the company, is carried out otherwise than through the proper exercise of its powers by its officers. It has been stated by the Court of Appeal that in the interest of avoiding confusion, the use of the phrase ultra vires should be rigidly confined to describing acts which are beyond the corporate capacity of the company.[2] The two badges of a transaction which is ultra vires are (1) that the transaction is wholly void and (2) that it is irrelevant whether or not the third party had notice. An ultra vires transaction cannot become intra vires by means of estoppel, lapse of time, ratification, acquiescence or delay.[3]

The principles which govern the determination of any issue as to whether a transaction is ultra vires were summarised by Slade LJ in *Rolled Steel Products (Holdings) Ltd v British Steel Corpn* as follows:[4]

'1 The basic rule is that a company incorporated under the Companies Acts

---

1 The term 'company' is used to mean a company as defined by the Companies Act 1985, s 735.
2 *Rolled Steel Products (Holdings) Ltd v British Steel Corpn* [1986] Ch 246 at 297B (per Slade LJ) and 303A (per Browne-Wilkinson LJ), [1985] 3 All ER 52 at 87, 91, CA.
3 *York Corpn v Henry Leetham & Sons Ltd* [1924] 1 Ch 557 at 573 (per Russell J), cited with approval in *Rolled Steel*, supra, by Slade LJ at [1986] Ch 246 at 296, [1985] 3 All ER 52 at 86, CA.
4 [1986] Ch 246 at 295, [1985] 3 All ER 52 at 85, CA.

only has the capacity to do those acts which fall within its objects as set out in its memorandum of association or are reasonably incidental to the attainment or pursuit of those objects. Ultimately, therefore, the question whether a particular transaction is within or outside its capacity must depend on the true construction of the memorandum.

2 Nevertheless, if a particular act ... is of a category which, on the true construction of the company's memorandum, is *capable* of being performed as reasonably incidental to the attainment or pursuit of its objects, it will not be rendered ultra vires the company merely because in a particular instance its directors, in performing the act in its name, are in truth doing so for purposes other than those set out in its memorandum. Subject to any express restrictions on the relevant power which may be contained in the memorandum, the state of mind or knowledge of the persons managing the company's affairs or of the persons dealing with it is irrelevant in considering questions of corporate capacity.

3 While due regard must be paid to any express conditions attached to or limitations on powers contained in a company's memorandum (eg a power to borrow only up to a specified amount), the court will not ordinarily construe a statement in a memorandum that a particular power is exercisable "for the purposes of the company" as a condition limiting the company's corporate capacity to exercise the power; it will regard it as simply imposing a limit on the authority of the directors: see the *David Payne* case.'

In the *David Payne* case,[5] the liquidator of an insolvent company sought a declaration that a second mortgage debenture purportedly issued by the company was ultra vires and void. The objects clause in the company's memorandum included a sub-clause 'to borrow and raise money for the purposes of the company's business in such manner as the company shall think fit, and in particular by the issue of debentures or debenture stock ...'. The company executed the second mortgage debenture in order to obtain a loan which was to be applied for purposes other than those of the company itself. It was held that the debenture was a valid security on the grounds that (1) it was intra vires the company and (2) the lender had no knowledge of the intended misapplication of the loan monies. Buckley J, whose judgment was affirmed on appeal, said:[6]

'A corporation, every time it wants to borrow, cannot be called upon by the lender to expose all its affairs, so that the lender can say "Before I lend you anything, I must investigate how you carry on your business, and I must know why you want the money, and how you apply it, and when you do have it I must see you apply it in the right way." It is perfectly impossible to work out such a principle.'

(ii) Capacity to open and operate an account (in credit)

Subject to any limitation contained in its memorandum, every company whether trading or non-trading has the capacity to open and operate a bank account. Thus in *Serrell v Derbyshire, Staffordshire and Worcestershire*

---

5 [1904] 2 Ch 608, CA.
6 Ibid at 613.

Junction Rly Co,[7] it was conceded that a trading company had an implied power to draw cheques for its lawful purposes.

(iii) *Capacity to borrow and create security*

The capacity to borrow is often made express by the inclusion in the memorandum of a power to borrow, as in the *David Payne* case. However, as is apparent from first principle stated by Slade LJ, the absence of an *express* power does not mean that the company lacks the capacity to borrow. A power to borrow will be *implied* if borrowing is an act which is capable of being reasonably incidental to the attainment or pursuit of the objects stated in the memorandum. Subject to any limitation authorised in its memorandum, every *trading* company has an implied power to borrow for the purposes of its business.[8] But it would be unsafe to assume that this general proposition applies to non-trading companies.[9]

Where a company has power to borrow, then subject to any limitation contained in its memorandum, it has implied power to borrow in such manner as it thinks fit, and to give security over any of its property in support of such borrowing.[10] In *Den Norske Creditbank v Sarawak Economic Development Corpn*,[11] a case concerning the powers of a statutory company, it was held that a company's right to exercise powers (in that case, the power to guarantee loans) which are naturally expedient for the pursuit of its objects can only be restricted by clear words in the relevant Act.

There are certain statutory restrictions on borrowing which do not affect the validity of any transaction entered into by a company. The most important are: (1) s 117 of the Companies Act 1985, which renders unlawful the exercise of any borrowing powers by a company registered as a public company unless the registrar of companies has issued it with a s 117 certificate; (2) the Borrowing (Control and Guarantees) Act 1946 and regulations made thereunder, which impose restrictions on (inter alia) borrowing and the raising of money by the issue of shares or debentures.

(iv) *Companies Act 1985, s 35*

This section confers protection on third parties as regards questions of corporate capacity and the authority of directors to enter into particular transactions. The Act provides:

'(1) In favour of a person dealing with a company in good faith, any transaction decided upon by the directors is deemed to be one which it is within the capacity of the company to enter into, and the power of the directors to bind the company is deemed to be free of any limitation under the memorandum or articles.
(2) A party to a transaction so decided on is not bound to enquire as to the capacity of the company to enter into it or as to any such limitation on the powers of the directors, and is presumed to have acted in good faith unless the contrary is proved.'

7 (1850) 9 CB 811 at 820.
8 *General Auction Estate and Monetary Co v Smith* [1891] 3 Ch 432; *Re David Payne & Co Ltd* [1904] 2 Ch 608 at 612 (per Buckley J).
9 See *R v Reed* (1880) 5 QBD 483, esp at 488–489, CA.
10 *Australian Auxiliary Steam Clipper Co v Mounsey* (1858) 4 K & J 733; *Re Patent File Co* (1871) 6 Ch App 83. Statutory companies may stand in a different position – see *Bateman v Mid-Wales Rly Co* (1866) LR 1 CP 499 at 506.
11 [1989] 2 Lloyd's Rep 35, CA.

In *TCB Ltd v Gray*,[12] Browne-Wilkinson V-C said of the predecessor section (s 9(1) of the European Communities Act 1972) that what is now sub-s 35(2) abolishes the doctrine of constructive notice of the contents of a company's memorandum and articles. It being the obvious purpose of the subsection to obviate the commercial inconvenience and frequent injustice caused by the old law, the Vice-Chancellor expressed reluctance to construe it in such a way as to reintroduce, through the back door, any requirement that a third party acting in good faith must still investigate the regulating documents of a company.

The transaction must have been decided upon by 'the directors'. By s 6(c) of the Interpretation Act 1978, words in the plural include the singular unless the contrary intention appears. The contrary intention does appear in this case because 'the directors' equates to the word 'organs' in art 9 of Council Directive 68/151/EEC (the first Council Directive on company law).

(b) Authority to exercise the company's powers for a particular purpose

(i) Basic principles

The phrase 'ultra vires' being now rigidly confined to acts which are beyond the corporate capacity of a company, the validity of acts which are within its capacity but are entered into in furtherance of an improper purpose fall to be determined by the law of agency. The principles were summarised by Slade LJ in *Rolled Steel* as follows[13] (the numbering following on from the principles set out above in relation to corporate capacity):

'(4) At least in default of the unanimous consent of all the shareholders (as to which see below), the directors of a company will not have *actual* authority from the company to exercise any express or implied power other than for the purposes of the company as set out in its memorandum of association.
(5) A company holds out its directors as having *ostensible* authority to bind the company to any transaction which falls within the powers expressly or impliedly conferred on it by its memorandum of association. Unless he is put on notice to the contrary, a person dealing in good faith with a company which is carrying on an intra vires business is entitled to assume that its directors are properly exercising such powers for the purposes of the company as set out in its memorandum. Correspondingly, such a person in such circumstances can hold the company to any transaction of this nature.
(6) If, however, a person dealing with a company is on notice that the directors are exercising the relevant power for purposes other than the purposes of the company, he cannot rely on the ostensible authority of the directors and, on ordinary principles of agency, cannot hold the company to the transaction.'

It is clear from an earlier passage in the judgment[14] that the entitlement to assume in relation to intra vires business that a company's directors are

---

12 [1986] Ch 621, [1986] 1 All ER 587; affd on appeal without affecting this point [1987] Ch 458n, [1988] 1 All ER 108, CA. See also *International Sales and Agencies Ltd v Marcus* [1982] 3 All ER 551, esp at 559.
13 [1986] Ch 246 at 295–296, [1985] 3 All ER 52 at 86, CA.
14 [1986] Ch 246 at 291H–292F, and see also 307D.

properly exercising the company's powers derives both from the rule in *Turquand's* case[15] and from more general principles in the law of agency.[16]

The application of the above principles in the context of borrowing by companies is illustrated by two cases decided within a short time of each other. The first is *Charterbridge Corpn. Ltd v Lloyds Bank Ltd*.[17] The plaintiff company sought a declaration that a legal charge made between a third party company (Castleford) and Lloyds Bank was void. Castleford, one of a large group of companies, gave the charge to secure its liabilities to Lloyds Bank under a guarantee of all moneys and liabilities owing or incurred by another company within the group (Pomeroy). The objects clause in Castleford's memorandum included a sub-clause:

'To secure or guarantee by mortgages, charges or otherwise the performance and discharge of any contract, obligation or liability of [Castleford] or of any other person or corporation with whom or which [Castleford] has dealings or having a business or undertaking in which [Castleford] is concerned or interested whether directly or indirectly.'

The granting of the charge was therefore clearly within the capacity of Castleford and the claim that it was ultra vires was rejected. An alternative claim was advanced based on an allegation that in granting the guarantee and legal charge the directors had not acted with a view to the benefit of Castleford, ie that they had acted for an improper purpose. Pennycuick J held that the test to be applied was whether an intelligent and honest man in the position of a director of Castleford would, in the whole of the existing circumstances, have reasonably believed that the transactions were for the benefit of the company.[18] Applying that test, the allegation of improper purpose failed.

The second case is *Re Introductions Ltd*,[19] where a liquidator sought to set aside debentures granted by a company in favour of its bankers to secure a loan made for the purpose of a pig-breeding business, which was not a purpose authorised by its memorandum. The objects clause included a sub-clause 'to borrow or raise money in such manner as the company shall think fit and in particular by the issue of debentures'. It was held by the Court of Appeal that the debentures were void. Harman LJ, who gave the leading judgment, observed that borrowing is not an end in itself, and concluded:[20]

'... it is a necessary implied addition to a power to borrow, whether express or implied, that you should add "for the purposes of the company". This borrowing was not for a legitimate purpose of the company: the bank knew it and therefore cannot rely on its debenture.'

As analysed by the Court of Appeal in *Rolled Steel*, the ground on which Harman LJ based his judgment was not that the debentures had been granted by the company in excess of its corporate capacity, but that the bank knew that the directors of the company, in purporting to grant the debentures, had

---

15 (1856) 6 E & B 327, Ex Ch.
16 For a fuller discussion of the authority of company directors, see *Gore-Browne on Companies* ch 5; *Palmer's Company Law* ch 21.
17 [1970] Ch 62, [1969] 2 All ER 1185.
18 [1970] Ch 62 at 74E, [1969] 2 All ER 1185 at 1194E.
19 [1970] Ch 199, [1969] 1 All ER 887, CA.
20 [1970] Ch 199 at 211B, [1969] 1 All ER 887 at 890D, CA.

exceeded the authority conferred on them by the company by entering into a transaction for an improper purpose.[1]

(*ii*) Section 35 of the Companies Act 1985

Reference has already been made to this section in the context of corporate capacity (where the section is set out in full). As regards intra vires transactions, the section appears to confer protection unless the person dealing with the company has actual knowledge (or something very near to actual knowledge) that the directors are exercising their powers for an improper purpose. Where actual knowledge is proved, as in *Re Introductions Ltd*, supra, the third party remains unprotected.

It must not be overlooked that even where the protection of s 35 is unavailable, a lender may yet be protected by the rule in *Turquand's* case.[2]

(c) Form of company cheques and other negotiable instruments

These are two provisions in the Companies Act 1985 relating to the form of company cheques:

(*i*) Companies Act 1985, s 37

This is one of a group of sections dealing with formalities of carrying on business, and in particular the manner in which a company may make contracts, bills of exchange and promissory notes. By s 37:

'A bill of exchange or promissory note is deemed to have been made, accepted or endorsed on behalf of a company if made, accepted or endorsed in the name of, or by or on behalf or on account of, the company by a person acting under its authority.'

An equivalent provision has existed in the companies legislation since s 47 of the Companies Act 1862.[3] The effect of the section is that a bill of exchange or promissory note may be made (ie drawn), accepted or endorsed by a company in either of two ways. The first is the signing of the company's name without more. The view has been expressed in previous editions of *Paget* (see 9th edn, p 267) that bankers, while admitting that the mere name of a company is a sufficient indorsement in law, regard it in practice as irregular. This probably remains true to-day. The degree of exactness which is required in stating the name of a company has been considered in several cases under what is now s 349 of the Companies Act 1985 (see below). This body of case law is prima facie directly applicable to s 37.

The second way is to sign 'by or on behalf of or on account of' the

1 [1986] Ch 246 at 293G, 396E, [1985] 3 All ER 52 at 84g, 93h, CA.
2 (1856) 6 E & B 327, Ex Ch. For cases relating to the validity of bills of exchange or security where the rule has been successfully invoked, see *Re Land Credit Co of Ireland* (1869) 4 Ch App. 460; *Biggerstaff v Rowatt's Wharf Ltd* [1896] 2 Ch 93, CA; *Dey v Pullinger Engineering Co* [1921] 1 KB 77; *British Thomson-Houston Co Ltd v Federated European Bank Ltd* [1932] 2 KB 176, CA. For unsuccessful attempts to invoke the rule, see *A L Underwood Ltd v Bank of Liverpool and Martins* [1924] 1 KB 775, CA; *Alexander Stewart & Son of Dundee Ltd v Westminster Bank Ltd* (1926) 4 LDAB 40, CA; *Kreditbank Cassel GmbH v Schenkers Ltd* [1927] 1 KB 826, CA; *B Liggett (Liverpool) Ltd v Barclays Bank Ltd* [1928] 1 KB 48.
3 The legislative history of the section is reviewed in *Dey v Pullinger Engineering Co* [1921] 1 KB 77, decided under s 77 of the Companies (Consolidation) Act 1908. The section was reenacted in s 30 of the Companies Act 1929 and s 33 of the Companies Act 1948.

company. This is the most commonly used method. It is not a requirement of the section that one of the above representative expressions be used, but where a person intending to sign in a representative capacity omits to use such wording, or an equivalent expression such as 'per pro',[4] he runs the risk that he will be held personally liable on the instrument. This risk is, however, greatly diminished if the instruments bear the printed name of the company and, in the case of a cheque, its account number. On this form of instrument there can be no question of the company and the signatory being jointly liable, the manifest intention being that the liability is that of the company alone. Even if such an instrument is signed without the addition of any words indicating a representative capacity, the signatory can be said to adopt all the wording of the instrument, including the company's name and account number, and will in this event be under no personal liability.[5]

The signatory must be acting under the authority of the company. It was held in *Dey v Pullinger Engineering Co*[6] that the section is not limited to express authority, but includes implied authority and what is now usually described as ostensible authority. The facts of the case were that a company's articles of association empowered the directors to authorise the managing director to draw bills of exchange. The managing director drew a bill on behalf of the company without having in fact received any authority from the directors to do so. In an action on the bill against the company as drawer, the company was held liable. By the application of the rule in *Royal British Bank v Turquand*,[7] persons contracting with the company were entitled to assume that the managing director had been acting lawfully in what he did.

In practice, want of authority in the drawing of a cheque would be difficult, if not impossible, to establish against a bank where it has acted in accordance with the mandate governing the account. A company's mandate confers an express authority on the named signatories. Even where the bank pays a cheque drawn by a company in a manner which does not comply with the mandate, the bank is protected if it can establish that the company did in fact authorise or ratify the particular payment.[8]

Reference must also be made to s 91(2) of the Bills of Exchange Act 1882, which provides:

'(2) In the case of a corporation, where, by this Act, any instrument or writing is required to be signed, it is sufficient if the instrument or writing be sealed with the corporate seal. But nothing in this section shall be construed as requiring the bill or note of a corporation to be under seal.'

(ii) Companies Act 1985, s 349

This section (formerly s 108(1) of the Companies Act 1948), provides, so far as material:

'(1) Every company shall have its name mentioned in legible characters –

...

---

4 For a discussion of the 'per pro' indorsement, see pp 399–400, post.
5 See *Chapman v Smethhurst* [1909] 1 KB 927, CA; *Bondina Ltd v Rollaway Shower Blinds Ltd* [1986] 1 All ER 564, [1986] 1 WLR 517, CA.
6 [1921] 1 KB 77.
7 (1856) 6 E & B 327, Ex Ch.
8 See *London Intercontinental Trust Ltd v Barclays Bank Ltd* [1980] 1 Lloyd's Rep 241.

(c) in all bills of exchange, promissory notes, endorsements, cheques and orders for money or goods purporting to be signed by or on behalf of the company, . . .'

It is then provided that, if an officer of a company or a person on its behalf signs or authorises to be signed on behalf of a company any bill of exchange, promissory note, endorsement, cheque or order for money or goods in which the company's name is not mentioned as required by s 349(1), he is liable to a fine, and he is further personally liable to the holder of the bill of exchange, etc for the amount of it (unless it is duly paid by the company).

It is suggested that the interrelation between s 37 and s 349(1) is not entirely clear. If a bill of exchange or promissory note purports to be made, accepted or endorsed by signing *the name of the company*, failure to state the name with the requisite exactitude for the purposes of s 349(1) prima facie prevents the instrument from having been made, accepted or endorsed in its name for the purposes of s 37; but misdescription of a company's name would not appear to prevent an instrument from having been made, accepted or endorsed by or on behalf of the company by a person acting under its authority. Certainly, it appears to have been assumed in a number of cases decided under the predecessor to s 349(1) that the personal liability of the signatory is additional to, and not in substitution for, the liability of the company itself.

Personal liability claims against company officers have given rise to a number of cases in which the court has had to determine whether a particular instrument has stated the name of a company with sufficient exactitude. These authorities being prima facie applicable to s 37, they are summarised below.

In *Stacey & Co Ltd v Wallis*[9] Scrutton J held it to be sufficient that the name of the company was given on the instrument as addressee and drawee. Accordingly, two company directors and a company secretary who had accepted a bill without referring to the company's name were held to be not personally liable to the drawer.

In *Durham Fancy Goods Ltd v Michael Jackson (Fancy Goods) Ltd*,[10] a bill of exchange was drawn on a company named Michael Jackson (Fancy Goods) Limited, but was addressed on the face of the bill to 'M Jackson (Fancy Goods) Limited' and bore an inscription on the left-hand side of the paper: 'Accepted payable: . . . For and on behalf of M Jackson (Fancy Goods) Limited, Manchester'. It was held that the bill did not comply with the predecessor to s 349(1). In rejecting a submission that just as 'Ltd' is an acceptable abbreviation for 'Limited', so 'M' is an acceptable abbreviation for 'Michael', Donaldson J stated:[11]

'The word "Limited" is included in a company's name by way of description and not identification. Accordingly a generally accepted abbreviation will serve this

9 (1912) 106 LT 544. The case was decided under s 63(1) of the Companies Consolidation Act 1908, the wording of which (so far as material) is identical to s 349(1) of the Companies Act 1985.

10 [1968] 2 QB 839, [1968] 2 All ER 987. On the facts the plaintiff was held to be estopped from asserting breach of the section because it was the plaintiff who had inscribed the words of acceptance, thereby implying that acceptance of the bill in that form would be accepted by it as a regular acceptance. Cf *Lindholst & Co A/S v Fowler* [1988] BCLC 166, CA. In *Blum v OCP Repartition SA* [1988] BCLC 170, CA, a director unsuccessfully sought rectification of cheques which failed to comply with the Companies Act 1948, s 108(1). May LJ at p 175 reserved his position as to the *Durham Fancy Goods Ltd* case.

11 [1968] 2 QB 839 at 846, [1968] 2 All ER 987 at 990.

purpose as well as the word in full. The rest of the name, by contrast, serves as a means of identification and may be compounded of or include initials or abbreviations. The use of any abbreviation of the registered name is calculated to create problems of identification which are not created by an abbreviation of "Limited". I should therefore be prepared to hold that no abbreviation was permissible of any part of a company's name other than "Ltd" for "Limited" and, possibly, the ampersand for "and". However it is not necessary to go as far as this. Any abbreviation must convey the full word unambiguously and the initial "M" neither shows that it is an abbreviation nor does it convey "Michael".'

In *Hendon v Adelman*,[12] a company named 'L & R Agencies Limited' drew a cheque on which the company's name had in error been printed as 'L R Agencies Limited'. It was held that the drawers of the cheque were personally liable.

In *British Airways Board v Parish*[13] the managing director of a company named 'Watchstream Limited' was held personally liable as drawer of a cheque in which the name of the company appeared as 'Watchstream' with the omission of the word 'Limited'.

In *Maxform SpA v Mariani & Goodville Ltd*,[14] the sole director of a company named 'Goodville Limited' accepted bills drawn on the company's business name 'Italdesign', which had been registered pursuant to the Registration of Business Names Act 1916.[15] It was held that 'name' means registered corporate name, with the consequence that the director was personally liable.

In *Banque de l'Indochine et de Suez SA v Euroseas Group Finance Co Ltd*[16] two cheques drawn by Euroseas Group Finance Company Limited were signed by officers of a company on its behalf beneath printed words 'Per pro Euroseas Group Finance Co Ltd'. It was held by Robert Goff J, declining to follow the above dictum of Donaldson J in *Durham Fancy Goods Ltd v Michael Jackson (Fancy Goods) Ltd*, that the defendants were not personally liable. The learned Judge stated by way of general principle that:[17]

'where there is an abbreviation of a word which is not merely an accepted abbreviation but is treated as equivalent to that word, and where there is no other word which is abbreviated to that particular abbreviation, and where there is no question of the companies registrar accepting for registration two companies, both of which have the same name, except that one contains the full word and the other the abbreviated word, then in those circumstances there is absolutely no possibility of any confusion arising by reason of the abbreviation, and in those circumstances where the abbreviation is used it is proper to hold that the company has its name mentioned in the relevant document in legible characters, as required by [s 349(1)(c) of the 1985 Act].'

2 PARTNERS

A partnership is not a legal entity. The rights and responsibilities of a partnership are laid down in the Partnership Act 1890. Any partner has a prima facie right to draw on the firm banking account in the firm name and

12 (1973) 117 Sol Jo 631.
13 [1979] 2 Lloyd's Rep 361, CA.
14 [1979] 2 Lloyd's Rep 385.
15 Repealed by the Companies Act 1981, s 119(5), Sch 4.
16 [1981] 3 All ER 198.
17 [1981] 3 All ER 198 at 202e.

implied authority to bind the firm by cheque,[18] but not to post-date it.[19] A post-dated cheque drawn by one partner in favour of another and fraudulently negotiated was upheld in *Guildford Trust Ltd v Goss*[20] on the ground that there was nothing to put the transferees on inquiry. A partner has authority also to stop a cheque drawn in the name of a firm by another partner.[1] In *Backhouse v Charlton*,[2] Malins V-C, laid down that a surviving partner was entitled to draw on the account. He further held that where a bank had a partnership account and accounts of individual partners, the bank was under no duty to inquire as to the propriety of transfers between the accounts. Section 33 of the Partnership Act 1890[3] provides that, in the absence of agreement to the contrary, the death of any one partner works a dissolution of the partnership, though the surviving partners have power to bind the firm and continue business so far as is necessary for winding up its affairs.[4] The banker in such a case is safe in dealing with the surviving partners only to such an extent as is clearly within this purpose.[5]

Similarly, the bankruptcy of one partner dissolves the firm in the absence of any provision to the contrary in the partnership articles, and the bankrupt partner has thereafter no authority to bind it;[6] the bankruptcy necessarily involves all the partners. A bank has no lien on a partner's private account for an overdraft[7] on partnership account unless the partnership mandate so provides.[8] Most bank mandates now provide for joint and several liability of partners; see also the Civil Liability (Contribution) Act 1978, s 3. Where a bank holds security for a partnership debt, how the security will be dealt with will depend upon whether the security is partnership property or the property of an individual partner or of a third party, in relation to the extent of the partnership debt and perhaps the terms of the security documents.

A partner has, as such, no authority to open a banking account on behalf of the firm but in his own name.[9]

3 MARRIED WOMEN

(a) Capacity

There is now no distinction in contractual capacity between a married woman and a *feme sole* or a man.[10] A married woman may open a current account, and moneys standing to such account in the married woman's own name are

---

18 *Laws v Rand* (1857) 3 CBNS 442; *Backhouse v Charlton* (1878) 8 Ch D 444.
19 See *Forster v Mackreth* (1867) LR 2 Exch 163.
20 (1927) 136 LT 725.
 1 *Gaunt v Taylor* (1843) 2 Hare 413.
 2 (1878) 8 Ch D 444.
 3 32 Halsbury's Statutes (4th edn) 654.
 4 Section 38: 32 Halsbury's Statutes (4th edn) 657; cf. *Dickson v National Bank of Scotland* 1917 SC (HL) 50.
 5 *Re Bourne, Bourne v Bourne* [1906] 2 Ch 427, CA.
 6 Partnership Act 1890, ss 33, 38; 32 Halsbury's Statutes (4th edn) 654, 657.
 7 As to the implied power of a partner to borrow money on the credit of the firm, see *Lindley on Partnership* (15th edn, 1984) pp 299–300.
 8 *Watts v Christie* (1849) 11 Beav 546.
 9 *Alliance Bank Ltd v Kearsley* (1871) LR 6 CP 433.
10 Law Reform (Married Women and Tortfeasors) Act 1935, s 1; 27 Halsbury's Statutes (4th edn) 573.

deemed her own estate, so as to entitle her to deal with them. She also has power to contract with regard to her property as if she were a *feme sole*, so that she can draw bills and cheques[11] and borrow.

(b) Joint account between husband and wife

The nature of joint accounts is considered in Ch 11, post. It is, however, convenient to discuss at this point the issue of survivorship in relation to a joint account between husband and wife. Where an account is a joint account and one party dies, the survivor or survivors is or are in ordinary cases entitled to the whole amount, either under the law of devolution between joint owners or by custom of bankers or by express or implied agreement. The banker obtains a good discharge by paying the survivor. In the case of joint account of husband and wife, where there is authority to the wife to draw, on the death of her husband the question arises whether the wife was joined for the sake of convenience or for the purpose of providing for her in case she was the survivor. As to the differing conclusions arrived at on this basis, see *Husband v Davis*;[12] *Marshal v Crutwell*;[13] *Williams v Davies*;[14] *Hall v Hall*,[15] and other cases. In *Marshall v Crutwell* the husband was failing in health at the time of the opening of the joint account and it was held by Sir George Jessel MR that the intention was not to make provision for the wife, but merely to manage the husband's affairs conveniently, and thus she had no claim to the balance of the joint account when he died

In the High Court of Australia, in *Russell v Scott*[16] the views of Dixon and Evatt JJ are, perhaps, of the greatest interest. At pp. 451 and 453 they said:

'The right at law to the balance standing at the credit of the account on the death of the aunt was thus vested in the nephew. The claim that it forms part of her estate must depend upon equity. It must depend upon the existence of an equitable obligation making him a trustee for the estate.'

And again,

'As a legal right exists in him to this sum of money, what equity is there defeating her intention that he should enjoy the legal right beneficially? Both upon principle and upon English authority we answer, none. English authority is confined, so far as we can discover, to cases of husband and wife. But there is much authority to the effect that where a joint bank account is opened by husband and wife, with the intention that the survivor shall take beneficially ... that intention prevails ... although the deceased husband supplied all the money paid in and during his life the account was used exclusively for his own purposes.'

11 Bills of Exchange Act 1882, s 22; 5 Halsbury's Statutes (4th edn Reissue) 334.
12 (1851) 10 CB 645.
13 (1875) LR 20 Eq 328; applied in *Re Bishop, National Provincial Bank Ltd v Bishop* [1965] Ch 450, [1965] 1 All ER 249, in which Stamp J held that if there was no indication that the account was opened for some specific or limited purpose, each party might draw on it for his or her own purposes and any investments made by either were the property of the one into whose name they went.
14 (1864) 3 Sw & Tr 437.
15 [1911] 1 Ch 487.
16 (1936) 55 CLR 440 at 448; and see *Re Bishop, National Provincial Bank Ltd v Bishop* [1965] Ch 450, [1965] 1 All ER 249; and *Re Cameron* (1967) 62 DLR (2d) 389.

The learned judges then cited *Williams v Davies,*[17] *Owens v Greene,*[18] *Re Pattinson,*[19] *Marshal v Crutwell*[20] and *Re Harrison*[19] and continued, at p 453:

> 'The fact that these cases arose between husband and wife affects only the burden of proof. In a case where there is no presumption of advancement, satisfactory affirmative proof of an intention to confer a beneficial interest supplies the place of the presumption. Once it appears, as it does in the present case, that a definite intention existed that the balance at the credit of the bank account should belong to the survivor, these cases become in our opinion indistinguishable.'

In *Re Figgis, Roberts v Maclaren,*[1] Megarry J appeared to follow *Re Harrison* and *Re Pattinson* and expressed the view that *Russell v Scott* provided little help on the subject with which he was concerned, perhaps because that case was not one of husband and wife. It should be added that in the lower Australian court in *Russell v Scott*, it had been held that the survivor could not take because the provision was testamentary in nature and had not been made in accordance with the statutory requirements for wills.

4 MINORS

By the common law infants were, until 1 January 1970, persons under the age of 21, but the age of majority was reduced from 21 years to 18 by the Family Law Reform Act 1969.[2] By s 1(2) this applies for purposes of any rule of law and, generally, for the construction of 'full age', 'infant', 'infancy', 'minor', 'majority' etc. By s 12 a person who is not of full age may be described as a minor instead of an infant.

Two aspects of the relation between banker and a minor customer call for special consideration. First, the capacity of a minor to operate an account, even if kept in credit. Second, the enforceability of loans to a minor and security taken for such lending.

(a) Capacity to operate a current account

Arguments against opening or keeping a current account with a minor have been based on the alleged incapacity of a minor:

(i) to give an effective discharge for a debt; and
(ii) to draw a valid cheque.

Such arguments are, it is conceived, fallacious.

---

17 (1864) 3 Sw & Tr 437.
18 [1932] IR 225.
19 *Re Head, Head v Head (No 2)* [1894] 2 Ch 236; *Re Pattinson, Graham v Pattinson* (1885) 1 TLR 216; *Foley v Foley* [1911] 1 IR 281; *Re Harrison, Day v Harrison* (1920) 90 LJ Ch 186.
20 (1875) LR 20 Eq 328; applied in *Re Bishop, National Provincial Bank Ltd v Bishop* [1965] Ch 450, [1965] 1 All ER 249.
1 [1969] 1 Ch 123, [1968] 1 All ER 999.
2 6 Halsbury's Statutes (4th edn) 213.

(i) Discharge for a debt

'The disability of infancy goes no further than is necessary for the protection of the infant.'[3]

No doubt a minor cannot give an effective discharge for an unperformed obligation; he cannot, even by deed, release an unpaid debt. But where the discharge is merely the recognition of the performance of the obligation, such as a receipt, there is no rational ground for importing the disability. The case usually quoted in support of the proposition that an infant cannot give a valid discharge, *Ledward v Hassells*,[4] possessed exceptional features, turning as it did on the express words of a will, which made the payment of a legacy to a minor conditional on his ability to give a valid discharge, so that, in a sense, such discharge would have had to be given (if at all) for a legacy as yet unpaid.

The capacity of a minor to give a discharge for fulfilled obligations in ordinary cases appears to have been recognised by James LJ in *Re Brocklebank, ex p Brocklebank*[5] where he said:

'Cannot an infant give a receipt for wages or a salary due to him in respect of his personal labour?'

and, at 360,

'I am of opinion that an infant to whom a debt is due has the same rights as any other person, that he is entitled to enforce the payment of it by means of a debtor's summons and proceedings in bankruptcy – based thereon.'

Moreover, it is difficult to see how the question is of practical importance. The suggested danger is that the minor, after drawing out the whole of his current account, might, either before or on attaining majority, claim the money over again from the banker, on the ground of his own inability to give a valid discharge during minority. This is purely imaginary. Whatever the law where it is sought to enforce a contract against a minor or make him pay for goods purchased or repay money lent, when the positions are reversed and the minor is himself the moving party, the ordinary rules of justice and equity prevail.

'If an infant was to buy a thing, not being necessaries, he could not be compelled to pay for it, but having done so, he could not recover back the money'.[6]
'If an infant receives rents, he cannot demand them again when of age'.[7]

Valentini v Canali[8] is an authority to the same effect. It was followed in *Pearce v Brain*,[9] though with some hesitation.

---

3 Per Pearson J in *Burnaby v Equitable Reversionary Interest Society* (1885) 28 Ch D 416 at 424, distinguishing the disability of infancy from that of coverture.
4 (1856) 2 K & J 370.
5 (1877) 6 Ch D 358 at 359.
6 Per Lord Kenyon in *Wilson v Kearse* (1800) Peake Add Cas 196.
7 Per Lord Mansfield in *Earl of Buckinghamshire v Drury* (1762) 2 Eden 60.
8 (1889) 24 QBD 166.
9 [1929] 2 KB 310; and cf *Hamilton v Vaughan-Sherrin Electrical Engineering Co* [1894] 3 Ch 589.

(ii) Capacity to draw valid cheques

The Bills of Exchange Act 1882, s 22(1)[10] distinctly limits his capacity to contract an infant's liability as a party to a bill. Subsection 2 of the same section enacts that where a bill is drawn or indorsed by an infant the drawing or indorsement entitles the holder to receive payment of the bill and enforce it against any party thereto, other than the infant.

By s 22(2) of the Bills of Exchange Act 1882:

'Where a bill is drawn or indorsed by an infant ... having no capacity or power to incur liability on a bill, the drawing or indorsement entitles the holder to receive payment of the bill, and to enforce it against any other party thereto.'

A cheque is a bill of exchange drawn on a banker payable on demand.[11] Thus a cheque drawn by an infant possesses all the characteristics of a cheque drawn by a person of full age, save as regards the liability thereon of the drawer.

If the account is opened by a father or guardian paying in money to be drawn on by the infant, the banker can incur no risk by applying the money according to directions,[12] any more than does a trustee in paying money to an infant by way of allowance under the terms of a trust.

(b) Lending to minors

The law governing contracts of loan to minors was formerly contained in s 1 of the Infants Relief Act 1874, which provided that all contracts entered into by infants for (inter alia) the repayment of money lent or to be lent and all accounts stated with infants were absolutely void. This provision gave rise to a body of case law on the enforceability of guarantees of loans to infants which created fine and somewhat artificial distinctions.[13]

This heavily obsolete law was swept away by the Minors' Contracts Act 1987, which applies to all contracts made on or after 9 June 1987.[14] The Act affects the position of banks in three main respects:

(i) By s 1(a), the Infants Relief Act 1874 does not apply to any contract made by a minor after 9 June 1987;

(ii) By s 2, where a guarantee is given in respect of an obligation of a party to a contract made after 9 June, 1987, and that obligation is unenforceable against him (or he repudiates the contract) because he was a minor when the contract was made, the guarantee is not for that reason alone to be unenforceable against the guarantor;

(iii) By s 3, where a person ('the plaintiff') after 9 June 1987 enters into a contract with another ('the defendant'), and that contract is unenforceable against the defendant (or he repudiates it) because he was a minor when the contract was made, the Court may, if it is just and equitable to do so, require the defendant to transfer to the plaintiff any

10 5 Halsbury's Statutes (4th edn Reissue) 334.
11 Bills of Exchange Act 1882, s 73.
12 See *McEvoy v Belfast Banking Co Ltd* [1935] AC 24, HL.
13 See *Wauthier v Wilson* (1912) 28 TLR 239, CA; *Coutts & Co v Browne-Lecky* [1947] KB 104, [1946] 2 All ER 207; *Yeoman Credit Ltd v Latter* [1961] 2 All ER 294, [1961] 1 WLR 828, CA; and see *Paget* (9th edn) pp 32–33.
14 Ie the date on which the Act came into force: s 5(2).

property acquired by the defendant under the contract, or any property representing it.

As regards remedies against a minor, the effect of the Act is to place a bank which has entered a contract of loan in the same position as parties to any other type of contract with a minor.[15] Moreover, even if the contract is unenforceable against the minor (or he repudiates it), the court now appears to have jurisdiction to order restitution of any monies advanced by the bank pursuant to the contract.

As regards security in the form of guarantees, the Act removes the uncertainty which existed under the previous law. It is clearly not now a bar to enforceability that the principal debtor was a minor when the lending was made.

5 EXECUTORS

Executors and administrators in law constitute one person. In the absence of express provision, any one executor or administrator can operate on the executorship or administration account, and the death or resignation of one does not necessitate any modification of the course of administration. An example of an express provision is to be found in s 2(2) of the Administration of Estates Act 1925,[16] which provides that where there are two or more personal representatives a conveyance of real property shall not be made except with the concurrence of all or pursuant to an order of the court. By s 55 'conveyance' covers a charge or mortgage.

The powers of personal representatives in regard to the raising of money are governed by ss 39 and 40 of the Act. Section 39 would seem to cover the carrying on of the deceased's business for as long as may be necessary for the purpose of winding up the estate, of selling, for example, as a going concern: and to cover any borrowing necessary to this end.[17]

For any further carrying on of the business the personal representative must either have authority from the will by which he was appointed or obtain authority from all beneficiaries. Without this he cannot pledge the assets of the estate for this purpose,[18] but if authorised by will he may borrow and charge the assets. The above restrictions do not, however, fetter the normal right of a personal representative to borrow and charge assets for the payment of death duties or legacies, but in this latter case no charging is permissible until the creditors of the estate have been paid.

---

15 For a discussion of the enforceability under the general law of contracts made with minors, see *Chitty on Contracts* (25th edn) paras 532–592.
16 17 Halsbury's Statutes (4th edn) 260; see *Williams on Executors and Administrators,* (16th edn, 1982) 684, 790, 953.
17 See *Marshall v Broadhurst* (1831) 1 Cr & J 403; *Garrett v Noble* (1834) 6 Sim 504; *Edwards v Grace* (1836) 2 M & W 190.
18 See *Kirkman v Booth* (1848) 11 Beav 273 at 280; *Travis v Milne* (1851) 9 Hare 141.

6 TRUSTEES

(a) Delegation

Trustees stand on a different footing.[19] The appointment of several trustees is for the purpose of ensuring that the trust property shall be under their combined control.[20] Delegation by a trustee of his powers is not permitted,[1] especially when such delegation involves exclusive dealing with the property. The signatures of all the trustees should therefore be required on cheques unless modification of the rule is authorised by the terms of the trust. The Trustee Act 1925, s 25,[2] as amended by the Powers of Attorney Act 1971, s 9(4) allows delegation, which is subject to strict conditions.[3] It has been contended that s 23 authorises delegation by trustees so that they may appoint one or more of their number to sign cheques. This is not so.[4] Subsection 23(1) only authorises the employment of an outside agent of a specified class entitled to be paid, appointed by all the trustees, to do or carry through specific business. Subsection 23(2) authorises the similar appointment of an agent with larger powers, where the subject-matter is outside the United Kingdom.

The Act does, however, provide for the carrying on of trust business for the time being by the surviving trustees or trustee or the personal representatives of a last surviving trustee.[5]

(b) Borrowing

Authority to borrow is strictly limited.[6] Unless the will or trust deed gives authority or the sanction of s 16 can be pleaded, a trustee cannot borrow, save for certain specific purposes such as for purposes of the Settled Land Act 1925 (as applied to trustees for sale and to personal representatives). Where borrowing is effected by virtue of the provisions of the trust deed, those provisions must be strictly construed. Section 16 reads:

> 'Where trustees are authorised by the instrument, if any, creating the trust or by law to pay or apply capital money subject to the trust for any purpose or in any manner, they shall have and shall be deemed always to have had power to raise the money required by sale, conversion, calling in, or mortgage of all or any part of the trust property for the time being in possession.
>
> This section applies notwithstanding anything to the contrary contained in the instrument, if any, creating the trust. ...'

and by s 17:

> 'No purchaser or mortgagee, paying or advancing money on a sale or mortgage purporting to be made under any trust or power vested in trustees, shall be

---

19 As to when executors or administrators develop into trustees, see *George Attenborough & Son v Solomon* [1913] AC 76, HL.
20 Cf *George Attenborough & Son v Solomon* [1913] AC 76, HL.
 1 See *Re C Flower and Metropolitan Board of Works, Re M Flower and Metropolitan Board of Works* (1884) 27 Ch D 592; see also p 151, above re charity trustees.
 2 48 Halsbury's Statutes (4th edn) 245.
 3 Cf. *Green v Whitehead* per Eve J, (1929) *Times,* 13 July; affd though on somewhat different ground, [1930] 1 Ch 38, CA.
 4 *Green v Whitehead* [1930] 1 Ch 38, CA.
 5 S 18.
 6 S 17 of the Trustee Act 1925 probably does much to eliminate the need for inquiry.

concerned to see that such money is wanted, or that no more than is wanted is raised, or otherwise as to the application thereof.'

This may not, however, protect the banker where the borrowing is ultra vires. It has not been decided whether a banker may be liable, where, without the authority of the will and creditors of the testator, he allows the continuance of the account for the purpose of carrying on the business of the deceased. Without such authority, a trustee can continue the deceased's business during the process of administration only, for the purpose of selling the business as a going concern.[7]

The trustee's position as regards creditors has been emphasised in *Morton v Marchanton*.[8] It not infrequently happens that where a will gives authority to carry on a business for the benefit of beneficiaries under a trust, the trustees borrow for the purpose and charge assets of the trust estate. Unless, however, the trustees have fulfilled their duties as executors and paid the debts of the testator, the latter's creditors will rank before both the indemnity of the executors (the right to be exempt from liability for their act in continuing the business) and the mortgagees of the estate. It is essential, therefore, where bankers are asked to lend against assets of the estate for such a purpose that they ensure that the debts of the testator have been paid. This applies only to the creditors of the testator, not to those of the trustees as trustees, and only where the business is being carried on for the beneficiaries, as opposed to continuance for the purpose of effecting a sale in the winding-up. Nevertheless, executors have power to borrow and mortgage for purposes of winding-up of the estate.

(c) Deposit of documents for safe custody

By s 21

'Trustees may deposit any documents held by them relating to the trust, or to the trust property, with any banker or banking company[9] or any other company whose business includes the undertaking of the safe custody of documents, and any sum payable in respect of such deposit shall be paid out of the income of the trust property.'

(d) Charity trustees

Charity trustees may, subject to the trusts of the charity, confer on any of their body (being not less than two in number) a general authority or an authority limited in such manner as the trustees think fit to execute assurances, deeds and other instruments.[10] On its ordinary construction, the word 'instruments' includes cheques.[11]

---

7 See *Dowse v Gorton* [1891] AC 190, HL.
8 *Re Elijah Murphy Estate, Morton v Marchanton* (1930) 74 Sol Jo 321, 4 Legal Decisions Affecting Bankers 328.
9 As to the meaning of 'banker' and 'banking company' see Ch 6, ante.
10 Charities Act 1960, s 34(1).
11 The same view is taken in *Tudor on Charities* (7th edn, 1984) p 565.

7   UNINCORPORATED BODIES

The banking account of an unincorporated body having no legal status need cause the banker no difficulty if the account is kept in credit. Where the body is a club or similar association the committee or board of management merely administer moneys coming into their hands. Cheques are normally drawn on the banking account by authorised members of the committee or board and countersigned by the secretary. But if the body wishes to borrow the personal liability of those who operate the account is necessary or the bank must obtain security from a third party, and the borrowing should be supported by a resolution of the governing committee or board. If the body has assets which can be charged as cover for a borrowing, further considerations arise.

An unincorporated body can neither sue nor be sued in its own name; it is not a legal entity. As for internal disputes members with a grievance which could not be settled otherwise would have to sue the committee and could, if necessary, bring a class or representative action.[12]

The capacity of the members is the sum total of their capacities as limited by any restraint to which they agree to subject themselves. A committee or other governing body have no power to delegate their powers nor to go outside the authority given to them by the general body of members as laid down in the constitution and rules.[13] Their powers are what they choose to exercise in concert or to delegate to others.[14] The rules usually provide for delegation; thus the powers at any given time are those laid down in the rules in so far as they are by initial agreement given continuing force and according as, by virtue of their authority, they are altered or augmented. In *Flemyng v Hector*[15] Lord Abinger CB said:

> 'It appears to me that this case must stand upon the ground on which the defendant puts it, as a case between principal and agent. ... It is therefore a question here how far the committee who are to conduct the affairs of this club as agents are authorised to enter into such contracts as that upon which the plaintiffs now seek to bind the members of the club at large, and that depends on the constitution of the club, which is to be found in its own rules.'

Where the association is a club there may be another factor to take into consideration, that the liability of members may be limited to the amount of their subscriptions. Lord Lindley, in *Wise v Perpetual Trustee Co*[16] suggested that

> 'Clubs are associations of a peculiar nature. They are societies the members of which are perpetually changing. They are not partnerships; they are not associations for gain; and the feature which distinguishes them from other societies is that no member as such becomes liable to pay to the funds of the society or to anyone else any money beyond the subscriptions required by the rules of the club to be paid so long as he remains a member. It is upon this fundamental condition, not usually expressed but understood by everyone, that clubs are formed; and this distinguishing feature has often been judicially recognised.'

Property of the unincorporated body is usually held in the names of

---

12 See Megarry J in *John v Rees* [1970] Ch 345, [1969] 2 All ER 274.
13 *William Bean & Sons Ltd v Flaxton RDC* [1929] 1 KB 450, CA.
14 *Bradley Egg Farm Ltd v Clifford* [1943] 2 All ER 378, CA.
15 (1836) 2 M & W 172.
16 [1903] AC 139, PC.

trustees, who may be the governing body itself. However that may be, a bank lending against a charge on property must ensure that the power to borrow on behalf of the membership exists, that the signatories to the charge are authorised and that the purpose of the borrowing is within the authority given to the trustees, committee or board of management. These may contract only on behalf of the existing members and new members will not be bound unless by joining the club they signify their consent. The difficulties which may arise in regard to ownership of club property, when changes in the constitution of the club takes place, are illustrated by the decision in *Abbatt v Treasury Solicitor*.[17] The question was whether the property of a club which had ceased to function was held on trust for the Crown as bona vacantia or for the members of the old club or for the members of a new club which had been formed. It was held that once the old club had ceased to function .the rights of the existing members crystallised; and that the club belonged to and was distributable amongst the members of the club as at that date and the personal representatives of those of the members who had died since that date.

It is impossible, perhaps, to speak of unincorporated bodies generally with certainty, as they differ in their constitutions and rules, and perhaps the law is changing somewhat. In a trade union case[18] Farwell J said:

'Now, although a corporation and an individual or individuals may be the only entity known to the law who can sue or be sued, it is competent to the Legislature to give to an association of individuals which is neither a corporation nor a partnership nor an individual a capacity for owning property and acting by agents, and such capacity in the absence of express enactments to the contrary involves the necessary correlative of liability to the extent of such property for the acts and defaults of such agents. It is beside the mark to say of such an association that it is unknown to the common law. The Legislature has legalised it, and it must be dealt with by the courts according to the intention of the Legislature.'

In a much later case,[19] Lord Denning MR asked:

'What, then, is the legal status of the council? It is not, of course, a body corporate. But may it not be a body unincorporate? ... We have reached the point foreseen by Professor Dicey long ago: "When a body of twenty, or two thousand, or two hundred thousand men bind themselves together to act in a particular way for some common purpose, they create a body which by no fiction of law, but by the very nature of things, differs from the individuals of whom it is constituted" ...'

Sometimes unincorporated bodies become incorporated. In *Coutts & Co v Irish Exhibition in London*,[20] an account was opened with the plaintiffs by a group of people interested in the idea of an Irish exhibition, which account was overdrawn and secured. Later a company was formed for the purpose of the exhibition and the original group proposed to pass the responsibility for the account to the company, maintaining that they were not liable for the overdraft. It was held by the Court of Appeal that they were; the company could not be and it was absurd to think that the plaintiffs did not look to the group for the repayment of the advance.

17 [1969] 1 All ER 52, [1969] 1 WLR 561.
18 *Taff Vale Rly Co v Amalgamated Society of Railway Servants* [1901] AC 426 at 442, HL.
19 *Willis v British Commonwealth Universities' Association* [1964] 2 All ER 39 at 42, CA.
20 (1891) 7 TLR 313, CA.

8 SOLICITORS

(a) Rules as to opening and keeping of accounts

Solicitors' banking accounts are the subject of legislation in the Solicitors Act 1974. Section 32(1)(a) of the Act, as amended by the Building Societies Act 1986,[1] requires the Council of the Law Society, with the concurrence of the Master of the Rolls, to make rules 'as to the opening and keeping by solicitors of accounts at banks[2] or with building societies for clients' money'. By s 32(2)(a), the Council must also make rules as to the opening and keeping by solicitors of accounts at banks or with building societies for money comprised in 'controlled trusts', meaning 'a trust of which the solicitor is a sole trustee or co-trustee only with one or more of his partners or employees' (s 87(1)). The rules so made are the Solicitors' Accounts Rules 1986 and the Solicitors' Trust Account Rules 1986, both dated 11 December 1986.

Rule 4 of the Solicitors' Accounts Rules 1986 specifies the monies which may be paid into a client account, defined in r 2 as meaning:

'A current or deposit account at a bank or deposit account with a building society in the name of the solicitor and in the title of which the word "client" appears.'

Rule 3 requires every solicitor who holds or receives clients' money, or money which under r 4 he is permitted and elects to pay into a client's account, without delay to pay such money into a client account. This duty is subject to r 9, which relieves a solicitor of the obligation to pay into a client account specified clients' money held or received by him.

(b) Interest on clients' money

In *Brown v IRC*,[3] the House of Lords held that the client whose money was placed on deposit was entitled to the interest which it earned unless retained by the solicitor with his consent. It is sometimes impracticable for a solicitor to ascertain to which client such interest should go, and this point is now dealt with by s 33 of the Solicitors Act 1974 and the Solicitors' Accounts (Deposit Interest) Rules 1988. The Rules do not directly affect bankers, save that they entitle solicitors to hold clients' money in a separate designated account, and a solicitor must account for the interest on money so held (r 3(a)).

(c) Statutory protection for the banker

By s 85 of the 1974 Act:

'Where a solicitor keeps an account with a bank or a building society in pursuance of rules under section 32 –
(a) the bank or society shall not incur any liability, or be under any obligation to make any inquiry, or be deemed to have any knowledge of any right of any

1 Building Societies Act 1986, s 120, Sch 18 para 11(1), (2), Sch 19, Part I.
2 Except where the context otherwise requires, 'bank' means the Bank of England, the Post Office, in the exercise of its powers to provide banking services, or an institution authorised under the Banking Act 1987: Solicitors Act 1974, s 87(1) (as amended by the Banking Act 1979, s 51(1), Sch 6, Part I, para 9, and the Banking Act 1987, s 108(1), Sch 6, para 5, Sch 7, Part I). A body comprised in the new TSB group is a bank for the purposes of the Solicitors Act 1974: Trustee Savings Banks Act 1985, s 3(9), Sch 1, para 11(2)(b).
3 [1965] AC 244, [1964] 3 All ER 119.

person to any money paid or credited to the account, which it would not incur or be under or be deemed to have in the case of an account kept by a person entitled absolutely to all the money paid or credited to it;'

It was rightly observed of a predecessor to this provision (s 8(1) of the Solicitors Act 1933) that its effect is that a bank is not to be deemed to have any knowledge of the rights of third parties which it has *not in fact*,[4] ie the words 'any knowledge of any right' refer to actual knowledge.

In considering the ambit of the statutory protection conferred by s 85, reference must be made to its legislative history. Section 8(1) of the Solicitors Act 1933 contained the following proviso:

'Provided that nothing in this sub-section shall relieve a bank from any liability or obligation under which it would be apart from this Act.'

This proviso was seemingly in conflict with the body of the section. On the one hand, banks were to be unaffected by constructive notice of the rights of third parties. On the other, banks were not to be relieved from any obligation under which they would have been but for the Act. Thus the proviso appeared to leave open the possibility of a constructive trusteeship which the main body of the section appeared intended to eliminate.

Section 8(1) of the Solicitors Act 1933 was re-enacted in s 85(1) of the Solicitors Act 1957. In 1974, legislation was in preparation to consolidate the Solicitors Act 1957, the Solicitors Act 1965, and certain other enactments relating to solicitors. The passage of this consolidating legislation was delayed by a general election, and instead certain amendments were made to the existing law by the Solicitors (Amendment) Act 1974, which was subsequently repealed by the Solicitors Act 1974. By the Solicitors (Amendment) Act 1974, s 19(4) and Sch 2, para 32, there was substituted for s 85 of the Solicitors Act 1957 what is now s 85 of the Solicitors Act 1974. In other words, the statutory protection was modified by the *deletion* of the proviso. The manifest purpose of this deletion was to eliminate the possibility of banks being held liable as constructive trustees on the basis of anything less than actual knowledge.

Notwithstanding this legislative history, in *Lipkin Gorman v Karpnale Ltd*,[5] Alliott J held that the intention of the legislature in relation to s 85 of the 1974 Act was not to give banks a special advantage in maintaining and operating a client's account, but to ensure that there was no special disadvantage to bankers in so doing. It is submitted that this is not correct. If it were, the section would serve no purpose. The true position is that banks have been placed in a special position with respect to solicitors' client accounts, and for good reason: in the absence of such protection, the completion of conveyancing and other transactions might be delayed pending the making of enquiries. It was for this reason that in 1974 the Law Society advocated the deletion of the former proviso. It should be noted that by s 85(b), a bank with which a solicitor keeps an account in pursuance of rules under s 32 may not have any recourse or right against money standing to the credit of the account in respect of any liability of the solicitor to the bank, other than a liability in connection with the account.

4 Per Du Parcq J in *Plunkett v Barclays Bank Ltd* [1936] 2 KB 107 at 116, [1936] 1 All ER 653 at 657.
5 [1987] 1 WLR 987 at 997. The decision was reversed on appeal [1989] NLJR 76, CA without deciding this point.

(d) Bankers' Books Evidence Act

By s 86 of the Solicitors Act 1974, 'an application to, or enquiry or other proceeding before, the Solicitors Disciplinary Tribunal' is made a legal proceeding for the purposes of the Bankers' Books Evidence Act 1879.

(e) Collection of cheques for a solicitor

In considering whether a bank was negligent in collecting for a solicitor customer a cheque to which he was not entitled, MacKinnon LJ in *Penmount Estates Ltd v National Provincial Bank Ltd*[6] treated as a relevant consideration the fact that the customer was a solicitor, taking the view that the need for strict enquiry was rather less than it might have been for someone other than a solicitor.

9   ESTATE AGENTS

Estate agents, ie those who perform estate agency work as defined in s 1(1) of the Estate Agents Act 1979, also are required to keep a client account (s 14) for moneys 'held or received by them as agent, bailee, stockholder or in any other capacity' (s 12(1)). A 'client account' means a current or a deposit account which, by s 14(2),

(a) is with an institution authorised for the purpose of this section, and
(b) is in the name of a person who is or has been engaged in estate agency work; and
(c) contains in its title the word 'client'.

Section 14(3) authorises the Secretary of State to make regulations which may specify '(a) the institutions which are authorised for the purpose of this section'. Regulations so made[7] have specified (inter alia) 'recognised banks and licensed institutions within the meaning of the Banking Act 1979'. This must presumably now be read as referring to authorised institutions within the meaning of the Banking Act 1987.

Section 13 provides that clients' moneys are trust moneys and it would seem that bankers must hold estate agents' client accounts in much the same way as solicitors' client accounts.

10   FSA AUTHORISED PERSONS

(a) The Financial Services (Clients' Money) Regulations 1987

By s 55(1) of the Financial Services Act 1986 ('the FSA'), the Secretary of State has power to make regulations with respect to clients' money which authorised persons may hold in such circumstances as are specified in the regulations. 'Authorised person' in the FSA means a person authorised under Chapter III of Part I (ss 7–34) of the Act (s 207(1)). The Securities and Investment Board Ltd, in exercise of delegated powers,[8] has made the Finan-

---

6 (1945) 5 Legal Decisions Affecting Bankers 418 at 422.
7 Estate Agents (Accounts) Regulations 1981, SI 1981/1520.
8 FSA, s 114; FSA 1986 (Delegation) Order 1987, SI 1987/942; Financial Services (Transfer of Functions Relating to Friendly Societies) Order 1987, SI 1987/925.

cial Services (Clients' Money) Regulations 1987, which came into force on 29 April 1988. These regulations have already been considered in Ch 3, ante.

(b) Statutory protection in favour of bankers

Section 55(4) of the FSA confers statutory protection in favour of any institution (including an authorised institution under the Banking Act 1987) with which an account is kept in pursuance of regulations made under s 55(1). This provision has also been considered in Ch 3, ante.

11 LOCAL AUTHORITIES

Local authorities are corporate bodies subject to the direction, control and supervision of ministers of the Crown to the extent authorised by statutes. In their relations with banks the questions which arise are mainly the capacity of a local authority to borrow and create security, and the authority of persons purporting to act on behalf of the authority in respect of such matters.

As regards capacity, s 111(1) of the Local Government Act 1972 provides:

'Without prejudice to any powers exercisable apart from this section but subject to the provisions of this Act and any other enactment passed before or after this Act, a local authority shall have power to do any thing (whether or not involving the expenditure, borrowing or lending of money or the acquisition or disposal of any property or rights) which is calculated to facilitate, or is conducive or incidental to, the discharge of any of their functions.'

Given that borrowing is not an independent function of a local authority, every borrowing must, unless specifically authorised by some other statutory provision, satisfy the requirements imposed by s 111.

Section 172 and Sch 13, Part I of the 1972 Act confer specific powers of borrowing which are expressly 'without prejudice to s 111'. Paragraph 1(a) of the Schedule authorises the authority to borrow for the purpose of lending to another authority and paragraph 1(b) provides that the authority may borrow money for any other purpose or class of purpose approved by the Secretary of State in accordance with conditions subject to which the approval is given.

As regards temporary borrowing, para 10(1) of Sch 13 provides that:

'A local authority may, without the approval of the Secretary of State under para 1(b) above, borrow by way of temporary loan or overdraft from a bank or otherwise any sums which they may temporarily require –
(a) for the purpose of defraying expenses (including the payment of sums due by them to meet the expenses of other authorities) pending the receipt of revenues receivable by them in respect of the period of account in which those expenses are chargeable;
(b) for the purpose of defraying, pending the raising of a loan which the authority have been authorised to raise, expenses intended to be defrayed by means of the loan.'

Further, the Schedule, para 3 is to the effect that:

'The power of a local authority to borrow money by any means includes power to raise money by those means outside the United Kingdom or in a foreign currency, but only with the consent of and in accordance with any conditions specified by the Treasury.'

Paragraph 2(1) of the Schedule sets out the ways in which the money may be raised, which include mortgage and the issue of debentures.

The functions of a local authority may be discharged by a committee or sub-committee of the authority or by any other local authority. Committee and officers are appointed by the council, which is empowered to delegate (s 101(10)), for instance, to a finance or similar committee whose duty, inter alia, is to determine who shall sign on the banking account and the extent of their authority in relation to it. The resolution delegating this authority should be given to the bank and will constitute the bank's mandate.

By Sch 13, para 20:

'A person lending money to a local authority shall not be bound to inquire whether the borrowing of the money is legal or regular or whether the money raised was properly applied and shall not be prejudiced by any illegality or irregularity or by the misapplication or non-application of that money.'

There would appear to be no limitation on the absoluteness of that provision.

12   MENTALLY DISABLED CUSTOMERS

Where a person is mentally disabled and the banker knows of it, he has no mandate on which to act; though if he collects a cheque for the mentally disordered person, it is likely that he could claim that he collected for a 'customer'; otherwise any balances and securities he may have with the bank are tied, to be dealt with on the directions of the Court of Protection or by the depositor if he recovers and again becomes capable of contracting. Yet difficulties arise. In *Scarth v National Provisional Bank Ltd*,[9] the bank paid to the wife the balance standing to her husband's credit, he having been certified and she having paid her husband's debts to a greater amount. Humphreys J held that the equitable doctrine as stated by Wright J in *B Liggett (Liverpool) Ltd v Barclays Bank Ltd* applied.[10] This is in line with the decision in *Re Beavon, Davies, Banks & Co v Beavan*,[11] that money lent by a bank to meet necessaries for a mentally disordered person's household and estate may be recovered by right of subrogation; but it was further held that claims for interest and charges would not lie.

9 (1930) 4 Legal Decisions Affecting Bankers 241.
10 [1928] 1 KB 48. See further, pp 230–231, post.
11 [1912] 1 Ch 196.

CHAPTER 10

RELATIONSHIP OF BANKER AND CUSTOMER

1 INTRODUCTION

The relationship of banker to customer is one of contract.[1] It consists of a general contract, which is basic to all transactions, together with special contracts which arise only as they are brought into being in relation to specific transactions or banking services. The essential distinction is between obligations which come into existence upon the creation of the banker-customer relationship and obligations which are subsequently assumed by specific agreement; or, from the standpoint of the customer, between services which a bank is obliged to provide if asked, and services which many bankers habitually do, but are not bound to, provide. Services such as standing orders, direct debits, banker's drafts, letters of credit and foreign currency for travel abroad probably fall into the second category of services which the bank is not bound to supply, but this has not been judicially determined.[2]

It was remarked by Bankes LJ in *Joachimson v Swiss Bank Corpn*[3] that in the ordinary case the relationship of banker to customer depends 'entirely or mainly upon an implied contract'. Save that the mandate for accounts maintained by certain types of customer is normally agreed in writing, it remains relatively unusual for the terms of the general contract to be expressly agreed, still less to be reduced to writing. Conversely, special contracts commonly incorporate a bank's printed terms and conditions. Thus (1) a customer's request to issue a letter of credit is normally made on a pre-printed application form containing, inter alia, an express indemnity; (2) travellers' cheques are normally issued subject to standard terms and conditions; (3) cash cards, credit cards and cheque cards are also normally issued subject to standard terms and conditions.

In accordance with general principles of the law of contract, a banker cannot vary the terms of the contract by printed conditions unless the customer is given reasonable notice of, and accepts, such conditions. This is illustrated by *Burnett v Westminster Bank Ltd*,[4] where a bank issued its

---

1 *Foley v Hill* (1848) 2 HL Cas 28; and see 'The General Contract', post.
2 The point was expressly left open by Staughton J in *Libyan Arab Foreign bank v Bankers Trust Co* [1988] 1 Lloyd's Rep 259 at 272.
3 [1921] 3 KB 110 at 117.
4 [1966] 1 QB 742, [1965] 3 All ER 81.

customer with a cheque book containing cheque forms for a branch operating the magnetic ink character recognition system (which automatically directs a cheque to the drawee branch). On the front cover of the cheque book, there were printed two sentences in clear and easily legible black type: 'The cheques and credit slips in this book will be applied to the account for which they have been prepared. Customers must not, therefore, permit their use on any other account.' It was held that these sentences had not varied the contract. The relevant factors were that (a) the defendant could not establish that the plaintiff had read the printed words; (b) cheque book covers had not previously been used for the purpose of containing contractual terms and therefore the recipient could reasonably assume that they contained none; and (c) the plaintiff had maintained an account with the defendant for some time under the manual punched-card or paper-tape input systems which had prevailed down to the issue of the new cheque book.[5]

An attempt was made to superimpose a special relationship upon that of the ordinary banker and customer relationship in *Midland Bank Ltd v Conway Corpn*,[6] in a matter arising under s 343 of the Public Health Act 1936. The bank had the account of the freeholder of premises who was ordinarily resident in Peru, received the rent from the tenant, credited the freeholder's account and paid the rates to the council. A nuisance abatement notice was served on the bank. The question which arose was whether the bank received the rent as 'agent or trustee' of the owner within s 343. It was held that it did not. Lord Parker CJ said that:

'Granted that the cashier may have received sums representing rent, when they were physically handed over the counter, the bank did not in my judgment receive such sums as agent in the sense in which that word is used in the Act.'

It was impossible to say that there were special circumstances which 'would bring these bankers into such a special relationship with the freeholder as to constitute them her agents for the purposes of this section.'

2   COMMENCEMENT OF RELATIONSHIP

The relationship of banker and customer may be said to begin the moment the parties enter into relations or negotiations which are to be considered part of the contract ultimately concluded. The negotiations must be part of the process and lead directly to agreement; negotiations without agreement cannot establish the relationship. Ordinarily, a person asks a bank to open an account for him; he may or may not offer cash for credit or a cheque for collection and credit. However that may be, it is submitted that from the opening of an account both he and the banker are entitled to the benefits and subject to the obligations to which the relationship gives rise. The relationship may, however, come into existence even before the opening of an account. This is illustrated by *Woods v Martins Bank Ltd*,[7] in which the relationship was said to exist from the date of the acceptance by the bank of the plaintiff's instructions to collect moneys from a building society, to pay part to a

---

5 The earlier systems are described at [1966] 1 QB 745, [1965] 3 All ER 83–84; the relevant factors appear at 763 and 87 respectively.
6 [1965] 2 All ER 972, [1965] 1 WLR 1165
7 [1959] 1 QB 55, [1958] 3 All ER 166.

company in which he had become interested and to 'retain to my order the balance of the proceeds'. At the time he had no account with the bank.

3   THE GENERAL CONTRACT

(a) Definition

The classic description of the contract constituted by the relation of banker and customer is that of Atkin LJ in *Joachimson v Swiss Bank Corpn*:[8]

> 'The bank undertakes to receive money and to collect bills for its customer's account. The proceeds so received are not to be held in trust for the customer, but the bank borrows the proceeds and undertakes to repay them.[9] The promise to repay is to repay at the branch of the bank where the account is kept, and during banking hours.[10] It includes a promise to repay any part of the amount due against the written order of the customer addressed to the bank at the branch, and as such written orders may be outstanding in the ordinary course of business for two or three days, it is a term of the contract that the bank will not cease to do business with the customer except upon reasonable notice.[11] The customer on his part undertakes to exercise reasonable care in executing his written orders so as not to mislead the bank or to facilitate forgery.[12] I think it is necessarily a term of such a contract that the bank is not liable to pay the customer the full amount of his balance until he demands payment from the bank at the branch at which the current account is kept.'

(b) Demand necessary

The ratio of *Joachimson v Swiss Bank Corpn* is expressed in the final sentence of the above citation: it is an implied term of the contract that the banker is not liable to repay the customer until demand is made. Until then, there is no presently due debt owed by the banker to his customer. The ground of implication is not stated, but it is apparent from the judgment that the term was regarded as necessary to give the contract business efficacy.[13] If the doctrine of an immediately recoverable right were accepted, consequences would follow which the parties cannot reasonably intend and which would render banking a non-business proposition. One would be to entitle the banker to tender the amount of a credit balance to the customer at any moment, and at any place, and then dishonour outstanding cheques to the detriment of the customer, a position inconsistent with the customer's established right not to have his account summarily closed. Another consequence would be to justify the customer in demanding his money at any branch of the bank, irrespective of where his account is kept – a further

8 [1921] 3 KB 110 at 127.
9 See *Foley v Hill* (1848) 2 HL Cas 28; and see 'Current Account', ch 11, post.
10 See *Woodland v Fear* (1857) 7 E & B 519; *Prince v Oriental Bank Corpn* (1878) 3 App Cas 325 at 332–333, PC; *R v Lovitt* [1912] AC 212 at 219; *Garnett v McKewan* (1872) LR 8 Exch 10.
11 See *Prosperity Ltd v Lloyd's Bank Ltd* (1923) 39 TLR 372; and see further 'termination', infra.
12 See *London Joint Stock Bank Ltd v Macmillan and Arthur* [1918] AC 777.
13 See, in particular, [1921] 3 KB 110 at 121, per Bankes LJ ('It seems to me impossible to imagine the relation between banker and customer, as it exists today, without the stipulation that, if the customer seeks to withdraw his loan, he must make application to the banker for it'); and at 130, per Atkin LJ ('A decision to the contrary would subvert banking practice').

subversion of the established and legally recognised principles of banking. The earlier cases[14] which suggested that demand was not necessary were explained in *Joachimson* on the ground that the point was not directly in issue or necessarily involved in their decision.

It was further stated in *Joachimson* that in most cases where the question will in practice arise, the issue of a writ by the customer is a sufficient demand without any previous request for payment.[15]

(c) 'One contract'

The case advanced by the customer in *Joachimson* was essentially that the relation of banker and customer is that of debtor and creditor with super-added obligations, and that the customer enjoys the right of a lender to sue for his debt whenever he pleases. Atkin LJ rejected altogether this conception of a dual relation with the emphatic pronouncement that there is only one contract made between the bank and its customer.[16] This rejection did not of itself determine the point at issue – indeed, Bankes LJ reached the same decision as Atkin LJ whilst adhering to the notion of implied superadded obligations.[17] But Atkin LJ's concept of a single contract is the more convincing, and it is this concept which has prevailed.

In practice, the point appears to be of limited importance. In particular, it does not follow from the concept of an indivisible contract that the relation between a bank and a customer maintaining accounts with it in different jurisdictions is embodied in one contract governed by one proper law. It was held in *Libyan Arab Foreign Bank v Bankers Trust Co*,[18] that such a contract may be governed in part by one law and in part by another. This case is considered more fully below under the heading 'Proper Law'.

4 DUTY OF CARE

Atkin LJ's formulation in *Joachimson* incorporates the ratio of *Macmillan's* case,[19] that the customer undertakes to exercise reasonable care in executing his written orders so as not to mislead the bank or to facilitate forgery. Since *Joachimson*, other duties of care have been held to exist or not exist (as the case may be) both as between banker and customer, and banker and third parties. It is convenient to summarise here the main context in which such issues have arisen, and to cross-refer to the chapter where such duties of care are considered.

14 The earlier cases include *Foley v Hill* (1848) 2 HL Cas 28; *Pott v Clegg* (1847) 16 M & W 321; *Schroeder v Central Bank of London Ltd* (1876) 34 LT 735; *Re Tidd, Tidd v Overell* [1893] 3 Ch 154; *Bradford Old Bank Ltd v Sutcliffe* [1918] 2 KB 833, especially per Scrutton LJ at 848 ('Even if the word 'demand' is used in the case of a present debt, it is meaningless and express demand is not necessary, as in the case of a promissory note: *Norton v Ellam* (1837) 2 M & W 461'). It was, however, well established that a debt could be stipulated to be not payable except on demand – see *Walton v Mascall* (1844) 13 M & W 452 at 455.
15 [1921] 3 KB 110 at 115, per Bankes LJ.
16 [1921] 3 KB 110 at 127.
17 [1921] 3 KB 110 at 119.
18 [1988] 1 Lloyd's Rep 259 at 271.
19 [1918] AC 777.

(a) Duty of care in contract

(i) Duties owed by banker to customer

The existence and scope of an implied contractual duty of care owed by a banker to his customer has arisen principally in the context of (1) the execution of payment instructions, (2) the giving of advice and (3) the taking and realising of security. These matters are considered in, respectively, chs 12, 15 and 30, post. Some guidance as to the limits of the banker's implied contractual duty of care can perhaps be obtained from two cases in other contexts in which such a duty has been held not to exist. In the first, *Schioler v National Westminster Bank Ltd*,[20] it was held that the defendant bank did not owe the plaintiff customer a duty of care to advise or warn her of the possible tax repercussions of remitting to England for realisation a warrant denominated in Malaysian dollars. In the second case, *Redmond v Allied Irish Banks plc*[1], it was held that the defendant bank did not owe the plaintiff customer a duty of care to advise or warn him of the risks of paying in for collection a cheque crossed 'not negotiable – account payee only' in circumstances where he was not the named payee.

(ii) Duties owed by customer to banker

The main and perhaps only implied duty of care owed by the customer to his banker is that laid down in *Macmillan's* case, which is considered more fully in ch 11, post. Any wider duty of care on the part of the customer will not be recognised unless the term contended for satisfies the strict requirements for the implication of a contractual term. This appears from *Tai Hing Cotton Mill Ltd v Liu Chong Hing Bank Ltd*,[2] where the Privy Council rejected a submission that a wider duty than that upheld in *Macmillan* is to be implied as a necessary incident of the legal relationship between banker and customer. Lord Scarman, delivering the judgment, stated:[3]

'The argument for the banks is, when analysed no more than that the obligations of care placed on banks in the management of a customer's account which the courts have recognised have become with the development of banking business so burdensome that they should be met by a reciprocal increase of responsibility imposed on the customer, and they cite *Selangor United Rubber Estates Ltd v Cradock (No 3)* [1968] 2 All ER 1073, [1968] 1 WLR 1555 (Ungoed-Thomas J) and *Karak Rubber Co Ltd v Burden (No 2)* [1972] 1 All ER 1210, [1972] 1 WLR 602 (Brightman J). One can fully understand the comment of Cons JA that the banks must today look for protection. So be it. They can increase the severity of their terms of business, and they can use their influence, as they have in the past, to seek to persuade the legislature that they should be granted by statute further protection. But it does not follow that because they may need protection as their business expands the necessary incidents of their relationship with their customer must also change.'

20 [1970] 2 QB 719, [1970] 3 All ER 177.
 1 [1987] 2 FTLR 264.
 2 [1986] AC 80, [1985] 2 All ER 947, PC.
 3 Ibid at, respectively, 105H and 956e.

(b) Duty of care in tort

(i) As between banker and customer

Tai Hing also provides the leading modern statement on the imposition of a duty of care in tort where the parties are in a contractual relationship. In the words of Lord Scarman:[4]

'Their Lordships do not believe that there is anything to the advantage of the law's development in searching for a liability in tort where the parties are in a contractual relationship. This is particularly so in a commercial relationship. Though it is possible as a matter of legal semantics to conduct an analysis of the rights and duties inherent in some contractual relationships including that of banker and customer either as a matter of contract law when the question will be what, if any, terms are to be implied or as a matter of tort law when the task will be to identify a duty arising from the proximity and character of the relationship between the parties, their Lordships believe it to be correct in principle and necessary for the avoidance of confusion in the law to adhere to the contractual analysis: on principle because it is a relationship in which the parties have, subject to a few exceptions, the right to determine their obligations to each other, and for the avoidance of confusion because different consequences do follow according to whether liability arises from contract or tort, eg in the limitation of action.'

This principle was applied by the Court of Appeal in *National Bank of Greece SA v Pinios Shipping Co (No 1)*,[5] where mortgagor shipowners and a guarantor alleged that the plaintiff bank owed them a duty of care in contract and in tort to ensure that a managing agent did not under-insure the mortgaged vessel. The Court of Appeal rejected the implication of a contractual term as unnecessary and unreasonable.[6] The defendants having failed to establish a duty in contract, their claims necessarily failed in tort. As it was put by Lloyd LJ:[7]

'But so far as I know it has never been the law that a plaintiff who has the choice of suing in contract or tort can fail in contract yet nevertheless succeed in tort; and, if it ever was the law, it has ceased to be the law since *Tai Hing Cotton Mill Ltd v Liu Chong Hing Bank Ltd.*'

Nicholls LJ also applied *Tai Hing*:[8]

'Pinios entered into a written agreement with the bank and, echoing the words of Lord Scarman in *Tai Hing Cotton Mill Ltd v Liu Chong Hing Bank Ltd*, Pinios cannot rely on the law of tort to provide it with a greater protection against the bank than that for which, expressly or impliedly, it has contracted with the bank.'

The precise limits of the *Tai Hing* principle are still being worked out. It has already been applied in several cases.[9] However, there appear to be at least three situations in which the principle does not preclude the imposition of a duty of care in tort between parties who stand in a contractual relationship. These are:

1 One contracting party may be liable in tort to another for mis-

4 Ibid at, respectively, 107B and 957d.
5 [1989] 1 All ER 213, [1988] 2 Lloyd's Rep 126, CA.
6 See per Lloyd LJ at 220a, and see also Nicholls LJ at 232c.
7 Ibid at 223j.
8 Ibid at 232e.
9 See *Greater Nottingham Co-operative Society Ltd v Cementation Piling and Foundations Ltd* [1989] QB 71, [1988] 2 All ER 971, CA; and see the cases in notes 10–11, post.

representations or misstatements made before the signing of a written agreement (as in *Esso Petroleum Co Ltd v Mardon*[10]), or the entering into of a general contractual relationship such as that of banker and customer (as in *Woods v Martins Bank Ltd*[11]);

2 In a large class of cases it always has been and probably remains possible for a plaintiff to sue either in contract or in tort; in such cases, liability in tort is co-extensive with liability in contract;[12]

3 A duty of care in tort may be held to exist where the events which give to the duty are simply outside the range of matters which can realistically be treated as within the scope of the contract.[13]

(ii) As between banker and non-customer

The existence of a duty of care has arisen principally in the context of bankers' references, and the taking and realisation of security, which are considered in chs 15 and 30, post.

(c) Statutory protection conditional upon absence of negligence

The statutory protection available to the paying banker under s 80 of the Bills of Exchange Act 1882, and to the collecting banker under s 4 of the Cheques Act 1957, is conditional upon the banker having acted 'without negligence'. The sections effectively impose upon the paying and collecting banker a duty of care. The requirement to act 'without negligence' is considered in ch 24 (as regards the paying banker) and ch 28 (as regards the collecting banker).

(d) Exercise of reasonable care as a condition of the right to reimbursement

There are certain situations in which the banker's right to reimbursement is conditional upon his having exercised reasonable care. An obvious example is the right of the issuing bank of a letter of credit to be reimbursed by the applicant for payments made to the beneficiary or to a bank authorised to effect payment. By art 15 of the Uniform Customs and Practice for Documentary Credits (1983 Revision), banks are required to examine all documents with reasonable care to ascertain that they appear on their face to be in accordance with the terms and conditions of the credit. An issuing bank which negligently fails to identify a discrepancy in the documents is not entitled to be reimbursed unless the applicant takes up the documents.

---

10 [1976] QB 801, [1976] 2 All ER 5, CA; and see *Banque Financiere de la Cite SA v Westgate Insurance Co Ltd* [1988] 2 Lloyd's Rep 513 at 558, CA.

11 [1959] 1 QB 55, [1958] 3 All ER 166. Pre-contractual liability was based upon a finding of a fiduciary relationship (ibid, at 72–73), but it is thought that nowadays *Hedley Byrne* would provide a more obvious basis of liability.

12 See *National Bank of Greece SA v Pinios Shipping Co No 1* [1989] 1 All ER 213, CA, per Lloyd LJ at 222–223.

13 See *Banque Financiere de la Cite SA v Westgate Insurance Co Ltd* [1988] 2 Lloyd's Rep 513 at 558–559, CA.

5   BUSINESS DAYS AND HOURS

An element in the relationship of banker and customer consists of their respective rights and obligations in regard to the days and hours during which business is transacted. A customer is entitled to know when he may expect his business to be dealt with. Atkin LJ's formulation in *Joachimson* includes the banker's promise to repay at the branch of the bank where the account is kept *during banking hours,* and, a fortiori, on days on which the bank is open for business.

(a) Days of business

It is probably an implied term of the contract that the banker will be open for business from Monday to Friday inclusive subject to: (i) statutory bank holidays; (ii) variation of the contract by agreement; or (iii) reasonable notice of closing to the customer. Saturday is no longer a customer business day since the introduction by the clearing banks of Saturday closing on 1 July 1969 following the similar introduction by Scottish banks on 10 June 1968. Certain banks do now open specified branches on Saturday mornings, and this may create a contractual duty to transact business on Saturdays at branches which have announced Saturday opening, but not at other branches.

(b) Hours of business

Hours of business are published by the Committee of London Clearing Bankers on behalf of the clearing banks as a whole, and are notified in the press and by notices posted in bank offices. The banker is probably entitled to depart from such published hours upon reasonable notice to his customer.

The significance of hours of business lies in the right of customers in relation to cheques they have issued – the right to compliance with their mandate and the right to countermand it. The peculiar nature of banking places the banker as mandatory under risk of failing to comply with the mandate by paying someone other than the intended payee. Against this risk he is protected by the Bills of Exchange Act 1882 and the Cheques Act 1957, but the right to protection depends on his paying in the ordinary course of business or without negligence, into both of which conditions enters the question of hours of business. Payment out of business hours is not in the ordinary course of business. This expression has not been defined and is to be considered at the time any question as to the bank's action arises. In *Baines v National Provincial Bank Ltd*,[14] Lord Hewart LCJ found in favour of a bank which had paid a cheque five minutes after the advertised closing time. He said:

> 'The general question of the limits of time within which a bank may conduct business having prescribed, largely for its own convenience, a particular time at which the doors of the building will be closed, is a large question, not raised here.'

It is doubtful if it could be shown to be normal banking practice to pay cheques over the counter after the advertised hour for closing, except in cases where the presenters, reaching the banking office before that time, could not by the pressure on the bank staff be dealt with until after. Otherwise a banker would be bound so to organise himself that he can cope with any business

14 (1927) 96 LJKB 801.

such as the presentation of cheques by the advertised closing time. Yet no amount of foresight would necessarily enable him to cope.

Where a customer places bills of exchange in the hands of a banker for the purpose of presentment, the banker is bound to make provision for carrying out his contract and cannot avoid his obligation by closing.

6 TERMINATION

The relationship may terminate (i) by agreement between the parties, (ii) by unilateral act, as where the customer or the banker gives notice to terminate, or (iii) by operation of law.

Termination by agreement does not require comment. As to termination by notice, where it is the banker who gives notice to terminate an account in credit, such notice must be adequate to enable the customer to make other banking arrangements.[15] However, where a banker closes an account without giving reasonable notice, an application by the customer for an injunction restraining closure pending the period of reasonable notice is unlikely to succeed. A customer's application for such an injunction failed in *Prosperity Ltd v Lloyds Bank Ltd*[16] on the grounds, inter alia, that (a) an order would have amounted to specific performance of a contract to provide personal services of a most confidential character, and would have been a direction to the bank to constitute itself a borrower of the customer's money as and when paid in; and (b) damages were an adequate remedy.

In modern banking practice, personal services have been so far superseded by computerisation that the first ground above may no longer carry weight. But damages remain as adequate a remedy as they ever were, and this ground of the decision represents a substantial hurdle to a successful application for an injunction.

Where a current account is overdrawn the banker's demand for repayment prima facie terminates the relationship.

The question of determination by operation of law has arisen principally in the context of claims for interest, the rule being that there is no implied contract for payment of compound interest after an account has ceased to be current for mutual transactions. The relevant authorities are considered in ch 14, post.

7 LIMITATION OF ACTIONS

Atkin LJ pointed out in *Joachimson v Swiss Bank Corpn*[17] that:

> 'The practical bearing of this decision [as to the necessity for a demand] is on the question of the Statute of Limitations ... The result of this decision will be that for the future bankers may have to face legal claims for balances on accounts that have remained dormant for more than six years.'

By s 5 of the Limitation Act 1980, an action founded on simple contract may

15 *Prosperity Ltd v Lloyds Bank Ltd* (1923) 39 TLR 372; and see *Cumming v Shand* (1860) 5 H & N 95; *Buckingham & Co v London and Midland Bank* (1895) 12 TLR 70; *Joachimson v Swiss Bank Corpn* [1921] 3 KB 110, per Warrington LJ at 125, and per Atkin LJ at 127.
16 *Prosperity Ltd v Lloyds Bank Ltd.* supra.
17 [1921] 3 KB 110 at 130 and 131.

not be brought after the expiration of six years from the date on which the cause of action accrued. In an action for the recovery of a debt, time does not begin to run until there is a debt presently due and payable. It follows from *Joachimson v Swiss Bank Corpn* that in the case of a credit balance on current account, time does not begin to run against the customer until demand for payment has been made.

Section 6 of the Limitation Act 1980 introduces a new provision applicable to any contract of loan which (1) does not provide for repayment of the debt on or before a fixed or determinable date; and (2) does not effectively (whether or not it purports to do so) make the obligation to repay the debt conditional on a demand for repayment made by or on behalf of the creditor or on any other matter. Where a demand in writing for repayment of the debt due under any such contract of loan is made by or on behalf of the creditor (or, where there are joint creditors, by or on behalf of any one of them) s 5 of the Act applies as if the cause of action to recover the debt had accrued on the date on which the demand was made.[18] This reverses the position at common law.[19] However, this provision does not apply where, in connection with taking the loan, the debtor enters into any collateral obligation to pay the amount of the debt or any part of it (as, for example, by delivering a promissory note[20] as security for the debt) on terms which would exclude the application of s 6 to the contract of loan if those terms applied directly to repayment of the debt.[1]

The limitation period in respect of a claim for repayment of an overdraft appears to commence from the date on which demand for repayment is made and not from the date on which the overdraft was granted. The contrary view was taken by the Court of Appeal in *Parr's Banking Co Ltd v Yates*,[2] where a claim against a guarantor was held to be time-barred in respect of advances made more than six years before the issue of the writ. However, in modern banking practice, overdrafts are treated as repayable on demand, and it is therefore doubtful whether *Parr's* case represents the law today. In any event an unsecured overdraft which creates a debt the repayment of which is not conditional on demand appears to fall within s 6 of the Limitation Act 1980.

8   PROPER LAW

The bank's promise to repay is to repay at the branch where the account is kept. Accordingly, in the absence of an express choice of law, the proper law of the contract between the bank and its customer is generally the law of the place where the account is kept, this being the law with which the contract has its closest and more real connection.

Where a customer maintains only one account with a bank, the court is likely to require solid grounds for displacing the law of that place as the proper law. Where a customer maintains two or more accounts with branches of a bank in different jurisdictions, the position is more complex. This problem

18 Limitation Act 1980, s 6(3).
19 See, eg *Re Brown's Estate* [1893] 2 Ch 300, *Reeves v Butcher* [1891] 2 QB 509.
20 'Promissory note' has the same meaning as in the Bills of Exchange Act 1882: Limitation Act 1980, s 6(4).
 1 Ibid, s 6(2).
 2 [1898] 2 QB 460, CA.

arose in *Libyan Arab Foreign Bank v Bankers Trust Co*,[3] where two banks in a correspondent relationship set up a managed account arrangement comprising (1) a call account in London for investment of liquid funds and (2) a demand (current) account in New York for daily dollar-clearing activity. It was submitted by the customer that there existed (a) two separate contracts, of which one related to the London account and was governed by English law; or (b) one contract, governed in its entirety by English law; or (c) one contract governed by two proper laws, namely English law and the law of New York. It was submitted by the bank that there was one contract only, governed by New York law. It was accepted by the bank that it is possible, although unusual, for a contract to have a split proper law. The notion of two separate contracts was rejected by Staughton J as superficial and unattractive. He held instead that there was one contract, governed in part by the law of England and in part by the law of New York.[4] In so holding, he expressly rejected a submission that difficulty and uncertainty would arise if different parts of the same contract were governed by different laws.

9 EFFECT OF WAR[5]

The effect on the relationship of banker and customer of the outbreak of hostilities in the place where both parties operate received very full treatment by the House of Lords in *Arab Bank Ltd v Barclays Bank* (*Dominion, Colonial and Overseas*).[6] The decision was unanimous in dismissing an appeal from the judgment of the Court of Appeal, which had upheld that of Parker J. The appellants had contended that they had the right to demand at any of the respondents' offices the sum of £582,931 standing to their credit with the Allenby Square branch of the respondent bank in Jerusalem on the day at the end of which the British mandate in Palestine expired. The new state of Israel vested in a custodian all 'absentee' property – property of any person who after 29 November 1947 had gone outside Israel – and Barclays Bank in due course paid the balance in question to the custodian, the appellants having become absentee by the removal of their Jerusalem office to Amman.

The appellants asserted that before the mandate terminated they demanded payment of the balance and were refused and that even if this were not so, the banker-customer contract was frustrated by the hostilities and that thereupon there arose a simple debt payable without demand; that there arose, by operation of law, a new right to have the balance repaid to them as money had and received for a consideration which had wholly failed; finally, that this new right, being wholly independent of the contract between the parties, was free from the two limitations imposed upon the current account, viz., that the respondents were only bound to repay the balance on it (1) after demand made and (2) at the Allenby Square branch. Parker J found that no such demand as had been alleged had been made.

---

3 [1988] 1 Lloyd's Rep 259. See also *X AG v A Bank* [1983] 2 All ER 464, [1983] 2 Lloyd's Rep 535.
4 Ibid at 271. cf *Libyan Arab Foreign Bank v Manufacturers Hanover Trust Co* (1989) Times, 28 February.
5 As to the effect of war generally, see Lord McNair and A D Watts, *The Legal Effects of War* (4th edn, 1966).
6 [1954] AC 495, [1954] 2 All ER 226.

The decision of the House is well illustrated by the following extract from the opinion of Lord Morton of Henryton:

'I am quite satisfied that the right to be paid a credit balance is a right which survives [the outbreak of war]. It is a right which the creditor can assign or bequeath by his will; it passes on his intestacy and it is, in my opinion, an "accrued right" in the sense in which these words were used by Lord Dunedin in the *Ertel Bieber* case.[7] It was, therefore, suspended and not destroyed by the outbreak of war and immediately after the outreak it was locally situated in the newly created State of Israel. Thus it became subject to the legislation of that State, was vested in the custodian and was rightly paid to the custodian by the respondents.'

The House was not unanimous on the point whether the necessity for a demand survived the war. Lords Morton of Henryton, Reid, Asquith of Bishopstone and Cohen thought that it did, but Lord Tucker reserved for further consideration

'the question whether the necessity for demand before action in respect of sums standing to the credit of a customer's current account during the currency of the account, as decided in *Joachimson v Swiss Bank Corpn*[8] applied equally in all circumstances to the balance after the account has been closed and thereby ceased to be current.'

7 *Ertel Bieber & Co v Rio Tinto Co Ltd* [1918] AC 260 at 269.
8 [1921] 3 KB 110, CA.

CHAPTER 11

TYPES OF ACCOUNT

1 CURRENT ACCOUNT

The current account, despite the many mutual duties engrafted on the relation of banker and customer since 1848, the date of *Foley v Hill*,[1] is still the basic and predominant element in dealings between the parties. A recent development in banking services offered to the public is the introduction by several major banks of interest-bearing current accounts. Such accounts are governed by the same principles as those applicable to non-interest-bearing current accounts.

(a) Title to monies paid in

The current or drawing account may be either a credit or an overdrawn account. A credit account is made up of moneys paid in by the customer, the proceeds of cheques and bills collected for him, coupons collected, interest and dividends paid direct to the banker and from various other sources, less any moneys properly paid out. Moneys from different sources, once they have found their way into the current account, are treated as one entire debt.[2] Property in money generally passes with possession.[3] When moneys are paid into an account they are reckoned as belonging to the bank and, if paid in cash, title does not pass from the customer paying them in to the bank until they are received on the bank side of the counter and accepted by the cashier or teller who gives a receipt for them. So long as the moneys are on the customer's side of the counter, the property does not pass and the bank is not in any way responsible for them.[4] Similarly once money is paid over the counter to the presenter of a cheque, for instance, the money ceases to be the property of the bank and becomes that of the presenter.

---

1 (1848) 2 HL Cas 28.
2 Except, for instance, where the customer's moneys are mixed with trust moneys; see *Re Hallett's Estate, Knatchbull v Hallett* (1880) 13 Ch D 696.
3 *Sinclair v Brougham* [1914] AC 398 at 418.
4 *Balmoral Supermarket Ltd v Bank of New Zealand* [1974] 2 Lloyd's Rep 164, [1974] 2 NZLR 155.

(b) Relation of debtor and creditor

It was settled in *Foley v Hill*[5] that the purely debtor and creditor position
excludes any element or suggestion of trusteeship or fiduciary relation in the
banker with regard to current account. The implied agreement between
banker and customer as stated by Atkin LJ in *Joachimson's* case is that all
moneys coming to the banker's hands for the credit of current account are
to be taken as lent to the banker. In *Hirschorn v Evans (Barclays Bank Ltd
garnishees)*[6] Mackinnon LJ said that there is never any question of property
in the credit balance of a bank account; that the relation between the parties
is simply that of debtor and creditor. By 'simply' the learned judge probably
meant 'basically', for the simple relationship takes no account of the necessity
for demand by the creditor which distinguishes the relationship from the
normal debtor and creditor relationship.

The banker is free to use the money as his own, like any other borrower;
the customer has parted with all control over it, like any other lender,
retaining only his right to repayment. And as a consequence the banker is
not as a general rule concerned to inquire into the sources whence his
customer derived the money, or to pay heed to the claims of third parties
seeking to reach it in his hands as being by right theirs.[7] However, two first
instance decisions of 1968[8] and 1970[9] indicated that a banker can be a
constructive trustee of a company customer's moneys in account and be liable
if he breaches that trust in paying from the account even against a valid
mandate. The circumstances in which a constructive trust will be imposed
are considered in ch. 12, post. Nevertheless a bank is not normally concerned
with the nature of payments to an account or with the customer's title.

Knowledge that particular moneys were in respect of rent did not in
Midland Bank Ltd v Conway Corpn[10] constitute the bank the landlord's agents
for the collection or receipt of rent.

(c) No implied duty to check periodic bank statements

The relationship of banker and customer does not give rise either in contract
(by way of an implied term) or in tort to a duty owed by the customer to the
bank to check his monthly (or other periodic) bank statements so as to be
able to notify the bank of any items which were not, or may not have been,
authorised by him. It was so held by the Privy Council in *Tai Hing Cotton
Mill Ltd v Liu Chong Hing Bank Ltd*,[11] a case which has already been
considered in ch 10, ante, in relation to duties of care generally.

---

5 (1848) 2 HL Cas 28.
6 [1938] 2 KB 801 at 815, [1938] 3 All ER 491 at 498 and see per Devlin J in *Baker v Barclays
Bank Ltd* [1955] 1 WLR 822 at 831–2.
7 Cf *Bodenham v Hoskins* (1852) 21 LJ Ch 864; *Thomson v Clydesdale Bank Ltd* [1893] AC
282, on the first point; *Calland v Loyd* (1840) 6 M & W 26; *Gray v Johnston* (1868) LR 3 HL
1, on the second; and see also *John Shaw (Rayners Lane) Ltd v Lloyds Bank Ltd* (1945) 5
LDAB 396, and *Banque Commerciale Arabe SA v Republique Algerienne Democratique et
Populaire* [1974] 2 BGE 200.
8 *Selangor United Rubber Estates Ltd v Cradock (a bankrupt) (No 3)* [1968] 2 All Er 1073,
[1968] 1 WLR 1555.
9 *Karak Rubber Co Ltd v Burden (No 2)* [1972] 1 All ER 1210, [1972] 1 WLR 602.
10 [1965] 2 All ER 972, [1965] 1 WLR 1165.
11 [1986] AC 80, [1985] 2 All ER 947, PC. The numerous authorities (both English and foreign)
for and against this proposition of law can be found in the report of counsels' submissions

The importance of this ruling is readily appreciated from the facts of *Tai Hing* itself.[12] The plaintiff company maintained with each of the three defendant banks a current account. The banks honoured by payment on presentation some 300 cheques totalling approximately HK$5.5 million which on their face appeared to have been drawn by the company and to bear the signature of Mr Chen, the company's managing director, who was one of the authorised signatories to its cheques. The banks in each instance debited the company's current account with the amount of the cheque. The cheques, however, were not the company's cheques. They were forgeries. On each the signature of Mr Chen had been forged by an accounts clerk. Upon discovery of the fraud, the company brought proceedings for a declaration that the banks were not entitled to debit its accounts with the amount of the forged cheques. On appeal there was no challenge to the finding of the trial judge that, if there existed a duty to check bank statements, the company was in breach of that obligation.[13]

The banks relied upon breach of the alleged duty in support of three defences, namely: (1) set-off; (2) estoppel by negligence; and (3) estoppel by representation. In the Hong Kong Court of Appeal, the banks succeeded on (1) and (3) above, with the consequence that they emerged with total success. On appeal, as already stated, the Privy Council held against the banks on the alleged duty to check bank statements, so that there was no liability of the customer available for set-off against the liability of the banks. It was further held that as the company was not in breach of any duty owed to the banks, it was not possible to establish an estoppel from the company's mere silence and failure to act.[14] The reasoning by which an estoppel was rejected is clearly of general application.

(d) Bank statements not an account stated in absence of express agreement

(i) Nature and relevance of an account stated

Challenges by customers to entries in bank statements tend to arise in one of two situations. In the first, the customer challenges the accuracy of an entry. For example, he may dispute that any payment was in fact made such as to justify a particular debit entry. This situation arose in acute form in the wake of the dispute between certain American and Iranian banks following the Iranian hostage crisis in 1979–1980. In the unwinding of formerly close and complex banking relationships, certain Iranian banks sought explanation and justification of debit entries in their accounts going back several years. In the second situation, of which *Tai Hing* is in example, the dispute is not whether a debit entry reflects an actual payment, but whether the bank is entitled to debit the account at all.

In both situations the question arises whether there is an account stated. In the strict sense of the term, an account stated describes the position where

---

in *Tai Hing* [1986] AC 80 at 86–96. In *Canadian Pacific Hotels Ltd v Bank of Montreal* (1987) 40 DLR (4th) 385, the Supreme Court of Canada, having considered *Tai Hing*, came to the same conclusion.

12 This statement of facts is taken from the judgment of Lord Scarman at [1986] AC 80 at 97A, [1985] 2 All ER 947 at 949h.

13 [1986] AC 80 at 103A, [1985] 2 All ER 954c.

14 Mere silence or inaction cannot amount to a representation unless there exists a duty to disclose or act: *Greenwood v Martins Bank* [1933] AC 51, HL.

an account contains items both of credit and debit, and the figures are adjusted between the parties and a balance struck.[15] In *Laycock v Pickles*,[16] Blackburn J explained that the consideration for the payment of the balance is the discharge of the items on each side, and continued:

> 'It is then the same as if each item was paid and a discharge given for each, and in consideration of that discharge the balance was agreed to be due.'

(ii) No account stated in absence of express agreement

There being no duty on the part of the customer to check his statements, a fortiori the continued payment in and withdrawal of monies from a current account after the receipt of a bank statement does not constitute the customer's agreement, express or implied, to the balance shown on the statement. In no sense can it be said that a balance is struck between the parties.

(iii) Conclusive evidence clauses

It is, of course, always open to a bank to refuse to do business save upon express terms which incorporate an account stated provision. Such provisions have come to be called conclusive evidence clauses.

Although reliance upon a conclusive evidence clause can be forensically unattractive, there is a clear authority that, as a matter of principle, such a provision is binding according to its terms. This authority is *Bache & Co (London) Ltd v Banque Vernes et Commerciale de Paris SA*,[17] applying a decision of the High Court of Australia, *Dobbs v National Bank of Australasia Ltd*.[18] In both cases, a conclusive evidence clause was claimed to be contrary to public policy as tending to oust the jurisdiction of the court and in both, the submission was rejected. However, both cases involved claims against guarantors, and as was observed by all three members of the Court of Appeal in the *Bache* case, the decision did not lead to any injustice because if the figure certified to be due was erroneous, it was always open to the principal debtor to have it corrected by instituting proceedings against the creditor.

Support for the validity of conclusive evidence clauses can also be found in *Tai Hing*, supra, where the defendant banks relied upon printed terms and conditions pursuant to which the company's current accounts were operated. The relevant terms, and the facts relating to the three accounts, were as follows:

A. CHEKIANG FIRST BANK LTD

The bank's terms provided:

> 'A monthly statement for each account will be sent by the bank to the depositor by post or messenger and the balance shown therein may be deemed to be correct by the bank if the depositor does not notify the bank in writing of any error therein within 10 days after the sending of such statement ...'

---

15 See *Camillo Tank Steamship Co Ltd v Alexandria Engineering Works* (1921) 38 TLR 134 per Viscount Cave at 143; *Siqueira v Noronha* [1934] AC 332 per Lord Atkin at 337.
16 (1863) 4 B&S 497, cited with approval by Lord Atkin in *Siqueira v Noronha* [1934] AC 332 at 338.
17 [1973] 2 Lloyd's Rep 437, CA.
18 (1935) 53 CLR 643.

The company returned, upon receipt of its periodic bank statement, a confirmation slip signed by two authorised signatories. No cleared cheques were ever returned to the company.

B. BANK OF TOKYO LTD

The bank's terms provided:

'The bank's statement of my/our current account will be confirmed by me/us without delay. In case of absence of such confirmation within a fortnight, the bank may take the said statement as approved by me/us.'

Periodic bank statements were rendered by the bank, but cleared cheques were not returned. No bank statement relevant to the case was ever confirmed by the company.

C. LIU CHONG HING BANK LTD

The bank's terms provided:

'A statement of the customer's account will be rendered once a month. Customers are desired: (1) to examine all entries in the statement of account and to report at once to the bank any error found therein, (2) to return the confirmation slip duly signed. In the absence of any objection to the statement within seven days after its receipt by the customer, the account shall be deemed to have been confirmed.'

The bank never did send any confirmation slips to the company; nor did it return cleared cheques. The company never sent the bank any confirmation slip.

It was held by the Privy Council that none of the above contractual terms constituted a conclusive evidence clause. They were not such as to bring home to the customer either the intended importance of the inspection it was being invited to make or that they were intended to have conclusive effect if no query was raised on the bank statements. In the words of Lord Scarman, delivering the judgment of the Privy Council:[19]

'If banks wish to impose upon their customers an express obligation to examine their monthly statements and to make those statements, in the absence of query, unchallengeable by the customer after expiry of a time limit, the burden of the objection and of the sanction imposed must be brought home to the customer. In their Lordships' view the provisions which they have set out above do not meet this undoubtedly rigorous test. The test is rigorous because the bankers would have their terms of business so construed as to exclude the rights which the customer would enjoy if they were not excluded by express agreement. It must be borne in mind that, in their Lordships' view, the true nature of the obligations of the customer to his bank where there is not express agreement is limited to the *Macmillan* and *Greenwood* duties. Clear and unambiguous provision is needed if the banks are to introduce into the contract a binding obligation upon the customer who does not query his bank statement to accept the statement as accurately setting out the debit items in the accounts.'

The *Macmillan* and *Greenwood* duties are explained in ch 12, post.

19 [1986] AC 80 at 110A, [1985] 2 All ER 947 at 959d. See also *Stewart v Royal Bank of Canada* [1930] 4 DLR 694; *Keech v Canadian Bank of Commerce* [1938] 2 WWR 291; *B and G Construction Co Ltd v Bank of Montreal* (1954) 2 DLR 753; *Arrow Transfer Co Ltd v Royal Bank of Canada* [1971] 3 WWR 241.

(e) The pass book as an account stated

The pass book has long been replaced by loose-leaf bank statements. The essential difference is that bank statements are not intended to be returned to the bank. The original characteristic of the pass book, the passing to and fro, is therefore absent. In *Blackburn Building Society v Cunliffe, Brooks & Co*,[20] Lord Selborne spoke of this 'passing to and fro', and most of the earlier cases contemplated it. It was mainly this feature which lent colour to the argument that a pass book is an account stated.

The question whether a pass book constitutes an account stated is one on which there is extensive authority and learning. The matter has deservedly been given full consideration in previous editions of *Paget*.[1] However, in modern banking practice the point is essentially academic because pass books are no longer used. For this reason the matter is touched on only briefly.

There are two points still worthy of note. First, in law there undoubtedly can be an account stated between banker and customer. The point was put by Lord Wright in *Bishun Chand Firm v Seth Girdhari Lal*:[2]

'It has not been doubted that in law there can be a settled or stated account between banker and customer; what has been questioned is whether the acceptance by the customer without protest of a balance struck in the pass book constitutes a settled account, but the question has had reference merely to the issue whether such a settlement can be inferred as a matter of fact from the passing backward and forward of the pass book. The legal competence of such a settlement, if more, is not questioned.'

Secondly, the account stated principle cannot bind a customer to a borrowing beyond its capacity. In *Blackburn Building Society v Cunliffe Brooks & Co*, a building society borrowed ultra vires. In the Court of Appeal, Lord Selbourne LC, delivering the judgment of the court, said:[3]

'Nor can they (the bankers) have the benefit of the doctrine that a pass book passing to and fro is evidence of a stated and settled account; because, if the directors of this society could not borrow money, they could not ratify an illegal borrowing simply by returning a pass book.'

(f) Credits made in error

It was noted above that one of the situations which can give rise to an issue whether there is an account stated is where the customer challenges a long-standing debit to his account. The inverse situation is that where the bank claims reversal of a credit made in error to an account, or the repayment of monies paid in reliance upon such a credit. This situation is especially likely to arise if an account is mistakenly credited with the same sum twice over. The problem is essentially one of the recovery of money paid under a mistake of fact, and is considered in that context (ch 25, post). It may be noted at this point: (1) that the principle of account stated appears not to extend to an

---

20 (1882) 22 Ch D 61. In *Devaynes v Noble, Clayton's Case* (1816) 1 Mer 529, the Court of Chancery directed an inquiry into the nature and effect of a pass book. The report, at 535–537, was accepted by the Court (at 610). It appears from the report that even at that date there existed a practice of sending out statements of account to customers 'resident at a distance from the metropolis'.
1 See *Paget's Law of Banking* (9th edn) pp 104–111.
2 (1934) 50 TLR 465 at 468–449, PC.
3 (1882) 22 Ch D 61 at 72.

obvious clerical error, the bank being prima facie entitled to reverse a credit made in error if it has not been acted upon; but (2) that a bank is not entitled to dishonour cheques drawn bona fide and without negligence on the faith of an incorrect entry.

In *Holland v Manchester and Liverpool District Banking Co Ltd*[4] the plaintiff, a customer of the defendant bank, finding on examining his pass book that it showed a balance of £70 17s 9d in his favour, drew a cheque for £67 11s in favour of a firm to whom he owed that amount. On the cheque being presented by that firm, it was dishonoured by the defendants, as a result of which the plaintiff suffered damage, in respect of which he sued the defendants. From the evidence it appeared that at the time the plaintiff drew the cheque for £67 11s he had a balance at the bank of £60 5s 9d only, but that in his passbook one of the bank clerks had, in error, entered to the plaintiff's credit a sum of £10 12s twice, with the result that from the pass book the plaintiff appeared to be in credit to the amount of £70 17s 9d. Lord Alverstone CJ said that the bank had the right to have the entry subsequently corrected but not to dishonour cheques drawn on the faith of it so long as it remained uncorrected, and awarded damages for dishonour of such cheque. The pass book was prima facie evidence against the bank, on which the customer, in the absence of negligence or fraud on his part, was entitled to rely; and the learned judge found support for this view in the judgment of Lord Campbell LC in *Commercial Bank of Scotland v Rhind* where he said:[5]

'It would indeed be a reproach of the law of Scotland, if, there being satisfactory evidence that, by the mistake of a clerk, there had been in the pass book a double entry of the same sum to the credit of the respondent, the mistake could in no way be shown by the bank, and if he were entitled fraudulently to extort from them £80 beyond the amount of what is justly due to him.'

(g) Rights of third parties to trace monies into a bank account

(i) Tracing in general

It was at one time thought that once money had reached the hands of a banker or broker, it was absolutely merged, not traceable, and so not recoverable, whatever might be the claimant's rights against the customer. And the idea reappears in the doctrine of the appropriation of payments, by which earlier payments out are attributed to earlier payments in, possibly wiping out the impugned items (the rule in *Clayton's Case*[6]). It is obvious that these principles, if pushed to extremes, would work injustice. One of the injurious tendencies of the rule in *Clayton's Case* was neutralised in *Re Hallett's Estate, Knatchbull v Hallett*,[7] by the adoption of the charitable legal fiction that where a trustee or other person in a fiduciary capacity has paid trust money into his own private account there is a presumption that when he draws for his own use he draws his own rather than trust moneys, the rule in *Clayton's Case* not applying, and that any balance left is available to answer the trust.

---

4 (1909) 25 TLR 386, 14 Com Cas 241.
5 (1860) 3 Macq 643 at 648.
6 *Devaynes v Noble, Clayton's Case* (1816) 1 Mer 529 at 572.
7 (1880) 13 Ch D 696 (Jessel MR and Baggallay LJ, Thesiger LJ dissenting); see also *Sinclair v Brougham* [1914] AC 398, HL; *Re Diplock, Diplock v Wintle* [1948] Ch 465, [1948] 2 All ER 318.

But where the moneys of more than one person have been wrongfully mixed in a private current account the rule in *Clayton's Case* does apply as between two or more *cestuis que trust*.[8]

An early recognition of a right to trace monies into a bank account was the prerogative of the Crown in following Crown moneys into the accounts of persons into whose hands they came. In its broadest aspect, as laid down by Lord Lyndhurst in *R v Wrangham*,[9] any such person becomes at once a debtor to the Crown in respect of such moneys, whether he knew them to be Crown moneys or not; but the rule, at any rate as regards bankers, is probably confined to cases where the banker knew or ought to have known that the moneys were in fact Crown moneys.[10] In such cases the banker might even be liable to replace money already drawn out by the customer, unless the customer was authorised to pass the money to his private account.[11]

It is now firmly established that so long as money is traceable either in specie or in its proceeds or investment, equity will follow and lay hold of it, under what is known as a tracing order, for the benefit of the person who had been defrauded of it, parted with it under mistake of fact, or is otherwise rightfully entitled to it.

This procedure enables relief to be given in many cases where the narrower form of action for money had and received would fail. It is fully expounded by the House of Lords in *Sinclair v Brougham*,[12] and in a review of the authorities with 'exhaustive accuracy' by the Court of Appeal in *Re Diplock, Diplock v Wintle*.[13] Its operation is further exemplified and shown to affect money in the hands of a banker by *Banque Belge pour l'Etranger v Hambrouck*.[14] There a cheque had been obtained by fraud, the proceeds thereof subsequently transferred to a third person for no legal consideration, and by that person paid into a bank. The bank paid the money into court, and the question was between the defrauded party and the transferee of the proceeds. The Court of Appeal, adopting the line laid down in *Sinclair v Brougham*, held that the transferee could have no better title to the money than the fraudulent transferor had. They said that there was no immunity for bank accounts and that, if traceable, the money could have been followed into the bank. The rule in *Hallett's* case was introduced to meet cases where the money was not identifiable, because merged in the bank's assets. Atkin LJ said in *Banque Belge pour l'Etranger v Hambrouck*:[15]

'The case of *In Re Hallett's Estate* makes it plain that the court will investigate a banking account into which another person's money has been wrongfully paid, and will impute all drawings out of the account in the first instance to the wrongdoer's own moneys, leaving the plaintiff's money intact so far as it remains in the account at all.'

8 Per Fry J in *Re Hallett's Estate, Knatchbull v Hallett* (1880) 13 Ch D 696; *Re Stenning, Wood v Stenning* [1895] 2 Ch 433.
9 (1831) 1 Cr & J 408.
10 *Re West London Commercial Bank* (1888) 38 Ch D 364.
11 Ibid.
12 [1914] AC 398, in which Viscount Haldane LC, stated that where the receipt of money was ultra vires, it could only be recovered by an action in rem and not in personam for money had and received.
13 [1948] Ch 465, [1948] 2 All ER 318; and see Lord Simmonds in *Ministry of Health v Simpson* [1951] AC 251, [1950] 2 All ER 1137.
14 [1921] 1 KB 321.
15 [1921] 1 KB 321 at 333, 335.

And again:

'The question always was, Had the means of ascertainment failed? But if in 1815 the common law halted outside the banker's door, by 1879 equity had had the courage to lift the latch, walk in and examine the books: *In Re Hallett's Estate*. I see no reason why the means of ascertainment so provided should not now be available both for common law and equity proceedings ... the plaintiffs have the common law right to claim it [the money in the bank] and can sue for money had and received.'

These comments of Atkin LJ were approved by the Court of Appeal in *Re Diplock, Diplock v Wintle*:

'If it is possible to identify a principal's money with an asset purchased exclusively by means of it, we see no reason for drawing a distinction between a chose in action such as a banker's debt to his customer and any other asset.'

It is not the duty or interest of a banker to decide between conflicting claims to money in his hands; the course adopted in the above case, of obtaining the protection of the court and leaving the interested parties to fight the matter out, is obviously the wise one to pursue.[16]

(ii) Tracing money paid by mistake

The circumstances in which a person is entitled to recover monies paid under a mistake of fact are considered in ch 25, post. Where a right of recovery exists, the relation of banker and customer will not enable the banker to hold it against the person who paid it in, unless the banker received it as agent and has altered his position before he discovers or has notice of the mistake.[17] Where a banker pays over as an agent, it is immaterial that he is under a misapprehension as to the identity of his principal,[18] but the payment must be a real alteration of position.[19] Merely putting money to reduction of an overdraft is not sufficient unless it engenders or is accompanied by a forbearance to require repayment of the balance; making further advances on the strength of it probably would be.[20] There is no question of set-off; as Bailhache J said in *Scottish Metropolitan Assurance Co v P Samuel & Co*,[1] lien (sic) only affects the customer's money, which money paid to his account by mistake of fact is not.

In the case of *Admiralty Comrs v National Provincial and Union Bank of England Ltd*,[2] the plaintiff had made 22 monthly payments totalling £440 into the account of a former naval officer in the mistaken belief that he was still alive. The defendant bank had a balance remaining in its hands of some £417. The bank refused repayment on the ground that the legal personal representative of the customer had not been joined, with the consequence that the bank was liable to be sued over again. This defence was rejected,

16 See in this connection, *Fontaine-Besson v Parr's Banking Co and Alliance Bank Ltd* (1895) 12 TLR 121, CA.
17 *Admiralty Comrs v National Provincial and Union Bank of England Ltd* (1922) 127 LT 452.
18 *Gowers v Lloyds and National Provincial Foreign Bank Ltd* [1937] 3 All ER 55.
19 *Buller v Harrison* (1777) 2 Cowp 565; *Bavins Jnr and Sims v London and South Western Bank Ltd* [1900] 1 QB 270, 5 Com Cas 1.
20 Cf *Kleinwot, Sons & Co v Dunlop Rubber Co* (1907) 97 LT 263; *Kerrison v Glyn, Mills, Currie & Co* (1911) 81 LJKB 465.
1 [1923] 1 KB 348.
2 (1922) 127 LT 452.

and the bank was ordered to repay the £417. *Joachimson v Swiss Bank Corpn*[3] was cited for the defendants, but Sargant J said:

> 'The case of *Joachimson* has nothing to do with it. That only refers to the ordinary relation of banker and customer; the undertaking to honour cheques does not extend to amounts standing to the credit of current account if and so far as it was swollen by an inadvertent payment in mistake of fact.'

This view would appear to be supported by the decision of MacKenna J in *United Overseas Bank v Jiwani*[4] in which the bank by mistake credited the defendant's account twice. The learned judge held that if the defendant had been misled (which he had not), the bank would have been estopped from reclaiming the money if the defendant had so changed his position as the result of the crediting that it would be inequitable to require him to repay. In *Steam Saw Mills Co v Baring Bros & Co*,[5] money had been paid by the plaintiffs into the bank in the belief that the then Russian Government would pay the rouble equivalent to the exporters in Russia, which belief was confounded when the Russian Government was overthrown in 1917. The Court of Appeal held that the bank could keep the money but must undertake not to part with it without notice to the plaintiffs and without an order of the court, there having been no failure of consideration between the plaintiffs and the Russian Government, which was not represented.

(iii) Other circumstances giving rise to a tracing claim

Other circumstances in which moneys which have wrongfully found their way into the banker's hands may be reclaimed, include moneys collected for a wrongful holder of cheques and trust moneys mixed with non-trust moneys. The latter circumstance may include the payment into a buyer's account of the proceeds of a sub-sale where the original seller has, by virtue of a suitably drafted *Romalpa* clause,[6] title to such proceeds. In such cases the question is how far the seller may trace into a bank account on the ground that there is a trust relationship between the parties to the contract of sale, which would entail that part of the proceeds would represent trust moneys. It is submitted that until the banker has notice he cannot in any event be put upon inquiry and may deal with the account in the ordinary way; he may be put upon notice where the original seller asserts that part of the buyers' balance consists of moneys in which the seller has an interest.

As to freezing orders in aid of tracing claims, see ch 19, post.

(h) Assignment of credit balance

(i) Assignment of whole balance

Normally a credit balance on current account is as readily transferred by cheque as by assignment; it is only when what is to be transferred is not readily available, such as moneys on 'time' or 'notice' deposit, that the issue of a cheque is unavailing unless it is post-dated. Generally in these circumstances an assignment pursuant to the Law of Property Act 1925,

---

3 [1921] 3 KB 110, CA.
4 [1977] 1 All ER 733, [1976] 1 WLR 964.
5 [1922] 1 Ch 244 and *Archangel Saw Mills Co v Baring Bros & Co* [1922] 1 Ch 244.
6 See *Aluminium Industrie Vaassen BV v Romalpa Aluminium Ltd* [1976] 2 All ER 552, [1976] 1 WLR 676, CA.

s. 136 is the method of transfer. A cheque does not operate as an assignment of the sum for which it is drawn.[7]

In *Walker v Bradford Old Bank Ltd,*[8] the court held that the ordinary relation of debtor and creditor existed between the customer and his banker and consequently that moneys then or thereafter standing to the customer's credit were an accruing debt arising out of contract which was assignable under the Judicature Act. In *Schroeder v Central Bank of London Ltd,*[9] it was contended that a cheque operated as an assignment of the amount of the credit balance it represented. The contrary is, of course, settled by s 53(1) of the Bills of Exchange Act 1882. Brett J held that there was no debt on which any action against the banker could be founded until a sum was demanded and that, when the cheque was drawn, there was no debt which could be assigned, and consequently there could be no debt owing by the banker to the assignee. On this basis it might be argued that there can be no assignment of a current account balance, there begin no assignable debt till after demand. But the debt exists even though it is not enforceable and if, as laid down in the *Joachimson* case, a writ is a sufficient demand, this would seem to dispose of any difficulty. The assignment, if absolute and not by way of charge only, transfers all the assignor's rights to the assignee,[10] and this must include the right to demand payment.

As to the effect of assignment on rights of set-off, see ch 31, post.

(ii) Assignment of part

P. O. Lawrence J in *Re Steel Wing Co Ltd*[11] reviewed the cases on the assignment of part of a debt. He pointed out that in *Skipper and Tucker v Holloway and Howard*[12] Darling J held that part of a debt could be assigned under s. 25(6) of the Judicature Act 1873, but that in *Forster v Baker,*[13] Bray J dissented, holding that that subsection was not applicable on the ground that if it were:

> 'the consequence is that the assignee is able to sue the debtor without joining the assignor or the assignee of the other part of the debt, if there have been two assignments; and it might happen that if the debt had been split up into two, three or four parts, there might be two, three or four actions with different results. All sorts of difficulties would arise, and a great burden, an unnecessarily great burden, would be placed upon the debtor.'

P O Lawrence J further stated that in *Conlan v Carlow County Council*[14] Gibson and Boyd JJ concurred in the view of Bray J in *Forster v Baker.*[15] He

---

7 Bills of Exchange Act 1882, s 53(1).
8 (1884) 12 QBD 511, applied in *Bank of Nova Scotia and Diversified Industrial Services Ltd v Royal Bank of Canada* [1975] 5 WWR 610 – money in second bank account a book debt for purposes of an assignment of book debts.
9 (1876) 34 LT 735.
10 See *Hughes v Pump House Hotel Co* [1902] 2 KB 190.
11 [1921] 1 Ch 349.
12 [1910] 2 KB 630; the judgment was reversed by the Court of Appeal on the facts, but the point as to assignment was not decided.
13 [1910] 2 KB 636; observation of Bray J applied in *Green v Berliner* [1936] 2 KB 477, [1936] 1 All ER 199; in *Durham Bros v Robertson* [1898] 1 QB 765 and *Hughes v Pump House Hotel Co* [1902] 2 KB 190; the Court of Appeal gave no decision on the point.
14 [1912] 2 IR 535.
15 [1910] 2 KB 636.

also agreed with Bray J but held that such assignment operates in equity to transfer the part assigned and consequently constitutes the assignee a creditor in equity, who could not make an effective demand for payment without joining the assignor. In *Bank of Liverpool and Martins Ltd v Holland*[16] an assignment of debt for £285 included a promise that 'the amount recoverable ... shall not at any time exceed £150'. Wright J held that the assignment was an absolute legal assignment of the whole debt but that if the bank should recover more than the amount assigned they must hold the balance as trustees for the assignor. But, as he further stated, following *Re Steel Wing Co Ltd*, even if it were an assignment of part only it would still be a good equitable assignment. The point was considered by the Court of Appeal in *Williams v Atlantic Assurance Co Ltd*.[17] Greer LJ was the only member of the court to express an opinion and he held that an assignee of part of a debt was merely an equitable assignee.

> 'and at any rate, unless the equitable assignment be accompanied by a power to give a discharge, it is impossible for the assignee to succeed unless he sues in the name of the assignor.'

He referred to the assignment in *William Brandt's Sons & Co v Dunlop Rubber Co*[18] as 'giving the power to give a perfectly good receipt'. The decision of the Court of Appeal in *Walter and Sullivan Ltd v J Murphy & Sons Ltd*[19] – in which the assignment took the form of an irrevocable authority to pay the assignee, as in *Re Kent and Sussex Sawmills Ltd*,[20] is to the effect that an equitable assignor of part of a debt cannot sue without joining the assignee, s. 136 of the Law of Property Act 1925 not applying. If this is the case, then neither the 'payee' nor any transferee of an order for payment not being a cheque, such as a conditional order, can, without joining the drawer in the action, sue the drawee banker in respect of that part of the drawer's current account balance which is represented by the order.[1]

(i) Overdraft

(i) Nature of an overdraft

An overdraft is money lent: 'a payment by a bank under an arrangement by which the customer may overdraw is a lending by the bank to the customer of the money'.[2] A banker is obliged to let his customer overdraw only if he has agreed to do so or such agreement can be inferred from a course of business;[3] borrowing and lending are a matter of contract, express or implied.

An overdraft is repayable on demand and forms of charge over security

---

16 (1926) 43 TLR 29, 32 Com Cas 56.
17 [1933] 1 KB 81; and see *Re Griffin, Griffin v Griffin* [1899] 1 Ch 408.
18 [1905] AC 454.
19 [1955] 2 QB 584, [1955] 1 All ER 843, following *Re Steel Wing Co Ltd* [1921] 1 Ch 349.
20 [1947] Ch 177, [1946] 2 All ER 638.
 1 Bills of Exchange Act 1882, s 53.
 2 Per Harman J in *Re Hone (a bankrupt), ex p Trustee v Kensington Borough Council* [1951] Ch 85 at 89, [1950] 2 All ER 716 at 719.
 3 *Brooks & Co v Blackburn Benefit Society* (1884) 9 App Cas 857 at 864; *Cumming v Shand* (1860) 5 H & N 95 (course of business).

invariably provide accordingly.[4] Nevertheless the right to repayment on demand should be exercised so as not unduly to prejudice the borrower's interests, in the shape, for example, of outstanding cheques drawn in the belief that the facility was available, even if the limit of overdraft has already been reached.[5] There are clearly conflicting interests but, providing the banker is in possession of a document by which the customer agreed to repay on demand, the banker would normally be entitled to take any action necessary to safeguard his interests, even if it prejudiced those of his borrower.

The drawing a cheque or the accepting a bill payable at the bank, when the drawer knows that there are not sufficient funds in the account to meet it, may be taken as a request for an overdraft and also when the drawer is not, as he should normally be, aware of the lack of funds.

Some banks when lending for a specific period (a term loan) pursuant to a facility letter setting out the terms of the contract of loan provide either in the facility letter or in their security documents that the loan shall be repayable on demand. It is submitted that in the event of such conflicting provisions, if there is no breach by the borrower of the conditions on which the loan was granted, the provision for a term loan would take precedence. The right to repayment on demand is repugnant to the main object of the transaction.[6] In short, where a banker agrees to lend for a specific period, that agreement cannot, unless there is a breach by the borrower, be terminated by the bank purely on the strength of its alleged right to repayment on demand or on the strength of such a right given in its standard security document.

(ii) Interest

The subject of interest is considered in detail in chapter 14, post. In the present context it need only be noted that the customer is liable for interest on an overdraft from the moment it accrues and probably whether the interest is in effect compound or not. The effect of the practice of bankers in debiting interest to an overdrawn current account periodically and thereby increasing the capital sum was considered in *Yourell v Hibernian Bank Ltd*[7] in which Lord Atkinson said:

4 In *Titford Property Co v Cannon Street Acceptances Ltd* (1975) 22 May (unreported), Goff J said that an ordinary overdraft can be called in at any time; and see *Cripps v Wickenden* [1973] 2 All ER 606, [1973] 1 WLR 944.

5 On this subject the difficulty is, perhaps, illustrated by the judgment of Gibson J in *Williams and Glyn's Bank Ltd v Barnes* [1981] Com LR 205. The point seems not hitherto to have been judicially considered. The learned judge said:

'There is an obligation upon the bank to honour cheques drawn within the agreed limit of an overdraft facility and presented before any demand for payment or notice to terminate a facility has been given. That obligation, however, does not by itself require any period of notice beyond the simple demand. The bank may, by the contract, be required to honour cheques drawn within the agreed facility before the demand for repayment or notice to terminate but still be free to require payment by the customer of any sums previously lent, which will be increased by any further cheques which the bank must honour'.

See also *Johnston v Commercial Bank of Scotland* 1858 20 D 790; *Buckingham & Co v London and Midland Bank* (1895) 12 TLR 70.

6 See *Titford Property Co Ltd v Cannon Street Acceptances* (1975) unreported (Goff J); and see also the cases on fundamental breach culminating in *Photo Production Ltd v Securicor Transport Ltd* [1980] AC 827, [1980] 1 All ER 556.

7 [1918] AC 372.

'The bank, by taking the account with these half-yearly rests, secured for itself the benefit of compound interest. This is a usual and perfectly legitimate mode of dealing between banker and customer.'

Where the overdraft fluctuates considerably it may well be that the interest debited one day is paid by the operation of the rule in *Clayton's Case*[8] as applied to the account.

(j) Management charges and commissions

Bankers have been held entitled to recover management charges and commissions by the customer's acquiescence in the debiting thereof to an account. An example is *Spencer v Wakefield*,[9] where a customer was held liable for commissions on the ground that he had acquiesced in the charging thereof at each half-yearly rest on his account.

As is explained more fully in ch 14, post, acquiescence became entrenched in the law's analysis of the banker's rights in relation to entries in bank accounts as part of a fiction adopted to circumvent the usury laws before their repeal in 1854. Whether acquiescence in the sense of mere silence would today create an entitlement to management charges and commissions is considered doubtful, especially in the light of the fact that the customer is under no obligation to examine his bank statements. It is thought that a right to management charges and commissions must rest today on express or implied agreement, or the custom and usage of bankers, which custom and usage would have to be proved if disputed. Evidence was adduced in *Spencer v Wakefield* of the custom and usage of bankers in the north of England, but in the event the case was decided solely on the basis of the customer's acquiescence.

2 DEPOSIT ACCOUNTS

(a) Classes and nature of deposit accounts

Deposit accounts are normally one of three classes:

1 repayable at call or on demand;
2 withdrawable on specified notice;
3 for a fixed period.

The customer has no right to draw cheques against a deposit account of class 2 or 3, and probably not against a deposit account of class 1 although in *Hopkins v Abbott*,[10] and also in *Stein v Ritherdon*,[11] Mallins V-C expressed the view that a deposit account at call was liable to be drawn on by cheque. But the obligation to honour cheques is only part of the contract implied between banker and customer, and nowhere else has this ever been recognised as extending beyond the current account. It is clearly not contemplated in

---

8 *Devaynes v Noble, Clayton's Case* (1816) 1 Mer 529 at 572, applied in *Siebe Gorman & Co v Barclays Bank Ltd* [1979] 2 Lloyd's Rep 142.
9 (1887) 4 TLR 194.
10 (1875) LR 19 Eq 222 at 228.
11 (1868) 37 LJ Ch 369.

the summary of the banker's contractual duties by Atkin LJ in *Joachimson v Swiss Bank Corpn*.[12]

Where a depositor wishes to withdraw without waiting for the expiry of the agreed period of notice, it is usual to allow him to do so. He has no right to break the deposit contract; where this happens often a course of business may be established binding the banker and precluding his right to regard the balance as unavailable to the depositor. A course of business may also be established if the banker pays cheques drawn against the deposit balance.

Money paid into a deposit account is a loan to the banker, not a specific fund held by him in a fiduciary capacity.[13]

The account is one continuing contract; there is not a new contract every time money is paid in,[14] except where the fresh deposit is made the subject of a fresh contract.

An overdrawn deposit account cannot exist at law.[15]

A distinguishing feature between deposit and current account is that the former may be subject to a condition precedent to the withdrawal of the money, in which case the money is not withdrawable and there is no cause of action until the condition is complied with.[16] In *Re Tidd, Tidd v Overell*[17] North J appeared to understand Lord Esher's words in *Atkinson v Bradford Third Equitable Benefit Building Society*[18] as pointing to the necessity for the return of the receipt before the deposit could be withdrawn. The fact that a bank could not refuse to pay in the event of the receipt being lost, alluded to in *Re Dillon, Duffin v Duffin*,[19] does not affect the question, being merely an example of the exercise of the equitable jurisdiction with respect to lost instruments.[20]

(b) Deposit books and receipts

The Court of Appeal in *Birch v Treasury Solicitor*[1] held deposit *books* (rarely to be found in England today) to be 'the essential indicia of title'

'and its delivery a transfer of the chose in action to found a good *donatio mortis causa*.'

How far the depositor, by dealing with the deposit *receipt* (also rarely to be found in England to-day), may entitle a person to claim the money from the bank, or debar himself from disputing a payment thereon, is not very clear.

12 [1921] 3 KB 110 at 127.
13 *Pearce v Creswick* (1843) 2 Hare 286; cf *Re Head, Head v Head* [1893] 3 Ch 426; *Re Head, Head v Head (No 2)* [1894] 2 Ch 236; and see Lord Atkin in *Akbar Khan v Attar Singh* [1936] 2 All ER 545 at 548, PC. The remarks of North J in *Re Tidd, Tidd v Overell* [1893] 3 Ch 154 at 156 are somewhat ambiguous, but are insufficient to establish any fiduciary relation.
14 Per Lord Goddard CJ, in *Hart v Sangster* [1957] 1 Ch 329, [1957] 2 All ER 208.
15 Per Mocatta J in *Barclays Bank Ltd v Okenarhe* [1966] 2 Lloyd's Rep 87.
16 *Re Dillon, Duffin v Duffin* (1890) 44 Ch D 76, per Cotton LJ at 81.
17 [1893] 3 Ch 154 at 157.
18 (1890) 25 QBD 377.
19 (1890) 44 Ch D 76, per Cotton LJ at 81.
20 See *Pearce v Creswick* (1843) 2 Hare 286.
1 [1951] Ch 298, [1950] 2 All ER 1198.

A deposit receipt, per se, is not negotiable or even transferable.[2] The money deposited is a debt or chose in action assignable like any other, independent of the receipt and despite any restriction on the transferability of that receipt. As shown by *Re Griffin, Griffin v Griffin*,[3] even the receipt itself may be utilised as the basis of an equitable assignment. The same has been held where the receipt was indorsed 'Pay my son'. It makes no difference whether the debt is repayable at notice or at a fixed date, or that it cannot be claimed without returning the receipt. It is always there; always a chose in action, with the attributes of such, including assignability. There is no enforceable debt till the return of the receipt, no immediate cause of action, but the banker is not entitled to refuse to accept the receipt from an assignee. In *Woodhams v Anglo-Australian and Universal Family Assurance Society*,[4] Stuart V-C held that a deposit receipt passed by delivery and required no assignment, and upheld a direct claim against the company by a third party on a receipt of delivery, free from any set-off against the original depositor. In *Re Griffin, Griffin v Griffin*,[5] indorsement and delivery of a deposit note was held to consitute a good equitable assignment, notwithstanding the fact that the receipt bore in two places the words 'This receipt is not transferable.'

If the bank were to issue deposit receipts in a form inviting or authorising transfer, it would probably be estopped from disputing their transferability and power to carry the deposit. If payable to bearer on demand, such receipt would probably constitute an infringement of the Bank Charter Act 1844.

But payment to a third party on any form of deposit receipt alone is open to risk.[6] The mere possession of the deposit receipt, even indorsed by the depositor, is not conclusive evidence of an equitable assignment. Possession is consistent with circumstances other than intentional assignment, in which case payment to the holder would not necessarily discharge the bank from liability to the depositor.[7] A valid equitable assignment would, however, apparently constitute a good defence against a subsequent claim by the depositor.[8] A deposit receipt not being a negotiable instrument, if the depositor has lost the receipt the bank is not entitled to an indemnity from the depositor before paying him (in the absence of notice of assignment).

3   JOINT ACCOUNTS

(a) Privity of contract between bank and each joint account holder

In modern banking practice, it will normally be clear from the account mandate form that the bank is in privity of contract with each joint account holder. The question of privity has in the past arisen where there is no signed mandate form and the account is opened by a deposit made by one of the named account holders. The position arising from the deposit by one person of money on joint account was fully discussed in *McEvoy v Belfast Banking*

---

2 *Cochrane v O'Brien* (1845) 8 1 Eq R 241; *Moore v Ulster Banking Co* (1877) IR 11 CL 512; *Re Dillon, Duffin v Duffin* (1890) 44 Ch D 76; *Pearce v Creswick* (1843) 2 Hare 286.
3 [1899] 1 Ch 408.
4 (1861) 3 Giff 238.
5 [1899] 1 Ch 408.
6 See, in this connection, *Wood v Clydesdale Bank Ltd* 1914 SC 397.
7 Cf *Evans v National Provincial Bank of England* (1897) 13 TLR 429; *Wood v Clydesdale Bank Ltd*, supra.
8 See per Maule J in *Partridge v Bank of England* (1846) 9 QB 396.

Co Ltd.[9] That case decided that where A deposits money with a bank in the names of himself and of B, payable to either or to the survivor, B's right to claim the deposit and to sue the bank depends on whether A purported to make B a party to the contract. If he did, he must either have had authority to act as agent or B must have ratified. The facts were that A, being mortally ill, deposited £10,000 with the respondents in his own name and that of his son, an infant. The deposit receipt expressed the sum to be repayable to either the father or the son, or the survivor. By his will A directed his executors to hold the residue of his property in trust for B until he reached the age of 25 years and on his attaining that age for him absolutely. On A's death the executors withdrew the money and redeposited it in their own names. Over a number of years this sum became exhausted through being paid into the overdrawn current account of A's business, which the executors carried on and in the management of which B participated actively before and after he came of age. Soon after attaining the age of 25, B claimed that he was entitled to the money and brought an action against the respondents to recover that sum as having been paid to the executors wrongfully and without his authority. The members of the House of Lords all delivered judgment against B, but on differing grounds. Lord Atkin's opinion is perhaps of special interest:

> It is said that the effect of the contract created by the deposit of £10,000 by the father in the names of himself and his son, the opening of the joint deposit account and the giving and acceptance of the deposit receipt, was the formation of a contract between the father alone and the bank. Neither the father nor the bank, it is said, purported to contract for or with the son; the son was a third party who could acquire no rights against the bank. It was as though the father had opened an account in his own name making the sums payable to himself or his son, in which case it was said the son would clearly have to prove an independent contract between himself and the bank before he could sue the bank. My Lords, this contention seems to me to raise the one question of general importance in this case. It involves the whole question of the legal relations created by a bank deposit in this form. The argument, if correct, appears to me inconsistent with well-established banking practice and likely to impair the confidence in deposits made in joint names. I consider it to be quite unfounded. It is, I think, significant that there appears no trace of such an argument having been put forward in the courts below. It would not have been attractive hearing for customer or potential customer of the bank in Belfast. It seems to have been reserved for the rarer atmosphere of your Lordships' House.
>
> The suggestion is that where A deposits a sum of money with his bank in the names of A and B, payable to A or B, if B comes to the bank with the deposit receipt he has no right to demand the money from the bank or to sue them if his demand is refused. The bank is entitled to demand proof that the money was in fact partly B's, or possibly that A had acted with B's actual authority. For the contract, it is said, is between the bank and A alone. My Lords, to say that is to ignore the vital difference between a contract purporting to be made by A with the bank to pay A or B and a contract purporting to be made by A and B with the bank to pay A and B. In both cases, of course, payment to B would discharge the bank whether the bank contracted with A alone or with A and B. But the question is whether in the case put B has any rights against the bank if payment to him is refused. I have myself no doubt that in such a case B can sue the bank. The contract on the face of it purports to be made with A and B, and I think with

9 [1935] AC 24, 40 Com Cas 1, HL.

them jointly and severally. A purports to make the contract on behalf of B as well as himself and the consideration supports such a contract. If A has actual authority from B to make such a contract, B is a party to the contract ab initio. If he has not actual authority, then subject to ordinary principles of ratification B can ratify the contract purporting to have been made on his behalf and his ratification relates back to the original formation of the contract. If no events had happened to preclude B from ratifying, then on compliance with the contract conditions, including notice and production of the deposit receipt, B would have the right to demand from the bank so much of the money as was due on the deposit account.

In my view, therefore, if nothing had happened to prevent the son from ratifying the contract, he could sue the bank on the original deposit account. It would be no answer to say that the bank had paid the executors, for the contract was not to pay to the executors of either of the two names, but to the survivor. I think the case is rightly put on ratification, for I can find no sufficient evidence that the father had the actual authority of the son to enter into this contract on the son's behalf.'

The other members of the House were of opinion that the money deposited passed to the executors with the rest of A's estate and that they were entitled to receive and apply it in due course of administration as directed by the testator's will. They therefore considered it unnecessary to discuss the position of the son in relation to the contract with the bank.

The question is largely one of intention to be discovered from the circumstances. In *Young v Sealey*,[10] the question for decision was what was the intention of a Miss Jarman, who transferred certain moneys to deposit account in the joint names of herself and the defendant. Romer J after reviewing the cases, found that the transactions were neither voluntary settlements nor immediately effective gifts, nor *donationes mortis causa*; that there only remained the view that the gifts were intended to be postponed until Miss Jarman's death, which reasoning he refused to apply as it would mean that the disposition was of a testamentary nature and void under the Wills Act 1837. He held that the defendant Sealey was beneficially entitled, the gift being complete at the time the deposit was made. The mandate was the usual one providing for either party to sign, the balance to go to the survivor.

(b) Nature of the bank's obligation

A joint account is in law simply a debt owed to the account holders jointly.[11] That raises the obvious question as to the rights of one of the joint creditors if the bank wrongly pays the other.

(i) The law before Catlin's case

The decision of Bingham J in 1982 in *Catlin v Cyprus Finance Corpn (London) Ltd*[12] is a landmark in the law relating to joint accounts. To appreciate the importance of the decision, some description must be given of the law as it stood immediately before it.

For several years the leading authority on the nature of a bank's obligations in relation to a joint account was *Brewer v National Westminster Bank*,[13] a decision of McNair J in 1952. The facts were that a fraudulent executor

10 [1949] Ch 278, [1949] 1 All ER 92.
11 *Re Head, Head v Head (No 2)* [1894] 2 Ch 236.
12 [1983] QB 759, [1983] 1 All ER 809.
13 [1952] 2 All ER 650.

forged the signature of his co-executor to cheques on the executors' account, which was governed by a mandate authorising the bank to honour drawings if signed by both. On the innocent executor asking for a declaration that the account had been wrongly debited, McNair J held that although the debits to the account were unauthorised and the bank was in breach of its obligation under the mandate and obtained no discharge, nevertheless the plaintiff could succeed only if both parties were in a position to sue, the bank's obligation being a single one to the parties jointly. The fraudulent executor clearly could not sue. The case went to appeal, but was settled during the hearing, when Lord Denning commented that the bank now had a decision in its favour on the record.

The bank set up a number of defences which were rejected,[14] namely that:

1 they had paid cash on each of the cheques to the fraudulent executor and had obtained from him a discharge sufficient to entitle them to debit the account
2 the plaintiff had failed in her duty to supervise her co-executor and to examine the bank statements, and thereby negligently caused or contributed to the forgeries or caused the bank to be misled by her co-executor;
3 the bank statements delivered from time to time amounted to accounts stated;
4 by failing to make any complaint as to the bank statements the plaintiff had impliedly represented that they were correct and was estopped from contending that they were not correct;
5 by opening the joint executorship account the plaintiff and her co-executor had impliedly agreed jointly and severally that each of them would act honestly in the conduct of the account;

The steps in the successful defence were that:

(i) the contract for the opening of the joint account had been made by the plaintiff and the second defendant jointly;
(ii) the plaintiff had no rights under the joint contract except such as were held by her jointly with the second defendant;
(iii) the second defendant was a necessary party to any action to enforce any rights belonging to the account holders under the joint contract, as a plaintiff if he consented to be joined, as a defendant if he did not consent, in accordance with the practice established in *Cullen v Knowles*;[15]
(iv) the rights of the plaintiff and the second defendant under the joint contract were the same whether they were asserted in any action brought by the plaintiff and the second defendant jointly as co-plaintiffs, or whether they were asserted, as here, in an action brought by the plaintiff alone to which she had joined the second defendant as a defendant on the ground that he had refused to be joined as a plaintiff;
(v) no action could be maintained by the joint contractors on a joint contract unless each of them was in a position to sue thereon;

14 McNair J refused to accept the necessity for implying any of these terms. He quoted Lord Wright in *Luxor (Eastbourne) Ltd v Cooper* [1941] AC 108, [1941] 1 All ER 33 as citing with approval Scrutton LJ in *Reigate v Union Manufacturing Co (Ramsbottom)* [1918] 1 KB 592 at 605, that only if a term is necessary to give business efficacy to a contract will the courts imply it.
15 [1898] 2 QB 380.

(vi) no action could successfully be maintained by the plaintiff and the second defendant as co-plaintiffs against the first defendant, in which they alleged, as the plaintiff alleged here, that the second defendant had forged the plaintiff's signature as the drawer of cheques on the joint account, and in which rights were asserted and relief claimed against the first defendant solely on the basis of such allegation. The second defendant would not be in a position to maintain such an action, for he could not be heard to say that he had forged the plaintiff's signature and he could not be permitted to assert rights and claim relief on the basis of such allegation.[16]

It was agreed that the bank had been in no way negligent, the forgeries having been skilfully perpetrated. But as was pointed out in *Catlin's* case, the ratio of the decision covers the case of a bank acting in clear breach of mandate with no plausible excuse for doing so.

It was accepted by McNair J that the bank did not obtain a good discharge by paying against a forged signature.[17] The judge did not have cited to him authorities, in particular *Twibell v London Suburban Bank*,[18] to the effect that if a bank obtains no discharge, it is liable to the innocent account holder.

The decision in *Brewer* was widely criticised.[19] In *Welch v Bank of England*,[20] Harman J professed not to understand it, and it was not followed by the Supreme Court of Victoria in *Arden v Bank of New South Wales*,[1] nor by Park J in *Jackson v White*.[2]

(ii) Catlin's case

In *Catlin's* case, the court had to choose between these conflicting authorities. The facts were that the plaintiff and her husband had deposited funds in a joint account with the defendant bank on terms of an express mandate that no payment out of the account should be made save on the joint signature of both account holders. In breach of that mandate, and without the knowledge or authority of the plaintiff, the bank negligently transferred all the funds out of the account on the instructions of Mr Catlin and to his use. It was held that the plaintiff was entitled to damages equal to her half-share interest in the funds so transferred.

In declining to follow *Brewer's* case, Bingham J adopted the solution suggested by Sir Arthur Goodhart,[3] that although the bank in *Brewer* made an agreement with the executors jointly, it also made a separate agreement with each of the executors severally that it would not honour any drawings

16 The learned judge found support for his view in a statement by Slesser LJ, in *Hirschorn v Evans* [1938] 2 KB 801, [1938] 3 All ER 491 to the effect that 'if the bank had failed to meet its obligations the rights under this [a joint] account could only have been exercised by both the persons, the husband and the wife, joining in whatever claim might be appropriate under the account'.
17 McNair J accepted this on the basis of *Stone v Marsh* (1826) Ry & M 364; *Innes v Stephenson* (1831) 1 Mood & R 145; and *Hubbard v Davis* (1851) 10 CB 645.
18 [1869] WN 127; see also *Bale v Parr's Bank Ltd* (1909) 25 TLR 549; *Reade v Royal Bank of Ireland Ltd* [1922] 2 IR 22.
19 See (1952) 68 LQR 446 (Sir Arthur Goodhart); (1953) 16 MLR 232 (Glanville Williams); *Paget* (9th edn) pp 76–77.
20 [1955] Ch 508 at 532, [1955] 1 All ER 811 at 821.
 1 [1956] VLR 569.
 2 [1967] 2 Lloyd's Rep 68.
 3 In (1952) 68 LQR 446.

unless he or she had signed them. Bingham J explained the reasons for adopting this solution as follows:[4]

> 'The defendants agreed to honour instructions signed by both account holders. This no doubt imported a negative duty not to honour instructions not signed by both account holders. This duty also could, in theory, have been owed jointly, but it must (to make sense) have been owed to the account holders severally, because the only purpose of requiring two signatures was to obviate the possibility of independent action by one account holder to the detriment of the other. A duty on the defendants which could only be enforced jointly with the party against the possibility of whose misconduct a safeguard was sought, and where the occurrence of such misconduct through the negligent breach of mandate by the defendants would deprive the innocent party of any remedy, would in practical terms be worthless. Indeed, it would be worse than worthless, because a customer would reasonably rely on the two signature safeguard and refrain from active supervision of the account, only to find when loss (allegedly irreparable) has resulted that the reliance was misplaced.'

The adoption of this solution also disposed of an objection taken by the bank that the non-joinder of Mr Catlin invalidated the proceedings.

Bingham J observed that it is highly undesirable that the issues raised by *Brewer's* case should continue to be litigated. It is to be hoped that *Catlin's* case will be accepted as having finally laid *Brewer's* case to rest.

(iii) Measure of damages

It will be noted that the plaintiff in *Catlin's* case recovered damages measured by reference to her half-share interest in the account. Similarly in *Twibell's* case, ante, the plaintiff recovered damages representing an appropriate moiety of the sum for which the cheque was drawn. This is the measure of damages which compensates the plaintiff for his loss.

Damages are liable to be reduced if the plaintiff has benefited from the wrongful payment. Such a deduction can be justified either on the basis that the plaintiff did not in fact suffer loss to the extent of any benefit received, or by parity with the rule in *Liggett's* case.[5]

(iv) Either to sign

A joint account is no less a joint account where the mandate under which it is operated provides for the bank to act on the sole signature of either account holder. This was accepted as the position in *Hirschorn v Evans*.[6]

(c) The principle of survivorship

On the death of one joint account holder the funds in ordinary cases pass to the survivor, although the principle of survivorship can be overridden by equity. Questions as to the applicability of the principle have arisen mostly in connection with joint accounts maintained by spouses, and it is in that context that the matter is considered (see 'Special Customers – Married Women', ch 9, ante).

---

4 [1983] QB 759 at 771C, [1983] 1 All ER 809 at 816j.
5 [1928] 1 KB 48. See ch 12, post. An example of the application of the principle in the present context is *Jackson v White* [1967] 2 Lloyd's Rep 68 at 80–81.
6 [1938] 2 KB 801, [1938] 3 All ER 491.

(d) Borrowing on joint account

Where there is a borrowing on joint account, the parties may now be sued separately or together. The earlier rule that parties in joint account had to be sued jointly, failing which the party not sued was released if judgment was obtained against the other, has been abrogated by s 3 of the Civil Liability (Contribution) Act 1978.

4 TRUST ACCOUNTS

(a) Trust accounts generally

Where a banker has knowledge that an account with him is the account of a trust, or information which should lead him to understand that the account is that of a trust, he must avoid being a party to breach of the trust, as by wrongfully paying away or otherwise dealing with the trust moneys. His difficulty often lies in his inability to know the nature of an account in this connection. Accounts headed, for distinguishing purposes, in terms not definitely indicating a trust, have been held proof that the banker was aware of the fiduciary nature of the account – for instance, in *Re Gross, ex p Kingston*,[7] 'police account' was held to constitute an account so headed a trust account.

If the banker has notice, however received, that an account is affected with a trust, express or implied, that the customer is in possession or has control of the money in a fiduciary capacity, he must regard the account strictly in that light. Of course, where there is no such notice, the mere fact that, unknown to the banker, moneys are held by the customer in a fiduciary capacity in no way affects the banker's right to treat them as the absolute property of the customer.[8] Nor is the mere fact that the person opening the account occupies a position which renders it probable that he has moneys of other persons in his hands sufficient to put the banker on inquiry;[9] but that fact may add significance to the heading under which the account is opened.

When once the banker is fixed with the fiduciary nature of the account he has to bear in mind two somewhat conflicting influences. He has to consider the interests of the persons beneficially entitled, perhaps including his own, and he has to recognise the right of his customer to draw cheques on the account and have them honoured. The banker obviously must not be a party or privy to any fraud, any misapplication of the trust fund. He could not, on the mere instruction of the customer, transfer trust moneys to private account, to wipe out or reduce an overdraft.[10]

It is with the cheque that difficulties arise. It is not the business or right of a banker, to whom a cheque is presented, to set up the claim of any third

7 (1871) 6 Ch App 632.
8 *Thomson v Clydesdale Bank Ltd* [1893] AC 282; *Union Bank of Australia Ltd v Murray-Aynsley* [1898] AC 693; *Bank of New South Wales v Goulburn Valley Butter Co Pty* [1902] AC 543, PC.
9 *Greenwood Teale v William Williams, Brown & Co* (1894) 11 TLR 56 (a solicitor); *Thomson v Clydesdale Bank Ltd* supra (a stockbroker).
10 Cf *John v Dodwell & Co* [1918] AC 563; The foregoing paragraphs were cited as a correct statement of the law by the learned judge in *Rowlandson v National Westminster Bank Ltd* [1978] 3 All ER 370, [1978] 1 WLR 798.

person against the mandate of his customer; at the same time, he cannot shelter behind his character of banker to cover complicity in a fraud.[11] Mere suspicion does not justify him in refusing payment of a cheque. The suggestion made in *Re Gross, ex p Adair*,[12] that a banker would rightly dishonour a cheque drawn by a customer on a trust account because it was payable to a person known to be that customer's tailor, is exaggerated, and is not supported by *Re Gross, ex p Kingston*,[13] which was the appeal from that decision. The same applies to some of the statements in *Re Wall, Jackson v Bristol and West of England Bank Ltd*.[14]

Circumstances which justify the imposition of a constructive trust in relation to payments out of non-trust accounts (see ch 12, post) must logically also found liability in relation to payments out of trust accounts.

(b) Banker benefiting from payment out of trust account

Cases have arisen where the banker has occupied the dual capacity of drawee of a cheque on an account known to be a trust account and at the same time banker to the payee of the cheque which is then paid into the payee's overdrawn account.

Decisions have somewhat varied as to the position in such cases. In *Foxton v Manchester and Liverpool District Banking Co*,[15] Fry J laid down that a bank could not retain the benefit of a cheque drawn on a trust fund known to be such and paid into an overdrawn private account. He said:

'Now it appears to be plain that the bank could not derive the benefit which they did from that payment, knowing it to be drawn from a trust fund, unless they were prepared to show that the payment was a legitimate and proper one, having reference to the terms of the trust. It is said that they did not know what the trust was at that time. That appears to me, I confess, to be immaterial, because those who know that a fund is a trust fund cannot take possession of that fund for their private benefit, except at the risk of being liable to refund it in the event of the trust being broken by the payment of the money.'

In *Coleman v Bucks and Oxon Union Bank*,[16] Byrne J carefully reviewed this case in the light of *Gray v Johnston*.[17] He quotes[18] significant passages from that case, in which Lord Cairns and Lord Westbury distinctly imply that the banker is not to be held privy to the fraud merely because, in the ordinary course of business, the cheque is carried to the private account and reduces an overdraft which, if a balance had been struck, would have been found to exist; but that to deprive the banker of it, the benefit must be one 'designed or stipulated for', as, for instance, where a balance has been struck and the customer pressed for payment or reduction of the ascertained overdraft on the private account. With regard to *Foxton's* case, he says:

'That was a case depending on the evidence. I need not go into all the circumstances,

---

11 *Gray v Johnston* (1868) LR 3 HL 1; applied in *John Shaw (Rayner's Lane) Ltd v Lloyds Bank Ltd* (1944) 5 LDAB 396.
12 (1871) 24 LT 198 at 203.
13 (1871) 6 Ch App 632.
14 (1885) 1 TLR 522.
15 (1881) 44 LT 406.
16 [1897] 2 Ch 243.
17 (1868) LR 3 HL 1.
18 See [1897] 2 Ch 243 at 248 and 249.

but there was a benefit designed for the bank, who had been calling on the parties having private accounts to reduce their overdrafts, and they did it with the intention of reducing their indebtedness.'

He then quotes the remarks of Fry J, reproduced above, and continues:[19]

'I am asked to say that that amounts to a decision to this effect: that wherever there is an account which upon the face of it is a trust account, and the customer draws a cheque upon that account and pays in the cheque to the credit of his private account, the bankers are bound to see and inquire (that is how I understand the proposition is put) that the customer is in point of fact entitled to the money which he so transfers from one account to another. I do not think that that was the meaning of the learned judge in that case. If bankers have the slightest knowledge or reasonable suspicion that the money is being applied in breach of a trust, and if they are going to derive a benefit from the transfer and intend and design that they should derive a benefit from it, then I think the bankers would not be entitled to honour the cheque drawn upon the trust account without some further inquiry into the matter.'

But he held that notwithstanding the fact that in point of law the money must, in the case before him, be regarded as having been applied in reduction of an overdraft, the bankers were not liable to refund it, although they had received the money from their London agents for the credit of A's trust account which they placed to his current account, there being no trust account. In *A-G v De Winton*,[20] Farwell J expressed approval of the view taken by Fry J. The stricter rule laid down by Fry J would be likely to be found correct today.

In *John v Dodwell & Co*,[1] the respondents' manager was authorised by power of attorney to draw cheques upon their account for the purposes of the business. He bought shares through the appellants as brokers and, in payment of the price, fraudulently gave cheques drawn upon the respondents' account. The appellant received such cheques without fraud, but with knowledge that the manager, without apparent authority, was drawing for his own purposes. The respondents were held entitled to recover the money as held in trust for them. Any third person taking from an agent a transfer of property with knowledge of the breach committed by him in making the transfer, must be taken to hold it under a fiduciary obligation to account for it to the principal.

In *British American Elevator Co Ltd v Bank of British North America*,[2] a bank agreed to furnish the company's agent with cash in exchange for drafts on the company. The cash, as the bank knew, was to be used in paying for grain to be purchased for the company by the agent. The bank, instead of giving cash for the drafts, credited them in whole or in part to the agent's private account, which was generally overdrawn. Held by the Privy Council that the bank having been party to a misapplication of trust funds it was liable to replace those funds. *John v Dodwell & Co* was followed and made the ground of decision in *Reckitt v Barnett, Pembroke and Slater Ltd*,[3] the case of an agent purchasing a motor car for himself with his principal's

19 [1897] 2 Ch 243 at 253.
20 [1906] 2 Ch 106.
 1 [1918] AC 563.
 2 [1919] AC 658.
 3 [1929] AC 176.

money. According to Lord Atkin, this case did not differ in principle from *Midland Bank Ltd v Reckitt,*[4] which was based on the receipt by the bank, in reduction of the overdraft of Lord Terrington, of a cheque drawn by him as attorney for Sir Harold Reckitt.

In the result, a banker must not be party to any transaction, on an account known to be a trust account, from which he would benefit; not even where acting on what would otherwise be a valid mandate, if the circumstances are such as to put him on inquiry as to the propriety of the transaction.

(c) Client accounts

A client account is essentially an account held on trust by the customer for his client. Reference has already been made to the client accounts required to be kept by authorised persons under the Financial Services Act 1986 (ch 3, ante) and to solicitors' and estate agents' client accounts (ch 9, ante). Reference can also be made in this context to s 430(10) of the Companies Act 1985, which applies to monies received by a company under s 430(5) (consideration paid or transferred by offeror to target company after offeror has exercised his s 429 right to buy out minority shareholders). By s 430(10), any sum so received by the target company must be paid into a separate bank account. Although this is not a client account in the strict sense, it has obvious parallels.

(d) Monies paid for a special purpose

(i) Co-existence of legal and equitable rights and remedies

Monies are sometimes paid to a banker to be applied for a special purpose, and often a special account will be opened to receive monies so paid. In *Barclays Bank Ltd v Quistclose Investments Ltd*[5] the question arose as to the rights of the payer in respect of such a transaction. The facts were that a company, Rolls Razor Ltd, which was in serious financial difficulties having an overdraft with Barclays Bank Ltd of some £484,000, needed to borrow a sum of £209,719 to meet an ordinary share dividend which it had declared. The company obtained a loan of that sum from Quistclose Ltd, who paid it on condition that it would be used to pay the dividend. A cheque drawn by Quistclose was paid into a separate account opened specially for the purpose with the bank, who knew of the purpose and conditions of the loan. Before the dividend had been paid, Rolls Razor went into voluntary liquidation. Quistclose claimed repayment of the £209,719, but this was refused by the bank, who applied the sum in reduction of the overdraft. It was submitted on behalf of the bank that the relationship between itself and Rolls Razor was one of loan, giving rise to a legal action in debt which necessarily excluded the implication of any trust enforceable in equity in favour of Quistclose. The House of Lords emphatically rejected this submission. In the words of Lord Wilberforce, delivering the leading speech:[6]

'I should be surprised if an argument of this kind – so conceptualist in character – had ever been accepted. In truth it has plainly been rejected by the eminent judges who from 1819 onwards have permitted arrangements of this type to be enforced,

4 [1933] AC 1.
5 [1970] AC 567, [1968] 3 All ER 651.
6 [1970] AC 567 at 581F, [1968] 3 All ER 651 at 655–656.

and have approved them as being for the benefit of creditors and all concerned. There is surely no difficulty in recognising the co-existence in one transaction of legal and equitable rights and remedies: when the money is advanced, the lender acquires an equitable right to see that it is applied for the primary designated purpose (see *Re Rogers* 8 Morr 243 where both Lindley LJ and Kay LJ recognised this): when the purpose has been carried out (ie, the debt paid) the lender has his remedy against the borrower in debt: if the primary purpose cannot be carried out, the question arises if a secondary purpose (ie, repayment to the lender) has been agreed, expressly or by implication: if it has, the remedies of equity may be invoked to give effect to it, if it has not (and the money is intended to fall within the general fund of the debtor's assets) then there is the appropriate remedy for recovery of a loan. I can appreciate no reason why the flexible interplay of law and equity cannot let in these practical arrangements, and other variations if desired: it would be to the discredit of both systems if they could not. In the present case the intention to create a secondary trust for the benefit of the lender, to arise if the primary trust, to pay the dividend, could not be carried out, is clear and I can find no reason why the law should not give effect to it.'

(ii) Existence of a trust

It is often a matter of difficulty to determine whether, on any given facts, the requisites for the creation of a trust are made out.[7] On one side of the line is *Re Kayford Ltd (in Liquidation)*,[8] where a company which carried on a mail-order business such that customers either paid the full purchase price or a deposit when ordering goods, got into financial difficulties. The managing director, who was concerned to protect customers who had sent and were sending money, was advised to open a special account to be called a 'Customers' Trust Deposit Account'. He accepted this advice, but then agreed with the company's bank to use for this purpose an existing, dormant deposit account with a small credit balance. Megarry J held that a trust in favour of the customers had been created. There was a sufficient manifestation of an intention to create a trust; its subject matter was pure personalty, so that writing, though desirable, was not essential; and each of the so-called 'three certainties' was present. This may be compared with *Re Multi Guarantee Co Ltd*, [9] where a company ('MG') was incorporated to market warranties for domestic appliances, which warranties provided insurance cover against failure of the goods after the expiry of the initial manufacturer's warranty. A company which owned a chain of shops operated the MG warranty scheme, and paid to MG premiums which it collected from its customers. The premiums were held by MG in a designated bank account. The retailing company became concerned that MG had not obtained proper insurance cover and, following negotiations, MG transferred the premium monies into a joint deposit account in the names of the parties' solicitors, and agreed to release the monies to the retailer. Before this could be done, MG went into voluntary winding-up and the retailing company then claimed that the premiums were held on trust in its favour. The Court of Appeal rejected this

---

7 The leading pre-1968 cases are reviewed in *Quistclose*, ante. As to subsequent cases, see *Re Kayford* [1975] 1 All ER 604, [1975] 1 WLR 279; *Re Chelsea Cloisters Ltd* (1980) 41 P&CR 98, CA; *Carreras Rothmans Ltd v Freeman Mathews Treasure Ltd* [1985] Ch 207, [1985] 1 All ER 155; *Re Multi Guarantee Ltd* [1987] BCLC 257, CA; *Re EVTR* [1987] BCLC 646, CA.
8 [1975] 1 All ER 604, [1975] 1 WLR 279.
9 [1987] BCLC 257, CA.

claim, holding that MG had never manifested a sufficient intention to create a trust, the requisite certainty of words being absent. Accordingly the premium moneys formed part of MG's general assets.

(iii) Notice of trust

The points made in relation to notice of trust accounts generally apply equally in context of monies paid for a special purpose. Thus in *Quistclose*, supra, it was common ground that a mere request to put the money into a separate account was not sufficient to constitute notice.[10]

Where a bank does not receive notice until after the payment in of monies impressed with a trust, the question arises whether the bank, by its promise to repay, has become a bona fide purchaser for value so as to take priority over the interests of the beneficiaries. In *Quistclose* in the Court of Appeal,[11] Russell LJ observed that, except in the technical sense of undertaking a repayment obligation, the bank gave no consideration for the receipt of the money; it gave no extension of credit to Rolls Razor on the faith of the payment; it did not credit any interest on the sum. In the House of Lords, Lord Wilberforce said that the bank had not in any real sense given value when it received the money or thereafter changed its position.[12] It appears from these observations that the bank's promise to repay will not of itself give the bank the status of a bona fide purchaser for value.

(iv) Effect of trust

Where a bank is on notice that monies paid for a special purpose are subject to a trust, the bank may not apply such monies to discharge indebtedness of the customer who is the trustee,[13] and the monies so paid will not form part of the customer's general assets so as to fall within assets charged to the bank under a debenture.[14]

5 NOMINEE ACCOUNTS

In *Re Willis, Percival & Co ex p Morier*[15] James LJ referred to what used to be called in the Privy Council a Bonamee[16] account, that is, 'an account put by one man into the name of another merely for his own convenience'. It is suggested that these words correctly define a nominee account in modern banking practice.

Where a banker and his customer agree that an account is to be treated as a nominee account, their respective rights of set-off will be determined on the basis that the account was in the name of the true owner. This is illustrated

10 [1970] AC 567 at 582C, [1968] 3 All ER 651 at 656F; and see *Union Bank of Australia Ltd v Murray-Aynsley* [1898] AC 693.
11 *Quistclose Investments Ltd v Rolls Razor Ltd* [1968] Ch 540, [1968] 1 All ER 613, CA.
12 [1970] AC 567 at 582C, [1968] 3 All ER 651 at 656E.
13 See, eg *Quistclose*, ante.
14 See, eg *Re EVTR*, ante.
15 (1879) 12 Ch D 491 at 496, CA.
16 In *Re Hett, Maylor & Co Ltd* (1894) 10 TLR 412, Chitty J stated that 'Bonamee' was a misspelling for 'Be-nami'.

by *Re Hett, Maylor and Co Ltd*,[17] where a company which contracted to construct a railway in one of the Philippine Islands maintained its account with the Manila Branch of the Chartered Bank of India, Australia and China in the name of its manager. This was done because by the laws of the Philippine Islands a public company was not recognisable.[18] The bank agreed to give credit to the company by crediting the proceeds of certain drafts to the nominee account. On the company's winding up, it was held that the credit balance on the account had to be brought into the statutory insolvency set-off of sums due in respect of mutual dealings between the bank and the company. Equally if the manager had become bankrupt, the bank could not have taken the credit balance on the nominee account in his name to discharge any debit balance on his private account.

17 (1894) 10 TLR 412. In *Bhogal v Punjab National Bank* [1988] 2 All ER 296 at 301, CA, Dillon LJ described *Re Hett, Maylor and Co Ltd* as 'a very plain case where the nomineeship of one account was known to both parties and undisputed'.
18 Then s 38 of the Bankruptcy Act 1883, which applied to company liquidations by virtue of s 10 of the Judicature Act 1875. See now Rule 4.96 of the Insolvency Rules 1986, and ch 31, post.

CHAPTER 12

THE PAYING BANKER

1 INTRODUCTION

In previous editions of *Paget,* the obligations of the paying banker have been considered in a group of chapters dealing solely with cheques and analogous instruments. Although much of the case law has developed around cheques, in modern banking practice the bank's obligation to repay falls to be performed in a far wider range of circumstances. There are today many methods of payment other than by cheque. These other methods are commonly used where a transfer is of a sufficiently large amount to make daily interest a relevant factor, or where payment has to be effected by a specified date (eg the payment of charter hire), or where funds are to be remitted abroad.

Accordingly, the banker's repayment obligation is considered at this point. This chapter includes a section on the payment of cheques, where consideration is given to those aspects of the repayment obligation which are peculiar to cheques. The statutory protection available to the paying banker, which protection is limited to the payment of cheques and analogous instruments, is considered in ch 24, post. The effect of garnishee orders, and of Mareva and other freezing orders, is considered in chs 18 and 19.

2 THE OBLIGATION TO REPAY

(a) The basic obligation

The paying banker's obligation is to honour his customer's payment instructions, including payment orders constituted by the drawing of cheques in legal form, provided that he has in his hands sufficient available funds to do so. The obligation is owed to the customer, not to the payee.[1]

The banker must, of course, act in accordance with the mandate governing the relevant account. He may, however, be protected even if he fails to do so. This is illustrated by *London Intercontinental Trust Ltd v Barclays Bank*

---

1 *Dublin Port and Docks Board v Bank of Ireland* [1976] IR 118; and see *National Westminster Bank Ltd v Barclays Bank International Ltd* [1975] QB 654 at 662f, [1974] 3 All ER 834 at 841b, but note that the premise for Kerr LJ's observation, namely that a mistake of fact must operate as between the payer and the payee, must now be considered doubtful: see ch 25, post.

Ltd,[2] where the defendant bank honoured a cheque drawn on one signature in breach of a mandate requiring two signatures, but the signatory had actual authority from the board of the plaintiff company to transfer the relevant sum. The company's claim against the bank was accordingly dismissed. The consequence of the bank's failure to observe the discrepancy between the cheque and the mandate simply had the consequence that the bank exposed itself to a risk that the signatory had not in fact been authorised.[3] It was further held the company had in any event ratified the payment.

In his formulation of the terms of the banker-customer contact in the *Joachimson* case,[4] Atkin LJ left open the question whether the demand for repayment must be in writing. It is submitted that the banker should be entitled to insist upon a written demand.

The obligation is to repay at the branch of the bank where the account is kept.[5]

(b) Sufficiency and availability of funds

The banker's obligation to pay cheques and honour other payment instructions is subject to the condition that there are in his hands funds of the customer sufficient and available for that purpose.

(i) Sufficiency of funds

The customer's funds must be sufficient to enable the banker to effect payment of the whole sum. If the funds are insufficient, the banker is not bound to effect partial payment of such funds as there may be. This proposition has been assumed to be correct in several cases.[6] It accords with the principle that a cheque is not an assignment of funds. Whether an order to pay, not being a cheque, may operate as an equitable assignment and, if so, what is the effect of demand by the payee, has not been decided.

Funds are sufficient if, notwithstanding the insufficiency of the credit balance on an account, the customer has the right to overdraw or otherwise borrow up to a given limit not yet reached. Furthermore the drawing of a cheque on an account the balance of which is not sufficient to meet it may be taken as authority to the bank to combine the account with another account sufficiently in credit in order that the cheque may be paid, but the bank is not obliged so to combine.[7]

Subject to contrary agreement, the funds must be sufficient at the date on which the banker is obliged to effect payment. In *Whitehead v National Westminster Bank,*[8] the defendant bank had accepted a standing order to pay a sum on a particular day to a payee until further order. On two occasions, there were insufficient funds on the specified day to meet the payment. The court rejected the customer's submission that the bank was under a duty to

2 [1980] 1 Lloyd's Rep 241.
3 Ibid at 249.
4 [1921] 3 KB 110 at 127, CA.
5 *R v Lovitt* [1912] AC 212; *Joachimson v Swiss Bank Corpn* [1921] 3 KB 110 at 127, CA.
6 See *Whitaker v Bank of England* (1835) 1 Cr M & R 744 at 749–750; *Marzetti v Williams* (1830) 1 B & Ad 415; *Carew v Duckworth* (1869) LR 4 Exch 313; *Whitehead v National Westminster Bank Ltd* (1982) Times, 9 June; and see also the summary of the banker customer contract given by Atkin LJ in *Joachimson v Swiss Bank Corpn* [1921] 3 KB 110 at 127.
7 See *Woodland v Fear* (1857) 7 E & B 519; *Garnett v M'Kewan* (1872) LR 8 Exch 10.
8 (1982) Times, 9 June.

keep the account under daily scrutiny so as to be able, whenever there was enough in the account, to pay the standing order.

It has been asked whether the holder of a cheque larger in amount than the funds available is entitled to pay in the difference to the customer's account and then withdraw the whole against the cheque. It is clear that the banker must not facilitate the operation by informing the holder how much the account is short of the amount of the cheque. That would be unjustifiable disclosure of the customer's affairs. Where a cheque is refused payment with a request to present again, it lies entirely with the holder whether he will do so or at once treat the cheque as dishonoured.[9]

The fact that one cheque has been refused on the ground that it overtops the available balance would not justify the banker in refusing payment of a cheque subsequently presented for an amount within the balance. Cheques should as far as possible be paid in the order in which they are presented if there be any question as to the sufficiency of the balance to cover them all.[10] When two or more cheques are presented simultaneously for payment and the balance is sufficient to satisfy one or some but not all, the bank should pay the one which the balance will cover. If there are two, each within the limit, but not enough money to pay both, or if there is enough money to pay two small ones but not one large one, the bank should pay the small ones, on the ground that their dishonour would have greater effect on the drawer's standing. The dilemma is the fault of the drawer, not the bank. But the banker is clearly not entitled to dishonour cheques presented because he knows of others to be presented shortly, unless he has special instructions from the customer to do so.[11] In *Dublin Port and Docks Board v Bank of Ireland*[12] there were delays in processing as the result of a backlog due to the bank officers' strike. Griffin J held that bankers should have paid in order of presentation 'subject to the interest of the customer being taken into account.'

(ii) Availability of funds

Funds may be sufficient but not available in at least two circumstances. The first is where the banker has a right to combine accounts (see Chapter 31, post). It was said in *Garnett v M'Kewan*[13] that the customer must be taken to know the state of each of his accounts and if the balance on the whole is against him or does not equal the cheques he draws, he has no right to expect those cheques to be cashed. The right of combination is, of course, subject to contrary agreement.

Secondly, money is not available immediately it is paid in. Even in the case of notes or cash, a sufficient period must be allowed to elapse to enable the bank to carry out the necessary book-keeping operations.[14] But as soon as notes or cash are credited, they are available for drawing.

The position with cheques is less clear. In *Capital and Counties Bank Ltd v Gordon*,[15] Lord Lindley said:

9 Cf *Sednaoni Zariffa Nakes & Co v Anglo-Austrian Bank* (1909) 2 LDAB 208.
10 *Sednaoni Zariffa Nakes & Co v Anglo-Austrian Bank*, ante.
11 *Sednaoni Zariffa Nakes & Co v Anglo-Austrian Bank*, ante.
12 [1976] IR 118. It was held that the *Sednaoni* decision, ante, is not an authority that a bank has a duty to the *payee* of a cheque to pay in order of presentation.
13 (1872) LR 8 Exch 10.
14 *Marzetti v Williams* (1830) 1 B & Ad 415.
15 [1903] AC 240 at 249.

'It must never be forgotten that the moment a bank places money to its customer's credit the customer is entitled to draw upon it, unless something occurs to deprive him of that right.'

This statement was obiter, because the customer had in fact been allowed to draw before the cheques were cleared, and the issue was whether the bank had received payment 'for a customer' so as to have available the protection of s 82 of the Bills of Exchange Act 1882. As is explained in ch 28, post, the decision in *Gordon's* case was heavily criticised and its effect was soon reversed by the Bills of Exchange Act (Crossed Cheques) Act 1906. It is suggested that the true position is that, by itself, crediting as cash does not give the customer the right to draw before the instrument is cleared. Thus in *Jones & Co v Coventry*[16] a Paymaster General warrant was handed to the owner's banker for collection and his account credited at once. It was held, in relation to a garnishee order nisi served the same day but after the crediting, that the balance was not liable to attachment as the moneys retained their character of retired pay until the warrant had been paid by the Paymaster General.

In modern banking practice, the point has assumed much less importance because banks normally reserve the right to refuse to pay against uncleared effects. In *Westminster Bank Ltd v Zang*,[17] the Court of Appeal held that a note to this effect on paying-in slips prevented there arising an implied agreement to allow drawings against uncleared effects. This decision was affirmed by the House of Lords.[18]

Subject to contrary agreement, if the crediting is communicated to the customer there can be no question that the amount can be drawn against.[19]

(c) Paying banker's duty of care

The paying banker owes his customer a contractual duty of care in carrying out payment instructions. The duty to act with reasonable care has been recognised on many occasions.[20] Furthermore, as has already been noted (see ch 10, ante) the availability of statutory protection and the right to be indemnified for payments made under letters of credit are both conditional upon the banker having acted with reasonable care.

The difficulty in this area is to define the precise relation between the banker's duty of care and the banker's duty to honour instructions given in accordance with the mandate. It has long been established that the banker must recognise the person from or for whom he received the money as the proper person to draw it, and the money as available for the purpose.[1] The

---

16 [1909] 2 KB 1029.
17 [1966] AC 182 at 196 (Lord Denning MR and Salmon LJ, Danckwerts LJ dubitante).
18 [1966] AC 182 at 215. See also *Re Keever* [1967] Ch 182, [1966] 3 All ER 631; *Barclays Bank Ltd v Astley Industrial Trust Ltd* [1970] 2 QB 527, [1970] 1 All ER 719.
19 *Akrokerri (Atlantic) Mines Ltd v Economic Bank* [1940] 2 KB 465, *Bevan v National Bank Ltd* (1906) 23 TLR 65; cf *Holt v Markham* [1923] 1 KB 504.
20 See the cases cited post; and see also *Westminster Bank Ltd v Hilton* (1926) 135 LT 358 at 362 (Atkin LJ) (revsd on appeal without affecting this point (1926) 136 LT 315, HL); *Royal Products Ltd v Midland Bank Ltd* [1981] 2 Lloyd's Rep 194 at 198 (Webster J).
1 *Calland v Loyd* (1840) 6 M & W 26; *Tassell v Cooper* (1850) 9 CB 509; *Fontaine-Besson v Parr's Banking Co and Alliance Bank Ltd* (1895) 12 TLR 121; *Szek v Lloyds Bank* (1908) Times, 15 January, and see *Banque Belge pour L'Etranger v Hambrouck* [1921] 1 KB 321; *Plunkett v Barclays Bank Ltd* [1936] 2 KB 107, [1936] 1 All ER 653; *John Shaw (Rayners Lane) Ltd v Lloyds Bank Ltd* (1945) 5 Legal Decisions Affecting Bankers 396; and *Stoney Stanton Supplies (Coventry) Ltd v Midland Bank Ltd* [1966] 2 Lloyd's Rep 373, in which the

banker cannot set up the claims of third parties or dispute his customer's title to money he has received from him or for his account.

In *Gray v Johnston,*[2] Lord Cairns LC said that it would be a serious matter if bankers were to be allowed, on grounds of mere suspicion or curiosity, to refuse to honour a cheque provided that the banker has money in his hands belonging to the customer.[3] He counterbalanced this observation by adding that it would be equally serious if bankers were to be allowed to shelter themselves under that title to say that they were at liberty to become parties to a breach of trust.

The law remained in a settled state until the decision of Ungoed-Thomas J in *Selangor United Rubber Estates Ltd v Cradock (No 3),*[4] which appeared to widen considerably the responsibility of a paying banker. The case concerned the purchase by Cradock of the capital of the plaintiff company using the company's moneys, a contravention of s 54 of the Companies Act 1948. The mechanics of the operation were that the National Bank (bankers to the plaintiff company) drew two drafts totalling £232,764 in favour of the District Bank (Cradock's bankers) to be placed in the plaintiffs' new account with that bank. A cheque for £232,500 was drawn on that account in favour of Woodstock Trust Ltd, by way of loan and Woodstock lent that sum to Cradock, the cheque being paid into Cradock's account. Cradock had obtained 79% of the plaintiff company's stock for £195,500, which was met from the sum of £232,500. The learned judge first dealt with an allegation that the bank was liable as a constructive trustee, and then considered the bank's liability in contract. Having recorded that it was common ground that any standard of care which puts a person on inquiry or notice was the same under both the equitable and common law claims,[5] he held that the bank had been negligent in honouring a cheque drawn on the plaintiffs' account without any or any sufficient inquiry as to the purpose for which it was being applied.[6] The standard of care set by the learned judge was undoubtedly a high one, and involved rejection of the submission that the bank is only liable if it actually knows of the drawer's lack of authority or, if from facts in the actual knowledge of the bank, the irresistible inference is that the cheque is so drawn.[7] The same high standard was applied by Brightman J in *Karak Rubber Co Ltd v Burden (No 2),*[8] where the duty of care was held to include the duty to make such inquiries as may, in given circumstances, be appropriate and practical if the banker has, or a reasonable banker would have, grounds for believing that the authorised signatories are misusing their authority for

---

moneys of R W Taylor (Coventry) Ltd found their way into an account opened on forged documents for the alleged purpose, inter alia, of a take-over by the plaintiff company of R H Taylor (Coventry) Ltd. McNair J after hearing evidence of current banking practice, refused to accept that the defendant bank had been negligent.

2 (1868) LR 3 HL 1.

3 Ibid at 11. Lord Cairns added on the facts of the case '... even although that customer might happen to be an administrator or executor.' This statement of Lord Cairns was cited by Dillon LJ as a clear rule of law in *Bhogal v Punjab National Bank* [1988] 2 All ER 296 at 300f. See also *Bank of New South Wales v Goulburn Valley Butter Co Pty Ltd* [1902] AC 543, PC, especially per Lord Davey at 550.

4 [1968] 1 WLR 1555, [1968] 2 All ER 1073.

5 Ibid at, respectively, 1591F and 1105E.

6 Ibid at, respectively, 1634E and 1138D.

7 Ibid at, respectively, 1609E and 1119H.

8 [1972] 1 All ER 1210, [1972] 1 WLR 602.

the purpose of defrauding their principal or otherwise defeating his true intentions.[9]

The decisions in *Selangor* and *Karak* did not pass without criticism.[10] This was noted by Steyn J in the recent case of *Barclays Bank plc v Quincecare,*[11] where the plaintiff bank's claims against a corporate borrower and its guarantor were resisted on the ground that the bank, in executing a payment order given on behalf of the company by its chairman, had been put on enquiry that the chairman was acting for his own benefit, or in any event, for an unauthorised purpose. In defining the paying banker's duty of care, Steyn J first gave careful consideration to the competing factors on either side, and then held that the fair balance between them was that a banker must refrain from executing an order if and for so long as he is put on inquiry in the sense that he has reasonable grounds (although not necessarily proof) for believing that the order is an attempt to misappropriate the funds of the company.

Having stated the governing principle in terms not dissimilar from the formulations in *Selangor* and *Karak,* the learned judge observed that factors such as the standing of the corporate customer, the bank's knowledge of the signatory, the amount involved, the need for a prompt transfer, the presence of unusual features and the scope and means for making reasonable inquiries may be relevant. He then identified the following factor as one which will often be decisive:

'That is the consideration that, in the absence of telling indications to the contrary, a banker will usually approach a suggestion that a director of a corporate customer is trying to defraud the company with an initial reaction of instinctive disbelief.'

The learned judge went on to observe that trust, not distrust, is the basis of a bank's dealings with its customers. These observations point in practice to a less onerous and fairer duty than that laid down in *Selangor* and *Karak*.

Quincecare was shortly followed by *Lipkin Gorman v Karpnale Ltd,*[12] where the scope of the paying banker's duty of care was considered by the Court of Appeal for the first time in many years. The appeal was by Lloyds Bank plc against a finding of liability as a constructive trustee and (apparently) for breach of contract. The basic facts were that a partner in a firm of solicitors was entitled to draw on the firm's client account on his sole signature. The partner was a compulsive gambler and stole monies from the clients' account in order to fund his addiction. The net loss to the clients' account was not less than £222,908.98.

The Court of Appeal dealt essentially with two issues, namely (1) the interrelation between the constructive trust claim and the claim for breach of contract and (2) the standard of care in contract. As to the first issue, the Court of Appeal accepted the bank's submission that if it was liable for breach of contract, the question whether it was liable as constructive trustee was irrelevant, and if it was not liable for breach of contract, it could not be liable as a constructive trustee.[13] This proposition prima facie holds good whenever the same basic facts are alleged by a customer to give rise to liability

9 Ibid at, respectively, 1231h and 629G.
10 See *Paget* (9th edn) p 225; *Goode* Commercial Law (1982) p 514.
11 [1988] 1 FTLR 507.
12 (1988) Times, 19 November.
13 See per Parker and Nicholls LJJ.

on the part of the paying banker for breach of contract and as a constructive trustee. As to the second issue, May LJ stated as follows:

'For my part I would hesitate to try to lay down any detailed rules in this context. In the simple case of a current account in credit the basic obligation on the banker is to pay his customer's cheques in accordance with his mandate. Having in mind the vast numbers of cheques which are presented for payment every day in this country, whether over a bank counter or through the clearing, it is in my opinion only when the circumstances are such that any reasonable cashier would hesitate to pay a cheque at once and refer it to his or her superior, and when any reasonable superior would hesitate to authorise payment without enquiry, that a cheque should not be paid immediately upon presentation and such enquiry made. Further, it would I think be only in rare circumstances, and only when any reasonable bank manager would do the same, that a manager should instruct his staff to refer all or some of his customer's cheques to him before they are paid.'

Parker LJ approached this question with the important observation that the reported authorities in which the question for decision has been whether a bank has failed in a duty of care must be approached with caution, for they are essentially no more than decisions of fact, ie of the application of the law to an endless variety of circumstances. In particular:

(i)   what may be held to be a breach of duty at one time may not be a breach of duty at another;[14]
(ii) cases relating to a collecting banker being sued in conversion and those relating to a paying banker being sued for breach of contract raise different considerations; and
(iii) the distinction between liability as a constructive trustee and liability for breach of contract is frequently blurred or unconsidered.

The standard of care was then formulated by Parker LJ as follows:

'The question must be whether if a reasonable and honest banker knew of the relevant facts he would have considered that there was a serious or real possibility albeit not amounting to a probability that his customer might be being defrauded. ... If it is established then in my view a reasonable banker would be in breach of duty if he continued to pay cheques without enquiry. He could not simply sit back and ignore the situation.'

Both *Quincecare* and *Lipkin Gorman* appear to set the contractual duty of care at a lower, and more realistic, standard than that applied in *Selangor* and *Karak*. It is submitted that this represents a fairer balance between the competing factors on either side.

(d) Proof of repayment

Reference has been made in ch 11, ante to the account stated principle. In the great majority of cases, that principle does not apply, and the question may then arise whether a particular sum has or has not been repaid. This is obviously a question of fact. An unusual example is *Douglass v Lloyds Bank Ltd*,[15] where the plaintiff claimed in an action heard in 1929 repayment of the balance of a deposit placed in May 1866. The judge held that although

---

14 Citing *Marfani & Co Ltd v Midland Bank Ltd* [1968] 2 All ER 573 at 579D, [1968] 1 WLR 956 at 972G, CA, per Diplock LJ.
15 (1929) 34 Com Cas 263. The judgment of Roche J gives a fascinating insight into the banking crisis in 1866.

the bank could produce no evidence of repayment, the proper inference was that the money must have been repaid. The point is of interest in that the question is raised whether want of any record in the books of a bank can be material evidence of the non-existence of the debt; obviously much could depend on when the deposit is alleged to have been made, for banks cannot keep records for ever.

(e) Forged and unauthorised signatures

The banker is not protected if he acts upon a forged or unauthorised payment instruction. The law in this regard has developed almost exclusively in relation to signatures on cheques, and it is in that context that the matter is considered (see p 211).

3   THE PAYMENT OF CHEQUES

(a) Regular and unambiguous in form

The cheque must be regular and unambiguous in form. Prior to the *Macmillan* case,[16] the only direct authority on this point was a dictum of Lord Blackburn in *Cunliffe Brooks & Co v Blackburn Benefit Society*[17] to the effect that the banker was only bound to pay 'cheques properly drawn'. But judgments both in the *Macmillan* and the *Joachimson*[18] cases explicitly declare that it is part of the contractual relation that the customer shall issue and the banker receive his mandate, embodied in the cheque, in plain, unmistakable terms. In the *Macmillan* case Lord Haldane said:[19]

'The customer contracts reciprocally that in drawing his cheques on the banker he will draw them in such a form as will enable the banker to fulfil his obligation, and therefore in a form that is clear and free from ambiguity.'

and

'The banker as a mandatory has a right to insist on having his mandate in a form which does not leave room for misgiving as to what he is called on to do'

and Lord Shaw enunciates much the same rule with regard to a cheque which suggests that it has been tampered with.[20]

As regards ambiguity in the mandate the recognised rule is that an agent who has adopted a reasonable course in face of ambiguity in the principal's instructions cannot be made liable whether such ambiguity arises from the method of expression or the medium of communication.[1] The banker is entitled to the benefit of this rule, but must also bear in mind the limits to its operation, including (1) that once a person enters into a contract, he is bound by its terms, which, in the event of dispute, will fall to be construed objectively; (2) that a party relying on his own interpretation of the relevant instrument

16 [1918] AC 777, HL.
17 (1884) 9 App Cas 857 at 864, HL.
18 [1921] 3 KB 110, CA.
19 [1918] AC 777 at 814 and 816.
20 Ibid at 824.
 1 *Ireland v Livingstone* (1872) LR 5 HL 395; *Curtice v London City and Midland Bank Ltd* [1908] 1 KB 293.

must have acted reasonably in all the circumstances in so doing, and, if the ambiguity is patent on the face of the document, it may well be right, especially with the facilities of modern communications, for an agent to have his instructions clarified by his principal, if time permits, before acting on them.[2]

It was recognised in the *Macmillan* case that the customer has no right to put upon the banker, and the banker is not bound to accept, any risk or liability not contemplated in or essentially arising out of the ordinary routine of business.

The rights of the banker to decline unusual risks, clearly recognised since the *Macmillan* case, are not confined to those arising directly from ambiguity of the mandate. It is a fair reading of the contractual obligation that not only shall the customer not impose, but the banker need not undertake, exceptional risks. In banking practice contingencies arise where, in the interests of banker and customer alike, the only reasonable course is to 'postpone' payment in appropriate and innocuous terms, as for instance where a cheque or draft is negotiated abroad and on which appears a special indorsement in Arabic or other Oriental characters, conveying absolutely nothing to the drawee bank.[3] By issuing such a cheque the customer must be taken to empower the banker to act reasonably for his own protection in any contingency such as foreign negotiation which may arise in connection with the cheque. The dictum of Maule J in *Robarts v Tucker*[4] that a banker might defer payment of a bill until he had satisfied himself that the indorsements thereon were genuine was expressly disapproved by the House of Lords in *Vagliano's* case, Lord Macnaghten laying down that a banker must pay off-hand and as a matter of course bills presented for payment, duly accepted and regular and complete on the face of them.

Ungoed-Thomas J in *Selangor United Rubber Estates v Cradock (No 3)*[5] recognised

> 'the very limited time in which banks have to decide what course to take with regard to a cheque presented for payment without risking liability for delay, and the extent to which an operation is unusual or out of the ordinary course of business.'

(b) Rules of the London Bankers' Clearing House

The rules of the London Bankers' Clearing House require that a bank dishonouring a cheque presented through the General (not the Town) clearing shall return it to the branch or office into which it was paid; it must be returned direct, not through the London office. Where these rules apply, a bank neglecting to adopt this course may be held to have paid the cheque[6] having represented that the cheque was paid. The case concerned two members of the clearing house but does not touch the question whether a customer of a clearing bank is entitled similarly to rely on an alleged

2 *European Asian Bank AG v Punjab & Sind Bank* [1983] 2 All ER 508 at 517, 518, [1983] 1 WLR 642 at 656, CA.

3 See *Carlisle and Cumberland Banking Co v Bragg* [1911] 1 KB 489 overruled by *Saunders v Anglia Building Society* [1971] AC 1004, [1970] 3 All ER 961; *Arab Bank Ltd v Ross* [1952] 2 QB 216, [1952] 1 All ER 709.

4 (1851) 16 QB 560.

5 [1968] 2 All ER 1073 at 1118H, [1968] 1 WLR 1555 at 1608C.

6 *Parr's Bank Ltd v Thomas Ashby & Co* (1898) 14 TLR 563; *Riedell v Commercial Bank of Australia Ltd* [1931] VLR 382.

representation. In Australia it has been held that the plaintiff 'was entitled as between himself and his agent to have the benefit of the advantage arising from the use of the machinery of the clearing house'.[7] Even so, it is still an open question whether the payee of a cheque may so rely on the rules of a clearing house as to be entitled to take advantage of any breach of a rule. The banks alone are party to the agreement of the rules. Whether there is privity with a paying bank through the payee's (collecting) bank is also an unanswered question. In *Parr's Bank Ltd v Thomas Ashby & Co*[8] the presenting bank would have suffered loss if it had not been able to recover from the paying bank, but what of the case where there was no question of loss except to the payee of the cheque? It is submitted that the payee of a cheque collected through a clearing house may not be justified in assuming that the rules are made for his benefit so that he may attack a paying bank which fails to obey the rules.

Where a bank receives from a customer for collection a cheque drawn on another bank by a person having an account at a branch of the paying bank and the cheque is dealt with through the inter-bank system for clearing cheques, the presenting bank's responsibility to its customer in respect of the collection is discharged only when the cheque is physically delivered to that branch of the paying bank for decision whether it should be paid or not.[9]

(c) Cheques out of date

It is the practice of bankers not to pay cheques presented after a certain period has elapsed since their ostensible dates of issue. The justification for this course is not very obvious. If the drawer is not willing to allow the cheque to remain outstanding, he may stop it. The difference between the practice of various banks makes it difficult to set up a custom, which must be universal and uniform among, at least, the bankers of a particular locality; there cannot be one custom of bankers in the City of London and another in the West End.[10] 'It was either a custom of the trade or nothing'.[11] Nor does the practice of a particular bank bind even a customer until it develops into a course of business, as is discussed in a note to *Serle v Norton*.[12] The note is, of course, no authority and the case itself affords none, especially in the altered conditions of the Bills of Exchange Act. The drawer's liability holds good for six years, save in one contingency, that of the cheque not having been presented within reasonable time, the bank having failed within such reasonable time, and the drawer having lost money by reason of such failure and failure to present in time. In such case he is discharged to the extent of his loss and no further. Cheques are intended for speedy presentation, not prolonged negotiation or as continuing security; but that has no legitimate application beyond that of limiting the period a cheque may be held over to charge parties other than the drawer, the cheque differing herein from the ordinary bill on demand. The banker might justify refusal to pay on the

7 Per Mann J in *Riedell v Commercial Bank of Australia Ltd* [1931] VLR 382 at 384, 389.
8 (1898) 14 TLR 563.
9 *Barclays Bank plc v Bank of England* [1985] 1 All ER 385 (Bingham J sitting as an arbitrator).
10 Cf *Rickford v Ridge* (1810) 2 Camp 537 and *Lloyds Bank Ltd v Swiss Bankverein* (1913) 108 LT 143, 18 Com Cas 79.
11 *Lloyds Bank Ltd v Swiss Bankverein* (1913) 108 LT 143 at 145 per Farwell LJ.
12 (1841) 2 Mood & R 401 at 404, in which, incidentally, Lord Abinger said that if the jury thought the cheque was post-dated, it was void.

ground that the practice has become so general that payment after the allotted period would not be in the ordinary course of business, but again the varying length of that period presents difficulties.

The answer given on such cheques, such as 'Out of date', is in no way calculated to damage the customer's credit, and the question of the validity of the practice is, therefore, never likely to be raised.

Bankers generally call such cheques 'stale', a term more properly applied to a cheque which is negotiated after being on the face of it an unreasonable time in circulation and so is assimilated to an overdue bill by s 36(3) of the Bills of Exchange Act 1882. As to when a cheque becomes stale or overdue see *London and County Banking Co v Groome*,[13] in which the plaintiff bank took the cheque eight days after its date. The judge held that the lapse of eight days, though not conclusive, was a circumstance to be taken into consideration. In *Griffiths v Dalton*,[14] Macnaghten J said that he did not regard *Hague v French*[15] and *Giles v Bourne*,[16] as supporting

'the proposition that an undated cheque is an instrument which the banker on whom it is drawn is bound to honour'.

The disability attaching to the transfer of such an instrument is, however, probably not a bar to its payment 'at or after maturity' by the drawee banker.

(d) Marking of cheques

The marking of a cheque is the addition by a banker of words to the face of the instrument with the object of furthering its ready acceptance by affording evidence that it is drawn in good faith and that there are funds sufficient and available to meet it.[17]

(i) Marking at the instance of a customer

In the United Kingdom, marking at the instance of a customer is rare. In 1920 the Committee of London Clearing Bankers resolved

'That the practice of marking or certifying at the request of a customer his cheques or drafts upon a clearing bank be discontinued, and that if such a request be made, the banks should issue to their customer in exchange for his cheque either a draft on themselves or on the Bank of England'.

Although in *Gaden v Newfoundland Savings Bank*[18] and *Imperial Bank of Canada v Bank of Hamilton*[19] the Privy Council referred to the object and effect of marking a cheque at the instance of a customer as being to add the credit of the drawee bank to that of the drawer, it may be taken that in the United Kingdom the marking of a cheque at the instance of the customer does not involve any liability on the part of the banker to the payee or any subsequent holder. First, the marking does not possess the essential characteristics of an acceptance, required by the Bills of Exchange Act.[20] In

---

13 (1881) 8 QBD 288.
14 [1940] 2 KB 264.
15 (1802) 3 Bos & P 173.
16 (1817) 6 M & S 73.
17 See *Gaden v Newfoundland Savings Bank* [1899] AC 281, PC and *Imperial Bank of Canada v Bank of Hamilton* [1903] AC 49, PC.
18 [1899] AC 281, PC.
19 [1903] AC 49, PC.
20 Ss 2, 17, 21.

Keene v Beard[1] it was suggested that there was nothing to prevent a banker accepting a cheque if so disposed; but neither in form nor effect is marking an acceptance of which the payee or a holder can avail himself. This is supported by a Privy Council opinion delivered by Lord Wright in *Bank of Baroda Ltd v Punjab National Bank Ltd*[2] (see post) that marking a cheque was not the equivalent of an acceptance. This being so, marking at the instance of the customer does not render the bank liable to the payee or holder.

Secondly, as regards money had and received, in *Warwick v Rogers*[3] it was said that

'There are many cases which establish that no action for money had and received will lie against a banker or agent in respect of funds which his principal has ordered him to pay to any person, at the suit of the person in whose favour the order is made, where the banker or agent has not assented to the order and communicated his assent to the plaintiff.'

The intimation, if any, conveyed by the marking of a cheque is far too vague and indeterminate to operate as such admission.

Thirdly, in so far as any representation is involved the banker only certifies the state of the account of the customer. If this is right any representation to the payee or subsequent holder lies in the use made by the customer of the intimation conveyed by the marking when he issues the cheque.

(ii) *Marking at the instance of a payee or holder*

In England the practice, common in North America, of the payee or holder bringing a cheque to the drawee bank, not for payment, but to get it marked is practically unknown. But if a marked cheque were brought to the bank by the payee or a holder, and the bank were to undertake to pay the specific person who brought it, or admit that they held the money for his use, such admission or promise would seem to be sufficient to bind the bank and obviate any difficulty arising from the want of appropriation of a definite sum to the cheque (see *Prince v Oriental Bank Corpn*).[4] Undoubtedly that is so when the cheque is presented for payment and, for some reason or other, marked by the bank instead of being paid (cf *Re Beaumont, Beaumont v Ewbank*[5] in which the bank refused to pay the cheque because of doubt concerning the drawer's signature, though otherwise payment would have been made).

In *Bank of Baroda Ltd v Punjab National Bank Ltd*[6] the cheques were marked with the words 'Marked good for payment up to 20 June 1939'. The court declined to treat this as an acceptance but did not indicate precisely what effect it might have. It was obviously not an indorsement and thus, to quote Lord Wright, would appear to be nothing more than

'words of representation as to the genuineness of the cheque and of the signature.

1 (1860) 8 CBNS 372.
2 [1944] AC 176, [1944] 2 All ER 83.
3 (1843) 5 Man & G 340 at 374 per Tindal CJ; see also *Malcolm v Scott* (1850) 5 Exch 601; cf *W P Greenhalgh & Sons v Union Bank of Manchester* [1924] 2 KB 153.
4 (1878) 3 App Cas 325 at 331.
5 [1902] 1 Ch 889 at 895.
6 [1944] AC 176, [1944] 2 All ER 83.

If the cheque had not been post-dated the certification might also be held to include a representation as to the then sufficiency of the drawer's account.'

And again, if it

'amounted to a promise ... want of consideration would be fatal to its enforceability',

and further,

'Nor could the certification be construed as an estoppel ... because what is called the representation related to the future.'

Another form of marking is that brought to light in the much older Ceylon case of *Adaicappa Chetty v Thos Cook & Son (Bankers) Ltd.*[7] There the marking was 'Payment of this cheque on ... guaranteed, per pro Thos. Cook & Son (Bankers) Ltd, John Davis.' The Supreme Court held that this constituted an acceptance, but the Privy Council, deciding the case on the signatory's want of authority, said, per Lord Atkin,

'Anything less like the ordinary business conception of an acceptance in form and intention than this contract it would perhaps be difficult to find.'

(iii) *Marking as between bankers*

As between banker and banker, cheques received from customers by London Clearing banks too late for presentation through the Clearing House on the day of receipt used to be sent to the clearing bank on which they were drawn, and then marked. Such marking was legally recognised as importing a promise or undertaking to pay, not analogous to acceptance, but based on custom:

'Besides this, a custom has grown up among bankers themselves of marking cheques as good for the purposes of clearance by which they become bound to one another'.[8]

However, the practice of marking as between bankers has now been discontinued by the agreement of the Committee of London Clearing Bankers. The procedure now is to have the cheque specially presented.

(e) Forged or unauthorised signatures

(i) *Effect of a forged or unauthorised signature*

By s 24 of the Bills of Exchange Act 1882:

'Subject to the provisions of this Act, where a signature on a bill is forged or placed thereon without the authority of the person whose signature it purports to be, the forged or unauthorised signature is wholly inoperative, and no right to retain the bill or to give a discharge therefor or to enforce payment thereof against any party thereto can be acquired through or under that signature, unless the party against whom it is sought to retain or enforce payment of the bill is precluded from setting up the forgery or want of authority.

Provided that nothing in this section shall affect the ratification of an unauthorised signature not amounting to a forgery.'

It is deducible from the language of this section that a forgery cannot be

---

7 (1930) 31 Ceylon NLR 385, on appeal (1932) 34 Ceylon NLR 443.
8 *Goodwin v Robarts* (1875) LR 10 Exch 337 at 351, per Cockburn CJ.

ratified. Unless the banker can set up an estoppel (see post) or adoption,[9] he is unprotected against forgery or lack of authority in the *drawing* of a bill. The circumstances is which a banker is protected against a forged *indorsement* are considered in ch 24, post.

(ii) Meaning of 'forged' and 'forgery'

The use of the words 'forged' and 'forgery' in ss 24 and 60 of the Bills of Exchange Act without definition makes it inevitable that criminal enactments in force from time to time should to some degree be imported into civil actions relating to bills and cheques. This seems to have been tacitly accepted during the period in force of the Forgery Act 1913, which defined forgery as the making of a false document in order that it might be used as genuine (s 1(1)). The 1913 Act was repealed and replaced by the Forgery and Counterfeiting Act 1981, which defines the offence of forgery as follows:

'1. A person is guilty of forgery if he makes a false instrument, with the intention that he or another shall use it to induce somebody to accept it as genuine, and by reason of so accepting it to do or not to do some act to his own or any other person's prejudice'.

The offence of forgery is followed by a series of offences in relation to it, covering, inter alia, the making of a false instrument (as defined by s 9 of the Act), the copying of a genuine instrument (s 2), the use of a false instrument (s 3) with the intention (ss 4 and 5)

'that he or another shall use it to induce someone to accept it ... and by reason of so accepting it to do or not to do some act to his own or any other person's prejudice'.

Section 5 further sets out the instruments to which falsity may attach, including money and postal orders, cheques, travellers' cheques, cheque and credit cards.

Section 9 provides that an instrument is false (for the purposes of this part of the Act):

'(a) if it purports to have been made in the form in which it is made by a person who did not in fact make it in that form; or

(b) if it purports to have been made in the form in which it is made on the authority of a person who did not in fact authorise its making in that form; or

(c) if it purports to have been made in the terms in which it is made by a person who did not in fact make it in those terms; or

(d) if it purports to have been made in the terms in which it is made on the authority of a person who did not in fact authorise its making in those terms; or

(e) if it purports to have been altered in any respect by a person who did not in fact alter it in that respect; or

(f) if it purports to have been altered in any respect on the authority of a person who did not in fact authorise the alteration in that respect; or

(g) if it purports to have been made or altered on a date on which, or at a place at which, or otherwise in circumstances in which, it was not in fact made or altered; or

(h) if it purports to have been made or altered by an existing person but he did not in fact exist.

9 As to adoption, see *Greenwood v Martin's Bank Ltd* [1933] AC 51 at 57, per Lord Tomlin.

(2) A person is to be treated for the purpose of this Part of this Act as making a false instrument if he alters an instrument so as to make it false in any respect (whether or not it is false in some other respect apart from that alteration).'

By s 8, 'instrument' means

(a) any document, whether of a formal or informal character; and
(b) any disc, tape, sound track or other device on or in which information is recorded or stored by mechanical, electronic or other means.

(iii) Inapplicability of the rule in Turquand's case to cases of forgery

It was established by the House of Lords in *Ruben v Great Fingall Consolidated*[10] that the doctrine that a person is deemed to have notice of a company's articles of association and need not inquire whether the domestic arrangements necessary to carry out a power of delegation have been made, has no application where the document to which that principle is sought to be applied is a forgery. In the words of Lord Loreburn LC:[11]

'It is quite true that persons dealing with limited liability companies are not bound to inquire into their indoor management, and will not be affected by irregularities of which they had no notice. But this doctrine, which is well established, applies only to irregularities that otherwise might affect a genuine transaction. It cannot apply to a forgery.'

Some twelve years or so after the passing of the Forgery Act 1913, came the case of *Kreditbank Cassel GmbH v Schenkers*.[12] It appears to be the first case (if the case of *Alexander Stewart & Son of Dundee Ltd v Westminster Bank Ltd*,[13] is excepted) in which the effect of the Act on civil proceedings as to bills and on the doctrine of imputed delegated authority formed the ground of decision. Clarke, the local manager of a company, drew and indorsed bills in the company's name in representative form and his official capacity. There was in the articles a very wide power to delegate the drawing and indorsing of bills, probably wide enough to have covered delegation to the local manager, but rather on the border line in view of his position as a local manager only. Certain powers as to cheques had been delegated to him, but no power to draw or indorse bills. The judge in the court below found imputed delegated authority and bona fide holder for value, and gave judgment against the company. The Court of Appeal, while doubting the finding as to imputed authority did not overrule it, or the other finding. They reversed the judgment on the ground that the bills were forgeries within the 1913 Act, consequently void under the Bills of Exchange Act, and that the doctrine of imputed delegated authority did not apply where the document in question was a forgery. On the first point, Atkin LJ said the bills were 'forgeries, they were false documents and fraudulent documents, concocted for fraud'. Scrutton LJ said:[14]

'In the present case the bills are clearly forgeries within the Forgery Act 1913, as they contain a false statement – namely, that Clarke was acting for the company, and they purport to bind the company in fraud of the company.'

10 [1906] AC 439.
11 Ibid at 443.
12 [1927] 1 KB 826, CA.
13 [1926] WN 126; revsd [1926] WN 271. The case is not well reported on this point.
14 [1927] 1 KB 826 at 840.

He referred to *Ruben's* case and *Lloyd v Grace Smith & Co*[15] as being a little difficult to reconcile.

The *Shenkers* case can be compared with *Morison v London Country and Westminster Bank Ltd,*[16] which established that the fraudulent misuse of authority does not invalidate a negotiable instrument in the hands of an innocent holder, that an instrument cannot be valid for one purpose and invalid for another, genuine in the hands of one person but a forgery in the hands of another. Authority once exercised is not retracted by misuse of that authority.

As Phillimore LJ said in the *Morison* case:

'Where there is power to sign "per pro", a document so signed is not a forgery to the person to whom it is addressed and who can, or, a fortiori, must, act upon it and therefore is not a forgery at all. This misuse by an agent of his power of writing his principal's name, either as a simple signature or by signing "per pro", may, however, be indictable as some sort of fraud.'

(iv) *Raised or otherwise materially altered cheques*

By s 64 of the Bills of Exchange Act 1882:

'(1) Where a bill or acceptance is materially altered without the assent of all parties liable on the bill, the bill is avoided except as against a party who has himself made, authorised, or assented to the alteration, and subsequent indorsers.
Provided that,
   Where a bill has been materially altered, but the alteration is not apparent, and the bill is in the hands of a holder in due course, such holder may avail himself of the bill as if it had not been altered, and may enforce payment of it according to its original tenor.
(2) In particular the following alterations are material, namely, any alteration of the date, the sum payable, the time of payment, the place of payment, and, where a bill has been accepted generally, the addition of a place of payment without the acceptor's assent.'

As to when an alteration is apparent:

'An alteration in a bill is apparent within s 64 if it is of such a kind that it would be observed and noticed by an intending holder scrutinising the document, which he contemplated taking, with reasonable care.'[17]

It may be contended that the avoidance by material alteration obtains in its extreme rigour only against a party setting up the instrument either as ground of action or direct means of defence. But that is not consonant with the cases cited below, and is only most vaguely deducible from *Suffell v Bank of England.*[18] An alteration is not the less effective because, on the face of it, it is authorised. Possibly the banker's best contention would be that where it is a question of mere unauthorised addition or increase, where the genuine can be disentangled from the false, the customer's mandate still holds good pro tanto; in the same way as Lord Ellenborough 'with the eyes of the law' read the erased but still legible £57 instead of the substituted £66 in *Henfree v Bromley.*[19] But this contention would not help in cases where the cheque

15 [1912] AC 716.
16 [1914] 3 KB 356, CA.
17 Per Salter J *Woollatt v Stanley* (1928) 138 LT 620.
18 (1882) 9 QBD 555.
19 (1805) 6 East 309.

was so altered as completely to merge its identity and directly contravene the customer's mandate. A crossed cheque opened by 'Pay Cash' and the signature of drawer forged; a post-dated cheque in which the date is altered to an earlier one;[20] 'order' altered to 'bearer' and falsely initialled; all these are material alterations which eliminate the customer's mandate. The last instance is a particularly hard one, inasmuch as if the fraudulent person had left the 'order' but forged the indorsement, the banker would be protected by s 60.[1] See also *Slingsby v District Bank Ltd.*[2]

This question does not seem affected by the *Macmillan* case.[3] If, as there, no sum was filled in in writing, the whole raised amount could be debited, under either of the alternative grounds of Lord Finlay's judgment in the *Macmillan* case. If a sum had been filled in but raised, the matter would stand as stated above.

Where a customer has drawn a cheque without leaving blanks or affording other facilities for alteration or addition, and the cheque is subsequently fraudulently manipulated so as to show a higher face amount, which is paid by the banker, he clearly cannot charge his customer with the excess.[4]

As to the amount chargeable, in *Colonial Bank of Australasia Ltd v Marshall,*[5] as in the earlier raised cheque cases, the customer only took objection to being charged with the excess over the original amount. In the *Macmillan* case, the original sum was negligible and the point was not raised. There are, however, expressions in other cases which, taken strictly, would seem to suggest a doubt as to the banker's right to debit even the original amount, if he is precluded from debiting the excess:

'... any alteration in a material part of any instrument or agreement avoids it, because it thereby ceases to be the same instrument.'[6]

'The question is whether the alteration introduced made it a different note; if it be material it is a different note.'[7]

'But it is further to be considered whether the crossing was part of the cheque, so that the erasure of it would amount to a forgery of another and different cheque from that which the plaintiff drew; for if it had that effect, the plaintiff never drew the cheque that was paid, and the banker cannot claim credit for it.'[8]

'If unfortunately he (the banker) pays money belonging to the customer upon an order which is not genuine, he must suffer; and to justify the payment, he must show that the order is genuine, not in signature only, but in every respect.'[9]

See, however, this last case distinguished in a case of accidental destruction of numbers on a note or bill.[10]

20 Cf *Vance v Lowther* (1876) 1 Ex D 176.
1 [1918] AC 777.
2 [1932] 1 KB 544, 37 Com Cas 39.
3 [1918] AC 777.
4 *Hall v Fuller* (1826) 5 B & C 750; and see now s 64.
5 [1906] AC 559; in *Commonwealth Trading Bank of Australia v Sydney Wide Stores Pty Ltd* (1981) 55 ALJR 574 the High Court of Australia held that 'the principle enunciated in *Macmillan* is to be preferred to that stated in *Marshall*' (1981) 148 CLR 304.
6 *Master v Miller* (1791) 4 Term Rep 320.
7 *Knill v Williams* (1809) 10 East 431.
8 *Simmons v Taylor* (1857) 2 CBNS 528 at 539; see also 541; affd (1858) 4 CBNS 463.
9 *Hall v Fuller* (1826) 5 B & C 750 at 757; see also *Suffell v Bank of England* (1882) 9 QBD 555.
10 *Hong Kong and Shanghai Banking Corpn v Lo Lee Shi* [1928] AC 181, distinguishing *Suffell v Bank of England* (1882) 9 QBD 555.

However, in *Imperial Bank of Canada v Bank of Hamilton*,[11] the Judicial Committee treat a raised cheque as having been a good cheque for the original amount.

A person who without authority materially alters a bill or cheque within the meaning of s 64 of the Bills of Exchange Act 1882 would seem to be making a false instrument and accordingly guilty of forgery under s 1 of the Forgery and Counterfeiting Act 1981.

As regards the material alteration of a promissory note, an unsuccessful attempt was made in Ireland by the signatory to a promissory note to avoid liability on the ground that the signature was appended after the completion and issue of the note and therefore constituted a material alteration.[12] Gavan Duffy J held that the alteration was material, but saw 'no reason, either in logic or grammar, for making an actual signatory less liable because he was not an original party'. He cited *Gardner v Walsh*,[13] which was supported in *Bolster v Shaw*,[14] a Canadian case; but *Re Smith, ex p Yates*,[15] which is authority for holding an additional signature to be operative as an indorsement, was not referred to.

(v) Domiciled bills

A head of forgery involving danger to the banker is forged indorsement on bills accepted payable with him. With regard to these there is no statutory protection. Neither s 60 of the Bills of Exchange Act, nor s 19 of the Stamp Act 1853,[16] has any bearing on them inasmuch as the bill, even if payable on demand, is not drawn on the banker. The payment is made to the wrong person, and the banker is therefore not entitled to debit his customer.[17] There is no question of inchoate instrument, incomplete instrument, or holding out. The acceptor has no possible means of preventing forged indorsement. The duty of customer to banker applies, however, with full force to the payment of domiciled acceptances, as being definitely the exercise of the functions of a mandatory, and such protection as can be derived therefrom is undoubtedly open to the banker. In practice bankers normally take the customer's indemnity before agreeing to pay bills domiciled with them.

(vi) Estoppel

An estoppel by representation may arise by express representation or by silence in the face of a duty to speak. The latter type of representation is considered below in the context of the customer's duties to the paying banker.

An example of an estoppel by express representation can be found in *Bank of England v Vagliano Bros*,[18] where the drawer's name, as well as that of the supposed payee, was the work of the forger, and the instruments were not really bills at all. The House of Lords held that Vagliano, by writing an acceptance on such instruments, represented to the bank that they were

11 [1903] AC 49.
12 *Flanagan v National Bank Ltd* (1938) 72 ILT 63.
13 (1855) 5 E & B 83.
14 [1917] 1 WWR 431.
15 (1857) 2 De G & J 191.
16 See Ch 24, post.
17 *Robarts v Tucker* (1851) 16 QB 560; *Bank of England v Vagliano Bros* [1891] AC 107.
18 [1891] AC 107.

genuine bills and that, this representation being untrue, the bank were entitled to be indemnified.[19] Moreover, the inclusion of spurious instruments in letters of advice to the bank of bills coming forward for payment was an act of the customer directly tending to mislead the bank, though such letters could not be read as guaranteeing any indorsement.

A valuable feature in the case is the assertion of the right of bankers, acting as agents for the payment of domiciled bills, to all the protection, consideration and indemnities to which an ordinary agent is entitled as against his principal.

'... a principal who has misled his agent into doing something on his behalf which the agent has honestly done would not be entitled to claim against the agent in respect of the act so done'.[20]

'It is not ... disputed that there might, as between banker and customer, be circumstances which would be an answer to the prima facie case that the authority was only to pay to the order of the person named as payee upon the bill, and that the banker can only charge the customer with payments made pursuant to that authority. Negligence on the customer's part might be one of those circumstances; the fact that there was no real payee might be another; and I think that a representation made directly to the banker by the customer upon a material point, untrue in fact (though believed by the person who made it to be true), and on which the banker acted by paying money which he would not otherwise have paid, ought also to be an answer to that prima facie case. If the bank acted upon such a representation in good faith and according to the ordinary course of business, and a loss has in consequence occurred which would not have happened if the representation had been true, I think that is a loss which the customer, and not the bank, ought to bear'.[1]

The negligence on the part of the customer spoken of by Lord Selborne must, however, be understood as limited to negligence directly leading to the loss or 'enabling' it, in the legal sense of the phrase, to be committed.[2]

In *Brown v Westminster Bank Ltd*[3] the plaintiff expressly stated to the bank manager that certain cheques were genuine. The learned judge refused to accept that there could be no estoppel in regard to the cheques paid before the representation:

'... the plaintiff is thereafter debarred from setting up the true facts in relation to the cheques which had already been forged.'

It would seem clear that the detriment suffered by the bank in regard to the earlier cheques was the loss of the right to sue the forgers between the date of the representation and that when the forgeries first became known – and this, in spite of the fact that the bank could still sue the forgers.

---

19 See, especially, per Lord Macnaghten, ibid, at 158, 159; per Lord Halsbury, ibid, at 114.
20 Per Lord Halsbury, [1891] AC 107 at 114.
1 Per Lord Selborne, ibid, 123.
2 *Farquharson Bros & Co v King & Co* [1902] AC 325; *Bank of England v Vagliano Bros* [1891] AC 107 at 115.
3 [1964] 2 Lloyd's Rep 187, followed in *Tina Motors Pty Ltd v Australia and New Zealand Banking Group Ltd* [1977] VR 205; and see *Arrow Transfer Co Ltd v Royal Bank of Canada Bank of Montreal and Canadian Imperial Bank of Commerce* [1971] 3 WWR 241.

(f) Inchoate instruments

By s 20 of the Bills of Exchange Act 1882 (as amended):

'(1) Where a simple signature on a blank paper is delivered by the signer in order that it may be converted into a bill, it operates as a prima facie authority to fill it up as a complete bill for any amount, using the signature for that of the drawer, or the acceptor, or an indorser; and, in like manner, when a bill is wanting in any material particular, the person in possession of it has a prima facie authority to fill up the omission in any way he thinks fit.

(2) In order that any such instrument when completed may be enforceable against any person who became a party thereto prior to its completion, it must be filled up within a reasonable time, and strictly in accordance with the authority given. Reasonable time for this purpose is a question of fact.

Provided that if any instrument after completion is negotiated to a holder in due course it shall be valid and effectual for all purposes in his hands, and he may enforce it as if it had been filled up within a reasonable time and strictly in accordance with the authority given.'

Since *Lloyds Bank Ltd v Cooke*,[4] it has been generally recognised that estoppels with regard to bills and cheques are not confined to the specific cases of inchoate instruments provided for by the Bills of Exchange Act, as in s 20, but by virtue of s 97(2) include all estoppels known to the common law.[5] But it was commonly assumed that even the common law operated in favour of the person who takes a negotiable instrument as a holder or transferee, not necessarily by negotiation from a prior party; thus the payee would be included. The limitation in s 20 to the holder in due course, a source of difficulty in *Lloyds Bank Ltd v Cooke*[5] was thus got over.

The *Macmillan* case[6] greatly expanded both the range and the applicability of this doctrine. The instrument in that case was not strictly a blank stamped piece of paper. There was nothing at all in the space allotted to the amount in writing, but there was the '2' in the space for figures. Section 9(2) says:

'Where the sum payable is expressed in words and also in figures, and there is a discrepancy between the two, the sum denoted by the words is the amount payable';

here there was no sum payable expressed in words, therefore no discrepancy. Possibly this was in the minds of the House of Lords, for they treated the absence of any sum expressed in words as putting the cheque on the footing of a blank cheque, the blank stamped paper which is the ideal starting point of estoppel, whether under common law or the Bills of Exchange Act.

Lord Finlay said:[7]

'But further, it is well settled law that if a customer signs a cheque in blank and leaves it to a clerk or other person to fill it up, he is bound by the instrument as filled up by his agent. This has been suggested as the real ground for the decision in *Young v Grote*'.[8]

---

4 [1907] 1 KB 794 at 800. Collins MR thought it unnecessary to treat the rights of the parties to a promissory note in that case as having to be ascertained by reference to the Bills of Exchange Act because 'the common law doctrine of estoppel applies, and the rights of the parties may be decided by reference to that doctrine.'
5 Cf *Talbot v Von Boris* [1911] 1 KB 854.
6 [1918] AC 777. The facts of the case are set out under '4. Duties of care owed by customer'.
7 [1918] AC 777 at 811.
8 (1827) 4 Bing 253.

While the judge did not think it was the real ground, he proceeded:[9]

'But the principle is thoroughly established, and it seems to me to apply to the facts of the present case ... On this ground also, which on my view of *Young v Grote*[8] is independent of that decision, I am of opinion that this appeal should be allowed'.

Lord Haldane took the same line and laid considerable stress on the provisions of s 20 relating to cheques wanting in any material particular. Lord Parmoor's judgment is also founded on the general estoppel basis rather than on any breach of duty between banker and customer. Lord Shaw described the cheque in the *Macmillan* case as a very near approach to a blank cheque.

In *Garrard v Lewis*[10] an acceptance was delivered with the amount in figures in the margin but the body of the bill blank. It was held that the defendant acceptor was liable for the larger amount for which the bill was filled in and altered, on the ground that he clothed the person to whom he entrusted the bill with ostensible authority to fill it in as he pleased. It seems to have been taken for granted that, for the purpose of estoppel, the paying banker was in the same position as a transferee. The cheque, so far as the signature goes, is a mandate which the paying banker is bound to obey, and the customer must be taken to contemplate its effect on him as much as on a transferee, and the banker would seem entitled to the same protection.[11]

As regards s 20 whether the cheque be treated as the result of signing a blank stamped[12] paper or a bill wanting in a material particular, the instrument, if not filled up in accordance with the authority given and within a reasonable time, is only valid and effectual in the hands of a holder in due course, which normally the paying banker is not. In *Gerald Macdonald & Co v Nash & Co*[13] Lord Haldane LC held that s 20 enabled the drawers of bills to complete them by adding the name of themselves as payees, in pursuance of an agreement between them, the sellers, and the buyers.

The estoppel is in no way dependent on the existence of a duty or the breach of it; it is not a question of negligence, save possibly in the sense of a man's duty to the public.[14]

It may seem a contravention of Lord Bowen's well-known dictum about a negotiable instrument not being a gun, or a dangerous animal, but if a man chooses to deliver an inchoate negotiable instrument to an agent for the purpose of negotiating it or raising money on it, he is responsible to anybody who is injured by the agent's misuse of the instrument. It may be suggested that in the above proposition, the factor of deputing the filling-up, included by Lord Finlay, has been omitted, but there was no evidence or suggestion in the *Macmillan* case that Arthur, the partner who actually signed the cheque, gave any authority to the fraudulent clerk to fill it up; he was in a hurry and simply did not notice that it was not filled up for £2. The position, therefore,

9 [1918] AC 777 at 812.
10 (1882) 10 QBD 30.
11 And see per Lord Greene MR in *Wilson and Meeson v Pickering* [1946] KB 422, [1946] 1 All ER 394.
12 The Finance Act 1970 removed from s20 the word 'stamped' and the words 'the stamp will cover', stamp duty on bills having been abolished.
13 [1924] AC 625.
14 See per Pollack CB, in *Barker v Sterne* (1854) 9 Exch 684 at 687.

appears fairly stated as it is; the handing the inchoate instrument to another person for the purpose of negotiation or getting money must be taken to involve authority to complete it, whether the signatory knows it is incomplete or not.

However, the inchoate instrument should be delivered for negotiation or to get the money; if, as in *Smith v Prosser*,[15] it were merely handed over for safe keeping, awaiting further instructions, and the custodian wrongfully filled up and dealt with it, neither transferee nor drawee could avail himself of either the inchoate instrument or the holding-out. In *Smith v Prosser* the instrument was handed to an agent for a specific purpose; he used it for another and the transferee had notice of the transferor's want of authority. It would be unreasonable if the drawer's intention, uncommunicated and in fact contradicted by his own instrument, should prejudice an innocent transferee for value in good faith. Section 20(2) of the Bills of Exchange Act 1882 would seem unhelpful, except where the transferee can show (proviso to s 20(2)) that he is a holder in due course.

Another construction is that the emission of an inchoate negotiable instrument is a holding-out of it as a complete instrument, even when completed wrongfully, but if a transferee takes it in its inchoate state it is doubtful if he can have a complete title.

The consequences of the *Macmillan* case, especially the importation of s 20, are far-reaching, but it is not easy to predict the conditions and facts which will bring the section into play. It is enough that the principle is established. The issue of an inchoate instrument binds the drawer vis a vis the paying banker, the collecting banker and any transferee, by virtue of estoppel. The issue of an instrument so loosely drawn that it is invisibly raised in amount binds the drawer vis à vis the paying banker and any transferee, but it is not clear that he is bound as against an innocent collecting banker. Except in relation to an action against a collecting banker for conversion, there is virtually no distinction between an inchoate instrument and one so loosely drawn as in effect to be inchoate. It is not certain how far the judgments in the *Macmillan* case support this view, but the comments of Lord Shaw of Dunfermline go further than any other of the learned Law Lords. Speaking of the relative obligations of banker and customer he said:[16]

'... it appears to me that a crucial consideration in a case such as the present is this, namely, what is the point of time at which these respective obligations meet. The point of time is the presentation of the cheque. Not until that moment is the banker confronted with any mandate or order, and in my opinion the responsibility for the cheque and all that has happened to it between its signature and its presentation is not and ought not to be laid upon the banker.'

More importantly, perhaps, he said:[17]

'It may be true – it is true in this case – that what happened in the meantime to increase the nominal value of the cheque and to deceive all parties was a crime. But it was a crime brought about during the period of the customer's responsibility, and, as frequently happens in such cases, the crime of the customer's own servant. Accordingly the condition of the cheque has been altered, not only during the period of the customer's authority, but by the act of some person with whom he

15 [1907] 2 KB 735.
16 [1918] AC 777 at 824.
17 Ibid, at 825.

had left the document in charge. If it is suggested that this a hardship upon the customer (abating for the moment the obvious consideration that it is a still harder one for the banker), the answer in the general case is obvious, namely, that it is part of the customer's duty to fill up his cheque in such a way as to prevent roguery being made easy.

'My Lords, I do not here pronounce any judgment upon another type of case which may be figured. I refer to a case in which there has been no negligence on the part of the customer in the respect last alluded to, but in which erasures of great skill or deletions, say accomplished by chemical aid, have been made upon a cheque so as to undo all the care properly exercised by the customer in regard to its contents. Yet I cannot conceal from your Lordships that I should have the greatest doubt as to whether – this kind of roguery having been practised during that period of responsibility on the part of the customer to which I have referred – the customer would not also be liable.'

This concept of the drawer's 'period of responsibility' is wide. Lord Shaw does not apply his remarks to the collecting banker – the collecting banker was not in the picture in that case – but they are sufficiently wide to include him. Lord Finlay LC, quoted Pollock CB, in *Barker v Sterne*[18] as saying:

'... when a person issues a document of that kind *the rest of the world* must judge of the authority to fill it up by the paper itself.'

It should be emphasised that the *Macmillan* case was not that of an inchoate instrument within the meaning of s 20 of the Bills of Exchange Act 1882. Within s 3 of that statute it was complete in law when it was delivered by the partner's signing and handing it back to the clerk. It was a case of fraudulent alteration and the drawer's action treated as a breach of his contract with his banker.

4 DUTIES OF CARE OWED BY A CUSTOMER TO HIS BANK

In *Tai Hing Cotton Mill Ltd v Liu Chong Hing Bank Ltd*,[19] the Privy Council had to determine whether English law recognises today any duty of care owed by the customer to his bank in the operation of a current account beyond first, a duty to refrain from drawing a cheque in such a manner as may facilitate fraud or forgery, and secondly, a duty to inform the bank of any forgery of a cheque purportedly drawn on the account as soon as he, the customer, becomes aware of it. The first duty was clearly enunciated by the House of Lords in *London Joint Stock Bank Ltd v Macmillan*,[20] and the second was laid down, also by the House of Lords, in *Greenwood v Martins Bank Ltd*.[1] The duties contended for by the banks in *Tai Hing* were (1) a duty upon the customer to take reasonable precautions in the management of his business with the bank to prevent forged cheques being presented to it, and (2) a (narrower) duty to take such steps to check his periodic bank statements as a reasonable customer in his position would take to enable him to notify the bank of any debit items in the account which he had not authorised.

It has already been noted in ch 11, ante, that the Privy Council rejected the narrower duty. A fortiori, the wider duty was also rejected. It follows

18 (1854) 9 Exch 684 at 687.
19 [1986] AC 80, [1985] 2 All ER 947, PC.
20 [1918] AC 777.
 1 [1933] AC 51, HL.

that the customer's duties of care are limited to the *Macmillan* and *Greenwood* duties.

(a) The *Macmillan* duty

The facts in *Macmillan's* case were that Macmillan and Arthur had a clerk who prepared and presented for signature to one of the partners cheques for petty cash of small amount. On this occasion the clerk, with a view to fraud, wrote a cheque, inserting a 2 in the space for figures, with available blanks before and after the numeral, putting nothing where the sum in writing should appear. The cheque was to bearer and uncrossed. This inchoate instrument he tendered for signature to a partner who was just leaving the office and who, being in a hurry, failed to notice anything unusual. Being told it was for petty cash and that two pounds would be sufficient, he forthwith signed it. The clerk filled in 'One hundred and twenty pounds' in writing, inserted a 1 before the 2 and a 0 after it, presented it to the bank, received the £120 and absconded. The judge at the trial and the Court of Appeal decided against the bank; the House of Lords reversed this decision and gave judgment for the bank. They rehabilitated *Young v Grote*[2] and 'the modified doctrine of Pothier',[3] they swept away *Colonial Bank of Australasia Ltd v Marshall*[4] as a miscarriage of justice, and put the paying banker into a sound and rational position on much the same lines as those later described and defined by Atkin LJ in *Joachimson v Swiss Bank Corpn.*[5] Lord Finlay put it in the *Macmillan* case:

'If he (the customer) draws a cheque in a manner which facilitates fraud he is guilty of a breach of duty as between himself and the banker, and he will be responsible to the banker for any loss sustained by the banker as a natural and direct consequence of this breach of duty.

As the customer and the banker are under a contractual relation in this matter, it is obvious that, in drawing a cheque, the customer is bound to take usual and reasonable precautions to prevent forgery. Crime is, indeed, a very serious matter, but everyone knows that crime is not uncommon. If the cheque is drawn in such a way as to facilitate or almost to invite an increase in the amount by forgery if the cheque should get into the hands of a dishonest person, forgery is not a remote but a very natural consequence of negligence of this description.'

It is a question of degree whether neglect of ordinary precautions in issuing a cheque amounts to breach by the drawer of his contract with his banker. On the one hand there are the remarks of Bovill CJ in *Société Générale v Metropolitan Bank Ltd*[6] in which a 'y' was inserted in a slight blank left after an 'eight' in a bill, that 'it was the usual way of filling up blanks in a form', and that 'no man in the City would take notice of "eight" not being close to the next word'. At the other extreme is the *Macmillan* case itself, where the space for the amount in writing was left absolutely blank.

Where the alteration is obvious or discoverable by the exercise of reason-

2 (1827) 4 Bing 253.
3 Per Lord Halsbury LC in *Scholfield v Londesborough* [1896] AC 514 at 531.
4 [1906] AC 559, PC; the case governed the law in Australia up to August 1981 when the High Court, preferring the principle laid down in the *Macmillan* case, decided in favour of the Bank in *Commonwealth Trading Bank of Australia v Sydney Wide Stores Pty* (1981) 55 ALJR 574 Australian High Court, (1981) 148 CLR 304.
5 [1921] 3 KB 110.
6 (1873) 27 LT 849.

able care, or where the state of the cheque raises suspicion of its having been tampered with and payment is made without inquiry[7] the *Macmillan* case offers no relief.

The judgment in the *Macmillan* case is confined in terms to the drawing of a cheque. With regard to bills accepted by a customer payable at his bank, the relation of mandant and mandatory, of principal and agent, obtains at least as much as in the case of cheques. To domicile bills with a banker is an authority to pay them, though the banker is not bound to do so except perhaps, where a course of business has been established in which case there is a contractual relation or implied contract binding the banker to pay on behalf of the customer.[8] Moreover, as the banker has no statutory protection in paying bills, there is all the more reason for holding him entitled to indemnity from his customer. *Mutatis mutandis,* it might therefore be taken that the principle of the *Macmillan* case applies equally to domiciled bills. A difference to be borne in mind is that the drawer, not the acceptor, is master of the form of the bill. In this connection Lord Esher and Rigby LJ in the Court of Appeal in *Scholfield v Earl of Londesborough*[9] expressed the opinion that, admitting the acceptor's duty to take care, his omission to detect or notice available blanks in the bill tendered to him for acceptance was not negligence.

An extension of the duty of the drawer of a cheque, as laid down in *Macmillan's* case, to cover the point of leaving a blank space after the payee's name, was refused by the Court of Appeal in *Slingsby v District Bank Ltd*.[10] That case was of the material alteration of a cheque payable to John Prust & Co by the fraudulent addition to the payee's name of 'per Cumberbirch and Potts'. It was argued that the drawers of the cheque were negligent in their duty to the paying banker in not drawing a line in the blank after the payee's name and had thus enabled the fraud to be committed. Scrutton LJ was satisfied, however, that at that time it was not a 'usual precaution' to draw lines before or after the name of the payee:

'If that sort of case became frequent it might become a "usual precaution", but no banking witness had ever heard of a case like this before'.

As to this it need only be said that the precaution in question in *Macmillan's* case is probably no more 'usual' than the one it was attempted to plead in *Slingsby v District Bank Ltd.* But it is the principle which is important and today, with the education of the cheque-using public to which the banks devote no little time and money, another case on the lines of *Slingsby v District Bank Ltd* might well be decided differently.

(b) The *Greenwood* duty

The *Greenwood* duty is the duty to inform the bank of forgery. If a man knows or has reasonable ground for believing that his name has been forged on a bill or cheque he is bound with reasonable despatch to warn the drawee banker of the fact. If he does not, and the bank's position is thereby

---

7 *Scholey v Ramsbottom* (1810) 2 Camp 485.
8 See *Bank of England v Vagliano Bros* [1891] AC 107.
9 [1895] 1 QB 536, CA.
10 [1932] 1 KB 544.

prejudiced, he adopts the bill or cheque.[11] The same rule would seem to apply when the signature has been fraudulently obtained.[12] The facts of *Greenwood*[12a] were that a wife forged her husband's signature to cheques which she cashed and the proceeds of which she applied to her own uses. When the husband discovered the forgeries he did not at once inform the bank and no more forgeries were made. He later decided to tell the bank and the wife committed suicide. It was held that the husband was estopped from setting up the forgeries for, by his silence, he had prevented the bank from suing him and the wife for the latter's tort. Giving the opinion of the House, Lord Tomlin said:

> 'The sole question is whether in the circumstances of this case the respondents are entitled to set up an estoppel.
>
> The essential factors giving rise to an estoppel are I think:–
> (1) A representation or conduct amounting to a representation intended to induce a course of conduct on the part of the person to whom the representation is made.
> (2) An act or omission resulting from the representation, whether actual or by conduct, by the person to whom the representation is made.
> (3) Detriment to such person as a consequence of the act or omission.
> Mere silence cannot amount to a representation, but when there is a duty to disclose deliberate silence may become significant and amount to a representation.
> . . . .
> The deliberate abstention from speaking in those circumstances seems to me to amount to a representation to the respondents that the forged cheques were in fact in order, and assuming that detriment to the respondents followed there were, it seems to me, present all the elements essential to estoppel.'

And he refused to consider that the respondents' initial negligence made any difference:

> 'What difference can it make that the condition of ignorance was primarily induced by the respondents' own negligence? . . . For the purposes of the estoppel which is a procedural matter, the cause of the ignorance is an irrelevant consideration.'

The above doctrine is not confined to customers. Where the relation of banker and customer exists, there is the more tangible ground of duty arising out of the relation. In *M'Kenzie v British Linen Co*[13] there was no relation of banker and customer; *M'Kenzie* was not a customer of the bank. It is specially stated in the headnote that the bank had had no previous dealings with him and the case contains nothing limiting the principle to the relation of banker and customer. In *William Ewing & Co v Dominion Bank*[14] there was no relation of banker and customer. In *Ogilvie v West Australian Mortgage and Agency Corpn Ltd* the Judicial Committee said with regard to *M'Kenzie v British Linen Co* and similar cases:[15]

11 See, in addition to *Greenwood v Martin's Bank Ltd* [1933] AC 51, HL. *M'Kenzie v British Linen Co* (1881) 6 App Cas 82, particularly at 92, 101 at 109; *Ogilvie v West Australian Mortgage and Agency Corpn Ltd* [1896] AC 257 at 270; *William Ewing & Co v Dominion Bank* [1904] AC 806; *Leather Manufacturers' National Bank v Morgan* (1885) 117 US 96 (Supreme Court of the United States); *Morison v London County and Westminster Bank Ltd* [1914] 3 KB 356.
12 *Midland Bank v Lord Shrewsbury's Trustees* (1924) Times, 18 March.
12a [1933] AC 51.
13 (1881) 6 App Cas 82, although M'Kenzie was referred to as a customer in *Ogilvie v West Australian Mortgage and Agency Corpn Ltd* [1896] AC 257.
14 [1904] AC 806.
15 [1896] AC 257 at 268.

'The ground upon which the plea of estoppel rested in these cases was the fact that the customer, being in the exclusive knowledge of the forgery, withheld that knowledge from the bank until its chance of recovering from the forger had been materially prejudiced.'

The position in *Greenwood v Martins Bank Ltd,*[16] was just that indicated in the judgment of the Judicial Committee, above quoted.

The obligation and duty require that a man must not knowingly allow another or a body corporate to be prejudiced by the fraudulent use of a forged instrument to which he has set, or appears to have set, his hand, a 'duty required of him by the rules of fair dealing between man and man'.[17] It is immaterial whether the forged signature on the bill or cheque is that of drawer, acceptor, or indorser, and there seems no need to confine the doctrine to signatures.

Actual knowledge of the forgery is probably not essential. Lord Selborne, in *M'Kenzie v British Linen Co,*[18] speaks of 'reasonable grounds to believe'; a man must be treated as in possession of knowledge which, but for his own neglect, he could not have failed to acquire.[19]

Mere silence, without resulting injury or prejudice to the bank, does not work estoppel or adoption.[20] Prejudice or injury is not confined to payment; it may arise where the bank are precluded from protecting themselves against subsequent forgeries or lose the chance of taking proceedings against the forger. And it is immaterial whether proceedings against the forger would result in getting the money back or not.[1] In the case of *Greenwood v Martins Bank Ltd,*[2] the forger was the wife of the bank's customer, and the husband would thus have been liable for his wife's tort, so that he could not have succeeded in any event in recovering the money the bank had paid away on the forgeries. This liability of the husband was removed by the Law Reform (Married Women and Tortfeasors) Act 1935.

A dictum in *Imperial Bank of Canada v Bank of Hamilton,*[3] apparently treating as material the likelihood that the forger could not have paid anything, is probably immaterial.

This principle of estoppel or adoption is valuable to the banker, as, when it can be pleaded, it may affect all cheques previously forged by the same person, though the fraud may only have been discovered with regard to the last of the series.[4]

---

16 [1933] AC 51.
17 *Ogilvie v West Australian Mortgage and Agency Corpn Ltd* [1896] AC 257 at 269; *William Ewing & Co v Dominion Bank,* ante; for report below, see Canada Supreme Court Reports, vol xxxv, where the judgments of the majority are based solely on this view.
18 (1881) 6 App Cas 82 at 92.
19 Cf per Lord Watson, in *Scholfield v Earl of Londesborough* [1896] AC 514 at 543; *Jacobs v Morris* [1902] 1 Ch 816; *Morison v London County and Westminster Bank Ltd* [1914] 3 KB 356.
20 *M'Kenzie v British Linen Co* (1881) 6 App Cas 82 at 109, 111, 112; but see, in another connection and in relation to ratification, *Bank Melli Iran v Barclays Bank (Dominion Colonial and Overseas)* [1951] 2 TLR 1057, [1951] 2 Lloyd's Rep 367.
1 *M'Kenzie v British Linen Co* (1881) 6 App Cas 82, and Scottish cases cited there at 110; *Ogilvie v West Australian Mortgage and Agency Corpn Ltd* [1896] AC 257 at 270; *William Ewing & Co v Dominion Bank* [1904] AC 806; *Leather Manufacturers' Bank v Morgan* 117 US 96 (1886); cf *Knights v Wiffen* (1870) LR 5 QB 660. See also *Brown v Westminster Bank Ltd* [1964] 2 Lloyd's Rep 187.
2 [1933] AC 51; affg [1932] 1 KB 371.
3 [1903] AC 49 at 57.
4 See *Brown v Westminster Bank Ltd* [1964] 2 Lloyd's Rep 187.

5   DETERMINATION OF AUTHORITY TO PAY

The Bills of Exchange Act 1882, s 75, enacts that:

'The duty and authority of a banker to pay a cheque drawn on him by his customer are determined by (1) countermand of payment, (2) notice of the customer's death.'

In principle, the above specified events should determine the duty and authority of a banker to honour any payment instructions.

(a) Countermand

To be effective a countermand must come to the conscious knowledge of the banker, constructive countermand being unknown in mercantile matters.[5]

A stop to one branch of a bank is not an effective stop on a cheque drawn on another branch of the same bank.[6] As to the position where the stop gives the wrong number of the cheque and for an authoritative review of the whole matter, see *Westminster Bank Ltd v Hilton.*[7]

Where a cheque is presented over the counter and is paid, there can be no effective countermand. The drawer's right to countermand lasts up to the time when the banker must either pay or dishonour, as on, for instance, a special presentation by another banker. Where both drawer and payee bank at the same branch of the drawee bank and the cheque is crossed, the banker is entitled to hold it over until the close of business before paying or returning it, and until he does pay the drawer may countermand and neither a request for payment made by the payee nor his wish to know if he may regard the cheque as paid takes away the drawer's right. In these circumstances, the payee may ask for what amounts to a special presentation, in which case vis à vis the payee the banker is collecting, not paying.[8] Any one of several partners,[9] trustees or executors has power to stop a cheque given by any or all.[10]

(b) Death of customer

In the case of the customer's death the property in his account passes to his legal representatives and the banker is justified in paying cheques presented after the death but before he receives notice thereof.[11] But if the account is a joint account the balance may be the survivor's in the event of the death of one, in which case the bank could pay the survivor.

---

5 *Curtice v London City and Midland Bank Ltd* [1908] 1 KB 293; and see *Commonwealth Trading Bank v Reno Auto Sales Pty Ltd* [1967] VR 790; *Shapera v Toronto-Dominion Bank* (1971) 17 DLR (3d) 122; *Giordano v Royal Bank* (1973) 38 DLR (3d) 191.
6 *London Provincial and South-Western Bank Ltd v Buszard* (1918) 35 TLR 142.
7 (1926) 136 LT 315, HL.
8 The contrary argument was put to the court in *Capital Associated Ltd v Royal Bank of Canada* (1970) 15 DLR (3d) 234 and rejected.
9 *Gaunt v Taylor* (1843) 2 Hare 413.
10 *Twibell v London Suburban Bank* [1869] WN 127. *Curtice v London City and Midland Bank Ltd* [1908] 1 KB 293; *Reade v Royal Bank of Ireland Ltd* [1922] 2 IR 22; cf *Westminster Bank Ltd v Hilton* (1926) 136 LT 315, HL; and see *Burnett v Westminster Bank Ltd* [1966] 1 QB 742, [1965] 3 All ER 81.
11 Cf *Tate v Hilbert* (1793) 2 Ves 111.

(c) Mental disorder and contractual incapacity

If the customer becomes mentally disordered or otherwise loses contractual capacity the banker should not honour his cheques.[12] If the state of the customer's mind is such that he does not know what he is doing, he can give no mandate[13] and any existing mandate is revoked;[14] but if the banker has no knowledge and no reason to suspect, then the mandate is operative. What is sufficient to entitle a banker to refuse to obey his customer's mandate, on the ground that he is suffering from a mental disorder depriving him of mens rea, is not necessarily easy to define. The opinion of the customer's medical practitioner would be a guide but not conclusive, though if he advised positively that his patient was of sound mind, the banker would normally be justified in paying. Entry into hospital for observation or treatment is not in itself enough.

Part VII of the Mental Health Act 1983 deals with arrangements for the management of the property and affairs of mental patients, and the powers of a nominated judge in this respect are very wide. Where an order or direction issued by a judge under s 96, whether providing for the appointment of a receiver or not (s 99), covers moneys and other property in the hands of the banker or affects his relations with the customer in any other way, the banker's position will to that extent be clear. But the appointment of a receiver per se does not preclude the banker's continuing to deal with his customer unless he is aware of the receivership or that the customer is mentally incapable of acting for himself and of understanding what he is doing.

Where a bank allowed an overdraft for the purpose of meeting necessary outgoings of a lunatic's estate, they were held entitled under the doctrine of subrogation to stand in the shoes of the creditors paid, but not for interest and commission.[15] An order in lunacy did not affect previously acquired rights enforceable against a lunatic's property at law or in equity.[16]

(d) Insolvency

The effect of insolvency is considered in ch 17, post.

6 DAMAGES FOR BREACH OF CONTRACT AND LIBEL

(a) Breach of contract

The credit of a customer may be seriously injured by the wrongful dishonour of a cheque. Yet it is rare that a customer will be able to prove special damage. His claim is for general damages in respect of injury to his reputation. There is an important distinction in this respect between trading and non-trading

---

12 *Drew v Nunn* (1879) 4 QBD 661; cf *Daily Telegraph Newspaper Co v McLaughlin* [1904] AC 776; cf *Bradford Old Bank Ltd v Sutcliffe* (1918) 34 TLR 299, 23 Com Cas 299, per Lawrence J, affd on appeal, but this matter not dealt with, [1918] 2 KB 833.
13 *Imperial Loan Co Ltd v Stone* [1892] 1 QB 599.
14 *Drew v Nunn* (1879) 4 QBD 661; *Daily Telegraph Newspaper Co v McLaughlin Ltd* [1904] AC 776.
15 *Re Beavan, Davies, Banks & Co v Beavan* [1912] 1 Ch 196 followed in *Lloyd v Coote and Ball* [1915] 1 KB 242.
16 *Davies v Thomas* [1900] 2 Ch 462.

customers. As regards trading customers the law presumes injury without proof of actual damage. The special position of traders was recognised by the House of Lords in *Wilson v United Counties Bank Ltd,* where, after reviewing the authorities, Lord Birkenhead LC said:[17]

> 'The ratio decidendi in such cases is that the refusal to meet the cheque, under such circumstances, is so obviously injurious to the credit of a trader that the latter can recover, without allegation of special damage, reasonable compensation for the injury done to his credit'.

The position of non-traders was summarised by Lawrence J in *Gibbons v Westminster Bank Ltd* to be:[18]

> 'that a person who is not a trader is not entitled to recover substantial damages for the wrongful dishonour of his cheque, unless the damage which he has suffered is alleged and proved as special damage.'

This principle was recently applied by the Court of Appeal in *Rae v Yorkshire Bank plc,*[19] where a non-trader who was unable to prove special damage was awarded only nominal damages for the wrongful dishonour of his cheques.

In the *Gibbons* case, nominal damages were fixed at £2. In the *Rae* case, the judge at first instance awarded £20. It was observed by the Court of Appeal that £20 as nominal damages may well have been too high, but as there was no cross-appeal, the point was left open.

(b) Libel

Libel is a tort, the making of a defamatory statement in writing or printing which without justification disparages a man's reputation to a third party. When a cheque is dishonoured it is usual for the drawee bank to put a note on it indicating the reason for the dishonour. This is required by the rules of the General Clearing of the London Bankers' Clearing House, but it is not required by law. In complying with the rules a banker may be placed in some difficulty, trying to avoid an answer which could be considered damaging to the drawer's credit or reputation.

In *Sim v Stretch*[20] Lord Atkin said that if the words used tend to lower the plaintiff in the estimation of right thinking people generally, they are defamatory. What are right thinking people may not readily be defined, but it may be said that the common answer where a bank decides to dishonour a cheque conveys in many people's minds that he has no money in his account to meet it, or that he did not draw in good faith or that he drew recklessly or in fraud.

In *Ellaw Co Ltd v Lloyds Bank Ltd*[1] in which the libel claim was not proceeded with, Mackinnon J said that if he had come to the conclusion that there had been any breach on the part of the bank it would have been a question whether any damages beyond the most nominal sum could have been claimed in view of the fact that the whole of the plaintiffs' banking account was concerned with kite-flying operations and that on many other occasions their cheques had been rightly dishonoured.

17 [1920] AC 102 at 112.
18 [1939] 2 KB 882 at 888, [1939] 3 All ER 577 at 579.
19 [1988] BTLC 35, CA (O'Connor and Parker LJJ).
20 [1936] 2 All ER 1237, HL.
 1 (Unreported.)

In *Frost v London Joint Stock Bank Ltd*[2] the Master of the Rolls said that in order to found a libellous interpretation of an answer there must be extrinsic evidence that the answer was calculated to lead reasonable people to attach an injurious meaning to it. A cheque was returned unpaid with a slip attached bearing the words 'reason assigned' against which was written 'not stated'. It appeared that the plaintiff had failed to prove that the words would naturally be understood by reasonable persons as conveying the libellous interpretation alleged. The Court of Appeal laid down that where words are not obviously and directly defamatory the test is not what they might convey to a particular class of persons who, by reason of their calling, might attach a special significance thereto, but what they would ordinarily suggest to the mind of any person of average intelligence who read them. It may well be that some of the answers in daily use may have acquired a special meaning or significance to business men, but such technical construction is not enough to put a forced interpretation on words not in themselves defamatory.

The answer commonly given, in the absence of circumstances requiring a different one, is 'Refer to Drawer', sometimes abbreviated to 'R/D'. At one time this was not regarded as capable of a defamatory meaning, as witness the statement of Scrutton J in *Flach v London and South-Western Bank Ltd*[3] that it was not possible to extract a libellous meaning from what the bank said. This view was adopted by Du Parcq J in *Plunkett v Barclays Bank Ltd.*[4] Today, it is generally accepted that the term is capable of a defamatory meaning.

In *Jayson v Midland Bank Ltd*[5] at first instance the jury found that 'Refer to Drawer' was likely to lower the drawer's reputation in the minds of right thinking people; but the bank succeeded on the facts and the Court of Appeal upheld the decision. In relation to a bill of exchange, 'R/A' in *Millward v Lloyds Bank Ltd*[6] was held to be defamatory, the acceptor being a merchant.

The cases are not consistent in the conclusions reached; most decisions are judgments at first instance and judges are apt to draw somewhat individual conclusions on the facts as found. In *Davidson v Barclays Bank Ltd*[7] Hilbery J held that the words 'not sufficient' on a bookmaker's cheque were capable of being defamatory. In *Baker v Australia and New Zealand Bank Ltd*[8] 'present again' was held to be defamatory.

In *Russell v Bank of America National Trust and Savings Association,*[9] the plaintiff's cheques were dishonoured with the words 'account closed' after the customer had allegedly arranged that they should be referred to an account in Jersey. The judge ruled that the words were capable of a defamatory meaning.

The decisions are well reviewed in the decision of Black J in *Pyke v Hibernian Bank Ltd.*[10]

Claims in respect of dishonoured cheques are often brought both in con-

2 (1906) 22 TLR 760, CA.
3 (1915) 31 TLR 334.
4 [1936] 2 KB 107, [1936] 1 All ER 653.
5 [1968] 1 Lloyd's Rep 409, CA.
6 (1920) unreported.
7 [1940] 1 All ER 316.
8 [1958] NZLR 907.
9 (1977) unreported.
10 [1950] IR 195.

tract and libel. If the claim for breach of contract fails, ie if the refusal to pay is justified, the claim for libel must also fail.

7   UNAUTHORISED PAYMENTS WHICH DISCHARGE A CUSTOMER'S DEBTS

It is a principle of equity that a person who has paid the debts of another without authority is allowed to take advantage of his payment.[11] A classic statement is that of Lord Selborne in *Blackburn Building Society v Cunliffe, Brooks & Co* who referred to:[12]

> '... the general principle of equity, that those who pay legitimate demands which they are bound in some way or other to meet, and have had the benefit of other people's money advanced to them for that purpose, shall not retain that benefit so as, in substance, to make those other people pay their debts.'

The application of this principle in the context of cheques arose in *A L Underwood Ltd v Bank of Liverpool and Martins*.[13] The defendant bank was held liable for conversion of the plaintiff's cheques which had been indorsed and paid by its sole director into his own account with the defendant. There was evidence that some of the proceeds of the cheques had been used to discharge the company's liabilities. The Court of Appeal ordered an inquiry to ascertain if that was so. The Court of Appeal did not expressly state what the position would have been if debts of the company had been discharged, but appeared to consider, without deciding the point, that the plaintiff's damages would have been reduced pro tanto.[14]

Underwood's case concerned a *collecting* bank. Shortly after, in *Liggett (Liverpool) Ltd v Barclays Bank Ltd*,[15] the question arose whether the equitable principle affords a defence to a *paying* banker. The defendant bank had paid cheques drawn on the plaintiff's account in breach of a mandate requiring two signatures. The plaintiff brought an action for money had and received. Wright J held that the bank was entitled to invoke the equitable principle. Insofar as the account had been *overdrawn* at the relevant dates, the case fell squarely within a line of authority in which the principle had been applied to unauthorised borrowings.[16] Insofar as the account had been *in credit* at the relevant dates, there was no material distinction between an action in conversion (as in *Underwood's* case) and an action for money had and received. Wright J concluded:[17]

> 'Under these circumstances I think that the equity I have been referred to ought to be extended even in the case where the cheque which was paid was paid out of the credit balance, and was not paid by way of overdraft, so that the banker will be entitled to the benefit of that payment if he can show that that payment went

11 The principle was so formulated by Scrutton LJ in *A L Underwood Ltd v Bank of Liverpool and Martins* [1924] 1 KB 775 at 794, CA.

12 (1882) 22 Ch D 61 at 71, CA, affd sub nom *Cunliffe Brooks & Co v Blackburn and District Benefit Building Society* (1884) 9 App Cas 857, HL.

13 [1924] 1 KB 775; see also *Jackson v White* [1967] 2 Lloyd's Rep 68 at 80–81.

14 Ibid at 794–795 (per Scrutton LJ) and 799 (per Atkin LJ).

15 [1928] 1 KB 48.

16 See *Baroness Wenlock v River Dee Co* (1887) 19 QBD 155; *Bannatyne v MacIver* [1906] 1 KB 103; *Reversion Fund and Insurance Co v Maison Cosway Ltd* [1913] 1 KB 364.

17 [1928] 1 KB 48 at 64.

to discharge a legal liability of the customer. The customer in such a case is really no worse off, because the legal liability which has to be discharged is discharged, though it is discharged under circumstances which at common law would not entitle the bank to debit the customer.'

Liggett's case appears to have been accepted as correctly applying the equitable principle both in *Lloyds Bank Ltd v Chartered Bank of India, Australia, and China*,[18] and in *Re Cleadon Trust Ltd*.[19] The former case again recognised the applicability of the principle to the collecting banker.[20] The latter case limits the principle to cases where the money provided has been expended by a quasi-borrower or by an agent authorised by him to pay his legitimate debts. It does not apply to the case of money expended by an outsider with no authority, direct or indirect, to pay the quasi-borrower's debts.[1]

8 THE BANKER AS CONSTRUCTIVE TRUSTEE[2]

(a) Introduction

A bank may be an express and formally appointed trustee, liable in breach of trust to make restitution to the trust like any other express trustee. When a bank is not an express trustee, the law may nevertheless impose upon it the liability of a trustee. The bank is then said to be a 'constructive trustee.'

(i) Situations giving rise to a constructive trust

A bank may be a constructive trustee in two distinct situations. First, although the bank is a stranger to the trust, it may take upon itself the responsibility to act on behalf of the beneficiary without authority to do so. By this unauthorised intermeddling, the bank may be held to have usurped the role of trustee and to have constituted itself a 'trustee de son tort'.[3] For a bank this situation will be unusual. It is well established that the predominant relationship between a bank and its customer is that of debtor and creditor,[4] not trustee and beneficiary. A bank is not normally trustee for its customer of the amount standing to his credit in his bank account. A court will not readily infer that a bank has voluntarily assumed the role of trustee.[5]

Secondly, a constructive trust may be imposed in circumstances where a bank has acted with such a degree of complicity in a breach of trust that it is fair that the bank should make restitution to the trust. The degree of complicity required is a matter of controversy in the caselaw. Unlike trusteeship 'de son tort', a bank's liability as constructive trustee in this

18 [1929] 1 KB 40, CA.
19 [1939] Ch 286, [1938] 4 All ER 518, CA.
20 [1929] 1 KB 40 at 61, 75 and 79–80.
 1 [1939] Ch 286 at 327–328 (Clauson LJ). See also *Owen v Tate* [1976] QB 402, [1975] 2 All ER 129, CA.
 2 The editor gratefully acknowledges that this section on the banker as constructive trustee has been contributed by Mr Richard Slade, Barrister.
 3 See, eg *Mara v Browne* [1896] 1 Ch 199 at 209 (solicitor as trustee de son tort).
 4 See ch 10, ante.
 5 See, eg *Rowlandson v National Westminster Bank Ltd* [1978] 3 All ER 370 at 378c, [1978] 1 WLR 798 at 803C.

situation needs no voluntary assumption of responsibility as trustee prior to the breach of trust.

It is this second form of constructive trusteeship which is of most relevance to banks. Banks are here especially vulnerable to having the liability of a trustee imposed upon them. They hold company and trust accounts, available for use and potential abuse by fiduciaries. They participate in complex financial transactions. They assist in the rapid and frequent transfer of large sums into and out of accounts. More importantly, banks remain in funds and in the jurisdiction at times when guilty fiduciaries may be bankrupt or overseas.

(ii) Form of liability

The form or liability may be either proprietary or personal. The proprietary form means a liability upon the bank to restore the trust assets or their traceable equivalent which it holds. The personal form means a liability upon the bank to compensate the trust. The personal form requires no trust property in the possession of the bank. It is for this reason that the constructive trust may be described as 'nothing more than a formula for equitable relief'.[6]

There is importance in the distinction between the two forms of liability. Proprietary liability involves a determination of property rights by well-established rules – for instance, the equitable doctrine of notice. It is not necessarily appropriate to use the same rules to impose a personal liability upon a party that no longer holds identifiable trust property, or never held such property. It may be that the requirements for the imposition of a constructive trust should vary with the form of liability, proprietary or personal, that is sought.[7]

(iii) Knowing receipt and knowing assistance

The seminal statement of the liability of a stranger to a trust as constructive trustee appears in the judgment of Lord Selborne LC in *Barnes v Addy*:[8]

'Now in this case we have to deal with certain persons who are trustees, and with certain other persons who are not trustees. That is a distinction to be borne in mind throughout the case. Those who create a trust clothe the trustee with a legal power and control over the trust property, imposing on him a corresponding responsibility. That responsibility may no doubt be extended in equity to others who are not properly trustees, if they are found either making themselves trustees *de son tort,* or actually participating in any fraudulent conduct of the trustee to the injury of the *cestui que trust*.

But, on the other hand, strangers are not to be made constructive trustees merely because they act as the agents of trustees in transactions within their legal powers, transactions, perhaps of which a Court of Equity may disapprove, unless those agents receive and become chargeable with some part of the trust property, or unless they assist with knowledge in a dishonest and fraudulent design on the part of the trustees. Those are the principles, as it seems to me, which we must bear in mind in dealing with the facts of this case. If those principles were disregarded, I know not how any one could, in transactions admitting of doubt as to the view

6 *Selangor United Rubber Estates Ltd v Cradock (No 3)* [1968] 2 All ER 1073 at 1097H, [1968] 1 WLR 1555 at 1582A, per Ungoed-Thomas, J.
7 See further p 239, post.
8 (1874) 9 Ch App 244 at 251.

which a Court of Equity might take of them, safely discharge the office of solicitor, of banker, or of agent of any sort to trustees. But, on the other hand, if persons dealing honestly as agents are at liberty to rely on the legal power of the trustees, and are not to have the character of trustees constructively imposed upon them, then the transactions of mankind can safely be carried through; and I apprehend those who create trusts do expressly intend, in the absence of fraud and dishonesty, to exonerate such agents of all classes from the responsibilities which are expressly incumbent, by reason of the fiduciary relation, upon the trustees.'

As a result of Lord Selborne's statement, the law as to the liability of an agent to a trust as constructive trustee in the second situation described above has been split between:

(i) agents who receive and become chargeable with some part of the trust property; and
(ii) agents who assist with knowledge in a dishonest and fraudulent design on the part of the trustees.

The shorthand names for these categories are 'knowing receipt' and 'knowing assistance'.

The existence of separate categories has unfortunately bred discrepancies in the law, and distracted from the essential principle asserted by Lord Selborne, that to be held liable as a constructive trustee an agent must have behaved dishonestly.

Most of the recent caselaw on the bank as constructive trustee has concerned Lord Selborne's second category of 'knowing assistance'. For this reason 'knowing assistance' will be considered before 'knowing receipt'.

(b) Knowing assistance

Four elements must be established to hold a bank liable as constructive trustee for assisting with knowledge in a dishonest and fraudulent design on the part of the trustees:[9]

(i) The existence of a trust. This need not be a formal trust. It is sufficient that there be a fiduciary relationship between the trustee and the property of another legal person (for example, a company director's fiduciary relationship between himself and the company).[10]
(ii) A dishonest and fraudulent design on the part of the trustee. 'Dishonest' and 'fraudulent' have their ordinary meaning. They go further than mere moral reprehensibility.[11] It will not be purely the perception of the trustee which decides if the design is dishonest.[12]
(iii) Assistance by the bank in that design.[13] This is a question of fact.
(iv) Knowledge by the bank of the trust, the dishonest and fraudulent design and of its own assistance in that design.[14]

At first sight this analysis seems simple. There is, however, much confusion

---

9 *Baden, Delvaux and Lecuit v Societe General pour Favoriser le Developpement du Commerce et de l'Industrie en France SA* [1983] BCLC 325 at 404.
10 Ibid.
11 *Belmont Finance Corpn Ltd v Williams Furniture Ltd* [1979] Ch 250 at 267, 274, [1979] 1 All ER 118 at 130, 135, CA; *Baden Delvaux* [1983] BCLC 325 at 407.
12 See *R v Ghosh* [1982] QB 1053 at 1064, [1982] 2 All ER 689 at 696.
13 *Baden Delvaux* [1983] BCLC 325 at 406.
14 Ibid at 407.

about the fourth element, the requisite degree of knowledge for constructive trusteeship.

In *Selangor United Rubber Estates Ltd v Cradock* (*No 3*), the facts of which have been stated above,[15] Ungoed-Thomas J concluded that the knowledge required to hold a bank liable as constructive trustee in a dishonest and fraudulent design was knowledge of circumstances which would indicate to an honest and reasonable man that such design was being committed or would put him on enquiry whether it was being committed.[16] This test is questionable for two reasons. First, it suggests that a negligent failure by a bank to recognise a transaction as dishonest is sufficient. This disregards the emphasis laid on dishonesty by Lord Selborne in *Barnes v Addy*. Secondly, the test suggests, contrary to authority,[17] that if a reasonable bank might suspect a dishonest design, the bank is bound to enquire to avoid potential liability as a constructive trustee.

Given the complexity of the transaction in *Selangor,* and the bank's complete good faith throughout, the decision against the bank was a harsh one. Nevertheless Brightman J in *Karak Rubber Co Ltd v Burden* (*No 2*)[18] was content to follow *Selangor*. *Karak* also concerned a takeover of the plaintiff company which involved the use of the plaintiff's own assets to buy out shareholders. Brightman J said of the defendant bank's assistant branch manager: 'I am completely satisfied that he entertained no suspicion whatever of any impropriety at any relevant time'.[19] Nevertheless the judge held that a reasonable banker would have been put on inquiry as to the propriety of a particular cheque. The defendant was accordingly held liable both for breach of its contractual duty of care and as constructive trustee.

Karak was followed by John Mills QC sitting as a Deputy Judge in *Rowlandson v National Westminster Bank Ltd*.[20] The case involved withdrawals from a trust account for a trustee's private purposes by cheques bearing only the signature of that trustee. On the facts it would appear that this was in breach of the mandate. In such circumstances recourse to the law of constructive trusts may have been unnecessary.

The most detailed exposition of the requisite degree of knowledge for 'knowing assistance' was provided by Peter Gibson J in the *Baden Delvaux* case.[1] The facts were that the defendant bank held a trust account containing $4 million. BCB was in a fiduciary position towards this account. The defendant knew that the account was a trust account and of BCB's fiduciary position. Amid unusual and confusing circumstances BCB's directors instructed the defendant to transfer the $4 million to Panama. The defendant did so. BCB's dishonest directors used the money transferred for their own purposes. The defendant was held to be not liable to account for the money as constructive trustee. Peter Gibson J reached this conclusion 'more willingly because [the defendant bank] acted honestly throughout and can in no real sense be said to have been party or privy to the fraud'.[2]

---

15 See p 203, ante.
16 [1968] 2 All ER 1073 at 1104F, [1968] 1 WLR 1555 at 1590E.
17 See, eg *Nihill v Nihill*, post.
18 [1972] 1 All ER 1210, [1972] 1 WLR 602.
19 Ibid at, respectively, 1221 and 617.
20 [1978] 3 All ER 370, [1978] 1 WLR 798.
 1 [1983] BCLC 325.
 2 Ibid at 445.

Although the decisions in *Karak* and *Selangor* placed onerous duties of analysis and inquiry upon banks, both as a matter of contract and as constructive trustee, in *Baden Delvaux,* it was not contended on the bank's behalf that *Selangor* and *Karak* were wrongly decided. Peter Gibson J accepted the plaintiff's submission that knowledge relevant for the purposes of constructive trusteeship can comprise one of five different mental states:[3]

(i)   actual knowledge;
(ii) wilfully shutting one's eyes to the obvious;
(iii) wilfully and recklessly failing to make such enquiries as an honest and reasonable man would make;
(iv) knowledge of circumstances which would indicate the facts to an honest and reasonable man;
(v)   knowledge of facts which would put an honest and reasonable man on enquiry.

This intriguing but complicated analysis of 'knowledge' seems questionable. First, a 'wilful shutting of eyes' under category (ii) is not a lesser degree of knowledge than actual knowledge, but evidence from which a court may infer actual knowledge.[4] Secondly, categories (iii), (iv) and (v) do not by any ordinary meaning of the word constitute 'knowledge'. However, category (iii) is distinguishable from (iv) and (v) because it does at least connote through the words 'wilful' and 'reckless' a degree of subjective awareness.[5] It is suggested that category (iii) catches the accessory to a breach of trust who believes that he is participating in a breach of trust but deliberately shuns the enquiry which might convert his belief into knowledge. To believe means more than to suspect.[6] It means at least to consider that a breach of trust is a probability. A bank cannot be rendered liable as constructive trustee from an awareness that breach of trust is a possibility, otherwise potential liability would arise, for example, in almost any instance where a bank allowed trustees to draw on a trust account.[7] It may be dishonest for a bank to shun enquiries despite its belief, but it is hard to see how any dishonesty can arise out of the negligent states of mind portrayed in categories (iv) and (v). In *Baden Delvaux,* Peter Gibson J accepted that, to have 'knowingly assisted', a constructive trustee must have had knowledge of a dishonest and fraudulent design on the part of the trustees. Such a requirement is without substance if so-called knowledge of categories (iv) and (v) be sufficient.

There are three reasons why in *Selangor, Karak, Rowlandson* and *Baden Delvaux* the court was able to conclude that constructive knowledge, that is, knowledge that would have been present in the mind of a reasonable bank who had drawn the appropriate inferences or made the appropriate inquiries, could be fixed upon a bank that had in reality honestly failed to draw such inferences or make such inquiries, and so render it liable as constructive trustee.

---

3 Ibid at 407.
4 *English & Scottish Mercantile Investment Co v Brunton* [1892] 2 QB 700 at 707; *Thomson v Clydesdale Bank Ltd* [1893] AC 282 at 291.
5 *Re Montagu's Settlement Trusts* [1987] Ch 264, [1987] 2 WLR 1192.
6 For an analogy in criminal law, see s 22(1) of the Theft Act 1968; *R v Hall* (1985) 81 Cr App Rep 260 at 264.
7 See *Nihill v Nihill,* post. Cf *Coleman v Bucks and Oxon Union Bank* [1897] 2 Ch 243.

First, in previous authorities 'knowledge' and 'notice' have been treated as if interchangeable.[8] They are not so,[9] since knowledge involves a degree of awareness and notice does not. The equitable doctrine of notice, long used to resolve whether a purchaser of property takes subject to an equitable interest, does not transpose easily into fixing a stranger with the liability of a fully fledged trustee.[10] Secondly, in many cases judges have found no actual knowledge and then added in emphasis that there were no grounds for such knowledge.[11] This has led to the contention that the presence of grounds for knowledge is itself enough for the imposition of a constructive trust. Thirdly, in many cases judges have charitably refrained from findings of actual knowledge in circumstances where they might easily have made such a finding.[12]

Since *Selangor,* however, the Court of Appeal has emphasised that the touchstone for the imposition of a constructive trust is a want of probity on the part of the constructive trustee. This want of probity cannot be derived from a state of mind that is negligent but honest. Sachs and Edmund-Davies LJJ made the point obiter in *Carl Zeiss Stiftung v Herbert Smith & Co (No 2):*[13]

'It does not, however, seem to me that a stranger is necessarily shown to be both a constructive trustee and liable for a breach of the relevant trusts even if it is established that he has such notice. As at present advised, I am inclined to the view that a further element has to be proved, at any rate in a case such as the present one. That element is one of dishonesty or of consciously acting improperly, as opposed to an innocent failure to make what a court may later decide to have been proper inquiry. That would entail both actual knowledge of the trust's existence and actual knowledge that what is being done is improperly in breach of that trust – though, of course, in both cases a person wilfully shutting his eyes to the obvious is in no different position than if he had kept them open. In becoming somewhat strongly inclined to that view before the *Selangor* case was cited [to us], I had been impressed by the recurrence of the close conjunction in textbooks and judgments of references to fraud and breach of trusts in the relevant passages.'

(Sachs LJ)

'Concepts may defy definition and yet the presence in or absence from a situation of that which they denote may be beyond doubt. The concept of "want of probity" appears to provide a useful touchstone in considering circumstances said to give rise to constructive trusts, and I have not found it misleading when applying it to the many authorities cited to this court. It is because of such a concept that evidence as to "good faith", "knowledge" and "notice" plays so important a part in the reported decisions.'

(Edmund-Davies LJ)

8 See, eg *Backhouse v Charlton* (1878) 8 Ch D 444 at 449; *Re Blundell* (1888) 40 Ch D 370 at 381–383.
9 *Carl Zeiss Stiftung v Herbert Smith & Co (No 2)* [1969] 1 Ch 276 at 296, [1969] 2 All ER 367 at 377, CA, per Sachs LJ.
10 *Re Montagu's Settlement Trusts* [1987] Ch 264 at 272.
11 See, eg *Williams v Williams* (1881) 17 Ch D 437 at 445; *Barnes v Addy* (1874) 9 Ch App 244 at 252; *Thomson v Clydesdale Bank Ltd* [1893] AC 282 at 287; cf *Gray v Lewis* (1869) LR 8 Eq 526 at 543.
12 *Bodenham v Hoskyns* (1852) 21 LJCh 864 at 873; *Shields v Bank of Ireland* [1901] 1 IR 222 at 229; *Lipkin Gorman v Karpnale Ltd* [1987] 1 WLR 987 (revsd on appeal without affecting this point) at 1005, explaining *Nelson v Larholt* [1948] 1 KB 339, [1947] 2 All ER 751.
13 [1969] 2 Ch 276 at 298 (Sachs LJ) and 301 (Edmund Davies LJ), [1969] 2 All ER 367 at 379, 381, CA.

In *Belmont Finance Corpn Ltd v Williams Furniture Ltd* Buckley LJ, with whom Orr LJ agreed, said:[14]

'The knowledge of that design on the part of the parties sought to be made liable may be actual knowledge. If he wilfully shuts his eyes to dishonesty, or wilfully or recklessly fails to make such inquiries as an honest and reasonable man would make, he may be found to have involved himself in the fraudulent character of the design, or at any rate to be disentitled to rely on lack of actual knowledge of the design as a defence. But otherwise, as it seems to me, he should not be held to be affected by constructive notice. It is not strictly necessary, I think, for us to decide that point on this appeal; I express that opinion merely as my view at the present stage without intending to lay it down as a final decision.'

Goff LJ expressed a similar view.[15] In *Nihill v Nihill*,[16] Slade LJ said:

'There is thus a strong expression of opinion of a majority of this court in the *Belmont* case, though without finally deciding the point, that constructive notice will not suffice to render a person liable as constructive trustee under this head, unless he has wilfully shut his eyes to dishonesty, or has wilfully or recklessly failed to make such inquiries as an honest and reasonable man would make.

Nevertheless, for present purposes, I for my part would be prepared to assume in favour of the plaintiff, though without deciding the point, that the onus of proof which she would have to satisfy in regard to knowledge on the part of the bank would be less onerous than that. I would be prepared to assume, without so deciding, that if there were facts known to the bank which ought to have alerted it to the *probability* that the first and second defendants were committing fraudulent breaches of trust, this would render the bank liable as constructive trustee, if it had assisted in such breaches by allowing the relevant moneys to be drawn out of the relevant account. I deliberately refer to probability rather than to possibility, because in my opinion on no footing could the bank have become liable as constructive trustee in allowing these monies to be drawn out of the trust account merely because it knew of the possibility that breaches of trust were being committed. If mere possibility sufficed to fix a bank with liability as constructive trustee in such circumstances, potential liability would arise in almost any instance were a bank allowed trustees to draw on a trust account.'

Dunn LJ described any extension to the rule in *Barnes v Addy* as undesirable:

'Applying Ungoed-Thomas J's test [in *Selangor*] to the facts of this case, it would mean that a paying banker would be obliged to monitor every cheque drawn on an account which he knew was operated by trustees. In my view this would be commercially impracticable and the law should not readily produce a result which has that effect.'

At first instance, too, the courts have declined to follow *Selangor, Karak* and *Baden Delvaux*. In *Re Montagu's Settlement Trusts*[17] Megarry V-C described the five types of 'knowledge' referred to in *Baden Delvaux* as 'useful guides',[18] but concluded that only types (i) to (iii) could show sufficient want of probity to justify imposing a constructive trust. Megarry V-C's decision has been followed in two subsequent decisions concerning banks, *Lipkin*

14 [1979] Ch 250 at 267, [1979] 1 All ER 118 at 130, CA.
15 Ibid at, respectively, 274 and 135.
16 Unreported, [1983] CA Transcript 276 (Civil Division).
17 [1987] Ch 264.
18 Ibid at 278H.

Gorman v Karpnale Ltd[19] and *Barclays Bank plc v Quincecare Ltd.*[20] In *Lipkin Gorman* Alliott J concluded that want of probity is a key aspect in the approach the court should take. He refused to follow *Selangor* and *Karak* in so far as those decisions held that knowledge of circumstances which would put an honest and reasonable man on inquiry was sufficient to impose a constructive trust. Steyn J endorsed this refusal in the *Quincecare* case: 'To that extent, and perhaps because of the imposition of liability in relation to the very complex series of transactions in *Selangor,* [the decisions of *Selangor* and *Karak*] caused consternation in banking circles'.[1]

In the most recent case, *AGIP (Africa) Ltd v Jackson,*[2] Millett J warned against over-refinement or too ready an assumption that Baden categories (iv) and (v) are necessarily cases of constructive notice only. The learned judge emphasised that the true distinction is between honesty and dishonesty.

In the light of the above line of decisions it is suggested that *Selangor* and *Karak* are now of little persuasive authority on the subject of the bank as constructive trustee.

(c) Knowing receipt

(i) The two limbs of knowing receipt

A bank may become liable as constructive trustee under this head if it receives trust property with knowledge that the transfer to it is in breach of trust, or else it deals with the property in a manner inconsistent with the trust after acquiring knowledge of the trust.[3]

On Lord Selborne's formulation in *Barnes v Addy,* ante, there is no need for a dishonest design on the part of the trustee to establish liability under this head. It is suggested, however, that there is no relaxation of the need for a want of probity as a condition of liability. This was the view taken obiter by Sachs and Edmund-Davies LJJ in the *Carl Zeiss* case cited above, and the point was re-stated by Megarry V-C in *Re Montagu's Settlement Trusts,* ante, both of which were knowing receipt cases.

As in the case of knowing assistance, a merely negligent failure to infer or make inquiries cannot normally be characterised as a want of probity sufficient to justify the imposition of a constructive trust. Only 'knowledge' of types (i), (ii) and (iii) in the *Baden Delvaux* categorisation suffice to establish liability.[4] The crucial distinction in 'knowing receipt' cases between an honest if negligent state of mind, and a dishonest state of mind, emerges clearly from Lord Watson's judgment in *Thomson v Clydesdale Bank Ltd.*[5] The facts were that a broker paid a cheque into his overdrawn account with the respondent bank. The bank knew that the cheque represented the proceeds of the sale of shares, but it did not know and did not ask, if the money was held by the broker as agent or in his own right. In fact the shares and the proceeds of

19 [1978] 1 WLR 987 (revsd on appeal without affecting this point).
20 [1988] 1 FTLR 507.
 1 Ibid at 516.
 2 (1989) Times, 5 June.
 3 As was pointed out in *Baden Delvaux* [1983] BCLC 325 at 403, the receipt of trust property for the purposes of the second limb may be lawful. See also *AGIP (Africa) Ltd v Jackson* (1989) Times, 5 June.
 4 *Re Montagu's Settlement Trusts* [1987] Ch 264 at 285.
 5 [1893] AC 282, HL.

their sale belonged to a trust fund. The House of Lords held that the bank was entitled to retain the money in discharge of the broker's debt. Lord Watson said:[6]

'The broker knew that he was insolvent, and that he was using his customers' money to pay his own debt to the bank without any reasonable expectation of his being able to replace it. That was an undoubted fraud upon the appellants; but, in my opinion, the broker's fraud is of no relevancy in this case, unless it is coupled with bad faith on the part of the respondents. The onus of proving that they acted in mala fide rests with the appellants. It is not enough for them to prove that the respondents acted negligently; in order to succeed, they must establish that the respondents knew, not only that the money represented by the cheque did not belong to the broker, but that he had no authority from the true owner to pay it into his bank account.'

Lord Shand said that the trustees had to show directly or by inference from facts proved that the bank was cognisant that the money was being misapplied.[7]

There is, however, at least some authority which suggests that a recipient of property transferred in breach of trust may be liable as constructive trustee through a negligent failure to infer or inquire rather than because he was wilfully participating in a breach of trust. In *Belmont Finance Corpn Ltd v Williams Furniture (No 2)*,[8] Goff LJ stated that to receive trust funds in such a way as to become accountable for them did not depend on fraud or dishonesty.[9] Buckley LJ said that if the directors of a company in breach of their fiduciary duties misapply the funds of their company so that they come into the hands of some stranger to the trust who receives them with knowledge (actual or constructive) of the breach, he cannot conscientiously retain those funds against the company unless he has some better equity; he becomes constructive trustee for the company of the misapplied funds.[10] In *International Sales and Agencies Ltd v Marcus*[11] Lawson J considered that a recipient of company funds transferred in breach of a director's fiduciary duties could be liable to account upon actual or constructive knowledge of the breach. He found actual knowledge on the facts, although he considered it would have been sufficient if the ordinary reasonable man in the position of the recipient ought to have known of the breach.

The suggestion that constructive knowledge is sufficient to impose liability as constructive trustee for 'knowing receipt' may arise from a confusion between the absence of *notice,* which shields a purchaser from a tracing claim and the absence of *knowledge* which will prevent the imposition of a constructive trust. The position was summarised by Megarry V-C in *Re Montagu's Settlement Trusts* as follows:[12]

'(1) The equitable doctrine of tracing and the imposition of a constructive trust by reason of the knowing receipt of trust property are governed by different rules and must be kept distinct. Tracing is primarily a means of determining the rights of property, whereas the imposition of a con-

6 Ibid at 290.
7 Ibid at 291.
8 [1980] 1 All ER 393, CA.
9 Ibid at 407.
10 Ibid at 405.
11 [1982] 3 All ER 551.
12 [1987] Ch 264 at 285.

structive trust creates personal obligations that go beyond mere property rights.

(2) In considering whether a constructive trust has arisen in a case of the knowing receipt of trust property, the basic question is whether the conscience of the recipient is sufficiently affected to justify the imposition of such a trust.

(3) Whether a constructive trust arises in such a case primarily depends on the knowledge of the recipient, and not on notice to him; and for clarity it is desirable to use the word "knowledge" and avoid the word "notice" in such cases.

(4) For this purpose, knowledge is not confined to actual knowledge, but includes at least knowledge of types (ii) and (iii) in the *Baden* case ([1983] BCLC 325, 407) ie actual knowledge that would have been acquired but for shutting one's eyes to the obvious, or wilfully and recklessly failing to make such inquiries as a reasonable and honest man would make; for in such cases there is a want of probity which justifies imposing a constructive trust.

(5) Whether knowledge of the *Baden* types (iv) and (v) suffices for this purpose is at best doubtful; in my view, it does not, for I cannot see that the carelessness involved will normally amount to a want of probity.'

In *Barclays Bank plc v Quincecare Ltd,* ante, Steyn J was satisfied that to render a bank liable as constructive trustee, whether for 'knowing assistance' or 'knowing receipt', only knowledge of types (i), (ii) and (iii) suffices.

(ii) *Inference of actual knowledge*

It has never been doubted that where a stranger to a trust has gained from the misapplication of trust funds, this will be strong evidence from which a court may infer that he had actual knowledge of the breach of trust.[13] This will especially be so in the case of a bank where the benefit is 'designed and stipulated for' by it.[14] For instance, there will clearly be more evidence from which to infer that a bank has wilfully participated in a breach of trust if a director uses company funds to pay off his private overdraft after the bank has insisted that the overdraft be reduced.

It has been said in the context of a third party's disobedience to a Mareva injunction that it is not possible to add together the innocent state of mind of two or more servants of a corporation in order to produce guilty knowledge on its part.[15] In principle the same should be true in relation to knowledge for the purposes of a constructive trust.

---

13 *Gray v Johnston* (1868) LR 3 HL 1 at 11, per Lord Cairns, LC; *Shields v Bank of Ireland* [1901] 1 IR 222 at 232.
14 *Gray v Johnston* (1868) LR 3 HL 1 at 13, per Lord Cairns LC; *Coleman v Bucks and Oxon Union Bank* [1897] 2 Ch 243 at 254.
15 *Z Ltd v A-Z and AA-LL* [1982] QB 558 at 581, [1982] 1 All ER 556 at 569, CA, per Eveleigh LJ, citing *Armstrong v Strain* [1952] 1 KB 232, [1952] 1 All ER 139, CA.

(iii) Interrelation between knowing receipt and knowing assistance

It was accepted in *Baden Delvaux* that a stranger who receives trust property can be made liable as a constructive trustee within the knowing assistance category if the plaintiff discharges the burden of proving that the stranger's conduct falls within the latter category.[16] Both *Selangor* and *Karak* illustrate this proposition.

It was also accepted in *Baden Delvaux* that a claim for knowing receipt does not lie if the recipient is a bona fide purchaser for value without knowledge of a breach of trust. On the facts, no claim was made under the head of knowing receipt because (i) the long and well-established principle is that a bank is not a trustee for its customer; (ii) a bank dealing with a customer only acts as agent of that customer; (iii) at the time that the recipient bank received the monies, it was a bona fide purchaser for value without notice of any breach of trust.[17]

(d) Statutory protection

Statutory protection is available to the banker in relation to constructive trust claims by s 85(a) of the Solicitors Act 1974 and s 55(4) of the Financial Services Act 1986, both of which provisions have been considered in ch 9, ante.

16 [1983] BCLC 325 at 404.
17 Ibid at 403.

CHAPTER 13

APPROPRIATION OF PAYMENTS

The law as to appropriation of payments, so far as it concerns bankers, is summarised in *Deeley v Lloyds Bank Ltd* in which Lord Shaw of Dunfermline adopted the statement by Eve J at first instance, to the effect that;[1]

'According to the law of England, the person paying the money has the primary right to say to what account it shall be appointed; the creditor, if the debtor makes no appropriation, has the right to appropriate; and if neither exercises the right of appropriation, one can look on the matter as a matter of account and see how the creditor has dealt with the payment in order to ascertain how in fact he did appropriate it. And if there is nothing more than a current account kept by the creditor, or a particular account kept by the creditor and he carries the money to that particular account, then the court concludes that the appropriation has been made; and having been made, it is made once for all, and it does not lie in the mouth of the creditor afterwards to seek to vary that appropriation.'

The bank had a mortgage as security for overdraft on current account. They received notice of a second mortgage on the same property. They did not break the account but carried it to moneys subsequently paid in. These being attributed under the rule in *Devaynes v Noble, Clayton's Case*[2] to the earlier drawings out, extinguished the secured debt and left the bank unsecured with regard to subsequent advances. The Court of Appeal, by a majority, upheld Eve J at first instance in favour of the bank on what they regarded as the intention of the parties; the House of Lords reversed this decision on the ground that the rule in *Clayton's Case* was not excluded by the conduct of the parties. In the Court of Appeal, Fletcher Moulton LJ, one of the majority, contended that *Devaynes v Noble, Clayton's Case*, only established a rule of evidence; that appropriation was a matter of intention and that it was absurd to attribute to a bank the intention to appropriate payments-in to a secured rather than an unsecured debt, and he ridiculed the recognition of a legal rule which the bank could circumvent by 'the simple formality of drawing two horizontal lines in their books and making believe to commence a new account'.

The moral is that the process ridiculed by Fletcher Moulton LJ should always be followed where it is desired to preserve a security on which further

---

1 [1912] AC 756 at 783; see also *Re Footman, Bower & Co Ltd* [1961] Ch 443, [1961] 2 All ER 161 and *Siebe Gorman & Co v Barclays Bank Ltd* [1979] 2 Lloyd's Rep 142.
2 (1816) 1 Mer 529, 572 at 608.

advances cannot be charged. The account should be ruled off, and a new account opened if further business is contemplated.[3]

In Canada, two banks were involved in a dispute as to the proceeds of the sale of a farmer's grain promised to both of them as security for loans.[4] The plaintiffs contended that following the rule in *Clayton's Case* the farmer's deposits into his current account with the defendants should have been used by them to offset the loans. It was held that in the absence of specific instructions from a customer, a bank was not duty bound under that rule to apply moneys deposited in a current account to offset or repay a loan on the ground that it was a debt prior to those debts created by the writing of cheques on the current account.

There are two contentions, not lacking in authority, which it would have been well to have had dealt with more definitely in *Deeley v Lloyds Bank Ltd*:

(1) That a creditor's right of appropriation is exercisable 'up to the very last moment', even when there is a current account, accounts rendered being only rebuttable evidence of such exercise;[5]

(2) That a creditor's appropriation does not bind him unless communicated to the debtor.[6]

Some of the cases on which these propositions are based were referred to in *Deeley v Lloyds Bank Ltd*[7] but no very definite ruling given with regard to them. There is no mention of any such qualification to the law as laid down by Lord Shaw. The rule published by the bank for the guidance of its staff was that:

'Wherever notice is received of a second mortgage or second charge on any security on which the banker holds a prior charge, the account must at once be ruled off and a separate account opened for subsequent transactions.'

Lord Shaw described the adoption of this rule as a mode of protection open to bankers as familiar and simple as could be imagined, by which the bank quite easily and naturally secures its own protection. It is usual to bring to the customer's notice the closing of the old account and the opening of the new one, which normally has to be conducted in credit or fresh security arrangements made regarding further advances.

'It is, of course, absolutely necessary for the application of this doctrine[8] that there should be one unbroken account, and entries made in that account by the person having the right to appropriate the payment to that account.'[9]

In *Re Diplock*[10] Lord Greene MR said 'we see no justification for extending the rule beyond the case of a banking account'.

3 See per Lord Shaw in *Deeley v Lloyds Bank Ltd* [1912] AC 756 at 785.
4 *Royal Bank of Canada v Bank of Montreal* (1976) 67 DLR (3d) 755 (Court of Appeal of Saskatchewan).
5 See *Cory Bros & Co v Turkish SS Mecca (Owners), The Mecca* [1897] AC 286 per Lord Macnaghten at 294; *Seymour v Pickett* [1905] 1 KB 715.
6 *Simson v Ingham* (1823) 2 B & C 65; *London and Westminster Bank v Button* (1907) 51 Sol Jo 466; cf. *Rekstin v Severo Sibirsko Gosudarstvennoe Akcionernoe Obschestvo Komseverputj and Bank for Russian Trade Ltd* [1933] 1 KB 47, CA.
7 [1912] AC 756 at 758.
8 The principle of *Clayton's Case* (1816) 1 Mer 529 at 572.
9 Per Lord Atkinson, in *Deeley v Lloyds Bank Ltd* [1912] AC 756 at 771, citing Lord Selborne in *Re Sherry* (1884) 25 Ch D 692 at 702, CA.
10 [1948] Ch 465 at 555, CA re the rule in *Clayton's Case*.

CHAPTER 14

DEMAND, INTEREST AND COSTS

Demand, interest and costs are to some extent interrelated, and it is convenient to consider them together in this Chapter.

1 DEMAND

The making of a valid demand is of practical importance in two contexts. First, the date of demand is normally the date from which interest is claimed on overdue amounts. Demand may cause interest to be claimable either de novo, and/or on an increased sum (as where demand causes outstanding principal and interest to capitalise), and in some cases at an increased rate, often described as a default rate. Second, the making of a valid demand is normally a pre-condition to the right to realise security.

(a) Peremptory character and unconditional

In *Re A Company*[1] Nourse J accepted as a fair working definition of a valid demand that given by Walker J in the Australian case of *Re Colonial Finance, Mortgage, Investment and Guarantee Corpn Ltd*:[2]

'... there must be a clear intimation that payment is required to constitute a demand; nothing more is necessary, and the word "demand" need not be used; neither is the validity of a demand lessened by its being clothed in the language of politeness; it must be of a peremptory character and unconditional, but the nature of the language is immaterial provided it has this effect.'

This definition has since been approved by the Court of Appeal.[3]

(b) Amount due need not be specified

The calculation of the precise amount due on a particular date can be an expensive and futile exercise. In *Bank of Baroda v Panessar*,[4] two associated companies executed in favour of the plaintiff a debenture which secured all

---

1 [1985] BCLC 37.
2 (1905) 6 SRNSW 6 at 9.
3 In *Bank of Credit and Commerce International SA v Blattner* (20 November 1986, unreported) Court of Appeal (Civil Division) Transcript No 1176 of 1986.
4 [1987] Ch 335, [1986] 3 All ER 751.

moneys owed. The plaintiff later made demand by a letter which simply stated:

> 'We hereby demand all monies due to us under the powers contained in the mortgage debenture dated 22 September 1981.'

Proceedings were then brought against guarantors of the companies who submitted that the demand, and the subsequent appointment of a receiver, were invalid because the demand had failed to specify the amount due. It was held by Walton J, following the Australian case of *Bunbury Foods Pty Ltd v National Bank of Australasia Ltd*,[5] that the demand was valid. The plaintiff had done precisely what, by the terms of his security he was entitled to do, ie to demand repayment of all moneys secured by the debenture. It was further observed that knowledge of the precise amount of the sum outstanding is only required in the exceptional case, because in most cases, the debtor has no real means of paying off the sum, and it would be idle to put the creditor to what might be very considerable expense in ascertaining the precise amount due when there is no likelihood that the sum will represent a realistic target at which the debtor can aim.[6] Although these observations were made in the context of a debenture which by its terms secured all moneys owing, they are clearly of wider application.

(c) Time for payment

An additional ground on which the receiver's appointment was challenged in *Bank of Baroda v Panessar*, supra, was that the companies had been given insufficient time for payment. The receiver had in fact been appointed only an hour after the making of the demand. Having reviewed the authorities Walton J concluded that English law has adopted a 'mechanics of payment' test, a clear statement of which is contained in the dictum of Blackburn J in *Brighty v Norton*:[7]

> 'I agree that a debtor who is required to pay money on demand, or at a stated time, must have it ready, and is not entitled to further time in order to look for it.'

The court in *Bank of Baroda v Panessar* specifically rejected the approach which has been adopted in certain other common law jurisdictions, that the debtor must be given a reasonable time for payment, regarding it as unfair to the creditor that the period should depend on all the circumstances of the case, some of which he may not know and may lack the means of knowing.

2 INTEREST

High interest rates and delays in the recovery of debts combine to make the law relating to interest a subject of some importance to bankers. The present law is the product of a long process of development described by Lord Brandon in *President of India v La Pintada Cia Navegacion SA*[8] as 'strange but hardly eventful'. Two factors have exerted a continuing influence. The first is the unavailability at common law of damages for the late payment of

5 (1984) 51 ALR 609.
6 [1987] Ch 335 at 347B, [1986] 3 All ER 751 at 759b.
7 (1862) 3 B & S 305 at 312, 122 ER 116 at 118.
8 [1985] AC 104, [1984] 2 All ER 773, HL.

a debt under limb one of the rule in *Hadley v Baxendale* (general damages) and, so it was thought until recently, limb two (special damages). The second is the gradual extension since 1833 of statutory remedies in respect of interest, to a position in which there now exists a discretionary remedy which covers the majority of cases where there is no contractual right to interest, but which remains subject to limitations which result in awards of interest providing less than full compensation for being kept out of money. The landmarks in this statutory development are:

1 the Civil Procedure Act 1833, which empowered juries to award interest to a creditor on debts or sums certain (s 28);
2 the Judgments Act 1838, which provides for judgment debts to carry interest from the time of entering up the judgment until satisfaction of the debt (s 17);
3 the Repeal of Usury Laws Act 1854, which removed the prohibition on contracts for compound interest;
4 the Law Reform (Miscellaneous Provisions) Act 1934, which empowered the Court to award interest in proceedings for the recovery of a debt or damages (s 3(1));
5 the Supreme Court Act 1981, which, as amended by the Administration of Justice Act 1982, re-enacted and extended the 1934 Act (s 35A).

(a) Interest pursuant to contract

(i) Express contract

Loan agreements and security documentation commonly contain express terms governing the payment of interest. The abolition of the usury laws removed the main limitation on freedom of contract in respect of interest. The principal limitations at the present day are (1) the doctrine of penalties (see infra) and (2) the Consumer Credit Act 1974 (see ch 5, ante).

1 INTEREST BEFORE DEMAND

An express contract for the payment of interest will normally specify the rate, and it may further specify the method of computing interest and whether interest is to be compounded.

The specification of a rate of interest per annum is often supplemented by the further specification of a particular basis on which interest is to be computed. There are three generally recognised bases:[9]

1 365/365. Under this method the rate of interest is divided by 365 to produce a daily interest factor. The number of days that the loan is outstanding is then multiplied by this factor. Under this method different amounts of interest are charged for months of different lengths.
2 360/360. Under this method each month is treated as having 30 days, with the consequence that interest for each month is the same. However, for a calendar year the interest is exactly the same as that calculated by using the 365/365 method.
3 365/360. This method is a combination of the first two. The interest rate

9 This description is taken from *American Timber and Trading Co v First National Bank of Oregon*, 551 F 2d 980 at 982 (US Ct of App, 9th Circ, 1974).

is divided by 360 days (30 days for each month) to create a daily factor. The number of days that a loan is outstanding is then multiplied by this factor. Interest charged for months of different lengths is different, and interest charged for a calendar year is greater than interest charged under the 365/365 or the 360/360 methods.

The *computing* of interest must be distinguished from *compounding*, which is the capitalisation of interest so that interest itself yields interest. Notwithstanding the removal of the former prohibition on compound interest, the law has traditionally leaned against it. A clear manifestation is the well established rule in the law of mortgage that in the absence of special agreement, simple interest only can be charged in a mortgage account.[10] This principle was recently applied by the Court of Appeal in holding that a mortgage under which the mortgagor covenanted to pay to a mortgagee bank all monies due 'so that interest shall be computed according to agreement or failing agreement to the usual mode of the bank' did not entitle the bank to compound interest, notwithstanding evidence that it was the bank's practice to charge it.[11]

2 INTEREST AFTER DEFAULT

Contractual provisions for the payment of interest after demand tend to fall into one of three categories.

1 Clauses which simply specify that interest is payable 'as well before or after demand', without any variation in the rate of interest, or the method of its computation or compounding (if any).
2 Clauses which provide for a default rate of interest, ie the payment of a higher rate of interest after default. Such a provision may constitute a penalty as being a stipulation for payment of money in terrorem of the offending party rather than a genuine pre-estimate of damage (propositions 2 and 3 in the speech of Lord Dunedin in *Dunlop Pneumatic Tyre Co Ltd v New Garage and Motor Co Ltd*[12]). The fact that the sum payable is characterised as a debt rather than damages appears to be immaterial. It was observed by the Court of Appeal in *The Angelic Star*[13] that a clause which provided that in the event of any breach of contract, a long-term loan would immediately become repayable and that interest thereon for the full term would not only still be payable, but would be payable at once, would constitute a penalty as being a payment of money stipulated in terrorem of the offending party. Such a provision would, of course, be far more obviously in terrorem than a mere increase in the rate of interest on outstanding amounts until payment. However, the practice in relation to

---

10 *Daniell v Sinclair* (1881) 6 App Cas 181, PC.
11 *Bank of Credit and Commerce International SA v Blattner* (20 November 1986, unreported) Court of Appeal (Civil Division) Transcript No 1176 of 1986.
12 [1915] AC 79 at 86, HL.
13 [1988] 1 Lloyd's Rep 122, CA, per Lord Donaldson MR at 125. In *National Bank of Greece SA v Pinios Shipping Co No 1, The Maira* [1989], 1 All ER 213, [1988] 2 Lloyd's Rep 126, the Court of Appeal awarded simple interest pursuant to a default interest provision. However, no point was taken on the default interest provision being penal. See also *Export Credit Guarantee Department v Universal Oil Products Co* [1983] 2 All ER 205, [1983] 1 WLR 399, HL.

mortgages (see (3) infra) raises a genuine doubt as to the validity of default interest provisions.

3 Clauses in mortgages which provide for a reduction in the rate of interest in the event of punctual payment. This transparent device for circumventing the doctrine of penalties received the approval of the House of Lords in *Wallingford v Mutual Society*, where Lord Hatherley said:[14]

> 'It is not a penalty on non-payment (though it seems a fine distinction) when you say that your contract shall be made for interest at 5% to be reduced, in the event of your punctual payment, to 4%; but it is a relaxation of the terms of that original contract, not taking it by way of penalty at all, but a relaxation of your contract which you would merit and purchase by paying at a definite and fixed time.'

3 CONTRACTUAL INTEREST AFTER JUDGMENT

It is commonly provided that interest is payable 'as well before or after judgment'. Where a plaintiff seeks an order for contractual interest to run after judgment (until payment), the question is 'whether the covenant for the payment of the interest is an independent covenant or a covenant which is merely ancillary to the payment of the principal money?' (per Lord Davey in *Economic Life Assurance Society v Usborne*[15]). If the agreement to pay interest is merely ancillary, the promise merges in the judgment.

(ii) Implied contract, acquiescence and custom

1 INTRODUCTION

Some contracts of loan commonly contain no express term as to payment of interest. The most striking example is the contract constituted by the customer's current account going into overdraft. The question then arises whether the bank is entitled to interest either by an implied contract, or by acquiescence or by custom. The law in this area has developed almost exclusively in the context of claims by bankers for payment of compound interest.

2 TERMINOLOGY

The word 'acquiescence' is now firmly embedded in the law of interest. The reason for this is not difficult to trace. It was explained in *National Bank of Greece SA v Pinios Shipping Co No 1, The Maira* by Nicholls LJ:[16]

> 'To facilitate the use of compound interest by banks despite the usury laws, which were not finally repealed until 1854, the Courts resorted to the fiction that a fresh agreement for the payment of interest was made on the occasion of each rest in a customer's account. An agreement, express or implied, to pay compound interest made when a customer opened an account with a bank would have been unlawful. But if on each occasion when a bank charged or credited interest to an account, the parties were to enter into a new agreement that the balance then struck would bear interest, that agreement would be lawful, because it would provide only for

---

14 (1880) 5 App Cas 685 at 702.
15 [1902] AC 147 at 152, HL, and see 149 (Earl of Halsbury LC). See also *Re Sneyd, ex p Fewings* (1883) 25 Ch D 338, CA; *Ealing London Borough v El Isaac* [1980] 2 All ER 548, [1980] 1 WLR 932, CA.
16 [1988] 2 Lloyd's Rep 126 at 147, CA.

the payment of simple interest on an agreed sum. Thus, on this analysis, over a period of years there would be a series of separate agreements between banker and customer, made at intervals of one year or six months or whenever, depending upon the manner in which the bank kept its accounts. That notion, of each debiting or crediting of interest being the subject of a separate, fresh agreement, was fundamental to the lawfulness of this practice. There was a succession of agreements, implied from the customer's acquiescence in the practice of the bank regarding the debiting and crediting of interest.'

This approach enabled the courts to uphold the custom of bankers by which interest was debited in a separate column in the account, and then added to outstanding principal at the end of the relevant period to form the first item in the next account.

Notwithstanding its artificiality, this analysis was adopted even after the repeal of the usury laws, when the rationale for it had disappeared.[17] The law remains that a claim for interest is justified by the customer's acquiescence in the charging of interest. Such acquiescence will justify the charging of compound interest or interest with periodic rests, so long as the relation of banker and customer exists, and the relationship is not changed into that of mortgagee and mortgagor.[18]

3 MERCANTILE ACCOUNT CURRENT FOR MUTUAL TRANSACTIONS

In *Fergusson v Fyffe*, decided before the repeal of the usury laws, Lord Cottenham LC said that generally a contract or promise for compound interest is not available in England except perhaps as to *mercantile accounts current for mutual transactions*.[19] This statement was approved and followed long after the repeal of the usury laws in *Deutsche Bank v Banque des Merchands de Moscou*.[20] It was doubted in *National Bank of Greece SA v Pinios Shipping Co No 1, The Maira*[1] whether an account recording outstanding indebtedness under a loan agreement could properly be characterised as such an account, and in *Minories Finance Ltd v Daryanani*,[2] leave to defend was granted under RSC Order 14 on the same issue.

4 TERMINATING EVENTS

An account which is current for mutual transactions ceases to be such an account by reason of any event which terminates the relationship of banker and customer. These events include:

17 See *Crosskill v Bower* (1863) 32 Beav 86; *Williamson v Williamson* (1869) LR 7 Eq 542; *London Chartered Bank of Australia v White* (1879) 4 App Cas 413 at 424, PC; *Spencer v Wakefield* (1887) 4 TLR 194; *Yourell v Hibernian Bank Ltd* [1918] AC 372, HL; *Deutsche Bank v Banque des Marchands de Moscou* (1931) 4 LDAB 293, CA. See also *IRC v Holder* [1931] 2 KB 81, CA; affd *sub nom Holder v IRC* [1932] AC 624, HL; *Paton v IRC* [1938] AC 341, [1938] 1 All ER 786, HL. As to cases where the analysis was applied before the repeal of the usury laws, see *Ex p Bevan* (1803) 9 Ves Jun 223, per Lord Eldon; *Lord Clancarty v Latouche* (1810) 1 Ball & B 420; *Gwyn v Godby* (1812) 4 Taunt 346, Ex Ch; *Fergusson v Fyffe* (1841) 8 Cl & Fin 121 at 140, HL, per Lord Cottenham LC.
18 See the cases cited in n 17, supra. This summary of the law was approved by Lloyd LJ in *National Bank of Greece v Pinios Shipping Co*, supra.
19 (1841) 8 Cl & Fin 121 at 140, HL.
20 (1931) 4 LDAB 293, CA.
1 [1988] 2 Lloyd's Rep 126 at 149, CA (O'Connor LJ); however, the point did not arise for determination, and was expressly left open by Nicholls LJ at 148.
2 (1989) Financial Times, 26 April, CA.

1 Death of the customer;[3]
2 Death of the banker;[4]
3 Insolvency of either banker or customer;[5]
4 Communication by customer of closing of the account;[6]
5 Demand by banker for repayment.[7]

It follows that once a banker or customer has unequivocally demanded immediate repayment from the other with the intention of ending their relationship, compound interest will normally cease to be payable, save where the contract expressly so provides. The usual formal letter, written by a bank before proceedings are started, would be typical of such a demand.[8]

5 CONVERSION INTO RELATION OF MORTGAGEE AND MORTGAGOR

The taking of a mortgage or charge to secure the fluctuating balance of an account is not so inconsistent with the relation of banker and customer as to preclude the charging of compound interest.[9] But the fact that a mortgage or charge has not itself been discharged does not determine whether the underlying account remains current for mutual transactions.[10]

6 IMPLIED TERMS AND CUSTOM

If interest cannot be recovered on the basis of acquiescence, it may yet be recoverable under an implied term of the contract, or by custom and usage. It would seem likely that evidence would be available to establish custom and usage conferring a right to compound interest before demand in relation to almost every kind of account.

In *Cook v Fowler*,[11] Lord Selborne stated that there is no general rule of law that upon a contract for the payment of money borrowed for a fixed period, on a day certain, with interest at a certain rate down to that day, a further contract is to be implied for the continuance of the same rate of interest after that day, until actual payment.

---

3 *Fergusson v Fyffe* (1841) 8 Cl & Fin 121, HL; *Re Russian Commercial and Industrial Bank* [1955] Ch 148, [1955] 1 All ER 75.
4 *Crosskill v Bower* (1863) 32 Beav 86 at 93.
5 *Crosskill v Bower* supra; *Deutsche Bank v Banque des Marchands de Moscou* (1931) 4 LDAB 293, CA.
6 *National Bank of Greece SA v Pinios Shipping Co No 1, The Maira* [1989] 1 All ER 213, [1988] 2 Lloyd's Rep 126, CA.
7 Ibid.
8 Ibid at 148, per Nicholls LJ.
9 *National Bank of Australasia v United Hand in Hand Band of Hope Co* (1879) 4 App Cas 391 in which the Privy Council remarked (409) that the Master 'seems to have acted correctly in allowing compound interest with half-yearly rests on the mortgage debt, that debt being the balance of a current banking account kept in that way'. See also *Corinthian Securities Ltd v Cato* [1970] 1 QB 377, [1969] 3 All ER 1168, CA, where it was held in the words of Cross LJ, that the plaintiffs were not bankers giving a client overdraft facilities but lenders making a loan on the security of property.
10 See *National Bank of Greece SA v Pinios Shipping Co No 1, The Maira* [1988] 2 Lloyd's Rep 126 at 143, CA (Lloyd LJ).
11 (1874) LR 7 HL 27 at 37; see also *Re Anderson's Seeds Ltd* [1971] 2 NSWLR 120.

(b) Interest pursuant to statute

(i) Interest before judgment

1 THE STATUTORY JURISDICTION

In the absence of a contractual right to interest, a claim for interest is almost invariably made pursuant to statute. The statutory jurisdiction in respect of debts generally is now contained is s 35A of the Supreme Court Act 1981. A claim for interest must be specifically pleaded (RSC Ord 18, r 8(4)); this rule is supplemented by a *Practice Direction*[12] on the manner of pleading of claims for interest in the Queen's Bench Division.

In *President of India v La Pintada Cia Navegacion SA*[13] Lord Brandon distinguished three cases in which loss or damage may be caused by the late payment of a debt. Case 1 is where a debt is paid late, but before any proceedings for its recovery have been begun. Case 2 is where the debt is paid late, after proceedings for its recovery have been begun, but before they have been concluded. Case 3 is where a debt remains unpaid until, as a result of proceedings for its recovery being brought and prosecuted to a conclusion, a money judgment is given in which the original debt becomes merged. The Law Reform (Miscellaneous Provisions) Act 1934 provided a discretionary remedy only in relation to Case 3. The 1981 Act extended the law so as to provide a discretionary remedy to cover Case 2 in addition to Case 3. There remains, however, no statutory remedy in respect of Case 1.

The 1981 Act appears to have further extended the law by permitting simple interest to be awarded on overdue contractual interest such as an unpaid instalment of loan interest. This is a consequence of the change in wording from the prohibition in the 1934 Act upon the giving of interest upon interest to the permissive provision in the 1981 Act that 'there may be included in any sum for which judgment is given simple interest . . .' (s 35A(1)). This permits a one-off capitalisation of outstanding interest as at the date of demand. If, for example, a banker demands repayment of an overdraft as regards which there exists no contractual right to interest after demand, the court may include in its judgment interest on the whole of the outstanding principal and interest as at the date of the demand for repayment. Interest may not, however, be awarded for a period during which, for whatever reason, interest on the debt already runs (s 35A(4)).

Although the 1981 Act has extended the jurisdiction to award interest, there remains the important and somewhat out-dated limitation that the court can award only simple interest.

2 RATE OF INTEREST

The rate of interest is in the court's discretion. In recent years there has been a welcome trend in commercial cases to award interest at a commercial rate. The court looks not at the profit which the defendant has wrongfully made out of the money withheld, but at the cost to the plaintiff of being deprived of the money which he should have had.[14] In giving effect to the principle of

---

12 [1983] 1 All ER 934, [1983] 1 WLR 377, set out in note 6/2/15 to RSC Ord 6.
13 [1985] AC 104, [1984] 2 All ER 773, HL.
14 *Tate and Lyle Industries Ltd v Greater London Council* [1981] 3 All ER 716 at 722d, [1982] 1 WLR 149 at 154B (Forbes J).

restitutio in integrum, the court is guided in deciding the appropriate rate of interest by the rate at which plaintiffs with the general attributes of the actual plaintiff could borrow the relevant sum. The rate is usually fixed by reference to base rate or LIBOR from time to time. A commonly awarded rate is base rate plus one per cent, and it has rightly been observed that there is much to be said for a practice, but not a rule, which is uniform and well known.[15]

3 INTEREST ON BILLS OF EXCHANGE

Interest on bills of exchange, cheques and promissory notes is recoverable under s 57(1)(b) of the Bills of Exchange Act 1882, which provides that where a bill is dishonoured, the holder may recover interest thereon from the time of presentment for payment if the bill is payable on demand, and from the maturity of the bill in any other case.

(ii) Interest after judgment

By s 17 of the Judgments Act 1838, every judgment debt carries interest from the time of entering up the judgment until the same shall have been satisfied, and such interest may be levied under a writ of execution. The rate of interest is fixed from time to time by statutory instrument.

(c) Interest as damages

The decision of the House of Lords in *London, Chatham and Dover Rly Co v South Eastern Rly Co*[16] was for a long time understood to have established a rule that damages are not recoverable at common law for the late payment of a debt. A major inroad into this previously accepted understanding was made by the Court of Appeal in *Wadsworth v Lydall*,[17] where it was held that the *London, Chatham and Dover Rly* case applied only to damages awarded under the first part of the rule in *Hadley v Baxendale* (general damages, ie damages arising naturally in the ordinary course of things), and does not apply to damages under the second part (special damages, ie damages in respect of special loss reasonably contemplated by the parties). *Wadsworth v Lydall* was subsequently approved by the House of Lords in *President of India v La Pintada Cia Navegacion SA*,[18] and as was observed by Lord Brandon, delivering the leading speech, the effect of *Wadsworth v Lydall* is to reduce considerably the scope of the *London, Chatham and Dover Rly* case. In practice, it is likely that damages under the second part of the rule in *Hadley v Baxendale* will normally be recoverable only in circumstances where the party in whose favour the award is made has in fact paid interest on the sum for which judgment is given.

3 COSTS AND EXPENSES

Bank documentation often provides that the bank is entitled to be paid on demand all its costs, charges and expenses incurred in enforcing or obtaining payment of sums of money owed to it. In the law of mortgage, the mortgagee's

15 *Buckingham v Francis* [1986] 2 All ER 738 at 744b, [1986] BCLC 353 at 360h, per Staughton J.
16 [1893] AC 429, HL.
17 [1981] 2 All ER 401, [1981] 1 WLR 598.
18 [1985] AC 104 at 127C, [1984] 3 All ER 773 at 787f.

entitlement to add to the mortgage debt all costs, charges and expenses reasonably incurred is well established.[19] In relation to non-proprietary security, the efficacy of such provisions remained untested until *Bank of Baroda v Panessar*,[20] where the point arose for decision in an action on two guarantees. It was held by Walton J (1) that the contractual provision in each guarantee for payment of all costs meant costs on an indemnity basis; but (2) that the provision was not binding on the court, which retained the discretion in any particular case to decide that it ought not to be given effect.[1]

A bank's position in relation to costs incurred in complying with or applying to vary freezing and discovery orders is considered in chs 19 and 20, post.

19 See *Fisher and Lightwood's Law of Mortgage* (15th edn, 1988), ch 36.
20 [1987] Ch 335, [1986] 3 All ER 751.
1 Ibid at 355E and 765e, respectively.

CHAPTER 15

SECRECY, BANKERS' REFERENCES, ADVISING ON INVESTMENTS

The relationship of banker and customer gives rise to a variety of obligations and services on the part of the banker, some of which latter he may undertake voluntarily; these include (1) the duty of secrecy; (2) the giving of information as to the credit and standing of a customer, commonly known as a banker's reference; (3) advising on investments.

1 SECRECY

(a) Nature of the duty

(i) The duty in general

The law on this subject was laid down by the Court of Appeal, especially by Bankes LJ, in *Tournier v National Provincial and Union Bank of England*[1] who described it as a difficult and hitherto only partially investigated branch of the law. The judgment established that the duty is a legal one arising out of contract, not merely a moral one. Breach of it, therefore, gives a claim for damages, substantial if injury has resulted from the breach. It is, however, not an absolute duty but qualified, being subject to certain reasonable exceptions. The Lord Justice said:

> 'In my opinion it is necessary in a case like the present to direct the jury what are the limits and what are the qualifications of the contractual duty of secrecy implied in the relation of banker and customer. There appears to be no authority on the point. On principle I think that the qualifications can be classified under four heads: (a) where disclosure is under compulsion by law; (b) where there is a duty to the public to disclose; (c) where the interests of the bank require disclosure; (d) where the disclosure is made by the express or implied consent of the customer.'

As instances he gave:

(a) the duty to obey an order under the Bankers' Books Evidence Act;
(b) (quoting Lord Finlay),[2] cases where a higher duty than the private duty is involved, as where danger to the state or public duty may supersede the duty of the agent to his principal;

---

1 [1924] 1 KB 461.
2 In *Weld-Blundell v Stephens* [1920] AC 956 at 965.

(c) of a bank issuing a writ claiming payment of an overdraft, stating on the face of it the amount of the overdraft;
(d) the familiar case where the customer authorises a reference to his banker.

In the common situation of a bank organising its business through a corporate structure involving a holding company and subsidiaries, disclosure by one company to another may constitute a breach of the duty of secrecy. Disclosure in such circumstances was regarded by the Court of Appeal in *Bank of Tokyo Ltd v Karoon*[3] as raising an arguable case of breach of contract.

(ii) Commencement and duration of the duty

The duty of secrecy arises only when the relationship of banker and customer is established. It does not cease the moment a customer closes his account. Bankes LJ says:

'Information gained during the currency of the account remains confidential unless released under circumstances bringing the case within one of the classes of qualification I have already referred to.'[4]

It probably continues after the customer's death. The duty applies whether the account is in credit or overdrawn. The confidence is not confined to the actual state of the customer's account; it extends to information derived from the account itself. In fact it is wide enough to cover all information acquired by the banker in his character as such, though, according to Scrutton LJ, not to

'knowledge which the bank acquires before this relation of banker and customer was in contemplation or after it ceased; or to knowledge derived from other sources during the continuance of the relation.'[5]

On the other hand, Atkin LJ thought that the obligation did extend

'to information obtained from other sources than the customer's actual account, if the occasion upon which the information was obtained arose out of the banking relations of the bank and its customers.'[6]

It may be that there is no conflict between these two views, but if there is, the view of Atkin LJ is to be preferred. Bankers would be well advised to put a liberal construction on the limitation.

Where a bank fills the double role of banker and trustee, its successors as trustees should be in no worse position as regards the obtaining of information concerning the trust bank account and the production of documents than if a third party had been the banker.[7]

---

3 [1987] AC 45n at 53, 54, [1986] 3 All ER 468 at 475, 476, CA; and see *Bhogal v Punjab National Bank* [1988] 2 All ER 296 at 305, CA.
4 *Tournier v National Provincial and Union Bank of England* [1924] 1 KB 461 at 473.
5 *Tournier v National Provincial and Union Bank of England* [1924] 1 KB 461 at 481.
6 Ibid at 485.
7 *Tiger v Barclays Bank Ltd* [1952] 1 All ER 85 at 88.

(b) The four heads

(i) Compulsion by law

1 DISCOVERY AND INSPECTION ORDERS

The range of jurisdictions to make discovery or inspection orders against banks is now so wide that the subject of discovery and inspection orders is considered separately in ch 20, post.

2 INQUIRIES NOT BACKED BY COMPULSION

Compulsion by law is confined to the exercise of proper authority deriving from statute or an order of the court. Casual inquiries by the police or government departments, for instance, place no obligation on a bank such as does an order under the Bankers' Books Evidence Act or a requisition by the Law Society under the Solicitors' Accounts Rules. Speaking of the contractual duty of confidence, Diplock LJ, in *Parry-Jones v Law Society*,[8] said:

'Such a duty exists not only between solicitor and client, but, for example, between banker and customer, doctor and patient, and accountant and client. Such a duty of confidence is subject to, and overridden by, the duty of any party to that contract to comply with the law of the land. If it is the duty of such a party to a contract, whether at common law or under statute, to disclose in defined circumstances confidential information, then he must do so, and any express contract to the contrary would be illegal and void. For example, in the case of banker and customer, the duty of confidence is subject to the overriding duty of the banker at common law to disclose and answer questions as to his customer's affairs when he is asked to give evidence on them in the witness box in a court of law. I think that similar provisions as to disclosure apply to doctors under the National Health Acts.'

(ii) Duty to public

This is, perhaps, the most difficult of Bankes LJ's instances of where a bank might be justified in disclosing, the dividing line between a state or public duty and a private duty being hard to define. The learned Lord Justice said that many instances of the second class might be given and cited Lord Finlay in *Weld-Blundell v Stephens*[9] to the effect that 'Danger to the state or public duty may supersede the duty of the agent to the principal.' Lord Chorley[10] suggests as an example the case where in time of war the customer's dealings indicate trading with the enemy. The giving of information to the police, for instance, in regard to a customer suspected of a crime would be unwarranted.[11] There appears to be only one reported case where a banker has thought himself under a duty to the public to disclose, namely *Libyan Arab Foreign Bank v Bankers Trust Co*,[12] where the defendant bank invoked the exception in relation to a disclosure made by it to, and at the request of, the Federal Reserve Bank of New York of payment instructions which the

8 [1969] 1 Ch 1 at 9, [1968] 1 All ER 177 at 180.
9 [1920] AC 956 at 965.
10 *Law of Banking* (6th edn, 1974) 23.
11 A point of view to which Bankes LJ, subscribed in the *Tournier* case [1924] 1 KB 461 at 474.
12 [1988] 1 Lloyd's Rep 259.

defendant had received from the plaintiff. Staughton J reached a tentative conclusion that the exception applied, but did not find it necessary to reach a final conclusion on the point.[13]

(iii) The bank's interest

As regards the case in which the bank's own interest justifies disclosure, the only time the matter has been before the court was in the case of *Sutherland v Barclays Bank Ltd.*[14] The bank had dishonoured the plaintiff's cheques, there being insufficient funds in the account to meet them, but the real reason for the refusal to pay was the knowledge that the plaintiff was betting. She complained to her husband who, during a telephone conversation with the bank, was told that most cheques passing through his wife's account were in favour of bookmakers. She sued for breach of duty to maintain secrecy. Du Parcq LJ thought that in the circumstances the interests of the bank required disclosure and that it had, moreover, the customer's implied consent. He went on to say that if his judgment had been for the plaintiff, he would have awarded only nominal damages. The plaintiff had suffered little damage, if any.

The learned Lord Justice gave as an example the case of the statement in a writ of the amount of a customer's overdraft; a necessary statement in a defence is in a similar category. Where disclosure is justified under this head, it must be limited to such as is strictly necessary to establish the point.

(iv) Authorised disclosure

Disclosure with the customer's consent needs no comment; the *Sutherland* case[15] may be said to be an example of this also.

2 BANKERS' REFERENCES

The most obvious example of Bankes LJ's fourth head is 'the familiar case where the customer authorises a reference to his banker.' Answering inquiries from another bank acting on behalf of a customer is within the scope of banking business,[16] and the practice may be regarded as implicitly authorised by most customers of banks.

This has to be considered from two points of view, that of the person, bank or customer, to whom information is given, and that of the customer about whom the inquiry is made.

13 Ibid at 286.
14 (1938) 5 LDAB 163.
15 (1938) 5 LDAB 163.
16 See *Swift v Jewsbury and Goddard* (1874) 9 LR QB 301; *Parsons v Barclay & Co Ltd* (1910) 103 LT 196.

(a) Liability to party to whom a reference is supplied

(i) Fraudulent misrepresentation

By s 6 of the Statute of Frauds Amendment Act 1828 (Lord Tenterden's Act):[17]

> 'no action shall be brought whereby to charge any person upon or by reason of any representation or assurance made or given concerning or relating to the character, conduct, credit, ability, trade, or dealings of any other person, to the intent or purpose that such other person may obtain credit, money, or goods upon, unless such representation or assurance be made in writing, signed by the party to be charged therewith.'

The section was supposed to enact that when a banker gave information to a customer or a third person as to the credit of a customer, he was not liable for false representation unless the representation was in writing and signed by the banker himself, the signature of a bank manager not being for this purpose that of his bank. This view was supported by *Swift v Jewsbury and Goddard*[18] and *Hirst v West Riding Union Banking Co Ltd*.[19]

In *Banbury v Bank of Montreal*[20] the House of Lords, though differing on other points, were unanimous that Lord Tenterden's Act had no bearing on the matter. As they pointed out, its wording, 'signed by the party to be charged therewith', and the circumstances of its enactment clearly show that the Act only applies to false and fraudulent representation. They cited with approval the words of Bramwell B in *Swift v Jewsbury and Goddard*:

> 'The effect of the statute is this, that a man shall not be liable for a fraudulent misrepresentation as to another person's means unless he puts it down in writing and acknowledges his responsibility for it by his own signature.'

In *UBAF Ltd v European American Banking Corpn*[1] the following propositions relating to s 6 were common ground:
(1) The section applies to fraudulent misrepresentations only: *Banbury v Bank of Montreal*.[2] Accordingly, the section has no application to alleged innocent but negligent misrepresentation. However, representations alleged to give rise to liability under s 2(1) of the Misrepresentation Act 1967 are also within Lord Tenterden's Act, because the person making the representation is liable only if he 'would be liable to damage in respect thereof had the misrepresentation been made fraudulently.' (2) The word 'person' in the section includes a corporation: *Banbury v Bank of Montreal*, approving *Hirst v West Riding Union Banking Co Ltd*.[3] (3) In order to be within the section the representation upon which the action is based must relate in some way to the credit or creditworthiness of a person: *Diamond v Bank of London and Montreal Ltd*.[4]

It was then held by the Court of Appeal that for the purposes of s 6, a written representation is made by a company if it is signed by its duly authorised agent acting within the scope of his authority.

17 11 Halsbury's Statutes (4th edn) 206.
18 [1874] LR 9 QB 301.
19 [1901] 2 KB 560.
20 [1918] AC 626.
 1 [1984] QB 713, [1984] 2 All ER 226, CA.
 2 [1918] AC 626.
 3 [1901] 2 KB 560.
 4 [1979] QB 333, [1979] 1 All ER 561, CA.

(ii) Negligence – Hedley Byrne v Heller & Partners

Prior to the decision of the House of Lords in *Hedley Byrne & Co Ltd v Heller & Partners Ltd*[5] the law limited action for negligent misrepresentation to cases where there was either a contractual or a fiduciary relationship between the parties.[6] The issue in this case was stated by Lord Morris of Borth-y-Gest as follows:

'In order to recover the damages they claim Hedleys must establish that the bank owed them a duty, that the bank failed to discharge such duty and that as a consequence Hedleys suffered loss.'

The facts were that through their bankers the plaintiffs made inquiry of the defendant bank as to the financial stability of customers of the defendants and, acting on the answer received, they incurred liabilities which ended in loss. McNair J at first instance held that the defendants were negligent but that they owed no duty to be other than honest in giving their reply. The Court of Appeal did not consider the finding of negligence, but upheld the judge below on the question of duty. The House of Lords were unanimous in holding that by reason of the defendants' disclaimer of responsibility there was no assumption of a legal duty of care.

What emerges from the decision is that there may be a special relationship between two parties deriving neither from contract nor from fiduciary responsibility, but from a relationship of proximity, which will give rise to a duty to take care in giving a reference; but that in the majority of banking cases – at least of those similar to the present case, which was the common case of a banker's reference – no such relationship arises; that, in any event a bank can safeguard itself by giving the information without responsibility.

The only case accepted as being based on a special relationship as visualised in *Hedley Byrne* was *Woods v Martins Bank Ltd*[7] but that was a case of banker and customer and the bank had held itself out as willing and competent to give advice, so that it was a matter of contract rather than of a special relationship. Lord Devlin seemingly distinguished the relation of banker and customer, 'a general relationship' from a particular relationship, in *Woods v Martins Bank Ltd*. Lord Pearce conceded that a duty of care was rightly found in that case. All the Law Lords appeared to be in agreement on the existence of the new category, Lord Read (by implication as he did not 'attempt to decide what kind of degree of proximity is necessary before there can be a duty ...'); Lord Morris ('irrespective of any contractual or fiduciary relationship and irrespective of any direct dealing, a duty may be owed by one person to another ...'); Lord Hudson ('a banker like anyone else may find himself involved in a special relationship involving liability'); Lord Devlin ('wherever there is a relationship equivalent to contract there is a duty of care ...'); Lord Pearce ('there is also in my opinion a duty of care created by

5 [1964] AC 465, [1963] 2 All ER 575; and see *Mutual Life and Citizens Assurance Co Ltd v Evatt* [1971] AC 793, [1970] 2 Lloyd's Rep 441.
6 See *Derry v Peek* (1889) 14 App Cas 337; *Le Lievre v Gould* [1893] 1 QB 491; *Nocton v Lord Ashburton* [1914] AC 932; and *Candler v Crane, Christmas & Co* [1951] 2 KB 164, [1951] 1 All ER 426. See also *Parsons v Barclay & Co Ltd* (1910) 103 LT 196, CA; *Robinson v National Bank of Scotland* 1916 53 SLR 390; *Evans v Barclays Bank and Galloway* [1924] WN 97, CA and *Batts Combe Quarry Co v Barclays Bank Ltd* (1931) 48 TLR 4, considered in *Paget* (9th edn) pp 156–157.
7 [1959] 1 QB 55, [1958] 3 All ER 166.

special relationships which, though not fiduciary give rise to an assumption that care as well as honesty is demanded.').

At pp. 528–529 Lord Devlin epitomises the position:

'I think, therefore, that there is ample authority to justify your Lordships in saying now that the categories of special relationships which may give rise to a duty to take care in word as well as in deed are not limited to contractual relationships or to relationships of fiduciary duty, but include also relationships which in the words of Lord Shaw in *Nocton v Lord Ashburton* are "equivalent to contract", that is, where there is an assumption of responsibility in circumstances in which, but for the absence of consideration, there would be a contract. Where there is an express undertaking, there can be little difficulty. The difficulty arises in discerning those cases in which the undertaking is to be implied. In this respect the absence of consideration is not irrelevant. Payment for information or advice is very good evidence that it is being relied upon and that the informer or adviser knows that it is. Where there is no consideration it will be necessary to exercise greater care in distinguishing between social and professional relationships, and between those which are of a contractual character and those which are not. It may often be material to consider whether the adviser is acting purely out of good nature or whether he is getting his reward in some indirect form. The service that a bank performs in giving a reference is not done simply out of a desire to assist commerce. It would discourage the customers of the bank if their deals fell through because the bank had refused to testify to their credit when it was good.

I have had the advantage of ... studying the terms which your Lordships have framed by way of definition of the sort of relationship which gives rise to a responsibility towards those who act upon information or advice and so creates a duty of care towards them. I do not understand any of your Lordships to hold that it is a responsibility imposed by law upon certain types of persons or in certain sorts of situations. It is responsibility that is voluntarily accepted or undertaken, either generally where a general relationship, such as that of solicitor and client or banker and customer, is created, or specifically in relation to a particular transaction. In the present case the appellants were not, as in *Woods v Martins Bank Ltd* the customers or potential customers of the bank. Responsibility can attach only to the single act, that is, the giving of the reference, and only if the doing of that act implied a voluntary undertaking to assume responsibility. This is a point of great importance because it is, as I understand it, the foundation for the ground on which in the end the House dismisses the appeal. I do not think it possible to formulate with exactitude all the conditions under which the law will in a specific case imply a voluntary undertaking any more than it is possible to formulate those in which the law will imply a contract. But in so far as your Lordships describe the circumstances in which an implication will ordinarily be drawn, I am prepared to adopt any one of your Lordships' statements as showing the general rule; and I pay the same respect to the statement by Denning LJ, in his dissenting judgment in *Candler v Crane, Christmas & Co*[8] about the circumstances in which he says a duty to use care in making a statement exists.'

It is thus pertinent to ask what, outside such a relationship as was found in *Woods v Martins Bank Ltd*,[9] it would take for a special relationship uncomplicated by that of banker and customer to arise. It may be that some indication is to be found in the judgment of the Privy Council in *Mutual Life and Citizens Assurance Co Ltd v Evatt*[10] though the facts differed in one important respect from those in *Hedley Byrne* in that the company's business

8   [1951] 2 KB 164.
9   [1959] 1 QB 55, [1958] 3 All ER 166.
10   [1971] AC 793, [1970] 2 Lloyd's Rep 441, PC.

did not cover the giving of advice on investments, nor did it claim to possess the skill and competence to do so. As Lord Diplock put it in the Privy Council the judgments in *Hedley Byrne* have lain at the heart of the argument in the Australian Courts in the *Evatt* case. The Court of Appeal of the Supreme Court of New South Wales by a majority dismissed the demurrer entered by the respondents who then appealed to the High Court of Australia, who by a majority dismissed the appeal. The respondents then appealed to the Privy Council who by a majority allowed the appeal. The facts were that the plaintiff, a policy holder in the defendant company, sought advice from it as to the financial stability of an associated company and acted on that advice to his loss. The majority of the Judicial Committee (Lord Hodson, Lord Guest and Lord Diplock, Lord Reid and Lord Morris of Borth-y-Gest dissenting) held that the company's duty was merely to give an honest answer to the inquiry. In giving the judgment of the majority in the *Evatt* case, Lord Diplock said that *Hedley Byrne*

> 'should not be regarded as intended to lay down the metes and bounds of the new field of negligence of which the gate is now opened. This will fall to be ascertained step by step as the facts of particular cases which come before the courts make it necessary to determine them'.[11]

He then gave the following lead:

> '... their Lordships would emphasise that the missing characteristic of the relationship which they consider to be essential to give rise to a duty of care in a situation of the kind in which Mr Evatt and the company found themselves when he sought their advice, is not necessarily essential in other situations – such as, perhaps, where the adviser had a financial interest in the transaction upon which he gives his advice (cf. *W. B. Anderson & Sons Ltd v Rhodes (Liverpool) Ltd*;[12] *American Re-statement of the Law of Torts*, 3rd Tentative Redraft).[13]

The minority judgment suggested that:[14]

> 'the appropriate question is whether this advice was given on a business occasion or in the course of the appellant's business activities. The solution of the question may be difficult where advice is given by an individual, but here the advice is alleged to have been given by a company. It must in fact have been given by some individual. If it was given by the company that must mean that the individual who gave the advice must have had general or special authority from the company to give it, or at least that the company must have held him out as authorised to give it ... So long as a company does not act ultra vires it is for the company to determine the scope of its business. It appears to be quite common practice for business to perform gratuitous services for their customers with the object of retaining or acquiring their goodwill. If they incur expense in doing so it has never so far as we are aware been suggested that such expense is not a business expense. And we think that where companies do perform such service both they and their customers would be surprised to learn that the company is under no obligation to take any care in the matter.'

The dissentients, Lord Reid and Lord Morris of Borth-y-Gest, refused to accept the view that a person cannot be under a duty unless he has some special skill, competence, qualification or information with regard to the

11 [1971] AC 793 at 809.
12 [1967] 2 All ER 850 applying *Hedley Byrne*.
13 [1971] AC 793 at 809.
14 Ibid at 810.

matter on which his advice is sought or the argument that a duty to take care was not the same for a specially skilled man and an unskilled. They were of opinion that it would be sufficient if the advice was given on a business occasion or in the course of the appellant's business activities. Again they refused to accept the 'holding out' argument: 'We can see no virtue in a previous holding out.' As to *Hedley Byrne* they said:[15]

'In *Hedley Byrne* their Lordships were not laying down rules. They were developing a principle which flows, as in all branches of the tort of negligence, from giving legal effect to what ordinary reasonable men habitually do in certain circumstances'

and they declined to construe the passages from their own speeches cited in the judgment of the majority in the way in which they are there construed.

The chief factor of the *Hedley Byrne* judgment is that there is a third category of case in which responsibility for negligence may give rise to damages, the case which, so far as banking is concerned, is dependent upon a special non-contractual, non-fiduciary, relationship: and, superimposed on that by the judgment in the Australian case, that that responsibility cannot arise if the defendant does not hold out as part of its business that it gives advice or claims the necessary skill and competence to give such advice. The question when and in what circumstances such responsibility arises is still open.

Ormrod LJ in *Esso Petroleum Co Ltd v Marden*[16] preferred the reasoning of the minority in the *Mutual Life*[17] case:

'If the majority view were to be accepted the effect of *Hedley Byrne* would be so radically curtailed as to be virtually eliminated.'

and

'There is no magic in the phrase "special relationship"; it means no more than a relationship the nature of which is such that one party, for a variety of possible reasons, will be regarded by the law as under a duty of care to the other.'

A decision of Lloyd J illustrates a further instance of the relationship. The branch manager in *Box v Midland Bank Ltd*,[18] answering a customer's request for an advance beyond the manager's discretionary limit told the customer that he (the manager) would have to get Head Office sanction, but had no doubt that approval would be given. The customer acted on this opinion and suffered loss. The judge, referring to Lord Devlin's speech in *Hedley Byrne*[19] pointed out that the manager was not obliged to predict the outcome of the application but, having done so, was under a duty to take reasonable care since he knew that his prediction would be relied on.

(iii) Disclaimer of liability for negligence

Information given is usually accompanied by an intimation that it is given in confidence and without responsibility on the part of the banker and bank officers. Such a disclaimer of responsibility was successful in protecting the

15 Ibid at 813.
16 [1976] QB 801 at 827, a case of pre-contractual negotiation concerning the throughput of petrol from a petrol station, applying *Hedley Byrne*.
17 [1971] AC 793, [1971] 1 All ER 150, PC.
18 [1979] 2 Lloyd's Rep 391. The Court of Appeal allowed an appeal as to costs: [1981] 1 Lloyd's Rep 434. See also *The Royal Bank Trust Co (Trinidad) Ltd v Pampellonne* [1987] 1 Lloyd's Rep 218, PC.
19 [1964] AC 465, [1963] 2 All ER 575 at 529 and 575–9.

banker in *Hedley Byrne & Co Ltd v Heller & Partners Ltd*. To be able to express an opinion without responsibility gives the banker a wide licence, but he must be honest in what he says if he is to avoid responsibility. This is not a matter of contract but of misrepresentation, perhaps fraudulent, as to which latter there is the decision of the High Court of Australia in *Commercial Banking Co of Sydney v R H Brown & Co*,[20] to the effect that if a representation is made fraudulently, in the sense that it could not have been made honestly, the fact that it is given without responsibility could not protect the defendant – a conclusion with which it is hard to complain, but which raises the question of when, apart from fraud, a representation may not be honest, a question which may depend upon the circumstances.

Up to 1977 the disclaimer of responsibility was effective. Today, the position is governed by the Unfair Contract Terms Act 1977, which was passed to

'impose further limits on the extent to which ... civil liability for breach of contract, or for negligence or other breach of duty, can be avoided by means of contract terms and otherwise. ...'

The meaning of this rather loose introduction becomes clearer when the Act itself is considered. Sections 2 and 3 provide:

2 (1) A person cannot by reference to any contract term or to a notice given to persons generally or to particular persons exclude or restrict his liability for death or personal injury resulting from negligence.
(2) In the case of other loss or damage a person cannot so exclude or restrict his liability for negligence except in so far as the term or notice satisfies the requirement of reasonableness.
(3) Where a contract term or notice purports to exclude or restrict liability for negligence a person's agreement to or awareness of it is not of itself to be taken as indicating his voluntary acceptance of any risk.

3 (1) This section applies as between contracting parties where one of them deals as consumer or on the other's written standard terms of business.
(2) As against that party, the other cannot by reference to any contract term –
    (a) when himself in breach of contract, exclude or restrict any liability of his in respect of the breach; or
    (b) claim to be entitled –
        (i) to render a contractual performance substantially different from that which was reasonably expected of him, or
        (ii) in respect of the whole or any part of his contractual obligation, to render no performance at all,
except in so far as (in any of the cases mentioned above in this subsection) the contract term satisfies the requirement of reasonableness.

For the purposes of the Act (and for s 3 of the Misrepresentation Act 1967) the requirement of reasonableness is stated in s 11(1) and (3) to the effect that

'(1) ... the term shall have been a fair and reasonable one ... having regard to the circumstances. ...'

and

'(3) ... in relation to a notice (not being a notice having contractual effect), that it should be fair and reasonable ... having regard to all the circumstances. ...'

20 [1972] 2 Lloyd's Rep 360.

It may be added that s 3 of the Misrepresentation Act 1967 is replaced by the following:

> '3 If a contract contains a term which would exclude or restrict –
>   (a) any liability to which a party to a contract may be subject by reason of any misrepresentation made by him before the contract was made; or
>   (b) any remedy available to another party to the contract by reason of such a misrepresentation,
> that term shall be of no effect except in so far as it satisfies the requirement of reasonableness as stated in section 11 (1) of the Unfair Contract Terms Act 1977; and it is for those claiming that the term satisfies that requirement to show that it does.'

In *Smith v Bush*,[1] the House of Lords held that a disclaimer of liability by a valuer who had prepared a valuation for mortgage purposes was a notice which purported to exclude liability for negligence and was therefore ineffective unless it satisfied the requirement of reasonableness provided by s 11(3). There appears to be no ground for distinguishing a disclaimer of liability in a banker's reference.

(b) Liability to customer about whom information is given

There remains to consider the position of the customer about whom the banker is expressing an opinion. This has two facets, that of breach of the obligation to maintain secrecy and that of liability for libel. The first is dealt with under the heading 'Secrecy', ante. With regard to the second, to which only the truth of the statement is a defence, the question of privilege arises. Though not in banking, it has been held in general terms that communication, if without malice and given bona fide, is privileged (*Waller v Loch* ,[2] *Robshaw v Smith*,[3] *London Association for Protection of Trade v Greenlands Ltd*).[4] In the last of these Lord Parker of Waddington said:

> 'It is therefore a principle of law that a person asked for information affecting the credit of another is justified in giving it provided (1) that he bona fide believes in the truth of the information he gives; (2) that he bona fide believes that the person making the enquiry has an interest which justifies it; and, (3) if *Macintosh v Dun*[5] is to be considered good law, that he is not actuated by motives of private gain or other motives, excluding the possibility of the communication being made under a sense of social duty.'

Where the advice the banker gives is at the request of one customer in respect of another the position is perhaps more delicate. The very fact, especially if there is any conflict of interest, would require him to dissociate himself from the matter if possible.

1 [1989] 2 All ER 514, [1989] 2 WLR 790, HL.
2 (1881) 7 QBD 619.
3 (1878) 38 LT 423.
4 [1916] 2 AC 15.
5 [1908] AC 390.

3 ADVISING ON INVESTMENTS

The question of advising on investments has no reference to the practice of bankers to pass stock exchange and similar inquiries to stockbrokers and other professional advisers and to pass the information given to their customer in such form that it is obvious that the banker is expressing no opinion of his own. This is no part of a banker's business; it is a service he offers as his customer's agent for which he does not make himself responsible.

It is a different matter if he assumes the responsibility of advising himself. If advising is within the scope of the business, the bank is under a duty to use reasonable care and skill, failure to do which would constitute negligence, of which one example is *Woods v Martins Bank*.[6]

In *Banbury v Bank of Montreal*[7] the plaintiff was not, though he previously had been, a customer; he was merely recommended to their kind offices by a customer. He was charged nothing for the advice he got as to the credit and standing of the company in which he invested and lost his money. The question narrowed down to whether it was part of a bank's business to advise on investments and if it was, whether a local manager had the necessary authority.

The case was treated as analogous to that of gratuitous services rendered by a person professing special knowledge and skill, say, a surgeon. Lord Finley LC said at 659:

'There is in point of law no difference between the case of advice given by a physician and advice given by a solicitor or banker in the course of his business'.

If the surgeon volunteers his aid and it is accepted, the confiding his body to him by the patient is sufficient consideration to raise a duty on the part of the surgeon to bring to the case such skill and care as are reasonably to be expected from a man of his position and pretensions. And to quote Lord Finlay LC again:[8]

'The limits of a banker's business cannot be laid down as a matter of law.[9] ... If he undertakes to advise, he must exercise reasonable care and skill in giving the advice. He is under no obligation to advise, but if he takes upon himself to do so, he will incur liability if he does so negligently.'

The question in *Banbury's* case, whether advising on investments was within the scope of the bank's business, depended on whether the local manager had authority to bind the bank, whether negligence on his part was negligence on the part of the bank. Two law lords, Finlay and Shaw, were in favour of the plaintiff and held that the authority extended to the local manager; of the three, Parker, Atkinson and Wrenbury, who had decided in favour of the bank, Lord Parker based his judgment mainly on the ground that there was no evidence on which a jury could find that the bank were bound by the act of the manager, and so the question of negligence did not

6 [1959] 1 QB 55; p 266, post.
7 [1918] AC 626.
8 Ibid at 652, 654: and see *Mutual Mortgage Corpn Ltd v Bank of Montreal* (1965) 55 DLR (2d) 164.
9 This view was adopted by Salmon J in *Woods v Martins Bank Ltd* [1959] 1 QB 55 at 70, [1958] 3 All ER 166. He continued: 'What may have been true of the Bank of Montreal in 1918 is not necessarily true of Martins Bank in 1958.' At this time Martins Bank were advertising their readiness to advise.

arise. Lords Atkinson and Wrenbury were more influenced by the consideration that advising on investments was not shown to be within the scope of the bank's business, and therefore there could be no authority to devolve. As Lord Wrenbury put it:[10]

'Either advising on investments was within the business of bankers or it was not. If it was, then not the head manager only, but the local manager, within his district, would also hold authority to do that business so as to bind his principals. If it was not, then the head manager could not do it, neither could he authorise the local manager to do it.'

Save for the authoritative exposition that Lord Tenterden's Act applies only to fraudulent representation, *Banbury's* case cannot be regarded as very conclusive.

Wilson v United Counties Bank Ltd[11] was an exceptional case. The plaintiff, a customer of the bank, was leaving for war service. It was agreed by him with the general manager that the local manager at B should supervise the plaintiff's business, see it carried on, particularly the financial side, and take all reasonable steps to maintain his credit and reputation. The jury found that the bank were negligent in performing their duties under this agreement and awarded £45,000 damages for loss to the plaintiff's estate, and £7,500 for injury caused to his credit and reputation. The House of Lords, reversing the Court of Appeal, restored the judgment for these amounts. Such a function as this can hardly be said to be within the scope of banking business. There seems to have been no special consideration for the agreement and no reference to the scope of banking business in the judgments. Lord Birkenhead LC said:

'If it is held that there is an irrebuttable presumption that the dishonour of a trader customer's cheque in the events supposed is injurious to him and may be compensated by other than nominal damages the conclusion would appear to follow almost a fortiori that such damages may be given where the defendant has expressly contracted to sustain the financial credit of a trading customer and has committed a breach of his agreement',

which points to breach of contract and not negligent performance of a duty due by a banker to his customer as being the ratio decidendi of the decision.

It seems probable that in any future case evidence would be forthcoming that advising on investments was the common practice of bankers, or if it were shown that they shared in the broker's commission, a court might find it to be a part of banking business.[12] In *Woods v Martins Bank Ltd*,[13] the bank had held itself out as willing to advise, and through its managers, though it pleaded that this was not part of the business of banking and that, therefore, the bank was under no duty and could not be responsible for any loss. Since it had advertised that it had 'six district head offices with boards of directors and general managers, so that the very best advice is available through our managers', and again, that the bank manager could be consulted

10 [1918] AC 626 at 715.
11 [1920] AC 102.
12 See in this connection, *Thornett v Barclays Bank (France) Ltd* [1939] 1 KB 675, [1939] 2 All ER 163.
13 [1959] 1 QB 55, [1958] 3 All ER 166; but see *Mutual Life and Citizens Assurance Co Ltd v Evatt* [1971] AC 793, [1971] 1 All ER 150, PC in which it was held that giving advice on investments was not part of the company's business.

freely on all matters affecting one's financial welfare, the bank's argument did not find favour with the learned judge, Salmon J. However, these were special facts, which may render the decision unsafe for general application. Each case will have to be considered on its own facts.

Whether a branch manager has authority to advise is a matter of fact. It is likely, however, that even where he is not authorised, advising is sufficiently within his ostensible authority to entitle a customer to assume that he is authorised and to found a claim for negligence if he falls short of the standard which the customer would be entitled to expect.[14]

14 For a case in which the authority of a bank employee was considered in a somewhat different context, namely the issue of a bank guarantee, see *Egyptian International Foreign Trade Co v Soplex Wholesale Supplies Ltd* [1985] 2 Lloyd's Rep 36, CA.

CHAPTER 16

SAFE CUSTODY

For the convenience of customers bankers assume charge of plate, securities and other valuables. The goods are said to be delivered to the banker for 'safe custody'. The banker thereby voluntarily becomes a bailee. Liability under a contract of bailment must be considered under two heads: negligence and conversion.

(a) Bailee's duty of care

(i) Existence and scope of the duty

A banker who accepts articles for safe custody is probably a bailee for reward rather than a gratuitous bailee.[1] This view was expressed in *Port Swettenham Authority v T W Wu and Co (M) Sdn Bhd* by Lord Salmon, delivering the advice of the Privy Council:[2]

> 'In any event, a bank which offers its customers, in the ordinary course of business, the service of looking after goods deposited with it, can hardly be described as a gratuitous bailee. The bank must realise that were it to refuse a customer such a service it would probably lose the customer who would have no difficulty in finding another bank which would be happy to render the service which is normally offered by banks to their customers.'

In practice, the distinction between a gratuitous bailee and a bailee for reward appears to make little difference to the existence and scope of the bank's duty of care, in that: (1) on a gratuitous bailment (as on a bailment for reward) the bailee may be liable for want of ordinary care;[3] (2) where bailed goods are lost from the custody of the bailee, then whether he was a gratuitous bailee or a bailee for reward, the onus is on him to prove that the loss was not due to his failure to exercise the care required by law;[4] (3) the standard of care required in providing a service for safe custody is unlikely to differ much, if at all, as between a gratuitous bailee and a bailee for reward,

---

1 For a fuller treatment of the law of bailment, see *Palmer on Bailment* (1st edn, 1979).
2 [1979] AC 580 at 589F, [1978] 3 All ER 337 at 340b, PC.
3 Per Lord Finlay LC in *Banbury v Bank of Montreal* [1918] AC 626 at 657; see also *Hedley Byrne & Co Ltd v Heller & Partners Ltd* [1964] AC 465 at 526, [1963] 2 All ER 575 at 608, HL (Lord Devlin).
4 *Port Swettenham Authority v T W Wu and Co (M) Sdn Bhd* [1979] AC 580, [1979] 3 All ER 337, PC, disapproving (as regards gratuitous bailees) *Giblin v McMullen* (1868) LR 2 PC 317.

especially in the light of Lord Salmon's observation set out above. The matter was put into proper perspective in *Houghland v R R Low (Luxury Coaches) Ltd* by Ormerod LJ who thought that:

'... to try to put a bailment, for instance, into a watertight compartment – such as a gratuitous bailment on the one hand, and bailment for reward on the other – is to overlook the fact that there might well be an infinite variety of cases which might come into one or the other category. The question we have to consider in a case of this kind, if it is necessary to consider negligence, is whether in the circumstances of this particular case a sufficient standard of care has been observed by the defendants or their servants.'[5]

The banker's knowledge or ignorance of the nature of the goods entrusted to him would seem not to affect his liability.

A banker is under no obligation to accept a parcel for safe custody and where he is asked to do so, could ask to know its contents and value in order to gauge the nature and extent of any possible liability; but it is submitted that he need not inquire.

(ii) Liability for dishonest acts of bank staff

The crux of the Court of Appeal decision in *Morris v C W Martin & Sons Ltd*,[6] in which a servant directed to clean a mink coat made away with it, was that the employee committed the fraud in the course of doing the class of acts which the company had instructed him to do, thus applying *Lloyd v Grace, Smith & Co*[7] and distinguishing *Ruben and Ladenburg v Great Fingall Consolidated Ltd*.[8]

'If the master is under a duty to use due care ... he cannot get rid of his responsibility by delegating his duty to another; and in the case of a bailee for reward the burden is on him to show that the loss or damage occurred without any neglect or default or misconduct of himself or of any of the servants to whom he delegated his duty.'[9]

On the basis of *Lloyd v Grace, Smith & Co*[10] responsibility for the wrongful acts of bank staff would seem to depend upon whether the act can be said to be within the scope of the servant's authority. In that case it was said by Lord Shaw of Dunfermline that:

'the fraud was committed in the course of, and within the scope of, the duties which the defendants had entrusted Sandles as their managing clerk ... they must in these circumstances be answerable for their agent's misconduct.'

5 [1962] 1 QB 694 at 698, [1962] 2 All ER 159 at 161.
6 [1966] 1 QB 716, [1965] 2 All ER 725, CA, applied in *Leesh River Tea Co Ltd v British India Steam Navigation Co Ltd* [1967] 2 QB 250, [1966] 3 All ER 593, CA, approved in *Port Swettenham Authority v T W Wu & Co* [1979] AC 580, [1978] 3 All ER 337, PC.
7 [1912] AC 716, overruling dictum of Lord Davey in *Ruben and Ladenburg v Great Fingall Consolidated Ltd* [1906] AC 439 at 465.
8 [1906] AC 439.
9 Lord Denning MR in *Morris v Martin, supra*.
10 [1912] AC 716. Cases such as *Giblin v McMullen* (1868) LR 2 PC 317, which were decided long before *Lloyd v Grace, Smith & Co* in days when it was thought to be the law that a master could not be liable for a theft by his own servant in any circumstances except where the master benefited from or connived at the theft, are now of doubtful authority. The *Giblin* case itself was disapproved in *Port Swettenham Authority v T W Wu and Co (M) Sdn Bhd* [1979] AC 580, [1978] 3 All ER 337, PC.

The decision was applied by the Privy Council in *United Africa Co Ltd v Saka Owoade*:[11]

'... the fair inference from the facts proved is that the goods were committed expressly to the respondent's servants and that they converted the goods whilst they were on the journey which the respondent had undertaken to carry out, and the conversion, therefore, was in their Lordships' view in the course of the employment of the respondent's servants. There is in their Lordships' opinion no difference in the liability of a master for wrongs whether for fraud or any other wrong committed by a servant in the course of his employment.'

The authorities were reviewed by the Court of Appeal in *Morris v Martin & Sons Ltd*[12] in which Lord Denning MR said that:

'From all these instances we may deduce the general proposition that when a principal has in his charge the goods or belongings of another in such circumstances that he is under a duty to take all reasonable precautions to protect them from theft or depredation, then, if he entrusts that duty to a servant or agent, he is answerable for the manner in which that servant or agent carries out his duty. If the servant or agent is careless so that they are stolen by a stranger, the master is liable. So also if the servant or agent himself steals them or makes away with them.'

Salmon LJ, at 78 said that:

'A bailee for reward is not answerable for a theft by any of his servants but only for a theft by such of them as are deputed by him to discharge some part of his duty of taking reasonable care. A theft by any servant who is not employed to do anything in relation to the goods bailed is entirely outside the scope of his employment and cannot make the master liable.'

The matter obviously depends in some degree upon the extent of the authority which the servant may be expected to have and, of course, on any knowledge in this respect of which the plaintiff may be possessed. The extent of the apparent or implied authority will depend in part upon the status of the staff officer concerned; as was said by the Privy Council in *Bank of New South Wales v Owston*:

'The duties of a bank manager would usually be to conduct banking business on behalf of his employers, and when he is found so acting, what is done by him in the way of ordinary banking transactions may be presumed, until the contrary is shown, to be within the scope of his authority; and his employers would be liable for his mistakes and, under some circumstances, for his frauds, in the management of such business'.[13]

The case was one of wrongful arrest and prosecution, as to which the Judicial Committee said:

'The arrest, and still less the prosecution, of offenders is not within the ordinary routine of banking business.'

11 [1955] AC 130 at 144.
12 [1966] 1 QB 716, [1965] 2 Lloyd's Rep 63, CA and see the warehouse cases: *Brooks Wharf and Bull Wharf Ltd v Goodman Bros* [1936] 3 All ER 696, 42 Com Cas 99; *Global Dress Co v W H Boarse & Co* [1966] 2 Lloyd's Rep 72; *British Road Services Ltd v Arthur v Crutchley & Co Ltd* [1968] 1 All ER 811, [1968] 1 Lloyd's Rep 271; *Mansfield Importers and Distributors Ltd v Casco Terminals Ltd* [1971] 2 Lloyd's Rep 73 (Supreme Court of British Columbia).
13 (1879) 4 App Cas 270 at 289. See also *Egyptian International Foreign Trade Co v Soplex Wholesale Supplies Ltd* [1985] 2 Lloyd's Rep 36, CA; *Russo-Chinese Bank v Li Yau Sam* [1910] AC 174, PC.

(b) Conversion

(i) Definition

Detinue was abolished by s 2(1) of the Torts (Interference with Goods) Act 1977. By s 2(2):

> 'An action lies in conversion for loss or destruction of goods which a bailee has allowed to happen in breach of his duty to his bailor (that is to say it lies in a case which is not otherwise conversion, but would have been detinue before detinue was abolished).'

'Wrongful interference' means conversion or trespass to goods, and negligence resulting in damage to goods. Contributory negligence is no defence in proceedings founded on conversion or intentional trespass (s 11(1)) and conversion includes the receipt of goods by way of pledge if the delivery is conversion (s 11(2)). Section 12 provides for the bailee's power of sale.

Atkin J in *Lancashire and Yorkshire Rly Co v MacNicoll*,[14] defined conversion in terms approved by Scrutton LJ in *Oakley v Lyster*,[15] and by Lord Porter in *Caxton Publishing Co Ltd v Sutherland Publishing Co Ltd*[16] as:

> 'a dealing with goods in a manner inconsistent with the right of the true owner ... provided that it is also established that there is also an intention on the part of the defendant in so doing to deny the owner's right or to assert a right which is inconsistent with the owner's right.'

But, as Lord Porter observed:

> 'Atkin J goes on to point out that when the act done is necessarily a denial of the owner's right inconsistent therewith, intention does not matter. Another way of reaching the same conclusion would be to say that conversion consists in an act intentionally done inconsistent with the owner's right though the doer may not know of or intend to challenge the property or possession of the true owner.'

Liability for conversion is independent of the distinction between commission and omission, between the active interference with the property involved in the voluntary handing over of the goods to a person not entitled to receive them, and the mere passive neglect of duty which may result in their loss. Authority for this proposition is not wanting. The cases have usually been those of carriers who have delivered goods to the wrong person. The earlier authorities are summarised in *Stephenson v Hart*,[17] Parke J saying:

> 'From the cases which have been cited it is clear that trover lies against a carrier for misfeasance in delivering a parcel to a wrong person. In *Ross v Johnson*[18] a distinction was taken between misfeasance and nonfeasance, and it was holden that trover would not lie where a carrier had lost goods by a robbery or theft, Lord Mansfield and Aston J considering that a case of mere omission. But in *Youl v Harbottle*,[19] Lord Kenyon, referring to *Ross v Johnson*, said that where the carrier was actor and delivered the goods to a wrong person he was liable in trover.'

14 (1919) 88 LJKB 601 at 605.
15 [1931] 1 KB 148.
16 [1939] AC 178, [1938] 4 All ER 389.
17 (1828) 4 Bing 476.
18 (1772) 5 Burr 2825.
19 (1791) Peake 68, NP.

(ii) Knowledge of adverse claims

The banker is primarily concerned to comply with the mandate pursuant to which he accepts the goods for safe custody. This is borne out by the judgment of Martin B in *Cheesman v Exall*[20] to the effect that:

> 'there are numerous cases in connection with wharfs and docks in which, if the party entrusted with the possession of property were not estopped from denying the title of the person from whom he received it, it would be difficult to transact commercial business.'

It is a nice question, dependent entirely upon the facts, when a banker is so vested with knowledge of a valid adverse claim to the property he holds as justifies him in refusing to redeliver to his bailor.

Where anyone other than the original depositor applies for re-delivery and cannot show his authority, the practical course would be to decline to deliver, but to this it is objected that the banker, if the application is genuine, is guilty of technical conversion of the goods, and that he would have to convince the court that he had reasonable grounds for suspicion, and had acted bona fide: or else suffer damages. The leading authority on the question is that of Blackburn J in *Hollins v Fowler*:[1]

> 'A demand and refusal is always evidence of a conversion. If the refusal is in disregard of the plaintiff's title and for the purpose of claiming the goods either for the defendant or a third person it is a conversion. If the refusal is by a person who does not know the plaintiff's title, and, having a bona fide doubt as to the title to the goods, detains them for a reasonable time for clearing up that doubt, it is not a conversion, *Isaack v Clark*;[2] *Vaughan v Watt*;[3] the principle being, as I apprehend, that the detention, which is an interference with the dominion of the true owner, is under such circumstances, excused, if not justified.'

The conclusion seems to be that there is conversion where the defendant asserts a title adverse to that of the true owner, either in himself or a third party,[4] or where he detains the goods from the rightful owner for an unreasonable time, thereby impliedly doing so. If the depositor himself applies, any delay is unreasonable, and refusal is a negation of his title.

Where a professing agent or messenger demands delivery there is, *ex necessitate rei*, a reasonable doubt as to his authority. The pseudo-messenger in *Langtry v Union Bank of London*[5] produced a most plausible document, written on Mrs Langtry's notepaper and with her signature forged. Mathew J in *London and River Plate Bank v Bank of Liverpool*,[6] finally disposed of the untenable contention that a banker is bound to know his customer's signature. It is said one is not bound to anticipate forgery; that ingenuous doctrine was rudely shaken in *London Joint Stock Bank Ltd v Macmillan and Arthur*.[7]

20 (1851) 6 Exch 341.
 1 (1875) LR 7 HL 757 at 766; and see Lord Abinger CB and Parke B in *Vaughan v Watt* (1840) 6 M & W 492 at 497, Fletcher Moulton LJ in *Clayton v Le Roy* [1911] 2 KB 1031 and Farnell LJ in *Burroughes v Bayne* (1860) 5 H & N 296 at 308.
 2 (1651) 2 Bulst 306 at 312.
 3 (1840) 6 M & W 492.
 4 Cf. *Warren v Baring Bros* (1910) 54 Sol Jo 720.
 5 (1896) 1 LDAB 229.
 6 [1896] 1 QB 7.
 7 [1918] AC 777.

It would seem that three courses are open to the banker-bailee when called upon to deliver; he must comply with his mandate or be excused by virtue of the *jus tertii* or he may be able to interplead. He cannot deny the bailor's title unless he has been evicted by a title paramount.[8] And he may, if necessary, delay delivery for such time as will enable him to satisfy himself as to the authority of the person seeking delivery.

(c) Joint bailors

Where chattels are deposited jointly by two or more persons, the authority of all is ordinarily requisite before they can be withdrawn.[9] In *Brandon v Scott*,[10] Lord Campbell CJ, dealt with the case where goods had been delivered by the bailee to one of three bailors:

> 'It is said that this is no defence, because the contract of bailment was not to deliver them except to the plaintiffs jointly. But as in fact one of the plaintiffs has got the goods, the question arises whether he can sue the defendants for giving them to himself. It would be contrary to all principle and the cases cited show that it would be contrary to all the decisions, if he could. I do not think that an action at law could be maintained against bankers in this position more than against others; but it is not to be supposed that they could therefore with impunity deliver up to one securities deposited with them to hold for several. I think in such a case they would stand in relation of trustees for all the joint bailees (sic); and there would be a clear remedy in equity for breach of trust in delivering joint property to one only of the cestuis que trust.'

Nowadays banks take specific mandates which may require the signature of all bailors as a prerequisite to withdrawal or give authority for delivery to less than all. But whatever the mandate many authorise, the banker's duty is to comply with it and this may give rise to difficulty as to the bank's responsibility (a) where the subject matter of the deposit is such as to pass upon death by the *jus accrescendi* and (b) where it is held in common.

The practice of banks in this matter is stated in the answer to question no. 44 in the 11th edition of *Questions on Banking Practice*[11] which asks whether a bank, having accepted from two or more persons in their joint names bearer securities, share certificates in joint names, deeds of which the depositors are joint mortgagees, conveyances to the depositors jointly and plate, jewellery or other chattels or a locked box or a sealed parcel, should on the death of one of the joint depositors allow the survivor or survivors to remove or deal with the articles deposited without the concurrence of the executors or administrators of the deceased. The answer given is that in regard to the first four the articles may be so delivered 'because the legal title passes to the survivor or survivors'; but that in regard to the plate etc. and locked boxes 'it is the practice to require the consent of the deceased's personal representatives.'

The banks take a mandate from joint depositors which provides for what is to happen upon the death of any; practice requires the discharge of both

8 *Ross v Edwards & Co* (1895) 73 LT 100 at 101; *Biddle v Bond* (1865) 6 B & S 225 (explained and distinguished in *Blaustein v Maltz Mitchell & Co* [1937] 2 KB 142, [1937] 1 All ER 497).
9 *May v Harvey* (1811) 13 East 197; *Atwood v Ernest* (1853) 13 CB 881; *Brandon v Scott* (1857) 7 E & B 234.
10 (1857) 7 E & B 234.
11 The Institute of Bankers 1978.

the survivor and the personal representatives of the deceased in the case of
chattels and, in the case of a locked box or a sealed envelope, that it be
opened in the presence of an officer of the bank and, if the contents include
chattels which may be held in common, a similar discharge. As to this it is
submitted that as a general rule the bank has no right to demand that the
contents of a box or envelope be disclosed; its sole duty is to comply with
the mandate pursuant to which the article is deposited. The matter is not one
of title but of authority. Where the property is joint, the relevant parties are
the survivors only; where the property is otherwise, compliance with the
mandate means obtaining the discharge of the deceased's personal representatives, unless the mandate binds the personal representatives as well.
A bare mandate is revoked by the death of a mandator and thus it must be
raised to the status of a contract which binds the personal representatives of
the deceased and does not determine on death; in the absence of such a
contract the discharge of the personal representatives must be obtained.

(d) Demand for delivery by transferee

If delivery is called for by a transferee of a chattel he has no direct claim
against the bailee until the bailee has attorned to him.[12] The banker is not
the debtor immediately affected by the assignment of a chose in action, nor
the person to receive notice if the assignment is under the Law of Property
Act 1925. He is a mere depositary. The banker is entitled to satisfy himself
regarding a derivative title.

(e) Removal of goods by banker

The banker must not remove the goods from the premises where they were
received for custody, if it is part of the agreement that they be stored at a
particular place. If he store them elsewhere, he may be liable for their loss or
destruction, apart from any question of negligence,

> 'even though he would have had a defence if goods had been lost by a similar peril
> while in the place where under the contract they should have been.'[13]

He would, however, be justified in removing them if danger threatened, as in
a case of national emergency, but would be wise to obtain the bailor's consent,
if possible.

(f) Banker's lien

Goods deposited for safe custody are not subject to the banker's lien. It was
so held in *Leese v Martin*.[14] To the extent that the decision rests upon (1)
Giblin v McMullen[15] (which has now been disapproved[16]), and (2) the plaintiff's failure to plead and prove a general custom amongst bankers to allow
their customers to deposit boxes in their strongrooms, these grounds must
now be regarded as suspect. However, the decision further rests upon (3) a

12 Cf *Dublin City Distillery Ltd v Doherty* [1914] AC 823 at 847.
13 Per Lord Wright in A/S *Rendal v Arcos Ltd* (1937) 43 Com Cas 1 at 14; *Lilley v Doubleday*
   (1881) 7 QBD 510; *Gibaud v Great Eastern Rly Co* [1921] 2 KB 426.
14 (1873) LR 17 Eq 224.
15 (1868) LR 2 PC 317.
16 See p 268, ante.

concession made, and approved by Lord Campbell, in *Brandao v Barnett*[17] and (4) general principle, and these additional grounds appear sound.

(g) Night safes

Night safes provide a service whereby a customer with money, cheques, et cetera in his possession after the banks are closed may place them in a wallet and deposit them into the fabric of the bank building. Customers availing themselves of this facility are required to enter into an agreement with the bank which provides that the relation of banker and customer in relation to the deposit shall not arise until the wallet is opened, either by the customer or his agent or by the bank on the customer's behalf, and deposited in the ordinary course of business. It is normally expressly stated in the agreement that until this takes place the relationship shall be that of bailor and gratuitous bailee.

(h) Conflicts of law

Two cases, decided by the House of Lords in October 1949, and resulting from the events which took place in Czechoslovakia after the war of 1939 to 1945, raise interesting questions. They are *Kahler v Midland Bank Ltd*[18] and *Zivnostenska Banka National Corpn v Frankman*[19], both of which were concerned with claims of the true owner of securities deposited, in the first case, with the defendant bank but to the order of a Czechoslovak bank, and in the second case with the London office of a Czechoslovak bank. In both cases it was held that Czechoslovak law applied and that the securities were deliverable only with the consent of the National Bank of Czechoslovakia, which consent was not forthcoming. There was no contractual relationship between the parties to the action. In the *Kahler* case, the plaintiff failed because he was not entitled to immediate possession. In the second case, the defendants being the London office of the foreign bank, Lord MacDermott said:

> 'that a customer who does business with one branch of a bank cannot, in the absence of some special provision, call as of right upon another branch to complete or clear that business.'

17 (1846) 12 Cl & Fin 787 at 808, HL.
18 [1950] AC 24, [1949] 2 All ER 621 (a decision by three members of the House to two); see also *Ratner v London Joint City and Midland Bank* (1922) 38 TLR 253.
19 [1950] AC 57, [1949] 2 All ER 671.

CHAPTER 17

INSOLVENCY OF CUSTOMER[1]

THE INSOLVENCY ACT 1986

The Insolvency Act 1986 introduced sweeping changes in insolvency law. Not only has the law relating to bankruptcy of individuals, receivership and winding up of companies changed, but the Insolvency Act has introduced new insolvency regimes such as administration orders in relation to companies, and voluntary arrangements between companies or individuals and their creditors. In this chapter particular consideration is given to aspects of insolvency law which are of concern to banks.[2]

1 ADMINISTRATION ORDERS

(a) Nature of an administration order

An administration order is an order directing that during the period for which the order is in force, the affairs, business and property of a company shall be managed by a licensed insolvency practitioner appointed by the court.[3] The order may be made if two conditions are satisfied, first that the company is or is likely to become unable to pay its debts,[4] and secondly that the court considers that an administration order would be likely to achieve at least one of four purposes set out in the Insolvency Act 1986.[5] There were divergent views between judges as to the second part of this test. In *Re Consumer and Industrial Press Ltd*[6] Peter Gibson J held that the phrase 'Likely to achieve' meant that the evidence before the court must be such as to enable the court

---

1 The Editor gratefully acknowledges that this Chapter was contributed by Mr Mark Phillips, Barrister.
2 For a full treatment of the new insolvency provisions see Peter Totty and Michael Jordan *Insolvency*; 7(2) Halsbury's Laws of England (4th edn); *Gore-Browne on Companies* (44th edn); Lightman and Moss *The Law of Receivers and Managers*; Muir Hunter on *Personal Insolvency*.
3 Section 8(2) of the Insolvency Act 1986.
4 Within the meaning given to that expression in s 123 of the Insolvency Act 1986. For the interpretation of that section see *Re a Company* [1986] BCLC 261; *Stonegate Securities Ltd v Gregory* [1980] Ch 576, [1980] 1 All ER 241, CA.
5 Section 8(1) of the Insolvency Act 1986.
6 [1988] BCLC 177.

276

to hold that the purpose or, if more than one, each of the purposes in question, is more probably than not achievable. This test was adopted by Harman J in *Re: Manlon Trading Ltd.*[7] In *Re Harris Simons Construction Ltd*[8] Hoffmann J held that the requirements of s 8(1)(b) were satisfied if the court considered that there was a real prospect that one or more of the purposes mentioned in s 8(3) might be achieved. It is now accepted by the court that the better view is that advanced by Hoffmann J.[9] The court's jurisdiction to specify a purpose in the order depends upon the test advanced by Hoffmann J being satisfied by each of the purposes so included. Even if satisfied that one or more of the specified purposes is likely to be achieved, the court has a discretion whether or not to make the order, and in exercising that discretion the position of secured creditors will be considered, although they will usually carry less weight than the interests of the unsecured creditors.[10]

An administration order must specify the purpose or purposes for which it is made. Frequently more than one purpose is specified, because there may be several alternatives depending for example upon the outcome of negotiations with prospective investors or purchasers of some or all of the company's assets. There are four possibilities:[11]

(a) 'The survival of the company, and the whole or any part of its undertaking as a going concern.' To achieve this purpose the company as a legal entity must survive together with at least part of its undertaking. It is not sufficient for part of the undertaking of the company to survive apart from the legal entity, so that a straightforward hive down would not fall within this purpose.
(b) 'The approval of a voluntary arrangement under Part I of the Insolvency Act 1986.'
(c) 'The sanctioning under s 425 of the Companies Act 1985 of a compromise or arrangement between the company and any such persons as are mentioned in that section.'
(d) 'A more advantageous realisation of the company's assets than would be effected on a winding up.' This is open to several interpretations. The first question is to whom must the realisation be advantageous. The second question is whether the advantage must in every case be financial. In the majority of cases this will be read as meaning a realisation for more money than would be effected on a winding up.[12] The specification of this purpose in an administration order should be of particular concern to banks who have security over some but not all of the company's assets, because, a 'more advantageous' realisation of the company's assets over which the bank does not have security may be effected in an administration in circumstances where those assets can be realised together with

7 (1988) 4 BCC 455.
8 [1989] 1 WLR 368.
9 See: *Re Primalaks UK Ltd* (1989) 5 BCC 710 (Vinelott J), and *Re SCL Builders Ltd* (1989) 5 BCC 74b in which Peter Gibson J followed Hoffmann J.
10 *Re Consumer and Industrial Press Ltd* [1988] BCLC 177; followed in *Re Imperial Motors (UK) Ltd* (1989) 5 BCC 214.
11 Section 8(3) of the Insolvency Act 1986.
12 In *Re Imperial Motors (UK) Ltd* (1989) 5 BCC 214 Hoffmann J held that there could be a more advantageous realisation where payment would be quicker in an administration even though the creditors would be paid in full under both an administration and a winding-up.

assets over which the bank has security. This arises by virtue of the administrator's powers to override that security.[13]

(b) The position of a debenture holder prior to the hearing

In its report on *Insolvency Law and Practice* the Review Committee[14] was satisfied that in a significant number of cases, companies had been forced into liquidation, and potentially viable businesses capable of being rescued had been closed down for want of a floating charge under which a receiver and manager could have been appointed. Administration orders were intended to fill that lacuna.[15] It follows from that underlying rationale that wherever an administrative receiver has been or might be appointed, the appointment of an administrator is unnecessary. The Insolvency Act 1986 provides that notice of an administration petition must be given to any person who has appointed or is or may be entitled to appoint an administrative receiver of the company,[16] and, where the court is satisfied that there is an administrative receiver of the company, the court must dismiss the petition save in particular circumstances.[17] Unless the debenture holder consents to short service, he has not less than five days between service of the petition upon him and the hearing of the petition to decide whether or not to appoint an administrative receiver.[18] Thus, provided that he has the power to appoint an administrative receiver, a debenture holder has an effective right to veto the making of an administration order. The circumstances in which the court may not dismiss the petition despite the fact that an administrative receiver has been appointed are that the person who has appointed the administrative receiver has consented to the making of the administration order, or that the security pursuant to which the administrative receiver was appointed was a transaction at an undervalue,[19] a preference,[20] or a floating charge liable to be avoided pursuant to s 245 of the Insolvency Act 1986. In practice it has proved difficult to have sufficient evidence that the charge fell within any of these avoidance provisions at the hearing of the petition, and this has meant that in practice the appointment of an administrative receiver by a debenture holder has resulted in the dismissal of the administration petition.

The power of a debenture holder who may appoint an administrative receiver to veto the making of an administration order has resulted in banks taking floating charges in circumstances where they were not taken in the past. During 1987 a new type of floating charge evolved, intended to deal

13 Pursuant to s 15 of the Insolvency Act 1986: see post.

14 *Insolvency Law and Practice* (Report of the Review Committee 1981, Cmnd 8558).

15 See the Report at paras 496 and 497.

16 Section 9(2)(a) of the Insolvency Act 1986. Section 437 and Sch 11, para 1(1) of the Insolvency Act 1986 provides that where any right to appoint an administrative receiver is contained in a debenture or floating charge granted before 29 December 1986 the conditions precedent to the exercise of that right are deemed to include the presentation of a petition applying for an administration order. For the definition of an administrative receiver see post.

17 Section 9(3) of the Insolvency Act 1986.

18 Rule 2.7 of the Insolvency Act 1986 provides that service of the petition shall be effected not less than five days before the date fixed for the hearing. The court has held that the person with power to appoint an administrative receiver should have an adequate opportunity to consider whether he wishes to exercise that power. The court has power to abridge the five-day period by virtue of r 12.9. In exceptional circumstances the court may abridge the five-day period despite opposition from the debenture holder. For both propositions see: *Re a Company (No 00175 of 1987)* [1987] BCLC 467.

19 Pursuant to s 238 of the Insolvency Act 1986.

20 Pursuant to s 239 of the Insolvency Act 1986.

specifically with administration petitions, but not intended to apply in other situations. It has been called the 'Fully Subordinated Floating Charge', and it is usually expressed to crystallise solely in the event of a petition being presented for the making of an administration order. In taking such a charge the bank must ensure that it has the power to appoint an administrative receiver and not merely a receiver or manager.[1] Before banks had any experience of administration orders, some commentators suggested that in general banks would oppose administration orders. In practice, that has not proved to be the case, and in many cases banks have been keen to support administration petitions. It is simplistic to suggest either that banks should in general oppose administration petitions, or that they should support them. Whether an administration order is in the interests of a bank will depend upon the circumstances of the case.

(c) The effect of an administration petition

After an administration petition has been presented the company cannot be put into liquidation, and it is protected from its creditors. In particular, no steps may be taken to enforce any security over the company's property, and no other proceedings or execution or other legal process may be commenced or continued without the court's leave and on such terms as the court thinks fit.[2] However, this does not prevent a debenture holder appointing an administrative receiver or, the carrying out by such receiver of any of his functions.[3] If an administrative receiver was appointed before the administration petition is presented, the company is not protected from its creditors by virtue of the presentation of that petition unless the debenture holder consents to the making of an administration order. If the debenture holder does consent to the making of an administration order, the company is protected from its creditors from the moment when the debenture holder gives that consent.[4]

A bank which is a creditor of the company, but is not entitled to appoint an administrative receiver, will be able to persuade the court that it should appear on the hearing of the petition,[5] but it will not be served with the petition, and, if the petition is heard shortly after presentation,[6] the bank is unlikely to know of or be represented at the hearing. The effect of an administration order is such, that banks should try to discover administration petitions which have been presented and the dates and venues of the hearing of any petitions concerning the bank's customers.

(d) The effect of an administration order

On the making of an administration order any winding up petition is dismissed and any administrative receiver of the company must vacate office.[7]

1 See post.
2 Section 10(1) of the Insolvency Act 1986. In *Re a Company (No 001992 of 1988)* [1989] BCLC 9 Harman J held that it was appropriate to allow a creditor to present a winding-up petition, but generally to restrain advertisement of the petition until after the hearing of the administration petition. This was followed in *Re: a Company* (No 001448 of 1989) (1989) 5 BCC 706.
3 Section 10(2) of the Insolvency Act 1986.
4 Section 10(3) of the Insolvency Act 1986.
5 Rule 2.9 (g) of the Insolvency Act 1986.
6 See p 278, ante.
7 Section 11(1) of the Insolvency Act 1986.

A receiver of part of the company's property must vacate office on being required to do so by the administrator.[8] In either case the remuneration and expenses and any indemnity to which the administrative receiver or receiver is entitled are charged on the property of the company which was in his custody or under his control at the time when he vacated office in priority to any security held by the person by or on whose behalf he was appointed.[9] While an administration order is in force the company cannot be wound up, no administrative receiver can be appointed, and no other steps can be taken to enforce any security over the company's property, and no proceedings, execution or other legal process may be commenced or continued except with the consent of the administrator or the leave of the court and subject to such terms as the court may impose.[10]

Once appointed the administrator of a company has extensive powers. From the moment he is appointed he may do all such things as may be necessary for the management of the affairs, business and property of the company, and he has all of the powers set out in Sch 1 of the Insolvency Act 1986.[11] Section 15 of the Insolvency Act 1986 gives the administrator power to dispose of property subject to security. If the property is subject to a security which as created was a floating charge the administrator may dispose of or otherwise exercise his powers in relation to that property as if it was not subject to the charge, and the debenture holder has the same priority in respect of any property of the company directly or indirectly representing the property disposed of as he would have had in respect of the property subject to the security.[12] If the property is subject to any other security the administrator may apply to the court, and if the court is satisfied that the disposal of the property subject to the security either with or without other assets would be likely to promote the purpose or one or more of the purposes specified in the administration order, the court may authorise the administrator to dispose of the property as if it were not subject to the security.[13] Any application under s 15 must be served on the secured creditor.[14] The order of the court authorising the administrator to dispose of the property must specify that certain sums, namely, the net proceeds of the disposal, must

8   Section 11(2) of the Insolvency Act 1986.
9   Section 11(4) of the Insolvency Act 1986.
10 Section 11(3) of the Insolvency Act 1986. In *Royal Trust Bank v Buchler* [1989] BCLC 130 Peter Gibson J dismissed an application by a bank for leave to enforce its charge against a freehold property owned by the company. The discretion to allow a secured creditor to enforce its security will be exercised in the light of all the circumstances, and in that case the administrator hoped to realise an enhanced price for the property for the benefit of the unsecured creditors, and there was evidence that the bank would be paid in full when the property was realised. In *Re: Barrow Borough Transport Ltd* (1989) 5 BCC 646 Millet J held that an application under s 404 of the Companies Act 1985 for an extension of time in which to register a floating change was not 'proceedings against the Company or its property' within s 11(3) of the Insolvency Act 1986.
11 Section 14(1) of the Insolvency Act 1986. Schedule 1 contains the powers of an administrator and of an administrative receiver. The manner in which the administrator may exercise his powers is to a certain extent limited by his duties contained in s 17 of the Insolvency Act 1986.
12 Section 15(1) (3) and (4) of the Insolvency Act 1986.
13 Section 15(2) and (3) of the Insolvency Act 1986. Section 15 also applies to goods in the possession of the company under hire-purchase, conditional sale, chattel leasing and retention of title agreements.
14 Rule 2.51 of the Insolvency Rules 1986.

be applied towards discharging the sums secured, and where those proceeds are less than such amount as may be determined by the court to be the net amount which would be realised on a sale of the property or goods in the open market by a willing vendor, such sums as may be required to make good the deficiency.[15] If there is more than one security on the property, the sum to be applied towards discharging the sums secured are applied in order of the priorities of the charges.[16]

In practice s 15 of the Insolvency Act 1986 does not enable an administrator to use the company's book debts if they are subject to a valid fixed charge in favour of the bank.[17] The fact that the proceeds of any disposal must be applied in discharge of the security is inappropriate where the secured asset is a debt. In practice, banks with fixed charges over book debts have found that they are in a strong position to influence the course adopted by an administrator who is keen either to use the book debts or to borrow money.

A bank considering whether to oppose an administration petition should have in mind that any debts and liabilities incurred by an administrator under contracts entered into by him or contracts of employment adopted by him, his remuneration and expenses properly incurred are a charge on the property of the company which is in his custody or under his control at the time when he vacates office. That charge ranks in priority to any charge which as created was a floating charge.[18] On the other hand where a receiver or manager vacates office the assets in his custody or under his control are subject to a similar charge which takes priority over any charge or other security held by the person on whose behalf he was appointed.[19]

(e) The bank's rights as a creditor in the administration

The administrator is subject to general duties[20] as well as specific duties such as sending notices,[1] laying his proposals before the creditors,[2] calling meetings of creditors[3] and providing information to a committee of creditors if one is established.[4] The administrator's general duties are to take into his custody or under his control all the property to which the company is or appears to be entitled,[5] and to manage the affairs, business and property of the company at any time before proposals have been approved in accordance with any directions given by the court, and at any time after proposals have been approved in accordance with the proposals.[6] These general duties do not affect the administrator if there are no approved proposals and no directions

15 Section 15(5) of the Insolvency Act 1986.
16 Section 15(6) of the Insolvency Act 1986.
17 As to which see ch 32, post.
18 Sections 19(2) (4) and 5 of the Insolvency Act 1986. Where an administration order is discharged upon the making of a winding-up order the company's property remains charged in the hands of the official receiver or liquidator: *Re Sheridan Securities Ltd* (1988) 4 BCC 200.
19 Section 37(4) and 45(3) of the Insolvency Act 1986.
20 Section 17 of the Insolvency Act 1986.
1 Section 21 of the Insolvency Act 1986.
2 Section 23 of the Insolvency Act 1986. Substantial revisions of those proposals are laid before the creditors pursuant to s 25 of the Insolvency Act 1986.
3 Sections 17(3), 23, 24, 25 of the Insolvency Act 1986.
4 Section 26 of the Insolvency Act 1986.
5 Section 17(1) of the Insolvency Act 1986.
6 Section 17(2) of the Insolvency Act 1986.

of the court. If proposals have been approved, but can no longer be achieved, and there is no time available to put revised proposals to the meeting of creditors, the court may give directions to the administrator.[7] In many administrations the creditors will have little control over the administrator's conduct. In particular, in many administrations the business of the company has had to be sold before it was possible to call a meeting of creditors to consider the administrator's proposals under s 23 of the Insolvency Act 1986.

If a bank which is a creditor of a company in administration wishes to challenge the acts of the administrator, there is little which it can do. Creditors do not have power to apply to the court for directions. If the bank, either alone or together with other creditors who wish to adopt the same course, represents more than 10% of the company's creditors it can require the administrator to call a meeting of creditors at which resolutions may be considered.[8] However, apart from any proposals approved under s 23 of the Insolvency Act 1986, the administrator is not bound to follow the wishes of the creditors, and this route is therefore not entirely satisfactory. The only remedy available to a creditor is to issue a petition pursuant to s 27 of the Insolvency Act 1986. While an administration order is in force a creditor can apply to the court on the ground that the company's affairs, business and property are being or have been managed in a manner which is 'unfairly prejudicial' to the interests of its creditors generally, or of some part of its creditors including at least himself, or that any proposed act or omission would be unfairly prejudicial.[9] This provision is similar to s 459 of the Companies Act 1985 which provides protection for the members of companies against unfair prejudice against them. However, the incorporation of 'unfair prejudice' into Part II of the Insolvency Act 1986 is unsatisfactory. Not only must a creditor prove that he is being prejudiced, but he must also establish that the prejudice was unfair to him. It follows that the creditor would have to show that the administrator was acting unfairly against him in favour of other creditors, or perhaps the members of some third parties. Unlike companies which have frequently been found to have conducted their affairs in a manner which is unfair to a minority shareholder,[10] it is unlikely that an administrator would be 'unfair' in that sense to the creditors as a whole, or to some part of them.

2   ADMINISTRATIVE RECEIVERS AND RECEIVERS

(a)   The meaning of 'administrative receiver' and 'receiver'

It is important to distinguish between administrative receivers and receivers because, not only may the ability to appoint an administrative receiver give the bank the power to veto the making of an administration order,[11] but

---

7 *Re Smallman Construction Ltd* [1989] BCLC 420.
8 Section 17(3)(a) of the Insolvency Act 1986.
9 Section 27(1) of the Insolvency Act 1986.
10 See for example *Re London School of Electronics Ltd* [1985] BCLC 273; *Re a Company (No 008699 of 1985) (1986)* 2 BCC 24; *Re a Company (No 005287 of 1985)* [1986] 2 All ER 253, [1986] 1 WLR 281; *Re Bird Precision Bellows Ltd* [1986] Ch 658, [1985] 3 All ER 523; *Re Cumana Ltd* [1986] BCLC 430; *Re Kenyon Swansea Ltd* [1987] BCLC 514. See also the decision of Harman J in *Re a Company (No 00370 of 1987)* [1988] BCLC 570.
11 See above.

whilst there are many provisions which apply both to administrative receivers and receivers,[12] there are provisions which apply only to administrative receivers[13] or to receivers.[14] An administrative receiver is a receiver or manager of the whole, or substantially the whole of a company's property appointed by or on behalf of the holders of any debenture of the company which, as created, was a floating charge, or by such a charge and one or more other securities, or, a person who would be such a receiver or manager but for the appointment of some other person as the receiver of part of the company's property.[15] A receiver or manager includes a receiver or manager of part only of the company's property.[16] A receiver includes a receiver of part only of the company's property or only of the income arising from that property or any part of it.[17]

(b) Appointment

A bank considering the appointment of a receiver or manager must first choose whom it wishes to appoint. A receiver cannot be a body corporate.[18] An undischarged bankrupt cannot be a receiver or manager.[19] Only a licensed insolvency practitioner can act as an administrative receiver.[20]

The appointment of a receiver or manager is normally permissable upon the happening of any of a number of events specified in the charge. One of those events is usually failure to meet a demand for repayment. Where the bank is entitled by the terms of the security to demand repayment of all monies secured, there is no need to specify the amount of the debt in the demand.[1] The demand must precede the appointment.[2] Unless there is clear evidence that the company did not have funds available to satisfy the demand the company is allowed sufficient time to implement the mechanics of payment before being in default, but that does not include time to raise the money if it is not there to be paid. In *Bank of Baroda v Panessar* Walton J said:

12 See for example s 33 to 36 of the Insolvency Act 1986, in relation to the appointment of a receiver and manager; liability for an invalid appointment; applications to the court for directions; and the courts power to fix remuneration; s 405 of the Companies Act 1985, in relation to the notification of the appointment; s 39 to 41 of the Insolvency Act 1986 in relation to notification on stationary that a receiver or manager has been appointed; payment of debts out of assets subject to a floating charge; and the enforcement of the duty to make returns.

13 See s 42 to 49 of the Insolvency Act 1986, in relation to the general powers of an administrative receiver, the power to dispose of charged property, agency and liability for contracts, vacation of office, information to be given to an administrative receiver, the statement of affairs, report to creditors and the creditors committee.

14 See s 37 and 38 of the Insolvency Act 1986 in relation to the liability for contracts and the receivership accounts to be delivered to the registrar of companies.

15 Section 29(2)(b) of the Insolvency Act 1986. For an analysis of the new status of administrative receivers see Adkins 'Company Receivers – A New Status' [1988] 5 JIBL 202.

16 Section 29(1)(a) of the Insolvency Act 1986.

17 Section 29(1)(a) of the Insolvency Act 1986.

18 Section 30 of the Insolvency Act 1986.

19 Section 31 of the Insolvency Act 1986.

20 Sections 388 and 389 of the Insolvency Act 1986.

1 *Bank of Baroda v Panessar* [1987] Ch 335 [1986] 3 All ER 751; *Cripps & Son Ltd v Wickenden* [1973] 2 All ER 606, [1973] 1 WLR 944; *Bunbury Foods Pty Ltd v National Bank of Australasia Ltd* (1984) 51 ALR 609.

2 *Windsor Refrigerator Co Ltd v Branch Nominees Ltd* [1961] Ch 375, [1961] 1 All ER 277, CA.

'English law, therefore, in my judgment has definitely adopted the mechanics of payment test. In order to see why this should be so, one has only to consider the case of a debtor who, perhaps for very legitimate reasons, keeps the money available to pay off his creditor – both he and the creditor being situate in London – in a bank in Scotland. It cannot possibly be the law that the debtor would have the right to the space of time necessary to journey to Scotland and back again before he was in default in complying with a demand for payment. There is no reason why he should not keep the money in Scotland but, if he does, he must then arrange for such mechanics of payment as are, under modern conditions available for the transfer of the money to his creditor, and, as is well known in these days of telex, facsimile transmission and other methods of communication and transfer of money, the time required for that is exceptionally short.'

In the circumstances of that case, Walton J held that the receiver was validly appointed one hour after the demand was served on the debtor.[3] If the bank failed to give the company sufficient time to effect the mechanics of payment, the appointment of a receiver or manager would be valid if the bank could show that the company did not have the funds available to satisfy the demand.[4]

In the absence of bad faith, a bank does not owe a duty of care to the company or any guarantors of the company's indebtedness to the bank in deciding whether to exercise its right to appoint a receiver or manager. It is extremely unlikely that there can be implied into a debenture a term that the bank shall be under a duty to consider all relevant matters before exercising that power, and in the absence of such a term, it has been held that no wider duty exists in tort.[5]

A receiver or manager must be appointed in accordance with the terms of the debenture[6] which usually requires the appointment to be made by writing. There is no requirement that the appointment should be under seal.[7] The appointment of a person as a receiver or manager is of no effect unless it is accepted by the proposed receiver before the end of the business day following that on which the instrument of appointment is received by him or on his behalf.[8] If it is accepted then the appointment is deemed to be made at the time at which the instrument of appointment is received by the receiver or manager or on his behalf.[9] The receiver or manager must confirm his acceptance of the appointment in writing to the bank within seven days.[10]

If the appointment is invalid the receiver or manager has to be withdrawn by the bank and reappointed.[11] A second appointment cannot be made until the bank has restored the company to possession of its assets and renewed its demand.[12] The risk of liability resulting from an invalid appointment may

3 [1987] Ch 335 at 348 F to H. See further, Ch 14, ante.
4 *R A Cripps & Son Ltd v Wickenden* (above) which was followed in *Bank of Baroda v Panessar* (above).
5 *Shamji v Johnson Matthey Bankers Ltd* [1986] BCLC 278, [1986] 1 FTLR 329, CA.
6 In *Cryne v Barclays Bank Plc* [1987] BCLC 548 Kerr and May LJJ held that in the absence of an express term which entitled the bank to appoint a receiver where they, on reasonable grounds, considered that their security was in jeopardy, such a term could not be implied into the debenture.
7 *Windsor Refrigeration Co Ltd v Branch Nominees* (ante).
8 Section 33(1)(a) of the Insolvency Act 1986.
9 Section 33(1)(b) of the Insolvency Act 1986.
10 Rule 3.1 of the Insolvency Rules 1986.
11 *R A Cripps & Son Ltd v Wickenden* (ante).
12 *R A Cripps & Wickenden* [1973] 1 WLR 944 at 957 A to B.

be overcome if the directors request that the bank should appoint a receiver or manager. The company will be estopped from relying upon an invalid appointment if it did not object to the defect at the time, or if by its conduct after the appointment it allowed or encouraged the receiver or the bank to assume that the appointment was valid.[13] If the appointment is invalid because of a defect in the debenture, or if an invalid appointment cannot be cured, the receiver is a trespasser in respect of all of the company's assets of which he takes possession.[14] However, the acts of the administrative receiver are valid notwithstanding any defect in his appointment, nomination or qualifications, but that does not apply to an appointment under an invalid debenture.[15] The receiver may take a contractual indemnity from the bank, but if he does not, the court may order the bank to indemnify the receiver against any liability which arises solely by reason of the invalidity of the appointment.[16]

If a bank appoints a receiver or manager, it must give notice of the fact to the registrar of companies within seven days, and the registrar enters that fact on the register of charges.[17] Registration of the appointment probably does not constitute notice of it. However, after his appointment a receiver or manager must put a statement that a receiver or manager has been appointed on every invoice, order for goods or business letter.[18] Where an administrative receiver is appointed he must advertise notice of his appointment, and within 28 days after his appointment he must send notice of his appointment to all the creditors of the company of whom he is aware.[19]

(c) Powers and duties of a receiver

Where a bank has a debenture, its appointment of a receiver usually provides that he shall be the agent of the company. An administrative receiver is deemed to be the agent of the company unless and until the company goes into liquidation.[20] If the receiver ceases to be the agent of the company he does not thereby become the agent of the bank,[1] although a bank may at any time be liable for the acts of the receiver if it interfered with his conduct of the receivership.[2] The relationship between the company and the receiver is not the relationship of an ordinary principal and agent because the receiver also owes duties to the debenture holder. This relationship has recently been considered by the courts. In *Gomba Holdings UK Ltd v Minories Finance Ltd*[3] Fox LJ said:[4]

'The agency of a receiver is not an ordinary agency. It is primarily a device to protect the mortgagee or debenture holder. Thus, the receiver acts as agent for the mortgagor in that he has power to affect the mortgagor's position by acts which,

13 *Bank of Baroda v Panessar* [1987] Ch 335 at 352.
14 *Re Goldburg (No 2)* [1912] 1KB 606.
15 Section 232 of the Insolvency Act 1986.
16 Section 34 of the Insolvency Act 1986.
17 Section 405 of the Companies Act 1985.
18 Section 19(1) of the Insolvency Act 1986.
19 Section 46(1) of the Insolvency Act 1986 and r 3.2 of the Insolvency Act 1986.
20 Section 44(1) of the Insolvency Act 1986.
 1 *Gosling v Gaskell* [1897] AC 575.
 2 *Standard Chartered Bank Ltd v Walker* [1982] 3 All ER 938, [1982] 1 WLR 1410.
 3 [1989] 1 All ER 261, [1988] 1 WLR 1231.
 4 At 1233 E to H.

though done for the benefit of the debenture holder, are treated as if they were the acts of the mortgagor. The relationship set up by the debenture and the appointment of the receiver, however, is not simply between the mortgagor and the receiver. It is tripartite and involves the mortgagor, the receiver and the debenture holder.

. . .

All this is far removed from the ordinary principal and agent situation so far as the mortgagor and the receiver are concerned. Whilst the receiver is the agent of the mortgagor he is the appointee of the debenture holder and, in practical terms, has a close association with him. Moreover he owes fiduciary duties to the debenture holder. . . .'

The directors of a company in receivership who are also agents of the company, have no powers over assets of the company which are in the possession or control of the receiver or manager.[5]

The appointment of a receiver or manager does not determine contracts entered into by the company before the appointment,[6] but the receiver need not cause the company to fulfil the contract.[7] However, if a contract is specifically enforceable, the receiver cannot resist a claim for specific performance.[8] A receiver or manager is personally liable on any contract entered into by him, and on any contract of employment adopted by him in the performance of his functions to the same extent as if he had been appointed by a court order.[9] In the 14 days after his appointment the receiver is not taken to have adopted a contract of employment by reason of any acts or omissions on his part.[10] If the receiver is personally liable on any contracts, he is entitled to an indemnity out of the assets of the company.[11]

A receiver or manager will have such powers as are contained in the debenture. The powers conferred upon an administrative receiver are deemed to include the powers specified in Sch 1 to the Insolvency Act 1986 unless those powers are inconsistent with the provisions of the debenture.[12] The powers contained in Sch 1 are the same as the powers of an administrator. It

---

5 Per Hoffman J in *Gomba Holdings UK Ltd v Homan* [1986] 1 WLR 1301 at 1307.
6 *Parsons v Sovereign Bank of Canada* [1913] AC 160; *Griffiths v Secretary of State for Social Services* [1974] QB 468, [1973] 3 All ER 1184.
7 *Airlines Airspares Ltd v Handley Page Ltd* [1970] Ch 193; *Re: Newdigate Colliery Co Ltd* [1912] 1 Ch 468, in which the Court of Appeal refused to give a receiver leave to repudiate forward contracts for coal. There is some doubt as to whether a receiver is liable for inducing a breach of contract. In *Lathia v Dronsfield Bros Ltd* [1987] BCLC 321 Sir Neil Lawson struck out a claim against the receivers for inducing a breach of contract between their principal and the plaintiff. The Court of Appeal in *Edwin Hill and Partners v First National Finance Corpn plc* [1988] 3 All ER 801, [1989] 1 WLR 225 suggested that a receiver will not be liable for inducing a breach of contract.
8 *Freevale Ltd v Metrostore (Holdings) Ltd* [1984] Ch 199 [1984] 1 All ER 495. The reasoning adopted in this case was applied in the context of an option granted to a third party in *Telemetrix plc v Modern Engineers of Bristol (Holdings) Ltd* [1985] BCLC 213.
9 Sections 37(1) and 44(1) of the Insolvency Act 1986. Prior to the introduction of these provisions, only a receiver who had ceased to be the agent of the company was personally liable: *Gosling v Gaskill* [1897] AC 575.
10 Section 37(2) and 44(2) of the Insolvency Act 1986. This prevents receivers allowing contracts of employment to continue but then refusing to pay the employees on the ground that the contracts were not 'entered into' by them: see *Nicholl v Cutts* [1985] BCLC 322. There is no judicial guidance as to what amounts to the 'adoption' of a contract. It is arguable that a failure to indicate that a contract is not being adopted by the receiver amounts to adoption. On the other hand it might equally be argued that the word 'adoption' implies that some active step should be taken by the receiver in order to 'adopt' the contract in question.
11 Section 37(1)(b) and 44(1)(c) of the Insolvency Act 1986.
12 Section 42 of the Insolvency Act 1986.

is unlikely that a bank would wish to limit or exclude the operation of the powers set out in Sch 1, which are likely to be wider than the powers provided in the debenture. A person dealing with an administrative receiver in good faith and for value is not concerned to inquire whether the receiver is acting within his powers.[13]

A receiver or manager, or a bank which has appointed him, has power to apply to the court for directions in relation to any particular matter arising in connection with the performance of the function of the receiver or manager.[14] This power has been used in order to ascertain whether a receiver or manager was an administrative receiver. The question of whether the receiver or manager has been properly appointed may also be the subject matter of an application although on a strict construction of the section a proper appointment is arguably a precondition of making an application under this section.[15]

An administrative receiver may apply to the court for an order authorising the disposal by him of property subject to a security which has priority over the security pursuant to which he was appointed.[16] The court may make the order if it is satisfied that the disposal of the property would be likely to promote a more advantageous realisation of the company's assets than would otherwise be effected.[17] This provision is similar to s 15 of the Insolvency Act 1986 which applies in the case of administrators. Its application in the context of an administrative receivership is curious, because, an administrative receiver is not interested in effecting a 'more advantageous realisation' of assets for the benefit of other secured creditors, or the unsecured creditors. The advantage should almost certainly be to the administrative receivership. The question which would then arise is whether the sale could be less advantageous to the secured creditor and still fall within this provision. It is arguable that it could, and in circumstances where a secured creditor, who must be served with the application,[18] objects to the sale, the court is likely to favour the administrative receiver. The reason for that is that in most cases the secured creditor is protected by the proviso to the order, namely that where the net proceeds of sale are less than such amount as may be determined by the court to be the net amount which would be realised on a sale of the property on the open market, the administrative receiver must pay the amount necessary to make up the deficiency in the net proceeds of sale.[19] However, the secured creditor would not be protected if he suffered a loss as a result of the timing of the sale.

A receiver owes a primary duty to the debenture holder who appoints him. In *Re B Johnson & Co (Builders) Ltd*[20] Lord Evershed MR said:[1]

'... it is quite plain that a person appointed as receiver and manager is concerned, not for the benefit of the company but for the benefit of the mortgagee bank to realise the security; that is the whole purpose of his appointment; and the powers

13 Section 42(3) of the Insolvency Act 1986.
14 Section 35 of the Insolvency Act 1986.
15 See Lightman and Moss *The Law of Receivers of Companies* p 43.
16 Section 43 of the Insolvency Act 1986.
17 Section 43(1) of the Insolvency Act 1986.
18 Rule 3.31 of the Insolvency Rules 1986.
19 Section 43(3) of the Insolvency Act 1986.
20 [1955] Ch 634, [1955] 2 All ER 775.
 1 At 644.

which are conferred upon him ... are really ancillary to the main purpose of the appointment, which is the realisation by the mortgagee of the security ... by the sale of the assets.'

Jenkins LJ agreed with Lord Evershed MR in the following terms:

'The primary duty of the receiver is to the debenture holders and not to the company. He is receiver and manager of the property of the company for the debenture holders, not manager of the company.'

Until recently, many commentators took the view that in exercising their powers receivers did not owe a duty of care to the company in tort. In *Cuckmere Brick Co Ltd v Mutual Finance Ltd*[2] the Court of Appeal held that a mortgagee when exercising his powers of sale owed a duty to the mortgagor to take reasonable care to obtain a proper price, and that included a duty to advertise the property, and to cancel an auction in order to advertise a sale. In *Standard Chartered Bank v Walker*[3] the Court of Appeal held that a receiver realising assets under a debenture owed a duty both to the borrower and to a guarantor of the debt to take reasonable care to obtain the best price that the circumstances permitted, and in choosing the time for the sale. If the receiver is negligent, and the acts complained of were carried out under the direction of the bank, the bank will be liable to the company and any guarantors for that negligence[4].

Where a receiver is appointed on behalf of the holder of any debenture secured by a charge which, as created, was a floating charge, and the company is not in liquidation, the preferential debts[5] must be paid out of the assets coming into the hands of the receiver in priority to any claims for principal or interest in respect of the debentures.[6] The preferential creditors only get priority in respect of the floating charge assets, and debenture holders do not lose their priority in respect of fixed charge security,[7] nor does the company lose its right to a surplus arising after the sale of fixed charge securities.[8]

In the course of a receivership, documents will be brought into being, many of which will be created for or by the bank which appointed the receiver. In *Gomba Holdings UK Ltd v Minories Finance Ltd*[9] the company sought orders for delivery up of all the receivers' documents on the ground that the receivers were the agents of the company, and that accordingly the documents created during the course of that agency were the property of the company. Hoffmann J held that only documents created in pursuance of the receivers' duty to manage the affairs of the company were the property of the company. That did not include documents created for the purposes of advising or informing the debenture holder, nor did it include documents created by the receivers to enable them to prepare such documents or perform such duties as they

2 [1971] Ch 949 [1971] 2 All ER 633. See also *Tse Kwong Lam v Wong Chit Sen* [1983] 3 All ER 54, [1983] 1 WLR 1349.
3 [1982] 3 All ER 938, [1982] 1 WLR 1410. Followed in *American Express International Banking Corpn Hurley* [1985] 3 All ER 564 [1986] BCLC 52; cited with approval in *Shamji v Johnson Matthey Bankers Ltd* (ante).
4 Applying *Standard Chartered Bank v Walker* (ante).
5 As defined in s 386 of and Sch 1 to the Insolvency Act 1986.
6 Section 40 of the Insolvency Act 1986. This provision derives from s 196 of the Companies Act 1985.
7 *Re Lewis Merthyr Consolidated Collieries Ltd* [1929] 1 Ch 498.
8 *Re G L Saunders Ltd* [1986] 1 WLR 215 [1986] BCLC 40.
9 [1989] 1 All ER 261, [1988] 1 WLR 1231.

were required to prepare or perform for the purposes of their professional duties to the debenture holders or the company. During the course of the receivership the receiver may refuse to divulge information which the company may be entitled to if he forms the view that disclosure would be against the interests of the debenture holder.[10] From the point of view of banks this is important, because if receivers had a duty to hand back to companies all of the documents created during the course of the receivership, first they would be wary of committing anything to paper, and secondly, companies may attempt to base proceedings against the receiver or the bank upon the documents once they were in the company's possession.

3   COMPANY LIQUIDATION

(a) Voluntary winding-up

There are two types of voluntary winding-up: members' voluntary winding-up and creditors' voluntary winding-up. The distinction between the two types of voluntary winding-up is that in a members' voluntary winding-up the directors of the company sign a declaration that the company will be able to pay its debts in full together with interest within 12 months of the commencement of the winding-up, and in a creditors' voluntary winding-up no such declaration is made.[11] A voluntary winding-up commences when the members of the company pass a resolution that the company be wound up,[12] and that resolution must be advertised in the *Gazette* within 14 days.[13] In a creditors' voluntary winding-up a meeting of the creditors of the company must be summoned within 14 days of the meeting at which the winding-up resolution was passed.[14] At the meeting of creditors the creditors consider the statement of affairs prepared by the directors,[15] vote for the appointments of the liquidator,[16] and, if they so wish, appoint a liquidation committee which may exercise control over certain powers of the liquidator.[17] If in a members' voluntary winding-up the liquidator forms the opinion that the company will not pay all of its debts within the 12 months specified in the declaration of solvency, he must call a meeting of creditors within 28 days.

---

10 *Gomba Holdings (UK) Ltd v Homan* (ante).
11 Section 90 of the Insolvency Act 1986.
12 Sections 84 and 86 of the Insolvency Act 1986.
13 Section 85 of the Insolvency Act 1986.
14 Section 98(1) of the Insolvency Act 1986.
15 Section 99 of the Insolvency Act 1986.
16 Section 100 of the Insolvency Act 1986 states that the liquidator is the person nominated by the creditors. The old law had been open to abuse, in that the members of the company could call a meeting at short notice and appoint a liquidator, but, because no meeting of creditors was held, there was no nomination by the creditors, and the members' choice of liquidator prevailed for the time being: *Re Centrebind Ltd* [1966] 3 All ER 889, [1967] 1 WLR 377. Section 166 of the Insolvency Act 1986 limits the powers of the liquidator nominated by the members pending the meeting of creditors, thereby preventing all of the company's assets being disposed of before the creditors' nominee is appointed liquidator.
17 Section 101 of the Insolvency Act 1986. Up to five persons may act on the committee of creditors. The liquidator's powers in a voluntary winding-up are set out in s 165 of and Sch 4 to the Insolvency Act 1986.

That meeting is treated as if it was a creditors' meeting in a creditors' voluntary winding-up, and the creditors may appoint a liquidator and a committee of creditors.[18]

After the passing of the resolution the company must cease to carry on its business, except so far as may be required for the beneficial winding-up of the company.[19] On the appointment of a liquidator the powers of the directors cease, except where authorised by the company in general meeting or the liquidator in a members' voluntary winding-up,[20] or by the liquidation committee of the creditors in a creditors' voluntary winding-up.[1] Accordingly, cheques drawn by directors or other instructions given by them after the liquidator is appointed are not binding on the company.[2] It has been argued that the directors may bind the company after the resolution has been passed but before the liquidator is appointed. However, this is extremely unlikely, because the standard form of the resolution to wind up a company includes the appointment of the liquidator. A bank discovering that a meeting has been called to consider a resolution to wind up the company should freeze all of the company's bank accounts, provided that it is entitled to do so on the relevant agreements between the bank and the company.

(b) Compulsory winding-up

The court has power to wind up a company incorporated under the Companies Acts in any of the circumstances specified in s 122(1) of the Insolvency Act 1988.[3] An unregistered company or partnership may be wound up in any of the circumstances specified in s 221(5) of the Insolvency Act 1986, and in the case of a partnership, upon certain further grounds set out in the Insolvent Partnerships Order.[4] The most usual ground upon which a winding-up petition is presented is that the company is unable to pay its debts, and that is deemed to be so if the company fails to comply with a statutory demand.[5] A company is also deemed to be unable to pay its debts if it is proved that the

---

18 Sections 95, 98 and 102 of the Insolvency Act 1986. Again, the creditors' choice of liquidator will prevail.
19 Section 87 of the Insolvency Act 1986.
20 Section 91(2) of the Insolvency Act 1986.
1 Section 103 of the Insolvency Act 1986.
2 *Re London and Mediterranean Bank, Bolognesi's Case* (1870) 5 Ch App 567.
3 They are: (a) the company has by special resolution resolved that the company be wound up by the court; (b) being a public company which was registered as such on its original incorporation, the company has not been issued with a certificate under s 117 of the Companies Act (public company share capital requirements) and more than a year has expired since it was so registered; (c) it is an old public company, within the meaning of the Consequential Provisions Act; (d) the company does not commence its business within a year from its incorporation or suspends its business for a whole year; (e) the number of the members is reduced below two; (f) the company is unable to pay its debts; and (g) the court is of the opinion that it is just and equitable that the company should be wound up.
4 See s 221 of the Insolvency Act 1986 in relation to unregistered companies. The circumstances are: (a) if the company is dissolved or has ceased to carry on business; (b) if the company is unable to pay its debts; (c) if the court is of the opinion that it is just and equitable that the company should be wound up. See: Insolvent Partnerships Order 1986, SI 1986/2142, regs 7, 8 and 12 and Sch 1 in relation to partnerships. Schedule 1 also provides that members of the partnership or the partnership may present a petition upon the two further grounds specified therein.
5 Section 123 of the Insolvency Act 1986. A statutory demand cannot be made by telex: *Re a Company* [1985] BCLC 37.

value of the company's assets is less than the amount of its liabilities, taking into account its contingent and prospective liabilities.[6]

A compulsory winding-up is deemed to begin at the time of the presentation of the petition, or if a voluntary resolution had previously been passed, from the time when that resolution was passed.[7] The banker's position will often be affected by the presentation of the petition by virtue of s 127 of the Insolvency Act 1986 which provides:

'In a winding-up by the court, any disposition of the company's property, and any transfer of shares, or alteration in the status of the company's members, made after the commencement of the winding-up is, unless the court otherwise orders, void.'

Unless validated under this section all payments into and payments out of a bank account are void.[8] A bank which allows a company to continue operating an account after the petition has been presented is therefore at risk that the payments into and out of the account will be declared void, and that the bank will be ordered to restore at least part of the monies paid away. Accordingly, upon receiving notice of a winding-up petition, banks should freeze the account, and insist that all future trading is carried out on a new account in respect of which a prospective validation order is obtained. It is not a disposition for assets which are subject to a charge to be realised and paid over to the bank,[9] but it is a disposition for the company to grant a charge over its assets.[10] It is not a disposition for a company to complete a contract which is specifically enforceable, but if the contract is conditional or voidable, any waiver, confirmation or variation of the contract may be a disposition.[11]

The court may validate a disposition either prospectively or retrospectively, but it does not necessarily follow that if the court would have made an order prospectively, it will make a retrospective validation order.[12] If a company makes a disposition of its assets which is not approved before it is made, the recipient will have to repay the money or restore the assets unless the court exercises its discretion to validate the disposition with retrospective effect. Vaisey J in *Re Steane's (Bournemouth) Ltd*[13] described the court's discretion in the following terms:

'The legislature, by omitting to indicate any particular principles which should govern the exercise of the discretion vested in the court, must be deemed to have left it entirely at large, and controlled only by the general principles which apply to every kind of judicial discretion.'

6 Section 123(2) of the Insolvency Act 1986 which introduced the balance sheet test of insolvency.
7 Section 129 of the Insolvency Act 1986.
8 *Re Gray's Inn Construction Ltd* [1980] 1 All ER 814, [1980] 1 WLR 711.
9 *Re Margart Pty Ltd, Hamilton v Westpac Banking Corpn* [1985] BCLC 314, a decision of the Supreme Court of New South Wales, approved by Vinelott J in *Re French's (Wine Bar) Ltd* [1987] BCLC 499.
10 See for example *Re Park Ward & Co Ltd* [1926] Ch 828.
11 *Re French's (Wine Bar) Ltd* [1987] BCLC 499.
12 *Re Gray's Inn Construction Ltd* (ante). In *Re McGuinness Bros (UK) Ltd* [1987] 3 BCC 571 Harman J relied upon the fact that prospective validation would have been refused as a reason to refuse retrospective validation.
13 [1950] 1 All ER 21, approved by the Court of Appeal in *Re Clifton Place Garage Ltd* [1970] Ch 477, [1970] 1 All ER 353; and in *Re Gray's Inn Construction Ltd* (ante).

In *Re Gray's Inn Construction Ltd*[14] Buckley LJ said that the discretion must be exercised in the context of the provisions governing liquidations. He went on to say:[15]

'It is a basic concept of our law governing the liquidation of insolvent estates ... that the free assets of the insolvent at the commencement of the liquidation shall be distributed rateably amongst the insolvent's unsecured creditors as at that date. ... There may be occasions, however, when it would be beneficial not only to the company but also for its unsecured creditors, that the company should be enabled to dispose of some of its property during the period after the petition has been presented but before the winding up order has been made. ... In considering whether to make a validating order the court must always, in my opinion, do its best to ensure that the interests of the unsecured creditors will not be prejudiced.'

Buckley LJ gave, as examples of dispositions which might be validated, the advantageous sale of a piece of property of the company, the completion of a contract, or, in appropriate circumstances, continuing trading generally.[16] In *Re Webb Electrical Ltd*[17] Harman J held that the court will only validate dispositions (in that case payments made out of the company's bank account) if the dispositions were made bona fide with a view to the assistance of the company, but, the authorities do not support such a restricted approach.[18] In *Re Tramway Building and Construction Co Ltd*[19] Scott J held that in exercising its discretion the court should have regard not only to the position of the unsecured creditors but also to the claims of beneficiaries of the disposition. A disposition carried out in good faith in the ordinary course of business at a time when the parties are not aware of the petition will normally be validated by the court.[20] In *Re Gray's Inn Construction Ltd*[1] the bank was treated as having notice of the petition on the day when it was advertised in the *Gazette* even though the bank had not seen the advertisement on that day, and the court validated credits paid into the company's bank account up to that date but not after. Banks should ensure that they are aware of the advertisement of a petition against their customer.

(c) Vulnerable transactions

The Insolvency Act 1986 prescribes three principle types of transaction which are vulnerable in a liquidation: transactions at an undervalue; preferences; and extortionate credit transactions. The provisions relating to those trans-

---

14 [1980] 1 All ER 814, [1980] 1 WLR 711.
15 At 717. Regarding the general purpose of the jurisdiction see also Oliver J in *Re J Leslie Engineers Co Ltd* [1976] 2 All ER 85, [1976] 1 WLR 292; *Re A I Levy (Holdings) Ltd* [1964] Ch 19 [1963] 2 All ER 556; *Re Sugar Properties (Derisley Wood) Ltd* [1988] BCLC 146.
16 See also *Re Repertoire Opera Co Ltd* (1895) 2 Mans 314, and *Re T W Construction Ltd* [1954] 1 All ER 744, [1954] 1 WLR 540 in which Wynn-Parry J validated repayment to the bank of monies lent by the bank after presentation of the petition to enable the company to pay wages and carry on its business.
17 [1988] BCLC 382.
18 See also *Re Clifton Place Garage Ltd* [1970] Ch 477, [1969] 3 All ER 892.
19 [1988] Ch 293, [1988] 2 WLR 640.
20 Arguably the court is applying the defence that the recipient was a bona fide purchaser for value without notice. Also see: *Re Wiltshire Iron Co* (1868) 3 Ch App 443; *Re Neath Harbour Smelting and Rolling Works* (1887) 56 LT 727; *Re Liverpool Civil Service Association* (1874) 9 Ch App 511.
1 [1980] 1 All ER 814, [1980] 1 WLR 711.

actions apply equally to administrations, and there are similar provisions in relation to personal insolvency.[2]

(i) Transactions at an undervalue

A company enters into a transaction at an undervalue if it makes a gift to another person or otherwise enters into a transaction on terms that it will receive no consideration, or alternatively, if the company enters into a transaction for a consideration the value of which, in money or money's worth, is significantly less than the value, in money or money's worth of the consideration provided by the company.[3] A transaction will only be caught if it is entered into at a relevant time. In the case of companies, the transaction must have been entered into two years preceding the administration petition or liquidation, or during the period between the presentation of an administration petition and the making of an administration order.[4] In addition, at the date when the translation is entered into the company must be unable to pay its debts[5] or, must become unable to pay its debts as a consequence of the transaction.[6] If the transaction was entered into with a connected person then it is presumed that the company was insolvent at the time.[7] A shadow director is a connected person,[8] which means that banks may find that they are caught by this presumption.[9] Section 238(5) prescribes that the court shall not make an order in the following circumstances:[10]

'(a) that the company which entered into the transaction did so in good faith and for the purpose of carrying on its business, and
(b) that at the time it did so there were reasonable grounds for believing that the transaction would benefit the company.'

The two types of transaction which will most frequently concern banks in this context are guarantees and charges. Banks which have taken guarantees from guarantors who become insolvent within the relevant time may find that the guarantees are set aside as transactions at an undervalue. The guarantor grants the bank a guarantee in consideration of the bank granting facilities to the debtor. Arguably the guarantor receives no consideration, or a consideration the value of which in money or money's worth is significantly less than the value in money or money's worth of the consideration provided by the guarantor. Even if it was successfully argued that consideration is received by the guarantor by the bank making advances to the principal

---

2 Sections 339 to 343 of the Insolvency Act 1986.
3 Section 238(4) of the Insolvency Act 1986. An individual may enter into a transaction at an undervalue if it is entered into in consideration of marriage: s 339(3)(b).
4 Section 240(1)(a) and (3) of the Insolvency Act 1986. In the case of individuals it is two years unless the bankrupt was insolvent at the date of the transaction, or was insolvent as a consequence of the transaction, in which case it is five years. If the transaction is entered into with an associate, the bankrupt is presumed to have been insolvent when the transaction was entered into: s 341 of the Insolvency Act 1986. The orders which might be made are set out in s 241 in relation to companies and 342 in relation to individuals (see post).
5 Within the meaning given in s 123 of the Insolvency Act 1986.
6 Section 240(2) of the Insolvency Act 1986, and in relation to individuals s 341(2).
7 Section 240(2) of the Insolvency Act 1986, and in relation to individuals, s 342(2).
8 Section 249 of the Insolvency Act 1986. Connected persons include associates of the company. The definition of who is an associate of the company is very wide, and appears in s 435 of the Insolvency Act 1986.
9 As to whether a bank is a shadow director see post.
10 There is no equivalent in the case of individuals.

debtor, the bank would face an additional hurdle if the guarantee was granted as security for past consideration. In the absence of any fresh advances, no consideration is given by the bank. If the past consideration is significantly greater than any fresh consideration passing from the bank, the transaction will, prima facie be caught as an undervalue. In most cases banks will rely upon the proviso contained in s 238(5) of the Insolvency Act 1986. Where cross guarantees have been given by several companies in the same group, it is likely that the bank will be able to establish that the guarantee was entered into in good faith and for the purposes of carrying on the company's business, and that there were reasonable grounds for believing that the transaction would benefit the company. Such an argument ought to succeed, because the requirement in s 238(5) that the transaction should benefit the company is wider than the requirement in s 238(4) that the company should receive consideration.

Banks which have taken charges from customers by way of security within the relevant time may find that the charges are challenged as transactions at an undervalue. If a charge is granted as security for past consideration (in which event it may also be a preference, or voidable floating charge[11]) then it is arguable that the company receives no consideration for the charge. It is likely that the consideration received by the company is the continuation of banking facilities. If the charge is granted by way of security for future and past debts, then, if the past debts are significantly greater than the future advances made by the bank, the transaction is prima facie a transaction at an undervalue. Again, it is likely that banks will rely upon s 238(5), and the fact that the company received the benefit of the bank continuing its banking facilities.

(ii) Preference

Section 239(4) of the Insolvency Act 1986 defines the circumstances in which a preference is given by a company in the following terms:[12]

'(4) For the purposes of this section and section 241, a company gives a preference to a person if –
(a) that person is one of the company's creditors or a surety or guarantor for any of the company's debts or other liabilities, and
(b) the company does anything or suffers anything to be done which (in either case) has the effect of putting that person into a position which, in the event of the company going into insolvent liquidation is better than the position he would have been in if that thing had not been done.'

Who is a creditor[13] or guarantor of the company is unlikely to cause any doubt, and frequently a bank will be a creditor. Under the Bankruptcy Act 1914 there was some doubt over who was a surety, and it was held to include a third party depositor of security even though he undertook no personal liability for the debt.[14] Whether or not the relevant act is a preference within subsection (b) is a matter of fact, but, in the majority of cases, it will apply

---

11 Section 245 of the Insolvency Act 1986.
12 Section 340 of the Insolvency Act 1986 makes similar provisions in relation to bankruptcy.
13 In *Re Blackpool Motor Car Co Ltd* [1901] 1 Ch 77 Buckley J held that the word 'creditor' means any person who was entitled to prove in the bankruptcy, and accordingly, included a surety.
14 *Re Conley, ex p Trustee v Barclays Bank Ltd* [1938] 2 All ER 127.

to payments made either to prefer the creditor[15] or to release the guarantor of the debt,[16] or charges granted by the company to the person preferred.

The preference must have been made at a relevant time, which in the case of a preference depends upon whether the person preferred is connected to the company or not.[17] If the person preferred was a connected person, then the relevant time can be two years prior to the presentation of an administration petition or prior to the commencement of the liquidation.[18] If not, then it is six months prior to the presentation of an administration petition or prior to the commencement of the liquidation,[19] or during the period between the presentation of a petition for an administration order and the order being made.[20] The act will not be a preference unless at the time when it was done the company was insolvent or it became insolvent as a consequence of the transaction.[1] However, insolvency is presumed where the person preferred is a connected person.[2]

The new preference provisions still require an element of intention or purpose to be proved, and it is this part of the test which banks will find most difficult to assess in relation to any transaction which is challenged. Section 239(5) of the Insolvency Act 1986 provides:

> 'The court shall not make an order under this section in respect of a preference given to any person unless the company which gave the preference was influenced in deciding to give it by a desire to produce in relation to that person the effect mentioned in subsection 4(b).'

This subsection requires that there must be a 'desire' to prefer the person. That connotes an element of intention, although it is arguably more subjective than the requirement for the company to have intended to give a preference. The difficulty with the use of the word desire is that in most cases a person only causes something to happen if he desires that it should happen. Arguably this will be satisfied unless the directors of the company do not know of the preference or do not realise that it will have the effect of preferring the creditor. In *New, Prance and Garrard's Trustee v Hunting*[3] Lord Esher said, in relation to fraudulent preference, that he did not think that the debtor should be taken to have intended the natural consequences of his acts, but that it depended upon what he actually intended. The better view is that this rationale should also apply in determining whether the company desired to

---

15 See for example *Re Cohen* [1924] 2 Ch 515.
16 See for example *Re F P & C H Matthews Ltd* [1982] Ch 257, [1982] 1 All ER 338; *Re Kushler Ltd* [1943] Ch 248, [1943] 2 All ER 22.
17 See p 293, n 8, ante.
18 Section 240(1) (a) and (3) of the Insolvency Act 1986. In relation to personal insolvency, the relevant time is extended to two years prior to the presentation of the bankruptcy petition where the person preferred was an associate of the individual: s 341(1)(b).
19 Section 240(1) (b) and (3) of the Insolvency Act 1986. In relation to individual insolvency see s 341(1)(c).
20 Section 240(1) (c) of the Insolvency Act 1986.
 1 Section 240(3) of the Insolvency Act 1986. Inability to pay debts is determined in accordance with s 123. In relation to individual insolvency see s 341(2) and (3).
 2 Section 240(2) of the Insolvency Act 1986. In relation to individual insolvency, the presumption applies to associates: s 341(2).
 3 [1897] 2 QB 19 at 27, cited with approval by Lord Halsbury LC in *Sharp v Jackson* [1899] AC 419 at 421, and by Lord Tomlin in *Peat v Gresham Trust Ltd* [1934] AC 252 at 262. See also *Re Lyons, Barclays Bank Ltd v Trustee* [1934] WN 195; *Re Cutts, ex p Bognor Mutual Building Society v Trustee in Bankruptcy* [1956] 2 All ER 537, [1956] 1 WLR 728, CA.

cause the preference. Accordingly, it will not be sufficient to rely upon the fact that a preference took place, but that it was intended that it should take place.

The more difficult question is how great the influence of the desire should be in causing the company to give the preference. The courts might follow the authorities decided in relation to fraudulent preferences under the old law, and conclude that the influence should be the dominant influence. In *Peat v Gresham Trust Ltd*[4] the House of Lords held that those who claim to avoid a transaction must establish that the debtor's dominant intention was to prefer, although that intention could be inferred.[5] However, the interpretation given to the words 'with a view of' was restrictive, and, the better view is that parliament used different wording in the Insolvency Act 1986 to ensure that the dominant purpose test is not followed.[6] In *Re F P & C H Matthews Ltd*[7] the Court of Appeal held that if the company, being unable to pay its debts as they arise, decides to pay one creditor in full ahead of the others the payment is made with a 'view of' preferring the creditor. It did not matter that the company's directors thought that the company would be able to pay its debts at some time in the future.

If the company has given a preference to a person connected with the company,[8] it is presumed that when the preference was given the company was influenced by the necessary desire.[9] Banks may be held to have been shadow directors of a company,[10] and there is a risk that a bank which exerts such pressure on the company that it cannot exercise a free will in doing the act alleged to be a preference of the bank will be a shadow director and, as a result, will have to disprove this presumption.

If the court declines to follow the dominant intention test, then some of the defences previously open to banks and persons preferred may not be available to them. For example, the fact that the bank has put considerable pressure on the company to make a payment does not necessarily mean that the company was not influenced by a desire to prefer the bank or a guarantor in making the payment. If a charge was created as part of a wider arrangement, then the company may have been influenced by a desire to prefer the person to whom the charge was granted in addition to intending to complete the transaction.[11] On the other hand, a company, in granting a mortgage to a bank may not intend to prefer the bank, but to ensure its survival with the continued assistance of the bank. In those circumstances the court should conclude that the company was not influenced by a desire to prefer the bank.[12] Whether or not a company which prefers a creditor pursuant to an earlier

4 [1934] AV 252 at 262.
5 Followed in *Re Eric Holmes (Property) Ltd* [1965] Ch 1052 at 1066; *Re F L E Holdings Ltd* [1967] 3 All ER 553, [1967] 1 WLR 1409.
6 *Gore-Browne on Companies* (44th edn) takes the view that the influence need not be the predominant influence: para 34.12.2.
7 [1982] Ch 257, [1982] 1 All ER 338.
8 As to which see ante.
9 Section 239(6) of the Insolvency Act 1986. In relation to individual insolvency, the same presumption applies to associates of the bankrupt: s 340(5).
10 In *Re a Company (No 005009 of 1987)* [1989] BCLC 13 Knox J refused to strike out a preference claim in which it was alleged that the bank was a shadow director. Knox J held that the allegation was not obviously unsustainable.
11 See *Re Eric Holmes (Property) Ltd* [1965] Ch 1052, [1965] 2 All ER 333.
12 This was the result in *Re F L E Holdings Ltd* [1967] 3 All ER 553, [1967] 1 WLR 1409.

contract or obligation will have been influenced by the necessary desire is unclear, although under the old law such a transaction would not have amounted to a fraudulent preference.

(iii) Orders which may be made

If the court finds that a transaction has been entered into at an undervalue or a preference given, it should make an order restoring the position to what it would have been if the company had not entered into the transaction or given the preference[13] and may include the following orders: (a) vesting property transferred in the company; (b) vesting the proceeds of any property transferred in the company; (c) releasing or discharging any securities granted by the company; (d) compensation for any benefits received; (e) reviving any obligations of sureties or guarantors released; (f) requiring security to be given for the performance of any obligations imposed by the court; and (g) directing the extent to which any person on whom obligations are imposed may prove in the liquidation.[14]

An order under s 241 of the Insolvency Act 1986 may affect persons who were not parties to the transaction or who were not preferred. Banks are most often affected by this provision when a payment is made to the bank which prefers a guarantor of the company's indebtedness to the bank. The bank is protected because the court can order that the guarantee discharged by the preference should be revived and, usually, guarantees provide that the guarantor remains liable to the bank in such circumstances. A person who receives an interest in property or a benefit from a transaction at an under-value or preference is protected if the benefit or interest was acquired in good faith and for value without notice of the relevant circumstances or derives from such an interest.[15] The relevant circumstances of which the person should have no notice are the circumstances by virtue of which an order could be made in relation to the transaction or preference.[16] This may protect banks who may receive a benefit from a transaction or preference in good faith and without notice.

(iv) Extortionate credit transactions

If a transaction involving the provision of credit to the company is extortionate and was entered into within three years of the administration order or the commencement of the liquidation, the court has power to grant relief to the liquidator.[17] Section 244(3) defines the circumstances in which a transaction is extortionate:

'(3) For the purposes of this section a transaction is extortionate if, having regard to the risk accepted by the person providing the credit –
(a) the terms of it are or were such as to require grossly exorbitant payments to be made (whether unconditionally or in certain contingencies) in respect of the provision of the credit, or
(b) it otherwise grossly contravened ordinary principles of fair dealing;
and it shall be presumed, unless the contrary is proved, that a transaction with

13 Section 238(3) of the Insolvency Act 1986, and s 339(2) in relation to bankruptcy.
14 Section 241 of the Insolvency Act 1986, and s 342 in relation to individuals.
15 Section 241(2) of the Insolvency Act 1986, and s 342(2) in relation to bankruptcy.
16 Section 241(3) of the Insolvency Act 1986, and s 342(4) in relation to bankruptcy.
17 Section 244 of the Insolvency Act 1986. In relation to individual insolvency see s 343.

respect to which an application is made under this section is or, as the case may be, was extortionate.'

This subsection adapts the provisions of the Consumer Credit Act 1974[18] for use in the context of insolvency. It is likely, but by no means certain, that the courts will follow decisions made under the Consumer Credit Act 1974 so far as possible. However, the Insolvency Act 1986 provides a narrower test than the Consumer Credit Act 1974. As regards the person providing the credit, s 244 of the Insolvency Act 1986 provides that the court should only have regard to the degree of risk accepted by him. Subsections (a) and (b) are very similar to s 138(1) of the Consumer Credit Act 1974, but there is no equivalent of sub-s (2), (3) or (4)(b) and (c) of that section in s 244 of the Insolvency Act 1986. The difference between the two acts is that the Insolvency Act directs the court to look at the financial circumstances of the transaction, but not to the particular circumstances of the debtor or creditor. It is likely that the circumstances of the debtor or creditor will only be material if it is alleged that the transaction grossly contravened the ordinary principles of fair dealing.

If the court finds that a transaction is extortionate it may set aside the whole or any part of any obligation created by the transaction; vary the terms of the transaction or the terms upon which any security is held; order that any person who was a party to the transaction should make payments to the liquidator; require anyone to surrender property held by way of security or direct accounts to be taken between anyone.[19]

(d) The liability of banks as shadow directors

Section 251 of the Insolvency Act 1986 defines a shadow director as a person in accordance with whose directions or instructions the directors of the company are accustomed to act. In *Re a Company (No 005009 of 1987), ex p Copp*[20] Knox J refused to strike out claims for preferences and for wrongful trading against the bank, both of which depended upon a finding that the bank was a shadow director. The facts which Knox J held could result in the bank being found to have been a shadow director were that when the bank discovered that the company was experiencing financial difficulties it started to exert pressure on the company; procured a debenture from the company and it commissioned a report which made several recommendations which, under pressure from the bank, the directors of the company followed.[1] Banks are faced with a very difficult dilemma. The scope of the words 'directions or instructions' has yet to be defined, and the courts may adopt a wide test. Companies in difficulty will often discuss their problems with the bank, which in many cases will have power, by virtue of its securities and importance to the company, to control the future conduct of the company's business. It is not clear whether a bank which indicates the terms upon which it is prepared to continue its support for the company will be a shadow director. Further uncertainty arises out of the possible control which a bank to a holding

18 As to which see ch 5, ante.
19 Section 244(4) of the Insolvency Act 1986.
20 [1989] BCLC 13.
 1 See [1989] BCLC at 18 b to f. Knox J declined to state his reasons for finding that the claim against the bank was not obviously unsustainable to avoid embarrassing the trial judge: see at 21 a to d.

company may have over subsidiaries of that holding company. Whether or not the subsidiary acts in accordance with the directions or instruments of its parent company's bankers could give rise to difficult questions of fact, which might be further complicated where there are cross guarantees between companies in the group. However, there are powerful arguments that the courts should be slow to find that a bank is a shadow director if the bank leaves the directors with a real choice whether or not to take a course which accommodates the bank.

If a bank is a shadow director, then in addition to the presumption which it will face in any proceedings claiming that a transaction is a preference,[2] the bank might find that it is liable for wrongful trading. Although the marginal note to s 214 of the Insolvency Act 1986 describes the 'offence' as 'wrongful trading', the section neither refers to nor depends upon the company having traded. A declaration that a person who is or was a director is liable to contribute to the assets of a company under section 214 may be made if the conditions in s 214(2) are satisfied:

'(2) This subsection applies in relation to a person if –
(a) The company has gone into insolvent liquidation,
(b) at some time before the commencement of the winding-up of the company, that person knew or ought to have concluded that there was no reasonable prospect that the company would avoid going into insolvent liquidation, and
(c) that person was a director of the company at that time; ...'

It will not be difficult to establish that the company has gone into insolvent liquidation. A company goes into insolvent liquidation at a time when its assets are insufficient for the payment of its debts and other liabilities and the expenses of the winding-up.[3] The time referred to in sub-s(b) is critical but establishing that time is not free from uncertainties. Although referred to in the section, the costs and expenses of the liquidation are unlikely to form part of what the director knew, and it is difficult to see how he ought to have concluded what they would be, because very few directors would know, or could be expected to know, what the costs and expenses of a liquidation are likely to be. Banks could be in a worse position than other directors because they could be expected to know what the likely expenses of a liquidation will be and therefore could be expected to realise earlier than other directors that the company will go into insolvent liquidation. However, in most cases the question will be whether the director knew that the company was likely to go into liquidation (other than a members' voluntary liquidation), or that he ought to have reached that conclusion.

If there is no evidence that the director knew that the company had no reasonable prospect of avoiding liquidation, then the liquidator will have to rely upon what the director ought to have concluded. Section 214(4) of the Insolvency Act 1986 sets out the standard to apply in order to determine both the facts which the director ought to know and the conclusions which he ought to reach. The director is taken to be a reasonably diligent person having both the general knowledge, skill and experience that may reasonably be expected of a person carrying out the same functions as are carried out by that director in relation to the company and the general knowledge, skill

2 Section 239(6) of the Insolvency Act 1986. Section 240 extends the relevant time to two years, see ante.
3 Section 214(6) of the Insolvency Act 1986.

and experience that that director has.[4] It is unclear how this provision would apply to a bank which was a shadow director because the bank does not have any formal functions qua director in relation to the company. The bank should only be found to have the knowledge which was in fact available to it, and should not be found to have information which it ought to have acquired by virtue of its office because it has no duty to inquire. Furthermore, the bank should be taken to have reached such conclusions as it should have reached based upon the information it had having regard to the expertise which banks ordinarily possess.

If the court concludes that the conditions in s 214(2) of the Insolvency Act 1986 are satisfied in relation to the bank, it will then have to consider the additional requirement in sub-s (3) which provides:

'(3) The court shall not make a declaration under this section with respect to any person if it is satisfied that after the condition specified in subsection (2)(b) was first satisfied in relation to him that person took every step with a view of minimising the potential loss to the company's creditors as ... he ought to have taken.'

The bank is required to take every step which it ought to have taken applying the same objective standards which are applied in determining what the bank ought to have concluded.[5] This does not require the directors or any shadow directors to cause the company to stop trading but to minimise the loss to creditors. One example of a situation where it could be wrongful trading to stop trading is where a company is party to a contract which if completed will yield a large profit but which if terminated would result in large damages claims. In such circumstances the directors should probably complete the contract, although they might also be liable for wrongful trading unless the contract is completed under the control of an administrator or administrative receiver. A bank which is a shadow director in such circumstances could be faced with a situation where the contract cannot be completed without further funding. However, it is their conduct qua directors and not their conduct qua banks which should be considered in this context. Arguably, if the bank refuses to lend money to the company (provided that it would be appropriately secured) it fails to take every step which it could take, and arguably which it ought to take. However, the courts should be reluctant to conclude that the bank is liable for wrongful trading in such circumstances because in deciding whether or not to lend money to the company the bank is acting qua bank and not qua director. In the more usual case, where the company's continued trading causes a loss to creditors, banks could be found liable as shadow directors if they fail to ensure that the company stops trading immediately.

If a bank is found liable for wrongful trading, the court may declare that it should make a contribution to the company's assets. The prima facie measure of loss is the difference between the position which the creditors were in on the date when the bank knew or ought to have concluded that the company would not avoid going into insolvent liquidation and their position when the company went into liquidation.[6] The court has wide powers to make such directions as it thinks proper to give effect to its declaration,[7] but

4 Section 214(4) of the Insolvency Act 1986.
5 Section 214(4) of the Insolvency Act 1986.
6 *Re Produce Marketing Consortium Ltd* (No 2) [1989] BCLC 520.
7 Section 215 of the Insolvency Act 1986.

in the case of banks the most usual order will be an order for payment by the bank to the liquidator.

(e) Distribution of the estate

(i) Secured creditors

A secured creditor is defined as a creditor who holds in respect of his debt any mortgage, charge, lien or other security,[8] and in many cases banks fall within one or more of these categories. Generally the rights of a secured creditor to the security is not affected in a liquidation.[9] Realisations from fixed charge securities are retained by the secured creditor, subject only to the costs of realising the security which might be paid either to a receiver or to the liquidator in the event that he realises the security with the approval of the secured creditor. If a secured creditor realises his security and there is a balance due to him from the company he may prove as an unsecured creditor for the balance due to him.[10] If part of the secured creditor's debt is preferential, then he may appropriate the sum realised from the security to pay the non preferential part of his debt, and maximise his claim to prove as a preferential creditor.[11] A secured creditor may surrender his security and prove as an unsecured creditor for the whole debt.[12] In many cases the secured creditor will submit a proof of debt for the amount by which the claim exceeds the value of the security. A proof of debt has to contain particulars of any security held, the date when it was given and the value which the creditor puts on it.[13] The valuation is not final and may be amended with the agreement of the liquidator or the leave of the court, provided that the secured creditor was not the petitioning creditor or voted in respect of the unsecured balance of his debt, in which case he must obtain the leave of the court.[14] If a secured creditor omits to disclose a security in his proof of debt he must surrender the security unless the court grants him relief on the ground that the omission was inadvertent or the result of honest mistake.[15]

A liquidator may give 28 days' notice to a secured creditor who has put in a proof of debt in which he has valued his security, that he will redeem the security at that value. The creditor then has 21 days in which to revalue his security if he wishes to do so. In order to avoid uncertainty, the secured creditor can give notice to the liquidator requiring him to elect whether to exercise his power to redeem the security. The liquidator has six months

---

8 Section 248 of the Insolvency Act 1986. A similar definition applies in relation to individual insolvency: see s 383.
9 In an administration or administrative receivership property given as security can be realised by the administrator or administrative receiver: see ss 15 and 43 of the Insolvency Act 1986, dealt with above. A lien on book debts is unenforceable if it would deny the office holder possession of any books, papers or other records of the company: s 246.
10 Rule 4.88 of the Insolvency Act 1986. In relation to individual insolvency see r 6.109.
11 *Re William Hall (Contractors) Ltd* [1967] 2 All ER 1150, [1967] 1 WLR 948.
12 Rules 4.88 and 6.109 of the Insolvency Rules 1986.
13 Rules 4.75 and 6.98 of the Insolvency Rules 1986.
14 Rules 4.95 and 6.115 of the Insolvency Rules 1986.
15 Rules 4.96 and 6.115 of the Insolvency Rules 1986. This discretion is wider than it was under the old law and, accordingly, it is unlikely that cases which held that amendment would not be allowed without proof that the liquidator had not changed his position ought not to be followed. See, for example, *Re Safety Explosives Ltd* [1904] 1 Ch 226.

either to redeem the security or to elect not to.[16] If the liquidator is not satisfied with the value put on the security he can require that the property be offered for sale.[17] If the property is realised the amount realised is substituted for the value given by the secured creditor in the proof of debt.[18]

(ii) Preferential claims

After payment of the expenses[19] the preferential debts[20] are paid in priority to all other debts.[1] The preferential debts ran equally amongst themselves and, if the assets are insufficient to meet them, they abate in equal proportions.[2] By virtue of paras 9 and 10 of Sch 6 to the Insolvency Act 1986 the following debts due to employees are preferential in relation to both companies and individuals: (a) remuneration which is owed by the company to an employee in respect of the period of 4 months before the relevant date[3] and (b) accrued holiday remuneration in respect of any period of employment before the relevant date. The present limit of any preferential claim for wages is £800.[4] By para 11 of Sch 6 to the Insolvency Act 1986 the following payments in respect of wages are preferential:

> 'So much of any sum owed in respect of money advanced for the purpose as has been applied for the payment of a debt which, if it had not been paid, would have been a debt falling within paragraph 9 or 10.'

A bank may claim that part of its debt is preferential if it can establish that it advanced money which was used to pay wages. In *National Provincial Bank Ltd v Freedman and Rubens*[5] Clauson J set out the facts as follows:

> '... cheques were not paid in until the company were pretty sure that they would receive the accommodation they required for meeting wages. Accordingly, every week a wages cheque was drawn, but the wages cheque was not paid until the manager (of the bank) was satisfied that there was being contemporaneously paid in, or there would be in due course of business in a few hours paid in, cheques which would have the result of reducing the overdraft to such an extent that the wages cheque would increase the overdraft back again to a figure not exceeding or not substantially exceeding the figure at which it stood at the beginning of the week.'

16 Rules 4.97 and 6.117 of the Insolvency Rules 1986.
17 Rules 4.98 and 6.118 of the Insolvency Rules 1986.
18 Rules 4.99 and 6.119 of the Insolvency Rules 1986.
19 In the relation to voluntary liquidation see s 115 of the Insolvency Act 1986. In relation to compulsory liquidation see s 156. The expenses are set out in rr 4.218 to 4.220. In relation to individual insolvency see s 324(i) of the Insolvency Act 1986.
20 They are defined in s 386 of and Sch 6 to the Insolvency Act 1986.
 1 Section 175 of the Insolvency Act 1986. In relation to individual insolvency see s 328.
 2 Sections 175(1) and 328(2) of the Insolvency Act 1986.
 3 The relevant date, by reference to which the preferential period is determined, is defined in s 387 of the Insolvency Act 1986. Where an administration order is in force the relevant date is the date of the administration order. In a receivership, the relevant date is the date of the appointment of the receiver. In a compulsory winding-up, the relevant date is the earlier of (a) the making of an administration order which immediately preceded the winding-up order; (b) the date of the resolution for voluntary winding-up if the compulsory liquidation followed a voluntary liquidation; (c) the appointment of a provisional liquidator or (d) the winding-up order. In a voluntary liquidation the relevant date is the date of the resolution. In a bankruptcy, the relevant date is the earlier of (a) the date when an interim receiver was appointed; or (b) the date of the bankruptcy order.
 4 Article 4 of the Insolvency Proceeding (Monetary Limits) Order 1986, SI 1986/1996.
 5 (1934) 4 Legal Decisions Affecting Bankers 444.

The question was whether or not the money which was paid out on the wages cheque was an advance by the bank for the purpose of paying wages, it having been alleged that in fact the wages were paid out of the cheques the company paid in. There was little evidence that this had been done in fact and Clauson J found for the bank. The rule in *Clayton's Case*[6] operated in favour of the bank, so that payments into the account discharged the oldest debts, some of which would not have been preferential by effluxion of time. Wynn-Parry J found for the bank in *Re Primrose (Builders) Ltd*[7] on facts similar to those in *National Provincial Bank Ltd v Freedman and Rubens*. He pointed out that there was no obligation on the banker to show that the moneys were advanced pursuant to any agreement or that his intention in so lending was to become a preferential creditor. He also found that the rule in *Clayton's Case* applied to the account, there being no evidence to the contrary.

A special wages account is frequently opened, although this is not essential if the facts are otherwise clear. Nevertheless, the advantage of a special account is that the possibility of reduction of the preferential claims by payments in, is avoided. Buckley LJ in *Re E J Morel (1934) Ltd*,[8] stressed that a claim under the provision then in force must be supported by evidence that money was advanced to pay wages; in that case there was a wages account which was in debit to the extent to which a No 2 account was in credit, and the interdependence of the two meant that the bank never made advances for wages.

In *Re James R Rutherford & Sons Ltd*,[9] Pennycuick J held that moneys transferred periodically from an overdrawn account to wipe out indebtedness on a wages account were moneys advanced for the payment of wages. The Judge agreed with Plowman J in *Re Yeovil Glove Co Ltd*[10] as to the operation of *Clayton's Case*. In *Re Rampgill Mill Ltd*[11] the bank had agreed that the company's cheques for wages and for other purposes might be cashed at another bank. The court gave a benevolent rather than a restrictive construction to the section and found as a fact that money was advanced for the purpose of paying wages.

The question whether a preferential claim in respect of advances for wages can be assigned is made even more uncertain by the omission in paragraph 11 of Sch 6 to the Insolvency Act 1986 of any reference to the person claiming preference being 'the person by whom the money was advanced'. Indeed the new wording, which refers to any sum owed in respect of money advanced, gives more support to the argument in favour of there being a power to assign the preferential claim.

(iii) Proof of unsecured claims: the rule against double proof

The unsecured creditors are entitled to share pari passu in the assets of the company[12] available after payment of the remuneration, expenses and liability

6 *Devaynes v Noble* (1816) 1 Mer 529.
7 [1950] Ch 561, [1950] 2 All ER 334; *Re Rampgill Mill Ltd* [1967] Ch 1138, [1966] 2 Lloyd's Rep 527.
8 [1962] Ch 21, [1961] 1 All ER 796.
9 [1964] 3 All ER 137, [1964] 1 WLR 1211.
10 [1963] Ch 528, [1962] 3 All ER 400.
11 [1967] Ch 1138, [1966] 2 Lloyd's Rep 527.
12 Section 107 of the Insolvency Act 1986, r 4.181 of the Insolvency Rules 1986. In relation to individual insolvency see s 328(3).

under any contracts of any administrator[13] or administrative receiver,[14] and after deduction of any sums payable to the holders of any floating charge. Banks which seek to prove as unsecured creditors often find that they are faced with problems arising out of the rule against double proof. In *Re Oriental Commercial Bank, ex p European Bank*[15] Mellish LJ described the principle in the following terms:[16]

> '... an insolvent estate, whether wound up in Chancery or Bankruptcy, ought not to pay two dividends in respect of the same debt ...'

Whether or not there is a risk of double proof does not depend upon a strict contractual analysis of the debts, but an analysis of their substance. In *Barclays Bank Ltd v TOSG Trust Fund Ltd*[17] Oliver LJ said:

> '... it is, as I think, a fallacy to argue ... that because overlapping liabilities result from separate and independent contracts with the debtor, that, by itself, is determinative of whether the rule can apply. The test is in my judgment a much broader one which transcends a close jurisprudential analysis of the persons by and to whom the duties are owed. It is simply whether the two competing claims are, in substance, claims for payment of the same debt twice over. ... the rule against double proofs in respect of two liabilities of an insolvent debtor is going to apply wherever the existence of one liability is dependent upon and referable only to the liability to the other and where to allow both liabilities to rank independent for dividend would produce injustice to the other unsecured creditors.'

It is not clear when the rule against double proof should be considered. Prima facie it should be the commencement of the liquidation, but, in *Barclays Bank Ltd v TOSG Trust Fund Ltd* Oliver LJ suggested that it is the point at which the dividend is to be paid which is relevant and not the point when the insolvency commenced. Oliver LJ said that at that point the question is whether, if the debtor had been solvent, one payment would discharge both claims.[18]

The rule against double proof has been considered by the courts in relation to the respective rights of creditors and sureties, although the cases are by no means clear. The creditor will only be able to prove in the insolvency of the debtor for the amount outstanding, and if monies are received from a surety, then the debt due from the debtor is reduced accordingly. However, banks usually have the power to deposit payments received from sureties into a suspense account. If that is done, then, until the payment is appropriated to the debt, it does not operate as a discharge of the principal indebtedness.[19]

---

13 Section 19(4) and (5) of the Insolvency Act 1986 secures by way of charge over the company's assets under his control when he ceases to hold office, the administrator's remuneration, expenses and liability under any contracts entered in by him. See: *Re Sheridan Securities Ltd* (1988) 4 BCC 200.
14 Section 45 of the Insolvency Act 1986 has similar effect to s 19, as to which see note 13, ante.
15 (1871) 7 Ch App 99. See also *Deering v Bank of Ireland* (1886) 12 App Cas 20, HL.
16 At 103.
17 [1984] AC 626 [1984] 1 All ER 1060. The Court of Appeal, approved in the House of Lords, held that on the facts of that case there was not a problem of double proof. The alleged debts due to the tourists were as a matter of fact discharged by the payments made out of the monies advanced by the banks pursuant to their indemnities. There were no debts due to the tourists (or assigned by them) which could compete with the banks' claims. Slade LJ said that he found no broad test of the rule against double proof entirely satisfactory (at 660 A to B).
18 *Barclays Bank Ltd v TOSG Trust Fund Ltd* [1984] AC 626 at 638 A, per Oliver LJ.
19 *Commercial Bank of Australia Ltd v Official Assignee of the Estate of John Wilson & Co* [1893] AC 181.

The creditor can then prove in respect of the whole debt. A surety is not entitled to payment where his claim remains wholly contingent, because the creditor's claim in respect of the same debt takes priority.[20] The proof of a surety cannot displace the proof of the principal creditor unless and until the surety has discharged all of his liabilities to the creditor.[1] If the surety has guaranteed part of the debt, and has paid that sum, then he is entitled to stand in the creditor's shoes and ranks for a dividend ahead of the creditor in respect of that part of the debt. If the surety has guaranteed the whole debt but limits his liability,[2] then, even if he pays the total amount due under his limited guarantee, he will not be treated as having discharged his liability and the creditor retains his right to prove.[3] However, the surety is entitled to receive the dividend which the debtor pays in respect of that sum which the surety has discharged.[4] This right to prove ahead of the creditor is usually excluded in bank guarantees by a provision that the security is to be in addition to and without prejudice to any other securities held from or on account of the debtor and that it is to be a continuing security notwithstanding any settlement of the account.[5]

The creditor is entitled to prove in the insolvency of a surety for the entire debt due without giving credit for any sums received from the other co-sureties since the date of the winding-up order, provided that he does not recover more than 100 pence in the pound.[6] The creditor's proof must give credit for any sums realised before proving, and for any dividends declared in the principal debtor's insolvency.[7] A surety may prove against the estate of a co-surety whether he has paid the debt in full or claims to be entitled under his right to contribution but he can only recover the just proportion which, as between the sureties, the co-surety is liable to pay.[8]

4 BANKRUPTCY

(a) The petition and bankruptcy order

Under the Insolvency Act 1986 acts of bankruptcy have been abolished. The doctrine of relation back of the trustee's title to the first available bankruptcy has also been abolished.[9] The law by which an individual may be made bankrupt is now similar to the law by which a company may be put into

---

20 *Re Fenton, ex p Fenton Textile Association Ltd* [1931] 1 Ch 85, CA.

 1 *Re Fenton* [1931] 1 Ch 85.

 2 In many cases the guarantor may be found to have guaranteed part only of the debt: see *Ellis v Emmanuel* (1876) 1 Ex D 157.

 3 *Re Rees, ex p National Provincial Bank of England Ltd* (1881) 17 Ch D 98; *Re Sass, ex p National Provincial Bank of England Ltd* [1896] 2 QB 12.

 4 *Ex p Rushforth* (1805) 10 Ves 409; *Gray v Seckham* (1872) 7 Ch App 680.

 5 *Re Sass, ex p National Provincial Bank of England* [1896] 2 QB 12.

 6 *Re Houlder* [1929] 1 Ch 205.

 7 *Re Blakeley, ex p Aachener Disconto Gesellschaft* (1892) 9 Morr 173; followed in *Re Amalgamated Investment and Property Co Ltd* [1985] Ch 349, [1984] 3 All ER 272.

 8 *Re Clark, ex p Stokes and Goodman* (1848) De G 618; *Re Parker* [1894] 3 Ch 400; *Wolmerhausen v Gullick* [1893] 2 Ch 514.

 9 Under s 37 of the Bankruptcy Act 1914. An available act of bankruptcy took place within the three months prior to presentation of the petition. The old law of bankruptcy is set out in *Williams and Muir Hunter on Bankruptcy* (19th ed.).

compulsory liquidation. A bankruptcy petition may be presented[10] against a debtor who is either (a) domiciled in England and Wales, or (b) is personally present in England and Wales on the day on which the petition is presented, or (c) at any time in the preceding three years has either been ordinarily resident[11] or has had a place of residence or has carried on business in England and Wales.[12] A creditor's petition may be presented to the court if the debt due to the petitioner exceeds £750; is liquidated and payable to the petitioning creditor immediately or at some future time and is unsecured.[13] The debt must be a debt which the debtor appears unable to pay, or to have no reasonable prospect of being able to pay.[14] A secured creditor can present a bankruptcy petition if he states in the petition that he will give up his security for the benefit of all of the bankrupt's creditors or if the security is value in the petition and the petition is in respect of the unsecured part of the debt.[15]

Usually, the debtor's inability to pay the debt is determined by the service of a statutory demand.[16] In *Re a Debtor (No 1 of 1987)*[17] the Court of Appeal refused to set aside a statutory demand on the grounds that it was perplexing because the debtor could not show that he had suffered any prejudice as a result.[18] In the judgment of the court, Nicholls LJ made the following general remarks about the new law:[19]

'I do not think that on this the new bankruptcy code simply incorporates and adopts the same approach as the old code. The new code has made many changes in the law of bankruptcy, and the court's task, with regard to the new code, must be to construe the new statutory provisions in accordance with the ordinary canons of construction, unfettered by previous authorities. Those authorities, on the setting aside of bankruptcy notices, were concerned with a different scheme, in that the operation of a bankruptcy notice was not, in all respects, the same as the effect of the new statutory demand.'

The demand in that case was on the wrong form, an affidavit served with the demand and referred to in the demand was inconsistent with the exhibits to that affidavit, and Counsel for the creditor needed an adjournment in order to understand the demand. But, it referred to a judgment, and the debtor

---

10 The persons who are able to present the petition are set out in s 264 of the Insolvency Act 1986, and include both a creditor and the debtor.
11 See for example *Re Brauch (A Debtor)* [1978] Ch 316, [1978] 1 All ER 1004, CA.
12 Section 265 of the Insolvency Act 1986. Section 265(2) prescribes an extended definition of what constitutes carrying on business. Under the Bankruptcy Act 1914 it was held that a debtor who had ceased trading, but had left trading debts unpaid, was carrying on business: *Theophile v Solicitor General* [1950] AC 186, [1950] 1 All ER 405; *Re Bird* [1962] 2 All ER 406, [1962] 1 WLR 686; *Re Brauch* (ante).
13 Section 267(1), (2) and (4) of the Insolvency Act 1986.
14 Section 267(2)(c) of the Insolvency Act 1986.
15 Section 269 of the Insolvency Act 1986. The trustee may later rely upon the valuation given in the petition and seek to redeem the security or require that it be sold or, in appropriate circumstances, it may be revalued: see ante.
16 Under s 268 of the Insolvency Act 1986. Inability to pay debts can also be established by proving an unsatisfied execution. A statutory demand can also require the debtor to prove that he will be able to pay a future debt when it falls due: s 268(2). If there is an application to set aside the statutory demand, then no petition can be presented on it: s 267(2)(d).
17 [1989] 2 All ER 46, [1989] 1 WLR 271.
18 The Court of Appeal approved the decision of Vinelott J in *Re a Debtor (No 190 of 1987)* (1988) Times, 21 May, in which the creditor mistakenly referred to a guarantee dated 21 July 1986 whereas it was in fact dated 21 July 1984.
19 At 276 G to H.

knew how much was due under the judgment. Creditors such as banks will find that they are not frustrated by spurious technical arguments advanced by debtors seeking to avoid the consequences of their insolvency. Whilst statutory demands should be drafted with care, they should not be set aside unless the debtor has a counterclaim, set-off or other cross claim which equals or exceeds the creditor's claim, or the debt is disputed on substantial grounds, or the creditor is secured, or if some real prejudice has resulted from a defect in the demand.[20] In *Re a Debtor (No 10 of 1988)*[1] Hoffman J held that a statutory demand was disputed unless the whole of the amount demanded was undisputed. However, the Court of Appeal's decision in *Re a Debtor (No 1 of 1987)* was not cited, and this case should not be treated as authority for the proposition that every dispute as to the amount claimed means that the statutory demand should be set aside. Whether or not a dispute as to part of the debt amounts to a dispute on substantial grounds will be a question of fact to be determined in each case. In the case before Hoffman J the creditor claimed that £15,727.17 was due, but the debtor disputed all but £2,426.26.

The old law by which a receiving order was made on the hearing of the petition and the bankrupt was adjudicated later on the application of the official receiver has also been repealed. On the hearing of the petition the court may make a bankruptcy order.[2] The court has a discretion to dismiss the petition if the debtor has made an offer to secure or compound for the debt which, if accepted, would have required the dismissal of the petition and the offer has been unreasonably refused.[3] In practice, the court has been reluctant to exercise this discretion. Usually a creditor is entitled to immediate payment and it is difficult to foresee the circumstances in which it would be unreasonable to refuse an offer for deferred payment or security against payment at a much later date.

The bankruptcy commences when the bankruptcy order is made,[4] and, depending upon the circumstances, will last for two or three years, unless an order is made extending the period of the bankruptcy until the bankrupt has complied with any obligations specified in the order.[5]

(b) Dispositions made by the bankrupt

Although the repeal of the doctrine of relation back has simplified the law regarding dispositions made by a bankrupt during the period immediately prior to the bankruptcy, the law relating to such dispositions, and in particular how it applied to banks, is still not free from uncertainty. In the period between the presentation of the petition and the date when the bankrupt's property vests in the trustee,[6] the validity of all dispositions of property and of any payments is governed by ss 284(1):

---

20 See r 6.5 of the Insolvency Rules 1986.
1 [1989] 1 WLR 405.
2 Section 271 of the Insolvency Act 1986. The court must be satisfied that the debt has not been paid or secured or compounded for or, if the debt is a future debt, that the debtor has no reasonable prospect of being able to pay it when it falls due.
3 Section 271(3) of the Insolvency Act 1986.
4 Section 278 of the Insolvency Act 1986.
5 Section 279 of the Insolvency Act 1986.
6 Section 284(3) of the Insolvency Act 1986.

'Where a person is adjudged bankrupt, any disposition of property made by that person in the period to which this section applies is void except to the extent that it is or was made with the consent of the court, or was subsequently ratified by the court.'

As this subsection applies until the bankrupt's property vests in the trustee, it will apply both to dispositions made before the bankruptcy order and to dispositions made after the bankruptcy order. The bankrupt's estate does not vest in the trustee until he is appointed,[7] which will occur either (a) at a meeting of creditors held for that purpose or (b) when the Secretary of State appoints a trustee or (c) from the date when the Official Receiver gives notice that he will be the trustee by operation of law.[8] If a payment is made to a bank, which is avoided by s 284(1), the bank holds the sum paid as part of the bankrupt's estate.[9]

The wording of s 284(1) is similar to the wording of s 127 of the Insolvency Act 1986 which makes void dispositions of a company's property made after the presentation of a winding-up petition. Accordingly, s 284(1) should apply to dispositions of the type caught by s 127.[10] It is also likely that the court will exercise its discretion under s 284(1), both before and after the disposition in question has been made, in a manner similar to the way in which it has exercised its discretion under s 127. The courts may treat as different banks which have notice of the presentation of the petition and banks which do not. Subsection (4) gives limited protection to banks which receive payments into an account after presentation of the petition but all payments out of an account will have to be ratified under s 284(1), and notice of the petition may be regarded as a relevant factor. It is an open question how the court will regard dispositions made after the bankruptcy order but before the trustee is appointed.[11] If the bank has actual notice of the bankruptcy order, then the court is likely to treat that as a reason to refuse to exercise its discretion in favour of the bank. A bank in such circumstances would know that the disposition cannot have been made in the ordinary course of the debtor's business, and that it may avoid the ordinary pari passu distribution of the bankrupt's assets.

Because s 284(1) affects dispositions made both before and after the bankruptcy order is made, the section has provided that it applies to all property belonging to the bankrupt regardless of whether that property would be comprised in the bankrupt's estate.[12] It follows that it applies equally to dispositions of after acquired property.[13] This provision is helpful to banks in that they do not have to consider whether monies paid into an account are after acquired property. All payments into and out of a bank account will be caught by s 284(1),[14] and the bank should refuse to allow the bankrupt to use his account without a validation order from the court.

---

7 Section 306 of the Insolvency Act 1986.
8 Sections 293 to 295 of the Insolvency Act 1986.
9 Section 284(2) of the Insolvency Act 1986.
10 See ante.
11 Subject to the specific provisions of s 284(5) which is considered below.
12 Section 284(6) of the Insolvency Act 1986.
13 Ordinarily, after acquired property would not form part of the estate unless the trustee gave notice under s 307 of the Insolvency Act 1986.
14 Applying *Re Gray's Inn Construction Ltd* [1980] 1 All ER 814, [1980] 1 WLR 711.

In addition to the discretion vested in the court by the section, s 284(1) is subject to the proviso in sub-s (4):

> The preceding provisions of this section do not give a remedy against any person –
> (a) in respect of any property or payment which he received before the commencement of the bankruptcy in good faith, for value and without notice that the petition had been presented, or
> (b) in respect of any interest in property which derives from an interest in respect of which there is, by virtue of this subsection, no remedy.'

This can only protect banks which received property or payments before the bankruptcy order. Unlike winding-up petitions, bankruptcy petitions are not advertised. The question of whether or not the bank had notice that the petition had been presented will not turn upon questions of constructive notice, but actual notice. Under the old law the bank was protected provided, inter alia, it did not have notice of an available act of bankruptcy.[15] The courts may be guided by cases under the old law in determining whether the bank had notice of the bankruptcy petition. Following those authorities the court is likely to conclude that the notice need not be express or precise, but that if information comes to the attention of the bank which ought to induce the bank to conclude that a bankruptcy petition has been presented, that is sufficient notice.[16] If a bank receives a payment with notice that the debtor has failed to comply with a statutory demand, it does not have notice of the petition but it is arguable that the bank does not receive the payment in good faith.[17] Subsection (4)(b) protects any person who takes title through another who is protected by sub-s 4(a). An example of when this could protect a bank is where it has received a bill of exchange for collection or where a bill has been indorsed in its favour by a third party after the presentation of the petition. The bank may be able to rely on sub-section 4(b) if the bill was negotiated to the third party by the bankrupt, in circumstances where the third party is protected by s 284(4).

When the bankruptcy order is made the Official Receiver will ordinarily take steps to recover the bankrupt's property.[18] In most cases he will give the bank notice of the order fairly quickly. The bank is also likely to get notice of the bankruptcy order when notice of the meeting of creditors is sent out.[19] The bankruptcy order will be advertised by the Official Receiver in a local newspaper unless the court makes an order suspending advertisement.[20] This usually occurs where the bankrupt makes an application to annul the bankruptcy order.[1] If that happens, and the Official Receiver does not tell the bank that the order has been made, then the bank may continue to pay

---

15 Under s 45 of the Bankruptcy Act 1914.
16 Cf *Hope v Meek* (1855) 10 Exch 829; *Re Dalton* [1963] Ch 336, [1962] 2 All ER 499.
17 In *Re Dalton* [1963] Ch 336, [1962] 2 All ER 499 it was held that knowledge of an available act of bankruptcy was not necessarily inconsistent with the creditor being bona fide under s 46 of the Bankruptcy Act 1914.
18 Under s 287 of the Insolvency Act 1986.
19 Section 293 of the Insolvency Act 1986 provides that unless a certificate for the summary administration of the estate has been issued, the Official Receiver has 12 weeks to decide either to summon a meeting of creditors to consider the appointment of a trustee, or to give notice to every creditor that he has decided not to summon a meeting.
20 Rule 6.34 of the Insolvency Act 1986.
1 The power to annul a bankruptcy order is contained in s 282 of the Insolvency Act 1986.

the customer's cheques. In *Re Wigzell, ex p Hart*,[2] a receiving order was made against the debtor but advertisement was postponed and all proceedings stayed. The bank received £165 to his credit and honoured cheques drawn by the debtor totalling £195. It was held that the bank was liable to the trustee for £165 without any credit for the £195 paid out.[3] Relief from this result is provided by s 284(5):

> 'Where after the commencement of his bankruptcy the bankrupt has incurred a debt to a banker or other person by reason of the making of a payment which is void under this section, that debt is deemed for the purposes of this Group of Parts to have been incurred before the commencement of the bankruptcy unless –
> (a) that banker or person had notice of the bankruptcy before the debt was incurred, or
> (b) it is not reasonably practicable for the amount of the payment to be recovered from the person to whom it was made.

The requirement that a debt should be incurred lends weight to the argument that this subsection only protects banks which have allowed the bankrupt to operate an overdraft. Payment out of an account in credit does not create a debt to the banker. On the other hand, it is arguable that the payment out of the account which is clearly a debit, creates a debt for the sum paid out. The effect of s 284(5) is that the debts created by payments out of the account are deemed to have been made prior to the bankruptcy order, and are therefore provable. In considering whether the bank had notice of the bankruptcy order, the court is likely to apply a similar test to the question whether the bank had notice of the petition under sub-s. (4).[4] However, the bank will not be able to rely upon s 284(5) after the bankruptcy order has been advertised.[5] If the bank had notice of the bankruptcy order, it may try to rely upon the second condition. That derives from s 4 of the Bankruptcy (Amendment) Act 1926. It was widely regarded as unsatisfactory and obscure under that Act, and its application under the Insolvency Act 1986 will also cause problems for banks which seek to rely upon it. The circumstances in which it is 'not reasonably practicable' to recover a payment from the recipient are unclear. If the recipient is insolvent, then, the test is probably satisfied. But if the recipient is difficult to sue, or his assets difficult to recover, possibly because he is abroad, then it is difficult to determine whether sub-s (5)(b) would apply. In practice it is unlikely that banks will rely upon this part of section 284(5).

A bank which has notice of either the presentation of a bankruptcy petition, or the making of a bankruptcy order should freeze the debtor's accounts pending an application to court for a prospective validation order. Banks which suspect that a petition has been presented or that a bankruptcy order has been made are in a more difficult position. On the one hand they might be fixed with constructive notice but, on the other, they should be careful before freezing the customer's account.

---

2 [1921] 2 KB 835.
3 See also *Re Wilson, ex p Salaman* [1926] Ch 21.
4 See ante.
5 *Re Byfield* [1982] Ch 267, [1982] 1 All ER 249.

(c) After-acquired property

The trustee may serve a written notice on the bankrupt claiming any property[6] for the bankrupt's estate which has been acquired by, or has devolved upon the bankrupt since the commencement of his bankruptcy.[7] The notice must be served within 42 days after the trustee discovered that the property had been acquired,[8] and in that regard a bankrupt is under a duty to inform his trustee of any property which is acquired.[9] The effect of such a notice is to vest the property in the trustee from the date when the property was acquired.[10] The protection afforded to banks against the avoidance of transactions entered into with a bankrupt in relation to his after-acquired property is set out in s 307(4):

'Where, whether before or after service of a notice under this section –
(a) a person acquires property in good faith, for value and without notice of the bankruptcy, or
(b) a banker enters into a transaction in good faith and without such notice,
    the trustee is not in respect of that property or transaction entitled by virtue of this section to any remedy against that person or banker, or any person whose title to any property derives from that person or banker.'

Under the Bankruptcy Act 1914 the bank was protected in certain circumstances even if it had notice of the bankruptcy.[11] However, under the new Act, banks with notice of the bankruptcy are not protected, and may find that the transaction is set aside. The courts are likely to apply the same test as to what constitutes notice under s 307 as that which applies under s 284 of the Insolvency Act 1986.[12] Accordingly, if a bank has notice of a bankruptcy it should not enter into any transactions concerning the property of the bankrupt.

(d) The avoidance of general assignments of book debts

If the bankrupt is engaged in business, a general assignment of book debts is void against the trustee of a bankrupt's estate as regards any book debts which were not paid before the presentation of the petition, unless the assignment has been registered under the Bills of Sale Act 1878.[13] An assignment includes an assignment by way of security or charge, but it will not be a general assignment if it is an assignment of specified debts or debts arising

6 The trustee cannot claim property which is otherwise excluded from the estate in bankruptcy: see s 307(2) of the Insolvency Act 1986. Because a bankrupt is entitled to carry on business and to retain the tools of his trade, there may be difficulties in establishing whether property acquired in the course of business can be caught by this section.
7 Section 307(1) of the Insolvency Act 1986.
8 Section 309 of the Insolvency Act 1986.
9 Section 333(2) of the Insolvency Act 1986. Rule 6.200(1) of the Insolvency Rules 1986 provides that the bankrupt has 21 days to give notice to his trustee.
10 Section 307(3) of the Insolvency Act 1986.
11 Under s 47 of the Bankruptcy Act 1914 any person dealing bona fide and for value with the bankrupt was protected.
12 See ante.
13 Section 344 of the Insolvency Act 1986. In substance this re-enacts s 43 of the Bankruptcy Act 1914.

under specified contracts.[14] Book debts are not defined in the section and, accordingly, the phrase will bear its common meaning.[15]

5 THE PRIVATE EXAMINATION OF BANKS

When its customer goes into administration, administrative receivership, liquidation or bankruptcy, the bank is often in a position to assist the office holder[16] in his investigations into the customer's dealings with his property and assets. Accordingly, banks are frequently made subject to orders under s 236 of the Insolvency Act 1986 [17] which enables the court, on the application of the office holder, to require any person to appear before it whom the court thinks capable of giving information concerning the promotion, formation, business, dealings, affairs or property of the company. The purpose of an examination under the predecessor to s 236 was considered by Buckley J in *Re: Rolls Razor Ltd*:[18]

> 'The powers conferred by s 268 are powers directed to enabling the court to help a liquidator to discover the truth of the circumstances connected with the affairs of the company, information of trading, dealings, and so forth, in order that the liquidator may be able, as effectively as possible and, I think, with as little expense as possible and with as much expedition as possible, to complete his function as liquidator, to put the affairs of the company in order and to carry out the liquidation in all its various aspects, including, of course, the getting in of any assets of the company available in the liquidation. It is, therefore, appropriate for the liquidator when he thinks that he may be under a duty to try to recover something from some officer or employee of a company, or some other person who is, in some way, concerned with the company's affairs, to be able to discover, with as little expense as possible and with as much ease as possible, the facts surrounding any such possible claim. Normally, it seems to me, the court should seek to assist the liquidator. . . .'

The power to require innocent third parties such as banks to attend for examination has been recognised to be an extraordinary power, and in one case it was even described as 'the star chamber clause'.[19] In *Re Rolls Razor Ltd (No 2)*[20] Megarry J said:

> '. . . the legislature has provided this extraordinary process so as to enable the requisite information to be obtained. The examinees are not in any ordinary sense witnesses, and the ordinary standards of procedure do not apply. There is here an extraordinary and secret mode of obtaining information necessary for the proper conduct of the winding-up.'

In exercising the discretion to make an order for a private examination, the courts are required to balance the views of the liquidator contained in his

14 Section 344(3) of the Insolvency Act 1986.
15 See Ch 32, post.
16 He may be the administrator, administrative receiver, liquidator or trustee. An order for an examination may also be sought by a provisional liquidator. It is unlikely that an administrative receiver would find it necessary to examine the bank which appointed him.
17 In an individual insolvency see s 366 of the Insolvency Act 1986.
18 [1968] 3 All ER 698 at 700.
19 Per Chitty J in *Re Grey's Brewery Co Ltd* (1883) 25 Ch D 400 at 403. See also *Re North Australian Territory Co* (1890) 45 Ch D 87.
20 [1970] Ch 576 at 591.

confidential report to the court,[1] to which great weight is attached, against the need to prevent any oppressive, vexatious or unfair use of the power.[2] Accordingly, in *Re Bletchley Boat Co Ltd*[3] Brightman J held that while it was not a conclusive objection to an order for an examination that proceedings had been commenced, the court ought not to allow an examination in such circumstances unless there is a good reason. The court was astute to ensure that the liquidator did not gain an unfair advantage in the litigation. This principle was followed by Slade J in *Re Castle New Homes Ltd.*[4] However, if the liquidator has not got a settled intention to sue the examinee, but merely issues a protective writ, that will not in itself be a reason to refuse an examination.[5]

An order under s 236 may be made either for an oral examination, or for the production of documents, or for the production of an affidavit.[6] If an oral examination is sought, there is no general rule that the examination should be preceded by written questions.[7] If an affidavit is sought, then the order should give sufficient particulars of the matters which the deponent is required to deal with.[8] Banks are usually asked to produce documents, either relating to the conduct of the company's account, or in some cases, the conduct of a third party's account. In that regard, the bank may find that documents are confidential, or that the use of those documents could prejudice the bank in unconnected transactions or proceedings. In *Re Esal (Commodities) Ltd*[9] a large number of documents were disclosed by the bank, some of which were confidential to present or former clients of the bank;[10] some of which were commercially sensitive, and could have been advantageous to the bank's competitors; and some of which could have been prejudicial to the bank in other proceedings. The Court of Appeal overrode all of those interests in favour of the liquidator. The liquidators were allowed to pass information obtained on the examination to other companies in the group to assist them in litigation against the examinee bank. In *Re Aveling Barford Ltd*[11] Hoffmann J held that solicitors could not exercise a lien over documents which the administrative receiver wanted to inspect. The same would apply to a banker's lien. The court has upheld claims to privilege. If documents are privileged, then the party claiming privilege is obliged to give the liquidator sufficient information to determine whether the claim to privilege is valid.[12] Accordingly, the bank is entitled to refuse to disclose all

---

1 The examinee is not entitled to see this report: *Re Gold Co* (1879) 12 Ch D 77; *Re Rolls Razor (No 2)* [1970] Ch 576, [1969] 3 All ER 1386; *Re Aveling Barford Ltd* [1989] BCLC 122.
2 *Re Rolls Razor Ltd (No 2)* (ante); *Re Spiraflite Ltd* [1979] 2 All ER 766, [1979] 1 WLR 1096; *Re Castle New Homes Ltd* [1979] 2 All ER 775, [1979] 1 WLR 1075; *Re John T Rhodes* [1987] BCLC 77; *Re Embassy Art Products Ltd* [1988] BCLC 1; *Re Esal (Commodities) Ltd* [1989] BCLC 59.
3 [1974] 1 All ER 1225, [1974] 1 WLR 630.
4 [1979] 2 All ER 775, [1979] 1 WLR 1075.
5 *Re John T Rhodes (No 2)* (1987) 3 BCC 588.
6 The rules governing the application for an examination and the manner in which an examination should be conducted are contained in Part 9 of the Insolvency Rules 1986.
7 *Re Norton Warburg Holdings Ltd* [1983] BCLC 235.
8 Rule 9.2 and 9.3 of the Insolvency Act 1986. *Re Aveling Barford Ltd* [1989] BCLC 122.
9 [1989] BCLC 59.
10 In *Re ACLI Metals (London) Ltd* (24 February 1989 unreported) Scott J upheld a claim to a common interest privilege maintained by a connected company.
11 [1989] BCLC 122.
12 *Re Aveling Barford Ltd* [1989] BCLC 122. See also *Re Highgrade Traders Ltd* [1984] BCLC 151, CA.

documents in respect of which it can claim privilege, for example where those documents contain or refer to legal advice given to the bank.

Even though the power should not be used in an oppressive, vexatious or unfair manner, the courts have been reluctant to refuse applications for private examinations, and have been ready to assist liquidators wherever possible. In order to do so, the court has recently extended the manner in which it exercises its jurisdiction. In *Re Oriental Credit Ltd*[13] Harman J granted an order restraining by injunction a person from leaving the jurisdiction until he had been examined. Harman J made the order under s 37 of the Supreme Court Act 1981. It follows that the court may grant Anton Piller relief and possibly even Mareva type relief in a private examination. If there is a fear that documents may be destroyed, the necessity for Anton Piller relief is clear. However, the circumstances in which a Mareva injunction might be appropriate are unclear. Arguably, the relief could be granted ancillary to any orders which may be made at the conclusion of the examination pursuant to s 237.[14] That section enables the court to order any person who, on the information obtained on the examination, appears to have any property of the company, or who is indebted to the company, either to deliver up the property or to pay the debt. But, in the context of an application for a private examination, there must be considerable doubt as to what evidence would be required before a Mareva type injunction could be granted. If there was a good arguable case that specific sums were owed by the examinee to the liquidator, then, it is arguable that the case is not suitable for examination following the *Bletchley Boat* line of cases.[15] On the other hand, if the evidence is not as strong as that, the courts should be reluctant to make such an order. The most difficult case will be where the liquidator can show that it is likely that he will bring successful claims against the examinee in due course, but the precise nature of those claims is not yet clear, and accordingly, he has not yet got a settled intention to sue the examinee. In such circumstances it is arguable that the Mareva injunction is granted in aid of the future proceedings and not in aid of the private examination. If that is right, then the Mareva injunction ought to be refused. It is doubtful whether orders in aid of private examinations can be made against third parties, even though s 237 applies both to the examinee and to any other person. It is inappropriate to grant injunctive relief in circumstances where the person against whom the relief is obtained is not a party to the proceedings.

If a bank is required to comply with an order made under s 236, then, in many cases it will incur substantial costs in complying with the order. That is particularly so if the bank's legal advisers have to consider whether documents are privileged, or should not be disclosed for any reason which the bank might wish to raise with the court. An examinee's right to such costs is unclear. Rule 9.6(4) provides:

'A person summoned to attend for examination ... shall be tendered a reasonable sum in respect of travelling expenses incurred in connection with his attendance. Other costs falling on him are at the court's discretion.'

---

13 [1988] Ch 204, [1988] 1 All ER 892.
14 In relation to individual insolvency the equivalent provision is s 367 of the Insolvency Act 1986.
15 See ante.

In *Re Aveling Barford Ltd*[16] Hoffmann J held that the court's discretion to make an order for costs is not limited to witnesses who attend for examination, but would extend to the costs of producing an affidavit, or disclosing documents.[17] But, there is no right to the payment of costs, and the courts rarely make orders of costs in favour of witnesses, relying upon the public duty to assist the liquidator in the performance of his functions. The courts should be astute to ensure that the burden of costs is not such as to make the examination oppressive or unfair. The difficulty for banks is that, save in cases where the costs are exceptional, it will be difficult to persuade the court that this argument applies to them.

16 [1989] BCLC 122 at 128.
17 In *Re Cloverbay Ltd* (1989) 5 BCC 732 Vinelott J held that the court's discretion to make an order for costs under r 9.4 extended only to oral examinations. The decision in *Re Aveling Barford Ltd* was not cited to the court.

PART III

INTERFERENCE BY THIRD PARTIES

SUMMARY OF CONTENTS

CHAPTER 18

ATTACHMENT

1 COURT'S JURISDICTION TO MAKE ATTACHMENT ORDERS

(a) Introduction

A useful summary of the nature of attachment proceedings under English law was given by Lord Denning MR in *Choice Investments Ltd v Jeromnimon*:[1]

'The word "garnishee" is derived from the Norman French. It denotes one who is required to "garnish", that is, to furnish a creditor with the money to pay off a debt. A simple instance will suffice. A creditor is owed £100 by a debtor. The debtor does not pay. The creditor gets judgment against him for the £100. Still the debtor does not pay. The creditor then discovers that the debtor is a customer of a bank and has £150 at his bank. The creditor can get a "garnishee" order against the bank by which the bank is required to pay into court or direct to the creditor – out of its customer's £150 – the £100 which he owes to the creditor.

There are two steps in the process. The first is a garnishee order nisi. Nisi is Norman-French. It means "unless". It is an order upon the bank to pay the £100 to the judgment creditor or into court within a stated time, *unless* there is some sufficient reason why the bank should not do so. Such reason may exist if the bank disputes its indebtedness to the customer for some reason or other. Or if payment to this creditor might be unfair to prefer him to other creditors: see *Pritchard v Westminster Bank Ltd*[2] and *Rainbow v Moorgate Properties Ltd*.[3] If no sufficient reason appears, the garnishee order is made absolute – to pay to the judgment creditor – or into court: whichever is the more appropriate. On making the payment, the bank gets a good discharge from its indebtedness to its own customer – just as if he himself directed the bank to pay it. If it is a deposit on seven days' notice, the order nisi operates as the notice.

As soon as the garnishee order nisi is served on the bank, it operates as an injunction. It prevents the bank from paying the money to its customer until the garnishee order is made absolute, or is discharged, as the case may be.'

Garnishee proceedings are a species of execution. There is therefore no jurisdiction to make a garnishee order if the judgment debt is not yet payable. In *White Son and Pill v Stennings*,[4] a judgment was given which contained

---

1 [1981] QB 149 at 154–155, [1981] 1 All ER 225 at 226–227, CA.
2 [1969] 1 All ER 999, [1969] 1 WLR 547, CA.
3 [1975] 2 All ER 821, [1975] 1 WLR 788, CA.
4 [1911] 2 KB 418. The application was made in the county court under Rules which were in all material respects to the same effect as the Supreme Court Rules.

an order that the judgment debt, and costs to be taxed, be paid into court fourteen days after taxation. The judgment creditor instituted garnishee proceedings before the period had expired. It was held by the Court of Appeal that there was no jurisdiction to entertain the application. Vaughan Williams LJ said:

> 'I think that garnishee proceedings are a species of execution and that a judgment creditor should not be allowed to take out a garnishee summons or get an order thereon under Order 45, rule 1, if the state of things is such that he cannot issue execution under the judgment.'

And Kennedy LJ says,[5]

> 'It is no argument, I think, to say that upon the view contended for by the plaintiffs, the county court judge can find some way of working out the rule so as to do no injustice to the judgment debtor; the question is whether, under the terms of the rule, there is jurisdiction to allow these summonses to be issued.'

(b) Effect of service of order

(i) *Attachment of whole balance*

The service of a garnishee order nisi on a bank was held by the House of Lords in *Rogers v Whiteley*[6] to attach and bind the *whole* of the judgment debtor's balance on current account, no matter what the amount of the judgment debt. The debtor having brought an action against the garnishee for refusing to honour cheques drawn against the balance over and above the amount of the debt, the House of Lords held that the order attached the whole of the moneys in the garnishee's hands and that he was right in dishonouring the cheques. It is immaterial whether the cheque is drawn before or after the making of the order. Service of a garnishee order nisi has been treated as binding any amount credited as cash on uncleared cheques;[7] in view of the decision in *A. L. Underwood Ltd v Barclays Bank*[8] that mere crediting as cash did not constitute the banker a holder for value, this would probably not hold good now unless, perhaps, the customer had the right to draw against uncleared effects.[9] In *Rekstin v Severo Sibirsko Gosudarstvennoe Akcionernoe Obschestro Komseverputj and Bank for Russian Trade Ltd,*[10] the bank on instructions from the Bureau, transferred the latter's balance to the account of the Trade Delegation of the USSR, which was not advised of the transfer. At the hearing of a garnishee order served after the transfer was effected, it was held that there having been no communication to the Delegation the instruction was revocable and the balance came under the attachment of the garnishee order, the latter operating as a revocation of the instruction.

It is today the practice for garnishee orders to require the attachment of debts due and accruing due up to a stated sum only; in such cases the banker

---

5 *White, Son and Pill v Stennings* [1911] 2 KB 418 at 431.
6 [1892] AC 118.
7 *Jones & Co v Coventry* [1909] 2 KB 1029.
8 [1924] 1 KB 775, 29 Com Cas 182.
9 *Fern v Bishop Burns* (1980) Financial Times, 3 July.
10 [1933] 1 KB 47; distinguished in *Momm v Barclays Bank International Ltd* [1977] QB 790, [1976] 3 Lloyd's Rep 341.

is free to part with any surplus he may hold on the customer's account, and he cannot later be made to refund any moneys paid from that surplus.

(ii) No transfer or assignment

A garnishee order does not create, as between garnishor and garnishee, any debt either at law or in equity. Accordingly: (1) a person who has obtained a garnishee order absolute is not entitled to petition for the winding-up of a garnishee company on its failure to obey the order;[11] (2) a judgment creditor ranks in priority behind the holder of a floating charge over all the property of the judgment debtor.[12]

In *Galbraith v Grimshaw and Baxter*[13] Farwell LJ said:

> 'The effect of the service of a garnishee order nisi in England was thus stated by Jessell MR in *In Re Stanhope Silkstone Collieries Co*:[14] "The attachment or garnishee order is a mode of enforcing by execution the payment of the debt in the original action; and the order that the debt be attached and that the garnishee, that is, the debtor of the original judgment debtor, shall appear to show cause why he should not pay the debt, does not operate to give the plaintiff in the original action any security until it is served." It is plain that Jessel MR means that as soon as the order is served it does give the judgment creditor some security. It does not, it is true, operate as a transfer of the property in the debt, but it is an equitable charge on it, and the garnishee cannot pay the debt to any one but the garnishor without incurring the risk of having to pay it over again to the creditor. That was decided in *Rogers v Whiteley*.'[15]

In *Cohen v Hale, The Midland Rly Co, Garnishees*[16] a garnishee order was made attaching a debt. At that time the garnishees had given the judgment debtor a cheque for the amount of the debt. Upon service of the order on the garnishees they stopped payment of the cheque, which had not been presented. It was held that the effect of the countermand was as if the cheque had never been given; there was therefore an existing debt capable of being attached, and the garnishee order was effectual.

(iii) Banking practice

The best course for a bank to pursue when an order is served is to open a new account, to which cheques presented for payment, if not dishonoured, should be debited and moneys paid in credited. Such payments-in are not affected by the garnishee order, inasmuch as the debt they constitute from the banker to the customer was not owing or accruing due at the time of the

---

11 *Re Combined Weighing and Advertising Machine Co* (1889) 43 ChD 99, CA. See also *Re Steel Wing Co* [1921] 1 Ch 349 at 355; *Pritchett v English and Colonial Syndicate* [1899] 2 QB 428, CA (action maintainable on garnishee order leading to petition based upon judgment).
12 *Norton v Yates* [1906] 1 KB 112; *Cairney v Back* [1906] 2 KB 746; cf *Vacuum Oil Co Ltd v Ellis* [1914] 1 KB 693, CA.
13 [1910] 1 KB 339 at 343 per Farwell LJ, affd [1910] AC 508.
14 (1879) 11 Ch D 160.
15 [1892] AC 118.
16 (1878) 3 QBD 371; but see *Elwell v Jackson* (1884) Cab & El 362, 1 TLR 61 and affd (1885) 1 TLR 454, CA, in which the cheque had not been presented, so that there was no debt actually due nor was there a debt *solvendum in futuro* as the cheque was ultimately paid; see also note 1 post.

service of the order.[17] The bank should communicate with the customer[18] stating that his account is stopped as far as the amount of the order is concerned, should appear in accordance with the order and, if the order is made absolute, pay over the amount of the judgment debt and costs.

A garnishee order nisi should make it plain to what account it refers and where there is a discrepancy or ambiguity in the order the banker is not bound to run the risk of attaching a particular account and dishonouring cheques pending the hearing of the summons, but should communicate with the solicitors serving the order in the endeavour to resolve the uncertainty. The address of the branch at which the account is kept should be stated in the supporting affidavit, but service should be on the head office, though it is obviously wise to serve a copy on the branch also.[19] In *Koch v Mineral Ore Syndicate (London and South Western Bank Ltd Garnishees)*[20] the bank, as a matter of courtesy, informed the judgment creditor's solicitors that they had no such account as was sought to be attached. They were asked to attach another account said to be that of the judgment debtor, but declined. The order nisi was amended, but the bank were not required to refund the amount of cheques paid during the interval.

(c) Debt 'due or accruing due'

(i) Debitum in praesenti, solvendum in futuro

The test of 'debt due' is whether it is one for which the creditor could immediately and effectually sue.[1] The definition of 'debt accruing due' given in *Webb v Stenton*[2] and adopted in many subsequent cases, is *debitum in praesenti solvendum in futuro*. In *Tapp v Jones*,[3] Lord Blackburn said,

> 'the meaning of accruing debt is *debitum in praesenti solvendum in futuro*, but it goes no further, and it does not comprise anything which may be a debt, however probable, or however soon it may be a debt.'

It follows from this that moneys paid into a banking account after the service of a garnishee order nisi are not attached by it. On this point *Webb v Stenton* was cited with approval of the Court of Appeal in *Heppenstall v Jackson and Barclays Bank Ltd*.[4] Lindley LJ in *Webb v Stenton*, says:

> 'An accruing debt is a debt not yet actually payable, but a debt which is represented by an existing obligation.'

Moneys represented by a bill of exchange are attachable when the bill matures.[5] Where a debt is payable by instalments the instalments can be attached as and when they fall due.

---

17 Cf *Jones & Co v Coventry* [1909] 2 KB 1029 at 1041–1043.
18 In *Plunkett v Barclays Bank Ltd* [1936] 2 KB 107, [1936] 1 All ER 653, du Parcq J suggested that it was a duty.
19 *Koch v Mineral Ore Syndicate (London and South Western Bank Ltd, Garnishees)* (1910) 2 Legal Decisions Affecting Bankers, 264.
20 Ibid.
 1 *Glegg v Bromley* [1912] 3 KB 474; and see *Elwell v Jackson* (1884) Cab & El 362 where a debtor paid his debt by cheque which was met and then was served with an order nisi; held that he was not under a duty to stop his cheque in the interim between the issue and payment.
 2 (1883) 11 QBD 518, CA.
 3 (1875) LR 10 QB 591.
 4 [1939] 1 KB 585, [1939] 2 All ER 10.
 5 *Hyam v Freeman* (1890) 35 Sol Jo 87.

There must, however, be an actual debt. The mere expectation of a debt is insufficient. In *O'Driscoll v Manchester Insurance Committee*,[6] which concerned fees earned by a doctor but not then paid, Bankes LJ said:

'It is well established that "debts owing or accruing" include debts *debita in praesenti solvenda in futuro*. The matter is well put in the Annual Practice 1915, p 808: But the distinction must be borne in mind between the case where there is an existing debt, payment whereof is deferred, and the case where both the debt and its payment rest in the future. In the former case there is an attachable debt, in the latter case there is not.'

(ii) Debts subject to a condition or contingency

Many debts are not payable either presently or in the future until the satisfaction of a condition or the occurrence of a contingency.

Prior to the Administration of Justice Act 1956, current account balances were different from deposit balances as regards garnishee proceedings in the sense that the latter were often subject to conditions precedent to their withdrawal which meant that they were not due or accruing due until the conditions had been fulfilled. Thus, if the return of a deposit receipt or a membership book was made a condition of repayment or withdrawal of money, no debt arose until its return.[7] And, when stipulated for, the giving of notice was held as much a condition precedent as the return of a membership book or deposit receipt in *Atkinson v Bradford Third Equitable Benefit Building Society*.[8] Therefore an unfilled condition precedent was none the less a bar to garnishee proceedings because it lay with the judgment debtor to perform it or not as he wished.

In *Cowley v Taylor, Ackers, Garnishees*,[9] the judgment creditor instituted garnishee proceedings against a friendly society of which the judgment debtor was a member, and in the funds of which he was interested. The rules provided that members desiring to withdraw funds from the society must give written notice of their intention. No such notice was given by the judgment debtor. It was held by Ridley and Darling JJ that where notice was required to be given in order to obtain a sum of money by the persons to whom it was due, such money was not recoverable by garnishee proceedings. If contingency be the only valid objection to a 'debt accruing due', this case shows that the exercise or non-exercise of a person's volition is a contingency.

In the case of a current account the only condition precedent to withdrawal is demand and it was held in the *Joachimson* case[10] that

'service of the garnishee order nisi is, by operation of law, a sufficient demand to satisfy any right the banker may have as between himself and his customer to a demand before payment of moneys standing to the credit of a current account can be enforced'.[11]

---

6 [1915] 3 KB 499 at 516, CA.
7 *Re Dillon, Duffin v Duffin* (1890) 44 Ch D 76, per Cotton LJ; *Re Tidd, Tidd v Overell* [1893] 3 Ch 154; *Bagley v Winsome and National Provincial Bank Ltd* [1952] 2 QB 236, [1952] 1 All ER 637.
8 (1890) 25 QBD 377.
9 (1908) 124 LT Jo 569.
10 *Joachimson v Swiss Bank Corpn* [1921] 3 KB 110 at 121, per Bankes LJ. The decision has been criticised in earlier editions of *Paget* (see 9th edn, pp 121, 124), but the law is now so well established as to make the point academic.
11 [1921] 3 KB 110.

The Court of Appeal accorded to it the same effect as if the demand had been made by the judgment debtor customer himself prior to the garnishee order nisi being applied for.

It was with deposit accounts that the difficulty lay before the passing of the 1956 Act. The provisions which meet this difficulty are now contained in s 40 of the Supreme Court Act 1981, as amended by the Banking Act 1987, s 108(1) and Sch 6, para 11, which provides:

'(1) Subject to any order for the time being in force under subsection (4) [ie any order including or excluding specified accounts], this section applies to the following accounts, namely:
(a) any deposit account with a bank or other deposit-taking institution.
(b) any withdrawable share account with any deposit-taking institution.
(2) In determining whether, for the purposes of the jurisdiction of the High Court to attach debts for the purpose of satisfying judgments or orders for the payment of money, a sum standing to the credit of a person in an account to which this section applies is a sum due or accruing to that person and, as such, attachable in accordance with rules of court, any condition mentioned in subsection (3) which applies to the account shall be disregarded.
(3) Those conditions are:
(a) any condition that notice is required before any money or share is withdrawn;
(b) any condition that a personal application must be made before any money is withdrawn;
(c) any condition that a deposit book or share-account book must be produced before any money or share is withdrawn; or
(d) any other prescribed condition.
. . . .
(6) In this section "deposit-taking institution" means any person carrying on a business which is a deposit-taking business for the purposes of the Banking Act 1987.'

(iii) *Flawed assets*

The term 'flawed asset' describes a protective mechanism which is widely employed in modern banking documentation. The essence of the mechanism is that an obligation to repay a debt is expressed to be conditional upon the occurrence of some specified event. For example, a parent company may place a deposit with its bank to facilitate a loan by the bank to its subsidiary. The agreement governing the deposit may contain a term that the bank is under no obligation to repay unless and save to the extent that the subsidiary has repaid the loan. The parent company's asset (the right to repayment of the deposit) would then be flawed.

In the light of the authorities which led to the 1956 Administration of Justice Act, a flawed asset arrangement appears to prevent any debt from being 'due or accruing due' within RSC Ord 49 until the occurrence of the event which constitutes the flaw. Such events are most unlikely to be within the conditions specified in s 40(3) of the Supreme Court Act 1981, ante.

(iv) *Margin payments*

Money deposited as margin is prima facie not attachable until after the closing and settlement of the transactions in respect of which it was paid. In

11 [1921] 3 KB 110.

Hutt v Shaw,[12] the judgment debtor, Tassie, was a client of the garnishee, Shaw, who was a stockbroker. Tassie had deposited with Shaw £150 as cover for certain speculations in stocks and shares. The judgment creditor, Hutt, served a garnishee order nisi on Shaw in respect of the £150 at a time when several transactions were open between Tassie and Shaw. If those transactions had been immediately closed, Shaw would have owed Tassie £70. It was held by the Court of Appeal that Hutt had no right to intervene and compel Shaw to close the transactions, and that until the transactions were closed and settled, there was no debt owing or accruing under the predecessor to Ord 49 (Ord XLV).[13]

(v) Debt situate outside the jurisdiction

RSC Ord 49, r 1(1) uses the expression '. . . and any other person *within the jurisdiction* ("the garnishee") is indebted to the judgment debtor'. Hence the garnishee must be within the jurisdiction.[14]

It was for a long time understood that the law required not only that the garnishee be within the jurisdiction, but also that the debt be situated and payable within the jurisdiction. This followed from the decision in *Richardson v Richardson*[15] that the words in the former Ord XLV 'any other person is indebted to the judgment debtor and is within the jurisdiction' meant 'is indebted within the jurisdiction and is within the jurisdiction'. However, in *S C F Finance v Masri (No 3)*[16] the Court of Appeal said, obiter, that there was no reason to read words in to the effect that the garnishee be indebted within the jurisdiction. The fact that the garnishee is not indebted within the jurisdiction goes to discretion, not jurisdiction.

(vi) Debts due in a foreign currency

In a logical development of the principle established in the *Miliangos* case[17] that an English court can give judgment in a foreign currency, the Court of Appeal has held that a debt payable in a foreign currency is attachable in accordance with the following procedure:[18]

'(1) So soon as reasonably practicable after the time of service of the order nisi, the bank must ascertain, at its then normal buying rate of exchange against sterling, the amount of the foreign currency balance of the judgment debtor as would, if converted at that rate, produce an amount equal to the sterling

---

12 (1887) 3 TLR 354, CA.
13 The rule then in force (Ord XLV) used the expression 'debt *owing* or accruing'. The wording was amended to 'debt *due* or accruing due' in 1967. The amendment appears to have been stylistic rather than substantive.
14 As to what constitutes presence within the jurisdiction, see *SCF Finance Co Ltd v Masri (No 3)* [1987] QB 1028, [1987] 1 All ER 194, CA.
15 [1927] P 228.
16 [1987] QB 1028 at 1044, [1987] 1 All ER 194 at 205 CA, citing *Swiss Bank Corpn v Boehmische Industrial Bank* [1923] 1 KB 673, CA. See also *Interpool Ltd v Galani* [1988] QB 738 at 741 D; [1987] 2 All ER 981 at 983j, CA; *Deutsche Schachtbau-und Tiefbohrgesellschaft GmbH v Ras Al Khaimah National Oil Co* [1987] 2 All ER 769 at 782a, [1987] 3 WLR 1023 at 1038G, CA; revsd in part on appeal without affecting this point [1988] 2 All ER 833, [1988] 3 WLR 230, HL.
17 *Miliangos v George Frank (Textiles) Ltd* [1976] AC 443, [1975] 3 All ER 801, HL.
18 *Choice Investments Ltd v Jeromnimon* [1981] QB 149, [1981] 1 All ER 225, CA.

judgment debt and costs, and that amount of foreign currency as ascertained must be attached;

(2) So soon as reasonably practicable after service of the order absolute, the bank must purchase at its then normal buying rate of exchange against sterling, the attached amount of foreign currency, or so much thereof as will by the application of that rate produce the sterling judgment debt and costs, and pay the same into court or to the judgment creditor;

(3) In order that the garnishee order absolute should express the obligation of the bank under the above procedure, the bank should inform the court of the amount of foreign currency attached and the rate of exchange used by the bank; and, when the order is made absolute, it should order the bank to pay the sterling equivalent of the foreign currency attached or the amount of the judgment debt and costs, whichever be the lesser.'

(d) Trust accounts and nominee accounts

The court has jurisdiction to make a garnishee order even where the debt is payable to the judgment debtor as trustee, but this is a matter which the court would be bound to take into account in exercising its discretion, and normally the order will not be made absolute.[19]

In *Plunkett v Barclays Bank Ltd*[20] Du Parcq J held that a solicitor's client account was attachable though known to be a trust account; that the bank was right in refusing to part with the balance and that it was its duty to inform the court of the claim of the person beneficially entitled. In this connection he cited *Roberts v Death*[1] to the effect that the court ought not to make an order absolute where there was reasonable ground for thinking that the money due to the execution creditor was trust money. He did not think that it was ever intended that the garnishee should be compelled to adjudicate on conflicting equities. As to the bank's obligation, the same view was expressed by Mackinnon LJ in *Hirschorn v Evans*.[2]

The courts have the power to go behind the ostensible ownership of an account, and would probably exercise it on cogent evidence that the account was in substance not the account of one of the parties, but of a third party.[3] In *Harrods Ltd v Tester*,[4] for instance, a garnishee order was served attaching an account of a woman whose husband supplied all the funds and who signed only with her husband's consent. The Court of Appeal held that, on the authority of *Marshal v Crutwell*,[5] there was in the circumstances a resulting trust in favour of the husband and that the creditors of the wife could not attach the husband's moneys by garnishee process, even though the account stood in her name.

---

19 *Deutsche Schachtbau- und Tiefbohrgesellschaft GmbH v Shell International Petroleum Co Ltd* [1988] 2 All ER 833 at 851g, [1988] 3 WLR 230 at 253E, HL, citing *Roberts v Death, post*.
20 [1936] 2 KB 107, [1936] 1 All ER 653; applied in *Re A Solicitor* [1952] Ch 328, [1952] 1 All ER 133.
1 (1881) 8 QBD 319.
2 [1938] 2 KB 801 at 815, [1938] 3 All ER 491 at 498.
3 Cf *Pollock v Garle* [1898] 1 Ch 1.
4 [1937] 2 All ER 236.
5 [1875] LR 20 Eq 328.

(e) Joint accounts

A current account credit balance in joint names is attachable to answer a joint debt only, irrespective of the mandate. As Pollock B put it in *Beasley v Roney*:[6]

'... the debt owing by a garnishee to a judgment debtor which can be attached to answer the judgment debt must be a debt due to the judgment debtor alone, and that when it is only due to him jointly with another it cannot be attached'.

This had previously been held to be the case in *Macdonald v Tacquah Gold Mines Co*,[7] and was approved by the majority of the Court of Appeal (Slesser and MacKinnon LJJ, Greer LJ dissenting) in *Hirschorn v Evans*.[8]

The liability of partners being joint, to attach a partnership debt the judgment on which a garnishee order is founded must be against the firm or the individual partners jointly. A judgment against an individual partner may form the basis of an attachment of his private account only.[9] But a judgment against a firm may serve to attach the private accounts of the partners.[10] A debt owing to a partnership is not garnishable in an action against a partner in his individual capacity.[11]

(f) Liquidator's account

A judgment obtained against a company in liquidation cannot form the basis for an order attaching the account of the liquidator; the liquidator was the only person who could sue the bank and there was no relationship of banker and customer between the bank and the company.[12] The Court of Appeal expressly dissociated themselves in that case from the decision of the court in *Gerard v Worth of Paris Ltd*[13] insofar as it held that the creditors of a company could attach an account in the name of the liquidator.

(g) Debts due to foreign sovereign state

Section 13(2)(b) of the State Immunity Act 1978 grants a general immunity from the enforcement jurisdiction of the United Kingdom courts to the property of a foreign sovereign state. This immunity is subject to an exception in s 13(4) in respect of property which is for the time being in use or intended for commercial purposes. In *Alcom Ltd v Republic of Columbia*,[14] an attempt was made to attach the credit balance on an account kept by a diplomatic mission with the London branch of a commercial bank for the purpose of meeting the expenditure of the day-to-day running of the mission. It was held by the House of Lords that words of s 13(4) were not apt to describe the credit balance on such an account and the debt was therefore not attachable. The debt owed is one and indivisible and is not susceptible of anticipatory

6 [1891] 1 QB 509 at 512.
7 (1884) 13 QBD 535.
8 [1938] 2 KB 801, [1938] 3 All ER 491.
9 *Fox v Mainwaring*, Henn Collins LJ in Chambers, 1891, 13 June following *Macdonald v Tacquah Gold Mines Co* (1884) 13 QBD 535, 53 LJQB 376 CA; and see RSC, Ord 81.
10 *Miller v Mynn* (1859) 1 E & E 1075.
11 *Hoon v Maloff (Construction and Builders Supplies Ltd)* (1964) 42 DLR (2d 770).
12 *Lancaster Motor Co (London) Ltd v Bremith Ltd, Barclays Bank Ltd (Garnishees)* [1941] 1 KB 675, [1941] 2 All ER 11.
13 [1936] 2 All ER 905.
14 [1984] AC 580, [1984] 2 All ER 6, HL.

dissection into the various uses to which moneys drawn on it might be used in the future. The judgment creditor has to show that the bank account is earmarked by the foreign state solely (save for de minimis exceptions) for being drawn upon to settle liabilities incurred in commercial transactions, for example reimbursement obligations in respect of letters of credit issued in payment of the price of goods sold to the state.[15]

2 FACTORS AFFECTING THE DISCRETION

Reference has already been made to two matters which may affect the discretion, namely (1) that the debt is payable outside the jurisdiction, and (2) that the judgment debtor is or claims to be a trustee. Without in any way attempting to identify all the factors which may be relevant in any given case, the additional factors referred to below are those which appear most likely to affect bankers.

(a) Rights of set-off

The principles seem to be as follows:

1 If no debt is due or accruing due from the judgment debtor to the garnishee bank, the order nisi will be made absolute. This applies even if the debt attached is payable in the future, so that a right of set-off might arise against the judgment debtor before the attached debt becomes payable. In *Tapp v Jones*[16] the garnishee owed the judgment debtor a sum of £590 payable by monthly instalments of £10 each. The garnishee objected that if the order were made absolute, the judgment creditor would be given a right greater than that enjoyed by the judgment debtor. Blackburn J rejected this argument:[17]

> 'It is obviously just that if a cross debt were due to the garnishee at the date of the attachment there should be a right of set-off in his favour, and I should strive hard to give effect to it if I could, though there would be difficulties in the way. But Mr Williams goes further, and maintains the right to set off debts accruing after the attachment. For this I see no ground. On the attachment the thing is absolutely fixed – and there is no clause of mutual credit or set-off. What would have been wise or just I do not say; but the legislature has certainly said no such thing as that contended for.'

The final two sentences refer to section 63 of the Common Law Procedure Act 1854, substantially re-enacted in RSC Ord 49, rr 1(1) and 4(1). *Tapp v Jones* is arguably inconsistent with the substantial body of authority to the effect that the judgment creditor must not be put in a better position than the judgment debtor – see, for example, *Sampson v Seaton Rly Co*[18] and *O'Driscoll v Manchester Insurance Committee*.[19]

2 If the debt owed by the judgment debtor to the garnishee (a) is presently payable, or (b) though payable in the future will accrue due *before* the debt attached accrues due, then, provided the two claims are capable of being

15 Ibid at 604 C and 13b, respectively.
16 (1875) LR 10 QB 591.
17 Ibid at 593.
18 (1875) LR 10 QB 28 at 30.
19 [1915] 3 KB 499 at 517.

set-off, the order nisi will not be made absolute. Authority for this proportion can be found in *Hall v Victoria Plumbing Co Ltd*, where Danckwerts LJ said:[20]

> 'It seems to me to be contrary to justice and sense to order that a garnishee should pay out money which it appears probably will not be due from him at all – because no proceedings have been taken by the judgment debtor against the garnishee. It seems to me contrary to justice that an order should be made for payment of moneys which on the face of it appear not likely to be due and which might perhaps be paid away irretrievably to a man or company who is in trouble.'

3 If a debt owed by the judgment debtor to the garnishee, whether presently due or payable in the future, could only form the basis of a counterclaim, not a set-off, the order will be made absolute – *Stumore v Campbell & Co.*[1] The rule appears to be a harsh one. If a counterclaim is successful, execution will only be levied for the balance. Accordingly this case, like *Tapp v Jones*, appears to worsen the position of the garnishee. *Stumore v Campbell* could possibly be distinguished if the garnishee could adduce good evidence that the judgment debtor would probably be unable to satisfy judgment on the garnishee's claim.

4 If a debt owed by the judgment debtor to the garnishee accrues due *after* the debt attached is or will become payable, the order will be made absolute because if the garnishee were to discharge his obligation promptly, no set-off could arise.

(b) Third party claims

Order 49, r 6 of the Rules of the Supreme Court provides that where it is alleged that the debt belongs to a third person or that any third person has a lien or charge on it, the judge may order that third person to appear and state his claim and may thereupon make such consequent order as he thinks fit. This procedure applies not only where it is alleged that the legal title to the debt is not vested in the judgment debtor, but also where it is so vested and the judgment debtor is alleged to be a trustee or a third party is alleged to be otherwise interested in the debt.[2]

A garnishee order is postponed to a prior equitable assignment[3] even in the absence of notice.[4] A receiver under a debenture containing a floating charge will take priority over a garnishor,[5] even though he is not appointed until after the order has been made absolute, if the judgment creditor has not actually been paid.[6] *Curran v Newpark Cinemas Ltd*[7] was a case in which the question for decision was whether there had been a valid prior assignment and whether a garnishee order was rightly made:

20 [1966] 2 QB 746 at 751, [1966] 2 All ER 672 at 673, CA.
 1 [1892] 1 QB 314, CA.
 2 See *Deutsche Schachtbau- und Tiefbohrgesellschaft GmbH v Shell International Petroleum Co Ltd* [1988] 2 All ER 833 at 851 g, [1988] 3 WLR 230 at 253E, HL; and see 'Trust accounts and nominee accounts', ante.
 3 *Holt v Heatherfield Trust Ltd* [1942] 2 KB 1, [1942] 1 All ER 404.
 4 *Yates v Terry* [1902] 1 KB 527.
 5 *Norton v Yates* [1906] 1 KB 112.
 6 *Cairney v Back* [1906] 2 KB 746; *Evans v Rival Granite Quarries Ltd* [1910] 2 KB 979.
 7 [1951] 1 All ER 295 at 300, CA. It is suggested that the word 'unless' should be 'if'.

'we think it clearly wrong, where the garnishee shows that he has notice of a prior assignment, to make an order against him unless (sic) he is able to prove strictly and conclusively that the assignment of which he has notice is a valid assignment.'

(i) Insolvency of the judgment debtor

An order for the compulsory winding-up of a company or a resolution of a company in general meeting for voluntary winding-up is, without more, a 'sufficient cause' for not making absolute a charging order nisi.[8] This accords with s 183(1) of the Insolvency Act 1986, which provides that where a creditor has (inter alia) attached any debt due to the company, he is not entitled to retain the benefit of the attachment unless he has completed the attachment before the commencement of winding-up. 'Completed' means, in the case of attachment, that there must be receipt of the debt.[9] Similar provisions apply in bankruptcy.[10]

A garnishee order ought not to be made absolute if payment would mean a preference of the judgment creditor, the judgment debtor being insolvent.[11]

3 RECEIVER APPOINTED BY WAY OF EQUITABLE EXECUTION

A situation analogous to attachment is the appointment of a receiver by way of equitable execution. Where a receiver is so appointed, a bank at which the judgment debtor has a deposit account can be brought into the proceedings, either on the application for a receiver or subsequently, and the order framed or a separate order made so as to affect the money in the hands of the bank. In *Giles v Kruyer*,[12] receivers were appointed by way of equitable execution on a judgment for £500 costs. The judgment debtor had a deposit account of £2,300 at a bank. The order appointing receivers was served on the bank on 17 April 1919, but they were not party to the proceedings. The bank, not having heard anything more of the matter, on 4 December 1919, paid the whole £2,300 to the judgment debtor. The receivers served the bank with a summons for an order that the bank should pay the receivers £500. Greer J dismissed the summons. He said that the order appointing receivers, made in the absence of the bank, was in personam the judgment creditor only, not in rem, and operated only as an injunction to restrain the judgment creditor from receiving the money, not the bank from paying it. He quoted Lord Esher in *Re Potts, ex p Taylor*:[13]

'If it (the order) had charged the money in the hands of the executors and had ordered them not to pay it to Potts, but to pay it to the receiver, although it might not create a common law charge, or a charge within the meaning of any of the statutes which create charges, it might still perhaps amount to an equitable charge.'

8 *Roberts Petroleum Ltd v Bernard Kenny Ltd* [1983] 2 AC 192, [1983] 1 All ER 564, HL.
9 Ibid, 213D and 576d, respectively. See also *Re Rainbow Tours Ltd* [1964] Ch 66, [1963] 2 All ER 820.
10 Insolvency Act 1986, s 346(1).
11 *George Lee & Sons (Builders) Ltd v Olink* [1972] 1 All ER 359, [1972] 1 WLR 214, applying *Roberts v Death* (1881) 8 QBD 319, CA; and see *Prichard v Westminster Bank Ltd* [1969] 1 All ER 999, [1969] 1 WLR 547.
12 [1921] 3 KB 23; and see RSC Ord 51/1/3.
13 [1893] 1 QB 648.

Receiver appointed by way of equitable execution 331

And he said that the plaintiffs had had opportunity from April to December to apply for an order directly affecting the bank.

CHAPTER 19

MAREVA INJUNCTIONS AND OTHER FREEZING ORDERS[1]

By s 37(1) of the Supreme Court Act 1981, the High Court has jurisdiction by order (whether interlocutory or final) to grant an injunction in all cases in which it appears to the court to be just and convenient to do so. In relation to the freezing of assets pending trial or execution of judgment, this jurisdiction is now exercised by the grant of injunctions of two types: Mareva injunctions and injunctions in aid of proprietary and tracing claims. These orders are an important aspect of modern banking because the majority are served on at least one bank. It has been aptly observed that banks bear by far the greatest burden of policing Mareva orders.[1a] Yet the jurisdiction to grant freezing orders is not wholly burdensome, for banks not infrequently obtain such orders on their own application, in particular in pursuit of funds of which they have been defrauded.

1   MAREVA INJUNCTIONS

(a) Nature of a Mareva injunction

A Mareva injunction[2] is an order of the court restraining a party to proceedings from removing from the jurisdiction of the court or otherwise dealing with assets located within the jurisdiction and, in more limited circumstances, from dealing with assets outside the jurisdiction.

The first Mareva order was made on an ex parte application in May 1975 by the Court of Appeal in *Nippon Yusen Kaisha v Karageorgis*.[3] The eponymous *Mareva Cia Naviera SA v International Bulkcarriers SA*,[4] also heard ex parte by the Court of Appeal, followed four weeks later. The Mareva has received statutory recognition in s 37(3) of the Supreme Court Act 1981, which provides:

'The power of the High Court under subsection (1) to grant an interlocutory injunction restraining a party to any proceedings from removing from the juris-

1 The Editor gratefully acknowledges the assistance of Mr Hodge Malek, Barrister, in the preparation of this chapter.
1a *Oceanica Castelana Armadora SA of Panama v Mineralimportexport* [1983] 2 All ER 65 at 71, [1983] 1 WLR 1294 at 1302, per Lloyd J.
2 For a fuller treatment of Mareva injunctions generally, see Gee and Andrews *Mareva Injunctions*, (1st edn, 1987).
3 [1975] 3 All ER 282, [1975] 1 WLR 1093, CA.
4 [1980] 1 All ER 213 (Note), [1975] 2 Lloyd's Rep 509, CA.

diction of the High Court, or otherwise dealing with, assets located within that jurisdiction shall be exercisable in cases where that party is, as well as in cases where he is not, domiciled, resident or present within that jurisdiction.'

The words 'or otherwise dealing with' are not to be construed ejusdem generis with 'removing from the jurisdiction'; they are to be given a wide meaning, and they include dissipation of assets within the jurisdiction.[5]

The words 'dealing with' are wide enough to include disposing of, selling, pledging or charging,[6] and although orders are frequently drafted with the inclusion of such words immediately before the words 'or otherwise dealing with', they appear to add nothing. The approved form of order at Annex A to the *Guide to Commercial Court Practice* appended to RSC Ord 72 uses the hybrid phrase 'disposing of or dealing with'.

The word 'assets', if used without limitation, includes chattels such as motor vehicles, jewellery, objets d'art and other valuables, as well as choses in action.[7] Mareva orders often specify particular assets to which the restraint applies, and in practice the assets most commonly so specified are bank accounts and interests in land.

(b) Purpose and operation of Mareva injunctions

The foundation of the Mareva jurisdiction is to prevent judgments of the court from being rendered ineffective whether by the removal of assets from the jurisdiction or by dissipation within the jurisdiction. In cases where a Mareva is granted over foreign assets, the purpose extends to preventing dissipation of assets outside the jurisdiction, or the transfer of assets from one foreign jurisdiction to another. An example of the latter is *Republic of Haiti v Duvalier*,[8] where the defendants' own evidence was that assets in their control had, when threatened with legal attachment proceedings, been removed from the foreign jurisdiction concerned to other foreign jurisdictions.

It is not the purpose of the Mareva jurisdiction in any way to improve the position of claimants in an insolvency. In particular: (1) a Mareva injunction is not a form of pre-trial attachment, but a relief in personam which prohibits certain acts in relation to the assets in question; (2) it is not the purpose of the Mareva jurisdiction to freeze a defendant's assets to ensure that there are funds available from which the plaintiff will be able to satisfy a judgment, regardless of the defendant's need to draw on the funds to meet his debts as they fall due.[9]

In *Z Ltd v A-Z and AA-LL* Lord Denning MR said, obiter, that a Mareva injunction is a method of attaching the asset itself, and that it operates in rem just as the arrest of a ship does.[10] These observations are difficult to reconcile with the established proposition that a Mareva injunction is an

5 *Z Ltd v A-Z and AA-LL* [1982] QB 558 at 571, [1982] 1 All ER 556 at 561, CA, per Lord Denning MR.
6 *CBS United Kingdom Ltd v Lambert* [1983] Ch 37 at 42, [1982] 3 All ER 237 at 241, CA.
7 Ibid.
8 [1989] 1 All ER 456, [1989] 2 WLR 261, CA.
9 *Cretanor Maritime Co Ltd v Irish Marine Management Ltd* [1978] 3 All ER 164, [1978] 1 WLR 966, CA; *Iraqi Ministry of Defence v Arcepey Shipping Co SA* [1981] QB 65, [1980] 1 All ER 480; *AJ Bekhor & Co Ltd v Bilton* [1981] QB 923 at 942, [1981] 2 All ER 565 at 577, CA: *K/S A/S Admiral Shipping v Portlink Ferries Ltd* [1984] 2 Lloyd's Rep 166, CA.
10 [1982] QB 558 at 573, [1982] 1 All ER 556 at 562.

order in personam, and it has since been remarked by Kerr LJ that they go too far in a number of respects.[11] Certainly, the analogy with the arrest of a ship is unpersuasive. A warrant of arrest places the ship under the safe arrest of an officer of the court pending trial; a ship will be released from arrest only upon provision of adequate security, eg a bank guarantee, bail or payment into court; an arrest is effective against a purchaser of the vessel, even a bona fide purchaser after issue of the writ but before service. A Mareva has none of these features.

(c) Extra-territorial limits to the jurisdiction

The wide power to grant Mareva injunctions is exercised as regards territorial limits in accordance with the following principles:

(i) Where the English court is properly seized of the dispute before it, the court will grant a Mareva over assets outside as well as within the jurisdiction, and both before and after judgment.[12]

(ii) Where the English court is not seized of the dispute, the court still has jurisdiction to grant a Mareva in cases falling within s 25 of the Civil Jurisdiction and Judgments Act 1982, by which the High Court has power to grant interim relief where (a) proceedings have been or are to be commenced in a contracting state other than the United Kingdom, and (b) they are proceedings whose subject-matter is within the scope of the 1968 Convention as defined by Art 1 (whether or not the Convention has effect in relation to the proceedings).[13] Where s 25 applies, the court may grant leave under RSC Ord 11, r 1(1)(b) to issue and serve originating process outside the jurisdiction.[14]

(iii) Where the English court is not seized of the dispute, and the case does not fall within s 25, the position is governed by *Siskina* (*Cargo Owners*) *v Distos Compania Naviera SA*,[15] the only case in which the Mareva jurisdiction has been considered by the House of Lords. It was held (a) that a Mareva injunction is interlocutory, not final; it is ancillary to a substantive claim for debt or damages; (b) that as such, a claim for Mareva relief is not a cause of action capable of standing on its own. It is a form of relief dependent upon there being a pre-existing cause of action against the defendant arising out of an invasion, actual or threatened by him, of a legal or equitable right of the plaintiff for the enforcement of which the defendant is amenable to the jurisdiction of the court.[16] Since it cannot by itself support an action within the jurisdiction, a fortiori it cannot by itself justify leave to serve out under RSC Ord 11.

11 See *Babanaft International Co SA v Bassatne* [1989] 1 All ER 433 at 438, [1989] 2 WLR 232 at 240. See also the statement of Lord Donaldson MR in *Derby & Co Ltd v Weldon* (*Nos 3 and 4*) that a Mareva injunction operates solely in personam: [1989] 1 All ER 1002 at 1011, [1989] 2 WLR 412 at 425.
12 See *Republic of Haiti v Duvalier* [1989] 1 All ER 456 [1989] 2 WLR 261, CA; *Babanaft International Co SA v Bassatne* [1989] 1 All ER 433, [1989] 2 WLR 232, CA; *Derby & Co Ltd v Weldon* [1989] 1 All ER 469, [1989] 2 WLR 276, CA; *Derby & Co Ltd v Weldon* (*Nos 3 and 4*) [1989] 1 All ER 1002, [1989] 2 WLR 412, CA.
13 *X v Y and Y Establishment* (1989) Times, 16 May 1989.
14 Ibid.
15 [1979] AC 210, [1977] 3 All ER 803, HL.
16 Ibid at 256 and 824, respectively.

(d) Guidelines for the grant of a Mareva

It is beyond the scope of *Paget* to give detailed consideration to this topic, but it may be helpful to give a summary of the guidelines which govern the grant of Mareva relief.[17]

1 The plaintiff should make full and frank disclosure of all material facts known to him or which would have been known to him had he made all such inquiries as were reasonable and proper in the circumstances.[18]

2 The plaintiff should give particulars of his claim against the defendant, stating the ground of his claim and the amount thereof, and fairly stating the points made by the defendant.

3 The plaintiff should give some grounds for believing that the defendant has assets in the relevant place; the existence of a bank account is enough, whether it is in overdraft or not.

4 The plaintiff should give some grounds for believing that there is a risk of the defendant's assets being removed or dissipated before the judgment or award is satisfied.

5 The plaintiff must give an undertaking in damages in case he fails in his claim or the injunction turns out to be unjustified; and in a suitable case this should be supported by a bond or security.

6 The plaintiff must establish a good arguable case.[19]

7 The difference between a good arguable case and a serious question to be tried, which is incapable of definition, does not affect the applicability of the general principle that it is no part of the court's function at the interlocutory stage to try to resolve conflicts of evidence on affidavit as to fact on which the claims of either party may ultimately depend, nor to decide difficult questions of law which call for detailed argument and mature consideration.[20]

8 The defendant should not be prevented from using his assets for a purpose which does not conflict with the policy underlying the Mareva injunction, eg for the making of payments which the defendant in good faith considers he should make in the ordinary course of business.[1]

9 The order should normally specify a maximum sum, that is to say it should restrain removal or dissipation of assets save in so far as such assets exceed a specified sum.[2]

10 The order should not be used to prevent a defendant from living as he has always lived, or from paying legal costs to defend the proceedings.[3]

---

17 Guidelines (1)–(5) are based upon *Third Chandris Shipping Corpn v Unimarine SA* [1979] QB 645 at 668–669, [1979] 2 All ER 972 at 984–985, CA, per Lord Denning MR, with modifications to take account of subsequent developments in the Mareva jurisdiction.

18 For the consequence of breach of these notices, see *Lloyds Bowmaker Ltd v Britannia Arrow Holdings plc* [1988] 3 All ER 178, [1988] 1 WLR 1337, CA; *Brink's Mat Ltd v Elcombe* [1988] 3 All ER 188, [1988] 1 WLR 1350; *Dormeuil Freres SA v Nicolian International (Textiles) Ltd* [1988] 3 All ER 197, [1988] 1 WLR 1362; *Behbehani v Salem* [1989] 2 All ER 143, CA.

19 *The Niedersachsen* [1984] 1 All ER 398 at 414–415, [1983] 1 WLR 1412 at 1417, CA.

20 *Derby & Co Ltd v Weldon (No 1)*, post.

1 *Iraqi Ministry of Defence v Arcepey Shipping Co SA* [1981] QB 65, [1980] 1 All ER 480.

2 See 'Maximum sum orders', post.

3 *PCW (Underwriting Agencies) Ltd v Dixon* [1983] 2 All ER 158, [1983] 2 Lloyd's Rep 197 (appeal allowed by consent without affecting this point [1983] 2 All ER 697); see also *Derby & Co Ltd v Weldon (Nos 3 and 4)* [1989] 1 All ER 1002 at 1007, [1989] 2 WLR 412 at 419.

11 The order should make reasonable provision for the protection of third parties.[4]

As regard the grant of worldwide Marevas, although it was originally said that the circumstances in which it will be appropriate to grant such a Mareva will be rare,[5] the position now appears to be that a Mareva over the defendant's assets outside the jurisdiction can properly be granted whenever his assets within the jurisdiction are insufficient.[6]

The grant of worldwide Marevas has given rise to difficult questions as to how third parties, and in particular banks, can best be protected from committing an unintended contempt of court. The problem was described by Lord Donaldson MR in *Derby & Co Ltd v Weldon (No 4)*:[7]

'Court orders only bind those to whom they are addressed. However, it is a serious contempt of court, punishable as such, for anyone to interfere with or impede the administration of justice. This occurs if someone, knowing of the terms of the court order, assists in the breach of that order by the person to whom it is addressed. All this is common sense and works well so long as the "aider and abettor" is wholly within the jurisdiction of the court or wholly outside it. If he is wholly within the jurisdiction of the court there is no problem whatsoever. If he is wholly outside the jurisdiction of the court, he is either not to be regarded as being in contempt or it would involve an excess of jurisdiction to seek to punish him for that contempt. Unfortunately, juridical persons, notably banks, operate across frontiers. A foreign bank may have a branch within the jurisdiction and so be subject to the English courts. An English bank may have branches abroad and be asked by the defendant to take action at such a branch which will constitute a breach by the defendant of the court's order. Is action by the foreign bank to be regarded as contempt, although it would not be so regarded but for the probably irrelevant fact that it happens to have an English branch? Is action by the foreign branch of an English bank to be regarded as contempt, when other banks in the area are free to comply with the defendant's instructions?'

The court has attempted to solve this problem by the insertion in Mareva orders over foreign assets of a proviso which has come to be known as the *Babanaft* proviso. Various forms have been suggested, the most recent being that adopted by the Court of Appeal in *Derby & Co Ltd v Weldon (No 4)*, above, which was as follows:

'PROVIDED THAT, in so far as this order purports to have any extra-territorial effect, no person shall be affected thereby or concerned with the terms thereof until it shall be declared enforceable or be enforced by a foreign court and then it shall only affect them to the extent of such declaration or enforcement UNLESS they are (a) a person to whom this order is addressed or an officer of or an agent appointed by a power of attorney of such a person or (b) persons who are subject to the jurisdiction of this court and (i) have been given written notice of this order at their residence or place of business within the jurisdiction, and (ii) are able to prevent acts or omissions outside the jurisdiction of this court which assist in the breach of the terms of this order.'

In relation to states which are parties to the European Judgments Convention, the procedure by which an order of the English Court is declared enforceable or enforced is that contained in Arts 25 to 45 of the Convention.

4 See the cases cited in note 13, ante; and see 'The banker's right to set-off', post.
5 See the cases cited in note 13, ante, up to *Derby & Co Ltd v Weldon*.
6 *Derby & Co Ltd v Weldon (Nos 3 and 4)*, ante.
7 Ibid at 1011–12 and 425, respectively.

In *Derby & Co Ltd v Weldon (No 4)* a receivership order was made over a company incorporated in Luxembourg. The order was then recognised by the Luxembourg court. On the above wording of the proviso, banks, whether English or foreign, with branches in Luxembourg become affected by the order upon such recognition.

The same proviso is to be inserted even if the defendant is resident or incorporated in a state which is not a convention state. Thus in *Derby & Co Ltd v Weldon (No 4)* a receivership order was made against a Panamanian company in the same terms (mutatis mutandis) as those made in relation to the Luxembourg company.

(e) Effect on a bank of a Mareva against a customer

(i) Searching for accounts maintained by the defendant

If the plaintiff is able to identify bank accounts maintained by the defendant, he should do so with as much precision as is reasonably practicable,[8] and normally any such account will be specified in the order itself.

If the plaintiff cannot identify a bank account, he has the following options:

(i) He may request the bank to conduct a search of a particular branch or branches, or of all its branches. If he does so, he will normally be required to agree in advance to pay the costs of the search.

(ii) He may simply serve a copy of the Mareva on the bank. This is tantamount to a request to search all branches, for it has been said that such service obliges a bank, as a matter of self-defence for the purpose of complying with the order, to carry out a search throughout all its branches in order to see whether it holds any assets of the particular defendant.[9] In practice, the bank will normally first check with the plaintiff's solicitors that the plaintiff intends a full search to be made. Whether or not the plaintiff requests a search, the bank is entitled to carry one out and to be indemnified in respect of its costs.

(iii) He may apply for a discovery order against the defendant or his agents requiring him to disclose the identity of all bank accounts maintained by him within the jurisdiction, whether in his own name, or jointly or in the name of a third party, or otherwise howsoever, and the credit balance (if any) on each such account.

(ii) Joint accounts and accounts in the name of a third party

In *Z Ltd v A-Z and AA-LL*, the Court of Appeal stated by way of general guideline that any Mareva order which it is intended to serve on a bank is not applicable to a joint account in the name of the defendant and of some other person or persons unless the order is so drafted as to make it clear that it is intended to apply to it, but this would only be justifiable in rare cases.[10] Where the other holder of a joint account is not a party, the order should include reference to the joint account, and a copy of the order should be served on the other holder. In principle these guidelines apply, mutatis

---

8 *Searose Ltd v Seatrain (UK) Ltd* [1981] 1 All ER 806, [1981] 1 WLR 894; *Z Ltd v A-Z and AA-LL* [1982] QB 558 at 575, [1982] 1 All ER 556 at 564, CA, per Lord Denning MR.
9 *Z Ltd v A-Z and AA-LL*, ante at 586 and 573, respectively per Kerr LJ.
10 Ibid, at 557, 591 and at 565, 576, respectively.

mutandis, to accounts maintained by the defendant in the name of third parties. The guidelines presuppose that a Mareva over a joint account restrains drawings by either account holder, even where the mandate provides either to sign. Although, strictly speaking, each account holder owns separate choses in action against the bank,[11] it is clearly preferable for Mareva purposes to treat the asset as being the fund itself. It is for this reason that the injunction should be extended to a joint account only if there are good grounds for suspecting that the account belongs in truth to the defendant alone.

In *SCF Finance Co Ltd v Masri* the position in relation to accounts in the name of a third party was summarised by Lloyd J as follows:[12] (1) Where a plaintiff invites the court to include within the scope of a Mareva injunction assets which appear on their face to belong to a third party, eg a bank account in the name of a third party, the court should not accede to the invitation without good reason for supposing that the assets are in truth the assets of the defendant. (2) Where the defendant asserts that the assets belong to a third party, the court is not obliged to accept that assertion without inquiry, but may do so depending on the circumstances. The same applies where it is the third party who makes the assertion, on an application to intervene. (3) In deciding whether to accept the assertion of a defendant or a third party, without further inquiry, the court will be guided by what is just and convenient, not only between the plaintiff and the defendant, but also between the plaintiff, the defendant and the third party. (4) Where the court decides not to accept the assertion without further inquiry, it may order an issue to be tried between the plaintiff and the third party in advance of the main action, or it may order that the issue await the outcome of the main action, again depending in each case on what is just and convenient.

This summary was approved by the Court of Appeal in *Allied Arab Bank Ltd v Hajjar*,[13] where the Court rejected a contention that where the third party has become a party to the action and is thus before the court, it is sufficient for the plaintiff to show that there is a serious issue to be tried, and that the court's approach to the matter should be the same as that laid down by the House of Lords in *American Cyanamid Co v Ethicon Ltd*.[14]

The principles stated in *SCF Finance Co Ltd v Masri* presumably apply mutatis mutandis to joint accounts.

(iii) Maximum sum orders

The normal form of Mareva order restrains the defendant from removing his assets from the jurisdiction or otherwise dealing with them within the jurisdiction save insofar as such assets exceed a specified sum. An order which specifies a sum in this way is often described as a maximum sum order.

Such an order is preferable to an order which imposes a freeze on the defendant's assets within the jurisdiction without limitation. As Kerr LJ observed in *Z Ltd v A-Z and AA-LL*,[15] there are two obvious reasons for this preference. First, it represents no more than what a plaintiff can justifiably request from the court. Second, an order which freezes all assets is, in the

11 See ch 11, ante.
12 [1985] 2 All ER 747 at 753, [1985] 1 WLR 876 at 884, CA.
13 [1989] Fam Law 68, CA.
14 [1975] AC 396, [1975] 1 All ER 504, HL.
15 [1982] QB 558 at 589, [1982] 1 All ER 556 at 575.

ordinary case, bound to lead to an outcry from the defendant and to the need for an adjustment, at any rate if he is resident within the jurisdiction. A general freezing order cannot be justified in principle, save in wholly exceptional cases, unless it is clear that (1) the defendant's assets within the jurisdiction are insufficient to meet the claim, and (2) he is neither resident nor carries on business within the jurisdiction.

In *Z Ltd v A-Z and AA-LL*, the Court of Appeal accepted the submission of the intervening bank that a maximum sum order is unworkable as far as a bank or other innocent third party is concerned, because it does not know what other assets the defendant may have or their value.[16] As a solution to this difficulty the Court of Appeal gave a guideline that the first paragraph of a Mareva order should restrain the defendant in general terms up to the maximum sum in question, but the second paragraph should then qualify the first by providing that, so far as any specified accounts are concerned, the defendant is not to be entitled to draw upon any of them except to the extent to which any of them exceed the maximum sum.[17] The advantage to a bank of an order in this form is the protection it confers from demands for repayment from an enjoined customer on the basis of the customer's assertion that he has other frozen funds exceeding the maximum sum. The order places the onus firmly on the customer to obtain a variation to permit payment by the bank. If the order has the effect of freezing assets in the hands of third parties exceeding the maximum sum, the defendant is adequately protected both by his right to apply for a variation, and by the plaintiff's undertaking in damages.

In practice, Mareva injunctions continue to be granted in the form of a restraint on removing or dealing with assets, in particular specified assets, save in so far as such assets exceed a maximum sum. The suggested unworkability of orders in this form appears not to have resulted in a flood of variation applications. It is thought that the difficulties caused by such orders may have been somewhat overstated given that however a maximum sum order is drafted, the bank will freeze funds up to the maximum sum.

In *Oceanica Castelana Armadora SA of Panama v Mineralimportexport*[18] a point arose as to whether, in calculating the amount not caught by a Mareva, a bank must make provision for future liabilities of the customer. The court gave the following example to illustrate the point. A bank holds assets of the defendant totalling $10,000,000. The defendant's future liabilities to the bank amount to $3,000,000. The Mareva is limited to a maximum sum of $2,000,000. Is the bank bound to freeze US$2,000,000 or US$5,000,000? It is, of course, to the plaintiff's considerable advantage for the bank to freeze the higher sum. If the bank freezes only $2,000,000, any subsequent set-off in respect of the $3,000,000 will reduce and eventually extinguish the $2,000,000. Conversely, if the bank freezes $5,000,000, the $2,000,000 is likely to be preserved intact, subject to any application by the defendant to vary the order to permit payments out of it.

In the example given, where the order specifies the lower sum, there is obviously no ground upon which the bank can be held bound to freeze the higher sum. This, however, does not answer the question of principle, which

16 Ibid.
17 Ibid at 590 and 575, respectively.
18 [1983] 2 All ER 65, [1983] 1 WLR 1294.

is whether the order ought to specify the higher sum so that, subject to any variation of the order on the defendant's application, funds will be available to satisfy the claims of both the bank and the plaintiff. It was held that the order should specify only the lower sum. Two reasons were given.[19] First, there is no ground on which the bank could, in the example given, have refused to repay $8,000,000 to its customer, in respect of which, ex hypothesi, it would have no existing right of set-off. This is true, but it surely begs the question. But for the order, the bank has no ground for refusing to repay any part of the $10,000,000. Second, that the extinction of the $2,000,000 by the exercise of the bank's right of set-off is 'an inevitable consequence of a defendant who is subject to a "maximum sum" Mareva, and who has no other free assets, being allowed to pay his debts as they fall due'. This reason pre-supposes that the defendant has no other free assets. However, in the example given, even if the order were to specify the higher sum, the defendant would have $5,000,000 free funds available for payment of debts owed to persons other than the plaintiff and the bank. Conversely, whatever the specified maximum sum, the other is liable to be varied if the defendant requires the frozen funds to pay his debts. The true position, it is submitted, is that there are powerful arguments, yet to be fully explored judicially, both for and against the grant of a Mareva over assets which are likely to be extinguished by set-off before the plaintiff obtains judgment.

Where the order is expressed in one currency, and the bank holds an account in another currency, the problem is to be resolved in the same way as in relation to garnishee orders; ie upon being served with the order, the bank should convert the credit balance into sterling at the then buying rate to the extent necessary to meet the sum stated in the order, and then put a stop on the account to this extent.[20] If the order expresses the maximum sum in a currency other than sterling, the conversion should presumably be made into that other currency.

(iv) Particular assets other than cash balances

The assets with which banks are primarily concerned are:

  (i) Letters of credit, performance bonds and bank guarantees of which the defendant is beneficiary.
 (ii) Bills of exchange and other negotiable instruments of which the defendant is payee.
(iii) Shares, title deeds, and articles held in safe custody.

1 LETTERS OF CREDIT ETC

Where the defendant is the beneficiary of a letter of credit, performance bond, or bank guarantee, the following questions arise:

1 Is the benefit of the issuing or confirming bank's undertaking an asset to which the Mareva applies?
2 If so, will an order be made restraining the issuing or confirming bank (in either case, 'the paying bank') from performing its undertaking to the defendant, or otherwise interfering with the contract between them?

---

19 Ibid at 71 and 1301, respectively.
20 *Z Ltd v A-Z and AA-LL* [1982] QB 558 at 593, [1982] 1 All ER 556 at 557–578 CA, per Kerr LJ.

3 If not, will the order restrain disposal of the proceeds as and when received by the defendant?

For these purposes there is no material difference between letters of credit, performance bonds and bank guarantees, and reference is made simply to letters of credit.

(i) Does the Mareva apply?

On the assumption that an irrevocable credit becomes binding once it is communicated to the beneficiary, the benefit of the issuing or confirming bank's undertaking is prima facie an asset to which a Mareva order in standard form will apply.

In *Z Ltd v A-Z and AA-LL*, it was noted that banks do not maintain a central register or other means of identifying the defendant as the beneficiary, even if he is a customer in whose name they hold accounts. This is of no concern if the credit proceeds are paid into a frozen account, for ex hypothesi the bank is on notice that those funds are subject to a Mareva. The difficulty arises if, for example, the defendant instructs the bank's letter of credit department to remit the proceeds direct to an overseas account. It was said, obiter, in *Z Ltd v A-L and AA-LL* that a Mareva drafted in the split form recommended for maximum sum orders would confine the effect of the order to the defendant's bank accounts, and not extend it to the defendant's assets generally (including letters of credit) insofar as they are under the control of a bank on which a copy of the order is served.[1] It is, however, difficult to see how the mere division of the order into paragraphs in the manner suggested can limit the ordinary meaning of the word 'asset'. In any event, many orders do not adopt the recommended drafting. In practice the instances of defendants attempting to circumvent Marevas by issuing remittance instructions in respect of credit proceeds are so few that it has not yet been necessary for the courts to consider the problem more fully.

(ii) Will the court restrain performance?

The court will not restrain the paying bank from performing its undertaking to the defendant as beneficiary. This accords both with the general principle that a Mareva will not be permitted to interfere with performance of an existing contract between a third party and the defendant,[2] and also with the general approach of the court to restraint of payment under letters of credit.[3]

The Mareva does, of course, restrain any transfer by the defendant of a portion of the credit or any assignment of the benefit thereof.

(iii) Does the order apply to the proceeds?

There is no objection to the order imposing a specific restraint in respect of the proceeds of a letter of credit as and when received by or for the defendant.[4] If the proceeds are paid into a frozen bank account, they are caught by the

1 Ibid at 591 and 576, respectively.
2 *Galaxia Maritime SA v Mineralimportexport* [1981] 1 All ER 796, [1982] 1 WLR 539, CA.
3 See ch 36, post.
4 *Intraco Ltd v Notis Shipping Corpn* [1981] 2 Lloyd's Rep 256, CA; *Power Cuber International Ltd v National Bank of Kuwait SAK* [1981] 3 All ER 607 at 613, [1981] 1 WLR 1233 at 1241–1242; *Z Ltd v A-Z and AA-LL* [1982] QB 558 at 574, 591, [1982] 1 All ER 566 at 563, 576, CA.

order whether or not the proceeds are specifically identified as an asset to which the order applies.

2 BILLS OF EXCHANGE AND OTHER NEGOTIABLE INSTRUMENTS

The principles stated above apply, so far as they are relevant, where the defendant is the payee of a bill of exchange or other negotiable instrument.

3 SHARES, TITLE DEEDS AND ARTICLES HELD IN SAFE CUSTODY

In *Z Ltd v A-Z and AA-LL* Kerr LJ said the following in relation to shares or title deeds which a bank may hold as security, or articles in a safe deposit which the bank may hold in the name of the defendant:[5]

> 'Unless these are either (sic) specifically referred to in the order, because they are in some way connected with the subject matter of the action, the order should not apply to such assets even if the bank in question is able, through some central register, to ascertain that they are held in the name of the defendant. The reason is that the bank may not, and generally will not, know their precise value, and that the bank should not be expected to try to assess this in some way; even at the plaintiff's expense, unless the terms of the order are specifically drafted so as to include them. The same applies to articles held in safe custody in the name of the defendant, with the additional complication that the bank may neither know the contents of the safe deposit or of some other container entrusted to it for safe-keeping, let alone the value of the contents; nor whether or not the contents in fact belong to the defendant or are held by him for someone else. Accordingly, the order should be so drawn as to make it clear that its terms do not apply to such assets, if any.'

In practice it is rare for orders to be so drawn because the plaintiff will normally not know whether the defendant has placed such assets with his bank. In the exceptional case where the plaintiff has such knowledge, he may well also be in a position to give a sufficient estimate of value to meet the suggested difficulty.

(v) Debits to the defendant's account

The bank's entitlement to debit the defendant's account has been considered in relation to:

(i) cheques drawn by the defendant;
(ii) transactions entered into by the defendant involving the use by him of a cheque card or credit card;
(iii) letters of credit, etc, as regards which the defendant is the applicant.

1 CHEQUES DRAWN BY THE DEFENDANT

As soon as a bank receives notice of a Mareva injunction, it must freeze the defendant's bank accounts up to the specified maximum amount (if any) and it must not allow any drawings to be made on the frozen funds, even by cheque drawn before the making of the order. The reason is because, if it allowed any such drawings, the bank 'would be obstructing the course of justice – as prescribed by the court which granted the injunction – and it would be guilty of a contempt of court'.[6] The dishonouring of cheques drawn

5 [1982] QB 558 at 590–591, [1982] 1 All ER 556 at 576.
6 Ibid at 574 and 563, respectively, per Lord Denning MR.

before the making of the order is typical of the damaging consequences which can result from the grant of a Mareva. This particular consequence could, of course, be avoided by a suitably worded proviso. The justification for the non-inclusion of such a proviso appears to be that a proviso might result in post-order cheques being deliberately ante-dated.[7]

A proviso permitting the defendant to pay specified expenses or to discharge pre-existing liabilities permits a bank to honour cheques in respect of such expenses or liabilities, whether drawn before or after the making of the order. This raises a fresh difficulty, discussed below, whether a bank has to satisfy itself that cheques purporting to be drawn pursuant to a proviso are in fact so drawn.

2 TRANSACTIONS INVOLVING THE USE OF A CHEQUE CARD OR CREDIT CARD

If a defendant has used a cheque card or credit card so as to give rise to obligations on the part of a bank to a third party, the bank is entitled and bound to honour such obligations to the third parties concerned.[8] This creates a fundamental distinction from the position relating to cheques, where the bank's obligation is solely to the defendant. The Court of Appeal has given a guideline that, in cases where the defendant might avoid the incidence of the freezing order by means of cheque and credit cards, the order should make it clear that it does not preclude the debiting of his account in respect of any cheque or credit card transaction effected by the defendant prior to the date when the order is served on the bank.[9]

In practice it is rare for an order to contain such a provision, and this reflects the fact that banks and credit card companies have not found it necessary to insist upon its inclusion. There are several reasons for this. First, in most cases where such a provision would otherwise be appropriate, the order will contain a more general proviso in respect of trading or living expenses, and/or pre-existing liabilities. Secondly, credit card companies are not generally entitled to debit the card holder's account, and therefore the recommended proviso would not assist them in any event. Thirdly, a plaintiff cannot properly use his Mareva to defeat a bank's contractual right to debit an account in respect of a pre-order card transaction, and so in practice, such debits are made with the plaintiff's consent.

It has been said that once the bank has been served, it will no doubt consider it prudent to take steps to withdraw the card facility from the defendant insofar as it is in its power to do so. This implies that failure to do so would be a material consideration on an application to vary a Mareva to permit the debiting of an account in respect of use of a card which could have been prevented, and that failure to prevent such use may amount to contempt of court. It is, however, thought doubtful whether either proposition survives analysis, especially where the order contains the usual proviso to cover living or trading expenses.

Where, before the making of an order, the bank accepts a draft drawn by the defendant, the bank's entitlement to debit the defendant's account is in principle the same as its position in relation to pre-order cheque card and credit card transactions.

7 Ibid at 592 and 577, respectively, per Kerr LJ.
8 Ibid at 592–593 and 576–577, respectively, per Kerr LJ.
9 Ibid.

3 LETTERS OF CREDIT, ETC

It has already been noted that where the defendant is the beneficiary of a credit, a Mareva will not be granted to restrain payment by the issuing or confirming bank. Consistent with this approach, and with the bank's position in relation to cheque card and credit card transactions, where the defendant is the applicant for the credit, the issuing bank, having paid the beneficiary (or reimbursed the paying bank), should be permitted to debit the defendant's account.[10]

(vi) The banker's right of set-off

All Mareva injunctions which are intended to be served on banks should contain in the original ex parte order a suitable proviso to enable the bank to exercise its right of set-off without the necessity of applying for a variation to the order. An approved form of wording[11] is:

> 'Provided that nothing in this order shall prevent [X Bank plc] from exercising any rights of set-off it may have in respect of facilities afforded by it to the Defendant prior to the date of this Order.'

If a bank is served with an order which does not contain a set-off proviso the question arises whether it is entitled to exercise its right of set-off without applying to the court for a variation. In *Oceanica Castelana Armadora SA of Panama v Mineralimportexport*,[12] Lloyd J held that the answer is 'no', or at the very least, that there is a doubt. In light of this observation, it would clearly be imprudent for a bank to effect a set-off without first making the appropriate application. If such an application is made, the bank is not required to disclose the state of its customer's accounts, nor to provide other information about its customer, eg the availability of other assets within the jurisdiction out of which to discharge the debit balance sought to be set-off.

2 INJUNCTIONS IN AID OF TRACING CLAIMS

There is a well-established jurisdiction to grant injunctions in aid of tracing claims. The jurisdiction is now embodied, at least in relation to identifiable finds, in RSC Ord 29, r 2(1) and (3).

In the recent exercise of this jurisdiction the court has tended to follow the robust approach taken in two unreported cases in 1978. In the first, *London and Counties Securities Ltd (in liquidation) v Caplan*[13] Templeman J granted in aid of a tracing claim an injunction which restrained the defendant from dealing not only with assets within the jurisdiction, but also assets outside the jurisdiction, including in particular any credit balances in accounts maintained with specified overseas subsidiaries of Lloyds Bank Ltd. In the second case, *Mediterranea Raffineria Siciliana Petroli Spa v Mabanaft GmbH*,[14] the

---

10 See ibid at 574 and 563, respectively, per Lord Denning MR.
11 RSC Ord 72, Appendix, Annex A.
12 [1983] 2 All ER 65, [1983] 1 WLR 1294.
13 5 May 1978 (ex parte application); 26 May 1978, unreported (inter parties hearing between plaintiff and Lloyds Bank Ltd).
14 (1978) CA (Civil Division) Transcript 816 of 1978.

Court of Appeal upheld discovery orders in aid of an injunction freezing certain sale proceeds in which the plaintiff claimed a proprietary interest.

The jurisdiction has since been exercised, or its exercise considered, in a number of reported cases. In *A v C*,[15] Robert Goff J granted an injunction in aid of a tracing claim restraining disposal of moneys in bank accounts up to a specified amount. He also granted a Mareva injunction restraining disposal of a much larger sum in aid of claims in personam.

In *Ashtiani v Kashi*,[16] a case involving a worldwide Mareva, Dillon LJ observed that the jurisdiction conferred by s 37(1) of the Supreme Court Act 1981 (ante) obviously covers an injunction in respect of foreign assets where the title to those assets is in question. In *Republic of Haiti v Duvalier*, Staughton LJ observed that the powers of the court to restrain dealing with assets outside the jurisdiction may be wider, and its discretion is certainly more readily exercised, if the plaintiff's claim is a proprietary claim.[17]

In *A v C*, supra, the bank which had received the monies which were the subject of the tracing claim was joined as a party to the action. It is thought that this is generally not necessary, save where a discovery order is sought. A bank which is on notice of a tracing claim could not safely pay away any such monies in its hands, even before the making of a freezing order against its customer. After notice of a freezing order, such payment would constitute a contempt of court.

In relation to the obtaining of freezing orders, a plaintiff with a proprietary claim enjoys certain advantages over a plaintiff with a claim in personam, namely: (1) an injunction over overseas assets will more readily be granted; (2) it is not necessary to prove a real risk of dissipation – it is sufficient to establish an arguable title to the monies; (3) ancillary relief by way of discovery and the appointment of a receiver is in practice more readily available; (4) if the defendant has other assets, the court may decline to permit payments out of the disputed fund to pay legal costs, trade debts, etc; (5) if the proprietary claim is established, the plaintiff's title prevails even in an insolvency.[18]

15 [1981] QB 956 (Note), [1980] 2 All ER 347.
16 [1987] QB 888 at 901, [1986] 2 All ER 970 at 977, CA.
17 [1989] 1 All ER 456 at 464, [1989] 1 WLR 261 at 270.
18 See *Chase Manhattan Bank NA v Israel-British Bank (London) Ltd* [1981] Ch 105, [1979] 3 All ER 1025.

CHAPTER 20

DISCOVERY AND INSPECTION ORDERS

1 DISCOVERY ORDERS IN AID OF FREEZING INJUNCTIONS

(a) Jurisdiction

The court has power to make discovery orders in aid of freezing orders, ie Mareva injunctions and injunctions in aid of tracing claims and it is a power which is frequently exercised.

The jurisdiction to grant discovery orders in aid of Mareva injunctions derives from s 37(1) of the Supreme Court Act 1981. Although the section does not expressly confer such power, there is inherent in the statutory power to grant a Mareva the power to make all such ancillary orders as appear to the court to be just and convenient to ensure that the exercise of the Mareva jurisdiction is effective to achieve its purposes.[1] There is, however, no power under the Rules of the Supreme Court to order discovery or interrogatories in aid of a Mareva injunction because the documents and information sought on such an application do not relate to any matter in question in the action.[2]

Where an injunction is granted in aid of a tracing claim, there exists the same inherent power to make ancillary discovery orders. If the order is sought against parties to the action the court also has jurisdiction to order discovery under RSC Ord 24 of documents relating to title to monies, if that is a matter in question in the action. In addition, the court has power to order discovery when an order is made under the jurisdiction conferred by RSC Ord 29 r 2(3) (order for the preservation of a specific fund in dispute) or pursuant to its inherent jurisdiction.[3]

(b) Discretion

The power to make ancillary discovery orders is discretionary. Issues of principle relating to the manner in which the discretion should be exercised were considered in the two unreported cases concerning tracing claims referred to in ch 19, ante. In the first, *London and Counties Securities (In*

---

1 *A J Bekhor & Co Ltd v Bilton* [1981] QB 923, [1981] 2 All ER 565, CA, approving (on this point) *A v C* [1981] QB 956n, [1980] 2 All ER 347.
2 Ibid.
3 See generally the cases decided under the *Anton Piller* jurisdiction, described in the notes to RSC Ord 29, r 2; and see also *A J Bekhor & Co Ltd v Bilton* [1981] QB 923 at 953–954, [1981] 2 All ER 565 at 586, CA.

346

Liquidation) *v Caplan*,[4] the court made a discovery order requiring Lloyds Bank Ltd to procure certain overseas subsidiaries to disclose statements of bank accounts maintained with them outside the jurisdiction. Templeman J acknowledged that it was not surprising that injunctions in those forms had caused both Lloyds Bank Ltd and its foreign subsidiaries considerable concern for two reasons: (1) an injunction of the English court would not be a complete answer to a civil action brought against them overseas for non-repayment of credit balances; (2) the English order might give rise to civil or even criminal liability for breach of the duty of secrecy. To meet these concerns, the ex parte order was varied in two respects. First, to minimise the possibility of civil liability in damages, the freezing order was varied so as to cease to bite if one of the overseas banks gave notice to the plaintiff that the defendant was seeking to withdraw money, but subject to the plaintiff having seven days in which to take action themselves abroad so as to obtain a corresponding order from the foreign court. Secondly, to minimise the possibility of criminal proceedings, the disclosure order was made subject to a proviso that the banks would not be guilty of contempt if their failure to comply with the order would render them liable to criminal process in the jurisdiction in which it was situate.

This solution to the problems raised by the extra-territorial nature of the order foreshadowed the *Babanaft* proviso (see ch 19 ante). But the protection conferred by the Babanaft proviso in its latest form seems to be wider because it has the effect that a foreign subsidiary of an English bank is not affected by a freezing or discovery order, since it is not a person who is subject to the jurisdiction of the English court. It remains to be seen whether a narrower form of proviso will be adopted in future tracing claims.

In the second unreported case, *Mediterranea Raffineria Siciliana Petroli Spa v Mabanaft GmbH*,[5] the Court of Appeal upheld an order for discovery and for an affidavit of documents made for the purpose of ascertaining not only the whereabouts of certain proceeds of sale to which the plaintiff asserted a proprietary title, but also the identity of persons who controlled a Panamanian company. In a statement which has often been cited, Templeman LJ said:

'A court of equity has never hesitated to use the strongest powers to protect and preserve a trust fund in interlocutory proceedings on the basis that, if the trust fund disappears by the time the action comes to trial, equity will have been invoked in vain. That is why orders of this sort were made long before the recent orders for discovery, and they are at the heart of the Chancery Division's concern, and it is the concern of any court of equity, to see that the stable door is locked before the horse has gone.'

In exercising its discretion to order discovery or further discovery in aid of a Mareva, the court will generally not make an order if it is clear upon what assets the freezing order operates. It goes beyond the legitimate purpose of an order for discovery in aid of a Mareva to make an order which is designed to establish the extent of breaches by the defendant of the order or any undertaking given by him. In exercising its discretion, the court can properly

---

4 5 May 1978 (ex parte application); 26 May 1978 (inter partes hearing between plaintiff and Lloyds Bank Ltd).
5 (1978) CA (Civil Division) Transcript 816.

take into account its power under RSC Ord 38, r 2 to order the defendant to attend for cross-examination on his affidavit evidence.[6]

(c) Procedure and costs

Where a discovery order is sought against a bank, the proper procedure is to join the bank as a defendant to the action, as in *A v C*.[7] This accords with the established practice that an injunction ought not to be granted against a non-party.[8] The order will normally contain an undertaking by the plaintiff to pay the bank's reasonable costs and expenses of compliance on an indemnity basis.

If, however, the bank is not joined as a party, it may apply for leave to make an application to vary or discharge in the existing action. It is not necessary to institute separate proceedings in order to seek such relief.[9] The plaintiff must expect to pay the costs of an innocent third party who applies to intervene. In *Project Development Co Ltd SA v KMK Securities Ltd*[10] an order was made that the intervener's costs were to be taxed in accordance with RSC Ord 62, r 29 (revoked) on a solicitor and own client basis but with a direction that, notwithstanding the terms of RSC Ord 62, r 29(1), it was for the intervener to establish that the costs had been reasonably incurred and were reasonable in amount. It appears that the equivalent direction under the new RSC Ord 62 would be for taxation in accordance with RSC Ord 62, r 12(2) on an indemnity basis but with a direction that, notwithstanding the terms of RSC Ord 62, r 12(2), any doubts as to whether the costs were reasonably incurred or were reasonable in amount are to be resolved in favour of the paying party.

(d) Use of documents for collateral purposes

Following the decision of the House of Lords in *Harman v Home Office*, a new rule (RSC Ord 24, r 14A) was introduced:

> '14A. Any undertaking, whether express or implied, not to use a document for any purposes other than those of the proceedings in which it is disclosed shall cease to apply to such document after it has been read to or by the Court, or referred to, in open court, unless the Court for special reasons has otherwise ordered on the application of a party or of the person to whom the document belongs.'

There is as yet little authority on the manner in which the court will exercise its direction 'to otherwise order'.[11] If a bank wishes to obtain the benefit of such an order in respect of documents produced by it pursuant to a disclosure order, the application must be made before the documents are read or referred

---

6 *A J Bekhor & Co Ltd v Bilton* [1981] QB 923, [1981] 2 All ER 565, CA.
7 [1981] QB 956n, [1980] 2 All ER 347.
8 See *Elliot v Klinger* [1967] 3 All ER 141, [1967] 1 WLR 1165.
9 In *London and Counties Securities (In Liquidation) v Caplan* the bank issued an originating notice of motion, but it was held that the application should be made in the existing action. For an example of a third party intervening, see *Project Development Co Ltd SA v KMK Securities* [1983] 1 All ER 465, [1982] 1 WLR 1470.
10 [1983] 1 All ER 465, [1982] 1 WLR 1470.
11 The matter has been considered in two cases, which take a somewhat different approach: *Bibby Bulk Carriers Ltd v Cansulex Ltd* [1989] QB 155, [1988] 2 All ER 820; *Derby & Co Ltd v Weldon (No 2)* (1988), Times, 20 October.

to in open court.[12] It is noteworthy that in *Bankers Trust Co v Shapira*,[13] decided before the new rule had been introduced, Waller LJ stated in the context of a discovery order against a bank in aid of a tracing claim, that there was to be an implied undertaking on the part of the plaintiffs not to use the information which they would obtain otherwise than for the purposes of the action.

2 DISCOVERY ORDERS UNDER *NORWICH PHARMACAL*

In *Norwich Pharmacal Co v Customs and Excise Comrs*[14] the House of Lords held that if a person through no fault of his own becomes involved in the tortious acts of others so as to facilitate their wrongdoing, he may incur no personal liability but he comes under a duty to assist the person who has been wronged by giving him full information and disclosing the identity of the wrongdoers. This jurisdiction overlaps considerably the jurisdiction under s 37(1) to make discovery orders in aid of tracing claims. It was applied in *Bankers Trust Co v Shapira*,[15] where the plaintiff claimed to have been defrauded by two individuals of US $1,000,000, of which US $708,203 had been credited to accounts maintained with Discount Bank (Overseas) Ltd. Upon discovery of the fraud some months later, the plaintiff instituted proceedings against the two individuals and the bank, and applied ex parte for freezing and discovery orders. The freezing orders were granted, but at first instance Mustill J declined to grant a discovery order against the bank, principally on the grounds that there was no need to forestall the disposition of money since the events in question had happened eight months earlier, and the individual defendants were not before the court, not having been served. The Court of Appeal, applying *Norwich Pharmacal*, allowed an appeal against the refusal to grant a discovery order. The Court recognised that it is a strong thing to order a bank to disclose the state of its customer's account and the documents and correspondence relating to it, and stated that this should only be done when there is good ground for thinking that the money in the bank is the plaintiff's money.

The categories of documents ordered to be disclosed by the bank were:

1 all correspondence passing between the bank and the first and second defendants (the two individuals) relating to any account at the bank in the names of either the first and/or second defendants;
2 all cheques drawn on any account at the bank in the names of either the first and/or second defendants;
3 all debit vouchers, transfer applications and orders and internal memoranda relating to any account at the bank in the names of either the first and/or second defendants;

in each case from the date of the alleged fraud, onwards.

An order of that breadth was held to be justified because, unless the fullest

12 *Derby & Co Ltd v Weldon*, ante.
13 [1980] 3 All ER 353, [1980] 1 WLR 1274, CA.
14 [1974] AC 133, [1973] 2 All ER 943, HL.
15 [1980] 3 All ER 353, [1980] 1 WLR 1274, CA.

possible information had been ordered, the difficulties of tracing the funds would have been 'well-nigh impossible'.

It has been said that the international jurisdictional limits of discovery under *Norwich Pharmacal* are the same as those of a subpoena duces tecum or an order under the Bankers' Books Evidence Act 1879.[16]

3   INSPECTION ORDERS UNDER THE BANKERS' BOOKS EVIDENCE ACT 1879

The Bankers' Books Evidence Act 1879 deals with two separate matters. First, it provides a convenient procedure for the proof of the contents of bankers' books without bank officers being compellable witnesses in legal proceedings to which the bank is not a party. Secondly, it confers a jurisdiction to make inspection orders against banks. It is convenient to deal with both matters in this chapter, even though the first is not strictly within its ambit.

(a) Proof of contents of bankers' books

The main object of the Act, the operation of which is governed by RSC Ord 38, r 13(2), is to avoid the inconvenience to bankers[17] of their being compellable to produce their books in legal proceedings to which they are not party.[18] The previous practice was vexatious, because in theory the books could be utilised only for refreshing the memory of the clerk or officer who made the entries and was summoned as a witness, and the real object of compelling their production was that they were in practice invariably but irregularly put forward and treated as substantive evidence in themselves.[19]

By s 3, in all legal proceedings, including arbitrations,[20] a copy of any entry in a banker's books, shall be received as prima facie evidence of the existence of such entry and of matters, transactions and accounts therein recorded. By s 9(2), as substituted by the Banking Act 1979, s 51(1) and Sch 6, Pt I, 'bankers' books include ledgers, day books, cash books, account books and other records used in the ordinary business of the bank, whether those records are in written form or are kept on microfilm, magnetic tape or any other form of mechanical or electronic data retrieval mechanism.' Such evidence is available against anyone; thus copies of entries in the books of defendant bankers can be used as evidence against the plaintiff.[21]

In *Barker v Wilson*[1] it was held by the Divisional Court that the definition of 'bankers' books' included microfilm of the bank's records. An entry in a banker's book included any form of permanent record by means made

16 *Mackinnon v Donaldson, Lufkin and Jenrette Securities Corpn* [1986] Ch 482 at 498–499, [1986] 1 All ER 653 at 661.
17 For the meaning of 'bank' and 'banker' in the Act, see ch 6, ante.
18 *Parnell v Wood* [1892] P 137.
19 See per Bowen LJ in *Arnott v Hayes* (1887) 36 Ch D 731 at 738.
20 Section 10; extended by Solicitors Act 1974, s 86 by the addition at the end of the definition of 'legal proceedings' of the words 'and an application to, or an inquiry or other proceeding before, the Solicitors' Disciplinary Tribunal or any body exercising functions in relation to solicitors in Scotland or Northern Ireland corresponding to the functions of that Tribunal.'
21 *Harding v Williams* (1880) 14 Ch D 197. In *London and Westminster Bank v Button* (1907) 51 Sol Jo 466 it was held that evidence produced under the Act was prima facie evidence against the world.
1   [1980] 2 All ER 81, [1980] 1 WLR 884.

available by modern technology (per Bridge LJ). Although cheques and paying-in slips constitute part of a bank's records used in the ordinary course of its business, the adding of an individual cheque or paying-in slip to a bundle of cheques or paying-in slips does not constitute the making of an entry in those records. A microfilm recording the payment of cheques by photographing the name of the payee appears to be an entry in a banker's books within the meaning of the Bankers' Books Evidence Act 1879.[2]

To be a book used in the ordinary business it does not have to be in use every day; it is sufficient if it be a book kept by the banker for reference if necessary.[3] For copies to be admissible in evidence, it must first be proved by a partner or officer of the bank, either orally or by affidavit, that the book from which the entries were copied was at the time of making such entries one of the ordinary books of the bank, as above defined, that the entry was made in the usual and ordinary course of business, and that the book is in the custody and control of the bank, or the successors of the bank in whose custody or control it was when the entry was made.[4] It must also be proved in like manner that the copy has been examined with the original and is correct.

The banker must give all reasonable facilities to a party authorised to inspect and take copies of entries by an order under s 7 of the Act;[5] only when the banker has complied with the requirements of the Act is he entitled to its protection.[6]

In *Douglass v Lloyds Bank Ltd*[7] Roche J allowed the bank to produce old deposit ledgers to show that they carried no trace of a deposit alleged to have been made in 1866 and not repaid. The bank could produce nothing earlier than 1873 and the learned judge held that 'the ignorance of the bank of the subsistence of this deposit as constituting a debt' confirmed his view that the deposit had been repaid. The learned judge relied upon s 3 in permitting such evidence to be adduced.

Where the bank itself is a party to the litigation, it can still be made to produce its books under *subpoena duces tecum*. It is no answer to such an order that the document is held by the bank on terms that its delivery up requires the authority of the depositors.[8]

(b) Inspection orders

(i) In general

By s 7 of the Act, on the application of any party to a legal proceeding a court or judge may order that such party be at liberty to inspect and take copies of any entries in a banker's book for any of the purposes of such proceedings. An order may be made either with or without summoning the bank or any other party, and must be served on the bank three clear days before the same is to be obeyed, unless the court or judge otherwise directs.

2 *Williams v Williams* [1988] QB 161 at 168, [1987] 3 All ER 257 at 261, CA.
3 *Idiots' Asylum v Handysides* (1906) 22 TLR 573.
4 Sections 4, 5.
5 *Waterhouse v Barker* [1924] 2 KB 759; *Williams v Summerfield* [1972] 2 QB 512, [1972] 2 All ER 1334.
6 *Emmott v Star Newspaper Co* (1892) 62 LJQB 77.
7 (1929) 34 Com Cas 263.
8 *R v Daye* [1908] 2 KB 333, 77 LJKB 659.

An order may be made under s 7 by a magistrate before whom criminal proceedings are being taken.[9] The granting or refusing of an application for inspection is discretionary[10] and the power to grant it will be exercised with great caution and only on clearly established and sufficient grounds.[11]

The power to make an order for inspection will seldom be exercised with regard to the accounts of third parties unless it be shown that such account is in substance really the account of one of the parties to the litigation, or kept on his behalf, so that the entries would be admissible in evidence.[12] Where it is sought to obtain inspection of the account of a third party, notice of such application must be given to such third party and to the bank concerned.

In *South Staffordshire Tramways Co v Ebbsmith*[13] Lord Esher MR said that:

'... if the court were satisfied that in truth the account which purported to be that of a third person was the account of the party to the action against whom the order was applied for, or that though not his account, it was one with which he was so much concerned that items in it would be evidence against him at the trial ... then they might order an inspection.'

This test was approved by the Court of Appeal in *Ironmonger & Co v Dyne*,[14] when inspection of a husband's account was ordered for the purpose of discovery concerning his wife's transactions in securities for which the husband's account was a cloak. The Act may not be used to increase facilities for discovery and s 7 'must be regarded as being subject to the scope of the Act in general.'[15] If made at all, the order should be strictly confined to relevant entries, of which copies would be admissible in evidence at the trial.[16] In *Williams v Summerfield*[17] the Divisional Court held that if legal proceedings were begun with the sole object of investigating a suspect bank account – a fishing operation – an application pursuant to s 7 should be rejected.

In Canada the British Columbia Court of Appeal approved the grant of permission to inspect the accounts of third parties since they might well be relevant to substantiate the plea of justification in defamation,[18] Davey JA refusing to accept as accurate the statement of principle by Smith LJ in

9 *R v Kinghorn* [1908] 2 KB 949.

10 *Emmott v Star Newspaper Co*, ante; *Waterhouse v Barker* [1924] 2 KB 759.

11 See *Arnott v Hayes* (1887) 36 Ch D 731, per Bowen LJ at 738; also *South Staffordshire Tramways Co v Ebbsmith* [1895] 2 QB 669 per Lord Esher MR at 674; see also *R v Andover JJ, ex p Rhodes* [1980] Crim LR 644, DC; *M'Gorman v Kierans* (1901) 35 ILT 84; *L'Amie v Wilson* [1907] 2 IR 130.

12 *South Staffordshire Tramways Co v Ebbsmith*, post; *Howard v Beall*, post; *Pollock v Garle* [1899] 1 Ch 1; *Ironmonger & Co v Dyne*, (1928) 44 TLR 579, CA. See also *Staunton v Counihan* (1957) 92 ILT 32, in which Dixon J refused to accept the view given obiter in *L'Amie v Wilson* [1907] 2 IR 130, that it was desirable to serve notice on the bank of an application to inspect.

13 [1895] 2 QB 669 at 675.

14 (1928) 44 TLR 579; and see *Re Marshfield, Marshfield v Hutchings* (1886) 32 Ch D 499.

15 Per Ridley J in *R v Bono* (1913) 29 TLR 635 at 636. In *Waterhouse v Barker* [1924] 2 KB 759, it was held by Bankes and Atkin LJJ (Scrutton LJ dissenting) that on an application under s 7, the court is guided by the general rules regulating the inspection of documents before trial.

16 *Arnott v Hayes* (1887) 36 Ch D 731; *Howard v Beall* (1889) 23 QBD 1; *Perry v Phosphor Bronze Co Ltd* (1894) 71 LT 854. See also *R v Marlborough Street Metropolitan Stipendiary Magistrate, ex p Simpson* (1980) 70 Cr App Rep 291.

17 [1972] 2 QB 512, [1972] 2 All ER 1334.

18 *Sommers v Sturdy* (*No 2*) (1957) 10 DLR (2d) 269.

Emmott's case[19] to the effect that inspection had never been ordered to enable a defendant to justify a libel.

When an order allowing inspection and copies to be taken has been made and served, there would seem no objection to the bank's supplying the requisite copies, if that be the more convenient course.[20]

(ii) Extra-territorial orders

A. ORDERS MADE BY THE ENGLISH COURT

An order whether under s 7 of the Bankers' Books Evidence Act or by subpoena, requiring the production by a non-party of documents held outside the jurisdiction concerning business transacted outside the jurisdiction should not, save in exceptional circumstances, be imposed upon a foreigner, and, in particular, a foreign bank. The principle is that a state should refrain from demanding obedience to its sovereign authority by foreigners in respect of their conduct outside the jurisdiction.[1]

In *R v Grossman*,[2] an order was made ex parte under s 7 of the Bankers' Books Evidence Act 1879 on Barclays Bank Ltd at its head office in London requiring it to allow the Inland Revenue to inspect and take copies of an account maintained by an Isle of Man company with Barclays Bank's branch in the Isle of Man. An application for a similar order had previously been made to the court in the Isle of Man and had been refused. The Court of Appeal set aside the inspection order. In the words of Lord Denning MR:

'I think that the branch of Barclays Bank in Douglas, Isle of Man, should be considered in the same way as a branch of the Bank of Ireland or an American bank, or any other bank in the Isle of Man which is not subject to our jurisdiction. The branch of Barclays Bank in Douglas, Isle of Man, should be considered as a different entity separate from the head office in London. It is subject to the laws and regulations of the Isle of Man. It is licensed by the Isle of Man government. It has its customers there who are subject to the Manx laws. It seems to me that the court here ought not in its discretion to make an order against the head office here in respect of the books of the branch in the Isle of Man in regard to the customers of that branch. ... Any order in respect of the production of the books ought to be made by the courts in the Isle of Man – if they will make such an order. It ought not to be made by these courts. Otherwise there would be danger of a conflict of jurisdictions between the High Court here and the courts of the Isle of Man. That is a conflict which we must always avoid. ... It seems to me that, although this court has jurisdiction to order the head office here to produce the books, in our discretion it should not be done.'

R v Grossman was applied in *Mackinnon v Donaldson, Lufkin and Jenrette Securities Corpn*[3] where the court set aside an ex parte order made against Citibank NA, which was not a party to the proceedings, requiring it to produce books and other papers held at its head office in New York relating to transactions which took place in New York on an account maintained

---

19 *Emmott v Star Newspaper Co* (1892) 62 LJQB 77.
20 Cf *Emmott v Star Newspaper Co* (1892) 62 LJQB 77.
 1 *Mackinnon v Donaldson, Lufkin and Jenrette Securities Corpn* [1986] Ch 482 at 493G, [1986] 1 All ER 653 at 658b, per Hoffmann J. This statement of principle was referred to with apparent approval in *Interpool Ltd v Galani* [1988] QB 738 at 742F, [1987] 2 All ER 981 at 984h, CA.
 2 (1981) 73 Cr App Rep 302.
 3 [1986] Ch 482, [1986] 1 All ER 653.

there by a Bahamian company. Hoffmann J, from whose judgment the statements of principle at the start of this section are taken, stated that orders concerned with documents outside the jurisdiction are so unusual that they should ordinarily be made on notice to the bank concerned so as to give it full opportunity to investigate the position.[4]

B. ORDERS MADE BY FOREIGN COURTS

The same principles apply in the inverse case of a subpoena issued by a foreign court requiring production of documents by non-parties relating to business transacted outside the jurisdiction of the foreign court. In *X AG v A Bank*[5] two corporate customers of the London branch of an American bank (the identity of which is not disclosed in the report) applied for an injunction to restrict the bank from producing documents relating to their accounts pursuant to a subpoena issued by a grand jury and upheld by the United States District Court for the Southern District of New York. The court granted an interlocutory injunction to restrain disclosure. The issue having arisen on an interlocutory application, it was dealt with in strict conformity with *American Cyanamid* principles. In considering the balance of convenience, Leggatt J made reference to the fact that the exercise of power by the United States court was, by English standards, excessive. The point of principle arose in more acute form in *FDC Co Ltd v Chase Manhatten Bank NA*,[6] where the parties agreed that the hearing of an application for an interlocutory injunction should be treated as the trial of the action. The case arose out of a subpoena issued by the New York District Court addressed to the defendant Bank in New York, but aimed at information within the jurisdiction of the Hong Kong courts. The Hong Kong Court of Appeal granted a final injunction restraining the bank from complying with the subpoena. It held that disclosure did not fall within any of the four exceptions to the duty of confidentiality stated in *Tournier's* case (see ch 15, ante). In dealing with the exception which permits disclosure by compulsion of law, Silke JA observed that the compulsion had to be that of the law of Hong Kong, ie the law governing the relevant account. Applying *R v Grossman*, ante, the court treated the Hong Kong branch of the bank as a separate entity from the head office in New York.

4   ORDERS UNDER THE EVIDENCE (PROCEEDINGS IN OTHER JURISDICTIONS) ACT 1975

By ss 1 and 2(1) of the above Act, where an application is made to the High Court, and the court is satisfied (1) that the application is made in pursuance of a request issued by or on behalf of a court or tribunal ('the requesting court') exercising jurisdiction in any other part of the United Kingdom or in a country or territory outside the United Kingdom; and (2) that the evidence to which the application relates is to be obtained for the purposes of civil proceedings which either have been instituted before the requesting court or whose institution before that court is contemplated, the court has power by

---

4 Ibid at 497E and 660h, respectively.
5 [1983] 2 All ER 464, [1983] 2 Lloyd's Rep 535.
6 (1984) unreported, Hong Kong CA.

order to make such provision for obtaining evidence in the part of the United Kingdom in which it exercises jurisdiction as may appear to it to be appropriate for the purpose of giving effect to the request in pursuance of which the application is made.

The manner in which the court's discretion should be exercised in relation to evidence the production or giving of which would lead to disclosure by a bank of confidential information relating to a customer was considered by the Court of Appeal in *Re State of Norway's Application*.[7] The position was summarised by Kerr LJ as follows:[8]

'The court must carry out a balancing exercise. In the scales on one side must be placed the desirable policy of assisting a foreign court, in this case supported by both parties to the litigation before it. On the other side there is the opposing principle that the court will give great weight to the desirability of upholding the duty of confidence in relationships in which, as here, it is clearly entitled to recognition and respect. Which way the balance then tilts depends upon the weight which is properly to be given to all the other circumstances of the case.'

On the facts of the case, the request was held to be in the nature of a roving investigation which might affect the private financial affairs of unknown persons who were entitled to expect that the highly reputable merchant bank to which they had entrusted their affairs would never be compelled to disclose those affairs except in circumstances of allegations of fraud or crime.[9] Exercising the discretion afresh, the Court of Appeal, by a majority, refused to accede to the request. However, in *Re State of Norway's Application (No 2)*,[10] the House of Lords upheld a redrafted request. Lord Goff, delivering the leading speech, recorded that both sides accepted that the question of confidentiality could only be answered by the court undertaking a balancing exercise of the sort described by Kerr LJ.[11]

5 DISCLOSURE UNDER THE INSOLVENCY ACT 1986, s 236

Disclosure under this section is considered in ch 17, ante.

6 DISCLOSURE TO INVESTIGATORS

The powers of the Bank of England under the Banking Act 1987 to obtain, inform and require production of documents have been considered in ch 1, ante. The Bank also has power under s 4(3) of the Bank of England Act 1946 to request information from bankers, provided that no such request is made with respect to the affairs of any particular customer of a banker.

The following additional statutory powers of investigation and seizure are subject to limited protection in favour of bankers:

1 The power conferred by ss 431 to 466 of the Companies Act 1985 to investigate a company and its affairs, as regards which s 452(1)(b) provides:

7 [1987] QB 433, [1989] 1 All ER 661, CA.
8 Ibid at 486G.
9 Ibid at 487D (Kerr LJ). See also Glidewell LJ at 490D.
10 [1989] 1 All ER 745, [1989] 2 WLR 458, HL.
11 Ibid at 762h and 479E, respectively.

'(1) Nothing in sections 431 to 446 requires the disclosure to the Secretary of State or to an inspector appointed by him:
(b) by a company's bankers (as such) of information as to the affairs of any of their customers other than the company.'

2 The power conferred by ss 447 to 451 of the Companies Act 1985 to requisition and seize books and papers of a company, as regards which s 452 (3) provides:

'(3) The Secretary of State shall not under section 447 require, or authorise an officer of his to require, the production by a person carrying on the business of banking of a document relating to the affairs of a customer of his unless either it appears to the Secretary of State that it is necessary to do so for the purpose of investigating the affairs of the first-mentioned person, or the customer is a person on whom a requirement has been imposed under that section, or under section 44(2) to (4) of the Insurance Companies Act 1982 (provision corresponding to section 447).'

3 The power conferred by s 105(1) of the Financial Services Act 1986 to investigate the affairs of any person relating to any investment business, as regards which s 105(7) provides:

'The Secretary of State shall not require an institution authorised under the Banking Act 1987 to disclose any information or produce any document relating to the affairs of a customer unless the Secretary of State considers it necessary to do so for the purpose of investigating any investment business carried on, or appearing to the Secretary of State to be carried on or to have been carried on, by the institution or customer or, if the customer is a related company of the person under investigation, by that person.'

4 The power conferred by s 177(1) of the Financial Services Act 1986 to investigate whether any contravention of ss 1, 2, 4 or 5 of the Companies (Insider Dealing) Act 1985 has occurred, as regards which s 177(8) provides:

'Nothing in this section shall require a person carrying on the business of banking to disclose any information or produce any document relating to the affairs of a customer unless:
(a) the customer is a person who the inspectors have reason to believe may be able to give information concerning a suspected contravention; and
(b) the Secretary of State is satisfied that the disclosure or production is necessary for the purposes of the investigation.'

7   DISCLOSURE TO INLAND REVENUE COMMISSIONERS

By s 24(1) and (2) of the Taxes Management Act 1970, a bank can be required to give information to the Commissioners of Inland Revenue as to the receipt of income from United Kingdom securities by persons other than the holders or from United Kingdom bearer securities. Tax inspectors have similar powers under s 17(1) of that Act.

By s 745(1) of the Income and Corporation Taxes Act 1988, the Commissioners of Inland Revenue have power by notice to require any person to furnish them within such time as they may direct, not being less than 28 days, with such particulars as they think necessary for the purposes of the tax provisions relating to the transfer of assets abroad (ss 739–746). However, by s 745(5), a bank is under no obligation to furnish particulars of any ordinary banking transactions between it and a customer carried out in the ordinary course of banking business unless the bank has acted or is acting on behalf of the customer in connection with (1) the formation or management of any body corporate resident or incorporated outside the United Kingdom which is, or if resident in the United Kingdom would be, a close company but not a trading company; or (2) the creation, or the execution of the trusts, of any settlement by virtue or in consequence of which income becomes payable to a person resident or domiciled outside the United Kingdom. The meaning of 'ordinary banking transactions' was considered in *Royal Bank of Canada v IRC* discussed in ch 6, ante.

8 DISCLOSURE PURSUANT TO CRIMINAL LAW STATUTES

(a) Drug Trafficking Offences Act 1986

Section 24 of the above Act provides, inter alia:

'**24. Assisting another to retain the benefit of drug trafficking** (1) Subject to subsection (3) below, if a person enters into or is otherwise concerned in an arrangement whereby:

(a) the retention or control by or on behalf of another (call him "A") of A's proceeds of drug trafficking is facilitated (whether by concealment, removal from the jurisdiction, transfer to nominees or otherwise), or

(b) A's proceeds of drug trafficking:

(i) are used to secure that funds are placed at A's disposal, or

(ii) are used for A's benefit to acquire property by way of investment,

knowing or suspecting that A is a person who carries on or has carried on drug trafficking or has benefited from drug trafficking, he is guilty of an offence.

(2) In this section, references to any person's proceeds of drug trafficking include a reference to any property which in whole or in part directly or indirectly represented in his hands his proceeds of drug trafficking.

(3) Where a person discloses to a constable a suspicion or belief that any funds or investments are derived from or used in connection with drug trafficking or any matter on which such a suspicion or belief is based:

(a) the disclosure shall not be treated as a breach of any restriction upon the disclosure of any information imposed by contract, and

(b) if he does any act in contravention of subsection (1) above and the disclosure relates to the arrangement concerned, he does not commit an offence under this section if the disclosure is made in accordance with this paragraph, that is:

(i) it is made before he does the act concerned, being an act done with the consent of the constable, or

(ii) it is made after he does the act, but is made on his initiative and as soon as it is reasonable for him to make it.'

'Property' is defined in s 38(1) to include, inter alia, money. The section appears not only to permit but to require disclosure by a bank of a *suspicion* that money in a bank account represents the proceeds of drug trafficking. By s 24(4) it is a defence for the accused to prove that he did not know or suspect that the arrangement related to any person's proceeds of drug trafficking or that by the arrangement the retention or control by or on behalf of A of any property was facilitated or used within s 24(1).

During the first 18 months of the 1986 Act being in force, banks and other financial institutions made disclosure to the National Drugs Intelligence Unit of some 500 transactions which had aroused their suspicion.[12]

(b) Police and Criminal Evidence Act 1984

Section 9 of the above Act empowers a constable to obtain access to specified material for the purposes of a criminal investigation by making an application under and in accordance with Sch 1 to the Act.

In *Barclays Bank plc v Taylor*,[13] two customers made counterclaims against their banks in respect of the banks' compliance with orders under s 9. It was alleged by the customer that the orders had been improperly made. The Court of Appeal struck out counterclaims alleging breach of contract by the banks in complying with the orders, on the grounds that: (1) a court order which was valid on its face was fully effective and demanded compliance unless and until it was set aside by the process of law, and therefore there had been no breach of the duty of confidentiality; and (2) there was no implied contractual obligation on the part of a bank to take action in support of the confidentiality of their customers' affairs by resisting a s 9 order and by informing a customer on learning that such an order was being sought.

12 (1988) Times, 24 June.
13 (1989) Times, 23 May, CA. See also *R v Manchester Crown Court* [1988] 2 All ER 769, [1988] 1 WLR 705, DC.

PART IV

CHEQUES AND OTHER ORDERS FOR PAYMENT

SUMMARY OF CONTENTS

CHAPTER 21

CHEQUES: GENERAL

1 DEFINITION

The cheque[1] is the customer's mandate and its payment or collection carries a serious responsibility for the bank concerned. The cheque remains the normal means by which a customer of a bank draws on his current account, and is defined by s 73 of the Bills of Exchange Act 1882 as 'a bill of exchange drawn on a banker payable on demand'. 'Banker' is not defined.[3]

In addition to being drawn on a banker, a cheque must conform to the requisites laid down by the Bills of Exchange Act as necessary to constitute a bill. By s 3(1), a bill is defined as:

'an unconditional order in writing addressed by one person to another, signed by the person giving it, requiring the person to whom it is addressed to pay on demand, or at a fixed or determinable future time, a sum certain in money to or to the order of a specified person or to bearer.'

(a) 'Unconditional order'

Instruments which require as a condition of payment the signing of a receipt are not cheques.[4] Where the condition is not imposed on the drawee-banker (the party to whom the order is given), but is addressed to and affects only the payee or holder, this does not make the cheque conditional.[5] The distinction is somewhat shadowy. A direction contained in the body of the instrument and running in terms such as:

'Pay John Jones on the attached receipt being duly signed'

---

1 For the general law as to cheques, see Bills of Exchange Act 1882, 5 Halsbury's Statutes (4th edn) 346; Cheques Act 1957, 5 Halsbury's Statutes (4th edn) 399; *Byles on Bills of Exchange* (25th edn,1988); *Chalmers' Digest of the Law of Bills of Exchange* (13th edn, 1964); 4 Halsbury's Laws (4th edn, Reissue) paras 163–190, 210–236.

3 As to the meaning of 'banker' at common law, see ch 6, ante.

4 See *Bavins Junior and Sims v London and South Western Bank* [1900] 1 QB 270; *Capital and Counties Bank Ltd v Gordon* [1903] AC 240.

5 *Nathan v Ogdens Ltd* (1905) 94 LT 126; *Thairlwall v Great Northern Rly Co* [1910] 2 KB 509; *Roberts & Co v Marsh* [1915] 1 KB 42. In the last-named case the word 'drawee' should read 'payee' throughout. See errata at beginning of the volume.

is addressed to the drawee and makes the document conditional; if it takes the form of a note such as:

'This receipt must be signed before presentment for payment'

it is taken to be addressed to and affect only the payee and not to impair the unconditional nature of the cheque, on the ground that it is only the *order* in a bill or cheque which must be unconditional under s 3 of the Bills of Exchange Act.[6]

To be unconditional a cheque must not be made payable out of a particular fund[7] or payable on a contingency.[8] In *Thairlwall v Great Northern Rly Co*[9] a dividend warrant bore a note to the effect that it would 'not be honoured after three months from the date of issue unless specially indorsed by the Secretary.' It was held that the bill was unconditional. The words were merely a definition by the directors acting within their authority as to what was a reasonable time within which the warrant had to be presented having regard to the nature of the instrument, the usage of trade and bankers, and the facts of the particular case. A cheque is none the less an unconditional order notwithstanding that by s 74 of the Bills of Exchange Act the drawer may be discharged if the cheque is not presented within a reasonable time.[10]

(b) 'Addressed by one person to another'

A cheque, like all bills of exchange, must be addressed by one person to another. There must be one person as drawer, another, a bank, as drawee.[11] The head office and branches of a bank constitute for general purposes only one concern or legal entity.[12] For this reason drafts drawn by one branch of a bank on another branch or the head office are not cheques or bills.

Section 5(2) of the Bills of Exchange Act enacts that:

'Where in a bill drawer and drawee are the same person ... the holder may treat the instrument at his option either as a bill of exchange or as a promissory note'.

This certainly appears to contemplate a bill in which drawer and drawee are the same person, as does, to a lesser extent, s 50(2)(c). The true interpretation of those sections is, however, that though such an instrument is not really a bill, the holder may treat it as such,[13] but even then need not give notice of

---

6 Instruments which combine cheque and receipt forms are subject to the public circular dated 23 September 1957 issued by the Committee of London Clearing Bankers. The effect of such instruments is dealt with below in ch 23 – 'Cheques: Instruments Analogous' post.

7 Bills of Exchange Act 1882, s 8, (3).

8 Bills of Exchange Act 1882, s 11.

9 [1910] 2 KB 509; for a full discussion of this instrument see *Paget* (8th edn) pp 219–223.

10 Ibid, per Lord Coleridge J at 520.

11 *Vagliano Bros v Bank of England* (1889) 23 QBD 243 at 248, CA; *London City and Midland Bank Ltd v Gordon* [1903] AC 240.

12 *Prince v Oriental Bank Corpn* (1878) 3 App Cas 325. The decision of Bailhache J in *Ross v London County Westminster and Parr's Bank Ltd* [1919] 1 KB 678 that a draft drawn by one branch of a bank on another branch of the same bank was a cheque is clearly wrong. Cf *Slingsby v Westminster Bank Ltd* [1931] 1 KB 173, where Finlay J held that an instrument drawn on the Bank of England and signed by the chief accountant was a cheque, because the Chief Accountant in appending his signature acted as agent of the government. The substance of the transaction was that the government was drawing on moneys in the hands of the Bank. See also Bigham J in *Brown Brough & Co v National Bank of India Ltd* (1902) 18 TLR 669 at 670.

13 *Re British Trade Corpn Ltd* [1932] 2 Ch 1, per Greer LJ at 11 and per Romer LJ at 14.

dishonour to the drawer. The right so to treat it is, in any event, confined to the holder.[14]

(c) 'On demand'

A cheque must be payable on demand. The omission of the words 'on demand' in the ordinary cheque form is justified by s 10 of the Bills of Exchange Act, which provides:

'A bill is payable on demand
(a) which is expressed to be payable on demand or at sight or on presentation, or
(b) in which no time for payment is expressed'.

Sometimes instruments in cheque form bear a note to the effect that they must be presented within a given period or they will not be paid. In *Thairlwall v Great Northern Rly Co,* ante, Bray J further held that the note on the warrant that it would not be honoured after three months from the date of issue did not prevent the instrument from being payable on demand.

(d) 'To a specified person or to bearer'

By s 7(1):

'Where a bill is not payable to bearer, the payee must be named or otherwise indicated therein with reasonable certainty.'

The normal cheque is one in which there is a drawer, a drawee banker and a payee, or no payee but bearer. The payee is, as the term imports, the person to whom the drawer primarily intends and directs payment to be made. Subject to crossings, it rests entirely with the payee whether he presents the cheque or negotiates it.

The section uses the expression 'not payable to bearer', as distinct from 'not payable to order or to bearer'. In *Gerald McDonald & Co v Nash & Co,*[15] bills were drawn payable to the drawer's order, and the question arose whether the instruments were complete bills in that form. In the event, the point was not finally determined because it was unanimously held by the House of Lords that even if the bills had been wanting in any material particular the drawers had validly filled up the omission pursuant to s 20(1) of the Act.[16] On the completeness of the bills, Lord Sumner doubted whether the bills were complete,[17] and further held that s 8(5), which provides that a bill expressed to be payable to the order of a specified person is nevertheless payable to him or his order at his option, does not deal with the conditions necessary for a complete bill or declare that a bill drawn in this form is complete. However, Viscount Haldane LC, relying upon s 8(5), held the bills complete in their original form,[18] and this appears the correct view.

---

14 *London City and Midland Bank Ltd v Gordon* [1903] AC 240.
15 [1924] AC 625, HL.
16 Section 20(1) provides, so far as material, that when a bill is wanting in any material particular, the person in possession of it has a prima facie authority to fill up the omission in any way he thinks fit.
17 Ibid at 652.
18 Ibid at 633.

2 PROBLEM CASES

(a) Fictitious or non-existing payee

By s 7(3):

'Where the payee is a fictitious or non-existing person, the bill may be treated as payable to bearer'.

It is first necessary to explain the relevance of this subsection. As between the drawer of a cheque and a third party to whom the proceeds have been paid, its relevance can be illustrated by the facts of *Clutton v Attenborough & Son*.[19] An employer was fraudulently induced by an employee to draw cheques in favour of a non-existent payee, whose indorsement was then forged by that employee in favour of a bona fide transferee for value. After discovery of the fraud, the drawer of the cheque claimed to recover the proceeds from the transferee. If the transferee's title had been dependent upon the fraudulent indorsement it would have been defective, because by s 24 of the Bills of Exchange Act a forged signature is wholly inoperative. However, by s 7(3) the bill became payable to bearer, and the transferee therefore did not have to rely upon the indorsement and was entitled to retain the proceeds.

As between banker and customer, s 7(3) has the consequence that payment by a bank in circumstances such as existed in *Clutton v Attenborough* is within the mandate, being payment of a valid cheque drawn by its customer payable to bearer.

As to what is fictitious or non-existing, the leading case is *Bank of England v Vagliano Bros*,[20] where, on the particular facts, the effect of s 7(3) was held to be that a bill may be treated as payable to bearer where the person named as payee and to whose order the bill is made payable on the face of it is a *real* person but has not and never was intended by the drawer to have any right upon it or arising out of it.

The House of Lords rejected the submission that the words 'where the payee is a fictitious person' apply only where the payee never had a real existence. In the words of Lord Herschell:[1]

'It seems to me, then, that where the name inserted as that of the payee is so inserted by way of pretence only, it may, without impropriety, be said that the payee is a feigned or pretended, or, in other words, a fictitious person.'

---

19 [1897] AC 90.
20 [1891] AC 107. The observation of Lord Halsbury LC at p 122 that the section is dealing with the form of the instrument appears incorrect. The form of a cheque is unaffected by the insertion of a fictitious or non-existing payee, unless the name inserted is such as to render the mandate uncertain.

The decision is far reaching because the instruments in question were not bills at all, the drawer's signature having been forged. As it is put in the headnote immediately following the above statement as to the effect of s 7(3): 'and this is so though the bill (so called) is not in reality a bill but is in fact a document in the form of a bill manufactured by a person who forges the signature of the named drawer, obtains by fraud the signature of the acceptor, forges the signature of the named payee, and presents the document for payment, both the named drawer and the named payee being entirely ignorant of the circumstances.' The wording of s 7(3) appears to require the existence of a bill. This difficulty was overcome by holding that Vagliano, as acceptor, was estopped from denying that the instrument was a bill.

1 [1891] AC 107 at 153.

Vagliano was followed by three further cases turning on s 7(3): (1) *Clutton v Attenborough & Son*,[2] supra, where the payee did not exist and the cheque was accordingly held by the House of Lords to be within the section; (2) *Vinden v Hughes*,[3] where a clerk fraudulently induced his employer to draw cheques in favour of customers, whose indorsements the clerk subsequently forged. It was held by Warrington J that at the time the cheques were drawn, the employer believed that they were being drawn in the ordinary course of business for the purpose of the money being paid to the named payees. Accordingly the payees were not fictitious; (3) *North and South Wales Bank Ltd v Macbeth*,[4] where the payee was an existing person who was intended to have the benefit of the cheque and it was accordingly held by the House of Lords that the payee was a real and not a fictitious person.

The following general principles can be extracted from the decisions:

1 The primary factor is the state of mind and intention of the drawer of the bill or cheque; if his mind is directed to a specific existing individual, whom he intends to receive the money, such a payee is not a fictitious or non-existing person, even though by reason of fraud on the part of a third party in obtaining the instrument, such individual never acquired or exercised any rights in relation thereto;

2 If, by fraud of a third party, a man is induced to draw a bill or cheque in which the name inserted as the payee's is that of an imaginary person (although people of that name may exist), such payee is 'a non-existing person' although the drawer contemplated someone of that name receiving the money;

3 Where a bill or cheque falls within the subsection, it may be treated as payable to bearer not only by a holder for value but by anyone else whose interest it is so to treat it, eg, a banker who has paid such a bill on a forged indorsement.

Section 7(3) authorises treating a cheque as payable to bearer only where the payee is a fictitious or non-existing '*person*', defined in s 2 as follows:

'"Person" includes a body of persons, whether incorporated or not.'

This could hardly apply to an impersonal payee.[5]

(b) 'Wages' or 'cash'

Instruments are often drawn on a cheque form to order but in favour of 'Wages' or 'Cash'; there is in these cases no payee and the instruments are not bills of exchange or cheques and thus s 7(3) has no application.

In *North and South Insurance Corpn Ltd v National Provincial Bank Ltd*,[6] an instrument in the form of a cheque drawn 'pay cash or order' was delivered by the drawer to a company in payment for services. The instrument was

---

2 [1897] AC 90, explained in *North and South Wales Bank Ltd v Macbeth*, post.
3 [1905] 1 KB 795, approved in *Coldman v Cox* (1924) 40 TLR 744.
4 [1908] AC 137, HL.
5 Cf *North and South Wales Bank Ltd v Macbeth* [1908] AC 137 at 140 and see Lord Mansfield in *Grant v Vaughan* (1764) 1 Wm Bl 485.
6 [1936] 1 KB 328, approved in *Orbit Mining and Trading Co Ltd v Westminster Bank Ltd* [1963] 1 QB 794; and see also *Cole v Milsome* [1951] 1 All ER 311, in which Lloyd-Jacob J at 313 came to the same conclusion in regard to an instrument which in all material respects was the same.

duly presented to the drawer's bank and paid. An action was subsequently brought by the liquidator of the drawer claiming that the bank had acted without authority in paying the instrument. It was first contended that the instrument was a cheque drawn to order and accordingly required endorsement. Branson J held that the instrument was not a cheque. In his view, the printed words 'or order' were to be disregarded, with the result that the instrument was a direction to pay cash. Accordingly the document was not drawn to pay any person at all, and not being payable to a specified person or bearer, failed to satisfy s 7 of the Act. It was then contended that if the instrument was not a cheque, it contained no mandate justifying its being acted upon as in fact it was. In rejecting this contention, Branson J held that the drawer had intended the bank to pay the person presenting the document and that the bank had properly interpreted the intention of the drawer, and accordingly the latter could not then question the transaction.

Such instruments are clearly not negotiable. However, they fall within ss 1(2)(a) and 4(2)(b) of the Cheques Act 1957 as being documents issued by a customer which, though not bills of exchange, are intended to enable a person to obtain payment from the banker of the sum mentioned in them.

A cheque payable to 'Wages or bearer', 'Petty cash or bearer', or in any such form where 'bearer' is used instead of 'order', is, of course, payable to bearer, and therefore there is a payee (bearer) within the meaning of s 3(1).[7]

(c) No payee

A cheque drawn 'Pay   order', indorsed by the drawer, would be a good cheque, the words being construed as equivalent to 'Pay to my order'.[8] A cheque payable to 'Pay   or order' is not a bill because there is no payee, as was held in *R v Randall*.[9] The question as to the effect of such a document, and in particular the nature of any estoppel arising out of its indorsement, was raised, but not decided, in *Chamberlain v Young and Tower*.[10] A banker to whom an instrument in this form is presented for payment would probably act wisely in declining to pay it. Nor could he be certain of bettering his position by requesting the holder to fill in his own name as payee because the authority to fill up a blank bill, given by s 20, is only a prima facie one and may have been revoked, and moreover the omission must be filled up within a reasonable time and in strict conformity with the authority given. However, as in *North and South Insurance Corpn Ltd v National Provincial Bank Ltd,* the fact that the instrument is not a cheque would not preclude the court from finding that the drawer intended his banker to effect payment to the person presenting the document, and moreover such an instrument would seem to fall within ss 1(2)(a) and 4(2)(b) of the Cheques Act 1957.

The common law doctrine of estoppel arising from delivery of a blank or incomplete negotiable instrument is supplemented by s 20 of the Bills of Exchange Act.[11] By the judgment of the House of Lords in *London Joint*

7 See also *Grant v Vaughan* (1764) 1 Wm Bl 485, where it was held that a draft payable to 'ship Fortune or bearer' was payable to bearer alone.
8 *Chamberlain v Young and Tower* [1893] 2 QB 206; cf *North and South Insurance Corpn Ltd v National Provincial Bank Ltd* [1936] 1 KB 328.
9 (1811) Russ & Ry 195; *R v Richards* (1811) Russ & Ry 193.
10 [1893] 2 QB 206.
11 See *Lloyds Bank Ltd v Cooke* [1907] 1 KB 794; *Smith v Prosser* [1907] 2 KB 735 distinguishing *Lloyds Bank Ltd v Cooke* on the ground that in that case the instruments were and were intended to be negotiable instruments.

Stock Bank Ltd v Macmillan and Arthur,[12] the operation of the estoppel is not confined to the payee or holder in due course of a cheque, but extends in fitting cases to cover the bank which pays it.

In *Daun and Vallentin v Sherwood,*[13] Kennedy J held that a promissory note without a payee, and which contained neither the words 'order' nor 'bearer', was payable to bearer 'because that is the natural legal effect'. The decision appears to conflict with the clear terms of s 7(1). The reasoning would in any event not apply in a case such as *Chamberlain v Young and Tower*[14] because the use of the words 'or order' negatives the idea of the cheque being payable to bearer.

(d) Post-dated cheques

A post-dated cheque is an instrument which bears a date later than the date of its issue. Such an instrument is undoubtedly a bill of exchange. This follows from s 13(2) of the Bills of Exchange Act 1882, which provides:

'A bill is not invalid by reason only that it is ante-dated or post-dated. . . .'[15]

The cases establish the validity and capacity for negotiation of a post-dated cheque between the date of its issue and its maturity date (ie the date it bears), and for a reasonable time thereafter.[16]

The more important question is whether a post-dated cheque is a cheque properly so called, ie a bill of exchange drawn on a banker payable *on demand*. The importance of this question is that if a post-dated cheque is not a cheque in the strict sense, then first, the protection of the Cheques Act 1957 may be unavailable,[17] and secondly, the drawer may be discharged in default of due presentment.[18]

There was formerly a third consequence, namely that bills other than cheques attracted ad valorem stamp duty. For this reason the status of post-dated cheques has tended to arise in the form of disputes as to the admissibility in evidence of instruments not bearing ad valorem stamp duty. The leading authority is *Royal Bank of Scotland v Tottenham.*[19] In upholding the admissi-

---

12 [1918] AC 777.
13 (1895) 11 TLR 211.
14 [1893] 2 QB 206.
15 The position before the 1882 Act was different – see *Emanuel v Robarts* (1868) 9 B & S 121, which proceeded on the basis that there were then doubts as to the legality of a post-dated cheque.
16 See *Hitchcock v Edwards* (1889) 60 LT 636; *Carpenter v Street* (1890) 6 TLR 410; *Royal Bank of Scotland v Tottenham* [1894] 2 QB 715; *Robinson v Benkel* (1913) 29 TLR 475. This statement (as it appeared in *Paget* (8th edn)) was cited with approval by the New South Wales Court of Appeal in *Hodgson & Lee Pty Ltd v Mardonius Pty Ltd* (1986) 5 NSWLR 496 at 498–499.
17 The question whether a post-dated cheque is a cheque strictly so called is not wholly determinative of the availability of protection under the Cheques Act 1957. There is an argument that such an instrument, even if not a cheque, is a document issued by a customer of a banker which, though not a bill of exchange, is intended to enable a person to obtain payment from that banker in the sum mentioned in the document (see ss 1(2)(a) and 4(2)(b)). This would involve construing the words 'though not a bill of exchange' as having the inclusive meaning 'even if not a bill of exchange'.
18 See the Bills of Exchange Act 1882, s 45, and *Hodgson & Lee Pty Ltd v Mardonius Pty Ltd* (1986) 5 NSWLR 496.
19 [1894] 2 QB 715.

bility in evidence of such an instrument, the Court of Appeal treated a post-dated cheque as a valid cheque at the relevant date, ie the date on which the cheque had been tendered in evidence, which date was after the date of the cheque itself. The Court of Appeal construed s 13(2) of the Bills of Exchange Act 1882 ('A *bill* is not invalid by reason only that it is ... post-dated. ....') to include the proposition that a *cheque* shall not be invalid by reason only of its being post-dated.[20]

A more detailed analysis of the problem was made by the New South Wales Court of Appeal in *Hodgson & Lee Pty Ltd v Mardonius Pty Ltd,*[1] where the drawer of a post-dated cheque sought to escape liability on the ground that the holder had failed to make due presentment. In rejecting this unmeritorious defence, the Court of Appeal analysed statutory provisions corresponding with ss 3, 10 and 11 of the Bills of Exchange Act 1882, and concluded convincingly that a post-dated cheque is not payable at a fixed or determinable future time, and must therefore be payable on demand. On this view, a post-dated cheque is a valid cheque not simply from the date it bears, but from the date of its issue.[2] It was rightly pointed out that in *Bank of Baroda Ltd v Punjab National Bank Ltd,*[3] Lord Wright, delivering the advice of the Judicial Committee, treated the post-dated cheque in question as a cheque and not as a bill of exchange payable at some later date.

3 NEGOTIABILITY AND TRANSFERABILITY

Cheques, being bills of exchange, are basically negotiable instruments, but there may be a perfectly good cheque which is not negotiable (apart altogether from the case of a cheque crossed 'not negotiable'), as where a cheque is made not transferable. This would be the case if a cheque were drawn payable to a specified person 'only' or where the words 'not transferable' were written prominently across the cheque. The mandate embodied in such a cheque would seem to place on the drawee banker the responsibility of ensuring that only the payee, and no-one else, was paid. A non-transferable or non-negotiable instrument should be capable of delivery to an agent purely for collection and it is hardly within the contemplation of the drawer that the payee must himself present the cheque, though the intention that he shall not negotiate it is clear. A corporate body can, of course, only act by a servant and payment to the servant would not be in breach of the mandate to pay the corporation 'only'.

If it is permissible to transfer to a collecting agent a cheque drawn payable to 'X only' it would be permissible to cross it; but a collecting banker should

---

20 See [1894] 2 QB 715 at 718, per Lord Esher MR ('On the other hand, s 13 of the Bills of Exchange Act 1882, says that a cheque shall not be invalid by reason only of its being post-dated'), and at 719, per Kay LJ ('The Bills of Exchange Act 1882, expressly says that a post-dated cheque is not for that reason only invalid').

1 (1986) 5 NSWLR 496. Cf *Brien v Dwyer* (1979) 141 CLR 378.

2 In *Royal Bank of Scotland v Tottenham, ante,* Lord Esher MR appears to have considered that during the period up to the date of the cheque, the instrument would not have been a cheque for the purposes of the Stamp Act 1891, but it is not clear whether he considered that the status of the instrument would have been the same during that period under the Bills of Exchange Act 1882.

3 [1944] AC 176, [1944] 2 All ER 83.

not collect for anyone other than X, though he might have a set-off against the proceeds in respect of any indebtedness of the drawer to him.[4]

It is deducible from the wording of s 8(1) that a bill which is not negotiable (as distinct from a cheque crossed 'not negotiable') is not only not negotiable, but not transferable; while it would seem from s 36(1) that a negotiable bill (not including the cheque crossed 'not negotiable') is not only transferable but, until restrictively indorsed or overdue, fully negotiable.

A cheque, 'Pay AB', without the addition of the words 'or order' or 'or bearer', is negotiable by indorsement of AB under s 8(4) of the Bills of Exchange Act.

A cheque payable to the order of AB is payable to him or his order at his option.[5]

The common form of cheque, 'Pay self or order', is justified by s 5(1):

'a bill may be drawn payable to or to the order of the drawer'.

4 NOTICE OF DISHONOUR

A cheque being a bill, the drawer is entitled to notice of dishonour and if it is not given and not excused by circumstances,[6] he is discharged from liability both on the cheque and on the consideration for which it was given.[7] It is anomalous that the drawer of a cheque should be entitled to notice of dishonour, seeing that he is the party primarily liable, and has no remedy over against anyone. In most cases, however, notice would be dispensed with.[8]

---

4 The effect of the crossing 'not negotiable' on a bill other than a cheque was discussed in *Hibernian Bank Ltd v Gysin and Hanson* [1939] 1 KB 483; and see p 376, post.
5 Section 8(5).
6 Bills of Exchange Act 1882, s 48; *Peacock v Pursell* (1863) 14 CBNS 728; *May v Chidley* [1894] 1 QB 451.
7 Bills of Exchange Act 1882, s 50(2)(c).
8 Bills of Exchange Act 1882, s 50(2); as to notice of dishonour by the collecting banker, see post, 'Collecting Banker'.

CHAPTER 22

CHEQUES: CROSSED[1]

The law relating to crossed cheques is mainly to be found in ss 76 to 81 of the Bills of Exchange Act 1882 – the crossed cheque sections – and in s 4 of the Cheques Act 1957. The Act authorises two types of crossing – general and special. By s 76(1), a general crossing is constituted by the addition across the face of a cheque of (a) the words 'and company', or an abbreviation thereof between two parallel transverse lines, either with or without the words 'not negotiable'; or (b) two parallel transverse lines simply, either with or without the words 'not negotiable'.

By s 76(2), a special crossing is constituted by the addition across the face of a cheque of the name of a banker, again either with or without the words 'not negotiable'. Any authorised crossing is a material part of a cheque (s 78) and if tampered with might fall foul of s 64 as being a material alteration.

1 EFFECT OF CROSSING

(a) General effect

The several crossings have different effect, but any crossing requires that if the paying banker is to obtain the protection conferred by s 80 he must pay only to another banker. Apart from requiring payment to another banker general crossings (except the 'not negotiable' crossing) have no effect on a bank. The 'not negotiable' crossing, however, is a very different matter; and last in the present context may be mentioned the marking on a cheque of the words 'a/c payee' or something similar. This latter is unauthorised by statute; the effect of its addition is dealt with later.

Apart from the 'not negotiable' crossing none of the authorised forms has any effect on the negotiability of the cheque. It is suggested that no transferee of a cheque crossed 'not negotiable' can be a holder in due course, but if the cheque is not affected by fraud and no party to it has a defective title, it is submitted that the transferee is in the same position as if the cheque were not so crossed. The crossing tells the transferee that he may not get a good title

---

1 The protection given by the statutes to the paying and collecting bankers, including the meaning of 'true owner', 'good faith' and 'without negligence', are dealt with in ch 24–26, post. For a history of the crossed cheques legislation see *Byles on Bills of Exchange* (26th edn, 1988).

by the transfer, that he takes a risk, but his title is as good as that of a holder in due course if the cheque is not affected by fraud or other defects of title.

(b) Crossed to two bankers

Section 79 deals with the case where a cheque is crossed to two bankers, i.e. it bears on its face the crossings of two bankers, in which case the drawee bank must refuse payment except only where one crossing is that of one bank acting as agent of the other.[2] Where the customer of the collecting bank has no title, failure to refuse renders the drawee bank liable to the true owner of the cheque for any loss he may sustain by reason of the wrongful payment. This is not unreasonable, for unless one of the crossings is that of an agent for collection known to the collecting bank to be such, the fact that there are two crossings ought to arouse suspicion in the mind of the drawee bank, though the ultimate collecting banker might feel happy to take whatever risk there might be on the strength of what it knew of the initial collecting bank. In *Smith v Union Bank of London*[3] a cheque was crossed to two bankers and was paid by the drawee bank to the holder in spite of the fact. The Court of Appeal held that the negotiability of the cheque was not affected and that the holder was a lawful holder. To meet this decision the 'not negotiable' crossing was introduced.

(c) Payment contrary to crossing

Section 79 requires a banker to refuse payment of a cheque crossed specially to more than one banker. The Act contains no corresponding prohibition on the payment of a generally crossed cheque otherwise than to another banker. However, s 80 has the effect that a banker on whom a crossed cheque is drawn is liable to the true owner unless in good faith and without negligence he pays it, if crossed generally, to a banker, and if crossed specially, to the banker to whom it is crossed, or to his agent for collection being a banker.

Payment contrary to the crossing is, apart from any statutory enactment, negligence on the part of the banker, and if loss ensues, the banker cannot charge the customer. In *Bellamy v Marjoribanks* in 1852,[4] at which date there was no crossed cheques legislation in existence but a custom to pay only to another banker, the court said:

> 'If the banker disregarded the custom, and paid the cheque to a private individual, that circumstance would be strong evidence against him in the event of his seeking to charge his customer with the payment, if the person actually presenting it was not the lawful holder and bearer of the cheque'.[4a]

The negligence is today obviously greater because of the statutory recognition and regulation of crossings.

In the face of the crossed cheques sections and the universal practice of bankers, no banker could for a moment contend that he did not understand what his customer meant by crossing the cheque. The customer does not do it to afford the banker statutory protection, but for his own protection. In

2 Section 79(2). As to the protection conferred by the proviso to s 79, see ch 24, post.
3 (1875) 1 QBD 31.
4 (1852) 7 Exch 389.
4a Ibid., at 404.

Aronowitz v R[5] the petitioner contended that the crossed cheque which he presented over the counter and which was refused payment on the ground of its being crossed was thereby dishonoured. This was obviously a hopeless contention for the cheque was not 'duly presented' within the meaning of s 47.

(d) Crossing by 'holder'

Subsections 77(1) to (4) deal with the crossing of cheques by the drawer or 'holder'. The holder need not be a holder for value. Section 2 defines 'holder' as the payee or indorsee of a bill who is in possession of it or the bearer thereof, not a lawful holder necessarily. The word 'lawful', which occurred in the Crossed Cheques Act 1876, is omitted in s 77 of the Bills of Exchange Act 1882. A thief in possession of a bearer cheque is a holder, as is an agent for collection. An innocent possessor for value of an order cheque under a forged indorsement is not a 'holder' except by estoppel against an indorser subsequent to the forgery;[6] he is not a holder within the Act, and accordingly it is submitted that he could not cross the cheque so as to provide any protection for the collecting or the paying banker. However, in *Akrokerri (Atlantic) Mines Ltd v Economic Bank*,[7] Bank A received from a customer for collection crossed order cheques on which the customer had forged the payees' indorsements. Bank A specially crossed these cheques to Bank B for presentation and payment. Bigham J treated this as a special crossing by a 'holder' and said that when the cheques reached Bank B they were specially crossed to that bank.

(e) Opening a crossing

It is not uncommon for a drawer to 'open' a crossing, as it is termed, in a sense neutralising it by writing 'Pay cash' and initialling the amendment, and the practice received some sanction from *Smith v Union Bank of London*.[8] Only the drawer can open and he may do so either before the cheque is delivered to the payee or at the request of the payee after delivery. Once the drawer has issued the cheque he cannot retract or neutralise his mandate to the prejudice of anyone who has taken the cheque on the faith of the instrument as delivered to him. Thus in *Smith v Union Bank of London*[9] where the cheque had been issued, indorsed by the payee and sold by a thief to a third party, the Court of Appeal contemplated opening of the crossing by the *joint* action by the drawer and lawful holder. Although the Act does not authorise the opening of a crossing, in principle it is within the capacity of the drawer to amend the instrument before issue, and to do so even after issue if the holder consents. Such an amendment is not an obliteration, addition or alteration of a crossing within s 78, for that section is concerned with unilateral acts after issue.

In *Smith and Baldwin v Barclays Bank Ltd*,[10] one of several cheques was

5 (1927) Times, 18 November.
6 Section 55(2).
7 [1904] 2 KB 465.
8 See (1875) 1 QBD 31 at 35.
9 (1875) 1 QBD 31.
10 (1944) 5 Legal Decisions Affecting Bankers 370 at 375.

crossed 'not negotiable' and superimposed on it were the words 'please pay cash'. Stable J said:

'It is conceded[11] that that alteration [the writing of the words 'please pay cash'] to the printed form does not make the instrument any the less a crossed cheque, so that in relation to that cheque as well as the others the defence of s 82 is open to the bank.'

It is not stated in the report on what basis this concession was made, and it is submitted that it was wrong. If, contrary to the above view, a cheque is a crossed cheque notwithstanding the crossing's being opened, the paying banker should never pay it over the counter unless satisfied that this was the drawer's intention.

Presumably the banker paying across the counter a cheque on which the crossing had been opened by his customer would be entitled to indemnity from the latter. But if the 'opening' is a forgery it is ineffective and the banker paying would pay contrary to his mandate.

On 7 November 1912 the Committee of London Clearing Bankers passed a resolution in the following terms:

That no opening of cheques be recognised unless the full signature of the drawer be appended to the alteration, and then only when presented for payment by the drawer or his known agent.'

The general practice of English banks is more or less in accordance with this regulation, though the full signature is often not required.

(f) Crossing by collecting banker

The power of crossing cheques given by s 77 to a 'holder' is not confined to a holder for value. The collecting banker is a 'holder' and, apart from the special powers given him under s 77(5) and (6), may exercise a holder's powers of crossing including the right to cross a cheque specially to himself. Today the anomaly which existed before the passing of the Cheques Act 1957 by which crossed and uncrossed cheques were very different in their effect on a collecting banker has been eliminated. Nevertheless, sub-ss (5) and (6) of s 77 of the Bills of Exchange Act 1882 have not been repealed and the benefit of crossing is still available to a banker transmitting a cheque for collection; the sub-ss are as follows:

(5) 'Where a cheque is crossed specially, the banker to whom it is crossed may again cross it specially to another banker for collection.'
(6) 'Where an uncrossed cheque or a cheque crossed generally is sent to a banker for collection, he may cross it specially to himself.'

It has been contended that sub-s (6) enabled a banker, by crossing a cheque sent to him uncrossed for collection, to obtain the protection of the statute, but this view was conclusively rejected in *Gordon v Capital and Counties Bank Ltd*;[12] today the Cheques Act 1957 makes no distinction between crossed and uncrossed cheques.

11 Whether by counsel in that case or by the learned judge himself is not clear.
12 [1902] 1 KB 242; affd [1903] AC 240.

(g) Crossing between branches

Cheques may be presented for payment crossed to two offices of the same bank, the cheque having been transmitted from one to the other for convenience of collection. The second crossing does not seem to fall exactly within either subsection. It may be a crossing 'to another banker', although for many purposes head office and branches constitute only one entity; but if this is wrong, the two crossings would presumably be regarded as one only and neither paying nor collecting banker would be prejudiced thereby.

2   THE 'NOT NEGOTIABLE' CROSSING[13]

(a) General effect

The 'not negotiable' crossing on a cheque is authorised by s 76 and a major effect of such a crossing is to be found in s 81 which provides:

'Where a person takes a crossed cheque which bears on it the words "not negotiable", he shall not have and shall not be capable of giving a better title to the cheque than that which the person from whom he took it had.'

The effect of the crossing is that the cheque remains transferable, but is deprived of the full character of negotiability. However honestly and for value a transferee may take it, he cannot acquire any better title to the cheque or its proceeds, or any better right against any prior party to it, than his transferor had. So long, however, as there is no defect of title, or failure of consideration, the cheque may pass from hand to hand just as if it was an open cheque or a simply crossed cheque, and each successive holder acquires full rights and title thereon.

(b) Affects cheque and proceeds

In *Great Western Rly Co v London and County Banking Co,* it was sought to establish a distinction between the cheque and its proceeds. It was contended that s 81 in terms only affected the title to the *cheque,* and that, therefore, if an innocent holder of such a cheque obtained the *proceeds* he could hold them as against the true owner of the cheque. The House of Lords, however, put the rational interpretation on the section; Lord Halsbury C, said:[14]

'The supposed distinction between the title to the cheque itself and the title to the money obtained or represented by it seems to me to be absolutely illusory. The language of the statute seems to me to be clear enough. It would be absolutely defeated by holding that a fraudulent holder of the cheque could give a title either to the cheque or to the money.'

And Lord Lindley:[15]

'... it is said that, although the bank had a defective title to the cheque, they have a good title to the money paid to them as holders of it. My Lords, so to construe the section would destroy more than half its utility; a cheque marked "not nego-

---

13 As to the effect of the 'not negotiable' crossing on the paying and the collecting bankers, see chs 24, 26, post.
14 [1901] AC 414 at 418.
15 Ibid., at 424. See also *Morison v London County and Westminster Bank Ltd* [1914] 3 KB 356 at 375.

tiable" would be no safer than any other cheque if once cashed, i.e., unless payment of it was stopped before it was presented ... Everyone who takes a cheque marked "not negotiable" takes it at his own risk, and his title to the money got by its means is as defective as his title to the cheque itself.'

(c) Title void or voidable

Where a fully negotiable instrument by reason, say, of the circumstances under which it has been obtained, is voidable but not void, even the person who has so obtained it has a temporary revocable property in it. If, prior to its revocation or repudiation, an innocent third party takes the instrument as holder for value, or even without value, subsequent revocation or repudiation cannot affect his rights or fix liability upon him.[16] However, in the case of a cheque marked 'not negotiable', it matters not whether the defect of title is such as to render the cheque void or merely voidable. In the *Great Western Railway* case, one Huggins, not a customer, falsely obtained from the plaintiffs a cheque in his own favour. It was argued that 'Huggins' title was voidable, not void, and could not be avoided after a bona fide transfer without notice. As to this Lord Lindley commented:[17]

'Whether the cheque was void or only voidable, as contended by Mr Lawrence, appears to me really immaterial. Be it void or be it voidable, it was not negotiable, and by s 81 of the Bills of Exchange Act 1882, Huggins was not capable of giving a better title to the cheque than he had himself.'

Thus where the voidable instrument is a cheque crossed 'not negotiable', the distinction between void and voidable is swept away. Subject to the statutory protection in favour of bankers, no rights countervailing repudiation of a voidable contract can be acquired through a cheque crossed 'not negotiable'. Each holder is put on precisely the same footing, depending upon the earliest title. On repudiation or revocation of a voidable contract affecting such cheque, the title of the true owner relates back to the date of the fraud or other circumstance which entitles him to repudiate. Every person who has taken or dealt with the cheque does so on the basis that his position is subject to possible revocation. Any of the successive holders can be sued for conversion, it being no defence that he has parted with the article converted. The document is in fact 'on much the same footing as an overdue bill'.[18]

(d) 'Not negotiable' must be combined with crossing

The words 'not negotiable' have no statutory effect by themselves. The cheque must be crossed if the words are to have the effect given by s 81, and without a crossing as defined in s 76(1), they have no effect on its negotiability. It would be incongruous to accord to those words, without a crossing, the effect conferred on them by statute when used in conjunction with a crossing. The meaning of s 81 cannot be given to the words by themselves, but they would seem to take effect by s 8(1) unless cheques are to be excluded from its

16 *Tate v Wilts and Dorset Bank* (1899) 1 Legal Decisions Affecting Bankers 286.
17 [1901] AC 414 at 424.
18 In early editions of *Paget*, this statement is attributed to Sir Mackenzie Chalmers. The status of a cheque crossed 'not negotiable' was defined along similar lines by Vaughan Williams LJ in *Great Western Rly v London and County Banking Co* [1900] 2 QB 464 at 474. Although the House of Lords reversed the Court of Appeal on other grounds, they took the same view on this point.

operation, s 81 referring to cheques, s 8 to bills. 'Bill' includes 'cheque', so s 81 must be regarded as an exception to s 8 so far as cheques are concerned. Instruments falling within both ss 8 and 81 are alike in that neither is negotiable; they differ in that those within s 8 are not even transferable, whereas those within s 81 are.

(e) Placing of 'not negotiable'

The Bills of Exchange Act does not require the words 'not negotiable' in order to be effectual to be between the two parallel transverse lines of a crossing. In s 76(1)(a), 'with or without the words "not negotiable"' seems more properly to be read with the words immediately preceding, viz 'two transverse parallel lines', than with 'and company or any abbreviation thereof', denoting that it is only the latter which must be between the lines. In s 76(1)(b) there is no mention of anything at all being between the lines. 'Transverse lines with or without the words "not negotiable"' is equally fulfilled whether the words, when used, are between the lines or not. In the case of specially crossed cheques, transverse parallel lines are not necessary and would be superfluous. Subsection (2) of s 76 does not prescribe them, and under s 77(3) a holder may, in the case of a cheque crossed generally, add the name of a banker, ie, cross it specially. So that in the case of the special crossing there may be no transverse parallel lines within which to put the words 'not negotiable'.

Section 81 does not prescribe that the words shall be on the face of the crossed cheque; it merely says 'bears on it'. It is submitted, however, that to constitute an effective 'not negotiable' crossing, the words must be in some reasonable collocation to the recognised crossing. It can hardly be contended that s 81 would be satisfied by the crossing being on the face of the cheque, and 'not negotiable' on the back. If 'bears on it' must be interpreted 'bears on the face of it', the words 'with or without' in s 76 and 'may add' in s 77(4) appear to point to the words, when used, being in some relation or connection with the authorised crossing, not, as is sometimes the case, printed across the extreme edge of the cheque, while the crossing is in or near the middle.

(f) Effect of 'not negotiable' on a bill other than a cheque

The words 'not negotiable' written across a bill of exchange other than a cheque mean that the instrument is not to be negotiable and do not carry the special meaning given them by s 81; thus Lewis J in *Hibernian Bank Ltd v Gysin and Hanson*.[19] The bank sued as holders for value of a bill, accepted by the defendants, drawn to the order of the payees 'only' and crossed 'not negotiable', and relied on *National Bank v Silke*.[20] The judge held that that case had no application to the one he was trying. It would seem from the facts of the case that the drawers of the bill intended that the instrument should not be transferable, and the decision gave effect to this intention. It is perhaps strange that the plaintiffs, in arguing that a bill drawn to order could not be deprived of its negotiability, did not contend that the words in dispute were by virtue of the statute tied to cheques and could thus have no significance whatever in relation to a bill which was not drawn on a banker.

19 [1938] 2 KB 384; affd. [1939] 1 KB 483.
20 [1891] 1 QB 435.

However, the fact that the bill was drawn to the order of the payees 'only' would seem sufficient to take it out of the category of negotiable instruments and the case might, perhaps, have been decided on this issue alone. In the words of Slesser LJ, in the Court of Appeal,[1] the bill

'is not a bill payable to order within the meaning of the Bills of Exchange Act'

and the bill never was a negotiable instrument.

It is submitted that the decision in *Hibernian Bank Ltd v Gysin and Hanson* has no application at all to an uncrossed cheque, for the words 'not negotiable', can have significance only in relation to a crossing and that if they appear on a cheque without a crossing must be construed as not transferable.

3 ACCOUNT PAYEE[2]

(a) General effect

It is not uncommon today to find adjacent to the crossing on a cheque or within the two parallel transverse lines, expressions such as 'account payee', 'account of AB' or 'account payee only'. Such an expression is not authorised or recognised by the Bills of Exchange Act. It has been suggested that if the words are included within the transverse lines and incorporated with the crossing they invalidate the cheque, or the crossing, or are contrary to s 78, which enacts that:

'a crossing authorised by this Act is a material part of the cheque; it shall not be lawful for any person to obliterate or, except as authorised by this Act, to add to or alter the crossing'.

It has, however, been held that the words are not in any sense an addition to the crossing.[3] A crossing is a direction to the *paying* bank to pay the money generally to a bank or to a particular bank as the case may be, and when this has been done the whole purpose of the crossing has been served. The words 'account payee' are 'a mere direction to the *receiving* bank as to how the money is to be dealt with after receipt'.[4]

National Bank v Silke[5] shows that such an addition to the crossing does not prevent the cheque from being transferable. In the judgment in that case the terms transferable and negotiable are used somewhat indiscriminately and no direct authority can be deduced from them as to the effect, if any, of such words as 'account of AB' on the negotiability of a cheque. However, the defence was based on the allegation that the cheque had been obtained by false representation and that the plaintiffs were not holders for value in due course. The defendant would have been entitled on that basis to judgment equally whether the cheque was not transferable or only not fully negotiable; and from the fact that the Court of Appeal affirmed the judgment in favour

1 [1939] 1 KB 483 at 489.
2 As to the effect of these words on the paying and the collecting banker, see chs 24, 26, post.
3 *Akrokerri (Atlantic) Mines Ltd v Economic Bank* [1904] 2 KB 465.
4 Ibid at 472.
5 [1891] 1 QB 435, CA; see also *Morison v London County and Westminster Bank Ltd* [1924] 3 KB 356, CA; *A L Underwood Ltd v Bank of Liverpool and Martins* [1924] 1 KB 775, CA; *Importers Co v Westminster Bank Ltd* [1927] 2 KB 297, CA, especially Atkin LJ at 307, approving Bigham J in *Akrokerri*; and *Universal Guarantee Pty Ltd v National Bank of Australasia Ltd* [1965] 2 All ER 98, PC.

of the plaintiffs it may be presumed that they did not consider the full negotiability of the cheque to have been in any way affected. Another ground for this view is that, if such words had the effect of limiting the negotiability of the cheque, the result would be precisely equivalent to that of the 'not negotiable' crossing; and it is not permissible to attribute to one set of words the effect exclusively attached by statute to another. In *A L Underwood Ltd v Bank of Liverpool and Martins*[6] Scrutton LJ definitely adopts the view that the words have no effect on the negotiability of a cheque, though they may have some effect in practice of restraining its transfer.

(b) 'Account payee only'

Sometimes the marking 'account payee' is extended to 'account payee only'. The cheque in *Sutters v Briggs*[7] was so marked, as were those in *Importers Co Ltd v Westminster Bank Ltd.*[8] Whether the word 'only' has any further significance has not yet been considered judicially though in *Importers Company Ltd v Westminster Bank Ltd*, Atkin LJ appeared to consider that it did not.[9]

It is probably the intention of the drawer in any of these cases to restrict transfer but if, as is today certainly the view of the courts, the marking 'account payee' is addressed to and binds a collecting banker, there would seem no good reason why the addition of 'only' should place any greater obligation on the collecting banker or raise one on the paying banker which he would not otherwise suffer. The same effect could, of course, be reached by drawing the cheque in favour of the payee 'only'.

It would seem wise for banks to discourage the use of the word 'only' and for the drawer to be content with the protection afforded by the use of 'account payee' simply, but it is likely that the practice is now too well established and banks would certainly not wish cheques to be drawn in favour of a named payee 'only'.

6 [1924] 1 KB 775, CA.
7 [1922] AC 1.
8 [1927] 2 KB 297, CA.
9 [1927] 2 KB 297 at 307.

CHAPTER 23

CHEQUES: INSTRUMENTS ANALOGOUS

The statutory protection relating to the payment and collection of cheques extends by virtue of the Cheques Act 1957, ss 1(2) and 4(2)[1] to certain instruments which, though not cheques, are analogous to cheques. These instruments are:

1 As regards the paying banker,
   (a) a document issued by a customer of his which, though not a bill of exchange, is intended to enable a person to obtain payment from him of the sum mentioned in the document;
   (b) a draft payable on demand drawn by him upon himself, whether payable at the head office or some other office of his bank.
2 As regards the collecting banker,
   (a) any document issued by a customer of a banker which, though not a bill of exchange, is intended to enable a person to obtain payment from that banker of the sum mentioned in the document;
   (b) any document issued by a public officer which is intended to enable a person to obtain payment from the Paymaster General or the Queen's and Lord Treasurer's Remembrancer of the sum mentioned in the document but is not a bill of exchange;
   (c) any draft payable on demand drawn by a banker upon himself, whether payable at the head office or some other office of his bank.

This chapter considers certain instruments analogous to cheques (some of which may in fact be cheques if drawn in the appropriate form) and whether the payment and collection of such instruments attracts the protection of the Cheques Act 1957.

(a) Dividend warrants

Dividend warrants are often cheques in a somewhat unusual form. A dividend warrant would not, however, be a cheque if made conditional, for instance, by making the counter-signature of the payee a condition of payment.

Section 95 of the Bills of Exchange Act 1882 provides that the crossed cheques provisions of the Act shall apply to 'a warrant for the payment of dividends'; and s 97(3)(d) provides that nothing in the Act shall effect the validity of any usage relating to dividend warrants or the endorsement

1 5 Halsbury's Statutes (4th edn, 1989 Reissue) 387.

thereof. This latter provision is probably directed to the custom of bankers to pay dividend warrants drawn in favour of two or more payees on the endorsement or discharge of one.

A dividend warrant which is not a cheque will ordinarily be a document intended to enable a person to obtain payment from a banker within s 1(2)(a) or s 4(2)(b) of the Cheques Act 1957.

(b) Interest warrants

The question has often been debated whether the provisions of ss 95 and 97(3)(d) extend to warrants for the payment of fixed interest, or are confined to dividend warrants strictly so termed; particularly, whether a banker is justified in paying an interest warrant, payable to two payees or order, on the indorsement of one of them, as he is in the case of a dividend warrant by the usage preserved by s 97(3)(d). The usage is in practice extended to interest warrants. In *Slingsby v Westminster Bank Ltd*[2] Finlay J held that a Bank of England interest warrant was a dividend warrant within the meaning of s 95 and that accordingly, applying the provisions of the Bills of Exchange Act as to crossed cheques, s 82 was available to the defendant bank. The ground was that the drawer of the warrant, the Chief Accountant of the Bank of England, was acting as agent of the Government and that the instrument was thus a cheque.

As in the case of dividend warrants, an interest warrant which is not a cheque will ordinarily fall within s 1(2)(a) or s 4(2)(b) of the Cheques Act 1957.

(c) Conditional orders for payment

Conditional orders for payment are instruments issued by a customer of and addressed to a bank imposing a condition of payment, commonly the signing by a payee of a form of receipt placed thereon or annexed thereto. Where this is a condition of payment, contained in the body of the instrument, addressed to and affecting the drawee banker, the instrument is not a bill of exchange and therefore not a cheque.[3]

(i) Negotiability of conditional orders for payment

Conditional orders for payment are frequently made payable to order or even to bearer, but this does not make them negotiable,[4] nor even transferable. If this were not so, incongruous results would follow. This becomes clear upon considering the position in the case of a purported transfer. The transferee (B) would only accept the instrument upon signature of the receipt by the payee (A), for otherwise B would be unable to tender the document in the appropriate form. This has the consequence, however, that if the instrument

---

2 [1931] 1 KB 173.
3 See *Bavins Junior and Sims v London and South Western Bank Ltd* [1900] 1 QB 270; *London, City and Midland Bank Ltd v Gordon* [1903] AC 240. The Revenue Act 1883 (repealed) treated conditional orders as non-negotiable instruments. The Cheques Act 1957, s 6(2) provides that its foregoing provisions do not make negotiable any instrument which, apart from them, is not negotiable.
4 See the judgment of the Court of Appeal in *Gordon v London, City and Midland Bank Ltd* [1902] 1 KB 242 at 275.

were paid, the bank would be paying to B money which A had already acknowledged to have been paid to him in accordance with the order.[5]

(ii) Statutory protection

Payment of conditional orders to pay was at one time protected by s 17 of the Revenue Act 1883, and is now protected by the Cheques Act 1957, the protection deriving from the fact that a conditional order for payment is a document within s 1(2)(a) or s 4(2)(b) of the 1957 Act. However, in the nature of conditional orders for payment, the protection may be of limited value. As regards the *paying* banker, s 1(2) only relieves him in respect of any absence of or irregularity in indorsement and then only if the payment is in good faith and the ordinary course of business. If he disobeys the mandate by paying a transferee from the payee or indorsee, he is treating the instrument as negotiable and it is doubtful if he can debit the drawer's account. If the condition embodied in the instrument is that the signature of the payee is required to a receipt, it is submitted that the paying bank must ensure that the signature is in fact that of the payee.

As regards the *collecting* banker, his statutory protection is conditional on receiving payment for a customer in good faith and without negligence. By s 4(3) of the Cheques Act, failure to concern himself with absence of or irregularity in indorsement does not render the collecting banker negligent. Whether there is negligence is a matter of fact. It is submitted that to collect a conditional order for a transferee from the payee or an indorsee would not, by itself, amount to negligence,[6] the mere fact that a non-negotiable instrument had been negotiated would not put the banker on inquiry.

(d) 'Cheque' requiring receipt

Cheques are sometimes issued bearing an indication[7] to the payee that there is a receipt which he is required to complete. Such instruments enjoy the statutory protection available to bankers, being either cheques in the strict sense, or documents within s 1(2)(a) or s 4(2)(b) of the Cheques Act 1957.[8] In considering the value of this protection, it is again necessary to distinguish the position of the paying banker from that of the collecting banker.

5 This obvious objection to the negotiation or transfer of conditional orders for payment appears never to have been raised in cases where it might have been, eg *Bavins Junior and Sims v London and South Western Bank*, above, or the *Gordon* case, above.
6 In *Bavins Jnr and Sims v London and South Western Bank* [1900] 1 QB 270, CA and in the *Gordon* case [1903] AC 240, conditional orders were collected for a transferee, but no objection seems to have been raised. As to negligence which deprives a collecting banker of the statutory protection, see ch 28, below.
7 See, eg *London and Montrose Shipbuilding and Repairing Co Ltd v Barclays Bank Ltd* (1925) 31 Com Cas 67 at 78–79 (revsd on appeal without affecting this point, (1926) 31 Com Cas 182, CA).
8 Prior to the coming into force of the Cheques Act 1957, the Committee of London Clearing Banks, issued a circular which included the statement that: 'A bold letter "R" on the face of a cheque is to be the indication to the payee that there is a receipt which he is required to complete.'

(i) The paying banker

The position of the paying banker is greatly affected according to whether the payee's receipt constitutes an indorsement. If it does, the paying banker has the benefit of s 1(2) of the Cheques Act 1957 relieving him of any liability incurred by reason only of the absence of, or irregularity in, indorsement.

It is submitted that the signature to the receipt is not an effective indorsement. There is no legal authority that indorsement can be effected by a signature which concurrently fulfils another purpose, ie the satisfaction of a condition stipulated by the drawer. No *animus indorsandi* can be predicated in such case. No doubt the payee's indorsement of an order cheque may be utilised as a receipt, but that is an incidental matter. It would seem, therefore, that a signature by way of receipt would not give the banker protection under s 60 if it proved to be a forgery. Bankers usually decline to allow customers to use instruments of this class except under indemnity.

(ii) The collecting banker

The drawer's mandate being addressed to the paying banker, the collecting banker can disregard the requirement for a receipt. If there was no signature to the receipt he might in practice well draw his customer's attention to the omission, for he would naturally doubt if the instrument would be paid; but he is under no duty to do so.

(e) Bankers' drafts[9]

Drafts drawn by one branch on another branch or on the head office of the same bank or vice versa are not cheques or bills, there being no distinct drawer and drawee.[10]

Bankers' drafts payable to order on demand were always thought to be within the protection of s 19 of the Stamp Act 1853.[11] In the *Gordon* case, some of the documents involved were bankers' drafts, drawn by the A branch of a bank upon its head office, payable to G and M or order. These were issued by the A branch to a customer who forwarded them to G and M. They were intercepted by J, who forged the indorsement of G and M and paid them uncrossed into his own account at the B branch of the same bank.

The House of Lords held that these documents were not cheques or bills within s 3 of the Bills of Exchange Act, there being no separate drawer and drawee as required by that section, and that the power given by s 5(2), to treat as a bill a document in which drawer and drawee are the same person is confined to the holder, as indeed, in terms, it is. They therefore held that the bank was not protected by s 60 of the Bills of Exchange Act, but was covered by the Stamp Act 1853, s 19. Since the passing of the Bills of Exchange Act (1882) Amendment Act 1932, however, the crossed cheques sections of the parent statute have applied to bankers' drafts as if they were cheques. Before that time any crossing was a nullity and refusal to pay over the counter, if solely on account of the crossing, was unwarranted dishonour.

---

9 For the history of the legislation relating to bankers' drafts see *Paget* (8th edn) p 272.
10 *London City and Midland Bank Ltd v Gordon* [1903] AC 240; and see further ch 21 above, sub-heading 'Addressed by one person to another'.
11 4 Halsbury's Statutes (4th edn, 1987 Reissue) 442. See *London City and Midland Bank Ltd v Gordon* [1903] AC 240.

The 1932 Act has now been repealed by the Cheques Act 1957, and its provisions re-enacted by ss 1 and 4 of that Act.

A banker's draft payable to bearer on demand would probably be an infringement of the Bank Charter Act 1844, s 11,[12] which was enacted in the national interest to prevent the excessive issue of notes by banks and to facilitate the ultimate transfer of the whole note issue to the central bank. The relevant part of the section – the remainder was repealed by the Currency and Bank Notes Act 1928 – reads:

> 'From and after the passing of this Act it shall not be lawful for any banker to draw, accept, make or issue in England or Wales, any bill of exchange or promissory note or engagement for the repayment of money to bearer on demand, or to borrow, owe, or take up in England or Wales any sums or sum of money on the bills or notes of such banker payable to bearer on demand'.

'Banker' is defined by s 28 as any person carrying on the business of banking.

(f) Foreign bankers' drafts

In the *Gordon* case,[13] Lord Lindley referred to the doubt whether s 19 of the Stamp Act 1853 applied to any except inland drafts or orders. It is conceived that the protection extends to all documents falling within its terms at the present day. Statutes are not to be confined to conditions existing at the date of their passing, if their wording is wide enough to include subsequent developments.[14] In *Brown, Brough & Co v National Bank of India Ltd*,[15] Bigham J in a case of a draft drawn in Madras on London, expressly stated that, but for the then existing ruling of the Court of Appeal in the *Gordon* case, subsequently reversed, he would have held the document to be within s 19 of the Stamp Act 1853. The House of Lords, in the *Gordon* case, referring to the decision in *Brown, Brough & Co v National Bank of India Ltd*, did not express dissent on the ground of the draft being foreign; but the question was not relevant to the drafts before them, which were inland drafts.

The Cheques Act 1957 does nothing to include a draft drawn abroad, but it does not exclude it and the argument that it is included would still seem valid.

(g) Travellers' cheques

Travellers' cheques may take any one of several forms, resembling cheques but often without the essential attributes of a cheque.[16] Whether any amounts

---

12 4 Halsbury's Statutes (4th edn, 1987 Reissue) 440. The section appears to have been judicially considered only in the case of *A-G v Birkbeck* (1884) 12 QBD 605, where it was held that the word 'issue' means the delivery of notes to persons who are willing to receive them in exchange for value in gold, in bills or otherwise, the person who delivers them being prepared to take them up when they are presented for payment: ibid at 611.

13 *London City and Midland Bank v Gordon* [1903] AC 240 at 251.

14 *A-G v Edison Telephone Co of London* (1880) 6 QBD 244.

15 (1902) 18 TLR 669.

16 For a detailed treatment of the subject, see Ellinger 'Travellers' Cheques and the Law' (1969) 19 University of Toronto LJ 132; Cowen *Law of Negotiable Instruments in South Africa* (5th edn, 1985) pp 295–313. For cases on the right to reimbursement of a holder of stolen travellers' cheques, all of which cases were decided on the construction of the particular written terms subject to which the cheques were issued, see *Fellus v National Westminster Bank Plc* (1983) 133 NLJ 766; *Braithwaite v Thomas Cook Travellers Cheques Ltd* [1989] 1

to a bill, cheque, a draft on a banker or other instrument within the Bills of
Exchange Act 1882 or the Cheques Act 1957, depends on its form and content
and, vis-à-vis the person to whom it is issued, on the conditions on which it
is issued. Some travellers' cheques are drawn by the person, usually a
customer, to whom they are issued, in favour of 'Self or order'; others, again,
are drawn by the drawee bank on itself. The first type could be a cheque, the
second a banker's draft; and both would be covered by the Bills of Exchange
Acts 1882, and the Cheques Act 1957, but in most cases the place for the
name of the payee is left blank, in which case they are not cheques at the
time of issue.

(h) Postal and money orders

Pursuant to the powers conferred by the Post Office Act 1969, the Post
Office today issues postal orders, money orders and drafts on the National
Girobank. The money order is virtually extinct; such as there are when paid
into a bank are paid by the Post Office without examination and 'if it is
found' that payment ought not to have been made the Post Office may deduct
the amount from subsequent collections by that bank in respect of money
orders (1969 Act, s 71(1)).[17] The bank's only remedy is to debit the customer
for whom they collected the impugned money order. Neither money orders
nor postal orders are negotiable;[18] if crossed they will be paid only to another
bank,[19] though the crossing does not bring them within the Bills of Exchange
legislation. As regards uncrossed orders, s 70 of the 1969 Act provides that
payment discharges the order when it is presented for payment by a banker
to whom it has been delivered for collection.

As regards postal orders, s 21(3) of the Post Office Act 1953 (as amended
by the 1969 Act) provides that:

'Any person acting as a banker in the British postal area who, in collecting in that
capacity for any principal, has received payment or been allowed by the Postmaster-
General (or the authority established by s 6 of the Post Office Act 1969) in account
in respect of any postal order, or of any document purporting to be a postal order,
shall not incur liability to anyone except that principal by reason of having received
the payment or allowance or having held or presented the order or document for
payment; but this sub-section shall not relieve any principal for whom any such
order or document has been so held or presented of any liability in respect of his
possession of the order or document or of the proceeds thereof.'

All ER 235, [1989] 3 WLR 212; *Elawadi v Bank of Credit and Commerce International SA*
   [1989] 1 All ER 242, [1989] 3 WLR 220.
17 *London and Provincial Bank v Golding* (1918) 39 Journal of Institute of Bankers 136.
18 *Fine Arts Society Ltd v Union Bank of London Ltd* (1886) 17 QBD 705.
19 The Post Office (Postal Order) Scheme 1971, para 8, made under the Post Office Act 1969,
   s 28.

CHAPTER 24

THE PAYING BANKER: PROTECTION

1 INTRODUCTION

(a) Sources of liability and their interrelation

The logical starting point in any discussion of the statutory protection available to the paying banker is to identify the sources of liability against which he needs to be protected. The position can be illustrated by the simple example of a cheque drawn by A payable to B or order in satisfaction of a debt. If B pays the cheque into his own account, there is a discharge of the instrument and of the debt. The cheque might, however, still be paid if it is stolen from B by C. Thus if C were to forge B's indorsement and pay the cheque into his own account, the cheque might appear entirely regular on its face, and be paid by A's banker in ignorance of the true facts. A's banker, D, then faces the risk of liability (in the sense of having to bear the loss himself) from two sources. First, A may dispute D's entitlement to debit his account, leaving D with an unreimbursed payment. Secondly, B may claim damages for conversion, or payment of the instrument.

The interrelation between these sources of liability was considered by the Court of Appeal in *Charles v Blackwell*.[1] The facts were that the defendants purchased goods from the plaintiffs and paid for them by a cheque made payable to the plaintiffs or their order. An agent of the plaintiffs, who had authority to receive payment for them but not to indorse cheques, indorsed the cheque and failed to account to the plaintiffs for part of the proceeds. The plaintiffs sued the defendants for (a) damages for conversion, (b) the price of goods sold, alternatively (c) an order for delivery up of the cheque so that the plaintiffs might duly indorse it and present it to the defendants' bankers for payment. By the following process of reasoning, the Court of Appeal rejected the plaintiffs' claims:

(i) as between the defendants' bankers and the defendants themselves, the bankers were justified in paying the cheque by s 19 of the Stamp Act 1853;

(ii) the cheque having reached the payee and having been paid to one to

1 (1877) 2 CPD 151.

whom the bankers were authorised to pay it by the operation of s 19, the plaintiffs had no action on the cheque itself;

(iii) the due payment of the cheque similarly defeated the plaintiffs' claim for the price of the goods;

(iv) the plaintiffs' claim in conversion (trover) failed because they no longer had any property in the cheque.

On this last point, Cockburn CJ, delivering the judgment of the Court of Appeal, said:[2]

'A cheque taken in payment remains the property of the payee only so long as it remains unpaid. When paid the banker is entitled to keep it as a voucher till his account with his customer is settled. After that the drawer is entitled to it as a voucher between him and the payee. If the cheque was duly paid, so as to deprive the payee of a right of action, either on it or in respect of the goods in payment for which it was given, they no longer have any property in it.'

It may thus be taken that whenever a banker pays a cheque without contravening any statutory enactment, and in such a manner that, either at common law or by virtue of any statute, that payment, though made to an unlawful holder or possessor, operates as a discharge of the cheque, he is under no liability to the true owner for conversion. If he pays contrary to statutory enactment, if for instance, he pays a cheque crossed specially to more than one banker, not an agent for collection being a banker, or where, contrary to the ordinary course of business, he pays a cheque with a forged indorsement, then his liability to the true owner remains, apart from any express right given to the true owner by statute.

It appears to be possible for a bank to pay the rightful owner of a cheque and yet not be entitled to debit the customer's account. This is illustrated by *Smith v Union Bank of London*,[3] where a cheque was drawn payable to the plaintiff or his order upon the defendant bankers. The plaintiff indorsed the cheque generally, and crossed it with the name of his bankers, 'London & County Banking Co.' The cheque was stolen, and passed for full value to a third party, who paid it into his bank. That bank was not the bank to which the cheque had been specially crossed. At the relevant date there was statutory prohibition against paying crossed cheques contrary to the crossing,[4] but no special remedy given to the true owner against the banker so paying. The position of the defendant bankers was that they had wrongfully paid the cheque contrary to the crossing, but to the rightful owner. The plaintiff's claim failed because the cheque remained negotiable notwithstanding the crossing, and, the plaintiff having indorsed the cheque so that the third party became bona fide holder before it was presented to the defendants, the plaintiff was not the holder and had no right of action against the defendants. In delivering the judgment of the Court of Appeal, Lord Cairns summarised the position as follows:[5]

'The plaintiff cannot maintain an action for conversion of the cheque, for he had no property in it. He cannot maintain an action on the ground that the defendants have paid the cheque contrary to the statute, because, though an action lies by the

2 Ibid at 162–163.
3 (1875) 1 QBD 31, CA.
4 21 & 22 Vict c 79, s 2 (An Act to amend the law relating to cheques or drafts on bankers (Drafts on Bankers Act 1858)).
5 (1875) 1 QBD 31 at 35–6.

person grieved where the provisions of a statute have been infringed, yet that is only when those provisions are for his direct benefit, and he has sustained loss by their infringement. Here the prohibition of payment except to a banker is for the direct benefit of the drawer, indirectly only for the benefit of any holder of the cheque. The drawer, if any, is the person aggrieved. As we have shown, the plaintiff is no loser by the cheque having been paid, as another person had become the lawful holder of it. Further, the drawers might refuse to be debited with it as having been paid contrary to their mandate as altered by the statute. It cannot be that in addition to this the defendants are liable to this action.'[6]

In so holding, the Court of Appeal affirmed the decision of the Court below, (Blackburn and Field JJ). In his judgment, Blackburn J said that the defendants would have been liable for a conversion of the cheque if they had paid it to anyone but the lawful holder.[7] These and similar remarks are in wide terms, but they should probably be confined to cases where the payment is made in contravention of some statutory provision, or in such a manner as to preclude it from being a statutory discharge.

If payment contrary to the crossing, even to the true owner, leaves the drawer liable on the consideration, it is reasonable that his banker should not be entitled to debit his account. A rare example of a case in which the action was brought by the drawer of the cheque instead of the payee from whom it had been stolen is *Bobbett v Pinkett*.[8] The plaintiff drew a cheque on his bankers payable to order, crossed it 'London and Country Bank', and sent it for value to the payee, from whom it was stolen and his indorsement forged. The defendant took the cheque bona fide in ignorance of the forgery, and gave it to his country bankers whose London agents, the London and Joint Stock Bank, presented and received payment for it. Meanwhile the plaintiff sent a second cheque to the original payee, and the plaintiff's account was debited with both cheques. The plaintiff then sued the defendant for money had and received. The jury found that all parties except the defendants had been negligent. It was nevertheless held that as the first cheque had been paid by the plaintiff's bankers improperly and without authority, the plaintiff was entitled to maintain the action against the defendant, who had no title.

(b) The multiplicity of protective statutory provisions

There is a multiplicity of statutory provisions conferring protection on the paying banker, and there is unfortunately considerable overlap between them. The difficulties to which this situation inevitably gives rise are not lessened by differences in terminology between the various provisions. For example, s 60 of the Bills of Exchange Act 1882 refers to payment 'in good faith and in the ordinary course of business', whereas s 80 refers to payment 'in good faith and without negligence'. Again, the effect of s 60 and of s 1(1) of the Cheques Act 1957 is that a payment is to be deemed to have been made 'in due course', but the effect of s 80 is that a payment is to be deemed to have been made 'to the true owner', and the effect of s 1(2) of the Cheques Act 1957 is that payment 'discharges the instrument'. There is a clear case for the

---

6 As to the present position where payment is made contrary to a special crossing, see Bills of Exchange Act 1882, s 79(2).
7 (1876) 1 Ex D 368.
8 (1875) LR 10 QB 291 at 295.

various overlapping provisions to be repealed and re-enacted in a single consolidating enactment.

The statutory provisions which protect the paying banker from constructive trust claims are considered separately in ch 12, above.

2   BILLS OF EXCHANGE ACT 1882, s 59

Payment of a bill of exchange, including a cheque, is governed by s 59 of the Bills of Exchange Act 1882, which reads:

> '(1) A bill is discharged by payment in due course by or on behalf of the drawee or acceptor. "Payment in due course" means payment made at or after the maturity of the bill to the holder thereof in good faith and without notice that his title to the bill is defective.'

(a) Meaning of 'payment'

'Payment' within the meaning of the Act is widely interpreted.[9] In *Meyer & Co Ltd v Sze Hai Tong Banking and Insurance Co Ltd*,[10] the Privy Council held that where a bank paid a crossed cheque across the counter by giving its own cheque on another bank, this was payment of the cheque within s 80.[11] Payment may take the form of the actual delivery of money to the presenter of the instrument or of transfer to the account of the payee whether in account with the paying bank or otherwise, or again, through a clearing; it is complete when the payer obtains a discharge. Where an English bank had the accounts of two German banks and was instructed by one to transfer £120,000 from its account to the account of the second, it was held that payment was complete when the English bank set in motion the computer processes for making the transfer. The dispute arose because the first bank failed on the day the transfer was to be made with its account in debit and the English bank revised the entries.[12] Where a payment by one bank to another on the instruction of charterers in respect of hire was made by a payment order used between bank and bank, it was held that as such an order was regarded by banks as equivalent to cash the hire was paid when the order was delivered to the receiving bank.[13] Where a cheque drawn on one branch of a bank was paid in at another and appeared as an item in balancing the accounts between the two branches, the branch on which it was drawn was held to have paid it within the meaning of s 60.[14]

The intimation, in response to inquiry, that a cheque would be paid, known as notifying its fate, though usually regarded as equivalent thereto as between bankers could hardly be regarded as payment within the Act. The courts regard the question and answer as to the fate of a cheque purely as a

---

9 See *Glasscock v Balls* (1889) 24 QBD 13 at 16, per Lord Esher MR.
10 [1913] AC 847.
11 5 Halsbury's Statutes (4th edn, 1989 Reissue) 334.
12 *Momm v Barclays Bank International Ltd* [1977] QB 790, [1976] 2 Lloyd's Rep 341.
13 *The Laconia* [1976] QB 835, [1976] 1 Lloyd's Rep 395, CA.
14 *Gordon v London City and Midland Bank Ltd* [1902] 1 KB 242 per Collins MR at 274–5; cf *Bissell & Co v Fox Bros & Co* (1885) 53 LT 193.

precaution taken by the collecting banker mainly for his own benefit;[15] but it may be at the request of the customer paying it in.

(b) Meaning of 'holder'

The holder is defined by s 2 as the 'payee or indorsee of a bill or note who is in possession of it, or the bearer thereof'. 'Bearer' is defined as 'the person in possession of a bill or note which is payable to bearer'. By s 8(3):

> 'A bill is payable to bearer which is expressed to be so payable, or on which the only or last indorsement is an indorsement in blank'.

(c) Payment to person claiming under forged indorsement

Payment to a person claiming under a forged indorsement is not protected by s 59 for two reasons. First, a forged indorsement is by s 24 wholly inoperative, and accordingly a person claiming under such an indorsement is not an indorsee of the bill. Secondly, s 59 refers to payment without notice that the holder's title is defective. A defective title must be distinguished from complete absence of title; a person who claims under a forgery has no title and can give none.[16]

(d) Payment of lost or stolen bearer cheques

The definition of holder in the Act requires only 'possession', not restricting it to lawful possession; and therefore a person in possession of a bearer cheque, even though he be the actual thief, is the holder. It follows that payment in due course by the banker of an uncrossed bearer cheque to anyone presenting it discharges not only the banker, but, if the cheque had reached the payee, the drawer also, both as to cheque and consideration. The position is clearly stated by Cockburn CJ, delivering the judgment of the Court of Appeal in *Charles v Blackwell*:[17]

> 'The matter is equally clear on principle, for where the banker paid the bearer of such a cheque, he obeyed the mandate of his customer, the drawer, and could charge him accordingly; while, on the other hand, the customer was protected, and this even though the bearer so paid had no property in the cheque, but was himself a thief who had stolen it. The drawer was entitled to say to the payee, "I gave you an instrument which you were willing to take in satisfaction of your debt if the drawee paid the amount to the bearer, and this the drawee has done".'

---

15 See eg *Bissell & Co v Fox Bros & Co* (1884) 51 LT 663; varied (1885) 53 LT 193; *Ogden v Benas* (1874) LR 9 CP 513 at 516.

16 This again follows from the Bills of Exchange Act 1882, s 24. An apparent exception to the inefficacy of a person in possession under a forged indorsement to constitute a holder is to be found in s 55(2)(b) of the Bills of Exchange Act 1882 which precludes an indorser from denying to a 'holder in due course' the genuineness and regularity of all indorsements. However, the subsection does not make the transferee a holder in due course. The term is there used to denote the character in which a person must have taken the bill, namely, in good faith and for value, and before it was overdue, in order to enable him to maintain a right of recourse by estoppel against an indorser subsequent to the forged indorsement. Such an indorser is in effect estopped from denying the genuineness of the drawer's signature to anyone who but for the forgery would be a holder in due course. Payment by drawee or acceptor to a person entitled to the benefit of the estoppel would be a valid discharge of the bill. See further *Smith v Union Bank of London* (1875) LR 10 QB 291 at 296 per Blackburn J; affd (1875) 1 QBD 31 at 35, per Lord Cairns.

17 (1877) 2 CPD 151 at 158. See also *Robarts v Tucker* (1851) 16 QB 560 at 576.

3   BILLS OF EXCHANGE ACT 1882, s 60

Section 60 of the Bills of Exchange Act reads:

'60. When a bill payable to order on demand is drawn on a banker, and the banker on whom it is drawn pays the bill in good faith and in the ordinary course of business, it is not incumbent on the banker to show that the indorsement of the payee or any subsequent indorsement was made by or under the authority of the person whose indorsement it purports to be, and the banker is deemed to have paid the bill in due course, although such indorsement has been forged or made without authority.'

A bill payable to order on demand drawn on a banker is a cheque.[18] The section requires that, to entitle him to its protection, the banker must pay the cheque 'in good faith and in the ordinary course of business'.

(a) 'Payable to order'

The instrument must be payable to order; this seems to involve the necessity that it must be negotiable, which is further emphasised by the reference to the indorsement of the payee and any subsequent indorsement which occurs in both enactments, a reference only applicable to an instrument negotiable by indorsement. The banker's draft in *Gordon's* case, though not a bill, because drawer and drawee were the same person, was yet an instrument which, both at common law[19] and under the Bills of Exchange Act, s 5(2), might be treated as negotiable, either as a bill of exchange or as a promissory note. The *Gordon* decision, therefore, does not militate against the restriction that the instrument must be negotiable. Anything which would be fatal to the character of an instrument as a negotiable bill is sufficient to exclude it from protection.

(b) Good faith

The payment must be 'in good faith and in the ordinary course of business'. It is difficult to conceive, still more to formulate, conditions involving absence of good faith on the part of a bank in relation to payment of cheques. Section 60 does not, as does s 80, make the absence of negligence a condition of the protection. Negligence is not incompatible with good faith. The Bills of Exchange Act, s 90, reads:

'A thing is deemed to be done in good faith within the meaning of this Act if in fact it is done honestly, whether it is done negligently or not.'

Negligence may, of course, be so gross as to be evidence of want of good faith, but that is not a principle likely to apply to a banker. In *Woods v Martins Bank Ltd*[20] Salmon J held the bank's branch manager to be honest though 'none of the advice which he gave the plaintiff comes within measurable distance of being reasonably careful or skilful'.

18 Bills of Exchange Act 1882, s 73.
19 *Miller v Thomson* (1841) 3 Man & G 576.
20 [1959] 1 QB 55, [1958] 3 All ER 166; as to good faith where a bill is taken at an undervalue, see *Jones v Gordon* (1877) 2 App Cas 616.

(c) Ordinary course of business

(i) Meaning of 'ordinary course of business'

As to ordinary course of business, there are some obvious derelictions – for example, payment of a crossed cheque contrary to the crossing. In the majority of cases, the usual course of business is a matter on which bankers are best qualified to judge and courts would be largely influenced by the evidence of persons experienced in banking on such questions.[1] But the 'ordinary course of business' must be the recognised or customary course of business of the banking community at large, not of any particular bank or group of banks.[2] The question whether a payment is made in the ordinary course of business must depend upon circumstances. Lord Halsbury in *Bank of England v Vagliano Bros*[3] said:

'I do not know what is the usual course, among bankers, and I should doubt whether in such a matter it would be possible to affirm that any particular course was either usual or unusual in the sense that there is some particular course to be pursued when circumstances occur necessarily giving rise to suspicion. I can well imagine that on a person presenting himself whose appearance and demeanour was calculated to raise a suspicion that he was not likely to be entrusted with a valuable document for which he was to receive payment in cash, I should think it would be extremely probable that, whether the document were a cheque payable to bearer for a large amount or a bill, the counter clerk and banker alike would hesitate very much before making payment.'

In *Auchteroni & Co v Midland Bank Ltd,*[4] where the bank had paid a bill for £876 9s. to the plaintiff's cashier over the counter, Wright J quoted Lord Halsbury in *Vagliano's* case and held the bank justified in paying. He agreed that a different course might reasonably be adopted if a bill for a larger amount was presented by, say, an office boy or a tramp. In *Baines v National Provincial Bank Ltd,*[5] a cheque was paid at 3.5 pm, closing time being 3 pm. Lord Hewart LCJ held such payment good but said:

'The general question of limits of time within which a bank may conduct business, having prescribed, largely for its own convenience, a particular time at which the doors of the building will be closed, is a large question, not raised here.'

In the *Joachimson* case,[6] Atkin LJ defined the banker's promise to repay as to pay 'during banking hours'; see ch 10, above.

It is uncertain whether the practice whereby customers may have their cheques encashed at branches other than those at which their accounts are kept is within the ordinary course of business of the paying banker. The encashment of cheques is not the payment of them except in the sense that the encasher is the agent of the drawee bank, which is the case only where the payment is in accord with instructions received and is not ad hoc. There

---

1 See per Denning LJ in *Arab Bank Ltd v Ross* [1952] 2 QB 216 at 227, [1952] 1 All ER 709 at 716; and *United Dominions Trust Ltd v Kirkwood* [1966] 1 QB 783, [1965] 2 Lloyd's Rep 195, affd [1966] 2 QB 431, [1966] 1 Lloyd's Rep 418; also *Jayson v Midland Bank Ltd* [1967] 2 Lloyd's Rep 563.
2 Cf *Rickford v Ridge* (1810) 2 Camp 537; *Lloyd's Bank Ltd v Swiss Bankverein* (1913) 108 LT 143.
3 [1891] AC 107 at 117.
4 [1928] 2 KB 294.
5 (1927) 96 LJKB 801, 32 Com Cas 216.
6 [1921] 3 KB 110.

would seem no good reason why payment should not be effected through an agent, but the drawee bank would stand or fall by what his agent did in the ordinary course of business or otherwise. Where a banker gives cash for a cheque on another branch, not pursuant to instructions received to do so, he probably becomes a holder for value of it.

Presentment for payment by post is sufficient where authorised by agreement or usage;[7] today there is none except between banker and banker in the case of a special collection.

(ii)   Relation between 'ordinary course of business' and negligence

It is an open point whether a bank may act in the ordinary course of business and yet be negligent. In *Brighton Empire and Eden Syndicate v London and County Bank*,[8] the bank had cashed, inter alia, an order cheque drawn by the plaintiffs on which the indorsement had been forged by a servant of theirs, whose handwriting was alleged to be well known to the bank and which it was said was negligence in the bank not to recognise. The Lord Chief Justice, Lord Alverstone, held that there was no case with regard to this cheque, as no want of bona fides was proved against the bank, who were therefore protected by s 60. Lord Alverstone must have considered that negligence did not preclude the protection of the section.

Conflicting views on this issue were subsequently expressed by the Court of Appeal in *Carpenters' Co v British Mutual Banking Co Ltd.*[9] Slesser and Mackinnon LJJ supported the view that a bank may act in the ordinary course of business and yet be negligent.[10] But Greer LJ considered that a bank could not be heard to say:[11]

'when acting negligently, that it was acting in the ordinary course of business within the meaning of s 60.'

(iii)   Words or indorsements in foreign characters

It sometimes happens that the name of a payee or special indorsee is expressed in English letters, while the indorsement is in Arabic, Hindustani, or some other totally different characters. Unless the banker has personal knowledge of the particular language, it would seem doubtful whether the mere placing on the cheque of hieroglyphics conveying nothing to his mind brings the case within s 60. He could hardly say that he paid in the ordinary course of business if it is not in the ordinary course to pay an instrument part of the writing of which he could not understand. As Buckley LJ said in *Carlisle and Cumberland Banking Co v Bragg*:[12]

'If a document were presented to me written in Hebrew or Syriac, I should for the purposes of the document be both blind and illiterate, blind in the sense that, although I saw some marks on the paper, they conveyed no meaning to my mind, and illiterate as regards the particular document, because I could not read it.'

7   Bills of Exchange Act 1882, s 45(8).
8   (1904) Times, 24 March.
9   [1938] 1 KB 511, [1937] 3 All ER 811, CA.
10   [1938] 1 KB 511 at 534, 536, [1937] 3 All ER 811 at 819, 821.
11   [1938] 1 KB 511 at 532, [1937] 3 All ER 811 at 818.
12   [1911] 1 KB 489 at 496, overruled by *Gallie v Lee* [1971] AC 1004, [1970] 3 All ER 961, but not on the subject of indorsement.

In *Arab Bank Ltd v Ross*[13] Denning LJ said:

'It was suggested that an indorsement in Arabic letters would be regular. I cannot accept this view. The indorsement should be in the same lettering as the name of the payee; for otherwise it could not be seen on the face of it to be regular'.

(d) Payment to person claiming under forged indorsement

Payment by the drawee banker in good faith and in the ordinary course of business of a cheque with a forged indorsement discharges the instrument and entitles the banker to debit his customer. In this important respect s 60 affords protection which is not available under s 59.

4   STAMP ACT 1853, s 19

Section 19 of the Stamp Act 1853 reads:

'... any draft or order drawn upon a banker for a sum of money payable to order on demand which shall, when presented for payment, purport to be indorsed by the person to whom the same shall be drawn payable, shall be a sufficient authority to such banker to pay the amount of such draft or order to the bearer thereof; and it shall not be incumbent on such banker to prove that such indorsement, or any subsequent indorsement, was made by or under the direction or authority of the person to whom the said draft or order was, or is, made payable, either by the drawer or any indorser thereof.'

(a) Purpose and scope of s 19

In *Charles v Blackwell*[14] the Court of Appeal said that:

'The purpose seems to have been to make the banker free of all responsibility in respect either of the genuineness or validity of the instrument whether purporting to be that of the payee or subsequent indorser on the one hand or of an authorised agent on the other.'

In the Gordon case, Lord Lindley stated:[15]

'I invite your Lordships' attention to the fact that s 19 of the Act of 1853 is left unrepealed by the Bills of Exchange Act 1882, although s 60 of that Act is evidently taken from s 19 of the Act of 1853, and made applicable to bills of exchange, and to cheques, as defined in ss 3 and 73 in the Bills of Exchange Act of 1882. The only conclusion which I can draw from these enactments is that s 19 of the Act of 1853 was purposely left unrepealed in order that it might apply to drafts or orders which did not fall within the definitions of bills of exchange or cheques in the codifying Act of 1882. These definitions are far more limited and scientific than the sweeping descriptions contained in the Stamp Acts; and s 19 of the Act of 1853 appears to me to be purposely preserved in order to protect bankers cashing drafts or orders on them, and which are not bills of exchange or cheques as defined in the Act of 1882, in the same way as s 60 of that Act protects them from cashing documents drawn on them, and which are bills of exchange and cheques as defined in it.'

13 [1952] 2 QB 216 at 228, [1952] 1 All ER 709 at 716.
14 (1876) 1 CPD 548; affd (1877) 2 CPD 151.
15 [1903] AC 240 at 251. These words were treated in *Carpenters' Co v British Mutual Banking Co Ltd* [1938] 1 KB 511, 43 Com Cas 38, CA, as meaning that s 19 is impliedly repealed by s 60 of the Bills of Exchange Act 1882 in the case of bills and cheques – see per Slesser LJ at 534 and per Greer LJ at 531. Cf *Bissell & Co v Fox Bros & Co* (1884) 51 LT 663; varied (1885) 53 LT 193.

(b) 'Draft or order drawn upon a banker'

The instrument must be a draft or order. The latitude of interpretation involved in the decision in the *Gordon* case[16] renders it difficult to define what instruments may fall within the extended scope of this category. An instrument may not be a cheque or bill, for want of some essential element, but the words 'draft or order', of which there is no authoritative definition, may supply the deficiency. The instrument must be drawn on a banker.[16] By the decision in *Gordon's* case this does not necessarily involve its being drawn by a customer. It may be drawn by a branch of a bank on another branch or on the head office, or by a beneficiary under a commercial credit drawing on the issuing bank. This requirement excludes bills accepted payable at a banker's or domiciled with him; such bills are not instruments drawn on a banker. It has already been noted under sub-heading (a) above that s 19 is impliedly repealed by s 60 of the Bills of Exchange Act 1882 in the case of bills and cheques. As to the requirement that the draft or order be 'payable to order', see the text under this sub-heading in the above section on s 60 of the Bills of Exchange Act 1882.

(c) Requirement of good faith

Section 19 does not expressly require that payment must be made in good faith, but this is undoubtedly a condition of the protection. The banker could never take advantage of his own wrong, and the necessity for good faith is distinctly postulated in *Hare v Copland*[17] and in *Smith v Union Bank of London.*[18]

(d) Payment not required to be in the ordinary course of business

The ordinary course of business, apart from the question of negligence, does not seem a factor. In *Bissell & Co v Fox Bros & Co*[19] a payment treated as doubtful under s 60 was held good under s 19. No condition that payment be in the ordinary course of business was included by Sir Mackenzie Chalmers in his *Digest of the Law of Bills of Exchange,* published before the passing of the Bills of Exchange Act, or insisted on by Blackburn J in the passage above referred to. Nor is it mentioned in *Charles v Blackwell.*[20] The instrument in the *Gordon* case[1] was a draft drawn by a branch bank on head office. The issue of such drafts is a recognised means of transmitting funds from abroad, and they are in common use; the subsequent payment might, therefore, fairly be regarded as being in the ordinary course of business, but the point was not raised or discussed.

(e) Effect of s 19

The section does not specifically provide that the banker who acts within its conditions shall be deemed to have paid the bill in due course, notwithstanding the forged or unauthorised indorsement, but the section does operate to give

---

16 *Capital and Counties Bank Ltd v Gordon* [1903] AC 240 at 252 per Lord Lindley.
17 (1862) 13 ICLR 426 at 433.
18 (1875) LR 10 QB 291 at 296.
19 (1885) 53 LT 193.
20 (1876) 1 CPD 548.
1 [1903] AC 240, 8 Com Cas 221.

a discharge of the draft or order,[2] with the same results as follow from compliance with s 60. The section, like s 60, has full effect though the indorsement is per pro. Indeed the decision in *Charles v Blackwell*[3] was on this section, being before the Bills of Exchange Act was passed.

5   PROVISO TO BILLS OF EXCHANGE ACT 1882, s 79

Section 79 concerns cheques crossed specially to more than one banker, and is discussed above in the chapter on crossed cheques.

By the proviso to s 79:

'... where a cheque is presented for payment which does not at the time of presentment appear to be crossed, or to have had a crossing which has been obliterated, or to have been added to or altered otherwise than as authorised by this Act, the banker paying the cheque in good faith and without negligence shall not be responsible or incur any liability, nor shall the payment be questioned by reason of the cheque having been crossed, or of the crossing having been obliterated or having been added to or altered otherwise than as authorised by this Act, and of payment having been made otherwise than to a banker or to the banker to whom the cheque is or was crossed, or to his agent for collection being a banker, as the case may be.'

The point covered by this proviso is of little practical importance. The requirement that payment be made 'in good faith and without negligence' is also a requirement of s 80, and it is in relation to that section that its meaning is considered.

6   BILLS OF EXCHANGE ACT 1882, s 80

Section 80 of the Bills of Exchange Act 1882 reads:

'Where the banker, on whom a crossed cheque is drawn, in good faith and without negligence pays it, if crossed generally, to a banker, and if crossed specially, to the banker to whom it is crossed, or his agent for collection being a banker, the banker paying the cheque, and, if the cheque has come into the hands of the payee, the drawer, shall respectively be entitled to the same rights and be placed in the same position as if payment of the cheque had been made to the true owner thereof'.

(a) 'Without negligence'

There is little guidance on what constitutes negligence within s 80. The reason is not hard to identify. Payment of a crossed cheque bearing a forged indorsement is protected not only by s 80, but also by s 60 and by s 1 of the Cheques Act 1957. A payment is protected under s 60 and s 1 if made 'in the ordinary course of business', and it has already been noted under s 60 that a payment may be in the ordinary course of business even if made negligently. Thus negligence does not preclude relief under s 60 or s 1, but conduct amounting to a violation of the ordinary course of business would amount to negligence and debar the banker from the benefit of s 80. Nor could the banker who paid a cheque with a forged indorsement contrary to the crossing or the

2 *Halifax Union v Wheelwright* (1875) LR 10 Exch 183 at 194.
3 (1876) 1 CPD 548.

ordinary course of business, set up against the true owner the line of defence suggested by *Charles v Blackwell*[4] that the instrument, if returned to the payees by the defendants whose bankers have paid it and were covered by the statute, would be valueless, inasmuch as its subsequent non-payment if re-presented would not be dishonour, because it had effectively been paid already, though to someone without title and that, therefore, there was no right of recourse against the drawer or any previous indorser.

(b) 'True owner'

The true owner of a cheque must be the party with an unassailable title to it whether in possession of it or not, for the reason that a cheque is a negotiable instrument. That party may not be the holder or last transferee; where forgery enters into the matter the true owner must be someone prior to the forgery, but if it is only a question of defective title, even though the transfer may have been affected by fraud, the transferee or holder may yet be the true owner. At the time the cheque is issued either the drawer or the payee is the true owner, the payee if he has not come by the cheque fraudulently and the drawer if the payee has been fraudulent; but if, before the fraud is known, the cheque is transferred to someone taking as a holder in due course within s 29 of the Bills of Exchange Act 1882 he is the true owner.

7   CHEQUES ACT 1957, s 1

The protection which this section offers is additional to that given by s 19 of the Stamp Act 1853 and ss 60 and 80 of the Bills of Exchange Act 1882, and the paying banker is entitled to whatever advantage he can gain from all or any. The section reads:

"1. (1) Where a banker in good faith and in the ordinary course of business pays a cheque drawn on him which is not indorsed or is irregularly indorsed, he does not, in doing so, incur any liability by reason only of the absence of, or irregularity in, indorsement, and he is deemed to have paid in due course.
(2) Where a banker in good faith and in the ordinary course of business pays any such instrument as the following, namely:
(a) a document issued by a customer of his which, though not a bill of exchange, is intended to enable a person to obtain payment from him of the sum mentioned in the document;
(b) a draft payable on demand by him on himself, whether payable at the head office or some other office of his bank;
he does not, in doing so, incur any liability by reason only of the absence of, or irregularity in, indorsement, and the payment discharges the instrument.'

Section 6 enacts that the Act shall be construed as one with the Bills of Exchange Act 1882. As to instruments within s 1(2), see ch 23, above.

(a) Relation between ss 60, 80, 19 and 1

Sections 60 and 80 of the Bills of Exchange Act 1882 and s 19 of the Stamp Act 1853 are concerned essentially with the problems of forged indorsements, a risk against which the paying banker is clearly entitled to be protected. Those sections do not, however, afford protection against risks which are

---

4 (1877) 2 CPD 151 at 159, the action being brought on s 19 of the Stamp Act 1853.

apparent on the face of a cheque, in particular, the absence of or irregularity in indorsement. Payment in such circumstances would not be in the ordinary course of business (within s 60), nor without negligence (within s 80); and the protection of s 19 does not extend to the payment of cheques. Accordingly, before the passing of the Cheques Act 1957, prudent banking practice required the paying banker to dishonour cheques which lacked indorsement or which were irregularly indorsed.

The avowed purpose of the Cheques Act 1957 was to eliminate the need for the indorsement of cheques and analogous instruments. It achieves this objective by preventing the paying banker from incurring liability by reason only of the absence of, or irregularity in, indorsement of the instruments mentioned in s 1(1) and (2).

There is a striking difference in the approach taken in the 1957 Act between the paying banker and the collecting banker. The protection of the collecting banker had previously existed by virtue of s 82 of the Bills of Exchange Act 1882. When this protection was extended in 1957, s 82 was repealed and re-enacted with modifications in s 4 of the Cheques Act 1957. In the case of the paying banker, the additional protection contained in s 1 of the 1957 Act was engrafted onto the existing law. From the standpoint of clarity, it is unfortunate that the protection available to the paying banker was not brought within the one enactment. Insofar as any inference can be drawn from the non-repeal of the earlier legislation, it is that the legislature intended that paying banks should not disregard altogether the indorsement of cheques and other orders to pay on demand. There do indeed remain circumstances in which the paying banker ought to require an indorsement (see 'Indorsement Required' below).

(b) Effect of s 1(1) and (2)

Subsections 1(1) and (2) cover much the same ground. The difference is that the one concerns cheques, and the other instruments analogous to cheques. As regards both, payment must be in good faith and in the ordinary course of business. There is, however, a curious difference in the drafting between the stated effect of the two subsections. As regards payment of cheques, the effect is that the banker is deemed to have paid in due course (s 1(1)), but as regards instruments analogous to cheques, the effect is that the instrument is discharged (s 1(2)). It is permitted to wonder why different language is used. Further, inasmuch as the protection offered by the section is directed to absence of or irregularity in indorsement, why could not s 1(1) have been combined with s 1(2) – unless discharge under the latter has not the same effect as payment in due course in s 1(1). Is not the banker under s 1(2) regarded as having paid in due course if the instrument is discharged? Another curious feature of the drafting is that s 1(2)(a) is not limited to instruments payable on demand, notwithstanding that the Act is dealing with cheques and analogous instruments. The probable explanation is that s 1(2)(a) replaced s 17 of the Revenue Act 1883, which extended the crossed cheques sections of the Bills of Exchange Act 1882 to certain 'documents' as if they were cheques, and, therefore, payable on demand. Moreover, it is hard to visualise an instrument falling within s 1(2)(a) which in the ordinary course of business would not be payable on demand.

(c) Indorsement required

Since the passing of the Act, however, the paying banker has required an 'indorsement' on cheques and other instruments cashed (i) at the counter including those cashed under open credits, or (ii) on combined cheque and receipt forms marked 'R', or (iii) on cheques payable to joint payees where offered for credit to an account to which all are not parties. This practice follows the circular dated 23 September 1957 issued by the Committee of London Clearing Bankers. The adoption of the practice prescribed by the circular may have established a new course of business, departure from which could be held to be not in the ordinary course of business. In other words 'the ordinary course of business' as understood by s 1 of the Act may, by reason of the universal practice of bankers, be different from that which it was before the Act was passed. It is probable that the signature obtained in the above cases is a receipt; but, if it is ever an indorsement as understood by the Acts, it is submitted that it must be regular to afford the banker a discharge and that if it is a forgery, s 1 may not protect him. Where an indorsement is demanded and a forged signature is the result it is submitted that there is no valid payment, no discharge, and that the protection of the section is not available, because payment is not in the ordinary course of business as practised by bankers in spite of the licence offered by the section. It may be argued that a forged indorsement is no indorsement; but this argument would fail for the same reason that it failed in regard to s 19 and s 60.

The Act makes no reference to cheques paid to a bank for the credit of the account of the payee and it does not readily appear that it was the intention of the legislature so to restrict the operation of the statute – rather the reverse, which view receives some support from the House of Lords' decision in *Westminster Bank Ltd v Zang*[5] although Lord Denning MR,[6] in the Court of Appeal, thought that a banker who receives a cheque for collection can only dispense with indorsement when it is to be credited to the account of the payee; he thought that the bankers interpreted the intention of the Legislature aright when they issued their memorandum.

8   REGULARITY OF AN INDORSEMENT

(a) Relevance

Payment against an irregular indorsement is not protected by ss 60 or 80 of the Bills of Exchange Act 1882, but is now protected by s 1 of the Cheques Act 1957. The regularity of an indorsement has therefore become less important since the passing of the 1957 Act. It is not, however, irrelevant because the protection of that Act is conditional upon payment being made in the ordinary course of business, and if this condition is not satisfied, it may be necessary to establish the regularity of an indorsement.

---

5 [1966] AC 182 per Viscount Dilhorne at 218 and Lord Reid at 222.
6 [1966] AC 182 at 202.

(b) Requisites of a regular indorsement

By s 32(1) of the Bills of Exchange Act 1882, an indorsement must be written on the bill itself and be signed by the indorser. The simple signature of the indorser on the bill, without additional words, is sufficient. A regular indorsement in the case of an *individual* is one which purports to be that of the payee or indorsee, by reproducing exactly the name as shown on the cheque. As Wright J said in *Slingsby v District Bank Ltd*:[7]

'But I think the paying bank ought to require a signature indicating the position exactly as it is indicated by the mandate describing the payee.'

The regularity of an indorsement by a *company* is governed by s 37 of the Companies Act 1985, discussed in ch 9, above.

(c) 'Per pro'; 'for'; 'on behalf of'

Cheques and other instruments are commonly signed by persons acting in a representative capacity. In such cases, the indorsement is not regular if the representative capacity stated is not reasonably compatible with authority to indorse. For example, an office boy or porter would not normally have authority to indorse a cheque on behalf of his employer.

The point has arisen in this connection whether there is a difference between a person signing 'per pro' another person, and a person signing 'for' or 'on behalf of' another. By s 25 of the Bills of Exchange Act 1882:

'A signature by procuration operates as notice that the agent has but a limited authority to sign, and the principal is only bound by such signature if the agent in so signing was acting within the actual limits of his authority.'

In his dissenting judgment in *McDonald & Co v Nash & Co*, Scrutton LJ said:[8]

'The other point is that F W Nash, who signed for Nash & Co, had no authority to sign in that way, and that the form "for" gave notice of agency and put the other parties on enquiry. This is the effect of the signature "per pro" under s 25 of the Act. On this point I refer to the careful judgment of Chief Baron Pigott in *O'Reilly v Richardson*, with which I agree. He limits the cases in which one is put on enquiry to cases where the form of signature shows a special and limited authority as "per procurationem" or "under power of attorney", and excludes cases of a general authority as "A for B".'

Pigott CB had said in *O'Reilly v Richardson*:[9]

'An acceptance "for Richardson & Son, Thomas Popple" is not equivalent in the law merchant to the form "per pro. Richardson & Son, Thomas Popple". The former does not, like the latter, import a special and limited authority to do a specific act; nor does it put the drawer of a bill, accepted in that form, upon discovery, whether the agent has exceeded his authority. Acceptance "for" is to be governed by the general rule of law applicable to principal and agent. Therefore the course of dealing by the agent acting for his principal with third parties is evidence to go to a jury towards determining the extent of the agent's authority'.

---

7 [1931] 2 KB 588 at 597, affd [1932] 1 KB 544, CA.
8 [1922] WN 272, CA; revsd on appeal [1924] AC 625.
9 (1865) 17 ICLR 74. This statement was also approved by Rowlett J in *Alexander Stewart & Son of Dundee Ltd v Westminster Bank Ltd* [1926] WN 126, revsd [1926] WN 271, 4 Legal Decisions Affecting Bankers 40, CA.

The same was held by Byles J in *Stagg v Elliott*,[10] citing *Alexander v M'Kenzie*, in which Maule J said: '... the extent of the authority is to be inferred from its exercise and the mode of exercising it does not import any limitation of the authority'.[11]

The other Lords Justices in *O'Reilly v Richardson*[12] decided on grounds which made this point immaterial, and they did not deal with it. It was a case of taking a bill as transferee, in which s 25 operates. In a similar case, *Alexander Stewart & Son of Dundee Ltd v Westminster Bank Ltd*,[13] Atkin LJ was disposed to agree with Scrutton LJ. But the wording of s 60, let alone the obvious impossibility of a paying banker going into questions of indorsements other than that of his own customer, excludes as regards a paying banker any importation of s 25. Section 25 was held in *Morison v London County and Westminster Bank Ltd*[14] not to affect s 82, Lord Reading LCJ appearing to suggest that the operation of s 25 was limited to the time before the instrument was honoured (though Lord Atkin in *Midland Bank Ltd v Reckitt*,[15] declined to limit the 'period within which alone the section affects legal rights').

(d) Position of 'per pro'

There are further differences of opinion as to the proper placing of a per pro signature. 'Per pro James Brown, John Smith', is said to be correct on a cheque payable to James Brown; 'James Brown, per pro John Smith' is said to be wrong. And yet, if the object is, as it must be, to get as near an actual signature as possible, one would think the latter form the more appropriate as meaning 'This is the signature of James Brown affixed, with his authority, by me, John Smith', whereas the former might be interpreted, 'By the authority of James Brown I sign myself John Smith'. This opinion was quoted with approval by Scrutton LJ in *Slingsby v District Bank Ltd*[16] in dealing with the indorsement of a cheque drawn in the form 'A per B'. It is to be noted that in *Charles v Blackwell*,[17] the very case to which bankers owe the extension of their immunity under s 60 to per pro indorsements, the words per pro occur between the two names, not before that of the principal. If the Latin of the per procurationem be extended to the signature, this seems to be the legitimate interpretation.

9   'NOT NEGOTIABLE' AND 'ACCOUNT PAYEE'

The general effect of these words has already been considered in ch 22. It is convenient to summarise here their effect on the paying banker.

10 (1862) 12 CBNS 373 at 381–2.
11 *Grant v Norway* (1851) 10 CB 665; *Attwood v Munnings* (1872) 7 B & C 278.
12 (1865) 17 ICLR 74.
13 [1926] WN 271.
14 [1914] 3 KB 356.
15 [1933] AC 1.
16 [1932] 1 KB 544.
17 (1877) 2 CPD 151.

(a) 'Not negotiable'

The not negotiable crossing means that no-one can get a better title to a cheque so crossed than his transferor. The paying bank is unaffected by the crossing. The fact that a cheque so crossed bears indorsements indicating negotiation does not put him on inquiry. Although the drawee banker is protected if he does effect payment, it is submitted that he would be justified in refusing payment of a cheque so crossed bearing indorsement on the ground that his mandate was ambiguous.

(b) 'Account payee' and subsequent indorsements

It has been suggested that the words 'account payee' are an indication to the drawee bank not to pay the cheque bearing them if when the cheque is presented it bears indorsements indicating that it has not been collected for the payee. But, unless the words are printed on the cheque, the banker has no means of knowing whether they were put on by the drawer, by the payee or some other person. Further, the drawer, even if he himself is responsible for the addition, has issued an instrument negotiable ad infinitum by indorsement, with nothing which in law tends to limit that negotiability. The mandate is contradictory and ambiguous and the banker therefore incurs no liability by acting upon a reasonable construction of it. If one of the indorsements was forged the true owner might contend that the paying banker was not protected by s 60 as not having paid the cheque 'in good faith and in the ordinary course of business' or by s 80, as not having paid it 'without negligence'; and the drawer might for the same reason object to be debited. It is, however, submitted that this argument is fallacious, the answer being that the instrument is negotiable, the marking 'account payee' having no effect in restraining the cheque's legal transfer.

CHAPTER 25

MONEY PAID BY MISTAKE[1]

1 INTRODUCTION

Typical instances of payments made by a bank under a mistake of fact are (1) payments made in the mistaken belief that a customer's purported signature is genuine, when in fact it has been forged; and (2) payments made in the mistaken belief that a payment instruction remains extant, when in fact it has been countermanded. In neither case is the bank entitled to be reimbursed by its customer, and the question then arises as to the bank's entitlement to recover the payment from the payee.

The principles underlying the law relating to the recovery of money paid by mistake have been variously stated over the years without any very clear expression emerging and the law is, perhaps, not clearly defined even today . Much has been clarified by the judgments of Kerr J in *National Westminster Bank Ltd v Barclays Bank International Ltd*[2] and of Robert Goff J in *Barclays Bank Ltd v W J Simms, Son and Cooke (Southern) Ltd*.[3] In the latter the judge said that the key to the problem of the recovery of money paid by mistake lay in a careful reading of the earliest and most fundamental authorities and in giving full effect to certain decisions of the House of Lords.

The claim is often for money had and received to the use of the claimant, which in *Holt v Markham*[4] Scrutton LJ tersely described as:

'... a troublesome instance of a particularly troublesome class of action. It is an action for money had and received to the plaintiffs' use, and is based upon the ground that the payment was made under a mistake of fact ... the whole history of this particular form of action has been what I may call a history of well-meaning sloppiness of thought.'

This he attributed to Lord Mansfield's judgment in *Sadler v Evans*[5] to the effect that:

---

1 The editor gratefully acknowledges that this chapter has been updated, and in large part rewritten, by Mr Richard McManus, Barrister. For an exhaustive treatment of this subject, see *The Law of Restitution* (3rd edn, 1986), by Lord Goff and Gareth Jones, chs 3 and 4.
2 [1975] QB 654, [1974] 3 All ER 834.
3 [1980] QB 677, [1979] 3 All ER 522.
4 [1923] 1 KB 504, CA.
5 (1766) 4 Burr 1984 at 1986.

'It is a liberal action, founded upon large principles of equity, where the defendant cannot conscientiously hold the money. The defence is any equity that will rebut the action.'

In 1938 Sir Wilfrid Greene MR in *Morgan v Ashcroft*[6] stated that:

'The nature of a claim to recover money paid under a mistake and the limits within which it can be made, have been the subject of much controversy and the difficulties involved in providing a comprehensive solution to these problems have not as yet been overcome.'

Fifteen years later Lord Wright said in the House of Lords in *Fibrosa Spolka v Alcyjna v Alcyjna Fairbairn Lawson Combe Barbour Ltd:*[7]

'It is clear that any civilised system of law is bound to provide remedies for cases of what has been called unjust enrichment[8] or unjust benefit, that is to prevent a man from retaining the money or some benefit derived from another which it is against conscience that he should keep. Such remedies in English law are generally different from remedies in contract or in tort and are now recognised to fall within a third category of the common law which has been called quasi-contract or restitution ... Payment under a mistake of fact is only one head of this category of the law ... The gist of the action is a debt, or obligation implied, or, more accurately, imposed by law.'

Even at that date and perhaps for some years after it could hardly be said that the law was much clearer. If unjust enrichment is the basis for recovery of money paid by mistake it is necessary to know what 'unjust' means and the same may be said to apply to 'enrichment', though this is probably less uncertain. If a defendant has been 'enriched' by money to which he was not entitled – in the sense that he could not have demanded it – and if his only loss in restitution would be these same moneys, then there would appear to be no good reason why he should not be liable to repay in an action for the return of money had and received; to retain it in these circumstances would be unjust to the payer. If every case could be brought within this simple instance, the history of this form of action would be immaterial.

In *Kiriri Cotton Co Ltd v Dewani*[9] Lord Denning said that the action was not an action in contract or imputed contract (as was at one time thought), but simply an action for restitution of money which the defendant has received but which the law says he ought to return. And in the *Fibrosa*[10] case Lord Wright said that all heads of money had and received, such as money paid under a mistake of fact or paid under a consideration that has wholly failed, or, again, paid by one who is not in pari delicto with the defendant, are only instances where the law says the money ought to be returned.

The basis of the right of recovery has also been variously stated as retention

6 [1938] 1 KB 49 at 62; and see Asquith J in *Weld-Blundell v Synott* [1940] 2 KB 107 at 112: 'It is notoriously difficult to harmonise all the cases dealing with payment of money under mistake of fact'.
7 [1943] AC 32 at 61.
8 'Unjust enrichment', as stated in *Goff and Jones* is, simply, the name which is commonly given to the principle of justice which the law recognises, and gives effect to in a wide variety of claims.
9 [1960] AC 192 at 204, PC.
10 [1943] AC 32, HL.

being 'against conscience'; or the receipt as being 'wrongful'; or based on the obligation on the recipient to repay because 'of the ties of natural justice and equity'; or on repayment being 'just and reasonable'; or, again, recovery being of money which 'rightly belongs' to the payer. However, as to this Hamilton LJ (later Lord Sumner) in *Baylis v Bishop of London*[11] said:

'To ask what course would be *ex aequo et bono* to both sides never was a very precise guide and as a working rule it has long since been buried in *Standish v Ross*[12] and *Kelly v Solari*[13].'

In the United States, in 1901[14] Chief Justice Holmes said that the ground for recovery for a payment under a mistake of fact is that the existence of the fact supposed was the conventional basis or tacit condition of the transaction, and the court applied the rule in *Price v Neal*.[15]

Yet it was put generally in *Brooks Wharf and Bull Wharf Ltd v Goodman Brothers*:[16]

'The obligation [to repay] is imposed by the court simply under the circumstances of the case and on what the court decides is just and reasonable having regard to the relationship of the parties. It is a debt or obligation constituted by the act of the law, apart from any consent or intention of the parties or privity of contract.'

As a general statement this is hard to question; nevertheless it leaves unsaid what is the act of the law by which a debtor obligation is constituted.

2   CONDITIONS FOR RECOVERY

In the last edition of *Paget*, the conditions for recovery were considered under nine principles.[17] In the light of *Barclays Bank Ltd v W J Simms, Son & Cooke (Southern) Ltd*,[18] this categorisation can now be simplified. The essential principles were summarised in the *Simms* case by Robert Goff J as follows:[19]

'(1) If a person pays money to another under a mistake of fact which causes him to make the payment, he is prima facie entitled to recover it as money paid under a mistake of fact. (2) His claim may however fail if (a) the payer intends that the payee shall have the money at all events, whether the fact be true or false, or is deemed in law so to intend; or (b) the payment is made for good consideration, in particular if the money is paid to discharge, and does discharge, a debt owed to the payee (or a principal on whose behalf he is authorised to receive the payment) by the payer or by a third party by whom he is authorised to discharge the debt; or (c) the payee has changed his position in good faith, or is deemed in law to have done so.'

The first proposition contains three elements:

11 [1913] 1 Ch 127, CA.
12 (1849) 3 Exch 527.
13 (1841) 9 M & W 54.
14 *Dedham National Bank v Everett National Bank* 177 Mass 392 at 395 (1901).
15 (1762) 3 Burr 1354.
16 [1937] 1 KB 534 per Lord Wright MR at 545, CA.
17 See *Paget* (9th edn) pp 286 et seq.
18 [1980] QB 677, [1979] 3 All ER 522.
19 Ibid at, respectively, 695 and 535.

1 The mistake must be one of fact, not one of law.
2 The mistake must have caused the payment.
3 The mistake must have been that of the payer, but not necessarily that of the payee.

If the foregoing conditions are satisfied, there is a prima facie right of recovery. This right may, however, be defeated in any of the three circumstances referred to in the second proposition.

(a) Mistake must be one of fact

(i) The general principle

The general principle is that the mistake must be one of fact, and not one of law. In the *Simms* case, Robert Goff J founded this proposition on three cases in the House of Lords, namely *Kleinwort, Sons & Co v Dunlop Rubber Co*,[20] *Kerrison v Glyn, Mills, Currie & Co*,[1] and *R. E. Jones Ltd v Waring and Gillow Ltd*.[2] The principle can be traced back to *Kelly v Solari*, decided in 1841, where Lord Abinger said:[3]

'The safest rule however is that if the party makes the payment with full knowledge of the facts, although under ignorance of the law, there being no fraud on the other side, he cannot recover it back again.'

(ii) Distinction between fact and law

The authorities contain numerous examples of mistakes of fact. In the context of banking, these include payment on a forged cheque,[4] payment of a cheque contrary to a stop instruction,[5] and payment to a person other than the person directed.[6] Examples of a mistake of law include payment under a mistaken construction of a statute[7] and payment in reliance upon a judicial decision which is subsequently overruled.[8]

The distinction between fact and law is, however, one which gives rise to difficulty in this area of the law, as it does in other areas. A particular difficulty is that of payments made under a mistaken construction of a covenant. There appears to be a rule that such payments are irrecoverable.[9] The leading modern authority is *Re Hatch*[10], where a husband and later his executors

---

20 (1907) 97 LT 263.
1 (1911) 81 LJKB 465.
2 [1926] AC 670.
3 (1841) 9 M & W 54.
4 *National Westminster Bank v Barclays Bank International Ltd* [1975] QB 654, [1974] 3 All ER 834.
5 *Barclays Bank Ltd v W J Simms, Son & Cooke (Southern) Ltd* [1980] QB 677, [1979] 3 All ER 522.
6 *Kleinwort, Sons & Co v Dunlop Rubber Co* (1907) 97 LT 263.
7 See, eg *Whiteley Ltd v R* (1909) 26 TLR 19 (monies paid by way of duty to the Commissioners of Inland Revenue on a mistaken construction of a statute held to be irrecoverable).
8 See, eg *Henderson v Folkestone Waterworks Co* (1885) 1 TLR 329 (monies paid pursuant to a water rating which was subsequently declared by the House of Lords to be unlawful, held to be irrecoverable).
9 See *Atwood v Lamprey* (1719) 3 P Wms 127 cited in a note to *East v Thornbury* (1731) 3 P Wms 126; *Currie v Goold* (1817) 2 Madd 163; *Denby v Moore* (1817) 1B & Ald 123; *Warren v Warren* (1895) 72 LT 628; *Shrewsbury v Shrewsbury* (1906) 23 TLR 100; *Re Hatch* [1919] 1 Ch 351; *Holt v Markham* [1923] 1 KB 504.
10 [1919] 1 Ch 351.

failed to make deductions for income tax in making covenanted payments to his wife. It was held that the overpayments were made under a mistake of law and could not be recovered. The case is not a strong one because it was conceded by counsel that the mistake was one of law,[11] albeit that the concession was accepted as having been rightly made by Sargent J. Further the mistake was not purely one of construction; the decision was underpinned by a question of law as to whether income tax was properly deductible. Virtually all the authorities on which the apparent rule is based have had in the background a similar legal question, that is, the application to particular facts of an Act of Parliament or some form of delegated legislation. *Re Hatch* was followed in the materially identical case of *Ord v Ord*,[12] and although it was criticised in *Re Diplock*,[13] that criticism was not in relation to the present point.

The existence of an apparent rule that misconstruction of a contract is a mistake of law is difficult to reconcile with the 'private rights' doctrine enunciated in *Cooper v Phibbs*.[14] There Cooper entered into an agreement with Phibbs to pay rent in respect of a fishery which Cooper already owned pursuant to various settlements (including a private Act of Parliament). It was held by the House of Lords that he was entitled to relief from the agreement as he had made a mistake as to his private rights. The decision is not considered in the cases relating to misconstruction of covenants.

Further the apparent rule rests uneasily with the rule that a misrepresentation as to the contents of a document is one of fact.[15] If it is a question of fact for the purposes of misrepresentation if ought equally to be so for the purposes of mistake. It is difficult to discern any legal policy behind a rule which would permit recovery of a payment by someone who relied upon a misrepresentation as to the contents of a contract, but would deny recovery to a person who made a payment having read a contract but honestly misconstrued its effect. The distinction between contents and construction is both artificial and difficult to draw in practice.

Despite these objections to the apparent rule that a misconstruction of a covenant is a mistake of law it would be unsafe to conclude that the rule is not established. It is, however, open to reconsideration.

(iii) Exceptional cases

In exceptional cases the courts have allowed recovery of repayments made under a mistake of law. Although their precise limits are far from clear, the main cases appear to be payments made by trustees or personal representatives, at least where the recovery is by way of deduction from future payments;[16] payments made to an officer of the court;[17] payments where there is an implied contract for repayment in certain circumstances;[18] payments of

11 Ibid at 354, 356.
12 [1923] 2 KB 432.
13 [1948] Ch 465 at 500, which observations were approved on appeal, [1951] AC 251 at 276.
14 (1867) LR 2 HL 149, especially per Lord Westbury at 170.
15 See, eg *Wauton v Coppard* [1899] 1 Ch 92.
16 *Dibbs v Goren* (1849) 11 Beav 483 at 484; *Livesy v Livesy* (1827) 3 Russ 287; *Re Musgrave* [1916] 2 Ch 417.
17 *Re Carnac, ex p Simmonds* (1885) 16 QBD 308.
18 *Sebel Products Ltd v Comrs of Customs & Excise* [1949] Ch 409, [1949] 1 All ER 729.

public monies without legal authority;[19] payments made pursuant to a court order which is reversed on appeal;[20] and payments induced by the payee's fraud, oppression, undue influence or breach of fiduciary duty, or received in bad faith.[1]

This last exception to the general rule was applied and extended by the Privy Council in *Kiriri Cotton Co Ltd v Dewani*[2] to enable the recovery by a tenant of an illegal premium, the duty of observing the law having been placed on the shoulders of one rather than the other.

(b) Mistake must have caused the payment

The mistake must have caused the payment, and the burden of so proving is on the payer.[3] This burden includes satisfying the court on the balance of probabilities that the relevant mistake was one of fact and not one of law, and ordinarily it will be necessary to identify and call the person acting on behalf of the payer who was mistaken. Although this was not done in *Avon County Council v Howlett*, Slade LJ sounded a warning that in the future this would be expected.[4]

Where the payment is induced by a mistake as to two matters, the dominant mistake has to be one of fact. The law was so stated by Lord Kingsdown in *Trigge v Lavallee*:[5]

'The rule, as we collect it, from the numerous authorities cited in the argument, appears to be this: – if the error relied on be in a matter of fact, ... and of such a character that it must be considered the determining motive of either of the parties entering into the agreement, its existence is regarded as a condition implied, though not expressed; and then, if the fact fail, the foundation of the agreement fails'.

Although *Trigge v Lavallee* turned exclusively on French law, the court expressed the view that the law of France had in effect been adopted by English law.[6]

In *Home and Colonial Insurance Co Ltd v London Guarantee and Accident Co Ltd*[7] payments were made under marine insurance contracts without stamped policies having been issued. The payer, a liquidator, was ignorant as to the fact that no stamped policies had been issued and also of the law that it was essential to liability that such policies had been issued. It was held by Wright J that the payment was irrecoverable:[8]

'Mr Barham [the liquidator] admitted that if he had been told that no stamped policies had been issued he would have regarded it as irrelevant. His mind was ignorant both of the fact and of the law, but the more important part of the

19 *Auckland Harbour Board v R* [1924] AC 318 at 326–327.
20 *Re Birkbeck Permanent Benefit Building Society* [1915] 1 Ch 91.
 1 *Rogers v Ingham* (1876) 3 Ch D 351.
 2 [1960] AC 192, [1960] 1 All ER 177, PC. See also *Harse v Pearl Life Assurance Co* [1904] 1 KB 558 at 564 per Romer LJ. The *Kiriri Cotton* case was applied by the Court of Appeal in *Shelley v Paddock* [1980] QB 348, [1980] 1 All ER 1009, CA.
 3 *Holt v Markham* [1923] 1 KB 504, CA; *Avon County Council v Howlett* [1983] 1 All ER 1073, [1983] 1 WLR 605, CA.
 4 [1983] 1 All ER 1073 at 1085b, [1983] 1 WLR 605 at 620A.
 5 (1862) 15 Moo PCC 270 at 298.
 6 Ibid at 303.
 7 (1928) 45 TLR 134.
 8 Ibid at 135.

ignorance was that of the law. If he had known that there were no stamped policies
his ignorance of the law would still have led him to act as he did in paying the
money. The onus was on a plaintiff claiming to recover money paid under mistake
of fact to show that he was induced to pay by his ignorance of the fact and by
nothing else and there was no right to recover money paid where knowledge of
the fact would not have affected his conduct.'

Wright J was following *Trigge v Lavallee*, and notwithstanding his reference
to the payer having been induced by nothing else than a mistake of fact, it is
submitted that the rule is that a mistake of fact must simply be the dominant
reason for the payment.

There is some suggestion in the authorities that it is not sufficient that a
payment was induced by a mistake of fact unless the mistake is fundamental
in the sense that it relates to a material fact which, if true, would make the
person paying liable to pay the money.[9] It was pointed out by Robert Goff
J in the *Simms* case that this proposition is inconsistent with the Privy
Council's decision in *Colonial Bank v Exchange Bank of Yarmouth, Nova
Scotia*,[10] and also with the three House of Lords cases referred to above in
considering the general principle that the mistake must be one of fact. It is
submitted that no such requirement exists.

(c) Mistake must be that of payer, but not necessarily that of payee

(i) The general principle

It is only necessary that the mistake be on the part of the payer; it is not
necessary that the payee be also mistaken,[11] and it is not material if he was
mistaken.

As was pointed out in *Lloyds Bank Ltd v The Hon Cecily K. Brooks*:[12]

'If the hand that pays the money, even though it is only that of an agent, is acting
under a mistake of fact, that payment is a payment made under a mistake of fact.'

This point was raised in *Secretary of State for Employment v Wellworthy
(No 2)*[13] in which Nield J said:

'It is submitted [by the employee] that the Secretary of State has failed to show
that the money was paid because of a mistake on his part, and he complained that
local officers had not been called who were best able to deal with this question and
he indeed submitted that the witnesses who were called were once or twice removed
from the persons who had the real knowledge of these matters. Mr Sumner,
however, on behalf of the Secretary of State points out rightly in my view that the
crucial time to be considered in this regard is the time when payment of the rebate
was made by the Secretary of State and thus it was wholly proper to call the officer
concerned at that time, who was Miss Micklethwaite, and her evidence is very
clear. She told the court she had initialled the RPI's:
 "and when I did so I did not know that any of the men had been reemployed
 by the defendants. ...."

9 See *Aiken v Short* (1856) 1 H & N 210 at 215, per Bramwell B; *Morgan v Ashcroft* [1938] 1
 KB 49, [1937] 3 All ER 92, CA; *Norwich Union Fire Insurance Society Ltd v Price Ltd* [1934]
 AC 455, 40 Com Cas 132, PC.
10 (1885) 11 App Cas 84.
11 See, eg *Westminster Bank Ltd v Arlington Overseas Trading Co* [1952] 1 Lloyd's Rep 211.
12 (1950) 6 LDAB 161 at 164, per Lynskey J.
13 [1976] ICR 13 at 22.

In my view there is certainly evidence to show that the Secretary of State made these rebate payments because of the mistaken beliefs which are pleaded.'

The mistake must therefore be made by the person who pays the money or authorises the payment of the money and the rule in *Kelly v Solari*,[14] that:

'the knowledge of the facts which disentitles the party from recovering must mean a knowledge existing in the mind at the time of payment'

and that:

'generally speaking the money may be recovered back however careless the party paying may have been in omitting to use due diligence to inquire into the fact' (Parke B at 59)

applies to the person actually paying and includes the absence of diligence in inquiring from other employees of the plaintiff.

(ii) Mistake as between payer and payee

There are several statements in the authorities that the mistake must be as to some matter between the party paying and the party receiving,[15] and this proposition was advanced in the last edition of *Paget*.[16] This led Kerr J, to state, obiter, in *National Westminster Bank Ltd v Barclays Bank Ltd*:[17]

'It is settled law that if a bank honours a cheque or bill in the mistaken belief that it has sufficient funds from its customer to do so, then the money cannot be recovered back, because a mistake of this nature only operates between the bank and its customer and not between the bank and the payee: see the authorities in *Paget's Law of Banking* (8th edn, 1972).'

However, in the *Simms* case,[18] Robert Goff J subjected the supposed rule that the mistake must be as between payer and payee to a searching analysis, and rejected it, observing that its reformulation by Asquith J in *Weld-Blundell v Synott*[19] and by Windeyer J in *Porter v Latec Finance (Queensland) Pty Ltd*[20] mean no more than that the mistake must have caused the payment. The decision in the *Simms* case is, of course, contrary to supposed rule of settled law referred to by Kerr LJ.

As Asquith J remarked in *Weld-Blundell v Synott*[1] it is extremely difficult to ascertain what the phrase 'as between the parties' is intended to mean. It has already been noted that there is no requirement that a mistake must relate to the liability of the payer to the payee to make the payment. It has also been noted that there is no requirement that the mistake must be shared by both parties.

The authorities which are said to support the supposed rule are weak. The

---

14 (1841) 9 M & W 54 per Lord Abinger at 58.
15 See *Rogers v Kelly* (1809) 2 Camp 123, per Lord Ellenborough; *Skyring v Greenwood* (1825) 4 B & C 281; *Chambers v Miller* (1862) 13 CBNS 125; *Deutsche Bank (London Agency) v Beriro & Co* (1895) 73 LT 669, 1 Com Cas 255; *Barclay & Co Ltd v Malcolm & Co* (1925) 133 LT 512; *RE Jones Ltd v Waring and Gillow Ltd* [1926] AC 670, especially at 692 (per Lord Sumner); *National Westminster Bank Ltd v Barclays International Bank Ltd* [1975] QB 654, [1974] 3 All ER 834.
16 See *Paget* (9th edn) pp 293–296.
17 [1975] QB 654 at 662 E, [1974] 3 All ER 834 at 841a.
18 [1980] QB 677 at 696C, [1979] 3 All ER 522 at 536e.
19 [1940] 2 KB 107.
20 (1964) 111 CLR 177 at 204.
1 [1940] 2 KB 107.

earliest is *Rogers v Kelly*.[2] That, however, was not an action by the payer to recover a mistaken payment. In *Skyring v Greenwood*,[3] the claim was defeated on the basis of estoppel and it does not appear to have been a ground for the decision that the mistake had to be as between payer and payee.

Chambers v Miller[4] was, as pointed out by Robert Goff J, also not a claim for recovery of a payment made under a mistake of fact, but an action for assault and false imprisonment. The question actually considered by the Court was whether the property had passed in money paid by a cashier under a mistake as to the sufficiency of the funds available in the customer's account. It was not relevant whether the money could be recovered back as paid under a mistake of fact. Only Erle, CJ stated (obiter) that a mistake had to be between the parties. Williams J stated that it was unnecessary to consider whether the money was recoverable as paid under a mistake of fact, albeit that he does appear to suggest that a mistake as to the state of the account would be insufficient to ground recovery. Byles J also stated that even if there had been a mistake of fact, the assault was unjustified. He expressed hesitation as to whether the money was recoverable and by inference suggested that a mistake as to the state of the account was insufficient, but the basis for this conclusion is not clear. Keating J expressly held that the question did not arise as to whether the money was recoverable, and even there was a right of recovery, that did not justify the assault.

In *Deutsche Bank v Beriro*[5] a bill was indorsed by a third party to the defendant, who indorsed it to the plaintiff. The plaintiff thinking mistakenly that the bill had been paid, sent a cheque to the defendant. It was held at first instance that the payment was irrecoverable. The appeal was dismissed on the facts without the Court of Appeal considering that part of the judgment of Matthew J which was based on the authorities.

In *Barclay & Co Ltd v Malcolm & Co*[6] the plaintiff bank paid the sum of £2,000 twice by mistake, believing that a letter confirming an original telegraphic instruction to make a payment was a further instruction. Roche J held that the money was irrecoverable because 'the mistake which was made concerned only the plaintiffs and the Warsaw Bank by whom the plaintiffs were instructed', and it was not a mistake with regard to the liability of one person to pay or the 'right of another to receive'. *Chambers v Miller* was the only case relied on, and the case was also dismissed on the basis that the payment had been ratified.

In the *Simms* case, Robert Goff J observed[7] that the supposed rule is inconsistent with the House of Lords decision in *Re Jones Ltd v Waring & Gillow Ltd*.[8] Nevertheless none of the authorities in support of the supposed rule were overruled. On the contrary, *Skying v Greenwood* and *Deutsche Bank v Beriro* were referred to in the speech of Lord Sumner without disapproval. It would therefore be unsafe to assume that the *Simms* case has settled the law on this issue.

2 (1809) 2 Camp 123.
3 (1825) 4 B & C 281.
4 (1862) 13 CBNS 125.
5 (1895) 73 LT 669, 1 Com Cas 255, CA.
6 (1925) 133 LT 512.
7 [1980] QB 677 at 649D, [1979] 3 All ER 522 at 534g.
8 [1926] AC 670.

(iii) Payment within the mandate

The above point is of considerable practical importance not only where there is a stop instruction, but also where a bank mistakenly believes there are sufficient funds in an account of its customer to meet a cheque drawn on it. If there does not have to be a mistake as between payer and payee, then prima facie a bank should be able to recover from the payee the sum mistakenly paid. In the *Simms* case, Robert Goff J analysed this issue by reference to the customer's mandate:

'The two typical situations, which exemplify payment with or without mandate, arise first where the bank pays in the mistaken belief that there are sufficient funds or overdraft facilities to meet the cheque, and second where the bank overlooks notice of countermand given by the customer. In each case, there is a mistake by the bank which causes the bank to make the payment. But in the first case the effect of the bank's payment is to accept the customer's request for overdraft facilities; the payment is therefore within the bank's mandate, with the result that not only is the bank entitled to have recourse to its customer, but the customer's obligation to the payee is discharged. It follows that the payee has given consideration for the payment; with the consequence that, although the payment has been caused by the bank's mistake, the money is irrecoverable from the payee unless the transaction of payment is itself set aside. Although the bank is unable to recover the money, it has a right of recourse to its customer. In the second case, however, the bank's payment is without mandate. The bank has no recourse to its customer; and the debt of the customer to the payee on the cheque is not discharged. Prima facie, the bank is entitled to recover the money from the payee, unless the payee has changed his position in good faith, or is deemed in law to have done so.'[9]

It is not clear why the fact that the payee gave consideration for the cheque should entail that the paying banker should not be entitled to recover. In most cases this point would not arise – it would be unknown to the paying banker – and the position would be the same no matter for what reason the cheque was given; there may be no debt due to the payee at the time of countermand. Whenever a customer draws a cheque, whether he has the money in account or not, and whether he is justified or not in drawing, it is not easy to see why the fact that the payee may have been entitled vis-à-vis the drawer should deprive the paying banker of the right to recover.

As to payment without a mandate, when payment is countermanded it is because the drawer does not want the cheque paid, yet consideration for it may well have been given by the payee.

The reasoning of Robert Goff J also involves the proposition that the bank can accept an offer without being aware that one is being made in circumstances where had it known the true facts, it would not have accepted it. However the general rule is that an acceptance in ignorance of an offer is of no effect.[10] It is submitted that it remains open to a court to hold that payment by a bank under a mistake as to the sufficiency of funds in the customer's account is prima facie recoverable.

---

9 [1980] QB 677 at 700, [1979] 3 All ER 522 per Robert Goff J at 535.
10 See Treitel *Law of Contract* (7th edn, 1987), p 29.

3 RECOVERABILITY OF PAYMENTS ON NEGOTIABLE INSTRUMENTS

There is some suggestion in the authorities that payments on negotiable instruments are the subject of special rules. Two special rules have been suggested: First, that a payer on a negotiable instrument who is negligent cannot recover a mistaken payment. Secondly, that a payment on a negotiable instrument cannot be recovered if the payee's position might, but not necessarily would, be affected if he had to refund the payment.

(a) Negligence on part of payer

Price v Neal[11] and *Smith v Mercer*[12] both support a rule that payment on a negotiable instrument which is negligent cannot be recovered. They are however both prior to *Kelly v Solari*,[13] which laid down a general rule that negligence is irrelevant. In *Imperial Bank of Canada v Bank of Hamilton*,[14] where payment was made on a fraudulently altered cheque and it was contended that payment had been negligent, Lord Lindley, giving the judgment of the Privy Council, held that the money was recoverable on the basis of *Kelly v Solari:*[15]

> 'As regards negligence in paying the cheque: it cannot be denied that when the Bank of Hamilton paid the cheque on January 27, it had the means of ascertaining from its own books that the cheque had been altered. But means of knowledge and actual knowledge are not the same; and it was long ago decided in *Kelly v Solari* that money honestly paid by mistake of facts could be recovered back, although the person paying it did not avail himself of means of knowledge which he possessed. This decision has always been acted upon since, and their Lordships consider it applicable to the present case.'

Lord Lindley did go on to state that there were no circumstances exciting suspicion. However, it is submitted that he was there simply dealing with an additional reason why the defence of negligence failed and not departing from the view which he had just expressed that a payer who fails to avail himself of means of knowledge is not thereby debarred from recovery. It might also be said that *Imperial Bank of Canada v Bank of Hamilton* is not an authority on the relevance of negligence to payment under a bill of exchange because there never was a valid bill of exchange by reason of the forgery. This argument is unsound because Lord Lindley treated the cheque as valid for $5, the amount for which it was drawn and certified.[16]

There is little assistance on this point in *National Westminster Bank Ltd v Barclays Bank International Ltd*[17] where the 'cheques' were total forgeries and not valid bills of exchange. Kerr J accepted that there was a prima facie right of recovery even if the payer had the means of discovering the mistake,

11 (1762) 3 Burr 1354.
12 (1815) 6 Taunt 76.
13 (1841) 9 M & W 54.
14 [1903] AC 49, PC.
15 Ibid at 56.
16 Cf *Kwei Tek Chao v British Traders and Shippers Ltd* [1954] 2 QB 459 at 476, [1954] 1 All ER 779 at 787F, per Devlin J.
17 [1975] QB 654, [1974] 3 All ER 834.

but also found it necessary to dispose of an argument that special collection implied something sinister or suspicious which should have put the paying bank on guard.[18]

In the *Simms* case,[19] Robert Goff J formulated the relevant principles without reference to negligence being a bar to recovery, but the point does not appear to have been argued before him.

On policy grounds, there appears to be no reason for excluding payments on negotiable instruments from the general rule that negligence is irrelevant, and it is submitted that the authorities do not establish any such exception.

(b) Recovery where payee's position might be prejudiced

There is a rule, derived principally from *Cocks v Masterman*[20] and *London and River Plate Bank v Bank of Liverpool*[1] that where money is paid on a negotiable instrument to a person innocent of any knowledge of mistake it cannot be recovered if the payee's position might, not necessarily would, be affected if he had to refund the payment. This suggests that while in all other cases, in resisting an action for recovery of money paid to him under a mistake of fact, the defendant must establish an estoppel on the basis of his having actually acted to his detriment, in relation to negotiable instruments the principle is that the defendant need only show that his position might be affected if he had to repay.

In *Cocks v Masterman* a bill which had a forged acceptance was paid on its due date in ignorance of this fact. The payer discovered the forgery on the following day, and gave notice to the payee and demanded repayment. It was held that the payer could not recover even though the holder was not bound to take any steps against the parties to the bill until the day after it was dishonoured. Bayley J, delivering the judgment of the court, laid down a strict rule:

'But we are all of the opinion that the holder of a bill is entitled to know, on the day when it becomes due whether it is an honoured or dishonoured bill, and that, if he receives the money and is suffered to retain it during the whole of that day, the parties who paid it cannot recover it back. The holder, indeed, is not bound by law (if the bill be dishonoured by the acceptor) to take any steps against the other parties to the bill till the day after it is dishonoured. But he is entitled so to do, if he thinks fit, and the parties who pay the bill ought not by their negligence to deprive the holder of any right or privilege. If we were to hold that the plaintiffs were entitled to recover, it would be in effect saying that the plaintiffs might deprive the holder of a bill of his right to take steps against the parties to the bill on the day when it becomes due.'

In *London and River Plate Bank v Bank of Liverpool*,[2] long recognised as the leading authority, Mathew J laid down the law to be derived from *Cocks v Masterman* in even broader terms than the general proposition contained in that judgment. He held that the ruling principle was not negligence or the banker's knowledge or means of knowledge, but the right to an immediate answer as to the fate of a cheque – which is an element essential to the negotiability of the instrument and imperatively demanded by the exigencies

18 Ibid at, respectively, 675 and 851.
19 [1980] QB 677 at 695, [1979] 3 All ER 522 at 535.
20 (1829) 9 B & C 902.
 1 [1896] 1 QB 7.
 2 [1896] 1 QB 7.

of business. A bill drawn in Montevideo on the plaintiffs in London, on which indorsements were forged, was paid by them to the defendants; some months later the forgeries were discovered and the action brought to recover the money as paid under a mistake of fact. Matthew J held it was not recoverable, and gave judgment for the defendants. It was agreed that there was no evidence of negligence on the part of the plaintiffs and that the defendants had acted throughout in perfect good faith. After reviewing the cases prior to *Cocks v Masterman* and expressing his opinion that the question of negligence was not, and could not be, the foundation of the judgment in any of them, Matthew J proceeds:

'In *Cocks v Masterman* the simple rule was laid down in clear language for the first time that when a bill becomes due and is presented for payment the holder ought to know at once whether the bill is going to be paid or not. If the mistake is discovered at once, it may be the money can be recovered back; but if it be not, and the money is paid in good faith, and is received in good faith, and there is an interval of time in which the position of the holder may be altered, the principle seems to apply that money once paid cannot be recovered back. That rule is obviously, as it seems to me, indispensable for the conduct of business. A holder of a bill cannot possibly fail to have his position affected if there be any interval of time during which he holds the money as his own, or spends it as his own, and if he is subsequently sought to be made responsible to hand it back. It may be that no legal right may be compromised by reason of the payment. For instance, the acceptor may pay the bill and discover on the same day that the bill is a forgery, and so inform the holder of it, so that the holder would have time to give notice of dishonour to the other parties to the bill; but even in such a case it is manifest that the position of a man of business may be most seriously compromised even by the delay of a day. Now that clear rule is one that ought not to be tampered with. It is one of the few rules of business which is perfectly clear and distinct at present, and, as it seems to me it is unimpeachable.'

The rule was also recognised in the case of *Mather v Lord Maidstone*.[3]

No convincing reason is given for the rule and it is not surprising that subsequent authorities have sought to limit its apparently broad application. In *Leeds and County Bank Ltd v Walker*,[4] it was held to have no application to a forged bank note.

The application of the rule was further restricted by the Privy Council in *Imperial Bank of Canada v Bank of Hamilton*, ante. The facts were that one Bauer drew a cheque for five dollars on the Bank of Hamilton, leaving a considerable space after the word 'five'. He got it marked by the Bank of Hamilton and then wrote in the word 'hundred' after the word 'five'. He opened an account with the cheque with the Imperial Bank of Canada and forthwith drew out the amount. The Bank of Hamilton paid the altered amount to the Imperial Bank. The Bank of Hamilton discovered the fraud the next morning, and immediately gave notice to the Imperial Bank, demanding repayment of 495 dollars. The Privy Council held that the money was recoverable, affirming the decision of the Canadian Courts. After stating that the Imperial Bank was not in fact prejudiced in any way by want of notice on the day of payment, Lord Lindley said that it appeared to them that the stringent rule laid down in *Cocks v Masterman* did not really apply to the case, and proceeded:

3 (1858) 18 CB 273.
4 (1883) 11 QBD 84, especially at 89.

'The cheque, as drawn and certified, ie for $5, was never dishonoured, and no question arises as to that. The cheque for the larger amount was a simple forgery; and Bauer, the drawer and forger, was not entitled to any notice of its dishonour by non-payment. There were no indorsers to whom notice of dishonour had to be given. The law as to the necessity of giving notice of dishonour has therefore no application. The rule laid down in *Cocks v Masterman* and recently reasserted in even wider language by Mathew J in *London and River Plate Bank v Bank of Liverpool* has reference to negotiable instruments on the dishonour of which notice has to be given to someone, namely, to some drawer or indorser, who would be discharged from liability unless such notice were given in proper time. Their Lordships are not aware of any authority for applying so stringent a rule to any other cases. Assuming it to be as stringent as is alleged in such cases as those above described, their Lordships are not prepared to extend it to other cases where notice of the mistake is given in reasonable time and no loss has been occasioned by the delay in giving it.'

The *Imperial Bank* decision was applied by Kerr J in *National Westminster Bank Ltd v Barclays Bank International Ltd*,[5] a case involving a forged cheque, and again by Robert Goff J in the *Simms* case, refusing to accept the criticism in the 8th edition of *Paget* of the law as laid down by Lord Lindley in the *Imperial Bank* case. Robert Goff J held:[6]

'It follows that in the case of a simple unendorsed cheque, payment of which is countermanded by the drawer, notice of dishonour is not required; and in such a case the payee cannot invoke the defence established in *Cocks v Masterman*.'

Cocks v Masterman and the *London and River Plate Bank* cases were referred to by the Court of Appeal without disapproval in *Morison v London County and Westminster Bank Ltd*.[7] The rule undoubtedly survives, but it is now strictly limited to cases where notice of dishonour is required to be given to preserve the rights of the holder.

4 RECOVERABILITY OF PAYMENTS MADE TO OR BY AN AGENT

(a) Money paid to an agent

Money paid under a mistake of fact to an agent will be recoverable from the agent up to such time as the agent has paid it over to the principal or has legitimately disposed of it on behalf of the principal, in which event it becomes recoverable from the principal. This proposition is derived from a line of cases starting with *Buller v Harrison*,[8] which decided that money paid to an agent but not paid over (though placed to the principal's account in the agent's books) is recoverable as money had and received. However, it is subject to certain qualifications. In *Rahimtoola v Nizam of Hyderabad*[9] Viscount Simonds said:

'I am not concerned to deny that in a suit in which private persons only are concerned the rule in *Buller v Harrison*, if I may call it so, may prevail, though I would suppose that, in any case, the principal should not be denied the opportunity of asserting that the money was not paid to his agent in consequence, for instance, of a mistake of fact.'

5 [1975] QB 654, [1974] 3 All ER 834.
6 [1980] QB 677 at 703A, [1979] 3 All ER 522 at 542c.
7 [1914] 3 KB 356, especially at 378, 383.
8 (1777) 2 Cowp 565.
9 [1958] AC 379 at 397, HL.

The principle as derived from *Buller v Harrison*[10] was discussed in the leading cases of: *Continental Caoutchouc and Gutta Percha Co v Kleinwort Sons & Co*[11] and *Kleinwort Sons & Co v Dunlop Rubber Co*,[12] which were cited in *Thomas v Houston Corbett & Co*,[13] and from those cases it is clear that a defendant will not succeed in avoiding repayment by establishing that he was acting as agent if:

(a) he had notice of the plaintiff's claim before paying the money to the principal or otherwise disposing of it on his behalf;
(b) in the course of the transaction he acted as the principal; or
(c) he received the money in consequence of some wrongdoing to which he was a party or of which he had knowledge.

In *Thomas v Houston Corbett & Co* it was said that the right to recover does not depend on any previous relationship between the parties, privity if necessary being established by proof that payment was made and that it would not have been paid but for this mistake. Then the obligation to repay is implied as a matter of law.

In *Admiralty Comrs v National Provincial and Union Bank of England Ltd*,[14] money was mistakenly paid into the bank to a customer's account. The bank refused to refund it without the consent of the representatives of the customer, he being dead. The bank contended, but failed, that it had incurred an obligation to honour cheques to the amount of the payment in, which absolved it from any liability to repay, citing *Joachimson v Swiss Bank Corpn*,[15] in support. Sargant J pointed out that the *Joachimson* case dealt only with the normal conditions of banker and customer, and that the undertaking to honour cheques did not extend to amounts standing to the credit of current account if and in so far as it was swollen by an inadvertent payment in mistake of fact. It follows that the banker cannot set up lien or set-off, which he could otherwise claim against his customer, even where the money has been paid to him as agent for that customer. Lien only extends to the property of the customer, which money paid in by mistake of fact is not; set-off only applies to debts between the same two parties; continuance of an overdraft is not necessarily a sufficient change of position.

(b) Money paid by an agent

In respect of money paid by an agent of the plaintiff under a mistake of fact the plaintiff may rely on the mistake provided that both the payment and the mistake were made by the same agent. In *Turvey v Dentons (1923) Ltd*,[16] Pilcher J said:

'... where ... a limited liability company is concerned and payments are made under a bona fide mistake of fact by an authorized agent of the company, the fact that some other agent of the company may have had full knowledge of all the facts does not disentitle the company to recover the money so paid provided that the

10 (1777) 2 Cowp 565.
11 (1904) 90 LT 474, 9 Com Cas 240, CA.
12 (1907) 97 LT 263, HL.
13 [1969] NZLR 151 at 162, 172.
14 (1922) 127 LT 452.
15 [1921] 3 KB 110, CA.
16 [1953] 1 QB 218 at 224 per Pilcher J.

agent with the full knowledge does not know that the payments are being made on an erroneous basis.'

And in *Lloyds Bank Ltd v The Hon. Cecily K. Brooks*[17] Lynskey J said:

'If the hand that pays the money, even though it be only that of an agent, is acting under a mistake of fact, that payment is a payment made under a mistake of fact.'

Therefore

(a) Payments made by an agent of the plaintiff may be recovered as money paid under a mistake of fact provided (i) the agent himself made the payment under the mistake, (ii) no other agent of the plaintiff, or the plaintiff himself, knew of the payment and knew that a mistake was being made.
(b) Where money is paid to an agent of the defendant, the defendant may resist a claim for money paid under a mistake of fact if (i) the money has not been paid to him or used on his behalf by an agent acting for him, (ii) the agent knew of the mistake or was party to some wrongdoing which makes the agent himself responsible, (iii) the agent knew of the mistake before parting with the money and again is himself responsible for repaying it.

It has to be borne in mind that the persons concerned where money is claimed to have been paid under mistake of fact are the person who has paid it and the person who has directly received it. The interests of third parties, say, the banker's customer, do not necessarily come into the matter at all. Nevertheless, there is the statement of Lord Mansfield in *Buller v Harrison*[18] to the following effect:

'Now, the law is clear, that if an agent pays over money which has been paid to him by mistake of fact he does no wrong; and the plaintiff must call on the principal.'

Sir Wilfrid Greene MR used words of much the same effect in *Gowers v Lloyds and National Provincial Foreign Bank.*[19]

5 ESTOPPEL

A plaintiff who is prima facie entitled to recover money paid under a mistake of fact will be estopped from doing so if:

(a) he made a representation of fact which led the defendant to believe that he was entitled to treat the money as his own;
(b) relying on this representation the defendant changed his position and in so doing acted to his detriment;
(c) the defendant was not at fault either in relation to the mistake being made or in subsequently acting to his detriment.

If an estoppel operates then it defeats the whole of the claim even though the

17 (1950) 6 LDAB 161 at 164.
18 (1777) 2 Cowp 565 at 568.
19 [1938] 1 All ER 766, CA at 773 per Sir Wilfrid Greene MR.

payee spent only part of the mistaken payment, as happened in *Avon County Council v Howlett*.[20]

The tendency in the recent authorities on money paid by banks under a mistake of fact has been to bring them into line with other persons paying money under a mistake of fact and to entitle them to recover the money on precisely the same considerations, so that in order to raise an estoppel the defendant cannot rely on the banks' once alleged duty to know the customer's signature or on any special duty to make inquiries.

(a) Representation

In each case, the defendant must prove a representation upon which he relied. *National Westminster Bank Ltd v Barclays Bank International Ltd*[1] establishes three important propositions with respect to representations in this field:

(i) Paying bank owes no duty to payee

The paying bank owes no duty of care to the payee in deciding whether to honour a customer's cheques, at any rate when it appears to be regular on its face.[2] This prevents an estoppel by negligence.

(ii) Paying bank does not represent that drawer's signature is genuine

In most of the earlier cases judges have talked about the banker being bound to know his customer's signature, failure being negligence on the banker's part such as to preclude recovery. The judgment of Mathew J[3] has sometimes been read as laying down that negligence had nothing to do with the question. The judge declined to recognise it as the ruling principle of any of the earlier cases, as was contended on behalf of the plaintiff bank. The case was one of forged indorsement, as to which no duty of recognition could be alleged, and it was admitted that the bank had not been negligent. In the earlier cases the instrument possessed some negotiability and Mathew J held that the real ground of those decisions was the same as that of the case he was trying, the maintenance of negotiability.

To suggest that a banker is bound to know his customer's signature is wrong; there can be no such obligation in law. The real position is that if the banker pays in reliance on the signature being his customer's he cannot charge his customer. Even if it were a duty to know the customer's signature, it could not possibly be a duty to the payee of a cheque.

The theory that the presenter of a bill or cheque warrants its genuineness was demolished in *Guaranty Trust Co of New York v Hannay & Co*,[4] a case concerning the genuineness of a bill of lading.

In *National Westminster Bank Ltd v Barclays Bank International Ltd* the plaintiff bank paid and later discovered that the instrument which it paid was a forgery (Barclays agreed to submit to whatever order the court might make).

---

20 [1983] 1 All ER 1073, [1983] 1 WLR 605, CA. See also *Greenwood v Martins Bank Ltd* [1933] AC 51.
1 [1975] QB 654, [1974] 3 All ER 834.
2 Ibid at, respectively, 662F and 841b. Cf *Skyring v Greenwood* (1825) 4 B & C 281, and *Holt v Markham* [1923] 1 KB 504, CA. See also *Weld-Blundell v Synott* [1940] 2 KB 107 at 114–115, per Asquith J.
3 *London and River Plate Bank v Bank of Liverpool* [1896] 1 QB 7.
4 [1918] 2 KB 623, CA.

The second defendant, Ismail, asserted that the plaintiffs were estopped by their negligence in honouring the cheque and that the payment gave rise to a representation that the cheque was genuine. On the representation point the judge found against Ismail. In the words of Kerr J:[5]

'None of the various rationes decidendi can however in my view be taken even as persuasive authority for the broad proposition that merely by honouring a forged cheque without negligence the paying bank impliedly represents to the payee that the signature is genuine so as to bar any right of recovery from him.'

and:

'I think that the law should be slow to impose upon an innocent party who has not acted negligently an estoppel merely by reason of having dealt with a forged document on the assumption that it was genuine.'

It appears from this case that one can now finally dispense with the idea that by paying money on a forged signature the payer is making any representation that it was genuine such as can entitle the defendant to rely on an estoppel.

(iii) No special rule relating to special collection

There is no special rule where a cheque is presented for special collection.[6] Although banks know that there are usually particular reasons for presenting a cheque for special collection, the usual reason for doubt as to whether or not a cheque will be honoured is uncertainty as to whether the funds are available to cover the cheque, and not as to whether or not the cheque is a forgery.

(b) Change of position and detriment

The mere spending of money does not amount to a sufficient change of position and detriment.

The view that payment to a principal whose change of position derived from mere receipt of the money is recoverable, received the support of Denning LJ in *Larner v LCC*,[7] where he said that:

'Speaking generally, the fact that the recipient has spent the money beyond recall is no defence unless there was some fault, as, for instance, breach of duty, on the part of the paymaster and none on the part of the recipient. In both *Skyring v Greenwood and Cox*[8] and *Holt v Markham*[9] there was a breach of duty by the paymaster and none by the recipient: see *R E Jones Ltd v Waring and Gillow Ltd*[10] per Lord Sumner.

But if the recipient was himself at fault and the paymaster was not – as, for instance, if the mistake was due to an innocent misrepresentation or a breach of duty by the recipient – he clearly cannot escape liability by saying that he has spent the money.'

In both *Lloyds Bank Ltd v The Hon Cecily K. Brooks*[11] and *United Overseas*

5 [1975] QB 654 at 672E and 674F, [1974] 3 All ER 834 at 849 and 850h.
6 Ibid at, respectively 675 and 851.
7 [1949] 2 KB 683, [1949] 1 All ER 964 at 967.
8 (1825) 4 B & C 281.
9 [1923] 1 KB 504, CA.
10 [1926] AC 670 at 697.
11 (1950) 6 LDAB 161 at 165.

Bank v Jiwani[12] the respective plaintiff banks made overpayments into the respective defendants' accounts and in both cases the defendants removed the money from their accounts and could thus be said to have altered their positions. However in the *Lloyds Bank* case the bank failed to recover in an action for money paid under a mistake of fact, whereas in the *United Overseas Bank* case the bank succeeded in recovering. Both defendants raised a defence of estoppel. In *Lloyds Bank Ltd v The Hon Cecily K. Brooks*[13] Lynskey J found:

> '(the defendant) was in fact under the belief she was entitled to this money.'

He went on to point out that:

> 'If I had taken the view that she knew she was not entitled to this money, then of course her defence would fail because there could be no estoppel under cir-cumstances where a person, knowing she was receiving money to which she was not entitled, does not repay it ... The next thing I have to decide is, did she act upon the representations which were made to her by the statements of account ... according to her own evidence she did. One would naturally expect her to do so in the ordinary sense. ... First of all a question of fact arises ... did she in fact spend more money because of those representations ... I am quite satisfied here that the defendant because of this increased credit which she apparently was receiving did in fact spend more money on matters for her own purposes than she otherwise would have done.'

Lynskey J then at 169 concludes:

> 'If as a result of a mis-statement by a bank a person is induced to spend more money than they have got to spend then it seems to me in the ordinary sense, from the factual point of view apart from the legal point of view, they are certainly acting to their detriment ...'

From the 'legal point of view' Lynskey J reconciled the conflicting authorities, on whether the recipient of an overpayment of money can be estopped from repaying it by virtue of having altered his position to the extent of spending the money, by reference to *Larner v LCC*[14] where Denning LJ at 688 said:

> 'Speaking generally the fact that a recipient has spent the money beyond recall is no defence unless there was some fault – as, for instance, breach of duty – on the part of the paymaster and none on the part of the recipient.'

So in *Lloyds Bank Ltd v The Hon Cecily K. Brooks*[15] it was found that the defence of estoppel succeeded because:

1 as a result of the bank's representation as to the state of her account Miss Brooks believed she was entitled to the money in it; and
2 acting on this representation she acted to her detriment;
3 she was in no way at fault;
4 the bank was at fault in not keeping her correctly informed.

In *United Overseas Bank v Jiwani*[16] MacKenna J set out three conditions that he required the defendant to satisfy in order to establish that the plaintiffs were estopped from claiming repayment of their overpayment into the defen-dant's account as follows:

12 [1977] 1 All ER 733, [1976] 1 WLR 964.
13 (1950) 6 LDAB 161.
14 [1949] 2 KB 683, [1949] 1 All ER 964.
15 (1950) 6 LDAB 161.
16 [1977] 1 All ER 733 at 737, (1976) 1 WLR 964 at 968.

'First, he must show that either the plaintiffs were under a duty to give him accurate information about the state of this account and that in breach of this duty they gave him inaccurate information, or that in some other way there was a misrepresentation made to him about the state of the account, for which the plaintiffs are responsible. Secondly, he must show that this inaccurate information in fact misled him about the state of the account and caused him to believe that the plaintiffs were his debtors for a larger sum than was the case and to make the transfer to Mr Pirani in that mistaken belief. Thirdly, he must show that because of his mistaken belief he changed his position in a way which would make it inequitable to require him now to repay the money.'

Having considered the evidence MacKenna J found at 970:

'... first that he has not proved that if he was misled by the plaintiffs he changed his position in such a way as would make it inequitable to require him to repay the money.'

In *Skyring v Greenwood*[17] the fact that the payee had had money for a considerable time and spent it in such a manner as to have altered his mode of living was held a sufficient change of position, but as was pointed out in *Avon County Council v Howlett*,[18] it may be very difficult for a payee to prove that he has altered his mode of living.

Other examples of change of position are paying the money over to a third party to whom the payee believed he had a duty to pay it and from whom there are no practical means of recovering it,[19] and investing money in a company which has since gone into liquidation.[20]

(c) No fault on the part of the defendant

A defence of estoppel cannot succeed if there has been no fault, misrepresentation or concealment of relevant facts made by the defendant at any time from the original transaction to the plaintiff's request for repayment, for any such fault will prevent the defendant succeeding.

The following observations of Lord Brampton in *George Whitechurch Ltd v Cavanagh*[1] set out this proposition in general:

'... in my judgment no representations can be relied on as estoppels if they have been induced by the concealment of any material fact on the part of those who seek to use them as such; and if the person to whom they are made knows something which, if revealed, would have been calculated to influence the other to hesitate or seek for further information before speaking positively, and that something has been withheld, the representation ought not to be treated as an estoppel.'

This passage was cited by Kerr J in *National Westminster Bank Ltd v Barclays Bank International Ltd*[2] and by Neild J in *Secretary of State for Employment v Wellworthy Ltd (No 2)*.[3] In the former case Kerr J held that no estoppel could protect the defendant as 'the circumstances in which the cheque came into (his) hands ... reeked with suspicion.'

17 (1825) 4 B & C 281.
18 [1983] 1 All ER 1073, [1983] 1 WLR 605, CA.
19 See, eg *Deutsche Bank (London Agency) v Beriro & Co* (1895) 73 LT 669, 1 Com Cas 255, CA.
20 See, eg *Holt v Markham* [1923] 1 KB 504, CA.
 1 [1902] AC 117 at 145, HL.
 2 [1975] QB 654 at 676, [1974] 3 All ER 834 at 852.
 3 [1976] ICR 13 at 25.

6 TRACING

A mistaken payment may in equity be traced and recovered if the circumstances warrant it, as where an American bank was required to pay into another New York bank for the credit of an English company and by mistake did so twice. The English company went into liquidation insolvent. Goulding J held that the plaintiff was entitled to recover; the payee was subject to a fiduciary duty in respect of the plaintiff's proprietary interest.[4] The facts, somewhat unusual, are sufficiently stated at the beginning of the judgment:

'This action concerns a sum of money paid by mistake. In July 1974 the plaintiff, Chase Manhattan Bank NA, and the defendant, Israel-British Bank (London) Ltd, were carrying on business as bankers, the plaintiff in New York and the defendant in London. On or before July 2 an Italian bank instructed the plaintiff to pay US $2,000,687.50 to Mellon Bank International, another bank in New York, for the defendant's account. The plaintiff duly made that payment through the New York clearing house system on July 3. Later on the same day, July 3, the plaintiff made a further payment of the same amount, also through the clearing system, to the same recipient, Mellon Bank International, again for the account of the defendant. This second payment purported to be made on the instructions of a bank in Hong Kong. But no such instructions had been given, and the second payment was a pure mistake. Its original cause was a clerical error made by a servant of the plaintiff earlier on July 3. That error, however, was discovered in good time by another servant of the plaintiff, who gave instructions to correct it. His instructions were executed only in part by his fellow employees, and their failure was the proximate cause of the mistaken payment.'

The claim was for a declaration that the defendant became a trustee for the plaintiff in the sum paid by mistake. The defendant was insolvent and in liquidation and unless the plaintiff could avail itself of the equitable remedy of tracing it would find itself in competition with the creditors of the defendant – in regard to moneys to which the defendant never had title. As Goulding J put it,

'It is common ground that if (as I have decided) there is a right in English law to trace money paid by mistake, it rests on a persistent equitable proprietary interest'

and again

(a) If one party P transfers property to another party D by reason of a mistake of fact, P has in general a right to recover it and D a duty to restore it. (b) P in general has a right to sue in equity for an order that D return the property, or its traceable proceeds, to P. Sometimes this requires actual retransfer by D, sometimes the court can use the alternative remedy of reformation, ie rectification of instruments, to produce the same result. P is said to retain an equitable title to the property notwithstanding it may have been legally transferred to D, and D is treated as a constructive trustee thereof. (c) In many cases P has also a common law right of action in quasi-contract to recover damages in respect of his loss. (d) The court will not, in its equitable jurisdiction, order specific restitution under (b) above where common law damages under (c) furnish adequate relief. (e) Accordingly where the property in question is money, equitable relief is not available to restore the sum paid by mistake if the payee D is solvent. But when D is insolvent P is entitled to a decree in equity for the purpose of tracing the money paid and recovering it or the property representing it. (f) Modern analysis concentrates

4 *Chase Manhattan Bank NA v Israel-British Bank (London) Ltd* [1981] Ch 105, [1979] 3 All ER 1025.

attention less on the protection of P than on preventing the unjust enrichment of D, thus bringing the law of mistake into a broad jurisprudence of restitutionary rights and remedies.'

CHAPTER 26

COLLECTING BANKER: GENERAL

1 COLLECTION OF BILLS

(a) General rights and duties

As agent the banker collecting bills for a customer is entitled to all the rights of a mandatory against his mandant, as defined in *London Joint Stock Bank Ltd v Macmillan and Arthur*.[1] Unless himself in fault, he can claim indemnity from his customer and can debit him with a dishonoured bill or with any amount for which he has been found liable to a true owner. He is not liable where he acts reasonably, though mistakenly, on ambiguous instructions. The principal must save him harmless from any loss into which he has led him by word, deed, or silence. The banker is bound to present the bills for acceptance and payment in accordance with the provisions of the Bills of Exchange Act and must give notice of dishonour to the customer or the persons liable on the bill.[2] If the banker employs a sub-agent for the purpose of collecting bills, he is responsible to the customer for negligence on the part of such sub-agent[3] and for moneys received by such sub-agent, apart from any question of account between banker and sub-agent.[4]

Where bills are lost or destroyed while in the hands of a banker purely for collection, the loss will fall on the customer if the banker is not at fault.[5]

(b) Presentment of bills for acceptance

Presentment of a bill for acceptance is necessarily a step in collection, though a banker may be employed for that purpose alone, returning the accepted bill to the customer. If the customer is indebted to the banker and has indorsed the bill, the banker has a lien and is entitled to exercise it, unless

---

1 [1918] AC 777.
2 Bills of Exchange Act 1882, s 49(13); 5 Halsbury's States (4th edn, 1989 Reissue) 362. *Bank of Van Diemen's Land v Bank of Victoria* (1871) LR 3 PC 526; *Bank of Scotland v Dominion Bank (Toronto)* [1891] AC 592.
3 *Mackersy v Ramsays, Bonars & Co* (1843) 9 Cl & Fin 818; *Prince v Oriental Bank Corpn* (1878) 3 App Cas 325; see also *Calico Printers' Association Ltd v Barclays Bank* (1930) 36 Com Cas 71; on appeal (1931) 145 LT 51, 36 Com Cas 197.
4 *Mackersy v Ramsays, Bonars & Co*, above; and see *Morris v Martin & Sons Ltd* [1966] 1 QB 716, [1965] 2 All ER 725, CA.
5 *Thompson v Giles* (1824) 2 B & C 422; *Re Wise, ex p Atkins* (1842) 3 Mount D & DeG 103.

precluded by any special arrangement with the customer. The duties of a banker presenting bills for acceptance are set out in s 41 of the Bills of Exchange Act 1882. Whether there is any responsibility on the part of the presenting banker to ensure that the signature to the acceptance is that of the drawee or written by his authority has not been the subject of decision but it is not done. However, unless not identifying the drawee has the implied authority of the principal it would seem that the presenting agent must be deemed negligent in not doing so. The weakness of not identifying the drawee is perhaps greater where the bill is a documentary bill and the documents are to be delivered against acceptance. It would be a breach of mandate to deliver them to anyone other than the drawee.

(c) Agent for remitting banker

But the banker receiving bills for collection from another banker is not agent for that banker's customer, but for the remitting banker; and, unless he has distinct notice that the bills are the property of the customer and are in the remitting banker's hands purely for collection, may treat them as that banker's property.[6] On this basis they would be subject to the lien of the sub-agent for any balance due to him from the remitting banker.[7] In *Akrokerri (Atlantic) Mines Ltd v Economic Bank*,[8] Bigham J with respect to cheques uses expressions implying that, in his opinion, collection was a special purpose inconsistent with lien; but this is clearly not the case.[9]

(d) Lien against customer

The collecting banker equally has a lien on bills handed to him for collection for any amount due from the customer at the time of receiving the bills or during their currency.[10] If the customer has indorsed the bill, the banker, as a holder for value, has a remedy against him to the extent of such indebtedness.[11] Mere indorsement for collection, without indebtedness on the part of the customer, gives no remedy on the bill against the customer in case of dishonour, there being no consideration;[12] if the account has been credited it may be debited and if the balance is insufficient to meet the debit the customer will be liable for the overdraft thus created – or the banker may debit a suspense account and preserve his rights on the cheque against all parties including the customer. Indorsement by the payee or by an indorsee is necessary for collection or for extra security in case of the exercise of any lien.

The question whether a banker takes a bill for collection, subject to any

6 *Johnson v Robarts* (1875) 10 Ch App 505; *Re Dilworth, ex p Armistead* (1828) 2 Gl & J 371.
7 *Re Parker, ex p Froggatt* (1843) 3 Mont D & DeG 322; *Prince v Oriental Bank Corpn* (1878) 3 App Cas 325; *Re Burrough, ex p Sargeant* (1810) 1 Rose 153.
8 [1904] 2 KB 465.
9 Cf *Misa v Currie* (1876) 1 App Cas 554 at 565, 569, 573; *Thompson v Giles* (1824) 2 B & C 422; and see *Re Keever v Midland Bank* [1967] Ch 182, [1966] 3 All ER 631.
10 *Giles v Perkins* (1807) 9 East 12; *Brandao v Barnett* (1846) 12 Cl & Fin 787, HL; *Re Firth, ex p Schofield* (1879) 12 Ch D 337; *Dawson v Isle* [1906] 1 Ch 633; *Re Keever, A Bankrupt, ex parte Trustee of the Property of the Bankrupt v Midland Bank* [1967] Ch 182, [1966] 3 All ER 631.
11 *Giles v Perkins*, above.
12 *Re Firth, ex p Schofield* (1879) 12 Ch D 337, per Brett LJ 343 and per James LJ 347.

lien or as a transferee for value, is irrelevant as his rights are the same in each case.

2   COLLECTION OF CHEQUES

(a) General rights and duties

Save that cheques are not presented for acceptance, the banker's general rights and duties are much the same as in relation to bills generally. It has been held in Australia that a bank is not obliged to collect a cheque if it might expose itself to an action for conversion in which no statutory defence would have been available.[13]

(b) Time for presentment

In the case of a cheque, the only limitation on the time for presentment is that it shall be presented for payment within a reasonable time after issue in order to charge the drawer, or within a reasonable time after indorsement to charge the indorser.[14] When the cheque is drawn on a bank in the same place, the banker should present it the day after he receives it.[15] When the cheque is on a bank in another place, it is sufficient if the banker either presents it or forwards it on the day following receipt.[16]

(c) Method of presentment

(i) Presentment through clearing

Presentment normally means presentment according to the rules of the clearing. The custom of the trade and of bankers today is to present cheques through the clearings, which have their own rules. Such forwarding may be to another branch or to an agent of the bank, who has the same time for presentation after receipt.[17] A non-clearing bank can thus use a clearing bank. Sections 45 and 74 of the Bills of Exchange Act import the custom of trade and the custom of bankers as elements in the determination of what is reasonable time for the presentation of a cheque. Section 49(13), dealing with bills in the hands of an agent when dishonoured, is applicable to cheques, and seems to recognise the intervention of a banker.

(ii) Presentment by one bank to another

Presentment by one bank to another is sufficient[18] but is done only for a special purpose. In such case it would seem that the paying bank receives the

---

13 *Tan ah Sam v Chartered Bank* (1971) 45 ALJ 770.
14 Bills of Exchange Act 1882, s 45(2), 5 Halsbury's Statutes (4th edn, 1989 Re-issue) 359; cf *Alexander v Burchfield* (1842) 7 Man & G 1061, where it was held that the recipient of a cheque was bound to present it the day after receipt.
15 *Rickford v Ridge* (1810) 2 Camp 537; *Alexander v Burchfield* (1842) 7 Man & G 1061; *Forman v Bank of England* (1902) 18 TLR 339; *Hamilton Finance Co Ltd v Coverley. Westray, Walbaum and Tosetti Ltd and Portland Finance Co Ltd* [1969] 1 Lloyd's Rep 53.
16 *Hare v Henty* (1861) 10 CBNS 65; *Prideaux v Criddle* (1869) LR 4 QB 455; *Heywood v Pickering* (1874) LR 9 QB 428.
17 *Prideaux v Criddle* (1869) LR 4 QB 455.
18 *Bailey v Bodenham* (1864) 16 CBNS 288 at 296.

cheque as agent for presentation to itself,[19] and so can hold it till the day after receipt.[18] If not paid, it must be returned the day after receipt.

(iii) Presentment by post

Presentment by post is sufficient only where authorised by agreement or usage,[20] and the usage of bankers does not authorise presentment by post except by a bank.

(d) Cheque drawn by one customer received from another customer of the same branch

When a cheque drawn by one customer of a bank is received from another customer of the same branch, it is a question of fact whether it is presented for payment or paid in for collection.[1] If the latter, the bank has the usual time of an agent for returning it and giving notice of dishonour.[2] In *Grace Chu Chan Po Kee v The Hong Kong Chinese Bank Ltd* the plaintiff, a customer of the defendant bank, delivered to the bank a cheque for HK$1,200,000 drawn on the bank by another customer for the credit of her loan account. Three weeks later the bank returned the cheque. It was conceded that this period exceeded 'the time established by the custom and practice of banks in Hong Kong within which paying banks decide the fate of a cheque which has not been presented to the paying banker through the Clearing House'. Judgment was given for the plaintiff.[3] If paid in for collection, the bank would deal with it as in the case of any other cheque but, as drawee banker also, must pay such cheque in preference to a debt due to itself from the drawing customer.[4] If, for instance, the drawer's account was overdrawn when the cheque was paid in but before it was returned the drawer paid in sufficient funds to cover it, not appropriated to other payments, the bank would have to pay the cheque, irrespective of its lien for the overdraft.

(e) Liability to customer for delay in presentment

If the collecting banker fails to present a cheque within the allotted time after it reaches him, he is liable to his customer for loss arising from the delay.[5] The indorser may thus be discharged by the omission to present the cheque within a reasonable time after indorsement. The drawer of a cheque is, however, in a different position in this respect from the drawer of a bill other than a cheque payable on demand; he remains liable on the cheque until action on it is statute-barred. However, the banker is further liable to his customer for damage to credit if he dishonours a cheque which there would

---

19 See opinion of Mr Arthur Cohen QC, and Sir Mackenzie Chalmers, *Questions on Banking Practice* (8th end) Question 388.
20 Bills of Exchange Act 1882, s 45(8).
1 Cf *Carpenters' Co v British Mutual Banking Co Ltd* [1938] 1 KB 511.
2 *Boyd v Emmerson* (1834) 2 Ad & El 184.
3 High Court of Hong Kong 9 January 1979; judgment provided by the courtesy of Mr Richard Yorke QC, Counsel for the plaintiff.
4 *Kilsby v Williams* (1822) 5 B & Ald 815.
5 *Lubbock v Tribe* (1838) 3 M & W 607; see also *Yeoman Credit Ltd v Gregory* [1963] 1 All ER 245, [1963] 1 WLR 343.

have been funds to meet if cheques paid in had been presented for payment without delay.[6]

3   NOTICE OF DISHONOUR

(a) Requirement for notice

The collecting banker must give notice of dishonour with regard to any bills or cheques dishonoured on presentation by him. So far as cheques are concerned, the need for notice of dishonour to the drawer is, as previously stated, somewhat of an anomaly, the drawer being the principal debtor on the instrument and having no right of recourse against any other party. But as drawer within s 48, he is entitled to notice, though in the majority of cases omission to give it would be excused under s 50(2)(c).

(b) To whom notice to be given

Under s 49(13), where a bill when dishonoured is in the hands of an agent, he may either himself give notice to the parties liable on the bill, or he may give notice to his principal; the latter would seem the preferable course for the collecting banker. There seems no reason why he should take upon himself the additional labour of notifying parties other than his own customer. If he were to give notice to, say, the last indorser only, that indorser might not pass it on, and other parties would consequently be discharged. In such case the banker might be liable to his customer.

(c) Notice by return of dishonoured bill to customer

Section 49(6)[7] enacts that:

> 'The return of a dishonoured bill to the drawer or an indorser is, in point of form, deemed a sufficient notice of dishonour.'[8]

However, the usual and natural practice of collecting bankers is to return the bill or cheque to their own customer which would seem to be covered by the sub-section only if the customer is the holder by indorsement. By s 49(13) notice of a dishonoured bill in the hands of an agent (such as a collecting banker) may be given to his principal, his customer, and, presumably, by the return of the instrument to him. Further the words 'return of a dishonoured bill' seem to point to the bill or cheque being restored to the source whence it came, to the customer.

(d) Form of notice

Save in the case of the return of the instrument itself, notice must be given in writing or by personal communication (s 49(5)). It may be sent by post. Notice by telegram seemed to be good. Willes J appears to have doubted this

---

6 *Forman v Bank of England* (1902) 18 TLR 339.
7 See *Westminster Bank Ltd v Zang* [1966] AC 182 and in the Court of Appeal, Lord Denning MR, ibid at 197.
8 *Chalmers' Bills of Exchange* (13th edn) 158: 'This subsection approves a common practice of collecting bankers which was previously of doubtful validity'.

in *Godwin v Francis*;[9] but in *Fielding & Co v Corry*,[10] A L Smith and Rigby LJJ expressed the opinion that such notice was sufficient, Collins LJ dissenting. But see *Lombard Banking Ltd v Central Garage and Engineering Co Ltd*.[11] If good notice could be given by telegram, the same is presumably true of notice by telex or fax.

No case has yet arisen as to the validity of notice by telephone. It might fairly be considered to come under the head of a personal communication, the actual voice being transmitted by the reciprocal vibrations of the discs induced by the current in the same way as by vibration of the air or intervening material in the case of ordinary speaking. However, in the *Lombard Banking* case, Scarman J held that:

'in the present case the prior oral or telephonic communication of the Westminster Bank to its principal was a warning of what was in the post and not the substantive notice of dishonour'.[12]

(e) Time for giving notice

The time allowances for giving notice, where a bill or cheque is in the hands of a bank for collection, are on a fairly liberal scale. By s 49(13), the banker has the same time to give notice to his customer as if he (the banker) were the holder, and the customer, upon receipt of such notice, has himself the same time for giving notice as if the banker had been an independent holder. Moreover, where the instrument has been forwarded by one branch to another, or by a branch to the head office, or vice versa, for collection, each such constituent of the entire bank is, for the purpose of giving notice of dishonour, regarded as a separate entity, and the same time allowed as if it were an independent holder.[13] However, except in the case of personal communication, the crucial time is the sending, not the receipt, of the notice (s 49(12)). Thus, where the parties reside in different places, the notice must be sent off on the day after the dishonour of the bill if there be a post at a convenient hour on that day, and if there be no such post on that day, then by the next post thereafter.

In *Fielding & Co v Corry*,[14] notice of dishonour was posted by mistake to the wrong branch of the presenting bank and a telegram sent the next day to the right branch was held equivalent to a redirection of the latter, and that the notice was good; but the decision seems open to criticism. In fact the decision was of two Lords Justice in three, Collins LJ holding that for the purpose of notice of dishonour the branches of a bank must be regarded as distinct; that, therefore, the notice was ineffective and out of time. In *London Provincial and South-Western Bank Ltd v Buszard*,[15] an order to stop a cheque, addressed to the wrong branch, was held ineffective.

---

9 (1870) LR 5 CP 295 at 303.
10 [1898] 1 QB 268.
11 [1963] 1 QB 220, [1962] 2 All ER 949.
12 [1963] 1 QB 220 at 232, [1962] 2 All ER 949.
13 *Clode v Bayley* (1843) 12 M & W 51; *Prince v Oriental Bank Corpn* (1878) 3 App Cas 325; *Fielding & Co v Corry* [1898] 1 QB 268.
14 [1898] 1 QB 268; and see *Eaglehill Ltd v J Needham Builders Ltd* [1973] AC 992, [1972] 3 All ER 895, HL where the House of Lords held that a notice of dishonour sent by post and delivered in the ordinary course of post is not 'given' until it is received.
15 (1918) 35 TLR 142.

In *Lombard Banking Ltd v Central Garage and Engineering Bank Ltd*[16] bills accepted payable with Barclays Bank Ltd in Porthcawl were handed by the plaintiff to Westminster Bank in London for collection. The latter sent them to Barclays for presentment to themselves. They were dishonoured, upon which Barclays advised the Westminster and returned the bills, which were received by the Westminster on the working day following dishonour. The same day, the Westminster notified the plaintiffs who, however, did not advise the defendant company until the bills were in their possession, ie that day or the first working day following receipt. The second and third defendants were directors of the defendant company. To the defence that notice of dishonour was not given within s 49(12) and (13), Scarman J held that the plaintiffs had acted reasonably in waiting to get the bills back before giving notice and that even if Barclays were the agents of the holders notice of dishonour was given in time, since the oral or telephonic communication of the Westminster was a warning of what was in the post and not the substantive notice of dishonour, which was the receipt by the plaintiffs of the dishonoured bills.[17]

4 DEBITING CUSTOMER'S ACCOUNT UPON DISHONOUR

The right to debit the customer with a returned cheque, notwithstanding that it has been credited as cash, was recognised by Lord Lindley when he said in the *Gordon* case:[18]

'It is no doubt true that if the cheque had been dishonoured, Jones [the customer] would have become liable to reimburse the bank the amount advanced by it to him when it placed the amount to his credit. This he would have to do where any cheque, crossed or not, was placed to his credit, and was afterwards dishonoured.'

Prior to the *Gordon* case, in *Re Mills Bawtree & Co, ex p Stannard*,[19] Vaughan Williams J speaking of cheques paid in by Stannard, said as follows:[20]

'The answer to this seems to me to be twofold. First, in all probability the cheques paid in were indorsed by Messrs. Stannard. This would give the bankers the right to debit their customer, even though they originally received the cheque as their property as a loan to them. Secondly, even if the cheque was not indorsed, the result in my opinion would be the same, because I think that, just as a cheque may operate as a conditional payment to be avoided if the cheque is not honoured, so a cheque may operate as a conditional loan, creating a debt by the recipient of the cheque to be avoided if not honoured.'

Where the account for which the cheque is collected is in debit at the time of dishonour the banker has the choice of increasing the overdraft or of debiting a suspense account with a view to reserving his rights against other parties. The effect of debiting the customer's account may be to relinquish the lien, as was evident in *Westminster Bank Ltd v Zang*[1] and the banker would not acquire a fresh lien by taking the cheque back, as it would not

16 [1963] 1 QB 220, [1962] 2 All ER 949.
17 [1963] 1 QB 220, [1962] 2 All ER 949; and see *Hamilton Finance Co Ltd v Coverley, Westray, Walbaum and Tosetti Ltd and Portland Finance Co Ltd* [1969] 1 Lloyd's Rep 53.
18 [1903] AC 240 at 248.
19 (1893) 10 Morr 193.
20 Ibid at 212.
1 [1966] AC 182, [1966] 1 Lloyd's Rep 49.

have come into his hands qua banker but, presumably, as a plaintiff in an action on the instrument. It is an interesting conjecture whether a banker could preserve his rights by returning the cheque to the customer as his agent, but it would seem not if, at the same time, the banker debited the customer's account. It is doubtful, too, whether the second taking could be as a holder in due course, for the banker would have had notice that the cheque had been dishonoured.

If the customer's account cannot meet the dishonoured instrument and the banker wishes to retain his rights against the parties, he can retain possession, give notice to all parties and debit the amount to a suspense account; but that is a matter of accounting.

5 COLLECTING BANKER AS HOLDER FOR VALUE

(a) Section 27(3)

Section 27(3) of the Bills of Exchange Act reads:

> 'Where the holder of a bill has a lien on it arising either from contract or by implication of law, he is deemed to be a holder for value to the extent of the sum for which he has a lien'

and by s 27(1)(b) 'value' (or 'valuable consideration') is constituted by 'An antecedent debt or liability',[2] and he is obviously a holder either by virtue of an indorsement in blank or by s 2 of the Cheques Act which speaks of delivery without indorsement.

The words 'he is deemed' must be construed according to the object of the enactment. Section 27(3) is one of the group dealing with consideration; its object is to establish the validity of an existing lien as consideration pro tanto. It applies only where the party holding the bill is suing on it; and the character of holder for value would seem to exist only for the purposes for which it is conferred. Lien, being the right to hold another man's property until a debt is paid, gives no right of property. The ordinary holder who has given value is the person in whom the absolute property in the bill is vested; the use of the word 'lien' points therefore to the artificial nature of the holding for value therein referred to. The judgment of Lord Birkenhead in *Sutters v Briggs*,[3] delivered on behalf of himself and Lords Buckmaster and Carson, says:

> '... if bankers are not holders of cheques for which they are agents for collection only, they derive no benefit from s 27, sub-s 3, as the subsection does not apply, even where there is a lien, to a person who is not a holder.'

It is thus clear that lien is not inconsistent with agency for collection.

A L Underwood Ltd v Barclays Bank Ltd[4] was a case of a managing director of a one-man company with full powers to indorse cheques payable to the company, doing so and paying them into his private account. The bank credited them at once but he did not draw on them before they were cleared. Scrutton LJ refers to this, but only incidentally. He repeats that he can see

2 Section 27(1)(b).
3 [1922] 1 AC 1 at 16.
4 [1924] 1 KB 775, CA.

no evidence of a binding agreement with the customer as to payment before clearing. The Court of Appeal decided against the bank. Scrutton LJ said:[5]

'The cases where an agent for collection becomes a holder for value must turn on an express or implied agreement between bank and customer that the latter may draw against the cheques before they are cleared.'

Atkin LJ said:[6]

'I think it sufficient to say that the mere fact that the bank in their books enter the value of the cheques on the credit side of the account on the day on which they receive the cheques for collection does not, without more, constitute the bank a holder for value. To constitute value there must be, in such a case, a contract between banker and customer ... that the bank will, before receipt of the proceeds, honour cheques of the customer drawn against the cheques ... neither that decision [the *Gordon* case] nor the statute [the 1906 Act] lay down the rule, judicial or statutory, that if a bank credits a cheque at once in its books, that fact, without more, makes the bank a holder for value.'

In *Alexander Stewart & Son of Dundee Ltd v Westminster Bank Ltd*[7] cheques endorsed per pro were drawn on before they were cleared. Rowlatt J found that while the bank had been negligent, it was a holder in due course; the Court of Appeal reversed this decision on the ground that s 25 as to signatures by procuration was fatal to the bank's contention.

However, the strongest support for the 'holder for value' contention comes from the House of Lords in *Sutters v Briggs*.[8] The question was whether a banker who collected a crossed cheque marked 'not negotiable, account payee only' was (a) a holder or (b) a holder for value, within the wording of s 2 of the Gaming Act 1835, as an assignee, indorsee or holder. The judgment was virtually unanimous. It had been contended for the appellant that s 82 showed that a collecting banker was an agent, not a holder. In his judgment Lord Birkenhead said:

'Nor does s 82 afford assistance to the appellant ... I cannot myself understand how any inference can be drawn from this section that a banker who receives payment as agent is not a 'holder'. On the contrary, the opposite inference is far more plausible, namely, that the protection became necessary because he is a holder and as such liable to an action for conversion. The appellant's attempt to draw such an inference is further shown to be baseless by the fact that the Bills of Exchange (Crossed Cheques) Act 1906, confers the same protection on bankers who by their action have made themselves not only "holders" but holders in due course (see *Capital and Counties Bank v Gordon*[9] and per Bowen LJ *National Bank v Silke*[10]). Moreover, if bankers are not holders of cheques for which they are agents for collection only, they derive no benefit from s 27, sub-s 3, as the section does not apply, even where there is a lien, to a person who is not a holder.'

In *A L Underwood Ltd v Barclays Bank Ltd*, *Sutters v Briggs* appears not to have been referred to, Atkin LJ saying that neither the *Gordon* case nor the 1906 Act lay down the rule that a bank becomes a holder for value by the mere crediting in its books. Lord Birkenhead's reference to the banker

---

5 [1924] 1 KB 775 at 804.
6 Ibid at 805.
7 [1926] WN 126 (Rowlatt J) and 271 (Court of Appeal).
8 [1922] 1 AC 1.
9 [1903] AC 240
10 [1891] 1 QB 435 at 439.

as holder in due course, implies that the banker not only gives value but takes the instrument he is asked to collect under the conditions of s 29 – in other words, in circumstances which do not put him on inquiry as to the title of the customer for whom he collected. In *Midland Bank Ltd v Reckitt*[11] Lord Atkin said:

> 'That [the bank] were holders for value [in respect of two cheques] to that extent is, I think, true, whether the value is said to be the payment of the antecedent debt (the overdraft) or to be the lien to the extent of the overdraft (Bills of Exchange Act 1882, s 27(3)). But the notice[12] already referred to defeats their rights to be considered holders in due course.'

(b) Section 2

Section 2 of the statute puts the banker in much the same position as if the payee had indorsed, and provides that:

> 'A banker who gives value for, or has a lien on, a cheque payable to order which the holder delivers to him for collection without indorsing it, has such (if any) rights as he would have had if, upon delivery, the holder had indorsed it in blank.'

Section 2 first came before the courts in 1962, in the unreported case of *Barclays Bank Ltd v Harding*.[13] The bank sued as holders for value and holders in due course of a cheque drawn by the defendant. Paull J found as a fact that the bank had given value for the cheque and were ipso facto holders for value. Next came *Midland Bank Ltd v R V Harris*,[14] in which the facts were not dissimilar. The defence was, first, that the section merely gave the rights, but not the status, of a holder and thus the bank could not be holders in due course, the second that by handing the dishonoured cheque back to the customer, the bank relinquished all rights on it, both of which Megaw J refused to accept. This latter point received further notice in the Court of Appeal in *Westminster Bank Ltd v Zang*,[15] in which the cheque was delivered back to the customer who paid it in, in order that he might sue the drawer. The action was abortive and the bank took the cheque back in order itself to sue. Both Lord Denning MR and Salmon LJ held that the bank lost its lien thereby and could not recover it even through the indorsement of the customer, for it was not delivered back for collection. The only title the bank could have by such redelivery was that of holder for value, assuming that it gave value, for it could not be a holder in due course as it would be vested with notice that the cheque had been dishonoured. The question of the effect of returning a dishonoured cheque to the customer and debiting his account was not dealt with by the House of Lords, it being regarded as unnecessary to do so in view of their finding that the bank had not given value. If the account will not support the debit and the bank is unwilling to allow an overdraft it would seem that the bank can retain any rights it has as a holder only by retaining possession or if, for whatever reason, it relinquishes possession, it reserves its rights. It may be that if it does no more than relinquish possession on terms, and does not recover by debiting the customer's account, it can retain its rights on the cheque.

---

11 [1933] AC 1.
12 Of matters which call for inquiry.
13 (1962) 83 Journal of the Institute of Bankers 109.
14 [1963] 2 All ER 685, [1963] 1 WLR 1021.
15 [1966] AC 182, [1965] 1 All ER 1023, affd [1966] AC 182, [1966] 1 Lloyd's Rep 49, HL.

The facts in *Zang*'s case were that one Tilley without indorsing it handed a cheque drawn in his favour to the bank for collection for the account of Tilley's Autos. The defence argued that (a) Tilley was not the holder; (b) the cheque was not delivered to the bank for collection for the account of the holder; (c) the bank did not give value for the cheque and (d) the bank ceased to have any rights when it handed the cheque back to Tilley in order that he might sue the drawer. All three members of the court found that Tilley was the holder; Lord Denning MR and Danckwerts LJ held that it was necessary in order that the bank might plead s 2 that the cheque should be paid in for the account of the holder unless he indorsed it, but Salmon LJ thought otherwise and his view was accepted by the House of Lords. On the question whether value had been given, all three judges thought not; but Danckwerts LJ was not convinced that the note on paying-in slips, to the effect that the bank reserved the right to refuse drawing against uncleared effects, prevented value arising in this case – this difference arose from their different views of the facts. Nevertheless, Salmon LJ said that value could be given by the honouring of a cheque drawn against uncleared effects, without any prior express or implied agreement. The House of Lords came to the conclusion that value had not been given. In his judgment, Lord Denning MR suggested that 'The words printed on the paying-in slip (reserving the right to refuse to pay against uncleared effects) also negative the existence of any such implied agreement.' His Lordship can have meant only that in the circumstances of the case no such agreement could be shown. The fact that a bank retains generally the right to refuse payment against uncleared effects and publishes the fact does not mean that a customer can never by agreement or a course of business be entitled to draw.

A banker may, by reason of overdraft, need to recover on a cheque paid in for collection which is returned dishonoured. Section 27 of the parent statute and s 2 of the Cheques Act enable him to sue. By s 27(3):

> 'Where the holder of a bill has a lien on it arising from contract or by implication of law, he is deemed to be a holder for value to the extent of the sum for which he has a lien.'

Subsection (1)(b) of s 27 defines 'valuable consideration' as 'an antecedent debt or liability'. So that if the account is overdrawn at the time the cheque is paid in, the banker automatically acquires a lien on it by which he is deemed to be a holder for value and as such can sue in his own name. Section 4 may now be important for him, for as a mere holder for value he may be defeated by 'defects of title of prior parties as well as mere personal defences available to prior parties among themselves' (ss 38(2) and 29(2)); but providing he has not been negligent in collecting, he may still plead s 4 in an action by the true owner. However, it is not clear why he cannot plead s 29 as a holder in due course, unless (which is absurd) the taking of the cheque for value means giving tangible value as where the cheque is bought or cash is given for it or, again, credit is given without recourse.

The last in this line of cases is *Barclays Bank Ltd v Astley Industrial Trust Ltd*[16] in which the bank sued in respect of cheques drawn by the defendants,

---

16 [1970] 2 QB 527, [1970] 1 All ER 719; see also *Re Keever, A Bankrupt, ex p Trustee of the property of the Bankrupt v Midland Bank* [1967] Ch 182, [1966] 2 Lloyd's Rep 475, and *Barclays Bank Ltd v Aschaffenburger Zellstoffwerke AG* [1967] 1 Lloyd's Rep 387.

the receipt of which by the bank prompted them to pay cheques of a customer which they would otherwise have dishonoured. Milmo J found that the bank took the cheques in good faith without notice of any defect in the payees' title, that it had given value and accordingly had a lien on the cheques. He held that the bank must be deemed holders for value within the meaning of s 27(3) of the Bills of Exchange Act 1882 and, having satisfied the conditions of s 29(1), were holders in due course, thus supporting the view suggested above.

Inter alia, the learned judge said:

> 'I am unable to accept the contention that a banker cannot at one and the same time be an agent for collection of a cheque and a holder of that cheque for value. It seems to me that the language of section 2 of the Cheques Act 1957 negatives this proposition since it presupposes that a banker who has been given a cheque for collection may nevertheless have given value for it.'

6   COLLECTING BANKER AS HOLDER IN DUE COURSE

If the banker is a holder in due course, he has no need of the protection of s 4 of the Cheques Act 1957. It is, therefore, strange that the cases seem mostly to have held the banker to be a holder for value when he could have pleaded that he was a holder in due course, for only then could his position be indefeasible if he collects for himself and is unable to plead the protective section. Want of title or a defective title in his customer will probably be fatal to the banker unless he can show not only that he is a holder for value, but a holder in due course, which means that there is nothing on the cheque or in the circumstances of its receipt to put him upon inquiry. In such a case the circumstances in which he took the cheque must, almost without exception, be such as to warrant his pleading the perfect title. As a holder for value he is liable to be defeated by:

> 'defect of title of prior parties, as well as ... mere personal defences available to prior parties among themselves.'[17]

Some banks insert in their cheque books or place on paying-in slips a notice to customers that cheques paid in cannot be drawn against until cleared. This would appear to have been unnecessary so far as s 82 as amended by the 1906 Act was concerned, and inconsistent with the 'holder for value' attitude. It may, however, be useful as rebutting the right to draw against the cheques at once, vide the *Gordon* case. This appears to be the view taken by Lord Denning in the particular circumstances of *Westminster Bank Ltd v Zang*.[18]

A man who has stolen a cheque can give a perfectly good title to another who takes it as a holder in due course.[19] In *Clutton v Attenborough & Son*[20] a fraudulent clerk obtained possession of cheques which he had persuaded his employers to sign; there was actual theft coupled with fraud which might well have been classed as larceny by a trick; the House of Lords decided in favour of the bona fide holder in good faith for value.

17 Bills of Exchange Act 1882, s 38(2).
18 [1965] 1 All ER 1023, [1965] 1 Lloyd's Rep 183; see also [1966] AC 182 at 203.
19 *Lloyd v Howard* (1850) 15 QB 995 at 997.
20 [1897] AC 90.

Entering as cash before receipt of payment of a bill payable at a future date tendered for collection has been held evidence of the banker's having taken the bill in his own right,[1] and as constituting an undertaking by the banker to honour cheques to the amount of the bill.[2] In *Re Mills, Bawtree & Co, ex p Stannard*,[3] Vaughan Williams J recognised the authority of *Thompson v Giles*, but said it had never been applied to an instrument payable on demand.

1 *Giles v Perkins* (1807) 9 East 12; *Thompson v Giles* (1824) 2 B & C 422; *Re Harrison, ex p Barkworth*, above; cf *Dawson v Isle* [1906] 1 Ch 633.
2 *Thompson v Giles*, above at 429, 431; cf *Re Mills, Bawtree & Co, ex p Stannard* (1893) 10 Morr 193.
3 (1893) 10 Morr 193.

CHAPTER 27

THE COLLECTING BANKER: CONVERSION; MONEY HAD AND RECEIVED

1 CONVERSION

(a) Definition

(i) Nature of conversion

A conversion is a wrongful interference with goods, as by taking, using or destroying them, inconsistent with the owner's right of possession. To constitute this injury, there must be some act of the defendant repudiating the owner's right, or some exercise of dominion inconsistent with it.[1] Intention is no element of conversion.

By s 1(a) of the Torts (Interference with Goods) Act 1977, conversion of goods (also called trover) is included in the definition of 'wrongful interference' and 'wrongful interference with goods' for the purposes of the Act.

A bill, note, or cheque, or the paper it is written on, is 'goods' within the above definition.[2] Where it is a negotiable instrument, the damages in conversion or for money had and received are its face value.[3] Even in the case of a non-negotiable instrument, it would seem that the person who has obtained money by means of it is estopped from alleging that its value is not the amount he has obtained by its means.[4]

There can be conversion of documents of title to goods. For example in

---

1 *Hollins v Fowler* (1875) LR 7 HL 757 at 795; *Clayton v Le Roy* [1911] 2 KB 1031; *Morison v London County and Westminster Bank Ltd* [1914] 3 KB 356, CA; *A. L. Underwood Ltd v Bank of Liverpool and Martins* [1924] 1 KB 775, CA, per Scrutton LJ.

2 See *Morison v London County and Westminster Bank Ltd* [1914] 3 KB 356, CA, per Lord Reading LCJ; *Lloyds Bank Ltd v Chartered Bank of India, Australia and China* [1929] 1 KB 40, CA, per Scrutton LJ: '... but a series of decisions binding on this Court, culminating in *Morison's case* and *Underwood's* case, have surmounted the difficulty by treating the conversion as of the chattel, the piece of paper, the cheque under which the money was collected, and the value of the chattel converted as the money received under it'.

3 *Morrison v London County and Westminster Bank Ltd* [1914] 3 KB 356, CA, per Phillimore LJ; *Bobbett v Pinkett* (1876) 1 Ex D 368; *Fine Art Society Ltd v Union Bank of London Ltd* (1886) 17 QBD 705; *Bavins Junr and Sims v London and South Western Bank* [1900] 1 QB 270, CA; *Macbeth v North and South Wales Bank* [1908] 1 KB 13, CA, affd on appeal sub nom *North and South Wales Bank Ltd v Macbeth* [1908] AC 137, HL.

4 See *Bavins Jnr and Sims v London and South Western Bank*, supra; *Morison v London County and Westminster Bank Ltd*, supra; *Fine Art Society Ltd v Union Bank of London Ltd*, above; *Lloyds Bank Ltd v Chartered Bank of India, Australia and China* [1929] 1 KB 40.

Midland Bank Ltd v Eastcheap Dried Fruit Co,[5] the plaintiff bank delivered documents of title to goods to the defendants with a request for payment, which for a variety of reasons was not forthcoming. The Court of Appeal upheld the view of McNair J that the defendants were liable for conversion.

Obvious examples of situations where the collecting banker may be liable in conversion are (1) the collection of a bill, note, or cheque with a forged indorsement, or to which the customer has no title;[6] and (2) the taking as holder for value of a bill or cheque with a forged indorsement, or a cheque marked 'not negotiable' to which the transferor's title is void or defective.[7]

(ii) Entitlement to immediate possession

It is generally agreed, in stating the position requisite for a plaintiff in conversion, that he must have been entitled to immediate possession of the chattel at the date of conversion.[8] Examples of the application of this principle in the field of banking include the following:

(1) *Robinson v Midland Bank Ltd*[9] where an account was opened in the name of, but not by, one Robinson and a cheque in favour of Robinson's solicitors and indorsed over by them was paid in to that account. Robinson sued for conversion and money had and received, but failed on the ground that he had neither possession nor any right of property in the cheque.

(2) *Arrow Transfer Co Ltd v Royal Bank of Canada, Bank of Montreal and Canadian Imperial Bank of Commerce,*[10] a Canadian case, in which it was held that there can be no conversion of an instrument on which the drawer's signature is forged. Robertson JA, with Taggart JA concurring, said that:

'... the plaintiff must be the true owner of the piece of paper qua cheque and not simply the owner of the piece of paper qua piece of paper.'

(3) *Midland Bank Ltd v Eastcheap Dried Fruit Co,* above.

---

5 [1962] 1 Lloyd's Rep 359, CA, applied in *Ernest Scragg & Sons Ltd v Perseverance Banking and Trust Co Ltd* [1973] 2 Lloyd's Rep 101, CA.
6 Eg *Bissell & Co v Fox Bros & Co* (1885) 53 LT 193, CA; *Kleinwort, Sons & Co v Comptoir National d'Escompte de Paris* [1894] 2 QB 157; *Great Western Rly Co v London and County Banking Co Ltd* [1899] 2 QB 172, revsd [1901] AC 414, HL; *Capital and Counties Bank Ltd v Gordon* [1903] AC 240, HL; *A L Underwood Ltd v Bank of Liverpool and Martins* [1924] 1 KB 775, CA; *Midland Bank Ltd v Reckitt* [1933] AC 1, HL; *Lloyds Bank Ltd v E B Savory & Co* [1933] AC 201, HL; *Motor Traders Guarantee Corpn v Midland Bank Ltd* [1937] 4 All ER 90; *Baker v Barclays Bank Ltd* [1955] 2 All ER 571, [1955] 1 WLR 822; *Marquess of Bute v Barclays Bank Ltd* [1955] 1 QB 202, [1954] 3 All ER 365; *Nu-Stilo Footwear Ltd v Lloyds Bank Ltd* (1956) 7 LDAB 121.
7 *Great Western Rly Co v London and County Banking Co Ltd* [1901] AC 414, HL; *Capital and Counties Bank Ltd v Gordon* [1903] AC 240, HL.
8 *White v Teal* (1840) 12 Ad & El 106 at 115, in which Lord Denman said that lien was inconsistent with the plaintiff's right of possession.
9 (1925) 41 TLR 402.
10 [1971] 3 WWR 241 at 258, affd on appeal sub nom *Arrow Transfer Co Ltd v Royal Bank of Canada, Bank of Montreal, Canadian Imperial Bank of Commerce and Secor* [1972] 4 WWR 70.

(b) Particular types of action

(i) Action by holder in due course of stolen negotiable instrument

A holder in due course of a stolen negotiable instrument has title to sue in conversion. An example is *Smith v Union Bank of London*,[11] where a cheque payable to bearer by endorsement by the payee was stolen and negotiated to a holder in due course. He, and not the person from whom it was stolen, was held to be the true owner.

(ii) Action by principal in respect of conversion by agent

A principal may sue in respect of the conversion of his agent. The agent must, however, have been acting beyond his authority. In *Australia and New Zealand Bank Ltd v Ateliers de Constructions Electriques de Charleroi*,[12] an agent paid his principal's cheques into his personal account, but it was held that there was no conversion because there was implied authority from the principal to the agent to use his private account for such purposes although the principal was in fact defrauded. Thus, although the banker was negligent in dealing with such cheques without specific authority, and would have lost his statutory protection, he escaped liability.

This can be contrasted with *Marquess of Bute v Barclays Bank Ltd*[13] where warrants of the Scottish Department of Agriculture drawn on the King's and Lord Treasurer's Remembrancer in favour of Mr D McGaw were collected for McGaw. In a box opposite the name McGaw were the words '(for the Marquess of Bute)'. McNair J held that in order to claim in conversion it is sufficient if the plaintiff can prove that at the time of the alleged conversion he was entitled to immediate possession, and stated that the test was the intention of the drawers as expressed in the instrument. He held that the words 'for the Marquess of Bute' were an essential part of the description of the payee. It had been argued that the plaintiff was estopped from claiming by reason of his representation that the warrant could be paid to McGaw; but McNair J held that the warrant contained no such representation.[14] This decision was approved by the Court of Appeal in *International Factors Ltd v Rodriguez*.[15]

A bill or cheque may, of course, be made payable to an agent in his own name or under his official designation, but without reference to his principal. This occurred in *Great Western Rly Co v London and County Banking Co Ltd*,[16] where a cheque was made payable to Huggins or order, he being a rate

11 (1875) 1 QBD 31, CA.
12 [1967] 1 AC 86, PC.
13 [1955] 1 QB 202, [1954] 3 All ER 365.
14 [1955] 1 QB 202 at 213, as to which see *Woodhouse AC Israel Cocoa Ltd v Nigerian Produce Marketing Co Ltd* [1971] 2 QB 23, [1970] 2 All ER 124, CA, affd [1972] AC 741, [1972] 2 All ER 271, HL.
15 [1979] QB 351, [1979] 1 All ER 17, CA.
16 [1901] AC 414, HL.

collector, in payment of rates falsely represented by him to be due from the Great Western Railway. Lord Halsbury LC said:[17]

'In this case it cannot be pretended that Huggins had any title to it at all'.

Lord Davey:[18]

'I am of opinion that Huggins never had any property in the cheque, which was handed to him only as the collector and agent of the overseers in payment of a debt alleged to be due to them. The appellants never intended to vest any property in him for his own benefit, but the property in the cheque was intended to be passed to his employers, the overseers, notwithstanding that it was made payable to Huggins' order. Huggins therefore had no real title to the cheque'.

If a cheque is wrongfully issued by an agent authorised to draw it for specific purposes, the principal remains the owner.[19]

(iii) Action based upon after-acquired title

In *Bristol and West of England Bank v Midland Rly Co*,[20] the Court of Appeal reviewed the authorities and held that it was no answer to a claim in conversion that at the date of wrongful delivery, the plaintiffs had not acquired their title to the goods.[1]

Where goods are in the hands of someone with a revocable title and before revocation or notice thereof are delivered to someone taking bona fide for value, conversion will not lie either at the suit of the original owner or of anyone deriving title from him. The same applies to cases in which bills, notes or cheques are held under a revocable title. It does not, however, apply to a cheque crossed 'not negotiable' because the effect of such crossing is to put each holder on precisely the same footing as the earliest title (see ch 22, above).

(iv) Action based upon title by avoidance

A. DISTINCTION BETWEEN VOID AND VOIDABLE NEGOTIABLE INSTRUMENTS

If a negotiable instrument is delivered as a contract, the property in the chattel passes, it may be only temporarily if the contract is revocable, not if there is no contract. Whether there is a contract or not depends on the existence or absence of a contracting mind. Where there is a contract, the result of its negotiable incidents is that third persons may acquire rights to the instrument which subsequent revocation will not prejudice or affect. The distinction is almost invariably brought forward by and in cases of fraud.

Where a man is fraudulently deceived into issuing a negotiable instrument in favour of one specific person in the belief that he is another specific person, an essential element of contract is lacking, and the result is that the instrument is void;[2] but where a man is induced by fraud to execute and issue a negotiable

---

17 [1901] AC 414 at 418.
18 [1901] AC 414 at 417.
19 *Morison v London County and Westminster Bank Ltd* [1914] 3 KB 356 at 364, 375; *Lloyds Bank Ltd v E B Savory & Co* [1933] AC 201, HL.
20 [1891] 2 QB 653, CA.
 1 Cf *London Joint Stock Bank Ltd v British Amsterdam Maritime Agency Ltd* (1910) 104 LT 143, 16 Com Cas 102.
 2 *Cundy v Lindsay* (1878) 3 App Cas 459, HL; *Tate v Wilts and Dorset Bank* (1899) 1 LDAB 286.

instrument, knowing what it is, the contract is not void, but voidable. The property and right of possession in and to the chattel are divested but, on repudiation of the contract, revert to the defrauded person, subject to any right acquired by third parties in the interval.[3] The distinction is, as suggested by Lord Penzance in *Cundy v Lindsay*,[4] between a man who, being deceived, enters into no contract, and a man who, being deceived, does enter into a contract. The doctrine of this case was held distinctly applicable to negotiable instruments by Lord Davey in *Great Western Rly Co v London and County Banking Co Ltd*,[5] and by the court in *Tate v Wilts and Dorset Bank*.[6]

B. COLLECTION FOR CUSTOMER WITH VOIDABLE TITLE

Apart from statute, however, collection for someone with a voidable title is protected if the money is paid away before notice of revocation is received (see *Bavins Junr and Sims v London and South Western Bank*).[7]

C. LOSS OF THE RIGHT TO AVOID

The right to avoid a negotiable instrument, and the right to bring an action based on avoidance, is lost if the instrument is taken by a holder in due course.[8] But a smaller right in the instrument than that of a holder in due course may also defeat the right to avoid. In *Tate v Wilts and Dorset Bank*[9] Channell J says:

'I take it the bankers were the holders of the cheque (whether they were holders for value does not matter), and they got payment of it in the regular way. It is admitted if that was so there was a fresh disposition of the cheque, and that thereupon the transaction could not be avoided so as to make the bank liable, ...'

This case appears to have been doubted in *Lloyds Bank Ltd v Chartered Bank of India, Australia and China*,[10] but not overruled. Sankey LJ said:

'Even if Tate's case can be held to be good law since the decision in *Morison v London County and Westminster* Bank ...'[11]

'Fresh disposition' is a very wide term, and would cover almost any legitimate dealing with a negotiable instrument. As exemplified in *Tate v Wilts and Dorset Bank*,[12] the doctrine protects the banker who has collected a cheque for a customer, where that customer holds it under a voidable title. The particular case would have been that of an uncrossed cheque, the property in which had passed to the payee or indorsee; if it were collected in good faith and without negligence or notice of revocation, the banker would have been protected, quite apart from s 82 of the Bills of Exchange Act 1882, having collected for the true owner.

---

3 *Clutton v Attenborough & Son* [1897] AC 90, HL; *Tate v Wilts and Dorset Bank* (1899) supra; *Cahn v Pockett's Bristol Channel Steam Packet Co* [1899] 1 QB 643, CA; *Whitehorn Bros v Davison* [1911] 1 KB 463, CA.
4 (1878) 3 App Cas 459 at 461, HL.
5 [1901] AC 414, HL.
6 (1899) 1 LDAB 286, 376.
7 [1900] 1 QB 270, CA.
8 *Clutton v Attenborough & Son* [1897] AC 90.
9 (1899) 1 LDAB 286 at 290.
10 [1929] 1 KB 40, CA.
11 [1914] 3 KB 356, CA.
12 (1899) 1 LDAB 286 at 290.

D. VOIDABLE INSTRUMENT EXCHANGED FOR BANKER'S DRAFT

In two Australian cases cheques drawn in fraud of principals by an agent (as in *Morison's* case) were exchanged for bankers' drafts issued by the drawee bank and paid into the agent's account with another bank. The Privy Council have twice decided that the collecting bank was not liable in conversion or for money had and received. In *Union Bank of Australia Ltd v McClintock*[13] and again in *Commercial Banking Co of Sydney v Mann*[14] it was held that the property in the drafts was never in the respondents and that they could not ratify the obtaining of the drafts by their agent without ratifying his subsequent dealing with them. The ratio of the judgments may be questioned, for the property in the cheques with which the drafts were obtained was surely in the respondents (they could hardly be in the fraudulent agent) and it is not obvious why their conversion into drafts should change the ownership unless the drafts were negotiated to a bona fide holder for value without notice. It is submitted that the contracts were voidable and could be repudiated until an indefeasible title vested in a third party. In the second of the two cases there was a third party, but it is not clear whether he was a bona fide holder or why the defendant bank gave cash for the drafts, although they had the account of the third party and the drafts were crossed 'not negotiable'. They could not plead s 88A of the Australian Bills of Exchange Act 1909–1971, because they collected for themselves, and though they gave value they were not holders in due course. In the earlier case the legislation relating to bankers' drafts had not been passed.

(v) Action where signature authorised for one purpose is used for another

Section 24 of the Bills of Exchange Act 1882, which deals with forged and unauthorised signatures, raises questions with regard to signatures authorised for one purpose but used for another. *Morison v London County and Westminster Bank Ltd*[15] decided that an authorised signature could not become a forgery if used for an illegitimate purpose; what was not a forgery quoad the paying banker could not be one as against the collecting banker. The decision of the Court of Appeal in *Alexander Stewart & Son of Dundee Ltd v Westminster Bank Ltd*[16] would seem to qualify this view, for the signature of Sir John Stewart was held to be unauthorised within the meaning of the section (24) which places forged and unauthorised signatures in the same category; and that s 25 was fatal to the collecting bank's contention that it was not put upon inquiry; *Morison's* case does not appear to have been cited. In the lower court Rowlatt J held that the signature to the indorsement was not a procuration signature within the meaning of s 25 but only a signature (as in fact it was) 'for and on behalf of' the company, with nothing to show that the agent was acting under a special authority. A limited company could only sign through a natural person as agent (citing *Re Land Credit Co of Ireland, ex p Overend, Gurney & Co*[17] and *Dey v Pullinger Engineering Co*).[18] He found that the bank, although negligent, were holders

13 [1922] 1 AC 240, PC.
14 [1960] AC 1, [1960] 3 All ER 482, PC.
15 [1914] 3 KB 356 per Lord Reading LCJ at 366, Phillimore LJ at 379–80.
16 [1926] WN 126; revsd, [1926] WN 271, 4 LDAB 40.
17 (1869) 4 Ch App 460.
18 [1921] 1 KB 77.

in due course, and thus not liable for conversion, on the ground that Sir John Stewart had been allowed to draw against the cheques before they were cleared. The Court of Appeal allowed the appeal, presumably on the ground of negligence. They held also that the signatures were unauthorised within the meaning of s 25 (quaere s 24) and declined to express any opinion on Rowlatt J's view that s 25 was limited to agency on behalf of a natural person.

Morison's case dealt only with the Forgery Act 1861. But the *Kreditbank Cassel* case[19] put a different complexion on the question, by importing the Forgery Act 1913, with its interpretation of the words 'false statement' used there as including the use of any form of deputed authority signature by a company official, imputedly, if not actually, qualified to sign for company purposes, when that signature is affixed with fraudulent intent deduced from the subsequent payment of the instrument into a private account. This interpretation would seem to apply equally to the word 'unauthorised' in s 24 of the Bills of Exchange Act, but this seems immaterial.

In *Underwood's* case,[20] Scrutton LJ distinguishes between cases where a representative signature is obviously used for private ends, as by payment into a private account, and cases where a company cheque has been negotiated and it is doubtful whether or not there has been a misappropriation. The collecting banker has no means of knowing who are authorised to draw or indorse for a company not his customer. 'There is, no doubt, considerable difficulty in defining the limits of conversion, where servants or agents do ministerial acts in relation to the goods in good faith and on behalf of the apparent owner'.[1]

(c) Debiting customer's account where banker liable

Liability in conversion is independent of any right to debit the customer; the banker may be liable in conversion and at the same time disentitled to debit his customer.

In *Redmond v Allied Irish Banks Plc*,[2] the plaintiff paid into his account certain cheques marked 'not negotiable – account payee only', one of which he had endorsed, in circumstances where he was not the named payee. The defendant bank was subsequently successfully sued by the true owner, and debited the plaintiff's account with the face amount of the cheques. The plaintiff then sued the defendant for breach of an alleged duty of care. The action failed on the ground that the defendant owed the plaintiff no duty of care to advise or warn him of the risks of carrying out the transaction. Concessions made by the plaintiff made it unnecessary to decide (1) whether a bank which collects such a cheque for a customer who is not the named payee is entitled to be indemnified by that customer for liability to the true owner; and (2) whether in presenting such a cheque for collection the customer impliedly warrants that he has a good title. However, Saville J expressed doubt as to whether such concessions had been properly made:

'... the whole case has proceeded upon the assumption that the defendants were entitled to be indemnified by the plaintiff. I am bound to say that, without hearing argument, I regard this assumption as prima facie questionable, at least in relation

19 [1927] 1 KB 826.
20 [1924] 1 KB 775.
 1 [1924] 1 KB 775 at 790.
 2 [1987] 2 FTLR 264.

to the cheques which Mr Redmond did not endorse: for the assumption would seem to involve the proposition that the plaintiff impliedly agreed to indemnify the bank against the consequences of their own negligence in agreeing to collect and pay an account payee only cheque into the account of another: for, without negligence, it would seem that the bank would be protected by s 4 of the Cheques Act 1957. Whether the principle of cases such as *Sheffield v Barclay* [1905] AC 392 and *Stanley Yeung Kai Yung v Hong Kong and Shanghai Banking Corpn* [1981] AC 787 extend to cover such a case seems to me to be debatable.'

2 MONEY HAD AND RECEIVED

(a) Nature of the action

In the words of Lord Wright in *Fibrosa Spolka Akcyjna v Fairbairn Lawson Combe Barbour Ltd*:[3]

'... the common law still employs the action for money had and received as a practical and useful, if not complete or ideally perfect, instrument to prevent unjust enrichment, aided by the various methods of technical equity which are also available as they were found to be in *Sinclair v Brougham*.'

Wherever conversion lies, and money has been received for the negotiable instrument converted, the plaintiff may waive the wrong and sue for money had and received to his use.[4] The claims are usually joined in the alternative, and this is the form in which the action is couched against a banker who has collected a cheque for someone without title. The joinder of a claim for money had and received does not operate as a waiver of the wrong so as to prejudice the claim in conversion, but leaves the plaintiff free to recover on either ground; and defences appropriate to each are open to the defendant.[5] The action for money had and received is not merely an alternative to conversion, or dependent on the existence of a conversion; it is an independent and widespreading form of action, and lies in many cases where conversion would not, as for the recovery of money paid for a consideration which has failed[6] or under a mistake of fact.[7] It is independent of the legal nature of the instrument. In *Bavins Junr and Sims v London and South Western Bank*[8] the instrument was in the form of a cheque, but bore a form of receipt which had to be completed as a condition of payment; it was therefore not a negotiable instrument. The Court of Appeal found against the bank; in the words of Vaughan Williams LJ:

'It was argued that, if the action is treated as one of trover, only nominal damages

3 [1943] AC 32 at 64, HL.
4 For what amounts to a waiver, see *United Australia Ltd v Barclays Bank Ltd* [1941] AC 1, [1940] 4 All ER 20, HL; in the Court of Appeal in this case Clauson LJ [1941] AC 1 at 10 said that the claim for money had and received involved the position that there had been a tortious acquisition of the money.
5 See, for instance, *Morison v London County and Westminster Bank Ltd* [1914] 3 KB 356,CA; and see per Lord Atkin in *United Australia Ltd v Barclays Bank Ltd* [1941] AC 1 at 19, HL; 'You may put them in the same writ; or you may put one in first, and then amend and add or substitute another'.
6 Eg, *Fibrosa Spolka Akcyjna v Fairbairn Lawson Combe Barbour Ltd* [1943] AC 32, [1942] 2 All ER 122, HL.
7 See aso *Burnett v Westminster Bank Ltd* [1966] 1 QB 742, [1965] 3 All ER 81; as to money paid by mistake, see ch 25, ante.
8 [1900] 1 QB 270, CA.

can be recovered, because the document converted in itself constituted no cause of action but was merely evidence of a debt in respect of which it was given. ... But in any case it seems to me to be clear that the plaintiffs are entitled to recover the amount received by the defendants upon the document as money had and received. Having received money by presenting the document which belonged to the plaintiffs they cannot in my opinion, if the plaintiffs choose to waive the tort, say that they did not receive the money on account of the plaintiffs; or at any rate they cannot say so after they have knowledge of the plaintiffs' title, unless before obtaining that knowledge they have altered their position for the worse so as to bring themselves within the doctrine of *Holland v Russell*.[9]

The dictum of the Privy Council, per Viscount Haldane in *John v Dodwell & Co*[10] that,

'The action for money had and received is, according to the law of England, in its nature one of assumpsit, founded on implied or imputed contract and depends on a waiver of any tort committed, and on the correlative affirmance of a contractual relation,'

if and in so far as it avers dependence on the existence and waiver of a tort, is probably incorrect.[11]

In *Sinclair v Brougham*,[12] Lord Sumner said it was hard to reduce to one common formula the conditions under which the law will imply a promise to repay money received to the plaintiff's use. It would seem to have been thought at that time that the law would imply or impute a promise by the defendant to repay. It might be a mere fiction of law which supplied the promise, and it could not be implied where, as in *Sinclair v Brougham*, it would, if actually made, have been ultra vires. The early idea was that the action was an importation of principles of equity into common law, and that the money was recoverable where it was unconscientious, contra aequum et bonum, for the defendant to retain it as against the plaintiff. Lord Sumner says:[13]

'There is now no ground left for suggesting as a recognisable "equity" the right to recover money in personam merely because it would be the right and fair thing that it should be refunded to the payer.'

Lord Denning has described[14] the error that the basis of assumpsit is an implied promise, and he refers in this respect to *Sinclair v Brougham*,[15] *Re Simms*[16], *Morgan v Ashcroft*[17] and *Re Diplock*.[18] He said the fallacy was exposed and the true position shown by Lord Simon and Lord Atkin in *United Australia Ltd v Barclays Bank Ltd*[19] and by Lord Wright in the

9 (1863) 4 B & S 14.
10 [1918] AC 563 at 570.
11 This view is supported by an article by Lord Denning in 65 LQR 40; and see *United Australia Ltd v Barclays Bank Ltd* [1941] AC 1, HL.
12 [1914] AC 398 at 453, HL.
13 [1914] AC 398 at 456.
14 65 LQR 39.
15 [1914] AC 398, HL.
16 [1934] Ch 1, CA.
17 [1938] 1 KB 49, [1937] 3 All ER 92, CA.
18 [1948] Ch 465, [1948] 2 All ER 318, CA.
19 [1941] AC 1, HL.

Fibrosa case.[20] See also the judgment of the Court of Appeal in *Holt v Markham*.[1]

It seems now to be accepted that the law imposes a debt. In *Fibrosa Spolka Akcyjna v Fairbairn Lawson Combe Barbour Ltd*[2] Lord Wright referred to Lord Mansfield's judgment in *Moses v Macferlan*[3] and said:

> 'Lord Mansfield does not say that the law implies a promise. The law implies a debt or obligation, which is a different thing. In fact, he denies that there is a contract; the obligation is as efficacious as if it were upon a contract. The obligation is a creation of the law, just as much as an obligation in tort. The obligation belongs to a third class, distinct from either contract or tort, though it resembles contract rather than tort.'

And he goes on to say that Lord Mansfield's statement has, notwithstanding criticism, been the basis of the modern law of quasi-contract.

(b) Waiver of tort

The question of waiver was treated in the judgment of the House of Lords in *United Australia Ltd v Barclays Bank Ltd* where Lord Atkin, speaking in the first person of the tortious taking of money, asserted that 'I sue him because he has the actual property taken' and protested,[4]

> 'that a man cannot waive a wrong unless he either has a real intention to waive it, or can fairly have imputed to him such an intention . . . These fantastic resemblances of contracts invented in order to meet requirements of the law as to forms of action which have now disappeared should not in these days be allowed to affect actual rights.'

(c) Action for money had and received against banker as agent

Where an agent is sued for money had and received,[5] it cannot be recovered from him if he received it in good faith and materially altered his position, as by paying it over to his principal before it was claimed, especially, in the case of the agent's being a collecting banker, if he received the money on a negotiable instrument.[6] But cases against bankers have, however, almost always been decided on the conversion claim.

In *Bavins Junr and Sims v London and South Western Bank*,[7] the mere fact that the bank had credited the customer's account with the proceeds of the cheque and that sums had been drawn out which, on the ordinary system of appropriation, exhausted those proceeds, was held not to preclude the true owner from recovering as money had and received, inasmuch as the state of the account was such as admitted of the bank debiting the amount to the

---

20 [1943] AC 32 at 62.
1 [1923] 1 KB 504.
2 [1943] AC 32 at 62, HL.
3 (1760) 2 Burr 1005 at 1012.
4 [1941] AC 1 at 29.
5 As in *Transvaal and Delagoa Bay Investment Co Ltd v Atkinson* [1944] 1 All ER 579.
6 See *Morison v London County and Westminster Bank Ltd* [1914] 3 KB 356, CA, per Phillimore LJ at 386. See also *Buller v Harrison* (1777) 2 Cowp 565, per Lord Mansfield at 568: 'now the law is clear, that if an agent pay over money which has been paid to him by mistake of fact, he does no wrong; and the plaintiff must call on the principal'. Cf *Rogers v Kelly* (1809) 2 Camp 123.
7 [1900] 1 QB 270.

customer, and therefore the bank were not, in fact, prejudiced, and had not irrevocably altered their position.

(d) Relevance of negligence on the part of the defendant

In some cases it seems to have been suggested that negligence might deprive the agent of the protection above referred to; but it will be noticed that in *Bavins Junr and Sims v London and South Western Bank*,[8] the Court of Appeal found that the bank had acted negligently, and the plaintiffs were entitled to recover the money had and received.

Some light may be thrown on this point by Lord Sumner in *R. E. Jones Ltd v Waring and Gillow Ltd*,[9] where in his view neither party acted negligently,

'that is, in the absence of any duty to one another, imprudently or without ordinary sanction. The point is probably immaterial.'

---

8 (1899) 5 Com Cas 1 per A. L. Smith LJ at 12, Collins LJ at 13, and Vaughan Williams LJ at 14 in the judgments reported in [1900] 1 QB 270, there is no mention of negligence, but see the note to the statement of facts at 272: The Court of Appeal was, however, of opinion tha there had clearly been negligence on the part of the defendants in receiving the document with the indorsement and the receipt signed in a name other than that of the payees ....'.
9 [1926] AC 670 at 693.

CHAPTER 28

THE COLLECTING BANKER: STATUTORY PROTECTION

1 HISTORY OF THE LEGISLATION

(a) Relevance

The history of the legislation conferring protection on the collecting banker is relevant for two main reasons:

1 The terms of the original protective provision (s 12 of the Crossed Cheques Act 1876) as re-enacted in s 82 of the Bills of Exchange Act 1882 were such as to give rise to a distinction between (a) the banker acting as collecting banker, in which the protection was available, and (b) the banker acting as holder for value, where it was not available. It has already been noted in ch 26, above that if a banker takes an instrument as holder in due course, he has no need of the statutory protection. Although there are differences between a holder in due course and a holder for value, cases decided under s 82 give at least some guidance as to when a banker will be held to have acted otherwise than as a mere agent for collection.

2 The history of the legislation enters the assessment of the modern relevance of cases decided under statutes earlier than the Cheques Act 1957.

(b) Bills of Exchange Act 1882, s 82

Statutory protection was introduced as a corollary to the duties imposed upon bankers in relation to crossed cheques.[1] Section 82 provided:

'Where a banker in good faith and without negligence receives payment for a customer of a cheque crossed generally or specially to himself, and the customer has no title or a defective title thereto, the banker shall not incur any liability to the true owner of the cheque by reason only of having received such payment.'

The phrase 'receives payment for a customer' gave rise to difficulty. There are certain cases where a bank clearly receives payment for a customer, in particular where the customer's account is not credited until the banker has received the proceeds of a cheque. There are other cases where it is equally

---

1 See the judgment of Collins MR in *Gordon v Capital and Counties Bank Ltd* [1902] 1 KB 242, CA, expressly approved in the House of Lords by Lord Macnaghten [1903] AC 240 at 246

clear that a banker has gone further than to act as a mere agent for collection. Such cases include those where a banker gives cash over the counter for a cheque which is not drawn on him,[2] or where he lends against a cheque delivered to him for collection, or where he agrees that the customer may draw on uncleared effects.[3] Between these instances lies the case of a banker simply crediting the customer with the face value of a cheque on receipt for collection and before clearing. The effect of such a crediting arose for determination in the historic case of *Capital and Counties Bank Ltd v Gordon*.[4] The House of Lords held that:

1 'Receives payment for a customer' meant 'receives payment as a mere agent for collection'. In the words of Lord Macnaghten:[5]

> 'But the protection conferred by s 82 is conferred only on a banker who receives payment for a customer, that is, who receives payment as a mere agent for collection. It follows, I think, that if bankers do more than act as such agents , they are not within the protection of the section'.

The section indicates agency pure and simple.[6] There is nothing in the legislation affecting crossed cheques which necessitates the intervention of the collecting banker in any capacity other than that of an agent. And the House applied here the canon of construction that the protection must be limited to the enhanced risks imposed by contemporary legislation. Lord Macnaghten[7] quotes with approval the words of Collins MR in the Court of Appeal:

> 'The protection afforded by s 82 must be limited to that which is necessary for the performance of the duty which by the legislation as to crossed cheques was imposed on bankers.'

2 Crediting as cash constituted the banker a holder for value, and a banker could not receive payment of a cheque as an agent if he be himself the holder for value.

Thus the legal conception of the collecting banker enunciated in the *Gordon* case was that of a mere conduit pipe (per Collins MR in the Court of Appeal), receiving the cheque from the customer, presenting it and receiving the money for the customer, and then, and not till then, placing it to the customer's credit, exercising functions strictly analogous to those of a clerk of the customer sent to a bank to cash an open cheque for his employer.[8] The House of Lords held that the bank had not acted as such conduit pipe, had not received payment for the customer in respect of certain crossed cheques and so had lost the protection of s 82.

The reason why the House of Lords held the bank not to have received payment for the customer but for itself was that it had credited the customer

2 See *Great Western Rly Co v London and County Banking Co Ltd* [1901] AC 414, HL.
3 See *Re Palmer, ex p Richdale* (1882) 19 Ch D 409, CA, per Jessel MR at 417; *Royal Bank of Scotland v Tottenham* [1894] 2 QB 715, CA, per Lord Esher MR at 717.
4 [1903] AC 240, HL.
5 [1903] AC 240 at 245.
6 See *Matthiessen v London and County Bank* (1879) 5 CPD 7, and the judgment of Collins MR in the *Gordon* case in the Court of Appeal, [1902] 1 KB 242, expressly approved by Lord Macnaghten in the House of Lords.
7 [1903] AC 240 at 246.
8 Ibid. at 246.

with the face value as cash on receipt for collection and before clearing. What the *Gordon* case primarily did was to deprive bankers of the protection of s 82 against the true owner with regard to crossed cheques with a forged indorsement or to which the customer had no title or a defective title, where such cheques had been credited as cash before receipt of the money.

The *Gordon* case generated much discussion and doubt as to the banker's position, and not surprisingly, it was not the last word on the matter. Very soon the courts took the view that to deprive the banker of protection there must be something more than mere crediting as cash in the bank's own books, for instance some undertaking or understanding with the customer that he could draw against the cheques at once.[9] The government brought in amending bills in 1903, 1904 and 1905, which were successively dropped; and finally in 1906 the Bills of Exchange (Crossed Cheques) Act 1906 (see below) was passed which neutralised the effect of the *Gordon* case.

Even the 1906 Act did not finally end the controversy. In *A L Underwood Ltd v Bank of Liverpool: Same v Barclays Bank Ltd*[10] Bankes LJ and presumably Scrutton LJ acquiesced in the view of Atkin LJ that neither the *Gordon* case nor the 1906 Act laid down the rule, judicial or statutory, that if a bank credits a cheque at once in its books, that fact, without more, makes the bank a holder for value. It is difficult to follow the court in its statement concerning the *Gordon* case. That part of the judgment dealing with the point of crediting as cash allows of no misunderstanding. Lord Birkenhead LC recognised the position in *Sutters v Briggs*:[11]

> 'It is, as is well known, usual for bankers, in the case of substantial customers at least, to constitute themselves holders in due course, as was the case in *Capital and Counties Bank Ltd v Gordon,* the result of which case led to the passing of the Bills of Exchange (Crossed Cheques) Act 1906'.

The true position is that the *Gordon* case was wrongly decided and that Atkin LJ in *Underwood's* case was correctly stating the law, but misapplying the *Gordon* decision. As recently as 1965, Lord Denning MR in *Westminster Bank Ltd v Zang*[12] said that *Underwood's* case has 'always been accepted as good law'.

(c) Amendments to s 82

(i) Revenue Act 1883

Section 17 of the Revenue Act 1883 provided:

> 'Sections 76 to 82, both inclusive, of the Bills of Exchange Act 1882 . . . shall extend to any document issued by a customer of any banker and intended to enable any person or body corporate to obtain payment from such banker of the sum mentioned in such document, and shall so extend in like manner as if the said document were a cheque. Provided that nothing in this Act shall be deemed to render any such document a negotiable instrument.'

This extended the statutory protection to instruments such as conditional orders for payment, which have already been considered in the context of the

---

9 See *Akrokerri (Atlantic) Mines Ltd v Economic Bank* [1904] 2 KB 465; *Bevan v National Bank Ltd* (1906) 23 TLR 65.
10 [1924] 1 KB 775, CA.
11 [1922] 1 AC 1 at 15.
12 [1966] AC 182 at 203

statutory protection available to the paying banker (ch 24). The protection it offered is now to be found, as regards collection, in s 4(2)(b) of the Cheques Act 1957. Section 6 (2) of the Cheques Act 1957 provides that nothing in ss 1 to 5 of the Act shall make negotiable any instrument which apart from them is not negotiable.

(ii) Bills of Exchange (Crossed Cheques) Act 1906

This Act contained only one operative provision, as follows:

'1. A banker receives payment of a crossed cheque for a customer within the meaning of section 82 of the Bills of Exchange Act, 1882, notwithstanding that he credits his customer's account with the amount of the cheque before receiving payment thereof.'

In *Re Farrow's Bank Ltd,*[13] Astbury J said:

'It is no longer arguable, if it ever was, that the mere crediting ...of a cheque paid into a customer's account, independently of any knowledge of the customer, or arrangement as between him and the bank, converts the bank into a holder for value as distinct from a recipient for the customer within the meaning of s 82 of the Bills of Exchange Act 1882. This is now laid down by the Bills of Exchange (Crossed Cheques) Act 1906.'

The 1906 Act was substantially re-enacted in s 4(1) of the Cheques Act 1957.

(iii) Bills of Exchange (1882) Amendment Act 1932

This Act also contained only one operative provision:

'1. Sections 76 to 82 of the Bills of Exchange Act 1882 (which relate to crossed cheques), as amended by the Bills of Exchange (Crossed Cheques) Act 1906, shall apply to a banker's draft as if the draft were a cheque.
    For the purposes of this section, the expression "banker's draft" means a draft payable on demand drawn by or on behalf of a bank itself, whether payable at the head office or some other office of the bank.'

Inasmuch as the amending Act specifically referred to the 1906 Act, bankers' drafts were clearly within the latter and the banker obtained the same protection, when crediting them as cash, as he had in respect of crossed cheques. The Cheques Act 1957 repealed the 1932 Act and s 4(2)(d) embraces the banker's draft today, which it defines as:

'any draft payable on demand drawn by a banker upon himself, whether payable at the head office or some other office of the bank.'

The reason for the slight change of language in the definition is not clear, except as bringing consistency by the use throughout of the word 'banker' instead of 'bank'.

13 [1923] 1 Ch 41 at 48. The case went to the Court of Appeal, [1923] 1 Ch 41 at 51, but there was no appeal on this point.

2   CHEQUES ACT 1957, s 4

Section 4 of the Cheques Act 1957[14] provides:

(1) Where a banker, in good faith and without negligence—
(a) receives payment for a customer of an instrument to which this section applies; or
(b) having credited a customer's account with the amount of such an instrument, receives payment thereof for himself;
    and the customer has no title, or a defective title, to the instrument, the banker does not incur any liability to the true owner of the instrument by reason only of having received payment thereof.
(2) This section applies to the following instruments, namely –
(a) cheques;
(b) any document issued by a customer of a banker which, though not a bill of exchange is intended to enable a person to obtain payment from that banker of the sum mentioned in the document;
(c) any document issued by a public officer which is intended to enable a person to obtain payment from the Paymaster General or the Queen's and Lord Treasurer's Remembrancer of the sum mentioned in the document but is not a bill of exchange;
(d) any draft payable on demand drawn by a banker on himself whether payable at the head office or some other office of his bank.
(3) A banker is not to be treated for the purposes of this section as having been negligent by reason only of his failure to concern himself with absence of, or irregularity in, indorsement of an instrument.'

(a) Introduction

Unless the banker can bring himself within the conditions formulated by this section, he is left with his common law liability for conversion or money had and received, in the event of the person from whom he takes the cheque for collection having no title or a defective title thereto. The onus is on the banker to disprove negligence:

'Section 82 is therefore not the imposition of a new burden or duty on the collecting bankers but is a concession affording him the means of avoiding a liability in conversion to which otherwise there would be no defence. As it is for the banker to show that he is entitled to this defence, the onus is on him to disprove negligence'.[15]

The Cheques Act 1957 was enacted to facilitate the elimination of indorsement of cheques. While, however, the opportunity was taken to bring the legislation as to cheques and analogous instruments within it and to introduce protection to bankers dealing with uncrossed and unindorsed or irregularly indorsed instruments, it would be reasonable to assume that no other change in the law was intended. Section 6 provides that the Act is to be construed as one with the Bills of Exchange Act 1882.

When a crossed cheque drawn by one customer is paid into the account of another, while the bank may be protected as *paying* banker as having paid to itself as a banker under s 80 or, in the case of forged indorsement of an order cheque, under s 60, as *collecting* banker this would not enable it to avoid its liability if it collected with negligence as in *Carpenters' Co v British*

14 5 Halsbury's Statutes (4th edn, 1989 Reissue) 387.
15 *Lloyds Bank Ltd v E B Savory & Co* [1933] AC 201, per Lord Wright.

Mutual Banking Co Ltd.[16] The bank is acting in two capacities and it cannot escape liability incurred in one capacity by setting up what might be a complete defence in the other.

It is stressed that today a collecting banker may collect for a customer, plead the protection of the statute and at the same time collect for himself; to put it another way, a banker may plead the protection of the statute even though he is holder in due course or a holder for value to the extent only of his lien: see per Milmo J in *Barclays Bank Ltd v Astley Industrial Trust Ltd.*[17] Prior to the passing of the Cheques Act 1957 the banker had either to have collected only for a customer or to rely on his own rights as a holder who, in some form or other, had given value, a somewhat anomalous situation from which the decisions of the courts only gradually rescued him.

(b) In good faith

The protected case is where:

'a banker in good faith and without negligence receives payment'.

The whole transaction from the taking of the cheque to the receipt and disposition of the money, must be in good faith and without negligence and even transactions with the customer prior to the collection.[18]

If it were only the actual receipt of payment which had to be in good faith and without negligence the section, from the true owner's point of view, would be of little value. The obligation and the protection must be correlative and co-extensive. If the words 'receives payment' are to be read as involving protection to the banker for all preliminary operations leading up to the receipt of the money, the condition precedent to that protection, viz, that the banker shall act in good faith without negligence, must cover the same ground. It is hard to visualise a condition of things in which a banker could take a crossed cheque negligently or in bad faith and yet receive the money for his customer in good faith and without negligence.

The Privy Council in *Taxation Comrs v English, Scottish and Australian Bank*[19], must not be read as seriously impugning this obvious proposition. Their Lordships, after pointing out that the words of the section are 'without negligence receives payment', say:[20]

'It is not a question of negligence in opening an account, though the circumstances connected with the opening of an account may shed light on the question of whether there was negligence in collecting a cheque'.

As will be seen hereafter, the opening of an account without inquiries has been treated as sufficient of itself to fix a bank with negligence under s 82. The contrary view expressed in *Ladbroke & Co v Todd*[1] was mentioned in the appellants' argument as being obiter but there is no mention of it in the judgment of the Privy Council; the question was whether or not the person

---

16 [1938] 1 KB 511.
17 [1970] 2 QB 527, [1970] 1 All ER 719. See also *Re Keever, A Bankrupt, ex p Trustee of the Property of the Bankrupt v Midland Bank* [1967] Ch 182, [1966] 3 All ER 631. See further The Collecting Banker: General, Ch 26, above.
18 In this respect see Diplock LJ in *Marfani & Co Ltd v Midland Bank Ltd* [1968] 2 All ER 573, [1968] 1 WLR 956, CA.
19 [1920] AC 683.
20 Ibid. at 688.
 1 [1914] WN 165, 19 Com Cas 256.

opening the account was a customer. If the dictum of the Privy Council were directed only to this one point, that the *punctum temporis* at which negligence becomes material is only that of the receipt of the money, one must respectfully differ.

(c) Without negligence

(i) Introduction

Section 4 of the Cheques Act 1957 is in very similar terms to s 82 of the Bills of Exchange Act 1882. Both sections require the banker to act 'without negligence', but neither statute defines it. The effect of s 6(1) of the Cheques Act, which enacts that 'This Act shall be construed as one with the Bills of Exchange Act 1882', is not necessarily to give the same interpretation to 'negligence' in s 4 as it had in s 82, but it is fair to assume that the same considerations which led the courts to their construction of 'negligence' within the repealed section would impel them to find similarly under s 4. On this assumption cases decided under s 82 are valid authorities for the purposes of s 4, subject to the important caveat that changes in banking practice may affect such questions as what facts ought to be known to the banker and what facts are sufficient to cause him reasonably to suspect that his customer is not the true owner.

The importation of negligence into this section is, in a sense, an anomaly; there can be no negligence without a duty.[2] There is no contractual relation between the collecting banker and the true owner which gives rise to a duty on the part of the former to the latter. The banker's only contractual obligation is to his own customer; and conduct beneficial to the customer at the expense of the true owner is no breach of that duty. The true exposition is that given by Denman J and the Court of Appeal in *Bissell & Co v Fox Bros & Co;*[3] the duty is a purely statutory one imposed on the banker in favour of the true owner and the negligence consists in the disregard of his interests, usually taking the form of ignoring (or perhaps not noticing) obvious indications that the customer for whom the banker is collecting may not be the true owner. The assumption of this duty and liability to a stranger must be regarded as the price paid by bankers for protection under statute. It is from the standpoint, then, of the true owner that questions of negligence under this section must be viewed.

(ii) The general standard of care

Broadly speaking, the banker must exercise the same care and forethought in the interest of the true owner, with regard to cheques paid in by the customer, as a reasonable business man would bring to bear on similar business of his own, a formula approved by Sankey LJ in *Lloyds Bank Ltd v Chartered Bank of India, Australia and China.*[4] In *A L Underwood Ltd v Bank of Liverpool*[5] Bankes LJ adopts the test suggested by Lord Dunedin in *Taxation Comrs v English, Scottish and Australian Bank,*[6] where he says that the bank's action must be in accordance with 'the ordinary practice of

---

2 *Scholfield v Earl of Londesborough* [1896] AC 514.
3 [1884] 51 LT 663; varied (1885) 53 LT 193.
4 [1929]1 KB 40 at 69, CA.
5 [1924] 1 KB 775, 29 Com Cas 182, CA.
6 [1920] AC 683 at 689.

bankers', and he went on '... a bank cannot be held to be liable merely because they have not subjected an account to microscopic examination'. In *Lloyds Bank Ltd v Chartered Bank of India, Australia and China,*[7] Sankey LJ approved the view taken by Bailhache J in *Ross v London County, Westminster and Parr's Bank Ltd,*[8] that he must attribute to the clerks and cashiers of the defendant bank the degree of intelligence and knowledge ordinarily required of persons in their position to fit them for the discharge of their duties, but that no microscopic examination of cheques paid in for collection was necessary. 'It is not expected', he said, 'that officials of banks should also be amateur detectives'.[9] In the same case, Scrutton LJ said, accepting the qualification expressed by Lord Dunedin in the *Taxation Comrs* case,[10] that:

> 'to require a thorough inquiry into the history of each cheque would render banking business impracticable'

and there are similar comments by Sellers and Harman LJJ in *Orbit Mining and Trading Co Ltd v Westminster Bank Ltd.*[11]

In *Lloyds Bank Ltd v EB Savory & Co* Lord Wright said:[12]

> 'The most obvious circumstances which should put the banker on his guard (apart from manifest irregularities in the indorsement and such like), are where a cheque is presented for collection which bears on its face a warning that the customer may have misappropriated it, as for instance where a customer known to be a servant or agent pays in for collection a cheque drawn by third parties in favour of his employer or principal. Such a case carries even a clearer warning if the cheque is indorsed per pro the employer or principal by the servant or agent ... at least where the new customer is employed in some position which involves his handling, and having the opportunity of stealing, his employer's cheques, the bankers fail in taking adequate precautions if they do not ask the name of his employers, and fail even in carrying out the rule which I have just quoted, because they fail to ascertain a most relevant fact as to the intending customer's circumstances'.

He points out that a precaution does not cease to be proper for purposes of s 82 merely because, though generally effective, it may in special circumstances be ineffectual. But not all the Law Lords went as far as Lord Wright. Lord Warrington[13] thought that:

> 'The standard by which the absence or otherwise of negligence is to be determined must in my opinion be ascertained by reference to the practice of reasonable men in carrying on the business of bankers and endeavouring to do so in such a manner as may be calculated to protect themselves and others against fraud.'

Lord Blanesburgh[14] in a dissenting judgment, gave the practice of bankers in making inquiries on opening an account a different significance. He thought that:

> '... inquiry as to the name of a customer's employer ... had no reference at all to the possible perpetration of frauds within the reach of a clerk as such. It was

---

7 [1929] 1 KB 40, CA.
8 [1919] 1 KB 678 at 685.
9 A view taken by Mackinnon LJ (sitting as an additional judge) in *Penmount Estates Ltd v National Provincial Bank Ltd* (1945) 173 LT 344.
10 [1920] AC 683.
11 [1963] 1 QB 794, [1962] 3 All ER 565, per Sellers LJ at 574 and Harman LJ at 579.
12 [1933] AC 201 at 229 and 231, HL.
13 [1933] AC 201 at 221.
14 Ibid at 218.

neither designed nor in its imperfect range was it calculated to be a check upon these... its only purpose, I am satisfied, was to test the proposing customer's respectability by reference to the status and position of the employer who had so far trusted him as to receive him into his service – information whose value for that purpose was in no way lessened by a mere change in that employment subsequently effected – information, therefore, which called for no later inquiries on the subject – its end, when it was given, being fully attained.'

The 'doctrine' underlying the *Savory* decision was described by Harman LJ in *Orbit Mining and Trading Co Ltd v Westminster Bank Ltd*[15] as a 'hard' one and he went on: 'It cannot at any rate be the duty of the bank continually to keep itself up to date as to the identity of a customer's employer'. Further:[16]

'It is never possible to lay down a rule as to what constitutes negligence and what avoids it. Each case depends on its own facts. Perhaps the most help is to be got from the decision of the Privy Council in *Taxation Comrs v English, Scottish and Australian Bank*[17] in which Lord Dunedin says: "... If, therefore, a standard is sought, it must be the standard to be derived from the ordinary practice of bankers not individuals".'

a view which is echoed by Diplock LJ in the *Marfani* case. The practice of bankers can hardly be proved other than by evidence of bankers themselves. If this may appear to be special pleading the safeguard must be that it would be rare for bankers to testify in support of acts done by a collecting banker, which he could not clearly approve in the circumstances of the case as applied to his own bank.

In *Marfani & Co Ltd v Midland Bank Ltd*[18] Diplock LJ distinguished the *Savory* decision in the following words:

'That case, as all other cases, depended on its own particular facts. The frauds had gone on for a very long time. There were many other matters calculated to arouse suspicion in the social conditions of the 1920s. It was decided upon expert evidence, not of what is now current banking practice, but of what it was 40 years ago. I find it no more than an illustration of the application of the general principle that a banker must exercise reasonable care in all the circumstances of the case.'

Diplock LJ further said:[19]

'The only respect in which this substituted statutory duty differs from a common-law cause of action in negligence is that, since it takes the form of a qualified immunity from a strict liability at common law, the onus of showing that he did take such reasonable care lies upon the defendant banker. Granted good faith in the banker (the other condition of the immunity) the usual matter with respect to which the banker must take reasonable care is to satisfy himself that his own customer's title to the cheque delivered to him for collection is not defective, i.e., that no other person is the true owner of it. Where the customer is in possession of the cheque at the time of delivery for collection, and appears upon the face of it to be the 'holder', i.e., the payee or indorsee or the bearer, the banker is, in my view, entitled to assume that the customer is the owner of the cheque unless there are facts which are known, or ought to be known, to the banker which would cause a reasonable banker to suspect that the customer is not the true owner. What facts ought to be known to the banker, i.e., what inquiries he should make,

15 [1963] 1 QB 794 at 824–825 [1962] 3 All ER 565.
16 [1963] 1 QB 794 at 822, [1962] 3 All ER 565 at 578.
17 [1920] AC 683 at 688.
18 [1968] 2 All ER 573 at 582B, [1968] 1 WLR 956 at 976E, CA.
19 [1968] 2 All ER 573 at 579, [1968] 1 WLR 956 at 972–973, CA.

and what facts are sufficient to cause him reasonably to suspect that the customer is not the true owner, must depend upon current banking practice, and change as that practice changes. Cases decided 30 years ago, when the use by the general public of banking facilities was much less widespread, may not be a reliable guide to what the duty of a careful banker, in relation to inquiries and as to facts which should give rise to suspicion, is today.

The duty of care owed by the banker to the true owner of the cheque does not arise until the cheque is delivered to him by his customer. It is then, and then only, that any duty to make inquiries can arise. Any antecedent inquiries that he has made are relevant only in so far as they have already brought to his knowledge facts which a careful banker ought to ascertain about his customers before accepting for collection the cheque which is the subject-matter of the action, and so have relieved him of any need to ascertain them again when the cheque which is the subject-matter of the action is delivered to him.

What the court has to do is to look at all the circumstances at the time of the acts complained of, and to ask itself: were those circumstances such as would cause a reasonable banker, possessed of such information about his customer as a reasonable banker would possess, to suspect that his customer was not the true owner of the cheque?'

One point taken by the plaintiff in *Marfani* was that a reference obtained by the bank was given after the bank had collected the cheque, when the conversion was in law complete. The judge at first instance had thought that this was answered by the bank's evidence that no payment would have been permitted until the reply to the inquiry had been received and found satisfactory. Diplock LJ thought this: 'much too technical an effect to give to a statute [the Cheques Act 1957] which was intended to apply to business transactions as they are carried on in real life'. And:

'At the relevant time, the banker was entitled to take into consideration the interests of his customer who, be it remembered, would in all probability turn out to be honest, as most customers are, and his own business interests and to weigh these against the risk of loss or damage to the true owner of the cheque in the unlikely event that he should turn out not to be the customer himself'.

The relevant time he held to be the time at which the banker pays out the proceeds of the cheque to his own customer (and he might have added 'or to his customer's order') and so deprives the true owner of his right to follow the money into the banker's hands.

Diplock LJ held that what the bank had done was in accordance with current banking practice; and with the words that 'this court should be hesitant before condemning as negligent a practice generally adopted by those engaged in banking business' he declined to accept that the court was entitled to examine that practice.

This by no means relieves bankers of their duty to true owners of cheques they collect, but it expresses a philosophy which in contrast to the trend shown by earlier decisions, and takes a realistic view of the limit of the responsibilities of a collecting banker.

It might be awkward for the banker to manifest suspicion of his own customer; but if he refrains from acting on suspicion, he might easily render himself liable to the true owner, as having neglected his duty to him; as Scrutton LJ said in *Underwood's* case,[20]

20 [1924] 1 KB 775.

'If banks for fear of offending their customers will not make inquiry into unusual circumstances, they must take with the benefit of not annoying those customers the risk of liability because they do not inquire'.

The burden is on the collecting banker to give:

'all facts and matters relied upon as establishing that your client bank acted without negligence and in particular... whether your client bank made any and if so what enquiries of their customer or any other persons as to the title to the cheques and each of them and with what result in each case';

thus Donaldson J in Chambers.[1]

(iii) General factors

A. FAILURE TO COMPLY WITH BANK'S INTERNAL RULES

Both in *Lloyds Bank Ltd v E B Savory & Co*[2] and in *Motor Traders Guarantee Corpn Ltd v Midland Bank Ltd,*[3] it was suggested on behalf of the plaintiffs that failure to comply with the regulations contained in the books of instruction was evidence of negligence. In the latter case, however, Goddard J put the matter in its right perspective. He said:[4]

'I again say that I am far from saying that the plaintiffs, or any other person whose property has been converted, are entitled to rely upon a literal performance, or are entitled to require a literal performance, by the bank of these regulations. The bank does not owe a duty to them to carry out this rule, that rule, or the other rule. Indeed, I doubt whether they owe their own customers the duty of carrying out all the rules which they may lay down as counsels of perfection. The question in every case is not whether the bank require a particular standard of conduct, but whether the particular acts which are done are enough to discharge the onus which is upon the bank either in respect of their own customer or in respect of some other customer.'

In *Orbit Mining and Trading Co Ltd v Westminster Bank Ltd*[5] it was held at first instance that the bank had fallen short of its own requirements as revealed in its written instructions, but the views of Goddard J as given in the *Motor Traders* case were approved by Sellers LJ:

'Such instructions are not of statutory effect but they are clearly a useful guide, and it was submitted to us on behalf of the bank that they had been built up on the courts' decisions. I hope they are based on a wider survey of the requirements of care and do not await a court's ruling'.

MacKenna J had remarked that it was implicit in the instructions that there should always be a scrutiny of the drawer's name, but Sellers LJ's comment was that the bank could not with reasonable care have known that the cheque was signed on behalf of *Orbit* by the fraudulent director for whose account the cheque was collected:

'I do not think it can be held that that in itself prevents the bank from being held to have acted without negligence'.

Harman LJ was of opinion that the bank's rules were:

1 *Griggs Bartlett Ltd v Coutts & Co* (1968) unreported.
2 [1932] 2 KB 122; and see [1933] AC 201 at 205, per Lord Buckmaster.
3 [1937] 4 All ER 90.
4 [1937] 4 All ER 90 at 96.
5 [1963] 1 QB 794, [1962] 3 All ER 565, CA.

'counsels of perfection but the fact that they are not always entirely complied with does not convict the bank of negligence, though, no doubt, where the rules are not kept the matter needs close attention'.

The latest pronouncement on the point is that of Donaldson J in *Lumsden & Co v London Trustee Savings Bank*[6] to the effect that the banks' instructions were not conclusive of the standard to be applied but they did offer some evidence of what could reasonably be expected.

B. SUDDEN FLUCTUATIONS IN BALANCES, AMOUNTS PAID IN OR AMOUNTS WITHDRAWN

The question has been raised whether if a man with an habitually small account or one on which the credit balance has steadily dwindled, or which is slightly overdrawn, suddenly pays in for collection a cheque for a large amount, should that put the banker on inquiry? Little or no guidance can be derived from the cases which have dealt with the point. In *Crumplin v London Joint Stock Bank Ltd*[7] Pickford J attached some weight to it. In *Taxation Comrs v English, Scottish and Australian Bank*,[8] an account was opened with £20, and the next day a cheque for £786 18s 3d payable to bearer was paid in. The Privy Council saw nothing in this to excite suspicion or invite inquiry. In *Morison v London County and Westminster Bank Ltd*,[9] Lord Reading CJ came to the conclusion that the yearly increase in payments would not of itself arouse doubt or suspicion, being consistent with increased salary or emoluments.

The opinion among bankers is that sudden fluctuations are not significant. This view acquires some sanction from *Thomson v Clydesdale Bank Ltd*.[10] But the opening of an account with a nominal sum, speedily followed by the payment in of a large one, is, perhaps, not so readily accounted for.

In *Slingsby v District Bank Ltd*[11] Scrutton LJ could not agree with the judge at first instance that the bank:

'were not negligent in making no inquiries as to why a cheque for a large amount [£5,000] apparently destined for Prust & Co [the payee] through the medium of Cumberbirch & Potts was paid into the private account not of that firm, but of a company of which Cumberbirch was chairman.'

C. FAILURE TO TAKE UP REFERENCES OR MAKE INQUIRIES ON OPENING OF ACCOUNT

In *Turner v London and Provincial Bank Ltd*[12] evidence was admitted, as proof of negligence, that the customer had given a reference on opening the account and that this was not followed up. In *Ladbroke & Co v Todd*[13] Bailhache J held the bank negligent because they did not make inquiries about a proposing customer, an ordinary precaution which other banks took.

6 [1971] 1 Lloyd's Rep 114.
7 (1913) 109 LT 856, 19 Com Cas 69.
8 [1920] AC 683.
9 [1914] 3 KB 356.
10 [1893] AC 282.
11 [1932] 1 KB 544 at 556.
12 [1903] 2 LDAB 33
13 (1914) 111 LT 43, 19 Com Cas 256.

Harding v London Joint Stock Bank Ltd[14] was a similar case, except that the bank on making inquiry as to why the cheque with which the account was opened was not drawn in favour of the prospective customer, were satisfied with confirmation from the drawers, actually written by the fraudulent person himself. The jury found the bank negligent.

The relevance of failure to make inquiries on the opening of an account by a person acting in a fiduciary capacity is further considered in the context of cheques drawn by fiduciaries (see below).

D. REQUEST FOR SPECIAL COLLECTION

In *Turner v London and Provincial Bank Ltd*[15] the fraudulent customer had asked for the cheques to be specially collected. Evidence was given that it is common for banks to make special collections of cheques for customers, though it is a matter for the banker's discretion. Special collection is desired for the purpose of learning quickly whether or not the cheque will be paid and a special presentation can hardly be said to render a bank liable. This case was mentioned in the judgment in *Marfani & Co Ltd v Midland Bank Ltd*[16] where the Midland Bank had made a special collection without being asked by their customer. The judge decided that this did not indicate that the bank's suspicions were aroused which would require further inquiry. He found that the bank decided upon the special collection for the reasons (a) that the cheque was for a large sum, so that it was in their interest to collect quickly and (b) that the customer, who was about to buy a restaurant, might require the proceeds quickly. In the Court of Appeal Diplock LJ said that the 'significance of the special clearance depends upon the Judge's assessment of the credibility of the bank officials who gave evidence'; and he saw no reason to differ from him.

E. FAILURE TO VERIFY INDORSEMENT

Before the passing of the Cheques Act 1957, failure to see that any indorsement was in order, at least ostensibly, had been recognised as negligence on the part of the collecting banker[17].

Today, as the result of the Cheques Act 1957, the position is different in that both paying and collecting bankers are, in certain conditions, free from liability if they pay or collect cheques on which there is no, or an irregular indorsement.[18] Nevertheless, the banks have adopted a practice whereby cheques presented over the counter for payment still have to be 'indorsed' by the payee and also cheques paid in for collection for an account other than that of the payee. The signature in the former case must be regarded as a receipt; it cannot be an indorsement within the meaning of the Act.

As regards collection, s 4(3) is somewhat strangely worded; it says that a banker is not to be treated as having been negligent by reason only of his 'failure to concern' himself with absence of or irregularity in indorsement.

---

14 (1914) 3 LDAB 81.
15 (1903) 2 LDAB 33.
16 [1968] 2 All ER 573, [1968] 1 Lloyd's Rep 411.
17 See, eg *Bissell & Co v Fox Bros & Co* (1884) 51 LT 663, varied (1885) 53 LT 193; *Bavins Junior and Sims v London and South Western Bank Ltd* [1900] 1 QB 270; *Turner v London and Provincial Bank Ltd* (1903) 2 Legal Decisions Affecting Bankers 33.
18 See in this connection Lord Dilhorne in *Westminster Bank Ltd v Zang* [1966] AC 182 at 218.

This can apply only where the banker does not insist on an indorsement. If he chooses to ask for it in spite of the dispensation offered by the statute, the indorsement he accepts must be regular; in waiving the dispensation he must be regarded as reverting to the position he would have been in but for it. Where the banker asks for an indorsement, it must surely be negligence, as it would have been under s 82, to collect a cheque bearing an irregular indorsement. On the other hand, the fact that a cheque, on which he would not under post-1957 practice require the payee's indorsement, is irregularly indorsed when it is handed to him for collection would not deprive him of the protection of s 4, because 'failure to concern' himself with it would not be negligence. If he asks for indorsement the banker can hardly say that he has not concerned himself with it.

If the instrument is one which calls for a receipt as a condition of payment the collecting banker should ask for the receipt to be completed, in which case it would seem that he must ensure that the signature to the receipt is regular.

F. ENQUIRY AS TO FATE OF A CHEQUE

Inquiry as to the fate of a cheque is of no help to anyone but the collecting bank; as pointed out in *Bissell & Co v Fox Bros & Co*[19] and *Ogden v Benas*[20] the inquiry is normally made by the collecting banker in his own interest and for his own benefit.

G. EXIGENCIES OF BUSINESS

A banker is not normally permitted to plead the exigencies of business as a defence to a charge of negligence. Negligence as meant by s 4 of the Cheques Act 1957 is negligence of the bank itself, though caused, as it must be, by a member of the staff. A bank impliedly represents its staff as competent for the particular work they are required to do and the bank is liable if a member of the staff fails to measure up to his responsibility; in such circumstances the bank may be negligent. In *Ross v London County Westminster and Parr's Bank Ltd*[1] Bailhache J recognised that the same standard of experience and care is not to be expected from a cashier as from a bank manager, but said:

'I must, however, attribute to the cashiers and clerks of the department the degree of intelligence and knowledge ordinarily required of persons in their positions to fit them for the discharge of their duties,'

a view adopted by Sankey LJ.

One school, of which perhaps Lord Bramwell was the protagonist, refused to give any countenance to this plea or make any allowance on this ground. In *Crumplin v London Joint Stock Bank Ltd*,[2] Pickford J said:

'It is no defence for a bank to say that they were so busy and had such a small staff that they could not make inquiries when necessary; they must take the consequences.'

Yet in a case which had nothing to do with collection of a cheque or with negligence, McNair J thought that a delay of six weeks, deriving from pressure

19 (1885) 53 LT 193, CA.
20 (1874) LR 9 CP 513 at 516.
 1 [1919] 1 KB 678.
 2 (1913) 109 LT 856, 19 Com Cas 69.

of work in the documentary credit department of a bank, in accepting or repudiating documents tendered under a documentary credit would not alone amount to a ratification of wrongful payment by the bank tendering the documents.[3]

(iv) Cheques paid by fiduciaries into private account

A. THE NEED FOR CAUTION

The practice of collecting banks not to collect for private account a cheque which on the face of it by indorsement bears evidence of being the property of or intended for the benefit of a company, firm or other person and which is tendered for collection by a person holding or purporting to hold a fiduciary or other position in or in relation to that company, firm or person, whether indorsed by him or not, and whether crossed or not, should be rigorously adhered to. The authorities which emphasise the importance of this pre-caution and the danger of neglecting it are numerous.[4]

The precaution is all the more important where a cheque is not only paid in by a fiduciary for his private account, but also drawn by him. An example is *Midland Bank Ltd v Reckitt*,[5] where the bank collected for Lord Terrington a cheque drawn by him as attorney for Sir Harold Reckitt and paid in in reduction of his (Lord Terrington's) overdraft; a letter addressed by Sir Harold to his bankers authorised the attorney to draw 'without restriction'. In the House of Lords, Lord Atkin held that the bank had notice from the form of cheque that the money was not Lord Terrington's.

B. CHEQUES PAYABLE TO A COMPANY

Banks generally forbid the acceptance for the credit of private accounts of cheques drawn in favour of limited companies, even where there is no con-nection between the payee and the persons for whom they are asked to collect. The authorities demonstrate the wisdom of this practice.[6]

In *Motor Traders Guarantee Corpn Ltd v Midland Bank Ltd*[7] Goddard J held that the bank had been negligent in collecting for a motor trader a

---

3 *Bank Melli Iran v Barclays Bank (Dominion, Colonial and Overseas)* [1951] 2 Lloyd's Rep 367.
4 *Hannan's Lake View Central Ltd v Armstrong & Co* (1900) 16 TLR 236, 5 Com Cas 188; *Morison v London County and Westminster Bank Ltd* [1914] 3 KB 356; *Souchette Ltd v London County, Westminster and Parr's Bank Ltd* (1920) 36 TLR 195; *Ross v London County, Westminster and Parr's Bank Ltd* [1919] 1 KB 678; *A L Underwood Ltd v Bank of Liverpool* [1924] 1 KB 775; *Lloyds Bank Ltd v Chartered Bank of India, Australia and China* [1929] 1 KB 40; *Slingsby v Westminster Bank Ltd* [1931] 2 KB 583; and see Scrutton LJ in *Slingsby v District Bank Ltd* [1932] 1 KB 544 at 556, 558; *Midland Bank Ltd v Reckitt* [1933] AC 1; *Lloyds Bank Ltd v E B Savory & Co* [1933] AC 201; *Motor Traders Guarantee Corpn Ltd v Midland Bank Ltd* [1937] 4 All ER 90; *Baker v Barclays Bank Ltd* [1955] 2 All ER 571, [1955] 1 WLR 822; *Nu-Stilo Footwear Ltd v Lloyds Bank Ltd* (1956) 7 LDAB 121; *Orbit Mining and Trading Co Ltd v Westminster Bank Ltd* [1963] 1 QB 794, [1962] 3 All ER 565, CA.
5 [1933] AC 1.
6 In *London and Montrose Shipbuilding and Repairing Co Ltd v Barclays Bank Ltd* (1926) 31 Com Cas 67 at 76, Mackinnon J refused to accept that wherever the named payee on a cheque was a limited company and the cheque had been indorsed to an indorsee by that company, the bank collecting on behalf of the indorsee was put on inquiry. On appeal (1926) 31 Com Cas 182, Mackinnon J was reversed in his finding that the bank had not been negligent.
7 [1937] 4 All ER 90.

cheque payable to a firm of motor dealers to which cheque the trader had no title. The decision appears to be based on the fact that the trader's account with the defendant bank had been unsatisfactorily conducted, several cheques having been dishonoured, principally for lack of funds, and that one trader was 'bringing in another trader's cheque'. The learned judge was of the view that this put the bank on inquiry and that the inquiry in fact made did not discharge the onus placed on the bank by s 82. There was no fiduciary relationship between the trader and either the plaintiffs (the drawers of the cheque) or the payees. The reason why the majority of people have their cheques dishonoured is that they have not at the time of presentment the wherewithal to meet them, not that they are dishonest. Bankers know this quite well and if they find that a customer is drawing cheques without having the funds in hand, simply in order to gain time, they very soon close his account. He is a nuisance, but no more until proved so to be.

In 1941 Lord Atkin in *United Australia Ltd v Barclays Bank Ltd,*[8] found it possible to say,

'In these days every bank clerk sees the red light when a company's cheque is endorsed by a company's official into an account which is not the company's',

– not into the official's account, be it noted, but any account other than the company's.

The circumstances in which a collecting bank has been held negligent have been so varied that it is difficult to draw a line between safety and liability. The unsatisfactory feature of the *Marquess of Bute* case[9] was that the plaintiff had not notified the Department of Agriculture for Scotland of his withdrawal of authority from a former agent, McGaw, in whose favour warrants were made out by the Department and to whom they were sent. But adjacent to McGaw's name were the words 'for Marquess of Bute' and the bank was held to have been negligent in collecting for McGaw. The inference from this decision is that the bank collecting the warrants was under a duty to read into the plain words of the warrant something which contradicted what was actually said. The way in which it was drawn indicated McGaw's right to receive or deal with the warrant. He could simply have handed it to the Marquess and, if he had, would the latter's bankers have collected it without McGaw's indorsement? In *Baker v Barclays Bank Ltd*[10] there was no question of fiduciary relationship, but Devlin J thought that if the cashier who took the cheques in had been less unsuspecting he might have thought that the customer was defrauding the true owner:

'of course, cheques are endorsed over to third parties, but usually for small amounts and only occasionally. When the bank manager sees it happening for large sums and quite regularly, I think he is put on enquiry.'

In *Nu-Stilo Footwear Ltd v Lloyds Bank Ltd,*[11] the plaintiffs manufactured ladies' footwear at Bridgend, South Wales. They suffered loss by frauds of their servant, Gerald Trevelyan Montague, at the time their secretary and works accountant. They sought to recover that loss from the defendant bank on the ground of the conversion of nine cheques for which the defendants

8 [1941] AC 1 at 23–34; and see per Scrutton LJ in *Slingsby v District Bank Ltd* [1932] 1 KB 544 at 556.
9 [1955] 1 QB 202, [1954] 3 All ER 365.
10 [1955] 2 All ER 571, [1955] 1 WLR 822.
11 (1956) 7 LDAB 121.

received payment for a customer who was in fact Montague but who had opened and operated an account at a different branch of the defendant bank, in the false name of Edward Bauer. When he opened the account he gave himself under his real name as a reference, stating that he was a freelance agent. The bank telephoned the referee and got a satisfactory reply, which included the statement that Bauer had recently come down from Oxford and intended setting up business on his own. The officer who opened the account asked the name of the referee's banker and wrote and obtained a satisfactory report on him. The cheques which were converted were drawn on the plaintiffs' account by two officers, one of whom was Montague. The first for £172 was payable to Bauer and no question arose on this. Sellers J drew attention in his judgment to what he regarded as two important facts, that the customer was commencing business on his own account; and 'that he had no more solid a business activity than that covered by the description "a freelance agent."' The bank was held liable on all but the first cheque.

The implication in this decision is that the bank must at all times be cognisant, through all its officers, present and future, who may have dealings by way of collection of cheques for any customer, of the information derived at the time the account was opened, that they are to be vested with this knowledge for all time, whether they were aware of it at the time or not—in case the customer should prove fraudulent. In the light of the trend of earlier decisions this may perhaps be regarded as appropriate; by any other standard it is not, but the judgments of Harman LJ in the *Orbit Mining* case[12] and of Diplock LJ in *Marfani & Co v Midland Bank Ltd*[13] indicate that the above view is too demanding.

In *Orbit Mining and Trading Co Ltd v Westminster Bank Ltd,*[15] one of the two signatures on behalf of the drawer-plaintiff was illegible, no indorsement was in the circumstances required, and it was into this signatory's account that the proceeds of the cheque went. The collecting bank had no information that their customer was connected with the plaintiff company. Accordingly, the Court of Appeal reversed a finding of negligence. But it seems likely that, if the link between the drawer-company and the fraudulent signatory for whom the cheque was collected had been established as within the knowledge of the bank, the decision might have been different.

A distinction was drawn between order and bearer cheques in *Souchette Ltd v London County Westminster and Parr's Bank Ltd.*[16] Greer J was satisfied that the bank were not negligent in this respect because they were entitled to suppose that the directors who drew these cheques drew them to 'bearer' for convenience in order that they might be dealt with by the bearer for the benefit of the company. It is doubtful if a similar result would be reached today.

C. CHEQUES PAYABLE TO A PARTNERSHIP

On the same principle, it is unsafe without inquiry to take a cheque made payable to a partnership for the private account of one of the partners.[17]

12 [1963] 1 QB 794.
13 [1968] 1 Lloyd's Rep 411 at 412.
15 [1963] 1 QB 794, [1962] 3 All ER 565 CA.
16 (1920) 36 TLR 195.
17 Cf *Re Riches and Marshall's Trust Deed, ex p Darlington District Joint Stock Banking Co* (1865) 4 De GJ & Sm 581; *Bevan v National Bank Ltd* (1906) 23 TLR 65.

Backhouse v Charlton,[18] which might be cited as an authority to the contrary, was not strictly a case of collecting; it was a transfer from partnership to private account by cheque drawn by one of the partners, which cheque the banker was under obligation to honour.[19]

In *Baker v Barclays Bank Ltd*[20] the plaintiff was in partnership with one Bainbridge, the plaintiff working from the Hinckley premises and Bainbridge from the Nuneaton under the name of Modern Confections. Bainbridge misappropriated cheques drawn in favour of Modern Confections, paying them not in to the partnership account at the Hinckley branch of the Midland Bank but to one Jones, a third party, who paid them into an account of his with the defendant bank. Devlin J found for the plaintiff on the grounds that both Bainbridge and Barclays had converted the cheques; that Barclays could not claim statutory protection because they were negligent in not making adequate inquiries; that the bank were not holders in due course since Bainbridge had been guilty of fraud and the bank had not discharged the burden of showing that they had subsequently given value for the cheques and that thinking that the cheques belonged to Bainbridge the bank did not give value by crediting to Jones' overdrawn account.

In *Smith and Baldwin v Barclays Bank Ltd,*[1] the bank manager collecting for a private individual cheques payable to the Argus Press (under which name the plaintiffs were trading) was held by Stable J to be rightly satisfied with production of the certificate of registration under the Registration of Business Names Act 1916, which his customer had obtained over twelve months earlier.

D. CHEQUES PAYABLE TO OFFICIALS

It would clearly be negligence to collect for a man's private account cheques made payable to him in his official capacity, such as 'Collector of Rates', 'Collector of Inland Revenue', or the like, unless the banker was satisfied that the customer had the authority of his superiors to deal with them; similarly where as in *Ross v London County, Westminster and Parr's Bank Ltd,*[2] it was obvious that the payee held the cheque in an official capacity and the cheque, although indorsed by him, is paid into a private account.[3]

E. FAILURE TO MAKE INQUIRIES OF PRINCIPAL OR EMPLOYER

Lloyds Bank Ltd v E B Savory & Co[4] brought to light a breach of duty which was hitherto unsuspected. The negligence imputed to the bank was that of failing, on the opening of the account, to make inquiries as to the customer's employers and, in the case of a woman, what her husband was and as to his circumstances. The difficulty of complying with the injunction laid down by Lord Wright in the House of Lords is obvious. Lord Wright speaks of the new customer being employed in a position in which he has the opportunity

---

18 (1878) 8 Ch D 444.
19 But see *Carpenters' Co v British Mutual Banking Co Ltd* [1938] 1 KB 511.
20 [1955] 2 All ER 571, [1955] 1 WLR 822; but see Diplock LJ in *Marfani & Co Ltd v Midland Bank Ltd* [1968] 2 All ER 573 at 582D, [1968] 1 WLR 956 at 976H.
 1 (1944) 5 LDAB 370.
 2 [1919] 1 KB 678.
 3 Ibid.
 4 [1933] AC 201.

of stealing his employer's cheques. It would seem to be the duty of a banker to ensure, firstly, that his opening inquiries disclose the nature of the employment and, secondly, that the information he receives is verified from time to time, an unreasonable burden. Lord Wright turns these points aside rather lightly; as to the chance of the customer's changing his employment he said:[5]

'It is useless to consider what might be the position if something had happened which did not happen'.

As to the female of the account holders to whose account some of the moneys went, Lord Blanesburgh, in a dissenting judgment, said:[5a]

'In these days of emancipation when female clerks, married as well as single, abound, a decision to the contrary is in danger of being invoked as authority for the proposition that when a man known to be married applies to a bank to open an account, the bank is negligent if it refrains from making similar inquiry with reference to his wife – a proposition which still strikes me as extravagant.'

Lord Russell[5b] of Killowen also dissented. In the course of his judgment he said:

'It seems, however, a very long step to take to say that because if banks know that a customer is employed by a firm whose cheque in favour of a third party he is paying in to his own credit, they should make inquiries before receiving payment of it, therefore banks are bound at the outset to ascertain the names of their customer's employers and are guilty of negligence if they do not ... I know of no case, and none was cited to us, in which it has been held that a bank which did not in fact know was liable upon the footing of negligence in not making the initial inquiry.'

With respect, the dissentient view is much to be preferred, for it is reasonable in its effect on the banker and maintains a reasonably balanced responsibility between him and the true owner of any instrument he is called upon to collect. The alternative view takes little account of the fact that banking is a business in which comfortable relations between banker and customer are essential.

F. PROCURATION INDORSEMENTS

Section 25 of the Bills of Exchange Act[6] enacts that

'A signature by procuration operates as notice that the agent has but a limited authority to sign ...'

'Signature by procuration' is not defined. Any signature which purports to be put on by delegated authority should for this purpose be regarded as a signature by procuration; the fine distinctions which have been drawn between 'per pro.' and 'for' or 'pro.' appear irrelevant in this connection.

How far a collecting banker is affected by notice of a signature by delegated authority is not clear, but it is likely that his responsibility requires him to take such a signature into account only where the cheque otherwise puts him on inquiry. It can hardly be said that the collection of a cheque drawn by a

5 Ibid at 233.
5a Ibid at 219.
5b Ibid at 225.
6 5 Halsbury's Statutes (4th edn, 1989 Reissue) 334.

delegated signature is, by itself, sufficient to put the collecting banker upon inquiry, and enough to deprive him of protection. On the other hand, such a signature either as drawer or indorser may take on a special significance where the collecting banker takes as holder for value.[6a]

The signature in *Midland Bank Ltd v Reckitt* was that of an attorney drawing on behalf of his principal. Referring to the judgment of Lord Reading CJ in *Morisons's* case,[7] Lord Atkin said:

'It seems to be suggested ... that the operation of this section was limited to the time before the instrument was honoured, but that after a bill so signed in excess of authority has been honoured s 25 did not confer a right to recover the proceeds. If the words used meant to mark off a definite period within which alone the section affects legal rights, I see no grounds for such a distinction. The effect of the statute is to give notice of limited authority on the face of the document and this operates as and when the document is negotiated or delivered. The legal consequence of such notice may be to prevent the holder who obtains payment from supporting his right to have received payment. The case of *Reckitt v Barnett, Pembroke and Slater Ltd*,[8] is a good instance. The rights in respect of a bill after payment are no doubt matters of special consideration; but whether before or after payment, the fact that the bill contains on the face of it notice of limited authority to place on it the particular signature continues to be a fact affecting pro tanto the rights of the parties both before and after payment. What effect, if any, such notice has on an intermediate holder for value it is unnecessary to discuss.'

(v) Cheques crossed 'not negotiable'

The nature and effect of the 'not negotiable' crossing have been considered in ch 21, above. It is submitted that the crossing has no bearing on the collecting banker as regards s 4 of the Cheques Act 1957.

There are however, suggestions in certain authorities decided under s 82 that the 'not negotiable' crossing may be relevant to the question of negligence. In *Great Western Rly Co Ltd v London and County Banking Co Ltd*[9] Lord Brampton said:

'that the respondents in good faith received payment of the cheque is beyond question. I am not, however, quite so sure that it was altogether without negligence, for I must assume the manager at Wantage knew the meaning and legal effect of the crossing with the words 'not negotiable'. This point, however, does not appear to have been raised, and certainly there was no finding upon it at the trial. I will reject it therefore for present purposes.'

The suggestion appears to be that to take a cheque marked 'not negotiable' from anyone but the payee is enough to put the banker on inquiry. Unfortunately, this view was, though somewhat hesitatingly, resuscitated by Lord Reading in *Morison v London County and Westminster Bank Ltd* where he said:[10]

'The addition of the words, "not negotiable", and in some cases "not negotiable, account payee", to some of the crossed cheques ... has, in my opinion, no bearing upon the matters to be decided in this case. The protection of s 82 is afforded to

6a *Midland Bank Ltd v Reckitt* [1933] AC 1 at 18 per Lord Atkin.
7 [1914] 3 KB 356. See also *Crumplin v London Joint Stock Bank Ltd* (1913) 109 LT 856, 19 Com Cas 69.
8 [1929] AC 176.
9 [1901] AC 414 at 422.
10 [1914] 3 KB 356 at 373; the dictum as to 'account payee' is clearly wrong.

crossed cheques marked "not negotiable" as well as to cheques not so marked. It is certainly not conclusive evidence of negligence against a banker who collects crossed cheques so marked. Even if I assume that the taking of a crossed cheque bearing these words would be some evidence of negligence it could not affect my decision upon the later cheques, as the other considerations to which I have referred would outweigh any value I could attribute to such evidence.'

In *Turner v London and Provincial Bank Ltd*,[11] evidence was given to show that at some banks special care is taken in dealing with cheques marked 'not negotiable'.

The view that the crossing has no bearing on the collecting banker is based upon the following considerations:

(1) The provisions of ss 81 and 82 were formerly combined in one section, s 12 of the Crossed Cheques Act 1876, the substance being as in s 81, with s 82 appearing as a proviso thereto. The whole controversy in *Matthiessen v London and County Bank*[12] was whether the proviso applied to cheques other than those crossed 'not negotiable'. The court held that it did, the proviso, though in that form, operating as a substantive enactment. It would be extraordinary if the Bills of Exchange Act, in emphasising this decision by reproducing the proviso as an independent section, had excluded from its operation the very class of crossing to which alone it had been contended it applied.[13]

(2) The whole scheme of s 76 makes the words 'not negotiable' part of the 'addition' which 'constitutes a crossing', which renders the cheque a crossed cheque. The words used are 'with or without the words 'not negotiable' '. When, therefore, s 82 used the phrase 'without negligence' in reference to a crossed cheque, it meant negligence independent of anything inherent in or related to the instrument.

(3) Again, where there is prior absence or defect of title the effect of the 'not negotiable' crossing is to render the customer's title null or defective, the precise contingency against which the banker used to be protected by s 82.

It is submitted that the 'not negotiable' crossing has nothing to do with the collecting banker unless he takes the instrument for value, in which case he gets no better title than had the customer who paid it in. Stable J in *Smith and Baldwin v Barclays Bank Ltd*[14] held that the protection of s 82 was available where a cheque crossed 'not negotiable' was marked 'please pay cash', the addition being signed by the drawers, on the ground that the instrument was no less a crossed cheque as a result of the alteration.

(vi) Cheques marked 'Account payee'

The effect of the words 'Account payee' have been considered in ch 21 above.

Conclusive evidence of negligence in the collecting banker is, without inquiry, to take a cheque marked with the words 'account payee', or 'account so and so', for an account other than that indicated. This has even been held to apply where the cheque was payable to a specified payee or bearer. The

11 (1903) 2 LDAB 33.
12 (1879) 5 CPD 7.
13 Cf per Pickford J in *Crumplin v London Joint Stock Bank Ltd* (1913) 109 LT 856, 19 Com Cas 69.
14 (1944) 5 LDAB 370 at 375.

only exception hitherto recognised is where the customer was a foreign bank, and the marking, 'account payee' or even, as in the *Importers Co* case,[15] 'account payee only', referred to the foreign banker's customer, as to whom it was obviously impossible for the English bank to know or find out anything. It is submitted, further, that it is also negligent to inquire and fail to obtain a satisfactory answer as, for example, getting an answer from someone whose interest would be suspect. It is not possible to draw the line, the point depending upon the particular circumstances.

The practice has been recognised so long that it would be hopeless for any collecting banker to allege that the expression conveyed no meaning or to justify his ignoring it. The cheque in *Bellamy v Marjoribanks*[16] had words of this nature upon it, and significance was attached to the fact; their addition is common, and the present practice is not to take in a cheque so marked for any account other than that indicated.

In the *Importers Co* case,[17] Atkin LJ, having approved the statement of Bigham J in the *Akrokerri* case that the addition of 'account payee' is a mere direction to the receiving bank as to how the money is to be dealt with after receipt, said:

'I agree that there is a duty upon the bank which takes a cheque in those circumstances to see that in fact, they are collecting money for the account of the payee and that the proceeds when received will go to the payee'.

In *Bevan v National Bank Ltd*[18] Channell J held that it would be negligence to take a cheque marked 'account payee' for an account other than that of the payee. In *Morison v London County and Westminster Bank Ltd*,[19] the point was not material, since the cheques so marked went into the designated account. Lord Reading CJ said:[20]

'The words "account payee" ... are only to be found on the crossed cheques made payable to Abbott or order, or Abbott or bearer, defendants or bearer, and defendants or order. The words "account payee" are a direction to the bankers collecting payment that the proceeds when collected are to be applied to the credit of the account of the payee designated on the face of the cheque.'

And in *Ross v London County, Westminster and Parr's Bank*,[1] Bailhache J said that his observations in regard to negligence in collecting 'apply to this cheque with even greater force than to the others'.

In *House Property Co of London Ltd v London County and Westminster Bank*,[2] Rowlatt J treated it as negligence to collect a cheque payable to a named payee or bearer marked 'a/c payee' for an account other than that of the named payee.

If an order cheque can be so treated, there is no logical reason why a bearer cheque should not be, each being by nature negotiable, though by different means.

15 *Importers Co v Westminster Bank Ltd* [1927] 2 KB 297.
16 (1852) 7 Exch 389.
17 [1927] 2 KB 297 at 309.
18 (1906) 23 TLR 65.
19 [1914] 3 KB 356.
20 [1914] 3 KB 356 at 374.
 1 [1919] 1 KB 678 at 687.
 2 (1915) 84 LJKB 1846.

(d) 'Receives payment'

(i) Additional words in the 1957 Act

Section 4 of the Cheques Act 1957 relieves the collecting banker of liability to the true owner of an instrument to which the section applies, where in good faith and without negligence he:

'(a) receives payment for a customer of an instrument to which this section applies; or
(b) having credited a customer's account with the amount of such an instrument, he receives payment thereof for himself.'

There is nothing in s 4 – any more than there was in s 82 – to indicate what is the meaning of 'receives payment for a customer', but whereas the 1906 Act made it clear that a banker did not lose the protection of the section by the mere fact of crediting his customer's account before receiving payment of a cheque, the point may now be in doubt, for s 4(1)(b) ties the protection to cases in which the banker, 'having credited a customer's account . . . receives payment for himself', which is also without explanation. The sub-clause makes sense only if it follows that having credited his customer's account and having received payment in good faith and without negligence, he 'does not incur any liability to the true owner by reason only of having received payment . . .', in which cases it is immaterial that he received payment for himself.

(ii) Dealings prior to receipt

If the receipt of the money is protected by the section, the protection covers all prior dealings with the cheque. The section deals only with the receipt of the money. As Lord Macnaghten says in the *Gordon* case:[3]

'The only question is, did the banks receive payment of these cheques for their customer? If they did, it is obvious that they are relieved from any liability which perhaps, might otherwise attach to some preliminary action on their part, taken in view and anticipation of receiving payment. The section would be nugatory, it would be worse than nugatory, it would be a mere trap, if the immunity conferred in respect of receipt of payment, and in terms confined to such receipt, did not extend to cover every step taken in the ordinary course of business and intended to lead up to that result.'

The same view was fully recognised in *Morison v London County and Westminster Bank*.[4]

(iii) Receiving payment for a customer whose account is overdrawn

In *Clark v London and County Banking Co*[5] the Divisional Court held that a bank received payment for its customer notwithstanding that the customer's account was overdrawn at the time. A banker is under obligation to the customer to receive for collection and present the cheque for payment; if in so doing a lien arises the banker may plead statutory protection and the status of a holder for value at one and the same time.

3 *Capital and Counties Bank Ltd v Gordon* [1903] AC 240 at 244.
4 [1914] 3 KB 356.
5 [1897] 1 QB 552; and see per Romer LJ in *Great Western Rly Co v London and County Banking Co Ltd* [1900] 2 QB 464 at 476.

(iv) '... having credited a customer's account'

The words of the Act, 'credits his customer's account', might be confined to crediting in the bank's own books; but it is submitted that this by itself is not enough. If the credit is communicated to the customer before the cheque is cleared, the banker goes beyond mere agency for collection. In *Akrokerri (Atlantic) Mines Ltd v Economic Bank*[6] Bigham J adverted to the distinction between crediting the bank's own books, an uncommunicated entry,[7] and crediting in the customer's pass book for his information.

(v) '... receives payment thereof for himself'

A collecting banker collects for himself whenever he receives a cheque and the customer for whom he collects is indebted to him or he otherwise gives value for the cheque.

A collecting banker may give value in a number of ways, some deliberate and others arising by operation of law. Instances of the former are:

(a) lending further on the strength of a cheque;
(b) paying over the amount of the cheque or part of it in cash or in account before it is cleared;[8]
(c) agreeing, either then or earlier, or as a course of business, that the customer may draw before the cheque is cleared;
(d) accepting the cheque in avowed reduction of an existing overdraft.

An instance of a banker being a holder for value by operation of law is where there is an antecedent debt within the meaning of s 27(1)(b) of the Bills of Exchange Act 1882.

(vi) Banker employing another bank as agent for collection

A collecting banker may employ another bank as his agent for collection (s 77(5)) and yet be receiving for a customer. The use of a clearing, by a non-clearing, bank was admitted by Bigham J in *Akrokerri (Atlantic) Mines Ltd v Economic Bank*,[9] to be an incident of the ordinary process of collection, and not to impair the protection. In that case the question arose whether the defendants, the transmitting bank, violated the character of an agent by subjecting the cheques to a lien of the receiving bank, the former being indebted to the latter. Bigham J held that there was no such lien, which is probably wrong. Incidentally, the indorsements were forged and yet the judge treated the collecting banker as holder. The question is, however, settled, that crossing by a banker is strictly consistent with agency, by the judgment of Lord Birkenhead LC in *Sutters v Briggs*,[10] delivered on behalf of himself, Lords Buckmaster and Carson, Lord Wrenbury concurring.

6 [1904] 2 KB 465. Cf *Gaden v Newfoundland Savings Bank* [1899] AC 281.
7 Cf. *Bevan v Capital and Counties Bank Ltd* (1906) 23 TLR 65.
8 *Midland Bank Ltd v Charles Simpson Motors Ltd* (1960) 7 LDAB 251.
9 [1904] 2 KB 465; and see also *Importers Co Ltd v Westminster Bank Ltd* [1927] 1 KB 869.
10 [1922] 1 AC 1.

(e) 'The customer has no title, or a defective title'

Section 4 confers protection where the customer has no title or a defective title.

It is submitted that s 4 applies even where the cheque collected bears a forged indorsement. In the *Gordon*[12] case itself there were forged indorsements, which goes to show that Lord Macnaghten contemplated their intervention. In *Souchette Ltd v London County, Westminster and Parr's Bank Ltd*,[13] a fraudulent employee obtained from his company cheques payable to creditors of the company for larger amounts than were due, forged the indorsements, and paid them into his private account, discharging the actual debts by his own cheque on the collecting bankers. The latter were held liable only for the difference.[14]

(f) Instruments to which s 4 applies

(i) Cheques

The statutory protection applies to the collection of cheques by virtue of s 4 (2)(a). It is, however, necessary to distinguish an instrument in the form of a cheque which is a nullity ab initio (as where the drawer's signature is forged) from one which is a valid cheque properly issued, but which is fraudulently altered.

A. NULLITY AB INITIO

An instrument in the form of a cheque to which the drawer's signature is a forgery is not a cheque and is not within s 4.

A decision of the Supreme Court of Ceylon[15] is an instance and is specifically stated to have been reached after a consideration of the English reports and of this textbook:

> 'It would appear from the English cases and the work on banking cited by learned counsel for the respondent that if this question had arisen for decision in England it would on the facts of this case be decided against the collecting banker.'

The facts were that one Kulatilleke was fraudulently persuaded by a servant to draw two cheques on the Mercantile Bank of India, which were subsequently raised in amount without the alteration being visible to the naked eye, and with which the servant opened an account with the Bank of Ceylon, which collected the cheques for him. Kulatilleke brought an action against the paying banker, but lost it on the ground that by loosely drawing his cheques he had so facilitated the alteration that he was in breach of his duty to the

---

12 [1903] AC 240. See *Sutters v Briggs* [1922] 1 AC 1, and also *Morison v London County and Westminster Bank Ltd* [1914] 3 KB 356, CA.
13 (1920) 36 TLR 195.
14 And see *Lloyds Bank Ltd v Chartered Bank of India, Australia and China* [1929] 1 KB 40, per Scrutton LJ at 61.
15 *Kulatilleke v Bank of Ceylon* (1957) 59 Ceylon NLR 188, disapproved by a divisional bench of the Supreme Court in *Daniel Silva v Johanis Appuham* (1965) 67 NLR 437, but approved by a bench of five judges in *De Costa v Bank of Ceylon* (1969) 72 NLR 457; and see Scrutton LJ, in *Slingsby v District Bank Ltd* [1932] 1 KB 544; Phillimore LJ in *Morison v London County and Westminster Bank Ltd* [1914] 3 KB 356; Devlin J in *Chao v British Traders and Shippers Ltd* [1954] 2 QB 459, [1954] 1 All ER 779.

bank. He then proceeded against the collecting banker, who was held liable. The basis of the decision was that the instrument collected was not a cheque.

B. FRAUDULENT RAISING OF AMOUNT

The unauthorised raising of the amount or other material alteration of a cheque gives rise to different considerations. The instrument is not a nullity, though by s 64 of the Bills of Exchange Act it is discharged as against any party who has not assented to the alteration, certain rights being reserved to a holder in due course. What this means is that even if the instrument is in the hands of a holder in due course the drawer is discharged except as regards the original amount of the instrument unless the instrument is so loosely drawn that it virtually authorises alteration. The alteration must not be 'apparent' or the drawer will be discharged altogether. It is fair to say that a collecting banker taking an instrument in which the alteration is 'apparent' in the sense of being obvious, might be able to look to his customer, for the statutory protection would not be available to him. Where the alteration is not apparent the question is, what is the nature of the instrument in the hands of a collecting banker; does it fall within s 4(2)(a) and (b) of the Cheques Act 1957? A holder in due course (or a transferee who has taken the instrument under the conditions set out in s 29 of the 1882 Act) may seemingly by the proviso to s 64(1) deal with the instrument as a cheque, though to the extent of the original drawing only; is there any reason why his agent for collection should be liable for conversion when the principal is not? If the principal is entitled to treat the instrument as a cheque, can the instrument change its character in the hands of a collecting agent?

It is not every raising of the amount of a cheque which can be attributed to negligent drawing. Anything similar to the raising in the *Macmillan* case[16] is obviously the responsibility of the drawer, who must be held liable for any loss thereby sustained. Breach of mandate concerns only the drawer and the paying banker; while there would seem to be no duty to the collecting banker, the latter is under duty to him, if he is the true owner. Where the negligence of the drawer is such as to relieve the paying banker, is the instrument as altered the instrument of the drawer or still a cheque sufficient to permit the collecting banker to plead the protection? It is submitted that the collecting banker may do so on the ground that he has collected an instrument falling within s 4(2)(a) and (b) without negligence or, if not, on the ground that the true owner, drawer or otherwise, is estopped from claiming against the banker by reason of his responsibility to anyone taking a transfer of an instrument inviting alteration.

There is also the question whether an instrument can be valid for certain purposes of the law relating to bills of exchange and a nullity for others. It was said in *Morison's* case[17] that a signature which was authorised for one purpose could not become a forgery if utilised for another, though the court in *Alexander Stewart & Son of Dundee Ltd v Westminster Bank Ltd*[18] seemed not to agree. However, if the proposition is to be supported it must be on

16 [1918] AC 777.
17 [1914] 3 KB 356.
18 [1926] WN 271.

the principle propounded by Devlin J in *Chao v British Traders and Shippers Ltd*,[19] that the question is whether the alteration:

'goes to the whole or to the essence of the instrument or not. If it does and if the forgery corrupts the whole of the instrument or its heart, then the instrument is destroyed; but if it corrupts merely a limb, the instrument remains alive, though no doubt defective.'

An instrument on which the amount is fraudulently raised remains alive for purposes of s 64. Nevertheless, it was such an instrument which Devlin J gave as an example of an utter nullity.

'For example, if a man adds two noughts to a cheque, that is the end of it. It is no longer a cheque for, let us say, £10, because the original figure of £10 has been destroyed by the addition of the two noughts. It is not a cheque for £1,000 because the figure of £1,000 is a forged figure. There is, therefore, nothing left of it and it must go. The same result would not necessarily follow, however, if a man were, for example, to forge the date on a cheque because he thought that, it being overdue, there was a possibility that awkward questions might be asked.'

The distinction may be between the raising of the amount and the forgery of an indorsement. The principle is well-established that if the drawer misleads his mandatory, he and not the mandatory is responsible and where also he delivers an inchoate instrument to an agent who completes it beyond his authority.[20] He cannot shield behind the actual authority he gave his agent.[1] He has let loose a thing which is capable of injuring and cannot avoid the consequences by placing the responsibility on an innocent intervener.[2] In the *Imperial Bank of Canada* case[2] the instrument was not strictly inchoate, in that it was complete when handed to the agent, though the drawing was so careless that the instrument could almost be said to be inchoate; there was implied authority to use the instrument in whatever way possible within the range of inchoateness represented by the loose drawing.

In *Lloyds Bank Ltd v Cooke*[3] it was held that the common law doctrine of estoppel by conduct applied, irrespective of s 20 of the Bills of Exchange Act 1882, the court following *Brocklesby v Temperance Permanent Building Society*[4] in which a father entrusted his son with securities for the purpose of borrowing against them and the son borrowed a larger sum than the father had authorised. It was held that the father could not recover the securities without paying the larger sum borrowed.

To sue the collecting banker in conversion the drawer must be entitled to the property in or possession of the instrument and unless the payee is fraudulent and responsible for the forgery, the drawer has neither. Once he accepts responsibility for it, he adopts what the forger has done or is limited to his rights on the cheque as originally drawn. The drawer may not approbate and reprobate at the same time. The forger or agent has abused his authority – the cheque was handed to him for a specific purpose and he applied it to another, which is what happened in *Morison's* case.[5] If the drawer does

19 [1954] 2 QB 459 at 476, [1954] 1 All ER 779 at 787.
20 *Gerald McDonald & Co v Nash & Co* [1924] AC 625.
 1 *Baxendale v Bennett* (1878) 3 QBD 525 at 531; *France v Clark* (1884) 26 ChD 257 at 262.
 2 See *Imperial Bank of Canada v Bank of Hamilton* [1903] AC 49.
 3 [1907] 1 KB 794.
 4 [1895] AC 173.
 5 [1914] 3 KB 356.

mislead and the collecting banker complies with the conditions in which he could ordinarily successfully plead protection, he should not be defeated by the claim that the instrument is no longer what it purported to be. The amount of the cheque as raised is probably 'the sum mentioned in the document' for the purposes of s 4(2)(b) of the Cheques Act 1957.

(ii) Instruments analogous to cheques

If an instrument analogous to a cheque is a document issued by a customer of a banker which, though not a bill of exchange, is intended to enable a person to obtain payment from that banker of the sum mentioned in the document, a collecting banker is protected by s 4(2)(b) of the Cheques Act 1957. These instruments were formerly within s 17 of the Revenue Act 1883 and the Bills of Exchange Act (1882) Amendment Act 1932. The nature of such instruments has already been considered in ch 23, above.

Whether they can safely be credited as cash, as in the case of cheques proper, appears not to have been judicially considered. It is, however, submitted that, as the Cheques Act is by s 6 to be construed as one with the Bills of Exchange Act 1882, it is likely that analogous instruments would be similarly treated by the courts. It would be absurd if because of crediting as cash, the protection of the statute were to be granted to cheques proper but not, for example, to dividend warrants. There is neither legal nor practical reason why they should not be brought within s 4.

(iii) Bills of exchange other than cheques

The banker appears to have no statutory protection with regard to the collection of bills proper. The Cheques Act 1957 is in terms confined to cheques and certain instruments analogous to cheques; protection in collecting is available only to those instruments mentioned in s 4(2). Bills of exchange proper are excluded from s 4(2)(b).

(g) Causation

In the *Marfani* case, Diplock LJ made the following observations on the question of causation:[6]

'There are dicta, which can be found collected in *Baker v Barclays Bank Ltd*[7] at pp 836 to 838, which suggests that, even if it could be proved that a failure to make a particular inquiry which a prudent banker would have made had no causative effect upon the loss sustained by the true owner, the banker would nevertheless be disentitled to the protection of s 4 of the Cheques Act 1957. For my part I think that these dicta are wrong. But it is obviously difficult to prove so speculative a proposition as what would have happened if inquiries had been made which were not made, and I do not think that the defendant bank has sustained the onus of proving it here. I prefer to put it in the alternative way I have already indicated. It does not constitute any lack of reasonable care to refrain from making inquiries which it is improbable will lead to detection of the potential customer's dishonest purpose, if he is dishonest, and which are calculated to offend him and maybe drive away his custom if he is honest.'

Devlin J in *Baker v Barclays Bank Ltd* refused 'in the light of the dicta I have

---

6 [1968] 2 All ER 573 at 582 C, [1968] 1 WLR 956 at 976 H.
7 [1955] 2 All ER 571, [1955] 1 WLR 822.

quoted' to speculate about what would have happened if the bank manager in that case had asked to see the person responsible for the frauds. The dicta were from *Jones v Williams,*[8] *A L Underwood v Bank of Liverpool,*[9] and *Lloyds Bank Ltd v E B Savory & Co.*[10] He held, in the words of the headnote, that where a bank manager failed to make the inquiries that he should have made, a very heavy burden rested on him of showing that such inquiries could not have led to any action which would have protected the interests of the true owner. The inquiry would have been why a partner in a confectionery business should be paying partnership cheques in to an account of a third party.

3 CONTRIBUTORY NEGLIGENCE

(a) Availability of the defence

As evidenced by the *Macmillan*[11] and other cases, negligence on the part of the drawer of a cheque amounting to a breach of the banker-customer contract has long been a defence to a *paying* banker. The Law Reform (Contributory Negligence) Act 1945[12] was not thought to have any bearing on the position of a *collecting* banker until the decision of Donaldson J in *Lumsden & Co v London Trustee Savings Bank.*[13] The case was of a fraudulent employee of a firm of stockbrokers who altered his employers' cheques and paid them into his account with the defendant bank. The court held first, that the defendants were bankers and were negligent and accordingly not entitled to the statutory protection; further, that the Law Reform (Contributory Negligence) Act 1945 was applicable to the tort of conversion. It was admitted that the plaintiffs were negligent in the loose manner in which they drew their cheques and on this basis the judge allowed a discount of 10%. The judge said that there was no English authority for the proposition that contributory negligence might have provided a complete defence to an action based on conversation and he referred to a contrary dictum of Lord Wright in *Lloyds Bank Ltd v E B Savory & Co,*[14] to the following effect:

'And just as in an action in conversion it is an immaterial averment that the conversion was only possible because of want of ordinary prudence on the part of the true owner, so that averment is equally immaterial if the issue arises under s 82.'

However, s 1 of the 1945 Act speaks of damage suffered by a person as the result partly of his own fault and partly of the fault of any other person. 'Fault' is defined in s 4 and is said to mean negligence, breach of statutory duty or other act or omission (a) giving rise to a liability in tort or (b) which would hitherto have given rise to the defence of contributory negligence.

The Torts (Interference with Goods) Act 1977, s 11(1) stated that:

8 (1857) 24 Beav 47 at 62.
9 [1924] 1 KB 775 at 789.
10 [1933] AC 201, especially per Lord Wright at 233 ('...it is useless to consider what might be the position if something had happened which did not happen').
11 [1918] AC 777.
12 31 Halsbury's Statutes (4th edn) 185.
13 [1971] 1 Lloyd's Rep 114; see also *Souhrada v Bank of New South Wales* [1976] 2 Lloyd's Rep 444.
14 [1933] AC 201 at 229.

'Contributory negligence is no defence in proceedings founded on conversion or on intentional trespass to goods.'

It was uncertain whether this provision, being concerned with goods, applied also to cheques. The point is now answered by s 47 of the Banking Act 1979, which provides:

'In any circumstances in which proof of absence of negligence on the part of a banker would be a defence in proceedings by reason of section 4 of the Cheques Act 1957, a defence of contributory negligence shall also be available to the banker notwithstanding the provisions of section 11 (1) of the Torts (Interference with Goods) Act 1977.'

This section remains in force notwithstanding the repeal of the greater part of the 1979 Act (see ch 1, above).

In *Bank Russo-Iran v Gordon, Woodroffe & Co Ltd*[15] Browne J held that the *Lumsden* case was no authority for the proposition that contributory negligence can be set up in answer to a claim for fraudulent misrepresentation.

(b) Lulling to sleep

The *Morison* case[16] which was, of course, decided before the recognition of the defence of contributory negligence to a claim in conversion, appeared to establish that a repeated practice permitted by the plaintiff amounts to condonation. The frauds in *Morison's* case extended over a number of years; some of them were known to the owner, others came to the knowledge of accounts staff employed by him. Some of the cheques which had been wrongfully dealt with had been the subject of subsequent arrangement between the fraudulent person and his employer, the plaintiff, and debited to the former in the books of the business; the employee had been re-employed after the earlier frauds had been discovered. None of this had been communicated to the defendant bank, the plaintiff's explanation being that he always believed that Abbott, the employee, was going to be honest for the future. The Court of Appeal recognised that there was no contractual duty owed by the plaintiff to the defendants, no obligation on the plaintiff to examine his own pass book. Even if the plaintiff had banked with the defendants, the existence and effect of any such duties might have been doubtful; *London Joint Stock Bank Ltd v Macmillan and Arthur*[17] had not then rescued the mandant and mandatory question from its state of chaos, and the efficacy of the pass book as a check on the customer was in law, negligible.

There being no duty owed by the plaintiff to the defendants, there could strictly speaking be no negligence, which is a breach of duty. However, in the *Morison* case the court decided for the bank in respect of the later cheques, largely on the ground that the frauds having gone on for so long the bank were misled into thinking that there was nothing wrong. As to the earlier cheques the court held that by his conduct and by withholding all information from the bank as to the employee's improper dealings with the cheques, the plaintiff must be held to have adopted them.[18] He had obviously done so in

15 (1972) 116 Sol Jo 921.
16 [1914] 3 KB 356, CA.
17 [1918] AC 777.
18 See also *Brown v Westminster Bank Ltd* [1964] 2 Lloyd's Rep 187.

the case of those cheques which he charged against the employee in his accounts with the business. And the court gave judgment for the bank on the whole claim.

The doctrine of reasonable interpretation of the attitude of the possible true owner as negativing negligence is applicable, possibly, only to protracted dealings. The decision, so far as it proceeded on the ground of reasonableness and thus absence of negligence, was independent of the exceptional features unknown to the bank; it took into account only those which were obvious or legitimate deductions.

The notion of 'lulling to sleep' was subsequently impugned. In *Lloyds Bank Ltd v Chartered Bank of India, Australia and China*,[19] Scrutton LJ said:

'I am not at all satisfied as to the grounds of such a decision [*Morison's*] It does not seem consistent with the decisions in *Bank of Ireland (Governor & Co) v Evans' Charities Trustees*[20] and *Swan v North British Australian Co*[1], that in order to act as an estoppel negligence must be the proximate cause of the loss. If my butler for a year has been selling my vintage wines cheap to a small wine-merchant, I do not understand how my negligence in not periodically checking my wine book will be an answer to my action against the wine-merchant for conversion.'

In the same case, Tomlin J said he thought that each repetition of the transaction was calculated to aggravate rather than to allay suspicion:

'There can be no presumption that every fraud must be discovered or that every discovery must be made within any given time and, except upon the basis of some such presumption, I am unable to see why the Chartered Bank should have been entitled to assume that the absence of complaint in respect of any one transaction established the regularity of that or any subsequent transaction.'

In *Lloyds Bank Ltd v E B Savory & Co*[2], Lord Wright found it:

'difficult to appreciate on what principle that case *(Morison's)* was decided in regard to this point; it can only be justified, if at all, on its special facts.'

---

19 [1929] 1 KB 40.
20 (1855) 5 HL Cas 389.
 1 (1863) 2 H & C 175.
 2 [1933] AC 201. See also *Carpenters' Co v British Mutual Banking Co Ltd* [1938] 1 KB 511, CA.

CHAPTER 29

CREDIT CARDS AND CHEQUE GUARANTEE CARDS

The Consumer Credit Act implications of credit cards and cheque guarantee cards are considered in ch 5, above. This chapter is concerned solely with the contractual consequences of such cards.

1 CREDIT CARDS

(a) Normal features of credit card transactions

The normal features of a credit card transaction were stated by Sir Nicholas Browne-Wilkinson V-C in *Re Charge Card Services Ltd*[1] to include the following: (1) There is an underlying contractual scheme which predates the individual contracts of sale. Under such scheme, the suppliers have agreed to accept the card in payment of the price of goods purchased: the purchasers are entitled to use the credit card to commit the credit card company to pay the suppliers. (2) The underlying scheme is established by two separate contracts. The first is made between the credit company and the seller: the seller agrees to accept payment by the use of the card from anyone holding the card and the credit company agrees to pay to the supplier the price of goods supplied less a discount. The second contract is between the credit company and the cardholder: the cardholder is provided with a card which enables him to pay the price by its use and in return agrees to pay the credit company the full amount of the price charged by the supplier. (3) The underlying scheme is designed primarily for use in over-the-counter sales, ie, sales where the only connection between a particular seller and a particular buyer is one sale. (4) The actual sale and purchase of the commodity is the subject of the third bilateral contract made between buyer and seller. In the majority of cases, this sale contract will be an oral, over-the-counter sale. Tendering and acceptance of the credit card in payment is made on the tacit assumption that the legal consequences will be regulated by the separate underlying contractual obligations between the seller and the credit company and the buyer and the credit company. (5) Because the transactions intended to be covered by the scheme would primarily be over-the-counter sales, the card does not carry the address of the cardholder and the supplier will have

1 [1988] 3 All ER 702 at 705, [1988] 3 WLR 764 at 768, CA.

no record of his address. Therefore the seller has no obvious means of tracing the purchaser save through the credit company.

For these purposes, there is no relevant distinction between credit cards and charge cards.

(b) Effect of payment by credit card or charge card

There is no general principle of law that, whenever a method of payment is adopted which involves a risk of non-payment by a third party, there is a presumption that the acceptance of payment through a third party is conditional upon the third party making the payment, and that, if he does not pay, the original obligation of the purchaser remains. It was so held in *Re Charge Card Services Ltd*, above. The presumption of conditional payment in relation to cheques and letters of credit rests not on any principle of general application, but on a consideration of the consequences of treating as absolute a payment made in those particular circumstances.

Whether the seller's acceptance of payment by a credit card or charge card is conditional or absolute depends on the terms of the agreement between the various parties. It was observed in *Re Charge Card Services Ltd* that the analogy between credit cards and cheques is not at all close[2]. Payment by cheque involves the unilateral act of the buyer and his agent, the bank on which the cheque is drawn. The position differs from that when payment is made by credit card in that (1) the buyer's basic obligation to pay the price is sought to be discharged through a third party (the bank) which is not in a contractual relationship with the seller, and (2) the seller has no say in the selection of the bank. The Court of Appeal regarded the analogy with letters of credit as closer, but not of great assistance. Although the bank is in a contractual relationship with the seller/beneficiary, there are fundamental differences: (1) A letter of credit is normally issued pursuant to a negotiated contract of considerable substance, whereas a credit card is used for small over-the-counter transactions between strangers. (2) It is usually the buyer who selects the bank issuing the letter of credit, whereas in credit card transactions the seller has decided long before the specific supply contract is made whether or not he accepts the cards of the credit company, and has entered into an overall contract with it. (3) With letters of credit it is the buyer who pays for the facility, whereas in credit card transactions, it is the seller who pays for the facility by allowing deduction of commission.

In *Re Charge Card Services Ltd,* the issue was whether payment by charge card for the purchase of petrol was absolute or conditional. This issue arose because the card issuing company went into creditors' voluntary liquidation, and sums collected from cardholders became the subject of rival claims made by the garages who supplied the fuel and by a factoring company to which the company's receivables had been assigned. It was held by the Court of Appeal that the cardholder's obligations to the garages were absolutely, not conditionally, discharged by the garage accepting the vouchers signed by the cardholder. The factors which held to this conclusion were as follows:[3]

1 The cardholder knew that, if he signed the voucher, the garage would be

2 [1988] 3 All ER 702 at 710h, [1988] 3 WLR 764 at 774 H.
3 [1988] 3 All ER 702 at 707–708, [1988] 3 WLR 764 at 772.

entitled to receive a payment for the petrol which would fully discharge the customer's liability for the price.

2 The cardholder might, depending on his sophistication, have known that the card issuing company would deduct commission in paying the garage.

3 The garage knew that on signing the voucher, the cardholder rendered himself liable to the card issuing company to pay the price of the petrol.

4 Before entering into the forecourt agreement, both the garage and the cardholder had entered into their respective contracts with the card issuing company, and they must have assumed that on completion of the sale, the parties' future rights and obligations would be regulated by those underlying contracts.

5 In the majority of cases, the garage had no record of the address of the customer and no ready means of tracing him.

6 The agreement between the card issuing company and the garage included an undertaking by the company to provide a guarantee of its obligations to the garage (although this guarantee was not in fact provided).

7 The agreement between the card issuing company and the cardholder imposed a liability on the cardholder to pay the company whether or not the company had paid the garage, so that if payment by charge card had been merely conditional, the cardholder might have been liable to pay twice over – once to the company and again to the garage.

The first five of the above factors will be present (mutatis mutandis) in most credit card or charge card transactions, and it would seem therefore that payment by credit card or charge card is likely to be treated as absolute payment of the price save in exceptional circumstances.

2 CHEQUE GUARANTEE CARDS

A cheque guarantee card, or cheque card, is a card issued by a bank to its customer for use in conjunction with cheques drawn by him. In *Re Charge Card Service Ltd*[4], Millett J at first instance described the obligation undertaken by the bank to the supplier, which it enters into through the agency of its customer when he uses the card, as being not to dishonour the cheque on presentation for want of funds in the account, with the consequence that the bank is obliged to advance moneys to the customer to meet it.

Both the use of a cheque card and the bank's guarantee of payment are normally subject to express conditions, which typically include the following: (1) The cheque must be signed in the presence of the payee. (2) The payee must write the card number on the reverse of the cheque. (3) The amount of the cheque must not exceed a specified amount. (4) No other cheque is to be used to settle the same transaction. (5) The cheque must be dated before the date on which the card expires.

The customer normally undertakes not to countermand payment of any guaranteed cheque. Any such countermand would probably be invalid, or would entitle the bank to damages from the customer equal to the amount of any payment under its guarantee to the supplier.

In *Re Charge Card Services Ltd,* Millett J at first instance stated, obiter, that the presumption that the giving of a cheque operates as a conditional

4 [1987] Ch 150 at 166, [1986] 3 All ER 289 at 301.

payment only would not be displaced merely by the fact that the cheque is accompanied by a bank card.[5] On appeal, this point was expressly left open.[6]

By exhibiting to the payee a cheque card containing the undertaking by a bank to honour cheques drawn in compliance with the conditions indorsed on the back, and drawing the cheques accordingly, the drawer represents to the payee that he has actual authority from the bank to make a contract with the payee on the bank's behalf that it will honour the cheque on presentment for payment.[7]

5 [1987] Ch 150 at 166, [1986] 3 All ER 289 at 301–302.
6 [1988] 3 All ER 702 at 711, [1988] 3 WLR 764 at 775.
7 *Metropolitan Police Comr v Charles* [1977] AC 177 at 182, [1977] 3 All ER 112 at 114, HL, per Lord Diplock.

PART V

SECURITY FOR ADVANCES

SUMMARY OF CONTENTS

CHAPTER 30

THE TAKING OF SECURITY[1]

The issues considered in this Chapter encompass a complex interrelation
between rules of common law and principles of equity. The common thread
is that each of them operates so as to affect the enforceability of an agreement
creating security. They concern matters which a bank needs to consider and
guard against when taking security; a failure so to do may result in the court
setting it aside. Challenges to security tend to arise most frequently in the
context of guarantees, and mortgages or charges over property, given by
individuals. However, the rules and principles considered below apply to all
forms of security agreement and whether given by an individual or by a
corporate entity.

In *Lloyds Bank Ltd v Bundy*[2] Lord Denning MR endeavoured to collate
the various categories in which the courts have set aside transactions into a
single principle of:

> '... inequality of bargaining power. By virtue of it, the English law gives relief to
> one who, without independent advice, enters into a contract upon terms which are
> very unfair or transfers property for a consideration which is grossly inadequate,
> when his bargaining power is grievously impaired by reason of his own needs or
> desires, or by his own ignorance or infirmity, coupled with undue influences or
> pressures brought to bear on him by or for the benefit of the other.'

The House of Lords in *National Westminster Bank Plc v Morgan*[3] rightly
disapproved this approach. The various rules and principles have developed
independently of each other and require separate consideration.

1 UNDUE INFLUENCE

The equitable doctrine of undue influence extends to cover both (1) those
cases in which the particular relationship of trust and confidence between the
parties leads the court to presume that undue influence has been exerted
without necessity for proof ('presumed undue influence'); and (2) those cases

---

1 The Editor gratefully acknowledges that this chapter has been contributed by Peter Havey,
  Barrister.
2 [1975] QB 326 at 339, [1974] 3 All ER 757 at 765.
3 [1985] AC 686 at 708, [1985] 1 All ER 821 at 830.

outside such relationships in which the court will uphold a plea of undue influence only if satisfied that such influence has been affirmatively proved on the evidence ('actual undue influence').[4]

The principle justifying the court in setting aside a transaction for undue influence is based specifically upon the victimisation of one party by another.[5] The court has been astute not to fetter the ambit of the doctrine by seeking to define the exact limits of its exercise.[6]

(a) Presumed undue influence

In cases of presumed undue influence, once it has been established:

1 that a relationship of influence exists between the parties; and
2 that a transaction has taken place between them which was wrongful in the sense that the party in a position of influence took an unfair advantage of the party subject to the influence which operated to the latter's manifest disadvantage;

a presumption arises that the transaction was procured by the exercise of undue influence.[7] The presumption may, of course, be rebutted by evidence to the contrary.

(i) Relationship of influence

There are certain categories of relationship which lead the court to presume from the relative status of the parties that a relationship of influence exists, eg parent/child,[8] doctor/patient,[9] solicitor/client[10] and religious or spiritual adviser/adherent.[11] The relationship of husband and wife[12] does not give rise to such a presumption, nor does the normal relationship between banker and customer.[13] Accordingly a bank will not be affected by this presumption except where it obtains a security from one of the above-mentioned weaker parties through the intervention of the stronger acting as its agent, or has knowledge that the security was obtained in this manner.[14]

Outside these particular relationships, the onus is on the party seeking to set aside the transaction to establish that a relationship of influence existed between himself and the party benefitting from it. It must be shown that the degree of trust and confidence between the parties is such that 'the party in whom it is reposed, either because he is or has become an adviser of the other

4 *Allcard v Skinner* (1887) 36 Ch D 145 at 171; *Goldsworthy v Brickell* [1987] Ch 378 at 400, [1987] 1 All ER 853 at 865, CA; *Bank of Credit and Commerce International SA v Aboody* [1989] 2 WLR 759 at 768–769, CA.
5 *Allcard v Skinner*, supra at 182–183; *National Westminster Bank Plc v Morgan*, supra at, respectively, 705 and 828.
6 See per Lord Chelmsford LC in *Tate v Williamson* (1866) 2 Ch App 55 at 61. See also *National Westminster Bank Plc v Morgan*, supra at 709 and 831.
7 *Allcard v Skinner*, supra at 171; *National Westminster Bank Plc v Morgan*, supra at 704 and 827.
8 *Archer v Hudson* (1844) 7 Beav 551.
9 *Dent v Bennett* (1839) 4 My & Cr 269.
10 *Gibson v Jeyes* (1801) 6 Ves Jun 266.
11 *Huguenin v Baseley* (1807) 14 Ves Jun 273; *Allcard v Skinner*, supra.
12 *Bank of Montreal v Stuart* [1911] AC 120, PC.
13 *National Westminster Bank plc v Morgan* [1985] AC 686 at 707, [1985] 1 All ER 821 at 829, HL; *Bank of Credit and Commerce International SA v Aboody* [1989] 2 WLR 759 at 769.
14 See p 489, infra.

or because he has been entrusted with the management of his affairs or everyday needs or for some other reason, is in a position to influence him into effecting the transaction of which complaint is later made'.[15] The relationship need not be one of domination of one party by the other.[16]

In *Lloyds Bank Ltd v Bundy*[17] the bank was held on the special facts of that case to have attained a relationship of influence with its customer. In view of the fact that the position of financial adviser to a customer is one to which many banks properly aspire, it may be not infrequent that a bank has such a relationship of influence with its customer. It is less likely that a bank would have such a relationship with a non-customer who merely offers security.

(ii) Manifest disadvantage

In *National Westminster Bank plc v Morgan* the House of Lords held that in order for the presumption of undue influence to operate, it must be shown that the transaction was wrongful in the sense that it operated to the manifest disadvantage of the person influenced.[18] Lord Scarman stated:[19]

'Whatever the legal character of the transaction, the authorities show that it must constitute a disadvantage sufficiently serious to require evidence to rebut the presumption that in the circumstances of the relationship between the parties it was procured by the exercise of undue influence. In my judgment, therefore, the Court of Appeal erred in law in holding that the presumption of undue influence can arise from the evidence of the relationship of the parties without also evidence that the transaction itself was wrongful in that it constituted an advantage taken of the person subjected to the influence which, failing proof to the contrary, was explicable only on the basis that undue influence had been exercised to procure it.'

It is clear that manifest disadvantage is not present where the transaction provides reasonably equal benefits for both parties.[20] Beyond this, there is no very clear guidance as to what is meant by the term. This is not surprising since the issue of manifest disadvantage is a mixed question of fact and law and, as concerns the facts, one of degree.[1] In each case, the court will objectively examine the facts, with particular reference to the terms of the transaction into which the parties entered, and, it is submitted, will conduct a balancing exercise weighing on the one hand any benefits derived by the party subjected to the influence, and on the other hand any worsening of his position suffered as a result of the transaction. Where the latter significantly outweighs the former, manifest disadvantage will be held to be present. The nature of the disadvantage is to be judged by the circumstances subsisting at the date of the transaction, though subsequent events may be considered as evidence of what may reasonably have been foreseen at that date.[2]

---

15 *Goldsworthy v Brickell* [1987] Ch 378 at 401 D, [1987] 1 All ER 853 at 865e, CA, per Nourse LJ.
16 *Goldsworthy v Brickell,* supra at, respectively, 404F and 868a.
17 [1975] QB 326, [1974] 3 All ER 757, CA.
18 *National Westminster Bank Plc v Morgan* [1985] AC 686 at 704, [1985] 1 All ER 821 at 827; *Bank of Credit and Commerce International SA v Aboody* [1989] 2 WLR 759 at 772–773.
19 *National Westminster Bank Plc v Morgan,* supra, loc cit.
20 *National Westminster Bank Plc v Morgan,* supra loc cit, disapproving an observation of Slade LJ in the Court of Appeal [1983] 3 All ER 85 at 92d.
1 *Midland Bank plc v Phillips,* (14 March 1986, unreported), CA.
2 *Bank of Credit and Commerce International SA v Aboody* [1989] 2 WLR 759, CA, at 780 D, per Slade LJ delivering the judgment of the Court.

Where a bank takes a security from a customer in respect of his own indebtedness, for example a charge over his property to secure his overdraft, it is unlikely that this will be held to be manifestly disadvantageous to the customer since the bank would in any event be able to call in the lending and, if it remained unpaid, obtain a monetary judgment and execute against such property. On the other hand, where a security is taken by the bank from a third party in respect of a customer's indebtedness, for example where a wife mortgages her interest in the matrimonial property to secure the overdraft of her husband's business, manifest disadvantage is more likely to be shown because she may be giving up something of substance without receiving any tangible benefit in return. However, the evidence may disclose that the wife's livelihood depended on the success of her husband's business and the bank's continued support for the business, and that therefore she received a benefit at least equal to the risk of jeopardy to her interest in the property.

It is, of course, axiomatic that in every case where a bank takes a security, there is a risk that the security will be enforced. The approach of the court to the question of whether such a risk is manifestly disadvantageous to the giver of security essentially involves the balancing of two factors, namely (a) the seriousness to the giver of the risk of enforcement, and (b) the benefits obtained by the giver in accepting that risk.[3]

(*iii*) *Rebuttal of the presumption*

For the purposes of rebutting the presumption, evidence must be adduced to satisfy the court that the transaction was the spontaneous act of the party subjected to influence acting in circumstances which enabled him to exercise an independent will, so as to justify the court in holding that he entered into the transaction after full, free and informed consideration.[4] The fact that the person alleged to have been influenced has taken and acted upon independent legal advice given with a knowledge of all the relevant circumstances by an honest adviser acting solely in the interest of his client will generally rebut the presumption, but independent legal advice is not the only way to do so.[5]

(b) Actual undue influence

Where the relationship between a bank and a giver of security is not such as to give rise to a presumption of undue influence, the security may nonetheless be set aside if the giver establishes that undue influence has in fact been exerted over him by the bank or its intermediaries or that the bank had knowledge of circumstances indicating that the security had been procured by undue influence.[6]

In *Bank of Credit and Commerce International SA v Aboody,* the Court of Appeal, while disavowing any intent to attempt a comprehensive definition of undue influence, was of the view that in order to establish a plea of actual undue influence it must be shown that:

3 *Bank of Credit and Commerce International SA v Aboody* [1989] 2 WLR 759, CA, at 780 E.
4 *Allcard v Skinner* (1887) 36 Ch D 145 at 171; *Zamet v Hyman* [1961] 1 WLR 1442 at 1446; *Goldsworthy v Brickell* [1987] Ch 378 at 408, [1987] 1 All ER 853 at 871.
5 See *Inche Noriah v Shaik Allie Bin Omar* [1929] AC 127 at 135.
6 As to notice of undue influence, see p 489, infra.

1 the party alleged to have brought about the transaction had the capacity
   to influence the complainant;
2 the influence was exercised;
3 its exercise was undue;
4 its exercise brought about the transaction;
5 the transaction was to the complainant's manifest disadvantage.[7]

This can be contrasted with the position in cases of presumed undue influence,
where it is necessary to establish only elements (1) and (5), the others being
presumed to be present. Manifest disadvantage has already been considered
above.

(*i*) *Position of influence*

All that it is necessary to establish is that by reason of some factor, even of
an instantaneous or transitory nature, the alleged influencer was in a position
which he could utilise to influence the complainant into giving the security.
There is no need to establish a relationship of trust and confidence as in cases
of presumed undue influence.

(*ii*) *Exercise of undue influence*

Elements (2) and (3) can conveniently be dealt with together. There must be
something in the nature of the conduct of the influencer which is unfair and
improper, whether it takes the form of coercion, overreaching or cheating.[8]
A somewhat extreme example of actual undue influence being exerted by a
bank is the case of *Williams v Bayley*.[9] There the bank coerced a father into
agreeing to give security for his son's debts by a threat to prosecute the son
for having forged his father's endorsements on some promissory notes given
by him to the bank. The transaction was set aside. However, the exercise of
influence need not necessarily take the form of active coercion or persuasion
in order to render it undue. It may be an indirect form of pressure such as
an appeal to the emotions[10] or may be wholly passive such as a failure to
disclose the risks involved in the transaction.[11] Nor need such influence be
accompanied by any malign intent in order to render it undue.[12]

(*iii*) *Causation*

If it can be positively established on the evidence that the party who gave the
security under undue influence would have done so in any event, even in the
absence of undue influence, the court will not exercise its jurisdiction to set
aside the security.[13] However, it is submitted that the exercise of undue

7 [1989] 2 WLR 759 at 782.
8 *Allcard v Skinner* (1887) 36 Ch D 145 at 181.
9 (1866) LR 1 HL 200. Cf *Lloyds Bank v Suvale Properties* (Unreported) (1981) CLY 271, CA,
   where it appears that the Court would not have granted equitable relief to parties who had
   defrauded the bank even if it had been established that security had been obtained from
   them by a threat to prosecute for the fraud. In *Williams v Bayley* the father was in no way
   implicated in the son's wrongdoing.
10 *Barclays Bank Plc v Kennedy* [1989] 1 FLR 356.
11 *Bank of Credit and Commerce International SA v Aboody* [1989] 2 WLR 759 at 783–784.
12 *Barclays Bank Plc v Kennedy,* supra; *Bank of Credit and Commerce International SA v Aboody*
   [1989] 2 WLR 759 at 784.
13 Ibid at 785.

influence having been proved, the burden on the influencer to establish that this was not causative of the transaction will inevitably be a heavy one.

(c) Circumstances in which a bank is affected by undue influence exerted by another

Undue influence exerted by a third party over the giving of security will generally have no effect on the validity of the security taken by a bank. However, there are two distinct grounds upon which a bank may be affected by such undue influence:

(i) where the bank has constituted the third party its agent for the purpose of procuring the execution of the security; and
(ii) where the bank has actual or constructive notice at the time of execution of the security that it has been procured by undue influence.[14]

(*i*) *Agency*

Where the transaction has been brought about by the undue influence of a person acting on behalf of a bank, the bank cannot rely on the transaction since, but for the wrongful acts of its agent, the transaction would not have taken place. The clearest statement of this principle is to be found in the judgment of Dillon LJ in *Kingsnorth Trust Ltd v Bell*:[15]

'... if a creditor, or potential creditor, of a husband desires to obtain, by way of security for the husband's indebtedness, a guarantee from his wife or a charge on property of his wife and if the creditor entrusts to the husband himself the task of obtaining the execution of the relevant document by the wife, then the creditor can be in no better position than the husband himself, and the creditor cannot enforce the guarantee or the security against the wife if it is established that the execution of the document by the wife was procured by undue influence by the husband and the wife had no independent advice.'

This principle is of general application to the situation where the creditor chooses to leave it to a third party to procure the execution of the security and is not limited to the field of husband and wife.[16] Nevertheless, since the principle applies both where the agent is presumed to have exerted undue influence as well as where he has actually exerted undue influence, the bank is peculiarly vulnerable in the husband and wife situation, since there will often be little difficulty in establishing that the relationship between them was such as to give rise to the presumption, which must then be rebutted by evidence.

Whether in any particular case a third party is acting as the bank's agent is a question of fact. However, there is no distinction in principle between the situation where a bank hands the security document to the third party to enable him to obtain its execution by the giver of security and where it is simply left to the third party to procure the attendance of the giver at the

14 *Bank of Credit and Commerce International SA v Aboody* [1989] 2 WLR 759 at 786.
15 [1986] 1 All ER 423 at 427c, [1986] 1 WLR 119 at 123. See also *Turnbull & Co v Duvall* [1902] AC 429; *Chaplin & Co Ltd v Bramall* [1908] 1 KB 233; *Bank of Credit and Commerce International SA v Aboody*, supra at 987. Cf *Coldunell Ltd v Gallon* [1986] QB 1184, [1986] 1 All ER 429.
16 *Avon Finance Co Ltd v Bridger* [1985] 2 All ER 281, CA; *Kingsnorth Trust Ltd v Bell* [1986] 1 All ER 423 at 427, [1986] 1 WLR 119 at 124.

bank's premises for the purposes of executing the security.[17] The issue of fact in both cases is whether it can be said that the bank 'left everything' to the third party as regards the obtaining of the execution of the security.[18]

Further, it is clear that agency is by itself sufficient to fix the bank with undue influence. There is no additional requirement that the bank must also have notice that undue influence would or might have been exercised by the person chosen to procure the execution of the security.[19]

(ii) Notice

If, at the time of execution of security, a bank has actual or constructive notice that the security has been procured by the exercise of undue influence, an equity is raised disentitling the bank from relying in any way upon it.[20] In *Bainbrigge v Browne*[1] Fry J put the matter thus:

'... against whom does this inference of undue influence operate? Clearly it operates against the person who is able to exercise the influence ... and, in my judgment, it would operate against every volunteer who claimed under him, and also against every person who claimed under him with notice of the equity thereby created or with notice of the circumstances from which the Court infers the equity.'

This equity has effect irrespective of any issue of agency.[2]

The circumstances constituting notice required to fix the bank with liability for another's undue influence depends on the nature of the undue influence alleged. Where actual undue influence is alleged, what must be shown is notice of the circumstances alleged to amount to actual exercise of undue influence or at least circumstances from which it can be inferred that undue influence was exercised. Where presumed undue influence is alleged, what must be shown is notice of circumstances from which the presumption of undue influence is alleged to arise or from which such presumption can be inferred.[3]

(d) Remedies

A successful invocation of the equitable principle of undue influence affords an equitable right to set aside the security. It affords no remedy in damages. Further, this equitable right is liable to be defeated by the equitable defences of laches, acquiescence and affirmation.[4] It is outside the scope of *Paget* to outline the nature of these equitable defences and reference should be made to the standard textbooks on equity.

17 *Barclays Bank plc v Kennedy* [1989] 1 FLR 356.
18 *Turnbull v Duvall*, supra at 435; *Bank of Credit and Commerce International SA v Aboody*, supra at 788.
19 *Bank of Credit and Commerce International SA v Aboody*, supra at 787.
20 *Kempson v Ashbee* (1874) 10 Ch App 15; *Bainbrigge v Browne* (1881) 18 Ch D 188; *Bank of Credit and Commerce International SA v Aboody*, supra at 787.
 1 (1881) 18 Ch D 188.
 2 *Bank of Credit and Commerce International SA v Aboody*, supra at 787.
 3 Ibid at 787–789.
 4 *Allcard v Skinner* (1887) 36 Ch D 145 at 196–199; *Goldsworthy v Brickell* [1987] Ch 378 at 411.

2 UNCONSCIONABLE TRANSACTIONS[5]

The equitable jurisdiction to set aside unconscionable transactions is independent of the principles as to undue influence. Under this jurisdiction a security taken by a bank may be held to be unenforceable if: (1) it was taken from a person under a special disadvantage or disability; (2) the transaction was disadvantageous to such person; (3) independent legal advice was not available.

Once these factors are established, the party seeking to defend the transaction must prove it was fair, just and reasonable.[6]

The invocation of this doctrine is likely to be rare and in recent times Australian courts have taken it up with greater enthusiasm than English courts.[7] Nevertheless, there may be scope for its application in cases where no question of undue influence arises but where a bank obtains security for the debt of its customer from a third party with no material interest in that indebtedness who is under a special disability such as infirmity, low intelligence or poor understanding of English, and that third party did not obtain independent legal advice before entering the transaction.

The position as regards remedies is the same as for undue influence.

3 DURESS[8]

Unlawful acts or threats to commit unlawful or improper acts directed against a party in order to induce that party to enter into a transaction may render the resulting transaction voidable for duress.[9] There is a clear overlap between duress and actual undue influence[10] and it is difficult to see any scope in the context of taking of security for the application of the doctrine of duress independent of undue influence. Possibly duress may provide a remedy in damages where the remedy of setting aside of the security for undue influence is not an adequate remedy or is liable to be defeated by the equitable defences.[11]

---

5 See generally *Snell's Principles of Equity* (28th edn) p 545; Meagher, Gummow and Lehane *Equity* (2nd edn) ch 16.
6 *Fry v Lane* (1888) 40 Ch D 312; *Cresswell v Potter* [1978] 1 WLR 255; *Commercial Bank of Australia v Amadio* (1983) 151 CLR 447.
7 *Commercial Bank of Australia v Amadio,* supra; *Nobile v National Australian Bank* [1987] ACLD 410. In both cases the special disability of the security giver was a poor understanding of English.
8 See generally *Chitty on Contracts* (25th edn) Vol I, pp 266–283.
9 *Pao On v Lau Yiu Long* [1980] AC 614, [1979] 3 All ER 65; *Atlas Express Ltd v Kafco (Importers and Distributors) Ltd* [1989] 1 All ER 641, [1989] 3 WLR 389.
10 Cf *Williams v Bayley* (1866) LR 1 HL 200; *Mutual Finance Ltd v John Wetton & Sons Ltd* [1937] 2 KB 389, [1937] 2 All ER 657.
11 See *Chitty* p 282.

4 MISREPRESENTATION AND NON-DISCLOSURE

(a) Misrepresentation

A contract of security, like any other contract, is liable to be avoided if induced by a material misrepresentation of fact made by the bank or its agent.[12] In addition, the giver of the security may have a remedy in damages if the misrepresentation is fraudulent or negligent, but if the misrepresentation is merely innocent, damages are available only in lieu of rescission.[13] Statements as to the terms and effect of the security document, although involving a representation as to the effect in law of the security, will nevertheless probably be classified as a representation of fact.[14]

(b) Negligent misstatements

Where a banker embarks on an explanation as to the terms and effect of a security document in circumstances where he knew or ought to have known that the person to whom the explanation is proferred would rely on it in deciding whether or not to execute the security, he is likely to come under a duty to that person to take reasonable care not to misstate the position.[15] If he does negligently misstate the position, whether by making a positive misrepresentation or by omitting to point out a material fact,[16] the bank may be liable in damages for negligence. The effect of the award in damages, intended as it is to return the parties to the position they would have been in but for the negligent misstatement, is likely to mean in practical terms that the bank loses the benefit of the security.

In accordance with the general law of principal and agent, a bank will be liable for a misrepresentation or negligent misstatement made by a third party to whom it has entrusted the task of procuring the execution of the security.

(c) Duty to proffer explanation

Cornish v Midland Bank Plc[17] is authority for the proposition that where a banker chooses to explain the nature and effect of a security document he must take care not to misstate the position.[18] However, in the same case, Kerr LJ went further and suggested tentatively that in certain circumstances a bank may owe a duty to the giver of security, at least if he is a customer,[19] to proffer some explanation as to the nature and effect of the security document to be executed.[20]

---

12 *MacKenzie v Royal Bank of Canada* [1934] AC 468 at 475; *Kingsnorth Trust Ltd v Bell* [1986] 1 All ER 423, [1986] 1 WLR 119.
13 S 2(2) of the Misrepresentation Act 1967. See generally *Chitty on Contracts* (25th edn) Vol 1, pp 225–244.
14 *Chitty* pp 214–215.
15 *Cornish v Midland Bank* [1985] 3 All ER 513 applying *Hedley Byrne & Co Ltd v Heller & Partners Ltd* [1964] AC 465 [1963] 2 All ER 575. See also *Midland Bank plc v Perry,* [1988] 1 FLR 161.
16 *Cornish v Midland Bank,* supra at 517a.
17 [1985] 3 All ER 513.
18 See supra.
19 In *O'Hara v Allied Irish Banks Ltd* [1985] BCLC 52 Harman J held that a bank is under no duty to explain the terms and legal effect of a guarantee to a potential guarantor who is not a customer.
20 [1985] 3 All ER 513 at 522–523.

In reaching this conclusion Kerr LJ placed particular reliance on the following passage in the judgment of Sir Erich Sachs in *Lloyds Bank Ltd v Bundy*:[1]

> '... it seems necessary to point out that nothing in this judgment affects the duties of a bank in the normal case where it is obtaining a guarantee, and in accordance with standard practice explains to the person about to sign its legal effect and the sums involved.'

Kerr LJ deduced that it appeared to be implicit from this passage that at any rate in relation to customers, banks may be under a duty to proffer an adequate explanation of the security. However, the passage is not confined to customers but extends to potential guarantors generally, and the implication of the passage would appear to be that duties arise if and when the bank proffers the explanation, rather than there being a duty to explain whenever a guarantee is taken.[2]

Kerr LJ does not elaborate on the source of the suggested duty. The fact that it is expressed to be confined to customers suggests it is contractual in nature, in which case it must be taken to arise as an implied term of the contract between banker and customer. However the implication of such a term is not so obvious as not to require express statement, nor is it necessary to give business efficacy to the contract, and it would run counter to the general principle that in the context of contractual negotiations there is no duty to speak.[3] If there is no duty in contract, there is unlikely to be a duty in tort.[4] It is submitted that the existence of the suggested duty must be regarded as doubtful.

If, however, such a duty does exist, then it would appear to be open to a bank to discharge it in one of two ways. Either it could endeavour to provide some adequate explanation of the nature and effect of the security document, the extent of which explanation would depend on the complexity of the security. Alternatively it could direct the customer to obtain independent legal advice. In view of the complexity of many security documents, it might well be prudent for the bank to adopt the latter course.

(d) Duty of disclosure

A contract creating security, whether it be a guarantee, mortgage or charge, is not a contract of utmost good faith requiring full disclosure of all material facts by both parties. There is a limited duty upon the creditor in contracts of guarantee to disclose to the intending surety any unusual features of the underlying transaction which affect the nature and degree of the surety's liability. This duty is considered in ch 35, below. It appears not to be applicable to other contracts creating security unless such contracts incorporate an obligation in the nature of a guarantee.

---

1 [1975] QB 326 at 347, [1974] 3 All ER 757 at 772.
2 This would be consistent with the above stated ratio of *Cornish v Midland Bank Plc*.
3 As regards contracts of guarantee there is an obligation to disclose unusual features of the principal transaction – see ch 35, below. This does not, however, appear to extend to the terms of the guarantee itself.
4 *Tai Hing Cotton Mill Ltd v Liu Chong Hing Bank Ltd* [1986] AC 80 at 107; *Banque Keyser Ullmann SA v Skandia (UK) Insurance Co Ltd* [1989] 3 WLR 25 at 106.

CHAPTER 31

LIEN AND SET-OFF

Set-off is a subject of immense importance in modern banking law. Day by day, banks in the City of London enter huge transactions in which rights of set-off are relied upon as conferring protection in the event of the counterparty's default.

Set-off is also a subject of great complexity. The objective of this Chapter is to identify those aspects of the law of set-off which most impinge on bank lending. It is logical to begin not with set-off, but with the banker's lien, the recognition of which led to the subsequent recognition of the banker's right of set-off. Consideration is then given to relevant aspects of set-off under the general law, including the vulnerability of rights of set-off to third party interference. This is followed by a section on contractual set-off provisions, ie provisions which are either contractual rights of set-off or provisions intended to reinforce rights of set-off under the general law.

1 THE BANKER'S LIEN

(a) Existence and nature of the banker's lien

(i) Existence of the lien

The banker's lien was recognised by the Court of King's Bench as early as 1794 in *Davis v Bowsher*.[1] In 1846 the House of Lords regarded its existence as indisputable in *Brandao v Barnett*,[2] where Lord Campbell said:

> 'Bankers most undoubtedly have a general lien on all securities deposited with them as bankers by a customer, unless there be an express contract, or circumstances that show an implied contract, inconsistent with lien.'

It was further stated by Lord Campbell that the banker's lien is part of the law merchant,[3] which courts of justice are bound to know and recognise.[4] Consequently the existence of the general lien need not normally be pleaded or proved. It must be remembered that the law merchant is not fixed and

---

1 (1794) 5 Term Rep 488; 101 ER 275.
2 (1846) 12 Cl & Fin 787 at 806.
3 For a description of the law merchant, see the Introduction to *Chalmers on Bills of Exchange* (3rd edn), reproduced at pp xli to xlvi of the 13th edn (1964).
4 Ibid at 805. See also Lord Lyndhurst at 810: 'There is no doubt that, by the law-merchant, a banker has a lien for his general balance on securities deposited with him.'

stereotyped. It is capable of being expanded and enlarged so as to meet the wants and requirements of trade in the varying circumstances of commerce.[5] Therefore if a bank relies upon some aspect of the lien which is not clearly established on the authorities, it is open to it to plead and adduce evidence of a general usage, and it is open to the court to recognise such usage as establishing the right relied upon.

(ii) The banker's lien as an implied pledge

In *Brandao v Barnett* Lord Campbell stated that the right acquired by a general lien is an implied pledge.[6] This observation was made in support of a ruling that the banker's lien exists if the banker has acted in good faith, even though the subject of the lien turns out to be the property of a stranger. This ruling is part of the ratio of *Brandao v Barnett,* for the subject of the lien, namely exchequer bills, had been deposited with the respondent bankers, not by the appellant, who was the owner, but by his London agent. The House of Lords rejected the appellant's submission that that circumstance was sufficient to negate a lien.

For present purposes, the essential difference between a lien and a pledge is that a lien confers a mere right of retention, whereas as pledge confers an implied authority to sell.[7] In fact in many cases a bank has no need to rely upon a power of sale, because the existence of the lien does not relieve it from the duty to present bills, notes or cheques at maturity.[8] However, the lien appears to extend to securities which do not require to be presented, and in relation to such securities, if a bank is to be empowered to sell without an order of the court, it may need to rely upon, and it appears to have, an implied power of sale. Where the securities are not to be presented for payment, it is prudent to obtain at the time of deposit an express power of sale.

Absolute property is inconsistent with the right of a lienee or pledgee. If the banker becomes holder in his own right of negotiable securities coming into his possession as banker, his right of lien or pledge is gone.

(b) Securities subject to lien

(i) Paper securities

What class of securities may be the subject of lien is not entirely clear. The words used in *Brandao v Barnett*[9] are 'all securities'. In *Davis v Bowsher*,[10] Lord Kenyon CJ uses first the words 'all the securities', but afterwards says:

> '... wherever a banker has advanced money to another, he has a lien on all the paper securities which come into his hands for the amount of his general balance.'

Gross J uses the term 'paper securities'. In *Wylde v Radford*,[11] Kindersley V-C said that:

5 Per Cockburn CJ in *Goodwin v Robarts* (1875) LR 10 Exch 337 at 346, affd (1876) 1 App Cas 476, HL.
6 (1846) 12 Cl & Fin at 806.
7 *The Odessa* [1916] 1 AC 145 at 159, PC. See also *Donald v Suckling* (1866) LR 1 QB 585.
8 See p 498, post.
9 (1846) 12 Cl & Fin 787 at 808, per Lord Campbell.
10 (1794) 5 Term Rep 488, 101 ER 275.
11 (1863) 33 LJ Ch 51 at 53.

'The cases refer to a deposit of documents which are in their nature securities, but there is some ambiguity in the term "securities". Anything may of course be deposited, and deeds or plate, after they have been deposited, may be said to be a security; but what is intended is such securities as promissory notes, bills of exchange, exchequer bills, coupons, bonds of foreign governments, etc, and the courts have held that if such securities are deposited by a customer with his banker, and there is nothing to show the intention of such deposit one way or the other, the banker has, by custom, a lien thereon for the balance due from the customer.'

The class of securities covered by these definitions cannot, on the one hand, be limited to fully negotiable securities. In *Re United Service Co, Johnstone's Claim*,[12] share certificates; in *Misa v Currie*,[13] an order to pay money to a particular person; in *Jeffryes v Agra and Masterman's Bank*,[14] a species of deposit receipt, were all held subject to the banker's lien, though none of them was negotiable. In *Re Bowes, Earl of Strathmore v Vane*,[15] it would seem to have been assumed that the lien would attach to a policy of insurance. On the other hand, the general lien cannot be said to extend to all classes of documents, even though they might otherwise be utilised as security.

(ii) Documents of title to land

The nature of the 'securities' subject to the lien is further deducible from the condition that they must come to the banker's hands in his capacity as banker, in the course of banking business. It is part of a banker's business to advance money and any class of property may by proper means be made the subject of security. But, save in the case of specific deposit as security, or by way of equitable mortgage, in which cases lien becomes immaterial, it is difficult to conceive how such things as leases or conveyances should come to the banker's hands in the course of his business, though they might change character while in his hands so as to set up a lien or charge.

In *Wylde v Radford*,[16] a customer deposited with his bankers a deed of conveyance of two distinct properties, giving them at the same time a memorandum, charging one of the properties as security both for a specific sum and also for his general balance. The bankers later claimed a general lien over the other property. This claim was rejected, but on the basis of the construction of the memorandum rather than on the ground that the general lien does not extend to conveyances. The case is therefore of little assistance. As Buckley J said of *Wylde v Radford* in *Re London and Globe Finance Corpn*:[17]

'All that Kindersley V-C held was that, upon the true construction of the memorandum, the result of the transaction in that case was that property B was never intended to be charged at all; that the deed was deposited because it contained property A, and not because it contained property B; and that as regarded B there was no security given.'

Kindersley V-C is not to be taken as having held that the lien does extend to conveyances. The better view would seem to be that in the admittedly rare

12 (1870) 6 Ch App 212.
13 (1876) 1 App Cas 554, HL.
14 (1866) LR 2 Eq 674.
15 (1886) 33 Ch D 586.
16 (1863) 33 LJ Ch 51.
17 [1902] 2 Ch 416 at 420.

cases in which a banker is entitled to refuse to re-deliver deeds until the depositor's debt to him is repaid, it is because an equitable charge over the deeds has arisen simultaneously and as a consequence of an implied change of character in which the deeds are held. Normally, deeds of property come into the banker's possession either when handed over as security or with the request that they be held for safe custody; thus they cannot ordinarily be the subject of lien. If the customer subsequently borrows from the bank the latter might properly retain the deeds until the debt is paid, as the result of a new implied contract taking the deeds out of the category of safe custody and giving the banker a charge by way of deposit. This, however, is not strictly lien.

(iii) *Money and credit balances*

Notwithstanding that money paid into a bank account becomes the property of the banker to do with as he likes, there are many statements, some of high authority,[18] to the effect that money paid in is subject to the banker's lien. This misuse of language was finally laid to rest in *Halesowen Presswork and Assemblies Ltd v Westminster Bank Ltd,* where Buckley LJ,[19] in a passage which was approved by the House of Lords,[20] observed that no man can have a lien on his own property, and that the term 'securities' used in *Brandao v Barnett* does not extend to the banker's own indebtedness to the customer.

(c) Relevant liabilities

(i) *The customer's general balance*

The banker's lien is for the general balance owed by the customer.[1] The term 'general balance' refers to all sums presently due and payable by the customer, whether on loan or overdraft or other credit facility.[2]

(ii) *Future or contingent liabilities*

Save in the event of the customer's insolvency, the banker is not entitled to retain money standing on current account to meet contingent liabilities of the customer to him. It is true that in *Bolland v Bygrave,*[3] Abbott LCJ, sitting at Nisi Prius, appears to have thought that the banker's lien attached to securities of the customer when the banker had discounted or accepted bills for the accommodation of the customer. However, in *Jeffryes v Agra and Masterman's Bank,*[4] Sir W Page Wood V-C said:

---

18 See eg Lord Hatherley in *Misa v Currie* (1876) 1 App Cas 554 at 569. See also *Roxburghe v Cox* (1881) 17 Ch D 520, CA.
19 [1971] 1 QB 1 at 46, [1970] 3 All ER 473 at 487–488, and see also Lord Denning MR at, respectively, 32 and 477.
20 [1972] AC 785 at 802 (Viscount Dilhorne) and 810 (Lord Cross), [1972] 1 All ER 641 at 646, 653.
 1 *Brandao v Barnett* (1846) 12 Cl & Fin 787, 8 ER 1622, per Lord Campbell at 806 (citing Lord Kenyon in *Davis v Bowsher,* supra) and Lord Lyndhurst at 810.
 2 See *Re European Bank* (1872) 8 Ch App 41, where it was conceded that the lien extended to a loan account.
 3 (1825) Ry & M 271. See also *Re Keever* [1967] Ch 182 at 190, [1966] 3 All ER 631 at 634, where Ungoed Thomas J treated *Bolland v Bygrave* as authority that the lien extends to an overdraft not yet due for payment but constituting a contingent liability.
 4 (1866) LR 2 Eq 674.

'... they say, further, that there were very heavy liabilities outstanding, and that they would have retained, when they became due, these balances as against those outstanding bills. I apprehend they never could do that in any court of law, and of course there is no equity of the kind; you cannot retain a sum of money which is actually due against a sum of money which is only becoming due at a future time ... at all times when the bills became due, they would have been entitled to set off any moneys actually due from him to the bank, whatever the account should be. As to mere liabilities, it is equally clear that they could not set them off.'

The point was settled by *Bower v Foreign and Colonial Gas Co Ltd, Metropolitan Bank, Garnishees,*[5] in which the customer had a credit balance of £751. The bank had discounted bills not yet due, for £500. A garnishee order having been served on the bank, the bank claimed to retain £500 of the current account against the liability on the bills, alleging that they had a lien to that extent. The court held that they had not, the fact that they had discounted bills which were still running being no ground for an implied agreement for lien on the balance; indeed it would be contrary to the object of such advances. Although Grove J said there was a great difference between the case of securities, as in the authorities cited (which included *Bolland v Bygrave*), and a drawing account, it would not be safe to assume that in the modern law of banking there is any relevant distinction between the banker's lien and the banker's right of set-off in relation to future and contingent liabilities.

The distinction between a contingent liability, and an actual liability which remains to be quantified, can be a fine one. An illustration is *Baker v Lloyds Bank Ltd,*[6] where the defendant bank had discounted twelve bills of exchange on which its customer was contingently liable in various different capacities, but as regards most bills, as indorser. Before the bills fell due, the customer by deed assigned to the plaintiff as its trustee all its real and personal property on terms that dividends were to be paid to creditors on a bankruptcy basis, and expressly preserving creditors' liens. At the date of the assignment the bank held shares as security for a specific advance, which shares were realised shortly after the assignment leaving a surplus of £812. It was held that the bank could retain and set off the £812 against the customer's liability on the bills. Wright J held that both by the rules of bankruptcy *and common law,* the customer's contingent liability on the bills became an actual liability at the date of the assignment. The customer's declaration that it was insolvent and unable to meet its liabilities amounted to a repudiation of its ability to perform its undertaking that the bills which it had indorsed would be paid at maturity. Although the *quantum* of liability was not ascertainable until the maturity of the bills, there existed an *actual* liability which founded a right to retain the £812.[7]

---

5 (1874) 22 WR 740.
6 [1920] 2 KB 322.
7 Although Wright J does not expressly so state, it follows from his finding of an actual liability that on ascertainment of the amount due in respect of the bills, the bank could have effected a set-off by virtue of its banker's right of set-off, in addition to its right of set-off under the then bankruptcy rules.

(d) Matters excluding lien

(i) Express or implied agreement inconsistent with lien

The lien may be excluded by express or implied agreement inconsistent with such a right. There are two common situations in which an inconsistent agreement may be found to exist, namely the deposit of securities for safe custody, and the deposit of securities as cover for a specific advance.

The deposit of securities for safe custody is normally inconsistent with a right of lien. This was the position in *Brandao v Barnett*,[8] where exchequer bills were deposited with bankers and kept in a tin box of which the depositor kept the key. In those circumstances the bills could not be considered as having been deposited with the bankers *as bankers,* but as bailees.

However, safe custody does not always exclude lien.

A lien may arise in relation to securities held for safe custody. The possession of anything essential to collection, though not itself to be collected, would be covered by the collection to which it was essential. A body which had to be produced whenever interest was paid would be subject to the lien if the bankers were instructed to collect the interest. Where bonds are deposited with the banker in order that he might cut off and collect the coupons, the lien would probably attach to the bonds as well as the coupons; but not if the customer himself cut off the coupons as they became due and, as to these latter, only if they were handed to the banker for collection. If bonds redeemable at a fixed time or by drawings were deposited with the banker to be presented for payment at the due date, or in the event of their being drawn, the lien would attach. The case of debenture or stock certificates deposited with a bank which is to receive the interest for the customer seems doubtful. The possession of them would not seem to be essential or instrumental to the receipt of the interest, and would seem more consistent with mere safe custody until they should be required on transfer. In *Re United Service Co, Johnstone's Claim*[9] James LJ appears to have considered that certificates deposited in such circumstances would be subject to the lien. Sir Mackenzie Chalmers, in an opinion given in 1882, expresses doubt, but inclined to the view above expressed, as being the natural inference from the transaction.[10]

In *Akrokerri (Atlantic) Mines Ltd v Economic Bank*,[11] Bigham J uses words which might be taken to imply that collection is a special purpose inconsistent with lien. This is not so. Collection is essentially in the way of a banker's business, and his lien over documents in his hands for that purpose has been repeatedly recognised.[12] In the words of Lords Birkenhead LC, Buckmaster and Carson in *Sutters v Briggs*:[13]

'... if bankers are not holders of cheques for which they are agents for collection only, they derive no benefit from s 27, sub-s 3, as the subsection does not apply even where there is a lien, to a person who is not a holder.'

It has even been held that, in the absence of special notice, a clearing

---

8 (1846) 12 Cl & Fin 787, 8 ER 1622.
9 (1870) 6 Ch App 212.
10 See the Institute of Banker's *Questions on Banking Practice* (8th edn) no 1111.
11 [1904] 2 KB 465.
12 Cf *Misa v Currie* (1876) 1 App Cas 554 at 565, 569, 573.
13 [1922] 1 AC 1 at 18.

banker has a lien over bills remitted for collection by his correspondent in respect of a balance due from the correspondent, though the bills were the property of the latter's customer.[14]

Where securities deposited to cover a specific advance yield a surplus on realisation, it is a matter of intention whether the surplus is available to meet the customer's general balance. There are cases on either side of the line. In *Wilkinson v London and County Banking Co*,[15] it was assumed that a customer depositing securities as cover for specific advances was entitled to have them back on repayment of those advances independent of the state of account between him and the banker. Conversely in *Re London and Globe Finance Corpn*,[16] Buckley J held that securities deposited as cover for specific advances, but after discharge thereof left in the banker's hands, became liable to the general lien. Similarly in *Baker v Lloyds Bank Ltd*, supra, surplus proceeds of sale of shares deposited as cover for an advance were held to be available to discharge the customer's general balance. The same conclusion was reached in *Jones v Peppercorne*,[17] a case involving the stockbroker's general lien.

A somewhat strange set of circumstances arose in *London and County Banking Co v Ratcliffe*.[18] The owner of land gave to the bank an equitable mortgage by deposit of deeds to secure the general balance of his account. The memorandum of deposit declared that the security should not be satisfied by the payment or liquidation of any sums to be thereafter from time to time due on the balance of the account, but should extend to cover all future sums which should at any time be or become due. This memorandum was cancelled subsequently and replaced by another in much the same terms, but the Lord Chancellor considered the case as if this had not taken place. The borrower thereafter sold one of the properties subject to and with notice of the mortgage, the purchaser paying in instalments. The bank continued to make advances after the purchaser had paid in full, but did not advise the purchaser. The conveyance to the borrower of the property he sold could not be given to the purchaser as it covered other properties also. It was held, on the principle of *Hopkinson v Rolt*,[19] that the bank had no charge for the further advances, that the initial advance had been discharged by the operation of the rule in *Clayton's Case*,[20] and that the purchaser was not bound to ask if further advances had been made. On the same basis the bank would presumably have had no lien either.

In *Re Bowes, Earl of Strathmore v Vane*,[1] a policy of life assurance was deposited with a bank with a memorandum stating it to be deposited as security for all moneys then or thereafter due on current account or otherwise, not exceeding in the whole at any one time the sum of £4,000. The customer died indebted to the bank in more than £4,000. North J held that the special agreement was inconsistent with a general lien for the balance of £1,000. This case and *Jones v Peppercorne* were, in *Re London and Globe Finance Corpn*,[2]

---

14 *Johnson v Robarts* (1875) 10 Ch App 505; *Re Dilworth, ex p Armistead* (1828) 2 Gl & J 371.
15 (1884) 1 TLR 63, HL.
16 [1902] 2 Ch 416.
17 (1858) John 430.
18 (1881) 6 App Cas 722.
19 (1861) 9 HL Cas 514.
20 (1816) 1 Mer 529.
 1 (1886) 33 Ch D 586.
 2 [1902] 2 Ch 416.

treated as establishing the law. The judgment of Buckley J in the latter case was thus based on the ground that the securities, being consciously left in the banker's hands after satisfaction of the specific advances, could be regarded as having come into his hands anew in the way of business or as impliedly repledged or redeposited. It might perhaps, be put another way: that where securities have been charged for an advance which is repaid and the securities left with the banker, he will have a lien on them for any other advance allowed subsequently or existing at the time, unless this is expressly excluded either by the original memorandum of charge if there was one or by some other agreement or arrangement such as that they had been specifically 'appropriated' to the advance, or that they were henceforth to be held for safe custody. This would be in accord with *Brandao v Barnett*.[3] It would further seem that where securities are jointly deposited to cover a joint liability, one of the depositors, on paying his share of the liability, is entitled to the return of a proportionate share of the securities.[4] This point is, however, usually covered by the memorandum or deed charging the securities.

Where security other than land has been given to cover specified indebtedness, and its realisation brings in more than enough to satisfy that indebtedness, and the banker is not affected with notice of any assignment of the depositor's remaining rights or any further charge on the security, he must, of course, pay over the surplus to the debtor or hold it at his disposal. If, however, the depositor is further indebted to the banker, say on general account, the banker can retain the surplus, or a sufficient part thereof, to cover such further indebtedness, by virtue either of his general lien or the right of set-off.[5]

It may at first sight seem strange that immunities attaching to the security itself should not extend to what is only a converted part thereof, but the authorities are clear.[6] In *Re Bowes, Earl of Strathmore v Vane*,[7] North J while holding that the bank had no general lien on the security itself, said that if the memorandum had given a power of sale, or if such power had been obtained from the court, the surplus proceeds would probably have been retainable by the bank by way of set-off for its further claim against the customer's estate. The explanation may be that the express or implied power of sale is an incorporated or inherent incident of the deposit, and its exercise terminates any fiduciary relation that may have existed with regard to the security itself.

(ii)   Securities belonging to a third party

The lien is excluded if, to the knowledge of the banker at the time of deposit, the securities in question belong to a third party.[8] But the lien is not excluded if the bank receives the securities in good faith and without knowledge that

---

3 (1846) 12 Cl & Fin 787.
4 *Coats v Union Bank of Scotland* (1928) SC 711.
5 See however, *London and County Banking Co Ltd v Ratcliffe* (1881) 6 App Cas 722.
6 *Jones v Peppercorne* (1858) John 430; *Re London and Globe Finance Corpn* [1902] 2 Ch 416 (recognising *Jones v Peppercorne*), in which it was stated as settled that brokers and bankers have a general lien on securities in their hands, as between themselves and the customer, for the balance due. The loan by brokers had been repaid, but the customer subsequently became liable for losses.
7 (1886) 33 Ch D 586.
8 [1909] 2 Ch 226, CA.

they in fact belong to a third party. This is illustrated by *Brandao v Barnett*[9] and *Jones v Peppercorne*.[10]

(iii) Notice of charge

A banker cannot rely on his banker's lien over property which was his customer's property when it first came into the banker's hands, but which the banker knows to have been subsequently assigned by the customer to a third party to the full extent of the customer's beneficial interest therein, if the purpose of relying on the lien is to reimburse the banker in respect of advances made by him to the customer after notice of the assignment.[11]

2 BANKER'S RIGHT OF SET-OFF

(a) Introduction

(i) Relationship between lien and set-off

It has already been noted that the inaccurate use of the term 'lien' to describe the banker's right over money paid into, and credit balances on, a customer's account was deprecated in the *Halesowen* case.[12] The judicially approved expressions are the banker's right of set-off or the banker's right to combine accounts, there being no difference between these two expressions.

It was rightly observed by Roskill J at first instance in the Halesowen case[13] that:

'... what is sometimes called the right of set-off and sometimes the right of combination or of consolidation of accounts is but the manifestation of or a right analogous to the exercise of the banker's right of lien, a right which is of general application and not in principle (apart from special agreement whether express or implied) limited to current or other similar accounts.'

In the House of Lords, Lord Cross observed that as a matter of history the recognition by the courts of the right of a banker to treat several accounts as one may have been influenced by their earlier recognition of the banker's lien.[14] The close connection between lien and set-off can be seen in the example of a cheque paid in for collection in circumstances where the customer's general balance is in debit. The bank has a lien over the cheque, but is not relieved of its duty to present the cheque for payment. It is submitted that the bank does not lose its lien by parting with the cheque for the purpose of presenting it for payment; the instrument is still in the bank's constructive possession until it is paid or, if dishonoured, returned to its actual possession. The lien, it would seem, must continue for that time. If the instrument is paid, and the proceeds credited to an account in credit, there is substituted for the lien a right of set-off.

There may be this difference between the scope of lien and set-off, that the lien arises if the customer is indebted on the general balance whether or not

9 (1846) 12 Cl & Fin 787, 8 ER 1622.
10 (1858) John 430.
11 Per Slade J in *Siebe Gorman & Co Ltd v Barclays Bank Ltd* [1979] 2 Lloyd's Rep 142 at 166.
12 See p 496, supra.
13 [1971] 1 QB 1 at 19E, [1970] 1 All ER 33 at 47g.
14 [1972] AC 785 at 810G, [1972] 1 All ER 641 at 653j.

there is an agreement to keep accounts separate, but if there is such agreement and the proceeds are paid into an account in credit, the banker cannot effect a set-off. This points to the distinction discussed immediately below between set-off and appropriation.

(ii) *Distinction between set-off and appropriation*

In the above example, the bank may wish to appropriate the proceeds of the cheque to the account in *debit* rather than to the account in *credit,* since this eliminates the need for a subsequent set-off by which the proceeds of the cheque are applied in reduction or extinction of the debt owed by the customer. The right of appropriation is generally that of the customer, and the payment in of a cheque for the credit of a specified account is prima facie an exercise of that right. It may be, however, that the customer's right of appropriation is displaced in favour of the bank's rights as holder for value of the cheque to the extent of its lien (s 27(3) of the Bills of Exchange Act 1882). If the banker has the right to exercise his lien, the customer's right of appropriation must surely have gone.

Nor does the existence of an agreement to keep accounts separate seem to bar appropriation by the bank. This must surely be the case where the banker is dealing with the property in the cheque in his own right, unless the agreement amounts to an undertaking by the banker not to exercise his right of set-off, and more, to forgo his right of lien.

(iii) *Distinction between set-off and accounting*

In the *Halesowen* case, Buckley LJ in the Court of Appeal,[15] drew a distinction between a set-off situation, which postulates mutual but independent obligations between the two parties, and an accounting situation, in which the existence and amount of the one party's liability to the other can only be ascertained by discovering the ultimate balance of their mutual dealings. The distinction is potentially important in any situation where rights of set-off are in dispute, in particular in the problem areas of set-off against assignees and set-off in insolvency. Buckley LJ gave as examples of accounting situations *Garnett v McKewan,*[16] *Re European Bank,*[17] *T & H Greenwood Teale v William Williams, Brown & Co,*[18] and *Mutton v Peat.*[19] He added that these authorities demonstrate that where there is a running account between the parties which in other respects is governed by the accounting principle, a particular transaction or series of transactions can by agreement be segregated from the other dealings between the parties so as to give rise to a separate indebtedness which is not to be taken into account in arriving at the balance on the general running account between them. If the indebtedness on the running account is one way and that in respect of the segregated dealings is the other way, the one indebtedness may be capable of being set off against the other, but the latter cannot be taken into account in ascertaining the amount of the former.

15 [1971] 1 QB 1 at 46E, [1970] 3 All ER 473 at 488b, cited with approval by Millett J in *Re Charge Card Services Ltd* [1987] Ch 150 at 173–174, [1986] 3 All ER 289 at 307.
16 (1872) LR 8 Exch 10.
17 (1872) 8 Ch App 41.
18 (1894) 11 TLR 56.
19 [1900] 2 Ch 79, CA.

Whether or not the authorities cited by Buckley LJ are truly examples of an accounting situation, it must be the case that certain bank accounts fall outside the accounting principle, not by agreement, but because their nature is such as to create obligations which are independent of those arising on current and loan accounts. This would probably be true of accounts maintained to record profits and losses on foreign exchange dealings, or to record cash deposits placed as cover for liabilities undertaken by the bank to third parties. The availability of such accounts for combination is uncertain, but on any common sense view the amounts due thereon are part of the general balance between banker and customer, and therefore, it is submitted, they ought to be available for combination.

(b) Extent of the banker's right of set-off

(i) Indebtedness available for set-off

In the absence of agreement, a bank cannot combine a debt presently due to the customer with a debt payable by the customer to the bank at a future date, still less with a contingent liability of the customer. Nor may the bank achieve the same result by retaining money presently payable to the customer so as to combine accounts at a future date. The law is as stated by Sir Page Wood V-C in *Jeffryes v Agra and Masterman's Bank*,[20] that 'you cannot retain a sum of money which is actually due against a sum of money which is only becoming due at a future time.'

(ii) Combination of two current accounts

The basic rule is that a bank may combine two current accounts at any time without notice to the customer, even though the accounts be maintained at different branches. It was so held in *Garnett v McKewan*,[1] which was approved by the Privy Council in *Prince v Oriental Bank Corpn*.[2] In *Garnett v McKewan* Kelly CB said:[3]

'In general it might be proper or considerate to give notice to that effect, but there is no legal obligation on the bankers to do so, arising either from express contract or the course of dealing between the parties. The customer must be taken to know the state of each account and if the balance on the whole is against him or does not equal the cheques he draws, he has no right to expect more cheques to be cashed.'

The rule has been affirmed more recently in the *Halesowen* case. In the Court of Appeal, Lord Denning posed the question whether a banker has a right to combine two accounts so that he can set off the debit against the credit and be liable only for the balance, and gave the following answer:[4]

'The answer to this question is: Yes, the banker has a right to combine the two

---

20 (1866) LR 2 Eq 674. A fuller citation from the judgment is set out at p 497, supra. See also *Bower v Foreign and Colonial Gas Co Ltd* (1874) 22 WR 740, considered in the text immediately following the citation from *Jeffryes v Agra and Masterman's Bank* at p 497.
1 (1872) LR 8 Exch 10.
2 (1878) 3 App Cas 325 at 333.
3 At p 13.
4 [1971] 1 QB 1 at 34, [1970] 3 All ER 473 at 477; revsd, without affecting this point, sub nom *National Westminster Bank v Halesowen Presswork and Assemblies Ltd* [1972] AC 785, [1972] 1 All ER 641, HL.

accounts whenever he pleases, and to set-off one against the other, unless he has made some agreement, express or implied, to keep them separate. This principle was stated and applied in two cases decided on the same day – November 8, 1872. One was *In re European Bank, Agra Bank Claim* (1872) 8 Ch App 41 in the Court of Appeal in Chancery. The other was *Garnett v McKewan* (1872) LR 8 Exch 10 in the Court of Exchequer. It has been applied several times since, such as *T & H Greenwood Teale v William Williams, Brown & Co* (1894) 11 TLR 56 and *In re Keever (A Bankrupt)* [1967] Ch 182.'

Lord Denning went on to disapprove a dictum of Swift J in *W P Greenhalgh & Sons v Union Bank of Manchester*[5] that a banker may not combine one account with another without the customer's consent; in the House of Lords, Lords, Lord Kilbrandon agreed with this criticism.[6]

A customer who maintains two current accounts has, in the absence of agreement, no corresponding right to draw a cheque on one on which the balance is insufficient to meet it and expect the cheque to be paid if the combined balance is sufficient.[7] But the customer does have a right to call on his bank to combine two accounts unless there is some agreement to the contrary.[8] If the banker customer relationship remains in existence, the customer's right to require a combination is self-evident. The instruction is simply to transfer a credit balance on one account to another account in debit. The existence of the right after the determination of the relationship is less obvious, but is illustrated by *Mutton v Peat*.[9] The facts were that stockbrokers deposited with their bankers securities which were clients' property. The deposit was made without authority, but the bankers did not know that the securities belonged to third parties, and therefore they had a valid security.[10] The stockbrokers maintained two accounts, a current account and a loan account. There was no agreement at the time of deposit that the securities were placed as cover only for one account, and therefore they stood as security for the general balance on both accounts. It was held that in dealing with the proceeds of the securities, the bankers were bound to combine the accounts so as to ascertain the general balance, and were not entitled to disregard the credit balance on the current account. Although *Mutton v Peat* turned on the construction of a particular agreement, the reasoning is applicable whenever securities are held (whether by lien or otherwise) to secure a general balance on two or more accounts.

(iii) *Combination of current account and loan account*

The leading authority on the combination of a current account and a loan account is the decision of the Court of Appeal in *Bradford Old Bank Ltd v*

5 [1924] 2 KB 153 at 164.
6 [1972] AC 785 at 819, [1972] 1 All ER 641 at 661.
7 *Direct Acceptance Corpn Ltd v Bank of New South Wales* (1968) 88 WN NSW 498, per Macfarlan J.
8 *Mutton v Peat* [1900] 2 Ch 79, CA; *Halesowen Presswork & Assemblies Ltd v Westminster Bank Ltd* [1971] 1 QB 1 at 34E, [1970] 3 All ER 473 at 477h, per Lord Denning MR; revsd on appeal [1972] AC 785, [1972] 1 All ER 641 without affecting this point.
9 [1900] 2 Ch 79, CA.
10 This accords with the position where a lien is asserted over securities which do not belong to the customer – see p 500, ante.

Sutcliffe,[11] the effect of which was summarised by Lord Cross in the *Halesowen* case:[12]

'If a banker permits his customer to have two accounts, one – sometimes called a "loan account" – which records the indebtedness of the customer to the bank in respect of advances made to him and the other a current account which the customer keeps in credit and uses for the purpose of his trade or business or ordinary expenditure, then, unless the bank makes it clear to the customer that it is retaining the right at any moment to apply the credit balance on the current account in reduction of the debt on the loan account, it will be an implied term of the arrangement that the bank will not, so long as it lasts, consolidate the two accounts. As Scrutton LJ pointed out in *Bradford Old Bank Ltd v Sutcliffe* [1918] 2 KB 833, 847, unless such a term is implied no customer could feel any security in drawing a cheque on his current account if he had a loan account greater than the credit balance on his current account.'

This dictum of Scrutton LJ was applied in *Re E J Morel (1934) Ltd*[13] in which Buckley J held that *Garnett v McKewan* was applicable only where the accounts were current accounts, that it did not apply where one of the accounts was a loan account. In this latter respect he thought that a current account which had been frozen and was no longer capable of being operated in the ordinary way as a current account partook of the nature of a loan account.

Where there exists an implied term which precludes combination of accounts, an issue may arise as to the circumstances in which the term ceases to be operative. Such an issue arose in the *Halesowen* case.[14] The facts were that in February 1968 the respondent company's loan (no 1) account with the appellant bank was overdrawn by £11,339. On 4 April, it was orally agreed between the company and the bank that the bank should freeze that account and that the company should open a trading account (no 2 account) to be maintained strictly in credit. The bank agreed that the arrangement should last for a period of four months 'in the absence of materially changed circumstances'. On 20 May 1968 pursuant to the Companies Act 1948, s 293, the company gave notice to the bank of a meeting of creditors on 12 June to consider a winding-up resolution. The bank, however, did not terminate the agreement and dealings on the no 2 account continued. On the morning of 12 June a cheque for £8,611 drawn in favour of the company, was paid into the no 2 account. That afternoon it was resolved at the creditors' meeting that the company be voluntarily wound-up. The company's liquidator then claimed the credit balance on the no 2 account. The bank contended that it was entitled to set off the balance on the no 2 account against the company's indebtedness to the bank on the no 1 account.

The liquidator's claim was based on the grounds (1) that the proceeds of the cheque were collected after the commencement of winding-up; and (2) that the parties had agreed that the bank would not consolidate the two accounts.

All three judges of the Court of Appeal were of opinion that the bank could have given notice to determine when the company called a meeting of

11 [1918] 2 KB 833, CA.
12 [1972] AC 785 at 809, [1972] 1 All ER 641 at 652–653.
13 [1962] Ch 21, [1961] 1 All ER 796.
14 [1972] AC 785, [1972] 1 All ER 641, HL.

its creditors, in which case a right of set-off would have arisen. Winn LJ said that he would not find it easy to say what period of notice would be required, which suggests that he thought time was necessary to allow the company to adjust itself to the changed conditions. Further, he did not think that the agreement was determinable without notice.[15] Lord Denning MR[16] appeared to be of the same view, for he said that if the bank had given notice to end the agreement, 'the company would no longer have been bound to pay in their trading cheques to the no 2 account' with the Westminster, but would probably have paid them into some other bank. Buckley LJ[17] was 'inclined to think that a notice taking immediate effect might have sufficed'.

In the House of Lords, Lord Cross dealt with the question of notice in the following terms:[18]

> 'I cannot agree ... that any period of notice was necessary for on receipt of such notice the company could have defeated the object with which it was given by at once drawing out the credit balance on the account. The choice as I see it lies between a notice taking immediate effect and no notice at all.'

He inclined to the view favoured by Buckley LJ that the bank could not consolidate the accounts on a material change of circumstances in the four months' period without notifying the company that it was doing so and also being subject to a liability to honour any cheques drawn up to the limit of the credit balance before the company received the notification.

In the Court of Appeal, the chief point appeared to be whether there was mutuality within the meaning of s 31 of the Bankruptcy Act 1914; Roskill J had not dealt with the point at first instance. Only Buckley LJ held that the section applied and his view was supported by the four members of the House of Lords. The latter's judgment included that the agreement to keep the accounts separate lasted only so long as the relationship of banker and customer continued, that this came to an end on the passing of the winding-up resolution, and that then the bank was entitled to combine.

The agreement in the instant case was brought to an end by the notice of the meeting to wind-up; why, then, was notice necessary to give the bank the right to set-off? This question may have been answered in the House of Lords when Lord Cross expressed the view that no period of notice was necessary.

The principles governing combination of a loan account and a current account can perhaps be summarised as follows:

1 An arrangement by which a bank permits its customer to have two accounts, one a loan account and the other a current account, normally contains an implied term that so long as the arrangement lasts, the bank will not combine the two accounts.

2 An agreement to keep two accounts separate will normally be operative only for so long as the accounts are 'alive' (the term used in *British Guiana*

---

15 [1971] 1 QB 1 at 38, [1970] 3 All ER 473 at 481. Winn LJ cited *Buckingham & Co v London and Midland Bank Ltd* (1895) 12 TLR 70, where the questions for the jury were framed by reference to the course of dealing between the plaintiff and his bank, and the jury found that the plaintiff was entitled to reasonable notice that the course of dealing would be discontinued.

16 Ibid, at, respectively, 35 and 478–479.

17 Ibid, at, respectively, 38 and 481.

18 [1972] AC 785 at 810, [1972] 1 All ER 641 at 653.

Bank Ltd v Official Receiver[19]), that is, while the relation of banker and customer continues in existence, but not once the relationship has been determined by death, insanity, liquidation, bankruptcy or for any other reason.[20]

3 It is a question of intention whether an agreement to keep accounts separate is determinable by notice, and if so whether notice may be given with immediate effect.

4 Where notice is required, the bank is prima facie subject to a liability to honour any cheques drawn up to the limit of the credit balance before the customer receives notification, and during any period of notice.

(iv) Combination on insolvency

In the *Halesowen* case, the customer went into creditors' voluntary winding up on 12 June 1968. The bank combined the company's two accounts on (at the earliest) 14 June 1968. The House of Lords held that the bank had a right of set-off on two independent grounds, namely (1) s 31 of the Bankruptcy Act 1914, which applied by virtue of s 317 of the Companies Act 1948, and (2) the banker's right of set-off. That these grounds were treated as independent is made clear in the speeches of Viscount Dilhorne[1] and Lord Cross:[2]

'The appellants also contended that, quite apart from section 31, they were entitled to set off one account against the other ... In my opinion the agreement [not to combine] came to an end when the winding-up resolution was passed. Could the bank then, the agreement being at an end, combine the two accounts? For reasons very clearly stated by Roskill J [1971] 1 QB 1, 23–25, in my opinion the answer is, "Yes".'
(per Viscount Dilhorne)

'... the bank has chosen to insist on its legal rights and I think that Roskill J was right in holding that it was entitled to consolidate the accounts, quite apart from the "set-off" provisions in section 31 of the Bankruptcy Act 1914.'
(per Lord Cross)

The independence of the grounds is also implicit in Lord Kilbrandon's formulation of the main issue as being whether as a matter of construction the agreement between the bank and the company was intended to, and did, provide that in the event of the company's winding up, the bank was to be deprived of the power, which in the absence of agreement it would have had, to combine the no 1 and no 2 accounts.[3]

The legal significance of there being independent grounds for set-off is much reduced by the further ruling in *Halesowen* that the statutory provisions for set-off in insolvency are mandatory, and parties may not contract out of them. It is difficult to postulate any cross-claims which would fall outside the statutory provisions, but within the banker's right of set-off. Nevertheless in

19 (1911) 27 TLR 454, PC, cited in *Halesowen* by Viscount Dilhorne, Lord Cross and Lord Kilbrandon, [1972] AC 785 at 807D, 811B and 820E, [1972] 1 All ER 641 at 651a, 654c and 662f.

20 See also *Halesowen* at first instance, [1971] 1 QB 1 at 24G, where Roskill J followed *Re Keever* [1967] Ch 182, [1966] 3 All ER 631, and declined to follow *Re E J Morel (1934) Ltd* [1962] Ch 21, [1961] 1 All ER 796. In the House of Lords, Viscount Dilhorne approved the reasoning of Roskill J at [1971] 1 QB 1 at 23–25: see [1972] AC 785 at 807E, [1972] 1 All ER 641 at 651b.

1 [1972] AC 785 at 807, [1972] 1 All ER 641 at 650–651.

2 Ibid at, respectively, 811 and 654.

3 Ibid at, respectively, 820 and 662.

practice, a bank may seek immediate confirmation that an exercise in an insolvency of its banker's right of set-off is effective, and in such a case the above-cited statements from *Halesowen* may be of importance.

(v) Combination of accounts maintained in different jurisdictions

Where accounts are maintained in different jurisdictions, it is first necessary to consider whether the accounts are governed by different contracts, or by one contract governed by different proper laws, or by one contract governed by one (and if so, which) proper law.[4] Even if both the accounts are governed by one contract with English law as its only proper law, there are two matters which make it uncertain whether an English court would uphold a combination of the accounts. First, this aspect of the right of set-off has not yet been judicially recognised, and may therefore have to be proved by evidence of usage. Secondly, the fact of the accounts being in different jurisdictions would provide a ready basis for a finding of an implied agreement not to combine. The prudent course for a bank seeking an entitlement to combine accounts maintained in different jurisdictions is to obtain the customer's express agreement at the time of opening the accounts.

(vi) Mode of exercise

Although the exercise of the banker's right of set-off will normally be evidenced by physical combination, ie by debiting one account and crediting another, it appears that a set-off may be effective without any such overt act. In the *Halesowen* case, the evidence disclosed that there had been no physical combination of the no 1 and the no 2 accounts; the bank simply claimed to prove in the customer's liquidation for the general balance on the accounts. At first instance, Roskill J held that the absence of physical combination did not defeat the bank's claim:[5]

'... I cannot think that the mechanics by which a bank seeks to exercise its right of lien are relevant, unless, of course, the bank by its action precludes itself from thereafter asserting that right. In the present case the bank acted promptly to assert its right vis-à-vis the liquidator. If it possessed that right, that right was asserted properly and timeously; if it did not possess that right then it had no right to assert. But the existence or absence of the right cannot, in a case such as the present, in my judgment turn upon the actual form in which the entries in the bank's books were made or upon the absence from those books of any physical consolidation or combination.'

This ruling appears not to have been challenged on appeal.

(c) Matters inconsistent with set-off

(i) Express or implied agreement excluding set-off

The right of set-off may be excluded by express or implied agreement. This point has already been discussed in considering combination of a current account and a loan account. Examples of agreements excluding set-off are *Bradford Old Bank Ltd v Sutcliffe*,[6] *W P Greenhalgh & Sons v Union Bank of*

4 As to the proper law of the contract, see ch 10, ante.
5 [1971] 1 QB 1 at 19F, [1970] 1 All ER 33 at 48b.
6 [1918] 2 KB 833, CA.

Manchester,[7] *Re E J Morel (1934) Ltd,*[8] *Re Keever*[9] and the *Halesowen* case.[10] As Roskill J observed at first instance in the *Halesowen* case,[11] the question to be asked in every case is 'what was the agreement?' and the ascertainment of the answer will involve also answering of the question 'what was the *duration* of the agreement?'. In both *Re Keever* and in the *Halesowen* case the agreement was held not to have been operative at the date of combination.

The facts of the *Halesowen* case have been described above. In *Re Keever,* a customer (Keever) maintained a current account and a loan account with the Midland Bank. A receiving order against Keever was made on 16 November 1962, pursuant to a petition presented on 12 October; on 15 November, Keever's current account was overdrawn some £350 and she was indebted to the bank on loan account in the sum of £1,000. On that same day she paid in for collection and credit to her account a cheque for £3,000; it was credited immediately. The following day, the day of the receiving order, the cheque was cleared. The question for decision was whether the bank was entitled to set-off the £3,000 against Keever's indebtedness. The bank argued that on 15 November, it had a lien on the cheque and that that lien constituted a 'contract dealing or transaction by or with the bankrupt for valuable consideration' within the meaning of s 45 of the Bankruptcy Act 1914. Ungoed-Thomas J agreed, and held that s 27 of the Bills of Exchange Act 1882 established that the lien was for valuable consideration within s 45 of the Bankruptcy Act 1914 and, therefore, that the bank were secured creditors. He further held that the bank were holders in due course of the cheque.

(ii) Accounts in different right

The right to combine does not exist where the accounts are not held in the same right, as where one is a trust account.[12] Knowledge of the fiduciary nature of an account, however acquired, will preclude the banker from utilising the account for his own benefit, as by combining it with the customer's overdrawn private account or asserting a lien over it for the customer's personal liabilities. Where, however, the customer has two accounts in his own name, one a purely private one, the other suggesting that someone else may have a proprietary interest in it, eg 'AB account CD' or 'AB re CD', it would seem that a balance on the purely private account might be utilised to cover a debit on the other.[13]

The above principle precludes set-off of monies which to the knowledge of the bank are impressed with a trust by reason of having been paid for a specific purpose.[14]

---

7 [1924] 2 KB 153. Note the criticism of Swift J's dictum at p 164 referred to at p 504, supra.
8 [1962] Ch 21, [1961] 1 All ER 796. Note that at first instance in *Halesowen* [1971] 1 QB 1 at 24, [1970] 1 All ER 33 at 52, Roskill J declined to follow *Re E J Morel (1934) Ltd* on the question of the effect of bankruptcy on an agreement not to combine, preferring instead to follow the conflicting decision in *Re Keever,* infra.
9 [1967] Ch 182, [1966] 3 All ER 631.
10 [1972] AC 785, [1972] 1 All ER 641, HL.
11 [1971] 1 QB 1 at 21B, [1970] 1 All ER 33 at 49c.
12 *Re Gross, ex p Kingston* (1871) 6 Ch App 632; see also *Union Bank of Australia Ltd v Murray-Aynsley* [1898] AC 693, PC; *Bank of New South Wales v Goulburn Valley Butter Co Pty Ltd* [1902] AC 543, PC. As to the circumstances in which a banker will be held to have had notice of the fiduciary nature of an account, see ch 9, ante.
13 Cf *Coutts & Co v Irish Exhibition in London* (1891) 7 TLR 313.
14 As to monies paid for a special purpose, see ch 11, ante. For an example of a set-off which

Similarly there is no right of set-off in respect of monies which would otherwise be recoverable by a third party as monies paid to the bank's customer under a mistake of fact.[15]

(iii) Accounts maintained in different currencies

It has not yet been judicially determined that the banker's right of set-off entitles a bank to set off accounts maintained (within the jurisdiction) in different currencies. This is therefore an aspect of the right which, if disputed, would require to be proved by evidence of usage. It is thought that such a usage may be difficult to prove because banks which foresee a requirement to combine accounts in different currencies usually take the obvious precaution of requiring the customer to execute a letter of set-off making the right so to combine a matter of express agreement.

It would seem, however, that the concept of the general balance owed by a customer ought as a matter of common sense to bring in current and deposit accounts maintained in foreign currencies. No doubt the existence of accounts maintained in foreign currencies may be evidence of an implied agreement not to combine but, as explained above, this is not the end of the matter; it leads to the further issue of the length of time for which such agreement is intended to operate. The fact that an account is maintained in a foreign currency is not of itself a convincing ground for holding that the account cannot be combined with another account (whether maintained in sterling, or in the same or a different foreign currency) on the termination of the banker customer relationship or the prior determination of any implied agreement not to combine.

3   RIGHTS OF SET-OFF UNDER THE GENERAL LAW

In this section, consideration is given to certain aspects of the general law of set-off which have particular relevance in the context of banking.[16]

Rights of set-off under English law fall into two broad categories: (1) rights of set-off before insolvency, and (2) rights of set-off after insolvency. This categorisation derives from the fact that the onset of insolvency triggers statutory set-off provisions which are both mandatory and materially different from pre-insolvency rights of set-off. Where rights of set-off are relied upon as a form of protection, it is in the context of insolvency that such rights are most likely to be needed. But this does not mean that pre-insolvency rights are unimportant. There are two situations bordering on insolvency, namely receivership and administration, where pre-insolvency rights continue to apply. Furthermore, pre-insolvency rights of set-off confer important

---

was disallowed on this ground, see *Barclays Bank Ltd v Quistclose Investments Ltd* [1970] AC 567, [1968] 3 All ER 651.

15 See *Admiralty Comrs v National Provincial and Union Bank of England Ltd* (1922) 127 LT 452, where Sargant J rejected the defendant bank's contention that it had incurred an obligation to its customer to honour cheques to the amount of the payment in, which obligation absolved it from any liability to repay.

16 For an exhaustive treatment of the law of set-off, see Wood *English and International Set-off* (1st edn, 1989). For an analysis of set-off in the context of specific banking transactions, including swaps, see the publication of the International Bar Association's Section of Business Law: *Using Rights of Set-off as Security: A Comparative Survey* edited by Francis Neate (1990).

protection in such pre-insolvency situations as assignment, attachment and Mareva orders.

(a) Rights of set-off before insolvency

(i) Legal set-off

Legal set-off is the set-off of mutual cross-debts which are due and payable in the same right at the commencement of an action. The description 'legal set-off' derives from the statutory origin of this form of set-off in the Statutes of Set-Off 1729 and 1735 (now repealed). Legal set-off is, of course, available to banks, but this form of set-off has no special application in the law of banking.

(ii) Equitable set-off

Equitable set-off refers to any form of set-off which before 1873 (the date of fusion of the systems of law and equity) was available in a court of equity but not in a court of law. Equity widened rights of set-off at law in two principal respects:

1 Equity came to permit a set-off of any cross-claim which impeaches the legal demand,[17] including cross-claims for unliquidated damages. Re-stated in modern terms, equity will permit set-off of mutual cross-claims which arise out of the same contract or out of closely connected contracts.[18]
2 Equity developed rules of set-off to govern tri-partite relationships such as exist between (a) trustee, beneficiary and third party, and (b) assignor, assignee and debtor.

The application of equitable set-off in the context of bank accounts has recently been considered by the Court of Appeal in *Bhogal v Punjab National Bank*[19] and *Uttamchandani v Central Bank of India*.[20] In the *Bhogal* case, the Court of Appeal heard appeals in two actions in both of which the defendant bank claimed to set-off in equity a credit balance on an account in the name of one customer with a debit balance on an account in the name of another customer. The bank alleged that the customers were nominees of a third party, and in one action (the *Basna* action) this allegation was held to raise an arguable issue of fact, whilst in the other (the *Bhogal* action), the two judge Court of Appeal (Dillon and Bingham LJJ) were divided on whether the evidence disclosed any such arguable issue of fact. However, in both actions the bank's appeal against summary judgment was dismissed on the ground that equitable set-off was not available. The ratio of the decision, as was stated by Lloyd LJ in the *Uttamchandani* case, is that a bank is not entitled to refuse payment of money deposited with it on the basis merely of an arguable case that some other debtor of the bank has an equitable interest in the money. The judgments of Dillon and Bingham LJJ both cite the

17 See *Rawson v Samuel* (1841) Cr & Ph 161, 41 ER 451.
18 See *Hanak v Green* [1958] 2 QB 9, [1958] 2 All ER 141, CA; *Federal Commerce & Navigation Co Ltd v Molena Alpha Inc* [1978] QB 927 at 974–975, [1978] 3 All ER 1066 at 1078b, CA, per Lord Denning MR, affd on appeal on different grounds [1979] AC 757, [1978] 1 All ER 307, HL; *BICC Plc v Burndy Corpn* [1985] Ch 232, [1985] 1 All ER 417, CA.
19 [1988] 2 All ER 296, CA.
20 (1989) 133 Sol Jo 262, CA.

512   *Lien and set-off*

following passage from the judgment of Scott J at first instance in the *Basna* action:

'The commercial banking commitment that a bank enters with a person who deposits money with it is just as needful of immediate performance as are a bank's obligations under a letter of credit or bank guarantee. I think it would be lamentable if a bank were able to defeat a claim by a person who had deposited money on such grounds as the bank is asserting in the present case. It is possible that this action will come to trial in some two to three years' time and that the bank will fail to make good the arguable case that it has set out before me. It would have succeeded in postponing for that considerable period its obligation to repay a customer who had made a simple deposit of money with it. That seems to me to be totally contrary to the basis on which banks invite and get money deposited with them. I hold that a bank is not entitled to refuse repayment of money deposited with it on the basis merely of an arguable case that some other debtor of the bank has an equitable interest in the money.'

Dillon LJ added the following observations on the law:[1]

'In the banking field there are clear rules of law. (1) It is the duty of the banker to pay within a reasonable time of presentment all cheques drawn by the customer in accordance with the mandate given to the banker provided that the banker has money in his hands belonging to the customer. As Lord Cairns LC stated in *Gray v Johnston* (1868) LR 3 HL 1 at 11, it would be a serious matter if bankers were to be allowed, on grounds of mere suspicion or curiosity, to refuse to honour a cheque drawn by their customer. He added on the facts of that case: "... even although that customer might happen to be an administrator or an executor." (2) As Scrutton LJ pointed out in *Bradford Old Bank Ltd v Sutcliffe* [1918] 2 KB 833 at 847, sums paid by a customer into his current account cannot be used by the bank in discharge of the customer's loan account without the consent of the customer, since no customer could otherwise have any security in drawing a cheque on his current account if he had a loan account greater than his credit balance on current account.'

Having distinguished *Re Willis Percival & Co ex p Morier*,[2] and *Re Hett Maylor & Co Ltd*,[3] Dillon LJ continued:

'It is one thing when the fact that a customer holds his accounts as nominee or bare trustee for a third party is clear and indisputable. It is quite another where the alleged nomineeship is very far from plainly made out and is strongly disputed. It would be wholly contrary to the rules of banking law, above indicated, if a bank could without warning dishonour a customer's cheque when there were funds to cover it in the account, on a tenuous, if just arguable, suspicion that the account was held by the customer as nominee for a third party who was indebted to the bank, and if the bank could then freeze the customer's account until it had been ascertained after full inquiry after a lengthy trial a year or more later whether the customer was indeed such a nominee. I can see no equity in the bank in such a case to override, in the words of Lord Wilberforce cited above,[4] the clear rules of law on which bankers and customers habitually deal with each other, especially as the bank in the present case has only itself to thank for not following ordinary banking practice and obtaining standard form security documentation before allowing the account ... to be seriously overdrawn.'

1 [1988] 2 All ER 296 at 300.
2 (1879) 12 Ch D 491, CA.
3 (1894) 10 TLR 412.
4 Ie, in *Aries Tanker Corpn v Total Transport Ltd* [1977] 1 All ER 398 at 404–405, [1977] 1 WLR 185 at 191.

The *Uttamchandani* appeal[5] arose on almost identical facts, and the Court of Appeal again rejected a bank's defence based on equitable set-off, holding that the claim that a customer holds an account as nominee or bare trustee does not provide a bank with a defence of equitable set-off unless the nomineeship or trusteeship is clear and indisputable.

An example of indisputable nomineeship founding a right of set-off is *Re Hett Maylor & Co Ltd,* supra, the facts of which have already been given at p 198, above, a case which Dillon LJ in *Bhogal* described as 'a very plain case where the nomineeship of one account was known to both parties and undisputed.'

The availability of set-off against assignees is considered at p 518, below in assessing the vulnerability of rights of set-off to third party interference.

(b) Rights of set-off after insolvency

Insolvency triggers statutory set-off provisions which are both mandatory and materially different from pre-insolvency rights of set-off.[6] Set-off in insolvency is self-evidently a matter of considerable importance in the context of banking, and accordingly there is given below a general description of insolvency set-off, in particular the availability of set-off in respect of contingent liabilities. The law described is that relating to the insolvency of companies within the meaning of the Companies Act 1985.

(i) Rule 4.90

The mandatory provisions for set-off in insolvency are contained, as regards companies, in Rule 4.90 of the Insolvency Rules 1986, which provides:

'4.90 Mutual credit and set-off
(1) This Rule applies where, before the company goes into liquidation there have been mutual credits, mutual debts or other mutual dealings between the company and any creditor of the company proving or claiming to prove for a debt in the liquidation.
(2) An account shall be taken of what is due from each party to the other in respect of the mutual dealings, and the sums due from one party shall be set off against the sums due from the other.
(3) Sums due from the company to another party shall not be included in the account taken under paragraph (2) if that other party had notice at the time they became due that a meeting of creditors had been summoned under section 98 or (as the case may be) a petition for the winding up of the company was pending.
(4) Only the balance (if any) of the account is provable in the liquidation. Alternatively (as the case may be) the amount shall be paid to the liquidator as part of the assets.'

Rule 4.90 is not designated 'CVL' or 'no CVL application', and it therefore applies both in a creditors' voluntary winding up (Rule 4.1 (2), (3), (4)) and in a winding up by the court (Rule 4.1 (2), (4)); it also applies in a members' voluntary (ie solvent) winding up (Rule 4.1 (1)).

The rule marks a departure from the pre-1986 regime whereby companies' insolvency legislation simply made applicable to every mode of winding up

---

5 (1989) 133 Sol Jo 262, CA.
6 For a fuller treatment of insolvency set-off, see Wood *English and International Set-off* (1st edn, 1989) ch 7.

the rules in bankruptcy as to the distribution of assets (Companies Act 1948, s 317; Companies Act 1985, s 612). The introduction of rules relating specifically to companies has removed the uncertainties which formerly existed as regards, for example, the corporate equivalent of an individual's acts of bankruptcy. However, the substance of mandatory set-off in insolvency remains the same for companies as for individuals because Rule 4.90 adopts identical wording (mutatis mutandis) to the bankruptcy provisions contained in s 323 of the Insolvency Act 1986.

The bankruptcy provision which applied in company insolvency before the enactment of Rule 4.90 was s 31 of the Bankruptcy Act 1914. Rule 4.90 (as well as s 323) has broken down into four paragraphs that which was formerly contained in one section, and in the process has made a number of changes in language. These changes appear not to have been intended to change the law, but rather to simplify and thereby improve the drafting of the former s 31. However, one change in wording has given rise to doubt. This change appears by comparing the words italicised below in the proviso to s 31 and in Rule 4.90 (3):

'... but a person shall not be entitled under this section to claim the benefit of any set-off against the property of a debtor in any case where he had, *at the time of giving credit to the debtor,* notice of an act of bankruptcy committed by the debtor and available against him,'   (s 31)

'Sums due from the company to another party shall not be included in the account taken under paragraph (2) if that other party had notice *at the time they became due* that a meeting of creditors had been summoned under section 98 or (as the case may be) a petition for the winding up of the company was pending.'
                                                                          (Rule 4.90 (3))

The above provisions are both exclusionary; they exclude by reference to a specified time claims which would otherwise be required to be set-off. Section 31 took as the relevant time the time of giving of credit to the insolvent, which is obviously correct in principle. This can be illustrated by the example of a bank giving credit to a corporate customer by issuing a letter of credit. If the bank issues the credit having received notice that its customer is insolvent, there is no injustice in the bank being disentitled from bringing into statutory set-off any claim in respect of the credit. Conversely, if the bank issues the credit without having received notice of insolvency, it would be arbitrary and unjust if the bank's right of set-off were to be dependent upon whether a drawing on the credit had been made before or after the time at which the bank received notice.

Rule 4.90 (3) defines the relevant time for notice as 'the time they (the sums due from the company to another party) became due.' At first sight the expression 'became due' appears to refer to a later time than 'the time of giving of credit.' It is submitted, however, that Rule 4.90 (3) did not change the law. The expression 'became due' relates back to the opening words of Rule 4.90 (3), 'Sums due from the company', which expression appears to refer to sums due from the company in respect of provable debts. By Rule 13.12 (1), 'debt' is given an extended meaning, such that the expression 'became due' is seemingly used in the sense of 'became incurred as debts within Rule 13.12 (1)'. It is, however, unnecessary to dwell further on this difficult point of construction because there is presently passing through Parliament a Companies Bill which, if enacted in its present form, will define rights of set-off in bankruptcy by reference to provable debts. A corresponding amendment to Rule 4.90 could then reasonably be expected.

(ii) The date of insolvency

Rule 4.90 applies where, *before the company goes into liquidation,* there have been mutual credits, etc. By s 247 (2) of the Insolvency Act 1986, a company goes into liquidation (a) if it passes a resolution for voluntary winding up, or (b) an order for its winding up is made by the court at a time when it has not already gone into liquidation by passing such a resolution.

As mentioned above, Rule 4.90 (3) contains an important exclusion in respect of dealings after notice of the summoning of a creditors' meeting or the presentation of a petition.

There is a further important limitation on rights of set-off arising out of s 127 of the Insolvency Act 1986. This renders void any disposition of the company's property made after *the commencement of winding up,* which is (a) in the case of a voluntary winding up, the time of the passing of the resolution for winding up (Insolvency Act 1986, s 86), or (b) in the case of a winding up by the court, the time of presentation of the petition for winding up or the time of the passing of any pre-presentation resolution for winding up (Insolvency Act 1986, s 129 (1), (2)). The general effect of s 127 has already been considered in ch 17, above. In the specific context of set-off, it should be noted that if there is any conflict between s 127 and Rule 4.90, s 127 appears to prevail.[7]

(iii) Mandatory nature of set-off in insolvency

It was held by the House of Lords in the *Halesowen* case[8] that the statutory provisions for set-off in insolvency (then contained in s 31 of the Bankruptcy Act 1914) are mandatory. It is therefore impossible for parties to contract out of insolvency set off. The mandatory language of s 31 is reproduced in identical form in Rule 4.90 (2).

(iv) Debts required to be set-off

Rule 4.90 (2) requires that sums due from one party shall be set-off against sums due from the other.

In ascertaining the meaning of 'sums due' in relation to the liabilities of an insolvent company to a creditor, reference must first be made to Rule 13.12, which provides (inter alia):

'13.12 "Debt", "liability" (winding up)
(1) "Debt", in relation to the winding up of a company, means (subject to the next paragraph) any of the following:
(a) any debt or liability to which the company is subject at the date on which it goes into liquidation;
(b) any debt or liability to which the company may become subject after that date by reason of any obligation incurred before that date; and
(c) any interest provable as mentioned in Rule 4.93 (1)
...
(3) For the purposes of references in any provision of the [Insolvency] Act [1986]

---

7 See *Barclays Bank Ltd v TOSG Trust Fund Ltd* [1984] BCLC 1 at 25–26. The point did not arise on appeal: [1984] AC 626, [1984] 1 All ER 628, CA, and [1984] 1 All ER 1060, HL.
8 [1972] AC 785, [1972] 1 All ER 641, HL.

or the [Insolvency] Rules [1986] about winding up to a debt or liability, it is immaterial whether the debt or liability is present or future, whether it is certain or contingent, or whether its amount is fixed or liquidated, or is capable of being ascertained by fixed rules or as a matter of opinion; and references in any such provision to owing a debt are to be read accordingly.

(4) In any provision of the Act or the Rules about winding up, except in so far as the context otherwise requires, "liability" means (subject to paragraph (3) above) a liability to pay money or money's worth, including any liability under an enactment, any liability for breach of trust, any liability in contract, tort or bailment, and any liability arising out of an obligation to make restitution.

Hence the debts in respect of which a person claiming to be a creditor must submit a proof of debt include contingent liabilities. Rule 4.86 imposes on the liquidator a duty to estimate the value of any debt which, by reason of its being subject to a contingency or for any other reason, does not bear a certain value.

(v) Set-off of contingent liabilities

The availability of set-off in respect of an insolvent's contingent liabilities is a matter of considerable importance in modern banking. Many transactions are so structured that in the event of the customer's insolvency there may exist an actual debt (whether or not presently payable) owed by the bank to the insolvent, and a contingent liability owed by the insolvent to the bank. Common transactions giving rise to contingent liabilities on the part of the customer include the issue of letters of credit and performance bonds, and the discounting of indorsed bills.

For several years the availability of set-off in respect of an insolvent's contingent liabilities was a fertile source of debate within the legal profession. However, two matters have largely laid this controversy to rest. First, in *Re Charge Card Services Ltd,*[9] Millett J subjected the authorities to an exhaustive analysis and convincingly concluded that a liability is not excluded from set-off merely because it was contingent at the relevant date (ie the date of the winding up order).[10] Secondly, the Companies Bill presently before Parliament will, if enacted, put the point beyond doubt by defining rights of set-off by reference to provable debts.

There are two additional aspects of the set-off of contingent liabilities which ought to be mentioned. The first is the availability of set-off where it is the *creditor's* liability which is contingent. There is a fundamental difference between the respective positions of the creditor and the insolvent in relation to contingent liabilities. As already stated, the insolvent's contingent liabilities give rise to an immediately provable debt, the value of which the liquidator is bound to estimate. There is, however, no corresponding procedure for the valuation of the creditor's contingent liabilities, and the insolvent has no immediate right against the creditor in respect of such liabilities. It might be thought that a creditor's contingent liabilities therefore fall outside the statutory set-off, but this is not so. A series of decisions going back over many years establishes that liabilities of the creditor which are future or contingent at the relevant date are available for set-off, provided that the

9 [1987] Ch 150, [1986] 3 All ER 289.
10 Ibid at, respectively 177 and 309.

relevant liability has matured into a presently due debt by the date of set-off.[11]

The second aspect of set-off is the requirement that the contingency shall have occurred. In *Re Charge Card Services Ltd*, Millett J stated:[12]

'In every case the claim to set-off requires that any contingency to which the liability was still subject at the date of the receiving order has since occurred.'

This observation was made in the course of analysing *Re Daintrey, ex p Mant*,[13] a case where the contingent liability was that of the creditor. As stated above, there being no procedure for the valuation of the creditor's contingent liabilities, set-off of such a claim has to await the occurrence of the contingency.

What is less clear is why the contingency must have occurred before set-off where the contingency liability is that of the insolvent. The creditor is entitled to submit a proof in respect of such a liability (Rule 4.73) and the liquidator is bound to estimate its value (Rule 4.86). Rule 4.90 applies where there have been mutual credits, etc, between the company and any creditor *proving or claiming to prove* for a debt in the liquidation. The value for purposes of proof of a contingent liability appears to be a sum due from the company which is required to be set-off. Indeed there are other passages in the judgment of Millett J in *Re Charge Card Services Ltd*,[14] which appear to accept that it suffices for set-off that a contingent liability has been quantified.

It will sometimes be in the interests of a creditor to wait and see whether the contingency occurs so as to avoid a valuation of his claim under Rule 4.86. It is unclear for how long a creditor is entitled to await the occurrence (or non-occurrence) of a contingency. It is also unclear whether, if a set-off is effected before the occurrence of the contingency, and the value of the creditor's claim is subsequently revised upwards upon its occurrence, a further set-off may be effected in respect of the additional quantum of proof.

(vi) The rule against double proof

The rule against double proof prevents two creditors each submitting a proof of debt in respect of the same liability, thereby doubling the dividend.[15] The rule has a well-established application in the context of guarantees, where there is an obvious risk that both the creditor and the surety will submit a proof in the event of the principal debtor's insolvency. The cases establish

11 See *Ex p Prescot* (1753) 1 Atk 230, 26 ER 147 (future debt); *French v Fenn* (1783) 3 Doug 257, 99 ER 642 (liability to account for the future sale of pearls); *Smith v Hodson* (1791) 4 Term Rep 211, 100 ER 979 (liability as the acceptor of bills payable after date of bankruptcy); *Booth v Hutchinson* (1872) LR 15 Eq. 30 (liability for rent in respect of post-bankruptcy occupation of demised premises); *Sovereign Life Assurance v Dodd* [1892] 1 QB 405 (liability for a future debt); *Palmer v Day & Sons* [1895] 2 QB 618 (liability to account for the future sale of pictures); *Re Daintrey, ex p Mant* [1900] 1 QB 546 (liability to pay a portion of the future profits of a business).
12 [1987] Ch 150 at 183F, [1986] 3 All ER 289 at 314e. See a similar observation at, respectively, 190D and 319f.
13 [1900] 1 QB 546.
14 [1987] Ch 150 at 180B, 182E, [1986] 3 All ER 289 at 311j, 313f.
15 See *Barclays Bank Ltd v TOSG Trust Fund Ltd* [1984] AC 626, [1984] 1 All ER 1060, HL. See further pp 303–305 above.

that the right to prove lies with the creditor. The guarantor may prove only if he pays before the creditor lodges a proof.[16]

It is beyond the scope of *Paget* to consider the rule in detail, but it should be noted that the rule is likely to operate so as to prevent submission of proof by the issuing bank of a standby letter of credit or performance bond before the credit or bond has been drawn on. Its application in the context of documentary letters of credit appears to be an open point.

(c) Vulnerability of general rights of set-off to third party interference

(i) Assignment

The authorities on the debtor's rights of set-off against an assignee were exhaustively reviewed by Templeman J in *Business Computers Ltd v Anglo-African Leasing Ltd,* who summarised the position as follows:[17]

'The result of the relevant authorities is that a debt which accrues due before notice of an assignment is received, whether or not it is payable before that date, or a debt which arises out of the same contract as that which gives rise to the assigned debt, or is closely connected with that contract, may be set off against the assignee. But a debt which is neither accrued nor connected may not be set off even though it arises from a contract made before the assignment.'

The meaning of the expression 'accrues due' in this citation is clear from the words 'whether or not it is payable before that date'. It includes debts which are presently payable and debts which are payable in the future, but not merely contingent liabilities.[18]

It will be readily apparent that the 'close connection' ground is of the utmost importance to banks. This can be illustrated by the example of a cash deposit placed as cover for the issue of a letter of credit. Until the credit is drawn on, the customer's reimbursement obligation to the issuing bank is a mere contingent liability. If the customer assigns the benefit of the deposit and the bank receives notice of assignment before any drawing, then even if the bank subsequently pays under the credit, it has no right of set-off against the assignee under the first ground of set-off referred to by Templeman J, the customer's liability not having accrued due before notice of assignment. The right of set-off, if any, rests on the closeness of the connection between the contract constituted by the application for the credit and the contract constituted by the placing of the deposit.

Some idea of the requisite degree of connection can be gleaned from *Business Computers* itself, where the court refused a set-off between (i) two debts totalling £6,587 due from the defendant to the assignor in respect of the defendant's purchase of two computers; and (ii) a debt of £30,000 due from the assignor to the defendant pursuant to the sale and lease-back of a third computer.

---

16 See *Re Fenton* [1931] 1 Ch 85, CA, per Lord Hanworth MR at 107 and Romer LJ at 118. And see generally Wood *English and International Set-off* (1st edn, 1989) paras 10.82ff.

17 [1977] 2 All ER 741 at 748b, [1977] 1 WLR 578 at 585.

18 See further *Watson v Mid-Wales Railway Co* (1867) LR 2 CP 593; *Re Pinto Leite & Nephews* [1929] 1 Ch 221.

(*ii*) *Attachment*

The subject of attachment has been considered in ch 18, above. The principles which apply when a garnishee opposes the making absolute of an order nisi on the ground of a right of set-off against the judgment debtor are fully considered in ch 18, above. The position in summary is that if no debt is due or accruing due from the judgment debtor to the garnishee, the order will be made absolute: *Tapp v Jones;*[19] but if there exists a presently payable debt from the judgment debtor to the garnishee, or a debt payable in the future but before the debt attached becomes payable, the order will not be made absolute: *Hale v Victoria Plumbing Co Ltd.*[20]

(*iii*) *Mareva injunctions*

The effect of a Mareva injunction on rights of set-off has already been considered in ch 19, above. In summary, the court will not permit a bank's rights of set-off to be prejudiced by the grant or continuance of a Mareva.

4 CONTRACTUAL SET-OFF PROVISIONS

Agreements in modern banking transactions commonly contain provisions which are either contractual rights of set-off or provisions intended to reinforce rights of set-off under the general law. It is appropriate to consider here some of the more common provisions, again distinguishing pre- and post-insolvency set-off.

Given that a right of set-off is not a proprietary security per se, the creation by a company of a contractual right of set-off appears unlikely to give rise to a registrable charge or to infringe typical negative pledge obligations. But it must always be remembered that a right of set-off may evidence a charge, being arguably one method by which a charge over a debt may be realised. Therefore care should always be taken to analyse the true nature of an arrangement incorporating a contractual right of set-off.

(a) Pre-insolvency provisions

(*i*) *Provisions which create an accounting situation*

The important distinction between an accounting situation and a set-off situation has already been mentioned at p 502, above. Within reasonable limits, a contract may be able to characterise a situation as one of accounting, and thereby create an even stronger right than set-off. A common type of transaction where there is scope for such characterisation is the deposit of cash cover. An early example is the Court of Appeal decision in *Hutt v Shaw.*[1] Money had been deposited with a stockbroker as cover for any loss upon speculations in stocks and shares. It was held that as long as the transactions were open there was no debt due or accruing from the stockbroker to the depositor. The case arose in the context of attachment proceedings and hence the relevant issue was whether a debt was due or accruing due. But if the context had been an action by the depositor for repayment, the non-existence

19 (1875) LR 10 QB 591.
20 [1966] 2 QB 746, [1966] 2 All ER 672, CA.
 1 (1887) 3 TLR 354, CA.

of a presently due debt would have required that the action be dismissed.

A more recent example is *Re Charge Card Services Ltd,* supra, which concerned a factoring agreement between two parties, one of whom became insolvent. The agreement contained a guarantee by the insolvent in favour of the factoring company that every debtor would duly and fully pay the receivables due from him before the end of the period of 120 days beginning with the date of issue of the relevant invoice (cl 3 (c)). The agreement also incorporated a condition which required the factoring company to maintain a current account to which there was to be debited, inter alia, the amount of any sum payable by the insolvent pursuant to the guarantee (cl 3A (ii) (D)). At the date of going into liquidation, the insolvent was contingently liable to the factoring company under its guarantee. The factoring company invoked a further condition (cl 3B) which provided, so far as is material:

'... [the factoring company] shall remit ... to ... [the insolvent] the balance for the time being standing to the credit of [the insolvent] in the current account up to the full amount thereof less any amount which [the factoring company] shall in its absolute discretion decide to retain as security for ... (iii) any amount *prospectively chargeable* to [the insolvent] as a debit [under Clause 3A (ii)].'(Emphasis added)

The liquidator objected to the validity of the factoring company's right of retention, alleging (inter alia) that it amounted to a contractual right of set-off which went beyond the statutory set-off in insolvency and was therefore void. This argument was rejected by Millett J:[2]

'... the short answer to these submissions is that [the factoring company's] right of retention under standard condition 3B (iii) in respect of any amount prospectively chargeable to the company as a debit to the current account is not a matter of set-off but of account.'

The efficacy of a contractual right to debit amounts prospectively due from a customer under, for example, a letter of credit is untested, but *Charge Card* suggests that such arrangements may be efficacious.

(ii) *Contractual rights of set-off*

Rights of set-off under the general law are commonly extended by contract to include: (a) a right of set-off in a tri-partite situation, as where a parent company agrees that a deposit placed by it with a bank may be set-off against debts due to the bank from a subsidiary company; (b) a right to set off presently due debts against future debts or contingent liabilities, or a right of retention pending the maturing of future debts or contingent liabilities; and (c) a right to set off accounts maintained in different currencies and/or different jurisdictions.

(iii) *Protection against assignees*

It is common for a contract to purport to deprive the benefit of a debt of the quality of assignability. In some contracts, the debt is expressed to be personal to a particular creditor. In others, the debt is expressed to be incapable of (for example) being assigned, mortgaged, charged or otherwise dealt with. The efficacy of such provisions is central to any assessment of the degree of

---

2 [1987] Ch 150 at 173G, [1986] 3 All ER 289 at 307d.

protection conferred by pre-insolvency rights of set-off, for inability to assign imports inability to create in favour of third parties rights by way of mortgage or charge. The manner in which such security can defeat rights of set-off is vividly illustrated by *Business Computers Ltd v Anglo-African Leasing Ltd,* considered at p 518, above, where the appointment of a receiver by debenture holders under a floating charge caused the incomplete assignment constituted by the debenture to become converted into a completed equitable assignment, thereby defeating a right of set-off.

There is no obvious reason in principle why parties should not be entitled to deprive a chose in action of the quality of assignability. Such authority as there is favours this entitlement. The case most in point is *Helstan Securities Ltd v Hertfordshire County Council.*[3] A contract between a county council and a road works contractor contained the following provision:

'(3) The contractor shall not assign the contract or any part thereof or any benefit or interest therein or thereunder without the written consent of the employer [the county council].'

In breach of this provision, the contractor purported to assign to the plaintiff the benefit of debts totalling £46,437 allegedly due from the county council. It was held that the assignee had no title to sue. Having reviewed the authorities, Croom-Johnson J stated:

'There are certain kinds of choses in action which, for one reason or another, are not assignable and there is no reason why the parties to an agreement may not contract to give its subject matter the quality of non-assignability.'

The application of this principle to the facts of *Helstan* is, however, open to doubt because the relevant provision did not in terms render the contract non-assignable, but simply contained a promise by the contractor not to assign.

In *British Eagle International Airlines Ltd v Cie Nationale Air France,*[4] Lord Cross, delivering the majority speech, stated:

'... for my part I am prepared to assume in favour of Air France that the legal rights against Air France which British Eagle acquired when it rendered the services in question were not strictly speaking "debts" owing by Air France but were innominate choses in action having some, but not all, the characteristics of "debts".'

The missing characteristic of the 'debts' owed by Air France was the creditor's right (before insolvency) to be paid them direct rather than through clearing. If a chose in action can be deprived of the quality of direct enforceability, it ought also to be capable of being deprived of assignability.

If the proposition stated in *Helstan* is sound, it appears to make no difference whether at the date of assignment the assignee knew of the non-assignability provision. The judgment in *Helstan* makes no reference to the assignee's state of knowledge at the date of assignment, and it is therefore to be inferred that the point was not regarded as material. Where the contract is contained wholly or partly in writing, the non-assignability provision should, of course, be made express on the face of the document.

Even if the *Helstan* proposition is not good law, all may not be lost in circumstances where the assignee can be shown to have known of a pro-

3 [1978] 3 All ER 262.
4 [1975] 2 All ER 390 at 409e, [1975] 1 WLR 758 at 778H.

hibition on assignment before the assignment was executed. In such a case, the debtor may be able to establish a cross-claim in damages for the tort of inducing breach of contract.

(b) Post-insolvency set-off provisions

It has already been noted that parties may not contract out of the mandatory insolvency set-off provisions. Nor is it possible to enlarge rights of set-off in insolvency by contract. The company's assets in a winding up must be distributed in satisfaction of its liabilities pari passu,[5] and the court will not give effect to an agreement which purports to provide for a different distribution.[6]

However, there are strong grounds for saying that a contract should be given effect if it goes no further than to make reasonable provision to fill a gap in the insolvency code. An example would be a provision conferring on a bank the right to convert (or not convert) foreign currency deposits the repayment of which is contingent upon an occurrence which has not yet occurred.

Insofar as the apprehended position on insolvency is that the insolvent's liability will be contingent, but that the liability of a lending bank will be actual, then for reasons explained in describing general rights of set-off in insolvency, present authorities suggest that set-off is available; but this is subject to the limitations and uncertainties described above, in particular the construction issue on Rule 4.90 (3), and the rule against double proof. Where, however, the apprehended position is that there will exist an actual liability owed by the bank to the insolvent, but that the relevant cross-liability will be owed not by the insolvent but by a third party (eg a subsidiary of the insolvent), there is no right of set-off under the general law, and it is impossible to create an enforceable right of set-off in insolvency by contract. In some cases, this difficulty can be resolved by creating mutuality between the bank and the depositor, as where a parent company places a deposit and gives a guarantee of the indebtedness to the bank of its subsidiary. In other cases, and for a variety of reasons, this solution is not available. The solution then commonly sought is to take a charge over the deposit, or to make the bank's obligation to repay the deposit conditional upon the third party's discharge of its liabilities to the bank. Both of these matters are considered in ch 32, post.

5 See the Insolvency Act 1986, s 107.
6 *British Eagle International Airlines Ltd v Cie Nationale Air France* [1975] 2 All ER 390, [1975] 1 WLR 758, HL.

CHAPTER 32

CHARGES OVER DEBTS, AND CONDITIONAL DEBT OBLIGATIONS[1]

It was pointed out at the conclusion of ch 31 that certain transactions give rise to exposures for which rights of set-off provide inadequate protection. Such transactions are often tri-partite. For example, a parent company may place a deposit with a bank as cover for a loan to its subsidiary; one bank may place a deposit with another in lieu of a formal sub-participation in a loan made by the depositee to a third party. Even in bi-partite transactions, rights of set-off cannot be regarded as watertight.

The limitations on set-off as a form of protection underline the importance of two other forms of protection which are widely used in modern banking transactions, namely charges over debts, and conditional debt obligations. It is common to find all three forms of protection contained in one and the same agreement.

1 CHARGES OVER BOOK DEBTS

Formal security by way of a mortgage or charge provides a lender with the surest protection. A secured creditor ranks ahead of the mortgagor's or chargor's unsecured creditors, and if a fixed security is perfected, it generally takes priority over any subsequent security over the same subject-matter of which the lender did not have notice at the date of making his advance.

(a) Mortgages and charges of book debts generally

(i) Method of creation

A debt is a chose in action. Formal security over a chose in action can be created by a mortgage or by a charge. The essence of a legal mortgage of a debt is the vesting of the legal estate in the mortgagee by assignment, subject to the mortgagor's entitlement to a re-assignment if the secured liabilities are

---

1 Certain passages in this chapter will also be published in a forthcoming publication of the International Bar Association's Section on Business Law: *Using Rights of Set-off as Security: A Comparative Survey* edited by Francis Neate, and are published here by kind permission of the IBA.

discharged. Such an assignment is absolute for the purposes of s 136 of the Law of Property Act 1925.[1a]

Subject to an exception which is not material for present purposes,[2] every charge, whether over a legal or equitable interest, must be equitable, there being no such thing as a legal charge. The essence of an equitable charge is that, without any conveyance or assignment to the chargee, specific property of the chargor is expressly or constructively appropriated to or made answerable for payment of a debt, and the chargee is given the right to resort to the property for the purpose of having it realised and applied in or towards payment of the debt. The availability of equitable remedies has the effect of giving the chargee a proprietary interest by way of security in the property charged.[3] A classic description is that of Atkin LJ in *National Provincial and Union Bank of England v Charnley*:[4]

> 'It is not necessary to give a formal definition of a charge, but I think there can be no doubt that where in a transaction for value both parties evince an intention that property, existing or future, shall be made available as security for the payment of a debt, and that the creditor shall have a present right to have it made available, there is a charge, even though the present legal right which is contemplated can only be enforced at some future date, and though the creditor gets no legal right of property, either absolute or special, or any legal right to possession, but only gets a right to have the security made available by an order of the court.'

(ii) Registration

By ss 395 and 396 of the Companies Act 1985, a charge created by a company registered in England and Wales must be registered if the charge is (inter alia) a charge on book debts of the company (s 396 (1) (e)), or a floating charge on the company's undertaking or property (s 396 (1) (f)). Unless the prescribed particulars of the charge together with the instrument (if any) by which the charge is created or evidenced, are sent to the registrar of companies for registration, the charge is, as far as any security on the company's property or undertaking is conferred by it, void against the liquidator or administrator and any creditor of the company (s 395 (1)). These provisions extend to charges on property in England and Wales which are created, and to charges on property in England and Wales which is acquired, by a company (whether or not a company within the meaning of the 1985 Act) incorporated outside Great Britain which has an established place of business in England and Wales (s 409 (1)).

It is beyond the scope of *Paget* to discuss these important provisions, and reference should be made to the standard works on company law.[5] For present purposes it need only be noted that the meaning of 'book debts' is a matter of some uncertainty, and the safest course is always to register a charge over a debt.

1a *Trancred v Delagoa Bay and East African Rly Co* (1889) 23 QBD 239, decided under the predecessor to s 136 (s 25 (6) of the Supreme Court of Judicature Act 1873).
2 The exception is a legal mortgage of land created by a charge by deed expressed to be by way of legal mortgage – see s 87 (1) of Law of Property Act 1925.
3 *Re Charge Card Services Ltd* [1987] Ch 150 at 176, [1986] 3 All ER 289 at 309, per Millett, J.
4 [1924] 1 KB 431 at 449. See also *Palmer v Carey* [1926] AC 703 at 706, PC, per Lord Wrenbury.
5 See *Gore-Browne on Companies*, ch 18; *Palmer's Company Law* (24th edn, 1987) ch 46.

(*iii*) *Priorities*

Where a mortgage or charge is taken without notice of a prior encumbrance, the priorities between competing mortgages and charges over book debts appear to be governed by the date on which notice of the mortgage or charge is given to the debtor. This principle derives from four propositions: (1) Priority between competing equitable assignments of choses in action is governed by the date of notice to the debtor.[6] (2) By s 136 (1) of the Law of Property Act 1925, notice in writing to the debtor is a requirement for a legal assignment of a chose in action, and therefore in practice the priority between competing legal assignments is also governed by the date of such notice. (3) By s 136 (1) a legal assignee takes subject to equities, and accordingly, even if a legal assignment is effected for value without notice of a prior equity, priorities between an equitable assignee and a subsequent legal assignee fall to be determined as if both assignments had been equitable.[7] (4) Although an equitable charge over a debt is created without any immediate assignment to the chargee, the chargee obtains an immediate proprietary interest such that the reasoning which underlies the rule in *Dearle v Hall* applies with the same force as to an immediate assignment.

(*iv*) *Further advances*

The existence of a mortgage or charge does not necessarily confer protection in relation to advances made after notice of a subsequent charge. Whether a charge has priority in relation to such advances depends upon the chargor's right to 'tack' subsequent advances on to his security. The subject of tacking is more fully considered in ch 34, post, in the context of mortgages over interests in land. The uncertainties over the construction of s 94 of the Law of Property Act are compounded in relation to mortgages over book debts by doubts as to the application of s 94 to mortgages other than mortgages of land. Since, however, rights of tacking before 1925 were wider than those now permitted under s 94, it is likely that a right to tack will exist if the relevant provision satisfies the terms of s 94, regardless whether s 94 is in fact applicable.

(b) Mortgages and charges of book debts in favour of the debtor

In *Re Charge Card Services Ltd*,[8] Millett J held that a creditor cannot create in favour of a debtor a charge over the debtor's own indebtedness to the chargor. A 'charge' of this type is sometimes called a 'charge-back', ie a charge by a creditor back in favour of a debtor. Millett J described such a charge as 'conceptually impossible'.

The decision in *Charge Card* was received by many practitioners with surprise. It has generated a large volume of legal literature,[9] and, unless reversed by statute, seems almost certain to be the subject of challenge on some future occasion. However, it remains, until reversed, the leading English authority on the point, and must be assumed to be correct.

---

6 *Dearle v Hall* (1828) 3 Russ 1.
7 *E Pfeiffer Weinkellerei-Weineinkauf Gmbh & Co v Arbuthnot Factors Ltd* [1988] 1 WLR 150 at 162.
8 [1987] Ch 150, [1986] 3 All ER 289.
9 For a penetrating criticism of *Charge Card,* see Wood *English and International Set-Off* (1st edn, 1989) paras 5–179 to 5–181. The contrary view is advanced by Professor R M Goode *Legal Problems of Credit and Security* (2nd edn, 1988) pp 127–128.

The grounds of the decision were as follows:

1 It was conceded by the creditor that a debt cannot be *assigned* in whole or in part to the debtor, since such an assignment operates wholly or partially as a *release*. Likewise, it was conceded that a debt cannot be made the subject of a legal or equitable *mortgage* in favour of the debtor, since this requires a conveyance or assignment of property by way of security, and this operates as a *conditional release*.[10]

2 It was accepted by the court that no conveyance or assignment is involved in the creation of an equitable charge, but this distinguishing feature between a mortgage and a charge was held to be irrelevant because the objection to such a charge was held *not* to be the process by which it is created.[11]

3 The objection to such a charge was held to be 'the result'. A debt is a chose in action; it is the right to sue the debtor. This can be assigned or made available to a third party, but not to the debtor, who cannot sue himself. Once any assignment or appropriation to the debtor becomes unconditional, the debt is wholly or partially released. The debtor cannot, and does not need to, resort to the creditor's claim against him in order to obtain the benefit of the security; his own liability to the creditor is automatically discharged or reduced.[12]

The essential reasoning is that upon the occurrence or fulfilment of a condition (which is not defined, but is presumably the chargor's default in payment of the indebtedness for which the security was given), the purportedly charged debt is *automatically released* to the extent of the sum in default. It is submitted that this betrays a failure to identify the true intention of the parties. Their manifest intention is that if the chargor defaults, the chargee shall be entitled to set off the debt owed by him to the chargor against the chargor's debt owed to him. This, it is submitted, is not only conceptually possible, but self-evident. Automatic release does not reflect the intention of either party, and if there is no automatic release, the chargee can, and does need to, effect a set-off (ie 'resort to the creditor's claim against him') in order to obtain the benefit of the security.

There is undoubtedly a question mark over this aspect of the decision in *Charge Card*. It is partly because of this that 'charge-backs' are still commonly included in security documentation governed by English law. Where this occurs, the charge should be sent to the Registrar of Companies for registration. On 28 March 1988 the Registrar issued a statement that, having regard to *Charge Card,* he considered that securities created by an account-holder in favour of its banker which are expressed to be by way of charge are not registrable. However, the Registrar went on to state that in view of the doubts which exist as to the correctness of the decision, he will register such securities if presented for that purpose. An annex to this statement headed 'Administrative Consequences' states (inter alia) that:

'If a security created over its account by an account holder in favour of its banker is expressed to be by way of charge or mortgage, or contains provisions which, disregarding the fact that the property charged is an account held with the chargee,

10 [1987] Ch 150 at 175D, [1986] 3 All ER 289 at 308d.
11 Ibid at, respectively, 176D and 309b.
12 Ibid at, respectively, 176E and 309b.

would be capable of creating a charge, it will be registered and a certificate issued. If the security is not expressed to be by way of charge and it appears to the Registrar that it is in a form which would be incapable in any circumstances of giving rise to a charge, he will return the instrument. If, however, a presentor considers that a security should be registered on the basis set out in this letter, there is nothing to prevent him making representations which will of course be considered by the Registrar.'

It must be emphasised that the Registrar's practice on registration of such charges has changed, and it is not safe to assume that his practice will not change again at some future date.

Millett J added in *Charge Card*[13] that it does not follow that an attempt to create an express mortgage or charge of a debt in favour of a debtor would be wholly ineffective. Equity looks to the substance, not the form, and a purported mortgage or charge may give a right of set-off which will be effective against the creditor's liquidator provided that it does not purport to go beyond what is permitted by the statutory set-off provisions in insolvency. Given this limitation, the treatment of a purported charge as a contractual right of set-off is of little practical value to the creditor.

2 CONDITIONAL DEBT OBLIGATIONS

(a) Nature of conditional debt obligations ('flawed assets')

Conditional repayment obligations are often referred to as 'flawed asset' arrangements. If A places with B a deposit as regards which the obligation to repay is conditional upon performance by a third party, C, of an obligation owed to B, the asset owned by A (the right to repayment of a deposit) is flawed in the sense that its value is dependent upon the payment of monies by C to A's debtor, B. A typical flawed asset agreement will provide that B shall be under no obligation to repay A unless and save to the extent that C shall have repaid B. This entitles A to pro tanto repayment in accordance with payments made by C to B. The agreement does not, however, involve any assignment by B to A. Their relation is that of debtor and creditor. There can equally be a bi-partite flawing arrangement, as where B's obligation to repay A is conditional upon the discharge by A of an obligation owed to B.

A flawed asset arrangement prima facie creates a valid contract under English law even if the agreement is not under seal. B's promise to repay the deposit appears to be sufficient consideration to create a contract notwithstanding the flaw in A's rights, and if additional consideration be needed, it can be found in B's advancing of monies to C at the implied request of A.

Accordingly, as regards the formal validity of the contract, the point to be considered by B is the capacity of A to enter into such an arrangement. Its effect is analogous to the creation by A of a charge over the deposit or the granting of a guarantee of C's liabilities. If A has the capacity to create a charge or to grant a guarantee, it would be surprising if A did not have the capacity to accept a flawing of its rights even though A's objects clause is unlikely to refer to flawed asset arrangements in terms.

13 Ibid at, respectively, 177A and 309g.

(b) Enforceability of tri-partite flawed asset arrangements

The adequacy of a flawed asset as a form of protection for B depends upon its efficacy in the event of A's insolvency. There are two potential sources of vulnerability – public policy, and the Insolvency Act 1986.

(i) Public policy

The leading authority on public policy in the context of insolvency is *British Eagle International Airlines Ltd v Cie Nationale Air France*,[14] a decision of the House of Lords. British Eagle was a member of the IATA clearing house, which provided a facility to its members by which liabilities arising out of individual transactions were settled not directly between the members concerned but through a clearing house which effected a clearance every month. British Eagle went into creditors' voluntary winding up in circumstances where (a) airlines had claims against British Eagle, (b) British Eagle had claims against airlines, including Air France, and (c) British Eagle was on the balance of the above claims in debit to the clearing house. The liquidator of British Eagle brought a test action against Air France claiming repayment of the net amount due from Air France as a result of mutual dealings between the two airlines. By a majority of 3–2 the House of Lords held that the liquidator was not bound by the clearing house arrangements, and was therefore entitled to recover debts owed by debtor airlines, leaving creditor airlines to prove in the winding up. The reasoning of the majority speech delivered by Lord Cross was as follows:

1 The power of the court to go behind agreements the results of which are repugnant to insolvency legislation is not confined to cases in which the parties' dominant purpose is to evade its operation.[15]
2 A contracting out of the Companies Act 1948, s 302 (now the Insolvency Act 1986, s 107), which provides that the property of a company shall, on its winding up, be applied in satisfaction of its liabilities pari passu, is contrary to public policy.[16]
3 It was irrelevant that the parties to the clearing house arrangements had good business reasons for entering into them and did not direct their minds to the question how the arrangements might be affected by the insolvency of one or more of the parties.[17]
4 It was immaterial whether the obligations of the debtor airlines to British Eagle were debts in the strict sense.[18]
5 The creditor airlines were in substance claiming that they ought not to be treated in the liquidation as ordinary unsecured creditors but that they had achieved by the medium of the clearing house agreement a position analogous to that of secured creditors without the need for the creation and registration of charges on the book debts in question.[19]

It is to be noted that, *British Eagle* was not decided on the short ground that the 'mini-liquidation', involving as it did a multiple set-off of debts

14 [1975] 2 All ER 390, [1975] 1 WLR 758.
15 Ibid at, respectively, 410–411 and 780F.
16 Ibid at, respectively, 411c and 780H.
17 Ibid, loc cit.
18 Ibid at, respectively, 409d and 778H.
19 Ibid at, respectively, 410h and 780E.

between member airlines and British Eagle, contravened s 317 of the Companies Act 1948, the provision for statutory insolvency set-off. The provision on which the rule of public policy was based was identified not as s 317 (set-off), but s 302 (pari passu distribution of assets). This was no oversight. The relevance of s 317 was expressly considered, and rejected, in the majority speech of Lord Cross:[20]

> 'Some reference was made in argument to s 31 of the Bankruptcy Act 1914 – the mutual credits section – which is made applicable to the liquidation of companies by s 317 of the Companies Act 1948. The liquidator rightly applied that section in framing his claim against Air France which he limited to the excess in the value of the services rendered by British Eagle to Air France over the value of the services rendered by Air France to British Eagle during the periods in question. But so far I can see the section has no bearing on anything that we have to decide in this appeal. It is therefore unnecessary for us to say anything about the recent case in this House of *National Westminster Bank Ltd v Halesowen Presswork and Assemblies Ltd.*'

In considering the relevance of the above reasoning to flawed asset arrangements, it is logical to begin with an example as close as possible to the facts of British Eagle. Without resorting to absurd examples, the closest analogy is a tri-partite arrangement under which B (British Eagle) borrows a sum of money from C (creditor airline) and lends it to A (Air France) on condition that A shall not be obliged to repay B unless B repays C. From the standpoint of B's liquidator, this arrangement seeks to achieve a result which is for all practical purposes identical to that of the IATA clearing house regulations, namely that B is not entitled to claim repayment from A whilst leaving C to prove in the winding up as an unsecured creditor. It will be noted that from the standpoint of A and C the intended result of the arrangement is the very opposite of the clearing house arrangement. If B's liquidator elects not to repay C, C's claim remains wholly unsatisfied, and it is A who reaps the benefit. A tri-partite flawing arrangement of this nature is therefore in practice limited to cases where A and C are related companies.

It can be argued with some force that the above flawing arrangement does not contravene the mandatory pari passu provisions now contained in the Insolvency Act 1986, s 107 for the reason that there is no application of an asset to discharge a liability. However, even if this proposition is correct, it would be too simplistic to conclude that the arrangement does not contravene public policy. The pari passu distribution of assets is but one part of a wider statutory scheme in which the first step is the collection of assets. In a winding up by the court, there is an express provision for collection of assets in the Insolvency Act 1986, s 148 (1), which provides that as soon as may be after a winding up order, the court shall cause the company's assets to be collected. A corresponding duty is placed on the liquidator by s 143 (1) and Rule 4.179 of the Insolvency Rules 1986. As regards voluntary winding up, the duty to get in assets is implicit in the express duty to realise and apply them pari passu and to declare dividends – see the Insolvency Act 1986, s 107, and Rule 4.186(1).

It would, moreover, be surprising if parties could achieve indirectly by a tri-partite flawing arrangement a result which they cannot achieve by the more direct route of contractual set-off; but as has already been noted, the statutory set-off provisions were regarded in *British Eagle* as irrelevant.

20 Ibid at, respectively, 411 and 781.

For these reasons, it seems unlikely that a tri-partite flawing arrangement would be upheld in a situation analogous to *British Eagle*. However, it by no means follows that a tri-partite flawing arrangement will contravene public policy in the deposit arrangements of the type described at the beginning of this chapter ((i) placement of deposit by parent A with bank B as cover for loan to subsidiary C; (ii) deposit by A with B in lieu of formal sub-participation in loan to C). These deposit arrangements are without doubt factually distinguishable from the situation in *British Eagle*. This appears clearly by identifying the position occupied by the party whose insolvency is being postulated. In the British Eagle situation, the insolvent party is B, which both owns an asset (the claim against a debtor airline) and is subject to a liability (the obligation to pay a creditor airline). The intended effect of a mini-liquidation via clearing, and of tri-partite flawing, is to deprive B of its asset for the exclusive benefit of one particular third party. In the other two cases, the party whose insolvency is postulated is A. A owns an asset, but is not subject to any liability. Hence (i) there is no question of any unsecured creditor of A obtaining directly or indirectly the benefit of A's asset; (ii) the arrangement is not one which elevates an unsecured creditor into the position of a secured creditor without the creation and registration of a charge; (iii) nor is it one which involves a set-off or analogous arrangement going beyond the statutory set-off in insolvency. It is submitted that those differences suffice to take these two cases outside the rule of public policy applied in British Eagle. It is true that each contract fetters the liquidator's ability to get in an asset, but in this respect the company's rights are similar to those under any contract where the right to receive performance is conditional upon an act being performed by the company itself or by a third party.

Where a tri-partite transaction does create a creditor of a party who becomes insolvent, if a security document includes both a charge-back and a flawed asset arrangement, a powerful argument on behalf of the lender is that at least one of these two provisions must be effective. The decision in *British Eagle* relied heavily on the proposition that the creditor airlines were claiming that they had achieved by the medium of the clearing house agreement a position analogous to that of secured creditors without the need for the creation and registration of charges on book debts. It was assumed by the majority that valid charges were capable of creation (see the observation of Lord Cross: 'Moreover, if the documents had purported to create such charges, the charges – as the judge saw – would have been unenforceable against the liquidator for want of registration under s 95 of the Companies Act 1948'[1]). It would be illogical to hold both that a charge cannot be created and that a flawed asset arrangement is contrary to public policy on the ground that a party has attempted to achieve a position analogous to that of a secured creditor without the creation and registration of a charge.

(ii) *Insolvency Act 1986*

In assessing the efficacy of a flawed asset arrangement, consideration must also be given to the Insolvency Act 1986, in particular to s 238 ('Transactions at an undervalue'). Section 238 applies in the case of a company where an

---

1 [1975] 2 All ER 390 at 410g, [1975] 1 WLR 758 at 780D.

administration order is made or the company goes into liquidation (s 238 (1)). Where the company has at a relevant time (in the case of unconnected persons, at a time in the period of six months ending with the onset of insolvency) entered into a transaction with any person at an undervalue, the court has power on the application of the insolvency office-holder to make such order as it thinks fit for restoring the position to what it would have been if the company had not entered into that transaction (s 238 (2) (3)). A company enters into a transaction with a person at an undervalue if, inter alia, it enters that transaction for a consideration the value of which, in money or money's worth, is significantly less than the value in money or money's worth, of the consideration provided by the company (s 238 (4)). There is as yet little judicial guidance on the interpretation of these new provisions. It appears strongly arguable that the consideration provided in the above examples by the depositor, A, is significantly more than the money value of the consideration provided by B. A's pre-transaction absolute and beneficial title to the amount of the deposit is transmuted into a mere conditional right to repayment. On the relevant factual hypothesis, ie where C has defaulted, leading B to refuse repayment to A's insolvency office-holder, the monetary value of the consideration provided by A and B respectively is likely to appear significantly unequal. However, even if the transaction was at an undervalue and was entered into at a relevant time, it may yet be saved by s 238 (5), which provides that the court shall not make a restoring order if it is satisfied (a) that the company which entered into the transaction did so in good faith and for the purpose of carrying on its business, and (b) that at the time it did so there were good grounds for believing that the transaction would benefit the company.

Reference should also be made to s 239 ('Preferences'), but this appears unlikely to be relevant in the examples given because the bank does not become a creditor of the depositor until after the terms of the deposit have been agreed.

(c) Enforceability of bi-partite flawed asset arrangements

The points made above in relation to tri-partite arrangements apply here with at least equal force. Flawed asset arrangements in the context of mutual dealings between the parties seem further removed from the rule of public policy identified in *British Eagle* than tri-partite flawed asset arrangements. There is nothing akin to a mini-liquidation by which one unsecured creditor receives an excess distribution out of a debt owed to the insolvent by a third party; and if analogy with set-off is relevant, the arrangement is not alien to statutory set-off. Nor, if *Charge Card* is right, is a creditor seeking to achieve the position of a secured creditor without the need for the creation and registration of a charge – such a charge is a conceptual impossibility.

CHAPTER 33

PLEDGES OF GOODS, DOCUMENTS OF TITLE AND NEGOTIABLE INSTRUMENTS

Pledge and lien are both types of security founded on possession.[1] The difference between the two lies in the method whereby the security is created. A pledge arises as a result of a deliberate act on the part of the customer. A lien can arise automatically, without any conscious intention of the customer.

The simplest example of a pledge is that of the poor widow delivering her wedding ring to a pawnbroker. The mere fact of delivery provides the pawnbroker with all the security he needs, provided, of course, the ring belongs to the widow: he can retain it until the loan is repaid and sell it if the loan is not repaid, and there is no risk of anyone acquiring a prior right to the ring as long as he retains it. These are the fundamental elements of the pledge: a security created by delivery of possession by or with the consent of the owner, coupled with a right of retention and, in the event of default, a right of sale.

1 GOODS AND DOCUMENTS OF TITLE TO GOODS

(a) Possession

(i) The requirement for possession

A pledge, being created by and based upon the delivery of possession, is a security limited by the extent of the pledgee's possession. Thus, if he loses possession, he loses his security. The security extends only to what is in his possession, and no further; and the security is incapable of extending to anything which is not capable of being possessed. Thus, delivery of the title deeds to land may constitute a pledge of the title deeds, but cannot constitute a pledge of the land itself; and delivery of a share certificate cannot constitute a pledge of the underlying shares, not merely because the certificate does not represent the underlying shares but is merely evidence of title to them, but because possession of shares (being intangible assets, or choses in action) is an impossibility. Both transactions may constitute pledges of the relevant documents, which of themselves are of little or no value to the person in possession of them, and they may also constitute (or be taken as evidence of

---

1 The editor gratefully acknowledges that this chapter has been revised by Mr Francis Neate of Slaughter and May.

an intention to create) equitable mortgages of the underlying assets (land and shares), but they cannot constitute pledges of those assets.

The pledge is, therefore, a security of limited application, being founded upon actual physical possession. The rule that the pledgee loses his security if he loses possession seriously limits the usefulness of the pledge as security. Banks are not in the business of warehousing or trading in goods, and are not equipped to do so. Furthermore, the bank's customer will want to retrieve the goods in order to be able to sell them, and the bank will wish to facilitate this without jeopardising its security. However, the value of the pledge as a security and the extent of its application has been increased by a number of legal devices, notably the concept of constructive possession (and the related concept of documents which represent the goods themselves), the trust receipt and the concept of negotiability.

(ii) Constructive possession

1 IN GENERAL

A pledge of goods is not complete unless and until there has been actual or constructive delivery of the goods. Actual delivery to a bank is impractical, so constructive delivery is what is normally relied upon. In the older cases, this is usually described as the handing over of the key to the warehouse where the goods are stored. In modern practice, constructive delivery will usually consist either of delivery of a valid document of title which represents the goods, such as a bill of lading (as to which see below), or of an acknowledgment (called an attornment) by the warehouse-keeper that he holds the goods to the order or at the disposition of the bank. It is by no means clear that any other form of constructive delivery is effective. The position is lucidly explained by Lord Wright in *Madras Official Assignee v Mercantile Bank of India Ltd*:[2]

'At the common law a pledge could not be created except by a delivery of possession of the thing pledged, either actual or constructive. It involved a bailment. If the pledgor had the actual goods in his physical possession, he could effect the pledge by actual delivery: in other cases he could give possession by some symbolic act, such as handing over the key of the store in which they were. If, however, the goods were in the custody of a third person, who held for the bailor so that in law his possession was that of the bailor, the pledge could be effected by a change of the possession of the third party, that is by an order to him from the pledgor to hold for the pledgee, the change being perfected by the third party attorning to the pledgee, that is acknowledging that he thereupon held for him; there was thus a change of possession and a constructive delivery: the goods in the hands of the third party became by this process in the possession constructively of the pledgee. But where goods were represented by documents the transfer of the documents did not change the possession of the goods, save for one exception, unless the custodier (carrier, warehouseman or such) was notified of the transfer and agreed to hold in future as bailee for the pledgee. The one exception was the case of bills of lading, the transfer of which by the law merchant operated as a transfer of the possession of, as well as the property in, the goods. This exception has been

---

2 [1935] AC 53. It should be remembered that this case was decided on the Indian Code, under which it was then possible for the owner of goods to obtain a loan on the pledge of documents of title without giving notice to the custodian and obtaining his attornment.

explained on the ground that the goods being at sea the master could not be notified; the true explanation may be that it was a rule of the law merchant, developed in order to facilitate mercantile transactions, whereas the process of pledging goods on land was regulated by the narrower rule of the common law and the matter remained stereotyped in the form which it had taken before the importance of documents of title in mercantile transactions was realised. So things have remained in the English law; a pledge of documents is not in general to be deemed a pledge of the goods; a pledge of the documents (always excepting a bill of lading) is merely a pledge of the ipsa corpora of them; the common law continued to regard them as merely tokens of an authority to receive possession, though from time to time representations were made by special juries that in the ordinary practice of merchants' transfers of documents were understood to pass possession, as for instance in 1815, in *Spear v Travers*.[3] The common law rule was stated by the House of Lords in *M'Ewan Sons & Co v Smith*.[4] The position of the English law has been fully explained also more recently in *Inglis v Robertson and Baxter*[5] and in *Dublin City Distillery Ltd v Doherty*.[6] But there also grew up that legislation which is compendiously described as the Factors Acts, the first in 1823, then an Act in 1825, then an Act in 1842, then an Act in 1877, and finally the Act in 1889 now in force. The purpose of these Acts was to protect bankers who made advances to mercantile agents: that purpose was effected by means of an inroad on the common law rule that no one could give a better title to goods than he himself had. The persons to whom the Acts applied were defined as agents who had in the customary course of their business as such authority to sell goods or to consign goods for sale or raise money on the security of goods; in the case of such persons thus intrusted with possession of the goods or the documents of title to the goods, the possession of the goods or documents of title to the goods was treated in effect as evidence of a right to pledge them, so that parties bona fide and without notice of any irregularity advancing money to such mercantile agents on the goods or documents were held entitled to a good pledge, even though such mercantile agents were acting in fraud of the true owner. Section 3 of the Factors Act 1889, provides that "a pledge of documents of title to goods shall be deemed to be a pledge of the goods". It has been held that this section only applies to transactions within the Factors Act: *Inglis v Robertson and Baxter*.

Thus the curious and anomalous position was established that a mercantile agent, acting it may be in fraud of the true owner, can do that which the real owner cannot do, that is, obtain a loan on the security of a pledge of the goods by a pledge of the documents, without the further process being necessary of giving notice of the pledge to the warehouseman or other custodier and obtaining the latter's attornment to the change of possession.'

For constructive delivery of goods to take place, the goods must, of course, be specific and ascertained. There cannot be an effective delivery (whether actual or constructive) of goods which cannot be identified.

It appears that the one person who cannot effect a constructive delivery of goods, as opposed to actual delivery, is the owner himself, because any document issued by him to the bank undertaking to hold to the order of the bank is likely to fall foul of the Bills of Sale Acts (see below). In *Dublin City Distillery Ltd v Doherty*,[7] the owners issued a delivery order to the bank. Lord Atkinson said:

3 (1815) 4 Camp 251.
4 (1849) 6 Bell App 340.
5 [1898] AC 616, HL.
6 [1914] AC 823, HL.
7 [1914] AC 823, HL.

'... delivery of a warrant such as those delivered to the respondent in the present case is in the ordinary case, according to Parke B, no more than an acknowledgment by the warehouseman that the goods are deliverable to the person named therein or to anyone he may appoint. The warehouseman holds the goods as the agent of the owner until he has attorned in some way to this person and agreed to hold the goods for him; then and not till then does the warehouseman become a bailee for the latter, and then and not till then is there a constructive delivery of the goods. The delivery and receipt of the warrant does not *per se* amount to a delivery and receipt of the goods.'

Lord Parker in the same case summarised succinctly how constructive delivery can usually be effected:

'When the goods are not in the actual possession of the pledger, but of a third party as bailee for him, possession is usually given by a direction of the pledger to the third party requiring him to deliver them to or hold them on account of the pledgee, followed either by actual delivery to the pledgee or by some acknowledgement on the part of the third party that he holds the goods for the pledgee. The form in which such direction or acknowledgement is given is immaterial. Where the third party is a warehouseman, the direction usually takes the form of a delivery order and the acknowledgement of a warrant for delivery of the goods or an entry in the warehouse books of the name of the pledgee as the person for whom the goods are held.'

Thus, the delivery to the bank by the bailee, at the direction of the owner, of any document which has the effect of constituting him bailee for the bank, ought to be sufficient to constitute an attornment and, therefore, to amount to a constructive delivery. Whether or not this would extend to a warehouse warrant made out to bearer is not clear: it seems that delivery of such a warrant to the bank by the warehouse-keeper would constitute an attornment, whereas delivery of such a warrant by the warehouse-keeper to the owner and thence by the owner to the bank might not.

2 DOCUMENTS OF TITLE TO GOODS

Only two classes of documents of title to goods merit specific consideration in the present context, namely statutory warrants and bills of lading. This is because they are the only documents recognised by the law to represent the goods themselves, so that transfer of the document can, of itself, constitute a transfer of possession of, or property in, the goods to which it relates. Although it may be customary for banks to take, as security, possession of other documents relating to goods, such as non-statutory warehouse warrants or delivery orders, it seems that possession of such a document cannot, of itself, amount to possession of the goods to which it relates. Other documents, such as letters of hypothecation and letters of trust, may constitute bills of sale (see below), in which case they will be of even less value to the bank looking to possession or constructive possession of goods for its security. Constructive possession of goods through possession of documents relating to the goods can normally be achieved only if the documents in question are statutory warrants or bills of lading.

Statutory warrants are warrants issued under various special Acts of Parliament, for example the Port of London Act 1968 (s 146), the Mersey Docks Acts Consolidation Act 1858 (s 200), the Liverpool Mineral & Metal Storage Company Limited (Delivery Warrants) Act 1921 (s 3), the Trafford Park Act 1904 (s 33). Reference must be made to the provisions of the relevant statute to determine the rights of the holder of such a warrant. However, statutory warrants are thought to be, in practice, now largely obsolete.

Bills of lading are the only documents recognised by the common law as having an exceptional, if not clearly defined, status. It is well-established that they represent the goods to which they relate, so that the transfer of the bill of lading (in proper form and manner) of itself constitutes a transfer of the goods themselves. The transfer may, of course, be merely a transfer of possession, for example by way of pledge, or a transfer of property by way of sale, depending upon the parties' intentions. What is not so clear is whether or not bills of lading have the special characteristic of negotiability. Negotiability, according to Scrutton,[8] is that characteristic of an instrument which is capable of conferring on the transferee a better title than that possessed by the transferor. As such, it is to be distinguished from mere transferability. (For a further discussion of negotiability see p 546 below.) The special verdict on the second trial of *Lickbarrow v Mason*[9] found that, by the custom of merchants, bills of lading were 'negotiable and transferable by the shipper's indorsement', but this was a jury verdict in which the word 'negotiable' may have been used in its more general, less technical sense. Bowen LJ said in *Burdick v Sewell*:[10]

'the words of the special verdict in *Lickbarrow v Mason* admittedly overstate the law ...'.

The judgment of Lord Campbell in *Gurney v Behrend*[11] probably still represents the law:

'A bill of lading is not, like a bill of exchange or promissory note, a negotiable instrument, which passes by mere delivery to a bona fide transferee for valuable consideration, without regard to the title of the parties who make the transfer. Although the shipper may have indorsed in blank a bill of lading deliverable to his assigns, his right is not affected by an appropriation of it without his authority. If it be stolen from him or transferred without his authority, a subsequent bona fide transferee for value cannot make title under it as against the shipper of the goods. The bill of lading only represents the goods; and in this instance the transfer of the symbol does not operate more than a transfer of what is represented.'

However, one feature akin to negotiability possessed by bills of lading is their capacity to defeat the unpaid vendor's right of stoppage in transitu, when transferred to a bona fide transferee for value. Under s 47 (2) of the Sale of Goods Act 1979, re-enacting in somewhat fuller terms s 10 of the Factors Act 1889:

'... where a document of title to goods has been lawfully transferred to any person as buyer or owner of the goods, and that person transfers the document to a person who takes the document in good faith and for valuable consideration, then (a) if such last-mentioned transfer was by way of sale, the unpaid seller's right of lien or retention or stoppage in transitu is defeated; and (b) if such last-mentioned transfer was by way of pledge or other disposition for value, the unpaid seller's right of

---

8   *Scrutton on Charterparties and Bills of Lading* (19th edn, 1984). Scrutton asserts the general proposition that bills of lading are not negotiable; nevertheless, he cites certain instances when they appear to be (p 185, note 6).
9   (1794) 5 Term Rep 683.
10   (1884) 13 QBD 159 at 173, CA.
11   (1854) 3 El & Bl 622 at 633.

lien or retention or stoppage in transitu can only be exercised subject to the rights of the transferee.'

Section 1 of the Bills of Lading Act 1855 provides:

'Every consignee of goods named in a bill of lading, and every endorsee of a bill of lading, to whom the property in the goods therein mentioned shall pass upon or by reason of such consignment or endorsement,[12] shall have transferred to and vested in him all rights of suit, and be subject to the same liabilities in respect of such goods as if the contract contained in the bill of lading had been made with himself.'[13]

It was decided in *Sewell v Burdick*[14] that these liabilities do not attach to one who takes the bill of lading by way of pledge only.

(*iii*) *Trust receipts*

As already mentioned, the rule that the pledgee loses his security if he loses possession seriously limits the usefulness of the pledge as security. The bank's customer will want to retrieve the goods in order to sell them. The trust receipt was conceived in order to enable the bank to facilitate this without unduly jeopardising its security.

Where the depositor of documents of title under pledge requires their return to him in order that he may obtain and warehouse or sell the goods covered by the documents, the re-delivery of the documents may be said to substitute for the bank's pledge the right to have the documents and the goods they represent held in trust for the bank and the right to the proceeds of sale, at any rate to the extent of the pledgor's indebtedness. If the purpose of the pledgor is to obtain delivery of the goods, he undertakes in the letter to have the goods warehoused in the bank's name. By a letter of trust a bank is able to preserve its security rights, except in the case of fraud on the part of the borrower to whom the documents are returned. The common law rule, that relinquishing possession of goods or the documents of title to them destroys the title underlying the pledge to which they were subject, does not apply where the re-delivery is for a specific limited purpose. The point was made clear by the House of Lords in *North Western Bank Ltd v John Poynter, Son and Macdonalds*,[15] Lord Herschell LJ asserting:

'There can be no doubt that the pledgee might hand back to the pledgor, as his agent for the purpose of sale, as was done in this case, the goods he had pledged without in the slightest degree diminishing the full force and effect of his security.'

The House of Lords decided that the law in both England and Scotland was the same. To the same effect is *Re David Allester Ltd.*[16]

The letter of trust does not embody a charge and, therefore does not require

---

12 Property does not pass by indorsement to the indorsee of a bill of lading unless the property is specific and ascertainable. See *The Aramis* [1989] 1 Lloyd's Rep 213, CA.
13 A bill of lading is not in itself the contract between shipper and shipowner, but is evidence of its terms. See *Ardennes (SS) (Cargo Owners) v Ardennes (SS) (Owners)* [1951] 1 KB 55, [1950] 2 All ER 517.
14 (1884) 10 App Cas 74, HL.
15 [1895] AC 56 at 67, 68; see also *Mercantile Bank of India Ltd v Central Bank of India Ltd* [1938] AC 287, [1938] 1 All ER 52; compare *Lloyds Bank Ltd v Bank of America National Trust & Savings Association* [1938] 2 KB 147, [1938] 2 All ER 63 which appears to be inconsistent with it.
16 [1922] 2 Ch 211.

registration under the Companies Acts. An attempt was made in *Re David Allester Ltd* to challenge its validity. A bank had re-delivered bills of lading covering seed to the borrowers, on their undertaking to hold the goods and the proceeds as trustees for the bank. The company went into liquidation and the liquidator challenged the bank's right to the goods. It was argued by the bank that letters of trust were 'documents used in the ordinary course of business as proof of the possession or control of goods' within the exceptions to the definition of a bill of sale in s 4 of the Bills of Sale Act 1878 (see below). Astbury J held that the documents were not bills of sale at all, that the bank's pledge did not arise from the letters of trust, but existed before they were executed, that they were merely records of trust authorities given by the bank setting out the terms on which the pledgor was authorised to realise the goods on the pledgee's behalf. He pointed out that letters of trust were not issued for the purpose of creating a security at all; the security already existed. He also held that the letter of trust was not a charge on book debts of the company. This decision and that in *North Western Bank Ltd v John Poynter, Son and Macdonalds*[17] dismiss the argument that a pledge is lost if the subject-matter of the pledge is returned to the pledgor. There is obviously no good reason why it should be unless third parties are likely to be prejudiced by it; a bona fide purchaser for value without notice of the trust will be protected, and creditors of a company in liquidation are no worse off than they would be if the bank employed a third party to sell the goods. It is the purpose of the re-delivery which determines its effect.

The reasoning of Astbury J in *Re David Allester Ltd*[18] has been described in detail because it both defines and limits the scope of the trust receipt. The fundamental requirement is that the documents must be the subject of a *pre-existing pledge* in favour of the bank, so that when they are released on trust, there is something for the trust to bite on, namely the bank's right of possession and the special property in the goods conferred by the pledge. The reasoning is subtle, but arrives at a desirable, practical result. There are dangers, however, in attempting to extend the reasoning beyond this limited application. Other documents purporting to create security in goods, sometimes also called trust receipts, more often called letters of hypothecation, letters of lien or letters of trust, if used in other circumstances, are likely to be bills of sale, in which case they may have little or no value to the bank as security (as to which see p 541, below).

(iv) Letters of hypothecation, lien or trust

1 LETTERS OF HYPOTHECATION

Letters of hypothecation, letters of lien and letters of trust are all documents used by banks in circumstances where their effectiveness as security is questionable. There is no generally accepted meaning for any of these terms. The very narrow basis for the effectiveness of the trust receipt has already been explained (supra). Hypothecation is a term more often found in the civil law. According to *Stroud*,[19] the contract of hypothecation is to be distinguished from pledge in that a pledge entails delivery of possession whereas a hypo-

17 [1895] AC 56 at 67, 68.
18 [1922] 2 Ch 211.
19 *Judicial Dictionary* (5th edn, 1986) p 1953, under 'Pledge'.

thecation does not. Both constitute an equitable charge.[20] Letters of hypo-thecation to a bank are often a notification and promise that the bank shall have a charge on any movables – goods, documents of title, bills of exchange, etc – which come into the hands of the bank from the signatory or with his consent or approval. Clearly, when this occurs, the bank will have a lien or pledge by virtue of its possession, but if the document creates an equitable charge prior to that time, the question must arise as to whether or not it constitutes a bill of sale or (if created by a company) a floating charge.

2 LETTERS OF LIEN

A letter of lien has been described as a document by which a bank can take goods as security which are not in the possession of the owner but, for instance, in that of someone in possession for processing.[1] An owner, though he cannot himself pledge by any document other than a bill of lading, may by agreement attempt to change his possession into that of bailee for the pledgee by means of a document using the expression 'we hold on your account and under lien to you'. Such a document may also be regarded as an equitable agreement to pledge subsequently. It would certainly appear to be an attempt to create a pledge without an attornment to the pledgee by the person actually in possession of the goods or a delivery of actual possession; and since a lien is a security based on possession, it is difficult to understand the effect of a document which purports to create such a security without conferring possession.

3 LETTERS OF TRUST

A letter of trust, if not a trust receipt falling strictly within the narrow scope of *Re David Allester Ltd*,[2] would seem only too likely to fall foul of the Bills of Sale Acts as constituting 'a declaration of trust without transfer'.

(b) Bills of Sale Acts

(i) Definition

A Bill of Sale is defined in s 4 of the Bills of Sale Act 1878 as follows:

'The expression "bill of sale" shall include bills of sale, assignments, transfers, declarations of trust without transfer, inventories of goods with receipt thereto attached, or receipts for purchase moneys of goods, and other assurances of personal chattels, and also powers of attorney, authorities, or licences to take possession of personal chattels as security for any debt, and also any agreement, whether intended or not to be followed by the execution of any other instrument, by which a right in equity to any personal chattels, or to any charge or security thereon, shall be conferred, but shall not include the following documents; that is to say, assignments for the benefit of the creditors of the person making or giving the same, marriage settlements, transfers or assignments of any ship or vessel or any share thereof, transfers of goods in the ordinary course of business of any trade or calling, bills of sale of goods in foreign parts or at sea, bills of lading, India warrants, warehousekeepers' certificates, warrants or orders for the delivery

---

20 *Re Slee, ex p North Western Bank* (1872) LR 15 Eq 69.
1 See *Re Hamilton Young & Co, ex p Carter* [1905] 2 KB 772, CA.
2 [1922] 2 Ch 211.

of goods or any other documents used in the ordinary course of business as proof of the possession or control of goods or authorising or purporting to authorise, either by indorsement or by delivery, the possessor of such document to transfer or receive goods thereby represented.'

One statutory exception to the definition of a Bill of Sale in the Bills of Sale Act 1878 which ought to be mentioned for completeness, although of limited application, is s 1 of the Bills of Sale Act 1890 (as amended by the Bills of Sale Act 1891) which provides as follows:

'An instrument charging or creating any security on or declaring trusts of imported goods given or executed at any time prior to their deposit in a warehouse, factory or store, or to their being reshipped for export, or delivered to a purchaser not being the person giving or executing such instrument, shall not be deemed a bill of sale within the meaning of the Bills of Sale Acts 1878 and 1882.'

Section 9 of the Bills of Sale Act (1878) Amendment Act 1882 provides:

'A bill of sale made or given by way of security for the payment of money by the grantor thereof shall be void unless made in accordance with the form in the schedule to this Act annexed.'

The registration and other formalities required by the Bills of Sale Acts were so cumbersome that they effectively destroyed the usefulness of the chattel mortgage as a basis for securing consumer credit, and thereby in due course led to the development of hire purchase for this purpose. So far as companies are concerned, ss 395 ff of the Companies Act 1985 and the equivalent sections of previous Companies Acts have since at least 1900 required registration of:

'a charge created or evidenced by an instrument which, if executed by an individual, would require registration as a bill of sale.'

In practice, banks seldom register security taken over goods, so that the effect of the Bills of Sale Acts has been to cast doubt on the effectiveness of any security over goods taken by a bank other than a pledge or lien founded on possession (or constructive possession) of the goods themselves.

The purpose of the Bills of Sale Acts was to prevent or avoid the retention of possession of goods by the owner after he had sold or charged them. The bank seeking security on goods should, therefore, be cautious about any arrangement which does not involve the transfer of possession to the bank, although the strict legal issue is whether the document by which the security is created falls within the definition of a 'Bill of Sale' in s 4 of the 1878 Act quoted above. Neither a pledge, nor a document recording a pledge and setting out the rights of the pledgee as regards sale of the pledged goods etc, will constitute a bill of sale; whereas a document creating an enforceable right to call for a pledge at a later date may well do so.

In short, if the security which the bank purports to take is a Bill of Sale and is not registered, it will be void.

However, this will be changed if the present Companies Bill (printed as Bill 174 by order of the House of Commons on 29 June 1989) becomes law. Under cl 89, s 396 of the Companies Act 1985 would be altered so that registration under Part XII of that Act would be required, inter alia, of:

'a charge on goods or any interest in goods, other than a charge under which the chargee is entitled to possession either of the goods or of a document of title to them.'

While the draftsman may have been attempting to simplify the law, the proposed section is extremely unclear, in that there is nowhere a definition of 'documents of title' and no guidance as to the meaning of 'entitled to possession'.

What is tolerably clear is that the purpose of the Bills of Sale Acts may be defeated in relation to companies as, for instance, trusts without transfer may not in future be registrable.

(ii) Application to letters of hypothecation, lien or trust

The issue in relation to letters of hypothecation, lien or trust is whether or not the document in question (whatever it may be called) is one 'used in the ordinary course of business as proof of the possession or control of goods', within the exception to the definition of a bill of sale in s 4 of the Bills of Sale Acts 1878 (supra). The authorities are confusing: it is difficult to draw out of them any principles of general application and dangerous to rely upon them as support for the effectiveness of any document not strictly on all fours with that considered in the particular case. In *Re Slee*[3] the facts were that Slee pledged wool in his own warehouse to the bank and undertook to deliver warrants; he absconded and the bank took the keys of the warehouse and possession of the wool. The wool belonged to third parties who did not claim as they were indebted to Slee, now bankrupt. It was held that the letter (of pledge) created a good equitable charge not registrable pursuant to the Bills of Sale Acts as it was a document used in the ordinary course of business; that it was not a declaration of trust without transfer. By way of contrast, in *R v Townshend*[4] a hypothecation given to a bank, undertaking to hold goods in trust for it and to hand over the proceeds when received, was held by Day J to be 'a declaration of trust without transfer'. However, the document was nevertheless held to be within the exceptions to the definition in s 4 of the 1878 Act because, in that particular case, the goods were at sea.[5]

The documents in *Re Hamilton Young & Co, ex p Carter*,[6] were what Vaughan Williams LJ, described as 'letters of lien'. They arose when traders sent goods to bleachers and packers for bleaching and packing respectively before export. The traders drew on their bank for a loan against the goods, and their letter of notice and request read:

'As security for this advance we hold on your account and under lien to you the under-mentioned goods in the hands of ... as per their receipt enclosed.'

The word 'lien' is an obvious misnomer, for the bank had neither goods nor documents of title; the goods were in fact hypothecated to it. In this case the firm became bankrupt and the trustee claimed that the documents (a) were bills of sale and void for non-registration and (b) that at the crucial date the goods were:

'in the possession, order, or disposition of the bankrupts, by the consent and permission of the true owners'

3 (1872) LR 15 Eq 69.
4 (1884) 15 Cox CC 466.
5 See also *Mercantile Bank of India Ltd v Chartered Bank of India, Australia and China and Strauss & Co Ltd (in liquidation) (No 2)* [1937] 4 All ER 651, in which instruments headed 'trust receipt' were held by Porter J not to create a trust and, therefore, not to be registrable under the Indian Trusts Act 1882, but created an equitable charge.
6 [1905] 2 KB 772, CA.

within s 38 of the Bankruptcy Act 1914.

Both in the lower court (Bigham J)[7] and the Court of Appeal[8] it was held that the documents came within the exceptions in s 4 of the Bills of Sale Act 1878, being documents:

> 'used in the ordinary course of business as proof of the possession or control of goods.'

Vaughan Williams LJ held that this applied in spite of the fact that Hamilton Young & Co could deal freely with the goods after processing for shipment to the East. The control of the bank, he thought, continued all along. Stirling LJ doubted this but accepted the view of Bigham J and it is certainly not easy to see how the bank had any control at all until attornment. Cozens-Hardy LJ thought that the letter of lien, coupled with the deposit of the bleachers' receipt, was a 'document used in the ordinary course of business as proof of the control of goods':

> 'It enabled the bank to prevent the bankrupts by injunction from dealing with the goods in any manner inconsistent with the arrangements contemplated by the parties – an arrangement which would result in the handing over of bills of lading when goods were ready for shipment to Calcutta. It thus gave the bank a "control" of the goods.'

Discussing this case in *Madras Official Assignee v Mercantile Bank of India Ltd*,[9] Lord Wright said:

> 'There was in that case notice by the bank of their lien to the bleachers shortly before the insolvency, but the statement of the bankers' rights in equity as against the debtors, and consequently as against the trustee in bankruptcy, is not made with reference to any question of notice. The rights between the immediate parties do not depend on notice, just as in the case of an equitable assignment of a debt notice is not necessary to complete the equitable right as between assignor and assignee.'

Applying the broad principles of equity, it is easy to understand that documents of the nature considered in these cases create an equitable charge. It is far less easy to understand how the courts were able to take them outside the definition of a bill of sale in s 4 of the 1878 Act. The decisions can only be explained as being based on a finding of fact that the particular documents in question were documents 'used in the ordinary course of business as proof of the possession or control of goods' and thus within the exception to s 4. It is thought unsafe to rely on them.

(c) Nemo dat quod non habet

This fundamental principle of English law is, of course, applicable to a pledge in the same way as it applies to any other disposition of property. Thus, a valid pledge of goods or of documents can normally be created only by or with the consent of the true owner. There are, however, exceptions to the rule which are more commonly encountered in the context of sale than of pledge, but may nevertheless be of assistance to the bank which has taken a pledge without the consent of the true owner. The principal exceptions fall

---

7 [1905] 2 KB 381.
8 [1905] 2 KB 772, CA.
9 [1935] AC 53 at 65, PC.

into two main categories: those arising under the Factors Act 1889 and Sale of Goods Act 1979, and those arising by virtue of the concept of negotiability.

(*i*) *The Factors Act 1889*

The Factors Acts (the first was enacted in 1823) were intended to overcome the weakness arising from the inability of a bona fide transferee of goods or of documents of title to goods to obtain a good title where his transferor had none. They made a breach in the common law rule *nemo dat quod non habet* by introducing, as Chalmers put it, a partial application of the French maxim: *en fait de meubles, possession vaut titre*. It was felt unreasonable, where goods were entrusted by the owner to someone else who, in fraud of the owner, sold or pledged them to a third party, that the third party should suffer if he gave value and took in ignorance of the fraud. As put by Blackburn J in *Cole v North Western Bank*:[10]

'The legislature seem to us to have wished to make it the law, that, where a third person has entrusted goods or the documents of title to goods to an agent who in the course of such agency sells or pledges the goods, he should be deemed by that act to have misled any one who bona fide deals with the agent and makes a purchase from or an advance to him without notice that he was not authorised to sell or procure the advance.'

The Acts remedied this weakness where the goods were entrusted to what was eventually called a 'mercantile agent',[11] which is defined by s 1 of the Factors Act 1889 as:

'a mercantile agent having in the customary course of his business as such agent authority either to sell goods or to consign goods for the purpose of sale, or to buy goods, or to raise money on the security of goods.'

In *Lowther v Harris*,[12] Wright J (as he then was) described a mercantile agent as:

'an agent doing a business in buying or selling, or both, having in the customary course of his business such authority to sell goods.'

Blackburn J in *Lamb v Attenborough*,[13] thought that:

'the agent contemplated by the statute is an agent having mercantile possession, so as to be within the mercantile usage of getting advances made.'

Raising money on the security of goods means pledging them. 'Pledge' is described in s 1 (5) as including:

'any contract pledging, or giving a lien or security on, goods, whether in consideration of an original advance or of any further or continuing advance or of any pecuniary liability.'

It is s 2 of the Act from which the 'interest', the 'special property', of the lender to a mercantile agent derives. Subsection (1) reads:

'Where a mercantile agent is, with the consent of the owner, in possession of goods or of the documents of title to goods, any sale, pledge, or other disposition of the

---

10 (1875) LR 10 CP 354 at 372.
11 *National Employers Mutual General Insurance Association v Jones* [1988] 2 All ER 425, [1988] 2 WLR 952, HL per Lord Goff.
12 [1927] 1 KB 393.
13 (1862) 31 LJQB 41.

goods, made by him when acting in the ordinary course of business of a mercantile agent, shall, subject to the provisions of this Act, be as valid as if he were expressly authorised by the owner of the goods to make the same; provided that the person taking under the disposition acts in good faith, and has not at the time of the disposition notice that the person making the disposition has not authority to make the same.'

It is essential that the agent has 'authority to sell or consign for sale or buy or raise money on goods', per Lord Alverstone CJ in *Oppenheimer v Attenborough & Son*.[14] The consent of the owner is presumed in the absence of evidence to the contrary (s 2 (4)). It is clear that the protection s 2 offers to a lender is limited by conditions the fulfilment of which it would often be difficult, if not impossible, for a bank to verify – which simply emphasises the necessity, as always, of knowing the borrower. Section 3 of the statute provides that:

'A pledge of the documents of title to goods shall be deemed to be a pledge of the goods.'

This applies only to pledges by mercantile agents, according to Lord Herschell in *Inglis v Robertson and Baxter*,[15] and only for money lent at the time of the pledge or subsequently:

'... the pledgee shall acquire no further right to the goods than could have been enforced by the pledgee at the time of the pledge.'

'Document of title' to goods is defined in s 1 (4) of the Factors Act 1889 as:

'any bill of lading, dock warrant, warehousekeeper's certificate and warrant or order for the delivery of goods and any other document used in the ordinary course of business as proof of the possession or control of goods, or authorising or purporting to authorise, either by endorsement or by delivery, the possessor of the document to transfer or receive goods thereby represented.'

This definition is the same as in s 61 of the Sale of Goods Act 1979 and almost the same as that found in the list of exceptions to the definition of a Bill of Sale in s 4 of the Bills of Sale Act 1878.

The definition is so broad that it seems the legislature intended the combined effect of ss 1 (4) and 2 of the Factors Act 1889 to be to enable a mercantile agent to create a valid pledge by a method not available to the true owner, eg by delivery of a warehousekeeper's warrant without an attornment from the warehousekeeper. Support for this view can be found in the wording of s 3 of the Act (supra) and it was clearly the view of Lord Wright, albeit obiter, at the end of the passage quoted on p 542, above from his judgment in *Madras Official Assignee v Mercantile Bank of India Ltd*. The safer view may nevertheless be that the Act represents no more than a statutory recognition of the principle of estoppel, in that the owner by entrusting the goods or documents of title to a mercantile agent has held him out as entitled to deal with them; but the bank must still ensure that the pledge is perfected and maintained as if it were dealing with the owner. In any event, as a practical matter, this is the only safe course for the bank to adopt, because it cannot be sure that it is dealing with a mercantile agent

14 [1908] 1 KB 221; applied in *Newtons of Wembley Ltd v Williams* [1965] 1 QB 560, [1964] 3 All ER 532, CA.
15 [1898] AC 616 at 630.

who is in possession of goods with the consent of the owner: if it can be sure of this, then it can presumably take a pledge from the owner as easily as from the mercantile agent.

Another question arises from the use of the word 'other' in the definition of 'documents of title' in s 1 (4). The implication is clear that the specific documents mentioned – bills of lading, dock warrants, warehousekeepers' certificates and warrants and orders for the delivery of goods – are regarded as documents 'used in the ordinary course of business as proof of the possession or control of goods.' What is not so clear is whether a further implication of the use of the word 'other' is that the category of such documents is closed, or that it can be expanded to include documents created to fit modern commercial needs. Even less clear is how broad is the effect of the last words of the definition, which refer to 'any other document ... authorising or purporting to authorise ... the possessor of the documents to transfer or receive goods thereby represented.'

(ii) The Sale of Goods Act 1979

Former Sales of Goods Acts have for a long time contained provisions enabling the seller or buyer in possession of goods to pass good title without the consent of the true owner. These provisions are now contained in ss 24 and 25 of the Sale of Goods Act 1979, which provide as follows:

'24 Where a person having sold goods continues or is in possession of the goods, or of the documents of title to the goods, the delivery or transfer by that person, or by a mercantile agent acting for him, of the goods or documents of title under any sale, pledge, or other disposition thereof, to any person receiving the same in good faith and without notice of the previous sale, has the same effect as if the person making the delivery or transfer were expressly authorised by the owner of the goods to make the same.

25 (1) Where a person having bought or agreed to buy goods obtains, with the consent of the seller, possession of the goods or the documents of title to the goods, the delivery or transfer by that person, or by a mercantile agent acting for him, of the goods or documents of title, under any sale, pledge, or other disposition thereof, to any person receiving the same in good faith and without notice of any lien or other right of the original seller in respect of the goods, has the same effect as if the person making the delivery or transfer were a mercantile agent in possession of the goods or documents of title with the consent of the owner.

(2) For the purposes of subsection (1) above –

(a) the buyer under a conditional sale agreement is to be taken not to be a person who has bought or agreed to buy goods, and

(b) "conditional sale agreement" means an agreement for the sale of goods which is a consumer credit agreement within the meaning of the Consumer Credit Act 1974 under which the purchase price or part of it is payable by instalments, and the property in the goods is to remain in the seller (notwithstanding that the buyer is to be in possession of the goods) until such conditions as to the payment of instalments or otherwise as may be specified in the agreement are fulfilled.'

While it is clear that these provisions of the Factors Act 1889 and the Sale of Goods Act 1979 may assist a bank which has mistakenly taken a pledge of goods or documents of title to goods from a person who was not the true owner, they provide little comfort to the bank which, at the time of making an advance, wishes to be satisfied as to the value and effectiveness of its security. At that stage, like the buyer of goods, the bank has no alternative but to take its security from or with the consent of the true owner, and not to extend credit if in any doubt on that score.

2   NEGOTIABLE INSTRUMENTS

The view has already been expressed[16] that bills of lading do not have the special characteristic of negotiability. Certain statutory warrants to bearer[17] may have this characteristic, if conferred by the statute under which they are issued, but the importance of these has declined in modern times. Accordingly, the introduction of the concept of negotiability leads away from the subject of goods and documents of title to goods, to the subject of choses in action, which as already explained[18] are not normally capable of being possessed or, therefore, susceptible to being pledged. Negotiable instruments are, however, a special category. A negotiable instrument is a document which itself embodies a cause of action, without more, title to which can be transferred by delivery, or by indorsement and delivery, in such a way that a holder for value without notice can obtain a good title notwithstanding defects in the title of his transferor.[19] Having these characteristics, a negotiable instrument is peculiarly suitable for a pledge, since the person in possession of it has, or can have, all the rights embodied in it. The principal examples of negotiable instruments are bills of exchange, cheques and promissory notes.

(a) Bills, cheques and notes

The pledgee of a bill, cheque or note has the same rights as he would have had under a lien. Unless the instrument bears a forged indorsement or is a cheque crossed 'not negotiable', he acquires an independent title and right to sue and to hold the instrument against the true owner until his debt is satisfied. As to sale, see under Realisation below.

(i) Pledge and discount distinguished

The discount of a bill is the purchase of it, normally with a right of recourse and for a sum less than its face value. The discountee, having bought it, is free to deal with the instrument as he pleases. Discount is a negotiation. Other things being equal, there is no practical or legal distinction between the ordinary negotiation of a bill and its being discounted, except in the amount paid for it. Discounting is a means of raising money, but is not a borrowing, as is the case with a pledge. If the pledge produces a surplus, it must be treated in the same way as a realisation under any other pledge; a bank which is a holder for value of a cheque collected may sue for the whole amount as it is suing on a negotiable instrument; but if it holds under lien or pledge, it must account for any excess received over its debt.

In *Barclays Bank Ltd v Aschaffenburger Zellstoffwerke AG*[20] the defendants

16 Supra.
17 Supra.
18 Supra.
19 Among the proposals of the *Review Committee on Banking Services Law,* set up in January 1987, which reported in February 1989 (Cm 622) was a new Negotiable Instruments Act, which would update the law in a number of ways including the introduction of a legal definition of 'negotiability', which would apply to all negotiable instruments.
20 [1967] 1 Lloyd's Rep 387, CA.

had paid for machinery supplied and erected by the drawers and payees of the bills of exchange, by accepting those bills. The goods were faulty, and payment on the bills by the acceptors to the payees was subject to a claim for set-off being pursued in arbitration proceedings overseas. The payees discounted the bills to the plaintiff bank for just under 75% of their face value. The bank sued the acceptors on the bills. Judgment was given for the bank for the whole sum, subject to a stay for 25% pending the outcome of the arbitration proceedings which would quantify the set-off. This result was reached because there was an agreement between the bank and the payees under which the bank would recover the first 75% for itself, but pay the remaining 25% over to the payees. So, although the bank had a better title than the payees, in that the bank's claim was free of the set-off, the bank was in fact claiming the 25%, as trustees for the payees, and the set-off could operate against that proportion.

In *Re Firth, ex p Schofield*,[1] bills were indorsed to the bank which, intending to discount the bills, held them while the status of the acceptors was examined. In the meanwhile the bank lent money to the indorser on the security of the bills held 'pending discount'. It was held that the bank had not yet bought the bills, so the indorsement was not by way of transfer, but merely by way of affording the additional security of the pledgor's name in a transaction which was really one of pledge only.

As to the complications which may arise where a 'stiffening' indorsement is taken from a person not a party to the bill, see the series of cases starting with *Steele v M'Kinlay* in 1880,[2] down to *Gerald McDonald & Co v Nash & Co*, in the House of Lords.[3]

Where a bill is deposited as security for an advance, it may mature and have to be dealt with before the advance is repaid; in such a case, the depositor must either withdraw the bill and present it himself, if necessary otherwise securing the advance in the meantime, or instruct the bank to present it for him, in which case the bank has a lien on it and a set-off against the proceeds. The bank is not entitled to negotiate the bill in these circumstances, though if it does so a bona fide holder for value without notice of the limitation on the bank's freedom of action would obtain a good title.

(ii) *No suspension of remedy on the instrument*

A bill or note deposited as security or pledged to cover an advance or overdraft does not, as does a bill or note or cheque given for a debt, suspend the remedy for the debt. There is nothing in law to prevent a bank suing for an overdraft during the currency of a note or bill at a fixed date which it has taken as security.[4]

(iii) *Satisfaction of debt not payment of instrument*

Nor is satisfaction of the debt necessarily payment of the bill or note. To discharge a bill there must be payment to the holder[5] in due course, which

---

1 (1879) 12 Ch D 337.
2 (1880) 5 App Cas 754, HL; and see *Byles on Bills of Exchange* (26th edn, 1988) pp 195 ff.
3 [1924] AC 625, HL; see also *McCall Bros Ltd v Hargreaves* [1932] 2 KB 423 and *Yeoman Credit Ltd v Gregory* [1963] 1 All ER 245, [1962] 2 Lloyd's Rep 302.
4 *Peacock v Pursell* (1863) 14 CBNS 728.
5 Bills of Exchange Act 1882, s 59.

must be by or on behalf of the drawee or acceptor. Application of moneys by the holder himself does not constitute payment in due course; for instance in *Jenkins v Tongue*,[6] the secretary of an institution had given a promissory note to secure an advance; part of the advance was stopped, with his consent, out of his salary: it was held that this would not support a plea of payment pro tanto of the promissory note. And in *Glasscock v Balls*,[7] a promissory note was given to secure an advance, and property mortgaged as further security. The mortgage was realised, and the mortgagee paid himself the advance out of the proceeds. The Court of Appeal were of the opinion that this did not constitute payment of the promissory note, which had been transferred for value to a bona fide transferee.

Lord Esher expressed himself as not being clear what were the rights of the person giving the bill or note in such a case. He suggested that he might be entitled to a perpetual injunction restraining the holder from negotiating or parting with the instrument.

It is difficult to see why, on satisfaction of the debt, however made, the giver of the note or bill is not entitled to claim the instrument, like a redeemed pledge. It is only Lord Esher's silence as to this obvious course that suggests a doubt. If the note or bill is, after satisfaction of the debt, left in the holder's hands, a bona fide holder for value, taking it before it is overdue, can acquire a good title,[8] and the satisfaction of the debt would be no defence against him when suing on the instrument.

(iv) Fully negotiable securities

Fully negotiable securities other than bills or notes may be deposited as cover with or without an accompanying memorandum. The lender becomes pledgee; if he takes the instrument bona fide and for value he acquires a title against all the world and may hold it until the obligation it was given to cover is discharged.[9] The test of good faith is the same as is applied in the case of the transferee of a bill. An antecedent debt forborne by express or implied agreement on deposit of the security is sufficient consideration.[10]

Fully negotiable instruments such as bonds to bearer, recognised as negotiable by The Stock Exchange and the mercantile community, are from a legal standpoint a sound security. No question of forged indorsement can arise; and by their nature there is no danger that they may have been obtained by fraud. A negotiable security of this class may be stolen from its true owner, and yet the pledgee, if he takes it bona fide and for value, can hold it against him.

Absolute negotiability admits of no qualifications.

(b) Pledge by an agent

The theory that a bank was affected with constructive notice if it took instruments, however fully negotiable, by way of pledge from an agent or

---

6 (1860) 29 LJ Ex 147.
7 (1889) 24 QBD 13.
8 *Glasscock v Balls* (1899) 24 QBD 13.
9 *London Joint Stock Bank v Simmons* [1892] AC 201, HL; *Bentick v London Joint Stock Bank* [1893] 2 Ch 120.
10 *Glegg v Bromley* [1912] 3 KB 474, CA.

broker was dispelled by the case of *London Joint Stock Bank v Simmons*.[11] The previous decision of the House of Lords in *Earl of Sheffield v London Joint Stock Bank Ltd*,[12] was not unreasonably understood as laying down that if negotiable securities were tendered as cover by a person who, from the nature of his business, was likely to have securities of other persons in his possession, it was the duty of the bank to inquire into the nature and extent of his authority to deal with the securities; that the omission to make such inquiry might preclude the bank from claiming to be a holder in good faith and for value; and further that, though the agent might have authority to pledge the securities of each principal separately, this would not avail the bank if the securities of various principals were pledged en bloc to secure one advance.

In *London Joint Stock Bank v Simmons*,[13] the House of Lords declared that *Earl of Sheffield v London Joint Stock Bank Ltd*[14] was decided purely on the particular facts of the case, which in their opinion were such as to affect the bank with either actual or constructive notice of the limited right of property of the person with whom they were dealing, and of the fact that, in pledging the securities as he did, he was exceeding such right of property or any authority reposed in him. They repudiated the idea that any new principle of law was laid down by that case, and emphatically affirmed the right of a bank or any other person to take as security negotiable instruments from a person known to be an agent without inquiring into his authority, provided always that there were no extrinsic circumstances reasonably calculated to arouse suspicion. The guiding principle must therefore be derived from *London Joint Stock Bank v Simmons*[15] irrespective of any supposed general propositions which may have appeared deducible from the *Sheffield* case. Lord Halsbury, in *London Joint Stock Bank v Simmons*, expressly says that there is nothing in the position of broker and customer which makes it a reasonable inference that the broker is exceeding his authority, or raises a doubt on the subject;[16] that the inferences arrived at in the *Sheffield* case have no relation to the course of business which brokers habitually pursue towards their own clients, and for their own clients, when dealing with banks with which they deposit securities; and he proceeds:[17]

'The deposit of securities as "cover" in a broker's business is as well known a course of dealing as anything can possibly be, and the phrase that they are deposited en bloc seems to me to be somewhat fallacious. That they are, in fact, deposited by the broker at one time, and to raise one sum, may be true. It does not follow, and I do not know, that the banker could reasonably be expected to presume that they belonged to different customers, and that the limit of the broker's authority was applied to each individual security by his own client.'

He proceeded:

'To lay down as a broad proposition that in every case you must inquire whether

11 [1892] AC 201, HL.
12 (1888) 13 App Cas 333.
13 [1892] AC 201, HL.
14 (1888) 13 App Cas 333.
15 [1892] AC 201, HL; see also *Fuller v Glyn, Mills, Currie & Co* [1914] 2 KB 168, 19 Com Cas 186; *Lloyds Bank Ltd v Swiss Bankverein* (1913) 108 LT 143, 18 Com Cas 79, CA.
16 The case of a solicitor and his client may well be different; see *Jameson v Union Bank of Scotland* (1913) 109 LT 850.
17 [1892] AC 201 at 211.

a known agent has the authority of his principal would undoubtedly be a startling proposition, and certainly nothing said in *Lord Sheffield's* case could justify so novel an idea. The broad proposition laid down by Chief Justice Abbot,[18] that whoever is the holder of a negotiable instrument "has power to give title to any person honestly acquiring it", seems to me to be decisive of this case.'

Lord Herschell dwelt strongly on the absurdity which would result if negotiable securities could not be as readily taken by way of pledge from an agent as documents of title to goods are by virtue of the Factors Act:[19]

'What ground is there for the position that in regard to a pledge the case is different; that one may safely take a negotiable instrument by way of sale from an agent without inquiry, but cannot so take it by way of pledge? It is surely of the very essence of a negotiable instrument that you may treat the person in possession of it as having authority to deal with it, be he agent or otherwise, unless you know to the contrary, and are not compelled, in order to secure a good title to yourself, to inquire into the nature of his title or the extent of his authority.'

And concluding his judgment he sums up in words which concede all that any bank could reasonably ask. He says:[20]

'But I desire to rest my judgment upon the broad and simple ground that I find, as a matter of fact, that the bank took the bonds in good faith and for value. It is easy enough to make an elaborate presentation, after the event, of the speculations with which the bank managers might have occupied themselves in reference to the capacity in which the broker who offered the bonds as security for an advance held them. I think, however, they were not bound to occupy their minds with any such speculation. I apprehend that when a person whose honesty there is no reason to doubt offers negotiable securities to a banker or any other person, the only consideration likely to engage his attention is whether the security is sufficient to justify the advance required. And I do not think the law lays upon him the obligation of making any inquiry into the title of the person whom he finds in possession of them; of course, if there is anything to arouse suspicion, to lead to a doubt whether the person purporting to transfer them is justified in entering into the contemplated transaction, the case would be different. The existence of such suspicion or doubt would be inconsistent with good faith. And if no inquiry were made, or if on inquiry the doubt were not removed, and the suspicion dissipated, I should have no hesitation in holding that good faith was wanting in a person thus acting.'

The principle involved here is not restricted to the case of an agent, but applies also to that of someone who professes to deal with the securities as an independent owner.[1]

---

18 *R v Bishop of Peterborough* (1824) 3 B & C 47.
19 [1892] AC 201 at 217.
20 [1892] AC 201 at 223.
 1 Cf *Jones v Peppercorne* (1858) John 430; *Eckstein v Midland Bank Ltd* (1926) 4 Legal Decisions Affecting Bankers 91. Under the rules of The Securities Association (TSA, Part III, Section 10, 100:01 (c)) if such a pledgor is a member of the TSA he is forbidden from pledging securities except in certain circumstances. Nevertheless, in practice, this restriction is unlikely to affect the decision in *London Joint Stock Bank v Simmons*.

(c) Negotiability

(i) Incidents of negotiability

The rights and immunities accorded to the bank in the *Simmons* case were dependent on the full negotiability of the instruments pledged. It is necessary, therefore, to consider what are the tests of negotiability.

To be negotiable, an instrument must embody a promise or ground of action in itself.[2] Foreign government bonds may embody a promise but there may be no enforceable ground of action.[3] A negotiable instrument must purport to be transferable by delivery or by indorsement and delivery; it must, either by statute or by the custom of the mercantile community of this country, be recognised as so transferable and as conferring, upon a person who takes it honestly and for value, independent and indefeasible property in, and right of action on, it.[4] Blackburn J says a negotiable instrument must be 'transferable, *like cash*, by delivery', but he does not mean it must always pass at its face value; he is speaking merely of the method of transfer. The admission made in the *Simmons* case was that the bonds in question passed from hand to hand on The Stock Exchange; and Bowen LJ points out the difference between transferability and true negotiability, and that the admission was consistent with the bonds being transferable, but not legally negotiable. The House of Lords, coupling this admission with a somewhat general statement made in evidence that the bonds so passed as 'negotiable securities', held their legal negotiability proved. Lord Macnaghten, indeed, seemed desirous of minimising, or even obliterating, the difference between transferability and negotiability, by deprecating the setting up of 'refined distinctions which are not understood or are uniformly and persistently ignored in the daily practice of The Stock Exchange'.[5]

(ii) Recent recognition sufficient

The recent origin of a mercantile custom to treat a particular class of instrument as negotiable is no bar to its validity.[6] This is disputed by those who advocate the view that the negotiability of certain instruments was recognised by, and incorporated in, the ancient law merchant, and that, save by statute, no addition can therefore be made to the category. The judgment of Kennedy J in *Bechuanaland Exploration Co v London Trading Bank Ltd*,[7] in which the earlier and somewhat conflicting decisions are carefully reviewed, is very convincing in the opposite direction; and it was followed by Bigham J in *Edelstein v Schuler & Co.*[8]

An illustration of comparatively recent origin is the so-called negotiable certificate of deposit issued by banks in the United Kingdom. They are on the

---

2 *Jones & Co v Coventry* [1909] 2 KB 1029.
3 *Goodwin v Robarts* (1875) LR 10 Exch 337; *Crouch v Credit Foncier of England* (1873) LR 8 QB 374 at 384.
4 Cf per Blackburn J in *Crouch v Credit Foncier of England* (1873) LR 8 QB 374 at 381; per Lord Herschell, in *London Joint Stock Bank v Simmons* [1892] AC 201 at 215; and especially the lucid statement of the true rule by Bowen LJ, in *Simmons v London Joint Stock Bank* [1891] 1 Ch 201 at 294.
5 *London Joint Stock Bank v Simmons* [1892] AC 201 at 224.
6 *Kum v Wah Tat Bank Ltd (Malaysia)* [1971] 1 Lloyd's Rep 439, PC.
7 [1898] 2 QB 658.
8 [1902] 2 KB 144.

face of them stated to be payable to bearer but normally require presentation through the medium of a recognised bank as a prerequisite to payment. They pass either by mere delivery or by indorsement and delivery. There is little doubt that the courts would today hold these instruments fully negotiable; and see below, as to estoppel by character of document.

(iii) Must be negotiable here

The negotiability of a foreign instrument in the country of its origin is no evidence that it is negotiable here. As Bowen LJ said in *Picker v London and County Banking Co:*[9]

> 'Then is evidence that an instrument or piece of money forms part of the mercantile currency of another country any evidence that it forms part of the mercantile currency in this country? Such a proposition is obviously absurd; for, if it were true, there could be no such thing as a national currency. For the same reason, as it appears to me, that a German dollar is not the same thing as its equivalent in English money for this purpose, and that the barbarous tokens of some savage tribe, such as cowries, are not part of the English currency, evidence that the instrument would pass in Prussia as a negotiable instrument does not show that it is a negotiable instrument here.'[10]

The instruments in *Picker's* case were Prussian bonds issued with detached coupons. The evidence was that they were treated in Prussia as negotiable by delivery apart from the coupons, but it was not proved that they were so treated in the English market. The question subsequently arose whether the absence of, say, one coupon not yet due, from an otherwise negotiable instrument, affects its negotiability. Mathew J in *Rothschild & Sons v IRC*,[11] held coupons negotiable per se. He did not distinguish between those due and those accruing. It is conceivable that a man might wish to realise future coupons without parting with the capital. The independent negotiability of the coupons would seem to imply that of the bond without them.

(iv) Negotiability by estoppel

Sometimes securities are said to be negotiable by estoppel, or quasi-negotiable. Both terms are misleading, the latter particularly so. Willis J expressed himself as follows:[12]

> 'Title by estoppel is what men mean when they speak of negotiability by estoppel, but title by estoppel is a different thing altogether from negotiability ...'.

The so-called doctrine of negotiability by estoppel would hardly suffice to give a power of sale on the pledge of documents not otherwise negotiable. The estoppel goes rather to the authority of the agent to deal with the document than to its nature, of which the pledgee is as competent to judge as the pledgor.

The phrase 'negotiable by estoppel' is used by Bowen LJ in *Easton v London Joint Stock Bank*;[13] but he is most careful to explain that it is a mere convenient figure of speech, and that the real underlying principle is that of personal

9 (1887) 18 QBD 515, CA.
10 Cf *Williams v Colonial Bank* (1888) 38 Ch D 388 at 404.
11 [1894] 2 QB 142.
12 *Law of Negotiable Securities* (5th edn, 1930) p 13.
13 (1886) 34 Ch D 95 at 113–114.

estoppel by conduct, representation, or holding out an agent as having certain authority, of which the instrument is an element of evidence, not the attribution of partial or fictitious negotiability to the instrument itself.

There is no case of this nature which is not either actually explained on this basis or is not so explainable.

In *Goodwin v Robarts*,[14] Lord Cairns put the position thus:

'The plaintiff bought in the market scrip which, from the form in which it is prepared, virtually represented that the paper would pass from hand to hand, and that anyone who became bona fide the holder might claim for his own benefit the fulfilment of its terms from the foreign government. The appellant might have kept this scrip in his own possession, and, if he had done so, no question like the present would have arisen. He preferred, however, to place it in the possession and under the control of his broker or agent, and, although it is stated that it remained in the agent's hands for disposal or to be exchanged for the bonds when issued, as the appellant should direct, those into whose hands the scrip would come could know nothing of the title of the appellant, or of any private instructions he might have given to his agent. The scrip itself would be a representation to anyone taking it, a representation which the appellant must be taken to have made or to have been a party to, that, if the scrip were taken in good faith and for value, the person taking it would stand to all intents and purposes in the place of the previous holder. Let it be assumed, for the moment, that the instrument was not negotiable, that no right of action was transferred by the delivery, and that no legal claim could be made by the taker in his own name against the foreign government; still the appellant is in the position of a person who has made a representation, on the face of his scrip, that it would pass with a good title to anyone on his taking it in good faith and for value, and who has put it in the power of his agent to hand over the scrip with this representation to those who are induced to alter their position on the faith of the representation so made. My lords, I am of opinion that, on doctrines well established, the appellant cannot be allowed to defeat the title which the respondents have thus acquired.'

Though they vary in form and expression, that is really the substance of all the cases which have given rise to the theory of quasi-negotiability or negotiability by estoppel.

(v) *Title by estoppel*

Bowen LJ in *Easton v London Joint Stock Bank*,[15] though for convenience he uses the ambiguous term 'negotiability by estoppel', clearly shows that the ground of his decision is the principle enunciated by Lord Cairns. Bowen LJ says:[16]

'... if these bonds are not strictly negotiable and do not possess the incidents of negotiable instruments which are recognised as such, nevertheless a further question arises: whether Lord Sheffield, by the way he has treated these bonds, has not estopped himself from denying their negotiability, whether he has not – by placing for disposal, and with the intention that they should be transferred, in the hands of an agent of his own, bonds which on their very face purport to create a liability quite independent of anterior equities between the company and the person who takes them – really chosen to treat these bonds as negotiable and to authorise his agent to treat them as such. If the negotiability of these bonds by estoppel, so to speak, arises, that disposes of all difficulty that would arise owing to the seal being

14 (1876) 1 App Cas 476 at 489.
15 (1886) 34 Ch D 95, CA.
16 Ibid, at 113.

attached to these bonds; because it is no longer a question whether they are, strictly speaking, negotiable, but whether Lord Sheffield has chosen to treat them as such. This second way of looking at the matter may be dealt with from two points of view, but practically they run into one another. You may say that Lord Sheffield, having placed in the hands of his agents these bonds with the intention that they should be transferred beyond these agents and held his agents out to the world as clothed with authority to transfer them as negotiable, cannot afterwards, by any unknown dealing, or any limitation of authority which he has conferred on his agents, prejudice those who took the bonds which have so been floated. Or you may say, which I think is a sound way of putting it, that as regards Lord Sheffield and the bank these bonds have become negotiable by estoppel, and therefore Lord Sheffield is precluded from saying the legal title to these bonds is not in the bank.'

The same principle is briefly expressed by Lord Herschell in *Colonial Bank v Cady and Williams*:[17]

> 'If the owner of a chose in action clothes a third party with the apparent ownership and right of disposition of it, he is estopped from asserting his title as against a person to whom such third party has disposed of it, and who received it in good faith and for value.'

(vi) Estoppel by conduct

The decision in *Colonial Bank v Cady and Williams* indicates factors which must be present to render the representation effective or justify a person in acting on it so as to acquire title by estoppel. The instrument must be complete; no further formality may be required to entitle the taker to full rights and title. If, for instance, it is a blank transfer, it must, on the face of it, purport to pass ipso facto, in its then condition, and without the necessity of any further step, all rights and title to a person taking it bona fide and for value.[18] Possession by an agent must, taken in connection with the nature and condition of the instrument, be consistent only with intention on the part of the principal that the agent shall have power to transfer it by way of sale or pledge. Their possession does not, as in the case of fully negotiable instruments, carry the right to dispose of the instrument. If the agent's possession is ambiguous, ie compatible equally with authority to transfer and another purpose, the taker has no right to assume the former. As Lord Halsbury points out in *Colonial Bank v Cady and Williams*,[19] mere custody, apart from what the instrument, upon the face of it, represents to any person to whom it might be exhibited, is not a representation of authority to transfer. Only when the document itself, in the condition in which it was entrusted to the agent, represents that the agent is entitled to deal with it can a transferee rely on the apparent authority. The real test is whether the principal has represented the agent as invested with disposing power.[20] It is liability by the holding out of the instrument, the agent or both.

A somewhat analogous case is that of a person who entrusts another with title deeds for the purpose of raising money on them for the principal's benefit. In such case the owner is estopped from disputing the title of any person who honestly lends money on the security, notwithstanding that the agent utilised the deeds to borrow money on his own account and beyond

17 (1890) 15 App Cas 267 at 285.
18 Cf *Fuller v Glyn, Mills, Currie & Co* [1914] 2 KB 168.
19 (1890) 15 App Cas 267 at 273.
20 Per Lord Halsbury, in *Farquharson Bros & Co v King & Co* [1902] AC 325 at 330.

the limit imposed by his principal.[1] The same principle is clearly expressed with regard to an incomplete cheque in *London Joint Stock Bank Ltd v Macmillan and Arthur*.[2]

(vii) Estoppel by character of document

Estoppel may arise from representation of the character of the document as conveyed by its terms. If a company, for instance, issues instruments such as debentures in a form whereby it binds itself to pay the amount to bearer, it may be estopped by such representation from asserting any equities of its own affecting a previous holder, as against a person who has taken the instrument bona fide and for value on the faith of such representation.[3]

Theoretically a pledgee may part with the possession of the securities to a third party or even to the pledgor himself for a temporary specific purpose not involving the creation of any conflicting right or interest, the securities being returned to the pledgee.[4] He may re-pledge the securities but only to the extent of his own interest, so long as he does not purport to pledge or charge the whole property.[5] But parting with possession may mean loss, for the same conditions which render them good in the bank's hands render them good in anybody else's hands as against the bank. If they are negotiable, anyone who takes them bona fide and for value obtains title; if not strictly negotiable, he may claim a holding out. As an illustration, in *Lloyds Bank Ltd v Swiss Bankverein*,[6] the plaintiff bank lent money on bearer bonds to bill brokers who, subsequently, repaid the loan by cheque and received back the bonds which they charged to the defendant bank. The cheque was dishonoured and the plaintiffs sued the defendants, who had received the bonds honestly. The Court of Appeal held that the question whether value had been given was immaterial. Notice, if any, was constructive. The alleged ground of action was that the bonds were impressed with a trust in favour of the plaintiffs. The Court of Appeal held that it was repugnant to the nature of negotiable instruments to seek to impress them with vendor's lien, implied trust or constructive notice, and that the plaintiffs' claim failed. Farwell LJ said,

'the bankers give up their securities and take the broker's cheque, and the risk is theirs on the broker's cheque.'

A strange question arose in *Crerar v Bank of Scotland* in the Court of Session.[7] A Miss Crerar deposited with the bank as security for advances 2,775 ordinary shares of J & P Coats Ltd which, following the usual custom, were transferred into the names of the bank's nominees. After some 15 years, the advances were repaid and Miss Crerar claimed to have retransferred to

---

1 *Brocklesby v Temperance Building Society* [1895] AC 173, p 365, ante; *Rimmer v Webster* [1902] 2 Ch 163; *Lloyds Bank Ltd v Cooke* [1907] 1 KB 794, CA; *Smith v Prosser* [1907] 2 KB 735, CA; *Re Burge Woodall & Co, ex p Skyrme* [1912] 1 KB 393, following *Perry-Herricke v Attwood* (1857) 2 De G & J 21 and *Rimmer v Webster*.
2 [1918] AC 777, HL.
3 See *Re Imperial Land Co of Marseilles, ex p Colborne and Strawbridge* (1870) LR 11 Eq 478, a case of a promissory note to bearer.
4 Cf *North Western Bank Ltd v Poynter, Son and Macdonalds* [1895] AC 56, HL; Cf Trust Receipts, p 9–12, supra.
5 *Halliday v Holgate* (1868) LR 3 Exch 299.
6 (1913) 108 LT 143, CA.
7 1922 SC (HL) 137 (1922) 3 LDAB 248; Journal of the Institute of Bankers, vol xliii, 50.

her name the identical shares which she had originally deposited. The bank always held sufficient shares to enable them at any moment to retransfer but it would be very unlikely that any customer would receive back the shares originally deposited, as no regard was paid to the individual numbers.

The Court of Session upheld Miss Crerar's contention that the bank was bound to identify and return the specific shares deposited by customers; but gave judgment for the bank on the ground that in this particular case the plaintiff had acquiesced in the course adopted by the bank. Probably this is right in theory: on payment a pledgor has a right to the return of the thing pledged, whether the pledgee be a bank or a pawnbroker, and the shares in this case were identifiable by number. Still the application of the principle to shares is unreasonable. Specific return, instead of damages, is not ordered unless the article is of unique or very special value, such as the Puzey horn or the Greek altar, the classic examples. Whether the claim is in conversion or breach of contract, Miss Crerar's injury and measure of damages could normally only be the value of equivalent shares at the market price on the day of judgment.[8]

3 REALISATION

(a) Power of sale

Where goods have been pledged, either actually, or constructively by means of the documents of title, or where securities have been pledged, as by deposit, with or without a memorandum, the pledgee has on default a power of sale without the necessity of resorting to the court. A pledgee's only remedy is to sell; he cannot foreclose with a view to acquiring the absolute property in the thing pledged.[9] An expression of opinion which might be interpreted as contrary to the right to sell is that of Lord Herschell in *North Western Bank Ltd v John Poynter, Son and Macdonalds*,[10] where he said:

'In the paragraph from which I have quoted these words it is pointed out that a pledge gives only a right of detention of the goods, and gives no right to sell. Where, as in the present case, the delivery of the goods is accompanied by a grant of an absolute right of sale to the pledgee, he is certainly something more than an ordinary pledgee: he has a right which a mere pledge does not convey.'

The paragraph quoted by Lord Herschell was from a textbook on Scots law published in 1871; the power of sale, as shown by the terms of the memorandum from the bank accepted as the basis of the transaction by the borrowers, was 'an immediate and absolute power of sale', independent of any default; and it must be either to Scots law or to this exceptional right of sale that Lord Herschell was really referring. He seems to emphasise the word 'absolute'.

The authorities for the power to sell on default appear conclusive. In *Burdick v Sewell*,[11] Bowen LJ said: 'The pledgee of goods is entitled to sell

---

8 *Rosenthal v Alderton & Sons Ltd* [1946] KB 374, [1946] 1 All ER 583, CA; *Sachs v Miklos* [1948] 2 KB 23, [1948] 1 All ER 67, CA; *Munro v Willmott* [1949] 1 KB 295, [1948] 2 All ER 983.
9 *Carter v Wake* (1877) 4 Ch D 605.
10 [1895] AC 56 at 69.
11 (1884) 13 QBD 159 at 174, CA.

them upon default'. In *Re Morritt, ex p Official Receiver*,[12] Cotton, Lindley and Bowen LJJ said:

'A contract of pledge carries with it the implication that the security may be made available to satisfy the obligation, and enables the pledgee in possession (though he has not the general property in the thing pledged, but a special property only) to sell on default in payment and after notice to the pledgor, although the pledgor may redeem at any moment up to sale.'

(b) Notice to pledgor

Where the debt is repayable at a fixed date, the default occurs on non-payment at that date, but notice to the pledgor of intention to sell is apparently also necessary. Where the advance is for an indefinite period, demand for payment, with notice that if not complied with within a certain reasonable time the pledged goods will be sold, is sufficient. In *Re Richardson, Shillito v Hobson*,[13] Fry LJ said:

'The pawnee would have a right to sell the chattel pawned, either in default of payment at the time fixed, if there be a time fixed, or in default of payment after reasonable notice if no time be fixed.'

The proposition in *Re Morritt, ex p Official Receiver*, above quoted, is in no way limited to pledges for advances repayable at a fixed date. *Deverges v Sandeman, Clark & Co*[14] clearly recognises the principle, but suggests that the notice ought to fix a definite day, at a reasonable future date, for repayment to obviate sale. From this case it would appear that when the transaction is strictly a pledge a month's notice would be sufficient.

If the pledge does not realise sufficient to cover the debt, the balance of the debt is still recoverable.

(c) Realisation of pledge held as cover for acceptances

The bank which holds bills of lading or other documents of title to goods as cover for acceptances of a customer's bills, is a pledgee of the goods, the consideration for the pledge being the liability assumed on the bills at the customer's request, and the object of the pledge being indemnification against that liability.

In such a case, there is no particular event which constitutes a default entitling the bank to realise. Either a default is inferred from the bank having to pay the acceptances, or a power of sale is implied after payment as being essential to the indemnity. It is beyond question that, having paid, the bank can realise its security.[15] In *Banner v Johnston* references to the bank selling in order to put itself in funds to pay the bills must be read in the light of the fact that the drawers had agreed that the bank should not lend for that purpose which, as pointed out by Lord Hatherley,[16] could only be achieved by realising before the bills of exchange became due.

Probably the right to realise would also accrue if the drawer had undertaken to put the bank in funds to meet the bills at a specified time before maturity

12 (1886) 18 QBD 222 at 232, CA.
13 (1885) 30 Ch D 396 at 403, CA.
14 [1902] 1 Ch 579, CA.
15 Cf *Re Barned's Banking Co, Banner v Johnston* (1871) LR 5 HL 157.
16 Ibid, at 167.

and had failed to do so, as this would constitute a default, but in the absence of some such agreement or of a definite power to sell the bank would not be entitled to realise until it had paid the bills. Even then it would seem desirable to apply to the customer for reimbursement, and give notice that failure to do so within a limited time would result in realisation of the securities.

With regard to any surplus realised by the sale of goods or securities pledged to cover acceptances, it was expressly declared in *Inman v Clare*[17] that the surplus, if any, was subject to the general lien of the bank which paid the acceptances. The drawer's only right is to have the goods or securities or their proceeds applied to the bills, so that no liability, either direct or by increased debit, shall accrue to him in respect of those bills. The drawer's right is assignable by agreement collateral to and independent of the bills, but the assignee can clearly take no better right to the surplus than his assignor.[18]

17 (1858) John 769 at 776.
18 *Inman v Clare* (1858) John 769; *Re Suse, ex p Dever* (1884) 13 QBD 766, CA.

CHAPTER 34

MORTGAGES OF LAND[1]

It is scarcely practicable in a work on banking to dwell at length on matters of land law or conveyancing practice but the law relating to mortgages of land[1a] is, inevitably, a product of both of these.[2] There is also an historical dimension to it that is important but which has to be largely ignored for present purposes.[3] This short chapter tries to draw attention to some of the basic concepts and to refer to some areas where the law is uncertain or unsatisfactory.[4]

1 BACKGROUND

Before the Law of Property Act 1925 ('the LPA') there were two principal ways of creating a legal mortgage of land.[5] The first involved the borrower transferring the property to the lender and the lender covenanting to transfer

---

1 The Editor gratefully acknowledges that this chapter has been contributed by David Beales of Slaughter and May.
1a This chapter is restricted to mortgages of legal interests in land in England and Wales. It does not deal with security taken over equitable interests or the rule in *Dearle v Hall* (1823–28) 3 Russ 1 which governs the priority between mortgagees of such interests, as to which see, for example, P V Baker and P St J Langan *Snell's Principles of Equity* (1982). Floating charges are dealt with at p 279, above, of this work.
2 The standard land law texts all contain useful sections on mortgages, eg the traditional approach of R E Megarry and H W R Wade *The Law of Real Property* (1984) ('*M & W*') and J T Farrand *Emmet on Title* (1986) ('*Emmet*') or the more modern style, placing land law in its social context, of Kevin Gray *Elements of Land Law* (1987) ('*Gray*'). The leading practitioners' text remains E L G Tyler *Fisher & Lightwood's Law of Mortgages* (1988) ('*F & L*'). P B Fairest *Mortgages* (1980) ('*Fairest*') makes a useful starting point.
3 For an account of the history, see C H M Waldock *The Law of Mortgages* (1950), and Holdsworth *History of English Law*.
4 The Law Commission's Working Paper No 99 *Land Mortgages* (1986) ('*LCWP*') includes a number of proposals for reform, the most radical of which is that the existing methods of mortgaging interests in land should be abolished and a new statutory form of Formal Land Mortgage should be created into which statute would incorporate a new set of standard conditions. The Paper also provides an analysis of the defects in the present law. See also P Jackson *The Need to Reform the English Law of Mortgages* (1978) 94 LQR 571.
5 There were of course others. *F & L* refers to a Welsh mortgage under which the property was conveyed to the lender and the lender took the income from it in satisfaction of the mortgage debt and interest. There was no condition for payment and therefore no equity of redemption. See also LPA, ss 85 (3) and 86 (3) for 'the mortgage expressed to be made by way of trust for sale or otherwise.'

it back again when the debt was paid.[6] Prior to repayment the lender had the legal estate so he had all he needed to sell the property free from the borrower's interest. However the outright transfer of the property was not always convenient. For example, in the case of leasehold property the lender would not want to take an assignment of the lease because that would mean he became liable on the covenants in the lease and responsible for payment of the rent. The alternative was the mortgage by demise which involved the borrower granting the lender a lease of the property, again with a proviso that the lease would cease when repayment was made.[7] In the case of leaseholds, the lease to the lender took the form of an underlease thus avoiding any relationship being created between the landlord and the lender. Of course, if there was a default the lender would want to be able to sell not just the lease or the underlease vested in it but also the borrower's reversionary interest as well. This was done by having the borrower declare himself trustee of his interest in the property for the lender giving the lender power to appoint himself as the trustee and thus deal with the property. Alternatively the lender could be given a power of attorney enabling him to transfer the property in the borrower's name.

The mortgage would state a date on or before which the borrower was to repay the loan if he wanted to recover the property. This was known as the legal date for redemption of the loan and was usually six months after the date of the mortgage. The parties never really intended that the loan was going to be repaid then but it was a convenient (if highly artificial) way of ensuring that if the lender ever needed to exercise his enforcement powers he could show that there had been an event of default and that the powers had arisen. Meanwhile the courts of equity would protect the borrower's position as against the lender so long as the borrower complied with the real commercial agreement with the lender by making the appropriate payments and complying with any other conditions that might have been imposed. This right of the borrower to pay off the loan after the legal date for redemption had passed was known as the equitable right to redeem and the interest which this gave the borrower in the property was the equity of redemption.

It is still common for mortgages to be drafted so as to include a legal date for redemption just six months after the date of the mortgage and the expression 'equity of redemption' is still used even though as noted in the next section, after 1925 the borrower retains full legal ownership of the mortgaged property and he no longer needs to depend on a re-conveyance from the lender.

(a) Legal mortgages of the legal estate

After 1925 a legal mortgage of a legal estate or interest in land cannot be created by a conveyance with a proviso for reconveyance. The legislation introduced the 'charge by deed expressed to be by way of legal mortgage'

6 This form of mortgage had become the usual form of mortgage of land by the time the LPA was introduced. It continues to be the usual form of a legal mortgage of assets other than land after 1925.
7 The mortgage by demise was used until the early nineteenth century. It had the advantage that freeholds and leaseholds could be mortgaged by the same instrument. There were however doubts about whether the mortgagee was entitled to the title deeds and in the case of enforcement a reversionary interest was left with the borrower unless one of the devices referred to in the text was employed.

more usually referred to as the 'legal charge' or the 'charge by way of legal mortgage'. A legal mortgage of a freehold can now only be created by demise or by a legal charge.[8] An attempt to create a mortgage by conveyance results in the mortgagee taking a term of three thousand years.[9] Similarly, a legal mortgage of a leasehold is only capable of being effected either by a sub-demise or by a legal charge.[10] The legislation tidied up the former dis-advantage of the mortgage by demise by making it clear that the mortgagee had the right to the title deeds[11] and could dispose of the reversionary interest if he ever came to enforce its security.

The rights available to the mortgagee under a legal charge are defined in the LPA by reference to the rights available under a mortgage by demise. The relevant subsection provides:

'87 (1) Where a legal mortgage of land is created by a charge by deed expressed to be by way of legal mortgage, the mortgagee shall have the same protection, powers and remedies (including the right to take proceedings to obtain possession from the occupiers and the persons in receipt of rents and profits, or any of them) as if –

(a) where the mortgage is a mortgage of an estate in fee simple, a mortgage term for three thousand years without impeachment of waste had been thereby created in favour of the mortgagee; and

(b) where the mortgage is a mortgage of a term of years absolute, a sub-term less by one day than the term vested in the mortgagor had been created in favour of the mortgagee.'

Although the legal chargee has no term of years[12] he can go into possession of the mortgaged premises and he can collect rents from tenants. He is also able to exercise the security powers of a mortgagee by demise so he can sell the property and he can let it. The legal charge of land is therefore unlike any other kind of charge in as much as it confers on the chargee many of the benefits of a mortgage.[13]

(b) Equitable mortgages of the legal estate

Prior to 1926, in those cases where a first mortgage was taken by way of a conveyance with a proviso for reconveyance, second and subsequent mort-gages were necessarily equitable only. The legal estate was with the first mortgagee with the consequence that subsequent mortgagees had to settle for less. By introducing the legal charge, the LPA allowed the creation of successive legal mortgages of the same legal estate and in all ordinary

8 LPA, s 85 (1).
9 LPA, s 85 (2).
10 LPA, s 86 (1).
11 LPA, ss 85 (1), 86 (1).
12 As to the nature of the interest see *Weg Motors Ltd v Hales* [1962] Ch 49, [1961] 3 All ER 181, CA; *Cumberland Court (Brighton) Ltd v Taylor* [1964] Ch 29, [1963] 2 All ER 536; and *Regent Oil Co Ltd v J A Gregory (Hatch End) Ltd* [1966] Ch 402, [1965] 3 All ER 673.
13 The mortgage is a security interest that can be created over assets other than land. Its characteristics are exhibited by the pre-1926 mortgage of land – the transfer of the legal title to the asset to the lender with the covenant for re-transfer to the borrower or cesser on payment of the debt. The charge is a much weaker security interest and involves no more than the appropriation (by one means or another) of the asset to the debt. The chargee may well need the assistance of the court to force a sale of the asset because title is not transferred to it at the outset of the transaction. The legal charge of land is a wholly exceptional creation of statute.

circumstances legal security properly protected by possession of the title documents or by registration is to be preferred.

Notwithstanding that it is inferior as a security interest, banks will still take equitable security. It is frequently regarded as simpler to create than legal security and is deemed more appropriate as a short term measure. At the time when stamp duty was payable on mortgages the informality was perhaps understandable and of course perfecting legal security on registered land may still require the payment of a significant land registry fee. Nevertheless, the bank should appreciate that it could find itself in difficulties in preserving its priority and enforcing its security which would not arise if it took a legal charge.

Equitable security can be created very simply. An agreement to create a legal mortgage will be enough to constitute an equitable mortgage as long as the agreement is itself enforceable. To be enforceable it is necessary to have a note or memorandum in writing evidencing the agreement in order to meet the requirements of section 2 of the Law of Property (Miscellaneous Provisions) Act 1989. The depositing of the deeds by the borrower with the lender will be sufficient act of part performance but the purpose of making the deposit must be clear. There is no need for a document under seal or otherwise.

In practice the bank is going to want a written agreement with its customer so that there is no doubt about why the bank holds the deeds or about exactly what is secured. This agreement will usually include an undertaking on the part of the customer to execute a legal charge if called upon to do so and a power of sale for the mortgagee so it will need to be under seal.

(c) Registered land

The Land Registration Act 1925 (as amended) ('the LRA') provides that the proprietor of registered land may by deed charge the land with the payment of any principal sum of money either with or without interest.[14] The charge may be in any form as long as the charge does not refer to any other interest or charge affecting the land which would have priority over it and is not registered or protected on the register and is not an overriding interest.[15]

The charge must be completed by the registrar entering on the register the person in whose favour the charge is made as the proprietor of the charge and particulars of the charge.[16] On a simultaneous purchase and charge the application for registration of the chargee's interest will usually be submitted at the same time as the application for the registration of the purchaser as the proprietor of the land. While the charge remains in effect, the land certificate will be kept in the registry and a charge certificate will be issued to the chargee.

Until registration is completed the charge only takes effect as between the parties[17] and the chargee does not acquire a legal estate. He cannot exercise rights against third parties so he has no power of sale and he does not have the power to appoint a receiver to collect the rents from the property.[18]

14 LRA, s 25 (1) (a).
15 LRA, s 25 (2).
16 LRA, s 26 (1).
17 *Grace Rymer Investments Ltd v Waite* [1958] Ch 831, [1958] 2 All ER 777 and *E S Schwab & Co Ltd v McCarthy* (1975) 31 P & CR 196.
18 *Lever Finance Ltd v Needleman's Trustees* [1956] Ch 375, [1956] 2 All ER 378.

The proprietor of registered land may create a charge on the land in any manner which would have been permissible if the land had not been registered.[19] He can also create equitable security by the deposit of the land certificate.[20]

2 PROTECTION AND PRIORITIES

Occasionally a property will be mortgaged to a number of different mortgagees and the aggregate of the amounts secured will exceed the value of the property. If the property has to be realised and the mortgagees cannot all be paid in full, there is no question of the mortgagees sharing the proceeds between them and each taking a proportion of the loss. The way in which they share the loss is determined by their priority and this is considered in this section. In ordinary circumstances a mortgagee who ranks first will be entitled to recoup the whole of his debt out of the proceeds of sale before the second mortgagee recovers anything. However, there may be circumstances which disturb this. The mortgagee may have advanced further funds to the mortgagor after he had received notice of a later mortgage and this can limit his right to recover. He may rank first in point of security but not necessarily be first in point of payment. The rules governing this are considered later.

It might reasonably be thought that principles as fundamental to the law relating to mortgages as these would be clear and reliable and that the parties ought to be in no doubt about where they stand if things go wrong. Unfortunately this is not the case and the law is far from straightforward. This lack of clarity arises from the 1925 legislation itself and is not the result of judicial intervention.

(a) Priorities in unregistered land

The LPA permitted successive legal charges on the same legal estate in a way that was not previously possible. Accordingly the emphasis that was previously placed on the distinction between legal and equitable mortgages gave way to a system which depends on possession of the title deeds to the mortgaged property and on registration of mortgages on the land charges register.

In the case of unregistered land the position appears to be clear. Section 97 of the LPA provides:

'Every mortgage affecting a legal estate in land made after [1925] whether legal or equitable (not being a mortgage protected by the deposit of documents relating to the legal estate affected) shall rank according to its date of registration pursuant to the Land Charges Act [1972].'

Subject to what is said below, a mortgagee whether legal or equitable who has the documents can therefore depend on them for priority. But what happens if he parts with them? Does he need to register a land charge to preserve his priority until he gets them back again?[1] And what happens if there are two mortgagees each of whom has some of the documents relating

---

19 Sometimes known as the 'Section 106 mortgage' from LRA, s 106 which preserves the right.
20 LRA, s 66.
1 See *Fairest* p 133 and *M & W* p 997.

to the legal estate?[2] Since neither of them can register a land charge how are priorities to be determined? These questions are not answered by the legislation and would fall to be decided under the pre-1926 rules.[3]

For present purposes then, the possibilities as far as unregistered land are concerned are as follows:

1 legal mortgage protected by deposit of title deeds,
2 legal mortgage not protected by deposit of title deeds,
3 equitable mortgage of the legal estate protected by deposit of title deeds, and
4 equitable mortgage of the legal estate not protected by deposit of title deeds.

Mortgages in category (1) are straightforward: they are not registrable under the Land Charges Act 1972 ('LCA'). Those in category (2) are defined in the LCA as puisne mortgages and are registrable as Class C (i) land charges.

Mortgages in categories (3) and (4) are rather problematic. The approach of the legislation generally seems to be that possession of the title documents should be a sufficient protection and that registration should not be necessary.[4] On this basis, mortgages in category (3) would not be registrable and mortgages in category (4) would be general equitable charges as defined in the LCA and registrable as Class C (i) land charges. However, in as much as an equitable mortgage constitutes an agreement to create a legal mortgage, there is the possibility that mortgages in categories (3) and (4) might fall within the definition of estate contracts and therefore be registrable as Class C (iv) land charges. If a category (4) mortgage is registrable as a Class C (iv) land charge it is outside the definition of a general equitable charge and therefore cannot be registered as a Class C (iii) land charge. The distinction is important because a failure to register a Class C (iv) land charge makes the interest void against a purchaser for money or money's worth of the legal estate whereas the effect of non-registration as a Class C (iii) land charge is, as noted later, void against a purchaser of *any* interest in the relevant land.[5]

These issues have not been considered by the courts or by the legislature.[6] The general view of the leading texts[7] is that the logic of registering equitable mortgages as estate contracts is compelling. On the other hand, they draw attention to the widespread practice of not registering mortgages in category

2 See (1950) 13 MLR 534 (Hargreaves), *M & W* p 928 and *Lacon v Allen* (1856) 3 Drew 579.
3 Having two separate sets of priority rules, one of which evolved in an earlier age out of a different structure of legal and equitable interest seems unnecessarily complicated. See LCWP p 41.
4 Quite apart from the argument referred to in the text, the equitable mortgagee who relies on possession of the deeds and does not register could lose priority to a subsequent legal mortgagee if the legal mortgagee did not know about the earlier equitable mortgage and had accepted some reasonable excuse for the mortgagor's inability to produce the title documents. See for example *Hewitt v Loosemore* (1851) 9 Hare 449, *M & W* p 991 and cases there cited.
5 See *McCarthy and Stone Ltd v Julian S Hodge & Co Ltd* [1971] 2 All ER 973, [1971] 1 WLR 1547.
6 The courts can of course only consider the issues that are presented to them. However, the legislature was advised by the Report of the Roxburgh Committee on Land Charges (1956) Cmd 9825 that the Land Charges Act system was 'fundamentally unsound'. The LCWP adds that the Law Commission expressed similar views in Transfer of Land: Report on Land Charges Affecting Unregistered Land (1969) Law Com No 18 and repeats them.
7 *M & W* p 998, *F & L* p 72.

(3) at all and registering category (4) mortgages in Class C (iii) and suggest that the courts might be reluctant to put forward a construction which would be contrary to existing practice and would adversely affect existing security rights.[8] Against this background the prudent view for the time being must be that all mortgages in categories (3) and (4) should be registered as Class C (iv) land charges and those in category (4) should additionally be registered as Class C (iii) land charges.[9]

Section 4 (5) of the LCA provides that a puisne mortgage or a general equitable charge created after 1925 is 'void as against a purchaser of the land charged with it, or of any interest in such land, unless the land charge is registered in the appropriate register before the completion of the purchase'. In the LCA 'purchaser' means 'any person (including a mortgagee or lessee) who, for valuable consideration, takes any interest in land or a charge on land' unless the context otherwise requires. The general scheme of the land charges legislation is to make knowledge of the purchaser or the mortgagee irrelevant and to replace it with a strict system of registration. Thus as between mortgagees, the mortgagee who is later in time may know all about the earlier mortgage but, if it should have been registered as a land charge and was not, he will not be prejudiced by it.[10] The earlier mortgage may be legal and the later merely equitable but the lack of registration will still result in priority being accorded to the later.

Of course things can go wrong. Even apart from the complications caused by fraudulent mortgagors and negligent mortgagees, mortgagees occasionally forget to register and this causes great difficulties if subsequent charges are created. It produces a set of conundrums, two of which are set out below. It is important not to lose sight of the fact that they are only relevant as between mortgagees who are not protected by the deposit of title deeds and that the successive charging of the legal estate which they contemplate is comparatively rare.

The conundrums exploit the apparent conflict between s 97 of the LPA and s 4 (5) of the LCA.[11]

Take the consequences of the following events:

1 January	Customer grants registrable mortgage to X Bank
1 February	Customer grants registrable mortgage to Y Bank
1 March	X Bank registers
1 April	Y Bank registers

Very simply, s 97 says that the mortgages rank according to the date of their registration (ie X Bank takes priority) whereas s 4 (5) says that the earlier mortgage is void as against Y Bank because it was not registered when Y Bank took its mortgage (ie Y Bank takes priority). The prudent banker must have considerable sympathy with Y Bank which has not done anything to prejudice its position whilst X Bank has clearly caused the mischief by not

---

8 It is suggested that the agreement to grant the legal estate would be void but that the equitable charge (properly so called) would survive. See 7 CLJ 252.

9 For the rest of this chapter, the possibility that mortgages in category (3) should be registered is not taken into account.

10 LPA, s 199 (1) (i); *Coventry Permanent Economic Building Society v Jones* [1951] 1 All ER 901.

11 See *M & W* pp 996 ff and the arguments and articles referred to particularly (1940) 7 CLJ 255 (R E Megarry).

registering promptly. Legal writers are divided on the issue and it has not come before the courts.

The second example introduces another mortgagee and causes the system to break down:

1 January	Customer grants registrable mortgage to X Bank
1 February	Customer grants registrable mortgage to Y Bank
1 March	X Bank registers
1 April	Customer grants registrable mortgage to Z Bank

As between X Bank and Y Bank, X Bank's mortgage was not registered when Y Bank took its mortgage and so, according to s 4 (5), X Bank's mortgage is void and Y has priority. As between Y Bank and Z Bank, exactly the same principles apply – Y Bank's mortgage was not registered so Z Bank has priority. But what about Z Bank and X Bank? X Bank's mortgage was registered by the time Z Bank took its mortgage so X Bank's mortgage will have priority.

(b) Priorities in registered land[12]

Subject to any entry to the contrary on the register, registered charges[13] on the same land as between themselves rank in point of security according to the order in which they are entered on the register, and not according to the order in which they are created.[14] This produces the rush to registration although it should be noted that the mortgagee who first submits his mortgage to HM Land Registry could be displaced by a later applicant lodging his mortgage within the priority period conferred by an official search pre-dating that of the first applicant.

LRA, s 106 preserves the possibility of creating security over registered land by depositing the land certificate, with or without a memorandum of deposit. Such security is necessarily equitable only and is capable of being overreached but it has the merit of being quick, cheap and easy to create.

The charges can rely on possession of the land certificate as against any later legal mortgagee or any purchaser from the registered proprietor because each of these needs to produce the land certificate in order to register his interest substantively. However the chargee will not have protection against the chargor granting leases of 21 years or less because they take effect free of interests not protected on the register and do not need to be perfected by registration.

A charge, which is not a registered legal charge, may be protected on the register in three different ways:

(a) by notice of the charge as a land charge under s 49 of the LRA, or
(b) by a notice of deposit or of intended deposit under the Land Registration Rules, rr 239–242, or
(c) by a caution under s 54 of the LRA which will take effect as an ordinary caution against dealing.

However, there is no general provision in the LRA to say that the order of registration determines the order of priority. Normally of course, as between equitable interests, the first in time would prevail. For example:

---

12 See generally D J Hayton *Registered Land* (3rd edn) and 93 LQR 541 'The Priority of Competing Minor Interests in Registered Land' (R J Smith).

13 The general scheme of the LRA supposes that only legal charges are capable of registration but this is not referred to specifically. See Lord Denning MR in *Re White Rose Cottage* [1965] Ch 940, [1965] 1 All ER 11, CA.

14 LRA, s 29.

1 January	Customer grants legal charge to Bank. Bank does not seek to protect its interest on the register but the land certificate is deposited with it.
1 February	Customer sells the property to T. T pays over all the purchase price and protects the sale contract by registering a caution.
1 March	Bank applies for the substantive registration of its charge.

On substantially these facts, the Court of Appeal found that the Bank's charge had priority over T's interest because the Bank was first in time[15].

Protection by way of notice may be more effective. LRA, s 52 provides:

'(1) A disposition by the proprietor shall take effect subject to all estates, rights and claims which are protected by way of notice on the register at the date of the registration or entry of notice of the disposition but only if and so far as such estates, rights, and claims may be valid....'

It may be that the section affords a degree of supremacy to the register and displaces the normal rule that the first in time prevails. An alternative approach would be for the courts to accept that a prior encumbrancer who had not taken steps to protect his interest ought to be estopped from asserting his interest against someone who had taken the trouble to register properly or at very least that the equities between them were not equal. Registering a notice is rather more difficult than registering a caution but clearly there are strong policy considerations for not having one rule for notices and another for cautions.

No useful purpose is served by having three different ways of protecting the chargee's interest[16]. The Law Commission have suggested that there should be only one method of protecting the chargee's interest but were not prepared to encourage a strict system of registration to replace the usual first in time rule.

(c) Further advances[16a]

The principles discussed earlier were directed to the issue of how priority in point of security is determined between a number of competing mortgages of the legal estate. The present section is concerned with how priority of payment is determined between them, that is to say, what happens when a mortgagee makes further advances after the mortgagor has mortgaged the property again to someone else. The original mortgagee is going to want to say that his earlier mortgage, which is undoubtedly prior in point of security, entitles him to priority in point of payment not just for his original loan but also for the further funds he advanced. He is said to want to 'tack' the further advance onto the original loan to enable it to rank ahead of the sums secured by the later mortgage.

A preliminary point to be addressed is a simple one of construction. It is necessary to decide exactly what the earlier charge secures. It is not uncommon to find in a charge a definition of 'the secured sums' and to find that they are defined as the amounts due to the bank under a particular loan agreement. Clearly such a charge is not going to secure amounts under

15 *Barclays Bank Ltd v Taylor* [1974] Ch 137.
16 There have only been two reported cases on this area of the law. See *Re White Rose Cottage* [1965] Ch 840 [1965] 1 All ER 11, CA and *Barclays Bank Ltd v Taylor* [1974] Ch 137, [1973] 1 All ER 752, CA. In both of them the courts decided that the wrong method of protection was used and raised more questions than they resolved.
16ᵃ (1958) 22 Conv (NS) 44 (Rowley).

an entirely separate loan agreement. Equally clearly there are going to be difficulties if the agreement that has been identified is amended. The security which a bank will usually take will attempt to secure all monies due from the customer to the bank on whatever account, whether as principal or as surety and will include all costs, charges and commission. Assuming therefore that the further monies that are being laid out by the lender are, on a proper construction, covered by the charge the question arises of the priority to be accorded to them as against sums secured by the later charge.

(i) Unregistered land

In respect of unregistered land[17] the position as between mortgagees is contained in s 94 of the LPA. Subsection (1) provides:

'After 1925, a prior mortgagee shall have a right to make further advances to rank in priority to subsequent mortgages (whether legal or equitable) –
(a) if an arrangement has been made to that effect with the subsequent mortgagee; or
(b) if he had no notice of such subsequent mortgages at the time when the further advance was made by him; or
(c) whether or not he had notice as aforesaid, where the mortgage imposes an obligation on him to make such further advances.
This sub-section applies whether or not the prior mortgage was made expressly for securing further advances.'

No distinction is drawn between legal and equitable mortgagees[18] or between those that are protected by deposit of deeds and those that are not. Thus unless he is under an obligation to make the advance, the right of the prior mortgagee to tack turns simply on the question of notice.[19] This is one of the principal reasons why a mortgagee should always give immediate notice to any prior mortgagees – to put an end to this right of prior mortgagees to advance further funds and to tack them on to the original advance.

But written notice aside, the effect of ss 197 and 198 of the LPA is to affix the prior mortgagee with deemed actual notice of everything which is registered as a land charge. This deemed actual notice is just as much notice for the purpose of sub-s (1) as if the later mortgagee had given written notice. Therefore, subject to what is said below in relation to sub-s (2), a mortgagee proposing to make a further advance on the security of unregistered land should always make a search of the land charges register in case something has been registered which will stop him tacking the further advance.

Sub-section (1), on its own, would cause problems for the banks. It would mean that they could not rely on the security they took for their customers' overdrafts. An example may assist:

1 January	Customer creates a mortgage in favour of X Bank to secure customer's overdraft and takes a deposit of the title deeds
1 February	Customer creates mortgage in favour of Y Bank

17 LPA, s 94 also applies to mortgages of registered land which are not substantively registered under the Land Registration Act 1925 ie to those which are protected on the register by means of a notice, a caution or a notice of deposit.
18 Thus the doctrine of *tabula in naufragio* which, as between competing equitable mortgagees, enabled the mortgagee who acquired a legal estate in the mortgaged property to prevail over the other was abolished. The doctrine remains important for resolving conflicts between other equitable interests eg *McCarthy and Stone Ltd v Julian S Hodge & Co Ltd* [1971] 2 All ER 973, [1971] 1 WLR 1547.
19 As prior to 1926, *Hopkinson v Rolt* (1861) 9 HL Cas 514.

| 1 March | Y Bank registers under Land Charges Act 1972 |
| 1 April | X Bank clears customer's cheque increasing the over-draft by £5,000 |

At the time X Bank made the further advance to the customer by honouring his cheque, it was deemed to have notice of Y Bank's mortgage because of the registration. Thus it would not be able to tack the further £5,000 to the amounts originally secured and the amount which Y Bank had advanced would gain priority. To avoid this happening X Bank would have to make a search of the land charges register against its customer and, having discovered the existence of the later mortgage, agree the priorities with Y Bank before it honoured the cheque. Clearly this would be impracticable and would make it all but impossible to take effective security for a running account.

Sub-section (2) of s 94 was introduced to deal with this situation and is sometimes called the banker's clause. As amended by the Law of Property (Amendment) Act 1926 it provides that:

'In relation to the making of further advances after [1925] a mortgagee shall not be deemed to have notice of a mortgage merely by reason that it was registered as a land charge ... if it was not so registered at the time when the original mortgage was created or when the last search (if any) by or on behalf of the mortgagee was made, whichever last happened.

This sub-section only applies where the prior mortgage was made expressly for securing a current account or other further advances.'

Therefore as long as the mortgage provides expressly that it is made to secure a current account or other further advances and the bank has done a search for land charges at the outset and found nothing, it is not going to be prejudiced by later mortgages until it has actual notice of them or does another search and finds out about them that way.[1]

Section 94 (2) is another key sub-section that has not been tested in the courts and where there is some speculation about its effectiveness. Although it protects the mortgagee from having deemed notice of later mortgages it does not apply to other encumbrances that may be registered on the land charges register.[2] The example usually given is of an option to sell the property to a third party for an amount sufficient to discharge the original indebtedness. This option is duly registered as an estate contract before the mortgagee makes the further advance. The fear must be that the mortgagee could be compelled to release its security in favour of the purchaser on payment of the option price thus leaving the mortgagee without security for the further advance. Concern has also been expressed about the possible limiting effect of the reference 'to current accounts or other further advances'. Here the fear is that the further advances have to be of the kind that a bank makes when it honours a customer's cheque drawn on a current account. In practice lenders will advance further sums on ordinary loan account in reliance on s 94 (2). For the time being however, the uncertainty must remain.

Finally, before leaving this subject of how a mortgagee might be affixed with notice of a later charge, mention must be made of s 395 of the Companies Act 1985 which provides that in the case of a corporate mortgage any charge which it creates over land will be void against the liquidator and creditors unless particulars of the charge and the charge itself are delivered to the registrar of companies within 21 days of the creation. In due course the

---

1 There is of course no obligation to search after the original mortgage was created.
2 Or indeed to some of the matters that may be registered as charges on the local land charges register.

particulars will be available for public inspection and the question arises whether this means that the original mortgagee is to be deemed to have notice of the later charge. Whereas the LPA specifically provides that registration as a land charge is deemed to be actual notice to everyone interested in the land, there is no equivalent provision in the Companies Act and no equivalent of s 94 (2). For the moment, the authorities indicate that registration is only going to be deemed to be notice in those cases where it would be reasonable to expect the mortgagee to search and the practicalities clearly dictate that expecting the mortgagee to search at the Companies Registry prior to honouring each cheque is not reasonable.[3] Therefore although registration may constitute notice for other purposes it is not regarded as notice for the purpose of s 94 (2).

The bank, or indeed any lender on a fluctuating account, also needs to have regard to the question of notice because of the effect of the rule in *Clayton's Case*.[4] This is the rule that says that when a bank operates a fluctuating account for a customer sums received into the account must be applied against the liabilities in order of priority.[5]

This means that cash that the customer pays in reduces the debt that was originally outstanding and cash that goes out when the customer's cheques are honoured are treated as new advances. The effect of this on the bank's security is disastrous even if the mortgage specifically provides that it is made to secure further advances. The debt that was outstanding when the bank received notice of the later charge and for which its charge has priority is frozen. All cash coming in reduces this debt. All cash going out is new money and ranks after the amount secured by the later charge. This process will eventually extinguish the original debt altogether and the bank will have lost priority. The solution in these circumstances is for the bank to rule off the customer's account when it receives notice of the later charge and not to credit any further amounts to it. It is common for banks' security documents to provide that this shall be deemed to have been done even if, in practice, the bank does not get around to it.

Section 94 (1) (c) specifically preserves the position of the mortgagee who is obliged by the terms of the mortgage to make further advances. He can make advances and tack them to the original advance even after he has received actual written notice of a later mortgage.

This is the commercial objective a bank would seek to achieve under any facility where it expected to be called upon to advance funds in the future eg a loan to enable a developer to meet building costs as and when they become due or a facility which the parties agreed should be fully revolving with a notional re-paying and re-drawing on every interest payment date. Unfortunately s 94 (1) (c) does not fit comfortably with modern banking practice. To begin with, such commitment as the bank gives is unlikely to be in the mortgage.[6] It is more likely to be in a separate loan agreement which may or

3 As to the effect of such registration generally see (1974) 38 Conv 315 (Farrar) and R M Goode *Commercial Law* (1982) pp 771 ff.
4 (1816) 1 Mer 572. For a more extended treatment of the rule see p 177, above.
5 *Deeley v Lloyds Bank* [1912] AC 756.
6 It is even more unusual to find the commitment given in the mortgage. In the example given on p 568, above X Bank may have agreed with its customer that it would honour his cheque and then have received actual notice of Y Bank's charge. X Bank's agreement with its customer would not be in the mortgage and the further advance would not gain priority even if the mortgage expressly covered further advances.

may not be expressly referred to in the mortgage. More fundamentally, the commitment which a bank gives to make further advances will usually be heavily qualified and will say that it is subject to there being no breach of the loan agreement and to no material adverse change having occurred. In such circumstances it may be doubted whether there is ever a meaningful obligation to make further advances as the bank will usually have a fairly subjective discretion in deciding whether there has been a breach or an adverse change. Even if the obligation is there at the outset, it is likely that technical defaults occurring during the term of the loan would relieve the bank of the obligation to make the further advances so later advances will not be made pursuant to the obligation. A certain amount can be achieved by making it clear that the obligation continues until the bank takes some positive step to bring it to an end but it is difficult to avoid the conclusion that a bank which seeks to rely on s 94 (1) (c) after it has received actual notice of a later charge is running a degree of risk not usually associated with prudent banking.

(ii) Registered land

Registered charges on registered land are outside s 94 of the LPA and further advances on the security of such charges are dealt with in s 30 of the LRA. Sub-section (1) provides:

> 'Where a registered charge is made for securing further advances, the registrar shall, before making any entry on the register which would prejudicially affect the priority of any further advance thereunder, give to the proprietor of the charge, at his registered address, notice by registered post of the intended entry, and the proprietor of the charge shall not, in respect of any further advance, be affected by such entry unless the advance is made after the date when the notice ought to have been received in due course of post.'

The registered land system therefore preserves some of the features of the unregistered land equivalent – the charge has to be made for securing further advances[7] and the proprietor can continue making advances until he receives notice. However, what constitutes notice is considerably simplified. There is no question of notice being given by registration at Companies Registry or, apparently, by express notice from the later mortgagee himself. Notice comes from the registrar and compensation is payable if the proprietor of the original charge suffers any loss as a result of a failure by the registrar or the Post Office.

It therefore becomes all the more important to lodge the later mortgage at HM Land Registry as soon as possible and, from the original mortgagee's point of view, to identify notices coming in from the land registrar.

Although not dealt with in s 30 of the LRA priority for advances made under a registered charge after registration of a subsequent charge can be obtained by the later chargee agreeing to postpone his charge. Any such agreement should be noted on the register so that there is no doubt that it binds transferees of the charges.

Section 30 (3) of the LRA which was added by the Law of Property (Amendment) Act 1926 endeavours to preserve the position of the mortgagee who has agreed to make further advances:

> 'Where the proprietor of a charge is under an obligation, noted on the register, to make a further advance, a subsequent registered charge shall take effect subject to any further advances made pursuant to the obligation.'

---

7 Cf 'a current account or other further advances' in LPA, s 94 (2).

Again, the need to establish that the advance is made pursuant to a continuing obligation makes reliance on the sub-section unattractive and again it would be hoped that priority was obtained against all subsequent encumbrances not just subsequent registered charges.

3 LEASEHOLD PROPERTY

A mortgagee taking security over leasehold property has to accept that as well as the mortgagor there is a third party/landlord with an interest in the property. He also has to accept that the mortgagor/tenant owes obligations to the third party/landlord as well as to the mortgagee and that the breach of those obligations will give the third party/landlord various remedies which will affect the security.[8]

In the first place, the tenant may need the landlord's consent to create the security. Leases commonly contain covenants which exclude or restrict the tenant's ability to deal with the property. These can be in 'absolute' or 'qualified' form. An absolute covenant prohibits the tenant from dealing with the property altogether, whereas a qualified covenant permits dealings only with the landlord's consent. By statute[9] any qualified covenant against assigning, underletting, charging or parting with possession will be deemed to be subject to a proviso that the landlord's consent is not to be unreasonably withheld. The tenant's position has been further strengthened by the Landlord and Tenant Act 1988 which effectively places the burden of proving that a refusal is reasonable on the landlord. If there is no restriction on dealing, or if there are matters not covered by the clause, the tenant normally has the right to deal with the property[10] and no consent will be necessary to the creation of the security.

A covenant against sub-letting, assigning or parting with the property will be broken by a mortgage by sub-demise[11] but not by a deposit of the lease by way of equitable mortgage as the covenant is taken to refer only to a dealing with the legal interest.[12] A mortgage by way of sub-demise will not be a breach of a covenant against assignment.[13]

A mortgage which is created by a charge expressed to be by way of legal mortgage, should in theory not breach a prohibition against assignment or against sub-letting as it does not operate as a transfer of title but simply gives 'the same protection power and remedies ... *as if*' a term had been created.[14] The point has come in for consideration by the court but was expressly left open, the court recognising 'the view generally held in the profession that a chargee by way of legal mortgage does not have to obtain the consent of the landlord to a charge'[15] except of course where charging is specifically referred to.

---

8 *Grand Junction Co Ltd v Bates* [1954] 2 QB 160, [1954] 2 All ER 385.
9 Landlord and Tenant Act 1927, s 19 (1) (a). As to leases originally granted for more than 40 years in consideration wholly or partially of the carrying of building works where the landlord is not a public body, see s 19 (1) (b) (no consent required except in the last seven years but notice must be given). But see s 19 (4) as to application to agricultural holdings and mining leases.
10 *Leith Properties Ltd v Byrne* [1983] QB 433, [1983] 2 WLR 67.
11 *Sergeant v Nash, Field & Co* [1903] 2 KB 304.
12 *Doe d Pitt v Hogg* (1824) 4 Dow & Ry KB 226, *Ex p Drake* (1841) 1 Mont D & De G 539; *Gentle v Faulkner* [1900] 2 QB 267.
13 *Crusoe d Blencowe v Bugby* (1771) 3 Wils 234; *Grove v Portal* [1902] 1 Ch 727.
14 LPA, s 87 (1).
15 *Grand Junction Co Ltd v Bates* [1954] 2 QB 160, [1954] 2 All ER 385.

Then, the mortgagee may need the landlord's consent to enable him to enforce the security. There is a potential breach of a covenant against parting with possession if the mortgagee goes into possession. If the landlord consented to the grant of the mortgage then he could be said to have consented to the action that the mortgagee can take under it. If consent was not required eg to the creation of a legal charge it may be that the landlord can be said to have impliedly waived the right to object.

On the exercise of the power of sale, there is a further possibility of a breach of a covenant against assignment but the mortgagee does have a certain amount of assistance from the statute. Section 89 (1) of the LPA provides that 'where a licence to assign is required on a sale by a mortgagee, such licence shall not be unreasonably withheld'. There is no authority as to whether this is dealing with an absolute covenant that prohibits all assignments or whether it relates to the qualified form that allows assignments with the landlord's consent. On principle and by analogy with s 19 of the Landlord and Tenant Act 1927 there is no reason why a landlord should not be allowed to insist on a complete prohibition against assignment and the better view is probably that s 89 (1) is not attempting to interfere with this. Thus a sale by a mortgagee will be a breach of an absolute covenant against assignment unless the landlord had consented to the creation of the security in the first place in which case he may be said to have impliedly consented to the consequences of the exercise of the power of sale.

Any event which enables the landlord to put an end to the lease by re-entry or forfeiture places the mortgagee's security at risk. The most common events are of course the tenant's breach of covenant or the tenant's insolvency. In these circumstances there is an inevitable conflict between the mortgagee who wishes to keep the lease in existence and the landlord who wants to have the breaches of covenant remedied (where possible) or otherwise be rid of an unsatisfactory tenant. The solution adopted by the legislation is to allow the mortgagee the right to seek relief against the forfeiture through the court. However, there are certain shortcomings in the arrangements of which the mortgagee ought to be aware.[16]

Historically, failure to pay rent has been distinguished from other breaches of covenant. One of the purposes of right of re-entry was to secure the payment of rent, so if the rent was paid with appropriate interest and costs the courts could assume that no harm was done and relief from forfeiture should be given. This attitude survives so far as tenants are concerned under the current legislation. If a landlord starts proceedings for forfeiture, the tenant has an absolute right to stay the proceedings if he pays the arrears of rent and costs before the hearing. After the hearing has taken place the tenant has six months to apply for discretionary relief.[17] The landlord may prefer to re-enter peacefully and not take proceedings for forfeiture,[18] in which case the tenant can apply to the court to exercise its residual equitable jurisdiction to determine disputes between the parties on the same basis as would apply

16 The Law Commission's Paper *Codification of the Law of Landlord and Tenant: Forfeiture of Finances* 1985, (Law Com No 142) draws attention to some of the defects in the present state of the law and proposes new legislation introducing the concept of 'termination order events' and requiring due process through the courts in all cases.
17 Supreme Court of Judicature Act 1981, s 38.
18 There are of course restrictions placed on the landlord's power to do so where the tenant is protected by the Rent Act 1977 or the Housing Act 1985.

and the time limit of six months will not be relevant.[19] A mortgagee of the lease is also able to take advantage of this.[20]

If the breach is of a covenant other than a covenant to pay rent, the tenant must seek relief from forfeiture under s 146 (2) of the LPA.[1] Section 146 (4) affords a remedy to an underlessee in the situation where a tenant has himself underlet the property and enables an underlessee to apply for relief against forfeiture of the headlease whether on the ground of non-payment of rent or other breach. In s 146 (4) 'underlessee' includes a mortgagee, as a mortgagee by sub-demise has a legal term of years and a mortgagee by way of legal charge has all the rights and remedies as if he had been granted a term.[2] To this extent the mortgagee has rights which are analogous to those of the tenant.

Although it is now clear that s 146 provides a complete code[3] setting out the courts' jurisdiction to grant relief against forfeiture of leases otherwise than for non payment of rent, the inherent jurisdiction of the court remains. This can be particularly important in circumstances where the mortgagor's interest falls short of being a lease and is limited, for example, to an agreement for lease where the lease will not be granted until conditions in the agreement for the completion of building works are fulfilled. A breach of these conditions can lend to an attempt to forfeit and to deprive the mortgagor of the value of work already carried out. It is common in such circumstances for the agreement for lease to attempt to incorporate s 146 expressly as if the agreement were actually a lease. Alternatively some third party might be given jurisdiction to determine disputes between the parties on the same principles that the court would use in s 146 proceedings. Failing these, the mortgagor and the mortgagee might both need to rely on the inherent jurisdiction.

One of the shortcomings in the arrangements in s 146 both as far as tenants and mortgagees are concerned is that relief can only be given where a landlord is proceeding by action or otherwise to enforce a right of re-entry or forfeiture through the court. The prospects of the mortgagee being told what is happening improved with the changes in the County Court Rules 1981[4] and in the Rules of the Supreme Court 1965[5] which now require a landlord which is taking action through the courts to advise the mortgagee. However, there is no requirement of due process and if the landlord chooses to resort to self-help measures it need not have recourse to proceedings and can instead peaceably re-enter the premises and bring the lease to an end. If he succeeds in completing the forfeiture, the right to relief can be lost before the mortgagee even becomes aware of the situation. This has been described as just one of the 'rules of the game' which the mortgagee of leasehold property is expected to appreciate.[6]

The tenant who obtains relief under s 146 (2) is back where he started. It is as if the lease had never been forfeited.[7] Any mortgage he has given stays

---

19 Common Law Procedure Act 1852, s 210. See *Lovelock v Margo* [1963] 2 QB 786, [1963] 2 All ER 13.
20 *Ladup Ltd v Williams & Glyn's Bank plc* [1985] 2 All ER 577, [1985] 1 WLR 851.
1 For the modern basis of the jurisdiction see *Shiloh Spinners v Harding* [1973] AC 691, [1973] 1 All ER 90.
2 *Official Custodian for Charities v Mackey* [1985] Ch 168, [1984] 3 All ER 689.
3 *Official Custodian for Charities v Parway Estates Developments Ltd* [1985] Ch 151, [1984] 3 All ER 679.
4 The County Court (Amendment No 2) Rules 1986, r 2.
5 The Rules of the Supreme Court (Amendment No 2) 1986, r 2.
6 For a discussion of some of the practical problems when the tenant is insolvent (pre-Insolvency Act 1986) see 1985 Blundell Memorial Lecture *The Conflicting Claims of Landlord and Bank in Receivership and Insolvency* (Beer).
7 *Cadogan v Dimovic* [1984] 2 All ER 168, [1984] 1 WLR 609, CA.

in place as do any sub-tenancies. However, the mortgagee who obtains relief under s 146 (4) is not in the same position at all. To begin with, the mortgagee will become the new tenant so it will take on personal liability under the covenants in the lease. Secondly, it is clear that the lease that is vested in the mortgagee by the order is an entirely new lease[8] and that its effect is not back-dated to the original forfeiture. This prompts the question of what happens in the twilight period between the service of the writ for forfeiture of the old lease and the vesting in the mortgagee of the new. More particularly who gets the benefit of any rents payable by the sub-tenants. In the final episode of long running litigation in which many of the points affecting the rights of the landlord, the tenant and the mortgagee in these circumstances were explored the court found that the landlord had no right to recover these rents from the receiver appointed by the mortgagee of the old lease.[9]

4 RIGHTS OF OCCUPATION[10]

Perhaps more than any other decision of the courts in recent years, the ruling of the House of Lords in *Williams & Glyn's v Boland*[11] in 1980 caused concern to the lending institutions. The protection which the House of Lords were prepared to give to the occupiers of the property against the 'monied might'[12] of the bank appeared revolutionary and threatened to take away much of the security which the banks thought they had obtained for themselves when their borrowers executed the standard mortgage forms. It was because the facts of *Boland* were so commonplace that the decision caused such anxiety. The bank agreed to make cash available to Mr Boland for the purpose of his business and it required him to mortgage the matrimonial home by way of security. The house was registered solely in his name so his wife did not have to sign anything. Mr Boland defaulted and the day came when the bank wanted to take possession and enforce its security. At this stage, Mrs Boland claimed that she had rights in the house that were not affected by the mortgage and that her right to occupation should prevail against the bank's right. The fact that by asserting her own rights she managed to keep the roof over the head of her defaulting husband merely added to the bank's discomfort in the particular case and the institution's concerns generally.

The decision in *Boland* has its roots in the principle that there can be rights affecting land which are not discernible from an examination of the title deeds but which will nevertheless bind third parties who acquire interests in the land. Those third parties can be purchasers or tenants or mortgagees. In the case of unregistered land, the principle finds expression in the rule in *Hunt v*

8 *Cadogan,* supra and *Official Custodian for Charities v Mackey* [1985] Ch 168, [1984] 3 All ER 689.
9 *Official Custodian for Charities v Mackey (No 2)* [1985] 2 All ER 1016, [1985] 1 WLR 1308.
10 This section does not deal with the issues arising where in the *scintilla temporis* between acquiring legal title and mortgaging it, 'tenancies' granted by the borrower before it acquired title are perfected. These tenancies by estoppel will bind the mortgagee. See *Church of England Building Society v Piskor* [1954] Ch 553, [1954] 2 All ER 85. Discussed at *Fairest* p 47.
11 *Williams & Glyn's Bank Ltd v Boland and William & Glyn's Bank Ltd v Brown* [1981] AC 487, [1980] 2 All ER 408, HL (*'Boland'*).
12 Lord Denning MR in *Boland* in the Court of Appeal [1979] Ch 312, [1979] 2 All ER 697. In his view the court 'should not give monied might priority over social justice' and the bank was 'not entitled to throw these families out into the street – simply to get the last penny of the husband's debt.'

Luck.[13] If the third party visits the property and finds someone unexpected there, he is going to be put on notice that something may be wrong and that he ought to start asking questions. If he does not visit the property or does not ask questions he is nevertheless deemed to have constructive notice of whatever his enquiries would have elicited. It was acknowledged in *Hunt v Luck* that this manifestation of the principle had to be kept within bounds. The law does not favour imputing to people knowledge which they do not actually have and the whole scheme of the Land Charges Act 1972 is to compel people to register their interests as land charges or face the risk that a third party will take free of them.

The courts had struggled to keep the notice principle within bounds for some years but they had particular difficulty with a series of cases in the early 1970s. The Matrimonial Proceedings and Property Act 1970 already provided that a spouse making a substantial contribution to the improvement of the home was to be regarded as having either acquired a share or an enlarged share in it. The courts were faced with a number of cases where people other than spouses who had made substantial contributions or who had assisted in other ways in purchasing or improving property asserted their claims to a share in the property concerned.[14] In a period of very rapidly rising property prices the 'contributor' would fare considerably better if the law found that he had an interest in the property rather than a mere personal right to be reimbursed with his expenditure. A variety of approaches were adopted by the courts, but generally it would be found that the legal owner of the property held it on trust for the legal owner and the contributor in shares which the court would determine.[15] Frequently the legal owner would be the husband and the imposition of a trust would require him to account to his wife for part of the proceeds of sale. Difficulties begin to arise when a third party arrives on the scene and the courts have to consider whether the third party is going to be affected with notice of the trust arrangements.

Prior to *Boland* the leading case was concerned with unregistered land.[16] On facts which were remarkably similar to those which were assumed to apply in *Boland,* the court considered the question of notice by asking, in effect, would the third party visiting the property find anything unusual or untoward that ought to prompt him to start asking further questions. The court found that the wife's presence[17] in the property was 'wholly consistent with the sole title offered by the husband to the bank'. In reaching this

13 [1901] 1 Ch 45, affd [1902] 1 Ch 428.
14 Eg *Cooke v Head* [1972] 2 All ER 38, [1972] 1 WLR 518; *Hussey v Palmer* [1972] 3 All ER 744, [1972] 1 WLR 1286; and *Eves v Eves* [1975] 3 All ER 768, [1975] 1 WLR 1338.
15 Ie a trust for sale (but see Lord Denning MR in *Boland*). It would be one answer to the problem to find that there is a true trust for sale in this situation and to apply the doctrine of conversion so that the interest of the 'contributor' is limited to an interest in the proceeds of sale: see (1969) 33 Conv (NS) 254 (Hayton) but the courts have been inclined to dismiss this as a little unreal. The crucial step in the reasoning was to find that the interest of the 'contributor' under the trust for sale carried a right to the occupation of the property. For the origin of this right see *Bull v Bull* [1955] 1 QB 234, [1955] 1 All ER 253 a decision of Denning LJ followed by Lord Denning MR in *Boland* in the Court of Appeal. See particularly Ormrod LJ [1979] Ch 312 and *Elias v Mitchell* [1972] Ch 652, [1972] 2 All ER 153.
16 *Caunce v Caunce* [1969] 1 All ER 722, [1969] 1 WLR 286.
17 It was doubtful whether she had 'actual occupation' on the basis of the law as it was understood at the time. See *Bird v Syme Thompson* [1978] 3 All ER 1027, [1979] 1 WLR 440: 'when a mortgagor is in actual occupation of the matrimonial home, it cannot be said that his wife also is in actual occupation.'

decision the court was very aware of the burden that would be placed on the bank if it did have to investigate.[18] It might have been different if the husband had not been there,[19] but as it was there was nothing to put the bank on notice that the wife might have an interest in the property. Therefore, the bank did not take subject to her rights and could require her to vacate the property.

In the case of registered land, effect is given to the principle by s 70 (1) of the LRA which deals with overriding interests. These are interests which will bind the purchaser even though they do not appear on the register. Section 70 (1) provides that overriding interests include:

'(g) The rights of every person in actual occupation of the land or in receipt of rents and profits thereof, save where enquiry is made of such person and the rights are not disclosed.'

This paragraph accords protection on the basis of occupation and it is not necessary to have recourse to concepts of constructive notice. If there was ever any doubt about what the paragraph meant, *Boland* made it clear. Mrs Boland was in actual occupation and the bank should have asked her what her rights were.[20] It is no good asking the legal owner of the property what the rights of the other occupiers are.[1] An untruthful answer from the legal owner may very well give the bank a right of action against him but this will not prejudice the position of the occupier. To be on the safe side, the enquiries have to be very specific because if they are not, there is every possibility that the person to whom the enquiries are being directed will not understand what they are being asked. Obtaining answers from people who are not of full age or who otherwise lack legal capacity is obviously problematical and as subsequent development of the law has shown 'actual occupation' is not quite the simple factual concept it was once thought to be and a good deal of detective work may be required to find all the relevant people.[2]

The rights which can be protected by actual occupation are not defined in the Land Registration Act and it has been left to the courts to decide. They have looked at the general law and have concluded that the rights which can subsist as overriding interests are those which 'have the quality of being capable of enduring through different ownerships of the land, according to

18 Stamp J in *Caunce,* supra referred to 'how unworkable and undesirable it would be if the law required such an enquiry [it would be] as embarrassing to the enquirer as [it would be] intolerable to the wife and the husband.'
19 See *Hodgson v Marks* [1971] Ch 892, [1970] 3 All ER 513.
20 The fact that this would add to the burdens of purchasers and mortgagees was dismissed. 'Bankers and solicitors exist to provide the service which the public needs. They can – as they have successfully done in the past – adjust their practice, if it be socially required': per Lord Scarman in *Boland.*
 1 'Reliance upon the untrue *ipse dixit* of the vendor will not suffice': (Russell LJ in *Hodgson v Marks* [1971] Ch 892, [1971] 2 All ER 684. Cf in unregistered land (pre *Boland*) *Goody v Baring* [1956] 2 All ER 11, [1956] 1 WLR 448.
 2 Whether they can ever hope to catch some of the transients that the courts are prepared to recognise as 'actual occupiers' must be open to doubt, eg in *Kingsnorth Trust Ltd v Tizard* [1986] 2 All ER 54, [1986] 1 WLR 783 the husband invited the mortgagee's agent to inspect on a Sunday afternoon. The wife did not sleep in the house when the husband was there and on the day in question the husband had eliminated all sign of her occupation. Nevertheless the agent should have found out about her so the mortgagee was bound. In *Rosset* 'actual occupation' was achieved by a wife who was flitting in and out of the semi-derelict property at the relevant time supervising the building works. There is at least the possibility here that the builders did the occupying for her. See also *Abbey National Building Society v Cann* [1989] Fam Law 314 where the Court of Appeal seemed unhappy that actual occupation could be established in the *scintilla temporis* at completion: see (1989) Conv 158 (Beaumont).

normal conceptions of title to real property'.[3] They have been prepared to recognise as overriding interests, a tenant's option to purchase the reversion,[4] the interest of a beneficiary under a bare trust,[5] the right to specific performance of an agreement for purchase,[6] the right of a tenant to deduct from future instalments of rent the costs of repairs which he has carried out[7] and the right to have a conveyance rectified on the basis of mistake.[8] All of these rights are capable of binding the mortgagee and of severely limiting the value of its security. Finally, and probably to most people's surprise, their Lordships in *Boland* also recognised Mrs Boland's right which was the right of a beneficiary under a trust for sale to occupy the property.

Although *Boland* was concerned with registered land, and in particular with s 70 (1) (g) of the LRA, there was never very much doubt that it would be applied to unregistered land.[9] This is now beginning to happen.[10] The earlier decisions on unregistered land were so heavily criticised that they were unlikely to survive. Any lingering doubts that there may have been about whether the interest of the beneficiary under a trust for sale carries a right of occupation now seem to have been swept away[11] and it is reasonable to suppose that rights in registered and unregistered land will be treated in the same way albeit for reasons that are legally different.

Immediately after *Boland* it was predicted that the cost of lending would be increased and that mortgagees would be plagued with fraudulent defences concocted by defaulting mortgagors and co-operative 'contributors' which they would be unable to challenge. Plenty of people were prepared to say that in balancing the interests of social justice on the one hand against conveyancing certainty on the other, their Lordships had come to the wrong conclusion. In the years since *Boland* mortgagees have been rather more careful to identify third party rights. On new purchases, most lending institutions will now urge husband and wife to acquire the legal title jointly so that both of them enter the mortgage.[12] They also make careful enquiries as to the source of the balance of finance for the purchase and as to the intended occupiers. These enquiries are frequently addressed not only to the borrower but also to the borrower's solicitors in case he has any information that might be relevant. If there is a third party who might acquire an interest in the property the institution insists that the third party either acknowledges his interest ranks after the mortgagee[13] or charges his interest as well.[14]

---

3 *National Provincial Bank Ltd v Hastings Car Mart Ltd* [1964] Ch 665, [1964] 1 All ER 688. In *Paddington Building Society v Mendelsohn* [1987] Fam Law 121, 50 P & CR 244 reference is made to rights which by their 'inherent quality' are enforceable at the date of the relevant transfer or mortgage.

4 *Webb v Pollmount Ltd* [1966] Ch 584, [1966] 1 All ER 481. Cf position for unregistered land *Hollington Bros Ltd v Rhodes* [1951] 2 All ER 578n, [1951] 2 TLR 691.

5 *Hodgson v Marks*, supra.

6 *Grace Rymer Investments Ltd v Waite* [1958] Ch 831, [1958] 2 All ER 777.

7 *Lee-Parker v Izzet* [1971] 3 All ER 1099, [1971] 1 WLR 1688.

8 *Re Beaney* [1978] 2 All ER 595, [1978] 1 WLR 770.

9 And that *Caunce Trust* was no longer to be regarded as good law.

10 *Kingsnorth Provincial Bank Ltd v Tizard* [1986] 2 All ER 54, [1986] 1 WLR 783.

11 *City of London Building Society v Flegg* [1988] AC 54, [1987] 3 All ER 435.

12 This of course has the further advantage that equitable interests will be overreached. See *Flegg*, supra in the House of Lords after an aberration in the Court of Appeal.

13 Any release or consent has to be clear and unambiguous if it is to be effective: *Zamet v Hyman* [1961] 3 All ER 933, [1961] 1 WLR 1442.

14 See *National Westminster Bank plc v Morgan* [1985] AC 686, [1985] 1 All ER 821 to the effect that in an ordinary banking transaction the bank is under no obligation to ensure that a wife who is asked to join in a charge in these circumstances obtains independent legal advice. But see *Kingsnorth Trust Ltd v Bell* [1986] 1 All ER 423, [1986] 1 WLR 119; *Avon Finance*

The courts have not treated *Boland* as opening the floodgates. Had they been prepared to do so it would have been seen first in an increased willingness to find that people had become 'contributors' and entitled to an interest in the property. In *Boland* it was assumed that Mrs Boland had a beneficial interest and this is why the court found that her husband was not solely entitled and that he held it on trust for sale. The indications are that the courts are very cautious in finding a beneficial interest in circumstances which cannot be properly investigated and which happen to favour the position of a husband and wife against a creditor who is claiming possession.[15]

The courts have also been looking at the conduct of the people in Mrs Boland's position, ie the beneficiaries under the trust for sale, who in some cases have stood by knowing the property was being mortgaged by the legal owner and who have not disclosed their interest.[16] These people, so the argument goes, have been content to take the benefit of the loan but they then seek to avoid the consequences. In what can only be seen as an attempt to limit the effect of *Boland,* the courts have been prepared in circumstances where the beneficiary clearly knew what was going on, to find that by their conduct they have led the mortgagee to make the advance and that in these circumstances they ought to be estopped from asserting their interest against the bank.[17]

The courts have also assisted the mortgagee in the context of registered land by clarifying the date at which the relevant enquiries have to be made for the purpose of identifying the rights of the occupier. Previously the view was that the relevant date was the date that the charge was lodged at HM Land Registry for registration.[18] Clearly it is all but impossible to raise enquiries at this time and there is a real risk of people going into occupation after completion about whom the mortgagee knows nothing at all. The court has now considered the matter[19] and found that it is the date the charge is executed and delivered, ie completion itself, that is relevant not the date the papers are lodged at HM Land Registry. The uncertainties are not removed by this but they must be lessened.

5 REMEDIES OF A LEGAL MORTGAGEE

The legal mortgagee has a number of powerful remedies which it can bring to bear if there is a default. With the exception of foreclosure, they are cumulative and generally they do not need to be preceded by a judgment of the court. Not surprisingly, the legislature and the judiciary have, from time

---

Co Ltd v Bridger [1985] 2 All ER 281; Coldunell Ltd v Gallon [1986] QB 1184, [1986] 1 All ER 429, CA and Cornish v Midland Bank plc [1985] 3 All ER 513.

15 *Midland Bank plc v Dobson* [1986] 1 FLR 171.

16 See for example *Midland Bank Ltd v Farmpride Hatcheries Ltd* (1980) 260 Estates Gazette 493.

17 See *Knightly v Sun Life Assurance Society Ltd* (1981) Times, 23 July and *Bristol and West Building Society v Henning* [1985] 2 All ER 606, [1985] 1 WLR 778. But against this there is *Boland* itself. *Paddington Building Society v Mendelsohn* [1987] Fam Law 121, 50 P & CR 244 may also be regarded as a restrictive decision shifting the burden onto the beneficiary to make the beneficial interest known rather than sitting back and waiting for the purchaser to enquire. Failure to do so may result in a conceding of priority.

18 *Re Boyle's Claim* [1961] 1 All ER 620, [1961] 1 WLR 339 and the Land Registration Rules, r 83 (2).

19 *Lloyds Bank plc v Rosset* [1988] 3 All ER 915, [1988] 3 WLR 1301.

to time, tried to control or exclude the powers. Important controls introduced by the Consumer Credit Act 1974 are considered elsewhere in this work and judicial attempts are noted in this section.

The legal mortgagee's remedies are as follows:

(a) An action on the covenant to pay

Almost all mortgage deeds are going to contain an express covenant on the part of the mortgagor to repay the secured sums. In the case of registered land a covenant is implied on the part of the mortgagor with the proprietor for the time being of the mortgage that the mortgagor will pay the secured sums.[20] The simplest remedy for the mortgagee is to sue on the covenant in exactly the same way as it would sue to recover any other debt. If the mortgaged property has been sold and has not realised enough to discharge the sums due to the mortgagee he has little alternative. The right to sue for the shortfall survives the exercise of the power of sale.[21]

(b) Possession[1]

By triumph of legal theory over commercial reality the mortgagee is, as against the mortgagor, entitled to possession of the mortgaged property.[2] The right arises 'before the ink is dry on the mortgage'[3] and has nothing to do with whether there has been a default or whether the mortgage money is due. The courts might be ready to find that the right has been impliedly excluded but there must be something upon which to hang such a conclusion[4] and they show no readiness to abandon the idea simply as a legal technicality.[5] In practice, the mortgage will usually confer on the mortgagee the right to enter the mortgaged property to inspect and perhaps to carry out repairs if the mortgagee is in default and this will usually be enough for the mortgagee. It is only going to be interested in asserting its right to possession if there has been a default and it wants to sell the property with vacant possession.

As a preliminary to realising the best price for the property the mortgagee may need to evict the mortgagor. Normally the mortgagor is regarded as a tenant at sufferance and not entitled to notice but it used to be the practice to have the mortgagor in the mortgage deed 'attorn tenant to the mortgagee'

---

20 LRA, s 28 (1). It is therefore necessary to have this implied covenant negatived by an entry on the register in circumstances where a mortgagor is charging property to secure the debts of a third party without intending to become personally liable for their repayment.

21 *Rudge v Richens* (1873) LR 8 CP 358.

1 As to whether the mortgagee's right to possession is more appropriately conceptualised as a paramount right rather than as a discretionary remedy, see *Gray* p 610. The former is thought to be the better view.

2 *Four Maids Ltd v Dudley Marshall (Properties) Ltd* [1957] Ch 317, [1957] 2 All ER 35; *Alliance Perpetual Building Society v Belrum Investments Ltd* [1957] 1 All ER 635, [1957] 1 WLR 720. See also s 95 (4) of the LPA which acknowledges the right but does not confer it.

3 Per Harman J in *Four Maids*, supra.

4 *Esso Petroleum Co Ltd v Alstonbridge Properties Ltd* [1975] 3 All ER 358, [1975] 1 WLR 1474. Building society mortgages commonly do confer a right of possession as in *Birmingham Citizens Permanent Building Society v Caunt* [1962] Ch 883, [1962] 1 All ER 163.

5 Eg *Western Bank Ltd v Schindler* [1977] Ch 1, [1976] 2 All ER 393 where the Court of Appeal unanimously upheld the mortgagee's right to possession even though there had been no financial default. There was clearly something wrong with the drafting of the mortgage in the particular case but the enthusiasm for the mortgagee's 'common law right ... which should not be lightly treated as abrogated or restricted' is striking.

that is to say to acknowledge the mortgagee as landlord. This was an artificiality and certainly was not intended to comfort the mortgagor who had been alarmed by the prospect of the mortgagee's immediate right to possession.[6] The attornment clause did not confer on the mortgagor rights under the Rent Acts or the Agricultural Holdings Act.[7] The point of it was that it gave the mortgagee of a dwelling house access to the simplified procedure of the Small Tenements Recovery Act 1838 when it wanted to evict the mortgagor. By making the rent under the notional tenancy equal to the interest payable under the mortgage the mortgagee/landlord also gained a power of distress. Both of these advantages have now disappeared[8] but the attornment clause continues to appear in mortgages and to give rise to problems.[9]

The right of a mortgagee to possession is restricted where the mortgaged property consists of or includes a dwelling house. Where a mortgagee seeks possession through the court,[11] Section 36 of the Administration of Justice Act 1970 (as amended by s 8 of the Administration of Justice Act 1973) confers on the court a wide power to adjourn the possession proceedings or to postpone the date for the giving of possession if it appears to the court that 'the mortgagor is likely to be able within a reasonable period to pay any sums due under the mortgage'.[12] The sums concerned, in the case of a mortgage where the mortgagor is entitled or is to be permitted to pay the principal sum secured by instalments or otherwise to defer payment of it (ie an instalment or an endowment mortgage),[13] are the actual payments which are in arrears. The court does not take into account the fact that repayment of the whole of the loan may have been triggered by the original default.[14]

6 As to the nature of the interest created, see *Regent Oil Co Ltd v J A Gregory (Hatch End) Ltd* [1966] Ch 402, [1965] 3 All ER 673.
7 *Steyning and Littlehampton Building Society v Wilson* [1951] Ch 1018, [1951] 2 All ER 452; *Peckham Mutual Building Society v Register* (1980) 42 P & CR 186. As to the possible requirement for four weeks' notice in accordance with the Protection from Eviction Act 1977, see *Alliance Building Society v Pinwill* [1958] Ch 788, [1958] 2 All ER 408; Vaisey J to the effect that the legislation only protects 'a real tenant against a real landlord under a real "residential letting"'.
8 As to a possible new use for the attornment clause in enforcing restrictive covenants on the mortgagor's part against its successors, see *Regent Oil,* supra but also (1965) 81 LQR 341 and (1966) 82 LQR 21.
9 Eg *Hinckley and Country Building Society v Henny* [1953] 1 All ER 515, [1953] 1 WLR 352.
11 There would normally be no obligation on the mortgagee to proceed through the court if it can peaceably retake possession without doing so. For the argument that s 36 creates a requirement of due process see [1983] Conv 293 (A Clarke). As to the applicability of the section when there has been no default, *Western Bank v Schindler* [1977] Ch 1, [1976] 2 All ER 393.
12 As to the section generally see [1979] Conv 266 (Smith), [1984] Conv 91 (Tromans) and *Gray* p 891. The section was introduced after *Birmingham Citizens Permanent Building Society v Caunt* [1962] Ch 883, [1962] 1 All ER 163 had all but put a stop on the inherent jurisdiction of the court in possession proceedings being exercised to ensure that 'in proper cases the wind was tempered to the shorn lamb, time being given for payment and so forth': per Clauson LJ in *Redditch Benefit Building Society v Roberts* [1940] Ch 415, [1940] 1 All ER 342 and followed the recommendations of the Payne Committee Report on the Enforcement of Judgment Debts, 1969, Cmd 3909.
13 *Governor and Company of the Bank of Scotland v Grimes* [1985] QB 1179, [1985] 2 All ER 254, CA.
14 S 8 of the Administration of Justice Act 1973. In *Halifax Building Society v Clark* [1973] Ch 307, [1973] 2 All ER 33 the court took the view that s 36 as drafted meant that *all* sums, ie the accelerated borrowings as well, had to be considered. Clearly a mortgagor who had defaulted on a few instalments was hardly likely to have access to sufficient capital to

The legislation does not fit comfortably with the kind of arrangement a bank will make with its customer over the customer's secured overdraft. Such an arrangement will not normally entitle the customer to pay by instalments or to defer the repayment of the debit balance. On the contrary, it will usually be crystal clear that the bank expects to be repaid on demand. The Court of Appeal has held that the legislation has no application to a mortgage given as security for a bank overdraft under which no money was due unless and until repayment was demanded by the bank[15] but a more recent decision emphasises the social purpose of the legislation and if this more liberal view prevails protection could easily be extended to the defaulting customer.[16]

The mortgagee's right to possession of the mortgaged property carries with it certain responsibilities. If the mortgagee goes into possession he will incur liabilities. He will owe a duty of care to third parties like any other person who has control of premises and he will be treated as the owner of the property for the purpose of certain statutes, eg the Highways Act and the Public Health Act 1936. Most importantly he will owe duties to the mortgagor and to anyone else interested in the equity of redemption such as later mortgagees of whom he has notice.[17] In the case of a property which is let, so that the mortgagee is entering into receipt of rent, he is obliged to account for what he receives[18] or what he could have received but for his gross default, mismanagement or fraud. If the mortgagee itself goes into actual possession of the property, otherwise than for the purposes of a sale within a reasonable time,[19] he must give credit for a full occupational rent and if he lets the property he must endeavour to obtain an open market rent. A mortgagee who lets the property at less than a market value because he takes some collateral benefit will be required to account on the basis of what he could have received had he managed the property with due diligence, not on the basis of his actual receipts.[20] He will also be liable if having obtained a possession order he does not take reasonable steps to secure the premises against vandals.

Whether or not this obligation to account on the basis of wilful default is quite so onerous as is sometimes suggested,[1] most mortgagees will not contemplate going into possession. The modern practice is for the mortgagee to appoint a receiver, either under the statutory powers or pursuant to an express power in the mortgage, in almost all cases where any income is receivable from the property.

(c) Power of sale

The mortgagee did not have the right to sell the mortgaged property free from the mortgagor's interest either at common law or in equity. He could always sell the benefit of the interest vested in him, ie the mortgage term and the right to receive the mortgage debt but no-one was going to buy this if the mortgagor was in default. To give value to the security the mortgagee had

discharge the whole of the original loan so s 36 was rendered almost useless and further legislation was required.

15 *Habib Bank Ltd v Tailor* [1982] 3 All ER 561, [1982] 1 WLR 1218.
16 *Bank of Scotland v Grimes*, supra. See also *Centrax Trustees Ltd v Ross* [1979] 2 All ER 952.
17 *Parker v Calcraft* (1821) 6 Madd 11.
18 *Lord Trimleston v Hamill* (1810) 1 Ball & B 377.
19 *Norwich General Trust v Grierson* [1984] CLY 2306.
20 *White v City of London Brewery Co Ltd* (1889) 42 Ch D 237.
 1 See Goff J in *Western Bank v Schindler*, supra.

to be able to sell the mortgaged property itself free from the mortgagor's right to redeem. The right to foreclose might be available but this was a cumbersome and unreliable remedy and it could only be exercised through the courts.

The solution was to give the mortgagee an express power of sale in the mortgage. This gave way to a statutory power of sale which was to be implied in certain kinds of mortgage. The relevant provisions are now to be found in the LPA. Section 101 (1) deals with when the power *arises* and provides that:

'A mortgagee, where the mortgage is made by deed shall by virtue of the Act, have the following powers, to the like extent as if they had been in terms conferred by the mortgage deed, but not further (namely):
(i) A power, when the mortgage money has become due, to sell, or to concur with any other person in selling, the mortgaged property, or any part thereof, either subject to prior charges, or not, and either together or in lots, by public auction or by private contract, subject to such conditions respecting title, evidence of title, or other matter, as the mortgagee thinks fit, with power to vary any contract for sale, and to buy in at an auction, or to rescind any contract for sale, and to re-sell, without being liable for any loss occasioned thereby.'

Section 103 deals with when the statutory power[2] is *exercisable*. The mortgagee is not permitted to exercise the power of sale unless and until:

(a) notice requiring payment has been served on the mortgagor demanding payment and the mortgagor has not complied for three months, or
(b) some interest under the mortgage is in arrears and unpaid for two months after becoming due, or
(c) there has been a breach of some other provision in the mortgage.

The distinction between the power arising and its being exercisable is critical. The LPA provides that a prospective purchaser of the mortgaged property from the mortgagee is not concerned to see or enquire whether the power is being properly or regularly exercised.[3] He is merely interested in whether it has arisen and he can usually ascertain this by inspecting the mortgage. As long as the mortgage is by deed and there is no contrary intention expressed, the power arises when the mortgage money has become due, ie on the legal date for redemption.[4] If the mortgage purports to sell the property before the power of sale arises he will only succeed in transferring his own limited interest. If he does so after the power arises but before it becomes exercisable, the purchaser will obtain a good title to the mortgaged property but the mortgagor will have a remedy in damages against the mortgagee based on the abuse of the power.[5] The mortgagor will not be able to get his property back because the relevant provision expressly provides that the purchaser's title is unimpeachable.[6] The only exception found here is that the courts will not allow any statute to be used for fraudulent purpose

2 The pre-conditions to the exercise of the statutory power are frequently excluded by the mortgage deed so that power is exercisable without the need to give notice. In the case of registered land, the mortgagee must be registered as proprietor of the charge: *Lever Finance, supra*.
3 LPA, s 104 (2).
4 For a defective mortgage where there was no proviso for redemption and no power of sale in case of default see, *Twentieth Century Banking Corpn Ltd v Wilkinson* [1977] Ch 99, [1976] 3 All ER 361. Also *Payne v Cardiff RDC* [1932] 1 KB 241.
5 LPA, s 104 (2).
6 LPA, s 104 (2).

and if the mortgagee can demonstrate that the purchaser knew that the power of sale was being improperly exercised they may be prepared to set the transaction aside.[7]

Where a mortgagee of freehold land[8] sells under his statutory or an express power of sale, Section 88 (1) of the LPA provides that:

'(a) the conveyance by him shall operate to vest in the purchaser the fee simple in the land conveyed subject to any legal mortgage having priority to the mortgage in right of which the sale is made and to any money thereby secured, and thereupon;

(b) the mortgage term or the charge by way of legal mortgage and any subsequent mortgage term or charges shall merge or be extinguished as respects the land conveyed.'

By this piece of statutory magic, the mortgagee is able to confer the legal estate in the mortgaged property to the purchaser even though it has never been vested in the mortgagee. The purchaser even takes the mortgaged property free from contracts entered into by the mortgagor after it created the mortgage notwithstanding that they have been registered against the mortgagor in the register of land charges.[9]

The mortgagee exercising his power of sale has to take a certain care.[10] This is not a duty that is imposed by the LPA[11] but a duty which has been imposed by the courts faced with complaints by various parties about the way sales have been conducted. It is clear that it is not a fiduciary duty and that the mortgagee is perfectly entitled to look to its own interests but at the same time a balance has to be struck between the mortgagee's concern to recover the outstanding debt as soon as possible and the interests of the mortgagor[12] in seeing that a full price is obtained.

The courts have chosen to express this duty in a variety of ways. There have been high points of judicial laissez-faire in favour of the mortgagee and high points of anxiety for the mortgagor's position – more it has to be said of the former than the latter – and there has been a shift in emphasis in recent years. A consistent principle has been the obligation for the mortgagee to act in good faith.[13] It is this principle which prevents a mortgagee selling the

---

7 Whether the courts would be prepared to do so will depend on how they treat s 104 (2), supra in the light of cases such as *Lord Waring v London and Manchester Assurance Co Ltd* [1935] Ch 310 and *Selwyn v Garfit* (1888) 38 Ch D 273. See also *Bailey v Barnes* [1894] 1 Ch 25: the purchaser must not 'wilfully shut his eyes and abstain from making inquiries which might have led to a knowledge of impropriety or irregularity.'

8 As to leasehold land, see LPA s 89 (1) to the same effect.

9 *Duke v Robson* [1973] 1 All ER 481, [1973] 1 WLR 267. The mortgagor will presumably be liable to the party with whom it contracted since it will no longer have any estate and is bound to be in breach of contract. In the case of registered land see *Lyus v Prowse Developments Ltd* [1982] 2 All ER 953, [1982] 1 WLR 1044 where Dillon J is of the view that it is irrelevant that the mortgagee consented to the contract concerned. See also LRA, s 34 (4).

10 The modern authorities have as their starting point *Cuckmere Brick Co Ltd v Mutual Finance Ltd* [1971] Ch 949, [1971] 2 All ER 633, CA.

11 But as to building societies see s 13 (7) of the Building Societies Act 1986: reasonable care to ensure that the property realises the best price that can reasonably be obtained.

12 And others interested in the amount realised. The 'proximity' of a guarantor was found to be sufficient for the mortgagee to owe him a duty of care in *Standard Chartered Bank Ltd v Walker* [1982] 3 All ER 938, [1982] 1 WLR 1410 contrary to previous authorities.

13 Thus, at one time a careless mortgagee could well escape liability. *Pendlebury v Colonial Mutual Life Assurance Society Ltd* (1912) 13 CLR 676. It was only if the sale price was so

mortgaged property to himself or his nominee even for full value[14] and why sales to people or companies connected with the mortgagee come under special scrutiny. Thus while there is no absolute rule preventing a sale by the mortgagee to a company in which he has an interest there does have to be a true sale and the mortgagee may be required to justify the course of action it adopted.[15] The courts have now begun to emphasise an obligation to act reasonably.

There has been a certain amount of discussion about whether the duty to act reasonably is just part of the duty to act in good faith[16] but the important message is that the courts are now applying the 'neighbour principle' found elsewhere in the law and are seeking to give the mortgagor rather more protection than was formerly the case. This need not cause great alarm amongst mortgagees who seek to exercise their powers conscientiously. As long as they take reasonable steps to ascertain the value of the property and to expose it to the market and generally act in the way a prudent vendor would who was selling on his own behalf they are not going to suffer. There has to be some exposure for a mortgagee in agreeing to a 'crash sale' and the mortgagee may well have to make out a case for doing so[17] but there is certainly no obligation to actually hold back and wait for a rising market[18] or to put the property up for auction. Similarly there is no obligation to keep the mortgagor advised of the progress of the sale although failure to do so may suggest a lack of good faith.

(d) Appointment of a receiver

In addition to the power of sale, Section 101 (1) of the LPA confers on the mortgagee:

'(iii) A power, when the mortgage money has become due, to appoint a receiver of the income of the mortgaged property, or any part thereof; or, if the mortgaged property consists of an interest in income, or of a rent charge or an annual or other periodic sum, a receiver of what property or any part thereof.'

The power becomes exercisable when the mortgagee is entitled to exercise the power of sale[19] and the duty of care which the mortgagee owes in exercising it is broadly similar. A receiver appointed under the statutory power or under an express power in the mortgage is frequently referred to as a 'LPA receiver'

---

low that it was evidence of fraud that the court would intervene: *Warner v Jacob* (1882) 20 Ch D 220.

14 *Martinson v Clowes* (1882) 21 Ch D 857; *ANZ Banking Group Ltd v Bangadilly Pastoral Co Pty Ltd* (1978) 19 ALR 519; and *Farrar v Farrars Ltd* (1888) 40 Ch D 395. But see Housing Act 1985, Sch 17, para 1 (1).

15 This reversal of the burden of proof is shown in *Tse Kwong Lam v Wong Chit Sen* [1983] 3 All ER 54, [1983] 1 WLR 1349 where it was stated that the mortgagee 'must show that the sale was in good faith and that the mortgagee took reasonable precautions to obtain the best price reasonably obtainable at the time.'

16 Salmon LJ in *Cuckmere,* supra, describes the mortgagee as 'owing both duties'.

17 *Predeth v Castle Phillips Finance Co Ltd* (1986) 279 Estates Gazette 1355 (see [1986] Conv 442 (M P Thompson)).

18 *Bank of Cyprus (London) Ltd v Gill* [1980] 2 Lloyd's Rep 51, CA.

19 LPA, s 109 (1). See also *Twentieth Century Banking,* supra. It does not matter that the mortgagee has already gone into possession: *Refuge Assurance Co Ltd v Pearlberg* [1938] Ch 687, [1938] 3 All ER 231, CA. In the case of registered land, the mortgagee must be registered as proprietor of the charge: *Lever Finance,* supra.

to distinguish him from the receiver and manager appointed under a debenture or an administrator or an administrative receiver appointed under the Insolvency Act 1986. The activities and the jurisdiction of an LPA receiver are likely to be much more restricted than these other kinds of receiver. It is common practice to extend the statutory power to give him wide powers of management and to give him a power of sale but his role will usually be confined specifically to the land which is the subject of the mortgage.

A receiver appointed under the statutory power is deemed to be the agent of the mortgagor and the mortgagor will be responsible for what he does.[20] An express power in the mortgage will usually provide for this as well. Thus the mortgagee of income producing property or property which requires active management will almost always choose to appoint a receiver to collect the rents and deal with the management because this will preclude the possibility of the mortgagee being in possession and incurring the strict obligations owed by the mortgagee in those circumstances.[1] Similarly, receipt of rent by the receiver will not create a tenancy by estoppel which binds the mortgagee.[2] There is a good deal of artificiality in this because the receiver will be the mortgagee's man – chosen by him and representing his interests.[3] The receiver will look to the mortgagee for his remuneration and may very well expect to be indemnified by the mortgagee against any liability incurred in carrying out his receivership. His primary duty, which he owes to the mortgagee, is to see to the reduction of the mortgage debt. The receiver's agency comes to an end when the corporate mortgagor is wound up[4] but this does not affect the receiver's power to deal with the mortgaged property and does not result in his automatically becoming the agent of the mortgagee.

(e) Foreclosure

The essence of foreclosure is that it enables the mortgagee to take the mortgaged property and treat it as his own, free from any right for the mortgagor to redeem the mortgage. The right to sue the mortgagor on the covenant to pay continues, notwithstanding the foreclosure, as long as the mortgagee retains the property.[5] A foreclosure order absolute vests the mortgagor's interest in the property in the mortgagee subject to any legal mortgage having priority to his mortgage.[6] The mortgage term or the legal charge merges and the interests of subsequent mortgagees who are made party to the proceedings are extinguished. The mortgagee stands to make a profit

---

20 LPA, s 109 (2). See generally *White v Metcalf* [1903] 2 Ch 567; *Jefferys v Dickson* (1866) 1 Ch App 183; *Law v Glenn* (1867) 2 Ch App 634; and *Gaskell v Gosling* [1896] 1 QB 669.
1 The mortgagee will normally refrain from interfering with the receiver's exercise of his powers in case his privileged position is eroded: see *American Express International Banking Corp v Hurley* [1985] 3 All ER 564.
2 *Lever Finance,* supra.
3 See *Re B Johnson & Co (Builders) Ltd* [1955] Ch 634, [1955] 2 All ER 775, CA.
4 *Gaskell v Gosling,* supra.
5 *Kinnaird v Trollope* (1888) 39 Ch D 636. However, attempting to sue on the covenant will give the mortgagor a new right to redeem and enable him to reclaim the property if he can pay off the debt: see *Perry v Barker* (1806) 13 Ves 198. If the mortgagee has sold he cannot reopen the foreclosure and thus cannot sue on the covenant: see *Palmer v Hendrie* (1859) 27 Beav 349. Also *Lloyds and Scottish Trust Ltd v Britten* (1982) 44 P & CR 249.
6 LPA, ss 88 (2) and 89 (2). In the case of registered land the proprietor of the charge in respect of which foreclosure has been obtained is re-registered as the proprietor of the land and the charge is cancelled LRA, s 34 (3).

from this if the property is worth more than the amount outstanding so it is a remedy that can only be exercised through the court and it is hedged around with procedural protections for the mortgagor.

Once the mortgagor's legal right to redeem has passed it is open to the court to grant an order for foreclosure. There are two stages to this. First the court will make a nisi order giving the mortgagor a fixed period, usually six months, to pay off the mortgage. The mortgagee's power of sale will be suspended during this period. If the mortgagor does not pay off the mortgage in the prescribed period, the order will be made absolute. Before the order is made absolute it is open to the mortgagor or any other person interested to apply to the court for an order directing the sale of the property rather than a foreclosure.[7] After the order absolute has been made it can in limited circumstances be opened up and the mortgagor's right to redeem will revive.[8]

The bank might foreclose on the mortgage in every good Victorian melodrama but given the willingness of modern courts to order a sale and the uncertainties caused by the ability to open up a foreclosure order absolute it is unlikely to find it an attractive remedy to pursue today.[9]

6   REMEDIES OF AN EQUITABLE MORTGAGEE OF THE LEGAL ESTATE

The remedies available to an equitable mortgagee are less extensive than those available to a mortgagee. By definition, the equitable mortgagee does not have a legal estate in the property. He is not therefore going to be able to collect rents from the tenants as of right because he is not the legal reversioner.[10] Similarly he cannot rely on a legal estate as entitling him to possession of the mortgaged property. It has been argued[11] that he has an alternative right to immediate possession but in any event a court will have little hesitation in ordering the mortgagor to give possession if there is any difficulty.[12] What the equitable mortgagee does have is the benefit of an agreement on the part of the mortgagor to create a legal mortgage and one of the remedies he has available is to obtain an order from the court perfecting this agreement by vesting in the mortgagee a legal term of years so that he is in the same position as a legal mortgagee.[13]

Otherwise, in addition to the personal right to take action against the mortgagee on the promise to pay, the equitable mortgagee has the following remedies:

---

7 LPA, s 91 (2).
8 See *Campbell v Hoyland* (1877) 7 Ch D 166.
9 But see *Twentieth Century Banking Corpn Ltd v Wilkinson* [1977] Ch 99, [1976] 3 All ER 361 where it was apparently all that was left.
10 *Vacuum Oil Co Ltd v Ellis* [1914] 1 KB 693.
11 See (1955) 71 LQR 204 (H W R Wade) and *Barclays Bank Ltd v Bird* [1954] Ch 274, [1954] 1 All ER 449. Also *F & L* p 332 and *M & W* p 951 and the materials referred to in each case.
12 LPA, s 90 (1) and *Ladup Ltd v Williams & Glyn's Bank plc* [1985] 2 All ER 577, [1985] 1 WLR 851.
13 LPA, s 90 (1).

(a) Power of sale

There is a statutory power of sale where the mortgage is made by deed.[14]
This is why the memorandum accompanying a deposit of deeds should always
be taken under seal. The power of sale extends to property which is the
subject of the mortgage[15] but there is room for doubt whether the property
concerned is anything more than the equitable interest vested in the mortgagee
by the equitable mortgage[16] so two conveyancing devices are commonly
employed to enable the mortgagee to deal with the legal estate.

First, the mortgagor may give the mortgagee a power of attorney. Such a
power, if given to secure the performance of an obligation owed to the
mortgagee and expressed to be irrevocable, is not revoked by the death,
incapacity or bankruptcy of the mortgagor.[17] On enforcing the security the
mortgagee sells the legal estate and conveys it by using the power of attorney.[18]

Secondly, the mortgagor may declare itself as trustee of the legal estate for
the mortgagee[19] and acknowledge that the mortgagee can change the trustee
at anytime. The instrument appointing the new trustee will divest the mortgagor of the legal estate and vest it in the new trustee who could quite easily
be the mortgagee or a nominee for the mortgagee.

Where the mortgage is not made by deed or does not contain one or both
of these devices the mortgagee will need an order from the court directing a
sale.[20]

(b) Appointment of a receiver

An equitable mortgagee has always had a right to apply to the court for the
appointment of a receiver. Where the mortgage is executed under seal the
mortgagee can take advantage of the statutory power to appoint a receiver
without the need for an application to the court.

(c) Foreclosure

The court has power to order foreclosure of an equitable mortgage or to
order a sale in lieu.

---

14 LPA, s 101 (1) (i).
15 LPA, s 104 (1).
16 *Re Hodson and Howes' Contract* (1887) 35 Ch D 668 but see Lord Denning MR in *Re White
    Rose Cottage* [1965] Ch 940 at 951 who has no difficulty in finding that the power already
    extends to the legal estate.
17 Powers of Attorney Act 1971, s 4 (1).
18 In *Re White Rose Cottage,* supra the conveyance purported to be a sale by the mortgagor
    so the purchaser took the property subject to certain interests subsequent to the charge. Had
    the sale been by the mortgagee the purchaser would have taken free of them.
19 *London and County Banking Co v Goddard* [1897] 1 Ch 642.
20 LPA, s 91 (2).

CHAPTER 35

GUARANTEES AND LETTERS OF COMFORT[1]

1 GUARANTEES

(a) Nature of guarantee

(i) General

A guarantee is a promise to be answerable for the debt of another. As such, it is a secondary obligation, depending for its meaning and existence upon the primary obligations of the principal debtor.

Guarantees are one of the commonest forms of banking security. They are sought, typically, from one individual in respect of the debts of another individual, from an individual in respect of banking facilities made available to the company in which he is the only or a major shareholder, and from a company in respect of banking facilities made available to an associated or subsidiary company. A guarantee does not in itself confer on the creditor direct recourse to assets, but merely adds the covenant of the guarantor (who may be regarded by the bank as the more credit-worthy party) to that of the principal debtor.

A contract of guarantee is not intrinsically complex, and in many cases it is possible for highly complicated obligations of a principal debtor which require lengthy documentation to be guaranteed in a simple and brief document. Many banks have their own standard form of guarantee which, with some variations depending upon whether the guarantor is a company or an individual and upon the nature of the debt guaranteed, will be used for virtually all of the guarantees which they receive in connection with their day-to-day business.

(ii) The secondary nature of the contract

This is perhaps the most difficult aspect of the law relating to guarantees. As a secondary obligation, a guarantee cannot exist apart from the primary obligation to which it relates. If that obligation is for any reason void, then the guarantee is also void. Further, if that primary obligation is discharged for any reason, the guarantee is also discharged.

1 The Editor gratefully acknowledges that this chapter has been revised, and expanded to include a section on letters of comfort, by Ruth Fox of Slaughter and May.

Consequently, many of the provisions which are to be found in the forms of guarantee used by banks are designed to avoid the consequence of this analysis of the nature of the guarantee by turning the guarantee into a contract of indemnity: that is, a primary obligation whereby the surety undertakes as his own principal obligation that the creditor will be paid.

The distinction between guarantees and indemnities was formerly of considerable importance in the context of lending to minors. There are authorities[2] which suggest that at common law, a guarantee of a minor's overdraft is unenforceable, whereas an indemnity in respect of lending to a minor can be enforced. The position in relation to indemnities was explained by Harman LJ in *Yeoman Credit Ltd v Latter:*[3]

'Where all concerned know that the first promisor is an infant, so that as against him the promise cannot be enforced, the court should incline to construe the document signed by the adult (the second promisor) as an indemnity, for that must have been the intention of the promisee and the second promisor. Both know that the first promise has no legal validity; it may be that both hope that the first promisor will honour his engagement, but with the knowledge that he cannot be obliged to do so it must have been their intention that the promise of the adult promisor should have an independent validity. Otherwise the whole transaction is a sham.'

The distinction between guarantees and indemnities has been rendered far less significant in this context by the Minors' Contracts Act 1987 (see ch 9, ante), s 2 of which provides that where a guarantee is given in respect of an obligation of a party to a contract made after 9 June 1987, and that obligation is unenforceable against him (or he repudiates the contract) because he was a minor when the contract was made, the guarantee is not for that reason alone to be unenforceable against the guarantor.

In *Garrard v James*,[4] where debts had been incurred in breach of the borrowing powers of the company and were therefore ultra vires, the view was taken by the court that it was a question of construction as to whether the guarantor had intended to be liable for non-payment by the principal debtor only by reason of his inability to pay, or for any other reason (including contractual incapacity).

A further distinction between contracts of guarantee and contracts of indemnity lies in the effect of a discharge of the principal debtor. Where the liability of a third party is secondary (to answer for the debts, or certain of the debts, of X) and X no longer owes any such debts then it follows that the guarantor has no further liability. Where the liability of a third party is primary (to ensure that certain sums are paid) then the fact that X, who was also primarily liable in respect of those debts, has been discharged does not affect the claim of the creditor against the third party. The consequences of the distinction were illustrated by the decision in *Lloyds & Scottish Trust Ltd v Britten*[5] where the documentation did not contain the provision, now very common in bank guarantees, whereby the guarantor agrees that sums which may not be recoverable from the borrower by reason of legal limitation, incapacity or any other fact or circumstance will nevertheless be recoverable

2 A review of the authorities can be found in *Paget* (9th edn, 1982) pp 499–500.
3 [1961] 2 All ER 294 at 299, [1961] 1 WLR 828 at 835, CA.
4 [1925] Ch 616.
5 (1982) 44 p & Cr 249.

from the guarantor as if the same had been incurred by the guarantor as sole and principal debtor. The lender had the benefit both of a mortgage over certain property of the borrower and of the personal guarantee of two of the company's directors. Having obtained a foreclosure order and sold the property for less than the sum owing, the lender sought to make a claim against the directors under their guarantee but failed because the effect of the foreclosure order was to discharge entirely the claim of the lender against the borrower, and in the absence of any claim against the borrower, the lender could not sustain a claim against third parties who had undertaken to be answerable for such claims.

In *Moshi v Lep Air Services Ltd*[6] the House of Lords held that where a debt was to be repaid by instalments the wrongful repudiation by the debtor of a contract which included the guarantee was a breach by the guarantor of his undertaking which rendered him liable in damages. As Lord Simon put it, Lep accepted the company's (Rolloswin Investments Ltd) fundamental breach as repudiation of the contract and were entitled to sue the guarantor for the total sum guaranteed.

(iii) Disclosure

1 CREDITOR'S DUTY TO DISCLOSE UNUSUAL FEATURES

The contract of guarantee is not a contract uberrimae fidei, requiring full disclosure of all material facts by one or both of the parties.[7] Non-disclosure by a bank, to a guarantor of a customer's overdrawn account, of facts from which the bank suspected that the customer was defrauding the guarantor was held in *National Provincial Bank of England Ltd v Glanusk*[8] and *Royal Bank of Scotland v Greenshields*[9] not to invalidate the guarantee.

The banker is not bound to volunteer to a proposing guarantor information as to the customer's financial position or business habits, however material such information might be. In *Hamilton v Watson*[10] Lord Campbell held that disclosure would otherwise be a duty only where what had taken place between the bank and the principal debtor was not naturally to be expected; or, as it was put by Sir E M Pollock MR, referring, in *Lloyds Bank Ltd v Harrison*,[11] to Lord Campbell,

'... the necessity for disclosure only goes to the extent of requiring it where there are some unusual features in the particular case relating to the particular account which is to be guaranteed'.

Hamilton v Watson was cited with approval by Vaughan Williams LJ in *London General Omnibus Co Ltd v Holloway*[12] and the Court of Appeal in *Lloyds Bank Ltd v Harrison*; see also *Westminster Bank Ltd v Cond*[13] and

---

6 [1973] AC 331; and see *Hyundai Heavy Industries Co Ltd v Papadopoulos* [1980] 2 All ER 29, [1980] 1 WLR 1129, HL.
7 *Davies v London and Provincial Marine Insurance Co* (1878) 8 Ch D 469 at 475.
8 [1913] 3 KB 335.
9 1914 SC 259.
10 Ibid, but see Lord Campbell in *Railton v Matthews* (1844) 10 Cl & Fin 934 at 942, HL.
11 (1925) 4 LDAB 12, CA.
12 [1912] 2 KB 72, CA.
13 (1940) 46 Com Cas 60.

Cooper v National Provincial Bank Ltd.[14] In this last case Lawrence LJ thought that where the account to be guaranteed was not really that of the person in whose name it stood, but of an undischarged bankrupt, the bank, if aware of the fact, might be under duty to disclose. It would, however, be unwise to be dogmatic on the point, which could easily turn on the special facts.[15]

2 BANKS IMPLIED AUTHORITY TO DISCLOSE

If questioned by the intending surety, on a point which might have a material bearing on his entering or not entering into the guarantee, the banker must give the information[16] honestly and to the best of his ability, the occasion justifying disclosure or the customer's authority for such disclosure being implied in the introduction of the surety.

(iv) Misrepresentation

A guarantor may rescind a contract of guarantee if he was induced to enter into it by a material misrepresentation of fact. This principle was clearly stated by the Privy Council in *MacKenzie v Royal Bank of Canada*[17] in which the plaintiff successfully repudiated her guarantee on the ground that the bank had misrepresented to her the position concerning some shares which she had earlier charged as security. The facts appear from the judgment of Lord Atkin giving the decision of the Board:

'A contract of guarantee, like any other contract, is liable to be avoided if induced by material misrepresentation of an existing fact, even if made innocently. In this case it is unnecessary to decide whether contracts of guarantee belong to the special class where, even at common law, such an innocent misrepresentation would afford a defence to an action upon the contract. The evidence conclusively establishes a misrepresentation by the bank that the plaintiff's shares were still bound to the bank with the necessary inference, whether expressed or not, and their Lordships accept the plaintiff's evidence that it was expressed, that the shares were already lost, and that the guarantee of the new company offered the only means of salving them. It does not seem to admit of doubt that such a representation made as to the plaintiff's private rights and depending upon transactions in bankruptcy, of the full nature of which she had not been informed, was a representation of fact. That it was material is beyond discussion. It consequently follows that the plaintiff was at all times, on ascertaining the true position, entitled to avoid the contract and recover her securities. There were subsequent renewals of the guarantee before the plaintiff was advised of the true facts, but counsel for the bank very properly conceded that they would be in the same position as the original guarantee. There is no difficulty as to *restitutio in integrum*. The mere fact that the party making the representation has treated the contract as binding and has acted on it does not preclude relief. Nor can it be said that the plaintiff received anything under the contract which she is unable to restore'.

In *Solle v Butcher*[18] Denning LJ cited *MacKenzie v Royal Bank of Canada* in support of the view that:

14 [1946] KB 1, [1945] 2 All ER 641.
15 In this connection see *Goad v Canadian Imperial Bank of Commerce* (1968) 67 WWR (2d) 189, Ontario High Court.
16 *Hamilton v Watson* (1845) 12 Cl & Fin 109, HL, cited with approval in *Goodwin v National Bank of Australasia Ltd* (1968) 42 ALJR 110.
17 [1934] AC 468, PC and 475 as to independent advice.
18 [1950] 1 KB 671 at 695.

'the lease (in *Solle v Butcher*) was induced by an innocent misrepresentation by the plaintiff. It seems to me that the plaintiff was not merely expressing an opinion on the law; he was making an unambiguous statement as to private rights and a misrepresentation as to private rights is equivalent to a misrepresentation of fact for this purpose.'

Three years after *MacKenzie's* case, came *Trade Indemnity Co Ltd v Workington Harbour and Dock Board.*[19] Lord Atkin expressed himself as follows:

'There may be a question whether in the formation of a contract of guarantee there is an obligation on the promisee to make a disclosure of material facts which would not exist in the formation of an ordinary contract ... But it is clear that in whatever way any duty to disclose arises and whether the promisee is under a positive duty to disclose material facts, which is one view, or is supposed to represent that the transaction sought to be guaranteed has no unusual or abnormal characteristics, making him the author of a misrepresentation innocent or fraudulent as the case may be, which is another view, the duty or the implied representation will depend upon the particular circumstances of each transaction.' *eg to a wife/non bus. prop*

Entrusting the guarantee to the principal debtor to get it executed by the surety, as was done in *Carlisle and Cumberland Banking Co v Bragg,*[20] is not common today. In that case the jury found that the principal debtor was not the agent of the bank. It may be difficult to differentiate between an emissary or messenger and an agent. If the form of guarantee were taken to the surety by a bank messenger who was simply to bring it back, there could be no question of agency, even if he took upon himself to make representations as to it. But where it is given to the principal debtor to get signed, one gets nearer to agency, with the possible risk of a material misrepresentation.

Negligence on the part of the signer is sufficient to debar him from setting up that it is not his act and deed, or that he was misled by the representation.[1]

(v) *Form and construction of the contract*

1 THE STATUTE OF FRAUDS 1677

Section 4 of the Statute of Frauds 1677[2] provides that 'no action shall be brought ... whereby to charge the defendant upon any special promise to answer for the debt default or miscarriage of another person ... unless the agreement upon which such action shall be brought or some memorandum or note thereof shall be in writing and signed by the party to be charged therewith or some other person thereto by him lawfully authorised.'

An agreement to give a guarantee is within the Act and so is subject to the rule.[3]

In practice, in the case of guarantees given to banks, the documentation will generally be more than sufficient to constitute a memorandum for these purposes. Difficulties can arise under the Act, however, in relation to amendments and limitations to guarantees. For example, parol evidence by a guarantor limiting the operation of the guarantee is inadmissible. In *Hawrish*

---

19 [1937] AC 1 at 17 HL.
20 [1911] 1 KB 489 overruled by *Saunders v Anglia Building Society* [1971] AC 1004, [1970] 3 All ER 961, HL.
1 *Saunders v Anglia Building Society,* supra.
2 11 Halsbury's Statutes (4th edn) 205.
3 *Mallet v Bateman* (1865) LR 1 CP 163.

v Bank of Montreal,[4] the Supreme Court of Canada applied *Heilbut, Symons & Co v Buckleton*[5] and *Hoyt's Proprietary Ltd v Spencer*[6] in deciding that a collateral agreement cannot be admitted where it is inconsistent with or contradictory to a written agreement. The guarantee in the case contained, inter alia, the acknowledgement by the guarantor that (a) no representation had been made to him on behalf of the bank; and (b) his liability was embraced in the guarantee.

In *Perrylease Ltd v Imecar AG*,[7] however, it was held that extrinsic objective evidence was nevertheless admissible to explain the meaning of terms used in a guarantee. Scott J quoted from Halsbury's Laws:

'The principles of construction governing contracts in general apply equally to contracts of guarantee. Dealing with a guarantee as a mercantile contract the court does not apply to it merely technical rules but construes it so as to reflect what may fairly be inferred to have been the parties' real intention and understanding as expressed by them in writing, and so as to give effect to it rather than not.'

Since Scott J was satisfied that in this case there was a complete written contract satisfying the requirements of s 4 of the Statute of Frauds extrinsic evidence could be admitted to explain the meaning of the words used in that contract.

2 THE STATUTE OF FRAUDS AMENDMENT ACT 1828

The Statute of Frauds Amendment Act 1828 (Lord Tenterden's Act)[8] provides:

'No action shall be brought whereby to charge any Person upon or by reason of any Representation or Assurance made or given concerning or relating to the Character, Conduct, Credit, Ability, Trade or Dealings of any other person, to the Intent or Purpose that such Person may obtain Credit, Money or Goods upon, unless such Representation or Assurance be made in Writing, signed by the Party to be charged therewith.'

It is established that this section only applies to fraudulent misrepresentations. It would appear that such a representation as to the creditworthiness of a debtor made to induce a third party to give a guarantee in respect of the debtor's obligations may be actionable only if the representation was in writing signed by the author of the representation.

The application of this section to a document signed on behalf of a company by one of its employees was considered in *UBAF Ltd v European American Banking Corp*,[9] where Ackner LJ held that a representation signed by a duly authorised agent acting within the scope of his authority or an employee acting in the course of his duties in the business of the company constituted a representation by the company and signed by it.

---

4 (1969) 2 DLR (3d) 600.
5 [1913] AC 30, HL.
6 [1919] 27 CLR 133 (HC Aust).
7 [1987] 2 All ER 373, [1988] 1 WLR 463.
8 11 Halsbury's Statutes (4th edn) 206.
9 [1984] QB 713, [1984] 2 All ER 226, CA.

3 CONTRA PROFERENTEM

Because the bank will in most cases require the guarantor to execute its guarantee in a form prepared by the bank for its own benefit, in the event of any ambiguity or doubt a court will construe the contract 'contra pro- ferentem' in favour of the guarantor. In response, the tendency of the drafts- man is to spell out in ever-increasing detail the rights of the bank so as to avoid any disadvantageous construction. Many provisions which are com- monly found in banks' forms of guarantee reflect unfavourable decisions in the past: for example, where there is to be more than one guarantor, it will usually be provided that the failure of any one of the proposed guarantors duly to execute the guarantee will not affect the liabilities of the others, reflecting the decision in *Hansard v Lethbridge*.[10]

The Unfair Contract Terms Act 1977[11] (considered in ch 30, below) may have increased the risk for a bank that its standard form of guarantee will be viewed unfavourably by a court.

(b) Matters for which contracts of guarantee commonly provide

There are certain matters for which contracts of guarantee commonly provide. Consideration has already been given to two such matters, namely interest, and conclusive evidence clauses.[12] The matters discussed below are not intended to constitute an exhaustive list of common provisions, but simply to indicate certain fundamental issues which ought to be considered in the drafting of a guarantee.

(i) Consideration

A guarantee should state that it extends to an existing overdraft or debt, if any, as well as to future advances. The consideration for covering past indebtedness is the grant of future advances. A usual expression is 'in con- sideration of your making or continuing advances or otherwise giving credit ...'. It is not essential that the consideration should be stated;[13] and any statement is not conclusive. Another consideration may be shown by external evidence. The real consideration, where further advances are not stipulated for, is the forbearance of the creditor to sue or press the debtor:

'... where a creditor asks for and obtains a security for an existing debt, the inference is that but for obtaining the security he would have taken action which he forbears to take on the strength of the security.'[14]

This has also been implied from the nature of the transaction as between business men.[15] But, in the absence of a statement in writing, it must always remain a matter of deduction whether any claim was contemplated, and if so, whether it was forborne at the request of the guarantor.[16]

The Northern Ireland Court of Appeal, deciding *Provincial Bank of Ireland*

10 [1892] 8 TLR 346.
11 Halsbury's Statutes (4th edn) 214.
12 See ch 14, ante.
13 Mercantile Law Amendment Act 1856, s 3, 11 Halsbury's Statutes (4th edn) 207.
14 Per Parker J in *Glegg v Bromley* [1912] 3 KB 474 at 491, CA.
15 See per North J in *Re Clough, Bradford Commercial Banking Co v Cure* (1885) 31 Ch D 324 at 326; and *Fullerton v Provincial Bank of Ireland* [1903] AC 309 at 316, HL.
16 *Miles v New Zealand Alford Estate Co* (1886) 32 Ch D 266, CA.

Ltd v Donnell,[17] held that the guarantee in the case was unenforceable for lack of consideration, because the agreement could (1) not be construed as a forbearance to sue, and (2) only amount to an intimation that the bank might make further advances, that it was not bound to do so and that, in fact, it did not. The guarantee was given for the payment of premiums on an insurance policy charged to cover an overdraft which was dormant.

Where, therefore, the only consideration is the forbearance to press for an existing debt, the guarantee should clearly show the time for which such forbearance is to last. It is always open to the surety to challenge the validity of the debt or obligation he has guaranteed.

The disadvantage of the consideration being merely 'continuing the existing account' is illustrated in the Privy Council decision in *National Bank of Nigeria Ltd v Oba MS Awolesi*[18] in which a new account was opened without the consent of the guarantor. It was held that this constituted a breach of the contract with the guarantor so that he was discharged. In *United Dominions Trust v Beech, Savan, Tabner and Thompson*[19] the plaintiffs sought to recover under a guarantee given in consideration of the extension of 'banking facilities ... by means of advances of cash on negotiable instruments and for any other form of security or by any other means'. Geoffrey Lane LJ held that block plan or block discounting facilities were not banking facilities.

(ii) Guaranteed liabilities

1 SPECIFIC OR CONTINUING

Guarantees may be either specific or continuing. The former is where provision is made for the advance of a specified sum or for a specific purpose. Repayment of the specified sum or the achievement of the specific purpose discharges the guarantee. The continuing guarantee is the commoner form, designed to cover a fluctuating or running account and securing the debit balance at any time, after allowing for payments-in.

In *Westminster Bank Ltd v Sassoon*[20] the Court of Appeal (Bankes, Scrutton and Sargant LJJ) dismissed the appeal of the guarantor from a decision of Rowlatt J, given for the bank. The guarantor guaranteed the account of the principal debtor for £1,700, undertaking to hold herself liable for a year only. The guarantee was signed on 3 July 1924, and at the end of the document were added the words: 'This guarantee will expire on 30 June 1925'. In October 1925 the bank called on the defendant to pay. In reply to her contention that the guarantee was for a limited period and that the defendant was not liable for claims made after that date, it was held that the guarantee was a continuing one and that she was liable to the extent of £1,700 for the debt on the principal debtor's account.

The words 'ultimate balance' are sometimes used, meaning the balance on all accounts taken together[1] but if the guarantee is intended to apply exclusively to one account, this should be made clear.

---

17 [1934] NI 33.
18 [1964] 1 WLR 1311, [1965] 2 Lloyd's Rep 389.
19 [1972] 1 Lloyd's Rep 546.
20 (1926) 5 LDAB 19, quaere, whether the result would be the same today if the bank's understanding of the words 'This guarantee will expire on 30 June 1925' were not made clear to her. There might easily be a misconception.
 1 See *Mutton v Peat* [1900] 2 Ch 79, CA.

2 MEANING OF 'FURTHER ADVANCE'

In *Burnes v Trade Credits Ltd*[2] the guarantee of a debt included a provision for further advances to be made unless the guarantor gave notice that she would not guarantee them. Without her consent the defendants agreed to vary the terms of a mortgage by which the debt was secured and provided that the rate of interest should be increased and the term of the mortgage extended. The Privy Council held that 'advance' meant the furnishing of money and that the changes were not within the terms 'further advance' and 'other indulgence or consideration' and did not cover the increase in the rate of interest or the extension of the term of the mortgage.

3 'DUE OR OWING'

A continuing guarantee is usually drawn to apply to the debt 'now or at any future time due or owing from' or, preferably, to moneys advanced and not repaid by the principal debtor. Although the former seems to have raised no objection in some cases[3] the decision in *Re Moss, ex p Hallet*,[4] points to the danger of using such words as 'debt' and 'due or owing', for it might well be held that on the bankruptcy of the principal debtor the debt is extinguished, so that the guarantor is released. The case directly decides that interest guaranteed on money due or owing from the principal debtor ceases to be recoverable as from his bankruptcy,[5] To avoid this result, the liability of the guarantor should be defined as being for all moneys advanced to or paid for or on account of the principal debtor and interest thereon remaining unpaid or until repayment thereof, or words to that effect.[6]

The better view is that of the Supreme Court of Newfoundland in *Bank of Montreal v McFatridge*,[7] in which *Re Moss* was distinguished, to the effect that bankruptcy did not extinguish the debt, but merely suspended any right of action on it. In *Re Moss* interest only was guaranteed and it was held discharged where the principal debt no longer existed.

4 ADVANCES AFTER NOTICE OF DETERMINATION

A much discussed question is whether, in the absence of any provision, purely voluntary advances within the limit of the guarantee, made during the currency of the notice to determine are recoverable against the guarantor.

This is obviously a matter for which the guarantee should provide, though whether such provision would be effective is by no means clear. There are two ways of looking at the matter; on the one hand there is the duty of the guaranteed party to behave equitably towards the guarantor, recognised in *Hollond v Teed*,[8] and the difficulty of seeing where the object or sense of giving notice comes in, if the guaranteed person on receiving it is free to run the account up to the extreme limit. The object of notice is to enable the

---

2 [1981] 2 All ER 122, [1981] 1 WLR 805, PC.
3 Eg *Re Rees, ex p National Provincial Bank of England* (1881) 17 Ch D 98, CA; *Re Sass, ex p National Provincial Bank of England* [1896] 2 QB 12.
4 [1905] 2 KB 307.
5 Cf *Stacey v Hill* [1901] 1 KB 660, CA.
6 Cf *Re Fitzgeorge, ex p Robson* [1905] 1 KB 462; and see *Coutts & Co v Browne-Lecky* [1947] 1 KB 104, [1946] 2 All ER 207.
7 (1959) 17 DLR (2d) 557.
8 (1848) 7 Hare 50.

guarantor to circumscribe his loss; the banker would not normally be prejudiced by not being able to increase that loss. The position is somewhat analogous to that, apart from s 94 of the Law of Property Act 1925,[9] of a first mortgagee for advances, who receives actual notice of a second mortgage. On the other hand, there could be legitimate reasons for advances during the period of notice which, if not permitted, might seriously prejudice the principal debtor and the bank. The principal debtor may have made engagements and undertaken liabilities on the faith of being able to obtain credit up to the full amount of the guarantee; the banker's duty is to his own customer rather than to the guarantor. Further, if the parties care to contract accordingly can there be any objection? Certainly, if licence to take this course is wanted, the right should be clearly expressed and should include obligations undertaken pending the notice but not maturing till after its expiration, as well as those maturing during its currency. Just as the entering into the guarantee is a matter for agreement between the two, so also ought to be that of determination, at any rate as regards the period of notice.

Whether the liability of a joint and several guarantor for future advances would be affected by the determination of the liability of his co-guarantor should depend upon the agreement between the parties as expressed in the guarantee. The death of one cannot relieve the other but unilateral termination is another matter. Where the sureties are joint only it is an open question whether the death of one stops the liability of the other for subsequent advances;[10] if joint and several the death of one guarantor does not affect the liability of the other for subsequent advances.[11] In *Egbert v National Crown Bank*[12] a joint and several continuing guarantee was to continue 'until the undersigned or the executors or administrators of the undersigned shall have given the bank notice in writing to make no further advances on the security of this guarantee'. Held, that it could not be determined by one of them, that each and all must combine to determine it. But the decision turned on the wording. Lord Dunedin said:

'It is not necessary to examine what is the law in the case of death when nothing is said in the guarantee about its continuation or not.'

Joint liability is today covered by the Civil Liability (Contribution) Act 1978. Neither determination by nor the death of one co-surety is to have any effect on the continuing liability of the other for past or future advances.

(iii) *Extent of guarantor's liability*

A guarantor's liability may be limited to a given sum. Normally, however, the guarantee is drawn so that the surety is made responsible for the whole debt, for all moneys, notwithstanding that his liability is limited.[13] This has the advantage that if the principal debtor becomes bankrupt the bank may prove for the whole debt even though the surety has paid the full sum for which he is liable.[14] Otherwise the surety, having met his liability, is entitled

---

9 37 Halsbury's Statutes (4th edn) 72.
10 *Re Sherry, London and County Banking Co v Terry* (1884) 25 Ch D 692 at 703, 705; and see the Civil Liability (Contribution) Act 1978.
11 *Beckett v Addyman* (1882) 9 QBD 783, CA.
12 [1918] AC 903, PC.
13 See *Ellis v Emmanuel* (1876) 1 Ex D 157, CA.
14 *Re Houlder* [1929] 1 Ch 205.

to dividends on the amount paid.[15] The effect of the former is illustrated by the decision in an Irish case in which the two individual sureties paid the sums to which their liability was limited, the moneys being placed to a suspense account. The bank demanded payment from the principal debtor of the difference between this sum and the liability on the account and then sued him for the whole amount disregarding the moneys in the suspense account. It was held that the payments by the guarantors did not discharge the principal debt *pro tanto* and that the bank were not estopped by demanding the smaller sum since the borrower had not acted on the demand to his detriment.[16]

A slight variation in the wording is sufficient to assign the liability to one category or the other, and it is therefore always desirable to supplement the statement of the liability, and anticipate any question, by adding a clause or proviso, such as proved so efficacious in both *Re Rees* and *Re Sass,* under which the surety contracts himself out of any such possible equity in plain and distinct terms.

Any limitation should be and normally is to the amount guaranteed not the amount advanced, for in the latter case a lending beyond the amount of the surety's limit might render the guarantee void.

(iv) Determination

1 NOTICE GIVEN BY GUARANTOR

A continuing guarantee should provide for its determination. Without determining the guarantee a guarantor is not entitled to call upon the principal debtor to release or indemnify him.[17] He is, in ordinary cases, entitled to determine the guarantee as to future advances at any time by notice, and by paying, if required, what is then due on or within the limit of his guarantee.[18] Even if the guarantee is for a specified period, or is under seal, this right probably exists in equity, if not at law,[19] unless the banker were bound to make further advances to the principal debtor.[20] It may be provided that the liability of each guarantor shall be determinable only on the expiration of specified notice, to be given by him in writing, and on payment of all sums outstanding at the date of receipt of such notice, or subsequently accruing by virtue of any engagement entered into prior to receipt of such notice which, if notice had not been given, would have been covered by the guarantee. An instance is that of a bill accepted by the bank on the faith of the guarantee prior to receipt of notice, but not falling due until after it had expired.[1]

In *Kalil v Standard Bank of South Africa Ltd*[2] several persons signed a continuing guarantee to a bank as security for the obligations of a company

---

15 See *Re Rees, ex p National Provincial Bank of England* (1881) 17 Ch D 98, CA; *Re Sass, ex p National Provincial Bank of England* [1896] 2 QB 12.
16 *Ulster Bank v Lambe* [1966] NI 161, applying *Harvie's Trustee v Bank of Scotland* (1885) 12 R 1141.
17 *Morrison v Barking Chemicals Co Ltd* [1919] 2 Ch 325.
18 *Beckett v Addyman* (1882) 9 QBD 783 at 791, CA.
19 *Re Crace, Balfour v Crace* [1902] 1 Ch 733 at 738.
20 Cf *Lloyd's v Harper* (1880) 16 Ch D 290 at 314, CA.
 1 Cf *Hollond v Teed* (1848) 7 Hare 50, where the form of the guarantee was held to cover such bills.
 2 [1967] 4 SA 550 (AD).

and the question arose whether one guarantor could by himself determine
the guarantee which was in the form:

> '... this guarantee shall remain in force as a continuing guarantee ... until ... the
> bank shall have received notice from us terminating the same. ....'

It was held that, as the bank had failed expressly or implicitly to stipulate for
the removal of the right of an individual surety, he could determine.

2 FORMAL NOTICE OF DEATH OF GUARANTOR

Again, in the case of individual guarantors, provision should be made for
formal notice of the death of a surety before the liability of his estate for
subsequent advances terminates. The mere fact of the death probably does
not put an end to the guarantee, which is a contract. *Bradbury v Morgan*[3] is
a direct authority to this effect. But later cases are less positive on the point.
In *Harriss v Fawcett*,[4] Mellish LJ says:

> 'As mere matter of law, although it is not necessary, perhaps, positively to decide
> it, I am of opinion that this guarantee was not determined by the death. If one
> were to suppose a case, which might very easily happen, where a bank holding
> such a guarantee was not aware of the death, I should think it very hard upon the
> bank to hold that a guarantee worded like this was terminated by the death of the
> guarantor.'

In *Coulthart v Clementson*,[5] Bowen J implies that constructive notice of the
death would prevent the bank claiming further advances against the estate
of the deceased. In *Re Silvester, Midland Rly Co v Silvester*,[6] Romer J
dissented from this view, but did not touch the question of the effect of the
death. Joyce J in *Re Crace, Balfour v Crace*,[7] agreed with Romer J.

The legal representatives of a guarantor may after his death determine
as to future advances by reasonable notice. The provision for notice of
determination should provide for both the guarantor and, on his death, his
legal representatives to determine. This would exclude any question as to
constructive notice, or acting on the footing of the guarantee being determined.[8] Mental disorder of the guarantor determines his liability for future
advances.[9]

(v) Reservation of creditor's rights

1 RIGHT TO DEAL WITH PRINCIPAL DEBTOR

A guarantee should provide for the danger of releasing a surety by dealings
with the principal debtor or a co-surety.[10] Most bank forms of guarantee
today cover the risk by providing that the surety's liability shall not be
affected by any indulgence granted by the bank to the principal debtor to a

---

3 (1862) 1 H & C 249.
4 (1873) 8 Ch App 866 at 869.
5 (1879) 5 QBD 42.
6 [1895] 1 Ch 573.
7 [1902] 1 Ch 733 at 739.
8 See *Re Silvester, Midland Rly Co v Silvester* [1895] 1 Ch 573.
9 *Bradford Old Bank Ltd v Sutcliffe* [1918] 2 KB 833, at the trial, not mentioned in the Court
   of Appeal.
10 See *Barclays Bank Ltd v Trevanion* (1933) *The Banker* vol. xxvii 98; and *National Bank of
   Nigeria Ltd v Oba MS Awolesi* [1964] 1 WLR 1311, [1965] 2 Lloyd's Rep 389, PC.

co-surety or to anyone else. Even so, a surety may be released in spite of this provision. Where the guarantee does not constitute an indemnity, but is entirely secondary in nature, the release of the principal debtor always discharges the sureties because the debt is extinguished[11] and no agreement between the debtor and the creditor to reserve remedies against the sureties can have effect. But an agreement by the creditor not to sue the debtor, with a reservation of rights against the sureties will not release the latter.[12] And even though the agreement purports to contain a release but, by reservation of right against sureties, it appears that the intention of the agreement was that the debtor should not be sued, it will be interpreted as such agreement, and the sureties will not be released.[13]

The novation of a debt by importing a new debtor in place of the old is a release of the latter, and of the sureties.[14] A surety cannot be liable for a debt due from someone he had never undertaken to guarantee. If the obligation is to be so shifted, a new guarantee must be taken for the existing debt, and the consideration expressed therein.

'There can be no doubt that a novation by which the original debtor is released from his debt discharges the surety'.[15]

But the release of the principal debtor may not release the surety if the guarantee is so worded as to cover this contingency. It was so held in *Perry v National Provincial Bank of England*,[16] where the guarantee provided that the bank should be at liberty to give time for payment, accept compositions and make arrangements with debtors. In *Union Bank of Manchester Ltd v Beech*[17] the guarantee provided that no composition with the principal debtor should discharge the liability of the guarantor, and the surety was held bound though the creditor had discharged the principal debtor.

The case of *Lep Air Services Ltd v Rolloswin Investments Ltd*[18] provides an example of a claim by a surety that he was released by the acceptance by the plaintiffs of the first defendants' wrongful repudiation of their contract with the plaintiffs, which the second defendants had guaranteed. 'The acceptance of a wrongful repudiation is a right given to the creditor by virtue of the law of contract,' and the exercise of that right does not extinguish the guarantor's liability.

Giving time to the principal debtor releases the surety if the time is given by a binding agreement arrived at for good consideration, and the rights against the surety are not reserved.[19] The agreement to give time need not be in writing to be binding; it may even be implied. It usually arises where the principal is pressed for further security, the giving of which constitutes consideration for the giving of time.[20]

11 *Commercial Bank of Tasmania v Jones* [1893] AC 313 at 316, PC.
12 *Price v Barker* (1855) 5 E & B 760.
13 *Green v Wynn* (1869) 4 Ch App 204 at 206; *Re Whitehouse, Whitehouse v Edwards* (1887) 37 Ch D 683 at 694; *Duck v Mayeu* [1892] 2 QB 511 at 514, CA.
14 *Commercial Bank of Tasmania v Jones* [1893] AC 313, PC.
15 Pickford LJ, in *Bradford Old Bank Ltd v Sutcliffe* [1918] 2 KB 833.
16 [1910] 1 Ch 464, followed in *Bank of Adelaide v Lorden* (1970) 45 ALJR 49.
17 (1865) 3 H & C 672.
18 [1971] 3 All ER 45, [1971] 1 WLR 934, CA.
19 Per Lord Herschell in *Rouse v Bradford Banking Co* [1894] AC 586 at 590, 594, HL.
20 See *Overend, Gurney & Co (Liquidators) v Oriental Financial Corpn (Liquidators)* (1874) LR 7 HL 348 at 361.

So also the taking a bill from the principal debtor would constitute a giving of time, unless it were clearly shown that it was taken merely as collateral security, not suspending any remedy on the debt.[21] Time given to the principal debtor does not discharge the surety if given after judgment recovered against both principal debtor and surety.[1]

There is some authority for holding that the surety will not be discharged if his remedies are not diminished or affected. But in view of the judgment in *Ward v National Bank of New Zealand*[2] it would be unwise to rely on this. The Judicial Committee there said:[3]

'In pursuance of this principle, it has been held that a surety is discharged by giving time to the principal, even though the surety may not be injured and may even be benefited thereby.'

The surety is the only judge whether a variation of the contract without his consent is for his benefit or detriment, except possibly in self-evident cases, as, for instance, the creditor agreeing to take a cheque for £500 in full discharge of a debt of £1,000.[4]

In respect of reservation of rights, there is the opinion of Lord Eldon, who held in *Boultbee v Stubbs*[5] that a reservation of rights against the surety is of no avail if the contract for reservation prevents the surety's remedy against the principal.

In order to avoid these questions the guarantee should in the plainest terms secure to the creditor the right to give time to the principal debtor in any way he may deem advisable.[6]

2 RIGHT TO TAKE FURTHER SECURITY

The guarantee should also provide that it is to be in addition and without prejudice to any other securities then or thereafter held or to be held by the creditor for past or future advances; and full power should be reserved to take, vary, exchange, or release such securities, renew bills, and so forth, without prejudice to the guarantee.

It has been held that the taking of additional security does not, unless it involves the giving of time, of itself discharge the surety,[7] but any such question should be anticipated by the guarantee.

Apart from the question of giving time, the risk of releasing a surety by taking securities for the debt affects cases where the suretyship takes the form of a note executed by principal and sureties rather than those where a formal guarantee is given. In so far as the doctrine is based on merger, it is not easy to see what can merge the guarantee, unless it were another one by the same parties under seal. But it might be contended that other securities, though taken primarily for the debt, were in substitution for the security afforded by

21 See *Croydon Gas Co v Dickinson* (1876) 2 CPD 46, CA.
1 *Re A Debtor* (*No 14 of 1913*) [1913] 3 KB 11.
2 (1883) 8 App Cas 755 applied in *Canadian Imperial Bank of Commerce v Vopni and Chicken Delight of Canada Ltd* [1978] 4 WWR 76.
3 (1883) 8 App Cas 755 at 763.
4 Cf *Polak v Everett* (1876) 1 QBD 669, CA.
5 (1811) 18 Ves 20.
6 Cf *Union Bank of Manchester Ltd v Beech* (1865) 3 H & C 672.
7 *Overend, Gurney & Co* (*Liquidators*) *v Oriental Financial Corpn* (*Liquidators*) (1874) LR 7 HL 348 at 361.

the guarantee or, by merging or suspending the debt, affected the liability of the surety.

The converse situation arose in *TCB Ltd v Gray*,[8] where the guarantor Gray argued unsuccessfully that his personal guarantee of a loan made to a company of which he was a director and the majority shareholder was invalid on the grounds that it had been intended that the loan should also be secured by a debenture to be executed by an associated company, which debenture was in fact invalid. It was held that where a guarantor wished to make his guarantee dependent on the giving of some other valid collateral security, he had to establish that this formed part of the contract under which the guarantee was given.

3 RIGHT TO CLOSE ACCOUNT ON DETERMINATION

The right to close the account on the determination of the guarantee and open a fresh one, to which moneys paid in by the customer and not otherwise allocated by him, can be carried, instead of being applied in reduction of the guaranteed account, is established by *Re Sherry, London and County Banking Co v Terry*,[9] and recognised in *Deeley v Lloyds Bank Ltd*,[10] but the right is usually reserved in the guarantee.

(*vi*) *Effect of release where liability joint and several, or several only*

Where the liability of the sureties is joint and several, the release of one surety releases the others, 'the joint suretyship of the others being part of the consideration of the contract of each'[11] even though a joint and several judgment has previously been recovered against them.[12] The effect of the agreement between the creditor and one joint debtor was that there was an accord and satisfaction equivalent to a release from the joint and several judgment debt, and therefore, no debt remained against the other defendant to the judgment. It may be mentioned that Romer LJ in this case contented himself with an expression of doubt. But for the opinion of the other members of the court, Collins and Rigby LJJ, he would have considered that the instrument by which one guarantor was discharged did not amount

> 'to a discharge of the debt itself, but only as a discharge of the particular debtor from the liability as against himself personally: in other words, as an agreement by the bank not to sue him.'

In *Barclays Bank Ltd v Trevanion*[13] Swift J held that the guarantee did not contain words entitling the bank to release two of three guarantors and retain their rights against the third. The guarantee was a joint and several guarantee having clauses which the bank thought protected it in such circumstances as gave rise to the case, in particular one by which the sureties agreed between themselves that any sum which, for any reason, should not be 'recoverable

---

8 [1987] Ch 458, [1988] 1 All ER 108, CA.
9 (1884) 25 Ch D 692, CA.
10 [1912] AC 756, HL.
11 *Ward v National Bank of New Zealand* (1883) 8 App Cas 755 at 764, PC, applied in *Canadian Imperial Bank of Commerce v Vopni and Chicken Delight of Canada Ltd* [1978] 4 WWR 76; *Re EWA* [1901] 2 KB 642, CA; quaere the impact of the Unfair Contract Terms Act 1977.
12 *Re EWA* [1901] 2 KB 642, CA.
13 (1933) *The Banker* vol. xxvii 98.

... on the footing of a guarantee' should 'nevertheless be recoverable ... as sole or principal debtors'.

In *James Graham & Co (Timber) Ltd v Southgate Sands*[14] a joint and several guarantee was purportedly signed by three parties. In fact, the signature of one of the parties was forged and the question for the court was whether one of the other purported guarantors (the third having become bankrupt) was liable under the guarantee. It was held that he was not. O'Connor LJ decided that a joint guarantor under a guarantee which shows on its face that other joint guarantors are intended to be parties is not liable if the signatures of one of those others is forged since at law there is no contract of guarantee unless all the anticipated parties to the contract in fact become bound.

Accordingly, it is wise to provide in a guarantee that failure by any of the proposed guarantors duly to execute the same will not affect the liabilities of the other parties thereto. But where the liability of the co-sureties is several only, not joint and several, the release of one does not discharge the other, unless that other had a right to contribution in equity and that right is taken away or injuriously affected by the release of the co-surety.[15] Theoretically a several surety has the same right of contribution as a joint surety[16] but, if alleging release, the burden is on him to show not only the right but the loss of or injury to it.

It was held by the Privy Counsel in *Scholofield Goodman & Sons Ltd v Zyngier*[17] that the right of a surety to obtain contribution from a co-surety is founded on equitable principles, not contract, and exists independently of whether the sureties are bound by the same or different instruments or whether one surety has become bound with or without the knowledge of his co-surety, unless the contract of suretyship expressly limits the scope of the suretyship in such a way as to preclude contribution.

(vii) Reinstatement

A guarantee should provide for the reinstatement of the claims of the bank against the guarantor in the event that any payment made by the principal debtor or a co-surety is set aside or revoked. Where a payment is made by an insolvent debtor, notwithstanding that it is made in good faith in the belief that the debtor is solvent, it may be liable to be set aside as a preference.[18] Accordingly, a bank should exercise great care before granting an express release of a guarantee, since the fact that it has received payment from the principal debtor may not in itself conclude the matter, and any such release should always expressly preserve the provision for reinstatement.

---

14 [1986] QB 80, [1985] 2 All ER 344, CA.
15 *Ward v National Bank of New Zealand* (1883) 8 App Cas 755 at 765, 766, PC.
16 Ibid; *Whiting v Burke* (1871) 6 Ch App 342.
17 [1986] AC 562, [1985] 3 All ER 105, PC.
18 *Re F P and C H Malthews* [1982] Ch 257, [1982] 1 All ER 338; Insolvency Act 1986, s 239 and s 340, 4 Halsbury's Statutes (4th edn) 889 and 947.

(c) Rights of guarantor

(i) Right to sue principal debtor

The surety had the right in equity, where the debt had accrued, even before
he had paid in respect of his liability, to sue the principal debtor, a rule which
was confirmed by the decision in *Ascherson v Tredegar Dry Dock and Wharf
Co Ltd*[19] in which it was held that where there is an accrued debt and one
surety for it admits liability for the amount he has guaranteed, he has the right
to compel the principal debtor to relieve him of his liability by paying off his
debt. The decision was applied in *Thomas v Nottingham Incorporated Football
Club Ltd*[20] in which Goff J said that the *Ascherson* principle is not dependent
on demand being made where the suretyship contract requires a demand:

'once the account is closed and there is an accrued fixed liability the surety is
entitled to his quia timet relief whether the case be one in which no demand was
required to be made or one in which it was and a demand has been made or one
in which it was and no demand has been made.'

In *Owen v Tate*[1] it was held that where, without request, a person assumes
an obligation or makes a payment for the benefit of another, he will have a
right of indemnity only if he can show that there was necessity for his doing
so and that reimbursement would be just and reasonable. A guarantor having
voluntarily undertaken liability behind the backs of the defendants to oblige
a third party could not recover. Ormrod LJ expressly reserved his opinion as
to guarantors who guarantee without the request of the principal debtor.

(ii) Right to securities

On payment, the surety, if his payment discharges all obligations of the
principal to the creditor, is entitled to all securities held by the creditor, in
addition to the guarantee, whether they were held at the time the surety
became bound or have been subsequently acquired, and whether the surety
knew of them or not.[2] The banker, if absolutely recouped by the surety,
would have no further need of the securities.

But cases may exist where security is held for a debt, for part only of which
the surety is liable. On discharging that liability, the surety is entitled to a
proportionate part of the security.[3] The apportionment of the security might
be difficult, for the security might not be divisible. In *Goodwin v Gray*,[4] the
surety appears to have been satisfied with a proportionate share of the
dividends on the debtor's shares which constituted the security, but it is
conceived that he was also entitled to a share in or at least a charge on the
shares themselves.[5]

If the surety is surety for the whole debt, as is customary, but his liability
is limited, it would appear from *Re Sass, ex p National Provincial Bank of*

19 [1909] 2 Ch 401, applied in *Tate v Crewdson* [1938] Ch 869, [1938] 3 All ER 43; and *Watt v
   Mortlock* [1964] Ch 84, [1963] 1 All ER 388; see also *Re Anderson-Berry, Harris v Griffith*
   [1928] Ch 290, CA.
20 [1972] Ch 596.
 1 [1976] QB 402, CA.
 2 *Duncan, Fox & Co v North and South Wales Bank* (1880) 6 App Cas 1, HL.
 3 *Goodwin v Gray* (1874) 22 WR 312.
 4 (1874) 22 WR 312.
 5 Cf *Coats v Union Bank of Scotland* 1928 SC 711.

England,[6] that he has no claim against the securities or any part of them until the whole debt is satisfied.

The inclusion in a guarantee of a clause to the effect that all securities held against the debtor's liability were to secure payment of the ultimate balance outstanding would remove any doubt in either case.[7] Provision is also made for the bank to receive dividends in bankruptcy and other payments without prejudice to the liability of the surety for the ultimate balance; such provision was found efficacious in *Re Sass, ex p National Provincial Bank of England*.[6]

(iii) *No right to call on creditor to resort first to securities*

The creditor is entitled to sue the guarantor without first resorting to securities, although there are certain indications to the contrary in *Duncan, Fox & Co v North and South Wales Bank*[8] where Lord Watson says[9] that, seeing that the real conflict of interest was between the acceptor and the indorsers, he thought it would be inequitable to compel payment from the indorsers (who stood in the place of sureties) until the securities given by the acceptor (treating him as principal) to the bank had been exhausted; and he further says that he is satisfied that it is a settled rule of equity that, in circumstances analogous to those of that case, the creditor is bound to take payment from that one of his debtors who is inter eos primarily liable for his debt.

The bank had discounted bills for and indorsed by Duncan, Fox & Co accepted by Radford & Co who stopped payment before the bills became due. The bills were dishonoured and Duncan, Fox & Co became liable to the bank. The bank held securities from Radford & Co to cover advances and other liabilities, but their only liability was in respect of the bills. Duncan, Fox & Co, having got to know of the securities, applied to the bank either to realise them and apply the proceeds in payment of the amounts due on the bills, or to render an account of what was due from Radford & Co, and on payment of that amount by Duncan, Fox & Co to transfer to them securities of equal value out of those in their hands. The bank declined to do anything but undertook to do whatever the court ordered.[10]

The order originally made, ultimately restored by the House of Lords, was that the bank should hand over the securities to Duncan, Fox & Co on payment by them of the balance remaining due to the bank.[11] The question was whether Duncan, Fox & Co, as indorsers, were entitled to the same rights as sureties on paying the bills; and, save for the words of Lord Watson quoted above, there is nothing in the judgments to support the proposition that a surety can decline to pay till the creditor has exhausted securities placed in his hands by the principal debtor.

On the contrary, the right to sue the guarantor without resorting to the securities is clearly recognised by Lord Selborne,[12] and by Lord Blackburn.[13] In the Scottish case of *Ewart v Latta*,[14] Lord Westbury C, says:

6 [1896] 2 QB 12.
7 Cf *Waugh v Wren* (1862) 1 New Rep 142.
8 (1880) 6 App Cas 1, HL.
9 (1880) 6 App Cas 1 at 22, HL.
10 (1880) 6 App Cas 1 at 8, 10, HL.
11 See (1879) 11 Ch D 88 at 91, CA.
12 (1880) 6 App Cas 1 at 10, 14, HL.
13 Ibid, at 18, 20, HL. See also *Re Howe, ex p Brett* (1871) 6 Ch App 838 at 841, where Mellish LJ, lays down the broad rule that a surety has no right or interest in securities until he has paid the debt.
14 (1865) 4 Macq 983 at 987, HL.

'Until the debtor has discharged himself of his liability, until he has fulfilled his own contract, he has no right to dictate any terms, to prescribe any duty, or to make any demand on his creditor. The creditor must be left in possession of the whole of the remedies which the original contract gave him, and he must be left unfettered and at liberty to exhaust those remedies, and he cannot be required to put any limitation upon the course of legal action given by him by his contract by any person who is still his debtor, except upon the terms of that debt being completely satisfied.'

Further on he says:[15]

'The same principle prevails also in the law of England, that if a debt be due from A and B, and B be the surety, B has no right in respect of that debt as against the creditor unless he undertakes to pay and actually does discharge it.'

It may therefore fairly be assumed that Lord Watson's remarks above quoted were intended to be, or must be, confined to cases where no claim or objection is raised by the holder of the securities; and that no general proposition is to be deduced from them.

There appears, therefore, no absolute necessity for the creditor to reserve in the guarantee the right to resort to the surety without first realising securities held from the principal, although it is nonetheless common to do so.

Where securities charged by a borrower in respect of his overdraft are sold by the bank, a guarantor has no claim against the bank in regard to the alleged negligent disposal of the security. The bank owed no duty to the guarantors to take reasonable care and skill to obtain the best price reasonably obtainable for the property.[16]

(iv) Right of set-off

The surety is entitled to a set-off of debts due from creditor to the principal debtor arising out of the transaction on which his own liability is founded.[17] This principle is not likely to operate in the case of a guarantee to a bank. There would be no credit balance on the guaranteed account, and credits on another account are outside the question.[18]

Normally a surety is liable for the 'ultimate' balance in respect of a borrowing on current account. This necessitates combining all accounts of the principal debtor in order to determine the sum for which the surety is liable.

(v) Right to call on creditor to sue

The surety who has paid his liability has a theoretical right to call on the creditor to sue the debtor. If the creditor refuses, the surety may, on indemnifying the creditor, sue in his name,[19] although the surety can just as well himself sue the debtor on the basis of indemnity or money paid for him. However, this right of the surety is invariably excluded in bank forms of guarantee today. Where the creditor sues the surety, the latter may join the principal debtor as a third party.[20]

15 (1865) 4 Macq 983 at 989, HL.
16 *Barclays Bank Ltd v Thienel and Thienel* (1978) 122 Sol Jo 472.
17 *Bechervaise v Lewis* (1872) LR 7 CP 372.
18 *York City and County Banking Co v Bainbridge* (1880) 43 LT 732.
19 See Mercantile Law Amendment Act 1856, s 5; 11 Halsbury's Statutes (4th edn) 208.
20 RSC, Ord 16, r 1.

(vi) No right to appropriate payments made by principal debtor

The fact that a debt on current account is covered by a guarantee does not constrain the banker to any particular system of appropriation of payments-in, so long as he deals with the accounts in the ordinary course of business. In the absence of express agreement, a surety has no right to control the right of appropriation possessed by the person making the payments or, in the absence of such appropriation, the payee.[1] Payments-in may be appropriated to a pre-existing debt of which the surety has no knowledge,[2] or to a new account opened on the closing of the guaranteed account.[3]

Where there is a mere unbroken current account, part of which is covered by a guarantee, there is, in the absence of appropriation, no presumption that moneys paid in are to be allocated to the unsecured rather than the secured portion, or otherwise than in the usual sequence of payments in and out in order of date.[4]

Where the guarantee is a continuing one to secure an ultimate balance, the question of appropriation does not arise, except in the sense suggested by Cotton LJ in *Re Sherry, London and County Banking Co v Terry*,[5] namely, that credits could not be carried to a new account during the currency of the guarantee so as to deprive the surety of the benefit of them in estimating the ultimate balance for which he was liable.[6] In a case[7] in which the consideration for a guarantee was the continuance of 'the existing account' of the principal debtor, the Privy Council held that the surety was discharged because, unknown to him, the bank opened a fresh account for the principal debtor into which all subsequent credits were paid. As to this it may be said that the guarantee was not in the form used in the United Kingdom, for it failed to provide the wide discretion commonly given.

The remedies of the surety who has to pay against the principal debtor or the co-sureties do not concern the banker and are not addressed here.

(vii) Limitation of action[8]

As to the effect of the Limitation Act on a continuing guarantee, in *Hartland v Jukes*[9] it was contended that the six years began to run in favour of the guarantor as soon as the principal debtor became indebted to the bank, inasmuch as there was then a right of action against the guarantor; but Pollock CB said:

'It was contended before us that the statute began to run from the 31st of December 1855, by reason of the debt of £179:1:11 then due to the bank; but no balance was then struck, and certainly no claim was made by the bank upon the defendant's testator (the guarantor) in respect of that debt; and we think the mere existence of

1 *Williams v Rawlinson* (1825) 3 Bing 71; *Re Sherry, London and County Banking Co v Terry* (1884) 25 Ch D 692, CA.
2 *Williams v Rawlinson,* supra.
3 *Re Sherry, London and County Banking Co v Terry,* supra, recognised in *Deeley v Lloyds Bank Ltd* [1912] AC 756, HL; but see *National Bank of Nigeria Ltd v Oba MS Awolesi* [1964] 1 WLR 1311, [1965] 2 Lloyd's Rep 389 PC.
4 *Deeley v Lloyds Bank Ltd* [1912] AC 756, HL.
5 (1884) 25 Ch D 692 at 706, CA.
6 Cf *Mutton v Peat* [1900] 2 Ch 79, CA; *Bradford Old Bank Ltd v Sutcliffe* [1918] 2 KB 833, 24 Com Cas 27, CA.
7 *National Bank of Nigeria Ltd v Oba M S Awolesi* [1964] 1 WLR 1311, [1965] 2 Lloyd's Rep 389 PC.
8 See generally, the Limitation Act 1980, 24 Halsbury's Statutes (4th edn) 629.
9 (1863) 1 H & C 667.

the debt, unaccompanied by any claim from the bank, would not have the effect of making the statute run from that date.'

On the other hand, in *Parr's Banking Co Ltd v Yates*,[10] the Court of Appeal appear to have taken the opposite view. It is true that in that case the account, so far as drawing on it went, had been practically closed more than six years prior to the commencement of the action, but the court treated the statute as beginning to run in respect of each item on the debit side from the date it came into the account. Vaughan Williams LJ said that the right of action on each item of the account arose as soon as that item became due and was not paid, and the statute ran from that date in each case, in favour of both principal and surety.

Hartland v Jukes is cited with approval in *Bradford Old Bank Ltd v Sutcliffe*.[11] *Parr's Banking Co Ltd v Yates* was quoted by Swinfen Eady J in *Ascherson v Tredegar Dry Dock and Wharf Co Ltd*.[12]

There can be little doubt but that *Hartland v Jukes* is the better authority. If the account in *Parr's Banking Co Ltd v Yates* had been a running account and not dormant, the debts on it would have been extinguished by appropriation pursuant to the rule in *Clayton's Case*[13] and new debts would have arisen; so that there might have been no question of limitation of action. The limitation period is long enough for the question not to be important in relation to an operative current account. This case appears to have been distinguished by the Privy Council in *Wright v New Zealand Farmers' Cooperative Association of Canterbury Ltd*,[14] the guarantee in which stated that it was to be 'a continuing guarantee and shall apply to the balance that is now or may at any time hereafter be owing ...'. Lord Russell of Killowan, giving the opinion of the Board, said:

> 'It is difficult to see how effect can be given to this provision except by holding that the repayment of every debit balance is guaranteed as it is constituted from time to time, during the continuance of the guarantee, by the excess of the total debits over the total credits. If that be the true construction of this document, as their Lordships think it is, the number of years which have expired since any individual debit was incurred is immaterial. The question of limitation could only arise in regard to the time which had elapsed since the balance guaranteed and sued for had been constituted.'

The House were satisfied that the *Parr's Banking Co* case 'has no application to the rights and liabilities of the parties to the guarantee' before them. It was pointed out that A L Smith LJ in that case said that no advances had been made for a period of more than six years before the date of the writ in the action and therefore the plaintiff was statute barred.

The view taken in *Parr's Banking Co Ltd v Yates* is altogether inconsistent with the intention and effect of a continuing guarantee. The object of such guarantee is the extension of a working credit to the principal debtor. There could be no right of action against the guarantor unless there was also one against the principal debtor, and the guarantee would be meaningless if the creditor could demand and enforce repayment of every overdraft within twenty-four hours or less from the time it was granted.

10 [1898] 2 QB 460.
11 [1918] 2 KB 833 at 839.
12 [1909] 2 Ch 401 at 406.
13 *Devaynes v Noble, Clayton's Case* (1816) 1 Mer 529.
14 [1939] AC 439, [1939] 2 All ER 701, PC.

Lord Herschell said in *Rouse v Bradford Banking Co*:[15]

'It is obvious that neither party would have it in contemplation that when the bank had granted an overdraft it would immediately, without notice, proceed to sue for the money; and the truth is that, whether there were any legal obligation to abstain from so doing or not, it is obvious that, having regard to the course of business, if a bank which had agreed to give an overdraft were to act in such a fashion, the results to its business would be of the most serious nature.'[16]

There is another consideration which makes the question one of little practical importance. In *Bradford Old Bank Ltd v Sutcliffe*,[17] it was pointed out that the contract of the surety was a collateral, not a direct, one and that in such case demand was necessary to complete a cause of action and set the statute running. Moreover, bank guarantees invariably specify that the liability of the surety is to pay on demand, and in this connection the words are not devoid of meaning or effect, even with reference to this statute, as is the case with a promissory note payable on demand, but make the demand a condition precedent to suing the surety, so that the statute does not begin to run till such demand has been made and not complied with. This in no wise runs counter to the decision in *Joachimson v Swiss Bank Corpn*;[18] indeed the principle is fully recognised there.

Payment of interest or on account of principal by the debtor does not keep alive the liability of the surety, not being made on his behalf.[19]

(d) Effect of change in constitution of parties

(i) Partnerships

A surety's rights, his liability even, may be affected by changes in the constitution of the party to or for whom a guarantee is given.

It is specifically stated in s 18[20] of the Partnership Act 1890, that any change in the constitution of the firm for or to which the guarantee is given revokes the guarantee as to future advances 'in the absence of agreement to the contrary', and the same Act repeals s 4 of the Mercantile Law Amendment Act 1856, which admitted 'necessary implication from the nature of the firm or otherwise'.

The Partnership Act 1890, deals specifically with 'firms', without defining them but from the nature of the Act the term must, however, be taken as equivalent to 'partnerships'. The principle involved is a general one, that change in the identity of the person to or for whom the guarantee is given revokes it as to future advances.

(ii) Companies

A bank is rarely a partnership; it is usually a corporation, a legal entity, apart from the members composing it. Internal changes such as transfer of shares, election of directors, and so on, do not work any change in the corporation;

---

15 [1894] AC 586 at 596, HL.
16 Cf *Re Clough, Bradford Commercial Banking Co v Cure* (1885) 31 Ch D 324 at 326, per North J.
17 [1918] 2 KB 833, 24 Com Cas 27, CA.
18 [1921] 3 KB 110, 26 Com Cas 196, CA.
19 See *Bradford Old Bank Ltd v Sutcliffe* [1918] 2 KB 833, CA.
20 32 Halsbury's Statutes (4th edn) 636.

they are not a change of identity. And the opening of new branches is no change in constitution. The corporation remains the same. Branches and the head office constitute a single undertaking.[1] There is nothing to change the status of the corporation so as to affect the liability of a surety.

1 ABSORPTION

The absorption of another bank whereby its identity is lost would, as regards guarantees given to the absorbing bank, stand on the same footing as the opening of a new branch.[2] There is, again, no change of identity.

With regard to guarantees held by the absorbed bank, these, so far as a definite amount is due at the time of absorption, can be made available in the hands of the absorbing bank. In *Bradford Old Bank Ltd v Sutcliffe*,[3] a guarantee was held by bank A, which was absorbed by bank B. In a sense the account was continued with bank B, but it was dormant at a fixed figure. No notice of any change was given to the surety. He contended that he had been discharged by novation, the debtor having accepted bank B as his creditor. The Court of Appeal held that there had been no novation because there was not the assent of all the parties and in the absence of such assent, no evidence that the rights of the absorbed bank were to come to an end. Accordingly, the surety was not discharged. Pickford LJ said, at 842:

'There can be no doubt that a novation by which the original debtor is released from his debt discharges the surety, but a transfer of an existing and ascertained debt to another creditor stands on a different footing. In order to discharge the surety it must affect a material alteration in his position. ... In either case the transferee of the debt, whether by novation or assignment, is the person with whom the surety has to deal, and as the liability is already ascertained, it is a matter of no consequence to whom he has to pay it.'

The court further held that it made no difference whether notice were given to the surety. Bankes LJ said that a creditor may assign his debt or his securities without releasing the surety and Scrutton LJ ended his judgment, at 852, with the words:

'... I am not at present satisfied, though I do not wish to express a final opinion on the point, that even a novation of a creditor for the original debt would necessarily have discharged the surety.'

The court further held that it made no difference whether or not notice were given to the surety.

This judgment is limited to the particular debts. There can be neither assignment nor novation of debts which, by reason of the elimination of the guaranteed bank, cannot come into existence and the principle is therefore inapplicable to subsequent advances by the absorbing bank. It could not be argued that the surety had guaranteed advances from bank B when it was bank A he had agreed with, and he knew nothing of the change.[4] He might fairly contend that moneys paid in and not otherwise allocated by the principal should be attributed to the guaranteed debt, leaving subsequent advances uncovered.

1 *Prince v Oriental Bank Corpn* (1878) 3 App Cas 325, PC.
2 *Capital and Counties Bank v Bank of England* (1889) 61 LT 516; *Prescott, Dimsdale, Cave, Tugwell & Co Ltd v Bank of England* [1894] 1 QB 351, CA.
3 [1918] 2 KB 833, 24 Com Cas 27, CA, approving *Wheatley v Bastow* (1855) 7 De G M & G 261; in the former, the guarantee was not in favour of the bank or successors or assigns.
4 Cf per Lord Eldon, in *Ex p Kensington* (1813) 2 Ves & B 79 at 83.

Pickford LJ continued his remarks by saying:

'The case would be different if it were sought to make the surety liable for a debt arising out of dealings between the new creditor and the debtor. ...'

However that may be, there would seem to be no reason why the contract between a bank and a borrowing customer should not be assigned by the bank provided the borrowing was for a fixed figure. This would bind a guarantor, to whom it would be of no concern whether his fixed liability was to one bank or another; he could, however, discharge his liability or be required to do so if he objected to the novation.

2 AMALGAMATION

Amalgamation, as distinct from absorption, stands on a different footing.

'An amalgamation between two banks need not necessarily cause the business thereafter carried on to be the same as was theretofore carried on by either; it must depend upon the nature and character of the businesses amalgamated and how the amalgamated business was subsequently carried on. In each case it must be a question of fact.'[5]

There are two cases where a bond given by way of guarantee to a railway company was held not to be discharged, as to the future, by the amalgamation of the company with another, only on the ground that the Act of Parliament effecting such amalgamation contained special clauses preserving such rights.[6] The security in both cases was for the faithful service of an employee, but the principle is equally applicable to a guarantee for advances.

Guarantees to either of the amalgamated banks would apparently stand good in the hands of the combination for ascertained debts due at the time of the amalgamation and assigned by either to the joint body, on the principle of *Bradford Old Bank Ltd v Sutcliffe*. Dicta, such as those in *Royal Bank of Scotland v Christie*,[7] as to implied novation on amalgamation, must be confined to such existing debts. Advances subsequent to the amalgamation would not, in the absence of special provision, be covered by guarantees to either of the amalgamated banks, and the danger of the existing debt being wiped out by later payments-in, unless the account be ruled off and a new one opened, would be as likely as in the case where the guaranteed bank is absorbed by another.

Debts and other choses in action can be assigned but, save in cases where the personality of the parties is wholly immaterial, neither the benefit nor the obligation of a contract can be handed over to someone else, without the assent of the other party. Assignability of contracts has been carried far.[8] Whether it goes far enough to cover the substitution of a different creditor for the one to whom the surety undertook to be liable, for a future unascertained debt, seems open to doubt.

Lord Lindley appears to be of opinion that this contingency may be provided against in anticipation by fitting terms. An astute draftsman might

5 Per A L Smith LJ, in *Prescott, Dimsdale, Cave, Tugwell & Co Ltd v Bank of England* [1894] 1 QB 351 at 365, CA.
6 *London, Brighton, and South Coast Rly Co v Goodwin* (1849) 3 Exch 320; *Eastern Union Rly Co v Cochrane* (1853) 9 Exch 197.
7 (1841) 8 Cl & Fin 214, HL.
8 Cf *Tolhurst v Associated Portland Cement Manufacturers* (1900) [1903] AC 414, HL.

devise a clause whereby the guaranteed bank was constituted the attorney of the surety to transfer the benefit of the guarantee, as to future advances, to any bank into or with which that other bank might be absorbed or amalgamated. However, almost all bank security forms are drawn in favour of the bank, its 'successors and assigns'. Forms of guarantee often embody an indemnity as well as a surety liability and in such case the surety is bound.[9] Whether he is bound otherwise as a matter of contract may depend upon circumstances. In *First National Finance Corpn v Goodman*,[10] a guarantee defined 'the Bank' to include its successors and assigns and any company with which it might amalgamate. The original creditor amalgamated with its parent company, which, unknown to the defendant guarantor, made further advances to the principal debtor. The defendant was held liable on his guarantee, the parent company being the subsidiary's successor and/or a company with which it had amalgamated.

Possibly, however, the safer plan is to get a new guarantee to the new bank, or an indorsement on the old guarantee, transferring all obligations thereunder to that bank. A verbal agreement would be no good; a guarantee must be in writing and signed, and no oral terms can be engrafted on or added thereto.

Given the practical difficulties involved in assigning the benefit of, or novating, significant numbers of contracts, some reorganisations of large banks in recent years have been effected by means of private Acts of parliament.[11] Such acts, which are obviously capable of overriding the contractual relationships between the original bank and its customers, have provided for the 'undertaking' (defined as covering all of the business, property and liabilities) of the original bank to vest by virtue of the statute and without further assurance in the new bank. Since 'property' in this context has included all guarantees and other securities, the effect has been to confer on the new bank the benefit of all guarantees which were given in favour of the original bank (coupled with all the obligations of the original bank to its customers in respect of which such guarantees were given).

The Lloyds Bank (Merger) Act 1985 provided specifically that any security (including any guarantee):

'which extends to future advances or liabilities shall, on and from the appointed day, be available to [the new bank] ... as security for the payment or discharge of future advances and future liabilities to the same extent and in the same manner in all respects as future advances by, or liabilities to [the original bank] ... were secured thereby immediately before that day.'

In these circumstances, the difficulties encountered in *Bradford Old Bank Ltd v Sutcliffe* clearly do not arise.

(e) Release of surety

The acts or defaults which would release the surety, apart from those generally provided for, are such as a bank can readily avoid, if it bears in mind that there must be no variation of the contract, no dealing with the principal, or a co-surety, or with the securities for the debt, behind the back of the surety, or without his consent, either given by anticipation in the guarantee or prior

9 *British Union and National Insurance Co v Rawson* [1916] 2 Ch 476, CA.
10 [1983] BCLC 203, CA.
11 For example, the Barclays Bank Act 1984 and the Lloyds Bank (Merger) Act 1985.

to such dealing; and that, save in self-evident cases, the surety is the only judge whether such dealing or variation is or is not for his benefit.[12]

In *Bank of India v Trans Continental Commodity Merchants Ltd*,[13] the Court of Appeal affirmed the judgment of Bingham J at first instance that mere irregular conduct on the part of a creditor, even if prejudicial to the interests of the surety, does not necessarily discharge the surety. In that case the creditor bank had allowed certain foreign exchange contracts that had been guaranteed by the guarantor to remain unsigned by the customer, but the guarantor was nonetheless held liable. Bingham J listed the circumstances in which a surety may be discharged as follows:

1　if the creditor acts in bad faith towards him;
2　if the creditor is guilty of concealment amounting to misrepresentation;
3　if the creditor causes or connives at the default by the debtor in respect of which the guarantee is given; or
4　if the creditor varies the terms of the contract in such a way as to prejudice the surety unless the surety has consented to, or the contract or guarantee authorised, the variation,

but it was emphasised in the Court of Appeal by Robert Goff LJ that this list of circumstances was not exclusive.

2　LETTERS OF COMFORT

Although they have come to the notice of the courts relatively recently, letters of comfort have been in use in commercial transactions for some years in circumstances where a company or other entity is unable or unwilling to provide a guarantee but is prepared to offer 'comfort' to a lender in the form of an assurance as to such entity's continuing interest in or commitment to the relevant debtor.

For example, a parent company may be unwilling to guarantee a loan facility made available by a bank to the company's subsidiary either because the contingent liability in respect of such guarantee would be required by its auditors to appear in its balance sheet or because such a guarantee would have to be taken into account in determining the usage of its borrowing powers. A government agency might lack the power to give a guarantee in respect of the obligations of a particular entity, or find it politically unacceptable to do so. In any of these circumstances, the parent company or agency may be prepared to give to the lender its assurance that, for example, it will continue to hold the controlling interest in the borrower and to procure that the borrower conducts its business and affairs in such a way as to be in a position to meet its obligations to the lender, or even that it will ensure that the borrower has the resources to meet its obligations to the lender.

In determining whether a letter of comfort is acceptable in circumstances where it might otherwise have required a guarantee, a bank must understand the nature and extent of the commitment which is being given. While it might be thought that the considerations which generally give rise to the use of a

12　See *Ward v National Bank of New Zealand* (1883) 8 App Cas 755 at 763, 764, PC, applied in *Canadian Imperial Bank of Commerce v Vopni and Chicken Delight of Canada Ltd* [1978] 4 WWR 76; and see *National Bank of Nigeria Ltd v Oba MS Awolesi* [1964] 1 WLR 1311, [1965] 2 Lloyd's Rep 389.
13　[1982] 1 Lloyd's Rep 506 at 515; affd [1983] 2 Lloyd's Rep 298, CA.

comfort letter rather than a guarantee are such that the giver would necessarily wish to ensure that the comfort letter did not in itself constitute a legally binding commitment, it appears that the courts will in fact treat such letters as being capable of constituting binding obligations unless the opposite intention is clearly expressed. In *Chemco Leasing SpA v Rediffusion plc*[14] Staughton J held that a parent company was liable as guarantor of the liabilities of its subsidiary company on the basis of a paragraph in a letter of comfort in the following terms:

> 'We assure you that we are not contemplating the disposal of our interests in [subsidiary company] and undertake to give Chemco prior notification should we dispose of our interest during the life of the leases. If we dispose of our interest we undertake to take over the remaining liabilities to Chemco of [subsidiary company] should the new shareholders be unacceptable to Chemco'.

In the event, the parent company was held not liable because Chemco had failed to comply with an implied obligation to give reasonable notice that the new shareholders were not acceptable to it.

The language of the letter of comfort in the Chemco case did contain something akin to a guarantee ('. . . we undertake to take over the remaining liabilities . . .'). The same cannot be said of the language of the letter of comfort which was considered in *Kleinwort Benson Ltd v Malaysian Mining Corpn Bhd*.[15] In that case, a letter written by a Malaysian parent company to a bank which was proposing to lend to its subsidiary stated:

> 'It is our policy to ensure that the business of [subsidiary company] is at all times in a position to meet its liabilities to you under the above arrangements.'

At first instance, Hirst J referred to *Rose & Frank Co v J R Crompton & Bros Ltd*[16] in which Scrutton LJ observed that in business matters there was a presumption that an agreement was intended to create legal relations although this presumption could be rebutted if the intention so to rebut was expressed with sufficient clarity. Hirst J held that the presumption had not been rebutted in this case, and that the bank was accordingly entitled to damages equal to the whole amount of the loan on the insolvent default of the subsidiary, because:

1 the wording of the paragraph was not ambiguous but completely apt to constitute a contractual undertaking;
2 it did not follow that once a formal guarantee had been rejected by the parent company, there was no further scope for a contractually binding obligation;
3 the bank had acted in reliance, inter alia, on the paragraph when agreeing to make the advances to the subsidiary;
4 it was of paramount commercial importance to the bank that the parent company would ensure that its subsidiary was at all times in a position to meet its liabilities and that the bank should have a contractually binding ability to have recourse to the parent company should the subsidiary default; and
5 it was also treated as a matter of importance by the parent company as was shown by the formal board resolution which had been passed approving the execution of the letter of comfort.

14 [1987] 1 FTLR 201, CA.
15 [1988] 1 All ER 714, [1988] 1 WLR 799; revsd on appeal, [1989] 1 All ER 785, [1989] 1 WLR 379, CA.
16 [1923] 2 KB 261.

The Court of Appeal disagreed with Hirst J's approach, preferring to treat the relevant statement in the letter of comfort as merely a statement of the parent company's present policy which could be changed at any time in the future. Thus, the words did not constitute a promise but a mere representation of fact, and only a moral obligation on the part of the parent company. In arriving at this decision, Ralph Gibson LJ noted in particular that no express words of contractual promise were used in the relevant sentence, which had to be looked at in the light of other statements in the same letter (for example, an agreement by the parent company not to reduce its financial interest in the subsidiary company, which would have been of no significance if in fact the sentence in dispute had constituted a promise to keep the subsidiary company in funds) and the fact that the parent company had refused throughout the course of the negotiations to assume legal liability for repayment by the subsidiary company.

In the light of the uncertainty generated by the decision at first instance in the *Kleinwort Benson* case, it is likely that many letters of comfort will in future contain an express statement to the effect that they do not confer legally enforceable rights on the recipient.

From the point of view of a bank, however, even if the legally binding nature of a letter of comfort can be established, it is necessary in each case to consider carefully the wording of the letter. In particular, the distinction, noted by Ralph Gibson LJ in the *Kleinwort Benson* case, between a letter which contains an undertaking as to the future ('... we will procure that ...') and a mere statement of present intention ('... it is our policy to ensure that ...') must be borne in mind. In the latter case, provided that the intention so expressed was honestly held, a subsequent change in intention will not constitute a breach entitling the recipient of the letter to damages. In every case, the meaning and effect of the letter will be a matter of construction of its wording.

For a bank dealing with a company or group of companies which it knows well, it may of course be acceptable to the bank to receive a letter which is neither a guarantee nor a legally binding commitment on the part of the relevant company to ensure that the subsidiary is able to meet the bank's claim, but which simply assures the bank of the intentions of the parent company regarding the conduct of its subsidiary business. The bank may take the view that, having given such assurances, the parent company will be compelled by 'commercial morality' to ensure that its subsidiary does not default. On the other hand (and apart from considerations as to whether, if commercial morality is actually the source of the bank's comfort, the position is in any way improved by the writing of a letter of comfort) it has to be noted that letters of comfort are not now used only in the circumstances of a close banking relationship but also in circumstances where a bank may not have had previous dealings with the companies concerned or the opportunity to form any view as to the likelihood that its management will treat the statements made in such a letter as moral, if not legal, commitments. In these circumstances, there can be no doubt that it should be the objective of the bank to obtain a legally binding commitment.

The taking of proceedings on a letter of comfort may be more complex than the making of a claim for a debt under a guarantee since, depending on the precise nature of the 'comfort' given, it may be necessary for the bank to establish a causal link between its loss and the breach by the writer of the obligations that it undertook.

PART VI

LETTERS OF CREDIT AND PERFORMANCE BONDS

CHAPTER 36

LETTERS OF CREDIT[1] AND PERFORMANCE BONDS

1 LETTERS OF CREDIT

(a) Introduction

A function of bankers which gained tremendously in importance between the wars and has remained important since then is the financing of foreign trade by commercial documentary credit.[2] The banker lends his name and his standing to overcome the seller's lack of knowledge of, or of confidence in, the buyer, or uncertainty regarding a political situation in the country of the buyer. The commercial credit transaction was simply put by Denning LJ, in *Pavia & Co SPA v Thurmann-Nielsen*[3] as follows:

> 'The sale of goods across the world is now usually arranged by means of confirmed credits. The buyer requests his banker to open a credit in favour of the seller and in pursuance of that request the banker, or his foreign agent, issues a confirmed credit in favour of the seller. This credit is a promise by the banker to pay money to the seller in return for the shipping documents. Then the seller, when he presents the documents, gets paid the contract price. The conditions of the credit must be strictly fulfilled, otherwise the seller would not be entitled to draw on it.'

In *United City Merchants (Investments) Ltd v Royal Bank of Canada*,[4] Lord Diplock observed that an international sale of goods transaction to be financed by means of a confirmed irrevocable documentary credit involves four autonomous though interconnected contractual relations:

> '(1) The underlying contract for the sale of goods, to which the only parties are the buyer and the seller; (2) the contract between the buyer and the issuing bank under which the latter agrees to issue the credit and either itself or through a confirming bank to notify the credit to the seller and to make payments to or to the order of the seller (or to pay, accept or negotiate bills of exchange drawn by the seller) against presentation of stipulated documents; and the buyer agrees to reimburse the issuing bank for payments made under the credit. For such

---

1 It would be out of place in a work such as *Paget* to attempt a comprehensive treatment of the subject; for a fuller treatment see Gutteridge and Megrah *The Law of Bankers' Commercial Credits* (7th edn, 1984).

2 For specimen letters of credit and forms pertaining to them, see Gutteridge and Megrah *The Law of Bankers' Commercial Credits* (7th edn, 1984) Appendix E.

3 [1952] 2 QB 84 at 88, CA.

4 [1983] 1 AC 168 at 182, [1982] 2 All ER 720 at 725, HL.

618

reimbursement the stipulated documents, if they include a document of title such as a bill of lading, constitute a security available to the issuing bank; (3) if payment is to be made through a confirming bank the contract between the issuing bank and the confirming bank authorising and requiring the latter to make such payments and to remit the stipulated documents to the issuing bank when they are received, the issuing bank in turn agreeing to reimburse the confirming bank for payments made under the credit; (4) the contract between the confirming bank and the seller under which the confirming bank undertakes to pay to the seller (or to accept or negotiate without recourse to drawer bills of exchange drawn by him) up to the amount of the credit against presentation of the stipulated documents.'

For many years past the practice relating to commercial documentary credits has been subject to a body of rules formulated by the International Chamber of Commerce to which the United Kingdom and the countries of the British Commonwealth did not, at first, subscribe, largely because they felt it important to retain complete freedom of action in a matter which seemed to defy unification. But in 1962, a revised edition of the rules was accepted by them and today the rules, revised again in 1974 and in 1983, are observed by banks in almost every country in the world. Almost invariably, forms of application for the issue of credits and the credits themselves state that they are subject to the rules ('the UCP').

The 1983 Revision is embodied in ICC Brochure 400 entitled the Uniform Customs and Practice for Documentary Credits,[5] and came into effect on 1st October 1984.

The credits to which the UCP apply are specified in Arts 1 and 2.

'General provisions and definitions

Article 1

These articles apply to all documentary credits, including, to the extent to which they may be applicable, standby letters of credit, and are binding on all parties thereto unless otherwise expressly agreed. They shall be incorporated into each documentary credit by wording in the credit indicating that such credit is issued subject to Uniform Customs and Practice for Documentary Credits, 1983 revision, ICC Publication No 400.

Article 2

For the purposes of these articles, the expressions "documentary credit(s)" and "standby letter(s) of credit" used herein (hereinafter referred to as "credit(s)"), mean any arrangement, however named or described, whereby a bank (the issuing bank), acting at the request and on the instructions of a customer (the applicant for the credit),

(i) is to make a payment to or to the order of a third party (the beneficiary), or is to pay or accept bills of exchange (drafts) drawn by the beneficiary, or

(ii) authorises another bank to effect such payment, or to pay, accept or negotiate such bills of exchange (drafts),

against stipulated documents, provided that the terms and conditions of the credit are complied with.'

5 Copies are obtainable in England from ICC United Kingdom, Centre Point, 103 New Oxford Street, London WC1A 1QB. For a comparison between the 1974 and the 1983 Revisions, see 'UCP 1974 1983 Revisions Compared and Explained', ICC publication No 411.

In *Forestal Mimosa Ltd v Oriental Credit Ltd*,[6] the Court of Appeal had to consider the effect of a marginal insertion in a credit which incorporated the UCP 'except so far as otherwise expressly stated'. If the relevant provision of the UCP (Art 10 (b) (iii)) had not been incorporated, the defendant confirming bank had an arguable defence for Ord 14 purposes on the ground that the applicant had refused to accept 90-day drafts which were stipulated in the credit and duly presented by the beneficiary. The Court of Appeal held that it was wrong to approach the question of construction by looking at the credit first without reference to the UCP. The credit contained no express provision excluding the Uniform Customs, and the words in the credit which would have founded an arguable defence without reference to the UCP were in fact explicable by reference to, and consistent with, Art 10 (b) (iii) and 11 of the 1983 Revision. Accordingly, adopting the correct approach to the question of construction, the defendant bank was held to have no arguable defence on that ground.

The reference to standby letters of credit was first introduced in 1983 following a decision of the ICC's Banking Commission in 1977 that the term 'documentary credit' in the 1974 Revision included a standby credit.[7] The essential difference between a letter of credit strictly so called and a standby credit is that the former is intended to secure payment to the beneficiary in respect of his *performance* of the underlying contract, whereas the latter is intended to secure the beneficiary against *non-performance* by the applicant.

The remaining articles of the UCP under the heading 'General Provisions and Definitions' set out certain fundamental principles:

'*Article 3*
Credits, by their nature, are separate transactions from the sales or other contract(s) on which they may be based and banks are in no way concerned with or bound by such contracts, even if any reference whatsoever to such contract(s) is included in the credit.

Article 4
In credit operations all parties concerned deal in documents, and not in goods, services and/or other performances to which the documents may relate.

Article 5
Instructions for the issuance of credits, the credits themselves, instructions for any amendments thereto and the amendments themselves must be complete and precise. In order to guard against confusion and misunderstanding, banks should discourage any attempt to include excessive detail in the credit or in any amendment thereto.

Article 6
A beneficiary can in no case avail himself of the contractual relationships existing between the banks or between the applicant for the credit and the issuing bank.'

The UCP then contain four further groups of articles headed Form and Notification of Credits, Liabilities and Responsibilities, Documents, and Miscellaneous Provisions.

Where the UCP are incorporated into a credit, it is generally no longer necessary to refer to the common law as regards matters which are the subject

6 [1986] 2 All ER 400, [1986] 1 WLR 631, CA.
7 See *Decisions (1975–1979) of the ICC Banking Commission* (ICC publication No 371) p 11.

of express provision.[8] However, the Code does not provide an exhaustive statement of the rights and duties of each of the parties to a credit transaction, and where gaps exist, resort must be had to the general law of contract and agency.

(b) The issue, amendment and transfer of credits

(*i*) *Issue*

1 THE APPLICATION FOR A CREDIT

A credit comes into being as the result of a formal written application by the applicant, usually the buyer of goods, which is at the same time a request, a mandate and an indemnity. It requests the banker to issue or 'open' the credit, sets out the conditions on which he is to act and holds him covered in respect of his doing so. While in principle these applications have a common form, they nevertheless differ in detail from country to country and often from bank to bank and, naturally, according to the subject matter of the underlying transaction of purchase and sale. As the application is the foundation on which the credit itself is based it is essential, in the interests of both buyer and banker that it should be couched in precise and unambiguous language. The UCP expressly provide in Art 5 that instructions for the issuance of credits must be complete and precise. They should take account of the practical implications and possible consequences of the bank's compliance with the mandate it embodies, so far as they can be foreseen.

2 THE ISSUE OF A CREDIT

The formal requirements for the issue of a credit are contained in Art 12, which provides so far as material:

'(a) When an issuing bank instructs a bank (advising bank) by any teletransmission to advise a credit or an amendment to a credit, and intends the mail confirmation to be the operative credit instrument, or the operative amendment, the teletransmission must state "full details to follow" (or words of similar effect), or that the mail confirmation will be the operative credit instrument or the operative amendment. The issuing bank must forward the operative credit instrument or the operative amendment to such advising bank without delay.

(b) The teletransmission will be deemed to be the operative credit instrument or the operative amendment, and no mail confirmation should be sent, unless the teletransmission states "full details to follow" (or words of similar effect), or states that the mail confirmation is to be the operative credit instrument or the operative amendment.

(c) A teletransmission intended by the issuing bank to be the operative credit instrument should clearly indicate that the credit is issued subject to Uniform Customs and Practice for Documentary Credits, 1983 revision, ICC Publication No 400.
...'

The word 'teletransmission' replaces the expression in the 1974 Revision 'cable, telegram or telex'. The 1983 revision also contains in Art 11 important new provisions to give effect to the principle that a credit should clearly state

---

8 In previous editions of *Paget* extensive reference has been made to cases which establish propositions now contained in the Code. Given the almost invariable incorporation of the UCP, these cases have for the most part now been relegated to footnotes.

the method and the bank by which it is available, and to clarify the effect of the issuing bank's nomination of another bank. Art 11 provides:

'(a) All credits must clearly indicate whether they are available by sight payment, by deferred payment, by acceptance or by negotiation.

(b) All credits must nominate the bank (nominated bank) which is authorised to pay (paying bank), or to accept drafts (accepting bank), or to negotiate (negotiating bank), unless the credit allows negotiation by any bank (negotiating bank).

(c) Unless the nominated bank is the issuing bank or the confirming bank, its nomination by the issuing bank does not constitute any undertaking by the nominated bank to pay, to accept, or to negotiate.

(d) By nominating a bank other than itself, or by allowing for negotiation by any bank, or by authorising or requesting a bank to add its confirmation, the issuing bank authorises such bank to pay, accept or negotiate, as the case may be, against documents which appear on their face to be in accordance with the terms and conditions of the credit, and undertakes to reimburse such bank in accordance with the provisions of these articles.'

It is further provided by Art 14 that if incomplete or unclear instructions are received to issue, confirm, advise or amend a credit, the bank requested to act on such instructions may give preliminary notification to the beneficiary for information only and without responsibility. Even when the necessary instructions are received, the credit will only be issued, confirmed, advised or amended if the bank is prepared to act upon such instructions.

The purpose of Art 14 is to protect a bank which declines to act upon incomplete or unclear instructions. A different problem arises where instructions are ambiguous, and the banker acts upon them, most probably having failed to detect the ambiguity. It is an established principle that if the instructions given by the customer to the issuing bank as to the documents to be tendered are ambiguous or capable of covering more than one kind of document, the banker is not in default if he acts upon a reasonable meaning of the ambiguous instructions, or if he accepts any kind of document which fairly falls within the description used.[9] Similarly the paying banker who acts upon an ambiguous mandate is protected.[10]

However, a party such as an agent acting upon his own interpretation of a document must act reasonably in all the circumstances in so doing. Accordingly, if the ambiguity is patent on the face of the document, it may well be right, especially with the facilities of modern communications, to have the instructions clarified if time permits.[11]

(ii) Types of credit

The UCP make provision for two types of credit, the revocable and the irrevocable credit, and for confirmation of the latter.

9 *Midland Bank Ltd v Seymour* [1955] 2 Lloyd's Rep 147; *Commercial Banking Co of Sydney Ltd v Jalsard Pty Ltd* [1973] AC 279, [1972] 2 Lloyd's Rep 529.
10 *Equitable Trust Co of New York v Dawson Partners Ltd* (1927) 27 Ll L Rep 49, HL; *Samuel Montagu & Co v Banco de Portugal* (1924) 19 Ll L Rep 99, HL; *Ireland v Livingston* (1862) LR 5 HL 395; *Miles v Haselhurst & Co* (1906) 23 TLR 142, 12 Com Cas 83; *M A Sassoon & Sons Ltd v International Banking Corpn* [1927] AC 711, PC. In principle the position is the same as between issuing and confirming bank.
11 *European Asian Bank AG v Punjab & Sind Bank* [1983] 2 All ER 508 at 517, 518, [1983] 1 WLR 642 at 656, per Robert Goff LJ.

1 REVOCABLE AND IRREVOCABLE CREDITS

The UCP provide as follows:

'*Article 7*
(a) Credits may be either
  (i) revocable, or
  (ii) irrevocable.
(b) All credits, therefore, should clearly indicate whether they are revocable or irrevocable.
(c) In the absence of such indication the credit shall be deemed to be revocable.'

A revocable credit may be amended or cancelled by the issuing bank at any moment and without prior notice to the beneficiary.[12] Accordingly such credits confer little or no protection upon the beneficiary and are so rare in practice that it is not necessary to consider them further.

The legal effect of an irrevocable credit is stated in Art 10 (a):

'*Article 10*
(a) An irrevocable credit constitutes a definite undertaking of the issuing bank, provided that the stipulated documents are presented and that the terms and conditions of the credit are complied with:
  (i) if the credit provides for sight payment – to pay, or that payment will be made;
  (ii) if the credit provides for deferred payment – to pay, or that payment will be made, on the date(s) determinable in accordance with the stipulations of the credit;
  (iii) if the credit provides for acceptance – to accept drafts drawn by the beneficiary if the credit stipulates that they are to be drawn on the issuing bank, or to be responsible for their acceptance and payment at maturity if the credit stipulates that they are to be drawn on the applicant for the credit or any other drawee stipulated in the credit;
  (iv) if the credit provides for negotiation – to pay without recourse to drawers and/or bona fide holders, draft(s) drawn by the beneficiary, at sight or at a tenor, on the applicant for the credit or on any other drawee stipulated in the credit other than the issuing bank itself, or to provide for negotiation by another bank and to pay, as above, if such negotiation is not effected.'

2 UNCONFIRMED AND CONFIRMED CREDITS

Where the services of an intermediary banker (ie between issuing banker and beneficiary) are advisable or necessary, as is usually the case, the instructions from the issuing bank may require the intermediary merely to advise the beneficiary of the credit, without any commitment on his (the intermediary's) part, or may require him to add his confirmatory undertaking to it, in which case he becomes directly liable to the beneficiary. Confirmation usually takes

---

12 UCP, Art 9 (a). This accords with the position at common law; see *Cape Asbestos Co Ltd v Lloyds Bank Ltd* [1921] WN 274; *International Banking Corpn v Barclays Bank Ltd* (1925) 5 Legal Decisions Affecting Bankers 1, CA; *M A Sassoon & Sons Ltd v International Banking Corpn* [1927] AC 711, PC. By Art 9 (b) the issuing bank is bound to reimburse a branch or bank with which a credit has been made available for sight payment acceptance or negotiation for any payment acceptance or negotiation made by such branch or bank against conforming documents prior to receipt of notice of amendment or cancellation. This also accords with the position at common law – see *Gelpcke v Quentell* 74 NY 599 (1878). Where a revocable credit takes the form of an authority to purchase drafts, any bank acting on the strength of the authority must be deemed to know its terms – see *Chartered Bank of India, Australia and China v P Macfadyen & Co* (1895) 64 LJQB 367, 1 Com Cas 1.

the form of an advice to the beneficiary of the direct promise of the issuing bank together with the undertaking of the intermediary in similar terms; but a similar result may be obtained by the intermediary banker's issuing his own credit to the beneficiary, in which case the beneficiary can then look to him alone.

The legal effect of a confirmed credit is stated in Art 10 (b):

'(b) When an issuing bank authorises or requests another bank to confirm its irrevocable credit and the latter has added its confirmation, such confirmation constitutes a definite undertaking[13] of such bank (the confirming bank), in addition to that of the issuing bank, provided that the stipulated documents are presented and that the terms and conditions of the credit are complied with: [There are then set out identical obligations mutatis mutandis to those in Art 10 (a).]'

If a bank is authorised or requested by the issuing bank to add its confirmation to a credit but is not prepared to do so, it must so inform the issuing bank without delay.[14]

The negotiation of bills by an intermediary bank is not a confirmation of the credit, nor does it make that bank the agent of the issuing bank.[15]

The intermediary banker is normally the agent of the issuing banker, but may also act as principal in relation to him. Where, for instance, the issuing banker's instructions to him are merely to advise the credit to the beneficiary and the credit calls for drafts to be drawn either on the issuing banker or on the buyer, the intermediary banker may negotiate the seller-beneficiary's drafts provided that negotiation is not restricted to another bank. He then stands in relation to the issuing banker as principal to principal, having either stepped into the shoes and succeeded to the rights of the beneficiary under the credit or, if he has negotiated solely on the strength of the credit, as having accepted the offer it contains.

Where the intermediary banker either pays or negotiates the beneficiary's drafts, he is the issuing banker's agent, entitled to the indemnity of an agent, provided he pays or negotiates in accordance with the conditions of the credit.[16]

Where the intermediary banker confirms the credit, he does so as the agent of the issuing banker; if he confirms by issuing his own credit, the effect vis-

---

13 The terms of the Uniform Customs, coupled with the general acceptance by banks that letters of credit give rise to binding obligations, renders somewhat academic the question of consideration. There is clear authority that the promise of the issuing bank is supported by good consideration – see *Urquhart, Lindsay & Co Ltd v Eastern Bank Ltd* [1922] 1 KB 318 at 321, per Rowlatt, J; *Donald H Scott & Co Ltd v Barclays Bank Ltd* [1923] 2 KB 1 at 14, CA, per Scrutton LJ; and see *Anglo-European SS Co Ltd v Blane & Co Ltd* (1922) 12 Ll L Rep 67 at 69, and *Dexters Ltd v Schenker & Co* (1923) 14 Ll L Rep 586. There is no authority on the position between the confirming bank and the beneficiary, although in *United City Merchants (Investments) Ltd v Royal Bank of Canada* [1983] 1 AC 168 at 182 Lord Diplock treated it as trite law that the confirming bank and the seller are in a contractual relationship. For a fuller discussion, see Gutteridge and Megrah, *The Law of Bankers' Commercial Credits* (7th edn, 1984). There is ordinarily no privity between the intermediary bank and the buyer – see *Johnson v Robarts* (1875) 10 Ch App 505; *Calico Printers' Association v Barclays Bank Ltd* (1931) 39 Ll L Rep 51, CA; *Equitable Trust Co of New York v Dawson Partners Ltd* (1927) 27 Ll L Rep 49, HL.
14 Art 10 (c).
15 *Maran Road Saw Mill v Austin Taylor & Co Ltd* [1975] 1 Lloyd's Rep 156.
16 See Art 11 (d) and Art 16 (a).

à-vis the issuing banker is the same, provided the terms of his credit are the same.

The terms 'irrevocable' and 'confirmed' were for long taken as synonymous. For example in *M A Sassoon & Sons Ltd v International Banking Corpn*,[17] Lord Sumner said that there was no distinction from a legal point of view between an irrevocable credit and a confirmed credit, and that both were concluded contracts; but he was presumably referring to the legal effect of each, which, as regards the beneficiary, is the same in the sense that in both cases he has the irrevocable promise of a banker.[18]

3 REVOLVING CREDITS

A credit may also be a 'revolving' credit, of which one type is that in which sums drawn may be added to the balance so as to keep the amount available always up to the total of a permitted figure.[19] The original amount is often not restored until advice is received of reimbursement of the previous drawing.

(iii) Effect of issue

1 AS BETWEEN ISSUING BANK AND NEGOTIATING BANK

Credits are sometimes addressed to a named banker and restricted to that banker for negotiation; others, however, are available to any banker to whom the credit has been shown by the beneficiary and who cares to negotiate on the strength of it and, as soon as that banker acts on the invitation, there is then a binding contract enforceable against the issuing banker[20] if the conditions of the credit are met. Similarly, if the credit requests payment to be made or money advanced apart from acceptance of bills, and such payments or advances are made to the beneficiary on production of the request, the issuing banker becomes liable to the banker making them.[1] This happens in the case of credits, sometimes called 'anticipatory' credits, bearing the so-called 'red clause', which authorises advances to be made to the seller before shipment. In every case the party claiming must act strictly within the terms and limitations of the credit,[2] and possession of the credit is not, per se, conclusive evidence that the person presenting is the beneficiary.[3]

---

17 [1927] AC 711 at 724, PC.
18 See eg *Stein v Hambro's Bank of Northern Commerce* (1921) 9 Ll L Rep 433 at 507; reversed (1922) 10 Ll L Rep 529, CA; and *Panoutos v Raymond Hadley Corpn of New York* [1917] 2 KB 473, CA, where the Court of Appeal throughout assumed that a confirmed credit was necessarily irrevocable.
19 See *Nordskog & Co v National Bank* (1922) 10 Ll L Rep 652; *J W Mitchell Ltd v Ivan Pedersen Ltd* (1929) 34 Ll L Rep 310.
20 See UCP Art 11; and see *Maitland v Chartered Mercantile Bank of India, London and China* (1869) 38 LJ Ch 363; *Union Bank of Canada v Cole* (1877) 47 LJQB 100, 109, CA, per Brett LJ; *Re Agra and Masterman's Bank, ex p Asiatic Banking Corpn* (1867) 2 Ch App 391; *Urquhart, Lindsay & Co Ltd v Eastern Bank Ltd* [1922] 1 KB 318. And see *M A Sassoon & Sons Ltd v International Banking Corpn* [1927] AC 711, PC (distinguishing *Re Agra and Masterman's Bank, ex p Asiatic Banking Corpn* (1867) 2 Ch App 391).
1 See *Morgan v Larivière* (1875) LR 7 HL 423.
2 *Brazilian and Portuguese Bank Ltd v British and American Exchange Banking Corpn Ltd* (1868) 18 LT 823; *Union Bank of Canada v Cole* (1877) 47 LJQB 100, CA; *Donald H Scott & Co Ltd v Barclays Bank of Canada Ltd* [1923] 2 KB 1, CA; and cf *Chartered Bank of India, Australia and China v P Macfadyen & Co* (1895) 64 LJQB 367, 1 Com Cas 1.
3 *Orr and Barber v Union Bank of Scotland* (1854) 1 Macq 513, HL; *British Linen Co v Caledonian Insurance Co* (1861) 4 Macq 107, HL.

By UCP Art 11 (d), by nominating a bank other than itself, or by allowing for negotiation by any bank, or by authorising or requesting a bank to add its confirmation, the issuing bank authorises such bank to pay, accept or negotiate, as the case may be, against documents which appear on their face to be in accordance with the terms and conditions of the credit, and undertakes to reimburse such bank in accordance with the provisions of these articles.[4]

2   AS BETWEEN BUYER AND SELLER

In a contract which provides for payment by irrevocable credit, the credit, in the absence of express stipulation, must be made available to the seller at the beginning of the shipment period,[5] for the reason that the seller is entitled to know, before he ships the goods, that payment will be forthcoming when he does so.[6]

Where the sales contract provides for payment by irrevocable credit, the question arises whether the issue of the credit constitutes absolute or merely conditional payment of the price.

The matter appears to have first come before the courts in New Zealand in *Hindley & Co v Tothill, Watson & Co*,[7] when the view that the credit constituted absolute payment was rejected. In 1956, in the course of his judgment in *Newman Industries Ltd v Indo-British Industries Ltd*,[8] Sellers J said:

'The action is against the buyer, not against the bank, and the question of importance is whether the seller must look only to the bank who issued the letter of credit; that is, whether the method of payment agreed releases the buyer from direct liability for payment under the contract of sale. There does not seem to be any direct authority on the matter. Where it has been agreed that payment is to be by bill of exchange, the payment would normally be a conditional payment and it

4 See further 'Reimbursement', p 643, infra.
5 Per Denning LJ in *Pavia & Co SpA v Thurmann-Nielsen* [1952] 2 QB 84, [1952] 1 All ER 492, CA; and see in this connection *Sinason-Teicher Inter-American Grain Corpn v Oilcakes and Oilseeds Trading Co Ltd* [1954] 3 All ER 468, [1954] 2 Lloyd's Rep 327, CA; *Etablissements Chainbaux SARL v Harbormaster Ltd* [1955] 1 Lloyd's Rep 303; *Baltimex Baltic Import and Export Co Ltd v Metallo Chemical Refining Co Ltd* [1955] 2 Lloyd's Rep 438; affd [1956] 1 Lloyd's Rep 450, CA; *British Imex Industries Ltd v Midland Bank Ltd* [1958] 1 QB 542, [1958] 1 All ER 264; *Ian Stach Ltd v Baker Bosley Ltd* [1958] 2 QB 130, [1958] 1 All ER 542; *Soproma SpA v Marine and Animal By-Products Corpn* [1966] 1 Lloyd's Rep 367; *Toprak Mahsulleri Ofisi v Finagrain Cie Commerciale Agricole et Financiere SA* [1979] 2 Lloyd's Rep 98, CA.
6 *Pavia & Co SpA v Thurmann-Nielsen* [1951] 2 All ER 866, affd, [1952] 2 QB 84, [1952] 1 All ER 492.
7 (1894) 13 NZLR 13.
8 [1956] 2 Lloyd's Rep 219 at 236; and see *Sinason-Teicher Inter-American Grain Corpn v Oilcakes and Oilseeds Trading Co Ltd* [1954] 2 All ER 497, [1954] 1 Lloyd's Rep 376; affd [1954] 3 All ER 468, [1954] 2 Lloyd's Rep 327, CA; *Saffron v Société Minière Cafrika* (1958) 100 CLR 231; *Soproma SpA v Marine and Animal By-Products Corpn* [1966] 1 Lloyd's Rep 367 at 385–6; *Alan (W J) & Co Ltd v El Nasr Export and Import Co* [1972] 2 QB 189, [1972] 2 All ER 127, CA; *Man (EF & D) Ltd v Nigerian Sweets & Confectionery Co Ltd* [1977] 2 Lloyd's Rep 50; *Ficom SA v Sociedad Cadex Ltda* [1980] 2 Lloyd's Rep 118; and see also in this connection *Re London, Birmingham and South Staffordshire Bank* (1865) 34 LJ Ch 418; *Re Romer and Haslam* [1893] 2 QB 286, CA; and *Gunn v Bolckow Vaughan & Co* (1875) 10 Ch App 491.

would require very clear terms to make it an absolute payment. Here payment was to be by a draft drawn on the bank issuing the credit and it was, therefore, to be made by a negotiable instrument. Originally the payment of the price was to be guaranteed by a bank and the letter of credit was only taken subsequently in substitution at the request of the defendants and with the agreement of the plaintiffs. I do not think there is any evidence to establish, or any inference to be drawn, that the draft under the letter of credit was to be taken in absolute payment. I see no reason why the plaintiffs ... should not look to the defendants, as buyers, for payment.'

However, to speak of a letter of credit as conditional payment of the price does not make clear what the condition is or how it works. In *Shamsher Jute Mills Ltd v Sethia (London) Ltd*[9] Bingham J summarised the position in the following propositions.[10]

1 If the buyer establishes a credit which conforms or is to be treated as conforming with the sale contract, he has performed his part of the bargain so far.
2 If the credit is honoured according to its terms, the buyer is discharged even though the credit terms differ from the contract terms.[11]
3 If the credit is not honoured according to its terms because the bank fails to pay, the buyer is not discharged because the condition has not been fulfilled.[12]
4 If the seller fails to obtain payment because he does not and cannot present the documents which the terms of the credit, supplementing the terms of the contract, require, the buyer is discharged.[13]
5 In the ordinary case, therefore, the due establishment of the letter of credit fulfils the buyer's payment obligation unless the bank which opens the credit fails for any reason to make payment in accordance with the credit terms against documents duly presented.

(iv) Amendment of credits

The undertakings constituted by the issue and confirmation of a credit can be neither amended nor cancelled without the agreement of the issuing bank, the confirming bank (if any) and the beneficiary; partial acceptance of amendments contained in one and the same advice of amendment is not effective without the agreement of all the above parties.[14]

(v) Transfer and assignment of credits

1 TRANSFER

Credits are not negotiable,[15] but Art 54 of the UCP makes provision for their

9 [1987] 1 Lloyd's Rep 388.
10 Ibid at 392.
11 *Alan (W J) & Co Ltd v El Nasr Export and Import Co,* supra.
12 *Man (EF & D) Ltd v Nigerian Sweets & Confectionery Ltd,* supra. This makes good sense: 'For the buyers promised to pay by letter of credit, not to provide by a letter of credit a source of payment which did not pay', as Stephenson LJ put it in the *Alan* case at p 220G.
13 *Ficom SA v Sociedad Cadex Ltda* [1980] 2 Lloyd's Rep 118.
14 UCP Art 10 (d).
15 There is no English authority for this proposition, but in the United States a credit has been held not to be a negotiable instrument, *Schaffer v Brooklyn Gardens Apts* 20 UCC Rep Serv 1269 (1977) (Minn Sup Ct).

transfer. Transfer is the making available of a credit in whole or in part to one or more parties other than the original beneficiary. These other parties are referred to in Art 54 as 'second beneficiaries'. Article 55 preserves the right to assign the proceeds of a credit by providing that the fact that a credit is not stated to be transferable shall not affect the beneficiary's right to assign any proceeds to which he may be, or may become, entitled under such credit, in accordance with the provisions of the applicable law.

Transfer or assignment may assist the seller to finance the underlying export transaction. In particular, the transfer of a fraction of the credit may enable the beneficiary to procure a contract for the manufacture of the goods or the supply of materials.

The main provisions of Art 54 are as follows:

1 A credit can be transferred only if it is expressly designated as 'transferable' by the issuing bank. Terms such as 'divisible', 'fractionable', 'assignable', and 'transmissible' add nothing to the meaning of the term 'transferable' and should not be used.[16]

2 The bank which is requested to effect a transfer (transferring bank), whether it has confirmed the credit or not, is under no obligation to effect such transfer except to the extent and in the manner expressly consented to by such bank.[17]

3 A transferable credit can be transferred once only. Fractions of a transferable credit (not exceeding in the aggregate the amount of the credit) can be transferred separately, provided partial shipments are not prohibited, and the aggregate of such transfers will be considered as constituting only one transfer of the credit.[18]

4 The credit can be transferred only on the terms and conditions specified in the original credit, with the exception of the amount of the credit, of any unit prices stated therein, of the period of validity, of the last date for presentation of documents in accordance with Art 47 and the period for shipment, any or all of which may be reduced or curtailed, or the percentage for which insurance cover must be effected, which may be increased in such a way as to provide the amount of cover stipulated in the original credit, or in the UCP.[19] This provision enables the first beneficiary to transfer an amount less than the full credit amount and thereby preserve his right to draw on the credit for the balance representing his profit.

5 The name of the first beneficiary may be substituted for that of the applicant for the credit, but if the name of the applicant for the credit is specifically required by the original credit to appear in any document other than the invoice, such requirement must be fulfilled.[20] This provision is necessary to enable the second beneficiary to draw on the credit by presenting documents made out to the first beneficiary.

6 The first beneficiary has the right to substitute his own invoices (and drafts if the credit stipulates that drafts are to be drawn on the applicant for the credit) in exchange for those of the second beneficiary, for amounts not in excess of the original amount stipulated in the credit and for the original

16 Art 54 (b).
17 Art 54 (c).
18 Art 54 (e).
19 Ibid.
20 Ibid.

unit prices if stipulated in the credit, and upon such substitution of invoices (and drafts) the first beneficiary can draw under the credit for the difference, if any, between his invoices and the second beneficiary's invoices.[1] This provision enables the first beneficiary to obtain the second beneficiary's invoices and thereby prevent the applicant from ascertaining the first beneficiary's profit on the transaction.

7 When a credit has been transferred and the first beneficiary is to supply his own invoices (and drafts) in exchange for the second beneficiary's invoices (and drafts) but fails to do so on first demand, the paying, accepting or negotiating bank has the right to deliver to the issuing bank the documents received under the credit, including the second beneficiary's invoices (and drafts) without further responsibility to the first beneficiary.[2] This provision enables the paying, accepting or negotiating bank promptly to remit the documents to the issuing bank notwithstanding delay by the first beneficiary.

Thus the actual mechanics of transfer may take one of two forms, to some extent dependent on the purpose to be achieved. The credit can be transferred *in toto* to a single transferee or piecemeal to a number of transferees, according as to whether there is an ultimate single supplier or a number of them. The original credit having been advised to the beneficiary by the intermediary bank with a form of request for transfer and the beneficiary having requested transfer and returned the credit to the intermediary bank, the latter will notify the named transferee of the terms on which transfer is permitted. The second method is that in which the intermediary bank passes the original credit to the transferee under cover of a letter setting out the terms on which the intermediary will give effect to the proposed transfer.

The legal effect of transfer on the issuing banker, the beneficiary and the transferee has not been defined. The right to tender documents against payment of the price would appear to be transferred from the original or first beneficiary to the transferee but the transferee's right to payment are dependent on strict compliance with the terms of the credit issued to him, as were those of the prime beneficiary. The intermediary banker and the transferee are in privity as the result of the former's promise as given in the substituted credit. The intermediary banker is relieved of his earlier obligation to the prime beneficiary except that, having accepted the latter's instructions to transfer (on the authority of the buyer as embodied in the credit or in an amendment), he does so on the prime beneficiary's terms, which must not conflict with the terms of the credit. What this amounts to is that the prime beneficiary is entitled to exchange his own invoice for that of the transferee and to receive his profit, being the difference between the amounts of the original and substituted credits. On the other hand, as transfer in this form is a substitution of parties and not an assignment of a contract, it would seem to follow that once it has taken place the prime beneficiary is under no further responsibility to the intermediary banker. The buyer agrees to the substitution of a third party for the prime beneficiary in circumstances in which the latter may have to obtain the goods from someone else. This is essential, for instance, if the prime beneficiary is a middleman. The buyer expects and in

1 Art 54 (f).
2 Ibid.

fact receives the prime beneficiary's invoice and usually has no knowledge of the transferee. It is the prime beneficiary to whom he looks for fulfilment of the sales contract.

The intermediary banker is clearly under no duty whatever to question the particular transfer or transferee; once it is authorised, the intermediary banker is free to act on the prime beneficiary's instructions, providing only that when he pays, he pays against the documents for which the credit calls and within the period of time permitted. It would seem also that he cannot refuse to act without breaching his contract with his principal. It is as if the credit had originally been issued to the transferee. It would appear to follow that so long as there is no breach of his mandate as embodied in the credit, the intermediary banker is impliedly indemnified as an agent for any loss which may be suffered as the result of his acting on the authority to transfer.

2 ASSIGNMENT

The only reference in the UCP to assignment is in Article 55, which provides:

> 'The fact that a credit is not stated to be transferable shall not affect the beneficiary's rights to assign any proceeds to which he may be, or may become, entitled under such credit in accordance with the provisions of the applicable law.'

There appears not to be any special advantage in assigning the whole benefit of a credit rather than transferring the credit as provided for in Article 54, but where, for instance, a beneficiary is being financed it may be useful to assign the whole rights under the credit to the financing agent.[3]

3 BACK-TO-BACK CREDITS[4]

A means of achieving a similar purpose as a transferable credit is what is known as a back-to-back credit, which arises where the beneficiary is not the supplier and has no authority to transfer. By producing his credit to his own banker the beneficiary may, on the strength of it, obtain a credit in favour of the proposed supplier. No legal problem arises, however, from this method but the banker issuing the back-to-back credit must obviously be in a position to satisfy himself that the conditions of the 'original' credit will be met, which in practice means issuing the second credit in the same terms and satisfying himself that the documents tendered to him are such as exactly meet the requirements of the first credit.

(c) Conformity of documents

There is no more difficult aspect of the operation of documentary credits than the determination of whether documents are in accordance with the

---

3 See *Singer and Friedlander v Creditanstalt Bankverein,* Austrian Commercial Court, 1981 Com LR 69. Assignments of credits have figured in two English cases, *United City Merchants (Investments) Ltd v Royal Bank of Canada* [1983] 1 AC 168, [1982] 2 All ER 720, HL and *Kydon Compagnia Naviera SA v National Westminster Bank Ltd* [1981] 1 Lloyd's Rep 68, but consideration of the effect of the assignment was not called for.

4 See *Ericksson v Refiners Export Co* 264 App Div 525, 35 NYS 2d 829 (1st Dept 1942); *King of Sweden v New York Trust Co* 197 Misc 431, 96 NYS 2d 779 (1949); *Ian Stach Ltd v Baker Bosley Ltd* [1958] 2 QB 130, *Meb Export v National City Bank* 131 NYLI 4 (1954); and *Commercial Banking Co of Sydney Ltd v Patrick Intermarine Acceptances Ltd* (1978) 52 ALJR 404.

terms and conditions of a credit.[5] It is necessary to consider first, some general principles, and then the specific provisions of the UCP.

(i) General principles

The basic principle is that the documents must comply strictly with the terms and conditions of the credit. This principle is expressed in the classic statement of Lord Sumner in *Equitable Trust Co of New York v Dawson Partners Ltd*:[6]

> 'It is both common ground and common sense that in such a transaction the accepting bank can only claim indemnity if the conditions on which it is authorised to accept are in the matter of the accompanying documents strictly observed. There is no room for documents which are almost the same or which will do just as well. Business could not proceed securely on any other lines. The bank's branch abroad, which knows nothing officially of the details of the transaction thus financed, cannot take upon itself to decide what will do well enough and what will not. If it does as it is told, it is safe; if it declines to do anything else, it is safe; if it departs from the conditions laid down, it acts at its own risk.'

From time to time this general principle has been supplemented and elaborated by more specific statements relating to particular aspects of compliance. The following propositions are supported by authority.

1 Where the documents are those for which the credit stipulates, the banker is under no duty to consider their legal effect,[7] nor is he concerned as to whether the documents serve any useful commercial purpose or as to why the customer called for tender of a document of a particular description;[8]

2 Where a credit stipulates for shipping documents, it is essential that they should "so conform to the accustomed shipping documents as to be reasonably and readily fit to pass current into commerce".[9]

3 The buyer is entitled to documents which substantially confer protective rights throughout the period during which the goods are at his risk.[10]

4 The buyer is not buying litigation, and furthermore the documents have to be taken up or rejected promptly and without any opportunity for prolonged inquiry,[11] so that a tender of documents which, properly read and understood, invites litigation or calls for further inquiry is a bad tender.[12]

---

5 See generally, Professor Clive Schmitthoff, 'Discrepancy of Documents in Letter of Credit Transactions' [1987] JBL 94.

6 (1927) 27 Ll L Rep 49 at 52. See also Greer J in *Skandinaviska Akt v Barclays Bank* (1925) 22 Ll L Rep 523; and *Kydon Compania Naviera SA v National Westminster Bank Ltd* [1981] 1 Lloyd's Rep 68.

7 *National Bank of Egypt v Hannevig's Bank* (1919) 1 Ll L Rep 69, CA; and see Devlin J in *Midland Bank Ltd v Seymour* [1955] 2 Lloyd's Rep 147 at 154; and Salmon J in *British Imex Industries Ltd v Midland Bank Ltd* [1957] 2 Lloyd's Rep 591 at 597.

8 *Commercial Banking Co of Sydney Ltd v Jalsard* [1973] AC 279 at 286, per Lord Diplock.

9 Per Lord Sumner in *Hansson v Hamel and Horley Ltd* [1922] 2 AC 36 at 46. A banker cannot, for instance, be compelled to accept a bill of lading which does not contain the name of the shipper and which is indorsed in an illegible manner – *Skandinaviska Akt v Barclays Bank* (1925) 22 Ll L Rep 523.

10 *Hansson v Hamel and Horley Ltd*, supra, at 46. The words 'the period during which the goods are at his risk' have been added.

11 Ibid. See also *Commercial Banking Co of Sydney Ltd v Jalsard* [1973] AC 279 at 286.

12 Per Donaldson J in *M Golodetz & Co Inc v Czarnikow-Rionda Co Inc* [1980] 1 WLR 495 at 510.

5 The fact that a document contains something unusual is not a ground of rejection, if, when properly read and understood, the document does not call for further enquiry.[13]
6 The effect of the different treatment under the UCP of on the one hand, transport documents, insurance documents and commercial invoices, and on the other, all other documents, is that the former are subject to stricter requirements than the latter.[14]
7 Where an alleged discrepancy is not covered by any of the above propositions or by the UCP, the test appears to be whether there is any ground upon which the alleged discrepancy can reasonably be regarded as material.[15]
8 An obvious typographical error is not a valid ground for rejection.[16]

The position in relation to forged and fraudulent documents is considered separately below.

It is expressly provided by Art 15 of the UCP that documents which appear on their face to be inconsistent with one another will be considered as not appearing on their face to be in accordance with the terms and conditions of the credit.

---

13 Ibid.
14 This is illustrated by *Kydon Compania Naviera v National Westminster Bank Ltd* [1981] 1 Lloyd's Rep 68, where Parker J held (a) that the commercial invoice had to follow the strict wording of the credit, with the result that even if the words used in the invoice have, as between buyers and sellers, exactly the same meaning as the words in the credit, the invoice does not conform unless it follows the exact wording of the credit; but (b) that in relation to other documents there is not the same need to follow the strict wording of the credit, with the result that a bill of sale which certified a vessel to be free of encumbrances was held to conform to a credit stipulating for a bill certifying the vessel to be free of *all* encumbrances.
15 An illustration is *Netherlands Trading Society v Wayne and Haylitt Co* (1952) 6 Legal Decisions Affecting Bankers 320. A credit called for presentation of a draft accompanied by (inter alia) an 'original weight certificate' and an 'original jute mills certificate'. The beneficiary in fact tendered seven certificates covering the required total number of bags, each being a *combined* 'weight and jute mill certificate'. The plaintiff bank accepted these certificates, but the applicant refused reimbursement on the ground (inter alia) that the bank should not have accepted combined certificates. The court held in favour of the bank on the ground that it had not been and could not have been alleged that the certificates did not contain everything that jute mill certificates and weight certificates ought to contain. In other words, the court construed the credit as requiring the certification of certain matters, but not as requiring such certification to be in separate documents for jute mills and weight; for it was impossible to point to any reason why the mere combining of the certificates could be material. Of course if the credit had stipulated for a jute mill certificate to be issued by A, and a weight certificate to be issued by B, the credit would have required separate certificates. See also *Gian Singh & Co Ltd v Banque de l'Indochine* [1974] 1 WLR 1234 at 1240 where Lord Diplock stated with reference to minor differences between the description in the credit of the certificate required and the wording of the certificate actually presented: 'The relevance of minor variations such as these depends upon whether they are sufficiently material to disentitle the issuing bank from saying that in accepting the certificate it did as it was told.'
16 See, for example, *Forestal Mimosa Ltd v Oriental Credit Ltd* [1986] 2 All ER 400 at 407–408, where a date on a declaration of shipment which appeared to be '2 July' was held to be a plain mistyping of '22 July', the two figures '2' having been superimposed.

(*ii*) Transport documents

1 DOCUMENTS OTHER THAN MARINE BILLS OF LADING

Transport documents are covered by Art 25–34 of the UCP. The 1983 Revision introduced important changes in relation to transport documents in recognition of the increasing volume of goods carried by containerised and combined transport methods. This has led to a new article, Art 25, which provides:

'Unless a credit calling for a transport document stipulates as such document a marine bill of lading (ocean bill of lading or a bill or lading covering carriage by sea), or a post receipt or certificate of posting:

(a) banks will, unless otherwise stipulated in the credit, accept a transport document which:

   i appears on its face to have been issued by a named carrier, or his agent, and

   ii indicates dispatch or taking in charge of the goods, or loading on board, as the case may be, and

   iii consists of the full set of originals issued to the consignor if issued in more than one original, and

   iv meets all other stipulations of the credit.

(b) Subject to the above, and unless otherwise stipulated in the credit, banks will not reject a transport document which:

   i bears a title such as "Combined transport bill of lading", "Combined transport document", "Combined transport bill of lading or port-to-port bill of lading", or a title or a combination of titles of similar intent and effect, and/or

   ii indicates some or all of the conditions of carriage by reference to a source or document other than the transport document itself (short form/blank back transport document), and/or

   iii indicates a place of taking in charge different from the port of loading and/or a place of final destination different from the port of discharge, and/or

   iv relates to cargoes such as those in Containers or on pallets, and the like, and/or

   v contains the indication "intended", or similar qualification, in relation to the vessel or other means of transport, and/or the port of loading and/or the port of discharge.

(c) Unless otherwise stipulated in the credit in the case of carriage by sea or by more than one mode of transport but including carriage by sea, banks will reject a transport document which:

   i indicates that it is subject to a charter party, and/or

   ii indicates that the carrying vessel is propelled by sail only.

(d) Unless otherwise stipulated in the credit, banks will reject a transport document issued by a freight forwarder unless it is the FIATA Combined Transport Bill of Lading approved by the International Chamber of Commerce or otherwise indicates that it is issued by a freight forwarder acting as a carrier or agent of a named carrier.'

The opening words of this Article indicate the manner in which the UCP now divide transport documents into three categories, namely (i) marine bills of lading, (ii) post receipts or certificates of posting and (iii) all other transport documents. It will be noted that Art 25 (a) specifies features of the document which are mandatory; Art 25 (b) specifies additional features which are not mandatory, but are permitted; Art 25 (c) specifies additional features which are not permitted and lead to rejection. The provisions here and elsewhere in the UCP are prefaced by the words 'unless otherwise stipulated in the credit', reflecting the exporter's entitlement vis à vis the issuing bank to frame the credit according to his requirements.

2 MARINE BILLS OF LADING

Marine bills of lading are now governed by Art 26, the structure of which closely follows Art 25:

If a credit calling for a transport document stipulates as such document a marine bill of lading:
(a) Banks will, unless otherwise stipulated in the credit, accept a document which:
    i appears on its face to have been issued by a named carrier, or his agent, and
    ii indicates that the goods have been loaded on board or shipped on a named vessel, and
    iii consists of the full set of originals issued to the consignor if issued in more than one original, and
    iv meets all other stipulations of the credit.
(b) Subject to the above, and unless otherwise stipulated in the credit, banks will not reject a document which:
    i bears a title such as "Combined transport bill of lading", "Combined transport document", "Combined transport bill of lading or port-to-port bill of lading", or a title or a combination of titles of similar intent and effect, and/or
    ii indicates some or all of the conditions of carriage by reference to a source or document other than the transport document itself (short form/blank back transport document), and/or
    iii indicates a place of taking in charge different from the port of loading, and/or a place of final destination different from the port of discharge, and/or
    iv relates to cargoes such as those in Containers or on pallets, and the like.
(c) Unless otherwise stipulated in the credit, banks will reject a document which:
    i indicates that it is subject to a charter party, and/or
    ii indicates that the carrying vessel is propelled by sail only, and/or
    iii contains the indication "intended", or similar qualification in relation to
        ●the vessel and or the port of loading – unless such document bears an on board notation in accordance with article 27 (b) and also indicates the actual port of loading, and/or
        ●the port of discharge – unless the place of final destination indicated on the document is other than the port of discharge, and/or
    iv is issued by a freight forwarder, unless it indicates that it is issued by such freight forwarder acting as a carrier, or as the agent of a named carrier.

A delivery order is not a good tender under a credit calling for a bill of lading,[17] nor is a ship's release;[18] nor is a bill of lading where the credit calls for a delivery order.[19] Where a contract provided for payment 'cash against documents or delivery order', it was held that the tender of a delivery order without the other documents normally required under a cif contract was not

---

17 *Forbes, Forbes, Campbell & Co v Pelling, Stanley & Co* (1921) 9 Ll L Rep 202.
18 *Heilbert, Symons & Co Ltd v Harvey, Christie-Miller & Co* (1922) 12 Ll L Rep 455.
19 *National Bank of South Africa v Banca Italiana di Sconto and Arnhold Bros & Co* (*Oleifici Nationale of Genoa, Third Parties*) (1922) 10 Ll L Rep 531, CA.

enough.[20] A tender of goods in lieu of documents is not sufficient.[1] The bill of lading must cover the transit from the port of origin to the port of destination.[2]

3 ACCEPTABILITY OF 'RECEIVED FOR SHIPMENT' TRANSPORT DOCUMENTS

The 1983 Revision introduced a further major change by departing from the principle that a bill of lading must show that the goods have been loaded on board or shipped on a named vessel, permitting instead a 'received for shipment' notation.[3] Article 27 provides:

'(a) Unless a credit specifically calls for an on board transport document, or unless inconsistent with other stipulation(s) in the credit, or with Article 26, banks will accept a transport document which indicates that the goods have been taken in charge or received for shipment.

(b) Loading on board or shipment on a vessel may be evidenced either by a transport document bearing wording indicating loading on board a named vessel or shipment on a named vessel, or, in the case of a transport document stating "received for shipment", by means of a notation of loading on board on the transport document signed or initialled and dated by the carrier or his agent, and the date of this notation shall be regarded as the date of loading on board the named vessel or shipment on the named vessel.'

A notation is an addition to the bill as distinct from words constituting part of the original documents presented to a ship's agents for signature and signing by them.[4] It was held by the Privy Council in *Westpac Banking Corpn v South Carolina National Bank*[5] that Art 27 (b) is a deeming provision; it does not follow that goods have in fact been received for shipment or shipped on the deemed date.

4 CLEAN DOCUMENTS

By Art 34 (a), a clean transport document is one which bears no superimposed clause or notation which expressly declares a defective condition of the goods and/or the packaging. Some cases are clear beyond question, as where bills of lading which bore clauses that:

'so dealt with the condition of the meat or with what the ship said as to the condition of the meat for shipment as to seriously affect its price and its acceptability.'

20 *Re Denbigh, Cowan & Co and R Atcherley & Co* (1921) 90 LJKB 836, CA.
1 *Orient Co Ltd v Brekke and Howlid* [1913] 1 KB 531, DC.
2 *E Clemens Horst Co v Biddell Bros* [1912] AC 18, HL; *Landauer & Co v Craven and Speeding Bros* [1912] 2 KB 94; *Brazilian and Portuguese Bank Ltd v British and American Exchange Banking Corpn Ltd* (1868) 18 LT 823; *Hansson v Hamel and Horley Ltd* [1922] 2 AC 36, HL, and *Holland Colombo Trading Society Ltd v Alawdeen and others* [1954] 2 Lloyd's Rep 45, 53.
3 For the position at common law, see *Diamond Alkali Export Corpn v Bourgeois* [1921] 3 KB 443; *Donald H Scott & Co Ltd v Barclays Bank Ltd* [1923] 2 KB 1, CA; *British Imex Industries Ltd v Midland Bank Ltd* [1958] QB 542, [1957] 2 Lloyd's Rep 591. But see *Marlborough Hill (Ship) v Alex Cowan & Sons Ltd* [1921] 1 AC 444, PC.
4 *Westpac Banking Corpn v South Carolina National Bank* [1986] 1 Lloyd's Rep 311 at 314–315.
5 Ibid at 316.

were held not to be clean.[6] In *British Imex Industries Ltd v Midland Bank Ltd*[7] Salmon J entirely agreed with the view of Bailhache J in the *National Bank of Egypt* case:

'when a credit calls for bills of lading, in normal circumstances it means clean bills of lading;'

Scrutton on Charterparties[8] describes a clean bill of lading as:

'one in which there is nothing to qualify the admission that so many packages are shipped in good order and well conditioned.'

As Donaldson J pointed out in the *Golodetz* case,[9] the UCP definition of a clean bill does not specify the time with respect to which the notation speaks. He further said that if the notation refers to the state of affairs upon completion of shipment the bill is clean, as it shows that the goods were in apparent good order and condition on shipment. Article 34 (b) is to the effect that:

'(b) Banks will refuse transport documents bearing such clauses or notations unless the credit expressly stipulates the clauses or notations which may be accepted.'

The question whether bills of lading are 'clean' or 'unclean' is in practice as well as in law a vexed one. To tie the question to the goods and packing may be too narrow. A buyer has the right to a bill of lading which is usual in form and appropriate to the particular trade and which carries no greater liability than the usual form of bill. That is what he intends and expects to receive and his expectation may be vitiated by two factors, not necessarily running counter to the declaration as to good order and condition: first, the reservation as to good order may be such as to leave a reasonable doubt whether it is such a reservation or not, and second, if there is no doubt, it may express or imply a reservation which, nevertheless, may be deleterious to the interest of the buyer and to which he had not obliged himself. It may, perhaps, be thought that, wherever a shipowner qualifies his bill by a superimposed assertion which is a reservation of responsibility as opposed to a statement of fact or opinion concerning the goods or packing, the bill cannot be a good tender under the credit whether or not 'clean' bills are impliedly or expressly called for. Whether or not such a bill is a good tender under a cif contract is a different question. A paying or negotiating banker has to decide whether or not the bill is one which he is authorised to accept; and if he is in any doubt he must be justified in refusing to pay except under reserve or indemnity and without being liable to an action by the seller-beneficiary. London practice, at any rate, is in line with this view; for instance

6 *Westminster Bank Ltd v Banca Nazionale di Credito* (1928) 31 Ll L Rep 306 at 311, per Roche J.
7 [1958] 1 QB 542 at 551.
8 (19th edn, 1984) p 177 (note 1) citing *Restitution SS Co v Sir John Pirie & Co* (1889) 61 LT 330 at 333 and referring to *Canada and Dominion Sugar Co Ltd v Canadian National (West Indies) Steamships Ltd* [1947] AC 46, PC.
9 In *M Golodetz & Co Inc v Czarnikow-Rionda Co Inc* [1979] 2 All ER 726, [1979] 2 Lloyd's Rep 450 there was a fire in the ship after loading; the bill of lading covering the sugar damaged by fire contained a notation to that effect; it was held that the notation did not affect the acknowledgment in the bill that the goods were shipped in apparent good order and condition, did not make the bill of lading unclean and that it was a good tender. Donaldson J's decision was approved by the Court of Appeal: [1980] 1 All ER 501, [1980] 1 WLR 495.

bills of lading containing ice and congestion clauses or, for a cif shipment, 'Freight paid by cheque', are not accepted.

5 DESCRIPTION OF GOODS

By Art 41 (c) the goods may be described in all documents other than the commercial invoice in general terms not inconsistent with the description of the goods in the credit. There is, however, a real distinction between an identification of goods and a description of goods. The latitude in relation to other documents extends only to description, and however general the description, the identification must be unequivocal.[10] A distinction exists between words of description and words relating to the condition of the described goods.[11] Linkage between documents is not, as such, necessary provided that each directly or indirectly refers unequivocally to the goods.[12]

It was at one time thought that at common law the bill of lading must conform strictly to the credit as regards description of the goods also, though in *Guaranty Trust of New York v Van Den Berghs Ltd*,[13] Scrutton LJ thought that:

'the bill of lading and the certificate of origin together complied with the letter of credit.'

The credit asked for documents covering Manila coconut oil, whereas the documents were for coconut oil simply, the missing link being supplied by the certificate of origin.[14] Where a credit called for bills covering a shipment of Manila hemp and the bank paid against documents for 'general merchandise contents unknown', it was held in America that the bank could recover in respect of that part of the shipment only which consisted of Manila hemp.[15] Where a bank refused to pay against bills of lading covering 'machine-shelled groundnut kernels' under a credit calling for 'Coromandel ground nuts', its refusal was upheld,[16] though in the trade the two expressions seemed to be synonymous. Where also a bank paid against documents in respect of trucks described as 'in new condition' and 'new, good', under a credit calling for 'new' trucks, it was saved only by the fact that the banker issuing the credit was held to have ratified the irregular payments.[17]

10 *Banque de l'Indochine et de Suez SA v J H Rayner (Mincing Lane) Ltd* [1983] QB 711 at 732, [1983] 1 All ER 1137 at 1142, 1143, CA, where Sir John Donaldson MR observed that the Uniform Customs and Practice for Documentary Credits (1983 Revision) art 41 (c) is less strict than the common law, which requires that the description in other documents must be consistent and *only* consistent with the commercial invoice and the credit.
11 *Astro Exito Navegacion SA v Chase Manhattan Bank NA* [1986] 1 Lloyd's Rep 455 at 458; affd on appeal without affecting this point [1988] 2 Lloyd's Rep 217, CA.
12 *Banque de l'Indochine et de Suez SA v J H Rayner (Mincing Lane) Ltd* [1983] QB 711 at 732, [1983] 1 All ER 1137 at 1142, 1143, CA.
13 (1925) 22 Ll L Rep 447, CA.
14 (1925) 22 Ll L Rep 447 at 454, CA.
15 *International Banking Corpn v Irving National Bank* 283 F 103 (1922).
16 *J H Rayner & Co Ltd v Hambro's Bank Ltd* [1943] KB 37, [1942] 2 All ER 694, CA; see also *Netherlands Trading Society v Wayne and Haylitt Co, Chan Soon Fat* (1952) 6 Legal Decisions Affecting Bankers 320, in which it was held by the Hong Kong Supreme Court that a bill of lading for '375 bales, gunny bags' should have been rejected under a credit calling for documents covering '375 bales, each containing 400 pieces New Indian Heavycee Bags ...'.
17 *Bank Melli Iran v Barclays Bank (Dominion, Colonial and Overseas)* [1951] 2 Lloyd's Rep 367; and see, further, *Netherlands Trading Society v Wayne and Haylitt Co, Chan Soon Fat* (1952) 6 LDAB 320.

However, the frequent impossibility of the bill of lading's containing all the descriptive terms of the credit is evident and providing the bill of lading describes the goods in general terms and identifies them and that there is no conflict between that description and the credit description, the bill is a good tender under a credit. This view received the sanction of Devlin J in *Midland Bank Ltd v Seymour*:[18]

'... all the documents between them – that is the set of documents – must contain all the particulars. That, of course, is subject to this obvious qualification, that each document (if it is not to contain all the particulars) must contain enough to make it a valid document.'

He said later that 'the documents must be consistent between themselves,' which, it is submitted, can be taken to mean that there must be no conflict and in the light of earlier decisions, no apparent conflict.

6 MISCELLANEOUS PROVISIONS

The UCP contain detailed provisions regarding loading on deck (Art 28), transhipment (Art 29), posting of goods (Art 30), freight and transportation charges (Art 31), the 'shipper's load and count' and similar notations (Art 32) and the identity of the consignor (Art 33).

7 LATEST DATE FOR SHIPMENT

There is no requirement to specify a latest date for shipment. If no date is stipulated, banks must reject transport documents indicating a date of insurance later than the expiry date stipulated in the credit (Art 48 (b)).

If the credit stipulates for a particular time, or date, of shipment, the stipulation must be complied with;[19] it is a condition precedent.[20]

8 LATEST DATE FOR PRESENTATION OF TRANSPORT DOCUMENTS

By Art 47 (a), in addition to stipulating an expiry date for presentation of documents, every credit which calls for a transport document(s) should also stipulate a specified period of time after the date of issuance of the transport document(s) during which presentation of documents for payment, acceptance or negotiation must be made. If no such period of time is stipulated, banks must refuse documents presented to them later than 21 days after the date of issuance of the transport document(s). In every case, however, documents must be presented not later than the expiry date of the credit (see below).

Provision as to the date on which a transport document is deemed to have been issued are contained in Art 47 (b), and further provisions as to the method of computing periods of time are contained in Art 51.

---

18 [1955] 2 Lloyd's Rep 147.
19 *Stein v Hambro's Bank of Northern Commerce* (1922) 10 Ll L Rep 529, CA, and see *Re General Trading Co and Van Stolk's Commissiehandel* (1911) 16 Com Cas 95; *Taylor & Sons Ltd v Bank of Athens* (1922) 91 LJKB 776, 27 Com Cas 142.
20 *J Aron & Co (Inc) v Comptior Degimont* [1921] 3 KB 435 per McCardie J at 441.

(iii) Insurance documents

The UCP provisions governing insurance documents are contained in Articles 35–40. An important change made in the 1983 Revision concerns 'all risks' insurance. Article 39, which replaces Art 30 in the 1974 Revision, provides:

'Where a credit stipulates "insurance against all risks", banks will accept an insurance document which contains any "all risks" notation or clause, whether or not bearing the heading "all risks", even if indicating that certain risks are excluded, without responsibility for any risk(s) not being covered.'

This accommodates changes made in 1982 to the standard form Institute of London Underwriters all risks clause, which now refers to excluded risks.

Unless the credit authorises their acceptance, brokers' cover notes are not a good tender;[1] nor is an open cover.[2] By Art 36 of the UCP, unless otherwise stipulated in the credit, or unless it appears from the insurance document(s) that the cover is effective at the latest from the date of loading on board or dispatch or taking in charge of the goods, banks must refuse insurance documents presented which bear a date later than the date of loading on board or dispatch or taking in charge of the goods as indicated by the transport document(s).

Article 38 requires that credits should stipulate the type of insurance required and, if any, the additional risks which are to be covered. Imprecise terms such as 'usual risks' or 'customary risks' should not be used; if they are used, banks must accept insurance documents as presented, without responsibility for any risks not being covered. Failing specific stipulations in the credit, banks must accept insurance documents as presented, without responsibility for any risks not being covered. These provisions render obsolete much of the caselaw on insurance documents, but reference to this caselaw is retained below for completeness.

At common law, the policy must insure the goods specified in the credit for the voyage contracted for,[3] and no other goods.[4] Where 'all risks' cover was called for, it has been held that the policy must be without franchise.[5] A policy to pay 'total loss by total loss of vessel only' was held inadequate in the meat trade in which it was customary to tender an 'all risks' insurance.[6] A policy is not unusual in peace-time merely because it does not cover war risk.[7] Where the policy covers a greater quantity than that contracted for, the buyer may reject;[8] it must be actionable and not voidable by reason of non-disclosure of material facts[9] and where, owing to outbreak of war, it has

---

1 UCP Art 35 (b); and see, as to insurance certificates and cover notes at common law, *Manbre Saccharine Co v Corn Products Co* [1919] 1 KB 198; *Diamond Alkali Export Corpn v Bourgeois* [1921] 3 KB 443. But *quaere*, if the certificate embodies the terms of the insurance; see *Donald H Scott & Co Ltd v Barclays Bank Ltd* [1923] 2 KB 1 at 15, CA, per Scrutton LJ.
2 *South African Reserve Bank v Samuel & Co Ltd* (1931) 40 Ll L Rep 291, CA.
3 *Landauer & Co v Craven and Speeding Bros* [1921] 2 KB 94.
4 *May and Hassell Ltd v Exportles of Moscow* (1940) 45 Com Cas 128.
5 *Vincentelli & Co v John Rowlett & Co* (1911) 105 LT 411, 16 Com Cas 310.
6 *Borthwick v Bank of New Zealand* (1900) 17 TLR 2, 6 Com Cas 1.
7 *C Groom Ltd v Barber* [1915] 1 KB 316.
8 *Hickox v Adams* (1876) 34 LT 404, CA.
9 *Cantiere Meccanico Brindisino v Constant* (1912) 106 LT 678, 17 Com Cas 182; see also *A C Harper & Co v Mackechnie & Co* [1925] 2 KB 423.

become illegal, it is not acceptable.[10] The buyer may reject a policy which has obviously been altered;[11] but a banker paying in good faith against a forged policy is not liable to his principals for any loss.[12]

(iv) Commercial invoices

By Art 41 of the UCP:

'(a) Unless otherwise stipulated in the credit, commercial invoices must be made out in the name of the applicant for the credit.

(b) Unless otherwise stipulated in the credit, banks may refuse commercial invoices issued for amounts in excess of the amount permitted by the credit. Nevertheless, if a bank authorised to pay, incur a deferred payment undertaking, accept, or negotiate under a credit accepts such invoices, its decision will be binding upon all parties, provided such bank has not paid, incurred a deferred payment undertaking, accepted or effected negotiation for an amount in excess of that permitted by the credit.[13]

(c) The description of the goods in the commercial invoice must correspond with the description in the credit. In all other documents, the goods may be described in general terms not inconsistent with the description of the goods in the credit.'

Article 41 (c) has already been considered under the heading of bills of lading. The wording of the description in the invoice must follow the words of the credit, and this is so even where the beneficiary uses an expression which, although different from the words of the credit, has, as between buyer and seller, the same meaning as such words.[14]

(v) Other documents

Apart from a specific provision regarding attestations of certificates of weight (Art 42), the UCP contain no specific provisions concerning documents other than transport documents, insurance documents and commercial invoices, save for Art 23:

'When documents other than transport documents, insurance documents and commercial invoices are called for, the credit should stipulate by whom such documents are to be issued and their wording or data content. If the credit does not so stipulate, banks will accept such documents as presented, provided that their data content makes it possible to relate the goods and/or services referred to therein to those referred to in the commercial invoice(s) presented, or to those referred to in the credit if the credit does not stipulate presentation of a commercial invoice.'

This replaces Art 33 in the 1974 Revision with a far clearer statement of the position in relation to other documents.

---

10 *Arnhold Karberg & Co v Blythe, Green, Jourdain & Co* [1916] 1 KB 495, CA.
11 *Re Salomon & Co and Naudszus* (1899) 81 LT 325.
12 *Basse and Selve v Bank of Australasia* (1904) 90 LT 618; followed in *Gian Singh & Co Ltd v Banque de l'Indochine* [1974] 2 All ER 754, [1974] 2 Lloyd's Rep 1, PC; *Ulster Bank v Synnott* (1871) IR 5 Eq 595; see further, 'Forged and fraudulent documents', infra.
13 See also *Donald H Scott & Co Ltd v Barclays Bank Ltd* (1923) 28 Com Cas 253 at 263, CA, per Scrutton LJ.
14 *Kydon Compania Naviera SA v National Westminster Bank Ltd* [1981] 1 Lloyd's Rep 68 at 76.

(vi) Quantities and amounts

By Art 43, the words 'about', 'circa' or similar expressions used in connection with the amount of the credit or the quantity or the unit price stated in the credit are to be construed as allowing a difference not to exceed 10% more or 10% less than the amount or the quantity or the unit price to which they refer. Unless a credit stipulates that the quantity of the goods specified must not be exceeded or reduced, a tolerance of 5% more or 5% less will be permissible, even if partial shipments are not permitted, always provided that the amount of the drawings does not exceed the amount of the credit. This tolerance does not apply when the credit stipulates the quantity in terms of a stated number of packing units or individual items. In this event, the doctrine of strict compliance is rigidly applied. The *de minimis* principle does not apply in such a situation,[15] unless, perhaps, a discrepancy is so miniscule that no reasonable banker would regard it as material.[16]

(vii) Credit specifying state of fact but no document

It is not uncommon for credits to contain a requirement that a state of fact should exist without specifying the documents to be presented. This breaks the rule that parties deal in documents alone, and in such a case the bank to whom the documents are presented is entitled to call for reasonable documentary proof.[17]

(viii) Expiry date for presentation of documents

By Article 46, all credits must stipulate an expiry date for presentation of documents. It is not always clear beyond question to what transaction a date in a credit applies. In *Midland Bank Ltd v Seymour*[18] the credit was issued in London in respect of shipments of duck feathers from Hong Kong; it stated that it was to be valid until a given date and 'available meanwhile by drafts at 90 days' sight against delivery of' certain documents and available at Hong Kong. Drafts were negotiated in Hong Kong before the date given in the credit and presented to the bank in London after the credit had expired; they were paid and the defendant claimed that they were paid out of time. The argument for the bank was that 'available' meant available for negotiation. Devlin J held otherwise, that:

> 'the terms of the confirmed credit have nothing to do with negotiation as such ... If the acceptance of the offer [embodied in the credit] is the act of presenting the bill and documents to the credit-granting bank or its agent, everybody will know where they are, but if it is an act of negotiation before acceptance, uncertainty will prevail.'

This comment is not easy to follow. On the assumption that the documents are in order, the seller is satisfied and the intermediary banker knows that he

---

15 See *Moralice (London) Ltd v ED and F Man* [1954] 2 Lloyd's Rep 526.
16 See *Astro Exito Navegacion SA v Chase Manhatten Bank NA* [1986] 1 Lloyd's Rep 455 at 460–461, affd on appeal without affecting this point [1988] 2 Lloyd's Rep 217, CA.
17 *Banque De L'Indochine et de Suez SA v J H Rayner (Mincing Lane) Ltd* [1983] QB 711 at 719 (Parker J) and 728 (Sir John Donaldson MR); *Astro Exito Navegacion SA v Chase Manhatten Bank NA* [1986] 1 Lloyd's Rep 455 at 462, and on appeal [1988] 2 Lloyd's Rep 217 at 220.
18 [1955] 2 Lloyd's Rep 147, applied in *Commercial Banking Co of Sydney Ltd v Jalsard Pty Ltd* [1973] AC 279, PC.

may rely on the credit, having done what he was authorised to do. There remain only the issuing banker and the buyer, neither of whom can complain. The learned judge seemed to regard it as serious that:

> 'the credit-granting bank may know nothing of the negotiation, and so may not know that its offer had been accepted.'

Nevertheless, it must know that it was liable up to a given date to pay against specified documents. It was further argued that unless the expiry date stated in the credit applied to acceptance in London, the issuing bank would again not know where it stood. It is not easy to see, however, what it could lose thereby; its obligation was quite clear or, to put it at its lowest, the view it was entitled to take of its obligation was quite clear and it would at any time subsequently to the expiry date have informed itself, by reference to its Hong Kong correspondents, as to the position. However, the matter was one of construction of a mandate, a great part of which was in the bank's own wording and it was held that the bank were in breach in accepting the drafts after the expiry date; they could have been accepted in Hong Kong. There is, of course, nothing to prevent acceptance by an agent, but the seller in Hong Kong would not know whether the Hong Kong correspondent of the issuing bank had authority to accept; it would be a most unusual transaction and any doubt might well vitiate the whole transaction.

The case points to the need for the clearest wording of forms of application for credits and of credits themselves.

(d) Examination and rejection of documents

(i) Examination of documents

By Art 15 of the UCP:

> 'Banks must examine all documents with reasonable care to ascertain that they appear on their face to be in accordance with the terms and conditions of the credit. Documents which appear on their face to be inconsistent with one another will be considered as not appearing on their face to be in accordance with the terms and conditions of the credit.'

By Art 16 (b), the issuing bank must determine on the basis of the documents alone whether to take up such documents or to refuse them. This gives effect to the basic principle, now embodied in Art 4, that all parties concerned deal in documents and not in goods, services and/or other performances to which the documents may relate. This principle was recognised in England[19]

---

19 See per Bankes LJ in *Belgian Grain and Produce Co Ltd v Cox & Co (France) Ltd* (1919) 1 Ll L Rep 257, CA; Rowlatt J's view in *Urquhart, Lindsay & Co Ltd v Eastern Bank Ltd* [1922] 1 KB 318 was adopted in *Dexters Ltd v Schenker & Co* (1923) 14 Ll L Rep 586. See also *Stein v Hambro's Bank of Northern Commerce* (1921) 9 Ll L Rep 433 at 507; revsd without affecting this point (1922) 10 Ll L Rep 529, CA; *National Bank of South Africa v Banca Italiana di Sconto and Arnhold Bros & Co (Oleoifici Nazionale of Genoa, Third Parties)* (1922) 10 Ll L Rep 531, CA; and *Donald H Scott & Co Ltd v Barclays Bank Ltd* [1923] 2 KB 1 at 14, CA, per Scrutton LJ (obiter).

and elsewhere[20] long before the introduction of the Uniform Customs. The position is different if the sales contract on which the credit is based is in some measure incorporated into the credit,[1] but this would require express agreement for Art 3 of the UCP provides that banks are in no way concerned with the underlying contract even if reference to such contract is included in the credit.

It is further provided by Article 16 (c) that the issuing bank shall have a reasonable time in which to examine the documents and to determine whether to take up or to refuse them. In modern banking practice a reasonable time for examination of documents is probably in the order of two to three working days, depending upon the amount of the drawing and the complexity of the documentation.[2] In practice these factors tend also to determine the number and status of employees who check the documents.

In relation to both examination and rejection of documents, the UCP deal only with the position between the issuing bank and the bank authorised to effect payment. In *United City Merchants (Investments) Ltd v Royal Bank of Canada*,[3] it became necessary to determine whether the confirming bank owes the beneficiary a duty matching that owed by the issuing bank to the confirming bank. It was held by the House of Lords that it does, with the consequence that a confirming bank owes the beneficiary an obligation to pay the sum stipulated in the credit upon presentation of apparently conforming documents notwithstanding that the confirming bank is on notice of forgery by a third party.

(ii) Reimbursement

Reference has already been made[4] to Art 11 (d). By Art 16 (a):

'If a bank so authorised effects payment, or incurs a deferred payment undertaking, or accepts, or negotiates against documents which appear on their face to be in accordance with the terms and conditions of a credit, the party giving such authority shall be bound to reimburse the bank which has effected payment, or incurred a deferred payment undertaking, or has accepted, or negotiated, and to take up the documents.'[5]

20 For a similar line of authority in the United States, see *American Steel Co v Irving National Bank*, 266 F 41; *Imbrie v D Nagase & Co* 196 App Div 380, 383 NYS 692, 695 (2d Dept 1921); *Dixon, Irmaos & Cia Ltda v Chase National Bank of the City of New York* 144 F 2d 759 (2d Cir 1944), cert denied 324 US 850; and see also *Davis O'Brien Lumber Co Ltd v Bank of Montreal* [1951] 3 DLR 536, where the Appeal Division of the New Brunswick Supreme Court declined to construe a credit which called for documents evidencing a shipment 'in accordance with contract dated 22.12.47, no. 47450' as adding to the normal obligation of the banker.
1 See *Chartered Bank of India, Australia and China v P Macfadyen & Co* (1895) 64 LJQB 367, 1 Com Cas 1; *Union Bank of Canada v Cole* (1877) 47 LJQB 100, CA; cf *Maitland v Chartered Mercantile Bank of India, London and China* (1869) 38 LJ Ch 363.
2 For a review of this issue, see Professor E P Ellinger 'Reasonable Time for Examination of Documents' [1985] JBL 406.
3 [1983] 1 AC 168 at 184–185, [1982] 2 All ER 720 at 726. See also *Co-operative Centrale Raiffeisen-Boerenleenbank BA v Sumitomo Bank Ltd* at first instance, [1987] 1 Lloyd's Rep 345 at 352, where it was held that a confirming bank owes the beneficiary a duty in the event of rejecting the documents to issue a notice in the form required as between issuing and confirming bank by Art 16 (d). On appeal it was found unnecessary to determine the point, and it was expressly left open: [1988] 2 Lloyd's Rep 250 at 256.
4 See p 622, above; and see also Art 21 as to reimbursement instructions.
5 This accords with the common law rule that the intermediary banker must obey strictly the

The UCP do not provide for the applicant's obligation to reimburse the issuing bank, but this will normally be the subject of express provision in the credit application form. In the absence of express agreement, a buyer who instructs his banker to issue a credit impliedly undertakes to reimburse the banker for any payment effected within his authority, although the banker must comply strictly with the instructions.[6] If the buyer provides funds in advance, the banker is bound to apply them to that purpose.[7]

In *Co-operative Centrale Raiffeisen-Boerenleenbank BA v Sumitomo Bank Ltd*[8] ('the *Rabobank* case'), it was accepted by all parties that, in the absence of contrary agreement, the issuing bank's obligation is to reimburse the confirming bank with funds of the same value date as the date of payment. The applicant's obligation to the issuing bank is in principle identical.

(iii) Rejection of documents

1 PROCEDURE ON REJECTION

The requisite procedure on rejection of documents is set out in Art 16 (d):

'If the issuing bank decides to refuse the documents,[9] it must give notice to that effect without delay by telecommunication or, if that is not possible, by other expeditious means, to the bank from which it received the documents (the remitting bank), or to the beneficiary, if it received the documents directly from him. Such notice must state the discrepancies in respect of which the issuing bank refuses the documents and must also state whether it is holding the documents at the disposal of, or is returning them to, the presentor (remitting bank or the beneficiary, as the case may be). The issuing bank shall then be entitled to claim from the remitting bank refund of any reimbursement which may have been made to that bank.'

Thus there are two requirements of the notice, viz (i) identification of discrepancies and (ii) a statement as to disposal of the documents. A statement:

'Please consider these documents at your disposal until we receive our Principal's instructions concerning the discrepancies mentioned in your schedules ...'

---

instructions he receives – see *Rayner & Co Ltd v Hambro's Bank Ltd* [1943] KB 37 [1942] 2 All ER 694, CA; *Bank Melli Iran v Barclays Bank (Dominion, Colonial and Overseas)* [1951] 2 Lloyd's Rep 367.

6 *Equitable Trust Co of New York v Dawson Partners Ltd* (1927) 27 Ll L Rep 49, HL; *South African Reserve Bank v Samuel & Co Ltd* (1931) 40 Ll L Rep 291, CA; *J H Rayner & Co Ltd v Hambro's Bank Ltd* [1943] 1 KB 37; *Moralice (London) Ltd v E D and F Man* [1954] 2 Lloyd's Rep 526; *Soproma SpA v Marine and Animal By-Products Corpn* [1966] 1 Lloyd's Rep 367; *Commercial Banking Co of Sydney Ltd v Jalsard Pty Ltd* [1973] AC 279, [1972] 2 Lloyd's Rep 529.

7 *Farley v Turner* (1857) 26 LJ Ch 710. If the banker becomes insolvent before this is done, the buyer has only a right to prove, *Re Barned's Banking Co Ltd, Massey's Case* (1870) 39 LJ Ch 635, unless the buyer can establish that the monies were impressed with a trust – see *Barclays Bank Ltd v Quistclose Investments Ltd* [1970] AC 567; *Carreras Rothmans v Freeman Mathews* [1985] Ch 207, [1985] 1 All ER 155; *Re Multi Guarantee Co Ltd* [1987] BCLC 257; see further p 195, ante.

8 [1987] 1 Lloyd's Rep 345 at 348; varied on appeal without affecting this point [1988] 2 Lloyd's Rep 250.

9 It has been said that it is the banker's duty to refuse documents which do not conform with the credit: *English, Scottish and Australian Bank Ltd v Bank of South Africa* (1922) 13 Ll L Rep 21 at 24, per Bailhache J; *Soproma SpA v Marine and Animal By-Products Corpn* [1966] 1 Lloyd's Rep 367 — but this means simply that a banker who pays against discrepant documents does so at his own risk.

was held in the *Rabobank* case[10] to be a valid notice of rejection within the predecessor to Art 16 (d).

2 NO DUTY TO IDENTIFY ALL DISCREPANCIES

The notice need only identify the discrepancies in respect of which the documents are rejected on that particular occasion. There is no wider duty to identify each and every discrepancy. Accordingly the statement of a particular reason or reasons for rejecting documents is not alone enough to found a representation, waiver or promissory estoppel in respect of other discrepancies,[11] although special circumstances may give rise to an estoppel. The position was succinctly stated by Parker J in *Kydon Compania Naviera v National Westminster Bank Ltd*:[12]

> 'It cannot, as a matter of general principle, be right that a bank can never be estopped any more than it can that a bank by stating one reason impliedly represents that the documents are otherwise in order or impliedly promises that if the stated defect is rectified it will pay.'

Special circumstances founding an agreement or estoppel were held to exist in *Floating Dock Ltd v HongKong and Shanghai Banking Corpn*,[13] where employees of the issuing bank reached an agreement with the beneficiary regarding amendment of two credits in circumstances such that the beneficiary could reasonably assume that the bank would not rely upon a particular ground of rejection.

3 REJECTION ON INVALID GROUNDS WHERE VALID GROUNDS EXIST

At common law a bank which rejects documents on invalid grounds would appear to be entitled if its rejection is challenged to rely upon all valid grounds which it might have taken, this being analogous to the assertion of a valid ground for terminating a contract after termination on an invalid ground. The UCP contains no express provision on this point and accordingly the common law rule prima facie applies even where the UCP have been incorporated. There is, however, a difficulty in reconciling this position with the requirement that the issuing bank is required to specify in a rejection notice the discrepancies in respect of which the documents are refused. If discrepancies are required to be stated, it is difficult to see how such a requirement is satisfied in any commercially sensible way if none of the stated discrepancies in fact exist; in practice, the beneficiary is then no better off than if no discrepancies had been stated at all, and in the latter event Art 16 (e) provides an estoppel. Notwithstanding this difficulty, it is submitted that the mere statement of invalid grounds of rejection does not give rise to an estoppel preventing the raising of valid grounds. To hold otherwise would be an unwarranted departure from the basic rule that the beneficiary is entitled to be paid only if he presents conforming documents.

10 [1988] 2 Lloyd's Rep 250, CA.
11 *Skandinaviska Akt v Barclays Bank* (1925) 22 Ll L Rep 523; *Kydon Compania Naviera v National Westminster Bank Ltd* [1981] 1 Lloyd's Rep 68; and see *Bank of Taiwan v Union National Bank of Philadelphia* 1 F2d 65, 66 (1924) (3rd Cir); *Siderius Inc v Wallace Co Inc* 583 SW 2d 852 (1979).
12 [1981] 1 Lloyd's Rep 68 at 79.
13 [1986] 1 Lloyd's Rep 65.

4 ESTOPPEL IN CASES OF DEFECTIVE REJECTION

The specific requirements in Art 16 (d) as to the form of rejection of documents are given sanction by Art 16 (e):

'If the issuing bank fails to act in accordance with the provisions of paragraphs (c) and (d) of this article and/or fails to hold the documents at the disposal of, or to return them to, the presentor, the issuing bank shall be precluded from claiming that the documents are not in accordance with the terms and conditions of the credit.'

This provision reflects the fundamental principle that the parties to a credit transaction are not entitled both to retain the documents and to refuse payment. The consequence of Art 16 (e) is that defective rejection amounts to deemed acceptance, which has the same legal effect as waiver. It has been said, rightly it is submitted, that the position is then just the same as if there had been no discrepancies in the first place.[14]

(iv) Payment under reserve

In a significant percentage of cases,[15] the documents tendered by the beneficiary contain or are alleged to contain discrepancies, but in only a small percentage of cases are the documents in fact rejected. This important result is normally achieved either by an amendment to the credit, or by the applicant's waiver of the discrepancies. It is in connection with waiver that payment under reserve plays an important role, for it facilitates remittance of the documents for consideration by the applicant.

---

14 Per Gatehouse J in the *Rabobank* case, [1987] 1 Lloyd's Rep 345 at 353. On appeal, [1988] 2 Lloyd's Rep 250, the point did not arise because the Court of Appeal overturned the finding of waiver. The UCP refer to the issuing bank's election as being to 'take up' or 'refuse' the documents, ie accept or reject them. It is submitted that the word 'waiver' is consistent with this terminology. Before the UCP became so widely adopted, the term used was not waiver, but ratification. An example is *Westminster Bank Ltd v Banca Nazionale di Credito* (1928) 31 Ll L Rep 306 at 312, where Roche J stated that if parties keep documents for an unreasonable time, that may amount to a ratification of what has been done as being within the mandate. Given that the relationship between the issuing and confirming bank is that of principal and agent, it is not difficult to see why the courts adopted this approach. As to what amounted to ratification, in *Bank Melli Iran v Barclays Bank (Dominion Colonial and Overseas)* [1951] 2 Lloyd's Rep 367, McNair J seemed to think that delay in rejecting the documents might be a matter to be judged by reference to the efficiency of the administration of a bank so that a bank whose letter of credit department was under pressure of work would not have ratified an unauthorised payment by a delay of six weeks before rejection. This approach is, of course, not open under the UCP, where the question is simply whether the issuing bank took a reasonable time to examine the documents. An approach which takes into account purely internal matters such as pressure of work suffers the obvious weakness that it introduces uncertainty and lays the more efficient bank open to the subterfuge of the less efficient. Moreover it conflicts with Lord Sumner's classic statement in *Hansson v Hamel and Horley Ltd* [1922] 2 AC 36 at 46, that documents have to be taken up or rejected promptly and without any opportunity for prolonged enquiry, and with the similar statement of Lord Diplock in *Commercial Banking Co of Sydney Ltd v Jalsard Pty Ltd* [1973] AC 279 at 286.
15 In both *Banque de l'Indochine et de Suez v J H Rayner (Mincing Lane) Ltd* [1983] QB 711, [1983] 1 All ER 1137 and the *Rabobank* case [1987] 1 Lloyd's Rep 345, on appeal [1988] 2 Lloyd's Rep 250, CA, expert evidence was adduced that a majority of tenders contain discrepant documents. A study of 1,215 sets of documents presented over a random three-week period in 1983 revealed that the total failure rate of first presentations was 49% – see Professor Clive Schmitthoff 'Discrepancy of Documents in Letter of Credit Transactions' [1987] JBL 94.

The expression 'payment under reserve' in fact refers to two different procedures. Under the first, payment is effected by the confirming bank in the ordinary way save that the payment is simply designated as being made 'under reserve'. This procedure is commonly followed where the confirming bank is dealing with a valued customer whose integrity is established. Under the second procedure, the confirming bank does not effect payment until it has received from the beneficiary a written indemnity or guarantee in respect of the consequences of paying against discrepant documents. Under both procedures the confirming bank remits the documents to the issuing bank and will normally draw its attention to the discrepancies in reliance on which unconditional payment was refused.

The system of payment under reserve is recognised and provided for by Art 16 (f) of the UCP:

> 'If the remitting bank draws the attention of the issuing bank to any discrepancies in the documents or advises the issuing bank that it has paid, incurred a deferred payment undertaking, accepted or negotiated under reserve or against an indemnity[16] in respect of such discrepancies, the issuing bank shall not be thereby relieved from any of its obligations under any provision of this article. Such reserve or indemnity concerns only the relations between the remitting bank and the party towards whom the reserve was made, or from whom, or on whose behalf, the indemnity was obtained.'

Thus the issuing bank remains under an obligation itself to examine the documents with reasonable care and, in the event of rejection, to give notice to that effect in accordance with Art 16 (d).

The following propositions are put forward in relation to these important procedures:[17]

1 There is in general no material difference between payment under reserve and payment against an indemnity or guarantee.[18] This is implicit in Art 16 (f). Hereafter, reference is made simply to 'payment under reserve'.
2 Payment under reserve brings into existence a contract whereby, in consideration for the payment, the beneficiary agrees to repay the money on demand in the event that the issuing bank rejects the documents in reliance upon some or all of the discrepancies alleged by the confirming bank. It was so held in the leading case of *Banque de l'Indochine v J H Rayner (Mincing Lane) Ltd.*[19]
3 After the expiry of a reasonable time to examine the documents, the issuing bank must decide whether to accept or reject them. If the issuing bank decides to reject, but fails to give a notice in accordance with Art 16 (d),

16 The word 'indemnity' was introduced in the 1983 Revision to replace the less accurate word 'guarantee' in the 1974 Revision.
17 Certain of these propositions derive support from the judgment at first instance of Gatehouse J in the *Rabobank* case [1987] 1 Lloyd's Rep 345. On appeal, [1988] 2 Lloyd's Rep 250, the points of principle determined by Gatehouse J largely fell away in the light of the Court of Appeal's finding that the issuing bank had accepted a re-tender of a discrepant sanitary certificate, and had not (as Gatehouse J held) waived the discrepancy in the document originally tendered.
18 However, in the *Rabobank* case, [1988] 2 Lloyd's Rep 250, the Court of Appeal appears to have considered that there was a material difference (notwithstanding the evidence of expert witnesses for both parties that there was not, but this is not fully explained in the judgments.
19 [1983] QB 711, [1983] 1 All ER 1137, CA.

it is in breach of its obligations to the confirming bank, and the confirming bank is thereby put in breach of a matching obligation to the beneficiary.[20] In such a case the issuing bank is precluded by Art 16 (e) from claiming against the confirming bank that the documents were not in accordance with the terms and conditions of the credit,[1] and the confirming bank is similarly precluded as against the beneficiary.[2]

4 It remains an open point whether the confirming bank may demand payment in the event that the issuing bank rejects the documents in reliance upon discrepancies not specified by the confirming bank itself.[3]

(v) Damages for breach of contract

It is thought that where a banker is liable for breach of contract to pay under a credit, the measure of damages is that which it could reasonably have been foreseen would flow[4] from the breach.[5] But special considerations, unless known to him or which he ought to have known, will not give rise to the special damages which may flow from them.[6] In *Trans Trust SPLR v Danubian Trading Co Ltd*,[7] it was held that damages for failure to open an irrevocable credit, would, in view of the fact that the buyers knew that the sellers could not get the goods unless the credit was opened, include loss of profit. The damages are not simply the damages for non-payment of money,[8] but for breach of contract.

In principle the beneficiary under a credit must do what he can to minimise damages, but there are views to the contrary.[9]

(vi) Documents as security

Throughout the working out of a credit the banker in possession of the documents of title has a security interest; he may even acquire such an interest before the documents come into his possession. The intermediary banker, whether acting pursuant to a mandate or negotiating on his own account, is

20 As to matching obligations, see p 643, ante.
 1 Art 16 (e) is made applicable by Art 16 (f).
 2 This latter proposition is implicit in the judgment of Gatehouse J in the *Rabobank* case (see note 17, supra).
 3 In *Rayner's* case, Kerr LJ inclined to the view (without deciding the point) that the issuing bank's grounds of rejection would have to include at least one ground relied upon by the confirming bank – [1983] QB 711 at 734. It is submitted that this view is correct.
 4 On the basis of the decision in *Hadley v Baxendale* (1854) 9 Exch 341; cf *Victoria Laundry (Windsor) Ltd v Newman Industries Ltd* [1949] 2 KB 528, [1949] 1 All ER 997, CA, applied in *Aruna Mills Ltd v Dhanrajmal Gobindram* [1968] 1 QB 655.
 5 *Prehn v Royal Bank of Liverpool* (1870) LR 5 Exch 92.
 6 *Hammond & Co v Bussey* (1887) 20 QBD 79, CA; *British Columbia and Vancouver's Island Spar, Lumber and Saw Mill Co Ltd v Nettleship* (1868) LR 3 CP 499; *Hydraulic Engineering Co Ltd v McHaffie, Goslett & Co* (1878) 4 QBD 670, CA; *Re R and H Hall Ltd, and W H Pim Junior & Co's Arbitration* (1928) 139 LT 50, 33 Com Cas 324, HL.
 7 [1952] 2 QB 297, [1952] 1 Lloyd's Rep 348, CA; *Prehn v Royal Bank of Liverpool* (1870) LR 5 Ex Ch 92; *Urquhart, Lindsay & Co Ltd v Eastern Bank Ltd* [1922] 1 KB 318; *Ozalid Group (Export) Ltd v African Continental Bank Ltd* [1979] 2 Lloyd's Rep 231.
 8 *Urquhart, Lindasy & Co Ltd v Eastern Bank Ltd* [1922] 1 KB 318 at 323; but see the judgment of Rowlatt J in *Stein v Hambro's Bank of Northern Commerce* (1921) 9 Ll L Rep 433, 507; revsd (1922) 10 Ll L Rep 529, CA, but not affecting this point.
 9 See *Stein v Hambro's Bank of Northern Commerce* (1921) 9 Ll L Rep 433, 507; revsd (1922) 10 Ll L Rep 529, CA, without affecting this point; and *Urquhart, Lindsay & Co Ltd v Eastern Bank Ltd* [1922] 1 KB 318 at 323.

entitled to reimbursement by the issuing banker as a condition of delivering the documents to him; similarly the issuing banker vis-à-vis the buyer. Both bankers have, therefore, by implication, a security interest in the documents, a pledge as soon as the documents are delivered to them.[10]

Both may, moreover, have a direct charge on the documents or may acquire a lien on them. It may be that the intermediary banker is already the creditor of the seller-beneficiary before the credit is issued; or he may have advanced to him purely on the strength of the credit or by virtue of the direct authority it contains to make pre-shipment advances, such as is common in the case of Australasian and South African 'anticipatory' credits, under the so-called 'red' clause. As soon, therefore, as the documents are handed to him, he has a pledge; prior to this, the goods may have been hypothecated to him. Similarly, the buyer may be indebted to the issuing banker, in which case the banker would have a lien on the documents as soon as they came into his hands, or he may have advanced expressly against hypothecation of the goods or documents.

(e) Fraud and restraint of payment

(i) Forged or fraudulent documents

By Art 17 of the UCP, banks assume no responsibility 'for the form, sufficiency, accuracy, genuineness, falsification or legal effect of any documents'. Accordingly a bank is bound to pay against apparently conforming documents which, unknown to it, contain an ingenious forgery, and having paid, the bank is entitled to be reimbursed by the applicant even after the forgery has been discovered. This is illustrated by *Gian Singh Ltd v Banque de l'Indochine*,[11] where the credit called for 'a certificate signed by Balwant Singh, holder of Malaysian passport E-13276'. The beneficiary presented a certificate on which the signature of Balwant Singh had been forged. The applicant failed to make out a case of negligence against the issuing bank or the advising bank in failing to detect the forgery. It was accordingly held that the issuing bank had been bound to pay against the documents tendered, and that the applicant was bound to reimburse the issuing bank. The Privy Council did not address the question whether the document was a complete nullity and if so, how it could be said that a certificate had been presented at all. This did not arise because the credit was construed as requiring that the certificate should be *signed* by Balwant Singh, not that it should be the certificate *of* Balwant Singh.

In the converse case where the bank discovers fraud before effecting payment, it is necessary to distinguish fraud committed by the beneficiary from fraud committed by third parties. As regards fraud by the beneficiary, the law is authoritatively stated by Lord Diplock in *United City Merchants (Investments) Ltd v Royal Bank of Canada*.[12] Having referred to the principle

10 *Re Barned's Banking Co, Banner v Johnston* (1871) LR 5 HL 157; *Rosenberg v International Banking Corpn and Far East Gerhard and Hey Co* (1923) 14 Ll L Rep 344 at 347 per Scrutton LJ; *Ross T Smyth & Co Ltd v T D Bailey Son & Co* [1940] 3 All ER 60 at 68, HL. See also the citation from the speech of Lord Diplock in *United City Merchants (Investments) Ltd v Royal Bank of Canada* at pp 618–619, ante.
11 [1974] 2 All ER 754, [1974] 1 WLR 1234.
12 [1983] 1 AC 168, [1982] 2 All ER 720, HL.

that the seller and confirming bank deal in documents, not in goods, he continued:[13]

'To this general statement of principle as to the contractual obligations of the confirming bank to the seller, there is one established exception: that is, where the seller, for the purpose of drawing on the credit, fraudulently presents to the confirming bank documents that contain, expressly or by implication, material representations of fact that to his knowledge are untrue. Although there does not appear among the English authorities any case in which this exception has been applied, it is well established in the American cases of which the leading or "landmark" case is *Sztejn v J Henry Schroder Banking Corpn* (1941) 31 NYS 2d 631. This judgment of the New York Court of Appeals was referred to with approval by the English Court of Appeal in *Edward Owen Engineering Ltd v Barclays Bank International Ltd* [1978] QB 159, though this was actually a case about a performance bond under which a bank assumes obligations to a buyer analogous to those assumed by a confirming bank to the seller under a documentary credit. The exception for fraud on the part of the beneficiary seeking to avail himself of the credit is a clear application of the maxim ex turpi causa non oritur actio or, if plain English is to be preferred, "fraud unravels all". The courts will not allow their process to be used by a dishonest person to carry out a fraud.'

Where the bank's knowledge relates to fraud committed by a third party, the position may differ according to whether the affected document is capable of having legal effect or is a complete nullity. *United City Merchants* was concerned with the former. The bills of lading bore a fraudulently dated 'on board' notation. The fraud was that of a third party (the loading brokers) and neither the sellers nor their transferees were parties or privy to the fraud. The bills were far from being a nullity: they were valid transferable receipts for the goods giving the holder a right to claim them at their destination, and were evidence of the terms of the contract of carriage. The confirming bank refused to pay on the ground that it had information in its possession 'which suggested that shipment was not affected as it appears in the bill of lading'. The House of Lords, overruling the Court of Appeal, held that the bank's rejection on this ground was unjustified. The bill of lading appeared on its face to accord with the terms and conditions of the credit, and fraud by third parties was held not to fall within the fraud exception. It would have been otherwise if the seller had known of the fraud at the time of presentation.

Where a third party fraudulently brings into existence a document which is a complete nullity, the position may be different because it can then be argued that the tender lacked that particular document and was therefore incomplete. This point was expressly left open in *United City Merchants*.[14]

(ii) Restraint of payment

In *Bolivinter Oil SA v Chase Manhattan Bank NA*,[15] the Court of Appeal made the following observations on the grant of ex parte injunctions restraining payment under letters of credit, performance bonds and guarantees:

'Before leaving this appeal, we should like to add a word about the circumstances

13 Ibid at, respectively, 183 and 725.
14 Ibid at, respectively, 188A and 728h.
15 [1984] 1 All ER 351, [1984] 1 WLR 392, CA, reported in full at [1984] 1 Lloyd's Rep 251.
    See also *Hamzeh Malas & Sons Ltd v British Imex Industries Ltd* [1958] 2 QB 127, [1958] 1 All ER 262, CA.

in which an ex parte injunction should be issued which prohibits a bank from paying under an irrevocable letter of credit or a purchase bond or guarantee. The unique value of such a letter, bond or guarantee is that the beneficiary can be completely satisfied that whatever disputes may thereafter arise between him and the bank's customer in relation to the performance or indeed existence of the underlying contract, the bank is personally undertaking to pay him provided that the specified conditions are met. In requesting his bank to issue such a letter, bond or guarantee, the customer is seeking to take advantage of this unique characteristic. If, save in the most exceptional cases, he is to be allowed to derogate from the bank's personal and irrevocable undertaking, given be it again noted at his request, by obtaining an injunction restraining the bank from honouring that undertaking, he will undermine what is the bank's greatest asset, however large and rich it may be, namely its reputation for financial and contractual probity. Furthermore, if this happens at all frequently, the value of all irrevocable letters of credit and performance bonds and guarantees will be undermined.

Judges who are asked, often at short notice and ex parte, to issue an injunction restraining payment by a bank under an irrevocable letter of credit or performance bond or guarantee should ask whether there is any challenge to the validity of the letter, bond or guarantee itself. If there is not or if the challenge is not substantial, prima facie no injunction should be granted and the bank should be left free to honour its contractual obligation, although restrictions may well be imposed upon the freedom of the beneficiary to deal with the money after he has received it. The wholly exceptional case where an injunction may be granted is where it is proved that the bank knows that any demand for payment already made or which may thereafter be made will clearly be fraudulent. But the evidence must be clear, both as to the fact of fraud and as to the bank's knowledge. It would certainly not normally be sufficient that this rests upon the uncorroborated statement of the customer, for irreparable damage can be done to a bank's credit in the relatively brief time which must elapse between the granting of such an injunction and an application by the bank to have it discharged.'

Although these observations were directed to ex parte injunctions, they apply with equal force where the application is inter partes. There are two major hurdles to be cleared by the applicant for an injunction restraining payment: (1) to establish a serious issue to be tried that the fraud exception applies; (2) to establish that the balance of convenience is in favour of the grant of an injunction. The circumstances in which both propositions can be established will be exceedingly rare.[16]

As to establishing a serious issue to be tried, on an interlocutory application for relief based on the fraud exception, what has to be established is a good arguable case that the only realistic inference is fraud.[17] The fraud must be that of the beneficiary, and, as stated in *Bolivinter Oil,* it must be clearly established both as to the fact and as to the bank's knowledge. The court will generally expect the beneficiary to have been given an opportunity to answer the allegation of fraud and to have failed to provide any adequate

16 There are numerous reported cases where applications for an injunction have failed, but none where an application has been successful. See, eg *R D Harbottle (Mercantile) Ltd v National Westminster Bank Ltd* [1978] QB 146, [1977] 2 All ER 862; *Howe Richardson Scale Co Ltd v Polimex-Cekop* [1978] 1 Lloyd's Rep 161, CA; *Edward Owen (Engineering) Ltd v Barclays Bank Ltd* [1978] QB 159, [1978] 1 All ER 976, CA; *Bolivinter Oil SA v Chase Manhattan Bank NA,* supra; *United Trading Corpn SA v Allied Arab Bank Ltd* [1985] 2 Lloyd's Rep 554; *Tukan Timber Ltd v Barclays Bank Plc* [1987] 1 Lloyd's Rep 171.
17 *United Trading Corpn SA v Allied Arab Bank Ltd* [1985] 2 Lloyd's Rep 554 at 561 and 565, CA.

answer in circumstances where one could properly be expected.[18] The bank's knowledge must be shown to have existed prior to payment to the beneficiary.[19] It appears not to be the case that the only relevant time at which the state of knowledge of the bank falls to be considered is when the documents are first presented or the demand for payment is first made.[20]

As to the balance of convenience, the applicant will almost invariably be faced with the submission that the balance of convenience is against the grant of an injunction because: (i) if the injunction is granted in circumstances where the fraud exception is not subsequently made out at trial, the bank will have suffered damage to its reputation which will be both irreparable and incapable of precise quantification; whereas (ii) if the injunction is refused, but the applicant does go on to establish the fraud exception at trial, he will have suffered no loss because the bank's claim against him for reimbursement will fail. Other factors will, of course, be thrown up by the facts of particular cases, but in practice it is very difficult to tip the balance in favour of granting an injunction.[1]

The court will generally decline to recognise the order of a foreign court restraining payment under a letter of credit on the application of the buyer where the foreign court, applying a law which is not the proper law of the credit, has made a restraining order contrary to the above principles. This is illustrated by *Power Curber International Ltd v National Bank of Kuwait SAK*,[2] where the Court of Appeal refused to recognise a 'provisional attachment' of sums payable to the plaintiff by the defendant bank granted by a Kuwaiti court (and upheld by the Kuwaiti Court of Appeal). The Court of Appeal (in England) instead granted the plaintiff summary judgment.

2   PERFORMANCE BONDS

It was observed by Lord Diplock in *United City Merchants (Investments) Ltd v Royal Bank of Canada*[3] that by issuing a performance bond or performance guarantee a bank assumes obligations to a buyer or other beneficiary analogous to those assumed by a confirming bank to the seller under a documentary credit.

The UCP are expressed to apply 'to all documentary credits, including, to the extent to which they may be applicable, standby letters of credit' (Art 1). There appears to be no material difference between a standby letter of credit, a performance bond and a performance guarantee; all three expressions describe an instrument which is intended to protect the beneficiary in the event of the applicant's default in performance. Reference will be made hereafter to 'performance bonds'.

In practice, performance bonds issued by English banks rarely incorporate the UCP, and the UCP have limited application to such instruments.

In words which have often been cited, Lord Denning MR in *Edward Owen*

---

18 Ibid at 561.
19 Ibid at 560.
20 See *Bolivinter Oil SA v Chase Manhattan Bank NA* [1984] 1 Lloyd's Rep 251 at 256.
 1 See the cases cited in note 16, supra.
 2 [1981] 3 All ER 607, [1981] 1 WLR 1233, CA.
 3 [1983] 1 AC 168 at 184, [1982] 2 All ER 720 at 725H.

Engineering Ltd v Barclays Bank International Ltd[4] described performance bonds as 'virtually promissory notes payable on demand'; Geoffrey Lane LJ agreed that performance bonds have much more of the characteristics of a promissory note than of a guarantee.[5] These observations point to the essential characteristics of a performance bond. It constitutes an unconditional obligation to pay the beneficiary upon demand and upon presentation of such additional documents (if any) as may be specified. A bank is not in the least concerned with the relations between the beneficiary and the applicant; nor with whether the beneficiary has performed his contractual obligations.[6] A fortiori, the various equitable defences available to a guarantor are not available to the issuer of such a bond.

The characterisation of an instrument as a performance bond or a guarantee is therefore a matter of considerable importance. Performance bonds tend to be issued by banks on the application of a party in one country in favour of a beneficiary in another, and they are generally significantly shorter than standard form bank guarantees for signature by customers, often being only a few lines in length. But these features obviously cannot themselves determine the legal characterisation of an instrument. If the instrument is payable upon 'first written demand', this points strongly to a performance bond. Difficulties on construction tend to arise where instruments containing such a provision bring in references to the event upon the occurrence of which the bond may be drawn on. An example is *Esal (Commodities) Ltd v Oriental Credit Ltd*,[7] where an instrument described as a performance bond provided:

'We undertake to pay the said amount of your written demand in the event that the supplier fails to execute the contract in perfect performance'.

It was submitted on behalf of the applicant that on a true construction of the bond (i) there was no liability save in the event of an established breach of the contract referred to in it; alternatively (ii) the bond required the beneficiary to assert in his demand that the supplier had failed properly to execute the contract. The Court of Appeal rejected the first submission. As to the second, Ackner LJ held that such an assertion was required, and observed that the requirement that the beneficiary must when making his demand for payment also commit himself to claiming that the contract has not been complied with, may prevent some of the many abuses of the performance bond procedure that have undoubtedly occurred.[8] However, Neill LJ expressly left open this question, expressing reluctance to introduce into this field any rule which provides scope for argument that the qualifying event has not been sufficiently identified (or, presumably, not stated to have occurred).[9]

The payment obligation of the issuer of a performance bond is subject to the fraud exception discussed at pp 649–652, above. Not surprisingly, most of the cases cited there involved allegedly fraudulent demands on performance bonds.

4 [1978] QB 159 at 170, [1978] 1 All ER 976 at 983, CA.
5 Ibid at, respectively, 175 and 986.
6 See *Edward Owen Engineering Ltd v Barclays Bank International Ltd* [1978] QB 159, [1978] 1 All ER 976 CA; approving *R D Harbottle (Mercantile) Ltd v National Westminster Bank Ltd* [1978] QB 146, [1977] 2 All ER 862.
7 [1985] 2 Lloyd's Rep 546, CA.
8 Ibid at 550.
9 Ibid at 554.

Index

All references are to page numbers